FUNDAMENTALS OF RISK AND INSURANCE

NINTH EDITION

EMMETT J. VAUGHAN
THERESE M. VAUGHAN

JOHN WILEY & SONS, INC.

Acquisitions Editor	Leslie Kraham
Marketing Manager	Charity Robey
Senior Production Editor	Patricia McFadden
Design Director	Madelyn Lesure
Production Management	Hermitage Publishing Services
Cover Photo	Kurt C. Vanderhoef

This book was set in 10/12 Times Ten Roman by Hermitage Publishing Services and printed and bound by R. R. Donnelley and Sons. The cover was printed by Lehigh Press.

This book is printed on acid-free paper ∞.

Includes copyrighted material used with permission of the Insurance Services Office.

ISBN 0-471-21687-9

Printed in the United States of America

10 9 8 7 6 5 4 3 2

ABOUT THE AUTHORS

Emmett J. Vaughan holds the Partington Professorship in Insurance at the University of Iowa, where he is Partington Professor of Insurance. Professor Vaughan received his undergraduate degree in economics from Creighton University and his M.A. and Ph.D. in economics and insurance from the University of Nebraska.

Therese M. Vaughan is currently Commissioner of Insurance for the State of Iowa. Commissioner Vaughan received her undergraduate degree in economics and insurance from the University of Iowa and her Ph.D. in insurance from the Wharton School of Business.

PREFACE

This ninth edition of *Fundamentals of Risk and Insurance* marks the thirtieth anniversary of the first edition, published in 1972. At the time the first edition was published, the field of insurance was quite different from what it is today. Many of the current forms of insurance coverage did not exist; the world seemed a simpler place. Medicare was not yet ten years old, and Richard Nixon was president of the United States. Automobile no-fault was an experiment that had been adopted by a single state (Massachusetts) and only three states had compulsory automobile insurance (New York, North Carolina, and Massachusetts). The 1943 Standard Fire Policy was the standard form of coverage for most commercial entities and the Family Auto Policy was the standard for personal automobile insurance. Universal life insurance was not yet on the drawing board and endowment policies were a staple for the life insurance agent. There was no such thing as long-term care insurance, no individual retirement accounts, and ERISA was not yet a gleam in a Congressperson's eye. The Social Security tax base was $9000 and the Medicare Part B premium was $5.60 a month.

The world has changed dramatically since 1972, and the field of insurance has changed with it. As insurance has changed, so too has *Fundamentals of Risk and Insurance*. A new co-author has been added and, regretfully, the book has lengthened. (The two are not related, although there is a temptation to plead that two authors have twice as much to say.) Although our editors have urged, with every edition, that we attempt to avoid expanding the book, there is, quite honestly, more to say in 2002 than there was in 1972. The book has grown in length from the modest 24 chapters in the first edition to 34 in this edition.

Although the book has changed over the years, its purpose, organization, and approach remain essentially the same. The original goal was to create a consumer-oriented text, and we have maintained this orientation in the present edition. The first edition of this book was written in response to a perceived need for an insurance textbook that addressed the principles of risk management without abandoning the discussion of insurance. The reception to the book over the past three decades has been gratifying. At least a part of the book's success is due to the fascinating subject matter it deals with. Experience indicated that insurance can be an exciting subject. University surveys repeatedly show that insurance courses usually score near the top in enrollment popularity, and students often rank the insurance courses they have taken as the most useful ones in college. This comes as no surprise to those of us who find this field so fascinating. It is satisfying, however, to find that our excitement can be shared by our students.

SCOPE OF THE SUBJECT

As a point of departure, it may be helpful to describe briefly exactly what the book is all about. As the title indicates, the ninth edition of *Fundamentals of Risk and Insurance* is about *risk* and about *insurance*. Its objective is to summarize the pervasive nature of pure risk on the individual and on society, and to illustrate the way in which insurance can be used to deal with the problems posed by such risk. It is a book on insurance theory as well as on how students can use insurance personally.

The intent from the beginning has been to create a text that is consumer oriented. The main emphasis is on the insurance product and the use of insurance within the risk management framework. The traditional fields of life insurance, health insurance,

property and liability insurance, and social insurance are treated in terms of their relationship to the wide range of insurable risks to which the individual and the business firm are exposed.

The text is designed for use in a college-level survey of the area of risk and insurance. As an introduction to the subject, it is intended for students who have had little or no prior education in insurance. It may serve as the basis for more advanced texts for those students who intend to specialize in the field of insurance, and at the same time it constitutes a compendium of what an informed citizen and consumer should know about the subject.

WHY STUDY INSURANCE?

The reasons for studying insurance are varied. For some, the study is undertaken in preparation for a career in the field. Others study to improve their knowledge of the subject to become more knowledgeable consumers. The average individual will spend a significant percentage of his or her disposable income on insurance over a lifetime, and one of the logical reasons for studying insurance is to learn how it can be used in personal financial planning. Still others study insurance as a part of the discipline of risk management, the managerial function that aims at preserving the operating effectiveness of the organization.

Although each of these reasons is adequate justification for the study of insurance, whether that study should be considered *essential* for business students depends on the approach and the specifics of what is studied. Some have argued that the study of insurance per se is a narrow specialty, yet the broader discipline of risk management—of which insurance buying is only a part—is clearly a function that all future managers should understand. A proper understanding of the methods of dealing with exposures to loss is essential to organizational leaders. Although insurance is only one of the techniques that can be used to deal with pure risks, risk management decisions presuppose a thorough understanding of the nature and functions of insurance.

We believe that insurance and risk management is a subject that needs to be taught in colleges and universities. Far from being the narrow specialty it is sometimes characterized as, the study of insurance has a breadth that few disciplines equal. As you progress through the book, you will encounter applications from economics, statistics, finance, accounting, law, decision theory, and ethics.

Because the study of risk management and insurance draws on these different disciplines, it is sometimes considered a subset of one of them. Thus, in many colleges and universities, insurance and risk management are a part of the finance curriculum, reflecting the financial nature of the risk management function. In other schools, it is considered a part of economics, while in still others it is located in another department. This organizational ambiguity reflects the confusion concerning what the study of risk management and insurance entails.

In fact, risk management and insurance is a separate and distinct discipline, which draws on and integrates the knowledge from a variety of other business fields. In a micro sense, it is a discipline in which a variety of methodologies are brought to bear on a significant problem.

Viewed from a macro perspective, the study of insurance addresses a variety of important issues facing society today: the high cost of medical care, crime, the tort system, pollution and the environment, and the broad subject of ethics. Indeed, it is not an exaggeration to say that the debates in the insurance arena address questions of what kind of society we will have and who will pay for what. Debates over the cost of insurance and the way in which insurance prices should be determined have intensified over the past two decades. Increasingly, the debate over insurance availability and affordability have come to center stage as the debate over the cost of automobile insurance, access to health care, responsibility for pollution, product liability, and medical malpractice have become crises. As consumers, we are all dramatically affected by the way in which insurance operates.

Finally, the study of risk management and insurance is a fertile field for considering the subject of ethics in business and in society. Indeed, the ubiquitous presence of ethical problems in the field of insurance transactions raises an important question: is ethics something to be studied and learned, or is it something innate in the individual?

ORGANIZATION OF THE BOOK

This book is divided into three major sections. In the first section, we examine the concept of risk, the nature of the insurance device, and the principles of risk management. This section also provides an overview of the insurance industry and the manner in which it operates.

The second section examines the traditional fields of life and health insurance as solutions to the risks

connected with the loss of income. The Social Security system, workers' compensation, and other social insurance coverages are discussed in this section to permit students to integrate the coverage under these programs in planning income protection.

The final section deals with the risks associated with the ownership of property and legal liability. The coverages applicable to the individual or family are treated in chapters that are separate from those designed for the business firm, permitting those instructors who prefer to concentrate on insurance for the individual to give only slight treatment to commercial coverages.

The book is designed to fit a one-semester or two-quarter course, but it may be adapted to longer and shorter sequences. We have composed what we consider to be a logical sequence of subject matter, but the book can be used flexibly. Sections Two and Three in particular may be taken in different order.

CHANGES IN THE NINTH EDITION

The thirty years that have passed since the publication of the first edition of *Fundamentals of Risk and Insurance* have been marked by significant change in the field of insurance. The second through the eighth editions are a chronology of that change. As the field of insurance and the environment in which it operates continue to change, our purpose has been to capture the flavor of that change in each revision. Changes in the legal environment, revisions in policy forms and the introduction of new types of insurance, and a myriad of new problems continue to make insurance an exciting field of study, but a challenge to the authors of textbooks.

One recent development that helps to mitigate the problems posed by the constantly changing nature of the insurance field is the increase in the resources available on the Internet. In the eighth edition we added Web site listings at the end of each chapter. In this edition, we have continued and expanded references to insurance-oriented Web sites. Most students will not need to be told about the significant impact that the Internet and World Wide Web have had on education. There are numerous insurance-related Web sites and the number continues to grow. These Web sites can be a valuable source of information on the changes that continue to occur in both government-sponsored programs and in the insurance industry. Although the authors have visited each of the sites listed, Web sites tend to come and go and the URLs

may change over time. Despite these impediments, the Web sites listed at the end of each chapter are a useful point of departure for exploring this valuable resource.

In the first through the sixth editions, we included sample policy forms as appendixes, bound with the text. As policy forms have grown in length (with larger type and simplified language), the number of pages devoted to sample policy forms increased, compounding the length problem. In the seventh and eighth editions, the policy forms that were printed in the bound volume in the first six editions were printed in a separate booklet. A number of users had suggested the separate booklet for policy forms, but the response from most users persuaded us that this was an unsatisfactory arrangement. In this edition, we are providing the sample policy forms on a CD, in an Acrobat format. We hope that this will prove to be a convenient arrangement for the students and for those instructors who prefer that students have policy forms in hand during the discussion.

CHANGES IN ORGANIZATION

The major changes in organization and presentation of the material are in Section I. We have divided the chapter on risk management from the first eight editions into two chapters. This allowed for a modest increase in the material on risk management, and also resolved a thirty-year dilemma about the order of the chapters that introduce risk management and insurance. In the first through eighth editions, we chose to introduce the concept of insurance first, and then risk management, on the premise that understanding something about the way that insurance works made it somewhat easier to understand the significance of risk management. With the separation of the material on risk management into two chapters, we can introduce the basic concept of risk management, then explain the concept of insurance, and then return to the discussion of risk management to discuss specific applications of the principles. To accommodate the expanded discussion of risk management, we have condensed (slightly) our earlier discussion of the fields of insurance and combined this material with the chapter that introduces the concept of insurance.

CHANGES IN MATERIAL

In addition to the organization changes, other changes update the material to reflect the changes in

the field of insurance since 1999, when the eighth edition was published. Those changes have been both numerous and significant. In 1999, Congress enacted the Financial Services Modernization Act, removing the Depression-era restrictions on the combination of banking and insurance and prompting what will very likely be change in the structure of the insurance industry. The presidential election of 2000 witnessed a more than lively debate over the future of Social Security, with frequent references to a lockbox and what was referred to as the risky scheme of privatization. A new homeowners policy was introduced in the year 2000, along with new commercial property forms, a new commercial crime program, and significant changes in other forms of coverage. In 2001, Congress passed and the president signed the Economic Growth and Tax Relief Reconciliation Act of 2001, with significant changes in the federal estate tax and qualified retirement plans.

ACKNOWLEDGMENTS

We have been supported and encouraged in this revision by many people. First and foremost are the members of our families, all of whom sacrificed much to assist us. We thank them all for their help, but, more important, for their understanding.

As a book progresses through successive editions, the number of persons to whom an author is indebted increases geometrically, since the efforts of so many people become a part of the work. First, we owe much to our teachers, whose influence left an indelible mark on us and on this book. In addition, we owe a debt of gratitude to the many reviewers and users who have helped to shape the book. Although much has been altered as the book moved through successive editions, our debt continues to colleagues and students who provided criticism and suggestions on the earlier editions. As a result, there are many people to whom special thanks are due. They include our colleague, Professor Michael Murray, who has shared his insights with us over the years and whose influence has been significant. The reviewers of the first eight editions, whose contributions to those editions helped to shape this one as well, were Tom Auippa, Richard C. Allgood, Garth H. Allen, Albert L. Auxier, W. Oscar Cooper, Robert W. Cooper, Richard Corbett, Bill Feldhaus, Roger A. Formisano, John W. Haney, Kenneth J. Krepas, E. J. Leverett, Joseph R. Morrin,

Robert J. Myers, John J. O'Connell, Mike Thorne, S. Travis Pritchett, Dede Pahl, Gary K. Stone, and Robert Witt.

In addition, we owe a debt of gratitude to the reviewers of this edition, who offered valuable suggestions that helped to shape the final work. They were Darlene Dicco of Hofstra University, Aaron Lieberman of the University of Central Florida, and Jim Milanese of the Bryan School of Business and Economics.

We owe special thanks to Mandell S. Winter, Jr. and Michael Snowden of the College for Financial Planning, for their assistance in reviewing the seventh, eighth, and ninth editions. Their suggestions and insights helped us to clarify many concepts and to avoid errors that would otherwise have marred the book. Mr. Winter's contributions to the seventh and eighth editions and Mr. Snowden's assistance in this edition went far beyond that of a reviewer and we are grateful for their assistance.

We also offer thanks to all of our former students. Their many comments and intelligent questions contributed to the design of the book and to the examples and illustrations used. Each of the past graduate teaching assistants at the University of Iowa who have shared with the senior author the pleasant task of teaching the basic insurance course at the University of Iowa contributed significantly to the earlier editions and to this one. They are Lois Anderson, Phillip Brooks, Robb Fick, Tim Hamann, Terry Leap, Lacy McNeill, Joseph Panici, Mark Power, Lori Rider, Roger Stech, Ellen Steele, Mike Steele, Patrick Steele, Art Cox, Robert Carney, and Changsu Ouh.

We also thank the users of the first eight editions who took time to write to us with their suggestions and comments.

From the teachers who will use this book as a text, we will be grateful to receive advice concerning any errors that should be corrected and any material that should be added or omitted when it is again revised. To the students who will be compelled to read it, we extend the hope that the material presented will seem as exciting and interesting as it has seemed to us.

Emmett J. Vaughan
Iowa City, Iowa

Therese M. Vaughan
Des Moines, Iowa

January 2002

CONTENTS

Chapter 15 The Life Insurance Contract— Other Provisions 263

Chapter 16 Special Life Insurance Forms 277

Chapter 17 Buying Life Insurance 288

Chapter 18 Annuities and Pension Benefits 306

Chapter 19 Managing the Retirement Risk 330

Chapter 20 Health Insurance: Disability Income Insurance 344

CHAPTER 1

THE PROBLEM OF RISK

"When I use a word," Humpty Dumpty said, in a rather scornful tone,
"it means just what I choose it to mean—neither more nor less."
"The question is," said Alice, "whether you can make
words mean so many different things."
"The question is," said Humpty Dumpty, "which is
to be master, that's all."

— LEWIS CARROLL
Through the Looking Glass

CHAPTER OBJECTIVES

When you have finished this chapter, you should be able to

- Define and explain the meaning of the term *risk*
- Distinguish among the terms *risk, peril,* and *hazard*
- Identify and explain the classes of hazards
- Differentiate between pure risk and speculative risk
- Differentiate between fundamental and particular risk
- Describe the categories into which pure risk may be subdivided
- Identify and explain the principal methods of handling risk

You see the mangled metal of two cars that have collided on an interstate highway. A fire engine with its siren screaming roars down the street. A building in your neighborhood burns or you see an ambulance racing to the hospital. All these tragic events arouse your interest and emotions. After the noise and excitement have died down, you are grateful that the loss did not happen to you and you may even feel sorry for whoever suffered the loss. But you're glad that it wasn't you. Losses like these happen to some people, while others go along happily, free from misfortune. The fact that these losses or similar events could happen to you, and the fact that you can't tell for sure whether or not they will, is a condition we

call risk. Risk is a pervasive condition of human existence. Although our instinctive understanding of the concept of risk is clear enough, terms that have a simple meaning in everyday usage sometimes have a specialized connotation when used in a particular field of study. In this chapter we will examine the concept of risk as the fundamental problem with which insurance deals. In addition, we will also examine several related concepts.

THE CONCEPT OF RISK

It would seem on the surface that the term *risk* is a simple enough notion. When someone states that there is risk in a particular situation, the listener understands what is meant: that in the given situation there is uncertainty about the outcome and the possibility exists that the outcome will be unfavorable. This loose, intuitive notion of risk, which implies a lack of knowledge about the future and the possibility of some adverse consequence, is satisfactory for conversational usage, but for our purpose a somewhat more rigid definition is desirable.

Economists, statisticians, decision theorists, and insurance theorists have long discussed the concepts of risk and uncertainty in an attempt to construct a definition of risk that is useful for analysis in each field of investigation. So far, they have not been able to agree on a single definition that can be used in each field. A definition of risk that is suitable for the economist or statistician may be worthless as an analytic tool for the insurance theorist. The fact that each group treats a different body of subject matter requires the use of different concepts. Although the statistician, the decision theorist, and the insurance theorist all use the term *risk,* they may each mean something entirely different.

Insurance is still in its infancy as a body of theory. As a result, we find contradictory definitions of risk throughout the literature dealing with this phenomenon from an insurance point of view. One reason for these contradictions is that insurance theorists have attempted to borrow the definitions of risk used in other fields. Surprising as it may seem, insurance text writers have not been able to agree on a definition of this basic concept.

To compound the problem, the term *risk* is used by people in the insurance business to mean either a peril insured against (e.g., fire is a risk to which most property is exposed) or a person or property protected by insurance (e.g., many insurance companies feel that young drivers are not good risks). In this text, however, we will use the term in its general meaning, to indicate a situation where an exposure to loss exists.

Current Definitions of Risk

If we were to survey the best-known insurance textbooks used in colleges and universities today, we would find a general lack of agreement concerning the definition of risk.[1] Although the insurance theorists have not agreed on a universal definition, there are common elements in all the definitions: indeterminacy and loss.

- The notion of an indeterminate outcome is implicit in all definitions of risk: the outcome must be in question. When risk is said to exist, there must always be at least two possible outcomes. If we know for certain that a loss will occur, there is no risk. Investment in a capital asset, for example, usually involves a realization that the asset is subject to physical depreciation and that its value will decline. Here the outcome is certain and so there is no risk.

- At least one of the possible outcomes is undesirable. This may be a loss in the generally accepted sense, in which something the individual possesses is lost, or it may be a gain smaller than the gain that was possible. For example, the investor who fails to take advantage of an opportunity "loses" the gain that might have been made. The investor faced with the choice between two stocks may be said to "lose" if he or she chooses the one that increases in value less than the alternative.

Our Definition of Risk

We define *risk* as a condition of the real world in which there is an exposure to adversity. More specifically,

[1] The term *risk* is variously defined as (1) the chance of loss, (2) the possibility of loss, (3) uncertainty, (4) the dispersion of actual from expected results, or (5) the probability of any outcome different from the one expected.

Risk is a condition in which there is a possibility of an adverse deviation from a desired outcome that is expected or hoped for.

Note first that in this definition risk is a condition of the real world; it is a combination of circumstances in the external environment. Note also that in this combination of circumstances, there is a *possibility* of loss. When we say that an event is possible, we mean that it has a probability between zero and one; it is neither impossible nor definite. Note also that there is no requirement that the possibility be measurable; only that it must exist. We may or may not be able to measure the degree of risk, but the probability of the adverse outcome must be between zero and one.[2]

The undesirable event is described as "an adverse deviation from a desired outcome that is *expected* or *hoped for.*" The reference to a desired outcome that is either expected or hoped for contemplates both individual and aggregate loss exposures. The individual hopes that adversity will not occur, and it is the possibility that this hope will not be met that constitutes risk. If you own a house, you hope that it will not catch fire. When you make a wager, you hope that the outcome will be favorable. The fact that the outcome in either event may be something other than what you hope constitutes the possibility of loss or risk.

In the case of an insurer, actuaries predict some specified number and amount of losses and charge a premium based on this expectation. The amount of predicted losses is the desired outcome that is expected by the insurer. For the insurer, risk is the possibility that losses will deviate adversely from what is expected.

Uncertainty and Its Relationship to Risk

Because the term *uncertainty* is often used in connection with the term *risk* (sometimes even interchangeably), it seems appropriate to explain the relationship between the terms *risk* and *uncertainty.*

The most widely held meaning of *uncertainty* refers to a state of mind characterized by doubt, based on a lack of knowledge about what will or will not happen in the future. It is the opposite of certainty, which is a conviction or certitude about a particular situation. A student says "I am certain I will get an A in this course," which means the same as "I am positive I will get an A in this course." Both statements reflect a conviction about the outcome. Uncertainty, on the other hand, is the opposite mental state. If one says "I am uncertain what grade I am going to get in this course," the statement reflects a lack of knowledge about the outcome. Uncertainty, then, is simply a psychological reaction to the absence of knowledge about the future.[3] The existence of risk—a condition or combination of circumstances in which there is a possibility of loss—creates uncertainty on the part of individuals when that risk is recognized.

The individual's conviction or lack thereof (certainty or uncertainty) about a specific fact or situation may or may not coincide with the conditions of the real world. The student who says "I am certain I will get an A in this course" may actually get a B, a C, a D, or even an F. Uncertainty varies with the knowledge and attitudes of the person. Different attitudes are possible for different individuals under identical conditions of the real world. It is possible, for example, for a person to experience uncertainty in a situation in which he or she imagines that there is a chance of loss, but where no chance of loss exists. Similarly, it is possible for an individual to feel no uncertainty regarding a particular risk when the exposure to loss is not recognized. Whether or not a risk is recognized, however, does not alter its existence. When there is a possibility of loss, risk exists

[2] We measure probability on an imaginary ruler, marked at one end with a zero and unity at the other. The high end of the scale, marked unity, represents absolute certainty. Any proposition about which there is no doubt whatsoever finds its place at this point on the scale. For example, the probability that the reader will eventually die is equal to 1, because it is absolutely certain that we will all die some day. Using the letter p to stand for probability, we would write $p = 1$. The bottom end of the scale, marked zero, represents absolute impossibility. The probability that the reader could run a mile in 30 seconds is zero, because failure would be absolutely certain. The statistician here would write $p = 0$. Events that are neither certain nor impossible lie between the two ends of our imaginary ruler, and are assigned values that vary with the likelihood of their occurrence. Thus, the probability of drawing the ace of spades from a deck of cards is 1/52 or .019. The probability of drawing any ace is 1/13, or the probability of drawing a black card is 1/2 or .5.

[3] In addition to its meaning as a psychological phenomenon, a second possible meaning of the term *uncertainty* relates to probability and is contrasted with a second meaning of *certainty:* a situation in which the probability of an event is 100 percent. An event may be said to be impossible (probability = 0), certain (probability = 1), or uncertain. Used in reference to the likelihood of an event, uncertain simply means that the probability is judged to be between 0 and 1.

whether or not the person exposed to loss is aware of the risk.[4]

The Degree of Risk

It is intuitively obvious that there are some situations in which the risk is greater than in other situations. Just as we should agree on what we mean when we use the term *risk,* we should agree on the way(s) in which risk can be measured. Precisely what is meant when we say that one alternative involves "more risk" or "less risk" than another?

It would seem that the most commonly accepted meaning of *degree of risk* is related to the likelihood of occurrence. We intuitively consider those events with a high probability of loss to be "riskier" than those with a low probability. This intuitive notion of the degree of risk is consistent with our definition of risk. When risk is defined as the possibility of an adverse deviation from a desired outcome that is expected or hoped for, the degree of risk is measured by the probability of the adverse deviation. In the case of the individual, the hope is that no loss will occur, so that the probability of a deviation from what is hoped for (which is the measure of risk) varies directly with the probability that a loss will occur. In the case of the individual, we measure risk in terms of the probability of an adverse deviation from what is hoped for. Actuarial tables tell us, for example, that the probability of death at age 52 is approximately 1 percent and that at age 79 it is about 10 percent. At age 97, the probability of death increases to nearly 50 percent. Using the probability of an adverse deviation from the outcome that is hoped for, we view the risk of death at age 79 as greater than that at age 52, but less than that at age 97. The higher the probability that an event will occur, the greater the likelihood of a deviation from the outcome that is hoped for and the greater the risk, as long as the probability of loss is less than one.

In the game of Russian roulette, there is more risk when there are two bullets in a revolver's six chambers than when there is one bullet. Adding a third bullet increases the risk, as does adding the fourth bullet and the fifth bullet. Adding the fourth and fifth bullets increases the probability of a deviation from the hoped-for outcome. If a sixth bullet is added, the player can no longer expect or even hope that the outcome will be favorable. The sixth bullet makes the outcome certain, and risk no longer exists. If the probability of loss is 1.0, there is no chance of an outcome other than that which is expected and, therefore, no hope of a favorable result. Similarly, when the probability of loss is zero, there is no possibility of loss and therefore no risk.

In the case of a large number of exposure units, estimates can be made about the likelihood that a given number of losses will occur, and predictions can be made on the basis of these estimates. Here the expectation is that the predicted number of losses will occur. In the case of aggregate exposures, the degree of risk is not the probability of a single occurrence or loss; it is the probability of some outcome different from that predicted or expected. Insurance companies make predictions about losses that are expected to occur and charge a premium based on this prediction. For the insurance company, then, the risk is that its prediction will not be accurate. Suppose that based on past experience, an insurer estimates that 1 out of 1000 houses will burn. If the company insures 100,000 houses, it might predict that 100 houses will burn out of the 100,000 insured, but it is highly unlikely that 100, and only 100, houses will burn. The actual experience will undoubtedly deviate from the expectation, and insofar as this deviation is unfavorable, the insurance company faces risk. Therefore, the insurance company makes a prediction not only with respect to the number of houses that will burn, but also estimates the range of error. The prediction might be that 100 losses will occur and that the range of possible deviation will be plus or minus 10. Some number of houses between 90 and 110 are expected to burn, and the possibility that the number will be more than 100 is the insurer's risk. Students who have studied statistics will note that when one of the standard measures of dispersion (such as the standard deviation) is used, risk is measurable, and we can say that more risk or less risk exists in a given situation, depending on the standard deviation.

[4] Some authors equate our notion of uncertainty with subjective risk, which is a person's perception of risk. An individual may perceive risk where it does not exist. (Navigators in Columbus's day perceived a risk of falling off the edge of the world.) They may also fail to perceive risk when it does exist. The distinction between objective risk and subjective risk (i.e., between risk and uncertainty) is important because subjective risk affects the decisions people make. Ideally, they should make decisions based on actual risk (i.e., objective risk). Better information reduces uncertainty (improves subjective risk estimates) and leads to better decisions.

At times we use the terms *more risk* and *less risk* to indicate a measure of the possible size of the loss. Many people would say that there is more risk involved in a possible loss of $1000 than in that of $1, even though the probability of loss is the same in both cases. The probability that a loss may occur and the potential severity of the loss if it does occur contribute to the intensity of one's reaction to risk. It seems, therefore, that a measurement of risk should recognize the magnitude of the potential loss. Given two situations, one involving a $1000 exposure and the other a $1 exposure, and assuming the same probability in each case, it seems appropriate to state that there is a greater risk in the case of the possible loss of $1000. This is consistent with our definition of risk, since the loss of $1000 is a greater deviation from what is hoped for (i.e., no loss) than is the loss of $1. On the other hand, given two situations where the amount exposed is the same (e.g., $1000), there is more risk in the situation with the greater probability of loss.

While it may be difficult to relate the size of the potential loss and the probability of that loss in the measurement of risk, the concept of expected value may be used to relate these two facets of a given risk situation. The expected value of a loss in a given situation is the probability of that loss multiplied by the amount of the potential loss. If the amount at risk is $10 and the probability of loss is 0.10, the expected value of the loss is $1. If the amount at risk is $100 and the probability is 0.01, the expected value is also $1. This is a very useful concept, as we will see later.

Risk Distinguished from Peril and Hazard

It is not uncommon for the terms *peril* and *hazard* to be used interchangeably with each other and with *risk*. However, to be precise, it is important to distinguish these terms. A peril is a cause of a loss. We speak of the peril of fire, or windstorm, or hail, or theft. Each of these is the cause of the loss that occurs. A hazard, on the other hand, is a condition that may create or increase the chance of a loss arising from a given peril. It is possible for something to be both a peril and a hazard. For instance, sickness is a peril causing economic loss, but it is also a hazard that increases the chance of loss from the peril of premature death. Hazards are normally classified into three categories:

- *Physical hazards* consist of those physical properties that increase the chance of loss from the various perils. Examples of physical hazards that increase the possibility of loss from the peril of fire are the type of construction, the location of the property, and the occupancy of the building.

- *Moral hazard* refers to the increase in the probability of loss that results from dishonest tendencies in the character of the insured person. More simply, it is the dishonest tendencies on the part of an insured that may induce that person to attempt to defraud the insurance company. A dishonest person, in the hope of collecting from the insurance company, may intentionally cause a loss or may exaggerate the amount of a loss in an attempt to collect more than the amount to which he or she is entitled. Fraud is a significant problem for insurance companies and increases the cost of insurance.

- *Morale hazard,* not to be confused with moral hazard, acts to increase losses where insurance exists, not necessarily because of dishonesty, but because of a different attitude toward losses that will be paid by insurance. When people have purchased insurance, they may have a more careless attitude toward preventing losses or may have a different attitude toward the cost of restoring damage. Morale hazard is also reflected in the attitude of persons who are not insureds. The tendency of physicians to provide more expensive levels of care when costs are covered by insurance is a part of the morale hazard. Similarly, the inclination of juries to make larger awards when the loss is covered by insurance—the so-called *deep-pocket syndrome*—is another example of morale hazard. In short, morale hazard acts to increase both the frequency and severity of losses when such losses are covered by insurance.

In addition to these three traditional types of hazard, a fourth hazard—the legal hazard—should be recognized. *Legal hazard* refers to the increase in the frequency and severity of loss that arises from legal doctrines enacted by legislatures and created by the courts. Jurisdictions in which legal doctrines favor a plaintiff represent a hazard to persons or organizations who are sued at tort. Although legal hazard is greatest in the field of legal liability, it also exists in the case of property exposures. In jurisdictions where building codes require that new buildings conform to statutory requirements, the destruction of a building that does not meet the requirements may force an

owner to incur additional costs in reconstruction, thereby increasing the exposure to loss.

Classifications of Risk

Risks may be classified in many ways; however, there are certain distinctions that are particularly important for our purposes. These include the following.

Financial and Nonfinancial Risks In its broadest context, the term *risk* includes all situations in which there is an exposure to adversity. In some cases this adversity involves financial loss, while in others it does not. There is some element of risk in every aspect of human endeavor, and many of these risks have no (or only incidental) financial consequences. In this text we are concerned with those risks that involve a financial loss.

Static and Dynamic Risks A second important distinction is between static and dynamic risks.[5] *Dynamic risks* are those resulting from changes in the economy. Changes in the price level, consumer tastes, income and output, and technology may cause financial loss to members of the economy. These dynamic risks normally benefit society over the long run, since they are the result of adjustments to misallocation of resources. Although these dynamic risks may affect a large number of individuals, they are generally considered less predictable than static risks, since they do not occur with any precise degree of regularity.

Static risks involve those losses that would occur even if there were no changes in the economy. If we could hold consumer tastes, output and income, and the level of technology constant, some individuals would still suffer financial loss. These losses arise from causes other than the changes in the economy, such as the perils of nature and the dishonesty of other individuals. Unlike dynamic risks, static risks are not a source of gain to society. Static losses involve either the destruction of the asset or a change in its possession as a result of dishonesty or human failure. Static losses tend to occur with a degree of regularity over time and, as a result, are generally predictable. Because they are predictable, static risks are more suited to treatment by insurance than are dynamic risks.

Fundamental and Particular Risks The distinction between fundamental and particular risks is based on the difference in the origin and consequences of the losses.[6] *Fundamental risks* involve losses that are impersonal in origin and consequence. They are group risks, caused for the most part by economic, social, and political phenomena, although they may also result from physical occurrences. They affect large segments or even all of the population. *Particular risks* involve losses that arise out of individual events and are felt by individuals rather than by the entire group. They may be static or dynamic. Unemployment, war, inflation, earthquakes, and floods are all fundamental risks. The burning of a house and the robbery of a bank are particular risks.

Since fundamental risks are caused by conditions more or less beyond the control of the individuals who suffer the losses and since they are not the fault of anyone in particular, it is held that society rather than the individual has a responsibility to deal with them. Although some fundamental risks are dealt with through private insurance,[7] usually, some form of social insurance or government transfer program is used to deal with fundamental risks. Unemployment and occupational disabilities are fundamental risks treated through social insurance. Flood damage or earthquakes make a district a disaster area eligible for federal funds.

In the final analysis, whether a risk is considered fundamental or particular depends on current public opinion concerning the responsibility for the causes and consequences of the risk. In the aftermath of the terrorist attack on the World Trade Center on September 11, 2001, congress and the insurance industry debated the question of whether terrorist attacks are a fundamental or particular risk. Reinsurers—the insurers that provide insurance to insurance companies—announced their intent to exclude acts of terrorism from the coverage they provide to other insurers. Faced with the loss of backup coverage, the insurers that deal with the public developed an endorsement for their policies excluding loss from

[5] The dynamic–static distinction was made by Willett. See Alan H. Willett, *The Economic Theory of Risk and Insurance* (Philadelphia: University of Pennsylvania Press, 1951), pp. 14–19.

[6] The distinction between fundamental and particular risks is based on C. A. Kulp's discussion of risk (which he referred to as "hazard"). See C. A. Kulp, *Casualty Insurance,* 3rd ed. (New York: Ronald Press, 1956), pp. 3, 4.

[7] For example, earthquake insurance is available from private insurers in most parts of the country, and flood insurance is frequently included in contracts covering movable personal property. Flood insurance on real property is available through private insurers only on a limited basis.

terrorist acts. In response to these developments, congress considered several bills to create a federal terrorism reinsurance program but by March 2002 had reached an impasse regarding the form that such a program should take.

Particular risks are considered to be the individual's own responsibility, inappropriate subjects for action by society as a whole. They are dealt with by the individual through the use of insurance, loss prevention, or some other technique.

Pure and Speculative Risks One of the most useful distinctions is that between pure risk and speculative risk.[8] *Speculative risk* describes a situation in which there is a possibility of loss, but also a possibility of gain. Gambling is a good example of a speculative risk. In a gambling situation, risk is deliberately created in the hope of gain. The student wagering $10 on the outcome of Saturday's game faces the possibility of loss, but this is accompanied by the possibility of gain. The entrepreneur or capitalist faces speculative risk in the quest for profit. The investment made may be lost if the product is not accepted by the market at a price sufficient to cover costs, but this risk is borne in return for the possibility of profit. The term *pure risk,* in contrast, is used to designate those situations that involve only the chance of loss or no loss. One of the best examples of pure risk is the possibility of loss surrounding the ownership of property. The person who buys an automobile, for example, immediately faces the possibility that something may happen to damage or destroy the automobile. The possible outcomes are loss or no loss.

The distinction between pure and speculative risks is an important one, because normally only pure risks are insurable. Insurance is not concerned with the protection of individuals against those losses arising out of speculative risks. Speculative risk is voluntarily accepted because of its two-dimensional nature, which includes the possibility of gain. Not all pure risks are insurable, and a further distinction between insurable and uninsurable pure risks may also be made. A discussion of this difference will be delayed until Chapter 2.

Classifications of Pure Risk While it would be impossible in this book to list all the risks confronting an individual or business, we can briefly outline the nature of the various pure risks that we face. For the most part, these are also static risks. Pure risks that exist for individuals and business firms can be classified under one of the following:

1. *Personal risks.* These consist of the possibility of loss of income or assets as a result of the loss of the ability to earn income. In general, earning power is subject to four perils: (a) premature death, (b) dependent old age, (c) sickness or disability, and (d) unemployment.

2. *Property risks.* Anyone who owns property faces property risks simply because such possessions can be destroyed or stolen. Property risks embrace two distinct types of loss: *direct loss* and *indirect* or "consequential" *loss.* Direct loss is the simplest to understand: If a house is destroyed by fire, the owner loses the value of the house. This is a direct loss. However, in addition to losing the value of the building itself, the property owner no longer has a place to live, and during the time required to rebuild the house, it is likely that the owner will incur additional expenses living somewhere else. This loss of use of the destroyed asset is an *indirect,* or "consequential," *loss.* An even better example is the case of a business firm. When a firm's facilities are destroyed, it loses not only the value of those facilities but also the income that would have been earned through their use. Property risks, then, can involve two types of losses: (a) the loss of the property and (b) loss of use of the property resulting in lost income or additional expenses.

3. *Liability risks.* The basic peril in the liability risk is the unintentional injury of other persons or damage to their property through negligence or carelessness; however, liability may also result from intentional injuries or damage. Under our legal system, the laws provide that one who has injured another, or damaged another's property through negligence or otherwise, can be held responsible for the harm caused. Liability risks therefore involve the possibility of loss of present assets or future income as a result of damages assessed or legal liability arising out of either intentional or unintentional torts, or invasion of the rights of others.

4. *Risks arising from failure of others.* When another person agrees to perform a service for you,

[8] Although the distinction between pure and speculative risk had been introduced earlier, Albert H. Mowbray formalized the distinction. See Albert H. Mowbray and Ralph H. Blanchard, *Insurance, Its Theory and Practice in the United States.* 5th ed. (New York: McGraw-Hill, 1961), pp. 6, 7.

he or she undertakes an obligation that you hope will be met. When the person's failure to meet this obligation would result in your financial loss, risk exists. Examples of risks in this category would include failure of a contractor to complete a construction project as scheduled, or failure of debtors to make payments as expected. With the development of the Internet and the rapid evolution of e-commerce, a variety of new risks relating to the failure of others have emerged.

THE BURDEN OF RISK

Regardless of the manner in which risk is defined, the greatest burden in connection with risk is that some losses will actually occur. When a house is destroyed by fire, or money is stolen, or a wage earner dies, there is a financial loss. When someone is negligent and that negligence results in injury to a person or damage to property, there is a financial loss. These losses are the primary burden of risk and the primary reason that individuals attempt to avoid risk or alleviate its impact.

In addition to the losses themselves, there are other detrimental aspects of risk. The uncertainty as to whether the loss will occur requires the prudent individual to prepare for its possible occurrence. In the absence of insurance, one way this can be done is to accumulate a reserve fund to meet the losses if they do occur.[9] Accumulation of such a reserve fund carries an opportunity cost, for funds must be available at the time of the loss and must therefore be held in a highly liquid state. The return on such funds will presumably be less than if they were put to alternate uses. If each property owner accumulates his or her own fund, the amount of funds held in such reserves will be greater than if the funds are amassed collectively.

Furthermore, the existence of risk may have a deterrent effect on economic growth and capital accumulation. Progress in the economy is determined to a large extent by the rate of capital accumulation, but the investment of capital involves risk that is distasteful. Investors as a class will incur the risks of a new undertaking only if the return on the investment is sufficiently high to compensate for both the

dynamic and static risks. The cost of capital is higher in those situations where the risk is greater, and the consumer must pay the resulting higher cost of the goods and services or they will not be forthcoming.

Finally, the uncertainty connected with risk usually produces a feeling of frustration and mental unrest. This is particularly true in the case of pure risk. Speculative risk is attractive to many individuals. The gambler obviously enjoys the uncertainty connected with wagering more than the certainty of not gambling—otherwise he or she would not gamble. But here it is the possibility of gain or profit, which exists only in the speculative risk category, that is attractive. In the case of pure risk, where there is no compensating chance of gain, risk is distasteful. Most people hope that misfortunes will not befall them and that their present state of well-being will continue. While they hope that no misfortune will occur, people are nevertheless likely to worry about possible mishaps. This worry, which induces a feeling of diminished well-being, is an additional burden of risk.

THE GROWING NUMBER AND VARIETY OF PURE RISKS

From the dawn of civilization, humans have faced the possibility of loss. Our ancestors confronted an environment characterized by incredible perils and hazards. The earliest perils giving rise to risk were those of nature and predators (including not only savage beasts but human predators as well). Humans learned to anticipate and prepare for adversity, both collectively and individually. They built shelter and they saved for the future. This provided protection from the elements and savage beasts, but it created new risks. Structures constructed for protection were vulnerable to damage and saving meant accumulation of wealth, which inevitably created new risks. Those who saved were exposed to the predatory inclinations of those who did not (an exposure that continues to the present day). Despite progress in learning how to deal with risks, the challenge of dealing with risk continued to grow. As new ways of addressing risk are found, new risks appear, often as a result of progress.

Harnessing energy has made life easier, but it created new risks. Until about 200 years ago, the major sources of energy were muscle (both human and animals), wind, and water, and the risks associated with

[9] One great danger of this approach is the possibility that a loss may occur before a sufficient fund has been accumulated.

energy sources were modest. Since the early 1800s, advances in technology have increased the sources of energy available to humankind and with each new source has come new risks. For example, the industrial revolution witnessed the application of steam to the production process, and with steam came new risks. The early steam engines were hazardous mechanisms and explosions were common. Not only was the risk of explosion great, steam power created other risks. Steam engines were far less prone to stoppage by obstructions than human-powered devices; they continued to grind away, oblivious to the hands and arms that got entangled in gears. Like steam, the introduction of electric power, the internal combustion engine, and nuclear power have all created new risks.

One can argue that the invention of the legal system was an effort to address risk. By defining individual rights and responsibilities, the legal system created a framework whose basic function was to protect those rights. At the same time, the legal system itself became a source of risk, by creating a system in which those who are injured or damaged by others may seek compensation. As the concept of rights and responsibilities has developed, new causes of action have emerged and many of the current legal risks were unknown a generation ago. These include potential liability for a profusion of new transgressions: environmental damage, discrimination in employment, sexual harassment, and violence in the workplace.

The most recent expansion of risks we face, like many previous expansions, is traceable to advances in technology. The information age in which we are now immersed embodies a variety of new exposures. Information has value and, as such, its exposure to loss represents risk. Information has, of course, always had value. What has changed is the way that information is collected, sorted, and communicated electronically. In an earlier era, when information was recorded on hard media, it was easier to protect. Equally important, it was easy to detect when the information security system had been breached. The interconnectivity of the Internet and electronic communication generally exposes valuable information to loss in ways not previously imagined. Pirates and thieves have been a constant source of potential loss throughout history. Hackers who commit vandalism and electronic larceny have replaced the bandits and pirates who threatened early traders. Modern thieves steal not only assets, but sometimes one's identity.

According to the FBI, *identity theft* is the fastest growing white-collar crime in the nation.[10]

With each advance in technology, new risks arise. Because many of the old risks remain, the inventory of risks that must be addressed increases geometrically. Daily newspapers indicate the simultaneous threat of new-age hazards and age-old perils of nature. The hazards posed by the nuclear age were demonstrated by the incident at the Three Mile Island nuclear facility in Pennsylvania in 1979 and the accident at the Soviet Union's Chernobyl plant in April 1987. The ravages that can be wreaked by nature are evidenced by Hurricane Andrew's $22 billion plus in damages, by the floods of near-biblical proportions that ravaged midwestern United States in 1993 and by earthquakes in California and Kobi, Japan, in 1993 and 1994. The bombings of the World Trade Center and the Oklahoma City Federal Building in 1993 and 1995 and the terrorist attack on the World Trade Center and the Pentagon on September 11, 2001 are stark reminders that it is not just nature than can cause death and destruction, but people as well. Although other losses are less momentous, it is only because they affect a single individual or firm. For the party who suffers the loss, they are no less devastating.

INCREASING SEVERITY OF LOSSES

As might be expected, with the increasing array of risks, the dollar amount of losses arising from accidents has also increased. Interestingly, however, the increasing dollar amount of losses is not solely a function of the increasing number of risks. Even those losses that arise from the perils of nature—windstorms, earthquakes and floods—have exhibited an increasing severity. Nor is the increasing severity merely a reflection of inflation; the dollar total from these losses continues to increase even when adjusted for inflation. Although the number of earthquakes,

[10] A headline-making example of identity theft occurred early in 2001 when a 32-year-old high school dropout, Abraham Abdallah, victimized more than 200 of the richest people in America, as listed by *Forbes* magazine, including Steven Spielberg, Ted Turner, Warren Buffet, Ross Perot, and Oprah Winfrey. Police alleged that Abdallah, using a computer at a Brooklyn library to access the Web, obtained detailed credit reports on the individuals and then used that information to assume their identities and gain access to their accounts at brokerage, bank, and credit-card accounts.

floods, and windstorms occur at essentially the same rate as in the past, each new catastrophe seems to exceed previous losses. The reason, of course, is that there is simply more wealth, more investment, and more assets exposed to loss. As business has become more capital intensive, as the technology of production equipment becomes more costly, capital investment increases. With the growth in capital investment, the risk of financial loss also increases.[11]

[11] The San Francisco earthquake of 1906 caused an estimated $24 million in direct earthquake damage, followed by $500 million in fire damage. The cost in 2002 dollars would have been about $9 billion. Damage from a quake of the same intensity as the 1906 earthquake would likely exceed $100 billion; San Francisco today is a dramatically different place from the San Francisco of 1906. Buildings are taller and more expensive to build and there are more of them. There are more people, more cars, and more "stuff" today than in 1906. As population and wealth increase, the exposure to loss is magnified. The richer we become as a society, the more wealth that is exposed to loss.

MANAGING RISK

There is no escape from the presence of risk, and humanity must accordingly seek ways of dealing with it. Some risks—generally of a fundamental nature—are met through the collective efforts of society and government. Municipal police and fire departments are good examples of the collectively financed approaches to dealing with risk, but countless others might be suggested. Although society and government can help to alleviate the burden of risks in many areas, there are some risks that are considered the responsibility of the individual.

Given the vast array of risks faced by individuals and businesses and the variety of possible ways to deal with them, a systematic approach is needed in dealing with risks. What can we do about the various risks we face? Which risks require attention first and how should they be addressed? In Chapter 2, we will begin our discussion of risk management and consider a systematic approach for dealing with pure risks faced by individuals and firms.

IMPORTANT CONCEPTS TO REMEMBER

risk	morale hazard	personal risk
uncertainty	deep-pocket syndrome	property risk
subjective risk	static risk	direct loss
degree of risk	dynamic risk	indirect loss
peril	fundamental risk	liability risk
hazard	particular risk	probability of loss
physical hazard	pure risk	expected value
moral hazard	speculative risk	

QUESTIONS FOR REVIEW

1. Define risk. In your definition, state the relationship between risk and uncertainty.

2. Risk may be subclassified in several ways. List the three principal ways in which risk may be categorized, and explain the distinguishing characteristics of each class.

3. The distinction between "pure risk" and "speculative risk" is important because only pure risks are normally insurable. Why is the distinction between "fundamental risk" and "particular risk" important?

4. Explain how pure risk has an adverse effect on economic activity.

5. List the four types of pure risk facing an individual or an organization and give an example of each.

6. The text discusses the "burden of risk." What are the two principal ways in which the impact of risk may be felt by an individual or an organization?

7. Distinguish between "perils" and "hazards" and give two specific examples of each.

8. Briefly distinguish among the three categories into which hazards may be divided and give an example of each.

9. Explain why the number of risks and the severity of losses increase over time.

10. With respect to each of the following, indicate whether you would classify the event or condition as a peril or a hazard: an earthquake, sickness, worry, a careless act, an economic depression.

QUESTIONS FOR DISCUSSION

1. Two 9-year-old boys are watching a television replay of a boxing match between Muhammad Ali and Joe Frazier on a program called "Great Fights of the Century." Since the fight took place before they were old enough to remember the outcome, neither knows who won and they bet on the outcome. Tom bets on Ali and Tim bets on Frazier. Does risk exist in this situation? For Tim? For Tom?

2. Mike says, "The possibility that my house may burn is a pure risk for me, but if I buy insurance, it is a speculative risk for the insurance company." Do you agree? Why or why not?

3. If risk is distasteful, how do you account for the existence of gambling, a pastime in which the participants indicate that they obviously prefer the risk involved to the security of not gambling?

4. What risks do you face as an individual? Which of these risks have you elected to retain and which have you transferred?

5. Both the probability of loss and its potential severity affect the intensity with which risk is felt by an individual. Would you find a 50 percent chance of losing $100 or a 5 percent chance of losing $1000 more distasteful? Why?

SUGGESTIONS FOR ADDITIONAL READING

Berenstein, Peter L. *Against the Gods—The Remarkable Story of Risk.* New York: John Wiley & Sons, Inc., 1996.

Denenberg, Herbert S. et al. *Risk and Insurance,* 2d ed. Englewood Cliffs, N.J.: Prentice-Hall, 1974. Chapter 1.

Hammond, J. D., ed. *Essays in the Theory of Risk and Insurance.* Glenview, Ill.: Scott, Foresman, 1968.

Head, G. L. "An Alternative to Defining Risk as Uncertainty." *Journal of Risk and Insurance,* vol. 34, no. 2 (June 1967).

Houston, D. B. "Risk, Insurance, and Sampling." *Journal of Risk and Insurance,* vol. 31, no. 4 (Dec. 1964).

Knight, F. H. *Risk, Uncertainty and Profit.* Boston: Houghton Mifflin, 1921.

Kulp, C. A., and John W. Hall. *Casualty Insurance,* 4th ed. New York: Ronald Press, 1968. Chapter 1.

Mowbray, A. H., R. H. Blanchard, and C. Arthur Williams. *Insurance,* 6th ed. New York: McGraw–Hill, 1969. Chapter 1.

Pfeffer, I. *Insurance and Economic Theory.* Homewood, Ill.: Richard D. Irwin, 1956.

Willet, A. *The Economic Theory of Risk and Insurance.* Philadelphia: University of Pennsylvania Press, 1951.

Wood, Oliver G., Jr. "Evolution of the Concept of Risk." *Journal of Risk and Insurance,* vol. 31, no. 1 (March 1964).

INTRODUCTION TO RISK MANAGEMENT

It is, generally speaking, all measures conferring security upon the undertaking and requisite peace of mind upon the personnel.

— HENRI FAYOL

CHAPTER OBJECTIVES

When you have finished this chapter, you should be able to

- Describe the evolution of modern risk management and identify the developments that led to the transition from insurance management to risk management
- Define and explain what is meant by the term *risk management*
- Identify the various reporting relationships that the risk management function may assume in an organization
- Identify the two broad approaches to dealing with risk that are recognized by modern risk management theory
- Identify the four techniques that are used in managing risk
- Describe risk management's contribution to the organization
- Distinguish risk management from insurance management and general management

Risk management is a scientific approach to the problem of pure risk, which has as its objective the reduction and elimination of pure risks facing the business firm. Risk management evolved from the field of corporate insurance buying, and is now recognized as a distinct and important function for all businesses and organizations. Many business firms have highly trained individuals who specialize in dealing with pure risk. In some cases this is a full-time job for one person, or even for an entire department within the company. Those who are responsible for the entire program of pure risk management (of which insurance buying is only a part) are risk managers. Although the term *risk management* is a recent phenomenon, the actual practice of risk management is as old as civilization itself. In the broad sense of the term, risk management is the process of protecting one's person and assets. In the narrower sense, it is a

managerial function of business, which uses a scientific approach to dealing with risks. As such, it is based on a specific philosophy and follows a well-defined sequence of steps. In this chapter, we will examine the distinguishing features of risk management.

THE HISTORY OF MODERN RISK MANAGEMENT

Although the term *risk management* may have been used in the special sense in which it was used here earlier, the general trend in its current usage began in the early 1950s. One of the earliest references to the concept of risk management in literature appeared in the *Harvard Business Review* in 1956.[1] In that article, the author proposed what, for the time, seemed a revolutionary idea: that someone within the organization should be responsible for "managing" the organization's pure risks. At the time that the term *risk manager* was suggested, many large corporations already had a staff position referred to as the "Insurance Manager." This was an apt title, since, in most cases, the position entailed procuring, maintaining, and paying for a portfolio of insurance policies obtained for the benefit of the company. The earliest insurance managers were employed by the first of the giant corporations, the railroads and steel companies, which hired them as early as the turn of the century. As the capital investment in other industries grew, insurance came to be a more and more significant item in the budget of firms. Gradually, the insurance-buying function was assigned as a specific responsibility to in-house specialists.

Although risk management has its roots in corporate insurance buying, the transition from insurance buying to risk management was not an inevitable evolutionary process. The emergence of risk management was a revolution that signaled a dramatic shift in philosophy. It occurred when the attitude toward insurance changed and insurance lost its traditional status as the standard approach for dealing with a corporation's risk. For the insurance manager, insurance had always been the standard accepted approach to dealing with risks. Although insurance management included techniques other than insurance (such as noninsurance or retention and loss prevention and control), these techniques had always been considered primarily as supplements to insurance.

The preeminence of insurance as a method for dealing with pure risks by corporate insurance buyers is probably understandable. Many of the earliest insurance buyers were skilled insurance technicians, often hired from an insurance agency or brokerage firm. They understood the principles of insurance and applied their knowledge to obtain the best coverage for the premium dollars spent. Traditional insurance textbooks had always preached against the dollar-trading practices that characterized some lines of insurance and most insurance buyers knew that economies could be achieved through the judicial use of deductibles. Despite these precursors of the risk management philosophy, the notion persisted that insurance was the preferred approach for dealing with risk. When insurance was generally agreed to be the standard approach to dealing with pure risks, the decision not to insure was courageous indeed. If an uninsured loss occurred, the risk manager would surely have been criticized for the decision not to insure. The problem was that not much consideration was given to whether or not insurance was the most appropriate solution to the organization's risk. The insurance managers' function was to buy insurance and they could hardly be criticized for doing so. After all, that was their job.

What caused the change in attitude toward insurance and the shift to the risk management philosophy? Although there is room for disagreement, it can be argued that the risk management philosophy had to wait for the development and growth of decision theory, with its emphasis on cost-benefit analysis, expected value, and the other tools of scientific decision making.

Whether it was an accident of timing or cause and effect, the risk management movement in the business community coincided with a revision of curriculum in business colleges throughout the United States. During the 1950s, two studies of the curriculum of business colleges were published in the United States: the Gordon and Howells Report and the Pierson Report.[2] Both studies concluded with

[1] See Russell B. Gallagher, "Risk Management: A New Phase of Cost Control," *Harvard Business Review* (September–October 1956).

[2] Robert A. Gordon and James E. Howell, *Higher Education for Business* (New York: Columbia University Press, 1959) and Franck C. Pierson et al., *The Education of American Businessmen* (New York: McGraw-Hill, 1959).

stinging criticisms of the curriculum at U.S. business colleges, arguing that it was outdated and did not help to prepare students for their future role as decision makers. Although some business faculty took issue with the conclusions of these reports, business schools began to change their curricula, adding new courses and changing the focus of others. The most significant changes in the curriculum were the introduction of *operations research* and *management science,* with a shift in focus from descriptive courses to normative decision theory.[3] Where previous courses described *how* and *why* people chose among options, prescriptive decision theory was introduced to focus on how choices *should* be made.

Not surprisingly, insurance faculty were among the first business academics to embrace decision theory. Many were trained in actuarial science, the mathematical underpinning of insurance. As the earliest quantitative specialists in business schools, they were knowledgeable in the methodologies of decision theory. Equally important, they had an inventory of interesting questions to which these tools could be applied in business situations—questions involving the choices among the techniques that could be used to address risk. Academics not only began to question the central role that had always been assigned to insurance, they developed the theoretical justification for the challenge.

Simultaneously—and independently—system engineers in the military and aerospace industry were developing new approaches to loss prevention and control that came collectively to be referred to as *systems safety.* Systems safety evolved in response to increasingly complex problems that needed to be solved and for which traditional approaches were inadequate. The initial stimulus for systems safety was the creation of the intercontinental ballistic missile (ICBM) system, which served as the key element in the nation's cold-war strategy of deterrence through the threat of nuclear retaliation. Later, systems safety was applied to the U.S. space program.

As the title indicates, systems safety views a process, a situation, a problem, a machine, or any other entity as a system—rather than as just a

process, situation, problem, or machine. An accident occurs when a human or a mechanical component of a system fails to function when it should and the objective of systems safety is to identify these failures and either eliminate them or minimize their effects. Systems safety rejects the notion that accidents are a matter of chance—something that simply happens. Instead, accidents are created events, enabled to happen by choices or decisions. Viewed from this perspective, accidents are not an inevitable part of the workplace, not *acts of God,* or simply unlucky breaks. If the causes of accidents can be identified, they can be eliminated and accidents can be prevented.[4]

As time passed, the influence of the changes in business college curriculum and systems safety began to spread through the insurance-buying community. Some corporate insurance buyers came to realize that there might be more cost-efficient ways of dealing with risk. It occurred to them that perhaps the most effective approach would be to prevent losses from happening in the first place, and to minimize the economic consequences of the losses they were unable to prevent. From this evolved the notion that management, having identified and evaluated the risks to which it is exposed, can plan to avoid the occurrence of certain losses and minimize the impact of others. This led to the conclusion that the cost of risk can be *managed,* and held to the lowest levels possible.

The risk management philosophy made sense, and it spread from organization to organization. When the insurance buyer's professional association decided to change its name to the Risk and Insurance Management Society (RIMS) in 1975, the change signaled a transition that was well under way. The Risk and Insurance Management Society publishes a magazine called *Risk Management* and the Insurance Division of the American Management Association publishes a wide range of reports and studies to assist risk managers. In addition, the Insurance Institute of America developed an education

[3] Decision theory is a branch of *management science,* a broad discipline that includes all rational approaches to decision making that are based on the application of scientific methodology. Decision theory is applied to complex problems in which the outcomes of the various choices are uncertain, including situations in which the probabilities of outcomes are unknown.

[4] For an interesting perspective on the development of the systems approach to risk management, see Vernon L. Grose, *Managing Risk: Systematic Loss Prevention for Executives* (Englewood Cliffs, N.J.: Prentice-Hall, 1987). Grose was a pioneer in the application of systems methodology to controlling risk managed risks in NASA's Projects Mercury, Gemini, and Apollo. In 1969, he was appointed to the NASA Safety Advisory Group for Space Flight. He later served as a member of the National Transportation Safety Board and the National Highway Safety Advisory Commission.

program in risk management with a series of examinations leading to a diploma in risk management. The curriculum for this program was revised in 1973, and a professional designation, Associate in Risk Management (ARM), was instituted.

As it exists today, risk management represents the merging of three specialties: decision theory, risk financing, and risk control. Decision theory has its roots in operations research and management science. The risk financing specialty came from the disciplines of finance and insurance, and the risk control specialty represents the merger of traditional safety management and loss prevention, as developed by the insurance industry, and systems safety from the military and aerospace industry.

RISK MANAGEMENT DEFINED

As a relatively new discipline, risk management has been defined in a variety of ways by different writers and users of the term. Although they vary in detail, most definitions offered thus far stress two points: first, that risk management is concerned principally with pure risk, and, second, that it is a process or function that involves managing those risks. We propose the following definition of risk management.

> Risk management is a scientific approach to dealing with pure risks by anticipating possible accidental losses and designing and implementing procedures that minimize the occurrence of loss or the financial impact of the losses that do occur.

Note first that risk management is described as a "scientific approach" to the problem of pure risks. Although risk management seeks to proceed in a scientific manner, it must be admitted that risk management is not a science in the same sense as the physical sciences are, anymore than management itself is a science. As the term is generally understood, a *science* is a body of knowledge based on laws and principles that can be used to predict outcomes. Scientists seek to discover and test these laws through laboratory experiments aimed at uncovering the principles that govern or control the events being studied. The standard method of physical sciences, for example, is the controlled experiment, but risk managers cannot use this method. Instead, risk management derives its rules (laws) from the general knowledge of experience, through deduction, and

from precepts drawn from other disciplines, particularly decision theory. Although risk management is not a science, it uses a scientific approach to the problem of pure risk. This scientific approach that distinguishes risk management from earlier approaches to risk decisions can be illustrated by contrasting it with those earlier approaches.

Humans have always found ways to deal with risks, and have reacted to adversity in a variety of ways. At the personal level, the natural instinct for self-preservation dictates an instinctive reaction to danger and hazards. Like most creatures, we react automatically to danger, taking whatever measures are available to avoid injury or loss. These instinctive reactions to risk situations are not decisions, but the innate self-preservation instinct.

In addition to our instinctive reactions to danger, much of what one might classify as personal risk management is a learned behavior. "Don't play with matches," "Don't tease the dog," "Don't run with scissors" are all axioms of risk management that are instilled in the individual from an early age.

Individuals acquire a body of principles that dictate patterns of action that are designed to protect and preserve. They become innate standards for behavior that, while sometimes violated, represent rules for personal loss prevention and control.

Another part of human behavior in responding to risk is institutionalized. Many insurance-buying decisions are dictated by legal, contractual, or societal conventions. The youthful driver does not really want to buy automobile insurance. He or she wants to drive a car. Most states require that, if you drive, you must have insurance. Similarly, while there are probably some consumers who must decide whether to purchase homeowners insurance, for the overwhelming majority, there really is little choice. Unless the individual can purchase the home for cash, there will be a mortgage, and the lender will insist on insurance. In short, many risk management and insurance decisions at the personal level are dictated by convention.

Often, the same institutional, legal, and societal pressures dictate risk management and insurance decisions in the business world. Business managers have found themselves responsible for the management of a firm's risks without any notion of how to go about the process. Bewildered by the confusing array of insurance coverages available, many business managers turned the problem of what to buy over to an outside party, such as an insurance agent. More often than not, the decision to delegate the

management of risk to an outside party is based on the misperception that insurance buying involves complicated decisions that the business manager is incapable of making. And because the agent does not want to be in a defensive position when a loss occurs, he or she recommends more rather than less insurance. The result is often dissatisfaction on the part of the buyer over "the high cost of insurance."

Risk management, by approaching the decisions related to pure risk scientifically, is a solution to the challenges in dealing with pure risks. In fact, the distinguishing feature of risk management is the way in which it approaches the decision-making process. Risk management seeks to make the "best" decision about how to deal with a particular risk. In Chapter 4, we will see how this is done.

RISK MANAGEMENT TOOLS

Our definition of risk management states that it deals with risk by designing and implementing procedures that minimize the occurrence of loss or the financial impact of the losses that do occur. This indicates the two broad techniques that are used in risk management for dealing with risks. In the terminology of modern risk management, the techniques for dealing with risk are grouped into two broad approaches: risk control and risk financing. Risk control focuses on minimizing the risk of loss to which the firm is exposed, and includes the techniques of *avoidance* and *reduction*. Risk financing concentrates on arranging the availability of funds to meet losses arising from the risks that remain after the application of risk control techniques, and includes the tools of *retention* and *transfer*.

Risk Control

Broadly defined, *risk control* consists of those techniques that are designed to minimize, at the least possible costs, those risks to which the organization is exposed. Risk control methods include risk avoidance, and the various approaches at reducing risk through loss prevention and control efforts.

Risk Avoidance Technically, avoidance takes place when decisions are made that prevent a risk from even coming into existence. Risks are avoided when the organization refuses to accept the risk, even for an instant. The classic example of risk avoidance by a business firm is a decision not to manufacture a partic-

ularly dangerous product because of the inherent risk. Given the potential for liability claims that may result if a consumer is injured by a product, some firms judge that the risk is not worth the potential gain.

Risk avoidance should be used in those instances in which the exposure has catastrophic potential and the risk cannot be reduced or transferred. Generally, these conditions will exist in the case of risks for which both the frequency and the severity are high and neither can be reduced.

Although avoidance is the only alternative for dealing with some risks, it is a negative rather than a positive approach. Personal advancement of the individual and progress in the economy both require risk taking. If avoidance is used extensively, the firm may not be able to achieve its primary objectives. A manufacturer cannot avoid the risk of product liability by avoiding the risk and still stay in business. For this reason, avoidance is, in a sense, the last resort in dealing with risk. It is used when there is no other alternative.

Risk Reduction Risk reduction consists of all techniques that are designed to reduce the likelihood of loss, or the potential severity of those losses that do occur. It is common to distinguish between those efforts aimed at preventing losses from occurring and those aimed at minimizing the severity of loss if it should occur, referring to them respectively as *loss prevention* and *loss control*. As the designation implies, the emphasis of loss prevention is on preventing the occurrence of loss; that is, on controlling the frequency. Prohibition against smoking in areas where flammables are present is a loss prevention measure. Similarly, measures to decrease the number of employee injuries by installing protective devices around machinery are aimed at reducing the frequency of loss. Other risk reduction techniques focus on lessening the severity of those losses that actually do occur, such as, the installation of sprinkler systems. These are loss control measures. Other methods of controlling severity include segregation or dispersion of assets and salvage efforts. Dispersion of assets will not reduce the number of fires or explosions that may occur, but it can limit the potential severity of the losses that do occur. Salvage operations after a loss has occurred can minimize the resulting costs of the loss.

Another distinction is sometimes made between the "engineering approach" to loss prevention and control, in which the principal emphasis is on the removal of hazards that may cause accidents, and the

"human behavior approach," in which the elimination of unsafe acts is stressed. This distinction is based on the focus of control measures and represents two schools of thought regarding the emphasis in loss prevention and control. The human behavior approach is based on the view that since most accidents result from human failure, the most effective approach to loss prevention is to change people's behavior. The engineering approach, in contrast, emphasizes systems analysis and mechanical design, aimed at protecting people from careless acts that are viewed as perhaps inevitable. National Safety Council ads on television and in-print media urging drivers not to drink typify the human behavior approach. Air bags in automobiles, which are activated without human intervention, typify the engineering approach.

A final way of classifying risk reduction measures is by the timing of their application, which may be prior to the loss event, at the time of the event, or after the loss event. Safety inspections and drivers' training classes illustrate measures that are designed to prevent the occurrence before losses occur. Seat belts and air bags are designed to minimize the amount of damage at the time an accident occurs. Post-event loss prevention measures related to auto accidents include negotiating with injured persons for an out-of-court settlement or a stern defense in litigation.

Risk Financing

Risk financing, in contrast to risk control, consists of those techniques that focus on arrangements designed to guarantee the availability of funds to meet those losses that do occur. Fundamentally, risk financing takes the form of retention or transfer. All risks that cannot be avoided or reduced must, by definition, be transferred or retained. Frequently, transfer and retention are used in combination for a particular risk, with a portion of the risk retained and a part transferred.

Risk Retention Risk retention is perhaps the most common method of dealing with risk.[5] Individuals, like organizations, face an almost unlimited number of risks; in most cases, nothing is done about them. Risk retention may be conscious or unconscious (i.e., intentional or unintentional). Because risk retention is the "residual" or "default" risk management technique, any exposures that are not avoided, reduced, or transferred are retained. This means that when nothing is done about a particular exposure, the risk is retained. Unintentional (unconscious) retention occurs when a risk is not recognized. The individual or organization unwittingly and unintentionally retains the risk of loss arising out of the exposure. Unintentional retention can also occur in those instances in which the risk has been recognized, but when the measures designed to deal with it are improperly implemented. If, for example, the risk manager recognizes the exposure to loss in connection with a particular exposure and intends to transfer that exposure through insurance, but then acquires an insurance policy that does not fully cover the loss, the risk is retained.

Unintentional risk retention is always undesirable. Because the risk is not perceived, the risk manager is never afforded the opportunity to make the decision concerning what should be done about it on a rational basis. Also, when the unintentional retention occurs as a result of improper implementation of the technique that was designed to deal with the exposure, the resulting retention is contrary to the intent of the risk manager.

Risk retention may be voluntary or involuntary. Voluntary retention results from a decision to retain risk rather than to avoid or transfer it. Involuntary retention occurs when it is not possible to avoid, reduce, or transfer the exposure to an insurance company. Uninsurable exposures are an example of involuntary retention.

Some forms of voluntary retention occur by default. When an organization purchases insurance that does not adequately cover the exposure, it retains the risk of loss for that part of the exposure that is inadequately insured. When a $5-million building is insured for $4 million, the organization retains a $1-million risk of loss. Similarly, in the case of liability insurance, an organization retains the risk of loss in excess of the limits of coverage that it carries. A business that carries a $5-million umbrella, for example, tacitly assumes the risk of all losses in excess of this limit. Although the risk manager may explicitly consider the decision in this context, selecting the $5-million limit is a decision to retain risks in excess of that limit.

[5] Some writers use the term risk *assumption* rather than retention. Since "to assume" implies that the object is somehow "taken on," retention, which implies that something is "kept," is more appropriate. The distinction is a semantic one, but risks are retained and the losses that occur are assumed.

A final distinction that may be drawn is between funded retention and unfunded retention. In a funded retention program, the firm earmarks assets and holds them in some liquid or semiliquid form against the possible losses that are retained. The need for segregated assets to fund the retention program will depend on the firm's cash flow and the size of the losses that may result from the retained exposure.

The form that risk retention may assume varies widely. Retention may be accompanied by specific budgetary allocations to meet uninsured losses and may involve the accumulation of a fund to meet deviations from expected losses. On the other hand, retention may be less formal, without any form of specific funding. A larger firm may use a loss-sensitive rating program (in which the premium varies directly with losses), various forms of self-insured retention plans, or even a captive insurer. The small organization uses deductibles, noninsurance, and various other forms of retention techniques. The specific programs may differ, but the approach is the same.

Risk Transfer Transfer may be accomplished in a variety of ways. Transfer of risk through the purchase of insurance contracts is, of course, a primary approach to risk transfer. In consideration of a specific payment (the premium) by one party, the second party contracts to indemnify the first party up to a certain limit for the specified loss that may or may not occur.

Another example of risk transfer is the process of hedging, in which an individual guards against the risk of price changes in one asset by buying or selling another asset whose price changes in an offsetting direction. For example, futures markets have been created to allow farmers to protect themselves against changes in the price of their crop between planting and harvesting. A farmer sells a futures contract, which is actually a promise to deliver at a fixed price in the future. If the value of the farmer's crop declines, the value of the farmer's future position goes up to offset the loss.[6]

Risk transfer may also take the form of contractual arrangements such as hold-harmless agreements, in which one individual assumes another's possibility of loss.[7] For example, a tenant may agree under the terms of a lease to pay any judgments against the landlord that arise out of the use of the premises. Risk transfer may also involve subcontracting certain activities, or it may take the form of surety bonds.[8]

RISK MANAGEMENT AS A BUSINESS FUNCTION

As noted earlier, risk management is a merger of the disciplines of decision theory, finance, insurance theory, and loss prevention and control specialties. Because risk management draws on these different disciplines, it is sometimes considered a subset of one of them. In many colleges and universities, insurance and risk management are a part of the finance curriculum, while in other schools they are located in another department. In fact, the study of risk management is a separate and distinct discipline, which draws on and integrates the knowledge from a variety of other business fields. The same ambiguity about the nature of risk management is reflected in the view of risk management within many organizations. In some organizations, it is viewed as a part of finance; in others it may be considered part of the safety organizations. In the organization, as in the academic environment, risk management is a distinct and separate function of business.

The famous French management authority, Henri Fayol, writing in 1916, divided all activities of industrial undertakings into six broad functions, including one (which Fayol called *security*) that is essentially equivalent to what we now call risk management. The six broad functions into which Fayol divided industrial undertaking were *technical activities* (such

[6] Hedging operations are made possible by speculators who buy and sell futures contracts in the hope of making a profit as a result of a change in price. The speculator attempts to predict the prices months in advance of delivery and buys and sells on the basis of these estimates. It is the speculator's willingness to buy and sell futures that makes possible the hedging process, and it is to the speculator that the risk is transferred.

[7] Although risk transfer by means of insurance constitutes risk financing, some transfers (such as hold-harmless agreements or other contractual transfers) are a form of risk control.

[8] Risk sharing is sometimes cited as a fifth way of dealing with risk. Risk is shared when there is some type of arrangement to share losses. Risk sharing may be viewed as a special case of risk transfer or risk retention. It is a form of transfer, because the risk of the individual is transferred to the group. It may also be viewed as a form of retention, in which the risks of a number of individuals are retained collectively. As we will see, one of the basic features of insurance is the sharing of risk by the members of the group.

as production and manufacturing), *commercial activities* (buying and selling), *financial activities* (finding sources of capital and managing capital flows), *accounting activities* (recording and analyzing financial information), *managerial activities* (organizing, planning, command, coordination, and control), and *security activities* (protecting the property and persons of the enterprise).[9]

While the other functions described by Fayol all developed as well-defined academic disciplines, and became divisions in the corporate structure headed by a vice president, "security" somehow got lost in the shuffle, and it was not until the 1950s that Fayol's six-function division of business activities was resurrected.

Distinguishing Characteristics of Risk Management

A better understanding of the risk management function and its place in the organization can be gained by distinguishing risk management from general management and from insurance management.

Risk Management Distinguished from General Management Initially, risk management should be distinguished from general management. Risk management differs from general management in its scope. Risk management deals with risk, but so too does general management. The difference, of course, is in the type of risks with which general management and risk management deal. General management is responsible for dealing with *all* risks facing the organization, including both speculative and pure risks.

The risk manager's area of responsibility is narrower in scope, and is limited primarily to pure risks only. General managers, who have stewardship of assets and income of the firm, are concerned with losses arising from both pure and speculative risks. They delegate to risk managers the duties associated with pure risks, and the risk manager becomes responsible for conserving the assets and the income of the organization from losses associated with pure risks. Thus, while the responsibility of "general" management is to conserve the assets of the organization and maximize profit, the risk manager is responsible

for a part of this general responsibility. More specifically, the risk manager is responsible for that segment of general management's mission that relates to pure risks.

Risk Management Distinguished from Insurance Management In addition to its relationship to general management, risk management should also be distinguished from insurance management. Risk management is broader than insurance management, in that it deals with both insurable and uninsurable risks and the choice of the appropriate techniques for dealing with these risks. Because risk management evolved from insurance management, the focus of some risk managers has been primarily with *insurable* risk. Properly, the focus should include all *pure* risk, insurable and uninsurable. In other words, the risk manager cannot ignore those pure risks that are not insurable. A good example is shoplifting losses. Although shoplifting losses represent a pure risk exposure, they are not generally insurable on an economical basis.

Risk management also differs from insurance management in philosophy. The insurance manager views insurance as the accepted norm or standard approach to dealing with risk, and retention is regarded as an exception to this standard. The insurance manager contemplates his or her insurance program and asks: "Are there any risks that I should retain?" "How much will I save in insurance costs if I retain them?" In viewing loss prevention measures, the insurance manager asks, "How much will this measure reduce my insurance costs?" "How long will it take for a new sprinkler system to pay for itself in reduced fire insurance premiums?" The risk manager, in contrast, views insurance as simply one of several approaches to dealing with pure risks. Rather than asking "Which risks should I retain?" the risk manager asks "Which risks must I insure?"

The difference is obviously one of emphasis. The insurance management philosophy views insurance as the accepted norm, and retention or noninsurance must be justified by a premium reduction that is, in some sense or another, "big enough." Under the risk management philosophy, it is insurance that must be justified. Since the cost of insurance must generally exceed the average losses of those who are insured, the risk manager believes that insurance is a last resort, and should be used only when necessary.

Risk management then, is something more than insurance management, in that it deals with both

[9] Henri Fayol, *General and Industrial Management* (New York: Pitman Publishing Corporation, 1949), p. 4. This is an English translation of the book originally published in French in 1916.

insurable and uninsurable risks, but it is something less than general management since it does not deal (except incidentally) with business risk.

Risk Management's Contribution to the Organization

Risk management can contribute to the organization's general goals in several ways. The first and most important one is in guaranteeing, insofar as possible, that the organization will not be prevented from pursuing its other goals as a result of losses associated with pure risks. If risk management made no contributions other than guaranteeing survival, this alone would seem to justify its existence. But risk management can contribute to corporate and organizational goals in other ways.

Risk management can contribute directly to profit by controlling the cost of risk for the organization—that is, by achieving the goal of economy. Since profits depend on the level of expenses relative to income, to the extent that risk management activities reduce expenses, they directly increase profits. There are several ways in which risk management activities can directly affect the level of costs. One, of course, is in the area of insurance buying. To the extent that the risk manager is able to achieve economies in the purchase of insurance, the reduced cost will increase profits. In choosing between transfer and retention, the risk manager will select the most cost-effective approach. This means that expenses for risk transfer will generally be lower in organizations in which the choice between transfer and retention considers the relative cost of each approach.

Risk management can also reduce expenses through risk control measures. To the extent that the cost of loss prevention and control measures is less than the dollar amount of losses that are prevented, the expense of uninsured loss is reduced. In addition, since loss prevention and control measures can also reduce the cost of insurance, risk control has a dual effect on expenses. Risk control measures that reduce the cost of losses include those measures that prevent losses from occurring as well as those that reduce the amount of loss when a loss does occur.

In addition to the reduction in expenses associated with losses, risk management can, in some instances, increase income. It can also be argued that when the pure risks facing an organization are minimized—through appropriate control and financing techniques—the firm has greater latitude in the speculative risks it can undertake. Although it is useful to distinguish between pure and speculative risks with respect to the manner in which they are addressed and the responsibility for dealing with them, there are inevitable trade-offs between pure and speculative risk in the overall risk portfolio of an organization. It has been argued that the total amount of risk that an organization faces is important, since firms with higher total risk are more likely to find themselves in financial distress than firms with lower total risk. When the organization faces significant pure risks that cannot be (or simply are not) reduced or transferred, its ability to bear speculative risk is reduced. By managing the amount of pure risk with which the organization must contend, risk management increases the firm's ability to engage in speculative risks.

Risk management can also permit an organization to engage in activities that involve speculative risk by minimizing the pure risks associated with such ventures. Consider, for example, the organization contemplating an entry into international markets. This decision will create both pure and speculative risks for that organization. If the combination of pure and speculative risks exceeds the risk threshold that management is willing to accept, the international venture may be abandoned. If, on the other hand, the risk manager can reduce the level of pure risk, the aggregate pure and speculative risk may be reduced to a level that management finds acceptable. To illustrate, suppose the corporation's top management is considering setting up a subsidiary in a politically troubled country. The threat of expropriation may appear to be too great and might cause management to reject the opportunity in favor of a safer but less profitable alternative. However, if the risk manager reports that political risk insurance is available and reasonably priced, management may decide in favor of the opportunity and thereby generate increased revenue and profits. The risk manager, who theoretically is responsible for managing all pure risks and can choose from many alternative risk treatment methods, is also in a position to contribute substantially to the operating results of the corporation.[10]

[10] See Marshall W. Reavis, "The Corporate Risk Manager's Contribution to Profit," *The Journal of Risk and Insurance*, vol. 36, no. 4 (September 1969), pp. 473–479.

The Risk Manager's Job

The term *risk manager* can be used in a functional sense to mean anyone who performs the risk management job, regardless of whether that person is an employee of the organization, an outside consultant, or an agent or broker. As the term will be used here, however, it will refer to an individual employed by the organization who is responsible for the risk management function.

Even when viewed from this perspective, every organization has a risk manager. The individual may not recognize that he or she is performing the risk management function, but in every organization someone must make decisions that relate to the pure risks facing the organization. In a large corporation, the risk manager is (or should be) a well-paid professional who has a specific title and job description that relates to the management of risks. In a small company, he or she may be the president or managing partner. In a moderate-sized company, he may be the chief financial officer or someone on an intermediate staff level.

The scope of the risk manager's job differs across organizations. In the broadest case, the risk manager has overall responsibility for all risk control and risk-financing activities, including the organization's employee benefit plan. Periodic surveys conducted by the Risk and Insurance Management Society reveal that the responsibility and duties of risk managers vary with the size of the organization. In some instances, the risk managers are also responsible for the firm's employee benefit plans, while, in other cases, their responsibility is limited to those risks that threaten the firm itself.

About one-fourth of risk managers reported having responsibility for some loss prevention activities within their organizations. A higher percentage reported more responsibility for safety and fire engineering, however, than for security, which seems to indicate some fragmentation in responsibility for loss prevention in organizations.

Position in the Organization In general, one usually finds risk managers in one of three corporate departments, depending on the history and development of risk management in the particular firm. In some organizations, the risk manager evolved from the insurance manager, who has traditionally been located in the finance division or under the comptroller. In these companies, risk management is viewed as a financial function and reports to the finance department. In companies in which the risk manager evolved from the employee benefits manager, the risk manager may be in the personnel division. Finally, in some companies, the risk manager will have developed from the safety function. Here, the risk manager will generally be located in the division that traditionally housed the safety director, usually the production division.

Most risk managers have a financial orientation, reporting to a vice president–finance, treasurer, or comptroller, although there is a growing school of thought that says he or she should be in a less specialized department, reporting to an executive vice president or even the president to illustrate the company-wide scope of risk management activities.

Risk Management and Speculative Risks

The term risk management is increasingly used to describe the management of speculative risk, particularly by persons in the field of finance. The U.S. Department of Agriculture, for example, uses the term risk management in reference to risks related to commodity market prices and the management of these risks by hedging, futures, options, and derivatives.[11] Similarly, banks and other financial institutions define the term *risk management* to include the management of such financial risks as interest rate risk and credit risk. To preserve the distinction between risk management in its original sense (as an approach for dealing with pure risk) and the management of financial risk, the term *financial risk management* is often used for the latter.

In recent years, there has been considerable discussion about the potential shift toward *enterprise risk management,* which would bring together the management of all risks—financial, operational, strategic, and traditionally insured hazards—into a single portfolio. Those who advocate a transition to enterprise risk management include some risk managers (and risk management scholars) who believe that the traditional focus of risk management on pure risk has been too narrow. They conclude that the convergence of responsibility for managing pure risks and other risks is a foregone conclusion and that the responsibility of risk managers should be

[11] Derivatives are financial instruments (investments) whose value is derived from the value of other assets, such as commodities or financial indexes.

expanded to include other risks, especially those relating to other facets of finance. "Risk is risk," they argue, "and the distinction between pure risk and speculative risk is an artificial one created and perpetuated by academics." Corporate managers are concerned (or should be) about the total risk portfolio of the firm and attempt to manage risks, regardless of the source. They buy insurance to protect against losses that may arise from pure risks, and they use commodity and financial futures to hedge against fluctuations in interest rates and foreign exchange rates. In most cases, the decisions about how the organization will deal with the various risks it faces have been made independently; one person (or department) deals with pure risks, another deals with the risk of interest rates and fluctuations in foreign exchange, and others deal with production and market risks. Critics make the case that since the separate decisions collectively affect the total risk of the firm, they should be integrated into a single framework that will determine the totality of risk, including both pure and speculative.

The counterargument is that whether the distinction between pure and speculative risk is real or artificial, the techniques used to address some types of risks differ significantly from those used to address others. Despite the arguments of those who would like to expand the concept of risk management, other authorities see clear and unequivocal distinctions among risks and have no problem in delineating pure risks from speculative risks. The reason that decisions about different risks have been made separately is not that the risks arise from different sources, but because the techniques that are used to deal with them are different. Corporate treasurers who deal with interest rate and currency risks refer to their activities as *risk management,* as indeed it is. But the expertise required for managing these risks is different from the expertise required for managing pure risks. Although some risk managers have the expertise to deal in the arena of hedging, futures, options and derivatives, there are others who feel sufficiently challenged by their existing responsibilities. For the foreseeable future, these risk managers will constitute the overwhelming majority of the profession.

Thus far, the concept of enterprise risk management is more theoretical that a reflection of practice. What remains unclear is who will have ultimate responsibility for managing a company's enterprise risk portfolio. The disagreement is not about whether financial risks susceptible to treatment by deriva-

tives, futures, and options should be managed, but whether they should be managed by the same person who manages the risks of fires, explosions, embezzlements, and legal liability. Nor is there disagreement that someone needs to manage the organization's total risk portfolio. The dispute is over whether this overall management of enterprise risk should be done by the risk manager. Skeptics who question whether the transition to enterprise risk management will actually occur argue that there is already an authority with the overall responsibility for managing enterprise risk, the CEO or chief executive officer.

MISCONCEPTIONS ABOUT RISK MANAGEMENT

Although risk management has become a popular topic of discussion, some of what is discussed reflects a misunderstanding of risk management. Some of these misconceptions reflect a misreading of the literature, while others reflect defects in the literature itself. The first misconception is that the risk management concept is applicable principally to large organizations. The second is that the risk management approach to dealing with pure risks seeks to minimize the role of insurance.

Universal Applicability

If one were to judge on the basis of much of the literature dealing with the concept of risk management, it would be easy to conclude that risk management has no useful application except with respect to the problems facing a large industrial complex. This misconception can easily result from the fact that many of the techniques with which writers have been preoccupied (e.g., self-insurance plans, captive insurers, etc.) *do* apply primarily to giant organizations. Most of the articles on risk management have been written by practicing professional risk managers. It is natural that they would write about the techniques they use in their own companies, and virtually all professional risk managers are employed by large organizations. But it cannot be overemphasized that the risk management philosophy and approach applies to organizations of all sizes (and to individuals as well), even though some of the more esoteric techniques may have limited application in the case of the average organization.

As the risk manager's position has grown within the corporate framework and *risk management* has become a recognized term in business jargon, the interest in risk management has increased in businesses of all sizes. It is obvious that the small firm cannot afford a full-time professional risk manager, yet the principles of risk management are as applicable to a small organization as to a giant international firm. As this text will illustrate, the principles of risk management are nothing more than common sense applied to the management of pure risks facing an individual or organization. The principles are applicable to organizations of all sizes, as well as to individuals and families. Although the techniques may differ in scope and complexity, the same risk management tools are used in either case.

Anti-Insurance Bias?

The second misconception about risk management—that it is anti-insurance in its orientation and seeks to minimize the role of insurance in dealing with risk—also stems from risk management literature. Much of the literature on risk management has also been preoccupied with topics related to risk retention, self-insurance programs, and captive insurance companies. Indeed, if one were to ask practitioners in the insurance field to describe the essence of risk management—that is, its philosophy—many would respond that the major thrust of risk management is on the retention of risk and on the use of deductibles. Although it is true that retention is an important technique for dealing with risks, this is not what risk management is all about.

The essence of risk management is *not* on the retention of exposures. Instead it involves dealing with risks by whatever mechanism is most appropriate. In many instances, commercial insurance will be the only acceptable approach. While the risk management philosophy suggests that there are some risks that should be retained, it also dictates that there are some risks that must be transferred. The primary focus of the risk manager should be on the identification of the risks that must be transferred to achieve the primary risk management objective. Only after this determination has been made does the question of which risks should be retained arise. More often than not, determining which risks should be transferred also determines which risks will be retained: the residual class that does not need to be transferred.

RISK MANAGEMENT AND THE INDIVIDUAL

Risk management evolved formally as a function of business. Insurance managers became risk managers, and with the transition certain principles of scientific insurance buying, which had always been used to some extent, were formalized. For the most part, these principles are commonsense applications of the cost-benefit principle, and they are equally applicable to the insurance buying decisions of the individual or the family unit. Like the business firm, the individual or family unit has a limited number of dollars that can be allocated toward the protection of assets and income against loss. Personal risk management is concerned with the allocation of these dollars in some optimal manner, and makes use of the same techniques as does business risk management. To achieve maximum protection against static losses, the individual must select from among the risk management tools of retention, reduction, and transfer.

THE RISK MANAGEMENT PROCESS

The risk management process can be divided into a series of individual steps that must be accomplished in managing risks. Identifying these individual steps helps to guarantee that important phases in the process will not be overlooked. Although it is useful for the purpose of analysis to discuss each of these steps separately, it should be understood that in actual practice the steps tend to merge with one another. The six steps in the risk management process are:

1. Determination of objectives
2. Identification of risks
3. Evaluation of risks
4. Considering alternatives and selecting the risk treatment device
5. Implementing the decision
6. Evaluation and review

Determination of Objectives

The first step in the risk management process is the determination of the objectives of the risk management program: deciding precisely what it is that the

organization would like its risk management program to do. Despite its importance, determining the objectives of the program is the step in the risk management process that is most likely to be overlooked. As a consequence, the risk management efforts of many firms are fragmented and inconsistent. Many of the defects in risk management programs stem from an ambiguity regarding the objectives of the program.

Mehr and Hedges, in their classic *Risk Management in the Business Enterprise,* suggest that risk management has a variety of objectives, which they classify into two categories: pre-loss objectives and post-loss objectives, and suggest the following objectives in each category.[12]

Post-Loss Objectives	Pre-Loss Objectives
Survival	Economy
Continuity of operations	Reduction in anxiety
Earning stability	Meeting externally imposed
Continued growth	obligations
Social responsibility	Social responsibility

Although all of the pre-loss and post-loss objectives suggested by Mehr and Hedges have relevance in the risk management effort, multiple objectives such as these naturally raise the question, which objective is primary.

Value Maximization Objectives One eminent scholar has argued that the ultimate goal of risk management is the same as the ultimate goal of the other functions in a business—to maximize the value of the organization.[13] Modern financial theory suggests that this value that is to be maximized is reflected in the market value of the organization's common stock. According to this view, risk management decisions should be appraised against the standard of whether or not they contribute to value maximization. It is a view difficult to disagree with; it is also a view that is not inconsistent with the objectives suggested by Mehr and Hedges. With limited exceptions, all the Mehr and Hedges objectives do, in one way or another, contribute to value maximization. Value maximization is the ultimate goal of the organiza-

tion, and is a reasonable standard for appraising corporate decisions in a consistent manner. It is also a logical objective for the individual or family. At the same time, the value maximization objective has some limitations for risk management. The most important is that it is relevant primarily to the business sector. For other organizations—nonprofit organizations and government bodies—value maximization is not particularly relevant.

The Primary Objective of Risk Management
The first objective of risk management, like the first law of nature, is survival—to guarantee the continuing existence of the organization as an operating entity in the economy. The primary goal of risk management is not to contribute directly to the other goals of the organization—whatever they may be. Rather it is to guarantee that the attainment of these other goals will not be prevented by losses that might arise out of pure risks. This means that the most important objective is not to minimize costs or to contribute to the profit of the organization. Nor is it to comply with legal requirements or to meet some nebulous responsibility related to social responsibility of the firm. It can and does do all of these things, but they are not the principal reason for its existence. The main objective of risk management is to preserve the operating effectiveness of the organization. We propose the following primary objective for the risk management function.

> The primary objective of risk management is to preserve the operating effectiveness of the organization; that is, to guarantee that the organization is not prevented from achieving its other objectives by the losses that might arise out of pure risk.

The risk management objective must reflect the uncertainty inherent in the risk management situation. Because one cannot know what losses will occur and what the amount of such losses will be, the arrangements made to guarantee survival in the event of loss must reflect the worst possible combination of outcomes. If a loss occurs and, as a result, the organization is prevented from pursuing its other objectives, it is clear that the risk management objective has not been achieved. While not immediately obvious, it is equally true that the risk management objective has not been achieved when there are unprotected loss exposures that could prevent the organization from pursuing its other objectives should the loss occur, even if the loss does not occur.

[12] Robert I. Mehr and Bob A. Hedges, *Risk Management: Concepts and Applications* (Homewood, Ill.: Richard D. Irwin, 1974), p. 4.
[13] Neil A. Doherty, *Corporate Risk Management* (New York: McGraw-Hill, 1985), Chapters 1 and 2.

For this reason, the objective refers to losses that *might* arise out of pure risks. The question is not only whether the organization survives, but whether it would have survived under a different combination of circumstances.

The Risk Management Policy Major policy decisions related to insurance should be made by the highest policy-making body in the organization—such as the Board of Directors—since these decisions are likely to involve large financial considerations, either in terms of premiums paid over the long term or risks assumed if hazards are not insured. In addition, it is the Board of Directors and the professional managers of the firm, after all, who are responsible for the preservation of the organization's assets. Once the objectives have been identified, they should be formally recognized in a risk management policy. A formal risk management policy statement provides a basis for achieving a logical and consistent program by offering guidance for those responsible for programming and buying the firm's insurance. Figure 2.1 is a sample of a corporate risk management policy.

Identifying Risk Exposures

Obviously, before anything can be done about the risks an organization faces, someone must be aware of them. In one way or another, someone must dig into the operations of the company and discover the risks to which the firm is exposed. In one sense, risk identification is the most difficult step in the risk management process. It is difficult because it is a continual process and because it is virtually impossible to know when it has been done completely.

It is difficult to generalize about the risks that a given organization is likely to face because differences in operations and conditions give rise to differing risks. Some risks are relatively obvious, while many can be, and often are, overlooked. To reduce the possibility of failure to discover important risks facing the firm, most risk managers use some systematic approach to the problem of risk identification.

Risk Identification Techniques The first step in risk identification is to gain as thorough a knowledge as possible of the organization and its operations. The risk manager needs a general knowledge of the goals and functions of the organization: what it does and where it does it. This knowledge can be gained through inspections, interviews with appropriate per-

sons within and outside the organization, and by an examination of internal records and documents.

Analysis of Documents The history of the organization and its current operations are contained in a variety of records. These records represent a basic source of information required for risk analysis and exposure identification. These documents include the organization's financial statements, leases and other contracts, asset schedules, inventory records, appraisals and valuation reports, buy-sell agreements, and countless other documents.

Analysis of the firm's financial statements, in particular, can aid in the process of risk identification. The asset listing in the balance sheet may alert the risk manager to the existence of assets that might otherwise be overlooked. The income and expense classification in the income statement may likewise indicate areas of operation of which the risk manager was unaware.[14]

Flow Charts Another tool that is useful in risk identification is a flow chart. A flow chart of an organization's internal operations views the firm as a processing unit and seeks to discover all the contingencies that could interrupt its processes. These might include damage to a strategic asset located in a bottleneck within the firm's operations or the loss of the services of a key individual or group through disability, death, or resignation. When extended to include the flow of goods and services to and from customers and suppliers, the flow chart approach to risk identification can highlight potential accidents that can disrupt the firm's activities and its profits.[15]

Internal Communication System To identify new risks, the risk manager needs a far-reaching information system that yields current information on new developments that may give rise to risk. Among the various activities that have relevance to the risk management function, some of the more important are new construction, remodeling, or ren-

[14] The "financial statement method" of risk analysis was proposed by the risk manager of a national corporation and has become a more or less standard approach to the risk identification problem. See A. Hawthorne Criddle, "A Theory of Risk Discovery," *National Insurance Buyer,* vol. 6, no. 1 (January 1959).

[15] The use of flow charts in risk analysis was suggested in the early 1960s. See A.J. Ingley, "Problems of Risk Analysis," *The Growing Job of Risk Management,* AMA Management Report No. 70 (New York: American Management Association, 1962), pp. 137–138.

<div style="border:1px solid">

Risk Management Policy

1. It shall be the policy of Iowa Pork Packers, Inc. to avoid, reduce, or transfer the risk of loss arising out of property damage, legal liability, and dishonesty in all cases in which the exposure could result in loss that would bankrupt or seriously impair the operating efficiency of the firm.

2. It shall be the policy of Iowa Pork Packers, Inc. to assume the risk of loss arising out of property damage, legal liability, and dishonesty in all cases in which the exposure is so small or dispersed that a loss would not significantly affect the operations or the financial position of the firm.

3. It shall be the policy of Iowa Pork Packers, Inc. to provide safe working conditions for its employees. Under no circumstances will the risk of serious injury or death of employees to be considered an acceptable risk.

4. Insurance will be purchased against all major loss exposures that might result in loss in excess of $100,000 or 10 percent of the projected annual working capital through the purchase of appropriate forms of property and liability insurance against the widest range of perils and hazards available.

5. Insurance will not be purchased to cover loss exposures below the amount of $10,000 unless such insurance is required by law or by contract, or in those instances in which it is desirable to obtain special services such as inspection or claim adjustment in connection with the insurance.

6. The administration of the risk management program will be under the direction of the Insurance Administrator, such responsibility to include placement of insurance coverages, maintenance of property appraisals and inventory valuations, processing of claims and maintenance of loss records, and supervision of loss prevention activities.

7. Safety and loss prevention recommendations by OSHA officials and insurance company loss prevention personnel will be given serious consideration and implemented whenever feasible. In those instances in which such recommendations are not implemented, a written justification for nonimplementation will be filed with the Board of Directors by the company officer making the decision.

8. Insurance will be placed only in insurance companies rated A+ or A in *Best's Policyholders Ratings*. Insurance placed in any other companies will require a written report of the particulars, such report to be filed with the Board of Directors by the Insurance Administrator.

</div>

FIGURE 2.1 Sample Risk Management Policy

ovation of the firm's properties, the introduction of new programs, products, activities, or operations, and other similar changes in the organization's activities.

Tools of Risk Identification Exposure identification is an essential phase of both risk management and insurance management. Because insurance management is the older field, the technique of identifying insurable exposures was already highly developed when the risk management movement began. Insurance companies created insurance policy checklists, which identify the various risks for which they offered coverage. They also developed extensive application forms for various types of insurance that elicited information about hazards that need to be reflected in rating and underwriting decisions. Although these tools naturally focused on the perils and hazards against which insurers offered protection, they provided a base on which risk identification methods could be constructed. Many of the tools that had been used by insurance agents and insurance managers to identify insurable exposures were expanded and adapted to aid in the identification of other risks for which the risk manager is responsible.

A few of the more important tools used in risk identification include risk analysis questionnaires, exposure checklists, and insurance policy checklists. These, combined with a vivid imagination and a thorough understanding of the organization's operations, can help to guarantee that important exposures are not overlooked.

Risk Analysis Questionnaires Risk analysis questionnaires, also sometimes called *fact finders,* are designed to assist in identifying risks facing an organization. They do this by leading the user through a series of penetrating questions, the answers to which indicate hazards and conditions that give rise to risk. Originally, such questionnaires were generic and were intended for use by a wide range of businesses. As a result, they did not address unusual exposures or identify loss areas that may be unique to a given firm. Today, risk analysis questionnaires are available for a wide range of specific industries.

Exposure Checklists A second important aid in risk identification and one of the most common tools for risk analysis is a risk exposure checklist, which is simply a listing of common exposures. Obviously, a checklist cannot include all possible exposures to which an organization may be subject; the nature and operations of different organizations vary too widely for that. However, it can be used effectively in conjunction with other risk identification tools as a final check to reduce the chance of overlooking a serious exposure.

Insurance Policy Checklists Insurance policy checklists are available from insurance companies and publishers specializing in insurance related publications. Typically, such lists include a catalogue of the various policies or types of insurance that a given business might need. The risk manager simply consults such a list, picking out those policies applicable to the firm. A principal defect in using insurance policy checklists for risk identification is that such checklists concentrate on insurable risks only, ignoring the uninsurable pure risks.[16]

Expert Systems With the advances in computer technology, many of the tools and techniques used in risk identification have been consolidated in computer software to create expert systems. An expert system used in risk identification incorporates the features of risk analysis questionnaires, exposure checklists, and insurance policy checklists in a single tool. The most sophisticated risk management expert systems include detailed, industry-specific risk questionnaires and exposure checklists. These survey questionnaires are detailed and assist in the identification not only of common exposures, but of those that may be unique to the specific industry.[17]

Combination Approach Required The preferred method of risk identification consists of a combination approach, in which all of the tools previously listed are brought to bear on the problem. In a sense, each of these tools can provide a part to the puzzle, and, combined, they can be of considerable assistance to the risk manager. But no individual approach or combination of these tools can replace the diligence and imagination of the risk manager in discovering the risks to which the firm is exposed.

Evaluating Risks

Once the risks have been identified, the risk manager must evaluate them. *Evaluation* implies some ranking in terms of importance, and ranking suggests measuring some aspect of the factors to be ranked. In the case of loss exposures, two facets must be considered: the possible severity of loss, and the possible frequency or probability of loss. Evaluation involves measuring the potential size of the loss and the probability that the loss is likely to occur.

A Priority Ranking Based on Severity One of the techniques used by scientists and engineers in the U.S. space program was *criticality analysis*—an attempt to distinguish the truly important factors from the overwhelming mass of unimportant ones. Given the wide range of losses that can occur, from the minute to the catastrophic, it seems logical that exposures be ranked according to their criticality. Certain risks, because of the severity of the possible loss, will demand attention prior to others, and in most instances there will be a number of exposures that are equally demanding.

[16] One of the most widely used policy checklists is a publication entitled *Coverages Applicable,* published by the Rough Notes Co. of Indianapolis.

[17] An expert system is a computer program for decision making that uses knowledge and analytical rules defined by experts in the field. Expert systems originated in the 1960s and are now used in a wide range of fields, including medicine, finance, insurance, and risk management.

Any exposure that involves a loss that would represent a financial catastrophe ranks in the same category, and there is no distinction among risks in this class. It makes little difference if bankruptcy results from a liability loss, a flood, or an uninsured fire loss. The net effect is the same. Therefore, rather than ranking exposures in some order of importance such as "1, 2, 3, etc.," it is more appropriate to rank them into general classifications such as critical, important, and unimportant. One set of criteria that may be used in establishing such a priority ranking focuses on the financial impact that the loss would have on the firm. For example:

- *Critical risks* include all exposures to loss in which the possible losses are of a magnitude that would result in bankruptcy.
- *Important risks* include those exposures in which the possible losses would not result in bankruptcy, but would require the firm to borrow in order to continue operations.
- *Unimportant risks* include those exposures in which the possible losses could be met out of the existing assets or current income of the firm without imposing undue financial strain.

Assignment of individual exposures into one of these three categories requires determination of the amount of financial loss that might result from a given exposure as well as the ability of the firm to absorb such losses. Determining the ability to absorb the losses involves measuring the level of uninsured loss that could be borne without resorting to credit and determining the maximum credit capacity of the firm.[18]

The Loss Unit Concept One of the most relevant measures of severity, which unfortunately has not been widely discussed, is the *loss unit*. The loss unit is the total of all financial losses that can result from a single event, taking into consideration the various exposures. It includes the loss for direct damage to property, the loss of income, and the liabilities that can result from a single occurrence. Computing the loss unit requires calculation of the maximum possible loss for each of these exposures and then aggregating the totals. The significance of the loss unit lies in the fact that while an organization might be able to retain certain of the exposures individually, there is no guarantee that losses will occur individually. The loss unit is an attempt to alert management to the potential catastrophe that could result under the worst possible conditions.

Probability and Priority Rankings Although the potential severity is the most important factor in ranking exposures, an estimate of the probability may also be useful in differentiating among exposures with relatively equal potential severity. Other things being equal, exposures characterized by high frequency should receive attention before exposures in which the loss frequency is low. Exposures that exhibit a high loss frequency are often susceptible to improvement through risk control measures. Having some notion of the loss frequency for different exposures can help determine where control efforts should be directed. Even broad generalizations about the likelihood of loss may be useful. One suggested approach is to classify probability as *almost nil* (meaning that, in the opinion of the risk manager, the event is probably not going to happen), *slight* (meaning that, while the event is possible, it has not happened and is unlikely to occur in the future), *moderate* (meaning that the event has occasionally happened and will probably happen again), and *definite* (meaning that the event has happened regularly in the past and is expected to occur regularly in the future).[19] Although probability estimates such as these may be of some help in risk management decisions, when the appropriate data is available, more precise mathematical estimates of the probabilities will be useful. Some organizations, by virtue of their size and the scope

[18] A classification based on these criteria would not be appropriate for all organizations. However, similar classifications can be structured on the basis of other measures related to the financial impact of the loss. For example, one midwestern municipality classifies as *critical* those exposures involving losses that would require the imposition of additional taxes, as *important* those exposures to loss that would require diversion of appropriated funds from planned activities, and as *unimportant* those exposures in which losses could be met out of current appropriations without modification of planned activities. In the case of a giant corporation, the division might be established according to the net impact of losses on shareholder earnings.

[19] See Richard Prouty, *Industrial Insurance: A Formal Approach to Risk Analysis and Evaluation* (Washington, D.C.: Machinery and Allied Products Institute, 1960).

of their operations, may be able to use probability estimates in risk financing decisions.

Consideration of Alternatives and Selection of the Risk Treatment Device

Once the risks have been identified and evaluated, the next step is consideration of the approaches that may be used to deal with risks and the selection of the technique that should be used for each one.

The Choice This phase of the risk management process is primarily a problem in decision making; more precisely, it is deciding which of the techniques available should be used in dealing with each risk. The extent to which the risk management personnel must make these decisions on their own varies from organization to organization. Sometimes the organization's risk management policy establishes the criteria to be applied in the choice of techniques, outlining the rules within which the risk manager may operate. If the risk management policy is rigid and detailed, there is less latitude in the decision making done by the risk manager. He or she becomes an administrator of the program rather than a policy maker. In other instances, where there is no formal policy or where the policy has been loosely drawn to permit the risk manager a wide range of discretion, the position carries much greater responsibility.

In deciding which of the techniques available should be used to deal with a given risk, the risk manager considers the size of the potential loss, its probability, and the resources that would be available to meet the loss if it should occur. The benefits and costs in each approach are evaluated, and then, on the basis of the best information available and under the guidance of the corporate risk management policy, the decision is made. Some of the important considerations in the selection of the most appropriate technique are discussed later in this chapter.

Implementation of the Decision

The decision is made to retain a risk. This may be accomplished with or without a reserve and with or without a fund. If the plan is to include the accumulation of a fund, proper administrative procedure must be set up to implement the decision. If loss prevention is selected to deal with a particular risk, the proper loss-prevention program must be designed and implemented. The decision to transfer the risk through insurance must be followed by the selection of an insurer, negotiations, and placement of the insurance.

Evaluation and Review

Evaluation and review must be included in the program for two reasons. First, the risk management process does not take place in a vacuum. Things change: new risks arise and old risks disappear. The techniques that were appropriate last year may not be the most advisable this year, and constant attention is required. Second, mistakes are sometimes made. Evaluation and review of the risk management program permit the risk manager to review decisions and discover mistakes, ideally before they become costly.

How does one review a risk management program? Basically, by repeating each of the steps in the risk management process to determine whether past decisions were proper in the light of existing conditions and if they were properly executed. The risk manager reevaluates the program's objectives, repeats the identification process to ensure, insofar as possible, that it was performed correctly, and then evaluates the risks that have been identified and verifies that the decision on how to address each risk was proper. Finally, the implementation of the decisions must be verified to make sure they were executed as intended.

Evaluation and Review as Managerial Control
The evaluation and review phase of the risk management process is the managerial control phase of the risk management process. The purpose of controlling is to verify that operations are going according to plans. Control requires (1) setting standards or objectives to be achieved; (2) measuring performance against those standards and objectives; and (3) taking corrective action when results differ from the intended results. In this context, it should be recognized that a disastrous loss need not occur for performance to deviate from what is intended. Because risk management deals with decisions under conditions of uncertainty, adequate performance is measured not only based on whether the organization has survived, but whether it would have survived under a

different set of more adverse circumstances. The existence of an inadequately addressed exposure with catastrophic potential represents a deviation from the intended objective. It is this type of deviation from objectives that the risk management control process is intended to address.

Quantitative Performance Standards Ideally, standards should be quantified whenever possible. One quantifiable measure of risk management performance that is frequently suggested is the *cost of risk,* which is the total expenditures for risk management, including insurance premiums paid and retained losses, expressed as a percentage of revenues. RIMS publishes annual studies on the *cost of risk,* which makes it convenient for the risk manager to compare the risk management costs of the organization with other firms in the same industry. The cost of risk varies from industry to industry, yet it generally averages in the neighborhood of 1 percent of revenues. Although the cost of risk may fluctuate because of factors over which the risk manager has no control, it is a useful standard when properly interpreted.

Quantitative performance standards are more prevalent in the area of risk control than for risk financing functions. Standard injury rates reflecting frequency and severity are available as benchmarks for measuring performance in the area of employee safety. Similarly, motor vehicle accident rates and other frequency and severity rates are useful benchmarks in measuring risk control measures.

Risk Management Audits Although evaluation and review is an ongoing process that is performed without interruption, the risk management program should periodically be subjected to a comprehensive review called a *risk management audit.* Most people are familiar with the term *audit* as it is used in the accounting field, where it refers to a formal examination of financial records by public accountants to verify the accuracy, fairness, and integrity of the accounting records. The term *audit* has a second meaning, which is any thorough examination and evaluation of a problem, and it is this second meaning that is implied in the term *risk management audit.* A risk management audit is a detailed and systematic review of a risk management program, designed to determine if the objectives of the program are appropriate to the needs of the organization, whether the measures designed to achieve those objectives are suitable, and whether the measures have been properly implemented.

Although risk management audits *may* be conducted by an external party, they may also be performed internally. When the risk management department has the required in-house expertise, it may establish a system for internal audits of the risk management function on a regularly scheduled basis. Although internal audits may lack the objectivity of external audits and are not substitutes for external audits, they can provide many of the same benefits. The benefits of internal audits will be maximized to the extent that they are conducted—to the extent possible—in the same way as an external audit.

IMPORTANT CONCEPTS TO REMEMBER

risk management	risk management process	important risks
risk control	determination of objectives	unimportant risks
risk avoidance	identification of the risks	risk management policy
risk reduction	evaluation of the risks	post-loss objectives
loss prevention	considering alternatives and	pre-loss objectives
loss control	selecting the risk treatment device	survival
risk financing	implementing the decision	cost of risk
risk retention	evaluation and review	maximum retention limit
risk transfer	insurance policy checklists	fact finders
risk sharing	risk analysis questionnaires	exposure checklists
security function	flow process charts	financial statement method
insurance management	critical risks	flow charts

QUESTIONS FOR REVIEW

1. According to the text, risk management represents the merging of three specialties. Identify these specialties and explain the contribution of each to modern risk management theory.

2. Identify the two broad approaches to dealing with risk recognized by modern risk management theory.

3. Identify and briefly describe the four basic techniques available to the risk manager for dealing with the pure risks facing the firm. Give an example of each technique.

4. The text states that the emergence of risk management was a revolution that signaled a dramatic shift in philosophy. What was this change in philosophy?

5. Briefly describe the development of risk management as a function of business in the United States. What, in your opinion, were the primary motivating forces and the strategic factors that led to the development of risk management?

6. Describe the responsibility of the risk manager and the risk manager's position within the organization.

7. What is the relationship between risk management and insurance management? In your answer you should demonstrate an understanding of the difference between the two fields.

8. Describe the relationship between risk management and general management. In what ways does a risk manager become involved in the overall supervision of the firm?

9. Identify two common misconceptions about risk management, and explain why these misconceptions developed.

10. Distinguish between risk management, financial risk management, and enterprise risk management.

QUESTIONS FOR DISCUSSION

1. In some sense, a risk manager must be a "jack of all trades," because of the breadth of his or her activities. Identify several areas in which a risk manager should be knowledgeable, and explain why this would be useful. What type of educational background should a risk manager have?

2. In a large, multidivision company, risk management may be centralized or decentralized. Which approach, in your opinion, is likely to produce the greatest benefits? Why?

3. The American Risk and Insurance Association has argued that risk management should be added to the required core of knowledge in business administration. To what extent do you agree or disagree that risk management should be a required course in a business curriculum?

4. Describe risk management's direct contribution to profit.

5. In your opinion, should the corporate risk manager's responsibility be expanded to include financial risk management?

SUGGESTIONS FOR ADDITIONAL READING

Doherty, Neil A. *Corporate Risk Management: A Financial Exposition.* New York: McGraw-Hill, 1985.

Fayol, Henri. *General and Industrial Management.* New York: Pitman Publishing Corporation, 1949.

Gallagher, Russel B. "Risk Management: A New Phase of Cost Control." *Harvard Business Review* (Sept.–Oct. 1956).

Grose, Vernon L. *Managing Risk: Systematic Loss Prevention for Executives* (Englewood Cliffs, NJ: Prentice-Hall, 1987).

Harrington, Scott E., and Gregory R. Niehaus. *Risk Management and Insurance.* New York: McGraw-Hill, 1998.

Head, George L., and Stephen Horn II. *Essentials of Risk Management,* 3rd ed., vols. 1 and 2. Malvern, Pa.: Insurance Institute of America, 1997.

Mehr, R. I., and B. A. Hedges. *Risk Management: Concepts and Applications.* Homewood, Ill.: Richard D. Irwin, 1974. Chapters 7–12.

Mehr, R. I., and B. A. Hedges. *Risk Management in the Business Enterprise.* Homewood, Ill.: Richard D. Irwin, 1963. Chapters 5–9.

Reavis, Marshall W. "The Corporate Risk Manager's Contribution to Profit." *Journal of Risk and Insurance,* vol. 36, no. 3 (Sept. 1969).

Skipper, Harold D., Jr. *International Risk and Insurance: An Environmental-Managerial Approach.* New York: McGraw-Hill, 1998.

Vaughan, Emmett J. *Risk Management.* New York: John Wiley & Sons, 1997.

Williams, C. Arthur, Peter C. Young, and Michael Smith. *Risk Management and Insurance.* 8th ed. New York: McGraw-Hill, 1998.

WEB SITES TO EXPLORE

International Risk Management Institute, Inc.	http://irmi.com
Nonprofit Risk Management Center	http://www.nonprofitrisk.org
Practical Risk Management	http://www.pracrisk.com/
Public Agency Risk Managers Association (PARMA)	http://www.parma.com
Risk and Insurance Management Society, Inc.	http://www.rims.org
RiskINFO	http://www.riskinfo.com/
Ultimate Insurance Links	http://www.barryklein.com/

CHAPTER 3

THE INSURANCE DEVICE

■

Bear ye one another's burden.

— NEW TESTAMENT, GAL. 6:2

CHAPTER OBJECTIVES

When you have finished this chapter, you should be able to
- Define insurance from the viewpoint of the individual and of society
- Identify and explain the two essential features in the operation of insurance
- Explain how the law of large numbers supports the operation of the insurance mechanism
- Identify and explain the desirable elements of an insurable risk
- Explain what is meant by adverse selection and why it is a problem for insurers
- Explain the economic contributions of insurance

THE NATURE AND FUNCTIONS OF INSURANCE

As we have seen, there are a number of ways of dealing with risk. In this book we are concerned primarily with the most formal of these various approaches. We turn now to an examination of the insurance device, focusing on its nature and the manner in which it deals with risk.

Risk Sharing and Risk Transfer

Insurance is a complicated and intricate mechanism, and it is consequently difficult to define. However, in its simplest aspect, it has two fundamental characteristics:

- Transferring or shifting risk from one individual to a group
- Sharing losses, on some equitable basis, by all members of the group

To illustrate the way in which insurance works, let us assume that there are 1000 dwellings in a given community and, for simplicity, that the value of each house is $100,000. Each owner faces the risk that his or her house may catch on fire. If a fire occurs, a financial loss of up to $100,000 could result. Some houses will undoubtedly burn, but the probability that all will burn is remote. Now, let us assume that the owners of these dwellings enter into an agreement to share the cost of losses as they occur, so that no single individual will be forced to bear an entire

loss of $100,000. Whenever a house burns, each of the 1000 owners contributes his or her proportionate share of the amount of the loss. If the house is a total loss, each of the 1000 owners will pay $100 and the owner of the destroyed house will be indemnified for the $100,000 loss. Those who suffer losses are indemnified by those who do not. Those who escape loss are willing to pay those who do not because by doing so they help to eliminate the possibility that they themselves might suffer a $100,000 loss. Through the agreement to share the losses, the economic burden of the losses is spread throughout the group. This is essentially the way insurance works, for what we have described is a pure assessment mutual insurance operation.

There are some potential difficulties with the operation of such a plan. Most obviously, some members of the group might refuse to pay their assessment at the time of a loss. This problem can be overcome by requiring payment in advance. To require payment in advance for the losses that may take place, it will be necessary to have some idea as to the amount of those losses. This may be calculated on the basis of past experience. Let us now assume that on the basis of past experience, we are able to predict with reasonable accuracy that 2 of the 1000 houses will burn. We could charge each member of the group $200, making a total of $200,000. In addition to the cost of the losses, there would no doubt be some expenses in the operation of the program. Also there is a possibility that our predictions might not be entirely accurate. We might, therefore, charge each member of the group $300 instead of $200, thereby providing for the payment of expenses and also providing a cushion against deviations from our expectations. Each of the 1000 homeowners will incur a small certain cost of $300 in exchange for a promise of indemnification in the amount of $100,000 if his or her house burns down. This $300 premium is, in effect, the individual's share of the total losses and expenses of the group.

Insurance Defined from the Viewpoint of the Individual

Based on the preceding description, we may define insurance from the individual's viewpoint as follows:

> From an individual point of view, insurance is an economic device whereby the individual substitutes a small certain cost (the premium) for a large uncertain financial loss (the contingency insured against) that would exist if it were not for the insurance.

The primary function of insurance is the creation of the counterpart of risk, which is security. Insurance does not decrease the uncertainty for the individual as to whether the event will occur, nor does it alter the probability of occurrence, but it does reduce the probability of financial loss connected with the event. From the individual's point of view, the purchase of an adequate amount of insurance on a house eliminates the uncertainty regarding a financial loss in the event that the house should burn down.

Some people seem to believe that they have somehow wasted their money in purchasing insurance if a loss does not occur and indemnity is not received. Some even feel that if they have not had a loss during the policy term, their premium should be returned. Both viewpoints constitute the essence of ignorance. Relative to the first, we already know that the insurance contract provides a valuable feature in the freedom from the burden of uncertainty. Even if a loss is not sustained during the policy term, the insured has received something for the premium: the promise of indemnification if a loss had occurred. With respect to the second, one must appreciate the fact that the operation of the insurance principle is based on the contributions of the many paying the losses of the unfortunate few. If the premiums were returned to the many who did not have losses, there would be no funds available to pay for the losses of the few who did. Basically, then, the insurance device is a method of loss distribution. What would be a devastating loss to an individual is spread in an equitable manner to all members of the group, and it is on this basis that insurance can exist.

Risk Reduction Through Pooling

In addition to eliminating risk at the level of the individual through transfer, the insurance mechanism reduces risk (and the uncertainty related to risk) for society as a whole. The risk the insurance company faces is not merely a summation of the risks transferred to it by individuals; the insurance company is able to do something that the individual cannot, and that is to predict within rather narrow limits the amount of losses that will actually occur. If the insurer could predict future losses with absolute precision, it would face no possibility of loss. It would collect each individual's share of the total losses and

expenses of operation and use these funds to pay the losses and expenses as they occur. If the predictions are not accurate, the premiums that the insurer has charged may be inadequate. The accuracy of the insurer's predictions is based on the law of large numbers. By combining a sufficiently large number of homogeneous exposure units, the insurer is able to make predictions for the group as a whole. This is accomplished through the theory of probability.

Probability Theory and the Law of Large Numbers Probability theory is the body of knowledge concerned with measuring the likelihood that something will happen and making predictions on the basis of this likelihood. It deals with random events and is based on the premise that, while some events appear to be a matter of chance, they actually occur with regularity over a large number of trials. The likelihood of an event is assigned a numerical value between 0 and 1, with those that are impossible assigned a value of 0 and those that are inevitable assigned a value of 1. Events that may or may not happen are assigned a value between 0 and 1, with higher values assigned to those estimated to have a greater likelihood or "probability" of occurring.

At this point, it may be useful to distinguish between two interpretations of probability:

- *The relative frequency interpretation.* The probability assigned to an event signifies the relative frequency of its occurrence that would be expected, given a large number of separate independent trials. In this interpretation, only events that may be repeated for a "long run" may be governed by probabilities.
- *The subjective interpretation.* The probability of an event is measured by the degree of belief in the likelihood of the given incident's occurrence. For example, the coach of a football team may state that his team has a 70 percent chance of winning the conference title, a student may state that she has a 50:50 chance of getting a B in a course, or the weather forecaster may state that there is a 90 percent chance of rain.

Both these interpretations are used in the insurance industry, but for the moment let us concentrate on the relative frequency interpretation.

Determining the Probability of an Event To obtain an estimate of the probability of an event in the relative frequency interpretation, one of two methods can be used. The first is to examine the underlying conditions that cause the event. For example, if we say that the probability of getting a "head" when tossing a coin is .5 or ½, we have assumed or determined that the coin is perfectly balanced and that there is no interference on the part of the "tosser." If we ignore the absurd suggestion that the coin might land on its edge, there are only two possible outcomes, and these are equally likely. Therefore, we know that the probability is .5. In the same manner, we know that the probability of rolling a six with a single die is ⅙ or that the probability of drawing the ace of spades from a complete and well-shuffled deck is 1/52. These probabilities are deducible or obvious from the nature of the event. Because they are determined before an experiment in this manner (i.e., on the basis of causality), they are called *a priori probabilities.*

These *a priori* probabilities are not of great significance for us except insofar as they can be used to illustrate the operation of the law of large numbers. Even though we know that the probability of flipping a head is .5, we also know that we cannot use this knowledge to predict whether a given flip will result in a head or a tail. We know that the probability has little relevance for a single trial. Given a sufficient number of flips, however, we would expect the result to approach one-half heads and one-half tails. We feel that this is true even though we may not have the inclination to test it. This commonsense notion that the probability is meaningful only over a large number of trials is an intuitive recognition of the *law of large numbers,* which in its simplest form states that

The observed frequency of an event more nearly approaches the underlying probability of the population as the number of trials approaches infinity.

In other words, for the probability to work itself out, a large number of flips or tosses is necessary. The greater the number of trials or flips, the more nearly the observed result will approach the underlying probability of .5.

Clearly, this *a priori* method of determining the probability of an event is the preferred method, but, except in the most elementary situations, determining causality is not practical. Therefore, another approach is employed. When we do not know the underlying probability of an event and cannot deduce it from the nature of the event, we can estimate it on the basis of past experience. Suppose that

we are told that the probability that a 21-year-old male will die before reaching age 22 is .00191. What does this mean? It means that someone has examined mortality statistics and discovered that, in the past, 191 men out of every 100,000 alive at age 21 have died before reaching age 22. It also means that, barring changes in the causes of these deaths, we can expect approximately the same proportion of 21-year-olds to die in the future.

Here, the probability is interpreted as the relative frequency resulting from a long series of trials or observations, and it is estimated after observation of the past rather than from the nature of the event as in the case of *a priori probabilities*. These probabilities, computed after a study of past experience, are called *a posteriori* or empirical probabilities. They differ from *a priori* probabilities, such as those observed in flipping a coin, in the method by which they are determined, but not in their interpretation. In addition, while the probability computed prior to the flipping of a coin can be considered to be exact, those computed on the basis of past experience are only estimates of the true probability.

The law of large numbers, which tells us that *a priori* estimates are meaningful only over a large number of trials, is the basis for the *a posteriori* estimates. Since the observed frequency of an event approaches the underlying probability of the population as the number of trials increases, we can obtain a notion of the underlying probability by observing events that have occurred. After observing the proportion of the time that the various outcomes have occurred over a long period of time under essentially the same conditions, we construct an index of the relative frequency of the occurrence of each possible outcome. This index of the relative frequency of each of all possible outcomes is called a *probability distribution,* and the probability assigned to the event is the *average rate at which the outcome is expected to occur.*

In making probability estimates on the basis of past experience or historical data, we make use of the techniques of statistical inference, which is to say that we make inferences about the population based on sample data. It is not usually possible to examine the entire population, so we must be content with a sample. We take a sample to draw a conclusion about some measure of the population (referred to as a parameter) based on a sample value (called a sample statistic). In attempting to estimate the probability of an event, the parameter of the population in which we are interested is the mean or average frequency

of occurrence, and we attempt to estimate this value based on our sample. Because only partial information is available, we confront the possibility that our estimate of the mean of the population (the probability) will be wrong.

We know that the observed frequency of an event will approach the underlying probability as the number of trials increases. It therefore follows that the greater the number of trials examined, the better will be our estimate of the probability. The larger the *sample* on which our estimate of the probability is based, the more closely our estimate should approximate the true probability.

Unfortunately, it is seldom possible to take as large a sample as we would like. Instead, we make an estimate (called a point estimate) of the mean of the population based on the mean of the sample and then estimate the probability that the mean of the population falls within a certain range of this point estimate. Put somewhat differently, we estimate the population mean on the basis of the sample, and then we allow a margin for error. The extent of the margin for error will depend on the concentration of the values that make up the mean and the size of the sample. The greater the dispersion of the individual values from the mean (i.e., the greater the variation in data on which the sample mean is based), the less certain we can be that our point estimate approximates the true mean of the population.

To illustrate this principle,[1] let us assume that an insurance company that has insured 1000 houses each year for the past five years examines its records and finds the following losses:

Year	Houses That Burn
1	7
2	11
3	10
4	9
5	13

Over the five-year period, a total of 50 houses have burned, or an average of 10 houses per year. Since the number of houses insured each year was

[1] This example is not intended as an illustration of the way insurance companies actually compute rates. As a matter of fact, industry rate-making practices bear little resemblance to the process described here. The example merely serves to show how the law of large numbers is the basis for the insurance mechanism.

1000, we estimate the chance of loss to be 1/100 or .01. In so doing, we are simply saying. "The average number of losses in our sample was 10 houses per 1000. If the mean of our sample approximates the mean of the entire population (all houses), the probability of loss is .01, and we predict that 10 houses will burn the sixth year if 1000 houses are again insured." But we cannot be certain that we are correct in our estimate of the probability. The mean of our sample (our estimate of the probability) may not be the same as the mean of the universe (the true probability). In other words, there is a possibility that the population mean is, say, eight houses burning per year, but we are observing an average of 10 houses for those particular years. The confidence we can place in our estimate of the probability will vary with the dispersion or variation in the values that make up the mean of the sample. Compare this second set of losses with the preceding set:

Year	Houses That Burn
1	16
2	4
3	10
4	12
5	8

The total number of losses over the five-year period is again 50, and the average or mean losses per year is again 10. However, there is a much greater variation in the number of losses from year to year. Even though the mean is the same in both groups, we would expect the mean of the first set of data to correspond more closely with the mean of the population. The greater the variation in the data on which our estimate of the probability is based, the greater we expect to be the variation between our estimate of the probability and the true probability. Since there is a relationship between the variation in the values that make up the sample mean and the likelihood that the sample mean approximates the population mean, it is useful to be able to measure the variation in these values.

Measures of Dispersion and Probability Estimate Statisticians have developed a number of measures of the dispersion in a group of values. For example, in the case of the first set of losses (7,11,10,9,13), the number of losses in any given year varied from 7 to 13; in the second set of losses (16,4,10,12,8), the num-

ber of losses varied from 4 to 16. This variation from the smallest number to the largest number is called the range, which is the simplest of the measures of *dispersion*. Another measure is the *variance*, which is computed by squaring the annual deviations of the values from the mean and then taking an average of these squared differences. For example, the variance of the two sets of losses under discussion here would be computed as follows:

Year	Average Losses	Actual Losses	Difference	Difference Squared
1	10	7	3	9
2	10	11	1	1
3	10	10	0	0
4	10	9	1	1
5	10	13	3	9
Summation of differences squared				20

$$\frac{\text{Summation of differences squared}}{\text{Number of years}} = \frac{20}{5} = 4$$

Year	Average Losses	Actual Losses	Difference	Difference Squared
1	10	16	6	36
2	10	4	6	36
3	10	10	0	0
4	10	12	2	4
5	10	8	2	4
Summation of differences squared				80

$$\frac{\text{Summation of differences squared}}{\text{Number of years}} = \frac{80}{5} = 16$$

The variance of the first set of losses is 4, and that of the second set is 16. The larger variance of the second set is simply an indication of the greater variation in the data that compose the mean.

The square root of the variance is called the *standard deviation*, which is the most widely used and perhaps the most useful of all measures of dispersion. Since the variance of the first group of losses is 4, the standard deviation of that group is 2. In the case of the second set, where the variance is 16, the standard deviation is 4. Like the variance, the standard deviation is simply a number that measures the concentration of the values about their mean. The smaller the standard deviation relative to the mean, the less the dispersion and the more uniform the values. To return to the question of the accuracy of our

point estimate of the probability based on the sample mean, the standard deviation is particularly useful in making estimates concerning the probable accuracy of this point estimate. In a sample with a lower standard deviation, we can be more confident in our estimate of the population mean.

Even if we know with certainty, however, that the population mean is 10 houses burning, that does not mean that 10 houses will in fact burn. In a normal distribution, 68.27 percent of the cases will fall within the range of the mean plus or minus one standard deviation. The mean plus or minus two standard deviations will describe the range within which 95.45 percent of the cases will lie, and the range of three standard deviations above and below the mean will include 99.73 percent of the values in the distribution. Using the sample mean as our point estimate of the probability, we can estimate the probability that the number of houses burning next year will be within a certain range of the sample mean, provided that we know the standard deviation of the distribution. In the case of the first set of losses, where the standard deviation was calculated to be 2, there is a 68.27 percent probability that the number of houses burning next year will be between 8 and 12 (i.e., 10 ± 2), a 95.45 percent probability that the number burning will be between 6 and 14 [$10 \pm (2 \times 2)$], and a 99.73 percent probability that the number will be between 4 and 16 [$10 \pm (3 \times 2)$]. In the case of the second set of data, where the values were more dispersed and the standard deviation was calculated to be 4, there is a 68.27 percent probability that the number burning will be between 6 and 14, a 95.45 percent probability that it will be between 2 and 18, and a 99.73 percent probability that it will be between 0 and 22.

Exactly what does all this mean? It means that uncertainty is inherent in our predictions. During the past five years, the average number of losses per 1000 dwellings has been 10, and on the basis of our estimate of the probability, we might predict 10 losses if 1000 houses are insured the sixth year, but we cannot be certain that our estimate of the probability is correct. Even if our estimate of the probability is correct, a different number of houses may burn next year. As a matter of fact, in the case of our first sample, our computations indicate that at best we can be 99 percent certain only that the true probability lies somewhere in the range of 4 to 16 losses per 1000 houses. The number of houses that may be expected to burn next year, other things being equal, is some number between 4 and 16. This means that actual results may

be expected to deviate by as much as 6 from the predicted 10. This represents a possible deviation of 60 percent (6/10) from the expected values.[2]

Other things being equal, the larger our sample, the more closely we will expect the mean of the sample to coincide with the mean of the population and the smaller will be the margin we must allow for error. This is reflected by the fact (which can be demonstrated mathematically) that the standard deviation of a distribution is inversely proportional to the square root of the number of items in the sample. For example, let us assume that we are able to increase the number of houses in our sample from 1000 to 100,000 per year and that we observe a 100-fold increase in losses.[3] The average number of losses observed per year will increase from 10 to 1000. The standard deviation will also have increased, but, and this is the critical point, it will not have increased proportionately, for the standard deviation increases only by the square root of the increase in the size of the sample. Thus, the standard deviation, which is calculated to be 2 at the 1000 exposure level, will increase to only 20 at the level of 100,000 houses. The new mean is 1000, and the mean plus or minus three standard deviations is now 1000 ± 60 and not 1000 ± 600. We can predict 1000 losses next year if 100,000 houses are insured, and we can feel 99 percent confident that the expected number of losses will fall somewhere between 940 and 1060. This represents a potential deviation of only 6 percent (60/1000) from the expected value. The area of uncertainty has decreased, because the size of the sample has increased. Note that in our example, neither the probability nor our estimate of it has changed. The number of losses expected per 1000 houses is the same, but we are more confident that our estimate approximates the true probability.

Dual Application of the Law of Large Numbers

Based on the preceding discussion, it should be apparent that the law of large numbers is important in insurance for two reasons. First, a large sample will

[2] This measure of uncertainty is somewhat related to the traditional statistical concept of the coefficient of variation, which is the standard deviation divided by the mean. The coefficient of variation at the 1000 exposure level in this example is 2/10 (20 percent).

[3] It is entirely possible that this larger sample might indicate a different number of losses per 1000 houses than the smaller sample, simply because our estimate based on the sample of 1000 was a poorer estimate of the true probability than that based on a sample of 100,000. For the purpose of simplification, we have assumed that the number of observed losses per 1000 does not change.

improve our estimate of the underlying probability. Even when we have estimated the probability on the basis of the sample of 100,000 houses per year, we cannot expect the narrower range of possible deviation if our estimate is applied to 1000 houses. As we have seen, even in the case of *a priori* probabilities where the probability is known, it must be applied to a large number of trials if we expect actual results to approximate the true probability. Therefore, in the case of empirical probabilities, the requirement of a large number has dual application:

- To estimate the underlying probability accurately, the insurance company must have a sufficiently large sample. The larger the sample, the more accurate will be the estimate of the probability.
- Once the estimate of the probability has been made, it must be applied to a sufficiently large number of exposure units to permit the underlying probability to work itself out.

In this sense, to the insurance company, the law of large numbers means that the larger the number of cases examined in the sampling process, the better the chance of making a good estimate of the probability; the larger the number of exposure units to which the estimate is applied, the better the chance that actual experience will approximate a good estimate of the probability.

In making predictions on the basis of historical data, the insurance company implicitly says: "If things continue to happen in the future as they have happened in the past, and if our estimate of what has happened in the past is accurate, this is what we may expect." But things may not happen in the future as they have in the past. As a matter of fact, it is likely that the probability involved is constantly changing. In addition, we may not have a good estimate of the probability. All of this means that things may not turn out as expected. Since the insurance company bases its rates on its expectation of future losses, it must be concerned with the extent to which actual experience is likely to deviate from predicted results. For the insurance company, risk (or the possibility of financial loss) is measured by the potential deviation of actual from predicted results, and the accuracy of prediction is enhanced when the predictions are based on and are applied to a large number of exposure units. If the insurance company's actuaries, or statisticians, could be absolutely certain that their predictions would be 100 percent accurate, there

would be no possibility of loss for the insurance company because premium income would always be sufficient to pay losses and expenses. Insofar as actual events may differ from predictions, risk exists for the insurer. To the extent that accuracy in prediction is attained, risk is reduced.

As a final point, it should be noted that although probability theory plays an important role in the operation of the insurance mechanism, insurance does not always depend on probabilities and predictions. Insurance arrangements can exist in which the participants agree to share losses and to determine each party's share of the costs on a post-loss basis. It is only when insurance is to be operated on an advance premium basis, with the participants paying their share of losses in advance, that probability theory and predictions are important.

Insurance Defined from the Viewpoint of Society

In addition to eliminating risk for the individual through transfer, the insurance device reduces the aggregate amount of risk in the economy by substituting certain costs for uncertain losses. These costs are assessed on the basis of the predictions made through the use of the law of large numbers. We may now formulate a second definition of insurance:

> From the social point of view, insurance is an economic device for reducing and eliminating risk through the process of combining a sufficient number of homogeneous exposures into a group to make the losses predictable for the group as a whole.

Insurance does not prevent losses,[4] nor does it reduce the cost of losses to the economy as a whole. As a matter of fact, it may very well have the opposite effect of causing losses and increasing the cost of losses for the economy as a whole. The existence of insurance encourages some losses for the purpose of defrauding the insurer, and, in addition, people are less careful and may exert less effort to prevent

[4] This statement is not intended to disparage the loss-prevention activities of insurance companies. In many forms of property and casualty insurance, attempts to reduce loss are perhaps the most important feature of all, but these loss-prevention activities are not essentially a part of the operation of the insurance principle. Insurance could exist without them, and they could and do exist without insurance. Insurance in and of itself does not favorably alter the probability of loss.

losses than they might if the insurance did not exist. Also, the economy incurs certain additional costs in the operation of the insurance mechanism. Not only must the cost of the losses be borne, but the expense of distributing the losses on some equitable basis adds to this cost.

Insurance: Transfer or Pooling?

The two definitions of insurance—from the viewpoint of the individual and from the viewpoint of society—reflect two different views of insurance, views that have divided insurance scholars for at least the past half century. The first view—that insurance is a device through which the individual substitutes a small certain cost for a large uncertain loss—emphasizes the transfer of risk. It does not attempt to explain how the risk is handled by the transferee. The second view—that insurance is a device for reducing and eliminating risk through pooling—emphasizes the role of insurance in reducing risk in the aggregate, which it does by pooling. Some writers maintain that the essential requisite in the insurance mechanism is the transfer of risk, while others argue that it is the pooling or sharing of risks.

Adherents of the "transfer" school point out that there are numerous examples of what are clearly insurance transactions, in which risks that are transferred to insurers are not pooled. There seems to be more or less general agreement on the point that insurance involves the transfer of risk. Even in risk-sharing mechanisms, such as post-loss assessment plans, risk is transferred from the individual to the group. Those who emphasize pooling of risk point out that it is this feature of insurance that distinguishes insurance from other risk transfer techniques. While they admit that pooling itself involves risk transfer (from the individual to the group), it is the pooling or combination of risks that makes the mechanism of insurance.

The definition of insurance from the perspective of the individual, as a device for the transfer of risk and the substitution of a small uncertain cost for a large uncertain loss, seems to be the better definition. It applies to all mechanisms we would call insurance, and it applies only to them. Since the pooling definition does not apply to all mechanisms that are considered insurance, it is somewhat less satisfactory. The *essential* feature of insurance is risk transfer. Pooling is an important technique available to the transferee, but it is not a requisite, and insurance transactions can occur in which the risk that is transferred is unique, and in which there is no pooling. Although insurance *generally* involves the reduction of risk in the aggregate, which is achieved by pooling, insurance transactions need not involve pooling.

Actually, both definitions are useful. The definition of insurance from the individual's perspective defines the essence of insurance, based on its essential component, transfer. The definition of insurance from the perspective of society is a functional definition, and explains how insurance usually achieves the transfer function.

Insurance and Gambling

Perhaps we should make one final distinction regarding the nature of insurance. It is often claimed that insurance is a form of gambling. "You bet that you will die and the insurance company bets that you won't" or "I bet the insurance company $300 against $100,000 that my house will burn." The fallacy of these statements should be obvious. In the case of a wager, there is no chance of loss, and hence no risk, before the wager. In the case of insurance, the chance of loss exists whether or not there is an insurance contract in effect. In other words, the basic distinction between insurance and gambling is that gambling creates a risk, while insurance provides for the transfer of an existing risk.

THE ECONOMIC CONTRIBUTION OF INSURANCE

Property that is destroyed by an insured contingency is not replaced through the existence of an insurance contract. True, the funds from the insurance company may be used to replace the property, but when a house or building burns, society has lost a want-satisfying good. Insurance as an economic device is justified because it creates certainty about the financial burden of losses and because it spreads the losses that do occur. In providing a mechanism through which losses can be shared and uncertainty reduced, insurance brings peace of mind to society's members and makes costs more certain.

Insurance also provides for a more optimal utilization of capital. Without the possibility of insurance, individuals and businesses would have to maintain relatively large reserve funds to meet the risks that they must assume. These funds would be in the form

of idle cash, or would be invested in safe, liquid, and low-interest-bearing securities. This would be an inefficient use of capital. When the risk is transferred to the professional risk bearer, the deviations from expected results are minimized. As a consequence, insurers are obligated to keep much smaller reserves than would be the case if insurance did not exist. The released funds are then available for investment in more productive pursuits, resulting in a much greater productivity of capital.

ELEMENTS OF AN INSURABLE RISK

Although it is theoretically possible to insure all possibilities of loss, some are not insurable at a reasonable price. For practical reasons, insurers are not willing to accept all the risks that others may wish to transfer to them. To be considered a proper subject for insurance, certain characteristics should be present. The four prerequisites listed next represent the "ideal" elements of an insurable risk. Although it is desirable that the risk have these characteristics, it is possible for certain risks that do not have them to be insured.

1. *There must be a sufficiently large number of homogeneous exposure units to make the losses reasonably predictable.* Insurance, as we have seen, is based on the operation of the law of large numbers. A large number of exposure units enhances the operation of an insurance plan by making estimates of future losses more accurate.[5]

2. *The loss produced by the risk must be definite and measurable.* It must be a type of loss that is relatively difficult to counterfeit, and it must be capable of financial measurement. In other words, we must be able to tell when a loss has taken place, and we must be able to set some value on the extent of it.

3. *The loss must be fortuitous or accidental.* The loss must be the result of a contingency; that is, it must be something that may or may not happen. It must not be something that is certain to happen. If the insurance company knows that an event in the future is inevitable, it also knows that it must collect a premium equal to the certain loss that it must pay, plus an additional amount for the expenses of administering the operation. Depreciation, which is a certainty, cannot be insured; it is provided for through a sinking fund. Furthermore, the loss should be beyond the control of the insured. The law of large numbers is useful in making predictions only if we can reasonably assume that future occurrences will approximate past experience. Since we assume that past experience was a result of chance happening, the predictions concerning the future will be valid only if future happenings are also a result of chance.

4. *The loss must not be catastrophic.* It must be unlikely to produce loss to a very large percentage of the exposure units at the same time. The insurance principle is based on a notion of sharing losses, and inherent in this idea is the assumption that only a small percentage of the group will suffer loss at any one time. Damage that results from enemy attack would be catastrophic in nature. There are additional perils, such as floods, which, while they would not affect everyone in the society, would affect only those who had purchased insurance. The principle of randomness in selection is closely related to the requirement that the loss must not be catastrophic.

Randomness

The future experience of the group to which we apply our predictions will approximate the experience of the group on which the predictions are based only if both have approximately the same characteristics. There must be a proportion of good and bad risks in the first group equal to the proportion of good and bad risks of the group on which the prediction is made. Yet, human nature acts to interfere with the randomness necessary to permit random composition of the current group. The losses that are predicted are based on the average experience of the older group, but there are always some individuals who are, and who realize that they are, worse than average risks. Because the chance of loss for these risks is greater than that for the other members of society, they have a tendency to desire insurance coverage to a greater extent than the remainder of the group. This tendency results in what is known as *adverse selection*. Adverse selection is the tendency

[5] The reader is no doubt aware of the much publicized instances in which Lloyd's writes insurance on the physical attributes of a rising starlet, or insures against loss from some unique event. While these exposures do not meet the desirable element of an insurable risk that there be a large number of exposures, the transactions are still insurance. The underwriters at Lloyd's are able to engage in such practices because they substitute mass underwriting (where a single risk is spread among many insurers) for the mass of exposures and because the premiums charged for such coverages are heavily loaded, that is, higher than probability requires.

of the persons whose exposure to loss is higher than average to purchase or continue insurance to a greater extent than those whose exposure is less than average. Unless some provision is made to prevent adverse selection, predictions based on past experience would be useless in foretelling future experience. Adverse selection works in the direction of accumulating bad risks. Given that the predictions of future losses are based on the average loss of the past (in which both good and poor exposures were involved), future losses will be worse than those of the past if the experience of the future is based on the experience of a larger proportion of bad risks, and the predictions will be invalid.

Adverse selection long caused private insurers to avoid the field of flood insurance. The adverse selection inherent in insuring fixed properties against the peril of flood is obvious. Only those individuals who feel that they are exposed to loss by flood are interested in flood insurance, and yet in the event of a flood, there is a likelihood that all these individuals would suffer loss. The element of the sharing of the losses of a few by the many who suffered no loss would not exist. Although some insurers have written coverage against flood on fixed properties, the coverage has not generally been available from private insurers for those who need it most.[6]

The "war-risk exclusion" that life insurance companies insert in their contracts during wartime is another example of the adverse selection principle. On the basis of past experience, it has been shown that deaths from combat have not been catastrophic, yet it is precisely because the insurance companies prevented adverse selection that they have not been. The war-risk exclusion is put into policies during wartime to prevent soldiers who would not otherwise have purchased insurance from doing so when they are exposed to a greater chance of loss. Policies that are sold before the war begins and do not have the war-risk exclusion cover deaths that result from war. If the policies purchased during the war were based on the same randomness as those sold in peacetime, the war-risk exclusion would not be necessary, but in the absence of such a provision, the randomness would not exist and the company would be selected against.

Economic Feasibility

Sometimes, an additional attribute is listed as a requirement of an insurable risk—that the cost of the insurance must not be high in relation to the possible loss or that the insurance must be economically feasible. We can hardly call this a requirement of an insurable risk in view of the fact that the principle is widely violated in the insurance industry today. The four elements of an insurable risk are characteristics of certain risks that permit the successful operation of the insurance principle. If a given risk lacks one of these elements, the operation of the insurance mechanism is impeded. The principle of "economically feasible insurability" is not really an impediment to the operation of the insurance principle, but rather a violation of the principles of risk management and common sense.

SELF-INSURANCE

The term *self-insurance* has become a well-established part of the terminology of the insurance field, despite disagreement as to whether or not such a mechanism is possible.[7] From a purely semantic point of view, the term *self-insurance* represents a definitional impossibility. The insurance mechanism consists of transfer of risk or pooling of exposure units, and since one cannot pool with or transfer to himself or herself, it can be argued that self-insurance is impossible. However, the term is widely used, and we ought therefore to establish an acceptable operational definition, semantically incorrect though it may be.

Under some circumstances, it is possible for a business firm or other organization to engage in the same types of activities as a commercial insurer dealing with its own risks. When these activities involve the operation of the law of large numbers and predictions regarding future losses, they are commonly referred to as "self-insurance."[8] To be operationally dependable, such programs must possess the following characteristics:

[6] After decades of agitation for the government to "do something" about flood exposure, a federal flood insurance program was enacted in 1968. This program is discussed in greater detail in Chapter 4.

[7] For example, see Matthew Lenz, Jr., "Self-insurance, Semantics, and Other Hang-ups," *CPCU Annals,* vol. 28 (June 1975).
[8] Technically, such programs are retention programs that employ insurance techniques. In spite of its semantic shortcomings, the term *self-insurance* is a convenient way of distinguishing the retention programs that utilize insurance techniques from those that do not.

- The organization should be big enough to permit the combination of a sufficiently large number of exposure units so as to make losses predictable. The program must be based on the operation of the law of large numbers.
- The plan must be financially dependable. In most cases, this will require the accumulation of funds to meet losses that occur, with a sufficient accumulation to safeguard against unexpected deviations from predicted losses.
- The individual units exposed to loss must be distributed geographically in such a manner as to prevent a catastrophe. A loss affecting enough units to result in severe financial loss should be impossible.

Even apart from its semantic shortcomings, *self-insurance* is an overworked term. Few companies or organizations are large enough to engage in a sound program meeting the requirements outlined here. In the majority of cases, risks are simply retained without attempting to make estimates of future losses. In many cases, no fund is maintained to pay for losses. Furthermore, until the fund reaches the size where it is adequate to pay the largest loss possible, the possibility of loss is not eliminated for the individual exposure units.

THE FIELDS OF INSURANCE

Insurance is a broad, generic term, embracing the entire array of institutions that deal with risk through the device of sharing and transfer of risks. Insurance may be divided and subdivided into classifications based on the perils insured against or the fundamental nature of the particular program. Basically, the primary distinction is between private insurance and social insurance. In addition to these two classes, we will also examine a third class of quasi-social insurance coverages called *public benefit guarantee programs*.

Private insurance consists for the most part of voluntary insurance programs available to the individual as a means of protection against the possibility of loss. This voluntary insurance is usually provided by private firms, but, in some instances, it is also offered by the government. The distinguishing characteristics of private insurance are that it is usually voluntary and that the transfer of risk is normally accomplished by means of a contract. *Social insurance,* on the other hand, is compulsory insurance, usually operated by the government, whose benefits are determined by law and in which the primary emphasis is on social adequacy. In general, the benefits under social insurance programs attempt to redistribute income based on some notion of "social adequacy." The largest of the social insurance programs in the United States is the Social Security system.

Unfortunately, there is no single criterion that can be used to distinguish private insurance from social insurance. Further complicating the situation, the designations *private* and *voluntary* are both slightly misleading: some "private insurance" is sold by the government, and not all compulsory insurance is social insurance. The following discussion of the fields of private insurance and social insurance will serve to distinguish them and will provide a basic introduction to the types of insurance to be discussed in later chapters.

Private (Voluntary) Insurance

As noted, private insurance consists of those insurance programs that are available to the individual as protection against financial loss. It is usually (but not always) voluntary, and generally (but not always) based on the concept of individual equity. Some private insurance coverages are compulsory, and, although the emphasis is on individual equity, private insurance for some classes of insureds is subsidized either by government or by other insureds. Furthermore, although most private insurance is sold by private firms, in a number of instances, it is offered by the government.[9]

Today, private insurance in the United States may be classified into three broad categories:

- Life insurance
- Health insurance
- Property and liability insurance

Life Insurance Life insurance is designed to provide protection against two distinct risks: premature death and superannuation. As a matter of personal preference, death at any age is probably premature,

[9] Examples of some types of private insurance sold by the government include life insurance, available through the Veterans Administration and federal crop insurance.

and superannuation (living too long) does not normally strike one as an undesirable contingency. From a practical point of view, however, a person can, and sometimes does, die before adequate preparation has been made for the future financial requirements of dependents. In the same way, a person can, and often does, outlive income-earning ability. Life insurance, endowments, and annuities protect the individual and his or her dependents against the undesirable financial consequences of premature death and superannuation.

Health Insurance Accident and health insurance (or, more simply, *health insurance*) is defined as "insurance against loss by sickness or accidental bodily injury."[10] The "loss" may be the loss of wages caused by the sickness or accident or it may be expenses for doctor bills, hospital bills, medicine, or the expenses of long-term care. Included within this definition are forms of insurance that provide lump-sum or periodic payments in the event of loss occasioned by sickness or accident, such as disability income insurance and accidental death and dismemberment insurance.

Property and Liability Insurance Property and liability insurance consists of those forms of insurance designed to protect against losses resulting from damage to or loss of property and losses arising from legal liability.[11] It includes the following types of insurance.

Property insurance, also sometimes referred to as *fire insurance,* is designed to indemnify the insured for loss of, or damage to, buildings, furniture, fixtures, or other personal property as a result of fire, lightning, windstorm, hail, explosion, and a long list of other perils. Originally, fire was the only peril insured, but the number of perils insured against has gradually been expanded over the years. Today, two basic approaches are taken with respect to the perils for which coverage is provided. Under the first approach, called *named-peril coverage,* the specific perils against which protection is provided are listed in the policy, and coverage applies only for damage arising out of the listed perils. Under the second approach, called *open-peril coverage,* the policy lists the perils for which coverage is not provided, and loss from any peril not excluded is covered.[12] Coverage may be provided for both direct loss (i.e., the actual loss represented by the destruction of the asset) and indirect loss (i.e., the loss of income and/or the extra expense that is the result of the loss of the use of the asset protected).

Marine insurance, like fire insurance, is designed to protect against financial loss resulting from damage to owned property, except that here the perils are primarily those associated with transportation. Marine insurance is divided into two classifications: ocean marine and inland marine.

Ocean marine insurance policies provide coverage on all types of oceangoing vessels and their cargoes. Policies are also written to cover the shipowner's liability. Originally, ocean marine policies covered cargo only after it was loaded onto the ship. Today the policies are usually endorsed to provide coverage from "warehouse to warehouse," thus protecting against overland transportation hazards as well as those on the ocean.

Inland marine insurance seems like a contradiction in terms. The field developed as an outgrowth of ocean marine insurance and "warehouse-to-warehouse" coverage. Originally, inland marine developed to cover goods being transported by carriers such as railroads, motor vehicles, or ships and barges on the inland waterways and in coastal trade. It was expanded to cover instrumentalities of transportation and communication such as bridges, tunnels, pipelines, power transmission lines, and radio and television communication equipment. Eventually, it was expanded to include coverage on various types of property that is not in the course of transportation, but that is away from the owner's premises.

Automobile insurance provides protection against several types of losses. First, it protects against loss resulting from legal liability arising out of the ownership or use of an automobile. In addition, the medical payments section of the automobile policy consists of a special form of health and accident insurance that provides for the payment of medical expenses incurred as a result of automobile accidents. Coverage is also provided against loss resulting from theft

[10] The Commission on Insurance Terminology of the American Risk and Insurance Association.

[11] Historically, property and liability insurance was referred to as *fire and casualty* (or sometimes *property and casualty*) insurance. The evolution of property and liability insurance is discussed in Chapter 5.

[12] This latter approach was formerly referred to as "all-risk" coverage, and you may still hear it called that. There is a concerted effort to avoid the term "all risk," however, because it was frequently misunderstood by insurance buyers. The term *open-peril* coverage is gradually replacing the term *all risk*.

of the automobile or damage to it from many different causes.

Liability insurance embraces a wide range of coverages. The form with which most students are familiar is automobile liability insurance, but there are other liability hazards as well. Coverage is available to protect against nonautomobile liability exposures such as ownership of property, manufacturing and construction operations, the sale or distribution of products, and many other exposures.

Workers compensation insurance had its beginning (in the United States) shortly after the turn of the century, when the various states began to pass workers compensation laws. Under these laws, the employer was made absolutely liable for injuries to workers that arose out of and in the course of their employment. Workers compensation insurance provides for the payment of the obligation these statutes impose on the employer.[13]

Equipment breakdown insurance (also referred to as boiler and machinery insurance) was introduced in the late 1800s to cover the explosion hazard inherent in early boilers. It was later expanded to include coverage for accidental breakdown of a wide range of types of equipment. More recently, with advances in automation, it was further expanded to include coverage for virtually all types of equipment. To prevent losses, equipment breakdown insurers maintain an extensive inspection service, and this service is a primary reason for the purchase of the coverage. Although the contract does not require them to do so, the insurers make periodic inspections of the objects insured. As a result, losses are reduced and the insured benefits.

Burglary, robbery, and theft insurance protect the property of the insured against loss resulting from criminal acts of others. Because a standard clause in these crime policies excludes acts by employees of the insured, they are referred to as "nonemployee crime coverages." Protection against criminal acts by employees is provided under fidelity bonds, which are discussed shortly.

Credit insurance is a highly specialized form of coverage (available to manufacturers and wholesalers) that indemnifies the insured for losses resulting from their inability to collect from customers. The coverage is written subject to a deductible equal to the normal bad-debt loss and with a provision requiring the insured to share a part of each loss with the insurer.

Title insurance is still another narrowly specialized form of coverage.[14] Basically, it provides protection against financial loss resulting from a defect in an insured title. The legal aspects of land transfer are rather technical, and the possibility always exists that the title may not be clear. Under a title insurance policy, the insurer agrees to indemnify the insured to the extent of any financial loss suffered as a result of the transfer of a defective title. In a sense, title insurance is unique in that it insures against the effects of some past event rather than against financial loss resulting from a future occurrence.

Fidelity and Surety Bonds Fidelity and surety bonds represent a special class of risk transfer device, and opinions differ as to whether bonds should be classified as insurance. As a matter of fact, there are certain fundamental differences between a bond and an insurance policy, and, strictly speaking, it can be argued that some bonds are not contracts of insurance. In general terms, a bond is an agreement by one party, the *surety,* to answer to a third person, called the *obligee,* for the debt or default of another party, called the *principal.* In other words, the surety guarantees a certain type of conduct on the part of the principal, and, if the principal fails to behave in the manner guaranteed, the surety will be responsible to the obligee.

Bonding is divided into two classes: *fidelity bonds* and *surety bonds.* Fidelity bonds protect the obligee against dishonesty on the part of his or her employees and are commonly called *employee dishonesty insurance.* In most respects they resemble insurance more closely than surety bonds do, and many authorities consider them a form of casualty insurance.

Most surety bonds are issued for persons doing contract construction, those connected with court actions, and those seeking licenses and permits. Basically, the *surety bond* guarantees that the principal is honest and has the necessary ability and financial capacity to carry out the obligation for which he or she is bonded. The surety obligates itself with the principal to the obligee in much the same manner

[13] As noted shortly, from the perspective of workers, workers compensation is considered a social insurance coverage.

[14] Title insurance is clearly a form of property insurance and whether it should be classified as "casualty" insurance is debatable. Historically, it has been written by specialty insurers, but it is generally classified as a casualty coverage by the state insurance codes.

that the cosigner of a note assumes an obligation with a borrower to a lender. The primary obligation to perform rests with the principal, but if the principal is unable to meet the commitment after exhausting all his or her resources, the surety must provide funds to pay for the loss. In this event, the surety may take possession of the principal's assets and convert them into cash to reimburse itself for the loss paid.

Although there is a difference of opinion as to whether bonds are actually insurance, insurance regulators normally include them within the framework of the contracts they regulate. Furthermore, property and liability insurers sell these bonds, and suretyship is normally considered a part of the property and liability insurance business.

Social Insurance

Social insurance differs from private insurance in a number of respects. In the case of social insurance, we use the insurance mechanism for transferring and sharing risk, but we do so on a somewhat qualified basis. Social insurance provides compulsory protection for personal risks—those that involve the possible loss of income or assets because of premature death, dependent old age, sickness or disability, or unemployment. Social insurance seeks to provide a "floor of protection" to persons who would not individually be able to cope with certain fundamental risks. It does this by providing benefits not only to those in need, but to others as well.

Modern social insurance originated in Germany in the 1880s under chancellor Otto von Bismarck. Over the period from 1884 through 1889, Germany constructed a model social insurance program composed of three elements. The first was *sickness insurance* for practically all employed persons, a nineteenth-century universal health insurance program. The second element was *accident insurance,* for work-related injuries—in effect, the first workers compensation program. The final element in the program was *insurance for invalidity and old age,* the equivalent of our Social Security system.[15] From

Germany, the idea of social insurance spread to other European nations and eventually to the United States.[16]

In the United States, the first social insurance program was the workers compensation system, which was adopted by the individual states during the early 1900s. A quarter of a century later, the Social Security Act of 1935 established the Old-Age, Survivors, and Disability Insurance Program, better known as the Social Security system. The Social Security Act also encouraged the states to enact unemployment insurance laws, which every state has done. In 1965, Medicare was added to the Social Security system, providing health insurance for persons over age 65. Finally, six jurisdictions (California, Hawaii, New Jersey, New York, Rhode Island, and Puerto Rico) have *enacted compulsory temporary disability laws* that require insurance against loss of income from nonoccupational disabilities. Thus, social insurance programs in the United States exist at both the state and federal level. State programs include workers compensation and unemployment insurance in all states and compulsory temporary disability insurance in six states. Federal programs include the Old-Age, Survivors, and Disability Insurance Program and Medicare.

Social Insurance Defined Any definition of social insurance must, by its very nature, be rather complex. The following definition of social insurance has been proposed:[17]

> Social insurance is a device for the pooling of risks by their transfer to an organization, usually governmental, that is required by law to provide pecuniary or service benefits to or on behalf of covered persons upon the occurrence of certain predesignated losses under all the following conditions:
>
> 1. Coverage is compulsory by law in virtually all instances.
> 2. Eligibility for benefits is derived, in fact or in effect, from contributions having been made to

[15] Interestingly, Bismarck's support for these programs was not motivated by an inclination toward social engineering. Rather, it was a shrewd political move designed to counter the rapid growth of socialism in Germany. One of the central themes of the social democrats' agenda was the promise of retirement benefits for workers. In effect, Bismarck simply outbid the socialists at their own game.

[16] Great Britain passed an old-age pension act in 1909 and added unemployment and health insurance in 1911. Other European nations followed in rapid succession: Luxembourg, 1911; Rumania, 1912; Sweden, 1913; Italy, 1919; Netherlands, 1919; Spain, 1919; Denmark, 1921; USSR, 1922; Belgium, 1924; Bulgaria, 1924; Czechoslovakia, 1924; France, 1928; Hungary, 1928; Greece, 1932; and Poland, 1933.

[17] The Commission on Insurance Terminology of the American Risk and Insurance Association.

the program by or in respect of the claimant or the person as to whom the claimant is dependent: there is no requirement that the individual demonstrate inadequate financial resources, although a dependency status may need to be established.

3. The method of determining benefits is prescribed by law.

4. The benefits for any individual are not directly related to contributions made by or in respect to him or her, but instead usually redistribute income so as to favor certain groups such as those with low former wages or large numbers of dependents.

5. There is a definite plan for financing the benefits that is designed to be adequate in terms of long-range considerations.

6. The cost is borne primarily by contributions that are usually made by covered persons, their employers, or both.

7. The plan is administered or at least supervised by the government.

8. The plan is not established by the government solely for its present or former employees.

Certain elements in the definition require clarification. First, the mere fact that a specific type of insurance is compulsory does not make it a social insurance program. Compulsory automobile insurance, for example, does not meet other conditions listed and, therefore, is not social insurance. Furthermore, although the government is usually the transferor in a social insurance plan, this is not a prerequisite. Workers compensation insurance is a social insurance coverage that is sold by commercial insurers.

The second of the conditions listed in the definition distinguishes social insurance from public assistance or welfare programs, in which eligibility for benefits is based on need. Because of the contributions made by or on behalf of the insureds under a social insurance program, the right to benefits is essentially a statutory right and is not based on "need" or a "means test."

More than any of the others, the fourth element in the definition distinguishes social insurance from private insurance. In private insurance, insurers attempt to distribute the loss costs equitably, in proportion to the loss-producing characteristics of the insureds. It would be considered inequitable, for example, to charge a 25-year-old person the same premium for life insurance as that charged to a 65-year-old person. In social insurance, individual equity is secondary in importance to the social adequacy of the benefits. Benefits are weighted in favor of certain groups so that all persons will be provided a minimum floor of protection. In the federal Social Security program, for example, the benefits are weighted in favor of the low-income groups, and persons with large families. Although benefits under social insurance programs are not directly proportional to contributions, they are at least loosely related to the earnings of the individual. Therefore, even though social adequacy rather than individual equity is stressed, there is at least a loose relationship between earnings and benefits.

The fifth condition, that there be a definite plan for financing the benefits that is designed to satisfy long-range considerations, merely requires that there be some sort of long-range planning. It does not demand that the obligations under the program be fully funded. In private insurance, insurers are required to maintain reserves to fund the future obligations they incur. In social insurance, the future obligations are rarely funded in full, but depend on the future taxing power of the government.

The sixth principle is known as the self-supporting contributory principle. This means that the costs are not financed from the general revenues of the Treasury, but are paid for primarily by those who expect to benefit from the programs. In most instances the support is derived from contributions by employees, employers, and the self-employed. This method of financing is unique to American social insurance programs, because in most other countries with extensive programs, a part or all of the financing comes from general government revenues.

Social Insurance Programs in the United States
Social insurance developed later in the United States than in European countries, but social insurance programs now exist at both the national and state levels. The principal social insurance programs under federal jurisdiction include the Old-Age, Survivors', and Disability Insurance program and the Medicare program, both administered by the Department of Health and Human Services, and the Railroad Retirement, Railroad Disability, and Railroad Unemployment insurance programs, administered by the Railroad Retirement Board. Social insurance programs under state jurisdiction include workers compensation, unemployment compensation, and compulsory temporary disability insurance laws.

Workers Compensation The first social insurance legislation in the United States was workers compensation laws, enacted by the individual states beginning in 1908. Workers compensation provides benefits to workers and their dependents when a worker suffers an occupational injury or disease. Workers compensation laws replaced a system of employers' liability, under which injured workers could recover for occupational injuries only through a lawsuit against the employer. Although workers compensation insurance is considered a form of social insurance, it is sold by private insurers and by state workers compensation funds. In addition, because workers compensation laws impose liability on the employer for program benefits, it is a form of private insurance from the employers' perspective.

Old-Age, Survivors', and Disability Insurance The Social Security Act of 1935 stands as the most comprehensive piece of social legislation of its kind in the history of this country. It established *the Old-Age, Survivors', and Disability Insurance Program* (OASDI), better known as Social Security, the largest of all government insurance programs in the United States.

Initially, the law provided only retirement benefits. It was modified to provide survivor benefits in 1939. Disability benefits were added in 1956, and in 1965 it was further expanded by the addition of the Medicare program. As presently constituted, the program provides life insurance, disability insurance, and retirement pensions to those covered under the program—virtually all gainfully employed persons in the nation and their dependents. The only exceptions are certain government employees who are covered under a civil service retirement system, railroad employees (protected under their own programs), and some persons engaged in irregular employment. By 2001, over 45.8 million people were receiving monthly benefits under the programs comprising OASDI. Annual taxes for the programs in the fiscal year of 2001 amounted to $421.3 billion, and benefits totaled $358.3 billion.[18]

Railroad Retirement, Disability, and Unemployment Programs Another U.S. government agency, the Railroad Retirement Board, administers and serves as the fiduciary for a comprehensive program of retirement pensions, survivor benefits, unemployment insurance, and disability coverage for persons employed by the railroads. In addition to their unique status with respect to retirement benefits, railroad workers are also covered under a separate unemployment compensation law, which includes coverage for occupational and nonoccupational disabilities as well as unemployment not connected with a disability.

Unemployment Insurance The Social Security Act of 1935 also initiated our system of unemployment compensation. Although some states had enacted unemployment laws, most states were reluctant to enact such programs because they feared that their industries would suffer a competitive disadvantage with other states unfettered by this kind of legislation. The Social Security Act used the power of the federal government to levy taxes to induce the several states to enact unemployment insurance plans. The Social Security Act of 1935 imposed a tax of 1 percent on the total payroll of most employers who had eight or more employees, but provided that employers would be permitted to offset 90 percent of the tax through credit for taxes paid to a state unemployment insurance program meeting standards specified in the law. In effect, this meant that any state that did not enact a qualified unemployment compensation law would suffer a financial drain. Not surprisingly, all the states elected to set up such programs and qualified for the tax offset. The tax has been altered several times since 1935.

Medicare The federal government's *Medicare* program, which is a basic part of the Social Security system, became effective on July 1, 1966. The program provides two forms of essential health insurance to virtually all citizens over 65 and to certain disabled persons. The first coverage, designated Part A, is compulsory hospitalization insurance, financed by payroll taxes levied on employers and employees. Part B is voluntary medical insurance, designed to help pay for physicians' services and other medical expenses not covered by Part A. This supplementary coverage is financed by monthly premiums shared by the participants and the federal government. More than 40 million persons are entitled to hospital insurance provided under Medicare, and over 37 million are enrolled for the supplementary medical insurance. During 2001, about $149 billion was paid in Medicare benefits, $93 billion in hospitalization

[18] The OASDI program dates from the enactment of the Social Security Act of 1935, which provided retirement benefits only. Survivors' benefits and disability benefits were added later. The OASDI program is discussed in greater detail in Chapter 11.

benefits, and $56 billion in supplementary medical insurance benefits.[19]

State Compulsory Temporary Disability Funds In addition to workers compensation and unemployment compensation, six jurisdictions (California, Hawaii, New Jersey, New York, Rhode Island, and Puerto Rico) have enacted *compulsory temporary disability laws* that require insurance coverage against loss of income from nonoccupational disabilities. These programs furnish a compulsory complement to the workers compensation laws, which cover occupational disabilities. In addition to requiring participation in the program and prescribing benefit levels, all the states also act as insurers. In Rhode Island, the state operates a monopolistic insurance program, while in the other jurisdictions state funds compete with private insurers providing the coverage.[20]

Is Social Insurance Really Insurance? One more aspect of social insurance, often expressed as a criticism, should at least be mentioned at this juncture— the question of whether social insurance is really insurance or whether it is merely a unique method of providing benefits without the use of the basic principles of insurance. Despite the rather substantial differences between the operational features of social and private insurance, it is our conclusion that the basic principles of insurance are just as applicable in one as in the other. As explained earlier, insurance is the mechanism by which the risk of financial loss is transferred by individuals (to a professional transferee or to a group), where loss costs are distributed in some equitable manner among the members of the group. Since social insurance uses both risk transfer and loss sharing, it is "insurance."

Critics who disagree with this conclusion maintain that social insurance programs are "actuarially unsound" and therefore cannot be insurance. The effectiveness of such an argument must, of course, depend on the definition of "actuarial soundness." To the critics, an insurance program is *actuarially sound* only if it is possible to measure the probability of loss with a high degree of accuracy and only if proper reserves are maintained to provide for future obliga-

tions. If this high degree of precision in measuring probabilities does not exist according to the argument, and if appropriate reserves are not maintained, the program should not be called insurance. For example, the OASDI program is affected by so many variables—population growth, the aging of the population, inflation, politics, and the like—that a precise prediction of long-range future obligations is not possible. Therefore, these critics would assume that the OASDI program is actuarially unsound and so is not insurance.

It is true, perhaps, that the success of the insurance principle must depend on the ability to obtain at least a reasonable approximation of the probability of loss. However, a precise prediction is not necessary. There are many forms of private insurance, such as windstorm, hail, earthquake, and even automobile, in which precise statistical calculations of probabilities are impossible. In some cases, probability calculations are nothing more than enlightened guesses. To the extent that a reasonable approximation of loss can be obtained, these types of private insurance are actuarially sound. To the extent that the future obligations under social insurance programs are capable of approximation for a reasonable time in the future, they are also actuarially sound. Actuarial soundness demands specifically a prediction of future obligations and has basically nothing to do with the maintenance of reserves. Therefore, an insurance program can be actuarially sound whether the future obligations are funded or not, just as long as there is sufficient income to pay for the obligations. The partial funding of many of our social insurance programs does not remove these from the category of insurance.

Public Guarantee Insurance Programs

In addition to the private insurance and social insurance coverages we have discussed, there are some insurance programs that do not fit precisely into either field. This third class of insurance programs consists of government-operated, compulsory, quasi-social insurance programs, mainly in connection with financial institutions holding assets belonging to the public. We have designated these as "public guarantee insurance programs." The best known of these programs is the Federal Deposit Insurance Corporation (FDIC), which insures depositors against loss resulting from failure of commercial banks.

Under these public guarantee insurance programs, government-funded agencies use the insur-

[19] The Medicare program is discussed in greater detail in Chapter 22.

[20] Rhode Island had the first such law, adopting it in 1942. California passed its law in 1946, New Jersey in 1948, and New York in 1949. There was no further similar legislation until 1968, when Puerto Rico enacted its law. Hawaii followed in 1969.

ance principle to provide protection to lenders, depositors, or investors against loss arising from the collapse of a financial institution holding deposits of the public or of some other type of fiduciary. Usually, as in the case of the FDIC, the insurance is closely allied with the function of regulation.[21]

Federal Public Guarantee Insurance Programs
Public guarantee insurance programs operate at both the state and federal level. There are four major federal public guarantee insurance programs.

The FDIC The modern prototype for this form of insurance, the FDIC, is a public corporation created by the federal government in 1933 to insure deposits in banks and thereby protect depositors against loss in case of bank failure. The FDIC currently insures accounts of any one depositor up to $100,000, providing protection against loss of the depositor's funds as a result of failure or insolvency of the bank. The FDIC was originally funded by an appropriation from general government revenues; its income is now derived from a $\frac{1}{12}$ of 1 percent annual assessment on the deposits of the banks covered. Although the FDIC has served successfully as a guarantor of depositors for over half a century, another federal instrumentality, the Federal Savings and Loan Insurance Corporation (FSLIC), ended in 1989 in the face of massive savings and loan failures.[22]

The National Credit Union Administration
Another organization, the National Credit Union Administration (NCUA), provides deposit insurance for members of credit unions. Like the FDIC, the NCUA affords protection up to $100,000 per depositor and derives its income from a $\frac{1}{12}$ of 1 percent annual assessment on the deposits covered.

Securities Investor Protection Corporation Comparable applications of this type of public insurer have been made in other fields. For example, following the failure of a large national securities brokerage firm with consequent losses to its clients, the federal government established an insurer designed to protect investors dealing with licensed security brokerage firms in case such firms did fold. The Securities Investor Protection Corporation, established in 1972, provides custodial account protection for those investors who allow their brokers to keep their securities for safety and trading convenience. All registered brokers must insure under the program, which protects each investor up to $500,000.

The Pension Benefit Guaranty Corporation The most recent of the public guarantee insurance corporations was established as a part of the far-reaching legislation known as the Employee Retirement Income Security Act of 1974 (ERISA). Congress had long been distressed by the inadequate performance of private pension plans, many of which were unfunded and offered little real security to workers. Although most have met their obligations, there have been notable examples of pension plans that have failed to meet their commitments, leaving workers stranded. Under the provisions of ERISA, Congress established a government insurer, the Pension Benefit Guaranty Corporation (PBGC), that offers insurance guaranteeing employees covered by private pension plans that they will receive their vested benefits up to a specified maximum if the plan is terminated.

State Public Guarantee Insurance Programs
Public guarantee insurance programs also exist at the state level. For example, some states maintain state funds similar to the FDIC to insure the deposits of state mutual savings banks. In addition, the following guarantee programs fit into this category.

State Insurer Insolvency Funds All states have funds designed to protect insurance policyholders from losses because of their insurer becoming insolvent. Most of these funds operate on a post-loss assessment basis, meaning the surviving insurers are assessed after an insolvency to pay the losses of the insolvent insurer. New York operates a pre-loss assessment fund for property and liability insurers. These funds are discussed in greater detail in Chapter 6.

Unsatisfied Judgment Funds Five states (Maryland, Michigan, New Jersey, New York, and North Dakota) have established *unsatisfied judgment funds*

[21] The public guarantee insurance concept had its inception with a law passed in New York State in 1829, under which banks were required to pay annual assessments into a safety fund to be used to pay the debts of any contributing bank that later became insolvent. By 1858, similar funds had been established in Michigan, Ohio, Iowa, Indiana, and Vermont. All these plans were short-lived and for various reasons had ceased operations by 1866. Between 1907 and 1917, eight other states established bank guarantee funds, but none of these was still in operation when the great wave of bank failures broke in the early 1930s.

[22] The FSLIC was a casualty of massive savings and loan failures in 1987, 1988, and 1989. Legislation enacted by Congress in 1988 as a part of the savings and loan "bailout" consolidated deposit insurance for savings and loan associations with that for commercial banks in the FDIC. The Government Accounting Office has estimated the cost of the savings and loan bailout to be $257 billion by 2021.

that provide for payment to persons injured in automobile accidents when the negligent party is unable to pay for the damages. The financing of these funds varies among the states. In North Dakota, the fund is financed by a uniform levy on each registered motor vehicle. In Maryland and New Jersey, a fee is also levied on each registered motor vehicle, but the amount is higher for uninsured drivers than for those who carry insurance. In addition, Maryland levies a tax of ½ percent of all auto premiums written by insurance companies in the state.

Public Guarantee Programs as Insurance
Despite occasional debates over whether these programs are actually insurance, all clearly utilize the basic insurance mechanisms of pooling and transfer of risk. Those who argue that the term *insurance* is misapplied to these plans point out that there is some question as to whether the individual programs meet the desirable elements of an insurable risk discussed in Chapter 2. For example, in some instances, it is doubtful whether the risks are in fact fortuitous. Furthermore, there is also an element of catastrophe, arising out of the dynamic nature of the credit exposure. Nevertheless, the programs all exhibit the basic characteristics of insurance, including the transfer of risk from the individual to a group and the sharing on some equitable basis of losses that do occur.

Similarities in the Various Fields of Insurance

As we have seen in this chapter, the term *insurance* encompasses a wide variety of approaches used by society for sharing risks. While attempting to distinguish among the various classes of insurance, we have focused on the differences. In closing, we should also note some of the similarities, lest the emphasis on differences obscure the common elements.

Although the actual details of operation may vary, all the programs examined in this chapter use some form of pooling of the exposure units exposed to risk. In every instance the possibility of loss is transferred from the individual to the group, where losses are shared on some prescribed basis. Each program calls for specific contributions made by the participants and is designed to meet the costs of the system. The basic concepts of pooling and sharing of losses and the individual's substitution of a small, certain cost for a large, uncertain loss are fundamental to all the programs.

IMPORTANT CONCEPTS TO REMEMBER

insurance defined from the viewpoint of the individual
randomness
insurance defined from the viewpoint of society
economic feasibility
a priori probabilities
statistical probabilities
a posteriori probabilities
law of large numbers
dispersion

adverse selection
standard deviation
relative frequency interpretation
subjective interpretation
sample
variance
elements of an insurable risk
self-insurance
private insurance
social insurance
public benefit guarantee program

ocean marine insurance
inland marine insurance
property insurance
health insurance
casualty insurance
liability insurance
surety bonds
surety
principal
obligee

QUESTIONS FOR REVIEW

1. List and explain each of the desirable elements of an insurable risk.
2. Explain the dual application of the law of large numbers as it pertains to the operation of insurance.
3. What is the effect of an increase in the number of observations in a sampling technique on:

a. the underlying probability of the event
b. our estimate of the probability
c. the standard deviation

4. Identify the two fundamental functions involved in the operation of the insurance mechanism.

5. How does insurance substitute certainty from the standpoint of the insured?

6. Give examples of three uninsurable exposures and indicate why each is uninsurable.

7. What are the costs to society of insurance and what are the contributions that insurance makes to society that justify these costs?

8. What are the specific conditions of a social insurance plan that distinguish it from private or voluntary insurance?

9. Briefly describe the three general categories into which private or voluntary insurance may be divided.

10. Briefly explain the fundamental difference between an insurance contract and a surety bond.

QUESTIONS FOR DISCUSSION

1. There are many strikes in the United States, bringing financial suffering to both employers and workers. Would you expect a commercial insurer to provide insurance protection to either the workers or the employers to cover losses resulting from these strikes? Why or why not?

2. Suppose that the members of your class enter into an agreement under whose terms all would chip in to pay for the damage to any automobile owned by a class member that was damaged in a collision. Explain if this is insurance and whether you would be willing to participate.

3. A friend tells you about a plan for the formation of an insurance company that will issue insurance policies to protect a person who buys stock against a decline in the value of that stock. Explain why you believe the scheme will or will not work.

4. "Other things being equal, one should prefer to purchase insurance from the largest insurance company possible." On what basis does the author of this statement probably draw this conclusion?

5. In the late 1980s, the U.S. economy witnessed widespread failures in the savings and loan industry. In the face of massive failures, the resources of the Federal Savings and Loan Insurance Corporation proved inadequate to meet losses, and a bailout of S & L depositors was enacted by Congress. To what extent does the failure of the FSLIC indicate anything about the extent to which public guarantee programs meet the desirable elements of an insurable risk?

SUGGESTIONS FOR ADDITIONAL READING

Denenberg, Herbert S. "The Legal Definition of Insurance." *Journal of Risk and Insurance,* vol. 30, no. 3 (Sept. 1963).

Faulkner, E. J., ed. *Man's Quest for Security.* Lincoln: University of Nebraska Press, 1966.

Kulp, C. A., and John W. Hall. *Casualty Insurance,* 4th ed. New York: Ronald Press, 1968. Chapter 1.

Lenz, Matthew, Jr. "Self-insurance, Semantics, and Other Hang-Ups." *CPCU Annals,* vol. 28 (June 1975).

Mowbray, A. H., R. H. Blanchard, and C. Arthur Williams. *Insurance,* 6th ed. New York: McGraw-Hill, 1969. Chapters 5, 6.

Rejda, George E. *Social Insurance and Economic Security,* 6th ed. Englewood Cliffs, N.J.: Prentice-Hall, 1998.

Smith, Barry D. *How Insurance Works: An Introduction to Property and Liability Insurance,* 2nd ed. Malvern, Pa.: Insurance Institute of America, 1994.

WEB SITES TO EXPLORE

Automation Management Group Links of Interest	http://www.taan.com/inssites.htm
Gamma Iota Sigma	http://members.tripod.com/gammagrand/sectioni.htm
Insurance News Network	http://www.insure.com/
RISKWeb	http://www.RISKWeb.com/
Ultimate Insurance Links	http://www.barryklein.com/

<div style="text-align:center">

CHAPTER 4

RISK MANAGEMENT APPLICATIONS

■

Things which matter most must never be at the mercy of things which matter least.

— GOETHE

</div>

CHAPTER OBJECTIVES

When you have finished this chapter, you should be able to

- Identify two decision models from the field of decision theory that may be used in risk management decision making and explain the circumstances in which each is applicable
- Identify the three rules of risk management and explain how they relate to the management science decision models
- Identify the common errors in buying insurance and explain how these errors can be avoided
- Select the appropriate technique for dealing with a particular risk, based on the characteristics of the risk
- Identify the factors that should be considered in the selection of an insurance agent and an insurance company
- Explain the advantages and disadvantages of self-insurance
- Describe the general nature of captive insurance companies

Now that we have examined the concepts of risk, risk management, and insurance, we turn to a discussion of risk management applications and the ways in which risk management concepts can be applied in actually managing risks. We begin with a discussion of the considerations in selecting the technique that will be used to address the various risks facing the individual or organization. Next, we will discuss the ways in which these considerations influence insurance-buying decisions. Finally, we will examine some of the alternatives to commercial insurance.

RISK MANAGEMENT DECISIONS

Once the risks have been identified and evaluated, the next step is the consideration of the techniques that should be used to deal with each risk. This phase of the risk management process is primarily a problem in decision making: more precisely, it is deciding which of the techniques available should be used in dealing with each risk. Numerous strategies have been suggested for this phase of the risk management process. Some have proven to be more productive than others.

Utility Theory and Risk Management Decisions

Some theorists have suggested that utility theory be used as an approach to risk management decisions, especially as regards retention and transfer.[1] They would use the expected value concept to compare an individual's preferences (utility) for different states of uncertainty (e.g., "Which would you prefer, a 10% chance of losing $1000 or a 1% chance of losing $10,000?"). Once the individual's preference for different states of uncertainty (his or her "utility function") has been derived, it is used in a calculation that multiplies utility units by the probability that each level of loss might occur. This calculation is made for each decision being considered and the decision that produces the lowest expected loss of utility is selected.

We will not discuss the process by which the utility function is derived primarily because we do not believe that it is a useful tool for risk management decisions. The theory of marginal utility was constructed by economists in an attempt to explain *why* people make the consumer choices they do. It does not and is not intended to provide guidance on the decisions people *should* make.[2] Using a utility func-

[1] For example, see Mark R. Greene and Oscar N. Serbein, *Risk Management: Text and Cases* (Reston, Virginia: Reston Publishing Company, 1983), p. 52.

[2] The seminal article on utility and choices involving risk was written to provide a theoretical explanation for the apparent inconsistencies in human behavior with respect to risk. Some people will purchase insurance, indicating a distaste for uncertainty, while other people gamble, indicating that they prefer risk to certainty. To explain this anomaly, Friedman and Savage hypothesized that people who buy insurance have a different utility curve from that of gamblers. See Milton Friedman and L. J. Savage, "Utility Analysis of Choices Involving Risk," *Journal of Political Economy,* LVI (August 1948), pp. 279–304.

tion (real or hypothetical) as the basis for risk-related decisions could conceivably lead to more consistent decisions, but there is no reason to believe that those decisions would be good. They might be consistent, but consistently bad decisions.

Decision Theory and Risk Management Decisions

The most appropriate approaches to risk management decisions are drawn from decision theory and operations research. The types of problems addressed by the decision theory approach to decision making are those for which there is not an obvious solution, a situation that characterizes many risk management decisions. The decision theory approach aims at identifying the *best* decision or solution to the problem.

Cost-Benefit Analysis In theory, each of the techniques of risk management should be used when it is the most effective technique for dealing with a particular risk. Further, each technique should be used up to the point at which each dollar spent on the measure will produce a dollar in savings through reduction in losses. This is simply cost-benefit analysis, which attempts to measure the benefit of any course of action against its costs.

Applying marginal-benefit marginal-cost analysis to the risk management problem is complicated by several factors. The first is that while costs are measurable, benefits may not be measurable. When there is uncertainty about what the benefits will be, the decision requires that one estimate the expected value of the benefits, computed from the potential payoffs and the probabilities of various outcomes.

Expected Value Decision theory literature suggests three classes of decision-making situations, based on the knowledge the decision maker has about the possible outcomes or results (called *states of nature*). The first is *decision making under certainty,* which defines the situation in which the outcomes that result from each choice are known (and therefore when benefit-cost analysis is appropriate). The second is *decision making under risk,* in which the outcomes are uncertain but probability estimates are available for the various outcomes. Finally, *decision making under uncertainty* means that the probability of occurrence of each outcome is not known.

In decision making under risk, where the probability of different outcomes can be predicted with

reasonable precision, expected values can be computed to determine the most favorable outcome. For example, a blackjack player with a count of 16 who "stands" against the dealer's ten will lose 78.8 percent of the time and win 21.2 percent of the time, for an expected value of –0.576. If the player "hits" the 16 against the dealer's ten, he or she will lose 77.9 percent of the time and will win 22.1 percent of the time, for an expected value of –0.557. Thus, the expected value is higher if the player hits 16 against the dealer's ten than if he or she stands.

In some situations, the expected value criterion that is used in decision making under risk can be used as a strategy for risk management decisions, such as the choice between retention and the purchase of insurance. A decision or choice is described in terms of a payoff matrix, a rectangular array whose rows represent alternative courses of action and whose columns represent the outcomes or states of nature. The expected value for a particular decision is the sum of the weighted payoffs for that decision. The weight for each payoff is the probability that the payoff occurs multiplied by the value.

For the purpose of illustration, assume a loss exposure of $100,000, for which the probability is estimated to be .01. Assume further that insurance against loss from this exposure will cost $1500 annually. The expected value for the two possible choices (insure and retain), given the two possible states of nature (No Loss and Loss Occurs), would be computed as follows:

	State 1 No Loss	State 2 Loss Occurs	Expected Value
Insure	–$1500 × .99	–$1500 × .01	–$1500
Retain	$0 × .99	–$100,000 × .01	–$1000

Applying the expected value criterion, the decision to retain is the most attractive. Adding the expected values the two possible outcomes (state 1 and state 2) for the decision *Insure,* the expected value of the decision is –$1500: (–$1500 × .01 + –$1500 × .99). For the decision *Retain,* the expected value is –$1000. If the decision is made on the basis of expected value, retention would be selected as the appropriate decision, since –$1000 is less than –$1500. It may be noted parenthetically that, given an accurate estimate of probabilities, the expected value criterion will always suggest retention over transfer through insurance. This is because the premium for insurance includes not only the expected value of the loss, but the cost of operating the insurance mechanism as well. Assuming that the insurer has an accurate estimate of probability, the cost of insurance is *always* greater than the expected value of a loss.

There are two problems with the expected value model for risk management decisions. The first is that the expected value model requires that the decision maker have accurate information on the probabilities, which is not available as often as desired. Second, and more important, even when accurate probability estimates are available, actual experience will deviate from the expected value. Although the *long-run* expected value of the retention strategy is –$1000, a loss of $100,000 *could* occur. If a $100,000 loss is unacceptable to management, the long-run expected value is irrelevant. There is little consolation following the bankruptcy that results from the uninsured $100,000 loss in the fact that the retention strategy would have been the cost-effective strategy in the long run if the firm had survived.

Pascal's Wager The defects in the expected value strategy suggested the need for a different strategy in some situations. Blaise Pascal, a seventeenth-century mathematician considered the situation in which the probability of an outcome is not known, and in which there is a significant difference in the possible outcomes. The question about which Pascal was concerned was the existence of God. For our purposes, the importance of Pascal's analysis of this question is not the question itself, but the logic of the analysis and its implications for risk management. The analysis led Pascal to what one author has cited as the beginning of the theory of decision making.[3]

According to Pascal, there is no way to estimate the probability or likelihood that God exists. One believes in God or one does not. The decision, therefore, is not whether to believe in God, but rather whether to act as if God exists or does not exist. The choice, in Pascal's view, is, in effect, a bet on whether or not God exists. According to Pascal's wager, if one bets that God exists, he or she will lead a good life. A person who chooses to lead an evil life is wagering that God does not exist. If God does not exist, whether you lead a good life or a bad one is immaterial. But suppose, says Pascal, that God does exist. If you bet against the existence of God (by refusing to

[3] Ian Hacking, *The Emergency of Probability: A Philosophical Study of Early Ideas about Probability, Induction, and Statistical Inherence* (London: Cambridge University Press, 1975), p. 62.

lead a good life), you run the risk of eternal damnation, while the winner of the bet that God exists has the possibility of salvation. Because salvation is preferable to damnation, for Pascal the correct decision is to act as if God exists.

"Pascal's Wager" introduces two significant principles for decision making. The first is that there are some situations in which the consequence (magnitude of the potential loss) rather than the probability should be the first consideration. Put somewhat differently, there are some situations in which one of the outcomes is so undesirable that its possibility is unacceptable. The second is that even when dependable estimates of the probability are not available, decisions made under conditions of uncertainty can be made on a rational basis.[4]

Minimax Regret Strategy In modern decision theory, the equivalent of Pascal's strategy is known as minimax (standing for minimize maximum regret). In the minimax regret strategy, the decision maker attempts to minimize the maximum loss or maximum regret. For problems such as those in the area of risk management, in which payoffs such as costs are to be minimized, the maximum cost of each decision for each of the possible outcomes is listed and the minimum of the maximums is selected as the appropriate choice, which gives rise to the term *minimax*. Returning to the $100,000 building with the $1500 insurance premium, an uninsured $100,000 loss represents the greater maximum loss and the choice "Insure" will minimize the maximum cost.

	State 1 No Loss	State 2 Loss Occurs	Maximum Loss
Insure	−$1500	−$1500	−$1500
Retain	$0	−$100,000	−$100,000

In risk management, the premise on which the minimax cost or minimax regret strategies are based is Pascal's contention that when the probability of loss cannot be determined, one should choose the option in which the potential for regret is the lowest. The minimax cost or minimax regret strategies are appropriate when the maximum cost associated with one of the possible states of nature is unacceptable to

management. This would be the case, for example, when the potential loss that might arise is beyond the firm's ability to bear; the situation in which one of the states of nature would result in bankruptcy and would result in failure to achieve the risk management objective.

It should be noted that while the expected value strategy will always suggest retention as the preferred approach, a *minimax* strategy will always suggest transfer. The obvious key, then, is to determine the situations in which each strategy should be applied.

The Rules of Risk Management

Both the expected value strategy and the minimax strategy have application in risk management decisions. Because the decisions recommended by these strategies are diametrically opposed (the expected value strategy will always suggest retention as the preferred approach and the *minimax* strategy will always suggest transfer), the obvious key is to determine the situations in which each strategy should be applied. This question was addressed in the first textbook on the subject of risk management. One of the earliest contributions to the risk management field was the development of a set of "rules of risk management."[5] These rules are simply commonsense principles applied to risk situations:

1. Don't risk more than you can afford to lose.
2. Consider the odds.
3. Don't risk a lot for a little.

Simple as they appear, these three rules provide a basic framework within which risk management decisions can be made. Unfortunately, they are sometimes misunderstood and are often neglected.

Don't Risk More Than You Can Afford to Lose
The first of the three rules—"Don't risk more than you can afford to lose"—is the most important. Although it does not necessarily tell us *what* should be done about a given risk, it does identify the risks about which *something* must be done. If we begin with the recognition that when nothing is done about a particular risk that risk is retained, identifying the

[4] This discussion of Pascal's wager is based on a discussion in Peter L. Bernstein, *Against the Gods — The Remarkable Story of Risk* (New York: John Wiley & Sons, Inc., 1998), pp. 69–71.

[5] These rules appeared in the first edition of Robert I. Mehr and Bob A. Hedges, *Risk Management in the Business Enterprise* (Homewood, Ill.: Richard D. Irwin, 1963), pp. 16–26.

risks about which something must be done resolves into determining which risks cannot be retained. The answer is explicitly stated in the first rule.

The most important consideration in determining which risks require some specific action is the maximum potential loss that might result from the risk. If the maximum potential loss from a given exposure is so large that it would result in an unbearable loss, retention is not realistic. The possible severity must be reduced to a manageable level or the risk must be transferred. If severity cannot be reduced and the risk cannot be transferred, it must be avoided. In decision theory terms, "Don't risk more than you can afford to lose" identifies the decisions for which the minimax cost or minimax regret strategy is appropriate.

Consider the Odds If an individual can determine the probability that a loss may occur, he or she is in a better position to deal with the risk than would be the case without such information. However, it is possible to attach undue significance to such probabilities, since the probability that a loss may or may not occur is less important than the possible severity if it does occur. Even when the probability of loss is low, the primary consideration is the potential severity.

This is not to say that the probability associated with a given exposure is not a consideration in determining what to do about that risk. Just as the potential severity indicates the risk about which something must be done (i.e., the risks that cannot be retained), knowing whether the probability that a loss will occur is slight, moderate, or quite high can assist the risk manager in deciding what should be done about a given risk (although not in the way that most people think).

A high probability is an indication that insurance is probably not an economical way of dealing with the risk. This is because insurance operates on the basis of averages. Based on past experience, the insurer estimates the amount that it must collect in premiums to cover the losses that will occur. In addition to covering the losses, it must cover the insurer's other expenses. Therefore, paradoxical though it may seem, the best buys in insurance involve those losses that are least likely to happen. The higher the probability of loss, the less suitable is insurance as a device for dealing with the exposure.

The best buys in insurance are those in which the probability is low and the possible severity is high.

The worst buys are those in which the size of the potential loss is low and the probability of loss is high. The most effective way to deal with those exposures in which the probability of loss is high is through loss prevention measures aimed at reducing the probability of loss.

The second rule of risk management, "Consider the odds," suggests that the likelihood or probability of loss may be an important factor in deciding what to do about a particular risk. But which risks? Logically, consideration of the odds is limited to those situations in which the first rule, "Don't risk more than you can afford to lose" does not apply. For decisions in which one of the possible states of nature is ruin, the minimax cost or minimax regret strategies are appropriate.

Having limited our application of probability to situations in which ruin is not one of the possible outcomes or states of nature, it should be noted that even in this limited set of decisions, situations in which probability theory is useful abound. Among the more fertile fields for analysis are the selection of deductibles, and the decision to insure or retain moderate losses.

Don't Risk a Lot for a Little Although the first rule provides guidance for those risks that should be transferred (those involving catastrophic losses in which the potential severity cannot be reduced) and the second rule provides guidance for those that should not be insured (those in which the probability of loss is very high), they leave a residual class of risks for which another rule is needed.

The third rule dictates that there should be a reasonable relationship between the cost of transferring risk and the value that accrues to the transferor. It provides guidance in two directions. First, risks should not be retained when the possible loss is large (a lot) relative to the premiums saved through retention (a little). On the other hand, there are instances in which the premium that is required to insure a risk is disproportionately high relative to the risk transferred. In these cases, the premiums represent "a lot" while the possible loss is "a little."

While the rule "Don't risk more than you can afford to lose" imposes a maximum level on the risks that should be retained, the rule "Don't risk a lot for a little" suggests that some risks below this maximum retention level should also be transferred. The maximum retention level should be the same for all risks, yet the actual retention level for some exposures may be less than this maximum.

Risk Characteristics as Determinants of the Tool

From the foregoing discussion, it is clear that there are some risks that should be transferred and some that should be retained. It is also clear that both transfer and retention are unsatisfactory in other cases, and that avoidance or reduction is necessary. What determines when a given approach should be used? It is the characteristic of the risk itself that determines which of the four tools of risk management is most appropriate in a given situation. Under what circumstances is each of the tools appropriate?

Based on the previous discussion, it is possible at this point to summarize a few general guidelines with respect to the relationship of the various tools and particular risks. The following matrix categorizes risks into four classes, based on the combination of frequency (probability) and severity of each risk. Although real world risks are not divided so conveniently, most exposures can be classified according to their frequency and potential severity.

	High Frequency	Low Frequency
High Severity		
Low Severity		

When the possible severity of loss is high, retention is not realistic and some other technique is necessary. However, we have also noted that when the probability of loss is high, insurance becomes too costly. Through a process of elimination, we conclude that the appropriate tools for dealing with risks characterized by high severity and high frequency are avoidance and reduction. Reduction may be used when it is possible to reduce either the severity or the frequency to a manageable level. Otherwise, the risk should be avoided.

Risks characterized by high severity and low frequency are best dealt with through insurance. The high severity implies a catastrophic impact if the loss should occur, and the low probability implies a low expected value and a low cost of transfer.

Risks characterized by low severity and high frequency are most appropriately dealt with through retention and reduction: retention because the high frequency implies that transfer will be costly, and reduction to decrease the aggregate amount of losses that must be borne.

Finally, those risks characterized by low severity and low frequency are best handled through retention. They seldom occur, and, when they do happen, the financial impact is inconsequential.

Although not all risks will fit precisely into the categories in the chart, most exposures can be classified according to their frequency and potential severity. In those instances in which the probability or severity is not "high" or "low" the principles may be modified by judgment.

The Special Case of Risk Reduction

From a theoretical perspective, decisions regarding the application of risk management techniques should be made on the basis of a marginal benefit–marginal cost rule. This means that from the viewpoint of minimizing costs, each of the techniques for dealing with risk should be utilized when that particular technique represents the lowest cost approach to the particular risk in question. Also, a given technique should be used only up to that point at which the last dollar spent achieves a dollar reduction in the cost of losses or risk and no further. However, this basic principle must sometimes be modified in the case of loss prevention and control methods. Humanitarian considerations and legal requirements sometimes dictate that loss prevention and control measures go beyond the optimal marginal cost-marginal benefit point. For example, the federal Occupational Safety and Health Act requires employers to incur expenses for job safety loss prevention and control measures that might not be justified on a pure cost-benefit basis.[6]

[6] Decisions with respect to loss prevention in connection with employee injuries have been greatly affected by OSHA. The Williams–Steiger Act of 1970, better known as the Occupational Safety and Health Act (OSHA), established a new agency within the U.S. Department of Labor, the Occupational Safety and Health Administration, which is empowered to set and enforce health and safety standards for almost all private employers in the nation. There are mandatory penalties under the law up to $1000 for each violation and optional penalties up to $1000 for nonserious violations. Penalties may be assessed for every day that an employer fails to correct a violation during a period set in a citation from OSHA. In addition, an employer who willfully or repeatedly breaks the law is subject to penalties up to $10,000 for each violation. Any willful violation of standards resulting in an employee's death, upon conviction, is punishable by a fine of up to six months' imprisonment or $10,000. The maximum penalty under the law is life imprisonment for killing an OSHA inspector.

BUYING INSURANCE

Although insurance is only one of the techniques available for dealing with the pure risks that the individual or the firm faces, many of the risk management decisions boil down to a choice between insurance and noninsurance. Although the basic principles of risk management have already been discussed, it may also be useful to examine the application of a few of these principles to the area of insurance buying.

Common Errors in Buying Insurance

In general, the mistakes that most people make when buying insurance fall into two categories: buying too little and buying too much. The first, which is potentially the more costly, consists of the failure to purchase essential coverages that can leave the individual vulnerable to unbearable financial loss. Unless the insurance program is designed to protect against the catastrophes to which the individual is exposed, an entire life's work can be lost in a single uninsured loss. On the other hand, it is possible to purchase too much insurance, buying protection against losses that could more economically be retained. The difficulty in buying the right amount of insurance is compounded by the fact that it is possible to make both mistakes at the same time. As a matter of fact, although most people spend enough to provide an adequate insurance program, too often they ignore critical risks, leaving gaping holes in the overall pattern of protection, while unimportant risks are insured, using valuable premium dollars that would be more effectively spent elsewhere.

Some insurance buyers turn the entire decision-making process over to an outside party such as an insurance agent or broker. In a sense, they delegate the responsibility for both policy decisions and administration to this outside party. While such a course of action may relieve the insurance buyer of the decision burden, it may not result in an optimal program. When the choices involved in the purchase of insurance are delegated to an outside party, there is often a tendency to insure exposures that might better be retained. An insurance agent does not enjoy being in a defensive position when a loss takes place and, when charged with the overall responsibility for the insurance decisions, may decide to protect himself or herself as well as the client by opting for more, rather than less, insurance. While a competent agent or broker is a valuable source of advice, the basic rules governing the decisions should be made by the person or persons most directly involved, since these decisions are likely to have large financial impact over the long run in either premiums paid or losses sustained if hazards are not insured.

Need for a Plan

The basic problem facing any insurance buyer is that of using the available premium dollars to the best possible advantage. To obtain maximum benefit from the dollars spent, some sort of plan is needed. Otherwise, there is a tendency to view the purchase of insurance as a series of individual, isolated decisions, rather than a single problem, and there are no guidelines to provide for a logical consistency in dealing with the various risks faced.

A Priority Ranking for Insurance Expenditures Such a plan can be formulated to set priorities for the allocation of premium dollars on the basis of the previously discussed classification of risks into *critical, important,* and *unimportant,* with insurance coverages designed to protect against these risks classified as *essential, desirable,* and *optional.*

- *Essential* insurance coverages include those designed to protect against loss exposures that could result in bankruptcy. Insurance coverage required by law is also essential.
- *Important* insurance coverages include those that protect against loss exposures that would force the insured to borrow or resort to credit.
- *Optional* insurance coverages include those that protect against losses that could be met out of existing assets or current income.

Large-Loss Principle: Essential Coverages First The primary emphasis on essential coverages follows the first rule of risk management and the axiom that the probability that a loss may or may not occur is less important than possible size. Since the individual must of necessity assume some risks and transfer others, it seems only rational to begin by transferring those that he or she could not afford to bear. One frequently hears the complaint, "The trouble with insurance is that those who need it most can least afford it." There is considerable truth in this statement. The need for insurance is dictated by the inability to with-

stand the loss in question if the insurance is not purchased, so while it is true that those who need insurance are those who can least afford it, it is also true that they are the ones who can least afford to be without it. In determining whether or not to purchase insurance in a particular situation, the important question is not "Can I afford it?" but rather "Can I afford to be without it?"

When the available dollars cannot provide all the essential and important coverages you want to carry, the question becomes where to cut. One approach is to assume a part of the loss in connection with these coverages. You can do this by adding higher deductibles to these coverages, thereby freeing dollars for others that you desire. In many lines of insurance, full coverage is uneconomical because of the high cost of protecting against small losses. If you exclude coverage for these losses through deductibles, the premium credits granted may permit you to purchase others that are desirable.

Insurance as a Last Resort: Optional Coverages

As we have seen, insurance always costs more than the expected value of the loss. This is because in addition to the expected value of the loss (the pure premium), the cost of operating the insurance mechanism must also be borne by the policyholders. For this reason, insurance should be considered a last resort, to be used only when absolutely necessary.

It is in connection with this latter aspect of insurance that many people fail to appreciate the appropriate function of the mechanism. The insurance principle should not be utilized to indemnify for small, relatively certain losses. These can more desirably be carried as a part of the cost of production in a business or as one small cost to an individual of maintaining self and family. Why should one want to collect from an insurance company for the two or three shingles blown off the roof during a windstorm? Why should any individual with any degree of affluence want a $100 deductible on an automobile? In many instances, these small, relatively certain losses can be eliminated from the insurance operation by specifically excluding them or by using a deductible. Insurance companies, in providing indemnity for such small losses in their contracts, are as guilty of the misuse of the insurance principle as are the insureds who buy them.

There is nothing intrinsically wrong with optional coverages. They are just not a very good way to spend the limited number of dollars that are available for

the purchase of insurance. If the individual's psychological makeup is such that he or she desires protection against even the smallest type of loss, optional coverages are probably all right. The real problem with such coverages is that the individual who insures against small losses often does so at the expense of exposures that involve losses that would be financially catastrophic. Although an individual or business firm might desire some optional coverages, they should be purchased only after all the important ones have been purchased. Of course, all essential coverages should be bought before premiums are spent on the less critical important coverages. In this way, the premium dollars will be spent where they are most effective—protecting first against those losses that could result in bankruptcy; next against those that would require resort to credit; and finally, when all other exposures have been covered, against those losses that could be met out of existing assets or current income.

Advantages of Deductibles It makes good sense to use the deductible in insurance contracts, whether bought by an individual or a business. The premium reduction normally more than compensates for the risk that is retained. Take the case of automobile collision insurance. The cost difference between a $200 deductible and a $500 deductible coverage may be substantial. The difference will depend on the rates applicable in the area and the age and value of the car, but, as an example, in a midwestern city, the cost of collision coverage on a medium-priced, late-model car, for a 23-year-old unmarried male operator, with a $200 deductible, is $722 per year. The cost with a $500 deductible is $613 a year, a difference of $109. With a difference of $109 a year, the individual is paying $109 for $300 in coverage. If the young man who purchases $200 deductible collision owned a car worth $300, and was offered collision coverage on it for $109—even without a deductible—he would reason that the premium is too high and that the car was not worth insuring. Why is it not also too high to pay $109 for $300 in coverage on a car that is worth more?

Other Considerations in the Choice Between Insurance and Retention

The choice between the risk financing alternatives— retention and transfer—is sometimes dictated by the first rule of risk management. When a risk exceeds

the organization's risk-bearing capacity, it must be reduced or transferred. In other cases, however, where the organization could afford the loss, there may still be advantages in transfer. It may be desirable, for example, to obtain the services of an insurance company for the investigation and settlement of liability losses or the inspection services that are offered in connection with boiler and machinery insurance. In addition, there are some instances in which risk transfer will produce economies despite the fact that the cost of insurance exceeds expected value. Two considerations in particular may affect the transfer-retention decision: the cost of financing risk and the tax treatment of insurance premiums and retained losses.

The Cost of Financing Risk The choice between transfer and retention and the way in which retention and transfer should be combined should recognize the distinction between the cost of financing losses and that of financing risk. A review of terminology may be helpful. A loss is a decline in or disappearance of value due to a contingency. Not all losses involve risk, which is the possibility of a deviation from what is expected or hoped for.

Consider a firm that owns buildings worth $1,000,000. Insurance on the buildings will cost $30,000. Assuming a loss ratio of about 65 or 66 percent, the expected loss (i.e., the average loss per insured) is roughly $20,000. In fact, let us also assume that the manufacturer's past losses have been about average, or $20,000 a year. If expected losses are $20,000 a year, but could be as much as $1,000,000, the risk is $980,000 ($1,000,000 minus $20,000). The $20,000 represents a predictable loss, while the remaining $980,000 represents "risk," which, like the cost of losses, can be transferred or retained.

If the firm decides to retain the entire risk of loss, it will presumably continue to incur $20,000 in losses annually. In addition, to protect against the possibility of a total $1,000,000 loss, it must maintain a liquid reserve of $980,000. The cost of the retention program will be the $20,000 in annual losses that must be paid plus the opportunity cost on the $980,000 reserve. This opportunity cost is measured as the difference between the return that will be earned on the reserve (which must be kept in a semiliquid form), and the return that could be realized if the $980,000 were applied to the firm's operations. If the average return on funds applied to operations is, say, 15 percent and the interest that can be earned on the

invested reserve is 6 percent, the opportunity cost is $88,200 ([15% minus 6%] × $980,000). Thus, the cost of insuring is $30,000, while the cost of retention is $108,200 ($20,000 in losses plus the $88,200 opportunity cost).[7] A more complete analysis would consider the effect of taxes on both costs. Assuming a combined state and federal marginal tax rate of 50 percent, the cost of insurance would be $15,000 and the cost of retention would be $54,100.

Tax Considerations In Risk Financing Decisions
One element that should be considered in the choice of the approach to risk financing for a particular risk is the impact that taxes may have on insurance costs and losses. In the case of a business firm, for instance, property and liability insurance premiums are a deductible business expense, as are uninsured losses. However, contributions to a *funded retention program* are not deductible. The inability to deduct contributions to a reserve fund does not eliminate the tax deductibility of self-insured losses—it only forces companies to wait until they actually incur a loss before taking the deduction. The decision to purchase insurance may be influenced by the fact that uninsured losses are deductible in the year in which they occur only to the extent of profit during that year and that the tax deduction resulting from the uninsured loss may be reduced by low profits in the year in which it occurs.[8]

Selecting the Agent and the Company

Although the selection of an insurance company is an important aspect of the insurance-buying process, in most cases the individual is probably well advised to focus primary attention on selecting the agent rather than the company. When an insurance policy is purchased, a part of the premium goes to the insurance company to pay for the protection. A second part is compensation to the agent for the service he

[7] If the firm decides that it will not maintain a reserve, but will borrow the required $980,000 if a total loss occurs, the net effect is the same, since it will need to maintain $980,000 of its line of credit free for use in the event of a loss. The opportunity cost is the same in either case.

[8] Unlike the case of the business firm, insurance premiums are not a tax-deductible expenditure for the individual. In addition, casualty losses sustained by an individual are deductible only to the extent that each loss exceeds $100 and the aggregate for all excess losses exceeds 10 percent of the individual's adjusted gross income.

or she provides to the insured. The most important part of this service consists of the advice the agent gives. Careful selection of the adviser is a fundamental part of insurance buying. From the point of view of the insured, the primary qualifications for a good agent are knowledge of the insurance field and an interest in the needs of the client. One indicator of a knowledgeable and professional agent is a professional designation; the Chartered Property and Casualty Underwriter (CPCU) designation and the Chartered Life Underwriter (CLU) designation both indicate that the agent is sufficiently motivated to work in a formal educational program for professional development. However, there are many competent and knowledgeable agents who do not have these designations.

The insured may receive assistance from the agent in selecting an insurer if the agent represents several companies. However, in the case of most life insurance agents and certain property and liability agents who represent only one company, the selection of the agent will automatically include the selection of the company. In choosing a company, the major consideration should be its financial stability. In addition, certain aspects of the company's operation, such as its attitude toward claims and cancellation of policyholders' protection, are important. Finally, cost is a consideration.

In view of the importance of the financial stability of the insurer in the selection process, a few comments relative to the determination of financial stability are in order. Actually, analysis of an insurance company's financial strength follows the same principles used in the financial analysis of any corporation. However, industry accounting practices require certain modifications, making the evaluation of an insurer's financial stability a somewhat more complicated procedure (see Chapter 8). For this reason, it is probably advisable for the layperson to consult an evaluation service rather than to attempt the analysis alone. Data on the financial stability of insurance companies are available from several sources that specialize in providing information on the companies' financial strength, the efficiency of their operation, and the caliber of management.

For many years, the principal rating agency for both property and liability insurers and life insurers was the Alfred M. Best Company. Recently, three firms that traditionally specialized in rating debt issues and preferred stocks entered the insurance rating field. They are Standard and Poor's Corporation, Moody's Investors Service, Inc., and Fitch, Inc.

(formerly Duff & Phelps). Finally, another recent entry into the insurer rating field is Weiss Ratings, Inc. Each of the rating services uses a slightly different classification system, and the categories have slightly different designations. All rating services, however, distinguish between insurers whose financial condition is deemed adequate and those insurers that are classified as vulnerable or weak. The ratings and the description assigned by the rating agency to the various classes are summarized in Table 4.1.

Standard and Poor's, Moody's, and Fitch and Weiss rate a far smaller number of companies than does Best's, and it is possible that a particular company in which a prospect is interested will not have been rated by these firms. A. M. Best, in contrast, assigns ratings to the vast majority of insurers, and assigns a "not rated" classification to those insurers that are not rated.[9]

Best's publishes separate reference guides for insurers in the property and liability and life insurance fields. In the property and liability field, *Best's Insurance Reports: Property-Liability*[10] is a comprehensive analysis of virtually all property and liability insurers. *Best's Key Rating Guide: Property-Liability*[11] is a smaller and less comprehensive book, but it offers sufficient information to assist in selecting a company in most cases. Both books include Best's ratings for all companies listed. Two ratings are assigned to each company: a "General Policyholders' Rating" and a "Financial Size Rating"; of these the General Policyholders' Rating is the more important.[12] The General Policyholders' Rating is based on an analysis of five

[9] In addition to the standard letter ratings listed in Table 4.1, which apply to approximately 70 percent of the insurers reviewed by Best's, about 30 percent of the companies are not rated, but are assigned to one of nine "Not Assigned" categories: NA-1 (Special Data Filing), NA-2 (Less Than Minimum Size), NA-3 (Insufficient Operating Experience), NA-4 (Rating Procedure Inapplicable), NA-5 (Significant Change), NA-6 (Reinsured by Unrated Reinsurer), NA-8 (Incomplete Financial Information), NA-9 (Company Request), and NA-11 (Rating Suspended).

[10] *Best's Insurance Reports: Property-Liability* (Morristown, N.J.: A.M. Best Company, annual).

[11] *Best's Key Rating Guide: Property-Liability* (Morristown, N.J.: A. M. Best Company, annual).

[12] The "Financial Size Rating" indicates Best's estimate of the safety factor of each company and is based solely on the financial resources of the insurer as indicated by the sum of net worth, conditional reserves, and the redundancy in liabilities. To avoid confusion with Best's "Policyholders Ratings," the financial ratings for property and liability insurers are represented by roman numerals, ranging from I for property and liability companies with $1 million or less in adjusted surplus to XV for companies with $2 billion or more in adjusted surplus.

factors: (1) underwriting results; (2) economy of management; (3) adequacy of reserves for undischarged liabilities; (4) adequacy of policyholders' surplus to absorb shocks; and (5) soundness of investments. From the analysis of these factors, the company is assigned 1 of 15 policyholders' ratings indicated in Table 4.1. The majority of property and liability companies are in the top four classifications.[13]

In the field of life insurance, Best's publishes *Best's Life Reports,*[14] which provide detailed financial and historical data on most life insurers. Life insurers are rated on the same basis (i.e., the same 15 classes from A ++ to F) as property and liability insurers. Less than a third of the life insurers that are rated are assigned ratings in the highest four categories.[15] The "Not Assigned" ratings for life insurers are the same as for property and liability insurers. As in the case of property and liability insurers, both a Policyholders' Rating and a Financial Size Rating is assigned to life insurers.[16]

When properly used, the ratings assigned by A. M. Best and the other rating services can be effective tools for avoiding delinquent insurance companies. In utilizing the ratings for both property and liability insurers and life insurers, the ratings should be checked for a period of years. If there has been a downward trend in the rating, further investigation into the cause of the change is warranted. For many years, the suggested standard was an A + rating from A. M. Best for a period of at least six years.[17] A current authority recommends that one should select a life insurance company that has very high ratings from at least two of the four rating firms other than Best. This seems like a reasonable standard for property and liability insurers as well.[18]

When comparing the ratings assigned by different rating services, the description of the rating assigned by each service should be reviewed. Although the agencies all divide insurers into approximately the same number of rating categories, the financial strength assigned to the categories varies, and insurers ranked in the top six categories by one service may represent a different evaluation than ranking in the top six categories of another service. Table 4.1 indicates the descriptions assigned to the categories by the rating agencies and the dividing line used by each service in distinguishing strong companies from weaker companies.

ALTERNATIVES TO COMMERCIAL INSURANCE

With the growth of risk management and the increased emphasis on finding the most appropriate technique for dealing with risk, alternatives to commercial insurance and to the traditional forms of retention have developed. These include self-insurance programs, captive insurers, risk-retention groups, and risk-sharing pools. The alternatives to commercial insurance have developed for a variety of reasons. In some cases, such as self-insurance programs for employer-provided health insurance, commercial insurance alternatives are available, but businesses and other organizations have found that they can achieve economies through self-insured programs. In other cases, the alternatives were adopted because of a perceived failure of the commercial insurance market. Faced with escalating insurance costs and, in some instances, the inability to obtain various types of liability insurance, some organizations opted to self-insure or simply "go bare," paying claims directly out of their income. Other organizations banded together to form group-owned captives or risk-retention groups. In the case of public entities, risk-sharing pools were formed in many states.

Self-Insurance

In the preceding chapter we noted that while self-insurance is technically a definitional impossibility, the term has found widespread acceptance in the business world. It is widely used (and understood) and there seems little sense in ignoring the widespread use of an

[13] In 2001, 60 percent of property and liability companies were assigned to the first four categories (A++ through A–).

[14] *Best's Life Reports* (Morristown, N.J.: A. M. Best Company, annual).

[15] In 2001, 57.4 percent of the rated life insurers were rated in classes A++ through A–.

[16] For life insurers, Best's Financial Size ratings range from class I for companies with $250,000 in surplus to class XV for companies with $100 million or more in surplus.

[17] See Herbert S. Denenberg, "Is 'A Plus' Really a Passing Grade?" *The Journal of Risk and Insurance,* vol. 34 (September 1967).

[18] Joseph M. Belth, "Financial Strength Ratings of Life-Health Insurance Companies," *The Insurance Forum,* vol. 21, nos. 3 and 4 (March/April 1994), p. 15.

TABLE 4.1 Rating Categories Used by Insurer Rating Agencies

A.M. Best		Fitch		Moody's		Standard & Poors		Weiss	
A++	Superior	AAA	Exceptional	Aaa	Exceptional	AAA	Extremely Strong	A+	Excellent
A+	Superior	AA+	Very Strong	Aa1	Excellent	AA+	Very Strong	A	Excellent
A	Excellent	AA	Very Strong	Aa2	Excellent	AA	Very Strong	A–	Excellent
A–	Excellent	AA–	Very Strong	Aa3	Excellent	AA–	Very Strong	B+	Good
B++	Very Good	A+	Strong	A1	Good	A+	Strong	B	Good
B+	Very Good	A	Strong	A2	Good	A	Strong	B–	Good
FPR 8	Strong	A–	Strong	A3	Good	A–	Strong	C+	Fair
FPR 7	Strong	BBB+	Good	Baa1	Adequate	BBB+	Adequate	C	Fair
FPR 6	Good	BBB	Good	Baa2	Adequate	BBB	Adequate	C–	Fair
FPR 5	Good	BBB–	Good	Baa3	Adequate	BBB–	Adequate	D+	Weak
B	Fair	BB+	Moderately Weak	Ba1	Questionable	BB+	Vulnerable	D	Weak
B–	Fair	BB	Moderately Weak	Ba2	Questionable	BB	Vulnerable	D–	Weak
C++	Marginal	BB–	Moderately Weak	Ba3	Questionable	BB–	Vulnerable	E+	Very Weak
C+	Marginal	B+	Weak	B1	Poor	B+	More Vulnerable	E	Very Weak
C	Weak	B	Weak	B2	Poor	B	More Vulnerable	E–	Very Weak
C–	Weak	B–	Weak	B3	Poor	B–	More Vulnerable	F	Failed
D	Poor	CCC+	Very Weak	Caa1	Very Poor	CCC	Currently Vulnerable	U	Unrated
E	State Supervision	CCC	Very Weak	Caa2	Very Poor	CCC	Currently Vulnerable		
F	In Liquidation	CCC–	Very Weak	Caa3	Very Poor	CCC	Currently Vulnerable		
S	Rating Suspended	CC	Very Weak	Ca	Extremely Poor	CC	Highly Vulnerable		
FPR 4	Fair	C	Very Weak	C	Lowest	CC	Highly Vulnerable		
FPR 3	Marginal	DDD	Distressed			CC	Highly Vulnerable		
FPR 2	Weak	DD	Distressed			R	Under Supervision		
		D	Distressed						

In addition to the letter ratings, Best assigns *financial performance ratings* (FPRs), ranging from FPR8 (the highest) down to FPR1. FPR ratings are assigned to companies with too few years of experience to qualify for Best's letter ratings.

Standard and Poor publishes two ratings. The first indicated above is the claims paying ability rating, which is computed at the insurer's request and is based on public and nonpublic data provided by the insurer. The second rating is computed from public information (and is designated with a "pi"). "Pi ratings" are assigned to many companies that have not requested ratings.

established and accepted term.[19] Although there are theoretical defects in the term self-insurance, it is a convenient way of distinguishing retention programs that utilize insurance techniques from those that do not. Self-insurance programs are distinguished from other retention programs primarily in the formality of the arrangement. In some instances this means obtaining approval from a state regulatory agency to retain risks, under specifically defined conditions. In other cases, it means the formal trappings of an insurance program, including funding measures based on actuarial calculations and the contractual definitions of the exposures, are self-insured. When the self-insurance involves third parties (as in the case of employees covered under an employer-sponsored health insurance program), there is a need for the formal trappings of insurance, such as certificates of coverage and premiums. It is in this limited sense that the term self-insurance is used in this section.

Over the past three decades, the use of self-insurance by businesses and other organizations in dealing with risk has grown significantly. In some areas, such as employer-sponsored health benefits for employees, it has become a major alternative to commercial insurance. Given the growing importance of this approach to dealing with risks, it seems appropriate that we consider some of the reasons for its growth.

Reasons for Self-Insurance Self-insurance—like any of the other risk management techniques—should be used when it is the most effective technique for dealing with a particular risk. The question is: under what circumstances is this the case? The main reason that firms elect to self-insure certain exposures is that they believe it will be cheaper to do so in the long run. This is particularly true when there is no need for the financial protection furnished by insurance. If losses are reasonably predictable, with a small likelihood of deviation from year to year, the risk can be retained.

1. First, as explained earlier, the cost of insurance must, over the long run, exceed average losses. This is a mathematical truism. In addition to the losses that must be paid, the insurance premium must include a surcharge to cover the cost of operating the insurance company and its distribution system. In addition, commercial insurance is subject to state premium taxes, which represent a cost that must be paid by buyers. Self-insurance avoids certain expenses associated with the traditional commercial insurance market. These include, among other things, insurer overhead and profit, agents' commissions, and the premium taxes paid by insurers.

2. The organization may believe that its loss experience is significantly better than the average experience on which rates are made, or that the rating system does not accurately reflect the hazards associated with the exposure.

3. In lines of insurance in which there are long delays between the time that a loss occurs and the time it is paid, insurers hold "reserves," which represent liabilities for unpaid losses. Some organizations believe that the investment income from these reserves is not adequately reflected in rates, and that they can reduce the cost of their insurance by capturing these investable funds through self-insurance.

4. Self-insurers can avoid the *social load* in insurance rates that results from statutory mandates that insurers cover certain exposures in which premiums are less than the losses for those insured. These underwriting losses are passed on to other insureds in the form of higher premiums than their hazards justify.

Disadvantages of Self-Insurance Offsetting the perceived advantages of self-insurance are certain disadvantages.

1. The greatest disadvantage of self-insurance is that it can leave the organization exposed to catastrophic loss. This disadvantage can be eliminated if the self-insurer purchases reinsurance for potentially catastrophic losses, much in the same way as insurers do.

2. Another disadvantage of a self-insurance program is that there may be greater variation of costs from year to year. When the variation in costs from year to year is great, the firm may lose the tax deduction for the losses that occur in years when there are no profits from which to deduct the losses.

3. Self-insurance of some exposures can create adverse employee and public relations. There may be advantages to the organization in having its claims handled by an insurer (as opposed to the staff of the employer organization).

[19] Many state laws, for example, refer to the "self-insurance" of the workers compensation exposure, usually under conditions that do not contemplate any of the requirements specified by textbook writers.

4. Loss of ancillary services. There are certain services provided by insurers that are lost when a company adopts a self-insurance program. Most of these relate to loss prevention and claims handling. These services can be purchased separately from an insurer (under an arrangement called *unbundling*) or from specialty firms. The cost of obtaining these services must be included in the cost of the self-insurance when a comparison is made with commercial insurance.

As self-insurance became more popular among large corporations, insurers developed loss-sensitive rating programs and retention programs to compete with self-insurance. These include programs with large deductibles, experience rating (in which the insured's own loss experience is a major factor in the cost of the insurance) and *cash-flow plans,* in which the premium payment arrangement allows the insured to retain premiums for investment until the funds are required for payment of losses.

Captive Insurance Companies

Captive insurance companies represent a special case of risk retention and, in some instances, risk transfer. A *captive insurance company* is an entity created and controlled by a parent, whose main purpose is to provide insurance to that parent. It is an insurance company that provides insurance to its corporate owner or owners. Within the context of this definition, two types of organizations may be considered.

1. Pure captives
2. Association or group captives

Pure Captives A pure captive is an insurance company established by a noninsurance organization solely for the purpose of underwriting risks of the parent and its affiliates. Although the term *captive* has sometimes been applied loosely to include other affiliated insurers, as used here the term does not include insurance subsidiaries whose purpose is to write insurance for the general public.[20]

Historically, many captives were formed in foreign domiciles, in part because their formation was easier in these jurisdictions. Most of these so-called offshore captives were chartered in Bermuda, where the business climate is receptive to their formation.

Association Captives An association or group captive is an insurance company established by a group of companies to underwrite their own collective risks. These organizations are also sometimes referred to as "trade association insurance companies" (TAICs) and also as "risk-retention groups." The term *risk-retention group* was added to the terminology of the captive field by the Risk Retention Acts of 1981 and 1986. A risk-retention group is simply a group-owned captive organized under the provisions of the Risk Retention Act.

Captive Domiciles Captives have traditionally been classified as onshore or offshore. An onshore captive is incorporated and conducts business as a licensed insurer under one of the laws of the states. Although a limited number of states have special legislation related to the formation of captives,[21] most U.S. captives have been domiciled offshore (in Bermuda or one of the other jurisdictions whose legal system encourages the location of captives). The main reason for organizing a captive offshore is to take advantage of the lower capital and surplus requirements and the less rigorous regulation that exist in these jurisdictions.

Growth of Captives There has been a steady growth in the number of captives since the 1950s, from a few hundred or so in the late 1950s to an estimated 4000 by 2002. Captives were conceived because they offered an alternative to the commercial market and because it was believed that certain tax benefits were available through captives that could not be attained through an internal retention program. Although the hoped-for tax advantages did not materialize, captives have been continued for other reasons.

[20] Under this definition, J. C. Penney Casualty Insurance, a subsidiary of J. C. Penney Company, Inc., would not be considered a captive, since it was not organized for the purpose of underwriting the exposures of its parent. Some pure captives have broadened into writing business of others and eventually moved from captives to ordinary insurance subsidiaries.

[21] Colorado was the first state to enact legislation (in 1972) designed to encourage the formation of captives, reducing some of the stringent requirements normally applied to insurers in such areas as capitalization, rating, pool participation, and surplus. Since Colorado's legislation authorizing captives, Arizona, Arkansas, Delaware, Florida, Hawaii, Illinois, Maine, New York, South Carolina, Tennessee, Vermont, Virginia, and the District of Columbia have also passed laws that encourage the formation of captives, and all have experienced some success. Vermont has been the most successful by far in attracting captives.

Tax Treatment of Captives One of the original rationales for captives was the hope that the parent company would be permitted to deduct premiums paid to the captive that would not be deductible as contributions to a self-insurance reserve. With the exception of certain group captives, the IRS rejected this strategy. From 1972 unil 2001, the IRS argued that with a captive, there is no shifting of risk and no loss of control of the premiums. Because the premiums paid to a single parent stayed within the *economic family*, the IRS held that they were nondeductible contributions to a self-insurance reserve. Although the courts have generally sustained the IRS position, they have generally done so on grounds other than the economic family doctrine.[22] In June 2001, the IRS reversed its position and announced that it would no longer routinely challenge deductions to single-parent captives based on the economic family doctrine.[23] Despite this concession, the IRS stated that it will continue to challenge captive transactions based on the actual facts and circumstances of each case. Challenges will likely continue in instances in which there is no real shifting of risk.

The situation regarding deductibility of premiums in the case of group captives has always been viewed differently by the IRS than for pure captives. The IRS position on group captives is that premiums are deductible because a large number of insureds creates a true element of insurance through spreading of risk.[24] The IRS has also indicated that a captive's assumption of outside risks is a factor in the taxpayer's favor and may permit a deduction of premiums paid by the parent when there is a true pooling of exposures.[25]

Taxation of Captive Income Although premiums paid to single-parent captives were considered nondeductible until 2001, the exceptions permitted for group-owned captives created a tax loophole for offshore association captives that was not addressed until the Tax Reform Act of 1986. Prior to TRA-86, the income of an offshore captive derived from premiums on U.S. exposures was taxed under complicated rules applicable to a "controlled foreign corporations" (CFC). Although the law defined a CFC as one in which 25 percent of the shareholders were U.S. residents, only shareholders owning 10 percent or more of the foreign corporation were counted in making the determination. This meant that an offshore captive owned by 20 participants, each with 5 percent of the stock, was not classed as a CFC and escaped taxation of its income, even though the parent recognized a deduction for the premiums paid to the captive. Under TRA-86, each U.S. shareholder who owns stock in a 25 percent or more U.S.-owned foreign corporation is subject to current taxation on a pro rata share of income of the foreign insurer arising from insuring risks of U.S. stockholders and related parties, regardless of the degree of ownership in the company.

In addition to state premium taxes and "excess and surplus lines" taxes that apply to traditional insurers, a federal excise tax may apply to premiums of a captive insurer domiciled outside the United States.[26]

Risk Retention Act of 1986

The most recent wave of captives followed enactment of the federal *Risk Retention Act of 1986*, which, in effect, exempted captives formed by groups for the purpose of sharing liability risks from much of state regulation, except in the state in which they are domiciled. This 1986 act expanded a 1981 act, which had applied to product liability only. The 1986 law expanded the provisions of the law to apply to most liability coverages except workers compensation and employers liability.

Like its predecessor, the Risk Retention Act of 1986 authorized two mechanisms for group treatment of liability risks:

1. Risk-retention groups for self-funding (pooling)
2. Purchasing groups for joint purchase of insurance

[22] The IRS formalized this position in Revenue Ruling 77-316 and was upheld by the courts in *Carnation Company v. Commissioner of Internal Revenue*, 71 T.C., no. 39, December 16, 1978; and *Clougherty Packing Co. v. Commissioner of Internal Revenue*, U.S.C.A., 9th, no. 85-7707, March 3, 1987.

[23] The decision was announced June 4, 2001, as Revenue Ruling 2001-31.

[24] Revenue Ruling 78-338.

[25] Revenue Ruling 78-277.

[26] Internal Revenue Code Section 4371 assesses a 4 percent tax on premiums (except life insurance) written directly with a foreign insurer and a 1 percent tax on reinsurance premiums placed with a foreign insurer.

Although there had been little activity under the 1981 Act, by 1997 there were 68 operating risk-retention groups and 620 insurance-purchasing groups.

Risk-Retention Groups A *risk-retention group* is essentially a group-owned insurer whose primary activity consists of assuming and spreading the liability risks of its members. As their name implies, risk-retention groups are formed for the purpose of retaining or pooling risk. They are insurance companies, regularly licensed in the state of domicile and owned by their policyholders, who are also shareholders. The members are required to have a community of interest (i.e., similar risks), and, once organized, they can offer "memberships" to others with similar needs on a nationwide basis. A risk-retention group can be licensed in only one state, but may insure members of the group in any state. The jurisdiction in which it is chartered regulates the formation and operation of the group insurer. Once it is chartered in its state of domicile, the risk-retention group may then operate in any other state simply by filing notice of its intent with the respective state insurance department.

Purchasing Groups In addition to risk-retention groups, the Risk Retention Act of 1986 also authorized *insurance-purchasing groups*. Insurance-purchasing groups are not insurers and do not retain risk. Rather, they purchase insurance on a group basis for their members. The coverage is purchased in the conventional insurance market, and state laws that prohibit the group purchase of property and liability insurance are nullified with respect to qualified purchasing groups.

Risk-Sharing Pools Risk-sharing pools are mechanisms that are closely related to and sometimes confused with association or group captives, but they actually constitute a separate technique. A group of entities may elect to pool their exposures, sharing the losses that occur, without creating a formal corporate insurance structure.[27] In this case, a separate corporate insurer is not created, but the risks are nevertheless "insured" by the pooling mechanism.

Viewed from one perspective, pooling may be considered a form of transfer, in the sense that the risks of the pooling members are transferred from the individuals to the group. Viewed from a different perspective, pooling is a form of retention, in which the entity's risks are retained along with those of the other pooling members. This dual nature of pooling stems from the sometimes-forgotten fact that in a pooling arrangement, members are both insureds and insurers.

[27] The laws in virtually all states currently permit public bodies such as municipalities and counties to form self-insurance or risk-sharing pools. The pools are generally deemed not to be insurance companies and are not subject to the provisions of the state's insurance laws, except as specifically provided by the statutes under which they are organized.

IMPORTANT CONCEPTS TO REMEMBER

cost-benefit analysis	minimax regret	important insurance coverages
utility theory	rules of risk management	optional insurance coverages
decision making under certainty	Don't risk more than you can afford to lose	large loss principle
decision making under risk	Consider the odds	insurance as a last resort
decision making under uncertainty	Don't risk a lot for a little	pure captive
expected value	essential insurance coverages	association captive
Pascal's wager		risk-retention group

QUESTIONS FOR REVIEW

1. Describe the two strategies that may be employed in risk management decisions and explain the situation in which each is appropriate.

2. Explain why it may be difficult or inappropriate to use utility theory, cost-benefit analysis, and expected value in making risk management decisions.

3. Explain how knowing the frequency and severity of loss for a given exposure to loss is helpful in determining what should be done about that exposure.

4. Three rules of risk management proposed by Mehr and Hedges are discussed in this chapter. List these rules and explain the implications of each in determining what

should be done about individual exposures facing a business firm.

5. Identify three categories into which insurance coverages may be priority ranked, indicating the nature of the exposures or risks to which each applies.

6. Describe the distinguishing characteristics of the risk-retention groups and insurance-purchasing groups authorized by the Risk Retention Act of 1986.

7. Why is the decision to use risk control measures sometimes made on grounds other than the rules of risk management?

8. Distinguish between the cost of financing risk and the cost of financing losses.

9. Identify the reasons for self-insurance and the disadvantages of self-insurance.

10. Distinguish between pure captives and group association captives.

QUESTIONS FOR DISCUSSION

1. The rules of risk management appear to be just plain common sense. In view of this fact, how do you account for the widespread violation of these rules in insurance buying today?

2. Explain the relationship, if any, among the statements: "Don't risk more than you can afford to lose," "Those people who need insurance most are those who can least afford it," and "Insurance should be considered as a last resort."

3. What are the implications of the observation that "the cause of a loss is less important than its effect?"

4. In what way does the cost of risk influence the decision to transfer or retain a particular risk?

5. In an effort to reduce insurance costs, the risk manager of a medium-sized manufacturing firm canceled the property insurance on the firm's $8.5-million plant and equipment, for which the annual premium was about $265,000. Two years later when the action was discovered, the risk manager was called on the carpet by a horrified vice president of finance. "What were you thinking of?" demanded the VP. "What if we had had a loss?" "But," responded the risk manager, "we didn't have a loss. The fact that I saved the firm over half a million dollars in the past two years is proof that the decision was the right one." If you agree with the risk manager, help her convince the VP that she is right. If you disagree, help the VP convince the risk manager that she is wrong.

SUGGESTIONS FOR ADDITIONAL READING

Denenberg, Herbert S. "Is A-Plus Really a Passing Grade?" *Journal of Risk and Insurance,* vol. 34, no. 3 (Sept. 1967).

Doherty, Neil A. *Corporate Risk Management: A Financial Exposition.* New York: McGraw-Hill, 1985.

Grose, Vernon L. *Managing Risk: Systematic Loss Prevention for Executives* (Englewood Cliffs, NJ: Prentice-Hall, 1987).

Harrington, Scott E., and Gregory R. Niehaus. *Risk Management and Insurance.* New York: McGraw-Hill, 1998.

Head, George L., and Stephen Horn II. *Essentials of Risk Management,* 3rd ed., vols. 1 and 2. Malvern, Pa.: Insurance Institute of America, 1997.

Mehr, R. I., and B. A. Hedges. *Risk Management in the Business Enterprise.* Homewood, Ill.: Richard D. Irwin, 1963. Chapters 5–9.

Ralston, August R., ed. *Risk Management Manual,* Santa Monica, Ca.: (loose-leaf service with monthly supplements). vol. 3, section 14.

Vaughan, Emmett J. *Risk Management.* New York: John Wiley & Sons, 1997.

Williams, C. Arthur, Peter C. Young, and Michael Smith. *Risk Management and Insurance.* 8th ed. New York: McGraw-Hill, 1998.

WEB SITES TO EXPLORE

A. M. Best Company	http://www.ambest.com
Captive Insurance Companies Association	http://www.captive.com
Fitch, Inc.	http://www.fitchratings.com
International Risk Management Institute, Inc.	http://irmi.com
Moody's Investors Service	http://www.moodys.com
Nonprofit Risk Management Center	http://www.nonprofitrisk.org
Practical Risk Management	http://www.pracrisk.com/
Public Agency Risk Managers Association (PARMA)	http://www.parma.com
Risk and Insurance Management Society, Inc.	http://www.rims.org
RiskINFO	http://www.riskinfo.com/
Self Insurance Institute of America	http://www.siia.org
Standard and Poor's Insurance Rating Services	http://www.standardandpoors.com/
Warren, McVeigh & Griffin Consultants	http://www.griffincom.com/
Weiss Ratings, Inc.	http://www.weissratings.com/

THE PRIVATE INSURANCE INDUSTRY

■

Tell me thy company, and I'll tell thee what thou art.

— MIGUEL CERVANTES
Don Quixote

CHAPTER OBJECTIVES

When you have finished this chapter, you should be able to

- Identify the categories of insurers classified by type of product
- Identify the major categories of insurers classified according to form of ownership
- Identify and describe the distinguishing characteristics of the different categories of insurers by form of ownership
- Identify the different distribution systems that are used in property and liability and life and health insurance
- Describe the major areas in which members of the insurance industry cooperate
- Identify and describe the major areas in which insurers cooperate
- Describe the evidences that indicate the extent of competition in the insurance industry

Despite the great benefits that accrue to society through operation of the insurance mechanism, it is self-evident that such a complicated and intricate device does not come into existence by itself. Someone must estimate the probability of loss, collect the funds necessary to compensate those who suffer loss, make payments for the losses that do occur, and provide for the general administration of the program. These are the functions performed by insurers.

A basic distinction may be made between private and government insurers. To a limited extent historically in this country, and to a considerable extent abroad, governmentally organized and managed insurance organizations have offered insurance to the public. Although the primary focus of this chapter is the private insurance industry, we will also review the limited activities of government insurers as providers of voluntary or private insurance.

Measured by any one of a number of standards, insurance in the United States is a large industry. More than 7900 insurance companies operate in this country. These firms employ more than 2.3 million persons and administer assets of more than $4 trillion. The industry is divided into three broad insurance categories: life, health, and property and liability. Total premiums written by all three segments of the industry in 2000 amounted to more than $1 trillion, or slightly more than 13.6 percent of the gross national product. Of this total, approximately $435 billion was life insurance and annuity premiums, about $340 billion went for health insurance, and roughly $300 billion was for property and liability insurance.[1]

We begin our examination of the insurance industry with a brief look at the development of insurance as a business. Although we are primarily concerned with insurance in this country, since insurance has its roots in the Old World, we will consider its development prior to the formation of the United States as well.

A BRIEF HISTORY OF PRIVATE INSURANCE

Because the historical development of insurance as a field of business helps to explain the division among the various lines of insurance, it may be helpful to take a very brief look at the historical development of insurance as an institution.

Insurance in Antiquity

There is evidence of practices resembling insurance in the ancient world. As early as 3000 B.C., Chinese merchants used the technique of sharing risk. These merchants shipped their goods by boat down river, and, because of treacherous rapids, not all the boats made it safely. To reduce the impact of losses on any one individual, the merchants devised the plan of distributing their goods on each other's boats. When a boat was dashed to pieces on the rocks, the loss was shared by all rather than one individual.

About 500 years later the famous *Great Code of Hammurabi* provided for the transfer of the risk of loss from merchants to moneylenders. A trader whose goods were lost to bandits was relieved of the debt to the moneylender who had loaned the money to buy the goods. Babylonian moneylenders undoubtedly loaded their interest charges to compensate for this transfer of risk. This innovation was adapted to the risks of sea trade by Phoenicians and then by the Greeks. Loans were made to shipowners and merchants engaged in trade, with the ship or cargo pledged as collateral. The borrower was offered an option whereby, for a somewhat higher interest charge, the lender agreed to cancel the loan if the ship or cargo were lost at sea.[2] In this way, the risk of loss was transferred from the owner of the boat or cargo to the lender. These contracts were referred to as *bottomry* contracts in those cases in which the ship was pledged and *respondentia* contracts when the cargo was the security.

The first evidence of anything resembling life insurance evolved from ancient benevolent societies, whose members contributed to a fund to aid less fortunate members of the group. As early as 2500 B.C., Egyptian stonemasons organized a club to provide funds for the burial of members. Later, around the third century B.C., Greek burial societies, funded by contributions of members, were common devices for meeting the expenses of burial and the needs of widows and orphans. Roman burial and benevolent societies known as the *Collegia* performed the same function. Although these examples indicate some features of insurance, the modern insurance business has its roots in the commercial revolution in Europe following the Crusades.

Origins of the Modern Insurance Business

Marine insurance, the oldest of the modern branches of insurance, appears to have been started in Italy sometime in the thirteenth century. From there it spread to the other countries on the continent and then to England through the Lombard merchants, who came to dominate British commerce and finance during the fifteenth century. This early marine insurance was written by individuals rather than by insurance companies as we know them. A shipowner or merchant who wanted protection for

[1] Insurance Information Institute, *Insurance Facts* (New York: III, 2001) and American Council of Life Insurance, *Life Insurance Fact Book* (Washington, D.C.: ACLI, 2001).

[2] The additional interest on such loans was called a "premium," and the term has become a part of insurance terminology, indicating the payment made by the insured.

the ship or cargo prepared and circulated a sheet with information describing the ship, its cargo, its destination, and other pertinent information. Those who agreed to accept a part of the risk wrote their names under the description of the risk and the terms of the agreement. This practice of "writing under" the agreement gave rise to the term *underwriter,* which has retained its meaning as one who selects and rejects risks. Shipowners seeking insurance and the individuals who organized themselves into groups of underwriters found the coffee houses of London convenient meeting places. One of the coffee houses, owned by Edward Lloyd, became the main meeting place because its proprietor made paper, pens, and information regarding shipping available. This coffee house eventually became Lloyds of London.

The second of the modern branches of insurance was life insurance. In 1536, a group of marine underwriters in London issued what appears to have been the first modern life insurance policy to a certain William Gybbons. The policy was a one-year term policy in the amount of £400. As an interesting footnote to history, Gybbons died within the year and the underwriters paid the £400. Other attempts similar to this were tried from time to time (although probably not by the underwriters who had insured Gybbons).

Although Edmund Halley (of Halley's comet fame) had prepared a mortality table as early as 1693, it was not until nearly 100 years later that any degree of accuracy was achieved in predicting mortality. The first modern life insurance company, the Society for the Assurance of Widows and Orphans, a London company founded in 1699, charged all insureds the same premium. It and several companies that followed it were unsuccessful. Then, in 1762, the Equitable Society for the Assurance of Life and Survivorship introduced the innovation of premiums that varied with the age of the insured and became immediately successful.

Fire insurance in the modern era dates from 1666 when the Great Fire of London occurred. The fire raged for five days, virtually destroying the city, and providing the impetus for modern fire insurance. An English physician named Nicholas Barbon (who had been relatively unsuccessful in medicine) entered the construction business during the rebuilding of the city and at the same time started the business of insuring the newly built houses against loss by fire. Other entrepreneurs soon followed his lead.

Insurance in the United States

During the colonial period, most insurance in the United States was marine insurance, placed with British insurers. The first successful insurer actually located in this country was a mutual fire insurance company founded in 1752 by Benjamin Franklin and a group of his associates, called the Philadelphia Contributionship for the Insurance of Houses from Loss by Fire.[3] The first capital stock insurance company in the United States was the Insurance Company of North America, which was founded as an association in 1792 and incorporated in 1794. Its charter gave it broad underwriting powers that permitted it to engage in all lines of insurance, but it limited its writings to fire and marine insurance.

The first life insurance company in America was founded in 1759. It was a stock company called the Corporation for Relief of Poor and Distressed Presbyterian Ministers and the Poor and Distressed Widows and Children of Presbyterian Ministers. This company is still in operation and is the oldest active life insurance company in the world. Between 1759 and 1835, several other stock companies were formed, but none survived. The first mutual life insurance company was New England Life, founded in 1835. It was followed by a dozen more companies that have survived to the present day.

In the mid-1800s, a new type of insurance called *casualty insurance* appeared. The earliest form of casualty insurance was accident insurance, and, like fire, marine, and life insurance, it originated in the Old World. The British Parliament chartered a company in 1848 to sell insurance against accidents to railroad passengers. A company formed in the United States to sell this type of insurance to travelers, the Travelers Insurance Company, wrote its first policy in 1864. The next type of insurance for accidents was boiler explosion coverage, which appeared in 1886. Boiler insurance was followed by employers liability insurance in 1886 and then elevator and public liability insurance in 1889. The first auto liability policy in the United States was written in 1898, and workers compensation insurance followed in 1910. As these new types of insurance appeared, they were offered by specialty companies that did not write fire,

[3] A company founded in Charleston, South Carolina, in 1735, the Friendly Society for Mutual Insuring of Houses, preceded the Philadelphia Contributionship. However, it lasted only a few years and very little is known about it.

marine, or life. The new forms of insurance (which generally covered losses arising from various types of accidents or casualties) came to be called *casualty insurance* and the companies that wrote them were called *casualty insurers.*

Monoline Organization in the United States Initially, insurers elected to specialize in a particular type of insurance. Then, as more and more states began to regulate insurance, state limitations on the companies' underwriting powers became common. A contributing factor to this trend was New York State's *Appleton Rule,* which required insurers operating in New York to follow the state's monoline law when operating in other states. The industry became organized on a monoline basis, with companies restricted by law to the writing of a single line of insurance. Under this system, three distinct classes of insurance developed: life insurers, fire insurers, and casualty insurers.

A company that wrote fire insurance was not permitted to write casualty insurance and a casualty company could not write fire insurance. Neither fire insurance companies nor casualty insurance companies could write life insurance, and life insurance companies were permitted to write only life insurance and health insurance.

There were three reasons for the compartmentalization of the American system. First, it was supposed that the monoline system would allow insurers to specialize in a particular field of insurance and develop greater proficiency in that field. Second, it was felt that the segregation of insurance by class would permit a more accurate appraisal of the financial qualification required for each type of insurance, and that regulatory requirements could be established to fit each class. Finally, insurance regulators feared that there was a danger in combining fire insurance, which seemed more subject to catastrophes, with life insurance. Various conflagrations, such as the New York fire of 1835, helped to reinforce this opinion.[4]

The Multiple-Line Transition In the late 1940s, individual states began to change their laws to allow multiple-line operations, permitting property and casualty insurers to cross the barriers that had separated them and write both property and casualty coverages. Insurers began a transition to *multiple-line underwriting,* the combination of property and casualty insurance in a single company. This allowed insurers to offer *package policies* that combine property and liability coverages.

Multiple-line legislation did not end underwriting compartmentalization. It merely permitted the companies in the property and casualty insurance fields to cross the traditional barriers when an insurer met the capital and surplus requirements of each line. It did not, in most cases, end the barrier between life insurance and property and casualty insurance.

CLASSIFICATION OF PRIVATE INSURERS

Insurers may be classified according to the type of insurance they sell, their licensing status, their legal form of ownership, or the marketing system they employ.

Classification by Type of Product

We can distinguish among three types of insurers based on their product. Life insurance companies sell life contracts and annuities and, in addition, write health insurance. Property and liability insurance companies market all forms of property and liability insurance (including health insurance), but do not write life insurance. Health insurers are a class of specialty insurers, concentrating on their one area of risk. Although there are other specialty insurers that write only a single line of property or liability insurance, these may be classed as property and liability companies.

Classification by Place of Incorporation and Licensing

A *domestic* insurer within any given state is an insurer that is incorporated in that state, or, if it is not incorporated, was formed under the laws of that state. A *foreign* insurer is one that is incorporated in another state of the United States or formed under the laws of another state. *Alien* insurers are incorporated or formed in another country.

[4] During the early years of the property insurance industry in the United States, catastrophe losses wiped out many companies. The most well known of these losses were the great New York City fire of 1835, which wiped out 23 of the 26 New York companies and almost wiped out New York; the 1871 Chicago fire, which made Mrs. O'Leary's cow famous; and the fire that accompanied the 1906 San Francisco earthquake.

A licensed (or *admitted*) insurer with regard to any particular state is an insurer that has been granted a license to operate in that state. An unlicensed (or *nonadmitted*) insurer is one that has not been granted a license. As a general rule, insurance agents are licensed to place insurance only with admitted insurers.[5]

Insurers Classification by Legal Form of Ownership

Broadly speaking, insurers can be classified into six categories based on their form of ownership.

1. Capital stock insurance companies
2. Mutual insurance companies
3. Reciprocals or interinsurance exchanges
4. Lloyd's associations
5. Health expense associations
6. Government insurers

Capital Stock Insurance Companies *Capital stock insurance companies* are organized as profit-making ventures, with the stockholders assuming the risk that is transferred by the individual insureds. If the actuarial predictions prove accurate, the premiums collected are sufficient to pay losses and operating expenses while returning a profit to the stockholders. The capital invested by the stockholders provides funds to run the company until premium income is sufficient to pay losses and operating expense. In addition, it provides a cushion to guarantee that obligations to policyholders will be met. The distinguishing characteristics of a capital stock company are (1) the premium charged by the company is final—there is no form of contingent liability for policyholders; (2) the board of directors is elected by the stockholders; and (3) earnings are distributed to shareholders as dividends on their stock.

Mutual Insurance Companies In contrast to a stock company, a *mutual insurance company* is owned by its policyholders. Normally, a mutual company is incorporated, and in many states this is a legal requirement. The distinguishing characteristics of a mutual insurer are its lack of capital stock and the distribution of earnings. Unlike the capital stock company, the mutual company has no paid-in capital as a guarantee of solvency in the event of adverse experience. For this reason, mutual insurers need to accumulate a surplus to protect against such adverse contingencies as heavy losses or a decline in investment return. Any money left after paying all costs of operation is returned to the policyholders in the form of dividends. Included in the concept of "costs" that must be paid is the addition to the surplus of the company.

A limited number of mutual insurers issue assessable policies, in which the insured has a contingent liability and is subject to assessment if losses exceed advance premiums.[6] However, all states permit mutual insurers to issue nonassessable policies when they have attained the same financial strength required of a capital stock company writing the same type of business. The advance premium that is collected is intended to be sufficient to cover all losses and expenses. If it is not, the additional costs are paid out of the accumulated surplus. All the larger mutual insurers in the United States operate on this basis. Unlike capital stock companies, the premium of a mutual insurer is not fixed, and the excess of premium income over costs may be returned to policyholders as dividends.

In the final analysis, there are few practical differences between a mutual company operating on an advance premium basis with nonassessable policies and a capital stock company. Although the policyholders own the mutual company in theory, there are no vested rights of ownership for these policyholders except in the case of liquidation. Policyholders acquire their ownership interest when they purchase a policy from the mutual insurer. They abandon that ownership when they nonrenew their insurance or are canceled by the insurer. Furthermore, while the policyholders theoretically control the company, this is equivalent to the theoretical

[5] When a prospective buyer cannot obtain required coverage from insurers who are licensed to do business in the state, state *excess and surplus lines laws* permit coverage to be placed in a nonadmitted insurer. In most states, only agents who hold a special license may place insurance in a nonadmitted insurer.

[6] Some mutual insurers operate on a post-loss assessment basis, in which premiums are payable after a loss occurs. The nuclear energy industry operates a post-loss assessment mutual to provide liability insurance for losses arising out of nuclear incidents. In addition, some mutuals charge an advance premium, but reserve the right to levy additional assessments if losses exceed the advance premiums collected. *County mutuals* authorized by the insurance laws of many states usually operate as advance premium assessable mutuals.

control of the stockholders over the management in a large corporation with many individual stockholders.

Demutualization and Mutual Insurance Holding Companies In recent years, a number of mutual insurance companies have demutualized. Demutualization refers to the process by which a mutual insurance company changes its organization structure, converting from the mutual form to a capital stock or modified capital stock form. Although there are several motivations for demutualization, the most important have been the need to access capital and the desire for diversification.

Mutual insurance companies have limited ways of raising capital. Whereas a stock insurer can issue shares of stock to acquire capital, a mutual insurer must generate it internally, from profits. Although mutual insurers can raise limited amounts of capital through subordinated loans (called surplus notes), they do not have access to equity funding. Increasingly, competition within the insurance industry has led to a greater emphasis on capital strength, and the inability to access capital markets can limit an insurer's growth and restrict its marketing strategies. In response to the need for increased flexibility, a number of mutual insurance companies have demutualized—they have converted into stock corporations. Because a mutual insurance company is owned by its policyholders, demutualization involves issuing stock to policyholders. As a general rule, policyholders have been offered a choice between stock in the new corporation or cash. Some policyholders have accepted stock while others have taken the cash.

In addition to total demutualization, some insurers have opted for a different approach: a mutual insurance holding company. About half of the states have adopted mutual insurance holding company laws, under which a mutual insurer converts to a stock insurer that is owned by a mutual holding company. The policyholders own the mutual holding company (similar to the way in which they owned the mutual insurer), while their contractual rights as insureds remain in the stock insurance company. This structure is more flexible than a mutual insurance company. The holding company can hold other subsidiaries, and may raise capital by issuing stock in the subsidiaries. State law generally requires that voting control remain with the holding company.

Fraternal Insurers Fraternal societies are specialized forms of mutual insurers. Basically, fraternal societies are nonprofit organizations that operate on the basis of "lodges," with a representative form of government. Fraternals have primarily concentrated their activity in the field of life insurance, although they sometimes sell sickness and accident insurance. Since fraternals are considered charitable institutions, they do not pay federal income tax or state premium tax.

Reciprocals The *reciprocal exchange* (also called an *interinsurance* exchange) is a particularly American innovation, and although reciprocals are only a small segment of the insurance industry (there are about 50 in existence), they are significant. A *reciprocal* is an unincorporated group of individuals, called subscribers, who exchange insurance risks. Each member (or subscriber) is both an insured and an insurer: as a member of the group, the individual is insured by each of the other members and, in turn, insures each of them. Reciprocal exchanges are sometimes confused with mutual insurers, and while there is a similarity, there is also a fundamental difference. Unlike a mutual insurer, in which members of the group assume their liability collectively; in a reciprocal exchange, each subscriber assumes his or her liability individually and not as a member of the group. This means that one member cannot be called on to assume the liability of a defaulting member.

The distinguishing characteristic of a reciprocal is the administrator, who is called the *attorney-in-fact*. This official derives authority through a power of attorney granted by each of the subscribers, which is used to commit the members as insurers of each other's property. The attorney-in-fact receives some percentage of the premiums paid by the subscribers (usually about 25 percent) to cover the expenses of operating the program. Reciprocals confine their operations to the property and casualty fields. The portion of the total premiums written through interinsurance exchanges is relatively small. In 1999, only about 6 percent of all property and casualty premiums were written through reciprocals.

Lloyd's Associations *Lloyd's associations* are yet another source of insurance coverage, although, strictly speaking, these organizations do not themselves underwrite insurance. Lloyd's associations include Lloyd's of London and American Lloyds.

Lloyd's of London Lloyd's of London is the oldest and perhaps the most famous insurance organization in the world. Generally speaking, Lloyd's is a

corporation for marketing the services of a group of individuals. The organization itself does not issue insurance policies or provide insurance protection. The actual insurance is underwritten by individual underwriting members, referred to as *"names,"* usually operating through syndicates. Technically, each name is a separate "insurance company," insuring risks separately or collectively with other members. In a sense, Lloyd's is similar to the New York Stock Exchange, in which the physical facilities are owned by the stock exchange and are made available to members for the transaction of business. Lloyd's is governed by a group known as The Committee of Lloyd's, which establishes standards with which members must comply.

Normally, policies written through Lloyd's are issued by a number of the individual underwriters, in which each underwriter assumes a fraction of the risk. The Lloyd's policy contains the statement, "Each for his own part and not for one another," indicating that the underwriters assume liability individually and that each underwriter is liable only for his or her own commitments. Historically, however, solvent members have assumed the liabilities of defaulting members for public relations reasons.[7]

Originally, each underwriter at Lloyd's conducted business as an individual proprietor or as a member of one of 170 syndicates. No corporations or other limitations on liability were permitted, and every member of Lloyd's exposed his or her entire personal fortune in addition to their business assets.[8] During the 1980s, membership at Lloyd's increased significantly, mushrooming from 6000 names at the start of the decade to 32,433 at the decade's close. This expansion in membership coincided with a period of disastrous losses experienced by Lloyd's underwriters, mainly in connection with pollution liability losses and claims for the occupational disease asbestosis, in which billions of dollars were lost. Most of the underwriting losses fell on the newest members of Lloyd's, many of whom were U.S. citizens who had been attracted to Lloyd's by what they thought was the potential for significant profits. Billions of dollars in losses were concentrated in about a third of the Lloyd's syndicates, while other syndicates, largely subscribed by Lloyd's insiders, achieved huge profits, in many cases in excess of 30 percent a year. Faced with disastrous losses, the U.S. investors filed complaints with U.S. regulators and initiated litigation in the courts, alleging that they had been misled.[9]

Although there was a serious question about whether Lloyd's would survive as the 1990s began, in May 1995, the management committee at Lloyd's unveiled a complex plan called the Reconstruction and Renewal plan (R & R plan), designed to close the books on the organization's past troubles. The R & R plan included three key features.

The first element was a settlement offer to the members at Lloyd's for the claims alleging mismanagement and fraud. The offer was for about £2.8 billion ($4.4 billion) and more than 90 percent of the names involved in the litigation eventually agreed to accept their share of a £3.2-billion settlement.

The second element in the plan was to isolate liability for losses prior to 1993 from liabilities incurred after 1993. This was done by reinsuring the liability from past losses with a new reinsurance company, Equitas, created for the purpose of assuming liability for unpaid losses that had accumulated during the period prior to 1985. Members who accepted the settlement offer applied their shares of the settlement to reinsure their old business with Equitas. They were thereby significantly protected—but not immune—from any further losses on business reinsured into Equitas.[10] Financing for the settlement drew on several sources, including a Lloyd's central fund of about $12 billion, a levy on members who continued trading, and the errors and omissions liability insurance of the agents and

[7] In addition to the individual liability, another problem arises from the severability of the underwriters. In the event of a dispute concerning coverage under the policy, it is technically necessary to sue each of the individual underwriters. As a matter of practice, however, if suit is brought against one underwriter under a contract and is successful, the remaining members pay their part of the loss without the necessity of further litigation.

[8] Standards for admission of underwriters are both severe and rigid. It not until 1968 that non-British members were admitted, and women were not allowed membership until 1969.

[9] For an interesting perspective, see Adam Raphael, *Ultimate Risk: The Inside Story of the Lloyd's Catastrophe* (New York: Four Walls Eight Windows, 1995), and Elizabeth Luessenhop and Martin Mayer, *Risky Business: An Insider's Account of the Disaster at Lloyd's of London* (New York: Scribner, 1995). See also Lloyd's Web site at *http://www.lloydsoflondon.co.uk/*.

[10] The Equitas Group is a group of limited liability companies independent of Lloyd's and outside the Lloyd's regulatory regime. Although Equitas was a key feature in Lloyd's of London's Reconstruction and Renewal program, Lloyd's no longer has an ownership interest in Equitas.

underwriters who were targets of the litigation.[11] After payment of the settlement offer, Lloyd's established a new central fund and also agreed to increase its trust funds in the United States. There are separate funds for direct premium business and reinsurance.

The third feature in the R & R plan was a revision of the financial standards for participation at Lloyd's. Corporate entities with limited liability were authorized and the financial requirements for individuals were increased. Although individual, unlimited liability was the sole mode of operation for most of Lloyd's history for more than 300 years, it is now the exception. By 2000, corporate capital accounted for the majority of underwriting capacity at Lloyd's, representing nearly two-thirds of the market's overall capacity. Although some observers believe that it is still too early to tell whether the changes at Lloyd's will be sufficient to prevent the reoccurrence of a debacle such as the one that triggered the reorganization, it is indisputable that the nature of Lloyd's of London has changed dramatically.

Although Lloyd's of London is famous throughout the United States, it is licensed in only two states, Illinois and Kentucky. Each Lloyd's policy issued in the United States contains a clause in which the underwriters agree to submit to the jurisdiction of either of these two states or any other court of competent jurisdiction in the United States.

Even though Lloyd's is licensed in only two states, it provides insurance in other states as well, under the provisions of state *excess and surplus line laws*. To accommodate the needs of individuals who desire protection not available from companies licensed in a state, all states allow the placement of insurance in nonadmitted or nonlicensed companies. Basically, an agent may secure coverage for a client with Lloyd's (or any other nonadmitted insurer) after a diligent effort to place the coverage with a licensed insurer has been unsuccessful.

American Lloyd's Associations The *American Lloyd's associations* are an attempt to copy the success of (and capitalize on the fame of) Lloyd's of London. An American Lloyd's is simply a group of individuals who operate an insurance mechanism using the same principles of individual liability of insurers as Lloyd's of London. Following the practice at Lloyd's of London, each underwriter assumes a part of a risk and is liable only for his or her portion of the risk. Individual underwriters have no obligation to cover losses for which a defaulting member is responsible. Although this is essentially the same system used by Lloyd's of London, many American Lloyd's lack the strict regulation that the original Lloyd's imposes on its members. Most states have laws prohibiting the organization or licensing of American Lloyd's. Those American Lloyd's that do exist operate almost exclusively in the property insurance field.

Insurance Exchanges In 1979, the states of Florida, Illinois, and New York enacted legislation authorizing the formation of "insurance exchanges," patterned after the method of operation used at Lloyds, in which a number of underwriters participate in providing insurance under a single contract. The exchanges were created to insure large, unusual, or hard-to-insure exposures. The Florida and New York exchanges encountered financial difficulties and both closed in 1988. The Illinois exchange continues to operate successfully.

Health Expense Associations *Health Expense Associations* are unique to the field of health insurance. They include Blue Cross and Blue Shield associations and managed care organizations. Blue Cross plans originated as nonprofit associations, usually organized by hospitals under special state-enabling legislation to provide for prepayment of hospital expenses. Blue Shield organizations were organized by state or local physicians associations to facilitate prepayment of physicians fees. The *Blues* pioneered the concept of service benefits in health insurance. Rather than providing a dollar indemnity when an insured is confined to a hospital, a Blue Cross contract would provide a semiprivate room in a member hospital and a Blue Shield contract would provide the services of a member physician.

Managed care organizations include *health maintenance organizations* (HMOs) and *provider sponsored*

[11] In response to the restructuring at Lloyd's to address the liabilities incurred in environmental and asbestos claims and similar restructuring of several U.S. insurers (most notably Cigna Property and Casualty), the NAIC established a liability-based restructurings working group that was charged with looking into restructurings such as Cigna Corp. performed with its property/casualty operations.

organizations (PSOs).[12] The insurance element in the operation of HMOs and PSOs derives from the manner in which they charge for their services, which is called *capitation*. Under the capitation approach, individual subscribers pay an annual fee and in return receive a wide range of health care services that is provided by the HMO or PSO. HMOs and PSOs differ from commercial insurers in that they are also health care providers. They are similar to commercial insurers because, by providing their services to enrollees for a fixed prepayment (capitation), they make possible the transfer and sharing of risk.

Government Insurers In addition to the social insurance programs they operate, federal and state governments also offer some forms of private (voluntary) insurance.[13] The private insurance programs of government have developed for diverse reasons. In some cases, the risks they cover do not lend themselves to private insurance, because either the hazards were too great or the private insurers were subject to adverse selection. In other instances, they originated because of the inability or reluctance of private insurers to meet society's needs for some form of private insurance. In some cases, government private insurance programs have been established as tools of social change and are designed to provide a subsidy to particular segments of society or to help solve social ills afflicting individual classes of citizens. Finally, government insurance programs have sometimes been founded on the mistaken notion that such programs could somehow repeal the law of averages and provide insurance at a lower cost than would be charged by private insurers.

Federal Private (Voluntary) Insurance Programs
Over the years, the federal government has engaged in a number of private insurance fields. In some programs, the government cooperates with private insurers, providing reinsurance or other forms of subsidy in meeting risks that the private insurance industry could not meet alone. The following are the federal programs that offer forms of private insurance.

1. Post Office insurance coverages. The U.S. Post Office sells insurance on registered mail and parcel post. The program is a convenience to occasional customers who desire insurance on property in the mail.

2. Federal crop insurance. Federal crop insurance has existed in one form or another since 1938. The current program dates from the Federal Crop Insurance Act of 1980, which established a new federal "multi-peril" crop insurance program.

3. Mortgage loan insurance. The federal government provides mortgage loan insurance through five agencies: the FHA, the VA, the Federal Home Loan Mortgage Corporation, the Federal Home Loan Bank Board, and the Farmers Home Administration. The coverage protects private financial institutions against loss from the borrower's default on a mortgage loan.[14]

4. National Flood Insurance Program. The 1968 Housing and Urban Development (HUD) Act, established a National Flood Insurance Program, which is conducted as a partnership between the federal government and the private insurance industry.

5. SBA surety bond program. Congress established the Small Business Administration (SBA) Surety Bond Guarantee Program in 1971. Under this plan the SBA reinsures private sureties that issue bonds to small contractors who would be unable to obtain a bond without this government backing.

6. Export-Import Bank. The U.S. Export-Import Bank, in cooperation with a group of private insurers known as the Foreign Credit Insurance Association (FCIA), offers U.S. exporters protection against *political risks,* such as expropriation or inconvertibility of the foreign currency into dollars, and credit losses resulting from war, insurrection, or revolution.

[12] A *provider sponsored organization* (PSO) is essentially an HMO that is organized by a partnership of health care providers, such as a hospital and a group of physicians. The terminology for *provider sponsored organizations* has been revised several times, as health care reformers reinvent the concept. At various times and in different proposals, provider sponsored organizations have been called *physician-hospital organizations* (PHOs) and *organized delivery systems* (ODSs). The PSO designation is used in the Tax Reform Act of 1997 in connection with new Medicare options and is likely to become the standard designation for these organizations.

[13] A *government insurer,* as used here, means an insurance enterprise operated by the state or nation, with the government or a government agency collecting premiums (or taxes in the case of some social insurance plans) and assuming liability for the payment of losses. It also includes instances in which the government provides reinsurance for other insurers or participates with them in assuming the risk of loss as a transferee. It does not cover self-insurance funds established for the protection of government property or insurance programs operated by the government exclusively for the benefit of its employees.

[14] Mortgage loan insurance is also available from private insurers, and it is estimated that they insure a greater dollar volume of loans than the FHA does. See Joseph E. Johnson and George B. Flanigan, "Private Mortgage Insurance," *CPCU Annals*, vol. 26, no. 4 (December 1973), and "Regulation of Private Mortgage Insurance," ibid., vol. 27, no. 2 (June 1974).

7. Overseas Private Investor Corporation. The Overseas Private Investor Corporation (OPIC) is a U.S. government agency organized to insure Americans who invest in foreign countries against loss by political risks such as war, revolution, insurrection, expropriation, or inconvertibility of foreign currency into dollars.

8. Servicemen's and veterans' life insurance. The U. S. Veterans Administration (VA) operates five separate life insurance programs, under which the government itself serves as the insurer. Only one program (Service Disabled Veterans Insurance) is still open to new issues.

The most recent consideration of a federal insurance program was occurring in March 2002, as Congress debated enacting a federal terrorism reinsurance program. In December 2001, worldwide reinsurers providing coverage in the United States announced that reinsurance contracts scheduled for renewal in January 2002 would exclude acts of terrorism. Faced with the unavailability of reinsurance for a potentially catastrophic exposure, U.S. insurers developed exclusions deleting coverage for acts of terrorism in their policies. Congress considered several versions of a federal terrorism reinsurance program but reached an impasse over program provisions, whether there should be a bar on punitive damage awards to victims of terrorist acts, a limit to other noneconomic damages, and a cap to attorneys' fees. It is conceivable that Congress will eventually act to address the terrorism exposure with a federal reinsurance program. Under the proposal that seemed to have the greatest support, the federal government would bear 80 percent of loss caused by terrorist acts up to $20 billion and the insurance industry would bear 20 percent. Losses that exceed $20 billion would be paid entirely by the government.

Other forms of private insurance that have been offered by the federal government in the past but that have been discontinued include war-risk insurance (during World Wars I and II), the Federal Riot Reinsurance Program (1968 to 1983) and the Federal Crime Insurance Program (1971–1997).[15]

State Private (Voluntary) Insurance Programs
Like the federal government, several individual states offer private or voluntary insurance, but the number and variety of state programs is far more limited. The state programs that do exist more often than not compete with those of the private insurance industry. About half the states sell workers compensation insurance.[16] In addition, the State of Wisconsin operates a state life insurance fund and Maryland operates a state automobile insurance fund. Finally, the states of California, Florida, and Hawaii have created state catastrophe funds to provide direct insurance and reinsurance for hurricane and earthquake losses.

MARKETING SYSTEMS

As noted, the agent is the central figure in the insurance marketing process. While this is true, the relationship between the agents and the companies they represent can be, and is often, quite varied. Through a process of evolution, several marketing forms have developed, each of which has as its goal the attainment of efficiency in distribution and service.

The Agent

With few exceptions, the marketing mechanism in the insurance industry revolves around the agent; however, his or her role varies in different lines of insurance. In the field of property and liability insurance, on the one hand, the *agent* is "an individual authorized to create, terminate, and modify contracts of insurance." In the area of life insurance, on the other hand, the agent's power is somewhat limited. Life insurance agents are appointed with the authorization to solicit and deliver contracts of insurance; however, they cannot, as can the property and liability agent, "bind" the insurance company to risk.[17]

The insurance agent is first and foremost the representative of the insurance company. An insurance *broker,* on the other hand, is a representative of the

[15] In addition to a federal terrorism reinsurance program, which remains under consideration, Congress has also considered several proposals to create a federal disaster reinsurance program, primarily as a result of the California earthquakes in 1989 and 1993 and Hurricane Andrew in 1992.

[16] State workers compensation funds are discussed in Chapter 11.

[17] "Binding" refers to the authority of an agent to commit his or her principal to a contract for the insurance. The authority of agents is discussed in Chapter 9.

insured. Although serving as the agent of the insured, the broker normally receives compensation in the form of a commission from the company. The fact that the broker is not an agent of the insurer means that he or she does not have the power to *bind* the company. The broker merely solicits business from clients and then places the business with an insurer. Brokers represent an important segment of the insurance marketing mechanism, particularly in large cities, where they control large segments of the market. In some instances, agents also act as brokers, placing coverage through the agents of companies they do not represent.

Historically, brokers rarely operated in the life insurance field, because most life insurers accepted business only from their own appointed agents. Today, there are many life insurance producers who operate as brokers, placing life insurance with a variety of insurers, rather than with a single company. Although life insurance agents do not have binding authority, the distinction between an agent and a broker can still be important in the life insurance field. Any information given to the agent of an insurance company is considered to have been given to the insurer, and the insurer is presumed to have knowledge of relevant facts known to its agent. This may have relevance in situations in which there is a question regarding the insured's disclosure of information pertinent to the underwriting decision. Because the broker is a representative of the insured rather than the company, information provided to the broker is not imputed to the company.

Consultants and Financial Planners In addition to insurance agents and brokers, there are a growing number of risk management and insurance consultants who do not represent insurers or sell insurance, but offer their services on a fee basis. Many states regulate the activities of these consultants and require that they be licensed.

In the personal lines field, there has been a rapid growth in the financial planning profession that focuses on the broad spectrum of an individual's or family's economic goals. It encompasses budgeting, planned accumulation of wealth, risk management, and tax minimization. Because protection of assets is a cornerstone of a financial plan, financial planners have become an important source of advice on personal risk management and insurance, especially for wealthy members of society. Although anyone can call him- or herself a financial planner, only persons who have met certain educational standards may use one of the financial planning industry's professional designations.[18]

Life Insurance Distribution System

With the exception of a small amount of life insurance that is sold through the mail, most life insurance is sold by agents or brokers. The agent may work through a general agency, a branch office, or a personal-producing general agent's office (discussed later). Most agents are independent contractors, but they may also be employees of the general agency or insurer. Life insurance companies originally insisted that individual agents represent them exclusively, but there is an increasing trend toward multiple company representation and brokerage of life insurance. Brokers place the insurance they write with a number of insurers, selecting the insurer most appropriate to the situation.

General agents are independent business people, empowered by the company they represent to sell life insurance in specified territories and to appoint subagents. The general agency receives an overriding commission on all business written by its subagents out of which it pays agency expenses. At one time, the general agents received no financial assistance from the companies they represented, but this has gradually changed, and now most general agents receive some sort of financial assistance from their companies in the form of a contribution toward the general agency expense. The fact that the general agent hires, trains, and compensates subagents makes the general agency a relatively inexpensive and riskless manner of starting in a new area.

In the *branch office system,* the sales force is supervised by a branch manager who, in contrast to the general agent, is a salaried employee of the insurance company. Expenses of the branch office are

[18] The Certified Financial Planner (CFP) designation is granted by the CFP Board to those persons who have met its educational standards, passed the CFP Board Comprehensive CFP Certification Exam, satisfied work experience requirements, and agree to follow the CFP Board Code of Ethics. The Chartered Financial Consultant (ChFC) designation is awarded by the American College to individuals who have passed 13 two-hour examinations. The ChFC designation is often held in conjunction with the CLU designation.

paid by the home office, for in reality the branch office is simply an extension of the home office. The agents assigned to a branch office may be employees of the insurer or independent contractors. At one time, the branch manager received only a salary, but in recent years this has been modified, and in many cases the branch manager now receives additional compensation on the basis of the productivity of the agents supervised.

The *personal-producing general agent* (PPGA) represents a unique arrangement between the insurer and selected agents. PPGAs are usually agents who have established a record of successful production and are granted a contract that gives them greater compensation than they received as agents. Like the general agent, the PPGAs absorb all their own expenses, including office facilities, clerical staff, and other overhead costs. Although most PPGAs have the authority to employ or appoint their own agents and/or to use independent brokers, such appointments are usually limited, since personal production is the PPGA's prime purpose.

Property and Liability Distribution Systems

In the field of property and liability insurance, companies may be classified into two groups based on their distribution system: (1) those who operate through the American Agency System and (2) the *direct writers*. The agents who operate through the American Agency System are known as independent agents, while those who represent direct writers are called captive agents.

The American Agency System *Independent agents* normally represent several companies, dividing the policies they sell among those companies according to their choice. They own their expirations, which means that they may place the renewals of sold policies with some other insurer if they choose to do so. This alternative often gives the independent agent strategic power to use to the benefit of clients. However, since even the independent agent is first and foremost a representative of the insurance company, he or she also has an obligation to the company. One implication of the ownership of renewals by the independent agent is that it prevents the insurance company from paying a lower commission on renewal business. If a com-pany represented by an independent agent were to attempt to pay a lower commission on renewal policies than on new ones, the agent could simply place the policy with a different company, making it new business for that company.

Direct Writers *Direct writers* operate through salaried representatives (as in the case of the Liberty Mutual Insurance Company) or through *exclusive* or *captive agents* (as in the case with Nationwide, State Farm, and Allstate).[19] The compensation of the salesperson may be in the form of a salary, or it may be a commission, based on the premium volume. In the case of the exclusive agent, it is normally a commission. The key point is that the agent or the salaried employee does not own the expirations. He or she has no choice as to where the policy is to be renewed. Since the agent cannot transfer the business written to another insurer, the direct-writing company can pay a small renewal commission or none at all.

The *ownership of renewals* is the most important difference between the two types of agents, and from this difference arise still other distinctions in the method of operation. Since the direct-writing agent receives little or no commission on renewals, the production of new business is of crucial importance. In a sense, the life insurance agent is in the same position; he or she is a captive agent, representing only one company. Since for the life insurance agent, like for the direct-writing agent in property and liability, the renewal commission is quite low, his or her income depends on the generation of new business. The independent agent, on the other hand, places greater emphasis on the retention of accounts currently serviced. As a matter of fact, the independent agent's interest in his or her obligation to clients is one of the fundamental themes of the advertising program of the independent agents.

Direct Response Distribution of Insurance Life insurance, health insurance, and property and liability insurance are all sold by insurers operating under a "direct response" system. These insurers do not use

[19] Technically, companies that operate through exclusive agents are not *direct writers* but rather *exclusive-agent companies*. However, the term *direct writer* is commonly used in reference to both companies operating through salaried representatives and those operating through exclusive agents.

agents, but promote the sale of insurance by mass media advertising, direct mail and, more recently, via the Internet. Historically, the direct response system has accounted for a small portion of the total insurance sold in this country, but this could change with the expansion of marketing over the World Wide Web.

Insurance Marketing and the World Wide Web

Despite a slow start, the insurance industry is rapidly establishing its presence in the electronic marketplace. By the close of the century, most U.S. insurers had established a presence on the Web, offering extensive information about their insurance products. A number had actually begun selling insurance online.[20] Given the success in marketing other products over the Web, it seems likely that the potential for marketing insurance via this medium is significant.[21] Insurance Web sales totalled $2.1 billion in 2001, mainly in the area of life insurance products and personal property and liability coverage. Some observers believe that significant growth will also occur in the commercial insurance area. Others disagree, arguing that commercial insurance coverages are too complex to be purchased via the Web by the vast majority of businesses.

Regulators are understandably concerned over the implications of Web-based marketing of insurance. In 1998, the NAIC adopted a white paper prepared by the Internet Marketing Issues Group of the Market Conduct and Consumer Affairs Subcommittee that addresses a variety of regulatory issues related to insurance sold over the Internet.

Corporate Combinations

To further explain the structure of the insurance industry, we should briefly examine some of its unique corporate relationships, which include insurance company groups and cooperating underwriting arrangements.

Insurance Company Groups Many insurance companies operate in groups, often called *fleets,* which consist of a number of insurance companies under common ownership and often under common management. Insurance company groups developed during the monoline era and were designed to permit the writing of both property and casualty coverages by insurers under a common management. Since a fire company could not write casualty coverages and a casualty company was forbidden to issue fire coverage, the logical solution was to form two companies and operate them in tandem. Although this reason for company fleets no longer exists, the form of operation persists, and the overwhelming preponderance of the property and liability insurance business is written by insurance companies that are members of a company group.[22]

Initially, company fleets limited their operations to the property and liability field, but over time these groups expanded to include life insurers. State Farm Mutual, founded in 1922, added a life subsidiary, State Farm Life Insurance Company, in 1929. One by one the other major property and liability insurers also acquired or formed life insurance company subsidiaries. Eventually, life insurance companies acquired or formed property and liability insurers. As a result, most insurance company fleets now include both property and liability and life insurers.

Underwriting Syndicates In addition to the other forms of cooperation, insurers sometimes join together in *underwriting syndicates* for the purpose of handling risks that would be beyond the capacity of an individual company. In these syndicates, which are found primarily in the property and liability field, insurers make use of the basic insurance principle of spreading risk and sharing losses.

[20] In November 2000, Allstate Insurance Company embarked on a program to emphasize the sale of insurance over the Internet, via its new *Good Hands Network,* where consumers will be able to get quotes and buy auto and homeowners insurance. With conversion of its Web site from an information site to an e-commerce site, Allstate converted all of its agents, some of which had been employees, into independent contractors. Customers who buy insurance through Allstate's Web system will deal with Allstate agents, who will earn a commission on Internet sales of 2 to 3.5 percent, compared with the 10 percent commission paid on agent-generated sales.

[21] Professor James R. Garven reports that insurers marketing via the World Wide Web have a 23 percent cost advantage over insurers that use the traditional agency system. *Insurance Online Marketing Report,* vol. 1, no. 1 (September 1999), p. 2.

[22] There are about 290 groups, composed of slightly more than 1100 insurers operating in the property and liability field, that write about 90 percent of the industry's total premiums.

The Associated Factory Mutual Insurance Companies The *factory mutuals* are a group of four direct-writing mutual insurers specializing in underwriting property insurance on highly protected exposures usually involving large concentrations of value.[23] Insurance purchased from one of the companies is shared on a percentage basis among all four companies. The basic emphasis of the factory mutuals is on loss prevention, and only high-grade and sprinklered risks are insured. Applicants are rigidly inspected both before and after the issuance of the coverage. Initial premiums are substantially higher than the amount anticipated to be needed for losses and expenses, with the excess premium returned to the policyholder as a dividend at the end of the year. Although the factory mutuals constitute only a small number of companies, the system is a significant factor in the insurance market, particularly for larger insureds.

Industrial Risk Insurers Industrial Risk Insurers (IRI) is an underwriting syndicate of about 45 stock insurers that was formed in December 1975 through the merger of two syndicates, the Factory Insurance Association (FIA) and the Oil Insurance Association (OIA). Like the factory mutuals, the IRI emphasizes loss prevention and specializes in large exposures. However, unlike the factory mutuals, in which the originating company issues the policy and then reinsures a portion with other insurers, the IRI itself issues the insurance, and the coverage is shared among the member companies on a predetermined basis.

Improved Risk Mutuals The Improved Risk Mutuals is an underwriting syndicate composed of 18 mutual insurance companies, which combine to write insurance on larger and higher valued properties than any one of the companies could individually insure. To a somewhat lesser extent than the factory mutuals and the IRI, the improved risk mutuals specialize in writing highly protected risks.

Nuclear Energy Pools Insurance for liability arising out of nuclear accidents is provided by an insurance industry pool, American Nuclear Insurers, up to $200 million. In addition, a mutual insurance assessment association, consisting of nuclear reactor operators, provides an additional $9 billion in coverage on a post-loss assessment basis.[24] Property insurance is provided by the nuclear pools and by two offshore industry mutual insurers, Nuclear Electric Insurance, Ltd., and Nuclear Mutual, Ltd. In 2000, the nuclear pools and industry mutuals provided over $1 billion primary and $1 billion excess property insurance.

Other Voluntary Syndicates In addition to the factory mutuals, the IRI, and the improved risk mutuals, several similar syndicates have been formed to deal with specialized exposures or concentrations of values in particular industries. For example, two syndicates, the Associated Aviation Underwriters and the United States Aircraft Insurance Group, offer insurance for aviation risks. The American Hull Insurance Syndicate represents its members in competition with international marine insurers, specializing in oceangoing ships of American registry. The Railroad Insurance Underwriters provides a market for insuring rolling stock and, in addition, insures fixed-location property owned by the railroads.

Banks and Insurance

As a result of legislation enacted during the Great Depression of the 1930s, the financial services in the United States have been divided into three broad segments: commercial banking, the insurance industry, and the securities brokerage field. The *Glass-Steagall Act of 1933* prohibited banks from owning insurance companies or security brokerage firms. In addition, federal banking laws, beginning with the *National Banking Act of 1864,* have prohibited banks from underwriting or selling insurance, except for

[23] The factory mutual concept dates from 1835, when Zachariah Allen, the owner of a textile mill, organized the Manufacturers Mutual Fire Insurance Company of Rhode Island. Allen, distressed because existing insurers granted no rate concessions to factories in which proper attention had been devoted to loss prevention and control, decided to organize a company that would recognize superior construction and loss-prevention efforts. The four factory mutuals currently in existence are the Allendale Mutual Insurance Company, Arkwright-Boston Manufacturers Mutual Company, Philadelphia Manufacturers Insurance Company, and the Protection Mutual Insurance Company. In addition, these companies own a stock company, the Affiliated Factory Mutual Insurance Company, that insures high-quality risks that do not meet the requirements of the factory mutuals.

[24] Nuclear reactor operators are subject to assessment up to $88.095 million per reactor. If coverage from the industry pools and assessments are inadequate to cover a catastrophic loss, Congress can appropriate additional funds and then tax the owners of the nuclear reactors to cover the appropriation.

specific limited exceptions. In 1916, Congress amended the National Banking Act to give banks in towns of fewer than 5000 inhabitants the power to sell insurance.[25] Then, in 1956, in the *Bank Holding Company Act,*[26] Congress authorized insurance agency affiliates of banks through the holding company mechanism, in which a bank holding company is allowed to own both a bank and an insurance agency. Thus, although some banks have been permitted to engage in insurance agency activities, their authorization is under a limited exception to the general rule separating banking and commerce.[27]

In 1999, after 20 years of debate, Congress repealed the *Glass-Steagall Act of 1933* and replaced it with the *Financial Services Modernization Act,* also known as the *Gramm-Leach-Bliley Act (GLBA).* This ended the compartmentalization of the financial services industry in the United States and allows full-scale affiliations among the three industries. The changes enacted in 1999 have been several decades in the making and occurred against a backdrop of convergence of the three segments of the financial services industry globally. The combination of banking and insurance in Europe has given rise to a phenomenon known as *bancassurance,* the full integration of retail banking and insurance operations.[28] Competition from foreign banks that can freely underwrite and distribute insurance products gave these insurers a competitive advantage over U.S. insurers, which could not offer the same wide mix of insurance, commercial banking, and investment banking services. The *Financial Services Modernization Act* was as much about international competition as it was about competition in the United States.

Originally, insurance companies, agents, and their trade associations opposed eliminating the barriers between banking and insurance. This opposition diminished after the U.S. Supreme Court ruled in two separate cases that the Office of the Comptroller of Currency (OCC)—not state insurance regulators—had authority over the insurance activities of federal banks.[29] The adverse effect of the decision was compounded by the *Chevron* doctrine, according to which the courts will give deference to the federal regulator when interpreting federal law.[30] Insurers dropped their opposition to the repeal of Glass-Steagal because of a provision in GLBA that ended the deference that the courts had granted to federal regulators.

With the repeal of Glass-Steagall, the financial services industry will change significantly. In fact, the changes began even before that repeal, as the industry anticipated congressional action.[31] Many authorities are predicting a rash of new affiliations between banks and insurers. Others believe that despite their long campaign for access to the insurance marketplace, banks will make limited incursions into the field, mainly in the life and annuity field.

COOPERATION IN THE INSURANCE INDUSTRY

Insurance by its very nature is cooperative. Despite the fact that insurance companies and agents compete vigorously with each other, there are many areas in which both companies and agents cooperate. In some cases, this arises out of economic necessity. Many cooperative organizations are formed and supported by groups of insurance companies to perform functions that would mean a duplication of effort if each company carried them out individually. In other instances, the cooperation is designed to spread risk among insurers, by sharing losses. In still other cases, the objective of the cooperation is improved public relations and personnel education. The nature and

[25] Act of Sept. 7, 1916 (Federal Statute), 39 Stat. 753, 12 U.S.C. 92.

[26] *Bank Holding Company Act of 1956* (P.L. 84-511, 70 Stat. 133).

[27] Congress reaffirmed this policy in the *Bank Holding Company Act of 1956* and extended it with the 1970 amendments to the same act. Congress again reaffirmed the separation of banking and insurance in the *Depository Institutions Act of 1982,* which expressly prohibited most bank holding company insurance activities.

[28] ING Group, the largest financial services group in the Netherlands, often is cited as a *bancassurance* success story. Although many European banks now sell insurance, ING was the first to implement wholesale mergers between banks and insurers.

[29] *NationsBank of North Carolina v. Variable Annuity Life Insurance Co.,* 115 Supreme Court 810 (1995) and U.S. Supreme Court No. 94-1837 *Barnett Bank of Marion County, N. A., Petitioner v. Bill Nelson, Florida Insurance Commissioner, et al.* [March 26, 1996].

[30] *Chevron U.S.A. Inc. v. Natural Resources Defense Council, Inc.,* 467 U.S. 837(1984).

[31] In April 1998, Citicorp and the Travelers Group announced plans to merge, a consolidation that was technically illegal at the time it was announced. Had it not been for the repeal of the Glass-Steagall Act, after a two-year grace period under the Bank Holding Company Act, Travelers would be required to divest itself of the activities that conflicted with the Glass-Steagall Act. In 2001, Citicorp announced that it will spin off and sell Travelers Property Casualty Corporation, and retain Travelers Life and Annuity Corporation.

extent of collaboration within the industry can best be shown by examining a number of the more important cooperative organizations.

Rating Organizations

One major area of cooperation among insurance companies is in ratemaking. As we have seen, the accuracy of an insurer's predictions increases with the number of exposures on which they are based. *Advisory organizations* (also called *rating bureaus*) are supported by insurance companies that furnish these organizations with their loss statistics as the raw material for producing rates. Some of the more important advisory organizations are the following:

1. *The Insurance Service Office* (ISO). The Insurance Service Office provides a wide range of advisory, rating, and actuarial services relating to property and casualty insurance, including the development of policy forms, loss information, and related services for multiple-line coverages. It computes and publishes trended loss data for most property and liability insurance lines other than workers compensation. ISO was originally owned and controlled by insurance companies. In 1994, ISO members approved a new structure in which the organization's board consists of seven noninsurers and four industry representatives.

2. *The American Association of Insurance Services* (AAIS). The American Association of Insurance Services performs approximately the same functions for its subscribers as does the ISO.

3. *The National Council on Compensation Insurance.* The National Council on Compensation Insurance develops and administers rating plans and systems for workers compensation insurance.

At one time, rating bureaus used the loss statistics reported by their members to compute advisory rates, which the bureaus then filed with state insurance departments on behalf of their members. Nonbureau companies either maintained their own loss statistics and filed their rates independently, or used the bureau rate as a point of departure, modifying it to reflect their own experience and expenses. Because insurers that used rates filed by bureaus charged the same rates for coverage, during the 1980s industry critics argued that the activities of rating bureaus constituted a form of "price-fixing" and that these activities permitted the industry to operate as a "cartel." Although it may be argued that the system of advisory rates did not pre-

vent the industry from operating in a highly competitive manner, major rating bureaus responded to the criticism in 1989 when they decided to discontinue filing advisory rates on behalf of their members.[32] In 1989, the ISO announced its decision to stop providing advisory rates to its members. Instead, it now provides insurers with trended loss costs only. Insurers develop and add their own factors for expenses, profits, and contingencies. In 1990, the National Council of Compensation Insurance and the Surety Association of America announced that they would follow the same practice.

There are no rating bureaus in the life insurance field. However, the Society of Actuaries, a voluntary association of actuaries, holds periodic meetings for the exchange of information with the goal of improving premium determination.

Distressed and Residual-Risk Pools

One of the most socially significant areas of cooperation among insurers is found in the techniques used to deal with certain classes of insureds that are unprofitable but that, for various reasons, must be insured. Property and liability insurers in all states are required to participate in *shared markets,* a euphemism for the involuntary markets in which insurance is provided to applicants that do not meet normal underwriting standards. In some instances, applicants are shared on some predetermined basis. In others, losses are shared. The following are a few of the more important programs that have been designed to deal with the problem of the high-risk insured.

1. *The automobile shared market.* Some drivers, because of their past records and the likelihood of future losses that those records indicate, are unacceptable to insurers in the normal course of business. However, because it is deemed socially undesirable to permit such drivers on the road without any insurance, the insurance industry has established special mechanisms to provide the necessary coverage. The most widely used approach is the *Automobile Insurance Plan* (formerly called assigned-risk plan), which is

[32] The accusation that advisory rates constituted a system of price-fixing ignores the fact that insurers were free to participate in bureaus or file their rates independently, thereby precluding the price-fixing and market-sharing activities of a cartel. As a matter of fact, a significant portion of the market is controlled by nonbureau companies, which develop their own rates and price their products individually.

currently used in 42 states. This plan functions by sharing applicants, with each automobile insurer operating in a state accepting a share of the undesirable drivers, based on the percentage of the state's total auto insurance that it writes. The remaining eight states use alternate plans designed to achieve the same purpose.[33]

2. *Workers compensation assigned-risk pools.* Shared-market plans also exist in the field of workers compensation insurance. Here, employers who are not acceptable to insurers in the standard market are assigned to insurers, based on each insurer's percentage of the standard market.

3. *Medical malpractice pools.* In the mid-1970s, because of deteriorating loss experience, many insurers withdrew from the medical malpractice insurance field, creating a *malpractice crisis,* in which many physicians found that they were unable to obtain professional liability insurance at any price. The reaction varied from area to area, but in many states a part of the response was the formation of mandatory participation reinsurance pools, in which all liability insurers in the state share in the premiums and losses associated with medical malpractice insurance.

4. *FAIR plans.* FAIR plans are insurance industry pools designed to provide insurance to property owners in inner-city and other high-risk areas who are unable to obtain insurance through normal market channels because of the location of their property or other factors over which they have no control. If a property owner cannot obtain insurance through normal markets, he or she makes application to the state FAIR plan. After inspecting the property, the FAIR plan assigns the property to a participating insurer or informs the owner what physical hazards must be corrected before the property will be insured.[34]

5. *Beach and windstorm pools.* Special *beach and windstorm plans* exist in seven states.[35] These plans provide property insurance to property owners along the Atlantic and Gulf coasts where vulnerability to hurricanes and other forms of severe windstorm damage is especially high. Like the automobile insurance and FAIR plans, the plans operate by sharing applicants, with each participating insurer accepting a share of the undesirable applicants proportionate to its premiums in the state.

6. *State health insurance plans.* A number of states have addressed the problem of availability of health insurance by creating subsidized state health insurance pools for the uninsurable.[36] Individuals who are not eligible for Medicare or Medicaid and who cannot buy private health insurance obtain coverage from the pools, usually at a subsidized rate. Although the plans differ in detail, the pools provide comprehensive medical coverage that includes in-hospital services, skilled nursing facility care, and prescription drugs. Although the pools are subsidized, even with the subsidy, premiums range from 125 percent to 150 percent of the state's average premiums. Costs in excess of the premiums are covered by a subsidy.[37]

Educational Organizations

The field of insurance demands continuing education on a scale matched by few occupations, and several educational organizations exist for the agent or company employee who wishes to become more knowledgeable and increase personal professionalism. In the life insurance field, the leading educational organization is the American College (formerly the American College of Life Underwriters). It sponsors the course of instruction leading to the professional designation *chartered life underwriter* (CLU), a symbol of professional attainment that relatively few achieve. The institution also offers advanced studies

[33] The operation of these programs is discussed in greater detail in Chapter 29.

[34] The term *FAIR* is an acronym for Fair Access to Insurance Requirements. State FAIR plans currently exist in Arkansas, California, Connecticut, Delaware, Florida, Georgia, Hawaii, Illinois, Indiana, Iowa, Kansas, Kentucky, Louisiana, Maryland, Massachusetts, Michigan, Minnesota, Mississippi, Missouri, New Jersey, New Mexico, New York, North Carolina, Ohio, Oregon, Pennsylvania, Rhode Island, Virginia, Washington, West Virginia, Wisconsin, and the District of Columbia. The FAIR plans were created as an adjunct to a federal riot reinsurance program created by Congress in the aftermath of an epidemic of urban riots that erupted in the summer of 1967 and in 1968. The reinsurance program, which was terminated in 1983, protected the private insurers against catastrophe losses from civil disorders. Participation in the reinsurance program was optional on a state-by-state basis, but if a state chose to participate, all property insurers operating in the state were required to join the state-supervised FAIR plan.

[35] Alabama, Florida, Louisiana, Mississippi, North Carolina, South Carolina, and Texas.

[36] By 1997, the following 30 states had created such pools: Alabama, Alaska, Arkansas, California, Colorado, Connecticut, Florida, Georgia, Illinois, Indiana, Iowa, Kansas, Louisiana, Maine, Minnesota, Mississippi, Missouri, Montana, Nebraska, New Mexico, North Dakota, Oklahoma, Oregon, South Carolina, Tennessee, Texas, Utah, Washington, Wisconsin, and Wyoming.

[37] The source of the subsidy varies by state, and includes state general revenues, a tax on hospital revenues, and assessments on health insurers. Most states fund their plans with an assessment on health insurers.

leading to a graduate degree, Master of Science in Financial Services. The college is supported by contributing life insurance companies.

The American Institute for Property and Liability Underwriters is the equivalent of the American College in the area of property and liability insurance. The designation granted by the Institute is *chartered property and casualty underwriter* (CPCU). The CPCU, like the CLU for life underwriters, is the highest symbol of attainment granted to a member of the property and liability insurance profession for educational development and professionalism.

In addition to the American Life College and the Institute for Property and Liability Underwriters, there are several other educational organizations. The Insurance Institute of America offers basic courses in preparation for the rigorous requirements of the CPCU study program. The Life Underwriters' Training Council provides similar instruction in the field of life insurance. The Insurance Company Education Directors Society (ICEDS) is a vehicle for exchange of ideas among the education directors of major insurance companies. A quite different organization, one that cuts across all industry lines, is the National Association of Insurance Women (International), a professional association of women engaged in insurance, which is dedicated to the three goals of service, fellowship, and education. Membership includes women from all fields of insurance and from all segments of the industry.

Insurance Trade Associations

Like many other industries, members of the insurance industry cooperate through trade associations. In the life insurance field, the leading insurer association is the American Council of Life Insurance, composed of legal reserve life insurance companies. It provides research and lobbying services for its member companies. The Health Insurance Association of America performs similar functions related to health insurance. In the property and liability field, insurers support the American Insurance Association, the Alliance of American Insurers, and the National Association of Independent Insurers.

Trade associations also exist at the agency level. In the property and liability field, many agents belong to local boards of insurance agents. These in turn are affiliated with a state association of insurance agents (e.g., the Independent Insurance Agents of Iowa, or the Professional Insurance Agents Association of Iowa). The state associations further collaborate by affiliating with one of two national associations, the Independent Insurance Agents of America or the National Association of Professional Insurance Agents.

In the area of life insurance, the basic cooperative organization is the local association of life underwriters; each local association affiliates with a state association (e.g., the Iowa Association of Life Underwriters). The national organization embracing the state associations is known as the National Association of Life Underwriters.

Insurance trade associations perform valuable functions for their members, particularly in supporting legislation of interest to the public and the insurance industry and guarding against legislation detrimental to members' interests.

Reinsurance Organizations

Reinsurance, the technique whereby an insurance company obtains insurance against catastrophic losses, is one of the most common forms of cooperation within the insurance industry.[38] In addition to individual contractual relationships among companies, there are a number of cooperative reinsurance bureaus. The best known of these include the Workers Compensation Reinsurance Bureau, which reinsures its capital stock members against catastrophe losses in its special area, and the American Mutual Reinsurance Bureau, which reinsures member mutual companies in all lines except life insurance.

COMPETITION IN THE INSURANCE INDUSTRY

The competition within the insurance industry today is intense, perhaps more so than at any time in history. Briefly, this rivalry takes place in two areas: price and quality.

Price Competition

Price competition in the insurance industry occurs primarily at the company level where rates are set.

[38] Reinsurance is discussed in greater detail in Chapter 8.

Insurance companies compete on the basis of price by attempting to offer a lower priced product than other companies dealing in the same line of insurance.

The agent does not (except in isolated cases) participate in setting the price of the product. Exceptions exist in the case of extremely large accounts on which the commission is negotiated, and the final commission agreed on is a factor in the final premium. In general, the pricing of the product by his or her companies is a factor outside the control of the agent. Price competition between agencies does, of course, take place, but it is based on the price competition between the companies that the agencies represent. There are differences in price among companies and in the selection of the companies that he or she will represent, the agent has control over the price of the contracts the agency sells. Agencies that want to compete on a price basis do so by entering into contracts with insurers whose marketing strategy also emphasizes price.

The price of insurance, like most prices, is a function of the cost of production, and to the extent that companies are successful in reducing their costs, they can also reduce their prices. The following costs are common to all insurance companies:

1. Losses and loss adjustment expense
2. Acquisition expense
3. Administrative expense (company overhead)
4. Taxes
5. Profit and contingencies

The first of the costs listed can be an area of considerable difference among companies. Some companies, through selective underwriting, have achieved significantly lower loss costs. It should be recognized, however, that lower premiums achieved by selective underwriting reflect a different *product*. The unique nature of price competition in insurance rests on the often neglected fact that the individual to whom an insurance policy is sold is, in a sense, the *product* that the insurer sells. It is the combination of hazards and loss-producing characteristics that the individual brings to the insured group that represents the risk transferred to the insurer. This means that two insurers selling policies to different individuals may be selling dramatically different products. If an insurer succeeds in selecting customers with lower than average probabilities of loss, it sells a product whose cost is lower and for which a lower premium may be charged.[39]

The second cost, acquisition expense, can also be altered to reflect substantial premium savings. The major part of the production costs have traditionally been agents' commissions. Some companies, especially direct writers, have been able to reduce premium costs by reducing or eliminating agents' commissions. Even in life insurance, where the agent's commission is usually a significant cost only in the first years, lower commissions permit lower premiums.

Administrative expense includes those expenses other than loss costs and acquisition expense that the insurer incurs in providing its product. Administrative expenses tend to be relatively fixed, and their influence on the final premium varies with the insurer's efficiency. This efficiency depends on the absolute level of overhead, the quality of the insurer's workforce, and the premium volume over which fixed costs are spread.

Although taxes represent only a small percentage of the total premium, some differences in cost are traceable to the tax element. Since the state premium tax is levied as a percentage of the total premiums written by an insurer and is added to the individual premiums, it tends to magnify the difference among companies in the other costs.

The final element, the allowance for profit and contingencies is a residual. In the rate-setting process, it is a hoped-for return on capital. In actual practice, it is a residual that exists only to the extent that projected premiums exceed the aggregate of the projected other expenses.

The differences that can exist in the common costs of insurers help to explain both the differences and the similarities in the premiums charged by insurers. If a company is successful in reducing any of its costs below those of its competitors, it is able to offer coverage at a lower price or derive a higher

[39] The unique nature of the insurance product, in which the individual insured is, in a sense, the product sold, serves as the foundation for a distinctive form of price competition in insurance markets. The existence of cooperative ratemaking, in which competitors charge the same price, is not inconsistent with a competitive market in which insurer's costs differ. In the traditional model of competition suggested by economists, market interaction forces prices downward to the level of costs. In the field of insurance, price competition can also occur in a second way. When prices are fixed and the insurer's costs differ from those on which the bureau rate is predicated, insurers adjust their costs to the market price by altering their underwriting standards.

profit on its operations. Insurers whose costs are excessive find it difficult to maintain an adequate market share.

Quality Competition

Quality competition takes place at two levels. Insurance companies compete by offering broader forms of coverage and prompt claim service. In some lines of insurance, service components of the insurance product include inspection and loss-prevention services offered by insurers. In general, however, quality competition occurs primarily at the agency or brokerage level where the service component can differ significantly.

It is possible to purchase insurance with or without the services of an agent or broker. If the consumer elects to purchase insurance from an agent rather than directly from a company, the cost may be somewhat higher, and the incremental cost that the consumer pays is compensation to the agent for the function he or she performs. Although the agent receives this payment from the insured in the form of a commission, the commission is available because consumers tacitly agree to pay the higher premium that the commission requires. When a consumer chooses to purchase insurance from an agent or broker at a higher cost than would be incurred in a purchase through the mail or directly from a company, he or she tacitly agrees to pay the higher premium because the benefits are equal to or greater than the cost. The benefits for which the consumer pays the higher premium consist, in the main, of the advice provided by the agent. This advice consists of an analysis of the client's insurance needs, recommendation of coverages, selection of an insurer, and assistance in processing claims at the time of a loss.

The insurance marketplace is characterized by numerous competitors offering products with different levels of cost and prices to consumers. Insurers have different levels of selectivity and, consequently, different levels of cost. They also have elected different distribution systems. The differing levels of selectivity in underwriting and the different distribution systems are reflected in the different prices at which insurers offer their products.

Is the Insurance Industry Really Competitive?

The decade of the 1980s witnessed a fierce debate over the question of whether or not the insurance industry is competitive. The protagonists in the debate are the insurance industry and a group of informed economists on the one hand and industry critics on the other. The real question in the debate is how insurance should be regulated, and the attack by many industry critics is aimed at creating a federal insurance regulatory system.

Industry critics base their attack that the industry is not competitive on the industry's partial exemption from the federal antitrust laws, which was enacted by Congress in 1945. But this criticism ignores the fact that the industry is regulated by the states. We will defer our discussion of the regulation of insurance until Chapter 6. For the present, let us consider the debate by examining whether or not the industry exhibits the characteristics of a competitive industry.

Hallmarks of a Competitive Industry Economists traditionally focus on market structure and market conduct as measures of competition within an industry. Important factors in the market structure include the number of competitors and the percentage of the market controlled by the largest firms. Market conduct is reflected by the ease of entry into the market and by changes in market share over time. To examine whether these conditions apply in the insurance field, let us briefly examine the structure of the industry.

Insurance Industry Market Structure Based on the number of competitors, freedom of entry into the market, and changes in market share over time, one would conclude that the industry exhibits the characteristics of a highly competitive industry.

- There are numerous competitors in each of the three major sectors in the insurance industry. Each field is highly decentralized, with no firm controlling as much as 10 percent of the market nationally. Consumers have a wide range of sellers from which to choose, offering differentiated products at different prices.

- Not only is the number of insurers operating in each field of insurance large, the number has grown over time, indicating freedom of entry into and exit from the market. There are few barriers to entry by new competitors—not only is it easy to form a new company or expand an existing one, but insurers face competition from alternatives to the traditional insurance market (e.g., risk-retention groups).

• Concurrent with the growth in the number of insurers, major shifts in market segments have occurred. In the property and liability field, the direct-writing companies, which controlled only about 8 percent of the total property and liability premiums in 1945, had boosted their share of the market to about 46 percent by the end of 1997. In the life insurance field, mutual insurers controlled 70 percent of the market in 1970, while capital stock companies wrote 30 percent of the business. By 1997, capital stock companies had captured 64 percent of the market, and the mutual insurers' share had declined to 36 percent. The shift in market share in health insurance has been from traditional health insurers to the 700-plus HMOs that have entered the market since 1970.

Based on structure and market conduct, all three segments of the insurance industry exhibit the characteristics of competitive markets.

Evidence of Intensity of the Competition In addition to features of the market structure, three additional factors indicate a highly competitive market and attest to the intensity of the competition in the property and liability field and, to a lesser extent, in the life and health insurance fields:

1. The industry is highly cyclical, a hallmark of a competitive industry, evidencing the inability of insurers to control output, prices, or profits.

2. Profits in recent years have consistently been below those for most other industries.

3. A number of insurer insolvencies attest to the intensity of the price competition in insurance.

To complete our discussion of competition in the insurance industry, we should briefly note three of these manifestations of industry competition: the insurance cycle, industry profitability, and the increasing number of insurer insolvencies during the 1980s. These effects of competition provide abundant and convincing evidence of the intensity of competition to all but the most obstinate critics.

The Insurance Cycle The property and liability industry is highly cyclical, and goes through periods of underwriting profit, followed by periods of losses: the insurance market is characterized as *hard* or *soft,* depending on the phase of the cycle. During periods when insurers are earning underwriting profits, the market is said to be *soft,* as insurers engage in price

cutting to increase their market share. The price cutting includes not only reduction in the absolute level of rates, but the loosening of underwriting standards. This has the natural result of generating losses, resulting in a "hard" market, during which insurers increase prices and tighten underwriting standards.

Although it is sometimes suggested that the underwriting cycle results from mismanagement within the insurance industry, this criticism ignores the fact that in a competitive market, competitors do not set the market price. Competitors accept the price that is set by the interaction of market forces. The pricing decisions of insurance companies are a response to the cycle, not a cause. Insurers cut prices not because they want to, but because they are required to by the pressure of market forces. Often, these pressures stem from forces outside the industry itself.

Cash-Flow Underwriting It has been said—only half in jest—that property and liability insurers are not so much insurance companies as investment companies that raise the necessary money for their investments by selling insurance. This observation was undoubtedly prompted by the size of the industry's investment portfolio and the importance of investment income in the overall operating profit of property and liability insurers. For the past three decades, property and liability insurers have about broken even or even lost money on underwriting, but investment income has provided an overall operating profit. The dependence on insurance premiums as funds for investment led to a phenomenon known as *cash-flow underwriting.* Cash-flow underwriting, as the term is generally understood, refers to the pricing practice aimed at maximizing written premium income rather than underwriting profit. In cash-flow underwriting, insurers price their products below the amount needed to cover losses and expenses to compete for premium dollars that can be invested. The rationale is that during periods of high interest rates, the investment income earned on additional premium volume will more than offset any underwriting loss that may be incurred. Insurers compete for dollars that can be invested at a higher rate than the cost of those funds. An insurer with a combined ratio of, say, 106 percent is, in effect, paying the policyholders 6 percent for the use of their money. If those funds can be invested at some rate greater than 6 percent, the leveraged investment will increase the return to stockholders. As a result, price competition in the

TABLE 5.1 **Insurer Insolvencies, 1980–2000**

Year	Life Insurer Insolvencies	Property and Liability Insolvencies
1980	9	5
1981	8	9
1982	10	8
1983	20	11
1984	11	27
1985	9	52
1986	14	32
1987	20	25
1988	19	42
1989	42	52
1990	41	43
1991	58	47
1992	32	59
1993	22	24
1994	11	22
1995	3	10
1996	6	9
1997	2	24
1998	4	7
1999	5	4
2000	8	14

Source: A. M. Best and National Association of Insurance Commissioners.

industry tends to be driven by the returns available in financial markets where insurers invest their funds.

Insurer Insolvencies Although some insolvencies are clearly a result of mismanagement, the increasing number of insurer insolvencies during the decade of the 1980s provides convincing evidence to all but the most intractable critics of the intensity of the competition in the insurance marketplace. Table 5.1 indicates the number of insurer insolvencies during the period since 1980 in both the life and health and property and liability fields.

Although the insolvency rate in the insurance field is significantly below that in the field of banking or other financial institutions, the historic number of insolvencies stands in mute testimony to the demands of a competitive marketplace. It also provides a convenient point of departure for our next chapter, which deals with the regulation of insurance.

Industry Profitability Because the property and liability insurance industry has been the most widely criticized, it has attracted the greatest interest from scholars. Numerous studies over the past two decades have examined the structure of the property and liability insurance industry. These studies were conducted by scholars from the academic world, by government commissions, by federal agencies, and by the U.S. Government Accounting Office. Using different methodology and different models, the researchers independently reached the same conclusions: (1) that the industry is competitively structured; (2) that there is no evidence of excessive profits; and (3) that the rate of return to firms in the industry is generally less than that for other industries with commensurate risk.[40]

[40] The most recent study, a 1989 Government Accounting Office study entitled *Insurance: Profitability of the Automobile Lines of the Insurance Industry,* concluded that the after-tax earnings on auto insurance over the period 1978 through 1987 produced an average 10.4 percent return on surplus. This is lower than the average rate of return on banks, utilities, and transportation for the same period.

IMPORTANT CONCEPTS TO REMEMBER

capital stock insurance company
mutual insurance company
assessment mutual
advanced premium mutual
assessible policy
fraternal insurer
reciprocals
demutualization
Lloyd's associations
insurance exchange
attorney-in-fact
excess and surplus line law
Blue Cross

Blue Shield
health expense associations
health maintenance organization
service contract
physician hospital organization
capitation
government insurer
Federal Crop Insurance Program
mortgage loan insurance
National Flood Insurance Program
Federal Crime Insurance Program
SBA Surety Bond Program
Federal Fidelity Bonding Program

Export–Import Bank
Overseas Private Investor
 Corporation
agent
broker
binding
American Agency System
direct writer
independent agent
captive agent
ownership of renewals
direct-response system
general agent

branch office system
personal-producing general agent
company groups
fleets
underwriting syndicate
factory mutuals
Industrial Risk Insurers

advisory organizations
rating bureaus
residual risk pool
assigned risk pool
Automobile Insurance Plan
FAIR Plan
beach and windstorm pool

CPCU
CLU
hard market
soft market
cash-flow underwriting

QUESTIONS FOR REVIEW

1. List the types of insurers as classified by legal form of ownership, and briefly describe the distinguishing characteristics of each type.

2. Distinguish between an insurance agent and an insurance broker. What is the significance of the distinction from the insured's viewpoint?

3. What is meant by the expression that independent agents "own their expirations"? Why is this of such great importance?

4. What are the characteristics of a health maintenance organization (HMO) that distinguish it from other types of insurers discussed in this chapter?

5. Briefly explain the sources of an insurance agent's authority. How does the authority of a life insurance agent differ from that of a property and liability insurance agent?

6. What are the general methods of operation of Lloyd's of London, and why does it receive such wide publicity?

7. Identify the various costs that are common to all insurers and explain the extent to which these costs may differ from one insurer to another.

8. How do you account for the fact that two insurers may charge significantly different premiums for identical coverage?

9. Describe the basic function of advisory organizations. In which lines of insurance are such organizations primarily found?

10. Government insurance programs may compete with those of private insurers, may involve cooperation between government and private insurers, or may be a monopoly. Give an example of a government insurance program in each of these three categories.

QUESTIONS FOR DISCUSSION

1. Adam Smith wrote, "People of the same trade seldom meet together, even for merriment and diversion, but the conversation ends in a conspiracy against the public, or in some contrivance to raise prices." To what extent do you believe that this observation holds true with respect to the various cooperative organizations in the insurance field?

2. "When an insurer is successful in its efforts to select insureds from the better than average classes, the gain in its competitive position is magnified by the impact of this success on its competitors." Explain what is meant by this statement.

3. Agents frequently emphasize "service" in their advertising. What services should a client legitimately expect from his or her insurance agent?

4. Some government insurers compete with private insurers. To what extent does a government insurer have an unfair advantage over a commercial one? How can competition of government insurers with private insurers be justified?

5. Government insurance programs frequently involve a subsidy to certain segments of society. To what extent do you feel that this is preferable to the provision of insurance on a subsidized basis through the mandatory participation pools operated by private insurers?

SUGGESTIONS FOR ADDITIONAL READING

American Council of Life Insurance. *Life Insurance Fact Book.* Washington, D.C.: American Council of Life Insurance, annual.

Adkins, Jason B. "The Policyholder Perspective on Mutual Holding Company Conversions." *Journal of Insurance Regulation,* vol. 16. no. 1 (Fall 1997), pp. 5–15.

Black, Kenneth, Jr., and Harold D. Skipper, Jr. *Life Insurance,* 12th ed. Englewood Cliffs, N.J.: Prentice-Hall, 1994. Chapters 29, 30.

Butler, Richard J., Yijing Cui, and Andrew Whitman, "Insurers' Demutualization Decisions," *Risk Management & Insurance Review,* vol. 3, no. 2 (Fall 2000), pp. 135–154.

Gibbs, D. E. W. *Lloyd's of London: A Study of Individualism.* New York: St. Martin's Press, 1975.

Greene, Mark R. "The Government As an Insurer." *Journal of Risk and Insurance,* vol. 43, no. 3 (Sept. 1976).

Health Insurance Institute. *Source Book of Health Insurance Data.* New York: Health Insurance Institute, annual.

Insurance Information Institute. *Insurance Facts, Property-Liability-Inland Marine-Surety.* New York: Insurance Information Institute, annual.

Nelli, H. O., and R. A. Marshall. *The Private Insurance Business in the United States,* Research Paper 48. Atlanta, Ga.: Bureau of Business and Economic Research, Georgia State College, June 1969.

Reinmuth, D. *The Regulation of Reciprocal Insurance Exchanges.* Homewood, Ill.: Richard D. Irwin, 1967.

Smallenberger, James A. "A Reply to Critics of Mutual Holding Companies." *Journal of Insurance Regulation,* vol. 16. no. 1 (Fall 1997), pp. 15–27.

WEB SITES TO EXPLORE

Alliance of American Insurers	http://www.allianceai.org
American Association of Insurance Services	http://www.aaais.org
American Association of Managing General Agents	http://www.aamga.org
American Institute for CPCU	http://www.aicpcu.org/
American Institute of Marine Underwriters	http://www.aimu.org/
American Insurance Association	http://www.aiadc.com
American Insurance Services Group	http://www.aisg.org/
Best's Review	http://www.ambest.com/review/
Factory Mutual System	http://www.factorymutual.com/
Federal Emergency Management Agency (FEMA)	http://www.fema.gov/
Independent Insurance Agents of America, Inc.	http://www.iiaa.org
Industrial Risk Insurers	http://www.industrialrisk.com/
Inland Marine Underwriters Association	http://www.imua.org/
Insurance Information Institute	http://www.iii.org
Insurance Institute of America, Inc.	http://www.aicpcu.org
Lloyd's of London	http://www.lloydsoflondon.co.uk/
National Association of Independent Insurers	http://www.naii.org
National Association of Insurance Brokers, Inc.	http://www.naib.org
National Association of Insurance Commissioners	http://www.naic.org
National Association of Insurance Women	http://www.naiw.org
National Association of Life Underwriters	http://www.agents-online.com/NALU/
National Association of Mutual Insurance Companies	http://www.namic.org
National Association of Professional Insurance Agents	http://www.pianet.com/
National Underwriter Company	http://www.nuco.com/
U.S. Small Business Administration	http://www.sba.gov/
Underwriters Laboratory	http://www.ul.com/

REGULATION OF THE INSURANCE INDUSTRY

The safety of the people shall be the highest law.

— CICERO

CHAPTER OBJECTIVES

When you have finished this chapter, you should be able to

- Identify and explain the reasons why insurance is subject to regulation
- Identify the major areas of insurer operations that are regulated
- Trace the history of insurance regulation and identify the landmark cases and laws that led to the current regulatory environment
- Identify the major aspects of insurance company operations that are subject to regulation
- Identify and explain the statutory requirements that exist with respect to insurance rates
- Describe the different approaches the states have taken toward the regulation of insurance rates
- Identify the arguments favoring state or federal regulation of insurance

THE WHY OF GOVERNMENT REGULATION OF INSURANCE

Before turning to the manner in which the insurance industry is regulated, it is appropriate that we examine the rationale for that regulation. Many of the original reasons for the regulation of the insurance industry are now being challenged, and new regulatory goals are being proposed. In analyzing the issues discussed in this chapter, it will be helpful if the reader is familiar with the general theory of regula-

tion that serves as the foundation for the theory of insurance regulation.

The Why of Regulation Generally

There are important differences of opinion among economists on the subject of government regulation, and much of the controversy concerning insurance regulation stems from these differences. Although there is little disagreement in principle on the need for some form of government control of business,

there is serious disagreement on the form that this control should take.

Some economists believe in the concept of an efficient market and maintain that competition will generally produce the greatest benefits to society. These economists agree that some form of government control is necessary, yet they would like the principal role of government to be maintaining competition. Other economists distrust the market, or at least have less confidence in its operation. They believe the lesson of history is that regulation is often needed to prevent abuse of consumers and should be imposed wherever there is a likelihood of market failure.

Approaches to Government Control of Business

Broadly speaking, government control of business takes one of two forms, paralleling the two economic philosophies just noted: antitrust and regulation. *Antitrust* concentrates on maintaining competition, whereas *regulation* involves the application of specific performance standards to the firms in an industry. The principal thrust of antitrust is to curtail monopoly power. It focuses on preventing collusion, opposing mergers that lead to excessive concentration, and abating market power. The theory of antitrust is that if the government prevents monopoly and unfair competition, competition will result in the public welfare.

Regulation represents a more direct involvement of government in the affairs of business. It usually consists of two types of actions by government: restricting entry into the market (usually because competition is thought to be infeasible, but sometimes on other grounds) and controlling prices so that the firms in an industry do not obtain excessive profits. In a sense, regulation replaces competition in industries that are natural monopolies or are considered to have special importance in size or influence.

Economic Theories of Regulation Having noted the attitudes of economists toward government control and the different forms that control may take, we will now examine three theories of regulation that will help in our interpretation of the current issues concerning insurance regulation. One theory provides an economic rationale for what regulation is intended to do; the other two theories attempt to explain why regulation does not always work as it is intended and why regulation sometimes fails to deal with the economic problems it is meant to solve.

The Market Failure Theory of Regulation The predominant theory of regulation is the *market failure theory,* which is based on the view that the purpose of regulation is to correct market failures.[1] A *market failure* occurs when the free market produces too much or too little of a product or a service at a price that is too high or too low. The classic example of a market failure occurs in the case of a monopoly with the incentive and the ability to produce too little and charge too much for a product. Another market failure is an unstable competitive process that leads to destructive competition. Still another is a lack of safety or security for consumers in financial markets or industries of a fiduciary nature. The role of regulation under the market failure theory is to restrict the actions of firms in an industry, forcing them to behave in a way that will produce results as near as possible to those that would occur in a competitive market.

Although the market failure theory provides an explanation of how regulation should work, casual observation shows that it does not always function the way the theory suggests. Regulatory systems are complicated, cumbersome, and costly, and there is a serious question whether they achieve their intended purpose. Indeed, it is clear that they sometimes produce objectionable results. Although proponents of regulation argue that the defects of regulation are due to legal and procedural problems that can be corrected by reform of the regulatory system, another view is that the market failure theory simply does not explain the way regulation works in the real world. This second view abandons the notion that correcting market failures is a serious goal of regulatory agencies and suggests that regulators operate under an entirely different set of incentives. Two views on the motivation of regulators have emerged: the capture theory of regulation and the public choice theory.[2]

[1] For a more complete discussion of the market failure view of regulation see C. F. Phillips, *The Economics of Regulation* (Homewood, Ill.: Richard D. Irwin, 1969). This draws heavily on the early work of A. C. Pigou, *The Economics of Welfare,* 4th ed. (London: Macmillan, 1932).

[2] The evolution of the capture theory and the public choice theory of regulation is revealed in George Stigler, "The Theory of Economic Regulation," *Bell Journal of Economics and Management Science,* vol. 2, no. 1 (Spring 1971), and Sam Peltzman, "Toward a More General Theory of Regulation," *Journal of Law and Economics,* vol. 19 (August 1976).

The Capture Theory of Regulation According to the *capture theory* of regulation, regulators often become "captured" by the industry they are responsible for regulating. They lose focus, and become more concerned about the success of the regulated industry than about consumers. Proponents of this theory observe that regulators often come from the industry to be regulated. In those cases in which the regulator does not come from the regulated industry, he or she is likely to accept a job with a regulated firm at the end of the regulatory appointment. The result, according to critics, is that regulatory agencies are characterized by revolving doors, in which regulators come from and return to the industry. Quite simply, the critics argue, these regulators place the interest of the industry they are supposed to regulate above the interest of consumers.

Although the capture theory of regulation has found many adherents, it does not seem to adequately explain regulation in the insurance field. If this theory actually prevailed, one would expect far different results in insurance regulation from those that exist. Further, the insurance industry, like most regulated industries, is not controlled by a regulatory agency alone. It is also regulated by the legislatures and by the courts. The theory does not explain how the industry succeeds in capturing the legislatures and the courts.

The Public Choice Theory of Regulation The public choice theory of regulation, like the capture theory, attempts to explain why regulation sometimes produces results other than those suggested by the market failure theory. The *public choice theory* views regulation as a part of a political-economic system that serves to reallocate wealth among competing groups based on preferences expressed in a political-economic marketplace. It is based on the fact that every regulation reallocates resources and in the process makes some individuals or groups richer and others poorer. Regulators perform the same functions as legislators in imposing *taxes* on some groups (the regulatory *taxpayers*) and dispensing *benefits* to others (the regulatory recipients). Any proposed regulation will attract the attention of both payers and beneficiaries, who will express their opposition or support through political and economic channels. The major goal of regulation is to transfer resources to groups that generate the most support for the program in a way that minimizes opposition to the regulatory tax.

The most important implication of the public choice theory is the conclusion that regulation will tend to favor (subsidize) relatively small and well-organized groups that have a high per capita stake in the regulation, at the expense of large, poorly organized groups with a lower per capita stake. Members of groups with a stake in proposed regulation must organize themselves to support or oppose the regulation. If the regulation involves a large tax or a large subsidy, there will be a strong incentive for the group to organize and oppose or support the regulation. When the tax or subsidy is small, there is less incentive. At the same time, the larger the group, the greater the cost of organizing and, therefore, the less likely is the group to be effectively organized.[3]

Importance of the Three Theories Both the market failure theory and the public choice theory of regulation are important in understanding the regulation of insurance. Although the market failure theory remains the standard against which regulatory programs should be measured, the public choice theory helps to explain why regulation in some areas departs from this standard.

Rationale for Regulation of the Insurance Industry

As noted, regulation is adopted as an alternative to antitrust in those instances in which competition is considered infeasible or in the case of industries that, because of monopolistic tendencies, must be subject to control. Natural monopolies, for example, are licensed and their pricing decisions controlled to protect the consumer from exploitation.

[3] Kenneth J. Meier offers still another view: that regulatory policies result from the interaction of four political institutions within an environment that influences their abilities to use their political resources effectively. The four players in the political process are regulators, consumers, the industry, and *political elites* (legislators, governors, federal officials, etc.). The major influence on the effectiveness of these parties in the politics of regulation is the nature of the regulatory issue. Meier suggests that regulatory issues can be characterized according to their *salience* and *complexity*. A *salient issue* is one in which large numbers of people feel that the issue affects them and that the political system is the way to address the issue. A complex issue is one in which specialized knowledge is required to understand the policy question. Where an issue is highly salient, consumers and political elites are more likely to become involved. Where an issue is highly complex, it is costly for them to be involved and regulators and the industry have a relative advantage. See Kenneth J. Meier, "The Politics of Insurance Regulation," *Journal of Risk and Insurance,* vol. 58, no. 4 (December 1991).

Cartelized industries are regulated for the same reasons. Here regulation is required because of a lack of competition; it seeks to generate results similar to those that would exist in a competitive industry. In insurance, the problem of monopoly is not significant, but there are still reasons for government restraint.

The rationale for regulation of insurance differs from that of monopolized or cartelized industries because the potential *market failures* are also different. The first of the potential market failures in insurance stems from the fiduciary nature of insurer operations; the second arises from the uncertainties inherent in the insurance pricing process.

Vested-in-the-Public-Interest Rationale The first rationale for the regulation of insurance is that it is an industry vested in the public interest. The courts have long held that insurance, like banking, is pervasive in its influence, and that failures in this field can affect persons other than those directly involved in the transaction.[4] Individuals purchase insurance to protect against financial loss at a later time, and it is important to the public welfare that the insurer promising to indemnify insureds for future losses fulfills its promises.

Classical economists held that competition serves the consumer by forcing inefficient firms out of the market. Contrary to this classical model, which held that the failure of some firms from time to time was a wholesome phenomenon, the public interest is not served by the failure of insurers, because of the resulting losses to policyholders and claimants. The *vested-in-the-public-interest* rationale for regulation of the insurance industry holds that the insurance industry, like any other business holding vast sums of money in trust for the public, should be subject to government regulation because of its fiduciary nature.

Besides the solvency issue, there are certain other *public interest* reasons that legislators have felt require regulation of the industry. The complex nature of insurance contracts makes them difficult for a consumer to understand. Regulation is therefore deemed necessary to ensure that the contracts offered by insurance companies are fair and that they are fairly priced.

Although the public interest rationale has a relationship to the area of pricing and competition, its implications are much broader. It implies a need for regulation of insurance in many areas, of which pricing is only one. The fiduciary nature of insurer operations and the extensive influence of insurance on members of society require regulation of entry into the market (i.e., the licensing of companies), the investment practices of insurers, and similar areas related to insurer solvency. In addition, the complexity of the insurance product requires regulatory scrutiny of contracts and the licensing of practitioners to ensure their competence. All of this means that because insurance is *vested in the public interest,* the industry would require regulation even if it were not for the second rationale for regulation discussed next.

Destructive-Competition Rationale The second rationale for the regulation of insurance—currently being challenged by some parties—is that competition in some fields of insurance, if left unregulated, would become excessive. Although regulation in many other industries aims at enforcing competition and preventing artificially high prices, insurance regulation was designed—at least initially—in the opposite direction: preventing excessive competition. It has long been argued that in the absence of regulation the natural tendency in the insurance industry would be toward the keenest sort of cutthroat competition. The assumption that the natural tendency in insurance pricing is toward destructive competition rests on two premises:

1. The cost of production is not known until the contract of insurance has run its full term.

2. Classes of desirable and undesirable insured exist. There is a danger that in attempting to compete, insurance companies might assume that their insureds are from the more desirable class and make unwarranted assumptions about their future costs.

As we will see later, there is considerable disagreement about these premises, and many are now questioning the validity of the argument. Nevertheless, those who argue that insurance regulation must be aimed at preventing too much competition maintain that the basic danger in the insurance industry is the possibility that, in vying for business, companies may underestimate future losses and as a result fail.

[4] The U.S. Supreme Court ruled that insurance is a business "affected with the public interest" in 1914. See *German Alliance Insurance Company v Lewis,* 233 U.S. 380 (1914).

Goals of Insurance Regulation

Originally, the goals of insurance regulation were clearly understood and generally agreed on by all concerned. The function of insurance regulation was to promote the welfare of the public by ensuring fair contracts at fair prices from financially strong companies. The *market failures* that insurance regulation was intended to correct were insolvencies (no matter what their source) and unfair treatment of insureds by insurers. In short, the dual goals of regulation were solvency and equity.[5]

Although the original goals still dominate the regulatory philosophy, new goals—still emerging—focus on the availability and affordability of insurance. Public dissatisfaction with the increasing cost of insurance, the inability of some consumers to obtain insurance at a price they are willing and able to pay, and a growing philosophy of entitlement have created pressure from some quarters for regulatory programs designed to guarantee the availability of insurance to all who desire it at affordable rates. Increasingly, those who cannot obtain insurance at a price they feel they can afford are demanding a subsidy from the rest of society. The traditional approach to this subsidy has been a residual-risk pool, such as the Automobile Insurance Plans, the FAIR plans, and the medical malpractice insurance pools. Here, insurers are compelled to write coverages at rates below those that would be required to cover losses and expenses. The losses sustained are passed on to other insureds as higher premiums. More recently, the availability/affordability demands have focused on a new issue: the manner in which insurance rates should be determined and the extent to which each insured's costs should reflect the hazards he or she brings to the pool of insured persons.[6]

A Brief History of Insurance Regulation

The earliest forms of insurance regulation were related to the premium taxes imposed by the states on out-of-state insurers and grew out of the registration and reporting requirements imposed for the purpose of determining insurers' tax liabilities. Although statutes dealing with insurance had been enacted by the states as early as the beginning of the nineteenth century, the history of modern insurance regulation begins shortly before the Civil War, when several states established bodies to supervise insurance operations within their borders. The New Hampshire Board of Insurance Commissioners, established in 1851, was the first of these bodies. Massachusetts followed shortly thereafter,[7] and New York instituted its board in 1859. The panic of 1857, which had been precipitated by the failure of a New York branch of the Ohio Life Insurance and Trust Company of Cincinnati, was probably the leading factor in the creation of the New York Commission as well as those of other states that followed.

Paul v. Virginia The case of *Paul v. Virginia* focused on the preeminence of the right of the states or federal government to regulate insurance. The U.S. Constitution gives the federal government the right to regulate interstate commerce, and the issue in *Paul v. Virginia* was whether insurance is interstate commerce. Samuel Paul was a native of Virginia who represented New York insurance companies in his home state. Paul challenged the right of the state to regulate insurance by selling policies without obtaining a state license. The state denied Paul a license, because his insurer would not comply with the demand of the state of Virginia for a security deposit. Likewise, a license for the insurer was denied on the same grounds. When Paul continued to sell insurance without a license, he was arrested and fined $50. The case was carried to the U.S. Supreme Court, where it was finally decided in 1869. In rendering its decision, the Supreme Court ruled that insurance was not interstate commerce:

> Issuing a policy of insurance is not a transaction of commerce. The policies are simply contracts of indemnity against loss by fire entered into between the corporations and the insured for a consideration paid by the latter. These contracts are not articles of commerce in any proper meaning of the

[5] These goals were articulated by Professor Spencer L. Kimball, who referred to them as the principles of *solidity* and *aequum et bonum*. See Spencer L. Kimball, *Essays in Insurance Regulation* (Ann Arbor, Mich.: Spencer Kimball, 1966), pp. 3–10.

[6] The availability/affordability debate is discussed in the chapter appendix.

[7] One member of the Massachusetts board was Elizur Wright, who is often called the father of insurance regulation. Wright was an abolitionist who turned his energies toward the elimination of unsavory practices in the insurance industry. He was an ardent proponent of federal regulation of insurance and viewed the state insurance department as a step toward a national insurance bureau.

word. They are not subjects of trade and barter, offered in the market as something having an existence and value independently of the parties to them. They are not commodities to be shipped or forwarded from one state to another and then put up for sale. They are like other personal contracts between parties which are completed by their signature and the transfer of considerations. Such contracts are not interstate transactions, though the parties may be domiciled in different states. The policies do not take effect—are not executed contracts—until delivered by the agent in Virginia. They are then local transactions, and are governed by the local law. They do not constitute a part of the commerce between the states any more than a contract for the purchase and sale of goods in Virginia by a citizen of New York, whilst in Virginia, would constitute a portion of such commerce.[8]

The decision of the U.S. Supreme Court that insurance was not interstate commerce and therefore was not subject to regulation by the federal government stood for 75 years.

Regulation from 1869 to 1944 During the years following the *Paul v. Virginia* decision, the insurance industry was regulated by the individual states. This was a period of rapid development and expansion for the entire economy, and the insurance industry was no exception. The quality of regulation varied from state to state, and it was inevitable that abuses would creep into the operation of the insurance business.

In the period after the Civil War, many life insurance companies were operated in a precarious manner. Unsound business practices were common, and advertising claims were greatly inflated. During the depression era of the 1870s, many of these poorly managed firms failed. In addition, many innovations were developed in the field of life insurance, some of which were detrimental to the insurance-buying public. One such innovation was the *tontine policy,* a life insurance contract with a higher than necessary premium that provided for the payment of dividends at some future time. Dividends on these policies were paid at the end of the tontine period (which was usually 10, 15, or 20 years). The dividends were paid only to those policyholders who survived to the end of the period, at the expense of those who had died or permitted their policies to lapse.

The Armstrong Committee Investigation Shortly after the turn of the century, big business was being condemned and investigated, and the rapid growth of the life insurance industry, including the previously mentioned abuses, attracted attention. In 1905, the New York State legislature appointed a committee to investigate the abuses in the life insurance industry. The committee was named after its chairman, Senator William W. Armstrong. The *Armstrong Investigation* turned out to be a sober, responsible examination of the life insurance industry. Many abuses were identified, and although the investigation caused a temporary loss of confidence among the insurance-buying public, legislation was enacted in New York following the investigation correcting these abuses, a result that proved to be a benefit to both the public and the life insurance industry.

The Merritt Committee Investigation In 1910, a second committee was appointed in New York, this time to investigate the property insurance industry. Edwin A. Merritt, Jr., was chairman of this committee, which became known as the *Merritt Committee.* The principal concern of the Merritt Committee was with the methods used by property insurers in making rates.

As we saw in Chapter 3, the accuracy of an insurer's predictions increases with the number of exposures on which the predictions are based. This principle led insurers to the practice of cooperative ratemaking, in which the experience of many insurers is pooled to increase the accuracy of insurers' predictions. The organizations that collect loss data and perform the actuarial calculations required to generate rates were called *rating bureaus.* From 1885 to 1910, over half of the states passed laws prohibiting cooperative ratemaking and outlawing rating bureaus. These *anticompact laws,* as they were called, prohibited insurance companies from joining together to make rates, a practice that the companies argued was necessary to achieve the accuracy inherent in the operation of the law of large numbers. Following the San Francisco fire of 1906, many fire insurance companies went bankrupt, in part because they had charged inadequate rates. Fire insurance rates then increased throughout the country in what appeared to be a concerted action. After an extensive study, the Merritt Committee made its recommendations, which became the basis for New York legislation. The committee opposed the anticompact laws and urged that rating bureaus

[8] *Paul v. Virginia,* 231 U.S. 495 (1869).

be recognized and, further, that a company be permitted to belong to a rating bureau, or to file its rates independently if it chose.

The Armstrong Committee and the Merritt Committee investigations were significant events in the development of the industry. Although they were state inquiries, the fact that many states patterned their laws after those of New York (plus the impact of the Appleton rule discussed in Chapter 5) made their effect pervasive.

South-Eastern Underwriters Association Case After a period of 75 years, another test of the authority of the federal government to regulate insurance was made. In 1942, the U.S. attorney general filed a brief under the Sherman Act against the South-Eastern Underwriters Association (SEUA), a cooperative rating bureau, alleging that the bureau constituted a combination in restraint of trade. In its decision of the SEUA case in 1944, the Supreme Court reversed its decision of *Paul v. Virginia,* stating that insurance is interstate commerce and as such is subject to regulation by the federal government.[9] This decision stands today.

Public Law 15 While the SEUA case was being decided and appealed, the insurance industry viewed with considerable alarm the prospect that the court might overturn *Paul v. Virginia.* This would have especially affected the property and casualty field, where concerted ratemaking through bureaus was the rule rather than the exception. Since it was clear that pooling loss information to generate standard industry rates constituted a form of price-fixing that would be illegal per se under the Sherman Act, the industry moved to obtain an exemption from the Sherman Act and other federal antitrust laws.

The insurance industry arranged to have bills introduced into Congress that would have exempted it from the federal antitrust laws, but these bills were all defeated. Finally, a law was drafted by the National Association of Insurance Commissioners that could be passed. This was *Public Law 15,* or the *McCarran-Ferguson Act,* which became law on March 9, 1945.

In the McCarran–Ferguson Act, Congress reaffirmed the right of the federal government to regulate insurance, but agreed that it would not exercise this right as long as the industry was adequately regulated by the states. The law declared a two-year moratorium on the regulation of insurance by the federal government, stating that the federal government would not regulate the industry until January 1, 1948, when the federal antitrust laws would be "applicable to the business of insurance to the extent that such business is not regulated by the states." In effect, the law explicitly grants to the states the power to regulate the insurance business—a power that the Supreme Court in the SEUA case had concluded was vested in Congress under the Commerce Clause of the Constitution. The exemption from federal law was not complete, however. The act provided that the Sherman Act would continue to apply to boycott, coercion, or intimidation.

REGULATION TODAY

Following enactment of Public Law 15, the states attempted to put their houses in order, passing rating laws, defining fair trade practices, and extending licensing and solvency requirements.

The Current Regulatory Structure

Insurance is presently regulated by the states through the three basic branches of our state governments: legislative, judicial, and executive.

Regulation by the Legislative Branch Each state enacts laws that govern the conduct of the insurance industry within its boundaries. These laws spell out the requirements that must be met by persons wishing to organize an insurance company in the state. As noted in the previous chapter, a company domiciled within the state (i.e., which has its home office in the state) is called a *domestic insurer.* The laws also specify certain requirements that a company domiciled in another state (called a *foreign insurer*) must meet to obtain a license to do business in the state.[10] In addition, the insurance code sets forth the standards of solvency that are to be enforced and provides for the regulation of rates and investments. It also regulates the licensing of agents.

[9] *United States v. South-Eastern Underwriters Association,* 322 U.S. 533 (1944).

[10] A company domiciled in a foreign country is called an *alien insurer.*

Regulation by the Judicial Branch The judicial branch exercises control over the insurance industry through the courts by rendering decisions on the meaning of policy terms and ruling on the constitutionality of the state insurance laws and the actions of those administering the law.

Regulation by the Executive Branch: The Commissioner of Insurance The central figure in the regulation of the insurance industry in each state is the commissioner of insurance.[11] In most states this official is appointed by the governor of the state and is charged with the administration of the insurance laws and the general supervision of the business. Although a part of the executive branch of the state government, the commissioner frequently makes rulings that have the binding force of law and exercises judicial power in interpreting and enforcing the insurance code.

National Association of Insurance Commissioners

The *National Association of Insurance Commissioners* (NAIC) has been an active force in the regulation of insurance since it was founded in 1871. Although it has no legal power over insurance regulation, it is an important influence. Through it, the nation's 55 insurance commissioners exchange information and ideas and coordinate regulatory activities.[12] Based on the information exchanged at its four annual meetings, the NAIC makes recommendations for legislation and policy. The individual commissioners are free to accept or reject these recommendations, but in the past most commissioners have seen fit to accept the recommendations appropriate for their particular states.

AREAS REGULATED

It is common to distinguish between two broad, but interrelated, areas of insurance regulation: solvency regulation and market regulation.

Solvency Regulation

Clearly, a primary focus on insurance regulation is on insurer solvency. Indeed, it has been argued that this should be the primary function of regulation. Regulatory interest in insurer solvency is concerned with the early detection of potential insolvencies and the prevention of consumer suffering when insolvencies occur.

Licensing of Companies In effect, when a company is licensed, the commissioner certifies the company with regard to its financial stability and soundness of methods of operation. Before licensing a firm to conduct business in the state, the commissioner must be satisfied that the company to be licensed meets the financial requirements specified in the insurance code of the state. To qualify for a license, the insurance company making application must have a certain amount of capital or surplus. The exact amount of capital and surplus required varies from state to state, being relatively small in some states and substantial in others. The amount of capital or surplus required also depends on the type of business the firm will conduct and whether the company is a stock or mutual carrier. These capital and surplus requirements usually apply to both individuals who wish to form an insurer in the state and to foreign companies that request a license to do business in the state.

Besides the capital and surplus requirement, the commissioner also reviews the personal characteristics of the organizers, promoters, and incorporators of the company to determine their competence and experience. The commissioner may deny the application for a license if the company's founders seem unworthy of public trust.

Reporting and Financial Analysis It has long been recognized that the key to protecting policyholders from insurer insolvencies lies in detecting potential failures before they occur. Insurance regulators rely on analysis of various insurer reports and financial examinations to detect potentially troubled companies.

Insurers are subject to significant regulatory reporting requirements. State insurance codes require every licensed insurer to submit annual and quarterly reports to the commissioner of insurance. These reports include information on the assets and liabilities of the company, its investments, its income, loss payments, expenses, and any other information

[11] Although the title *commissioner of insurance* is the most common, in some states the chief insurance regulator is referred to as the *director of insurance* or the *superintendent of insurance.*

[12] The 55 members of the NAIC include the 50 states plus the District of Columbia, American Samoa, Guam, Puerto Rico, and the U.S. Virgin Islands.

required by the commissioner. Actuaries must sign opinions attesting to the adequacy of reserves. Insurers must calculate and report their risk-based capital requirements annually. All of this information, along with other publicly available information about the company, is analyzed by state insurance departments on an ongoing basis.

The NAIC serves an important role in the financial analysis process. It maintains a database of financial information filed by insurers and automated tools to assist with financial analysis. In 1974, the NAIC adopted the Insurance Regulatory Information System (IRIS) to assist regulators in identifying potentially troubled insurers. Under IRIS, an insurer's performance on a series of financial tests is examined. Deviations from expected norms are taken as an indication that closer scrutiny of the insurer is needed. Currently, IRIS consists of 11 tests for property-liability insurers and 12 tests for life and health insurers. In the early 1990s, IRIS was expanded and enhanced to create the Financial Analysis Solvency Tracking System (FAST). Under FAST, a score is assigned to each company, based on its performance on a series of ratios and other financial indicators. The specific financial tests used and the company scores are kept confidential by the NAIC. Today, FAST is widely used by state regulators when prioritizing companies for further review. In addition to the many tools made available to the states, the NAIC has created the Financial Analysis Division (FAD) to monitor the financial performance of "nationally significant companies." This Division reports potential problems to the Financial Analysis Working Group of the NAIC, which coordinates with the commissioners in the company's state of domicile to resolve concerns.

Risk-Based Capital Risk-based capital (RBC) requirements are another tool used to detect companies that are potentially troubled. With RBC requirements, the amount of capital required for an insurer will vary, based on the specific risks facing the insurer, including risks associated with underwriting, the insurer's investment portfolio, and other risks not reflected by these factors. RBC standards enable regulators to more easily identify an insurer whose capital is inadequate to support the risks it has assumed.

In the 1990s, the NAIC developed risk-based capital (RBC) standards for life insurers (1992), property-liability insurers (1993), and health insurers (1997), and these models have been adopted widely across the country. Risk-based capital standards do not replace statutory capital and surplus requirements. Rather, the purpose of the RBC standards is to alert regulators to the need for closer scrutiny of insurers, based on an analysis of the insurer's capital and surplus, relative to the specific risks in its portfolio.

The RBC models require comparison between the insurer's total adjusted capital and the amount of capital required under risk-based capital. For a property and liability insurer, risk-based capital requirements recognize asset risk, underwriting risk, and off-balance sheet risks. Risks that the capital and surplus of a life insurer must protect and absorb are (1) risk of loss due to defaults in assets and variations in the market value of common stock; (2) risk of claims, expenses, and catastrophes; (3) risk of loss due to changes in interest rates; and (4) risks not otherwise reflected.

A deficiency in risk-based capital is indicated by the ratio of the company's actual capital and surplus and the required risk-based capital. Depending on the magnitude of the deficiency, the risk-based capital regulations will require specific action, ranging from corrective action by the insurer under a plan approved by the commissioner, to seizure of the company by the state insurance department.

Examination of Companies In addition to the annual report, insurance departments conduct periodic on-site examinations of each company conducting business in the state. The insurance commissioner may examine or inquire into the affairs of any company transacting business in the state at any time, but the insurance code normally requires examining of domestic companies at least once every five years. It is a detailed procedure, often lasting an extended period, during which the examiners scrutinize every aspect of the firm's operation. Targeted exams may be done more frequently and focus on a particular area of concern.

To eliminate duplication of effort, it has become the practice for each state insurance department to examine only those companies that are domiciled in the state. The state calling the exam invites participation from the other zones in which the company does business. (The NAIC is divided into four zones.) Other states in which the insurer does business typically accept the examination results, eliminating the need for separate exams of foreign insurers.

Regulation of Reserves Because insurers operate on the unusual plan of collecting in advance for a

product to be delivered at some time in the future, insurance laws require specific recognition of the insurer's fiduciary obligations. Life insurers are required to maintain *policy reserves* on outstanding policies, and to reflect these reserves as liabilities in their financial statements.[13] In the property and liability field, insurers are permitted to include premiums as income only as the premiums become earned—that is, only as the time for which protection is provided passes. In addition, the insurer is required to establish a deferred income account as a liability, called the unearned premium reserve, whose primary purpose is to place a claim against assets that will presumably be required to pay losses occurring in the future. In addition to the unearned premium reserve, property and liability insurers are required to maintain loss reserves. These include a reserve for losses reported but not yet paid and a reserve for losses that have occurred but have not yet been reported to the insurer because of a lag in claim reporting. The insurance code of most states specifies the manner in which the reserves must be computed.

The critical importance of the reserves in the financial stability and solvency of an insurer is apparent when we recognize that the reserves are true liabilities. They are an actuarial measurement of the company's liabilities to its policyholders and claimants that must be offset by assets. If the reserves are understated, the net worth of the company is overstated.

Investments To the extent that an insurer's promises depend on the value of its investments, those investments must be sound. For this reason, the insurance code of each state spells out the particular investments permitted to each type of insurance company in the state. The investments permitted are usually U.S. government obligations; state, municipal, and territorial bonds; Canadian bonds, mortgage loans, certain high-grade corporate bonds; and, subject to limitations, preferred and common stocks. In general, property and liability insurers are granted greater latitude in their investments than life insurers are. Life insurers are generally allowed to invest only a small percentage of their assets in common stocks. Consequently, common stocks account for less than 5

percent of the general account invested assets of life insurance companies, while about 25 percent of the assets of property and liability companies are in common stocks. Insurers must file their investments with the NAIC's Securities Valuation Office (SVO), which rates the credit quality of securities and establishes rules for valuing them.

Dealing with Insolvencies Although the principal thrust of insurance regulation is to avoid insolvencies, on occasion they do occur, and in such instances the commissioner of insurance must institute the necessary proceedings to have the insurer's assets taken over by an official liquidator. Usually, liquidation is a last resort, and the commissioner will often take steps to rehabilitate a company when an examination suggests that it is impaired or in a hazardous condition. In attempting to rehabilitate a company, the commissioner may direct that substantial portions of the firm's business be reinsured with other companies. Sometimes, the shaky firm may be merged with a stronger insurer. Often, the public is unaware that the company was threatened by insolvency.

When these efforts fail or when the company's position is too hazardous to attempt rehabilitation, it becomes necessary for the insurance department of the state in which the company is domiciled to handle the liquidation. In such circumstances, the commissioner may apply to a district court for permission to take possession of the company to conduct or close its business.

Although insurer insolvencies occur only infrequently, their impact is felt not only by the stockholders and policyholders of the company but by the claimants as well. Many of those who have claims against the company may be located in other states. Under such circumstances, dividing the assets that may be left among the company's claimants may be difficult. Many states have adopted the *Uniform Insurers Liquidation Act,* developed by the NAIC, which is designed to provide equitable treatment to all parties concerned when the insolvent insurer operates in several states. Under the provisions of this act, creditors in each state are afforded equal treatment and those located in the state of domicile are treated the same as those from other states.

State Insolvency Funds Insolvency guarantee funds designed to compensate members of the public who suffer loss because of failure of property and liability insurers or life and health insurers exist in all states. Generally, each claim covered by the

[13] The major liabilities of insurance companies are debts to policyholders; they are called *reserves*. In insurance accounting and insurance terminology generally, the term *reserve* is almost synonymous with *liability*.

guarantee fund is subject to a deductible (e.g., $100), and there is a cap on the amount that will be paid, requiring the policyholders and claimants to bear a part of the loss themselves.

Most of the property and liability insolvency guarantee funds date from the early 1970s, when they were established to forestall the formation of a federal agency, which had been proposed to perform the same function.[14] Most operate on a post-insolvency basis, in which insurers operating in the state are assessed their proportionate share of losses after an insolvency occurs. The New York plan for property and liability insurers is based on a pre-insolvency assessment. In some states, the assessments are allowed as tax offsets, permitting solvent insurers that have paid assessments to recoup these losses by reducing their premium taxes.

NAIC State Accreditation Program In 1990, the NAIC created its Financial Regulation Standards Accreditation Program, which is designed to assist state legislatures and insurance departments in developing an effective system of solvency regulation. The program provides for NAIC certification of states that meet the requirements of the accreditation program. The measures that must be adopted by a state to be accredited by the NAIC include a number of model laws and rules affecting regulation of insurance holding companies, managing general agents, reinsurance intermediaries, credit for reinsurance, examination processes, and liquidation proceedings. By August 2001, insurance departments in 47 states and the District of Columbia were accredited by the NAIC. In addition to the original certification, states must submit to an annual evaluation process and undergo recertification review every five years.

Market Regulation

A second major focus of insurance regulation is the fair treatment of policyholders. An insurer might be financially sound and yet indulge in practices that are detrimental to the public, such as unfairly discriminating against an insured or engaging in sharp claim practices. The commissioner attempts to control such activities. Market regulation encompasses such areas as advertising and other marketing issues, claims payment, underwriting, content of insurance policies, and rates charged.

Unfair Practices All states have Unfair Trade Practices Acts prohibiting an insurer from using unfair methods of competition or other unfair or deceptive acts or practices. States have also adopted laws governing claims settlement and prohibiting unfair claims settlement practices.

Unfair Trade Practices Acts prohibit unfair discrimination in underwriting, misrepresentation and false advertising, and twisting and rebating. *Rebating* consists of directly or indirectly giving or offering to give any portion of the premium or any other consideration to an insurance buyer as an inducement to the purchase of insurance. An example of unlawful rebating would be an offer by an insurance agent to give a part of his or her commission to a prospective insured.[15]

Twisting is the practice of inducing a policyholder to lapse or cancel a policy of one insurer in order to replace it with the policy of another insurer in a way that would prejudice the interest of the policyholder. Obviously, there is no crime in a complete comparison without misrepresentation an agent may make between a policy sold by his or her company and one sold by another company. It has been estimated that 30 to 40 percent of life insurance sales are replacements. This is unfortunate because there are a surprising number of cases when replacement of a contract does not benefit the policyholder.

Policy Forms Since the insurance product is a contract, by its very nature it is technical. In most cases,

[14] The earliest of the funds was established in New York (1947), New Jersey (1952), and Maryland (1965). However, these early funds did not pay claims on all lines of property and liability insurance, nor did they provide for the return of premiums that policyholders had paid to the insolvent insurer. These laws were revised in the 1970–1971 period when the rest of the plans were established.

[15] Although antirebating laws have been accepted without much question for about 70 years, they are now being challenged as anticompetitive in effect. Critics of the antirebate laws believe they represent anticompetitive laws, designed to prevent price competition among insurance agents. In fact, the original purpose of the laws was to complement the unfair discrimination provisions in the state rating laws. Legislators believed that it makes little sense to forbid insurers to charge different rates to persons with the same risk, and then permit the companies' agents to adjust the price at the point of sale. The original antirebate provisions of the New York Code—Sections 89 and 90—were titled *Discrimination Prohibited* and *Discrimination Against Colored People*. The first antirebate law was designed to protect blacks—"colored people" in the vernacular of the day—from discriminatory pricing. Nevertheless, we will undoubtedly see more challenges to the antirebate laws.

the customer is asked to purchase a product in which he or she becomes a party to a contract that the customer has not read or would understand if it were read. Because insurance contracts are complicated, they are subject to regulatory standards and must contain certain required provisions. In most cases, they must be approved by the regulatory authorities to ensure that the insurance-buying public will not be mistreated as a result of unfair provisions. In addition, the solvency of the insurers must be protected against unreasonable commitments they might make under stress of competition. In some states, new policy forms and endorsements need only be filed with the commissioner's office before they are put into use; if the commissioner does not approve of the form, it is then withdrawn. In most states, however, the law requires the approval of a form before it is adopted.

Competence of Agents Because of the technical complications in the insurance product, it is particularly important that those selling insurance understand the contracts they propose to sell. All states require a license from applicants to demonstrate by examination that they understand the contracts they propose to offer to the public and the laws under which they will operate. Also, the agents must be respected and responsible residents of their individual communities.

Consumer Complaints and Assistance All state insurance departments offer assistance to consumers in resolving disputes with insurers and insurance agents. During 2000, the states handled over 450,000 consumer compliants. In addition, most states have consumer information programs that provide educational brochures and other useful information.

Privacy and the Gramm–Leach–Bliley Act In 1999, Congress enacted the Financial Services Modernization Act, widely known as the Gramm–Leach–Bliley Act (GLBA), after its principle sponsors.[16] The primary purpose of GLBA was to relax the barriers between insurance, securities, and banking that had existed since the Great Depression. In the insurance area, GLBA permitted affiliations between banks and insurers and expanded the ability of national banks to sell insurance. It also defined the regulatory structure for these activities.

Although privacy was not the main focus of GLBA, the law contains important new privacy protections. During the debate over GLBA, many became concerned with the increasing ability of financial institutions to collect personal information about consumers and share it with others. Advancements in information systems and technology have increased the amount of information collected, and firms increasingly use this information to target their marketing. As more information is collected and it becomes easier to share with others, societal concerns about privacy have increased.

The consumer privacy protections in GLBA set some basic standards that all financial institutions—including insurance companies and agents—must meet. In general, the law requires insurers to notify consumers about their privacy policies and to give them the opportunity to prohibit the sharing of their protected financial information with nonaffiliated third parties. Information sharing between affiliated companies is not restricted. State insurance regulators are charged with enforcing the privacy provisions of GLBA as they apply to the insurance industry.

In response to GLBA, the NAIC adopted the Privacy of Consumer Financial and Health Information Model Regulation in September 2000. Recognizing the significance of health information in the insurance industry, the NAIC model regulates the privacy of both financial information and health information. For financial information, the model's requirements are consistent with those in GLBA. That is, the model requires the company to notify consumers about its privacy policies and to give consumers the opportunity to prohibit the company from sharing information with nonaffiliated companies. In the health information area, however, the NAIC established a higher standard of protection. A company may not share protected health information with affiliates or nonaffiliates without first obtaining the permission of the consumer.[17] Most states have adopted the NAIC model or amended their existing privacy laws to be consistent with the model.

In a related development, the U.S. Department of Health and Human Services finalized regulations in

[16] P.L. 106-102. The privacy provisions are found in Title V of the Act.

[17] The NAIC was particularly concerned about the health privacy issues raised by affiliations between banks and insurers—for example, the prospect that a health insurer might share protected health information with an affiliated bank that holds the consumer's mortgage.

April 2001 intended to protect the privacy of health records. These rules govern health plans (including health insurers and HMOs), health care clearinghouses, and health care providers. Covered entities must disclose their privacy policies, allow patients to have access to their medical records, and obtain consumer consent before releasing information to others. The standards must be met by April 2003, except for small health plans, which must comply by April 2004. To avoid application of both the NAIC health privacy protections and the HHS rules, the NAIC model exempts an insurer from its health privacy provisions if the insurer complies with the HHS rules.

Regulation of Rates

The original rationale for regulation of insurance rates was that such regulation was needed to achieve the dual goals of regulation (solvency and equity). To the extent that the insurer's promise depends on the price it charges for these promises, it was felt that these rates must be subject to government control. All states (except Illinois, which does not currently have a rating law) provide for the regulation of insurance rates, requiring that the rates must be adequate, not excessive, and not unfairly discriminatory.

Adequacy is the primary requirement. The rates, with interest income from investments, must be sufficient to pay all losses as they occur and all expenses connected with the production and servicing of the business.

In addition to being adequate, the insurance rates must *not be excessive*. Insurance has become regarded as a product that is essential to the well-being of society's members, and insurers may not take advantage of this need to realize unreasonable returns.

Finally, insurance rates must not *discriminate unfairly*. The emphasis in this requirement is on *unfairly*, since the very nature of insurance rates requires some degree of discrimination. By not being unfairly discriminatory, we mean that the insurance company may not charge a significantly different rate for two clients with approximately the same degree of risk. Any variation in rates charged must have an actuarial basis.

All states have legislation requiring that rates must be reasonable, adequate, and not unfairly discriminatory, yet the manner in which these requirements are enforced varies with different lines of insurance and from state to state.

Regulation of Life Insurance Rates Apart from making certain that the companies do not engage in price discrimination, most states do not exercise any form of direct control over the level of life insurance rates.[18] However, life insurance rates are regulated indirectly. Regulation of dividends and mutual insurers' accumulation of surplus represents an indirect control on maximum rates. In addition, legal limits on the expense portion of the premium help to control the cost of life insurance in those states that impose such limits.[19] Finally, state laws prescribe the mortality tables and interest assumptions that must be used in computing policy reserves, which means that the adequacy of life insurance rates is also indirectly regulated. If the insurer's rate structure is too low, premium income will be insufficient to generate the assets required to meet the required reserves.

Although these indirect forms of rate regulation do exist, they represent an extremely limited form of control. Most expenses are not controlled, and there are no limits set on profits (other than those imposed on mutual insurers in accumulating surplus). The chief justification for the absence of stricter regulation of life insurance rates has been the proposition that competition is an effective regulator and can be depended on to keep life insurance rates from being excessive. Informed authorities question this assumption, arguing that the pricing complexities in life insurance make determination of the true cost of the insurance

[18] Credit life insurance rates represent a special exception. In most states, the sale of credit life insurance is subject to special regulation, resulting from past abuses in the field characterized by a phenomenon called *reverse competition*. Credit life insurance is sold through lenders to a captive market. Reverse competition tends to increase rates and keep them high because of the insurance companies' practice of bidding for the lenders' business through the payment of excessive commissions whose cost is passed on to the consumer. Most states regulate rates for credit life, credit accident and health, and credit unemployment insurance under the terms of the NAIC Consumer Credit Insurance Model Act, originally adopted in 1958, but since amended a number of times. In June 2001, the NAIC adopted a new Credit Personal Property Insurance Model Act. This model applies when property insurance is written in connection with a personal credit transaction to cover the creditor's interest in collateral.

[19] New York, for example, limits the amount of commission payable to a soliciting agent in the first year of an ordinary life policy to 55 percent of the premium. Different limitations apply to other types of policies. Companies not licensed to sell in New York sometimes pay commissions as high as 125 percent of the first-year premium.

beyond even the sophisticated buyer.[20] This is because the combination of savings and protection in the life insurance policy tends to obscure both the cost of the protection and the return on savings.

Recognizing the inability of consumers to make informed decisions concerning the cost of life insurance without assistance, many states now insist that an insurer provide prospective buyers with cost disclosure information. In 1976, the NAIC adopted and proposed to the states the *Model Life Insurance Solicitation Regulation,* which was subsequently adopted by many states. This regulation requires insurers to make cost comparison information available to prospective buyers. The required information includes standardized cost indexes and dividend information.[21] The model regulation was revised in 1983, after critics, including the Federal Trade Commission, argued that it provided inadequate disclosure. Although the 1983 model regulation is an improvement over the original version, it too has been criticized as inadequate disclosure.[22]

Regulation of Property and Liability Rates
There is considerable diversity in the approaches taken by states to regulate property and casualty rates. In some cases, states exercise direct control over rates, requiring specific approval of rates before they can be used. In other cases, states follow the life insurance pattern, and exercise only indirect forms of regulation. Although there are other systems, the major approaches to rate regulation fall into four categories: prior approval, file and use, informational filing, and no filing.[23] The latter three are known collectively as *competitive rating* or *open rating*

systems.[24] In addition, we will briefly note a hybrid system known as "flexrating."[25]

The Prior Approval System Following the enactment of McCarran-Ferguson, most states adopted the *prior approval approach* to rate regulation, patterned after the *All Industry Model Rating Law,* developed by the NAIC in 1946. Under this system, the insurance company must obtain approval of its intended rates from the commissioner before they may be used, and the commissioner retains the right to disapprove the rates after they become effective. Insurers file statistical data in the form of trended loss experience and projected expenses with requests for approval of rates. An insurer may accumulate and file its own loss data, or it may authorize an advisory organization (i.e., *rating bureau*) to file industry-wide trended loss data on its behalf. In either case, the insurer must complete the filing data using its own projected expenses. If the commissioner is satisfied that the statistical data supports the proposed rate, it is approved. In most states, the law includes a *deemer* provision, which grants that if the rates have not been disapproved within a specified period of time (ranging from 15 to 60 days), they are *deemed* to have been approved.

The prior approval system has been the subject of considerable criticism. Insurers complain that the system tends to make the commissioner the justifier of rates to the public, so that the level of rates is often determined by political rather than actuarial considerations. Public pressure for containment of insurance prices may act to deny insurers needed rate increases. In some states, requests for rate increases are frequently denied or compromised, and sometimes they are delayed for unconscionable periods. The resulting rigidity of rates at inadequate levels produces the traditional market response to

[20] A study by Professor Joseph M. Belth has shown that wide differences exist in the cost of identical products in the life insurance field and that the consumer is not generally aware of the price he or she pays when buying life insurance. See Joseph M. Belth, *The Retail Price Structure in American Life Insurance* (Bloomington: Bureau of Business Research, Graduate School of Business, Indiana University, 1966).

[21] The required information is discussed in greater detail in Chapter 17.

[22] The 1983 version of the model regulation, like the 1976 model, has been criticized by consumer advocate Dr. Joseph M. Belth as *pseudo disclosure.* See *The Insurance Forum,* vol. 12, no. 2 (February 1985).

[23] In addition to these four basic systems and their many variations, there have been two other systems, state-made rates and mandatory bureau rates. State-made automobile rates are used in Massachusetts. Mandatory bureau rates are used in North Carolina for fire and automobile insurance.

[24] The term *competitive rating,* which has been used widely to identify the laws that do not require prior approval, has proven to be an unfortunate choice, for it has been interpreted by some to imply an absence of competition in states using the prior approval system. Because prior approval rate regulation is often used in other industries as an alternative to competition, some observers assume that this is also the case with insurance. The truth of the matter is that the industry is highly price competitive not only in those states with *competitive rating* laws but in the prior approval states as well.

[25] It is difficult to classify states with respect to their system of rate regulation because many states follow more than one system. A given state may use the prior approval system for some lines and a form of competitive rating for others.

an inadequate price level: a reduction in supply. Ironically, while insurers complain that the prior approval system results in inadequate rates, other critics argue that its effect is quite the opposite. A 1977 study by the U.S. Department of Justice, for example, concluded that the prior approval system is an unnecessary limitation on competition by insurers and has discouraged rate reductions.[26]

No Filing Although prior approval still remains a common approach to the regulation of property and liability rates, there is currently a trend toward eliminating prior approval requirements and adopting a competitive rating approach to rate regulation. One option is the so-called *no-file* law, also referred to as *open competition*. Under a no-file system, rates are not required to be filed with or approved by the state insurance department. However, the company must maintain records of experience and other information used in developing the rates and make these available to the commissioner on request.

The no-file approach follows the pattern of a California law, which existed from 1947 until it was repealed by Proposition 103 in 1987.[27] The California law made it clear that competition, not government authority, is the preferred governor of rates and that barring the existence of an anticompetitive situation or practice, the commissioner was not to regulate rates as such. In effect, the position of property and liability insurers under such a law is much the same as that of life insurers, which, as we have noted, are subject only to indirect control of their rates.

During the late 1960s and 1970s, a short-lived movement advocated replacing prior approval laws with open competition laws. No-file or open competition laws were passed in Florida, Georgia, Idaho, Illinois, Massachusetts, Missouri, and Montana.[28] The trend stalled in 1976 amid furor by consumer groups over the escalation in insurance costs. It was an accident of history that the no-file approach was gathering momentum when severe underwriting losses in

1974 and 1975 prompted insurers to increase their rate levels. Consumerists associated the increases with the absence of regulation and insisted that states control the level of rates.[29]

File-and-Use Laws A third system of rate regulation, *file-and-use* laws, represents something of a compromise between the prior approval system and the no-file system. Under the file-and-use approach, the insurer must file proposed rate changes, but may use the new rates immediately. However, the rates may subsequently be disapproved by the commissioner. The chief advantage of the file-and-use system is that there is no delay between the time a rate adjustment is needed and the time it becomes effective.[30]

Informational Filing The fourth system, *informational filing,* is considered by many authorities to be virtually identical in effect with the open competition approach. Rates may be used without regulatory approval, but they are filed with the regulator for information purposes.[31]

Flex-Rating The newest approach to rate regulation, known as *flex-rating,* combines elements of both the prior approval system and the open competition system. Under the flex-rating system, a range is established for insurance rates. Insurers are permitted to change their rates both up and down within the established range in response to market conditions and without prior approval. Increases above or decreases below the established range (e.g., 10 percent) require prior approval.

[26] U.S. Department of Justice, *A Report of the Task Group on Antitrust Immunities: The Pricing and Marketing of Insurance* (January 1977), passim.

[27] Proposition 103 repealed California's 40-year-old open competition law and replaced it with a prior approval system. Proposition 103 is discussed in the chapter appendix.

[28] The Florida law, which was one of the first competitive laws enacted since 1947, was repealed in 1971. After a one-year experiment with open competition in 1977, Massachusetts returned to state-made rates for automobile insurance in 1978.

[29] States using the no-file system for some lines in 2001 included Illinois, Nevada, and Wyoming. In addition, a number of states use a no-file approach for contracts written to cover large commercial insureds (e.g., Arkansas, Georgia, Indiana, Maine, Missouri, Nebraska, Pennsylvania, Rhode Island, and Virginia).

[30] The file-and-use system encompasses a wide range of rate regulatory systems, some of which are similar to the prior approval system, with others that in effect operate like the open competition system. For example, some states impose a waiting period before the rates may be used, and operate in much the same way as a prior approval law with a deemer period. In other states, rates may be used immediately on filing, but may subsequently be disapproved.

[31] *Use and file* is another approach, closely related to informational filing. Under use and file, rates may be used without regulatory approval, but an informational filing must be made within a specified period of time (e.g., 15 days) after the insurer begins using the rates. Generally, the commissioner retains the right to request supporting information where there is reason to believe the filing might violate statute, and the right to disapprove the rates prospectively based on review of the additional information.

Commercial Lines Deregulation Recent developments at the NAIC have led to renewed interest in competitive rating as an alternative to prior approval. In December 2000, the NAIC recommended improvements to the regulatory framework for commercial lines rates. Under the NAIC's recommendations, most commercial lines rates would be subject to informational filing only. Several lines would fall under a no-file system, including financial guaranty, aviation, ocean marine, directors and officers liability, boiler and machinery, nuclear insurance, and others. Filings made by advisory organizations would be subject to either file-and-use or prior approval, depending on the state. Prior approval rate regulation is recommended only in limited areas, including those lines in which the market is deemed to be noncompetitive. Many states are in the process of adopting the NAIC's recommendations.

Diversity as a Reflection of State Preference
Although it may be surprising that the states have taken such diverse approaches to the regulation of property and liability insurance rates, the truth is that there is still considerable disagreement about the proper role of regulation with respect to rates. Originally, prior approval laws were enacted to prevent insurers from engaging in cutthroat competition, which regulators viewed as the major threat. More recently, many prior approval laws have been administered under a different philosophy: The purpose of the regulation is to keep rates from becoming excessive. As a result, insurers have come to favor the no-file, informational filing, or file-and-use approaches to regulation.

Numerous arguments have been advanced in favor of free competition in property and liability insurance. It is argued, for example, that government attempts to regulate prices result in restrictions in the market. When price ceilings are imposed by regulators, insurers tend to compete in attracting only the better classes of insureds, leaving the less desirable ones without coverage. In addition, it has been argued that greater pricing freedom for insurers makes premium rates more responsive to changing conditions. Experience seems to indicate that the prior approval system exacerbates the underwriting cycle. Under the prior approval system, an insurer that discovers it is losing money faces a delay in adjusting its rates, whereas adjustments can be made immediately under the other systems. In prior

approval states, the changes tend to come less often but turn out larger.[32] This results in a more dramatic underwriting cycle. Finally, more competition, it is argued, will give insurers greater incentive to operate efficiently to cut costs and permit rate reductions.[33]

Risk-Retention Groups

As we noted briefly in Chapter 5, the Risk Retention Act of 1986 authorized groups with common exposures to band together and form *risk-retention groups* or purchasing groups. The major effect of the law was to carve out a federal exemption from state regulation for both risk-retention groups or purchasing groups. Risk-retention groups and purchasing groups are subject to regulation by the state in which they are formed, but are generally exempt from regulation by other states. Initially, the organizers of a risk-retention group submit a business plan or feasibility study to the insurance department of the chartering state and are regulated by that state. The group must submit copies of the plan or study to the insurance departments of all other states in which it will be doing business, but it need not be licensed to operate in other states. The group must file with the insurance commissioner in each state in which it does business a copy of the annual financial statement it files with the chartering state. In addition, risk-retention groups are subject to the unfair-claim settlement practice laws, residual market mechanisms (i.e., assigned risk pools), registration with the state insurance commissioner, and solvency examinations by insurance commissioners of the states in which they operate. Risk-retention groups are prohibited from

[32] A 1977 U.S. Department of Justice study suggested that insurers make smaller, but more frequent, rate changes in open competition states. U.S. Department of Justice, *The Pricing and Marketing of Insurance* (Washington, D.C.: U.S. Government Printing Office, 1977). Numerous other studies support the conclusion that the underwriting cycles are worsened under prior approval laws.

[33] Since the expansion of competitive rating systems during the early 1970s, a number of researchers have studied market performance under prior approval and open competition systems in an attempt to draw conclusions about the differences between the two rating systems. Harrington provides a detailed analysis of the many studies prior to 1984. After considering the results, he concludes, "A considerable amount of the evidence suggests that average loss ratios and prices did not differ between CR [competitive rating] and NCR [noncompetitive rating] states during the overall time period analyzed." See Scott Harrington, "The Impact of Rate Regulation on Prices and Underwriting Results in the Property-Liability Insurance Industry: A Survey," *Journal of Risk and Insurance* 51 (December 1984), pp. 577–623.

joining the state insolvency guaranty fund. In the event of insolvency of a risk-retention group, there is no source of recovery other than the assets of the members.

STATE VERSUS FEDERAL REGULATION

The prospect of federal regulation of the insurance industry has loomed since the SEUA case in 1944. Although the McCarran-Ferguson Act left regulation in the hands of the states, it did so with the implicit condition that the federal government would not regulate insurance as long as the states did a good job.

Pressure for Repeal of the McCarran–Ferguson Act

Bills to repeal or otherwise modify McCarran-Ferguson have been introduced in virtually every session of Congress since 1977. During the 1980s and early 1990s, the focus of most bills was on the insurance industry's federal antitrust exemption. Some bills would have made the insurance industry subject to federal antitrust laws without exception. Others would have granted a partial exemption from the antitrust laws, allowing insurers to engage in limited cooperation in ratemaking, primarily through exchange of loss data and in joint preparation and filing of policy forms. The insurance industry opposed both approaches, but generally found the partial exemption version less objectionable.[34]

More recent attempts to modify McCarran–Ferguson have gone to the heart of the system of state regulation. The *Gramm–Leach–Bliley Act,* enacted in November 1999, expanded the ability of national banks to engage in the insurance business. Since then, many large banks have taken an active interest in the system of insurance regulation. Given that national banks are already regulated by a federal

agency (the Office of the Comptroller of the Currency), it is not surprising that they would prefer a federal system of insurance regulation. Similarly, large insurers (particularly life insurers) have become more vocal in their criticism of state regulation. Both groups argue that it is inefficient and unnecessarily costly to comply with individual state laws, and they seek a federal regulatory system to achieve national uniformity.

Arguments Favoring Federal Regulation

Those who advocate repeal of the McCarran–Ferguson Act may be divided into two broad groups, diametrically opposed in their philosophies, but unanimous in their agreement that the law should be repealed.

The first group consists of those who argue that the states have done an inadequate job of regulating the industry. While these critics admit that some states have done a good job in regulating insurance, they point out that the quality of regulation nationwide has varied markedly. The result in some cases has been the failure of companies and public suffering. These advocates of federal regulation argue that the lack of consistency among the states has caused inconvenience, duplication of effort, and waste. There are 50 different insurance codes, each of which imposes restrictions and limitations on insurers. An insurance company seeking a rate adjustment or a change in policy form must obtain approval from each of the jurisdictions. A single federal system of regulation, it is argued, would provide uniformity and better quality regulation. In essence, it is argued that since insurance is interstate commerce, there should be one body to provide for uniform nationwide regulation.

The second group advocating the repeal of McCarran–Ferguson argue for its repeal on completely different grounds. A 1977 U.S. Department of Justice study, for example, argued that regulation of rates is unnecessary, and that the repeal of McCarran–Ferguson is desirable because it would subject insurers to the Sherman Act and other federal antitrust statutes. Some who advocate repeal of McCarran–Ferguson believe that the spread of open competition laws has been too slow and that repeal of the law is desirable for the purpose of ending the prior approval approach to rate regulation.

Interestingly, those who have suggested a change from state regulation to a federal system often see

[34] During the 1980s, three legislators in particular pushed for repeal or modification of McCarran-Ferguson: Senator Howard M. Metzenbaum (D-Ohio), Representative Jack Brooks (D-Texas), and Representative John Dingell (D-Mich.). Senator Metzenbaum did not seek reelection in 1994 and Representative Brooks was defeated in the November 1994 election. In the judgment of many observers, the likelihood of repeal or modification of McCarran-Ferguson is greatly diminished, at least for the time being.

this shift in different terms. Some favor the change because they feel that state regulation has been ineffective. Clearly, these advocates of federal regulation expect more, rather than less, regulation under a federal system. Other advocates of change, such as the Department of Justice, favor the shift because of a philosophical predisposition in favor of antitrust. Still others are concerned about consumer issues relating to availability and affordability and see a shift to a federal system of regulation as a solution to these contradictory goals. Finally, some people within the insurance industry view the prospect of the repeal of McCarran–Ferguson as an escape from the burdensome requirements of state regulation.

Arguments Favoring State Regulation

The opponents of federal regulation argue that the individual states have the experience and expertise necessary to meet and solve the critical issues, and that state regulatory authorities, being more familiar with location conditions and problems, are more responsive to local needs. They point to the assistance regulators give local consumers, and they argue that a federal system of regulation would of necessity be superimposed on the state system.

Perhaps the most impressive argument against federal regulation is the same as the one generally raised in favor of federal regulation—that a federal system would substitute a uniform system for the existing diversity under the states. Although the differences in approach to regulation taken by the states are often condemned as a defect of state regulation, *uniformity* is a neutral term, implying neither goodness nor badness. Given the performance of some regulatory agencies—at both the state and federal levels—the uniformity that it is claimed would exist under a federal system might be viewed as a defect rather than a benefit. State regulation provides the ability and freedom to innovate, experiment, and emulate. If a mistake is made in state regulation, it is limited to one jurisdiction and does not become national in scope. Federal regulation, with its uniformity, would eliminate the localized expressions of preference regarding the manner in which the industry should be regulated. To argue that there is something fundamentally wrong with differences in regulation among the various states is to quarrel with the entire concept of federalism and the legitimacy of individual states having independent powers and responsibilities.

Consequences of the Repeal of the McCarran–Ferguson Act

The effect of the repeal of the McCarran–Ferguson Act would depend on the nature of the regulatory system that evolved following such a repeal. Although it is impossible to determine precisely what that system might be, we can identify some possibilities.

Continuation of State Regulation Repeal of Public Law 15 would superimpose the federal system of regulation on a continuing state system. The leading proposals for repeal of McCarran–Ferguson would grant insurers the option of state or federal charters, and state-chartered companies would require retention of the state system of regulation. Even without alternative chartering, many insurers would not be subject to federal control because they operate on an intrastate basis and are not engaged in interstate commerce. In addition, the states would undoubtedly continue to license and regulate at least some agents, and would probably require reports from federally regulated insurers for premium tax purposes.

Possible Varieties of Federal Control Despite the considerable rhetoric on the subject, there is no way to predict the form that federal control would take. Yet most arguments for or against federal regulation have been based on some presumed system.

Although the pure antitrust approach suggested by the Department of Justice is one possible model, there are other systems of federal regulation as well. Federal regulatory agencies have used the prior approval approach in regulating the prices of natural gas, banks and other financial institutions, and the airline and trucking industries, and this approach could also be used under a federal system of insurance regulation. Despite the trend toward deregulation in other areas, there is a serious question whether Congress would permit insurers the freedom in pricing contemplated by a pure antitrust approach. It is becoming increasingly evident that consumers want some regulation of insurance rates. Although the original purpose of rate regulation was to prevent destructive competition, most consumers perceive its purpose to be that of controlling increases in rates. The public choice theory of regulation suggests that this attitude will play an important role in determining the system of insurance regulation under either a state or federal system.

Repeal of the McCarran–Ferguson Act as a States-Rights Issue

Because McCarran-Ferguson grants the industry an exemption from the federal antitrust laws, some advocates of repeal characterize their position as pro-competition and the position of those who oppose repeal as opposing competition. The truth of the matter is that repeal of McCarran–Ferguson is consistent with either a free-market or a market-intervention approach.

There are two issues related to the regulation of insurance. The first involves the question of whether an antitrust approach or regulation should be used with respect to insurer pricing; whether we should depend on market forces to control prices or resort to market intervention through regulation. This is not really the question in the debate over the repeal of McCarran-Ferguson. The debate is over where the decision of market intervention or nonintervention should be made. Repeal of McCarran–Ferguson is fundamentally a states-rights issue. McCarran–Ferguson does not exempt the industry from antitrust regulation, but only from *federal* antitrust laws. It was enabling legislation that allows the states to regulate as they choose. The states are free to choose between an antitrust, free-market approach or rigid regulation. As we have seen, the states have taken different approaches.

State versus Federal Regulation and Public Choice

The public choice theory of regulation suggests that the eventual decision with respect to state versus federal regulation will be determined by the intensity of efforts of *payers* and *beneficiaries*. Unfortunately, the issues in this controversy are not clearly understood by many of the debaters, and there is some uncertainty regarding exactly who will be payers and who will be beneficiaries.

We have noted that the principal supporters of federal regulation include the U.S. Department of Justice, some members of Congress, banks, and many large insurers. The supporters of state regulation include the National Association of Insurance Commissioners, most insurance agents and their associations, and a large number of insurance companies. In measuring the attitudes of insurance company managers, it should be remembered that most insurers are small regional organizations; it is logical that they would favor continuation of state regulation. Although it is an oversimplification to assume that the larger national companies all favor federal regulation and the smaller companies oppose it, a large insurer coping with 50 different insurance departments would be understandably more inclined to favor regulation than would the smaller, regional company.[35]

In the last analysis, the attitudes of the insurance industry itself should not be a major factor. The issue of state versus federal regulation should not be determined on the basis of the preferences of those who are being regulated. Nor should the decision be based on the preferences of state regulators or those who would run the federal system of regulation. Rather, it should be decided on the basis of the costs and benefits to the consumer under either system.

The controversy between the proponents of state regulation and those who advocate federal control will no doubt continue. The eventual result may well be a dual system of regulation, but even if this takes place, the debate regarding the superiority of one system over the other will not end.

[35] In 2001, several proposals for a system of federal charters were initiated by segments of the insurance industry. The American Bankers Association Insurance Association (which represents banks entering the insurance industry), the American Council of Life Insurers, and the American Insurance Association all developed legislation to create a dual system or regulation, with federally chartered insurance companies under the supervision of the Secretary of Treasury.

One of the newest areas of government concern, and also one of the most significant issues facing the insurance industry today, is the availability of insurance and the difficulty that some classes have experienced in obtaining insurance at affordable rates. Although there are many products that some members of our society cannot afford, it has been argued that insurance is fundamentally different from other products and that the insurance industry has a responsibility to make insurance *available* at *affordable* rates to all who want and need it. The issues in this debate are far-reaching and touch on such questions as the type of society we will have, and who will pay what in that society. In this appendix, we will examine some ways in which the demand for availability and affordability affects the insurance market and consider the implications of this debate.

THE ESSENCE OF THE DEBATE

From a regulatory perspective, the key issue in the debate over availability and affordability is whether availability and affordability problems that arise in insurance represent market failures that should be addressed by regulation.

Availability and *affordability* are concepts that economists know as supply and demand. Availability is a synonym for *supply,* and, like the economist's idea of supply, goods and services are *available* when the seller can obtain a price that will cover the cost of production.

Affordability refers to the ability of the consumer to pay for the insurance products that he or she requires. This is synonymous with the economist's definition of *effective demand,* defined as the willingness and the ability to pay. This means that there is an inevitable conflict between the goals of availability and affordability. When the cost of losses for a given group is low, it is clear that insurance will be available and affordable. Conversely, when the cost of losses for a given group is high, insurers will offer coverage to that group only at a high premium, which means that it may not be affordable without some type of

subsidy. This brings us to the real issue in the debate. In the final analysis, the debate over availability and affordability is a thinly veiled demand for cross-subsidies in the insurance market.

Existing Subsidies in the Insurance Market

Subsidies in the insurance market are not a new phenomenon. They have existed for many years. Insurance subsidies are provided in four different ways: (1) the shared markets, (2) mandated underwriting losses, (3) government programs, and (4) social pricing.

Shared Markets The most common approach to subsidizing high-risk insureds in the past has been the *shared markets,* a euphemism for the distressed-risk pools noted in Chapter 5. Property and liability insurers in all states are required to participate in this residual market, through automobile insurance plans (assigned risk plans), FAIR plans, and, more recently, joint underwriting associations established to provide medical malpractice insurance to physicians. Under each of these programs, unwanted insureds are assigned to insurers or are insured by an industry-wide loss-sharing pool. Almost without exception, losses and expenses incurred in the shared market exceed premiums by a substantial margin, and insurers pass the losses they sustain in the shared market on to other insurance buyers in the form of higher premiums.

Mandated Underwriting Losses A second approach to cross-subsidies in insurance arises when insurers are required to write a particular line of insurance at a loss, generally on the grounds that their overall operating results are satisfactory. Although cross-subsidies of this type are sometimes the unintended result of inaccuracies in the rating process, they also occur because of regulatory fiat. The question is whether insurers should overcharge buyers of homeowners insurance to subsidize the cost of automobile insurance, or whether premiums for fire and marine insurance should be loaded to cover losses under malpractice and product liability insurance.

Government Insurance Programs Government-operated insurance plans represent still another approach to subsidies in insurance. When applicants who are not insurable through normal market channels are insured under a government program at a loss, a subsidy is provided from taxpayers through the general revenues of the government body or through a special tax on some members of society. Subsidies of this type are expected in social insurance programs, but they also exist in private insurance programs operated by state and federal government.

A Related Issue: Social Pricing The debate over availability and affordability shifted to a different plane in the 1970s, with the introduction of the idea of *social rating*. The new disagreement was over what constitutes *equity* in insurance pricing. The protagonists in this debate were those who believe that the price of insurance should be based on the cost of production and that each segment of the insurance-buying public should pay the cost of losses for that segment, and those who argue that the rating system should be used to provide subsidies to some segments of the insurance market.

To appreciate the significance of the issue, it is necessary to understand how *social pricing* differs from the traditional *cost-based* approach. Under the traditional approach, insurers group insureds into reasonably homogeneous classes to predict the losses of the group and to charge all members of a given class the same price per unit of insurance. The criteria used to assign insureds to the respective rate classes are those that actuaries believe are related to claim frequency and severity. In automobile insurance, for example, these criteria have normally included age, sex, and marital status of the principal operator; the use of the auto; anticipated mileage; and the area in which the automobile is principally garaged. Thus, since young, unmarried males as a group have tended to have more auto losses per capita than do other policyholders, they are charged higher premiums. Policyholders living in heavily urbanized areas generally have higher losses than drivers living in other areas, and they too have been charged higher premiums. The philosophy of the system is based on the use of classification criteria that are demonstrably related to losses, and the premiums to be charged each class are a reflection of the losses of that class.

The proponents of social rating argue that it is unfair for insurance costs to vary because of group distinctions such as age, sex, or other factors "over which the individual has no control." These critics would like to change the system, maintaining that it is socially undesirable for the young, unmarried male driver, for example, to pay more for automobile insurance than other motorists, even though statistics show that these drivers have far more accidents than do other groups in the population.[36]

Gender-Neutral Rating The debate over social pricing is complicated by the fact that certain parties who favor social pricing are motivated by ideals other than availability and affordability. The issue in the debate over gender-neutral (unisex) rating, for example, is fundamentally different from the debate over availability and affordability. Although most advocates of social pricing are clearly arguing for a system of cross-subsidies, cost is not the primary consideration for many who support gender-neutral rating. In fact, women would actually pay more for their insurance in some cases, but the advocates of unisex rating view the changes in the distribution of costs as being of secondary importance. Unlike the other advocates of social pricing, the proponents of gender-neutral rating do not want to ignore costs: They simply want to reflect them differently. The arguments for gender-neutral rating stem from the philosophical premise that certain rating factors are unacceptable from a public policy perspective. Contemplating the many ways to divide people into groups for rating purposes, the advocates of gender-neutral rating argue that there are negative side effects to the use of sex as a rating factor. Implicit in their arguments is the notion that if you allow differentiation between men and women in insurance rating, the differentiation becomes manifest in other areas.

Those who oppose social rating (including gender-neutral rating) also argue from a fundamental principle. The question in their view is whether market intervention should be used. Should prices be determined by the market or by regulatory fiat? They argue that once the principle of market intervention is considered acceptable, it can be justified for disparate reasons. If intervention is acceptable to eliminate rates based on what some consider

[36] In 2000, for example, drivers under age 21 constituted about 6.8 percent of all drivers but were involved in 17 percent of all police-reported accidents and in 14.6 percent of all fatal accidents. Drivers under age 25 represented 13.5 percent of all drivers but were involved in 25.1 percent of all fatal accidents. National Highway Traffic Safety Administration.

socially unacceptable criteria, it may also be acceptable for other reasons.

The debate between the advocates of cost-based pricing and social pricing is far from academic. The traditional rating factors on which automobile insurance rates have been based in the past have been modified or eliminated in the states of California, Hawaii, Massachusetts, Michigan, Montana, North Carolina, and Pennsylvania and are being challenged in other states.[37] Montana enacted a full-scale unisex law in 1983, which became effective in 1985.[38]

Redlining Another important controversy in the debate over availability and affordability relates to the alleged practice of *redlining,* which refers to the policy decision by an insurer to avoid insuring property located in areas where the expected losses are higher than average. Generally, the areas in which it is alleged that redlining occurs are in urban centers where insurers have experienced excessive losses due to vandalism, arson, and riots. When insurers refuse to sell insurance in such areas, critics argue, insurance is simply not available. Even when they agree to write coverage, it is argued, the coverage is not affordable.[39]

Allegations of redlining and the availability of insurance in urban areas has been an issue since the riots in 1967 that occurred across the country in the aftermath of the assassination of Dr. Martin Luther King, Jr. Following these riots, property owners in some urban centers across the country reported diffi-

culty in obtaining insurance on their property. Congress responded by enacting the Federal Riot Reinsurance Program and the states created FAIR plans, which are designed to provide access to insurance for property owners who have difficulty in obtaining insurance because of the location of their property.

Concerns about availability and affordability of insurance in urban areas were renewed in the wake of the 1992 riots in Los Angeles. To address the problems related to availability, the NAIC established the Insurance Availability and Affordability Task Force, which reports to the Market Conduct and Consumer Affairs Subcommittee of the NAIC. The task force surveyed the states to determine the extent of the information and opinions on urban and rural availability problems. The task force is also charged with responsibility to study and make recommendations with respect to insurer underwriting and marketing practices as they relate to availability and affordability problems and to devise or suggest solutions.

The debate over redlining is based on the premise that redlining is an unfair restriction of insurance availability based on geographic location. All state insurance codes outlaw unfair discrimination in insurance. The issue, of course, is whether an underwriting decision based on the excessive hazard for a particular geographic area constitutes unfair discrimination. When the NAIC addressed the availability problem in mid-1992, several commissioners pointed out that availability and affordability problems also existed in rural areas where individuals and businesses experienced difficulty in obtaining property coverage because of the high incidence of weather-related catastrophes, such as tornadoes and hurricanes. Some industry critics argue that a fundamental difference exists between the refusal to write coverage in a geographic area because of excessive hazard arising from natural perils (such as windstorm and hail) and refusal when the excessive hazard arises from human perils (such as vandalism, arson, and riots). The latter, they argue, is a subterfuge for discrimination based on race or color.

In response to recent criticism about redlining, a number of insurers and insurer groups have actively pursued increased business in inner-city areas. They have added more agents, promoted consumer education, and sponsored programs to upgrade inner-city buildings and reduce loss exposures.

In 23 states, FAIR plans provide access to insurance for property owners who are unable to obtain coverage through normal market channels. To the

[37] Louisiana and Florida commissioners banned the use of sex and marital status in automobile insurance rates in 1979, but both were overturned by the courts. Regulatory orders in Wyoming (1978) and New Jersey (1981) to discontinue the use of sex and marital status were also challenged successfully by the insurance industry. Other states in which unisex automobile rating has been proposed include South Carolina (1979), Minnesota (1984), and New Mexico (1985).

[38] In 1989, the Montana legislature voted to repeal the unisex law, but the repeal was vetoed by the governor and the legislature failed to override the veto.

[39] The term *redlining* originated in the underwriting departments of insurers and has a historical basis in the "red lines" that were drawn on maps maintained by property insurance underwriting departments of insurers. In an effort to avoid unacceptable concentrations of risk, property insurers maintained maps (published by Sanborne and therefore referred to as *Sanborne maps*) on which underwriting personnel indicated the location of each building insured by the company. When the number of insured buildings in a particular area had reached a saturation point at which additional exposures might create a catastrophe exposure, the insurer declined to accept applicants from the area. In some cases, a red line was drawn around the area to alert underwriting personnel to the concentration of risks.

extent that redlining occurs, the FAIR plan provides access to the insurance market for property owners who are denied access to insurance because of the geographic location of their property. FAIR plans have been criticized for providing more limited coverage than that available in standard markets.

In a decision handed down in May 1993, the U.S. Supreme Court upheld the lower court ruling that the federal Fair Housing Act extends to cover racial discrimination in the sale of homeowners insurance. The decision upheld a decision by the Seventh U.S. Circuit Court of Appeals in Chicago, the first appellate court to apply the anti-redlining provisions of the Fair Housing Act to insurers. The ruling involved a class-action suit brought by eight black Milwaukee homeowners and the National Association for the Advancement of Colored People against American Family Mutual Insurance Co., of Madison, Wisconsin. In March 1995, American Family Mutual agreed to a settlement in which it agreed to provide more than $16 million to support programs aimed at improving housing in Milwaukee, the city in which the alleged redlining occurred.

California's Proposition 103 Any discussion of the affordability/availability debate would be incomplete without at least a brief mention of California's now-famous Proposition 103, an initiative enacted by the voters under California's referendum process on November 8, 1988. The principal effect of Proposition 103 was to change the way in which insurance rates are regulated in California, replacing the state's open competition law with a prior approval system. For California voters, however, the question of how rates are approved was an inconsequential consideration. The major appeal to voters was the Proposition 103 provision mandating a reduction in insurance premiums. The law required that insurance rates be reduced to the level at which they stood one year earlier, and then reduced by an additional 20 percent for those lines of insurance included under the law.[40] In addition to these reductions, the law further requires an additional 20 percent discount on private passenger auto policies for "good drivers" (defined as a motorist who has been licensed for three years and

who does not have more than one moving violation during the past three years). Finally, the law provided that for one year after enactment, insurance rates could not be increased unless the commissioner found that an insurer was substantially threatened by insolvency.

Although the suggestion that consumers could "vote" themselves a price reduction in insurance (or any other commodity) seemed to many observers to be totally inconsistent with the ideas of private property and a market economy, the industry held its collective breath as the law was challenged in the courts by the Association of California Insurance Companies (ACIC) and the Insurance Services Office, together with six major insurers.

The California Supreme Court Decision The California Supreme Court rendered its decision on the constitutionality of Proposition 103 on May 4, 1989.[41] Although the court upheld the constitutionality of Proposition 103 generally, it invalidated the most objectionable feature, the requirement that insurers write coverage at a loss unless their solvency was threatened. According to the court, this requirement would have—in effect—confiscated the assets of insurers (and thereby the assets of insurers' stockholders). The court held the insolvency standard unconstitutional because it did not make allowance for the insurer to obtain a fair rate of return. A *fair rate of return,* in the view of the court, should provide return to stockholders commensurate with the return to stockholders in entities facing corresponding risks. In a Solomon-like compromise, the court let the rate rollback stand, but established reasonable conditions for obtaining relief.[42] No insurer is required to charge the rates set by the initiative unless it is unable to prove that such rates would deprive it of a reasonable rate of return. It is enormously significant that the court said, among other things, that an inadequate rate is, by definition, confiscatory, and that insurers are entitled to a fair return on the business they write.

[40] Proposition 103 applies to all lines of insurance except life insurance, title insurance, certain types of marine insurance, disability insurance, workers compensation insurance, mortgage insurance, and insurance transacted by county mutual fire insurers.

[41] *CalFarm Insurance v. Deukmejian* (1989) 43 Cal.3d 805 (258 Cal.Rptr. 161).

[42] In October 1990, the 9th District U.S. Court of Appeals declared unconstitutional a 15 percent automobile insurance rate rollback that was scheduled to take effect in Nevada on October 1. The court ruled unanimously that the Nevada rollback statute violated insurance companies' constitutional guarantee to earn a "fair and reasonable return on their investment."

The Territorial Rating Issue Given the underlying premise of Proposition 103—that voters could vote themselves a price reduction in insurance—it is surprising that the proposition passed by only the narrowest of margins. The reason that the margin of approval was not greater was that the law also mandated a significant change in the way auto rates are determined, significantly reducing the influence of territory on rates. Under the provisions of Proposition 103, auto rates must be based on the following factors, which must be applied with descending weight: (1) the driver's safety record; (2) miles driven annually; (3) years driving experience; and (4) "other factors which the Commissioner adopts based on their substantial relationship to the risk of loss." Noteworthy by its absence in the permissible criteria is territory, which may be considered only under the fourth, "other factors," element. The proposal to significantly reduce the influence of territory as a rating factor pitted the residents of urban areas against nonurban residents.[43] With the passage of Proposition 103, automobile insurance costs in California have been redistributed. Whether this redistribution is equitable is a part of the availability/affordability debate.

Income Redistribution Effects of Subsidies in Insurance

When the insurers in a given jurisdiction are required to write insurance at a loss for classes that would otherwise be unacceptable, the losses must be passed on to other policyholders in the form of higher rates. This is true whether the losses are incurred in the shared market, through mandated underwriting losses, or through the rate structure. In these situations, the insurance industry serves as a tax-gathering, benefit-dispensing system that redistributes income among members of society.

The use of private insurers as a tax-gathering and income-redistribution mechanism is not something that was planned or rationally conceived. The industry moved into the system over time, accepting cross-subsidization as a solution first for one class, and then another. The first rate-subsidy mechanisms were the automobile assigned risk plans, which were voluntar-

ily established by insurers out of the fear that if the private insurance industry did not provide the insurance the government would, and because there was no reason to believe that if the government entered the insurance market it would limit its writings to the undesirable risks.

Although the main issue for some people today is still the method we should use to provide the subsidy to those who demand availability and affordability, the entire debate has prompted a reappraisal of the systems that have been used in the past to subsidize some buyers. Increasingly, some observers are suggesting that the distinctions among the approaches to subsidization are artificial and that it makes little difference if the subsidy is granted through an industry pool, the tax system, or the rating system. In each case, one group in society pays a part of the costs that would—without government interference—fall on a different group. For many, the question is no longer how we should provide the subsidy, but whether it should be provided at all. To address the question of whether subsidies in the insurance market are wise, we should look more closely at the reasons why availability and affordability problems sometimes exist in the insurance market.

Causes of Availability Problems

Insurance availability problems arise for three reasons. The first is that the absolute supply of insurance is limited. Insurers are limited in the aggregate amount of insurance they may write by regulatory standards that dictate the relationship between premiums written and insurers' surplus. Because insurers are limited in the volume of insurance they can write, they must select from among the risks offered to them. An underwriter who must accept some risks and reject others will accept those that have the greatest likelihood of yielding a profit.

Besides the finite supply of insurance, availability problems arise when the price at which the insurance may be sold is less than the costs that will be incurred by selling it. Even if insurers had unlimited surplus, there would still be some classes of insurance that they would reject. There are some lines of insurance that are demonstrably unprofitable for insurers. The reason that some lines of insurance are unprofitable is that the anticipated losses and expenses of providing the insurance exceed the premium the insurer can charge for the coverage. Usually, this occurs in markets where regulatory restrictions on insurer

[43] Proposition 103 passed narrowly, with 4,853,298 (51.2 percent) of the electorate voting in favor of the law, and 4,630,689 (48.8 percent) voting against, a margin of 222,609. Interestingly, the margin in Los Angeles County was 641,710. Excluding Los Angeles County, the proposition was defeated statewide by 419,101 votes.

prices are somewhat inflexible. Given the choice between insuring exposures on which they are almost guaranteed to lose money and those on which they can reasonably expect to earn a profit, insurance companies logically choose the latter.

Finally, the cyclical nature of the insurance industry creates periodic shortages of insurance. The insurance cycle results in changes in insurers' surplus and profit. When surplus falls, the supply of insurance is reduced. The reduction in insurer profit that results from the soft phase of the cycle makes insurers more restrictive in their underwriting, further restricting availability.

Some critics have suggested that availability problems in insurance indicate that the mechanism is somehow defective, and not working properly. In fact, availability problems are simply an indication that the insurance marketplace is highly competitive. It reflects the pressures on insurers to operate at a point of efficiency and the absence of excess profits that might permit insurers to offer coverage in areas where they would expect to lose money.

Causes of Affordability Problems

Affordability refers to the consumer's ability to pay for the insurance product he or she requires. What is *affordable* is determined by (1) the cost of the insurance and (2) the income of the buyer. Insurance is deemed not affordable when its cost is too high. But *high* is a relative term, and the premium may be too high in an absolute sense or a relative sense. A premium may be high in relation to the buyer's income, or it may be high in an absolute sense, reflecting an excessive hazard. The important question from a policy perspective is whether the premium is high only in relation to persons with low income or if it is high because it reflects an excessive hazard. To express the equation as a truism, some affordability problems arise because the insurance premium is too high, and some because the buyer's income is too low.

The first affordability problem results not from the absolute level of the insurance premium itself, but from the price of insurance relative to the low income of the buyer. A premium that is affordable to a consumer with one income level may be unaffordable to another consumer with a lower income level. This affordability problem is the same problem the poor face with respect to the affordability of food, housing, reasonable health care, education, and a wide range of other goods and services. It is an income distribution problem, not a flaw in the insurance mechanism.

The second affordability problem results from the absolute level of the insurance premium itself, which in turn results from the hazards associated with the risk for which insurance is required. Here the premium is too high and the insurance is unaffordable even for the consumer who is not in the low-income class. There are some groups who, because of the hazards they represent, have found insurance *unaffordable* because the potential costs they represent to the insurer require a premium that they are unable or unwilling to pay. In this case, the insurance is unaffordable not because the consumer's income is too low, but because the cost of the insurance is considered too high. These affordability problems are a signal that there is a societal problem that ought to be addressed.

The insurance mechanism provides a service to society when it prices protection based on hazard. Insurance is a mirror of society, and through its process of spreading losses, it helps to identify activities and exposures that are greater than the price society is willing to pay.

Two decades ago, trampoline centers dotted the national landscape. For a dollar or so, consumers could bounce on a trampoline until their hearts were content, or until they injured themselves. Trampoline centers have disappeared, primarily because the insurance mechanism, through the free-market pricing process, said that these trampoline centers imposed costs on society that were too great for the benefits.

When the affordability problem results from excessive hazard rather than low income, providing a subsidy may make the insurance affordable, but it hides the problem that the premium reflects. By hiding problems, it eliminates societal pressures to do something about them. Subsidies that make insurance affordable in those cases in which the unaffordability is a function of the high hazards are counterproductive.

Affordability problems that result from income distribution may be an appropriate realm for subsidies. There are some members of our society who cannot afford insurance they need to purchase. Like the other necessities of life that the unfortunate require but cannot afford, there are many who feel that we, as a society, have an obligation to help them to obtain insurance or otherwise satisfy this need. The important question is the manner in which a subsidy should be provided. A second question is how those entitled to a subsidy can be identified.

Identifying those entitled to a subsidy is a problem because whether essential insurance is affordable is a matter of opinion. Sometimes what one can "afford" is a psychological phenomenon. The view that insurance is unaffordable may reflect low income, or it may be a psychological reaction to the compulsion to purchase a commodity that the individual does not really want. In compulsory automobile insurance, for example, many buyers would clearly be disinclined to purchase the insurance in the absence of a legal requirement. Consumers who would not voluntarily purchase automobile insurance without a legal requirement may feel that automobile insurance is unaffordable because they cannot afford it and the other things they would prefer to purchase with the dollars that go to pay auto insurance premiums. This psychological affordability problem must be distinguished from the affordability problem that afflicts the poor.

The subsidy could, of course, be made available through the pricing system. But this is enormously complicated. It requires compulsion and a complex regulatory structure to ensure compliance. Also, there is no mechanism in the insurance pricing system for identifying affordability problems or for distinguishing affordability problems that result from low income from those that result from excessive hazard.

Most important, attempts to provide subsidies through the pricing system create distortions in the market that diminish the benefits of competition. Cross-subsidies in insurance pricing can result in a misallocation of resources, a luxury that the nation's economy can ill afford.

Finally, there is an additional objection to providing subsidies through the insurance pricing system, even more compelling from the perspective of those who advocate subsidies for humanitarian reasons. It is that cross-subsidies in the insurance pricing system are likely to fail in achieving the intended results. There is no guarantee that use of the insurance pricing system to effect subsidies will result in a more equitable burden of the insurance cost.

Although cross-subsidies in insurance are designed to provide an income transfer from one segment of society to another, they differ from most other income redistribution programs in one critical respect. There is a basic assumption—unstated perhaps, but assumed—that the cost of insurance coverage is beyond the means of the beneficiaries of the subsidy, and that cross-subsidization is necessary for them to obtain this modern necessity. This is obviously unproven. Indeed, the reverse may be true. It is conceivable that those persons accepted at standard rates, but who are required to subsidize the high-risk insureds, are those to whom social equity would dictate that income be redistributed.

Cross-subsidies that operate through the pricing system are just as likely to take a dollar from a person in need and give it to an affluent person as to take a dollar from the rich person and give it to the poor one. The assumption that persons whose exposures justify high premiums are by definition deserving or in need of a subsidy is unwarranted.

Many observers believe that if members of society require a subsidy for the purchase of insurance, the subsidy should be provided through the tax system in the same way that subsidies to the needy are provided for food, housing, and medical care. The tax system is designed to achieve income redistribution objectives, and the insurance mechanism is not. Under the tax system, mechanisms are already in place that determine whether a subsidy is needed. Also, the progressive tax structure helps to ensure that those who provide the subsidy are those who are able to.

This is not to suggest that availability and affordability of insurance are not appropriate goals for society. It merely expresses the truism that availability and affordability are mathematically incompatible and inconsistent with a competitive market. It also suggests that not all instances in which insurance is unaffordable are appropriate subjects for subsidies. Finally, it suggests that if a subsidy is to be provided, it should not be provided through the insurance pricing system.

Availability and Affordability and Public Choice

The outcome of the debate over the availability and affordability of insurance promises to be an interesting test of the public choice theory of regulation, which views regulation as a part of a political-economic system that serves to reallocate wealth among competing groups based on preferences expressed in a political-economic marketplace. It suggests that regulation will tend to favor (subsidize) relatively small and well-organized groups that have a high per capita stake in the regulation at the expense of relatively large, poorly organized groups with a lower per capita stake. The cross-subsidization that already exists in FAIR plans, automobile insurance plans, joint underwriting associations, and similar mechanisms is testimony to the operation of the public choice theory in the past.

IMPORTANT CONCEPTS TO REMEMBER

antitrust	McCarran–Ferguson Act	use-and-file law
regulation	National Association of Insurance	competitive rating law
market failure theory	Commissioners	no-file approach
capture theory	accreditation program	rebating
public choice theory	zone examination	twisting
vested-in-the-public-interest	insolvency guarantee funds	involuntary markets
Paul v. Virginia	postinsolvency assessment funds	social pricing
Armstrong Investigation	Insurance Regulatory Information	gender-neutral rating
Merritt Investigation	System	redlining
SEUA Case	risk-based capital	availability
domestic insurer	reverse competition	affordability
foreign insurer	legal requirements of insurance rates	cross-subsidies
alien insurer	prior approval law	
Public Law 15	file-and-use law	

QUESTIONS FOR REVIEW

1. Explain why the field of insurance has been regarded as a type of business that requires government regulation.

2. Precisely what is meant by the statement that insurance is an industry that is *vested in the public interest*.

3. Identify the landmark decisions and statutes that led to the present status of insurance as respects the federal antitrust laws.

4. Briefly outline the provisions of Public Law 15.

5. Describe the four principal approaches to rate regulation in the property and liability field.

6. List and briefly explain the statutory requirements with respect to insurance rates.

7. Distinguish among a *domestic* company, a *foreign* company, and an *alien* company.

8. Describe the operation of the state insolvency funds. To what types of insurers do they apply?

9. Briefly describe the arguments for and against federal regulation of insurance.

10. What arguments would probably be advanced by those opposing a change from a prior approval rating law to an open competition law? What arguments would be advanced by those who favored the change?

QUESTIONS FOR DISCUSSION

1. In most states, the office of commissioner of insurance is an appointive office. Do you feel that it would be better if it were elective? Why or why not?

2. Why is it necessary for insurance agents and brokers in many states to pass qualification examinations? Do you feel that these examinations in your state are too hard or too easy?

3. It is generally agreed that unrestricted price competition among insurers could be detrimental to the public, yet some people argue that antirebating laws represent an unnecessary restriction on price competition among insurance agents, and that such laws should be repealed. What is your opinion?

4. "Competition can be depended on to keep rates from being excessive, and good management will keep them from being inadequate; regulation of rates is an infringement on the right of management to make business decisions." Do you agree or disagree with this statement? Why?

5. What, in your opinion, are the major factors that should be considered in evaluating state regulation of insurance as opposed to federal regulation? What advantages do you see in each system?

SUGGESTIONS FOR ADDITIONAL READING

Belth, Joseph M. *Life Insurance: A Consumer's Handbook,* 2nd ed. Bloomington: Indiana University Press, 1985.

———. "Price Competition in Life Insurance." *Journal of Risk and Insurance,* vol. 33, no. 3 (Sept. 1966).

———. *The Retail Price Structure in American Life Insurance.* Bloomington: Bureau of Business Research, Graduate School of Business, Indiana University, 1966.

Black, Kenneth, Jr., and Harold D. Skipper, Jr. *Life Insurance,* 13th ed. Englewood Cliffs, N.J.: Prentice-Hall, 2000, Chapter 33.

Crane, Frederick G. "Insurance Rate Regulation: The Reasons Why." *Journal of Risk and Insurance,* vol. 39, no. 4 (Dec. 1972).

Decaminda, Joseph P. "Insurance Regulation: State or Federal?" *CPCU Journal,* vol. 41, no. 1 (March 1988).

Goodwin, David. "The Case for Abolishing Anti-Rebate Laws." *CPCU Journal,* vol. 43, no. 4 (Dec. 1990).

Hanson, John S., Robert Dineen, and Michael B. Johnson. *Monitoring Competition: A Means of Regulating the Property and Liability Insurance Business.* Milwaukee: National Association of Insurance Commissioners, 1974.

Holtom, Robert B. *Restraints on Underwriting: Risk Selection, Discrimination, and the Law,* 2nd ed. Cincinnati: National Underwriter, 1982.

Ippolito, Richard A. "The Effect of Price Regulation in the Automobile Insurance Industry." *Journal of Law and Economics,* vol. 22, no. 1 (April 1979).

Kimball, S. L. *Insurance and Public Policy.* Madison: University of Wisconsin Press, 1960.

Macey, Jonathan R., and Geoffrey P. Miller. *Costly Policies: State Regulation and Antitrust Exemption in Insurance Markets.* Washington, D.C.: The AEI Press, 1993.

Manders, John M. "Proposed Congressional Amendments to the McCarran-Ferguson Act: Their Impact on State Regulation." *Journal of Insurance Regulation,* vol. 9, no. 1 (Sept. 1990).

National Association of Insurance Commissioners. *Issues 1994.* Kansas City, Mo.: National Association of Insurance Commissioners, 1994.

Patterson, Edwin W. *The Insurance Commissioner in the United States, A Study in Administrative Law and Practice.* Cambridge, Mass.: Harvard University Press, 1927.

Peltzman, Sam. "Toward a More General Theory of Regulation." *Journal of Law and Economics,* vol. 19 (Aug. 1976).

Phillips, C. F. *The Economics of Regulation.* Homewood, Ill.: Richard D. Irwin, 1969.

State of New York. *Report of the Joint Committee of the Senate and Assembly of the State of New York, Appointed to Investigate Corrupt Practices in Connection with Legislation, and the Affairs of Insurance Companies, Other Than Those Doing Life Insurance Business.* Assembly Document No. 30, 1911, p. 76.

Stigler, George. "The Theory of Economic Regulation." *Bell Journal of Economics and Management Science,* vol. 2, no. 1 (Spring 1971).

U.S. Department of Justice. *A Report of the Task Force on Antitrust Immunities: The Pricing and Marketing of Insurance.* Washington, D.C.: U.S. Government Printing Office, 1977.

Using the NAIC Insurance Regulatory Information System: Life and Health and Fraternal Insurance (1978 ed.). Milwaukee: National Association of Insurance Commissioners, 1978.

Using the NAIC Insurance Regulatory Information System: Property and Liability Insurance (1978 ed.). Milwaukee: National Association of Insurance Commissioners, 1978.

Vaughan, Emmett J. "Economic Implications of the Repeal of the McCarran-Ferguson Act." *State Solutions for State Problems.* Tallahassee, Fla.: The Last Manifesto, 1980.

———, and Therese M. Vaughan. "Proposition 103: Repealing the Law of Supply." *CPCU Journal,* vol. 43, no. 1 (March 1990).

———. "The Case for Retaining Anti-Rebate Laws." *CPCU Journal,* vol. 43, no. 4 (Dec. 1990).

Wenck, Thomas L. "Insurer Insolvency: Causes, Effects and Solutions." *Journal of Insurance Issues and Practices,* vol. 10, no. 2 (June 1987).

Williams, C. A., Jr., and Andrew F. L. Whitman. "Open Competition Rating Laws and Price Competition." *Journal of Risk and Insurance,* vol. 40, no. 4 (Dec. 1973).

WEB SITES TO EXPLORE

Insurance Information Institute	http://www.iii.org/
Insurance News Network	http://www.insure.com/
Insurance Services Office, Inc.	http://www.iso.com
Journal of Insurance Regulation	http://www.naic.org/finance/research/jir/jirinfo.htm
National Association of Insurance Commissioners	http://www.naic.org
National Conference of Insurance Guaranty Funds	http://www.ncigf.org
National Council on Compensation Insurance	http://www.ncci.com
National Underwriter Company	http://www.nuco.com/
Shadow Insurance Regulation Committee	http://rmi.lsu.edu/shadow/

FUNCTIONS OF INSURERS

What I advise is that each contentedly practice the trade he understands.

— HORACE
Epistles

CHAPTER OBJECTIVES

When you have finished this chapter, you should be able to

- Identify and differentiate between the two broad approaches to ratemaking
- Explain the purpose of underwriting and describe the steps in the underwriting process
- Identify the principal sources of information on which an underwriter may rely
- Identify and differentiate among the various types of adjusters
- Identify and explain the steps in the loss adjustment process

As a part of our study of the insurance mechanism and the way in which it works, it will be helpful to examine some of the unique facets of insurance company operations. The unique nature of the insurance product requires certain specialized functions that do not exist in other businesses. In addition, financial record keeping of insurers deviates from common practices. In this chapter, we will examine some of the specialized activities of insurance companies, and in the next we will look at the financial aspects of their operations.

1. Ratemaking
2. Production
3. Underwriting
4. Loss adjustment
5. Investment

In addition to these, there are, of course, various other activities common to most business firms such as accounting, human resource management, market research, and so on.

FUNCTIONS OF INSURERS

Although there are definite operational differences between life insurance companies and property and liability insurers, the major activities of all insurers may be classified as follows:

RATEMAKING

An insurance rate is the price per unit of insurance. Like any other price, it is a function of the cost of production. However, in insurance, unlike other industries, the cost of production is not known when

the contract is sold, and it will not be known until some time in the future, when the policy has expired. One fundamental difference between insurance pricing and the pricing function in other industries is that the price for insurance must be based on a prediction. The process of predicting future losses and future expenses and allocating these costs among the various classes of insureds is called ratemaking.

A second important difference between the pricing of insurance and pricing in other industries arises from the fact that insurance rates are subject to government regulation. As we noted in the preceding chapter, virtually all states impose statutory restraints on insurance rates. State laws require that insurance rates must not be excessive, must be adequate, and may not be unfairly discriminatory. Depending on the manner in which the state laws are administered, they impose differing limits on an insurer's freedom to price its products.

The ratemaking function in a life insurance company is performed by the actuarial department or in smaller companies, by an actuarial consulting firm.[1] In the property and liability field, advisory organizations accumulate loss statistics and compute loss costs for use by insurers in computing final rates, although some large insurers maintain their own loss statistics. In the field of marine insurance and inland marine insurance, rates are often made by the underwriter on a judgment basis.

In addition to the statutory requirements that rates must be adequate, not excessive, and not unfairly discriminatory, there are certain other characteristics considered desirable. To the extent possible, for example, rates should be relatively stable over time, so that the public is not subjected to wide variations in cost from year to year. At the same time, rates should be sufficiently responsive to changing conditions to avoid inadequacies in the event of deteriorating loss experience. Finally, whenever possible, the rate should provide some incentive for the insured to prevent loss.

[1] Much of the discussion of ratemaking in this chapter pertains to property and liability insurance. Because of the long-term nature of life insurance contracts, special complications mark the life insurance ratemaking process. Life insurance ratemaking and the actuarial basis for life insurance are treated in greater detail in Chapter 13.

Some Basic Concepts

A *rate* is the price charged for each unit of protection or exposure and should be distinguished from a *premium,* which is determined by multiplying the rate by the number of units of protection purchased. The unit of protection to which a rate applies differs for the various lines of insurance. In life insurance, for example, rates are computed for each $1000 in protection; in fire insurance, the rate applies to each $100 of coverage. In workers compensation, the rate is applied to each $100 of the insured's payroll.

Regardless of the type of insurance, the premium income of the insurer must be sufficient to cover losses and expenses. To obtain this premium income, the insurer must predict the claims and expenses and then allocate these anticipated costs among the various classes of policyholders. The final premium that the insured pays is called the *gross premium* and is based on a *gross rate*. The gross rate is composed of two parts, one designed to provide for the payment of losses and a second, called a *loading,* to cover the expenses of operation. That part of the rate that is intended to cover losses is called the *pure premium* when expressed in dollars and cents, and the *expected loss ratio* when expressed as a percentage.

Although some differences exist among different lines of insurance, in general, the pure premium is determined by dividing expected losses by the number of exposure units. For example, if 100,000 automobiles generate $30 million in losses, the pure premium is $300:

$$\frac{\text{Losses}}{\text{Exposure Units}} = \frac{\$30,000,000}{100,000} = \$300$$

The process of converting the pure premium into a gross rate requires addition of the loading, which is intended to cover the expenses that will be required in the production and servicing of the insurance. The determination of these expenses is primarily a matter of cost accounting. The various classes of expenses for which provision must be made normally include

- Commissions
- Other acquisition expenses
- General administrative expenses
- Premium taxes
- Allowance for contingencies and profit

In converting the pure premium into a gross rate, expenses are usually treated as a percentage of the final rate, on the assumption that they will increase proportionately with premiums. Since several of the expenses do actually vary with premiums (e.g., commissions and premium taxes), the assumption is reasonably realistic.

The final gross rate is derived by dividing the pure premium by a *permissible loss ratio*. The permissible loss ratio is the percentage of the premium (and so the rate) that will be available to pay losses after provision for expenses. The conversion is made by the formula

$$\text{Gross Rate} = \frac{\text{Pure Premium}}{1 - \text{Expense Ratio}}$$

Using the $300 pure premium computed in our previous example, and assuming an expense ratio of 0.40.

$$\text{Gross Rate} = \frac{\$300}{1 - 0.40} = \frac{\$300}{0.60} = \$500$$

While the pure premium varies with the loss experience for the particular line of insurance, the expense ratio also varies from one line to another, depending on the commissions and the other expenses involved.

Types of Rates

The approach to setting rates is quite similar in most instances, but it is possible to distinguish between two different types of rates: class and individual.

Class Rates The term *class rating* refers to the practice of computing a price per unit of insurance that applies to all applicants possessing a given set of characteristics. For example, a class rate might apply to all types of dwellings of a given kind of construction in a specific city. Rates that apply to all individuals of a given age and sex are also examples of class rates.

The obvious advantage of the class-rating system is that it permits the insurer to apply a single rate to a large number of insureds, simplifying the process of determining their premiums. In establishing the classes to which class rates apply, the ratemaker must compromise between a large class, which will include a greater number of exposures and thereby increase the credibility of predictions, and one sufficiently

narrow to permit homogeneity. For example, a rate class could be established for all drivers, with one rate applicable regardless of the age, sex, or marital status of the driver or the use of the automobile. However, such a class would include exposures with widely varying loss potential. For this reason, numerous classes are established, with different rates for drivers based on factors such as those listed. Class rating is the most common approach today and is used in life insurance and most property and liability fields.

Individual Rates In some instances the characteristics of the units to be insured vary so widely that it is deemed desirable to depart from the class approach and calculate rates on a basis that attempts to measure more precisely the loss-producing characteristics of the individual. There are four basic *individual rating* approaches: judgment rating, schedule rating, experience rating, and retrospective rating.

Judgment Rating In some lines of insurance, the rate is determined for each individual risk on a judgment basis. Here the processes of underwriting and ratemaking merge, and the underwriter decides whether the exposure is to be accepted and at what rate. *Judgment rating* is used when credible statistics are lacking or when the exposure units are so varied that it is impossible to construct a class. This technique is most frequently applied in the ocean marine field, although it is also used in other lines of insurance.

Schedule Rating *Schedule rating,* as its name implies, makes rates by applying a schedule of charges and credits to some base rate to determine the appropriate rate for an individual exposure unit. In commercial fire insurance, for example, the rates for many buildings are determined by adding debits and subtracting credits from a base rate, which represents a standard building. The debits and credits represent those features of the particular building's construction, occupancy, fire protection, and neighborhood that deviate from this standard. Through the application of these debits and credits, the physical characteristics of each schedule-rated building determine that building's rate.[2]

[2] Schedule rating is used less frequently today than in the past. In 1976, the Insurance Services Office introduced a new class-rating program for many types of commercial buildings that had previously been schedule rated, leaving only the larger and more complex buildings to be schedule rated.

Experience Rating In *experience rating,* the insured's own past loss experience enters into the determination of the final premium. Experience rating is superimposed on a class-rating system and adjusts the insured's premium upward or downward, depending on the extent to which his or her experience has deviated from the average experience of the class. It is most frequently used in the fields of workers compensation, general liability, and group life and health insurance. Generally, experience rating is used only when the insured generates a premium large enough to be considered statistically credible.[3]

Although the exact method of adjusting the premium to reflect experience varies with the type of insurance, the general approach is usually the same. The insured's losses during the experience period are compared with the expected losses for the class, and the indicated percentage difference, modified by a credibility factor, becomes a debit or credit to the class-rated premium. The experience period is usually three years, and the insured's loss ratio is computed on the basis of a three-year average. The credibility factor, which reflects the degree of confidence the ratemaker assigns to the insured's past experience as an indicator of future experience, varies with the number of losses observed during the experience period.

The experience-rating formula used in general liability insurance illustrates the principle. The formula is:

$$\text{Modification} = \frac{\text{Actual Loss Ratio} - \text{Expected Loss Ratio}}{\text{Expected Loss Ratio}} \times \frac{\text{Credibility}}{\text{Factor}}$$

Assuming, for the purpose of illustration, that the expected loss ratio is 60 percent and that the insured has achieved a 30 percent loss ratio, and further that the credibility factor is .20, the computation would be:

$$\frac{0.30 - 0.60}{0.60} = 0.50 \times 0.20 = 10\%$$

The comparison of the actual loss ratio and the expected loss ratio indicates a 50 percent reduction in premium. However, the indicated reduction is tempered by the credibility factor, resulting in a 10 percent credit.

In most instances, the use of experience rating is mandatory for those insureds whose premiums exceed a specified amount.

Retrospective Rating A *retrospective-rating* plan is a self-rated program under which the actual losses during the policy period determine the final premium for the coverage, subject to a maximum and a minimum. A deposit premium is charged at the inception of the policy and then adjusted after the policy period has expired, to reflect actual losses incurred.[4] In a sense, a *retro plan* is like a cost-plus contract, the major difference being that it is subject to a maximum and a minimum. The formula under which the final premium is computed includes a fixed charge for the insurance element in the plan (the fact that the premium is subject to a maximum), the actual losses incurred, a charge for loss adjustment, and a loading for the state premium tax. Retrospective rating is used in the field of workers compensation, general liability, automobile, and group health insurance. However, only very large insureds will usually elect these plans.

Adjusting the Level of Rates When rates are initially established for any form of insurance, the rate is by definition an arbitrary estimate of what losses are likely to be. Once policies have been written and the loss experience on the policies emerges, the statistical data generated become a basis for adjusting the level of rates. Past losses are used as a basis for projecting future losses, and the anticipated losses are combined with estimated expenses to arrive at the final premium.

Any change in rate levels indicated by raw data is usually tempered by a *credibility factor,* which reflects the degree of confidence the ratemakers believe they should attach to past losses as predictors of future losses. The credibility assigned to a particular body of loss experience is determined primarily by the number of occurrences, following the statistical principle that the greater the sample size, the more closely will observed results approximate the underlying probability. To obtain a sufficiently large

[3] Many companies use a *merit-rating system* for automobile insurance, in which the individual insured's premium is based on that person's past driving record, as indicated by at-fault accidents and certain traffic violations. While this represents a form of experience rating in the broadest sense of the term, it is more accurately classified as a form of class rating, in which the class is defined as those drivers with no "points," those with one "point," and so on.

[4] Retrospective rating is illustrated in the appendix to this chapter.

number of observed losses for achieving an acceptable level of credibility, the ratemaker must sometimes include loss experience over a period of several years. The less frequent the losses in a particular line of insurance, the longer the period needed to accumulate loss statistics necessary to achieve a given level of credibility.

One of the principal drawbacks of a long experience period is that when the interval is too long, the underlying conditions that influence frequency and severity are likely to have changed, and adjustments reflecting such changes must be included in the ratemaking process. One approach is to weight the experience of the most recent years more heavily than that of the earlier years. Another technique is the use of trend factors. A *trend factor* is a multiplier calculated from the trend in average claim payments, the trend of a price index, or some similar series of data. The trend indicated by past experience is usually extended into the future to the midpoint of the period for which the rates will be used.

Catastrophe Modeling and Rate Making

Given the rash of catastrophes that have occurred during the past decade, some insurers have adopted a tool known as *catastrophe modeling,* originally for underwriting, but increasingly for rating purposes. Catastrophe modeling (also called *cat modeling*) uses computer simulations, based on experience and the insurer's known distribution of insured property. Insurers initially adopted catastrophe modeling to measure their exposure in areas where earthquakes and hurricanes are likely. Increasingly, they are suggesting that the catastrophe models may be an appropriate tool for ratemaking. For exposures such as earthquakes—characterized by low frequency and high severity—past experience may be an inadequate predictor of the future. One problem is that most of the catastrophe models that have been developed thus far are proprietary products and their designers are not prepared to divulge the programming on which the models are based. Some regulators have been concerned over the "black-box" nature of catastrophe modeling. Early in 1998, the Florida insurance commissioner rejected a rate increase requested by the state's windstorm pool, primarily because the increase was based on projections generated by a catastrophe model. In rejecting the risk, the commissioner stated, "I will not let the consumers of Florida become hostage to a computer." In addition to regulators, some scientists also question

cat models, arguing that the past disaster patterns on which they are based may not be appropriate guides to the future. In support of this contention, they cite evidence the global climate is changing, potentially causing more hurricanes and other bad storms. But traditional approaches to ratemaking are also subject to the criticisms that past experience may not properly reflect the future. It seems likely that catastrophe modeling will eventually find a place in property insurance rate making.

Legend of Actuarial Precision

Public opinion to the contrary, insurance ratemaking is not an exact science. The law of large numbers and the experience of the past permit actuaries to make estimates about future experience, but these must be qualified. When estimating future experience, the actuary implicitly says, "If things continue to happen in the future as they have in the past, this is what will happen…" But things do not happen in the future as they have happened in the past; some adjustment must be made to allow for changes that are likely to modify future losses. But even the adjustments to allow for deviations from past experience may be inadequate, particularly when the magnitude of the deviations is greater than anticipated. Of course, if the future differs from the past favorably, there is no great problem. However, if the deviation is adverse, the rate predicated on past experience may prove inadequate.

A major distinction between the fields of property and liability insurance and life insurance has been the differences in the deviation of present from past experience. In the case of life insurance, we have seen a continued improvement in life expectancy. This has benefited insurance companies in two ways. First, since people have been living longer than originally expected, the insurers have been permitted to delay payment of funds, which can thus continue to be invested. In addition, the people who have lived longer than anticipated have paid premiums on their policies longer than expected.

In the property and liability field, actual results have also deviated from those expected, but in this case the outcome has been less favorable for insurers. Inflationary pressures, which push up the cost of repairs and construction, rising medical costs, an increasing rate of automobile accidents, soaring liability judgments, and other similar factors have all acted to the detriment of insurance companies. Inflation does not affect the loss under a life insurance

policy because of the agreement to pay a fixed sum of dollars. In property and liability insurance, however, departures from past experience have caused severe difficulties.[5]

PRODUCTION

The production department of an insurance company, sometimes called the agency department, is its sales or marketing division. This department supervises the external portion of the sales effort, which is conducted by the agents or salaried representatives of the company. The various marketing systems under which the outside salespeople operate were discussed in Chapter 5.

The internal portion of the production function is carried on by the production (or agency) department. It is the responsibility of this department to select and appoint agents and assist in sales. In general, it renders assistance to agents in technical matters. *Special agents,* or people in the field, assist the agent directly in marketing problems. The *special agent* is a technician who calls on agents, acting as an intermediary between the production department and the agent. This person renders assistance when needed on rating and programming insurance coverages and also attempts to encourage the producers.

UNDERWRITING

Underwriting is the process of selecting and classifying exposures. It is an essential element in the operation of any insurance program, for unless the company selects from among its applicants, the inevitable result will be selection adverse to the company. As we noted in Chapter 2, the future experience of the group to which the rates are applied will approximate that of the group on which those rates are based only if both have approximately the same loss-producing characteristics. There must be the same proportion of good and bad risks in the group insured as there were in the one from which the basic statistics were taken. The tendency of the poorer-than-average risks to seek insurance to a greater extent than the average or better-than-average risks

must be blocked. The main responsibility of the underwriter is to guard against adverse selection.

It is important to understand that the goal of underwriting is not the selection of risks that will not have losses. It is to avoid a disproportionate number of bad risks, thereby equalizing the actual losses with the expected ones. In addition to this goal, there are certain other objectives. While attempting to avoid adverse selection through rejection of undesirable risks, the underwriter must secure an adequate volume of exposures in each class. In addition he or she must guard against congestion or concentration of exposures that might result in a catastrophe.

Few factors are as important to the success of the insurance operation as the underwriting function, for it is directly connected with the adequacy of rates. Actuaries compute the rates. The underwriter must determine into which of the classes, if any, each exposure unit should go. Poor underwriting may wipe out the efforts of the actuary, rendering a good rate inadequate. For this reason, those who perform the underwriting function must develop a keen sense of judgment and a thorough knowledge of the hazards associated with various types of coverage.

The underwriting process often involves more than acceptance or rejection. In some instances, an exposure that is unacceptable at one rate may be written at a different rate. In the life insurance field, for example, applicants may be classified as standard, preferred, substandard, and uninsurable. *Standard risks* are persons who, according to the company's underwriting standards, are entitled to insurance without a rating surcharge or policy restrictions. The *preferred-risk* classification includes those whose mortality experience, as a group, is expected to be above average, and to whom the insurer offers a lower than standard rate. The most common preferred class today consists of nonsmokers, for whom many insurers now offer a preferred-risk rate.

Substandard risks are persons who, because of a physical condition, occupation, or other factors, cannot be expected, on average, to live as long as people who are not subject to these hazards. Substandard applicants are insurable, but not at standard rates. Policies issued to substandard applicants are referred to as *rated policies* (or *extra risk policies*) and require a higher-than-standard premium rate to cover the extra risk where, for example, the insured has impaired health or a hazardous occupation. Usually, substandard risks will pay a percentage surcharge, a flat additional premium, or in some cases receive a

[5] An additional cause of these difficulties has been a degree of price inflexibility owing to the regulatory system.

policy subject to restrictions not included in the policies for standard risks. Most life insurers use a numerical rating system under which a point value is assigned for each type of physical disability or negative influence. The total of all points represents the expected mortality increase over that which is expected for standard or normal risks. The surcharge may apply only for a period of time and then disappear, or it may continue throughout the policy. In some situations, the policies issued to substandard risks may limit the death benefit during the first few years to the premiums paid.

Finally, there are some applicants that are simply *uninsurable*. The applicant may be uninsurable because of high physical or moral hazard, or if he or she suffers from a disease that is so rare or a situation so unique that the insurer does not have the experience to derive a proper premium.

The Agent's Role in Underwriting

Since the application for the insurance originates with the agent, this person is often called a field underwriter. The use of the term *underwriter* in reference to an agent is more common in the field of life insurance than in property and liability, which is surprising in view of the fact that the agent plays a far more important role in the underwriting process in the latter type of insurance. As a matter of fact, a part of the compensation of property and liability insurance agents is based on the profitability of the business they write. This is accomplished through a device known as a *contingency contract* or *profit-sharing contract,* the terms of which provide the agent with an additional commission at the end of the year if the business he or she has submitted has produced a profit for the company. The intent of these profit-sharing agreements is to encourage the agent to underwrite in his or her office.

Underwriting Policy

Underwriting begins with the formulation of the company's underwriting policy, which is generally established by the officers in charge of underwriting. The underwriting policy establishes the framework within which the desk underwriter makes decisions. This policy specifies the lines of insurance that will be written as well as prohibited exposures, the amount of coverage to be permitted on various types of

exposure, the areas of the country in which each line will be written, and similar restrictions. The desk underwriter, as the individual who applies these regulations to the applications is called, is usually not involved in the formation of the company underwriting policy.

Process of Underwriting

To perform effectively, the underwriter must obtain as much information about the subject of the insurance as possible within the limitations imposed by time and the cost of obtaining additional data. The desk underwriter must rule on the exposures submitted by the agents, accepting some and rejecting others that do not meet the company's underwriting requirements. When a risk is rejected, it is because the underwriter feels that the hazards connected with it are excessive in relation to the rate. There are four sources from which the underwriter obtains information regarding the hazards inherent in an exposure:

1. Application containing the insured's statements
2. Information from the agent or broker
3. Information from external agencies
4. Physical examinations or inspections

Application The basic source of underwriting information is the application, which varies for each line of insurance and each type of coverage. The broader and more liberal the contract, usually the more detailed the information required in the application. The questions on the application are designed to give the underwriter the information needed to decide if he or she will accept the exposure, reject it, or seek additional information.

Information from the Agent or Broker In many cases the underwriter places much weight on the recommendations of the agent or broker. This varies, of course, with the experience the underwriter has had with the particular agent in question. In certain cases the underwriter will agree to accept an exposure that does not meet the underwriting requirement of the company. Such exposures are referred to as *accommodation risks,* because they are accepted to accommodate a valued client or agent.

Information from External Agencies In most cases, the underwriter will request a report from an

external agency that specializes in providing information about individuals or organizations to their customers. These include credit bureaus, cooperative information bureaus within the insurance industry itself, and public agencies, such as a state department of motor vehicles. In the case of an application for commercial insurance, the underwriter may request a Dun & Bradstreet report. For the individual auto insurance buyer, the underwriter will request both a credit report and a copy of the individual's driving record from the state department of motor vehicles. Sometimes, the underwriter will request a report from a company that specializes in investigations. All the information is pertinent in the decision to accept or reject the application. For example, the financial status of the applicant is important in both the property and liability field and in the life insurance field, although for different reasons. In the property and liability field, evidence of financial difficulty may be an indication of a potential moral hazard. In life insurance, there is concern because an individual who purchases more life insurance than is affordable is likely to let the policy lapse, a practice that is costly to the company.

In addition to the information available from public sources and credit bureaus, the underwriter may seek information from one of the cooperative information bureaus the industry supports. The best example of this is the *Medical Information Bureau* (MIB), which maintains centralized files on the physical condition of applicants who have applied for life insurance in member companies.

Physical Examinations or Inspections In life insurance, the primary focus is on the health of the applicant. The medical director of the company lays down principles to guide the agents and desk writers in the selection of risks, and one of the most critical pieces of intelligence is the report of the physician. Physicians selected by the insurance company supply the insurer with medical reports after a physical examination; these reports are a very important source of underwriting information. In the field of property and liability insurance, the equivalent of the physical examination in life insurance is the inspection of the premises. Although such inspections are not always conducted, the practice is increasing. In some instances this inspection is performed by the agent, who sends a report to the company with photographs of the property. In other cases, a company representative conducts the inspection.

Postselection Underwriting

In some lines of insurance, the insurer has the opportunity periodically to reevaluate its insured. When the coverage in question is cancellable or optionally renewable,[6] the underwriting process may include *postselection* (or *renewal*) *underwriting,* in which the insurer decides if the insurance should be continued.

When a review of the experience with a particular policy or account indicates that the losses have been excessive, the underwriter may insist on an increased deductible at renewal. In other instances, the underwriter may decide that the coverage should not be continued and will decline to renew it, or even cancel it outright. Insurance companies differ in the extent to which they exercise their renewal underwriting options. In certain fields, such as auto insurance, some insurers are very selective and show little hesitation in refusing to renew or in canceling an insured who has demonstrated unsatisfactory loss experience.

Restrictions on Postselection Underwriting In addition to the fact that postselection underwriting is obviously possible only with policies that may be canceled or in which renewal is optional with the insurer, the ability of insurers to engage in postselection underwriting is considerably less in some lines today than in the past. Because cancellation or the refusal of the insurer to renew some forms of insurance can work an undue hardship on the insured, many states have enacted statutes or have imposed regulations that restrict the insurer's right to exercise these options.

Some laws merely require the insurer to give advance notice of its intent to refuse renewal. These laws were designed to prevent an insurer from canceling or from refusing to renew without providing adequate time for the insured to obtain replacement coverage. In some cases, the laws prohibit midterm cancellation, except for certain specified reasons, once a policy has been in effect for a designated period of time, such as 60 days. In addition, the laws of many states prohibit insurers from canceling or refusing to renew coverage because of an insured's age, sex, occupation, race, or place of residence. In most cases, the

[6] Cancellation is the process of terminating coverage prior to the normal expiration date.

laws require the insurer to furnish an explanation of the reason for cancellation or declination.

Although the restrictions on the right of a company to cancel or refuse to renew have been beneficial in many areas, they have also made it harder to obtain insurance. When legislative restraints are imposed on the insurers' ability to engage in postselection underwriting, insurers typically become increasingly selective before issuing a policy in the first place.

Credit Scoring

For the past 20 years, insurance companies have used *credit scoring* as a tool for underwriting auto and homeowners insurance, a practice that has recently become a point of controversy. Originally, credit scoring was developed for use by lenders in judging the credit risk of applicants for mortgages, car loans, and credit cards. Credit bureaus have long provided lenders with information on individuals' credit histories. Credit scoring goes further; it quantifies this history as a score, based on statistical correlation between such factors as the record of credit payments by groups of individuals and the likelihood of credit default. These scores, known as FICO scores, range from 375 to 900.

The leading provider of credit scoring information to the insurance industry is the Atlanta-based firm, ChoicePoint, an offshoot of the Equifax credit-reporting company. ChoicePoint maintains a database called CLUE (Comprehensive Loss Underwriting Exchange), which serves as the basis for the credit scores it generates. The statistical models used by ChoicePoint are based on generic scoring models developed by the California-based firm, Fair, Isaac and Co.

Critics argue that use of credit scoring for insurance underwriting decisions is totally inappropriate and that a person's credit history and driving are unrelated. Some insurers have also factored credit scores into their rating system, adding to the controversy. Insurers and independent actuaries respond that the correlation between credit scores and insurance loss ratios is indisputable and that the statistical models used in credit scoring allow insurers to segment applicants according to their likelihood of loss and price insurance with greater precision. ChoicePoint argues that the use of the term *credit score* is a part of the problem and that the scores it provides to the insurance industry are more appropriately referred to as *insurance bureau scores.*

Actually, the link between credit scores and the likelihood of insurance losses is not only plausible, it is also logical. In a sense, a credit score is a report card on how the individual has managed credit risks. It is reasonable to assume that one who is responsible in managing these credit risks will be responsible in managing his or her pure risks.

In 1997, the National Association of Insurance Commissioners issued a whitepaper, *Credit Reports and Insurance Underwriting,* which addresses some of the regulatory issues relating to unfair discrimination that may arise in the use of credit reports and credit scoring in insurance underwriting. A limited number of states have enacted legislation limiting the use of credit scores in insurance underwriting.[7] The use of credit scoring is also regulated by federal law, under the Fair Credit Reporting Act and the Equal Credit Opportunity Act, which prohibit consideration of ethnic group, religion, gender, marital status, nationality, age, income or address.

LOSS ADJUSTMENT

One basic purpose of insurance is to provide for the indemnification of those members of the group who suffer losses. This is accomplished in the loss-settlement process, but it is sometimes a great deal more complicated than just passing out money. The payment of losses that have occurred is the function of the claims department. Life insurance companies refer to employees who settle losses as claim representatives or benefit representatives. The nature of the difficulties frequently encountered in the property and liability field is evidenced by the fact that employees of the claims department in this field are called adjusters.

It is obviously important that the insurance company pay its claims fairly and promptly, but it is equally important that the company resist unjust claims and avoid overpayment of them. The view is rapidly increasing among insurers that prompt, courteous, and fair claim service is one of the most effective competitive tools available to a company.

[7] States in which legislation has been introduced or that have adopted regulations placing restrictions on the use of credit scoring in underwriting insurance are Colorado, Iowa, Indiana, Kansas, Nebraska, and Washington. In addition, Maryland is proposing a regulation restricting the use of credit reports in underwriting and rating.

Adjusters

Broadly speaking, an *adjuster* is an individual who investigates losses. He or she determines the liability and the amount of payment to be made. Adjusters include agents as well as staff, bureau, independent, and public adjusters. It is quite common for the agent to function as an adjuster in the case of small property losses. Many agents have been granted *draft authority* by their companies, which means that they are authorized to issue company checks in payment of losses up to some stipulated amount. Even in cases where the amount of the loss exceeds the draft authority, the agent may handle the settlement of the loss.

Most insurers employ adjusters who are salaried representatives of the company. The use of a company staff adjuster in a given area is dictated by the amount of work available. In a locality where the company has a large volume of claims, it will use a salaried staff adjuster in preference to an adjustment bureau or an independent adjuster. If the volume of claims is too small to support a full-time adjuster, the company will contract for adjusting service. It is not economically feasible to maintain an adjuster in every area in which the company writes insurance. Likewise, it would be too expensive to send an adjuster into a distant area simply for the purpose of adjusting one loss. In such cases, the insurer may use an adjustment bureau. The *adjustment bureaus* were originally organized and owned by insurers for the purpose of settling fire losses. Although the insurers that originally owned the bureaus have relinquished their ownership, the organizations continue to be referred to as *bureaus*. The largest of the adjustment bureaus is the General Adjustment Bureau, organized in 1896 by a group of insurance companies.[8]

As an alternative, the company may hire an *independent adjuster,* who does not work for a bureau, but instead contracts services directly to the insurance company. These adjusters normally do not handle claims for a single company, but work for any firm that is involved in the community and does not have a staff adjuster or adjusting bureau. The independent adjuster bills each company directly for the expense of adjustment.

The *public adjuster* is quite different from the other types discussed. Unlike the other adjusters, all of whom represent the insurance company in the loss-settlement process, the public adjuster represents the policyholder. A public adjuster is employed by an insured who has suffered a loss and does not feel able to handle his or her own claim. A public adjuster is a specialist available to the insured. The most common method of compensation for public adjusters is a contingency fee basis, under which the adjuster collects a percentage of the settlement; the usual fee is 10 percent of the amount recovered from the insurance company. In return for his fee, the public adjuster performs the actions normally required of the insured such as preparing estimates of the loss, presenting the amount of the claim to the insurance company, and negotiating the final settlement. A limited number of public adjusters hold one of two professional designations granted by the National Association of Public Insurance Adjusters. The Certified Professional Public Adjuster (CPPA) designation and the Senior Professional Public Adjuster (SPPA) designation are granted to public adjusters who pass a rigorous examination.

Courses of Action in Claim Settlement

Two basic courses of action are open to the company when confronted with a claim: pay or contest. In most cases there is little question concerning coverage, and payment of the loss is the most common procedure, but in those instances when the company feels that a claim should not be paid, it will deny liability and thereby contest the claim. The company might deny payment on two basic grounds: either because the loss did not occur or because the policy does not cover the loss. A loss might not be covered under the policy because it does not fall within the scope of the insuring agreement, it is excluded, it happened when the policy was not in force, or the insured had violated a policy condition.

Adjustment Process

In determining whether to pay or contest a claim, the adjuster follows a relatively set settlement procedure with four main steps: (1) notice of loss, (2) investigation, (3) proof of loss, and (4) payment or denial of the claim. The details of these steps vary with the type of insurance.

Notice The first step in the claim process is the notice by the insured to the company that a loss has occurred. The requirements differ from one policy to

[8] Following an investigation by the U.S. Department of Justice in 1970, the companies that owned the General Adjustment Bureau agreed to divest themselves of their stock in the company.

another, but in most cases the contract requires that the notice be given "immediately" or "as soon as practicable." Some contracts stipulate that notice be given in writing, but even in these, the requirement is not strictly enforced. Normally, the insured gives notice that a loss has occurred by informing the agent, and this satisfies the contract.

Investigation The investigation is designed to determine if there was actually a loss covered by the policy, and, if so, the amount of the loss. In deciding whether there was a covered loss, the adjuster must determine first that there was in fact a loss, and then whether the loss is covered by the policy. Determination as to whether there was a loss is the simpler of the two. There are, of course, instances in which the claimant attempts to defraud the insurer, and in some instances payment is undoubtedly made where there has not in fact been a loss. Once it has been determined that a loss has occurred, the adjuster must determine whether the loss is covered under the policy. First, was the policy in effect at the time of the loss? If the policy is newly issued, did the loss take place before the policy became effective? Or at the other end of the time spectrum, did the policy expire before the loss took place? Once it has been established that the loss took place during the policy period, there is still the possibility that the insured might have violated a condition that caused the suspension or voidance of the contract. If it appears that the policy was in effect at the time of the event and that there was a loss, was the peril causing the loss insured against in the policy? In the case of property insurance, does the property damaged or lost meet the definition of the property insured? The location of the property is still another question, because some contracts cover property only at a specific location, or are applicable only in certain jurisdictions. Finally, the adjuster must decide if the person making the claim is entitled to payment under the terms of the policy.

If the answer to all these questions is yes, the loss is covered. Yet to be determined is the amount of the loss, which in most cases can be far more complicated than the determination of whether or not coverage applied.

Proof of Loss Within a specified time after giving notice, the insured is required to file a proof of loss. This is a sworn statement that the loss has taken place and gives the amount of the claim and the circumstances surrounding the loss. The adjuster normally assists the insured in the preparation of this document.

Payment or Denial If all goes well, the insurance company draws a draft reimbursing the insured for the loss. If not, it denies the claim. The claim may be disallowed because there was no loss, the policy did not cover the loss, or the adjuster feels that the amount of the claim is unreasonable.

Difficulties in Loss Settlement

It is inevitable that there will be disagreements regarding loss settlements. In some instances, the insured will mistakenly feel that a loss should have been covered under the policy when in fact it is not. Adjusters, being human, also err, and there are occasions when a legitimate claim is denied. In addition to the question of whether the loss is covered, the amount of the loss is a continuing source of trouble. Value in most instances is a matter of opinion, and we should therefore not be surprised that the insured and the adjuster may differ regarding the amount of the loss. For these reasons the role of the adjuster is a delicate one. He or she must be fair, and yet must try not to leave the insured disgruntled. This is difficult when a loss is not covered.

On the surface, it would seem that an insured is relatively powerless against the insurance company in the event of a dispute. This is not the case. In those cases where the disagreement is over the amount of the loss, most policies provide for compulsory arbitration on the request of either party. In the case of a denial based on an alleged lack of coverage, the insured who feels unfairly treated may appeal to the state regulatory authority, which is charged with the protection of the consumer's interest. Finally, the insured has recourse through the courts. In some instances, the only alternative remaining to the insured is to bring suit against the insurer.

THE INVESTMENT FUNCTION

As a result of their operations, insurance companies accumulate large amounts of money for the payment of claims in the future. When these are added to the funds of the insurers themselves, assets total over $3.1 trillion. It would be a costly waste to permit these funds to remain idle, and it is the responsibility of the insurer's finance department or a finance committee to see that they are properly invested.

Because a portion of their invested funds must go to meet future claims, the primary requisite of insurance company investments is safety of principal. In addition, the return earned on investment is an important variable in the rating process: Life insurance companies assume some minimum rate of interest earnings in their premium computations. Increasingly, property and liability insurers are also required to include investment income in their rate calculations. It may be argued that even when investment income is not explicitly recognized, it subsidizes the underwriting experience and is therefore a factor in ratemaking in this field as well.

The percentage composition of investments for life insurers and property and liability insurers is indicated in Table 7.1. The largest component of the investment portfolio for both types of insurers is bonds. Life insurers invest slightly more than 70% of their general account assets in bonds, four-fifths of which are corporate bonds. Property and liability insurers invest 59 percent of their assets in bonds, with about two-thirds of these in state, federal, and municipal bonds. Life insurers invest less than 5 percent of their general fund assets in common stocks[9], while property and liability insurers invest nearly a quarter of their assets in stocks. Other differences are the mortgages, real estate investments and policy loans of life insurers and the receivables from agents of property and liability insurers.

MISCELLANEOUS FUNCTIONS

In addition to those already discussed, various other functions are necessary for the successful operation of an insurance company. Among these are the legal function, accounting, and engineering.

Legal

The legal department furnishes legal advice of a general corporate nature to the company. In addition, it counsels on such matters as policy forms, relations

TABLE 7.1 **Percentage Composition of Insurer Investments**

Type of Investment	Life Insurers	Property and Liability Insurers
Corporate Bonds	55.5	19.6
Government Bonds	14.9	39.8
Corporate Stocks	4.9	24.1
Mortgages	11.2	0.2
Real Estate	1.2	
Policy Loans	4.9	
Receivables from Agents		7.2
Miscellaneous	7.4	9.1
	100.0	100.0

Source: American Council of Life Insurers, Life Insurance Fact Book 2001 (Washington, D.C., ACLI, 2001), and A. M. Best and Company, *Best's Aggregates and Averages* (Morristown, N.J.: Best, annual).

with agents, compliance of the company with state statutes, and the legality of agreements. It may or may not render assistance to the claims department in connection with claim settlements. Many insurers have a separate legal staff as a part of the claims department, which is independent from the legal department.

Accounting

Historically, the primary function of the accounting department has been the recording of company operating results and the maintenance of all accounting records necessary for the company's periodic financial statements, especially the report to the commissioner of insurance. Insurance company accounting is a highly specialized field. In the past, the principal focus has been on external reporting, primarily because of the requirements of the report to the commissioner. Recently several companies have moved toward developing an internal information system, with greater emphasis on internal or managerial accounting.

Engineering

The engineering department, which is unique to the property and liability insurers, is charged with the responsibility of inspecting premises to be insured to determine their acceptability. In addition, the engineering department benefits the company's insured by making loss-prevention recommendations.

[9] In addition to their general account assets, life insurers maintain *separate accounts,* which are segregated from the insurers' general investment account and that are used primarily for retirement plans and variable life insurance products. About 80 percent of the assets in separate accounts are invested in equities, with another 12 percent invested in bonds.

Retrospectively rated programs are an approach to rating in which transfer and retention are combined in dealing with risk. Retrospective rating is an alternative to guaranteed-cost programs, and allows the premium for each period of protection to vary, depending on the loss experience for that period. It differs from guaranteed cost plans in the fact that the premium is variable, based on the insured's loss experience.

A retrospectively rated insurance policy is a self-rated plan under which the actual losses experienced during the policy period determine the final premium for the coverage, subject to a maximum and a minimum. A deposit premium is charged at the inception of the policy, and this premium is adjusted after the policy period has expired to reflect the actual losses incurred. The formula under which the final premium is computed includes a fixed charge for the insurance element in the program (i.e., the fact that the premium is subject to a maximum), the actual losses incurred, a charge for handling losses, and the state premium tax.

In a sense, a retrospectively rated policy is like a cost-plus contract; the major difference is that the premium is subject to a maximum and a minimum. Viewed from a slightly different perspective, a retrospective program is like a self-insured program up to the maximum premium. The lower the losses of the insured, the lower the final premium. The higher the losses, the higher the premium.

THE RETROSPECTIVE FORMULA

In order to provide a basis for the discussion of the retrospective approach to rating, it may be helpful to examine the retrospective rating formula that is used in workers compensation insurance. The basic formula used in this line of insurance is:

$$\text{Retrospective Premium} = \left[\text{Basic Premium} + \left(\text{Ratable Losses} \times \frac{\text{Loss Conversion}}{\text{Factor}} \right) \right] \times \text{Tax Multiplier}$$

The *basic premium* is the fixed-cost element in the plan, which does not vary with the level of losses. *Converted losses* are actual losses sustained, plus a percentage of losses for loss adjustment expense. The *tax multiplier* is a variable charge, equal to the premium that will be due to the state from the insurer, and is based on the total premium generated by the formula. The final premium for the year is determined by adding the basic premium to actual losses and loss adjustment expense, and then adding the amount of the premium tax that will be payable by the insurer to the state.

Although the terminology tends to be confusing, we can illustrate the elements in the retrospective rating formula by indicating one set of values for each of the elements in the formula. A large manufacturer with a workers compensation experience-rated premium of $100,000, for example, might elect a retrospectively rated plan under which the insurer would charge a fixed cost (the basic premium) of $20,000, plus the amount of all losses adjusted to include the cost of loss adjustment expenses (the loss conversion factor) and 3 percent of this total for the premium tax, all subject to a maximum of $150,000 and a minimum of $50,000. At the end of the policy period the final computation would generate a premium based on the amount of losses as illustrated by the schedule below.

(1) Incurred Losses	(2) Converted Losses (Losses + 14%)	(3) Basic Premium	(4) Basic Premium + Converted Losses	(5) Column (4) × 1.03 Tax Multiplier	
$ 20,000	$ 22,800	$20,000	$ 42,800	$ 50,000	Minimum
40,000	45,600	20,000	65,000	66,950	
60,000	68,400	20,000	88,400	91,052	
80,000	91,200	20,000	111,200	114,536	
100,000	114,000	20,000	134,000	138,020	
$120,000	$136,800	$20,000	$156,800	$150,000	Maximum

The insurer determines the final premium for the policy after the year is over by adding the basic premiums indicated above ($20,000) to actual losses incurred plus the cost of adjusting those losses. The cost of adjusting losses is indicated by the *loss conversion factor.* Losses are surcharged by 14 percent to cover loss adjustment expense (i.e., actual losses are multiplied by 1.14). After the charges for losses, loss adjustment expense and the basic premium are combined, this total is then increased by the amount of the premium tax that the insurer must pay to the state. In this way, the premium will vary directly with losses up to the point at which the maximum premium is reached. In this way, the premium varies directly with the loss experience during the policy period.

IMPORTANT CONCEPTS TO REMEMBER

rate	judgment rating	substandard risk
premium	schedule rating	uninsurable
gross rate	experience rating	rated policies
loading	retrospective rating	contingency contract
pure premium	credibility factor	profit-sharing contract
expected loss ratio	trend factor	accommodation risk
loss ratio	catastrophe modeling	postselection underwriting
expense ratio	special agent	benefit representative
permissible loss ratio	Medical Information Bureau (MIB)	staff adjuster
combined ratio	adjustment bureau	independent adjuster
class rating	standard risk	public adjuster
individual rating	preferred risk	

QUESTIONS FOR REVIEW

1. List and briefly explain the steps in the underwriting process.

2. What sources of information are available to the underwriter? Explain the importance of each source. Why are multiple sources necessary?

3. Sales representatives of property and liability insurance companies sometimes refer to the "sales prevention department." What department of the company are they referring to? Explain.

4. Why is the pricing of the insurance product more difficult than pricing of other products?

5. What is the difference between a premium and a rate?

6. List and briefly explain the steps in the loss-adjustment process.

7. Briefly explain the nature of retrospective rating plans and why they are used.

8. List several reasons for which a claim might be completely denied.

9. Name the various types of adjusters used by property and liability insurers.

10. Distinguish between an independent adjuster and a public adjuster.

QUESTIONS FOR DISCUSSION

1. How do you account for the feeling held by many people that there is something almost "immoral" about an insurance company canceling a policy in the middle of the policy term? Do you agree or disagree with this position?

2. Do you agree with legislation imposing restrictions on the right of an insurance company to engage in postselection underwriting?

3. At one time it was suggested that the problem of providing insurance protection against loss by flood be met by providing coverage against the flood peril as a mandatory part of the Standard Fire Policy. Do you agree with this solution? Why or why not?

4. Do you think that loss adjustment would be most difficult in the field of (a) life insurance, (b) property insur-

ance, or (c) liability insurance? What training would you recommend for adjusters in each of these three fields?

5. "Pricing is much more difficult in insurance than in other business fields, because the cost of production is not known until after the product has been delivered." To what extent is this statement true and to what extent false?

SUGGESTIONS FOR ADDITIONAL READING

Black, Kenneth, Jr., and Harold D. Skipper, Jr. *Life Insurance,* 13th ed. Englewood Cliffs, N.J.: Prentice-Hall, 2000. Chapters 23, 24, 32.

Donaldson, J. H. *Casualty Claims Practice,* 4th ed. Homewood, Ill.: Richard D. Irwin, 1984.

Holtom, Robert B. *Restraints on Underwriting: Risk Selection, Discrimination and the Law,* 2nd ed. Cincinnati: National Underwriter, 1982.

Kenney, R. *Fundamentals of Fire and Casualty Strength,* 4th ed. Dedham, Mass.: Kenney Insurance Studies, 1967.

Launie, J. J., J. Finley Lee, and Norman A. Baglini. *Principles of Property and Liability Underwriting,* 3rd ed. Malvern, Pa.: Insurance Institute of America, 1986.

Markham, James J., ed. *Property Loss Adjusting,* vol. 1 and vol. 2. Malvern, Pa.: Insurance Institute of America, 1990.

Markham, James J., Kevin M. Quinley, and Layne S. Thompson. *The Claims Environment.* Malvern, Pa.: Insurance Institute of America, 1993.

Webb, Bernard L., Connor M. Harrison, and James J. Markham. *Insurance Operations,* 2nd ed., vols. 1 and 2. Malvern, Pa.: American Institute for CPCU, 1997.

WEB SITES TO EXPLORE

Casualty Actuarial Society	http://www.casact.org
Claims Magazine	http://www.claimsmag.com/
Insurance Information Institute	http://www.iii.org/
Insurance Marketing Communication Association	http://connectyou.com/ins/imca.htm
Insurance Services Office, Inc.	http://www.iso.com
Medical Information Bureau	http://www.mib.com/
National Association of Public Insurance Adjusters	http://www.napia.com/
National Underwriter Company	http://www.nuco.com/
Property Loss Research Bureau	http://homepage.interaccess.com/~plrb/
Society of Actuaries	http://www.soa.org/

FINANCIAL ASPECTS OF INSURER OPERATIONS

■

Nobody was ever meant to remember or invent,
what he did with every cent.

— ROBERT FROST
The Hardship of Accounting

CHAPTER OBJECTIVES

When you have finished this chapter, you should be able to

- Explain the nature of insurance company reserves
- Explain the effect of statutory accounting requirements on the indicated profitability of insurers
- Describe the types of reinsurance and discuss the purposes of reinsurance
- Describe the ways in which insurance companies are taxed

In a general sense, the financial statements of insurance companies are similar to those of other business firms. However, state regulations require certain modifications of the traditional accounting practices in insurance accounting. These changes can distort the financial statements of insurers if they are not recognized. This chapter points out a few of the major differences between insurance accounting and accounting practices in other businesses and relates the implications of these differences to the financial operations of insurers.

STATUTORY ACCOUNTING REQUIREMENTS

The set of accounting procedures embraced by insurance regulators is referred to as the *statutory accounting system,* because it is required by the statutes of the various states. Virtually all insurance company accounting is geared to the National Association of Insurance Commissioners (NAIC) *Annual Statement Blank*—a standardized reporting format developed by the NAIC by which each company

must file an annual statement with the insurance department of its home state and with every other state in which it is licensed to do business. With minor exceptions, the required information and the manner in which it is to be submitted are the same for all states. There are two versions of the *Convention Blank,* one for property and liability insurers and one for life insurers. The information required in these documents and the procedures for recording that information (which are also spelled out by the NAIC) set the ground rules for insurance accounting.

Basically, the statutory system is a combination of a cash and an accrual method and differs from *generally accepted accounting principles* (GAAP) in a number of ways. Because the principal emphasis in statutory accounting is on reflecting the ability of the insurer to fulfill its obligations under the contracts it issues, statutory accounting is, in most areas, ultraconservative.

Differences between Statutory Accounting and GAAP

Before examining the specific requirements of statutory accounting and its applications to property and liability and life insurers, it may be helpful to note briefly some of the areas in which statutory accounting differs from GAAP. Since these differences apply to both the life and the property and liability fields, a brief overview will eliminate the need for repetition in the following discussion.

Admitted and Nonadmitted Assets The first difference between GAAP and statutory accounting lies in the criteria for inclusion of assets in the balance sheet. Although most noninsurance companies recognize all assets, insurance companies recognize only those that are readily convertible into cash. These are called *admitted assets,* and only they are included in the balance sheet of an insurance company. Assets such as supplies, furniture and fixtures, office machines and equipment, and premiums past due 90 days or more are nonadmitted assets and do not appear on the balance sheet. The elimination of these *nonadmitted assets,* whose liquidity is questionable, tends to understate the equity section of the balance sheet.[1]

Valuation of Assets Under GAAP, insurer assets have traditionally been valued on balance sheets at the lower of cost or market value or, in the case of debt securities (e.g., mortgages and bonds), at amortized value. The use of amortized value for debt securities was justified on the assumption that insurers would hold the investments to maturity and, therefore, changes in market value prior to maturity were not important. In reality, however, insurers did not hold all assets to maturity. In May 1993, the Financial Accounting Standards Board issued Statement No. 115, *Accounting for Certain Investments in Debt and Equity Securities,* which changed the reporting of many insurer assets on GAAP financial statements.[2] This standard affects GAAP accounting for marketable equity securities and all debt securities. The standard requires companies to classify securities as held-to-maturity, trading, or available-for-sale. Only assets in the held-to-maturity category may be valued at amortized cost. The held-to-maturity category is limited to debt securities (e.g., bonds and mortgages) that the company has both a positive intent and ability to hold to maturity. Securities in the other two categories are carried at fair market value.

Under the statutory system, stocks are carried at market value, as determined by the NAIC Valuation of Securities Task Force based on market values at the end of the year. Bonds not in default of interest or principal payments are carried at their amortized value.[3] (Bonds in default are carried at market value.) This means that changes in the market value of stocks held by insurers directly influence the equity section of the balance sheet, while changes in the market value of bonds do not. Unrealized capital

[1] In addition to the distinction between *admitted assets* and *nonadmitted assets,* insurance accounting also distinguishes between *ledger assets* and *nonledger assets.* Ledger assets are assets at cost as carried in the general ledger of the company. They are identical with the assets carried by any business firm. Nonledger assets include those not normally reflected in the balance sheet, such as the excess of market value over the cost of stocks owned. Admitted assets = Ledger assets + Nonledger assets – Nonadmitted assets.

[2] FASB No. 115 applies to all commercial enterprises. Given the large amount of debt and equity securities held by insurers and other financial institutions, it is likely to have a significant impact on those companies.

[3] Bonds are evidences of debt and promise to pay their face value at maturity. At maturity, the bond of a solvent corporation will be worth its face value, but the market value of bonds may vary from this face value over time, depending on the bond's interest rate compared with the market rate. For example, assume that a 20-year $1000 bond was issued 10 years ago with a 5 percent interest rate. Now assume that the market rate on bonds with similar risk increases to 10 percent. The bond in question will decrease in value, since a $500 investment will generate the same return as the $1000 bond. Conversely, if the interest rate falls, the market value of the bond will increase above its face value. If a bond is purchased in the market for other than its face amount, the book value will differ from the bond and must gradually be adjusted over time so that it will equal the face of the bond at maturity. The process of gradually writing the value of the bond up or down so that the book value will equal the face at maturity is called amortizing.

gains or losses on stocks under the statutory system are reported directly as changes in equity, but are not realized until the sale is made.

Matching of Revenues and Expenses A final major difference between statutory accounting and GAAP is in the matching of revenues and expenses. Under GAAP revenues and expenses are matched, with prepaid expenses deferred and charged to operations when the income produced as a result of incurring those expenses is recognized. Under statutory accounting, all expenses of acquiring a premium are charged against revenue when they are incurred, rather than being treated as prepaid expenses that are capitalized and amortized. The revenue generated, on the other hand, is treated as income only with the passing of the time for which protection is being provided. In the property and liability field, for example, commissions are generally payable when the policy is issued, and such expenses are charged against income at the time they are incurred. The related premium income, however, is deferred, and equal portions corresponding to the protection provided over time are recognized only as that time passes. Thus, while revenue is deferred until earned under the statutory system, there is no similar provision for the deferral of prepaid expenses; revenue is accounted for on an accrual basis, while expenses are accounted for on a cash basis. GAAP would dictate that both the revenue and the expenses related to the acquisition of that revenue be deferred and amortized over the life of the policy.

Other Differences In addition to the three major distinctions just outlined, there are certain other differences between statutory accounting and GAAP. However, those noted are the principal differences and also the ones that create the greatest distortions in the financial statements of insurers.

Terminology

Insurance accounting and finance also have their own established terminology along with the differences in conventions. Some of the specialized terminology will be dealt with later, but there are two important concepts that should be established at the outset.

Policyholder's Surplus The equity section of the balance sheet for any business consists of the excess of asset values over the liabilities of the firm. For an insurance company, it consists of either one or two

items. In the case of stock companies, it consists of the capital stock, which represents the value of the original contributions of the stockholders, plus surplus, which represents amounts paid in by the organizers in excess of the par value of the stock and any retained earnings of the company. Since there is no capital stock in mutual insurance companies, the total of the equity section is called surplus. In both stock and mutual companies, this is referred to as *policyholders' surplus,* indicating that this is the amount available, over and above the liabilities, to meet obligations to the company's policyholders.[4]

Reserves The major liabilities of insurance companies are debts to policyholders; they are called *reserves.* In insurance accounting and insurance terminology generally, the term *reserve* is synonymous with *liability.* Understanding insurance company finances will be greatly simplified if this point is clear.[5]

The NAIC Codification Project

Because the Securities Exchange Commission (SEC) requires companies with publicly traded stock to issue financial statements on the basis of generally accepted principles (GAAP), most stock insurers have historically issued two sets of financial statements, one based on statutory accounting principles and one based on GAAP. Mutual insurers, on the other hand, traditionally developed financial statements on the basis of statutory accounting principles. In the past, most mutual insurers did not issue financial statements on the basis of GAAP, and statutory statements were used for general purpose distribu-

[4] The modern trend in accounting terminology is away from the term *surplus.* The term *earned surplus* is gradually changing to *retained earnings,* and *paid-in surplus* is being replaced by the term *capital paid-in in excess of par.* Nevertheless, because of the statutory reporting requirements and the connotation that the policyholders' surplus is the total excess of assets over liabilities, the term *surplus* is, and will probably remain, acceptable in insurance terminology.

[5] The use of the term *reserve* to indicate a liability will undoubtedly make your accounting professor turn purple. This usage is probably misleading to the layperson and is contradictory to modern accounting terminology. In general connotation, the term *reserve* is a fund or asset accumulation. In addition, the term may refer to an asset valuation reserve, such as the *reserve for depreciation,* although this term is declining in favor of *accumulated depreciation.* Finally, *reserve* may refer to earmarked retained earnings. Unless otherwise specified, when used in insurance accounting, the term *reserve* always refers to a liability.

tion, including reports to both regulators and policy-holders.

Over the years, the question arose as to how the accounting profession would treat audits of statutory accounting statements. In the 1990s, the statutory accounting system came under criticism by independent public accountants, most notably, the AICPA, who argued that statutory accounting principles were not clearly articulated. They were not generally codified in state law, differences existed across states, and the sources of statutory accounting were found in numerous places (including instructions to the annual statement, the NAIC Accounting Practices and Procedures manuals, the Valuation of Securities manual, and individual state law, regulation and administrative rules). The conceptual framework for statutory accounting was not clear, critics argued, making unqualified opinions inappropriate. In 1993, the AICPA notified the NAIC that it would no longer issue unqualified audit opinions on statutory financial statements after 1994.

The NAIC responded to these criticisms of statutory accounting by initiating a project to more clearly define the principles underlying statutory accounting statements. The result is the replacement of the previous NAIC *Accounting Practices and Procedures Manuals* with a new, more comprehensive one—*Accounting Practices and Procedures Manual Effective January 1, 2001.* The new manual enables insurers to present their information in a manner that is more useful and meaningful to regulators and CPAs. The NAIC also developed a new statutory accounting model law for adoption by the states and made Codification of Statutory Accounting Principles a requirement for accreditation.[6] The AICPA has reversed its position and public accountants continue providing audit opinions for statements prepared on a statutory basis.

PROPERTY AND LIABILITY INSURERS

We will begin our discussion of the financial aspects of the operations of specific types of insurers with an analysis of the property and liability insurers, since the implications of statutory accounting tend to have more impact in this field. As a point of departure, we will discuss the unusual requirements of statutory

accounting that result in a combination of a cash and accrual system of accounting.

Concept of Earned Premiums

Most businesses count sales as income when the sale is made and make no provision for the possible contingency of return sales. Insurance, on the other hand, is unusual in that it collects in advance for a product that will not be delivered until some time in the future. Although premiums are paid in advance, the insurers' obligations under the contracts issued are all in the future. If the insurance company were permitted to use premiums currently being collected for future protection to meet obligations paid for in the past, it would be perpetrating a fraud on current purchasers. The only way that the advance premium form of operation can be safely administered is to require insurance companies to make some provision in their financial statements recognizing the fact that, although premiums have been collected, the company has not yet fulfilled the obligations they represent. This is done in two ways. First, insurers are permitted to include premiums as income only as the premiums become *earned*—that is, only as the time for which protection is provided passes. In addition, the insurer is required to establish a deferred income account as a liability, called the *unearned premium reserve,* the primary purpose of which is to place a claim against assets that will presumably be required to pay losses occurring in the future.

Unearned Premium Reserve The unearned premium reserve represents the premiums that insureds have paid in advance for the unexpired terms of their outstanding policies. Just as the insured carries *prepaid insurance premiums* as an asset on his or her books, so the insurance company enters them as a liability on its books. For each policy, the unearned premium reserve at the inception of the policy period is equal to the entire gross premium that the insured has paid. During the policy period, the unearned premium reserve for the policy declines steadily to zero by a straight mathematical formula.

The unearned premium reserve is computed by tabulating the premiums on policies in force according to the year (or month) of issue and the term. It is customary to assume that policies issued during any period were uniformly distributed over that time. If the income over the period is uniformly distributed, the result is the same as if the business had been

[6] States have until January 1, 2004 to adopt the model law.

written at the interval's midpoint. For example, annual premiums written during the first month of the year will almost have expired by the end of the year, while those written at year's end will still have 11 months to run. Thus, at the end of a given year, annual policies written during the calendar year are assumed to have been in force, on the average, for one-half of their term and still have one-half to run. To illustrate, if the insurance company writes $100,000 in premiums each month during the year, total premiums written that year will be $1.2 million. Assuming that all insurance sold consists of annual policies, the company will have earned $600,000 of the total written by the end of the year and will have an unearned premium reserve for these policies of $600,000.[7]

The unearned premium reserve is sometimes called the *reinsurance reserve* on the premise that it represents the amount that would be required to transfer the insurance in force to another insurer if the primary insurer should retire from the business. As we shall see, the amount that would actually be needed to reinsure existing policies is somewhat less than the full amount of the unearned premium reserve.

Incurred Losses

In calculating the losses sustained during a particular period, the statutory approach to accounting uses the matching concept, in that losses are compared with premiums earned. Because there may be delays between the occurrence of a loss and the time when it is actually paid, statutory accounting makes a distinction between *incurred* losses and *paid* losses. *Incurred losses* refer to those losses actually taking place during the particular period under consideration, regardless of when they are actually paid. *Paid losses* refer to losses paid during a particular period regardless of the time that the loss occurred. Recognition of the difference between paid and incurred losses is made through liability accounts called *loss* or *claim reserves.*

Loss Reserves There are two major classes of *loss reserves:* a reserve for losses reported but not yet paid and a reserve for losses that have occurred but

have not yet been reported to the insurance company. Reserves for losses reported but not yet paid can be established by an examination of each claim and an approximation based on what the loss will ultimately be. Alternatively, averaging formulas can be applied to blocks of outstanding claims. The reserve for losses incurred but not reported (losses the insurer presumes have already taken place but have not been submitted because of a lag in claim reporting) are usually estimated on the basis of the past experience of the insurer.

Expenses Incurred

For the purpose of statutory accounting, all commissions and other expenses in acquiring business are required to be charged against revenue when they are incurred. Experience has indicated that a very high portion of a company's expenses (perhaps as much as 80 to 90 percent) originates with the cost of writing new or renewal policies. Even though these expenses are charged against revenue when incurred, the insurer is required to establish an unearned premium reserve equal to the entire premium on a policy. This means that there is a redundancy in the unearned premium reserve; since expenses have already been paid, the unearned premium reserve is actually higher than need be. This, in turn, means that surplus is actually understated to the extent of the excess in the unearned premium reserve.[8]

Summary of Operations

There are two sources of profit or contribution to surplus for a property and liability insurer: underwriting gains and investments. The annual statement summarizes the results of operations in both of these areas.

Summary of Underwriting Results—Statutory Profit or Loss The combination of a cash basis of accounting for expenses and an accrual basis for premiums can, as one might suspect, create distortions in

[7] The most acceptable and most widely used method of calculating unearned premiums is called the monthly pro rata basis. Under this approach, 1/24 of the premium for an annual policy is considered earned during the month in which the policy is written, 1/12 is earned each month from month 2 through month 12, and 1/24 is earned in month 13.

[8] Those familiar with the property and liability insurance industry are aware of the inaccuracy in the figures presented in the insurer's balance sheets and make allowance for it. There is no universally accepted formula for doing this, but one method is to adjust surplus and the unearned premium reserve by the amount of the redundancy of the unearned premium reserve, usually considered to be about 35 percent.

the reported underwriting results of an insurer. Since expenses must be paid when the policy is written and before the premium income has been totally earned, and the premiums are included in the computation only as earned, the net effect is to understate profit whenever premiums written exceed premiums earned (when premium volume is increasing) and to overstate profit when premiums earned exceed premiums written (when premium volume is declining). This can be illustrated by an example:

The XYZ Insurance Company, a newly organized stock company, is about to go into business. At the time of its organization, its balance sheet looks something like this:

Assets	Liabilities and Net Worth	
Cash $1,000,000	Liabilities	None
	Net worth (policyholders' surplus)	
	Capital	$500,000
	Surplus	$500,000

We will assume that the expected and actual loss ratio on the policies written is 50 percent, that expenses incurred are 40 percent of premiums written, leaving a 10 percent profit.

During the first year of operation, the company writes $1 million in annualized premiums, distributed equally throughout the year. At the end of the year, one-half of these premiums will have been earned, and the unearned premium reserve will be $500,000. The income statement for the initial year of operation will indicate the following:

Premiums earned	$500,000
Expenses incurred	
(40% of premiums written)	−400,000
Losses incurred	
(50% of premiums earned)	−250,000
Statutory profit (loss)	($150,000)

Now, it is obvious that the company did not really lose money during the year, but under the assumptions required in the statutory computation, a loss of $150,000 is indicated. This loss is merely an illusion created by the fact that premiums are included in the computation only as they are earned but expenses are included as they are paid. Looking at the balance sheet, cash will have increased by

$350,000 ($1 million in premiums minus $400,000 in expenses minus $250,000 in losses), while liabilities will have increased by the amount of unearned premiums. The amount by which the increase in liabilities exceeds the increase in assets represents a reduction in the amount of the company's surplus. The balance sheet at the end of the first year of operation would appear as follows:[9]

Cash	$1,350,000	Unearned premium reserve	$500,000
		Policyholders' surplus	$850,000

To illustrate the effect of a decline in premium volume, let us assume that the insurer writes no new business in the second year and that the unearned premiums at the beginning of the year all become earned. The summary of operations for the second year would appear as follows:

Premiums earned	$500,000
Expenses incurred	
(40% of premiums written)	0
Losses incurred	
(50% of premiums earned)	−250,000
Statutory profit (loss)	$250,000

At the end of this second year, in which no new policies were issued, liabilities will have been reduced by $500,000 (the amount of unearned premiums that became earned), and cash will have been reduced by the amount of the $250,000 in losses paid. The resulting balance sheet would appear as follows:

Cash	$1,100,000	Unearned premium reserve	0
		Policyholders' surplus	$1,100,000

Several pertinent points can be recognized from the preceding simulation. First, it illustrates the manner in which statutory accounting distorts the actual results of an insurer's operations. During a year when premium volume is growing, the necessary increase

[9] For the sake of simplicity, it is assumed that all losses are paid when incurred. In actual practice the statement would also include loss reserves.

in the unearned premium reserve will result in an understatement of the underwriting gain and may even cause the company to report a statutory loss. The requirements of statutory accounting and the redundancy in the unearned premium reserve allow a company's operations to appear more profitable than they are during periods of declining business in force and less profitable in periods when business in force is increasing.

A second significant point is that an increase in premium writings, other things being equal, will result in a reduction in policyholders' surplus. The management of every insurer must constantly watch the growth of its business to make certain that a balance is maintained between its liabilities and its surplus to policyholders. Although there is no consensus on exactly what the ratio should be, agreement is widespread that there is some desirable ratio of policyholders' surplus to premiums written or to the unearned premium reserve.[10] This means that the drain on surplus created by the statutory accounting requirements places a limit on the ability of an insurer to write new business.

Investment Results The investment income of a property and liability insurer is composed basically of interest on bonds, dividends on stocks, and interest on collateral loans and bank deposits. Investment income is shown separately from the results of underwriting.

Statutory investment income does not include unrealized capital gains or losses. These result from the statutory requirement that stocks be carried by insurance companies at market value. If the market value of stocks held by the company increases, the company has unrealized capital gains; if the value of stocks held decreases, it has unrealized losses. These unrealized gains and losses are not included in the insurer's statement of operations but are entered directly as increases or decreases in policyholders' surplus.

[10] A rule of thumb that developed in the monoline era held that fire insurers should have $1 in surplus for every $1 of unearned premium reserve and that casualty companies should have $1 in surplus for every $2 in premiums written. This was known as the Kenney Rule, after Roger Kenney, an insurance financial analyst who formalized the axiom in 1948. For a revised discussion of the original concept, see Roger Kenney, *Fundamentals of Fire and Casualty Insurance Strength,* 4th ed. (Dedham, Mass.: The Kenney Insurance Studies, 1967). The National Association of Insurance Commissioners' IRIS System (discussed in Chapter 6) suggests premium writings of three times policyholders' surplus.

An Indicator of Underwriting Profitability—The Combined Ratio Clearly, statutory accounting procedures provide little in the way of an accurate picture regarding the true profitability of underwriting operations. A statutory loss may be the result of an increase in the amount of profitable business being written; on the other hand, it could also be the result of poor underwriting experience on a level or declining volume of business.

At this point, the reader may be wondering if insurance companies ever know whether or not they are really making a profit. The obvious answer is yes. However, instead of depending on the statutory figures, informed observers gauge the profitability of a given company on the basis of its *combined ratio,* which is derived by adding the loss ratio and the expense ratio for the period under consideration. The *loss ratio* is computed by dividing losses incurred during the year by premiums earned. The *expense ratio* is computed by dividing expenses incurred by premiums written. Because the loss ratio is computed on the basis of losses incurred to premiums *earned* and the expense ratio is based on premiums *written,* the combined ratio merges data that are not precisely comparable. Nevertheless, the ratio is widely used as an indication of the *trade profit* of an insurer. If the total of these two ratios is less than 100 percent for the year, underwriting was conducted at a profit, and in the degree indicated.

LIFE INSURANCE COMPANIES

The statutory accounting procedures applicable to life insurers, like those required of property and liability insurers, differ from GAAP. In addition, principally because of the long-term nature of life insurance contracts, the statutory procedures used in life insurance also differ from those used in the property and liability field. Life insurance policies usually run for many years from the date of issue and therefore entail a longer commitment on the part of the insurer that must be recognized in the accounting procedures.

Life Insurer Assets

One of the principal differences in the financial structure of life insurers and property and liability insurers is in the composition of assets. Like the property and liability segment, life insurers also distinguish

between admitted and nonadmitted assets. However, as we noted in the preceding chapter, the latter tend to concentrate their investments in bonds and mortgages, with only a small amount (less than 10 percent) of their total assets invested in stocks. Because the mortgages and most bonds are carried at amortized value, the listed or book value of a life insurer's assets tends to be more immune from fluctuations than does that of a property and liability company.

Life Insurer Liabilities

The principal liabilities of a life insurer, like those of a property and liability insurer, are its obligations to its policyholders. The major liabilities appearing on the balance sheet of a life insurance company include the following.

Policy Reserves Unearned premium reserves also arise in life insurance, but here they are called *policy reserves.* Under most forms of life insurance, the insured pays more than the cost of protection during the early years of the contract, and the insurer is required to set up policy reserves representing the amount of this overpayment. In addition, many forms of life insurance and annuities have a substantial savings or investment element, under which the insured accumulates cash values that will be paid out at some maturity date in the future. Policy reserves must also be established for these contracts.

Like the reserves in the property and liability field, life insurance policy reserves also contain an element of redundancy. In life insurance the redundancy arises from the fact that the rates and reserves are computed using interest assumptions that are lower than actual interest earnings and mortality assumptions that are higher than actual experience.[11]

Reserves on Supplementary Contracts Not all death claims or endowment maturities are paid out in a lump sum. In many instances the beneficiary may elect to leave the policy proceeds with the insurance company and draw only the interest, or interest and a part of the principal. These arrangements are evidenced by *supplementary contracts,* for which the insurer must establish a reserve recognizing its obligation to the beneficiary.

Dividends Left to Accumulate Life insurance policies frequently pay dividends, which represent the insured's participation in the divisible surplus of the company. Companies permit the insured several options in connection with these dividends, one of which is to leave them on deposit with the company, where they accumulate interest. When the insured elects to leave the dividends on deposit, the insurer establishes a reserve, recognizing its liability to the insured.

Reserves for Unpaid Claims As in the case of property and liability insurers, life insurance companies also establish reserves for unpaid claims. These include reserves for claims that have been reported to the company and are still in the process of settlement, and also a reserve for possible deaths that, because of a delay in reporting, may not yet be known to the company. Since life insurance claims tend to be settled quickly, the amount of these reserves is generally small.

Asset Valuation Reserve and Interest Maintenance Reserve Since 1951, life insurers have been required to include special liabilities in their annual statement to provide a cushion against adverse fluctuations in the value of assets held. The original requirement was for a Mandatory Security Valuation Reserve, which addressed stock and bond values. This was replaced in 1992 by two reserves: The Asset Valuation Reserve and the Interest Maintenance Reserve. The new reserves address all invested assets, not just stocks and bonds.[12]

Life Insurers' Policyholders' Surplus

The stability of life insurance operations does not require surplus in the same amounts as that of property and liability insurers. The policyholders' surplus of life insurers tends to represent a much smaller percentage of total assets than does that of property and liability insurers. Although the policyholders' surplus of property and liability insurers generally equals somewhere between 35 and 50 percent of total assets, policyholders' surplus of life insurers averages about 8 percent of total assets. Some states (e.g., New York) impose legal limits on the level of surplus.

[11] The computation of life insurance policy reserves is discussed in greater detail in Chapter 13.

[12] Property and liability insurance companies carry a *Special Valuation Reserve for Liabilities,* but this is not usually a liability account. Rather, it is an earmarked part of surplus.

Life Insurer Summary of Operations

The annual summary of a life insurer's operations, as contained in the Annual NAIC Convention Blank, includes three principal items of income and three major deductions from income:

Life Insurer Income	Deductions from Income
Premiums from policyholders	Contractual benefits to policyholders and beneficiaries
Considerations on supplementary contracts and dividends left with the company to accumulate	Increases in required reserves on policies in force
Investment income	Operating expenses and taxes

Income Although life insurers do not use the concept of *earned premiums* as do property and liability insurers, they accomplish the same end in a somewhat different manner. All premiums due or received are included as income during the year in which they are collected or become due, regardless of whether they represent payment for current or future protection. Then, in order to recognize the company's obligations in connection with premiums paid for future protection, the net increase in the legal reserves is deducted from income. The effect is to include as net income only those premiums received for present protection.

Similarly, when an insured dies or an endowment policy matures, the claim is treated as a deduction from income, regardless of whether or not the policy proceeds are actually paid out. When the policy proceeds are left with the company under a supplementary contract, the amount of the benefit is treated as the premium on the supplementary contract and is included as income. Dividends left with the company to accumulate at interest are handled in the same fashion. When a dividend becomes payable to an insured, it is treated as a deduction from income, even though the insured may elect to leave the dividend on deposit. Dividends left on deposit, after having been deducted from income as a contractual benefit paid to policyholders, are then included as income under dividends left on deposit.

The investment income of a life insurer is composed of interest on bonds; mortgage loans, collateral loans, and bank deposits; dividends on stocks; and real estate income. Investment income is reported on a *net basis,* after deduction of investment expenses and depreciation of investment real estate property. Investments generate a significant part of the income of life insurers, accounting for about 27 percent of total revenues for all companies in this industry sector.

Deductions from Income The largest deduction from income consists of benefits paid to policyholders, including death benefits, disability benefits, dividends, and cash surrender values. Such benefits amount to about 45.7 percent of income.

The second largest deduction from income is the deduction for required reserves, which amounts to about 33.4 percent of income. The deduction of the increase in required reserves on policies in force compensates for the inclusion of all premium income from policyholders in the income section of the statement.

Life insurance company operating expenses, based on industry aggregates, totaled about 11.9 percent of income during 2000, compared with 18 percent a decade earlier. Included in the 2000 total are about 6 percent of income for home office and field expenses and about 4.1 percent for commissions to agents. Taxes represent about 1.8 percent of income. Dividends to stockholders of stock life insurers were 2 percent of income.

Surplus Drain in Life Insurance

The surplus of a life insurance company is subject to a drain during periods of increasing sales similar to that of a property and liability insurer. As an incentive to their agents to produce new business continually, life insurance companies pay very high first-year commissions, sometimes more than 100 percent of the first-year premium. In a sense, it might be appropriate to view this first-year commission as an investment in the production of future premiums under the policy. However, under the statutory provisions governing life insurance accounting, all expenses of operation must be charged against income when they are incurred. This means that the sale of a new policy generally results in a reduction in surplus, since the commissions and other expenses together with the required contribution to legal reserves exceed the premium received. Unlike the problem in the property and liability field, state statutes have recognized this problem and permit life insurers to compensate for high first-year policy expenses through a modi-

fied reserving system. Under these modified reserving systems, the insurer is permitted to compensate for the initial expenses associated with the policy by deferring the establishment of the first-year reserve, thereby freeing the bulk of the initial premium for the payment of expenses.[13]

REINSURANCE

Nature of Reinsurance

Reinsurance is a device whereby an insurance company may avoid catastrophic hazard in the operation of the insurance mechanism. As the term indicates, reinsurance is insurance for insurers. It is based on the same principles of sharing and transfer as insurance itself. To protect themselves against the catastrophe of a comparatively large single loss or a large number of small losses caused by a single occurrence, insurance companies devised the concept of reinsurance. In a reinsurance transaction the insurer seeking reinsurance is known as the *direct writer* or the *ceding company,* while the company assuming part of the risk is known simply as the *reinsurer.* That portion of a risk that the direct writer retains is called the *net line* or the *net retention.* The act of transferring a part of the risk to the reinsurance company is called *ceding,* and that portion of the risk passed on to the reinsurer is called the *cession.*

Reinsurance had a very simple beginning. When a risk that was too large for the insurer to handle safely was encountered, the insurer shopped around for another insurance company that was willing to take a portion of the risk in return for a portion of the premium. A few current reinsurance operations are still conducted in this manner, which is called *facultative* or *street reinsurance.* In street reinsurance, each risk represents a separate case for the insurer, and the terms of reinsurance must be negotiated when the direct writer finds another insurer that will accept a portion of the risk. The ever-present danger is that a devastating loss might occur before the reinsurance

becomes effective. The cumbersome nature of the facultative system led to the development of modern reinsurance treaties.

Type of Reinsurance Treaties

Two types of reinsurance treaties are available: facultative and automatic. Under a *facultative treaty,* the risks are considered individually by both parties. Each risk is submitted by the direct writer to the reinsurer for acceptance or rejection, and the direct writer is not even bound to submit the risks in the first place. However, the terms under which reinsurance will take place are spelled out, and once the risk has been submitted and accepted, the advance arrangements apply; until then, the direct writer carries the entire risk.

Under an *automatic treaty,* the reinsurer agrees—in advance—to accept a portion of the gross line of the direct writing company or a portion of certain risks that meet the reinsurance underwriting rules of the reinsurer. The direct writer is obligated to cede a portion of the risk to which the automatic treaty applies.

Reinsurance in Property and Liability Insurance

There are two essential ways in which risk is shared under reinsurance agreements in the field of property and liability insurance. The reinsurance agreement may require the reinsurer to share in every loss that occurs to a reinsured risk, or it may require the reinsurer to pay only after a loss reaches a certain size. The first arrangement is called *proportional reinsurance* and includes quota share treaties and surplus line treaties. The second approach is called *excess-loss reinsurance.*

Quota Share Treaty Under a *quota share* treaty, the direct-writing company and the reinsurance company agree to share the amount of each risk on some percentage basis. Thus, the ABC Mutual Insurance Company (the direct writer) may have a 50 percent quota share treaty with the DEF Reinsurance Company (reinsurer). Under such an agreement, the DEF Reinsurance Company will pay 50 percent of any losses arising from those risks subject to the reinsurance treaty. In return, the ABC Mutual Insurance Company will pay the DEF Reinsurance Company 50 percent of the premiums it receives from the

[13] The general approach used in these modified reserving systems is quite similar. For example, one of the most direct approaches is the *full preliminary term method,* which uses the simple expedient of assuming that the policy is issued one year later for reserve purposes, thereby freeing all of the first-year premium (except the amount necessary to cover the policy's share of death claims) for the payment of expenses. For a more thorough discussion of the modified reserving systems, see any standard life insurance text.

insureds (with a reasonable allowance made to ABC for the agent's commission and other expenses connected with putting the business on the books).

Surplus Treaty Under a *surplus line* treaty, the reinsurer agrees to accept some amount of insurance on each risk in excess of a specified net retention. Normally, the amount the reinsurer is obligated to accept is referred to as a number of *"lines"* and is expressed as some multiple of the retention. A given treaty might specify a net retention of $10,000, with five *lines*. Under such a treaty, if the direct writer writes a $10,000 policy, no reinsurance is involved, but the reinsurer will accept the excess of policies over $10,000 up to $50,000. These treaties may be *first-surplus treaties, second-surplus,* and so on. A second-surplus treaty fits over a first-surplus treaty, assuming any excess of the first treaty, and so on for a third or fourth treaty. To illustrate, let us assume that the ABC Mutual Insurance Company (the direct writer), has a first-surplus treaty with a $10,000 net retention and five lines with the DEF Reinsurance Company and a second-surplus treaty with the GHI Reinsurance Company, also with five lines. If ABC sells a $100,000 policy, it must, under the terms of both agreements, retain $10,000. The DEF Reinsurance Company will then assume $50,000 and GHI will assume $40,000:

ABC Mutual Insurance Company	$10,000
DEF Reinsurance Company	50,000
GHI Reinsurance Company	40,000

Any loss under this policy would be shared on the basis of the amount of total insurance each company carries. Thus, ABC would pay 10 percent of any loss, DEF would pay 50 percent, and GHI would pay 40 percent. The premium would be divided in the same proportion, again with a reasonable allowance from the reinsurers to the direct writer for the expense of putting the policy on the books.

Excess-Loss Treaty Under an *excess-loss* treaty, the reinsurer is bound to pay only when a loss exceeds a certain amount. In essence, an excess-loss treaty is simply an insurance policy that has a large deductible taken out by the direct writer. The excess-loss treaty may be written to cover a specific risk or to cover many risks suffering loss from a single occurrence. Such a treaty might, for example, require the reinsurer to pay after the directwriting company had sustained a loss of $10,000 on a specific piece of property, or it might require payment by the reinsurer if the direct writer suffered loss in excess of $50,000 from any one occurrence. There is, of course, a designated maximum limit of liability for the reinsurer.

Pooling Still another method of reinsurance is pooling. The pooling arrangement may be similar to that used in aviation insurance, under the terms of which each member assumes a percentage of every risk written by a member of the pool. This pooling arrangement is similar to a quota share treaty. On the other hand, the pool may provide a maximum loss limit to any one insurer from a single loss, as is the case with the Workers Compensation Reinsurance Bureau. After a member of the pool has suffered a loss in excess of a specified amount (e.g., $100,000 as a result of one disaster), the other members of the pool share the remainder of the loss.

Reinsurance in Life Insurance

In the field of life insurance, reinsurance may take one of two forms: the term insurance approach and the coinsurance approach. Under the *term insurance approach,* the direct writer purchases yearly renewable term insurance equal to the difference between the face value of the policy and the reserve, which is the amount at risk for the company. The *coinsurance approach* to reinsurance in life insurance is quite similar to the quota share approach in property and liability. Under this approach, the ceding company transfers some portion of the face amount of the policy to the reinsurer, and the reinsurer becomes liable for its proportional share of the death claim. In addition, the reinsurer becomes responsible for the maintenance of the policy reserve on its share of the policy.

Functions of Reinsurance

Reinsurance actually serves two important purposes. The first, which is fairly obvious, is the spreading of risk. Insurance companies are able to avoid catastrophic losses by passing on a portion of any risk too large to handle. In addition, through excess-loss reinsurance arrangements, a company may protect itself against a single occurrence of catastrophic scope. Smaller companies are able to insure exposures they could not otherwise handle within the bounds of safety.

The second function reinsurance performs is not as immediately obvious: It is a financial function. As

we have seen, when the premium volume of an insurance company is expanding, the net result will be a drain on the surplus of the company. With a continually expanding premium volume, a company faces a dilemma. The business it is writing may be profitable, but because of the requirements of the unearned premium reserve, its surplus may be declining and may reach a dangerously low level. We say "dangerously low" because, although there is no absolute standard, the amount of new business a company may write is obviously a function of its policyholders' surplus. In the absence of some other alternative, a company could expand only to a certain point and would then be required to stop and wait for the premiums to become earned, freeing surplus.

Reinsurance provides a solution to this dilemma. When the direct-writing company reinsures a portion of the business it has written under a quota share or surplus line treaty, it pays a proportional share of the premium collected to the reinsurer. The reinsurer then establishes the unearned premium reserves or policy reserves required, and the direct writer is relieved of the obligation to maintain such reserves. Since the direct writer has incurred expenses in acquiring the business, the reinsurer pays the direct-writing company a commission for having put the business on the books. The payment of the ceding commission by the reinsurer to the direct writer means that the unearned premium reserve is reduced by more than cash is reduced, resulting in an increase in surplus. Thus, if the direct writer transfers $100,000 in premiums to the reinsurer, the unearned premium reserve of the direct writer is reduced by $100,000. The payment to the reinsurer is $100,000 minus a ceding commission of 40 percent, or $60,000. Since assets have been reduced by $60,000 and liabilities have been reduced by $100,000, surplus is increased by $40,000. When reinsurance is used on a continuing basis, the net drain on the surplus of the direct-writing company is reduced. In addition, the market is greatly increased, since excess capacity of one insurer may be transferred to another through reinsurance.

The Catastrophe Risk Exchange (CATEX)

The Catastrophe Risk Exchange, Inc. (CATEX) was founded in 1995 by former New Jersey Insurance Commissioner Samuel F. Fortunato and is licensed by the New York State Insurance department as a reinsurance intermediary. CATEX operates as a computer-based electronic market for the exchange of insurance risks by insurance companies and reinsurers. The exchange was conceived as a virtual trading floor in which participants can offer risks to be reinsured and exchanged.

CATEX does not function in any way as a risk-bearer, but merely operates a facility for the exchange of catastrophe risks among subscribers. Neither does CATEX represent any of the parties to an exchange, but restricts its activities to organizing and operating the mechanism and procedures required for the efficient exchange of risks. This is accomplished through a highly secure electronic system on which participants can advertise risks they want to exchange with other parties who have risks in different geographic locations. A typical swap, for example, could involve several units of Florida windstorm exposures for California earthquake exposures.

Although participation in the exchange is limited to subscribers (who pay a fee for membership and for each risk actually traded), CATEX allows insurers and self-insured companies to purchase reinsurance directly from CATEX subscriber reinsurers. Although CATEX has been in existence for a short time, the operation has been highly successful.

From its inception until mid-2001, over 3000 risks were posted on the CATEX exchange and nearly 1000 transactions were completed, representing over $5.5 billion of insured limit. Posted risks have included: facultative, casualty, property, aviation and aerospace risks, accident and health, marine, energy, political risk, weather, credit, auto liability and others. Although the main office of CATEX is in Princeton, New Jersey, it maintains offices in London and Bermuda.

Risk Financing Alternatives to Reinsurance

Our discussion of insurance company financial operations would not be complete without at least a brief mention of one of the most recent developments in insurance finance. This is the *securitization of insurable risk,* through which insurance risk is transferred to the financial markets.

Like reinsurance, securitization is designed to transfer a part of an insurer's underwriting risk to another party. To date, the vast majority of securitizations have dealt with the transfer of catastrophic risk. Securitization differs from reinsurance as an approach to risk financing by its direct link to the capital markets. Instead of transferring specific portfolios of risks to a reinsurer, insurers make what, in a sense, is a side

bet with another party—an investor or speculator—on whether a catastrophe loss will occur. These side bets take the form of securities traded in a market or, in some cases, private placements. The rationale for securitizing insurable risks is the contention by some members of the insurance industry that the industry needs additional capital. The most fervent advocates of securitization tout it as a source of external funding for the industry that can serve as a backstop to protect surplus against catastrophe losses. Currently, they argue, the property and liability industry has slightly less than $300 billion in surplus, which pales into insignificance when compared with the $19 trillion invested in securities markets. If insurance risks can be commoditized into tradable securities, the proponents of securitization argue that an enormous source of funds outside the industry can be tapped.

The question naturally arises as to why parties outside the property and liability insurance industry would be interested in investing in such securities. The advocates of insurance securitization suggest that there are several features that should appeal to the external market.

First, catastrophe-linked securities offer the potential for diversification; they fluctuate with a different pattern of gains and losses than stocks and bonds. The returns on catastrophe-linked securities are generally uncorrelated with the financial markets, but vary with the weather and would fluctuate with a different pattern of losses and gains than stock or bond markets.[14] This, coupled with a relatively high return (in years in which catastrophe losses are low) could make these securities attractive to institutional investors outside the insurance industry. In addition, there are times when investors believe that the stock market is overvalued and become nervous over the prospect of a serious decline. Here, again, the uncorrelated nature of catastrophe-linked securities—the zero beta investment—is an appealing feature.

Insurance securitization is accomplished using two types of financial instruments: *catastrophe bonds* (also called *act of God bonds* and *cat bonds*) and *insurance derivatives* such as futures and options. Derivatives are financial instruments whose value is derived (hence the name) from the value of commodity prices, interest rates, stock market prices, foreign exchange rates, and now insurance indexes.

Catastrophe Bonds Catastrophe bonds are issued by an insurance company with the repayment terms linked to the company's losses from disasters or acts of God. A loss exceeding a certain size automatically produces changes in the bonds' structure designed to enhance the issuing insurer's capital base. The nature of this change can vary, and several alternatives have been proposed. In each case, however, the bonds include a risk-transfer feature under which some or all of the principal or interest would be forgiven or subject to deferred payment in the event the issuing insurer suffers a disaster in excess of a specified amount. For stock insurers, the bonds may also be structured so that a disaster would provide for automatic conversion of the cat bonds into stock in the insurer.

The first major catastrophe bond transaction occurred in 1994, when Nationwide Mutual Insurance Company of Columbus, Ohio, issued $400 million in 30-year cat bonds. Nationwide used the proceeds from the sale of the bonds to buy Treasury securities, which were pledged as collateral for the bonds. In the event of a natural disaster, the bonds allow Nationwide to take the Treasury securities from the trust and substitute its own surplus notes, a type of IOU mutual insurers use to support borrowing. Nationwide pays bondholders about 2 percent over the rate on the government bonds in which the proceeds from the cat bonds are invested. In effect, this is the cost Nationwide incurs to guarantee the future rate at which funds may have to be borrowed.

A few smaller transactions followed during the next several years but several issues were offered and then withdrawn when they received a chilly reception in the market. Then, in 1997, USAA, a Texas-based insurer, created a special purpose reinsurance company called Residential Re that issued $477 million in cat bonds to 62 different investors.[15] A default was to

[14] As one industry spokesman has said, "A fall in the Hang Seng index doesn't cause an earthquake in California."

[15] The USAA cat bond issue consisted of two portions or *tranches*. Part A-1 was $164 million of notes with a coupon of 2.82 percent over the London InterBank Offered Rate (LIBOR), in which the coupon is at risk, but the full return of the principal was guaranteed. A-2 was $313 million of notes with a rate of 5.75 percent over LIBOR. The bonds' stated maturity was one year, maturing in June 1998. For the principal-protected portion of the issue (A-1), bonds would be extended for an additional 10 years, with no additional interest payable during the 10-year period. Although the proceeds from the issue totaled $477 million, $77 million was set aside for the purchase of zero-coupon bonds to pay the principal-protected investors at the end of the 10-year, no-interest deferred maturity. For the A-2 portion, the $1 billion in claims would trigger a default on the principal.

be triggered if a hurricane on the East Coast between July 15, 1997, and December 31, 1997 caused more than $1 billion of claims against USAA. The hurricane did not occur, and the bondholders received the return of both the principal and interest. Investors who purchase cat bonds are speculating that during a particular period, a catastrophic loss will not affect the regions covered by the bonds. If good weather prevails during the bond period, the investor wins. If a disaster strikes, the investor loses. It is the willingness of the speculator to make a side bet with the insurer that is the essential requirement for cat bonds.

Catastrophe Futures and Options A *futures contract* is a binding contract providing for the delivery of a specified quantity of some commodity or financial instrument at some future specified date. Futures originated as a means whereby the producers of agricultural products could hedge against a decline in the prices for their output, or by which a manufacturer could hedge against an increase in the price of raw materials. In the 1970s, a market developed in financial futures, and it was probably only a matter of time before insurance futures were devised. In December 1992, the Chicago Board of Trade (CBOT) began trading two versions of catastrophe insurance futures. The initial response was sluggish and in 1995 the CBOT shifted to a new line of catastrophe insurance *options* known as PCS options (because they are based on a benchmark of catastrophe loss estimates, provided by the firm *Property Claim Services*). The volume of trades in PCS options also proved to be disappointing and the CBOT discontinued these options at the end of 2000.[16]

The value of a catastrophe insurance option is directly linked to the industry's losses from natural disasters in a particular area over a specified period of time. The greater the losses, the higher the value of the cash settlement if the option is exercised. By acquiring call options—the right to buy futures contracts whose price is pegged to disaster losses—an insurer could earn a trading profit and thereby arrange a source of funds to pay claims for catastrophe losses. By taking the other side of the trade, investors could collect a favorable return during periods of favorable loss experience.

If this sounds like a win-lose situation, it is because it is. Hedging operations are made possible by speculators who buy and sell futures options in the hope of making a profit as a result of a change in price. For the speculator, the futures option is a speculative risk. Like stock index futures, insurance futures options will be a zero-sum game. For every winner, there will be a loser. When an insurer buys an insurance futures option in anticipation of increasing losses, the other half of the contract is filled by someone who is betting against the occurrence of a catastrophe.

The future of insurance securitization remains to be seen. Although securitization of risk activity has increased worldwide since the activity began in the mid-1990s, it still represents only about 1 percent of worldwide reinsurance volume. Although transactions continue to occur, the volume of trades transacted has been far below the levels originally predicted. According to estimates by Lehman Brothers, only 32 deals had been completed by June 2000, with about $2 billion in catastrophe-linked securities sold.[17]

For some insurers, the reluctance to use the futures market stems from a philosophic predisposition. In other cases, there has been some uncertainty regarding regulatory response. Given its long history, reinsurance is well understood from a regulatory, legal, and accounting basis, while insurance securitization arrangements are relatively new and untested. In addition, there are unresolved tax questions that impede the development of securitization arrangements in the United States. Finally, based on the transactions that have been made thus far, there do not seem to be any particular economies in securitization compared with traditional reinsurance.

TAXATION OF INSURANCE COMPANIES

Insurance companies, like all business corporations, are subject to federal, state, and local taxes. At the federal level, insurers are subject to the federal income tax. At the state level, they pay income and

[16] In 1997, the Bermuda Commodities Exchange (BCOE), which was incorporated in 1996, began trading insurance futures contracts and options. Like the CBOT, the BCOE offered members the opportunity to trade in option contracts based on an index of insured weather-related homeowners' losses in specific areas of the United States over specified periods of time. Like the CBOT it found inadequate market interest and suspended operations in 2000.

[17] National Underwriter Co., *Review Preview, Property/Casualty Edition 2001*

property taxes like other businesses and, in addition, are liable for a number of special taxes levied on insurers, the most important of which is the premium tax.

State Premium Tax

Taxation of insurance companies by the states grew out of the states' need for revenue and a desire to protect domestic insurers by a tariff on out-of-state companies. The premium tax spread from state to state as a retaliatory measure against taxes imposed by each state on outside insurance. As time went by, most states came to levy the premium tax on the premium income of both domestic and foreign insurers.[18]

Every state currently imposes a *premium tax* on insurers operating within its borders. In essence, this tax is a sales tax on the premiums for all policies sold by an insurer within the state. The amount of the tax varies among the states; the maximum in any state is 4 percent, with the most typical amount being 2 percent. The tax paid by the insurer is, of course, added to the cost of the insurance contract and is passed on to the policyholder. Most states tax all companies alike, but some states still apply the tax only to out-of-state companies, or they tax domestic companies at a preferential rate.[19]

In addition to the premium tax, the states also charge companies and agents license fees before they can solicit business in the state. The total revenue received by the insurance department of the states greatly exceeds the costs of operating these departments; this makes the insurance department in every state an income-producing agency. As a matter of fact, a critical concern of the states in the *state-versus-federal-regulation* issue is one of revenue. It has been said that "the power to regulate is the power to tax," and many state officials fear that should the federal government assume responsibil-

ity for the regulation of insurance, Congress would begin to look with growing interest at the state insurance tax revenues, which now amount to more than $1 billion annually.

Federal Income Taxes

For the purpose of taxation under the *Internal Revenue Code,* insurance companies are classified into three categories: life insurance companies, nonlife mutual insurance companies, and insurance companies other than life or mutual. In general, all three classes are subject to the same tax rates as are other corporations. However, they differ from other corporations, and from each other, in the manner in which taxable income is determined.[20]

Life Insurance Companies Life insurance companies are taxed at standard corporate rates on their *life insurance company taxable income* (LICTI), which is life insurance gross income minus deductions.[21] Life insurance gross income includes premiums, decreases in reserves, and other standard elements of gross income, such as investment income. Deductions include expenses incurred, death benefits, increases in certain reserves, policyholder dividends, and certain miscellaneous deductions.

Among the special deductions, the *Internal Revenue Code* (IRC) permits a *small-company* deduction to life insurers with less than $500 million in assets. The small-company deduction allows an eligible insurer to deduct 60 percent of its first $3 million in tentative LICTI, and the deduction is phased out as tentative LICTI reaches $15 million. If the phase-out of the deduction applies, the deduction is reduced by 15 percent of the excess of tentative LICTI over $3 million and is phased out when LICTI reaches $15 million.

[18] Since the levying of taxes on the premium income of insurers required a system of registration and reporting, the administrative requirements of taxation had a great deal to do with the development of regulation by the states.

[19] Most states have reciprocal or retaliatory premium tax laws. Under a retaliatory law, the purpose is to impose equally high taxes on the admitted companies of another state as that state imposes on the companies of the initial state doing business in the foreign state. For example, if Iowa taxes all companies doing business within its borders at the rate of 2 percent and Illinois taxes the companies organized in Iowa at the rate of 3 percent, companies from Illinois that are admitted to Iowa would be taxed 3 percent.

[20] Life insurers are taxed under *Code* Sections 801–820; mutual insurers other than life or marine are taxed under code Sections 821–826; and insurance companies (other than life and mutual) and mutual marine insurance companies are taxed under code Sections 831 and 832. Section 501(a) of the code provides that fraternal beneficiary societies, voluntary employees' beneficiary associations, federal employees' voluntary beneficiary associations, local benevolent life and mutual associations, and certain small property and liability mutuals are exempt from income taxation.

[21] The provisions of the *Internal Revenue Code* applicable to life insurers were substantially overhauled by the Life Insurance Tax Act of 1984. The provisions were further modified by the Tax Reform Act of 1986 and the Omnibus Budget Reconciliation Act of 1990.

Although life insurers are permitted to deduct increases in their reserves, the 1984 tax act dictates the method that must be used. Reserves for tax purposes cannot exceed the amount taken into account in computing statutory (annual statement) reserves.

The deduction for policyholders' dividends is also limited. Since 1984, the law has included a complex formula for determining the part of policyholders' dividends deductible by a mutual insurer in computing taxable income.[22] A mutual life insurance company must reduce the amount of its policyholder dividends by a *differential earnings amount,* which is, in effect, an imputed return on equity that is paid to policyholders as owners of a mutual insurer.[23]

The most recent change in the taxation of life insurers was enacted as a part of the Omnibus Budget Reconciliation Act of 1990 (OBRA). Under the new provisions introduced by OBRA, life insurers are required to capitalize and amortize policy acquisition expense. As you will recall from our discussion of life insurer finances, the high first-year commissions on life insurance policies produce an underwriting loss, which is recouped as future premiums are earned. The *IRC* now requires that deferral of the deduction, thereby increasing LICTI. The amount of premiums capitalized and amortized is determined by *proxy* based on a percentage of net premiums (that is, after deduction for dividends and reinsurance) for the first year of the policy and renewals.[24] The first $5 million of amortizable policy expenses may be amortized over 60 months. The next $5 million is amortized over 120 months. The amount subject to 60-month amortization is reduced dollar-for-dollar to the extent it exceeds $10 million.

Property and Liability Companies Property and liability insurers pay the usual corporate income tax on net underwriting profit and investment income. The manner in which taxable income is determined, however, reflects the unique conventions of statutory accounting. The Tax Reform Act of 1986 (TRA-86) substantially revised the provisions of the *Internal Revenue Code (IRC)* under which property and liability insurance companies (and Blue Cross and Blue Shield organizations) are taxed.[25] TRA-86 also eliminated certain provisions related to the taxation of mutual insurers and introduced new rules to reflect the anomalies of statutory accounting.[26]

The first feature of statutory accounting addressed by TRA-86 is the treatment of the unearned premium reserve that results in a mismatching of revenues and expenses. Under the provisions of TRA-86, only 80 percent of the increase in the unearned premium reserve in a given year is deductible in computing taxes.

TRA-86 also requires that property and liability loss reserves be discounted to reflect the time value of money. The annual deduction for incurred losses includes the increase in loss reserves, but the amount deducted is subject to statutory discounting. Any decrease in loss reserves results in income inclusion, also on a discounted basis. The discount rate used is based on the federal midterm rate.

Finally, the *IRC* disallows a portion (15 percent) of property and liability insurer's tax-exempt interest and dividends. This is accomplished by reducing the deduction for incurred losses by 15 percent of tax-exempt interest and deductible dividends.[27]

[22] Congress felt that the dividends to policyholders should be viewed at least in part as a return of the mutual life insurance company's profits for the year. In an effort to strike a competitive balance between stock and mutual life insurers, the 1984 act disallows as a deduction (via a complex formula approach) a portion of the dividends a mutual company pays to its policyholders.

[23] The differential earning rate is computed by the Treasury Department each year based on the earnings of the 50 largest stock life insurance companies.

[24] The percentages to be applied to the net premiums of specified insurance contracts are 1.75 percent for annuities, 2.05 percent for group life, and 7.7 percent for other life and noncancelable or guaranteed renewable accident and health insurance.

[25] Prior to the Tax Reform Act of 1986, Blue Cross and Blue Shield organizations were exempt from federal taxes. TRA-86 repealed this exemption for years after 1986 and provided for taxation of these organizations as property and liability insurers.

[26] Most mutual property and liability insurers were exempt from income taxes until 1942. From that time until 1962 they were taxed under special formulas that did not take into account their underwriting gains or losses. The Revenue Acts of 1962 and 1964 eliminated most differences in taxation of mutual and stock insurers, except for very small mutuals, which remained exempt from taxes. The Tax Reform Act of 1986 made both stock and mutual insurers eligible for exemption from income tax if the greater of their net or written premiums does not exceed $350,000.

[27] Generally, 80 percent of dividends received by corporations are deductible in computing taxable income.

IMPORTANT CONCEPTS TO REMEMBER

annual statement	loss ratio	surplus line reinsurance
statutory accounting	expense ratio	excess-loss reinsurance
GAAP	combined ratio	premium tax
admitted assets	written premiums	catastrophe insurance futures
nonadmitted assets	amortized value	catastrophe bonds
policyholders' surplus	policy reserves	mandatory security valuation
codification	supplementary contracts	reserve
earned premiums	reinsurance	surplus drain
unearned premium reserve	ceding company	net retention
reinsurance reserve	cession	retrocession
incurred losses	facultative treaty	life insurance company taxable
paid losses	automatic treaty	income (LICTI)
loss reserves	proportional reinsurance	
statutory profit (loss)	quota share reinsurance	

QUESTIONS FOR REVIEW

1. What characteristics of the insurance business make reserves necessary?

2. Is the life insurance policy reserve more analogous to an unearned premium reserve or a loss reserve in the property and liability field?

3. Define the unearned premium reserve and briefly explain how it is calculated. Why is the unearned premium reserve often referred to as the "reinsurance reserve"?

4. What does it mean to say that a reserve is redundant? What type of reserves are considered to be redundant? Why?

5. The XYZ Insurance Company had an unearned premium reserve of $20 million at the end of 2000. During 2001, it wrote $25 million in annual premiums. At the end of 2001, its unearned premium reserve was $23 million. What were the earned premiums during 2001?

6. The XYZ Insurance Company had loss reserves of $7 million at the end of 2000. During 2001, it paid $7 million in losses, and had loss reserves in the amount of $6 million at the end of 2001. What were the incurred losses for 2001?

7. The financial statements of the XYZ Property and Liability Insurance Company indicate the following:

Premiums written 2001	$10,000,000
Unearned premium reserve, Dec. 2000	9,000,000
Unearned premium reserve, Dec. 2001	11,000,000
Losses paid in 2001	6,000,000
Loss reserves, Dec. 2000	5,000,000
Loss reserves, Dec. 2001	4,000,000
Underwriting expense incurred	4,000,000

Compute the statutory profit or loss for the XYZ Company during 2001.

8. Give two specific reasons for reinsurance. Distinguish between *facultative* and *treaty* reinsurance.

9. The Tax Reform Act of 1986 introduced several new elements into the taxation of property and liability insurers. In what way did the TRA-86 deal with the mismatching of revenues and expenses of property and liability insurers? How did TRA-86 deal with the redundancy in loss reserves?

10. Explain two techniques that may be used to estimate the true underwriting profit or loss of a property and liability insurance company.

QUESTIONS FOR DISCUSSION

1. The primary emphasis in statutory accounting is supposedly on financial conservatism. However, some statutory techniques violate this principle. Discuss three ways in which statutory accounting is ultraconservative, and two areas where the principle of conservatism is violated.

2. The NAIC has staunchly defended its need to have an accounting system for insurance companies that differs from GAAP. On what basis have they argued for a different system? Do you agree or disagree that a separate system is needed?

3. A noted insurance authority stated, "The insured should prefer to purchase insurance from a company that has a high loss ratio, since this is evidence that the company is returning a high percentage of the premium dollars collected to its customers." Explain why you agree or disagree with this position.

4. To what extent does the movement of surplus of a property and liability insurer indicate the profitability of the company's operations? Would the same be true for a life insurer?

5. "In view of the relationship of surplus to premiums that may be written, a severe decline in the stock market is likely to serve as a brake on price-cutting practices." Explain the rationale behind this observation.

SUGGESTIONS FOR ADDITIONAL READING

Black, Kenneth, Jr., and Harold D. Skipper, Jr. *Life Insurance,* 13th ed. Englewood Cliffs, N.J.: Prentice-Hall, 2000. Chapters 32, 34.

D'Arcy, Stephen P., and Virginia Grace France. "Catastrophe Futures: A Better Hedge for Insurers." *Journal of Risk and Insurance,* vol. 59, no. 4 (December 1992).

Gart, Alan, and David J. Nye. *Insurance Company Finance and Investments,* 2nd ed. Malvern, Pa.: Insurance Institute of America, 1990.

Gastel, Ruth. *Reinsurance: Fundamentals and New Challenges,* New York: Insurance Information Institute, 1995.

Insurance Accounting and Systems Association. *Life Insurance Accounting,* 3rd ed. Durham, N.C.: IASA, 1994.

———. *Property-Liability Insurance Accounting,* 5th ed. Durham, N.C.: IASA, 1991.

Kenney, R. *Fundamentals of Fire and Casualty Strength,* 4th ed. Dedham, Mass.: Kenney Insurance Studies, 1967.

McDonald, Lee. "Investing in Risk Gets Real." *Best's Review—Property Casualty Edition* (April 1998), pp. 35–39.

Mooney, Sean, and Larry Cohen. *Basic Concepts of Accounting and Taxation of Property/Casualty Insurance Companies.* New York: Insurance Information Institute, 1995.

Munich Reinsurance Company. *Reinsurance and Reassurance.* New York: 1963–1966.

Phifer, Ross. *Reinsurance Fundamentals: Treaty and Facultative.* New York: John Wiley & Sons, Inc., 1996.

Reinarz, Robert C., Janice O. Schloss, Gary S. Patrik, and Peter R. Kensicki. *Reinsurance Practices,* vol. 1 and vol. 2. Malvern, Pa.: Insurance Institute of America, 1990.

Troxel, Terrie E., and George E. Bouchie. *Property-Liability Insurance Accounting and Finance,* 3rd ed. Malvern, Pa.: American Institute for Property and Liability Underwriters, 1990.

Webb, Bernard L., Connor M. Harrison, and James J. Markham. *Insurance Operations,* 1st ed., vols. I and II. Malvern, Pa.: American Institute for Property and Liability Underwriters, 1992.

Webb, Bernard L., Howard N. Anderson, John A. Cookman, and Peter R. Kensicki. *Principles of Reinsurance,* vol. 1 and vol. 2. Malvern, Pa.: Insurance Institute of America, 1990.

Zolkos, Rodd. "Catastrophe Bonds Take Risk Financing by Storm." *Business Insurance* (December 22, 1997), p. 18.

WEB SITES TO EXPLORE

Bermuda Commodities Exchange	http://www.bcoe.bm/
CATEX	http://www.catex.com/
Chicago Board of Trade	http://CBOT.com
Hedge Financial Products	http://www.hedgefin.com/
Independent Reinsurance Underwriters Association, Inc.	http://www.captive.com
Insurance Accounting and Systems Association	http://www.connectyou.com/ins/index.htm
Reinsurance Association of America	http://www.raanet.org

THE LEGAL FRAMEWORK

Even lawyers were children once.

— CHARLES LAMB

CHAPTER OBJECTIVES

When you have finished this chapter, you should be able to

- Identify and explain the essential elements of a contract
- Explain how the general law of contracts applies to insurance contracts
- Explain why the principle of indemnity is important to the operation of the insurance mechanism
- Explain the ways in which the principle of indemnity is enforced in insurance contracts
- Explain what is meant by the statements that insurance contracts are contracts of adhesion, aleatory contracts, conditional contracts, unilateral contracts, and contracts of utmost good faith
- Define and explain the nature of waiver and estoppel
- Explain the application of the doctrines of concealment and misrepresentation in the insurance transaction

The transfer of risk from the individual to the insurance company is accomplished through a contractual arrangement under which the insurance company, in consideration of the premium paid by the insured and his or her promise to abide by the provisions of the contract, promises to indemnify the insured or pay an agreed amount, in the event of the specified loss. The instrument through which this transfer of risk is accomplished is the insurance contract, which, as a contract, is enforceable by law.

A great deal of the law that has shaped the formal structure of insurance and influenced its content derives from the general law of contracts. But because of the many unique aspects of the insurance transaction, the general law has had to be modified to fit the needs of insurance. Our discussion will involve a combination of both general contract law and its modifications relative to insurance, but with particular emphasis on those principles that are peculiar to insurance.

INSURANCE AND THE LAW OF CONTRACTS

We begin our consideration of the legal aspects of insurance with a brief discussion of the general laws of contracts and the manner in which this special branch of law applies to the insurance transaction.

General Requirements of an Enforceable Contract

Insurance law is predominantly derived from the general law of contracts. Insurance policies, as is the case with all contracts, must contain certain elements to be binding legally. These elements of a contract are the following:

1. Offer and acceptance
2. Consideration
3. Legal object
4. Competent parties
5. Legal form

Offer and Acceptance To have a legally enforceable contract, there must be a definite, unqualified offer by one party, and this offer must be accepted in its exact terms by the other party. In the case of insurance, the *offer* is normally made by the prospect when applying for insurance. The *acceptance* takes place when the agent binds coverage or when the policy is issued. There is no requirement that the contract be in writing.

Under the Statute of Frauds, some types of contracts must be in writing to be enforceable. The only section of this statute that might be construed to apply to insurance contracts is that which requires written and signed proof of an agreement that by its terms is not to be performed within one year from its effect date. This provision has been interpreted to apply only to agreements that cannot possibly be performed within one year. Since the insurer's promise may be required to be fulfilled within one year, or even within one day, from the issue date of the policy, an insurance contract falls outside the statute. Hence, it may be said that in the absence of specific legislation to the contrary, an insurance

contract can be oral in nature.[1] However, most insurance contracts are written, and only rarely is an oral contract used.

An oral contract is just as binding on both parties as a written one. However, the difficulty of proving the terms of an oral contract, or even its existence, makes it advisable whenever possible to confine contractual agreements to those that are written. In certain instances, however, the situation may arise in which an oral contract of insurance may be necessary. When a prospective insured requests coverage from a property and liability agent, the agent may effect a contract orally, accepting the offer of the prospect. In such instances, coverage begins immediately. If a loss occurs before a written *binder* is issued,[2] or before the policy is issued, the company that the agent bound to the risk will be liable for the loss. However, the courts have ruled that if the agent represents more than one company, he or she must specify the company with which coverage is bound. The life insurance agent cannot bind the insurance company to a risk.

It is appropriate here to review the role of the insurance agent in the creation of a contract. In the property and liability field, in particular, the agent often acts for the insurer in accepting the insured's offer, thereby creating a contract. In addition to the power to "bind" the company to a risk by acceptance, the agent often acts on behalf of the insurer in other matters. Basically, the agent's authority to act on behalf of an insurer takes three forms, each derived from a somewhat different source: The authority of the agent may be *express authority, implied authority,* or *apparent authority.*

Express Authority *Express authority,* also sometimes called *stipulated authority,* is authority that is specifically granted to the agent. Agents are given express powers by their company in the agency agree-

[1] Of course, the states have the power to require that insurance contracts be in writing, and some states have done so. For example, the state of Georgia requires all contracts of insurance to be in writing. Other jurisdictions prohibit oral contracts in the fields of life, health, and, occasionally, property and liability insurance. In the absence of specific legislation specifying that an insurance contract be in writing, such contracts may be oral.

[2] A *binder* is a temporary contract, normally issued for 30 days, that an agent uses as evidence of accepting the offer of the prospect. The binder issued by the company is accepted by the insured with the understanding that it provides the same coverage as the policy form in use by the company.

ment or contract. The agency contract gives the agent express authority to represent the company, and generally contains clauses dealing with such things as the specific and general powers of the agent, the scale of commissions, and the ownership of the contracts sold, with a provision for cancellation of the contract.

Implied Authority In addition to those expressly granted powers, agents have certain *implied powers,* sometimes called *incidental authority.* Implied authority is the incidental authority required or reasonably necessary to execute the express authority. Although the agency contract may not specifically authorize the agent to advertise or to collect premiums from insureds, these are acts that are reasonably necessary to the duties expressly authorized.

Apparent Authority Finally, under the doctrine of *apparent authority* (also sometimes called *ostensible authority*) the courts have ruled that agents have those powers that the public has come to expect them to have. Because it is accepted by the public that property and liability agents can bind their company to a risk, they have this power, in spite of the fact that the company may not have granted it expressly. Let us say, for example, that the insurance company has told a particular agent not to sell any insurance on match factories, but the agent binds coverage on such an establishment. Despite the company's forbidding the agent to bind such coverage, it would be liable for any loss that occurred. As far as the public is concerned, an act by the agent is an act by the insurance company. He or she acts on behalf of the company in the insurance transaction, and under the laws of agency, these acts are deemed to be those of the company. If the agent binds the company to a risk, it is bound to that risk until such time as it effects cancellation of the contract.

Apparent authority arises only on the condition that the buyer has no way of knowing that the agent has exceeded his or her authority. Further, the agent's authority may be extended by ratification. If the agent exceeds his or her authority and the insurer acquiesces by acting as if the agent actually had authority (e.g., by accepting the premium on coverage the agent bound while exceeding express authority), the agent then does have the authority.

Consideration The binding force in any contract is the *consideration,* which is the items of value that each party gives to the other. Like all contractual arrangements, the insurance transaction requires that both parties exchange consideration if the contract is to have a proper legal status. The consideration of the insurance company lies in the promises that make up the contract, for example, the promise to pay if a loss should occur. The consideration on the part of the insured is the payment of the premium or the promise to pay it, plus an agreement to abide by the conditions of the contract. The promise to pay the premium is normally sufficient consideration for a legally binding contract in property and liability insurance. However, in life insurance, the first premium must be paid before the contract will take effect. And in a life insurance contract, only the first premium constitutes the consideration. This means that premiums subsequent to the first are not part of the legal consideration, since otherwise the contract could not come into existence until all the premiums were paid. The subsequent premiums, however, are conditions precedent to the continuance of the contract.

Legal Object A contract must be *legal* in its purpose. A contract in which one party agreed to commit murder for a specified amount would be unenforceable in court because its object is not legal. Likewise, an insurance policy that is actually a gambling contract would be unenforceable as contrary to public policy, as would a policy that promised to assume the consequences of the insured's criminal acts. Perhaps the most common example of such a contract is one in which insurable interest does not exist, which the courts have generally refused to enforce. However, lack of insurable interest is not the only possibility. For example, a business interruption policy written on the operations of an illegal whiskey still would not be enforceable. It is even possible that an insurance contract providing physical damage coverage on the contents of an illegal gambling establishment would not be enforceable, but legal opinion is divided. Some courts would hold the entire contract unenforceable. Some would hold it unenforceable just with respect to the equipment that can be used only for gambling purposes; other equipment, such as tables, chairs, beds, and the like, if destroyed, would be an enforceable obligation of the insurance company.

Competent Parties The parties to the agreement must be capable of entering into a contract in the eyes of the law. In most cases, the rules of *competency* are concerned with minors and the mentally incom-

petent. The basic principle is that some parties are not capable of understanding the contract they would enter into; therefore, the courts have ruled that they are not bound by such agreements.

In the absence of a statute to the contrary, a minor is considered to be a person under the age of 21, although the majority of states have passed laws lowering the age to 18 in recent years. In addition, the marriage of a person also creates full contractual competence under the law. The legal rule respecting a contract with a minor is that, except for contracts involving a reasonable value of necessities of life, the contract is voidable at the option of the minor. Since insurance has never been held to be a necessity of life by the courts, a minor could purchase insurance, repudiate the contract later, and receive a refund of all premiums. Several states, however, have enacted statutes conferring on minors of a specified age or over the legal capacity to enter into valid and enforceable life insurance contracts. The age limit varies from 14 and one-half to 18 years. But in the absence of such a statute, a minor could, for example, purchase a life insurance policy at age 15 and pay the premiums until age 20, then repudiate the contract, and receive a return of all the premiums paid. Most courts would probably not permit the insurance company even to make a deduction for the cost of the pure life insurance protection received while the contract was in force. Or a minor could purchase automobile insurance for a period of a year, and just before the expiration of the policy could repudiate the contract and receive a return of premium despite having had the protection while the contract was in existence.

Legal Form We have already noted that there is no requirement that the contract be in writing, but in many instances the form and content of a contract are rather carefully governed by state law. Many states, by law, use a standard fire insurance policy. In life insurance, a standard policy is not required in any state, but most insist on the inclusion of certain standard provisions in all life insurance policies. For example, the policy must provide that it will be incontestable after it has been in force during the lifetime of the insured for two years from the date of issue. Another standard provision also denies the life insurance company the right to void the policy because of a misstatement in age of the insured. In health insurance, the Uniform Law, adopted by practically all the states, demands that all individual and family health insurance contracts include 12 provisions specified and spelled out in the law.

In addition to the use of standard contracts and provisions, states require that all types of policies be filed with, and approved by, the state regulatory authorities before the policy may be sold in the state. This, of course, is to determine if the policy meets the requirements of the law, and to protect the policyholders from an unscrupulous insurance company that otherwise would take advantage of the public.

To be in *legal form,* then, the insurance contract must have the same wording as the legal standard policy, or must contain, in substance, the intent of the standard provisions. It must also follow the proper legal procedure of being filed and accepted by the state regulatory authority.

Void and Voidable

The terms *void* and *voidable* are sometimes incorrectly used interchangeably. Actually, to speak of a *void contract* is a contradiction in itself. A contract that is void is not a contract at all, but simply an agreement without legal effect. In essence, it lacks one of the requirements specified by law for a valid contract. A void contract cannot be enforced by either party. For example, a contract having an illegal object is void, and neither of the parties to the contract can enforce it. *A voidable contract,* in contrast, is an agreement that, for a reason satisfactory to the court, may be set aside by one of the parties. It is binding unless the party with the right to void it decides to do so. Assume, for example, that the insured fails to comply with a condition of the agreement. The company may elect, if it chooses, to fulfill its part of the contract, or it may elect to void it and revoke coverage. Or let us say that a 13-year-old purchases a life insurance contract. Although this contract would be binding for the company, in most cases it would be voidable at the option of the insured. A contract may be held to be voidable for any one of a number of legal reasons. If one party was forced into the contract under duress, or if there was an element of fraud involved, the contract may be voidable.

SPECIAL LEGAL CHARACTERISTICS OF INSURANCE CONTRACTS

In addition to those principles that apply to all contracts, certain legal characteristics are unique to insurance covenants.

Insurance Is a Contract of Indemnity

In many forms of insurance, particularly in property and liability, the contract is one of *indemnity*. This means that the insured is entitled to payment from the insurance company only if he or she has suffered a loss and only to the extent of the financial loss sustained. Put in its simplest terms, the principle of indemnity maintains that an individual should not be permitted to profit from the existence of an insurance contract but should be restored to the same financial condition that existed prior to the occurrence of the loss. Human nature being what it is, the ability to profit from the existence of an insurance policy would lead to the destruction of property, as well as to other more serious crimes. The principle of indemnity is enforced through legal doctrines and policy provisions designed to limit the amount the insured can collect to the amount of the loss. The four most important of these principles are (1) the doctrine of insurable interest, (2) the concept of actual cash value, and the (3) *other insurance* and (4) *subrogation* provisions of insurance contracts.

Insurable Interest The most important legal doctrine giving substance and support to the principle of indemnity is that of *insurable interest*. An insurance contract is legally binding only if the insured has an interest in the subject matter of the insurance and this interest is in fact *insurable*. In most instances, an insurable interest exists only if the insured would suffer a financial loss in the event of damage to, or destruction of, the subject matter of the insurance. To be more specific, an insurable interest involves a relationship between the person applying for the insurance and the subject matter of the insurance, such as a dwelling or a person's life, so that there is a reasonable expectation of benefit or advantage to the applicant from the continuation of the subject matter or an expectation of loss or detriment from its cessation. In property and liability insurance, this relationship requires a pecuniary interest, and insurable interest is limited to the extent of that pecuniary interest. In life insurance, it is broad enough to recognize a sentimental interest or one based on love and affection.

The doctrine of insurable interest was developed as a means of ensuring that the insurance contract would not be used for wagering purposes and also to mitigate the moral hazard. It should be obvious that if Smith can purchase insurance on Brown's house and collect if the house is damaged or destroyed, Smith would be profiting from the insurance. Smith might even be inclined to cause the damage. In the absence of the doctrine of insurable interest, an insurance policy might be used as a gambling contract and could be an inducement to commit arson.

The doctrine is used in life insurance as a means to control wagering with human lives. It is also intended to reduce the threat of murder just as it is used in property insurance to reduce the threat of willful destruction of property. If the class of persons who can legally insure the life of another is restricted to those who are closely related to the insured by blood or marriage, or who possess such a financial relationship to the insured that they stand to gain more by his or her continued life than by death, the temptation to murder the insured will be greatly curtailed.[3] There is even a requirement in a few states that the person whose life is to be insured by another must give consent to the transaction.

Insurable interest in property and liability insurance is established by means of a pecuniary relationship between the insured and the subject matter of the insurance. Perhaps the most obvious of these relationships is *ownership*. For example, if the insured owns an item of property such as a building or an automobile and if the property is destroyed, the insured will suffer a financial loss. Ownership, however, is not the only relationship that gives rise to insurable interest. If one has an interest in property for which title is held by another, then this interest may establish an insurable interest. An example would be property used as collateral for a debt. Thus, a mortgagee has an insurable interest in the property mortgaged, and a lienholder has an insurable interest in the property on which the lien is held. In both cases, damage to, or destruction of, the collateral could cause the creditor financial loss.[4] Legal liability for loss of, or damage to, property of others in the care of someone else may also establish an insurable interest. For example, the operators of an automobile

[3] Murder, of course, may still exist. Murder of the insured by the beneficiary will not relieve the insurance company of its obligation to pay the proceeds of the policy. The proceeds will not be paid to the murderer-beneficiary, obviously, but will be paid to a contingent beneficiary or to the estate of the insured.

[4] However, the insurable interest of the mortgagee or the lienholder does not extend to the full value of the property used as collateral, but only to the extent of the indebtedness. Obviously, the financial loss of the creditor would be limited to the balance of the debt, including unpaid interest.

storage garage could become legally liable for damage to, or destruction of, customers' cars in their care if the proximate cause of loss is their negligence. The fact that a bailee may become liable for the property of the bailor establishes an insurable interest that is of great importance. There are other relationships that will not be mentioned. As long as there is a relationship in which a financial loss would arise, it is a proper subject for a legally binding insurance contract.

An important aspect of the application of the doctrine to property and liability insurance involves the time at which the insurable interest must exist. The insurance contract will be valid only if the insurable interest exists at the time of the loss, regardless of whether it was or was not present at the inception date of the contract.

Insurable interest in life insurance requires a somewhat different relationship for its establishment, and it must exist at a different time. Here, a sentimental interest or one based on love and affection is sufficient to satisfy the requirement, even though a financial loss would not necessarily be involved. The family relationship of husband and wife is universally conceded, in and of itself, to satisfy the requirement. A number of courts, although perhaps a minority, have recognized the relationship of parent and child, of brother and sister, of grandparent and grandchild, and the like, as sufficient. But more remote kinships, such as cousins, have generally been rejected as insufficient unless a monetary loss would be involved. Other relationships growing out of affinity alone, such as the interest in the life of one's mother-in-law, are also insufficient. In other relationships, particularly those of a business nature, the death of the insured must give rise to the definite and measurable financial loss if insurable interest is to exist. Examples of the latter include the interest of a theatrical producer in the life of an actor, a professional baseball club in the lives of outstanding players, a corporation in the lives of key employees, a partner in the lives of the other partners, and creditors in the lives of debtors. There are many others, but these examples should be sufficient.

In contrast to the requirement in property and liability insurance, an insurable interest must exist at the inception of the life insurance contract for the contract to be legal, but it need not be present at the time of the insured's death. For example, if Jones and Smith are partners in a business operation, it is obvious that if Jones should die, the partnership must be dissolved. The heirs of the deceased partner are entitled to his share of the business, even though the sale of the assets will terminate the venture and may involve all concerned in substantial losses. Because of this possibility of financial loss, each partner has an insurable interest in the life of the other. But what happens to the life insurance policy Jones has purchased on Smith's life if a voluntary dissolution terminates the business? Since the rule in life insurance is that insurable interest is not required at the time of the occurrence of the event insured against, Jones could continue to maintain the policy and collect the proceeds at Smith's death. In the same manner, it is also possible for a creditor to maintain insurance on a debtor's life even though the debt has been paid off.

The extent of the insurable interest depends on a number of factors. First, and perhaps most important, it is assumed that an individual has an unlimited insurable interest in his or her *own* life. This is based on the principle that one should be able to dispose of one's human life value with the same freedom that one can exercise in disposing of other property after death. For example, if a man can find a company that will sell him $1 million worth of life insurance, and if he can pay the premiums on this amount, the contract would be legitimate, even though his death would not cause a financial loss to anyone. His insurable interest in his own life is without limit. The insured has the right to designate anyone he so desires as the beneficiary of his life insurance, and it is not required that the beneficiary have an insurable interest in the life of the insured. The beneficiary has a legal claim to a fixed sum of money on the occurrence of the insured's death and, as a consequence, need not prove that he sustained a financial loss because of the death. A third-party applicant for the insurance, who is to be the beneficiary, however, must possess an insurable interest, and the amount of the insurance must bear a relationship to the extent of the interest. For example, in most jurisdictions, the insurance procured by a creditor on the life of a debtor must not be disproportionate to the amount of the debt as it existed at the time the policy was issued or as it was reasonably expected to be thereafter. The purpose of this requirement is to prevent the use of a debt as a cloak for a wagering transaction.

Actual Cash Value The second doctrine that is used to enforce the principle of indemnity is the concept of *actual cash value*. No matter how much insur-

ance an individual purchases, the amount one may recover is limited to the amount of his actual loss. If Mr. Smith owns a dwelling worth $50,000 and he insures it for $100,000, in the event of a loss, he will be permitted to collect only the actual value of the house. Generally speaking, if persons were permitted to collect the face amount of their insurance contracts, regardless of the extent of the financial loss involved, this again would make the operation of the insurance principle impossible. Overinsurance would be common and would lead to willful destruction of property. As a result, it would upset any possibility of predicting losses with any reasonable degree of accuracy. Both results would be socially and economically undesirable.

The basis of measuring the financial loss of the insured varies with the type of contract and the circumstances surrounding the loss. In most types of property and liability insurance contracts, the measure is called *actual cash value*. This term, however, does not have a hard-and-fast meaning, and what constitutes actual cash value in one situation could not be used in another. Perhaps the most frequently used definition is "that amount of money necessary to replace the damaged or destroyed property with new materials at present-day prices, less depreciation." For example, let us assume that a dwelling was constructed in 1960 at a cost of $25,000. Today, the actual cash value of this structure would be the amount required to replace it with new materials at present prices, minus depreciation. If we assume that construction costs are four times as much as in 1960, then the replacement cost of the dwelling new today would be $100,000. If we assume that the structure has depreciated approximately 30 percent, then the actual cash value would be $70,000. This is the value that the insurance company would consider in determining the financial loss of the insured. If the policyholder had purchased physical damage insurance with a face value of $80,000 and a total loss occurred, only $70,000 would be paid, because this amount constitutes the actual cash value of the property.[5]

Although actual cash value is the basic measure of the financial loss of the insured in most types of property and liability insurance contracts, it is not the only measure used. In business interruption and in rent insurance, for example, the measure of financial loss is the insured's *loss of income* that arises because of inability to use and occupy the premises because of physical damage to the property. In extra-expense insurance, the measure is the amount of *abnormal expense* incurred to make possible the continued operation of a business in the event its premises have been damaged or destroyed by certain specified perils. In liability insurance, it would be the amount of damages the insured is obligated to pay a third party in cases in which the proximate cause of the injuries of the third party has been the negligence of the insured. But regardless of the method used in measuring the loss, the principle of indemnity is applicable. The insurance company will pay only if a loss has occurred and only to the extent of the financial loss of the insured, not exceeding the limits of coverage purchased, of course.

Valued Policies and Cash Payment Policies
These are other possible types of insurance contracts. They are not contracts of indemnity in the strict sense. Under the *valued policy* principle, the insurer agrees on the value of the property at the time the contract begins and in the event of a total loss must pay the face amount of the policy. This type of contract is characteristic of ocean marine insurance and insurance on fine arts. Life insurance contracts, on the other hand, are *cash payment* policies. There is not necessarily an agreement on the value of the life insured, but the company agrees to pay the face value of the policy on the death of the insured.

In ocean marine insurance, the valued policy is more a historical consequence than a modern necessity. Many years ago, if a ship were lost at sea, it could be many months before the loss became known, and in many cases it would be virtually impossible to determine exactly where the loss occurred. As a consequence, the disagreements arising from the attempts to determine the value of the destroyed property at the time and place of the loss were insurmountable. In addition, it is obvious that when a ship is lost at sea, there is no physical evidence that could be used to help establish the value at the time of the loss. The practical alternative to actual cash value was the use of an agreed value for insurance purposes. The principle of insuring on the basis of an agreed value was developed in ocean marine insurance in early times and it is still used today.

[5] Under some of the modern property forms, coverage is available on a "*replacement cost*" basis. Under the terms of these contracts, payment is made without a deduction for depreciation, provided that the insured maintains coverage equal to the full undepreciated value of the property. See Chapter 24.

In those cases where it would be difficult or impossible to determine the amount of the loss after it has taken place (as in the case of a rare or valuable work of art), the valued policy is used. Under these contracts, the face amount of the policy is paid in the event of a total loss, regardless of the actual amount of financial loss.

Valued Policy Laws In addition to its use in marine insurance, the *valued policy principle* has been enacted into law in some form or other in about half of the states.[6] The Nebraska law is an example:

> Whenever any policy of insurance shall be written to insure any real property in this state against loss by fire, tornado, or lightning, and the property insured shall be wholly destroyed, without criminal fault on the part of the insured or his assignee, the amount of the insurance written in such policy shall be taken conclusively to be the true value of the property insured and the true amount of loss and measure of damages.

This is an ill-conceived law and has little, if any, justification. Fortunately, however, it is limited in its application. The student should note carefully that it is applicable only to *real property,* only to the perils of *fire, tornado, or lightning,* and only if the loss to the real property is total.

A valued policy law is perhaps based on the mistaken assumption that if an insured pays for a certain amount of insurance, this is the amount that should be collected if a total loss occurs. If an insured has a dwelling with an actual cash value of $80,000 and purchases $100,000 coverage and the dwelling is totally destroyed by fire, the insurer will be obligated to pay the $100,000, even though this will yield the insured a profit of $20,000 and even though the contract promises to pay only the actual cash value of the destroyed property.[7] To permit the insured to profit through the existence of the insurance contract is in direct contradiction to the principle of indemnity and is contrary to public policy. Nevertheless, most valued policy laws have been in existence for many decades.

Cash Payment Policies The principle of indemnity is necessary in most forms of property insurance to prevent the insured from profiting on the insurance contract, but in life insurance the principle has limited application. Here, the insurance company contracts to pay a stated sum of money in the event of the insured's death, and this sum is payable without reference to any financial loss resulting from the death. The life insurance contract, therefore, is a cash payment policy. In life insurance, not only is it difficult to place a monetary value on a human life, but to the extent that it can be approximated, most individuals would be substantially underinsured. Overinsurance, with the possibility of profiting through the existence of the insurance contract, is not generally an important problem in life insurance.

The principle of indemnity is applicable only partially in the field of health insurance. Policies providing benefits for loss of income due to disability are cash payment contracts and not contracts of indemnity. The coverage is for a fixed amount, as in life insurance, and this amount will be paid if the insured becomes disabled, even though no financial loss is suffered or the amount of the financial loss is less than the insurance. For example, if X has a disability policy that will pay $600 per month in the event of total disability arising from sickness or bodily injury by accident, the insurance company must pay the $600 per month, even though the insured has not had employment for some time and suffers no loss of earnings because of the disability. The basic reasons for the use of the cash payment contracts rather than the indemnity principle are much the same in health as in life insurance. It is so difficult to place an exact monetary value on disability or freedom from it that any attempts to do so after a disability has occurred would be highly impractical.

Other Insurance Most insurance contracts, other than life and in most instances health, contain some clause relating to coverage by other insurance; the primary purpose of the restriction is that of preventing the insured from collecting for the same loss under two policies, and thereby profiting from the existence of duplicate insurance.

One of the most common of the other insurance clauses is one that is known as a *pro rata clause.* The provision in the basic fire insurance contract may be used as an illustration:

[6] Valued policy laws exist in Arkansas, California, Georgia, Kansas, Minnesota, Mississippi, Missouri, Montana, Nebraska, New Hampshire, North Dakota, Ohio, South Carolina, South Dakota, Texas, and West Virginia.

[7] The student is perhaps aware of the fact that, if there is a conflict between the provisions of a contract and a statute, the provisions of the statute will prevail.

This Company shall not be liable for a greater proportion of any loss that the amount hereby insured shall bear to the whole insurance covering the property against the peril involved, whether collectible or not.

An example will clarify the meaning. Let us assume that X has a dwelling with an actual cash value of $20,000. She purchases $10,000 fire insurance coverage from company A and $10,000 from company B, and then suffers a fire loss of $5000. If X could collect $5000 from each insurance company, which she has every intention of doing, she would obviously profit from the existence of the insurance. But under the provisions of the pro rata clause in each policy, each insurer will be obligated to pay only that proportion of the loss that its insurance bears to the total fire insurance on the property. Each company will pay $2500. This will rather effectively prevent the insured from profiting.

Another common type of other insurance clause is one that makes the insurance excess over other valid and collectible insurance. A partial statement of the other insurance clause in an inland marine personal property floater is as follows:

If at the time of the loss or damage, there is other valid and collectible insurance which would attach … had this policy not been effected, then this insurance shall apply as excess over all such other insurance and in no event as contributing insurance.

This clause is typical of inland marine insurance contracts and is also found to some extent in other property and liability insurance contracts. The excess other insurance clause is a method of distributing the insurance in those instances in which more than one policy covers a specific loss, and, similar in purpose with that of the pro rata clause, it prevents the insured from profiting through the existence of the insurance contract.

Yet another approach to other insurance is a provision in some contracts that makes the insurance inapplicable to property that is covered by other insurance. A common provision of this type states:

We do not cover articles separately described and specifically insured by other insurance.

Provisions of this type are referred to as *exculpatory clauses,* since they relieve the insurer of liability for loss.

The ocean marine contract provides still another contrast with the pro rata clauses used in property and liability insurance. Under the U.S. rule, if there is double insurance, the ocean marine policy with the earliest effective date is the primary insurance.[8] A policy with a subsequent effective date will be applicable only if the primary insurance is insufficient to provide full coverage for the loss.

Subrogation Another contractual provision designed to prevent the insured from making a profit is the *subrogation clause.* Here, if the insured collects indemnity under the policy and the loss has been caused by the negligence of some third party, the right to collect damages from the negligent party must be relinquished to the insurance carrier. However, relinquishment is required only to the extent of the amount paid by the insurance company. The right of subrogation is based on the principle that if it did not exist, the insured would be permitted to collect twice for the loss, once from the insurance company and once from the negligent party. This, of course, would be profiting from the existence of the insurance contract.

The doctrine of subrogation is applicable only in property and liability insurance. It is never applied in life insurance and seldom in health insurance. For example, if X has a $100,000 life insurance contract and is killed while crossing the street as the result of the negligence of the operator of a 10-ton truck, the widow-beneficiary can collect the $100,000 from the insurance company, and in addition can sue the driver and the trucking firm. The insurance company has no right to reimbursement from the negligent party. The inapplicability of the doctrine is based on the principle that in life insurance the policy is not a contract of indemnity. Support is also provided in the fact that in terms of one's economic value, most individuals will be substantially underinsured. Therefore, the possibility of profiting from the existence of a life insurance contract is relatively slight. The same principles are true in health insurance. For example, if X had a disability income contract that would provide a payment of $100 per week in the

[8] The English rule involved prorating regardless of the order of the dates on the contracts. Any company providing the insurance may become liable for the full amount of its coverage. However, if the insured collects from one specific insurer, the other companies would then be liable to this insurer for their pro rata share of the loss.

event of total disability, and if X is injured seriously as a result of the negligent operation of the 10-ton truck, he or she can collect the $100 per week from the insurance company and can also collect damages from the trucking firm without reference to the insurance coverage. The disability insurance company would have no rights against the negligent third party.

Insurance Is a Personal Contract

Although insurance coverage may apply to property, the risk is transferred to the company from an individual. While we speak of "insuring a house" or some other piece of property, the contract is between the company and a specifically named insured. If the insured should sell the property that is "insured," the protection is not binding in favor of the new owner of the property. Since the company has a right to decide with whom it will and will not do business, the insured cannot transfer the contract to someone else without the written consent of the insurer. The personal characteristics of the insured and the circumstances surrounding the subject matter of the coverage are important to the insurance company in determining whether it will issue the policy.

One important aspect of the application of the personal contract rule to insurance policies is the right of the insured to assign an insurance policy to another person. Since the general rule states that one cannot be forced to contract against one's will, the right of the insured to assign the policy must require the consent of the insurance company. Otherwise, the company could be legally bound on a contract with an individual to whom it would never have issued a policy originally, and on one in which the nature of the risk is altered substantially. For example, suppose an automobile owner decided to sell his or her car to a 17-year-old boy. If it were possible to assign the insurance policy to the boy without the consent of the insurance company, the company would then be in the position of contracting with a person with whom originally it would not have dealt. The insured has the right to assign his or her policy, but in most contracts the assigned policy will be legally binding only with the written consent of the insurance company.

There are instances in which an insured will assign the proceeds of the policy if a loss occurs, for example, to a mortgagee, a lienholder, or another creditor. This type of assignment is valid without the consent of the insurance company; it does not change the contracting parties or the nature of the risk; it merely makes the recipient entitled to a certain amount of money without making the person a party to the contract.

The requirement of written consent of the insurance company in the event of an assignment of the policy is not applicable to all insurance contracts. Life insurance policies are freely assignable without permission. The applicable rule is that anyone having an interest in a life insurance contract can transfer this interest, even to a person who does not have an insurable interest in his life and under circumstances in which no financial consideration is involved. Although no restrictions are placed on the right of the insured to assign a life insurance policy, the policy provides that the insurance company will not be bound by any assignment until it has received written notice of the assignment. This is simply for the protection of the company. An owner might, for example, assign the policy, and the company, not being aware of the fact, might make payment to someone other than the person to whom the policy was assigned. To avoid litigation and eliminate the possibility of being required to make a double payment, the company requires written notice of any assignment and is not bound by the assignment until the notice is received.

The difference in the application of the rule of assignment in life insurance as contrasted with its application in the property and liability field may be explained largely by the fact that an assignment of a life insurance policy does not alter the nature of the risk to the insurance carrier, but merely changes the ownership of the contract. The person whose life is insured is still the person insured, and the assignment should have no appreciable effect on the possibility of the insured's death. In property insurance, however, the assignment could have a substantial effect on the possibility of the occurrence of a loss.

Insurance Is a Unilateral Contract

Only one party to the contract is legally bound to do anything. The insured makes no promises that can be legally enforced. It is true that an insurance policy is a conditional contract, and if the insured violates certain conditions of the contract he or she may be prevented from collecting in the event of a loss.

Insurance Is a Conditional Contract

An insurance contract is said to be a conditional contract, which means that the conditions of the contract

are considered a part of the consideration by the insured. The insurer is obligated to fulfill its promises only if the insured has fulfilled his or her promises. As noted, since an insurance contract is a unilateral contract, the insured cannot be legally required to meet policy conditions. At the same time, if the conditions are not met, he or she may be prevented from collecting in the event of a loss. Although policy conditions are not obligations that the insured can be required to keep, they are requisites to recovery under the policy.

Insurance Is a Contract of Adhesion

A *contract of adhesion* is one prepared by one of the parties (the company) and accepted or rejected by the other (the insured). It is not drawn up through negotiation; the insured who does not particularly like the terms of the contract may choose not to purchase it, but if he or she does purchase it, it must be accepted as it is.

Because the insurance company has the right to draw up the contract, the courts have held that any ambiguity in the contract should be interpreted in favor of the insured. It is somewhat like the case of two small children and the device commonly adopted to settle the dispute as to which of the two gets the biggest piece of pie: "One child cuts and the other gets first pick." The company draws up the contract and the insured gets the benefit of any doubt.

The fact that the insurance policy is a contract of adhesion and the insured must accept or reject the terms as they are written makes the doctrine of "presumption of intent" rather important in the area of insurance. Under this doctrine, the courts have ruled that a person is bound by the terms of a written contract that he or she signs or accepts, whether he or she reads the contract or not. In other words, the court assumes that the insured reads the contract and agrees with the terms thereof.

Insurance Is an Aleatory Contract

Briefly, the term *aleatory* means that the outcome is affected by chance and that the number of dollars given up by the contracting parties will be unequal. The insured pays the required premium, and if no loss occurs, the insurance company pays nothing. If a loss does occur, the insured's premium is small in relation to the amount the insurer will be required to pay. In the sense that it is aleatory, an insurance contract is like a gambling contract.

Insurance Is a Contract of Utmost Good Faith

Partly due to the fact that the contract is aleatory, the insurer and the insured enter into an agreement in which mutual faith is of paramount importance. The legal principle of *uberrimae fidei* (utmost good faith) has deep historical roots in its application to insurance. In the early days of marine insurance, an underwriter was often called on to insure a ship that was halfway around the world and had to accept the word of the applicant that the ship was still afloat. The practical effect of the principle of utmost good faith today lies in the requirement that the applicant for insurance must make full and fair disclosure of the risk to the agent and the company. The risk that the company thinks it is assuming must be the same risk that the insured transfers. Any information about the risk that is known to one party should be known to the other. If the insured intentionally fails to inform the insurer of any facts that would influence the issue of the policy or the rate at which it would be issued, the insurer may have grounds for avoiding coverage. The courts have given meaning to the principle of *utmost good faith* through the evolution of the doctrines of misrepresentation, warranty, and concealment.

When disagreement concerning the conditions relating to an insurance contract arises, the insured or the insurer (or both) may turn to the courts for relief. In some cases, the court will be asked to interpret the contract when there is disagreement about its terms. In other cases, the parties may seek rescission or reformation of the contract. *Rescission* is the annulment or abrogation of the contact. The contract is repudiated and declared null from its beginning. The party seeking rescission of a contract must prove impossibility (usually not the case in insurance) or fraud, misrepresentation of a material fact, or concealment. In insurance, it is usually the insurer that seeks rescission of a contract, usually because of a misrepresentation or concealment of a material fact by the insured.

Reformation is a remedy when a written contract does not reflect the original intent of the parties. It is used to rectify mutual mistakes or unilateral mistakes coupled with fraud by the other party by rewriting the contract to express the original intent of the parties. The purpose of reformation is not to change the terms of the contract. It is to rectify a misstatement of those terms when they have somehow been incorrectly recorded.

Misrepresentation A representation is an oral or written statement made by the applicant prior to, or contemporaneously with, the formation of the contract. It constitutes an inducement for the insurer to enter into the contract. Normally, the representations are the answers to certain questions that are given by the applicant concerning the subject matter of the insurance. For example, in the negotiation of a life insurance contract, if the prospect states in answer to a question that he or she has never had tuberculosis, this statement is a representation. If the statement is false, a *misrepresentation* exists that may provide grounds for the insurer's avoidance of the contract later on. However, a misrepresentation may give grounds for rescission of a contract only if it involves what is known as a *material fact*. A material fact is information that, had it been known, would have caused the insurance company to reject the application or issue the policy on substantially different terms. Facts of minor importance, such as the age at which one's grandparents died, if misrepresented, would have had no influence on the terms of the contract had the truth been known and, therefore, would not provide a basis for rescission of the contract.

The doctrine of misrepresentation is applied with varying degrees of strictness. Since frequently in ocean marine insurance there is little chance for the insurer to inspect the subject matter of the insurance, the company must place greater reliance on the information supplied by the applicant than would be the case in domestic insurance. Therefore, it has always been a rule in ocean marine insurance that a misrepresentation of a material fact, even though there was no bad faith on the part of the insured, is grounds for rescission of the contract. In other words, even though fraud is not involved, the mere fact that certain conditions are misrepresented and exercise an improper influence is sufficient to exonerate the carrier from its contractual obligation.

In most other forms of insurance, the misrepresentation must be made with fraudulent intent before it can be used by the insurer as grounds for rescission of the contract. This application of the principle is, of course, based somewhat on the assumption that the subject matter of the insurance can be inspected by the insurance company. The company, then, is not obligated to depend so strictly for its knowledge on the information provided by the insured and therefore cannot have grounds for voidance of a contract unless it can prove a willful intent to defraud the company. For example, a provision in the basic fire insurance policy states:

> This entire policy shall be void if, whether before or after a loss, the insured has willfully concealed or misrepresented any material fact or circumstance concerning this insurance or the subject matter thereof.

Thus, the fire policy, by its provisions, requires a willful intent on the part of the insured to defraud the company before the policy can be voided.

Many applicants for insurance are inclined to misrepresent important facts. Naturally, the reason for this is to obtain insurance where otherwise no company would issue a policy at all or to obtain the coverage at a lower cost.

In some states there is a statutory requirement that the misrepresented or concealed material fact contribute to the loss before it can give grounds for voiding a policy. These are ill-conceived laws and have about as much justification as valued policy legislation. The illogical result of such legislation may be demonstrated rather easily. For example, in a nonmedical life insurance contract, the insured could misrepresent the fact that he has a serious heart impairment. If the insurer had known this fact, it would not have issued the policy. If the insured dies as a result of an automobile accident, and not because of the heart impairment, the company will be obligated to pay the proceeds of the policy because the misrepresented fact did not contribute to the loss. Such legislation seems to put a premium on fraud or at least make contracts based on fraudulent intent much more feasible. The rule followed in most states, that is, the possibility of voidance whether the misrepresented or concealed fact contributes to the loss or not, places the insurance contract on a much more logical and justifiable basis.

In life insurance, a misrepresentation may be used as grounds for voiding a policy only if the false information is a part of the written application and only if the application, or a photostatic copy thereof, is attached to the policy. In most other forms of insurance, the application is rarely a physical part of contractual arrangement; however, even though the application is not attached to the policy, the doctrine of misrepresentation is still applicable.

Some of the best examples of the operation of the doctrine of misrepresentation are found in automobile insurance. Many automobile insurance companies use a refined premium rating plan, in which the

premium will depend on several factors. The insured is required to fill out, and sign, a long application form. The signature attests to the fact that the applicant requests the company issue the policy and any renewals in reliance on the information provided. The company, then, obtains representations from the insured concerning such facts as the number of moving traffic violations of the insured and members of his or her household in the three years previous to the issuance of the policy, the ages of the operators in the household of the insured, previous cancellations of automobile insurance, and the like. Since the answers to these questions are representations of the insured and since automobile insurance is so important today, it would be desirable to see how far the courts have gone in permitting automobile insurers to void policies because of misrepresentations in the application.

In *Safeco Insurance Company v. Gonacha,* the Colorado Supreme Court held a policy to be void because of a misrepresentation by the insured that he had not had a previous cancellation or had not previously been refused insurance.[9] The court considered the false information to be material and grounds for voiding the policy, even though the application was not attached to and made a part of the policy. In other recent cases, it was held that a misstatement of age is material to the risk and therefore grounds for voiding the policy[10] and that a representation that the automobile would be principally garaged in a community that took a lower premium than the large city where it actually was located would also give grounds for voiding the contract.[11] In *Pittman v. West American Insurance Company,*[12] the court held that a misrepresentation in the application concerning previous accidents and major traffic convictions constituted material misrepresentations and could thus give grounds for voiding the policy. Here, the applicant stated that he had not had any accidents in the three years preceding the date of the application. However, shortly before applying for the

insurance, he had had an accident as a result of which he was fined for careless driving.

These cases emphasize the importance of the doctrine of misrepresentation and the necessity of providing complete and accurate information to the insurance company. Students should learn an excellent lesson from these cases particularly the one involving the representation of the place of principal use of the automobile. Remember that if you intend to leave the rural area or small town in which you reside and go to a relatively large city to attend college, it would be best to reveal this information to the insurance company. Otherwise, you may be driving an automobile around the college campus without any insurance coverage at all.

Warranties When a representation is made a part of the insurance contract, usually by physical attachment of the application to the policy, the statements of the insured then become warranties. Warranties, by definition, also include promises of the insured that are set forth in the policy. The promise to maintain certain protective devices, such as burglar alarms, in proper working order at all times would be an example. A *breach of warranty* may give grounds for voiding a policy, and most important, it may do so without reference to the materiality of the statement or promise. Therefore, whether the insurer was prejudiced by the untruth or nonfulfillment of the promise is not a consideration. The mere breach of warranty will provide grounds for voiding the contract. The warranty, therefore, is quite different from a representation in that (1) the warranty need not be material and (2) the warranty must be a part of the contractual agreement.

A breach of warranty as a means of avoiding a contract is in general much too harsh a doctrine to be applied to insurance contracts. As a consequence, its unqualified use is found only in ocean marine insurance. Here, for example, if the insured warrants that the ship will be used only in coastwise trade, any use otherwise, even though it would not materially increase the risk, would be a breach of warranty and could void the contract. However, in other forms of insurance, the use of the doctrine has been modified substantially. Courts have tended to look with disfavor on the strict application of the doctrine and, in most instances, have modified it by requiring that the breach of warranty materially increase the risk before it may be used to void an insurance contract. There have also been some statutory modifications

[9] 350 Pac. (2d) 189. Incorrect statements concerning previous cancellations have been held in other cases to be grounds for voiding coverage. *Draeosuich v. Allstate Insurance Company,* 118 N.E. (2d) 57, is typical.

[10] *State Farm Mutual Automobile Insurance Company v. Mossey,* 195 Fed. (2d) 56.

[11] *Purcell v. Pacific Automobile Insurance Company,* 64 Pac. (2d) 1114.

[12] 25 C. C. H. (Auto 2d) 349.

of the use of the doctrine. For example, in life insurance, the statements of the insured, regardless of the fact that they are part of the contract, can have the legal effect only of representations. This means that the breach of warranty must involve a material fact. Other statutory modifications provide that the breach of warranty will prevent recovery by the insured only if it increased the risk of loss, or only if it contributed to the loss. The disfavor into which warranties have fallen and the difficulties of enforcing their use are gradually leading to their abandonment except in ocean marine contracts. Instead of a promise in the form of a warranty, such as one requiring the insured to maintain certain protective equipment (e.g., burglar alarms) in proper working order at all times, the policy may provide an exclusion to the effect that the insurance coverage is not applicable while the equipment is in disrepair.

Concealment The disclosure of proper and accurate information is not all that is required if the knowledge of both parties of the material facts is to be equal. The applicant also has the obligation of voluntarily disclosing material facts concerning the subject matter of the insurance that the company could not be expected to know about. The failure of the insured to disclose such facts constitutes a *concealment,* and a willful concealment of a material fact will give grounds for voiding the policy.[13]

Since the insurance company cannot be expected to inquire about everything that may be material to the subject matter of the insurance, the insured has an obligation to disclose extraordinary facts within the scope of his or her knowledge. For example, a company normally would not ask the insured in the application whether there is a whiskey still in the basement of his or her home. However, if the insured has such an apparatus, this fact must be revealed to the company. If this is not done, the policyholder may be dismayed to discover that the insurance is without effect. Legislatures have also tampered with this doctrine, and, as is the case with representations, some states require that the concealed fact contribute to the loss before it will give grounds for voiding the policy. So if faulty wiring in the attic, rather than the still, were the cause of the loss, the policy would be valid. There are many other possibilities of conceal-

ments, yet this example should be sufficient for the student to recognize that any extraordinary fact related to the subject matter of the insurance, which the insurance company could not be expected to know, requires a disclosure of such fact to the insurance company.

Waiver and Estoppel Directly linked to the doctrines of concealment and misrepresentation are those of waiver and estoppel. These also relate directly to the law of agency and to the power of the agent.

Waiver is the intentional relinquishment of a known right. If the agent issues a contract, knowing that the conditions are being violated, that agent is deemed to have waived the violation. For example, let us assume that a man takes out an automobile liability policy, and in the application he states that no male drivers under 25 years of age will be operating the car, when the truth of the matter is that his 17-year-old son operates the car almost exclusively (probably in stock car races). Let us assume further that the agent knows full well that this is the case. Since the knowledge of the agent is presumed to be knowledge of the company, the agent is deemed to have waived this violation when issuing the policy.

Estoppel prevents a person from alleging or denying a fact the contrary of which, by his or her own previous action, the person has admitted. The waiving of a violation of the contract by the agent *estopps* the company from denying liability on the basis of this violation at some time in the future.

The powers of the life insurance agent, as we have said before, are somewhat more limited than are those of the property and liability agent. For the property and liability agent, however, make no mistake: The powers are extremely broad, and the power of waiver on the part of the agent has been extended by court decision. For example, in an attempt to protect themselves from actions on the part of their agents, insurance companies have inserted the following clause in the standard fire policy:

> No permission affecting this insurance shall exist or waiver of any provision be valid, unless granted herein or expressed in writing added hereto.

Does this clause really protect the companies from the waiver powers of agents? Let us suppose that an insurance agent receives a call from a client who says, "I just put a still in my basement and I wondered if this would affect my insurance." (Naturally it

[13] In ocean marine insurance the concealment does not have to be willful. In other forms of insurance, however, the material fact concealed must be with the intent to defraud.

would, for this is a provision in the policy suspending coverage at any time the hazard is increased by any means within the control of the insured.) The agent, however, says, "Don't worry about it—it's OK." If a fire occurs, will the insured be able to collect? The company will probably point to the clause stating that no waiver is valid unless expressed in writing, but this may not do much good. Some courts have ruled that the agent can waive the quoted clause along with any other clauses in the contract. In other words, the power of the agent is so strong that he or she can waive the very clause prohibiting waiver of any of the clauses in the contract!

The Parol Evidence Rule While on the subject of the interpretation of contracts, we should note in passing one of the important principles of law related to the interpretation of written contracts: the *parol evidence rule*. The parol evidence rule holds that when parties to a contract have committed their agreement to writing, the written contract is presumed to contain the agreement of the parties and that the contract cannot be modified or changed by parol (i.e., oral) evidence. In simple terms, this means that arguments about what the parties "agreed to" cannot be used to contradict what the written contract expresses as the agreement. There are a limited number of exceptions in which the parol evidence rule is not applicable and in which the terms of a written contract can therefore be modified by oral evidence. Parol evidence may be admissible in situations in which the terms of a written contract are incomplete, where the contract is ambiguous, or when there has been a mistake or fraud in the preparation of the written contract.

With respect to insurance contracts, a strict application of the parol evidence rule means that the written contract is the agreement of the parties, and that it cannot be modified by the insured's argument that the agent had agreed to provide coverage different from that in the contract.[14]

The Insurance Contract as a Contract

When members of society who have entered into a contractual arrangement disagree about the terms of the contract, or one of the parties questions the very existence of the contract, either party has recourse to the courts. The court will decide the issue in question and the decision will become a part of the body of common law. Common law is sometimes termed unwritten law to contrast it with statutory or written law, which consists of statutes and codes enacted by legislatures. Common law is unwritten in the sense that it can be found only in the various decisions of the courts. Under the doctrine of *stare decisis,* the courts, in attempting to decide an issue, look at previous decisions by other courts on the same point. If there is no precedent available, the court must decide the issue, and in doing so, it creates a precedent. At times the courts may deviate from previous precedents on the grounds that the circumstances are different, or that such deviation is necessary to serve the ends of justice.[16]

Reasonable Expectations We have already noted that, with respect to insurance contracts, any ambiguity is interpreted against the insurer. There is a second doctrine of policy interpretation with which the reader should be familiar, the doctrine of reasonable expectation. The doctrine of the insured's *reasonable expectations* represents an extension of the general rule that ambiguities are to be interpreted against the insurer. Under this doctrine, the courts interpret an insurance policy to mean what a reasonable buyer would expect it to mean. When it is applied, the *reasonable expectations* of the insured determine the coverage of the policy, even though policy provisions may deny those expectations. An important corollary of this doctrine is that policy language is to be interpreted as a layperson would understand it, and not as it might be interpreted by a lawyer or other person skilled in the law of insurance.[15]

Complexity of Insurance Contracts The complicated nature of the insurance contract has made it the butt of many jokes. "Why," people often ask, "doesn't the insurance company make the policy language simple enough for the layperson to understand?" "Why not cut out some of the excess wordage?" The answer to both questions is that the companies are in

[14] Although the insurer would not be held liable for the agent's agreement to obtain a different form of coverage than that which was written, the agent might be liable to the insured for negligent failure to obtain the appropriate coverage.

[15] See Robert E. Keeton. *Basic Text on Insurance Law* (St. Paul, Minn.: West, 1971), p. 357.

[16] The common law of this country is based to a large extent on English common law. The term common was originally applied to distinguish those doctrines that were common to all of England from those applied only on a local basis.

fact attempting to do precisely that. There is a trend within the industry toward simplified policy language, and much progress has been made in this area. However, it is a difficult task. As a contract enforceable by law, the insurance policy must set forth as clearly and as unambiguously as possible every condition and obligation of both parties. In addition, the insurer must attempt to define as precisely as possible the particular event against which protection is provided, while at the same time attempt to protect itself against misinterpretation by the courts. In spite of the fact that companies are attempting to simplify policy wording, the task is complicated by the stern realities of the law and the possibility that any ambiguity will be interpreted against the insurer.

Insurance and the Courts The courts play an important role in the operation of private insurance. Court decisions are important in the individual case because they decide the issue. More important from our point of view, they set precedents that are applied in future instances. Court interpretations of insurance policies make policy interpretation difficult in one sense, in that there is always the distinct possibility that the court will construe a contract in a way that the insurer had not considered. On the other hand, past decisions are useful in interpreting contracts, for they indicate the court's view of the policy's meaning. Since the insurer has the option of changing future contracts, court decisions often influence the drawing of insurance contracts.

Policy Construction

In the chapters that follow, we will examine a number of insurance contracts, and although all are different, they are similar in that they are all composed of four basic parts:

1. Declarations
2. Insuring agreement
3. Exclusions
4. Conditions

Declarations The declarations section contains the statements made by the insured. As we have seen, these are usually considered to be representations by the courts. Also included in this section is information about the location of the property insured, the name of the policyholder, and other matters relating to the identification of the person or property insured.

Insuring Agreements In this section, the company promises to pay for loss if it should result from the perils covered. Coverage may be provided in one of two principal ways. It is either on a *named-peril basis,* in which case the policy lists the perils insured against, or it is on an *open-peril basis.* Open-peril policies cover loss by any perils except those that are specifically excluded.

Exclusions In this section, the company states what it will not do. The number of exclusions has a direct relationship to the broadness or narrowness of the insuring agreement. If the policy is written on a named-peril basis, the exclusions may be few. On the other hand, open-peril policies require more exclusions to eliminate coverage for those perils that are uninsurable. The exclusions are a basic part of the contract and a complete knowledge of them is essential to a thorough understanding of the agreement. Certain perils must be excluded from insurance contracts either because they are not insurable or because the basic premium does not contemplate the exposure and the coverage must be obtained through the payment of an additional premium or under another more specialized contract.

Conditions This section spells out in detail the duties and rights of both parties. Most of the clauses contained in it are fairly standard; they relate to the duties of the insured in the event of loss and protect the insurance company from adverse loss experience through increases in the hazard within the control of the insured.

IMPORTANT CONCEPTS TO REMEMBER

requirements of an enforceable contract	apparent authority	binder
offer and acceptance	consideration	void contract
express authority	legal object	voidable contract
implied authority	legal form	contract of indemnity
	competent parties	insurable interest

actual cash value	unilateral contract	material fact
replacement cost	contract of adhesion	breach of warranty
valued policies	conditional contract	concealment
cash payment policies	aleatory contract	waiver
valued policy law	utmost good faith	estoppel
pro rata clause	*uberrimae fidei*	parol evidence rule
exculpatory clause	rescision	reasonable expectation
subrogation clause	reformation	
personal contract	misrepresentation	

QUESTIONS FOR REVIEW

1. We have noted several instances in which the principle of indemnity is not enforced in the various fields of insurance. List the exceptions to the principle of indemnity with which you are now familiar and explain why each is permitted.

2. Your roommate and you have automobile insurance policies written by the same insurance company, and with identical coverage. As a matter of fact, you both drive the same year and model car, but his premium is $220 less than yours. He tells you that he was able to obtain the insurance cheaper by having the automobile registered in his father's name and having his father purchase the insurance. Advise him.

3. What is meant by the expression, "The policyholder gets the benefit of the doubt," in connection with any interpretation of the provisions of the life insurance policy?

4. The principles of insurable interest, subrogation, actual cash value, and pro rata apportionment all stem from the broader principle of indemnity. Explain what is meant by the principle of indemnity, and indicate specifically in what way each of the four principles mentioned above helps to enforce the principle of indemnity.

5. In what ways have the doctrines of warranty and misrepresentation been modified in their application to the field of insurance in the United States?

6. What is the key factor in determining whether a fact is "material" in the application of the doctrines of misrepresentation and concealment?

7. Insurance contracts are said to be aleatory. What important additional feature of insurance contracts follows from this characteristic?

8. In what sense is an insurance contract conditional? In what sense is it unilateral?

9. Strictly speaking, life insurance is not a contract of indemnity. Nevertheless, there are certain applications of the principle of indemnity in this field. To what extent does the principle of indemnity apply to life insurance?

10. Identify and briefly describe the four basic sections of insurance contracts.

QUESTIONS FOR DISCUSSION

1. It was said that some people carried life insurance policies on the czar of Russia as a form of speculation. Although there was no insurable interest, presumably none of those carrying the insurance were in a position to cause intentional injury to the czar. Do you feel this form of speculation should have been considered objectionable?

2. Fred Schwartz is from Keokuk, Iowa. He is currently attending the College of Insurance in New York City. However, he purchases his automobile insurance from his hometown agent, giving his hometown address. Do you believe that the insurer could successfully deny liability in the event of an accident? On what grounds?

3. Rosie LaRue calls her insurance agent at 3:00 A.M. and asks the agent to increase the coverage on her house from $60,000 to $80,000. He agrees to do so. During the night the house burns to the ground, and the company denies liability for the additional $20,000 in coverage. On what grounds do you think the denial is based? Should the company be obligated to pay the original $60,000?

4. The subrogation provision enforces the principle of indemnity by preventing the insured from profiting from the existence of the insurance contract. What other beneficial effect might it have?

5. Jones tells the insurance company that his building is equipped with a sprinkler system and that a guard is on duty inside the premises when they are closed. Neither statement is true. The building is destroyed by a windstorm. Do you believe that an intentional misrepresentation by an applicant for insurance should permit the insurer to deny coverage for a loss even if the misrepresented fact had no relationship to the loss? Why?

SUGGESTIONS FOR ADDITIONAL READING

Black, Kenneth, Jr., and Harold D. Skipper, Jr. *Life Insurance,* 13th ed. Englewood Cliffs, N.J.: Prentice-Hall, 2000. Chapter 9.

Crawford, Murial L. *Life and Health Insurance Law,* LOMA Edition. New York: McGraw-Hill, 1997.

Grieder, J. E., and W. H. Beadles. *Law and the Life Insurance Contract,* 4th ed. Homewood, Ill.: Richard D. Irwin, 1979.

Horn, R. C. *Subrogation in Insurance Theory and Practice.* Homewood, Ill.: Richard D. Irwin, 1964.

Keeton, Robert E., and Alan I. Widiss. *Insurance Law – Student Edition.* St. Paul, MN.: West Publishing, 1988.

Lorimer, James J., et al. *The Legal Environment of Insurance,* 4th ed., vol. 1. Malvern, Pa.: American Institute for Property and Liability Underwriters, 1993.

McGill, D. M. *Legal Aspects of Life Insurance.* Homewood, Ill.: Richard D. Irwin, 1959.

Patterson, E. W., and W. F. Young, Jr. *Cases and Materials on the Law of Insurance,* 4th ed. New York: Foundation Press, 1961.

———. *Essentials of Insurance Law,* 2nd ed. New York: McGraw-Hill, 1957.

Vance, W. R., and B. M. Anderson. *Handbook on the Law of Insurance,* 5th ed. St. Paul, Minn.: West Publishing, 1951.

WEB SITES TO EXPLORE

Law Links on the World Wide Web	http://www.kahane.com/links.html
Law of Contracts (Cornell Law School)	http://www.law.cornell.edu/topics/contracts.html
Legal Information Institute (Cornell Law School)	http://www.law.cornell.edu/

MANAGING PERSONAL RISKS

■

Were it not for human life values there would be no
property values at all.

— S. S. HUEBNER

CHAPTER OBJECTIVES

When you have finished this chapter, you should be able to
- Identify the exposures that arise in connection with an individual's income
- Explain the concept of present value and why it is important in measuring life values
- Explain the human life value concept
- Describe how various lifestyles affect the risk of loss from premature death
- Explain the process of needs analysis
- Identify the sources of protection that may be available to an individual as protection in the event of premature death
- Explain how the risk of disability differs from the risk of premature death
- Explain the relationship between the risk of premature death and superannuation

We begin our study of specific types of insurance by looking at personal risks and insurance coverages designed to deal with them. As explained in Chapter 1, personal risks relate to the loss of the ability to earn income and include premature death, dependent old age (or superannuation), sickness or disability, and unemployment.

We treat these risks first to follow the philosophy of risk management. This entire text is designed to develop concepts that should be used in dealing with risks the individual faces. We noted in Chapter 4 that

losses with the greatest potential severity merit first attention. Following this principle, we turn first to the risk with the greatest potential severity for the individual and the family unit, the loss of income. A well-ordered personal insurance program should begin with protection of the individual's most valuable asset, income-earning ability. It is foolish to insure the property a person owns while neglecting to insure the asset that produces the property.

When designing a program to meet personal risks, individuals may already have some protection from a

number of sources. Social insurance programs, discussed in the next chapter, may provide an income in the case of death or disability. For example, Social Security provides some resources to meet the premature death, superannuation, and disability exposures. Workers compensation plans pay benefits to disabled workers and dependents of deceased workers if the death or disability arose out of employment. Many individuals also receive benefits from their employers. These may include employer-provided life insurance, pension plans, disability income plans, and medical expense insurance. Where government programs or employee benefits do not meet needs, the individual must make other arrangements, either through personal savings, insurance, or some combination.

This chapter will examine the exposures faced by the individual and family. The next chapter considers Social Security, workers compensation, and a number of other social insurance programs that may provide some resources when an individual dies or becomes disabled or unemployed. Finally, in later chapters, we will look at insurance products designed to deal with these risks.

We begin by focusing on those risks that arise from uncertainty concerning the time of death. The individual faces two mutually exclusive risks that arise from the uncertainty concerning the time of death: premature death and superannuation. Premature death occurs when the death takes place while others remain dependent on the individual's income. Superannuation is the risk of outliving one's income, that is, the risk of retiring without adequate assets to cover living expenses during the period of retirement.

The risk of *premature death* and the risk of *superannuation* are, in a sense, competing and diametric needs. If the individual dies prematurely, he or she will have no need for funds that were being accumulated for retirement. If the individual lives until retirement, provision made for premature death will not be used.

As we will see when we look at life insurance, some types of life insurance include an accumulating fund that can provide funds for retirement. This means that, although the basic function of life insurance is to provide protection against financial loss arising from premature death, it can also be used to insure against premature death and also as a vehicle for accumulating funds.

When no one is dependent on the individual and his or her death will not deprive anyone, there is no risk of financial loss, and protection against premature death is unnecessary. When protection against premature death is not needed, other approaches to accumulating funds for retirement will generally be more attractive than life insurance.

OBJECTIVES IN MANAGING PERSONAL RISKS

As in the case of risk management generally, the first step in managing personal risks is to establish objectives. Because personal risks involve the potential loss of income, the objectives in this area logically relate to the income that would be lost.

The first objective in managing personal risks is to avoid the deprivation of the individual and those dependent on him or her in the event of a loss that causes the termination of income. Achieving this objective generally means making arrangements to replace the income that would be lost as a result of death, retirement, disability, or unemployment. Insurance is a common approach to replacing such income.

In addition to this risk management objective, there may be other objectives derived from personal financial planning. One such objective is sometimes the goal of transferring the maximum wealth possible to dependents. Note that this second objective is fundamentally different from the goal of providing for those who are dependent and who would suffer deprivation if the income on which they are dependent were terminated. Eventually, offspring reach a point at which they are no longer dependent on their parents. The parents' concern for their children, however, may not end at this point. Usually, parents want to transfer wealth to their children (or other heirs) regardless of the children's need. To achieve this goal, they want to avoid the shrinkage that can occur as assets pass from generation to generation. Fortunately, there are measures that can minimize the shrinkage of the estate. These measures are generally referred to as estate planning.[1]

[1] Like the risk of income loss to dependents, premature death can also be a peril causing estate shrinkage. In the case of the estate, death is *premature* if it occurs before the individual has taken the appropriate steps to minimize the shrinkage of the estate. Although the process of estate planning is beyond the scope of this text, we will address those facets of the estate shrinkage exposure that have implications for life insurance purchases.

Finally, in addition to the objectives of protecting dependents from deprivation that would result from income producer's *premature* death and maximizing the wealth that is transferred to heirs, the individual may have other goals. These goals relate to the individual's plans for the future and things he or she hopes to achieve. They may include the education of children or grandchildren, charitable gifts, and other personal aspirations that might be frustrated by premature death.

OTHER STEPS IN MANAGING PERSONAL RISKS

The remaining steps in managing personal risks are the same as those discussed in Chapter 2: identifying the risks, measuring and evaluating those risks, selecting the risk management technique that will be used to address the risk, designing and implementing a plan to implement the decision, and evaluation and review. We have already noted the perils that give rise to personal risks: death, superannuation, disability, and unemployment. Because the risks relating to the loss of income may differ depending on the peril that threatens income, we will discuss the remaining steps in dealing with personal risks separately for each of the perils that threaten income.

MANAGING RISKS ASSOCIATED WITH PREMATURE DEATH

Death can be a source of loss in two ways. The first is in triggering the expenses associated with death itself. These consist primarily of funeral costs, payment of debts owed by the individual, and death transfer costs such as the cost of probate and estate taxes. The second loss occasioned by death is the loss of income that would have been earned by the deceased.

Identifying Risks Associated with Premature Death

On first consideration, it might seem that the risk of income loss resulting from premature death is universal. After all, no one lives forever. But death does not automatically result in financial loss. The individual who dies does not suffer financial loss; the financial loss is sustained by others who are dependent on

the income earned by the individual. The essential ingredient in the risk of income loss due to premature death is the existence of someone who would suffer deprivation as a result of the individual's death. The first step in determining whether the risk of lost income exists, then, is to determine whether anyone will suffer deprivation as a result of the death. When no one will be deprived of income as a result of death, there is no risk of financial loss due to premature death.

The expenses that arise directly from an individual's death, such as burial expenses, can be funded out of assets owned by the individual at the time of death. If the deceased had no assets at the time of death, burial costs must be paid by survivors or by the state. Overall, however, the costs created by death—the so-called last expenses—are usually modest and seldom require significant measures.[2] The loss of income that results from the individual's death may be significantly greater, and it is the loss of one's income-earning ability that is the major risk-management problem most people must deal with.

Measuring Risks Associated with Premature Death

Two approaches have been suggested to evaluate the risk of premature death: human life value and needs analysis. The human life value concept focuses on the earnings of the individual that would have been lost in cases of premature death. Needs analysis, on the other hand, focuses on the income and cash needs that must be met following an individual's premature death and compares those needs to resources already available.[3]

The Human Life Value The application of the concept of *human life value* to insurance purchase decisions is generally credited to S. S. Huebner.[4] Simply stated, the human life value is based on the individual's income-earning ability; it is the present value of

[2] Debts owed by the individual at the time of death represent a unique exposure. If an individual dies with debts that exceed assets, the loss falls on the creditors. Some people may feel a moral obligation to provide funds for payment of debts that exist at the time of their death, but there is no legal obligation.

[3] We cannot place a value on human life. What we attempt to measure is the income-producing capacity of the individual, which is something entirely different.

[4] S. S. Huebner, *The Economics of Life Insurance,* 3rd ed. (New York: Appleton-Century-Crofts, 1959), p. 5.

the income lost by dependents as a result of the person's death. Any attempt to measure the human life value must necessarily consider present value, a concept that will be familiar to students who have studied finance. Because an understanding of this concept is essential to a meaningful measurement of income flows, we will pause for our discussion to review the concept for those readers who have not encountered it in their previous studies. (The student who is familiar with the concept of present value and the time value of money can flip forward through the pages to the point where we resume our discussion.)

Time Value of Money and Present Value The term *time value of money* refers to the fact that $1 today is worth more than $1 a year from now (or at some other time in the future).[5] This is because $1 now can be invested at some positive rate of return and will be worth more in the future. If $1 can be invested at 6 percent, $1.06 is the future value of a present dollar in one year at 6 percent. If we assume that the $1.06 is reinvested at 6 percent, the future value of $1 invested at 6 percent for two years is $1.00 times 1.06 times 1.06, or, $1.1236. Continuing the computation, we can determine the future value of $1 invested for any number of years; this is called *compounding,* reflecting the fact that interest is paid on the interest earned in previous periods.

Just as it is sometimes useful to know the future value of a present dollar, we sometimes want to know the present value of a future dollar. The present value of a future dollar is simply the amount that will be required, invested at a specified rate of interest, to equal a dollar in a specified number of years. The present value of a future dollar one year from now is computed by dividing the present value of a present dollar ($1) by the future value of a dollar at the specified rate of interest. For example, $1 invested at 6 percent for a year will be worth $1.06 at the end of the year. How much must we have now, so that if we invest it at 6 percent it will equal $1 at the end of the year?

$$\frac{\$100}{\$106} = \$0.943396$$

This $0.943396 is the *present value of a future dollar* or *the discount factor.* If we invest $0.943396 at 6

percent, it will equal $1 at the end of a year. We can divide the present value of a dollar in one year by the future value of a future dollar in one year to determine the present value of a dollar now in two years:

$$\frac{\$0.943396}{\$1.06} = \$0.889996$$

Present value tables are available that indicate the present value of a future dollar for various numbers of years and at various rates. Table 10.1 indicates the present value of a future dollar at various interest rates from 1 to 40 years. It indicates the value of $1 to be received at the end of some specified number of years at various discount rates. It tells how much an individual would have to invest at a given rate of interest to receive $1 at some time in the future. Reading down the table, we can see that one must invest about $0.31 at 6 percent to have $1 at the end of 20 years.

Discounted Income Flows One of the most useful applications of the concept of present value is in discounting a flow of income to determine its present value. We can estimate the human life value by discounting the expected stream of income that would accrue to the dependents as a result of their breadwinner's continued employment. If we deduct the amount of the income that would be consumed by the producer personally and discount the remainder, we have a notion of the present value of the stream of income that would be lost.

Human Life Value Illustrated For the purpose of illustration, consider a 25-year-old person, who we will assume plans to work until age 65. If we estimate that his or her average earnings will be $60,000 annually and that two-thirds of the income will be consumed by dependents, the individual's economic value to dependents is $40,000 a year for 40 years. However, the life value at age 25 is not measured by this total figure, but by the amount that, invested at some conservative rate of interest, would yield an income of $40,000 per year for 40 years. We could compute this amount by discounting the $40,000 in each year by the appropriate discount rate for that year. Alternately, we can consult a table such as Table 10.2, which indicates the present value of $1 each year for different numbers of years. Table 10.2 shows that a present investment of $15.046 will yield an income of $1 per year for 40 years. By multiplying

[5] The expression "A bird in the hand is worth two in the bush" expresses the time value of birds, and suggests a discount rate of 0.5 as the present value of a future bird. Here we are doing the same thing with money.

TABLE 10.1 Present Value of $1 in N Years at Various Discount Rates

Year	1%	2%	3%	4%	5%	6%	7%	8%	9%	10%	11%	12%	13%	14%	15%
1	0.99010	0.98039	0.97087	0.96154	0.95238	0.94340	0.93458	0.92593	0.91743	0.90909	0.90090	0.89286	0.88496	0.87719	0.86957
2	0.98030	0.96117	0.94260	0.92456	0.90703	0.89000	0.87344	0.85734	0.84168	0.82645	0.81162	0.79719	0.78315	0.76947	0.75614
3	0.97059	0.94232	0.91514	0.88900	0.86384	0.83962	0.81630	0.79383	0.77218	0.75131	0.73119	0.71178	0.69305	0.67497	0.65752
4	0.96098	0.92385	0.88849	0.85480	0.82270	0.79209	0.76290	0.73503	0.70843	0.68301	0.65873	0.63552	0.61332	0.59208	0.57175
5	0.95147	0.90573	0.86261	0.82193	0.78353	0.74726	0.71299	0.68058	0.64993	0.62092	0.59345	0.56743	0.54276	0.51937	0.49718
6	0.94205	0.88797	0.83748	0.79031	0.74622	0.70496	0.66634	0.63017	0.59627	0.56447	0.53464	0.50663	0.48032	0.45559	0.43233
7	0.93272	0.87056	0.81309	0.75992	0.71068	0.66506	0.62275	0.58349	0.54703	0.51316	0.48166	0.45235	0.42506	0.39964	0.37594
8	0.92348	0.85349	0.78941	0.73069	0.67684	0.62741	0.58201	0.54027	0.50187	0.46651	0.43393	0.40388	0.37616	0.35056	0.32690
9	0.91434	0.83676	0.76642	0.70259	0.64461	0.59190	0.54393	0.50025	0.46043	0.42410	0.39092	0.36061	0.33288	0.30751	0.28426
10	0.90529	0.82035	0.74409	0.67556	0.61391	0.55839	0.50835	0.46319	0.42241	0.38554	0.35218	0.32197	0.29459	0.26974	0.24718
11	0.89632	0.80426	0.72242	0.64958	0.58468	0.52679	0.47509	0.42888	0.38753	0.35049	0.31728	0.28748	0.26070	0.23662	0.21494
12	0.88745	0.78849	0.70138	0.62460	0.55684	0.49697	0.44401	0.39711	0.35553	0.31863	0.28584	0.25668	0.23071	0.20756	0.18691
13	0.87866	0.77303	0.68095	0.60057	0.53032	0.46884	0.41496	0.36770	0.32618	0.28966	0.25751	0.22917	0.20416	0.18207	0.16253
14	0.86996	0.75788	0.66112	0.57748	0.50507	0.44230	0.38782	0.34046	0.29925	0.26333	0.23199	0.20462	0.18068	0.15971	0.14133
15	0.86135	0.74301	0.64186	0.55526	0.48102	0.41727	0.36245	0.31524	0.27454	0.23939	0.20900	0.18270	0.15989	0.14010	0.12289
16	0.85282	0.72845	0.62317	0.53391	0.45811	0.39365	0.33873	0.29189	0.25187	0.21763	0.18829	0.16312	0.14150	0.12289	0.10686
17	0.84438	0.71416	0.60502	0.51337	0.43630	0.37136	0.31657	0.27027	0.23107	0.19784	0.16963	0.14564	0.12522	0.10780	0.09293
18	0.83602	0.70016	0.58739	0.49363	0.41552	0.35034	0.29586	0.25025	0.21199	0.17986	0.15282	0.13004	0.11081	0.09456	0.08081
19	0.82774	0.68643	0.57029	0.47464	0.39573	0.33051	0.27651	0.23171	0.19449	0.16351	0.13768	0.11611	0.09806	0.08295	0.07027
20	0.81954	0.67297	0.55368	0.45639	0.37689	0.31180	0.25842	0.21455	0.17843	0.14864	0.12403	0.10367	0.08678	0.07276	0.06110
21	0.81143	0.65978	0.53755	0.43883	0.35894	0.29416	0.24151	0.19866	0.16370	0.13513	0.11174	0.09256	0.07680	0.06383	0.05313
22	0.80340	0.64684	0.52189	0.42196	0.34185	0.27751	0.22571	0.18394	0.15018	0.12285	0.10067	0.08264	0.06796	0.05599	0.04620
23	0.79544	0.63416	0.50669	0.40573	0.32557	0.26180	0.21095	0.17032	0.13778	0.11168	0.09069	0.07379	0.06014	0.04911	0.04017
24	0.78757	0.62172	0.49193	0.39012	0.31007	0.24698	0.19715	0.15770	0.12640	0.10153	0.08170	0.06588	0.05323	0.04308	0.03493
25	0.77977	0.60953	0.47761	0.37512	0.29530	0.23300	0.18425	0.14602	0.11597	0.09230	0.07361	0.05882	0.04710	0.03779	0.03038
26	0.77205	0.59758	0.46369	0.36069	0.28124	0.21981	0.17220	0.13520	0.10639	0.08391	0.06631	0.05252	0.04168	0.03315	0.02642
27	0.76440	0.58586	0.45019	0.34682	0.26785	0.20737	0.16093	0.12519	0.09761	0.07628	0.05974	0.04689	0.03689	0.02908	0.02297
28	0.75684	0.57437	0.43708	0.33348	0.25509	0.19563	0.15040	0.11591	0.08955	0.06934	0.05382	0.04187	0.03264	0.02551	0.01997
29	0.74934	0.56311	0.42435	0.32065	0.24295	0.18456	0.14056	0.10733	0.08215	0.06304	0.04849	0.03738	0.02889	0.02237	0.01737
30	0.74192	0.55207	0.41199	0.30832	0.23138	0.17411	0.13137	0.09938	0.07537	0.05731	0.04368	0.03338	0.02557	0.01963	0.01510
31	0.73458	0.54125	0.39999	0.29646	0.22036	0.16425	0.12277	0.09202	0.06915	0.05210	0.03935	0.02980	0.02262	0.01722	0.01313
32	0.72730	0.53063	0.38834	0.28506	0.20987	0.15496	0.11474	0.08520	0.06344	0.04736	0.03545	0.02661	0.02002	0.01510	0.01142
33	0.72010	0.52023	0.37703	0.27409	0.19987	0.14619	0.10723	0.07889	0.05820	0.04306	0.03194	0.02376	0.01772	0.01325	0.00993
34	0.71297	0.51003	0.36604	0.26355	0.19035	0.13791	0.10022	0.07305	0.05339	0.03914	0.02878	0.02121	0.01568	0.01162	0.00864
35	0.70591	0.50003	0.35538	0.25342	0.18129	0.13011	0.09366	0.06763	0.04899	0.03558	0.02592	0.01894	0.01388	0.01019	0.00751
36	0.69892	0.49022	0.34503	0.24367	0.17266	0.12274	0.08754	0.06262	0.04494	0.03235	0.02335	0.01691	0.01228	0.00894	0.00653
37	0.69200	0.48061	0.33498	0.23430	0.16444	0.11579	0.08181	0.05799	0.04123	0.02941	0.02104	0.01510	0.01087	0.00784	0.00568
38	0.68515	0.47119	0.32523	0.22529	0.15661	0.10924	0.07646	0.05369	0.03783	0.02673	0.01896	0.01348	0.00962	0.00688	0.00494
39	0.67837	0.46195	0.31575	0.21662	0.14915	0.10306	0.07146	0.04971	0.03470	0.02430	0.01708	0.01204	0.00851	0.00604	0.00429
40	0.67165	0.45289	0.30656	0.20829	0.14205	0.09722	0.06678	0.04603	0.03184	0.02209	0.01538	0.01075	0.00753	0.00529	0.00373

TABLE 10.2 Present Value of $1 Annually for N Years at Various Rates

Year	1%	2%	3%	4%	5%	6%	7%	8%	9%	10%	11%	12%	13%	14%	15%
1	0.99010	0.98039	0.97087	0.96154	0.95238	0.94340	0.93458	0.92593	0.91743	0.90909	0.90090	0.89286	0.88496	0.87719	0.86957
2	1.97040	1.94156	1.91347	1.88609	1.85941	1.83339	1.80802	1.78326	1.75911	1.73554	1.71252	1.69005	1.66810	1.64666	1.62571
3	2.94099	2.88388	2.82861	2.77509	2.72325	2.67301	2.62432	2.57710	2.53129	2.48685	2.44371	2.40183	2.36115	2.32163	2.28323
4	3.90197	3.80773	3.71710	3.62990	3.54595	3.46511	3.38721	3.31213	3.23972	3.16987	3.10245	3.03735	2.97447	2.91371	2.85498
5	4.85343	4.71346	4.57971	4.45182	4.32948	4.21236	4.10020	3.99271	3.88965	3.79079	3.69590	3.60478	3.51723	3.43308	3.35216
6	5.79548	5.60143	5.41719	5.24214	5.07569	4.91732	4.76654	4.62288	4.48592	4.35526	4.23054	4.11141	3.99755	3.88867	3.78448
7	6.72819	6.47199	6.23028	6.00205	5.78637	5.58238	5.38929	5.20637	5.03295	4.86842	4.71220	4.56376	4.42261	4.28830	4.16042
8	7.65168	7.32548	7.01969	6.73274	6.46321	6.20979	5.97130	5.74664	5.53482	5.33493	5.14612	4.96764	4.79877	4.63886	4.48732
9	8.56602	8.16224	7.78611	7.43533	7.10782	6.80169	6.51523	6.24689	5.99525	5.75902	5.53705	5.32825	5.13166	4.94637	4.77158
10	9.47130	8.98259	8.53020	8.11090	7.72173	7.36009	7.02358	6.71008	6.41766	6.14457	5.88923	5.65022	5.42624	5.21612	5.01877
11	10.36763	9.78685	9.25262	8.76048	8.30641	7.88687	7.49867	7.13896	6.80519	6.49506	6.20652	5.93770	5.68694	5.45273	5.23371
12	11.25508	10.57534	9.95400	9.38507	8.86325	8.38384	7.94269	7.53608	7.16073	6.81369	6.49236	6.19437	5.91765	5.66029	5.42062
13	12.13374	11.34837	10.63496	9.98565	9.39357	8.85268	8.35765	7.90378	7.48690	7.10336	6.74987	6.42355	6.12181	5.84236	5.58315
14	13.00370	12.10625	11.29607	10.56312	9.89864	9.29498	8.74547	8.24424	7.78615	7.36669	6.98187	6.62817	6.30249	6.00207	5.72448
15	13.86505	12.84926	11.93794	11.11839	10.37966	9.71225	9.10791	8.55948	8.06069	7.60608	7.19087	6.81086	6.46238	6.14217	5.84737
16	14.71787	13.57771	12.56110	11.65230	10.83777	10.10590	9.44665	8.85137	8.31256	7.82371	7.37916	6.97399	6.60388	6.26506	5.95423
17	15.56225	14.29187	13.16612	12.16567	11.27407	10.47726	9.76322	9.12164	8.54363	8.02155	7.54879	7.11963	6.72909	6.37286	6.04716
18	16.39827	14.99203	13.75351	12.65930	11.68959	10.82760	10.05909	9.37189	8.75563	8.20141	7.70162	7.24967	6.83991	6.46742	6.12797
19	17.22601	15.67846	14.32380	13.13394	12.08532	11.15812	10.33560	9.60360	8.95011	8.36492	7.83929	7.36578	6.93797	6.55037	6.19823
20	18.04555	16.35143	14.87747	13.59033	12.46221	11.46992	10.59401	9.81815	9.12855	8.51356	7.96333	7.46944	7.02475	6.62313	6.25933
21	18.85698	17.01121	15.41502	14.02916	12.82115	11.76408	10.83553	10.01680	9.29224	8.64869	8.07507	7.56200	7.10155	6.68696	6.31246
22	19.66038	17.65805	15.93692	14.45112	13.16300	12.04158	11.06124	10.20074	9.44243	8.77154	8.17574	7.64465	7.16951	6.74294	6.35866
23	20.45582	18.29220	16.44361	14.85684	13.48857	12.30338	11.27219	10.37106	9.58021	8.88322	8.26643	7.71843	7.22966	6.79206	6.39884
24	21.24339	18.91393	16.93554	15.24696	13.79864	12.55036	11.46933	10.52876	9.70661	8.98474	8.34814	7.78432	7.28288	6.83514	6.43377
25	22.02316	19.52346	17.41315	15.62208	14.09394	12.78336	11.65358	10.67478	9.82258	9.07704	8.42174	7.84314	7.32998	6.87293	6.46415
26	22.79520	20.12104	17.87684	15.98277	14.37519	13.00317	11.82578	10.80998	9.92897	9.16095	8.48806	7.89566	7.37167	6.90608	6.49056
27	23.55961	20.70690	18.32703	16.32959	14.64303	13.21053	11.98671	10.93516	10.02658	9.23722	8.54780	7.94255	7.40856	6.93515	6.51353
28	24.31644	21.28127	18.76411	16.66306	14.89813	13.40616	12.13711	11.05108	10.11613	9.30657	8.60162	7.98442	7.44120	6.96066	6.53351
29	25.06579	21.84438	19.18845	16.98371	15.14107	13.59072	12.27767	11.15841	10.19828	9.36961	8.65011	8.02181	7.47009	6.98304	6.55088
30	25.80771	22.39646	19.60044	17.29203	15.37245	13.76483	12.40904	11.25778	10.27365	9.42691	8.69379	8.05518	7.49565	7.00266	6.56598
31	26.54229	22.93770	20.00043	17.58849	15.59281	13.92909	12.53181	11.34980	10.34280	9.47901	8.73315	8.08499	7.51828	7.01988	6.57911
32	27.26959	23.46833	20.38877	17.87355	15.80268	14.08404	12.64656	11.43500	10.40624	9.52638	8.76860	8.11159	7.53830	7.03498	6.59053
33	27.98969	23.98856	20.76579	18.14765	16.00255	14.23023	12.75379	11.51389	10.46444	9.56943	8.80054	8.13535	7.55602	7.04823	6.60046
34	28.70267	24.49859	21.13184	18.41120	16.19290	14.36814	12.85401	11.58693	10.51784	9.60857	8.82932	8.15656	7.57170	7.05985	6.60910
35	29.40858	24.99862	21.48722	18.66461	16.37419	14.49825	12.94767	11.65457	10.56682	9.64416	8.85524	8.17550	7.58557	7.07005	6.61661
36	30.10751	25.48884	21.83225	18.90828	16.54685	14.62099	13.03521	11.71719	10.61176	9.67651	8.87859	8.19241	7.59785	7.07899	6.62314
37	30.79951	25.96945	22.16724	19.14258	16.71129	14.73678	13.11702	11.77518	10.65299	9.70592	8.89963	8.20751	7.60872	7.08683	6.62881
38	31.48466	26.44064	22.49246	19.36786	16.86789	14.84602	13.19347	11.82887	10.69082	9.73265	8.91859	8.22099	7.61833	7.09371	6.63375
39	32.16303	26.90259	22.80822	19.58448	17.01704	14.94907	13.26493	11.87858	10.72552	9.75696	8.93567	8.23303	7.62684	7.09975	6.63805
40	32.83469	27.35548	23.11477	19.79277	17.15909	15.04630	13.33171	11.92461	10.75736	9.77905	8.95105	8.24378	7.63438	7.10504	6.64178

TABLE 10.3 Economic Value of $10,000 Annual Income to Dependents

Age	Years Until Retirement	Present Value of $10,000 Per Year			
		At 5%	At 6%	At 7%	At 8%
20	45	177,740	154,588	136,055	121,084
25	40	171,590	150,462	133,317	119,246
30	35	163,741	144,982	129,476	116,545
35	30	153,724	137,648	124,090	112,577
40	25	140,939	127,833	116,535	106,747
45	20	124,622	98,182	114,699	105,940
50	15	103,796	97,122	91,079	85,594
55	10	77,217	73,600	70,235	67,100
60	5	43,294	42,123	41,001	39,927

$40,000 times $15.046, we obtain the sum that will yield $40,000 a year for 40 years, $601,840.[6]

Other things being equal, the economic value of the individual generally decreases over time and eventually disappears at retirement age. Table 10.3 indicates the declining economic value at different assumed rates of interest associated with an average annual income to dependents of $10,000. This table also illustrates the impact of the discount rate selected on the value indicated.

It should be obvious that this method of calculating the economic value of a life is fraught with many difficulties, the chief of which is estimating future changes in income. These changes may be expected as the individual progresses in his or her career, and are therefore important determinants of the life value. Estimates of future earnings can at best be nothing more than a projection based on present earnings in the person's occupation. Furthermore, as noted, the human life value will change if future earnings are discounted at a different rate.[7] Finally, the fact that the present value of an individual's income-producing ability is a given amount does not necessarily mean that this is the sum for which it should be insured. Where the loss of the individual's income would deprive no one, insurance is unnecessary. In addition,

a part of the income lost through the person's death may be replaced by other sources, such as Social Security or life insurance available under a group insurance program in connection with employment.

The amount of life insurance that an individual should purchase is properly determined by the so-called *needs approach,* which determines the amount of life insurance required based on analysis of the needs that would have to be met by dependents should the income producer die. While Huebner's life value concept focuses on the income that would be lost, the needs approach attempts to identify the allocation of that income and to determine the purposes to which it would have been put.

The effect of the income loss occasioned by premature death depends on the circumstances. These circumstances include how important the income is to the survivors and whether it can be replaced from other sources. If the survivors were not employed at the time of the income producer's death, they may be able to find employment to replace the lost income. If the income is not replaced, the survivors' standard of living may decline. The basic function of life insurance, then, is to replace the income that is lost by dependents if the income producer on whom they are dependent dies. The primary reason for the purchase of life insurance is to prevent a decline in the standard of living of dependents, and to permit the dependents to live in a manner that approximates the style they would have enjoyed if the income producer had not died.

Needs Analysis The needs approach attempts to determine the amount of life insurance that should be purchased based on analysis of the needs of those who would suffer financial loss. *Needs analysis* has

[6] The calculation can be performed on many calculators that include financial functions.

[7] The difficulties involved in the calculation do not, however, invalidate the concept. Even though considerable guesswork is required, this is still the most acceptable method of calculating the economic value of a human life. Although it is probably a defective technique for determining the amount of life insurance that should be purchased, it is widely used in determining the amount of damages payable in wrongful death and injury cases.

three basic steps. The first step is to identify the needs that would arise or continue to exist following the death of the individual. Second, resources already available to meet those needs must be identified. Potential resources at death might include savings, employer-provided life insurance, and various social insurance programs. Finally, the difference between needs and available resources represents unmet needs, and life insurance is one tool that may be used to meet this remaining need.

Although the concepts are different, there is a relationship between the human life value idea and the needs approach to determining the amount of insurance needed in a particular situation. In summarizing the needs that would exist if the wage earner should die, we are merely looking at the other side of the income-expenditure equation. While the life value concept focuses on the income that would be lost, the needs approach attempts to identify the allocation of that income and determine the purposes for which it would have been used. In addition, the needs approach attempts to recognize unusual or irregular expenditures that may result from the death of the individual and additional expenses that may accompany the period of readjustment following a wage earner's death.

For example, there may be a need to provide a source of funds to support the living expenses of surviving dependents. The amount of this need will vary, depending on marital status, the roles of husband and wife, the presence of children (or plans for children), and the employable skills of dependents. A variety of lifestyles are possible, each with different implications regarding the need for life insurance.

Lifestyles and the Needs Approach One way to illustrate the difference between the human life value approach and the needs approach to life insurance is to consider how different lifestyles affect the need for life insurance.

- *Single Individual* The single individual without dependents usually has little need for death protection. Unless there are parents (or others) who are dependent on a single person, there is no need to replace the income that might stop. Enough life insurance to cover any indebtedness and a fund for last expenses really constitutes the extent of the need. However, a young single person may still want to purchase life insurance because he or she may become uninsurable.

There are, of course, many single individuals who have dependents. These include widowed and divorced persons with children, single persons who support their parents, and single persons with other dependents. For these individuals, the need for death protection parallels that of the married couple with children.[8]

- *Childless Couple* Like the unmarried person, the need of a childless couple for death protection is modest, particularly if both are employed. When both spouses are employed outside the home, the need for death protection on the part of either is usually limited to an amount needed to meet any indebtedness and to cover final expenses. However, if the childless state is a temporary one and the couple intends to have children, they may need to buy life insurance to guarantee future insurability.

- *Persons with Children* When children enter the picture, the problem becomes somewhat more complicated. Both parents may be employed outside the home, or one parent may act as homemaker while the other produces income. In the first case, where both parents earn income, the standard of living may be threatened if either income is lost. Unless there is a willingness to reduce the family's standard of living in the event of a reduction in family income, the income of both spouses may have to be insured. When one parent works outside the home and the other acts as homemaker, the principal focus will be on insurance for the income-producing partner. The amount of insurance required in this case will depend, in part, on the ability and inclination of the homemaker spouse to obtain employment in the event of the income producer's death.

It is also important to recognize the contribution of the homemaking spouse. Clearly, such a spouse makes an economic contribution to the family, and the loss of the services he or she provides would create a financial burden for the family. When funds are available, this exposure should be insured, but such coverage ranks below coverage on an income-producing spouse.[9]

[8] Specific insurance applications relating to divorced persons will be discussed shortly.

[9] In addition to the loss of homemaking and child care services provided by the homemaking spouse, other losses result from his or her death. One seldom-recognized loss is the increase in income taxes to the surviving spouse resulting from the inability to use the joint return in filing federal income taxes.

In the case of a single parent with children, the situation is essentially the same as for the family with a single working spouse but without the "cushion" of a potentially employable surviving spouse. In addition, some plan should exist for the guardianship and care of the surviving children.

Divorce and Income Needs Divorce is a traumatic experience for the participants for a variety of reasons, not the least of which is the dramatic change in the financial situation of both parties. When one of the parties has been dependent on the income of the other, the divorce settlement may provide for continued support of that party through alimony, the money paid to a former spouse under a divorce or separation settlement. When there are minor children, the court will likely order child support payments. In such cases, the recipient of the alimony or child support payments faces the same risk associated with the premature death of the payer as before the divorce. The need for life insurance on the payer is therefore as great—if not greater—as in the case of the married couple. Insurance and annuities may be used to secure the obligations under a qualified domestic relations order or divorce decree.[10] Although income planning in a divorce situation involves many of the same considerations as income planning for the family unit, it differs in the sense that the decisions are often dictated by the court. Many of the decisions relating to needs are made for the parties, and the manner in which these needs will be met may also be specified by the court. Further, the arrangement may have tax implications for the parties. The tax ramifications relating to insurance in divorce proceedings are discussed in Chapter 16.

Classification of Needs The question often arises, how does one anticipate the amount that will be needed to replace the wage earner's income? Actually, there are two approaches. The first is to deduct from current expenditures the portion of family income that is consumed by the wage earner. The remainder is the amount that the family will require should the wage earner die. This approach, however, ignores the changes in expenditures that may occur as a result of the wage earner's death. The second approach, which

seems more logical, is to construct a household or family budget summarizing the expenditures that will be required. A family budget is simply a plan through which one establishes spending goals and monitors how well the household is doing in meeting these goals. Most budgets are based on historical expenditures and will include provision for weekly, monthly, quarterly, and annual expenditures. Many individuals have never constructed a budget for their day-to-day living and have, therefore, given little thought to the amounts that would be needed following the death of the wage earner. For those individuals who do not currently budget, constructing a needs-oriented *insurance program* may be the first attempt at budgeting. While a family budget is the starting point for determining needs, there are various ways in which needs may be classified; the traditional approach includes the following:

Cash Needs	*Income Needs*
Fund for last expenses and debts	Funds for readjustment
	Dependency period income
Emergency funds	
Mortgage payment funds	Life income for spouse
Educational funds	

The first group, cash needs, represents those needs for which a lump-sum amount is desirable at death. The nature of the *fund for last expenses,* also called the *cleanup fund,* is relatively obvious. Death may be accompanied by high medical expenses, funeral costs, and other unplanned outlays, and the fund for last expenses is intended to cover these. Ideally, medical expenses will be covered by a well-planned health insurance program. Whether specific funds should be provided for the payment of debts depends on the circumstances, but the planner should consider whether such funds should be provided as a part of the life insurance proceeds. Assuming that medical expenses associated with the last illness are covered by health insurance, something in the range of from $10,000 to $15,000 is usually adequate for the fund for last expenses.

The purpose of emergency funds is to provide the survivors with a cushion for unexpected expenses that may arise as the family makes its transition to life without the deceased and thereafter. Although the selection of the amount for an emergency fund is somewhat arbitrary in any case, a typical allowance is $5000 to $10,000.

[10] A qualified domestic relations order is a judgment or order that relates to the provision of child support, alimony or property rights to a spouse, a former spouse, or a child and which is made under a state's community property or other domestic relations law.

The mortgage payment fund may be a particularly effective way of reducing the amount of income needed during the dependency period. If the mortgage permits prepayment without penalty, substantial savings in future interest payments can be gained by paying off the loan at the death of the income producer. On the other hand, if the mortgage is not paid off, the payments may be met by providing a higher income during the years it has to run.

Although educational needs are typically listed as a separate need, this is arbitrary and parents may differ in attitude regarding the obligation to help finance a child's college education. Some parents provide considerable assistance in this respect, but there are countless students who finance their own college education through loans and part-time employment. If the parents plan to assist their children with college expenses, the income protection plan should specifically recognize these expenses as part of the income need. Provision for college expenses can take one or two forms: a specific lump sum can be made available to each child to help defray the cost of college, or the income of the dependency period can be extended to provide income throughout the college years.

The remaining three needs represent *income needs*. The need for continued income to support the family's lifestyle may be significantly greater than immediate cash needs, and it is the loss of one's income-earning ability that is the major risk management program with which most people must deal.

The income needs are classified into three groups, representing three different periods in the family's life cycle. Many experts recommend a separate readjustment period following the death of the wage earner, during which the family's income is higher than it will ultimately be. They believe that the family will have certain nonrecurring expenditures as it adjusts to its new way of life immediately following the death. Where the family will suffer a decline in standard of living following the death of an income earner, the readjustment period provides some time to accomplish that readjustment.

Income needs during the *dependency period* are the largest in most programs and consist of income required during the period for which others—generally children—would be dependent on the wage earner. The size of the dependency period income will usually depend on the number of children, their ages, and the relative contribution of the income producer to total family income. When both spouses are employed outside the home, the specifics of the situation will determine the percentage of each income that should be insured. The contribution of each income to family needs and the continuing needs that would have to be met will dictate whether both incomes, or a part of both, should be insured. When one spouse produces all family income, it will usually be necessary to insure a high percentage of that income. In either case, the important factor is the income producer's contribution to family welfare and the family needs that would have to be met from some other source if he or she dies. As we will see in the next chapter, the children and surviving spouse may be eligible for Social Security benefits following the death of the wage earner. (Typically, children are eligible for benefits as long as they are under age 18, and the surviving spouse is eligible until the youngest child reaches age 16.) By themselves, however, Social Security benefits are rarely sufficient to allow the family to maintain its previous standard of living.

The ability of a homemaker spouse to obtain employment in the event of the death of the income-producing spouse is also a factor. However, the net gain from such employment is generally much less than the wages that will be received. First, the spouse must pay taxes, including Social Security and income taxes on the earnings. Second, the spouse may lose Social Security benefits to which he or she was otherwise entitled, because earnings in excess of certain amounts allowed reduce the Social Security benefits.[11] There would also be additional costs incurred by working, including clothing, transportation, lunches, and child care. If life insurance provides adequate income, the surviving spouse may elect to work outside the home. Without it, he or she is compelled to do so.

Finally, when the children are grown, the spouse may still need to replace a part of the wage earner's income. This is particularly true if the surviving spouse is not employed outside the home and would have few employment opportunities if the income-producing spouse should die. Based on the structure of Social Security benefits, the spouse's life income may be conveniently divided into two parts. The first starts when the youngest child reaches 18, at which time Social Security benefits cease, and continues until the

[11] The exact amount of Social Security benefits that would be lost depends on the circumstances. Loss of Social Security benefits is discussed in the next chapter.

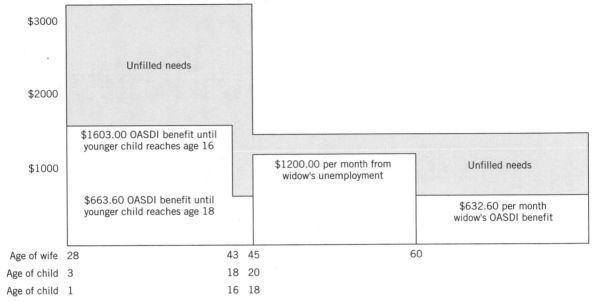

FIGURE 10.1 Needs Analysis Chart

spouse's Social Security benefits resume again at age 60 or 62. Because the spouse receives no Social Security benefits during this time, it is sometimes called the *blackout period*. During this period, the entire income must come from life insurance, employment, savings, or some other source. After the blackout period, Social Security benefits will resume, and a lesser amount of supplementary income will again be necessary.

Under the needs approach, these income requirements of the family are usually listed on a month-by-month basis over time. The presentation indicates the amount of income needed, the amount available from Social Security and other sources, and the extent of the unfilled need. This information may be summarized in graphic form, as shown in Figure 10.1. The chief benefit of this graphic analysis is that it helps the individual to visualize the amounts needed as a flow of income.

The perceptive student will note, however, that the needs presented in the chart are measured in constant dollars. Because actual needs will increase with inflation, the ideal approach is one in which the effects of inflation can be recognized. Various approaches have been used to address the problem of inflation in needs analysis with varying degrees of success. Today, with financial calculators and microcomputer spreadsheets, factoring inflation into the measurement of future income needs is much easier.

Determining future income needs combines the processes of compounding and discounting. First, to estimate future income needs, present needs are projected at an estimated inflation rate. Social Security benefits, which are subject to automatic adjustment for inflation, are projected at the same rate of inflation. If the spouse is employed, his or her income is also projected at an assumed rate for wage increases. The difference between the inflation-adjusted gross need and the inflation-adjusted sources of income represents the unfilled need. To determine the present value of this unfilled need, we discount the projected deficiency using a discount rate that represents the anticipated earnings on the funds that will be purchased to meet the unfilled need. Table 10.4 illustrates this process.

The current value of the remaining unmet needs in Table 10.4 is $153,768. This $153,768 amount summarizes the difference between projected income needs and the projected sources of funds to meet these needs. It is the present value of the difference between needs and available resources. To determine the portion of this amount that must be insured, existing resources should be considered. Suppose that the individual has $50,000 in life insurance available from his or her employer and savings of $20,000. This leaves a remaining unmet need of $83,768 ($153,768 minus $70,000) that may be covered by the purchase of additional life insurance.[12]

[12] There are a variety of assumptions in our calculations, any one or all of which may not be fulfilled. It should be recognized that despite the illusion of precision implied by the multidecimal calculations of our computers, the projections are a guess.

TABLE 10.4 Present Value of Inflation Adjusted Future Income Needs

Year	Age Tom	Age Mary	Age Junior	Age Francesca	Income Needs Projected at 3%	OASDHI Benefits Projected at 3%	Income From Mary's Employment at 4%	Projected Income Deficit	6% Discount Factor	Present Value of Projected Deficit
1	25	25	3	1	$40,000	$16,800	$20,000	$3,200	0.94340	$3,019
2	26	26	4	2	41,200	17,304	20,800	3,096	0.89000	2,755
3	27	27	5	3	42,436	17,823	21,623	2,981	0.83962	2,503
4	28	28	6	4	43,709	18,358	22,497	2,854	0.79209	2,261
5	29	29	7	5	45,020	18,909	23,397	2,715	0.74726	2,029
6	30	30	8	6	46,371	19,476	24,333	2,562	0.70496	1,806
7	31	31	9	7	47,762	20,060	25,306	2,396	0.66506	1,593
8	32	32	10	8	49,195	20,662	26,319	2,214	0.62741	1,389
9	33	33	11	9	50,671	21,282	27,371	2,018	0.59190	1,194
10	34	34	12	10	52,191	21,920	28,466	1,805	0.55839	1,008
11	35	35	13	11	53,757	22,578	29,605	1,574	0.52679	829
12	36	36	14	12	55,369	23,255	30,789	1,325	0.49697	659
13	37	37	15	13	57,030	23,953	32,021	1,057	0.46884	496
14	38	38	16	14	58,741	24,671	33,301	769	0.44230	340
15	39	39	17	15	60,504	25,412	34,634	459	0.41727	191
16	40	40	18	16	62,319	16,772	36,019	9,528	0.39365	3,751
17	41	41	19	17	64,188	17,275	37,460	9,454	0.37136	3,511
18	42	42		18	66,114	0	38,958	27,156	0.35034	9,514
19	43	43			68,097	0	40,516	27,581	0.33051	9,116
20	44	44			70,140	0	42,137	28,003	0.31180	8,732
21	45	45			72,244	0	43,822	28,422	0.29416	8,360
22	46	46			74,412	0	45,575	28,836	0.27751	8,002
23	47	47			76,644	0	47,398	29,246	0.26180	7,656
24	48	48			78,943	0	49,294	29,649	0.24698	7,323
25	49	49			81,312	0	51,266	30,046	0.23300	7,001
26	50	50			83,751	0	53,317	30,434	0.21981	6,690
27	51	51			86,264	0	55,449	30,814	0.20737	6,390
28	52	52			88,852	0	57,667	31,184	0.19563	6,101
29	53	53			91,517	0	59,974	31,543	0.18456	5,821
30	54	54			94,263	0	62,373	31,890	0.17411	5,552
31	55	55			97,090	0	64,868	32,223	0.16425	5,293
32	56	56			100,003	0	67,463	32,541	0.15496	5,042
33	57	57			103,003	0	70,161	32,842	0.14619	4,801
34	58	58			106,093	0	72,968	33,126	0.13791	4,568
35	59	59			109,276	0	75,886	33,390	0.13011	4,344
36	60	60			112,554	0	78,922	33,633	0.12274	4,128
										$153,768

Capital Liquidation versus Capital Conservation
Once future income needs have been estimated and combined into a total, the one question remains concerning the funding to meet the needs. There are two basic strategies, *capital conservation* and *capital liquidation*. The preceding illustration uses a capital liquidation approach, since it assumes that the principal will be consumed in meeting the projected income needs. Under the capital conservation approach, sufficient funding is provided so that investment earnings alone will supply the income stream without depleting the capital. Under this approach—also called capital needs analysis—the amount of funding required is an amount that is sufficient, together with other assets, to provide investment income that will cover the projected needs of the family. A capital conservation approach will always require a greater amount of capital than the capital liquidation approach, but the difference in the amount required for the two approaches will depend on the period for which the income stream must be provided and the return that will be earned on the capital. The longer the period and the higher the investment return, the smaller is the difference in the principal required under the capital conservation and capital liquidation approaches.[13]

The choice between the capital liquidation and capital conservation strategies relates to objectives. The capital liquidation approach is designed to meet the single risk management strategy of protecting dependents against deprivation that might result if the income stream on which they depend is interrupted. The capital conservation strategy seeks to also meet the personal financial planning objective of transferring wealth to heirs.

A Continuing Task The principal defect of both the life value and the needs approaches as they are generally used is that they rely on static analysis, determining the amount of insurance at a specific point in time. This results in the purchase of an amount of insurance that may be correct at that point in time, but that will be inaccurate as time goes by. Because the life value of the individual decreases over time as the end of the income-earning years approach, the fixed amount may be excessive. The needs of each individual will vary, depending on the age, the number of children, and financial assets. In addition, the wants of the individual may change over time, because during each period of life different needs appear more crucial.

The Estate Liquidity Need

As previously noted, one of the objectives in managing the risk of premature death may be the goal of transferring the maximum wealth possible to dependents. One of the impediments to achieving this objective arises from the fact that estates shrink as they pass from one individual to another. Several factors are responsible for this. First, there is the shrinkage that results from the debts of the decedent, for all debts must be paid before the estate may be passed on to the heirs. In addition, the costs involved in probate and administration generally amount to between 4 and 5 percent of the estate. Finally, and frequently the most burdensome, there are the federal estate tax and the state inheritance tax.[14] Although risk-control measures such as estate planning can reduce the amount of these costs, the need for liquidity in the estate to meet death costs that cannot be reduced represents a need that can be met with life insurance.

Estate Planning

Minimizing estate shrinkage is an area in which risk-control measures—generally referred to as *estate planning*—can be effective in reducing potential losses. Estate planning is the process through which one arranges one's affairs so as to yield the most effective accumulation, management, and disposition of capital and income. It involves decisions regarding how an individual's financial affairs will be managed following his or her death and who will do the managing. A major goal of estate planning is to reduce the shrinkage of an estate as it passes from one generation to the next. The greatest shrinkage of the estate has historically come from the federal estate tax, a tax that is imposed on the transfer of a taxable estate.

[13] For a discussion of the *capital needs analysis* concept, see Thomas J. Wolff, *Capital Needs Analysis—Basic Sales Manual* (Vernon, Conn.: Vernon Publishing Services, 1977).

[14] The estate tax is a tax on the right to transmit property at death; the inheritance taxes are levied by the states on the right of an heir to receive a bequest.

EGTRRA-2001 The federal estate tax, also known as a death tax, is simply a tax imposed on wealth transfers made at the holder's death. Virtually from the time it was enacted in 1916, there has been pressure for repeal of the federal estate tax.[15] Congress actually passed legislation repealing the estate tax in 2000, but President Clinton vetoed it. Then, in 2001, Congress passed and President Bush signed into law the Economic Growth and Tax Relief Reconciliation Act of 2001 (EGTRA-2001). Among numerous other changes, EGTRA-2001 contained provisions under which, beginning in 2002, the federal estate tax will be gradually reduced until January 1, 2010, when it will terminate. Then, on January 1, 2011, unless a future Congress passes another law, the estate tax will automatically revert to the system that existed in 2001, at the time EGTRA-2001 was enacted.

This bizarre scenario obviously creates challenging uncertainties for estate planners. It will take some time for the estate planning community to determine exactly how one should address these changes, but during the period over which the estate tax is phased out, the traditional estate planning techniques will remain relevant, albeit on a modified basis. This means that our discussion must address an estate tax environment that is constantly changing.

To understand the changes enacted in 2001, it is useful to know something about what it was that the legislation changed. The basic features of the estate tax in effect in 2001 were adopted by the Tax Reform Act of 1976, which unified the tax on three types of transfers: transfers at the time of death, gifts made prior to death, and generation-skipping transfers. The law requires that taxable gifts made during the lifetime of the deceased be combined with the decedent's estate to compute the taxable estate. The generation-skipping transfer imposes a tax on wealth that "skips" a generation (e.g., a bequest by a grandparent to a grandchild). EGTRRA-2001 includes changes that affect all three transfer taxes.

Estate Tax Changes The federal estate tax applies to one's entire *taxable estate*—the *gross estate* minus allowable deduction, but any tax payable is subject to a unified credit that reduces the actual tax payable. The unified credit was $220,550 in 2001, which exempted $675,000 from the estate tax.[16] Estates in excess of the exempt amount were taxed at rates from 37 percent to 55 percent (applicable to estates in excess of $3 million). A 5-percent surtax applies to estates from $10 million to $21 million.

EGTRRA-2001 phases out, repeals, and then resurrects the federal estate tax. The "repeal" process began in 2002, with a reduction in the maximum tax rate from 55% to 50 percent, elimination of the 5-percent surtax on estates over $10 million, and an increase in the exemption equivalent credit from $675,000 in 2001 to $1 million in 2002. Thereafter, as indicated in Table 10.5, the maximum tax rate will continue to decrease and the unified credit will increase until 2010, when the estate tax is repealed.[17] Then, in 2011, unless a future Congress acts to make the repeal permanent, a sunset provision in EGTRRA-2001 brings everything back to where it was in 2001. The maximum tax rate returns to 55 percent, the 5-percent surcharge tax is restored, and the estate tax credit returns to $675,000.

Generation-Skipping Transfer Tax Changes In 2001, generation-skipping transfers were taxed at the maximum estate tax rate of 55 percent. The generation-skipping transfer tax was subject to its generation-skipping transfer tax credit of $1 million, indexed for inflation. In 2001, this credit was $1,060,000.

Like the estate tax, the generation-skipping transfer tax is phased out over the period from 2002 to 2010. Generation-skipping transfers continue to be taxed at the maximum estate tax rate, which, as pre-

[15] The current federal estate tax was enacted in 1916 to help finance World War I. The pressure for repeal stems, in part, from historical precedent. A death tax has been imposed as a temporary expedient on three previous occasions, and repealed when the target funding had been raised. A death "stamp" tax was enacted in 1797 to pay for a naval buildup and abolished just five years later in 1802. The federal death tax was again enacted in 1862 to raise revenue for the Civil War. After the war ended, Congress repealed the tax in 1870. The third federal death tax was enacted in 1898 to finance the Spanish-American War. As before, the estate tax was abolished after the war in 1902. With the advent of World War I, the estate tax was reintroduced in 1916 and has existed in various forms since.

[16] The unified credit's equivalent exemption was set at $600,000 in 1997 with scheduled increases to $1 million in 2006. The scheduled increases were to $625,000 for decedents dying and gifts made in 1998; $650,000 in 1999; $675,000 in 2000 and 2001; $700,000 in 2002 and 2003; $850,000 in 2004; $950,000 in 2005; and $1 million in 2006. An additional estate tax credit was added in the TRA-97, making a family-business owner's total exemption from the estate tax to $1.3 million. This family-business credit was scheduled to decrease as the unified credit increased, so the combined unified credit and family business credit would remain at $1.3 million.

[17] The family-business credit is repealed in 2004 when the unified credit reaches $1.5 million.

TABLE 10.5 Phase-Out and Ultimate Repeal of Estate and GST Taxes

Year of Death	Estate Tax Exemption	Maximum Rates	
		Estate Tax	Gift Tax
2001	$675,000	55%	55%
2002	$1,000,000	50%	50%
2003	$1,000,000	49%	49%
2004	$1,500,000	48%	48%
2005	$1,500,000	47%	47%
2006	$2,000,000	46%	46%
2007	$2,000,000	45%	45%
2008	$2,000,000	45%	45%
2009	$3,500,000	45%	45%
2010	Tax repealed	0%	35%
2011	$675,000	55%	55%

viously noted, is scheduled to decrease and be repealed in 2010. The generation-skipping transfer credit increases from $1,060,000 in 2001 along with the increase in the estate tax credit until 2010, when both the estate tax and the generation-skipping transfer tax are repealed for one year.

Gift Tax Changes Prior to the Tax Reform Act of 1976 (TRA-76), estates and gifts were subject to separate taxes, each with its own exemption and progressive tax rates. TRA-76 combined these into a single *unified estate-gift tax* with the previously indicated unified credit. Gifts during one's lifetime that exceed $10,000 per donee per year (adjusted for inflation) are combined with the taxable estate and subject to a single credit and tax rate schedule.

Although EGTRRA-2001 phases out and repeals the estate tax and generation-skipping transfer tax, the gift tax is not repealed. Beginning in 2002, gift tax rates are reduced according to the schedule in Table 10.5. The unified credit exemption amount for gift tax purposes will be increased to, *and remain at,* $1 million. Once the estate tax is fully phased out, beginning in 2010, the top gift tax rate will be equal to the top individual tax rate (i.e., 35 percent under EGTRRA-2001).

Basis of Inherited Property One additional feature of EGTRRA-2001 requires comment, the provisions related to the tax basis of inherited property. Under current law (effective until 2010), heirs who receive property from a decedent are generally not required to carry over the decedent's income tax basis for that property for income tax purposes.

Rather, their basis for the property is equal to the fair market value at the date of the decedent's death (or six months after death in some cases). Thus, any appreciation that occurs from the time the decedent acquired the property until his or her death is permanently shielded from the capital gains tax. Under the new law, the availability of a date-of-death basis is severely limited. Only property up to $1.3 million in value is entitled to a date-of-death basis regardless of who inherits it. An additional bequest of $3 million to a surviving spouse will also qualify for a step-up basis (making the total property to a spouse eligible for the step-up basis $4.3 million).

One of the major concerns relating to the EGTRRA-2001 is the increased difficulty that it will pose for estate administrators in figuring out the cost basis for assets that were held by the decedent for an extended period of time. Information on the original cost of assets may not be available, posing enormous problems for those who inherit property.[18]

The Taxable Estate The taxable estate is determined by deduction of certain allowable exemptions from the gross estate. The gross estate includes the fair market value of all real and personal property owned by the individual at the time of death, including the individual's interest in any property that is owned jointly with another. In addition to other assets, the gross estate also includes the proceeds of life insurance policies on the individual's life, no matter how payable, if the deceased possessed any incidents of ownership in the policies. By *incidents of ownership* is meant such ownership rights as the right to change beneficiaries, to borrow against the cash value of the policies, or to collect the cash values. Inclusion of life insurance proceeds in an estate can be avoided if proceeds are payable to a named beneficiary such as a spouse, child, or friend and if the insured avoids incidents of ownership in the policy at death (and at any time within three years before death). If the insured has no incidents of ownership, the proceeds will be excluded from the taxable estate, even though the insured may have paid the premiums on the policy. The premium could be considered a gift to the beneficiary and subject to the $10,000 annual exclusion from the gift tax. Some

[18] The last time carryover basis was introduced was during the Carter Administration in the late 1970s. Because of implementation difficulties, it was retroactively repealed less than one year later.

individuals avoid incidents of ownership by having their spouses own policies on their lives and by giving up the right to change beneficiaries or to exercise any of the policy options.[19]

Deductions The gross estate is subject to certain deductions in determining the portion that is *taxable*. These include credit for death taxes paid to the states as well as foreign death taxes.[20] During the 2002 through 2011 estate tax phase-out period, the state death tax credit will be reduced from the 2001 level. The credit will be reduced from the 2001 level 25 percent in 2002, by 50 percent in 2003, by 75 percent in 2004. In 2005 the state death tax is completely repealed and replaced by a deduction for death taxes actually paid to any state or to the District of Columbia.

The most important deduction from the gross estate is the marital deduction. Since 1982, an unlimited marital deduction has been allowed for estate and gift tax purposes. This means that an individual may give his or her spouse gifts in any amount without gift tax liability, and property passing from one spouse to the other is not subject to the federal estate tax. However, the estate tax marital deduction applies only to the part of the estate that actually passes from the deceased to a surviving spouse.

A first strategy for reducing the estate tax is through the use of the marital deduction. This requires a brief digression into the subject of wills and the legal concept of intestacy. A will is the means by which an individual directs the disposition of the estate. Someone who dies without having left a will is said to have died *intestate*. In such cases, the individual may be deprived of some of the exemptions available under the federal estate tax law that would have limited the shrinkage of the estate. When an individual leaves no will, the property owned at the time of death is distributed in accordance with the fixed provisions of the laws in the state in which the person lived. Although this distribution may vary from state to state, in general it may be said that such distribution acts to the detriment of the survivors. In many states, if an individual dies without a will and is survived by a spouse and children, the spouse receives one-third and the remaining two-thirds is divided equally among the children.[21] This distribution deprives the estate of the full benefit of the marital deduction.

Although the unlimited marital deduction will protect an individual's entire estate from the federal estate tax, at the subsequent death of the surviving spouse, the spouse's estate (including amounts he or she received from the first partner to die) will be subject to the federal estate tax. This means that, in some cases, the marital deduction merely defers the taxation of the property, since property passed to a surviving spouse becomes a part of that spouse's estate and will be taxed without the benefit of the marital deductions when he or she dies.

An obvious strategy for the individual with a substantial estate is to arrange for the distribution of that estate in a manner that will maximize the use of the unified estate-gift tax credit. Consider, for example, the case of Bill and Mary Smith, who have now reached age 50. For the purpose of illustration, assume that Bill Smith has an estate in the neighborhood of $2 million. If he leaves his entire estate to Mary, it will pass without estate tax liability, but the tax is merely deferred. At Mary's death, there will be no marital deduction and the entire $2-million estate will be taxable, subject to the available unified tax credit. Instead of passing his entire estate to Mary, Bill might elect instead to pass a part of the estate to other heirs (such as children) in order to use part or all of the unified tax credit. If, for example, Bill dies in 2002, $1 million of his estate could pass to children or other heirs without tax liability. The remaining $1

[19] When incidents of ownership already exist, they may be transferred to another party, such as a spouse or child. If the transfer occurs within three years of the individual's death, the insurance proceeds may be brought back into the estate as a gift that was made *in contemplation of death*.

[20] Every state imposes an estate or inheritance tax on taxable estates. About two-thirds of the states have a "sop tax" or "sponge tax" law, so-called because it is limited to the allowable credit for state death taxes in the federal estate tax (i.e., the amount that will sop up or sponge up funds that would otherwise be payable as federal estate taxes). If those states that limit their estate or inheritance tax to the allowable credit for death taxes in the federal law take no action, these states will lose substantial revenue as the federal credit is repealed. If they replace the revenue by imposing separate taxes on estates, or by not recognizing the reductions, estates will see part of the benefit of the rate reduction and exemption increases taken away by the states.

[21] The *Uniform Probate Code* was revised in 1990, introducing significant changes in the provisions related to intestacy. By 1998, the 1990 version of the *Code* had been adopted, at least in part, by the following 19 states: Alaska, Arizona, California, Colorado, Florida, Hawaii, Idaho, Kentucky, Maine, Michigan, Minnesota, Montana, Nebraska, New Jersey, New Mexico, North Dakota, South Carolina, South Dakota, and Utah. In some cases the states have adopted the *Code* with significant modifications or in an incomplete form. Other states continue to follow the intestacy provisions of the previous version of the *Code*.

million may pass to Mary, or it may pass to the children or other heirs subject to the estate tax. If it passes to Mary, she will have the benefit of the unified estate-gift tax credit at the time she dies. By passing a part of his estate to heirs other than Mary, Bill Smith can maximize the effect of the unified credit.

In addition to the strategies of using the marital exemption effectively and maximizing the unified credit, there is a third strategy for reducing the value of the estate to be transferred by making gifts prior to death. Although lifetime gifts are combined with the taxable estate for the purpose of the unified tax, there is an annual gift tax exclusion, whereby assets may be transferred during one's lifetime without tax consequences. The annual gift tax exclusion was originally $10,000 per donee, but is adjusted for inflation since 1998 in $1000 increments; it increased to $11,000 in 2002.[22]

Trusts

A common tool for implementing estate-planning strategies and for the administration of an estate is a trust. A *trust* is an arrangement under which the holder (called the trustee) undertakes the management of another's property (called the *corpus* of the trust), for the benefit of designated persons. The person establishing the trust is called the grantor, trustor, or simply the creator of the trust. Those who receive income from the trust are known as beneficiaries, and persons to whom the corpus of a trust will pass at the death of the beneficiary or beneficiaries are called *remaindermen*.

The most widely used trusts are the *testamentary trust*, which is a part of the will and, as its name implies, takes effect after death, and the living or *inter vivos trust*, which is established during the lifetime of the creator and which may be revocable or irrevocable in nature.

Testamentary Trust A testamentary trust will not reduce estate taxes upon the death of the testator, nor will it lighten estate settlement costs. The potential trust property remains in the estate of the testator until distribution after the will has been probated. It is handled and taxed like all other property. However, it can reduce taxes and administration costs when the trust beneficiary dies. An individual who wishes to leave property to heirs other than a spouse

in order to maximize the impact of the tax credit, but who wants at the same time to provide adequately for a surviving spouse, may establish a testamentary trust with the spouse as the beneficiary of the trust and the other heirs as remaindermen. For estate tax purposes, the property in trust is not subject to the marital deduction, but instead uses all or part of the unified credit. Although the surviving spouse enjoys the income from the trust, the property will not be included in his or her estate at the time of death. This permits full use of the tax credit by the trust grantor, while at the same time providing an adequate level of income to the surviving spouse.

Living Trusts *Living trusts,* or *inter vivos trusts,* may be revocable or irrevocable. A *revocable inter vivos trust* is one in which the creator reserves the right to terminate the trust and acquire the property. The creator can reduce estate administration costs if the trust remains in force after his or her death for the property to pass outside the will. The beneficiaries will not have to wait until the will is probated to receive their allotted income and principal. The revocable trust does not, however, reduce the estate tax liability.

An *irrevocable inter vivos trust* is one in which the creator relinquishes the right to terminate the trust and acquire the property. An absolute and irrevocable trust takes the property out of the grantor's estate, thereby eliminating certain administrative costs. In addition, estate taxes may be reduced to the extent that the trust is established through gifts subject to exclusion from the federal gift tax (e.g., the annual $10,000 exemption per donee or the spouse gift exemption). Since such gifts are excluded from the gift tax, they are not subject to unification in computing the estate tax.

Irrevocable Life Insurance Trust One type of living trust that deserves special note is the *irrevocable life insurance trust* (ILIT), which is used to avoid the incidents of ownership in a life insurance contract that makes the insurance proceeds taxable under the federal estate tax. (If the policy beneficiary is a surviving spouse, the proceeds can escape estate taxation because of the unlimited marital deduction, but will be subject to tax in the estate of the surviving spouse.) An ILIT avoids incidence of ownership that would otherwise make the life insurance benefits taxable.

Under an ILIT, life insurance is purchased and managed by a trustee, subject to the instructions provided in a *life insurance trust agreement*. The trustee

[22] *IRC* Section 2503(b).

purchases a life insurance policy on the person to be insured, normally with the trust named as the beneficiary. At the insured's death, the life insurance proceeds are paid to the trust, and then distributed from the trust to the trust beneficiaries. The premiums are paid from funds transferred to the trust as gifts. Although the *IRC* exempts $11,000 in gifts per donee annually, the exemption applies to gifts of a *present interest,* while gifts to an irrevocable trust represent *future interest* gifts and usually do not qualify for the exemption. However, the annual gift tax exemption will apply if beneficiaries are given the right to withdraw amounts that are placed in the trust on a yearly, noncumulative basis.[23] Instead of making the gift directly to the beneficiaries, the grantor contributes funds to the trust for their benefit. The trustee then notifies each trust beneficiary that a gift has been received on his or her behalf and, unless the beneficiary elects to receive the gift now, the trustee will use the contribution to pay the premium on the life insurance policy. Obviously, a key feature of the ILIT is the willingness of the beneficiaries to not withdraw the gift, which they must have the right to do if it is to qualify as a gift.

In addition to addressing the issue of incidence of ownership, an ILIT also allows one to leverage the funds that are passed to family members as gifts through the purchase of insurance, the proceeds of which are an effective way to pay any estate taxes that remain after the maximum gifting has occurred.

THE RISKS ASSOCIATED WITH SUPERANNUATION

Superannuation—the risk of living too long—is probably less threatening than the threat of premature death. Still, it is a risk that deserves attention. The retirement risk is influenced by the increased hazard of physical disability as one grows older, and also by societal conventions. Many people consider age 65 the "normal" retirement age, but this is a relatively recent notion in human history. In earlier periods people usually worked until they died, or until they became physically incapable of working.

Today, retirement is a significant event in a person's life. Indeed, it may be said that people spend their entire lives preparing for retirement. As in the case of the biblical famine of ancient Egypt, resources are accumulated during the *income-fat* years to be consumed during the *income-lean* years. The amount that must be accumulated during the income-fat years depends on a variety of circumstances, and is influenced by the standard of living the individual wishes to maintain after retirement and the rate of inflation. A part of the risk associated with retirement is that the individual will not have accumulated sufficient assets by the time retirement arrives to afford an adequate standard of living. The second part is that the assets that have been accumulated will not last for the remainder of the individual's lifetime.

The Risk of Outliving the Retirement Accumulation

Before turning to the subject of accumulating funds for retirement, let us address the second part of the *retirement risk,* which is the easier of the two risks to manage—the risk that once funds have been accumulated, the individual may outlive those funds.

Except in unusual cases, the funds that will have been accumulated for retirement will be limited. Some strategy is needed to guarantee that the individual will not outlive the assets that have been accumulated. The conventional tool for this problem is a *life annuity,* under which a capital sum is converted into a stream of income over the individual's remaining life. An annuity may be defined as a periodic payment that continues for an individual's entire lifetime. The person whose life governs the duration of the payments is called the *annuitant.*

Annuities have been called "upside-down life insurance," and in a sense they are a reverse application of the law of large numbers as it is used in life insurance. The function of a life annuity is to liquidate a principal sum, regardless of how it was accumulated, over the lifetime of the annuitant. It may involve the liquidation of a sum derived from a person's savings (including the annuity itself) or the liquidation of life insurance cash values or death benefits in the form of a life income to the owner or beneficiary of the policy.

Under the annuity principle, the law of averages operates to permit a lifetime-guaranteed income to each annuitant. Some people who reach age 65 will

[23] The right to withdraw gifts to a trust is called "Crummey powers," after the individual involved in the case in which the principle was established. *Crummey v. Commissioner,* 397 F.2d 82 (9th Cir. 1968). President Clinton's 1998 budget proposal included a plan to legislatively override the Crummey decision.

die before they reach age 66. Others will live to be 100. Those who live longer than average will offset those who live for a shorter period than average, and those who die early will forfeit money to those who die later. Every payment the annuitant receives is part interest and part principal. In addition, each payment is part survivorship benefit, in that it is composed in part of the funds of group members who have died.[24]

Estimating the Accumulation Need

As with the premature death exposure, the individual may have a number of resources available to meet the superannuation exposure. Employer provided retirement plans and Social Security benefits are two important sources for most individuals. These benefits are usually payable over the lifetime of the individual, commencing at retirement. The individual must usually supplement these plans with personal savings or life insurance policies that include a savings element.

The need for retirement income can be measured in a way similar to that used in measuring death needs. The individual's income needs during retirement are projected at some assumed rate of inflation, together with Social Security benefits, which are deducted from the needs. If pension benefits will be available, they are also deducted in determining the postretirement need that must be met from savings. The remaining retirement income need may be met by purchasing a life annuity beginning at retirement age. In this case, sufficient funds must be accumulated by retirement age to cover the purchase price of the annuity.

In measuring the life insurance need, we discounted future income needs to determine the present value of future needs. Because the retirement need is a deferred need, the time value of money serves a different function in planning for retirement. In this case, we determine the amount that will be needed at some time in the future and calculate the contributions that will be required over time to reach the target accumulation, given some assumed rate of return. We can compute the future value of $1 contributed each year to an accumulating fund and invested at a specified rate and thereby determine the annual or monthly contribution that will be

required to meet a specific accumulation goal in a specified number of years at some assumed rate of return. We will defer our discussion of this process until Chapter 19, when we discuss the various options available to meet income needs during the retirement period.

THE RISKS ASSOCIATED WITH DISABILITY

In discussing the need for life insurance, we observed that there may be instances in which no one would suffer financial deprivation in the event of a person's death and there is no need for life insurance. The disability income need is fundamentally different. In the case of the disability exposure, the absence of dependents does not eliminate the need for income, since the disabled person will need income during a period of disability. As a matter of fact, the income need may be greater in the case of an individual without a spouse. When a disabled person has a spouse, the domestic partner may be able to provide some income for the couple. In addition, the nondisabled spouse will serve as a care provider. The single individual does not have the cushion of a spouse's income and will generally have to hire a care provider. This means that the percentage of a single person's income that must be replaced in the event of disability may be higher than that of a person with a spouse.[25]

For the individual with dependents, the family's income needs if the wage-earner becomes disabled are certainly as great as they would be if he or she died. In fact, they would probably be greater. As in the case of life insurance, the needs vary with the number of children in the family and with other responsibilities the insured may have. Also, as in the case of death, benefits available under employer-provided and social insurance plans should be considered in determining the need for other protection.

Some authorities argue that loss-of-income protection should come even before life insurance. When a wage earner is disabled, his or her earnings stop just as surely as if death had occurred. This "living death" of disability can be economically more severe than actual death. If the breadwinner of the

[24] Annuities are discussed in Chapter 18.

[25] In this sense, marriage represents a risk-sharing technique and the treatment of risk by combining a very small number of exposure units.

TABLE 10.6 Probability of Death and Disability at Various Ages

Age	Probability of Death Before Age 65	Probability of 90-Day Disability Before Age 65
25	24%	54%
30	23	52
35	22	50
40	21	48
45	20	44
50	18	39
55	15	32
60	9	9

Based on 1980 CSO Mortality Table.

Based on 1985 Commissioners Disability Table.

Source: McGill's Life Insurance, Edward E. Graves (ed.), (Bryn Mawr, Pa.: The American College, 1994).

family dies, the family's income stops; if he or she is disabled, not only does the income stop but expenses remain the same and usually increase. Because a disabled person—by definition—is one whose ability to work is impaired, he or she must depend on sources other than employment for income. When persons other than the disabled individual were also supported by the lost income, the problem is worse.

In addition to the fact that disability can be more burdensome financially to the individual and dependents than is usually supposed, the chance of loss at most ages is greater than the chance of death. Table 10.6 indicates the probability of death and disability at various ages.

As indicated by the data in the table, the probability of disability of at least 90 days is significantly higher at every age during the individual's working years than is the probability of death. Nearly half the people who reach age 35 will be disabled for at least three months before reaching age 65, and the average length of the disability will be more than five years.

Needs Analysis for the Disability Risk

A needs analysis for the *disability risk* is much like the needs analysis for premature death. First, income needs for each year are projected by examining the amount required to maintain the family in the event of disability. Usually the income needs of the family will not diminish much if the wage earner is disabled. There may be a modest reduction in some expenses associated with employment, such as the cost of com-

muting, business lunches, and perhaps a part of the clothing budget, but the reduction will probably be small. While there may be an increase in medical expenses, adequate medical expense insurance should be available to meet the increased medical care costs.

In determining disability income needs, careful consideration must be given to the need to continue to plan for the retirement years. In our discussion of disability income contracts, we will see that most insurers will provide coverage for disability arising out of accident for the individual's entire lifetime, but limit coverage for disability arising out of sickness until age 65. How, one may ask, do we provide for income beyond age 65 for the individual who is disabled as a result of sickness? The answer is that the income need after age 65 is treated as a part of the individual's retirement needs. The need for income after age 65 will exist whether or not the person is disabled, and prudent individuals accumulate funds to supplement Social Security benefits. Since insurers do not offer life-time disability coverage for illness, a disability protection program should provide benefits in an amount that will permit the disabled person to continue making contributions to his or her retirement program. In this way, the accumulation of funds intended for retirement will be there at age 65 whether or not the individual is disabled.

Resources Available to Meet the Disability Risk

After determining the needs, the next step is to identify any benefits available from existing sources. Several sources may provide protection against lost income during disability. For disability that arises out of and in the course of employment, most injured workers are entitled to benefits under their state workers compensation law. The amount of these benefits depends on the worker's earnings at the time of the injury and is specified by law. In addition, workers in California, Hawaii, New Jersey, New York, Rhode Island, and Puerto Rico are covered for nonoccupational disabilities by compulsory programs, under which the benefits are also prescribed by law. Finally, workers who are totally and permanently disabled and who meet special eligibility requirements qualify for disability benefits under the Social Security program. The eligibility requirements under this program are quite strict, and benefits are payable only if the individual is unable to engage in any "substantially gainful employment." This is much

more strict than the typical or individual disability income plan, and it is not uncommon for an individual to be eligible for private disability benefits but not for Social Security disability benefits. Usually, average earnings of $500 or more are considered substantial and will result in the discontinuation of the benefits under Social Security.[26]

Besides these government-sponsored or supervised programs, the most common source of recovery is through group or individual disability income policies. In some instances, employers self-insure a program of disability benefits for their employees, providing either cash benefits or paid sick leave. In others, the paid sick leave plans are integrated with disability income insurance purchased from commercial insurers.

Addressing Unmet Disability Income Needs

Unmet needs are determined by subtracting available resources from the needs that have been identified. Disability insurance may then be purchased to cover the unmet needs. The most important disability income need is long-term disability coverage for both occupational and nonoccupational disabilities to supplement Social Security. In addition, most people will need short-term disability coverage for disabilities that are not covered under Social Security (including the Social Security waiting period). A properly coordinated disability income program provides coverage for both occupational and nonoccupational injuries in an amount that meets the family's need for income during the entire period of disability. The coverage for occupational disability should supplement workers compensation benefits so that the combined workers compensation and disability income insurance provide the same level of coverage as for nonoccupational disabilities. Disability insurance is discussed in more detail in Chapter 20.

EVALUATING THE MEDICAL EXPENSE EXPOSURE

No personal risk management program is complete without some protection against medical expenses. The major consideration in the area of medical expense coverage should be protection against the catastrophic loss. A variety of plans are available, ranging from plans covering a specific class of medical expenses with a small deductible to plans covering a broad array of expenses with a larger annual deductible. Because of the variety of plans available and the fact that most individuals are covered for these expenses under employer-provided plans, we defer discussion to Chapter 21.

MANAGING THE RISK OF UNEMPLOYMENT

Three of the perils that threaten income—premature death, superannuation, and disability—have been addressed. It seems appropriate that we at least recognize the existence of the fourth peril and comment on the risk management alternatives available with respect to unemployment.

Although the techniques used in managing the *unemployment risk* are essentially the same as those used in managing the risk of other perils that threaten income, the range of alternatives is more limited. With respect to risk transfer, for example, there are limited options. State unemployment insurance programs exist in all states and most individuals will have some protection from this source. These programs are designed to provide protection against involuntary unemployment when the individual is available for work but is temporarily unemployed. The protection from this source is limited, both in duration and in amount.

In addition to the protection available under the state unemployment insurance programs, unemployment insurance is available on a limited basis in connection with installment credit. Usually, the coverage is vastly overpriced.

State Unemployment Insurance Programs

Because each state has enacted separate legislation and operates a separate program, the programs differ considerably in almost every respect. However, it will be useful to discuss their general nature.[27]

[26] Eligibility requirements for Social Security disability income benefits and workers compensation are discussed in Chapter 11.

[27] The student will no doubt want to look at the unemployment compensation act of his or her own state. One of the most up-to-date compilations of the laws of all the states is *The Unemployment Insurance Reporter,* a loose-leaf reporting service published weekly by the Commerce Clearing House in New York.

Eligibility for Benefits The eligibility requirements vary from state to state, but all call for previous employment in a covered occupation and continued attachment to the labor force as a prerequisite for benefits. In most states, the worker must also have earned a certain minimum income during the preceding year, referred to as the *base period.* Some states require that the worker must have been paid a stated dollar minimum during the base period, and a few demand a specified number of weeks of employment with a minimum amount of earnings each week. Most states require the employee to have earned some multiple of the weekly benefit amount that he or she will receive (e.g., 30 times).

Continued attachment to the labor force is also required. The basic philosophy of the unemployment compensation program is that only those workers who are legitimate members of the labor force are eligible for benefits. Therefore, unemployment must be involuntary before the worker can collect benefits, which means that the worker must be willing and able to work. This is the principal reason that benefits are payable through the state employment offices. The worker desiring to draw benefits must present himself or herself at the employment office to collect the money and must be willing to accept suitable work if it is offered.[28] The question of what constitutes suitable employment can be thorny, but normally the administrative staff of the state employment office decides whether the work is appropriate. The worker who feels that he or she has been unfairly treated is entitled to a hearing. Following the philosophy that only those who are involuntarily unemployed are entitled to benefits, most state laws deny or limit benefits to workers who quit without sufficient reason or who are discharged for misconduct.[29]

Benefits under State Unemployment Laws The worker who meets the requirements of previous employment and involuntary unemployment is enti-

tled to certain benefits as a matter of right, without the necessity of meeting a needs test. There is no uniformity among the states in the amount of benefits to which the qualified worker is entitled, and the benefits payable in some states are far higher than those in others.

In all states the amount of the benefits to which the worker is entitled is related to previous earnings. In most states the method of determining benefits is to take some percentage or fraction of the worker's wages during the quarter of highest earnings in his or her base year. One of the most commonly used fractions is 1/26. If the worker was fully employed during the quarter, the 1/26 benefit provides a weekly benefit equal to approximately 50 percent of his or her normal full-time earnings. The amount of the benefit is subject to a state weekly maximum and minimum. Most states now provide for an automatic adjustment of the benefit maximum to coincide with changes in the state's average weekly wage of those in covered employment. A few provide for a sliding maximum based on the number of dependents the unemployed worker has. The maxima in effect under the various state laws in mid-2001 varied from $195 to $603 a week. Most states provide for a one-week waiting period before benefits begin, but some states use a shorter waiting period, and in 10 states there is no waiting period.

In addition to imposing limits on the amount, all states stipulate a maximum period for which benefits are payable. In 44 states, this is 26 weeks, while in 6 states and the District of Columbia it is longer. The maximum in any state is 39 weeks.[30]

Retention and Risk Reduction

The limited range of transfer alternatives means that for most people, the alternatives for managing the risk of unemployment are retention and reduction. Unfortunately, the risk of unemployment is one of those risks that is involuntarily retained. As in the case of

[28] For example, students not available for work while attending school and women who quit their jobs because of pregnancy or to get married are not eligible for benefits. However, since 1978, states are prohibited from automatically disqualifying women from unemployment benefits solely on the basis of pregnancy.

[29] In such circumstances benefits may be completely or only partially forfeited. For example, under the Iowa law a worker discharged for misconduct forfeits from four to nine weeks of benefits. A worker who voluntarily quits a job forfeits all benefits for which he or she had accumulated credit in that particular job, but the benefits given up are those accumulated only during the job that was quit.

[30] In Alaska, California, Connecticut, Hawaii, and Oklahoma, benefits are extended under exclusively state funded programs when unemployment in the state reaches a specified level. In all states benefits may be extended during periods of high unemployment by 50 percent for up to 13 weeks under a federal-state Extended Unemployment Compensation Program. Extended benefits are triggered when the unemployment rate in a state averages 5 percent or more over a 13-week period and is at least 20 percent higher than the rate for the same period in the two preceding years.

other retained risks, recognizing the risk is a first step in dealing with it. The individual should do two things to address the risk of involuntary unemployment. The first is to recognize it as a retained risk and provide a cushion to cover the loss if it should occur.

Most authorities recommend an emergency or contingency fund, equal to the amount of three to six months' expenses. The purpose of this fund is to cover expenditures during a period of reduced income or unemployment. With an emergency fund of this type, the involuntary retention of the unemployment exposure is at least partially funded. The

emergency fund, combined with the modest benefits available from unemployment insurance, will provide a cushion for unemployment losses if they occur.

In addition to maintaining adequate funding for the retention of this risk, it also makes sense to reduce the likelihood that the loss will occur. In true-life practice, a comprehensive education and specialized work skills are still the most effective loss-prevention measures against the peril of involuntary unemployment. For students, this means selecting a career that is relatively immune to fluctuations in employment.

IMPORTANT CONCEPTS TO REMEMBER

premature death
superannuation
human life value
time value of money
present value
discounting
needs approach
capital needs analysis
insurance programming
fund for last expenses
cleanup fund
emergency fund

dependency period
capital liquidation strategy
capital conservation strategy
readjustment expense fund
premarital period
pre-child years of marriage
child-raising years
years approaching retirement
blackout period
estate planning
intestate
federal estate and gift tax rates

incidents of ownership
gross estate
taxable estate
trust
living trust
life insurance trust agreement
life annuity
retirement risk
disability risk
unemployment risk

QUESTIONS FOR REVIEW

1. Briefly explain how the human life value approach differs from the needs approach in determining the amount of life insurance an individual should purchase. What is the relationship between the two approaches?

2. What, if any, are the defects in using the human life value concept in determining the amount of life insurance an individual should purchase?

3. The need for life insurance varies with the individual's lifestyle. How does this need differ for single individuals, childless couples, and persons with children?

4. Identify the "needs" that are traditionally considered in determining the amount of life insurance required for a family.

5. Identify the sources other than life insurance that might provide resources to meet needs in the case of premature death.

6. One tool for dealing with the risk of outliving one's income is a life annuity. Briefly explain how a life annuity is able to do this.

7. Identify the resources that might be available to address the retirement risk.

8. Explain why the disability needs for a particular individual are likely to be even greater than the needs in the case of premature death.

9. How should one deal with the dilemma created by the fact that disability resulting from sickness may extend beyond age 65, but insurers are generally unwilling to provide coverage for such disabilities beyond age 65?

10. Identify the resources that may be available for an individual who experiences a disability.

QUESTIONS FOR DISCUSSION

1. The changing lifestyles of many Americans have modified some of the traditional principles of insurance buying. With an increase in the number of two-income families, do you think that the overall need for life insurance has (a) increased or (b) decreased? Why?

2. It is often stated that one of the most neglected areas in the life insurance field is that of insurance on the homemaker spouse. In facing the risk-management decision regarding life insurance for the family, where do you think that life insurance on a spouse who is not employed outside the home should fit?

3. What reasons can you suggest for providing a lifetime income to a spouse after any children have been raised?

Under what circumstances would you recommend against providing such a lifetime income?

4. "On first consideration, it might seem that the risk of income loss resulting from premature death is universal. After all, no one lives forever. But death does not automatically result in financial loss." Explain why you agree or disagree with this statement.

5. "The effect of the income loss occasioned by premature death depends on the circumstances." Describe a combination of circumstances in which the effect of income loss occasioned by premature death is insignificant.

SUGGESTIONS FOR ADDITIONAL READING

Aponte, J. B., and Herbert S. Denenberg. "A New Concept of the Economics of Life Value and the Human Life." *Journal of Risk and Insurance,* vol. 35, no. 3 (Sept. 1968).

Black, Kenneth, Jr., and Harold D. Skipper, Jr. *Life Insurance,* 13th ed. Englewood Cliffs, N.J.: Prentice-Hall, 2000. Chapters 1, 2, 13, 17.

Crawford, Murial L. *Life and Health Insurance Law,* LOMA ed. New York: McGraw-Hill. 1997.

Crowe, Robert M., and Charles E. Hughes, eds. *Fundamentals of Financial Planning,* 2nd ed. Bryn Mawr, Pa.: The American College, 1993.

Diamond Life Bulletins. Cincinnati: National Underwriter Company.

Hallman, G. Victor, and Karen L. Hamilton. *Personal Insurance: Life, Health & Retirement.* Malvern, Pa.: American Institute for CPCU, 1994. Chapters 3, 6.

Hofflander, A. E. "The Human Life Value: A Historical Perspective." *Journal of Risk and Insurance,* vol. 33, no. 3 (Sept. 1966).

Mehr, Robert I., and Sandra G. Gustavson. *Life Insurance Theory and Practice,* 4th ed. Austin, Tex.: Business Publications, 1987. Chapter 19.

Wolff, Thomas J. *Capital Needs Analysis—Basic Sales Manual.* Vernon, Conn.: Vernon Publishing Services, 1977.

WEB SITES TO EXPLORE

American College	http://www.amercoll.edu/
American Council of Life Insurance	http://www.acli.com/
American Society of CLU & ChFC	http://www.agents-online.com/ASCLU/web/index.html
Free Advice—Estate Planning	http://freeadvice.com/law/536us.htm
Institute of Certified Financial Planners	http://www.icfp.org/
Insurance News Network	http://www.insure.com/
Internal Revenue Service	http://www.irs.ustreas.gov/
International Association for Financial Planning	http://www.iafp.org/
Life Insurance Marketing and Research Association, Inc.	http://www.limra.com
Life Office Management Association (LOMA)	http://www.loma.org/
S.S. Huebner Foundation for Insurance Education	http://rider.wharton.upenn.edu/~sshuebne/
U.S. Gift and Estate Tax Law	http://www.law.cornell.edu/topics/estate_gift_tax.html

CHAPTER 11

SOCIAL INSURANCE
PROGRAMS

■

The essence of social insurance is bringing the magic
of averages to the rescue of millions.

— WINSTON CHURCHILL

CHAPTER OBJECTIVES

When you have finished this chapter, you should be able to

- Identify and describe the major classes of benefits in the Old-Age, Survivors', Disability, and Health Insurance Program (OASDHI)
- Identify the persons who are eligible for benefits under the Old-Age, Survivors', and Disability Insurance (OASDI) program and how eligibility for benefits is derived
- Explain how benefits under the OASDI program are financed
- Explain how the amount of benefits received under OASDI is determined and the circumstances that can lead to a loss of benefits
- Evaluate the financial soundness of the Social Security system and identify the proposals that have been suggested to improve that soundness
- Explain the rationale for workers compensation laws and outline the principles on which the workers compensation system is based
- Describe the operation of the workers compensation system, including the types of injuries covered and the types of benefits

In Chapter 10, we briefly noted how state unemployment insurance programs address the risk of income loss associated with unemployment. In this chapter, we turn to other social insurance programs that contribute to the security of the individual: the Social Security and workers compensation systems. We study these social insurance programs to acquire tools that may be used in dealing with the risks to income facing the individual. Although our examination will be brief, it will be sufficient to allow us to

relate the benefits under these programs to the over-all risk management problem facing the individual.

OLD-AGE, SURVIVORS', DISABILITY, AND HEALTH INSURANCE

The Old-Age, Survivors', Disability, and Health Insurance Program (commonly known as *Social Security*) protects eligible workers and their dependents against the financial losses associated with death, disability, superannuation, and sickness in old age. The benefits available under the program to the dependents of a deceased worker or to a disabled worker and his or her dependents are an important part of an individual's income protection program. The retirement benefits are also a fundamental element in the individual's retirement program. Any attempt to fit insurance to the needs of the family must consider the benefits available under OASDHI. There are four classes of benefits.

1. *Old-age benefits.* The old-age part of OAS-DHI provides a lifetime pension beginning at age 65 (or a reduced benefit as early as age 62) to each eligible worker and certain eligible dependents. The amount of this pension is based on the worker's average earnings during some period in the working years.

2. *Survivors' benefits.* Although the Social Security Act originally provided only retirement benefits, complaints that the system was unfair to workers who died before retirement (or after retirement) induced Congress to expand the program, extending benefits to the dependents of a deceased worker or retiree. The survivors' portion of the program provides covered workers with a form of life insurance, the proceeds of which are payable to their dependent children and, under some conditions, surviving spouses.

3. *Disability benefits.* Disability benefits were added to the program in 1956, when such benefits were extended to insured workers who became disabled between the ages of 50 and 64. In 1960, this coverage was broadened to all workers who meet certain eligibility requirements. A qualified worker who becomes totally and permanently disabled is treated as if he or she had reached retirement age and the worker and dependents become eligible for the benefits that would otherwise be payable at age 65.

4. *Medicare benefits.* The Medicare portion of the system was added in 1965. It offers people over 65 and certain disabled persons protection against the high cost of hospitalization, skilled nursing, hospice care, home health services, and other kinds of medical care. In addition, it provides an option by which those eligible for the basic benefits under the medical program may purchase subsidized medical insurance to help pay for doctors' services and other expenses not covered by the basic plan.[1]

All income benefits are subject to automatic adjustments for increases in the cost of living. Benefits for all recipients are increased automatically each January if the Consumer Price Index (CPI) shows a rise in the cost of living during the preceding year. Congress retains the right to legislate increases in benefit levels, but there is no automatic increase in any year for which Congress has legislated one.

Eligibility and Qualification Requirements

Initially, the act covered only about 60 percent of the civilian work force. The major classes not included were the self-employed, agricultural workers, government employees, and employees of nonprofit organizations. Coverage was gradually expanded until virtually all private employment and self-employment qualify for OASDHI. Today, more than 95 percent of the labor force is covered, most on a compulsory basis. Most of those not covered are state, local, or federal employees.[2]

To qualify for benefits, an individual must have credit for a certain amount of work under Social Security. Insured status is measured by *quarters of coverage,* and individuals earn these quarters by paying taxes on their wages. Some benefits are payable only if the worker has enough quarters of coverage to be considered *fully insured,* whereas other benefits are payable if the worker is merely *currently insured.*

[1] The original income-protection elements of Social Security (Old-Age, Survivor's, and Disability Insurance) are referred to as OASDI. The expanded system, which includes Medicare, is OAS-DHI. Medicare benefits are discussed in Chapter 22.

[2] Employees who are covered under a state or local government retirement system may elect to be included under OASDHI by referendum. Federal employees hired after December 31, 1983, are included in the OASDHI program.

Quarter of Coverage For most employment before 1978, an individual earned *one quarter of coverage* for each calendar quarter in which he or she paid the *Federal Insurance Contribution Act (FICA)* tax on $50 or more in wages. (A *calendar quarter* is any three-month period beginning January 1, April 1, July 1, or October 1.) Since 1978, the level of earnings on which FICA taxes must be paid for a quarter of coverage is adjusted annually, based on increases in average total wages for all workers. By 2002, one quarter of coverage was granted for each $870 of earnings, up to a maximum of four quarters per year. Further increases will take place as the average total wages for all workers increase.

Fully Insured Status Fully insured status is required for retirement benefits. To be fully insured the worker must have one quarter of coverage for each year starting with the year in which he or she reaches age 22, up to, but not including, the year in which the worker reaches age 62, becomes disabled, or dies. For most people, this means 40 quarters of coverage. No worker can achieve *fully insured* status with fewer than 6 quarters of covered employment, and no worker needs more than 40 quarters. Once a worker has 40 quarters of coverage, he or she is fully insured permanently.

Currently Insured Status To be *currently insured,* a worker needs 6 quarters of coverage during the 13-quarter period ending with the quarter of death, entitlement to retirement benefits, or disability. Basically, currently insured status entitles children of a deceased worker (and the children's mother or father) to survivor's benefits and provides a lump-sum benefit in the event of the worker's death.

Financing

The OASDHI program is administered by the Social Security Administration.[3] It is financed through a system of payroll and self-employment taxes levied on all persons in the program. For wage earners, a tax is paid on wages up to a specified maximum by both employers and the employee. In the original act of 1935, a tax rate of 1 percent applied to the first $3000 of an employee's wages, and the employer and employee were each liable for the tax up to a $30 annual maximum. When the Medicare program was added in 1965, a separate *Hospital Insurance tax* was added, which is combined with the Old-Age, Survivors', and Disability tax to make up the total FICA tax. Both the tax rate and taxable wage base to which it applies have increased over time as the program has expanded. The most recent change in the tax rate occurred in 1990, when the *Old-Age, Survivors', and Disability tax* was increased to 6.2 percent and the Medicare tax was increased to 1.45 percent, making a combined rate of 7.65 percent, payable by the employee and matched by the employer.

The Old-Age, Survivors', and Disability tax applies to a taxable wage base that automatically increases in the year following an automatic benefit increase. Like the automatic increases in benefit levels, congressional changes in the taxable wage base override the automatic adjustment provisions. Automatic increases in the earnings base are geared to the increase in average wages for all workers. With the legislated changes and automatic adjustments, the taxable wage base had increased to $84,900 by 2002 and will continue to increase in the future. Historically, the Medicare tax applied only up to the maximum taxable wage base. The 1993 Tax Reform Act eliminated the maximum wage base for the Medicare tax, and the tax now applies to total earned income without limit.

Self-employed persons pay a tax rate that is equal to the combined employer-employee contribution (i.e., 15.3 percent in 2002). Self-employed persons are allowed a deduction against income taxes equal to half the self-employment taxes paid for the year.

Some costs are financed from general funds of the U.S. Treasury. Among these are certain costs under the Medicare program and cash payments to some uninsured persons over age 72.

Amount of Benefits

Most OASDHI benefits are based on a benefit called the *primary insurance amount* (PIA). The PIA is the amount of the retirement benefit payable to a worker who retires at age 65. It is computed from the individual's *average indexed monthly earnings* (AIME), which is the worker's average monthly wages or other earnings during his or her computation years, indexed

[3] The Social Security Administration maintains an exceptionally useful Web page at http://www.ssa.gov/. The site provides current detailed information on all facets of the OASDI program with a link to the Health Care Financing Administration (HCFA), which administers Medicare. The HCFA Web site is http://www.hcfa.gov/.

to current wage levels. All monthly income benefits under OASDI to the worker and his or her eligible dependents are based on the PIA.

Computing the Primary Insurance Amount The first step in computing the primary insurance amount is to determine the average indexed monthly earnings. This is the average monthly earnings on which the worker paid FICA taxes, indexed to current wage levels. It is calculated by indexing prior earnings, dropping some low years, and calculating the average.

Indexing Earnings A worker's past earnings are indexed to wage levels in effect in the second year prior to eligibility, by comparing average wages covered by Social Security over the years. For example, consider an individual who reached age 60 in 1999 and is applying for benefits in 2001. Since individuals are first eligible for retirement benefits at age 62, prior earnings would be indexed to the year in which the person reached age 60, or 1999. Average earnings in 1999 ($30,469.84) were 3.5303 times average earnings in 1975, so wages earned in 1975 would be indexed by multiplying the worker's FICA-taxed wages in 1975 by 3.5303. Other years' wages would be similarly adjusted. Earnings after the index year are not adjusted.

Dropping Low Years After indexing prior earnings, the individual may be permitted to drop some low years of earnings. The number of years that must be included when computing the average depends on the age of the individual and the type of benefits for which he or she is applying.[4] An individual who works longer than the required number of years may be able to exclude some additional years of low earnings. On the other hand, if the individual was not employed at least the required number of years, some years of zero earnings must be included when calculating the average.

Computing the Primary Insurance Amount After dropping the allowed number of years of low earnings, total indexed earnings are divided by the

number of months included to produce the AIME. The AIME is converted to the PIA using a formula prescribed by law. The formula used in converting the AIME to the PIA provides for a higher percentage of the average indexed earnings at lower income levels than at higher income levels.[5]

Classes of Benefits

Retirement Benefits Workers who are fully insured are entitled to receive a monthly pension for the rest of their lives. If the worker retires at age 65, the benefit is equal to 100 percent of his or her PIA. Workers may elect to receive benefits as early as age 62, but the benefit is reduced 5/9 of 1 percent for each month prior to age 65 that benefits commence (a 20 percent reduction at age 62). The age at which full retirement benefits are payable—now age 65—is scheduled to increase to age 67 in gradual steps, beginning in the year 2000. Workers who delay retirement receive an increase in their PIA for each month between the ages of 65 and 72 that they delay retirement. This credit varies, depending on the date of birth. For individuals reaching age 65 in 1994, the increase is 3/8 percent for each month retirement is deferred. The credit will increase according to a legislated schedule until it reaches 2/3 percent per month in 2008.

In addition to the benefits received by the worker at retirement, others may receive benefits if the worker was fully insured. Total benefits received by the family, however, are subject to an overall maximum family benefit.

Spouse's Benefit The spouse of the retired worker (or a spouse divorced after 10 years of marriage) is entitled to a retirement benefit at age 65 equal to 50 percent of the worker's PIA. Like the retired worker, the spouse may choose a permanently reduced benefit as early as age 62. The benefit to the spouse of a retired worker is reduced 25/36 percent for each month prior to age 65 the benefit is received.[6]

[4] Calculating the number of years to include requires first calculating the number of *elapsed years*. Elapsed years are the years beginning the year in which the worker reached age 22 and ending with the year before the one in which the worker becomes 62, dies, or is disabled. Most workers must calculate the AIME using the years of earnings equal to the number of elapsed years minus 5. For workers applying for retirement benefits, this requires 35 years of earnings (40 minus 5). Fewer years may be included if the PIA is being calculated for a worker who has died or become disabled.

[5] For workers reaching age 65 in 2002, the PIA was computed on the basis of the following formula: 90 percent of the first $592 of AIME, plus 32 percent of the AIME from $592 to $3567, plus 15 percent of the AIME above $3567. The dollar amounts in the formula, known as *bend points,* are subject to adjustment based on changes in the national average monthly wages.

[6] A divorced spouse is entitled to receive a retirement benefit even if the worker on whose account the benefit is based continues working if both parties are at least age 62, were married for 10 years, and have been divorced for at least two years.

Children's Benefit The benefit for children of a retired worker is payable to three classes of dependent children: (1) unmarried children under age 18; (2) unmarried children age 18 or over who are disabled, provided that they were disabled before reaching age 22; and (3) unmarried children under age 19 who are full-time students in an elementary or secondary school. The benefit to each eligible child of a retired worker is 50 percent of the worker's.

Mother's or Father's Benefit A retired worker's spouse who has not yet reached age 62 may still be entitled to a benefit, if he or she has care of a child who is receiving a benefit. A *mother's benefit* is payable to the wife of a retired worker and a *father's benefit* is payable to the husband of a retired worker if either has care of child under 16 or a disabled child who is receiving a benefit.[7] This benefit is 50 percent of the worker's PIA.

Family Maximum All income benefits payable to a worker and his or her dependents are subject to a family maximum. The family maximum is based on a formula applied to the PIA.[8] If total family benefits are greater than the family maximum, each individual's benefit, except the retired worker's, is reduced.

Survivors' Benefits Benefits are payable to certain dependents of a deceased worker, provided that the worker had insured status, which varies for the different classes of survivors' benefits. Once again, total benefits are subject to an overall maximum family benefit. The benefits payable under this part of the program include the following.

Lump-Sum Death Benefit A $255 lump-sum death benefit is payable to the surviving spouse or children of the deceased worker.

Children's Benefit The *children's benefit* is payable to dependent children of a deceased worker in any of the three classes noted earlier. The benefit to each eligible child of a deceased worker is 75 percent of the worker's PIA.

Mother's or Father's Benefit A *mother's* or *father's benefit* is payable to the widow or widower of a deceased worker who has care of a child under 16 (or a disabled child over 16) who is receiving benefits. This benefit is 75 percent of the worker's PIA.

Widow's or Widower's Benefit The widow or widower of a deceased worker (or a worker's divorced wife of 10 years of marriage) is entitled to a retirement benefit at age 65 equal to 100 percent of the worker's PIA. The widow or widower may elect to receive a permanently scaled-down benefit as early as age 60. The *widow's* or *widower's benefit* is also payable to the spouse of a deceased worker who becomes disabled after age 50 and not more than 7 years after the death of the worker or the end of his or her entitlement to a mother's or father's benefit. A disabled widow or widower age 50 to 59 who is entitled to a benefit receives 71.5 percent of the PIA.[9]

Parents' Benefit The *parents' benefit* is payable to a deceased worker's parents who are over age 62, if they were dependent on the worker for support at the time of death. One parent is entitled to a retirement benefit at age 62 equal to 82.5 percent of the worker's PIA. The maximum benefit for two dependent parents is 150 percent of the worker's PIA (75 percent each).

Required Insured Status Under the survivor benefit program, the children's benefit, mother's or father's benefit, and lump-sum death benefit are paid if the worker is either fully or currently insured. All other benefits are payable only if the worker was fully insured.

Disability Benefits *Disability benefits* are payable to a worker and eligible dependents when a worker who meets special eligibility requirements is disabled within the meaning of that term under the law. Disability is defined as a "mental or physical impairment that prevents the worker from engaging in any substantial gainful employment." The disability must have lasted for 6 months and must be expected to last for at least 12 months or be expected to result in the prior death of the worker. Persons who apply for Social Security benefits are referred to the state agencies called *disability determination services* (DDSs)

[7] Prior to 1975, the law provided only for a "mother's" benefit (i.e., a benefit to the female spouse of a retired or deceased worker with a child in her care). The U.S. Supreme Court ruled that the provision of such a benefit to females only was unconstitutional and that it deprived working women of a form of protection afforded to working men.

[8] This formula, like the PIA formula, includes dollar *bend points* that are subject to adjustment based on increases in the average total wages of all workers.

[9] The widow's or widower's retirement benefit is reduced 19/40 of 1 percent for each month prior to age 65 that the benefits commence (thus, a benefit equal to $71^1/_2$ percent of the PIA at age 60).

to evaluate the disability. If the state agency is satisfied that the worker is disabled as defined by the Social Security Act, the individual is certified as such and benefits are paid. However, benefits do not start until the worker has been disabled for five full calendar months.

Qualification requirements for disability benefits depend on the worker's age. Workers who become disabled before reaching age 24 qualify if they have 6 quarters out of the 12 quarters ending when the disability began. Workers who became disabled between ages 24 and 31 must have 1 quarter of coverage for each 2 quarters beginning at age 21 and ending with the onset of disability. Workers over age 31 must be fully insured, and must have 20 out of the last 40 quarters in covered employment.

In general, disability benefits are payable to the same categories of persons and in the same amounts as retirement benefits, but subject to a special family maximum benefit. Total monthly payments for a disabled worker with one or more dependents are limited to the lower of 85 percent of the worker's AIME or 150 percent of the worker's disability benefit (but not less than 100 percent of the worker's PIA).[10]

The disability insurance program has a number of provisions designed to encourage beneficiaries to return to gainful employment. Beneficiaries may be referred to state vocational rehabilitation agencies for assistance. They are also permitted to return to employment for a "trial work period" without adversely affecting their benefits. After this nine-month period of employment, benefits will continue if average monthly earnings have not exceeded $500. (The nine months need not be consecutive.) If average earnings are greater than $500, benefits continue for a three-month grace period and then cease.

Summary of Qualification Requirements

Although the preceding discussion may seem complicated, the nature of the qualification requirements can be summarized concisely, and although all qualifications are important, some seem more so than others. The survivors' benefits payable to children and mother's or father's benefits require only that the worker have been fully or currently insured. To be eligible for any retirement benefits, the worker must have been fully insured. Table 11.1 summarizes the qualification requirements for the various categories of benefits under OASDHI.

Table 11.2 lists the actual dollar amount of benefits in effect in 2002. The PIAs are adjusted automatically each January (upward only) to match increases in the CPI. This means that the benefits shown in the table will be adjusted in January 2003, depending on the increase in the CPI from the first quarter of 2001 to the first quarter of 2002. In view of the automatic adjustment of benefit levels, the reader should check current Social Security Administration publications for the actual benefit levels in effect.

Loss of Benefits—the OASDHI Program

A person receiving benefits may lose eligibility for benefits in several ways. The most common causes of disqualification under the law are the following:[11]

1. *Divorce from a person receiving benefits.* For example, a retired worker's wife or husband who is receiving a benefit based on the qualification of that worker loses the right to the benefit after divorce, unless he or she was married to the worker for 10 years or longer.

2. *Attainment of age 18 by a child receiving benefits.* The benefit payable to the child of a deceased, retired, or disabled worker stops automatically when the child reaches age 18, unless the child is still in high school, in which case the benefit is payable until age 19. When the child reaches age 16, the mother's or father's benefit stops even though the child continues to receive a benefit. The child-raising widow or widower of a deceased worker, therefore, faces a period during which no benefits are payable. Between the time the youngest child turns 16 and the time the widow or widower reaches age 60, no benefits are payable. This period is commonly referred to as the *blackout period.*

3. *Marriage.* The rules governing the loss of benefits through marriage or remarriage are rather

[10] Disability benefits under OASDHI may be reduced if the individual also receives workers compensation benefits. The law limits combined benefits to 80 percent of the disabled person's recent earnings. Some states have reverse offset plans, under which workers compensation benefits are reduced if the worker is entitled to Social Security benefits.

[11] In addition to the causes of disqualification listed, benefits may also be lost because of conviction of treason, sabotage, or subversive activity; deportation; work in foreign countries, unless that work is also covered under OASDHI; and the refusal of rehabilitation by a disabled beneficiary.

TABLE 11.1 **Insured Status Required for OASDHI Benefits**

Benefit	Insured Status Required of Workers
Survivors' Benefits	
Children's benefits	Fully or currently insured
Mother's or father's benefit	Fully or currently insured
Dependent parent's benefit	Fully insured
Widow or widower age 60 or over	Fully insured
Lump-sum death benefit	Fully or currently insured
Retirement Benefits	
Retired worker	Fully insured
Spouse of retired worker	Fully insured
Child of retired worker	Fully insured
Mother's or father's benefit	Fully insured
Disability Benefits	
Disabled worker	Twenty of last 40 quarters fully insured or
Dependent of disabled worker	Six of last 12 quarters if under age 24
	One of every 2 quarters since age 21 if between 23 and 31
Medicare Benefits	Entitlement to cash benefits under Social Security or Railroad Retirement, or have reached age 65 before 1968, or meet special eligibility requirement

TABLE 11.2 **Old-Age, Survivors', and Disability Benefits – 2002**

	Percent of PIA	Low Earnings	Average Earnings	High Earnings	Maximum Earnings
Average Indexed Monthly Earnings (AIME)		$1045	$2322	$3590	$4770
Primary Insurance Amount (PIA)	100.00%	682	1127	1467	1660
Retired worker – age 65	100.00%	682	1127	1467	1660
Retired worker – age 62	80.00%	546	902	1174	1328
Disabled worker under 65	100.00%	682	1127	1467	1660
Spouse of retired worker at 65	50.00%	341	564	734	830
Spouse of retired worker at 62	37.50%	256	423	550	623
Child of retired or disabled worker	50.00%	341	564	734	830
Spouse under 65 with one child	50.00%	341	564	734	830
Widow or widower at age 65	100.00%	682	1127	1467	1660
Widow or widower at age 60	71.50%	488	806	1049	1187
Disabled widow or widower at age 50	71.50%	488	806	1049	1187
One surviving child	75.00%	512	845	1100	1245
Widow or widower with one child	125.00%	853	1409	1834	2075
Family maximum	Bend Points	1023	2095	2568	2906

Source: Social Security Administration (See Illustrative Benefit Tables at http//:www.ssa.gov/GACT/COLA/).

complicated. As a rule, if a person receiving a monthly benefit as a dependent or survivor marries someone who is not also a beneficiary, his or her payment stops. On the other hand, where both parties are beneficiaries, payments may continue. For example, a widow receiving mother's benefits (because of a child under 16) will not lose her benefits if she marries an individual receiving retirement or disability benefits. There are, of course, a number of exceptions to these rules.[12] Interested persons should contact their local Social Security office for a determination in specific situations.

4. *Adoption.* If a child receiving a benefit is adopted by anyone except a stepparent, grandparent, aunt, or uncle, the payment to the child stops.

5. *Disqualifying income.* Sometimes, persons receiving Social Security benefits continue to work. Some work full time, others only part time. The same is true with respect to dependents receiving benefits. The Social Security laws provide that if a person receiving benefits earns additional income, her or she may lose a part or all of his or her benefits, depending on the amount earned. Certain amounts of earnings are permitted, but earnings in excess of these amounts reduce the Social Security benefit.

Disqualifying Income For 65 years, from its inception in 1935 until 2000, the Social Security System enforced an "earnings test," under which benefits payable to beneficiaries could be reduced if the beneficiary had earned income. In 2000, faced with what most people agreed was a growing crisis in the system, Congress decided to eliminate the Social Security earnings test for persons over age 65. This means that a worker can now continue to work full-time and draw his or her full Social Retirement benefit.

For beneficiaries under age 65, the earnings test remains and Social Security benefits are reduced if the individual's earned income exceeds exempt amounts. The annual exempt amount of earnings increases each year, based on increases in national earnings. In 2002, the exempt earnings amount for persons under age 65 was $11,280. For earnings in excess of the exempt amount, $1 in benefits will be withheld for each $2 in earnings in excess of the exempt amount.

Because some earnings can reduce Social Security benefits, it is important to distinguish those types of income that do not affect Social Security benefits. Among the items that do not count as disqualifying income are (1) pensions and retirement pay, (2) insurance annuities, (3) dividends from stock (unless the person is a dealer in stock), (4) interest on savings, (5) gifts or inheritances of money or property, (6) gain from the sale of capital assets, and (7) rental income (unless the person is a real estate dealer or participating farm landlord).

Taxation of Benefits Social Security benefits were originally exempt from taxes. Beginning in 1984, however, beneficiaries who have significant income in addition to the Social Security benefits must pay taxes on a portion of their Social Security benefits. The amount of the benefits subject to tax depends on the *combined income* and the filing status of the individuals. *Combined income* is the sum of adjusted gross income, tax-exempt interest, and one-half of the Social Security benefits. If combined income for an individual is between $25,000 and $34,000, or for a couple filing jointly is from $32,000 to $44,000, 50 percent of the Social Security benefit may be taxed. For combined income above $34,000 for a single individual or $44,000 for a couple filing jointly, up to 85 percent of benefits may be taxed.

Because the provisions relating to taxation of Social Security benefits in the second tier were enacted later and are superimposed on the first tier, the system will become clearer if we discuss the two tiers in the sequence in which they became effective.

For the first tier, the amount of benefits subject to tax is the smaller of (1) one-half the Social Security benefits or (2) one-half of the amount by which *modified adjusted gross income* (adjusted gross income plus tax-exempt interest) plus one-half of the Social Security benefits exceed the so-called *base amounts,* namely, $25,000 for single taxpayers and $32,000 for married taxpayers filing jointly.[13]

Because the formula for even the first tier is confusing, let us consider an example. Abner, Baker, and Cole are all single taxpayers, and each receives $18,000 in Social Security benefits. Abner has $10,000

[12] For example, children under 18 lose their benefits if they marry, regardless of who they marry. Widows, widowers, and surviving divorced spouses lose their benefits based on the deceased worker's earnings if they remarry before age 60. Benefits to a surviving spouse or a divorced surviving spouse are not terminated if he or she remarries after age 60.

[13] The base amount for married taxpayers who file separate returns, but who live together at any time during the year, is zero.

in earned (taxable) income, Baker has $15,000 in earned income, and Cole has $30,000 in taxable income. In addition, each has $5,000 in tax-exempt interest. The determination of the portion of Social Security benefits that must be included as taxable income is made as follows:

	Abner	Baker	Cole
1. Earned income	$10,000	$15,000	$30,000
2. Tax-exempt interest	5,000	5,000	5,000
3. Modified adjusted gross income	15,000	20,000	35,000
4. Plus: One-half Social Security benefit	9,000	9,000	9,000
5. Combined income	24,000	29,000	44,000
6. Less: Base amount	25,000	25,000	25,000
7. Excess combined income over base	0	4,000	19,000
8. One-half of Social Security benefits	9,000	9,000	9,000
9. One-half excess of combined income over base	0	2,000	9,500
10. Amount taxable	0	2,000	9,000

As this chart shows, none of Abner's Social Security benefits will be included in taxable income. His combined income plus one-half of his Social Security benefit is less than the $25,000 base amount; since this is less than one-half of the Social Security benefit, none of his benefits is taxable. Baker's combined income plus one-half of his Social Security benefits exceeds the base amount by $4000; one-half of this $4000 is smaller than one-half of the Social Security benefits, so $2000 is includable in taxable income. Finally, Cole's combined income plus one-half of his Social Security benefits exceeds the $25,000 base amount by $19,000. Since one-half of the $19,000 is greater than one-half of his Social Security benefits, he will be taxed on one-half of the Social Security benefits.

Perhaps because the rules were not sufficiently complex, Congress added the second tax tier for tax years beginning in 1994. Under the new rules, persons whose modified adjusted gross income plus one-half the Social Security benefit exceeds $34,000 ($44,000 on a joint return) will be taxed on up to 85 percent of their Social Security benefit. These taxpayers must include in gross income the lesser of:

- 85 percent of the total benefits received, or
- 85 percent of the amount by which adjusted gross income plus one-half of the Social Security benefits exceeds the $34,000 or $44,000 threshold, plus the smaller of (1) the amount that would have been included under pre-1993 law or (2) $6000 on a joint return ($4500 on a single return).

Cole, who would have been required to include $9000 in Social Security benefits under prior law, is subject to the new threshold. Using the $34,000 threshold effective since 1994, determination of the benefits includable in Cole's taxable income is:

	Post 94	
Taxable income	$30,000	
Tax-exempt interest	5,000	
Modified adjusted gross income	35,000	
Plus: 50 percent of Social Security benefit	9,000	
Combined income	44,000	
Less: Base amount	34,000	
Excess combined income over base	10,000	
Includable in taxable income is		
— the lesser of 85 percent of Social Security benefit		15,300
or		
— the sum of 85 percent of the excess	8,500	
— plus the smaller of $4,500 or the amount includable under prior law	4,500	13,000

To compute the taxable income for persons whose combined income exceeds the higher thresholds, the amount that would have been includable under prior law must first be computed. The amount that is included is then the lesser of 85 percent of the Social Security benefit ($15,300) or 85 percent of the combined income in excess of the threshold ($8500) plus the smaller of $4500 or the amount that would have been includable under the previous rules ($9000). Since $8500 plus $4500 ($13,000) is less than $15,300, $13,000 will be includable in taxable income.

Social Security recipients now fall into three classes with respect to taxation of benefits: (1) persons whose Social Security benefits are not taxed; (2) persons who must include up to 50 percent of their Social Security benefits in taxable income; and (3) persons who must include up to 85 percent of their Social Security benefit in their taxable income. Revenues from the increased taxation of Social Security

benefits are transferred to the Medicare Hospital Insurance (HI) trust fund.

Soundness of the Program

One of the central issues in the debate over passage of the Social Security Act was the system's financing. Many authorities proposed that the federal government support the program out of general revenues; others maintained that it should be financed completely by the contributions of the workers and their employers. The decision was eventually reached that only revenues provided by Social Security taxes would be used to pay benefits. The intent at that time (and the principle that has, for the most part, been carried down to the present) was that the system should be self-supporting from contributions of covered workers and their employers. The bases for this decision were complex, but one of the primary reasons was to give the participants a legal and moral right to the benefits.[14]

Once the issue of a self-supporting program was settled, there was disagreement over whether to fund the program with a reserve similar to those used in private insurance or whether to operate it on a *pay-as-you-go* basis. The proponents of a pay-as-you-go approach eventually prevailed, creating the system currently in use.

Pay-as-You-Go System Under the *pay-as-you-go system,* those who are eligible receive benefits out of Social Security taxes paid by those who are working. In turn, today's workers will receive benefits after retirement from funds that are paid by the labor force at that time. The moneys collected are allocated to trust funds, from which the benefits are paid. There are separate trust funds for the Old-Age and Survivors' program, the Disability program, the Hospital Insurance program of Medicare, and the Supplementary Medical Insurance program. The trust funds were conceived as a contingency reserve to cover periodic fluctuations in income, but not to fund liabilities to future recipients.

The rationale for the pay-as-you-go system seems logical. Given a stable system with a high ratio of taxpayers to beneficiaries, modest tax rates can support relatively generous benefits. When current workers retire, their retirement benefits will be funded by a new generation of taxpayers (and a presumably larger one, if there is population growth). Moreover, those taxpayers will make contributions based on higher earnings as a result of improved national productivity. In theory, this results in an ever-increasing level of benefits.

Difficulties arise, however, when the relationship between the number of beneficiaries and the number of taxpayers changes adversely. If there are fewer taxpayers to support the benefits, tax rates must rise. That is, in fact, what has happened.

The combined Social Security contribution for employers and employees climbed from a modest $348 in 1965 to $12,990 for workers earning $84,900 in 2002, with further increases likely in the future. For the average wage earner, the greatest increase in the cost of living over the past 20 years has been the hike in Social Security taxes.

The increasing tax for workers covered under the program and the financial difficulties that are predicted stem from two causes: the increasing number of beneficiaries under the program and the increasing level of benefits. In 1947, when only retired persons and survivors were eligible for benefits, about 1 out of every 70 Americans received Social Security checks. With the expansion of the program to include disabled workers and their dependents, coupled with the changing age structure of the population, the ratio of beneficiaries to taxpayers had increased to about 1 to 3.3 by 1998. Over the next 32 years, as the large post–World War II baby boomers reaches age 65, the ratio will become even worse. In 2030, when the last baby boomers reach age 65, it is projected that there will be 2.3 taxpayers for each beneficiary.

While the proportion of the population entitled to benefits has grown, the level of those benefits has also increased. For most periods since the introduction of the automatic adjustment in benefits, average benefits paid to retired workers have increased at a faster rate than the CPI or the increase in wages. As benefits have increased, the percentage of preretirement income replaced by Social Security has also risen, from a replacement rate of about 31 percent in 1970 to more than 40 percent by 2001.

[14] As Franklin D. Roosevelt aptly put it, "Those taxes were never a problem of economics. They are politics all the way through. We put those payroll contributions there so as to give the contributors a legal, moral, and political right to collect their pensions and their unemployment benefits. With those taxes in there, no damn politician can ever scrap my social security program." Quoted in Arthur M. Schlesinger, Jr., *The Coming of the New Deal* (Boston: Houghton Mifflin, 1959), pp. 308ff.

With the growth in the number of recipients and the increasing level of benefits, the system reached a critical point in the late 1970s. In December 1977, Congress enacted a Social Security *bailout plan* to save the system from impending bankruptcy. It included the largest peacetime tax increase in the history of the United States up to that time. In signing the 1977 amendments, President Carter stated, "Now this legislation will guarantee that from 1980 to the year 2030, the Social Security funds will be sound." Unfortunately, the measures designed to save the system did not contain a sufficient margin of safety. As a result, the salvation was short-lived and another financing crisis occurred in 1981–1983. By 1981, the system's Board of Trustees warned in its annual report to Congress that, even under the most optimistic assumptions, the OASDI trust fund would be bankrupt by the end of 1982. In 1982, the Old-Age and Survivors' Trust Fund was forced to borrow from the Disability and Hospital Insurance trust funds to meet benefits obligations. Recognizing that corrective action was imperative, President Reagan appointed the bipartisan National Commission on Social Security Reform in December 1981 to review the system's financing problems and to recommend a solution. In mid-1983, Congress enacted legislation embodying the commission's proposals. The 1983 legislation included massive tax increases in 1988 and 1990, an increase in the retirement age beginning in the year 2000, and taxation of Social Security benefits for persons with incomes above a certain level.

In an effort to avoid a repetition that occurred as a result of faulty assumptions in the 1977 legislation, the changes enacted in 1983 were made on the basis of ultraconservative estimates. Recognizing the need to plan for the large numbers of individuals retiring in the next century, Congress enacted changes that would result in surpluses for a period of time, that is, revenues exceeding disbursements. Because the economy performed better than had been anticipated, the Social Security trust funds increased from modest contingency funds totaling about $45 billion in 1982 to more than $1 trillion in 2001. The trust fund is expected to peak at about $3.5 trillion in 2016. After 2016, large annual deficits will occur, depleting the fund by 2038.[15]

The dramatic growth in the trust funds that will occur over the next 25 years has led to a new concern over how those funds are invested. By law, the trust funds are invested in U.S. government bonds. In effect, the federal government is borrowing money from the trust funds to cover current operations and issuing IOUs to the funds. Of course, in the next century, these bonds will have to be redeemed as the trust fund balances are depleted. This leaves the question: Where will the money come from to redeem the bonds? Presumably, it will come from taxpayers at that time. In that case, the Social Security funding problem hasn't been resolved. Rather, it has been replaced by a massive new tax problem. This has led some critics to suggest abandoning the current attempt to accumulate large trust funds with high taxes, and to instead move closer to a system in which today's taxes are just enough to fund today's benefits. While that will lead to a day of reckoning, they argue, that day will come anyway, given how the funds are currently invested. Moreover, they argue, reduced payroll taxes could lead to greater economic growth.

Thus, there continues to be a basis for concern about the long-run soundness of the program. Although though the 1983 amendments appear to have solved the system's financial problems for the immediate future, some people believe that the means by which the solution was achieved—increasing the Social Security tax for workers—is a cure worse than the disease. Furthermore, the fundamental imbalance between workers and recipients will continue to grow, increasing the difficulty of funding benefits to future recipients. At the same time, the automatic cost-of-living adjustments will continue to push the amounts paid out to beneficiaries to higher and higher levels. With the growing imbalance between the number of workers and benefit recipients, the automatic cost-of-living benefit adjustments and wage base adjustments, and the scheduled tax rate increases, the cost of the program for workers cannot help but escalate even more. Meeting the obligations for benefits promised to workers entering the work force today will require higher payroll tax rates, including both the employer and the employee share, of up to 40 percent, compared to the current 15 percent.

Proposals for Change In the face of these prospective difficulties, a number of proposals have been made for changes in the system. Some suggest a revision in

[15] 2001 Annual Report of the Board of Trustees of the Old-Age and Survivors Insurance (OASI) and Disability Insurance (DI) Trust Funds.

the financing of the system; others call for a reevaluation of benefit levels.[16]

Proposals for Changes in Financing

The proposals for changes in financing the system have been many and varied. One approach suggests that the increased costs of the system be financed through higher taxes rather than through raising the earnings base. Proponents of this position argue that benefit increases should not be financed by the "painless" process of simply increasing the tax base. Higher tax rates would require all covered workers to share in the increased cost, thereby making the desirability of the increased benefits an issue to be considered by all.

Other proposals for changes in the system's funding take a directly opposite position, maintaining that the system is already highly regressive (most burdensome on low-income groups) and that the tax base should be eliminated completely, with Social Security taxes applying to all income earned. Others of this school have suggested that the system should be financed out of general revenues rather than through a separate tax.

Proposals for Changes in Benefit Levels

The Social Security system was originally developed on the principle that the amount of the social insurance benefit should be sufficient to provide a *floor of protection,* meaning an amount sufficient to maintain a minimum standard of living. This floor of protection was then to be supplemented by the individual through private insurance or other devices. Some critics believe that the system currently provides benefits to recipients far in excess of this *floor of protection* level. They have suggested that the level of benefits be limited.

A second proposal for changing the benefits structure focuses on the age for receiving full retirement benefits. When the Social Security Act was passed in 1935, the normal retirement age for benefits was 65. The 1983 amendments have instituted a gradual increase in this age to 67 years by the year 2022. Some critics argue that this compromise did not go far enough, and that there should be a significant and faster increase in the normal retirement age. They base this argument on the dramatic improvements in life expectancy since 1935, resulting in a much longer period of retirement for current retirees.[17]

Still another proposal argues that the solution to the problems is to permit workers to avail themselves of private alternatives to the Social Security system, through a system of credits for contributions to private retirement programs, such as individual retirement accounts (IRAs), and that the level of contribution to these programs should be increased.[18]

Privatizing Social Security

The most dramatic proposal for addressing the financial problems affecting Social Security is that it be privatized, with a change from the current pay-as-you-go system to a program with advance funding, in which contributions by workers and their employers are invested in the private sector. At one time, this would have been unthinkable. As long as Social Security was a "good deal" for participants and provided benefits that were substantially greater than the contributions they had made, a fundamental reform such as privatization was politically impossible. The current crisis in the system and the increasing imbalance between participant contributions and benefits has opened consideration to a variety of alternatives, including privatization, an idea that is gaining support.

One of America's most respected economists, Professor Martin Feldstein of Harvard University, makes a persuasive argument for privatization.[19] The problem, according to Professor Feldstein, is the pay-as-you-go system we use to finance the Social Security system. With benefits financed by current tax revenues, the 600 percent increase in the tax rate and the growth in the labor force since the Social Security Act was adopted has permitted the Social Security system to pay retirees significantly more in benefits than those retirees had paid in taxes during their working years. For current workers, and for those who will be entering the labor force, Social Security tax rates will have to increase to balance the aging of the population and the increasing number of retirees relative to those who are working. This means that the rate of

[16] For a summary of the many proposals for change, see Dorcas R. Hardy and C. Colburn Hardy, *Social Insecurity: The Crisis in America's Social Security System and How to Plan Now for Your Own Financial Survival* (New York: Villard Books, 1991).

[17] According to Hardy and Hardy, *Social Insecurity,* in 1935, the remaining life expectancy for a man retiring at age 65 was 11.9 years. (For a woman it was 13.2 years.) Today, the life expectancy of a 65-year-old is 16 years for a male and 19.2 years for a female.

[18] Peter J. Ferrara, *Social Security: The Inherent Contradiction* (Washington, D.C.: Cato Institute, 1984), and *Social Security: Averting the Crisis* (Washington, D.C.: Cato Institute, 1984).

[19] See "Time to Privatize Social Security," by Martin Feldstein, *Wall Street Journal,* March 8, 1996.

return that future workers will receive on their contributions is limited to the rate at which Social Security tax revenues will increase. This, it appears, will be limited to the increases that result from higher incomes and any growth in population. According to Feldstein, the implicit rate of return that is achievable from these sources is a modest 2.5 percent.

If the problem is a low rate of return, Feldstein argues, why not invest Social Security revenues where the return will be greater? Historically, over the past 30 years, funds that have been invested in stocks and bonds have earned a real pretax return of more than 9 percent. Shifting contributions from the current unfunded system to a funded program with IRAs or 401(k) plans would permit employees to earn that higher rate of return. Professor Feldstein estimates that if contributions were invested in a funded account earning a real return of 9 percent, the cost of financing Social Security benefits would be cut by about 80 percent.

Many other nations have already done precisely what Professor Feldstein has recommended, shifting from unfunded pay-as-you-go systems to funded privatized systems. Although the approach adopted by other countries differs in detail, the common thread is requiring that employer and employee contributions be invested in mutual funds or similar private assets.

The difficulty, of course, is that a privatized system could not be achieved immediately. There would be a transition period during which the Social Security Administration would have to continue to pay benefits to existing retirees while new funds are accumulated and invested through the individual accounts. There are several ways in which this could be done.

Report of the Advisory Council on Social Security
In January 1997, a special Advisory Council on Social Security appointed in 1994 to examine the long-term financing of Social Security issued its report. The council concluded that the program faces "serious problems in the long run," requiring attention in the near term. These problems, according to the council, are the funding deficit in the immediate future and beyond, the issue of equity from one generation to another, and the increasing skepticism among younger workers about the future of the system.[20]

All council members also agreed that the current pay-as-you-go system should be changed and recommended that there be partial advance funding for Social Security. Despite agreement about the problems facing the system, the council could not agree on a single proposal to address the system's financial problems. Instead the report offered three proposals, none of which was supported by a majority of the council. Although some strategies are common to all three proposals (i.e., accelerating the scheduled increase in the retirement age, decreasing benefit levels, and bringing state and local employees into the program), the most significant differences among the proposals relate to privatization. They serve as a convenient summary of current philosophical underpinnings in the debate over privatization.

One proposal—the *maintenance of benefits proposal*—recommended "a study of the possibility of investing up to 40% of Trust Fund assets in common stocks, corporate bonds, and other investments." Under this proposal, the surpluses that are accumulating in the Social Security trust funds would be invested directly in the stock market to increase the rate of the return on the funds (and, coincidentally, eliminate the future problem of repaying the government bonds in which the trust funds are now invested).

A second proposal—called the *individual account proposal*—would increase the FICA tax 1.6 percent to fund an individual account system to provide benefits in addition to the traditional Social Security benefit.

The third proposal—the *personal security accounts proposal*—would allow 5 percent of the current 12.4 percent payroll tax to be redirected to individual Private Security Accounts, which would not be taxed. Individuals would be permitted to direct the investment, choosing from among fund options provided by the federal government. Individuals could, if they choose, continue to allocate this part of their retirement program to government bonds.

Bush Commission to Strengthen Social Security
During the 2000 election campaign, candidate Bush argued strongly for a program of partial privatization, a plan labeled by his Democratic opponent as a risky scheme. In January 2001, almost immediately upon taking office, President George W. Bush appointed a new President's Commission to Strengthen Social Security to consider the future of Social Security. The commission was co-chaired by a long-time advocate of privatization, former Democratic senator from New York Daniel Patrick Moynihan and AOL Time

[20] An average worker born in 1915 and retiring at age 65 in 1980 could expect to collect about $60,000 more in benefits than the worker had paid into the system (adjusted for inflation and interest). Persons born in 1936 will just about break even. Persons born after 1960 can expect to pay at least $30,000 more in payroll taxes than they will ever receive in benefits.

Warner executive Richard Parsons (who previously served in the Ford administration).

In his charge to the Commission, President Bush requested that the Commission's recommendation adhere to several principles. The proposal was to include individually controlled, voluntary personal retirement accounts, and should not involve investment of the Social Security Trust funds in the stock market. The retirement benefits were not to change the benefits for retirees or near retirees, and the disability and survivors components must be preserved.

After eleven months of public hearings and debate, the Commission issued its final report in December 2001.[21] The Commission developed three separate models for consideration, all of which meet the mandate for voluntary private investment accounts. Participants would be allowed to divert a portion of the FICA tax they now pay into the private accounts, which would be owned by the participants and could be passed on to others as an inheritance. Arguing that the benefits currently paid to low-income workers are too low, the Commission included a provision in two of the three plans to significantly increase benefits for low-income workers.

In the introduction to the report, the co-chairs likened the Commission's proposals to the Thrift Savings Plan, a part of the retirement program for Federal Employees that was established in 1986. Under the federal employee plan, employees have three options for investing their retirement contributions, the G Fund, the F Fund, and the C Fund. The G Fund is invested in short-term Treasury securities, the F Fund is invested in a commercial bond index, and the C Fund is invested in an equity index fund. The annual compound rates of return on the three funds have been 6.7 percent, 7.9 percent, and 17.4 percent respectively. The intent of the privatization is to give nongovernmental workers the opportunity to invest a part of their Social Security taxes in the same types of options that federal employees have.

The report met with immediate disapproval from the opponents of privatization. Among other things, the Commission was criticized for proposing three models, rather than a single solution. Other commentators observed that the Commission's three models

represent a unanimity that contrasts sharply with the conflicting recommendations of the 1994 report. All three of the 2001 proposals call for voluntary private investment accounts and differ only with respect to the magnitude and the three share several features.

The Proposed Models The models differ in the magnitude of the contributions that would be allowed for private accounts, but contain other differences as well, including proposals to slow the rate of growth in future Social Security benefits. Members of the Commission stressed, however, that the changes in benefit growth are not intended to finance the personal accounts, but are required to bring Social Security toward solvency without tax increases.

Reform Model 1 establishes a voluntary personal account option but does not include any other changes in the Social Security benefit or revenue structure. Under this proposal, workers would voluntarily elect to invest 2 percent of their taxable wages in a personal investment account. In exchange, the individual's conventional Social Security benefits would be offset by the workers personal account contributions, compounded at an interest rate of 3.5 percent above inflation.

Reform Model 2 allows workers to redirect 4 percent of their payroll taxes up to $1000 annually to a personal account. The $1000 maximum would be indexed annually for inflation. The conventional Social Security benefit for the individual would be reduced by the annual contributions compounded at an interest rate 2 percent above inflation. In this plan, the minimum Social Security benefit paid to a worker with 30 years credit would be 120 percent of the poverty level. Similar minimums would apply to the disability and survivors' benefits. To slow the rate of growth in the traditional Social Security benefit, benefits would be indexed to inflation (instead of wages) starting for those who reach age 65 in 2009. Benefits for widows and widowers would be increased to 75 percent of couple benefits for low wage couples.

Reform Model 3 requires that workers who elect to participate in the personal account option contribute an additional 1 percent of their wages (up to the maximum taxable wage). The worker would be allowed to redirect 2.5 percent of their FICA tax up to an annually indexed $1000 maximum. The traditional Social Security benefit would be reduced by the annual contributions compounded at an interest

[21] The President's Commission to Strengthen Social Security established its website early in its proceedings. In addition to the final report, the site provides a record of the Commission's proceedings. See http://www.commtostrengthensocsec.gov/

rate 2.5 percent above inflation. Under this model, the minimum benefit payable to 30-year minimum credit worker would be 100 percent of the poverty level. For a 40-year minimum worker, it would be 111 percent of the poverty level. This model would increase the widows' and widowers' benefits in the same way as Model 2. To slow the growth rate in traditional benefits, benefits would be indexed to gains in average expectancy In addition to increasing the widow and widower benefits for low-income persons

Under all three proposals, additional revenues would be required to maintain the solvency of the Trust Fund. Under Reform Model 1, such revenues would be required starting in the 2030s. For Model 2, additional revenues would be required between 2025 and 2054. For the third model, additional revenues would be required between 2034 and 2064.

The commission concluded that Social Security cannot be rescued from the financial precipice it will reach by the middle of the next decade without cutting benefits for retirees and disabled Americans, using money from elsewhere in the federal budget, or both. In the Commission's view, whether additional funds are committed to the system or benefit levels are brought to a level that can be sustained within current projected revenues, private accounts will enhance retirement security.

The issue of privatization is highly contentious. Unquestionably, it involves the largest structural change in the program since its inception in 1935. It seems highly unlikely that an issue of such momentous magnitude will be resolved in the halls of Congress quickly and it is likely that the difficulties in financing the Social Security system will remain a haunting problem for our society.

WORKERS COMPENSATION

Workers compensation is a social insurance program that provides covered workers with protection against work-related disability and death. Workers compensation provides benefits for the cost of medical care and income to workers and their dependents when a worker is disabled or killed as a result of a work-related injury or occupational disease. The workers compensation system is based on statutes that exist in all states, which require covered employers to provide benefits specified by the law to covered workers and their dependents.

Historical Background

The workers compensation laws were enacted in response to a growing dissatisfaction with the system then in use for compensating injured employees and their dependents. Under English *common law,* which had developed in a society dominated by handicraft industries, certain legal principles evolved that made it difficult if not impossible for an injured worker to collect indemnity for an industrial injury. These doctrines were embodied in the special branch of law that had developed to deal with injuries to workers, called employers liability law. Under *employers liability law,* a worker who was injured on the job could collect for the injury only if he or she could prove that the injury resulted from the employer's negligence. To establish fault, the employee had to prove that the employer had violated one of five common-law obligations: (1) to provide the employee with a safe place to work; (2) to provide safe tools and equipment; (3) to provide sane and sober fellow employees; (4) to set up safety rules and enforce them; and (5) to warn of any dangers in the work that the worker could not be expected to know about.

Although these common law obligations established a basis for recovery of damages, the employer could interpose three common-law defenses that were often sufficient to defeat the worker's claim. The first was *contributory negligence.* Under this doctrine, if the employee's own negligence contributed to the accident in the slightest degree, he or she lost all right to collect damages. The second defense was the *fellow servant rule,* which held that the employer was not liable when the worker was injured by a fellow employee. Finally, the *assumption-of-risk doctrine* held that an employee was presumed to accept the normal risks associated with the job. If a worker continued employment while knowing, or when he or she might have been expected to discover, that the premises, tools, or fellow employees were unsafe, he or she was deemed to have assumed the risks connected with the unsafe conditions.

Although the severity of the common-law defenses was eventually softened, the modifications did not solve the fundamental problems inherent in a system based on the principle of negligence.[22] To establish

[22] The *doctrine of contributory negligence* was replaced by the *doctrine of comparative negligence,* under which the worker was allowed recovery in inverse relationship to his or her own negligence. The fellow servant doctrine was modified to the less severe *vice-principal rule,* which provided that supervisors did not fall under the fellow servant doctrine.

negligence, litigation was necessary, and in most cases, the worker did not have the resources to bring suit. Even if the worker won the suit, a substantial portion of the judgment went to the attorney who had accepted the case on a contingency basis. It was not unusual for the size of the attorney's fee to represent 50 percent of the amount of the judgment. Finally, there were some cases in which workers were injured where there was no employer negligence. Although there was no one the injured worker could sue, the financial loss in such instances was no less severe than when the employer was at fault. The unsatisfactory status of the worker under common law, and the social and economic consequences of industrial injuries, finally led to a new way of distributing the financial costs of industrial accidents.

Rationale of Workers Compensation Laws

The workers compensation principle is based on the notion that industrial accidents are inevitable in an industrialized society. Since the entire society gains from industrialization, it should bear the burden of these costs. Workers compensation laws are designed to make the cost of industrial accidents a part of the cost of production by imposing absolute liability on the employer for employee injuries regardless of negligence. The costs are thus built into the cost of the product and are passed on to the consumer. The basic purpose of the laws is to avoid litigation, lessen the expense to the claimant, and provide for a speedy and efficient means of compensating injured workers.

The first workers compensation laws were passed in Germany (1884) and England (1897). In the United States, workers compensation laws were enacted by the states shortly after the turn of the century. Workers compensation laws now exist in all 50 states.[23]

Principles of Workers Compensation

Although the laws of the various states differ somewhat in detail, the basic principles they embody are more or less uniform. There are five general principles on which all the laws are based.

Negligence Is Not a Factor in Determining Liability As a basic principle of law, liability for injury to another is generally based on the concept of negligence or fault. In general, without negligence, there can be no liability for injury to another.[24] Workers compensation laws represent an exception to this general principle and impose liability on the employer for injury to an employee that arises *out of and in the course of employment* regardless of fault. If the worker is injured, the employer is obligated to pay benefits according to a schedule in the law regardless of whose negligence caused the injury. The employer is considered liable without any necessary fault on his or her part and will be assessed the compensable costs of the job-connected injury, not because he or she was responsible for it, caused it, or was negligent, but simply because of social policy. Currently, all but two laws are compulsory and require every employer subject to the law to accept the act and pay the compensation specified.[25]

Indemnity Is Partial but Final The second principle of workers compensation involves the amount of the benefit. The indemnity to the worker is partial, meaning that the benefit is usually less than the employee might receive if he or she were permitted to sue and the employer were found to have been negligent. On the other hand, the worker is entitled to the benefits as a matter of right, without having to sue. In return for the entitlement to benefits regardless of the employer's fault, the worker gives up the right to sue the employer.[26]

Periodic Payments The third principle concerns the basis of payment of benefits, which is arranged to ensure a greater degree of security for the recipients. Usually, the indemnity is paid periodically instead of in a lump sum, although the periodic pay-

[23] There are also workers compensation laws in American Samoa, Guam, Puerto Rico, and the Virgin Islands in addition to three federal laws (applicable to civilian workers of the federal government, longshoremen and harbor workers, and nongovernment workers of the District of Columbia), making a total of 57 laws.

[24] The law dealing with liability for injuries arising out of negligence is called *tort law*. The law of torts is discussed in Chapter 20. Workers compensation laws represent an exception to the law of torts, since they impose liability on the employer for injuries to employees without regard to the question of fault.

[25] Coverage is elective in New Jersey and Texas. In these states either the employer or employee can choose to be exempt from the law.

[26] Employers liability law still applies to employments that are not covered under workers compensation. For example, in most states an injured farm worker or domestic servant has a remedy against the employer only under employers liability laws, which means that the negligence of the employer must be the cause of the injury and the employer would usually have the right to interpose the common law defenses.

ments may sometimes be commuted to a lump sum. The requirement of periodic rather than lump-sum settlement is designed to protect the recipient against financial ineptness and the possibility of squandering a lump sum.

Cost of the Program Is Made a Cost of Production Unlike many other social insurance coverages, the employees are not required to contribute to the financing of workers compensation coverage. The employer must pay the premium for the insurance coverage, or pay the benefits required by law, without any contribution by workers. The employer can predict the cost of accidents under a workers compensation program and build this into the price of the product, thereby passing the cost of industrial accidents on to the consumer.

Insurance Is Required As a general rule, the employer must purchase and maintain workers compensation insurance to protect against the losses covered under the law. All states require the employers coming under the workers compensation law to insure their obligations either through commercial insurance companies or a state fund or by qualification as a self-insurer. In 5 states the insurance must be purchased from a monopolistic state insurance fund. In 20 states the private insurance industry operates side by side with the state workers compensation insurance funds.[27] Under the workers compensation insurance policy, the insurer promises to pay all sums for which the insured (i.e., the employer) is obligated under the law.

Penalties for failure to insure are severe. Forty four states make failure to insure punishable by fines (ranging from $25 to $50,000 depending on the state), imprisonment, or both. Other laws provide that the employer may be enjoined from doing business in the state. In addition, about four-fifths of the states allow common lawsuits by the employee against a noninsuring employer.[28]

An Overview of State Workers Compensation Laws

Although it is difficult to generalize about state workers compensation laws, there are general similarities among the laws. The following discussion is intended to provide an overview of the laws and to identify the major areas in which the laws differ.[29]

Persons Covered under State Laws None of the state workers compensation laws covers all employees in the state. The most frequently excluded classes of employment are agricultural and domestic employees. Only 20 states cover agricultural workers on the same basis as other categories, and only 7 provide full coverage on domestic employees. About three-fourths of the states exclude *casual employees*—those whose work is occasional, incidental, or irregular.[30] In addition, about a fourth of the states have numerical limitations, providing that if the employer has fewer than a specified number of employees (ranging from two to five), the employees need not be covered under the act. The remainder of the states and the federal laws require the employer of one or more people to be covered under the law.

The laws usually permit the employer of persons omitted from the law to bring these workers under the law voluntarily. This applies to excluded classes of employment and to the employer with fewer than the number of employees specified in the law.

Injuries Covered The workers compensation laws stipulate that employee injuries are compensable only when connected with employment, requiring that the injury arise *out of and in the course of employment*. Usually, there is little difficulty in determining whether the injury is compensable, but problems do arise. The question may arise first whether the injured employee was actually "in the course of employment" at the time of the accident in cases where the injury was sustained while coming to or from the job or while the worker participated in social events connected with employment. The

[27] The 6 states that maintain monopolistic workers compensation programs are North Dakota, Ohio, Washington, West Virginia, and Wyoming. The 19 states in which the workers compensation fund operated by the state competes with private insurers are Arizona, California, Colorado, Idaho, Kentucky, Louisiana, Maine, Maryland, Minnesota, Missouri, Montana, Nevada, New Mexico, New York, Oklahoma, Oregon, Pennsylvania, Rhode Island, Texas, and Utah.

[28] States that allow common lawsuits against noninsuring employers give the employee the option of a common lawsuit or the benefits under the workers compensation law.

[29] Details regarding individual state laws may be found at http://www.workerscompensation.com/.

[30] Casual employment is usually excluded only if the employment is both casual and not for the purpose of the employer's trade or business. Unless both elements are present (i.e., the work is occasional, incidental, and irregular *and* not for the purpose of the employer's trade or business), the workers are not excluded. The courts tend to construe the meaning of "casual" employment against the employer to increase the coverage of the act.

greater problem frequently comes up when it is clear that the injury occurred in the course of employment, but there is a question whether it was caused by the employment. Generally, injuries sustained while at work are considered to arise out of the work, but there are exceptions. Injuries may be noncompensable if they are deliberately self-inflicted or result from intoxication.[31] In addition, there may be difficulties in such cases as heart attacks, mental or nervous disorders, or even suicide. Often, the only way these questions can be settled is by litigation, and litigation involving these issues has been almost endless. The courts have usually taken a liberal attitude and have done their best to compensate the injured worker or his or her dependents.

Occupational Disease In addition to the traumatic type of injury, all laws provide compensation for *occupational disease.* All states provide coverage for all occupational diseases, either under a separate occupational disease law or by defining injury broadly enough under the workers compensation law to include disease. Some states have specific conditions for particular diseases, such as silicosis, asbestosis, and AIDS.

Workers Compensation Benefits There are usually seven classes of benefits payable to the injured worker or his or her dependents under the workers compensation laws:

1. Medical expenses
2. Total temporary disability
3. Partial temporary disability
4. Total permanent disability
5. Partial permanent disability
6. Survivors' death benefits
7. Rehabilitation benefits

Medical Expense Benefits *Medical expense benefits* account for about 40 percent of total benefit payments under workers compensation. Medical expenses incurred through employment-connected injuries are covered without limit. In an effort to control costs, many states have established medical fee schedules that limit payments to providers of medical care, and

a number of states have placed limits on the employee's choice of physician.

Total Temporary Disability There are four classes of disability income benefits under the workers compensation laws. The most frequent type of disability is *total temporary disability,* which exists when the worker is unable to work because of an injury but will clearly recover and eventually return to work. All states provide for a waiting period before disability benefits are payable. This waiting period is a deductible, eliminating coverage for short periods of disability thereby reducing administrative costs. The normal waiting period is one week, although some states have waiting periods as short as three days. Normally, the waiting period does not apply if the disability lasts beyond some specified number of weeks, usually four.

The amount of the benefit is set by statute and varies with the worker's wage and in some cases with the number of dependents. The most frequently used percentage of the injured worker's wage is $66^2/_3$ percent, subject to a dollar maximum and minimum also imposed by the law. In some states, the dollar maximums and minimums are adjusted periodically by the state legislature, but in 40 states they are based on the state average weekly wage (SAWW). The minimums in these states range from 15 to 50 percent of the SAWW. Maximums range from 60 to 200 percent of the SAWW, with 100 percent being the most common. Some states provide for a sliding scale of benefits based on the number of dependents. More than 90 percent of the states provide benefits for the entire period of disability. In the remaining jurisdictions there is a time limit (ranging from 104 to 500 weeks) or a dollar limit on the benefits.

Partial Temporary Disability Many states provide disability benefits for *partial temporary disability,* to cover those cases in which the worker cannot pursue his or her own occupation but can engage in some work for remuneration. In these cases, compensation is based on a percentage of the difference between the wages received before the injury and those received afterward. This benefit is also subject to a maximum and minimum and is usually payable for the same period as total temporary disability.

Total Permanent Disability A worker is *totally and permanently disabled* when he or she is unable to obtain any gainful employment because of the injury and is expected to remain so. In practice, total perma-

[31] Normally, before it is considered a bar to recovery, the intoxication itself rather than some other factor must be the proximate cause of the injury.

nent disability benefits are payable to a worker who remains disabled after exhausting total temporary disability benefits. The benefit for total permanent disability is usually computed on the same basis as the total temporary disability benefit and is subject to the same minima and maxima, but the benefits are payable for life or, in some states, for a specified number of additional weeks.

In addition to the inability to obtain gainful employment, most laws specify that the loss of both hands, arms, feet, legs, or eyes, or any combination of two of these constitutes total and permanent disability.

Partial Permanent Disability An injury resulting from an industrial accident may be deemed a partial disability on one of two bases. In one instance, the loss of a member such as an arm or a leg is considered a *partial permanent disability*. In addition, the disability may consist of a disability of the body generally (e.g., an injured spine). In the case of a disability not involving the loss of a limb, a percentage disability is usually determined, and a benefit equal to some multiple of the weekly disability benefit as specified by law is payable for the various percentages so determined.[32] The compensation for the loss of a member such as an arm or leg is usually some multiple of the weekly disability benefit, which may be commuted and paid as a lump sum (for example, 230 weeks for an arm or 125 weeks for an eye). There are wide variations among the states in the amount of compensation for the various extremities and also in the stated value of one member as opposed to another.[33]

In most states, the compensation for scheduled injuries is payable in addition to any benefits otherwise given the injured worker under the total temporary disability benefit. However, some states limit the total temporary disability benefit when payment is made for a scheduled injury, and a few states deduct the amount paid under total temporary disability from the allowance for the scheduled injury.

Death Benefit Benefits are also payable when a worker is killed, and all laws allow two types of death benefits. Under the first, payment is made for the reasonable expenses of burial, not to exceed some maximum amount, ranging from $2000 to $15,000.

The second death benefit is a *survivors' benefit* payable to dependents. The survivors' benefit is usually paid as a weekly sum, determined by the usual formula. Although the definition of dependent varies from state to state, most laws provide that a dependent may be a spouse, a child of the deceased worker, or a dependent parent. A child is usually defined as under 18 years of age or physically or mentally incapacitated and receiving support from the worker. The child may be natural born, adopted, a stepchild of the deceased worker, or even an unborn child if conceived before the worker's injury.

Under about three-fifths of the laws, the survivors' benefit is payable to a surviving spouse for life or until remarriage, without limit. Five states provide for a maximum number of weeks (250 to 1040), and six others set an aggregate dollar maximum. In about half of the states, survivors' benefits are based on the number of dependents.

Rehabilitation Benefits Virtually all of the state laws contain specific rehabilitation *benefit provisions,* but even where state law does not enumerate such benefits, they are provided. Under these provisions, the injured worker may be entitled to additional compensation during a period of vocational training, transportation and other necessary expenses, artificial limbs and mechanical appliances, and other benefits. The funds for payment of the rehabilitation benefits may or may not come from the employer or its insurance company. In some cases, state funds are used. In others, funds come from insurers in death cases in which no surviving dependents receive benefits. Finally, the Federal Vocational Rehabilitation Act provides for federal funds to aid states in this program.

Second-Injury Funds Under most workers compensation laws, the loss of both arms, feet, legs, eyes, or any two thereof constitutes permanent total disability. As a result, situations may arise in which an injury that is partial in nature leaves a worker totally disabled; a worker who has lost an arm or a leg in an industrial accident and who has returned to work will

[32] The procedure varies among the states. Some use as a base the period for which total permanent disabilities are payable. Thus, if total permanent disability is payable for 500 weeks, and the worker is 50 percent disabled, the partial permanent disability benefit is payable for 250 weeks. In those states in which total permanent disabilities are payable for life, the law may specify a maximum number of weeks on which percentage disabilities are to be computed.

[33] For example, some states place a greater value on an arm than on a leg, while other states value a leg more highly. It would be interesting indeed to discover how the values were determined for the various parts of the body.

be totally incapacitated by another such accident. In all but three states *second-injury funds* have been established to meet the problem of injury to workers with preexisting industrially caused disabilities.[34] When a worker suffers a second injury that causes total permanent disability, and the injury is of a

nature that would constitute only partial permanent disability but for the previous injury, the employer is liable only for the benefits payable for the partial disability. The second-injury fund pays the difference between the partial and the total permanent disability. Second-injury funds are supported by required contributions from insurance companies operating in the state, either as a percentage tax or through payments into a fund in death cases in which there are no dependents.

[34] Alabama, Maine, and Wyoming.

IMPORTANT CONCEPTS TO REMEMBER

Social Security
social insurance
OASDHI
OASDI
Medicare
quarter of coverage
FICA tax
fully insured
currently insured
retirement benefits
survivors' benefits
disability benefits
children's benefit
mother's (father's) benefit

parents' benefit
widow's (widower's) benefit
lump-sum benefit
averaged indexed monthly earnings
 (AIME)
primary insurance amount
disqualifying income
pay-as-you-go system
floor of protection
common law
employers' common-law obligations
employers' common-law defenses
contributory negligence
fellow servant rule

assumption-of-risk doctrine
casual employee
out of and in the course of
 employment
medical expense benefits
total temporary disability
partial temporary disability
total permanent disability
partial permanent disability
rehabilitation benefits
second-injury fund
occupational disease
absolute liability

QUESTIONS FOR REVIEW

1. Identify and briefly describe the four classes of benefits available to those covered under OASDHI.

2. Explain how benefit levels are automatically adjusted under OASDHI. How are the increases in benefits financed?

3. Outline the requirements for *fully insured* status under OASDHI.

4. What benefits does a *fully insured* worker have that a *currently insured* worker does not?

5. What benefits does a worker who is only currently insured have?

6. Under what circumstances can a person who is entitled to Social Security benefits become ineligible for benefits?

7. Under what conditions is a *children's benefit* payable under Social Security? How is "child" defined for benefit purposes?

8. Explain the nature of the common-law obligations and the common-law defenses of employers liability. Are these obligations and defenses ever used today? Under what circumstances?

9. Identify and explain the five general principles on which workers compensation laws are based.

10. Identify and briefly describe the classes of benefits that are provided to injured workers under the workers compensation laws.

QUESTIONS FOR DISCUSSION

1. Social Security provides protection against financial loss to dependents resulting from premature death of the wage earner, and also provides wage earners with retirement benefits. Do you think that the enactment or expansion of the Social Security Act has adversely affected life insurance sales? Why or why not?

2. Many observers have voiced concern about the soundness of the Social Security system, pointing to the growing number of recipients and the increasing benefit levels. To what extent do you believe that the OASDHI system is still in trouble? What would you recommend in the way of corrective action?

3. The Old Age, Survivors', Disability, and Health Insurance program has been called "the greatest chain letter in history." To what aspect of the Social Security system does this probably refer? Do you agree or disagree with the observation and why?

4. The Social Security trust funds are invested in U.S. Treasury securities. Although there is little question regarding the safety of these instruments, many observers have expressed alarm over this arrangement. Do you believe that the current arrangement, in which the trust funds are invested in Treasury bonds is a good thing, a bad thing, or a matter of no consequence? Why?

5. Which, if any, of the three proposals contained in the report of the Advisory Council on Social Security released in 1997 do you personally prefer? Why?

SUGGESTIONS FOR ADDITIONAL READING

Black, Kenneth, Jr., and Harold D. Skipper, Jr. *Life Insurance,* 13th ed. Englewood Cliffs, N.J.: Prentice-Hall, 2000. Chapter 22.

Chamber of Commerce of the United States. *Analysis of Workers Compensation Laws.* Washington, D.C.: U.S. Chamber of Commerce, annual.

Hardy, Dorcas R., and C. Colburn Hardy. *Social Insecurity: The Crisis in America's Social Security System and How to Plan Now for Your Own Survival.* New York: Villard Books, 1991.

Matthews, Joseph L. *Social Security, Medicare and Pensions.* Berkeley, Calif.: Nolo Press, 1991.

Myers, Robert J. *Social Security,* 3rd ed. Homewood, Ill.: Richard D. Irwin, 1985.

———. "A Reappraisal of the Basic Purposes of Social Security." *Journal of the American Society of Chartered Life Underwriters,* vol. 31, no. 1 (Jan. 1977).

———. "Social Security's Health Is Really Robust." *Benefits Quarterly,* vol. 5, no. 4, 1989.

———. "Will Social Security Have Another Financing Crisis Soon?" *Benefits Quarterly,* vol. 1, no. 1 (First Quarter 1985).

Rejda, G. E. *Social Insurance and Economic Security,* 5th ed. Old Tappan, N.J.: Prentice-Hall, 1994.

———. "Social Security and the Paradox of the Welfare State." *Journal of Risk and Insurance,* vol. 37, no. 1 (March 1970).

Robertson, A. Haeworth. "Is the Current Social Security Program Financially Feasible in the Long Run?" *Benefits Quarterly,* vol. 1, no. 3 (Third Quarter 1985).

———. *Social Security: What Every Taxpayer Should Know.* Washington, D.C.: Retirement Policy Institute, 1992.

Schlesinger, A. M., Jr. *The Coming of the New Deal.* Boston: Houghton Mifflin, 1959.

State Workers Compensation Laws. Washington, D.C.: U.S. Department of Labor, revised annually.

Thomas, William W., III, ed. *Social Security Manual.* Cincinnati, Ohio: The National Underwriter Co., 2001.

Unemployment Insurance Reporter. A loose-leaf reporting service. New York: Commerce Clearing House.

Workmen's Compensation Law Reporter. New York: Commerce Clearing House, Biweekly.

WEB SITES TO EXPLORE

National Council on Compensation Insurance	http://www.ncci.com
Social Security Administration	http://www.ssa.gov/
The Cato Institute Project on Social Security Privatization	www.socialsecurity.org
President's Commission to Strengthen Social Security	http://www.commtostrengthensocsec.gov/
Workerscompensation.com	http://www.workerscompensation.com/

INTRODUCTION TO LIFE INSURANCE

A man's dying is more the survivors'
affair than his own.

— THOMAS MANN

CHAPTER OBJECTIVES

When you have finished this chapter, you should be able to
- Distinguish between the two broad types of life insurance contracts
- Explain how the cash value arises in some life insurance contracts
- Distinguish between participating and nonparticipating life insurance contracts
- Explain the importance of renewability and convertibility features in term life insurance policies
- Describe the distinguishing characteristics of universal life insurance, adjustable life insurance, and variable life insurance
- Identify and describe the four major marketing classes of life insurance
- Describe the distinguishing features of group life insurance and explain the basis for its cost advantages

We begin our study of specific types of insurance with life insurance. We do this for two reasons. First, the life insurance policy is one of the simplest of all the insurance contracts. The insuring agreement is straightforward and to the point, there are relatively few exclusions, and the conditions and stipulations are easily understood.

In addition, we treat life insurance before the wide range of other insurance coverages that may be needed by individuals because many college students will soon be considering the purchase of life insurance—some even before graduation. It is hoped that by treating life insurance at this point, some students may be able to avoid costly mistakes.

SOME UNIQUE CHARACTERISTICS OF LIFE INSURANCE

Life insurance is a risk-pooling plan, an economic device through which the risk of premature death is transferred from the individual to the group. However, the contingency insured against has certain characteristics that make it unique; as a result, the contract insuring against the contingency is different in many respects from other types of insurance. The event insured against is an eventual certainty. No one lives forever. Yet life insurance does not violate the requirements of an insurable risk, for it is not the possibility of death itself that is insured, but rather untimely death. The risk in life insurance is not whether the individual is going to die, but when, and the risk increases from year to year. The chance of loss under a life insurance contract is greater in the second year of the contract, as far as the company is concerned, than it was in the first year, and so on, until the insured eventually dies. Yet through the mechanism of the law of large numbers, as we shall see, the insurance company can promise to pay a specified sum to the beneficiary no matter when death comes.

There is no possibility of partial loss in life insurance as there is in the case of property and liability insurance. Therefore, all policies are cash payment policies. In the event that a loss occurs, the company will pay the face amount of the policy.

Life Insurance Is Not a Contract of Indemnity

The principle of indemnity applies on a modified basis in the case of life insurance. In most lines of insurance, an attempt is made to put the individual back in exactly the same financial position after a loss as before the loss. For obvious reasons, this is not possible in life insurance. The simple fact of the matter is that we cannot place a value on a human life.

As a legal principle, every contract of insurance must be supported by an insurable interest, but in life insurance, the requirement of insurable interest is applied somewhat differently than in property and liability insurance. When the individual taking out the policy is also the insured, there is no legal problem concerning insurable interest. The courts have held that every individual has an unlimited insurable interest in his or her own life and that a person may assign that insurable interest to any one. In other

words, there is no legal limit to the amount of insurance one may take out on one's own life and no legal limitations as to whom one may name as beneficiary.[1]

The important question of insurable interest arises when the person taking out the insurance is someone other than the person whose life is concerned. In such cases, the law requires that an insurable interest exists at the time the contract is taken out. There are many relationships that provide the basis for an insurable interest. Husbands and wives have an insurable interest in each other; so do partners. A corporation may have an insurable interest in the life of one of its executives. In most cases, a parent has an insurable interest in the life of a child, although the extent of this interest may be limited by statute. A creditor has an insurable interest in the life of a debtor, although this too is usually confined by statute to the amount of the debt or slightly more.

The question of insurable interest seldom arises in life insurance, because most life insurance policies are purchased by the person whose life is insured. In addition, the consent of the individual insured is required in most cases even when there is an insurable interest. The exception to this requirement exists in certain jurisdictions where a husband or wife is permitted to insure a spouse without the other's consent.

TYPES OF LIFE INSURANCE CONTRACTS

Based on their distinguishing characteristics, it is possible to identify six distinct types of life insurance contracts: (1) term insurance, (2) whole-life, (3) endowment, (4) universal life, (5) adjustable life, and (6) variable life policies. Term insurance, whole-life, and endowment contracts were the traditional forms of life insurance and have existed for many years. Universal life, variable life, and adjustable life insurance contracts are relatively recent innovations, and date from the 1970s. Ignoring the subtle differences among some of these types of policies for the moment, we can divide life insurance products into two classes: those that provide pure life insurance

[1] Although there is no legal limit, insurance companies often impose limits for underwriting reasons. Not only is the amount of insurance a company is willing to write on a life limited, but companies are also reluctant to issue a policy with a beneficiary where there is no apparent insurable interest.

protection, called *term insurance,* and those that include a savings or investment element, which we will call *cash value policies.* Based on this classification system, life insurance products are divided into two classes:

Term Insurance (Pure Insurance Protection)	Cash Value Insurance (Protection and Savings)
Term insurance	Whole-life insurance
	Endowment insurance
	Universal life insurance
	Adjustable life insurance
	Variable life insurance

Although there are important differences among the policies that we have classified together as cash value policies, these contracts are more similar than they are different. Later in the chapter, we will discuss the distinguishing characteristics of these contracts, but for the moment, let us focus on the difference between term insurance, which provides pure insurance protection, and cash value life insurance, which combines insurance with a saving element. Because whole-life insurance is the prototype cash value contract, it can serve as a representative in our discussion for cash value policies generally.

Reasons for Difference in Term and Cash Value Insurance

As a point of departure, let us examine the distinctions between policies that provide pure protection and those that combine insurance with an investment.

The simplest form of life insurance is yearly renewable term. This type provides protection for one year only, but it permits the insured to renew the policy for successive periods of one year at a higher premium rate each year, without having to furnish evidence of insurability at the time of each renewal. This is life insurance protection in its purest form.

The easiest way to understand the operation of any mechanism is to try it. In life insurance, as in other forms of insurance, the fortunate many who do not suffer loss share the financial burden of the few who do. In life insurance, each member of the group pays a premium that represents the member's portion of the benefit to be paid to the beneficiaries of those who die. Mortality data tell us that at age 21, 1.07 out of every 1000 females will die. To simplify

the mathematics, let us assume that there are 100,000 females in the group. On the basis of past experience, we may expect 107 of them to die, and if we wish to pay a death benefit of $1000 to the beneficiary of each woman who dies, we will need $107,000. Ignoring, for the present, the cost of operating the program and any interest that we might earn on the premiums we collect, and assuming that the mortality table is an accurate statement of the number who will die, it will be necessary to collect $1.07 from each individual in the group to provide the needed $107,000.[2] During the year, 107 members of the group will die and $107,000 will be paid to their beneficiaries.

The next year we would find that the chance of loss has increased, for all the members of the group are now older, and past experience indicates that a greater number will die per 1000. At age 25, it will be necessary to collect $1.16 from each member. At age 30, the cost will be $1.35. At age 40, the cost per member will have almost doubled from the cost at age 21, and it will be necessary to collect $2.42. By the time the members of the group reach age 50, we will have to collect $4.96 from each. At age 60, we will need $9.47, and at age 70, we will need $22.11 from each member. It does not take a great deal of insight to recognize that before long the plan is going to bog down, if it has not already done so before the members reach age 70. At age 70, when the probability of death is greater than ever before, the members of the group may find that they cannot afford the premium that has become necessary. At age 80, we will need $65.99 from each member, and at age 90, $190.75. The increasing mortality as the group grows older makes yearly renewable term impractical as a means of providing insurance protection at advanced ages. Yet many insurance buyers want coverage that continues throughout their lifetimes. Insurers have found a practical solution.

The Level Premium Concept

A practical method of providing life insurance for the entire lifetime of the insured is to use a level premium.

[2] The $1.07 indicated in our simplified calculation reflects mortality only. In actual practice, life insurance rates include two additional factors: *interest* and *loading.* Life insurers specifically recognize the investment income that will be earned on premiums by assuming that premiums will be paid at the beginning of the year and that deaths will occur at the end of the year. The discounted value of future mortality costs is called the net premium. A loading for expenses is added to the *net premium* to derive the *gross premium,* which is the amount the buyer pays.

The whole-life insurance policy was the original type of lifetime policy. It provides protection at a level premium for the entire lifetime of the insured. This lifetime protection is possible because the premium is set at a level that is higher than necessary to fund the cost of death claims during the early years of the policy, and the excess premiums are used to meet the increasing death claims as the insured group grows older.

The level premium for an ordinary life policy of $1000 purchased by a female at age 21 and the one for yearly renewable term insurance beginning at age 21 are illustrated in Figure 12.1. The line that constitutes the level premium is the exact mathematical equivalent of the yearly renewable term premium curve. This means that the insurance company will obtain the same amount of premium income and interest from a large group of insureds under either plan, assuming that neither group discontinues its payments.

The level premium plan introduces features that have no counterpart in term insurance. From a glance at Figure 12.1 it is clear that under the level premium plan, the insured pays more than the cost of pure life insurance protection during the early years the policy is in force. This overpayment is indicated by the difference between the term and the level premium lines up to the point at which the lines cross. The overpayment is necessary so that the excess portion, when accumulated at compound interest, will be sufficient to offset the deficiency in the later years of the contract. The excess payments during the early years of the contract create a fund that is held by the insurance company for the benefit and credit of the policyholders. The fund is invested, usually in long-term investments, and the earnings are added to the accumulating fund to help meet the future obligations to the policyholders. The insurer establishes a reserve or liability on its financial statement to reflect these future obligations.

Referring again to Figure 12.1, it appears that the reserve should increase for a time and then diminish. It also appears that the area of redundant premiums in the early years of the contract will never be sufficient to equal the inadequacy in the later years. In the case of a single individual, this would be true, but many insureds are involved, and the law of averages permits a continuously increasing reserve for each policy in force. Some insureds will die during the early years of the contracts, and the excess premiums that they have paid are forfeited to the group. The excess premiums forfeited by those who die, together with the excess premiums paid by the survivors, will

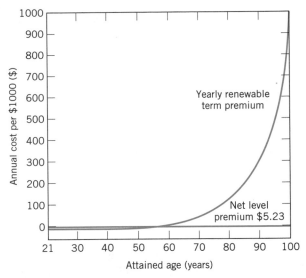

FIGURE 12.1 Comparison of Net Premiums per $1000 Yearly Renewable Term and Whole Life

not only offset the deficiency in later years but, with the aid of compound interest, will also continue to build the reserves on the survivors' policies until they equal the face of the contract at age 100. Death is bound to occur at some time, and in a whole-life policy, the insurance company knows that a death claim must ultimately be paid.[3] Aggregate reserves for the entire group of insureds increase and then decrease, but individual policy reserves continue to climb, mainly because the aggregate reserves are divided among a smaller number of survivors each year. Figure 12.2 shows the growth in the reserve on an ordinary life policy purchased at age 21.

The level premium plan introduces the features of the redundant premium during the early years of the contract and the creation of the reserve fund. The insured has a contractual right to receive a part of this reserve in the event the policy is terminated, under a policy provision designated the *nonforfeiture value* (discussed in Chapter 15). The contractual right to receive a part of the excess premiums that are paid under the level premium plan, therefore, represents an investment element in the contract for the insured. When a policyholder dies, the death benefit could be viewed as being composed of two parts—the portion

[3] The mortality table indicates that all policyholders will have died by age 100. If the insured has not died by this time, the insurance company will declare him dead and pay the face of the policy.

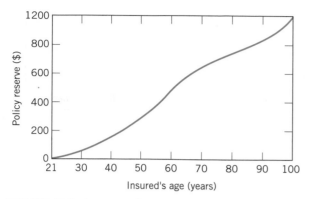

FIGURE 12.2 Increase in Reserve on Whole-Life Policy

of the reserve to which the insured would have been eligible and an amount of pure insurance. Under this view, the face amount of the policy is seen as a combination of a decreasing amount of insurance (the net amount at risk) and the increasing investment element (the growing reserve). The decreasing insurance and the increasing investment element always equal the face of the policy.

It should be stressed that the policy reserve is not solely the property of the insured. It is the insured's only if and when the policy is surrendered. If this occurs, the contract no longer exists, and the insurance company is relieved of all obligations on the policy. As long as the contract is in full force, the reserve belongs to the insurance company and must be used to help pay the death claim if the insured should die. As mentioned, the reserve must be accumulated by the company to take care of the deficiency in the level premium during the later years of the contract.

The preceding analysis suggests that there are two distinct advantages in the use of level premium insurance. First, by paying an amount in excess of the cost of pure life insurance during the early years of the contract, the insured avoids a rising premium in the later years; this will make it financially possible to maintain the insurance until the policyholder's death, even though it occurs at an advanced age. Second, if the insured survives, he or she has accumulated a savings fund that can be used for income in old age (or any other purpose the insured decides).

TAX TREATMENT OF LIFE INSURANCE

The accumulating fund that arises from the overpayment of premiums and the insured's right to withdraw the cash values based on these overpayments adds an investment element to the protection function of life insurance. Before continuing with our discussion, let us pause to examine the way in which this investment element and life insurance generally are treated for tax purposes.

Life insurance policies are granted favorable tax treatment in two ways. First, amounts payable to a beneficiary at the death of an insured are generally not included in taxable income.[4] In addition, income earned on the cash surrender value of life insurance policies is not taxed currently to the policyholder. The investment gain on a life insurance policy is taxed at the termination of the contract prior to death only to the extent that the cash value exceeds the policyholder's investment in the contract (i.e., the sum of all premiums paid on the contract). Since the total amount of premiums paid includes the cost of life insurance protection, this represents an understatement of the taxable gain. Both features of this tax treatment are obviously beneficial to the insured or beneficiaries.

Given the favorable treatment of the investment return arising from life insurance cash values, it was probably inevitable that entrepreneurial ingenuity would find a way to exploit that tax treatment. Over time, new forms of life insurance with greater and greater overpayments were developed to take advantage of the favorable tax treatment. It was also probably inevitable that Congress would eventually question whether the tax treatment of life insurance created unintended loopholes in the tax system. The issue arose because while the *Internal Revenue Code* (IRC) granted favorable tax treatment to life insurance, there was no statutory definition of the term *life insurance*. Congress concluded that the absence of a definition of life insurance allowed some products that were designed primarily as investment instruments to shelter what would otherwise be taxable income simply because the products were called life insurance. Congress therefore sought to construct a definition of life insurance that would preserve the favorable tax treatment of those instruments that are actually life insurance, but deny it to contracts that are essentially investment instruments.

[4] An exception exists in the case of *transfer for value*. An example of a policy transferred for value would be if A purchases from B an existing policy for $10,000 on B's life, paying B $3000 for the policy. If B dies, A will be taxed on the $7000 gain. The taxation of policies transferred for value does not apply if the transferee is the person insured, a partner of the insured, or a corporation of which the insured is a director or stockholder.

If the contract fails to meet the definition of life insurance at any time, the pure insurance portion of the contract (the difference between the face amount and the cash surrender value) will be treated as *term life insurance*. The cash surrender value will be treated as a deposit fund and income earned on the fund will be taxable currently. In addition, all income previously deferred will be included in the insured's income in the year the contract fails to qualify as a life insurance contract. The new definition of life insurance generally applies to policies issued after 1984.

Code Definition of Life Insurance

The 1984 act contains two tests for determining whether a contract is a life insurance contract. One test deals with a cash value accumulation; the second involves a guideline premium test and a cash value corridor test. Regardless which test is selected for a contract, it must be satisfied at all times for the life of the contract. Both tests are designed to limit the types of contracts that qualify as life insurance to those contracts that involve only a modest investment and yield a modest investment return.

The cash value accumulation test will be met if the cash surrender value of the contract at any time does not exceed the *net single premium* that is required to fund future benefits, assuming that the contract matures no earlier than age 95.[5] In general, the net single premium for this test is computed using the greater of a 4 percent annual effective rate of interest or the rate guaranteed when the contract is issued.

The second test has two requirements that must both be met: a *guideline premium test* and *cash value corridor test*. A contract can satisfy the guideline premium test if the sum of the premiums does not exceed the greater of two limitations: the guideline single premium or the sum of the guideline level premiums. The guideline single premium must use the greater of a 6 percent annual interest rate or the rate guaranteed when the contract is issued. The guideline level premium is the amount, over a period that does not end before age 95, necessary to fund future benefits. In effect, the guideline premium tests eliminate from the definition of *life insurance* those poli-

cies with premiums greater than the amount required to fund the contract's death benefits.

The cash value corridor test is designed to disqualify any contract that builds up excessive amounts of cash value in relation to the life insurance risk. The cash value corridor test will be satisfied if the death benefit at any time is not less than a percentage (supplied in the table contained in the 1984 act) of the cash surrender value. In general, the applicable percentages begin at 250 percent for an insured 40 years of age or less and decrease to 100 percent for an insured 95 years of age (see Table 12.1).

In applying the values in the table, the applicable percentage is decreased by a ratable portion for each full year. For each age bracket, the percentage is decreased by the same amount for each year in that bracket. For example, for the 55- to 60-year-old age bracket, the applicable percentage falls from 150 to 130 percent, or four percentage points for each annual increase in age. At age 57, the applicable percentage will be 142 (150 minus 8).

IMPACT OF THE 1984 RULES

Paradoxically, while the changes in the tax code were prompted by the introduction of the innovative forms of life insurance, the earliest victims were from the ranks of traditional life insurance contracts. Most traditional endowment contracts, for example, will not qualify as life insurance under the 1984 rules, because of their innate investment nature. In addition, certain

[5] The *net single premium* is the insured's share of the discounted value of future claims. The net single premium is discussed in Chapter 13.

TABLE 12.1 Percentages for Corridor Test

Insured's Age at Start of Contract Year		Percentage	
More than	But not more than	From	To
0	40	250	250
40	45	250	215
45	50	215	185
50	55	185	150
55	60	150	130
60	65	130	120
65	70	120	115
70	75	115	105
75	90	105	105
90	95	105	100

Source: Internal Revenue Code, Section 7702.

modified types of whole-life policies will not qualify, nor will a number of retirement-oriented life insurance policies.

Most companies marketing universal life policies have found little difficulty in coping with the new regulations. Although interest earnings in excess of the guaranteed minimum increase the cash value of the policy, and could therefore disqualify universal life policies as life insurance under the tax code, most universal life policies meet this problem by increasing the level of life insurance protection as the cash value increases. Otherwise, the excess accumulation in the cash value would accelerate the maturity of the policy, making it payable as an endowment at an earlier age and causing it to fail the tax tests. In this respect, universal life policies fall into two broad categories. Under one approach, increases in the cash value in excess of the guaranteed minimum are payable as an additional death benefit. Under the second approach, the insurer forestalls early maturity by maintaining a specified corridor between the cash value and the face amount of protection. When the cash value approaches the face of the policy, the insurer simply deducts a part of the cash value to pay for more term insurance.[6]

CURRENT LIFE INSURANCE PRODUCTS

Now that we have an idea about why term insurance differs from cash value life insurance, we can take a closer look at some of those differences as they are reflected in the insurance products from which consumers can choose. We will begin this examination by returning once again to term insurance.

Term Insurance

We already know that term insurance provides temporary protection. It is called *term* because the coverage is for a limited term. The period for which the coverage will be provided may be 1 year, 5 years, 10 years, or 20 years. It may be *term to expectancy,* which is term insurance for the period the insured is expected to live, according to the mortality tables.

In its purest form, a term policy is purchased for a specified period of time and the face is payable only if the insured dies during this period. Nothing is paid if the insured survives the term period. It is customary, however, for term policies to include provisions relating to renewability and convertibility.

Renewable Term *Renewable-term* policies include a contractual provision guaranteeing the insured the right to renew the policy for a limited number of additional periods, each usually of the same length as the original term period. For example, if the insured purchases a 10-year term policy at age 25 and survives this period, he or she has the option of renewing the policy for an additional 10 years without having to prove insurability. The level premium for this 10-year period will be higher than that for the first 10 years, because of the insured's more advanced age. The insured may renew the policy at age 45 and perhaps also at age 55. However, most insurance companies, because of the element of adverse selection, impose an age limit beyond which renewal is not permitted. A limited number of companies offer term policies that are renewable to age 100.

Convertible Term The *conversion provision* grants the insured the option to exchange the term contract for some type of permanent life insurance contract without having to provide evidence of insurability. The options to renew regardless of insurability and to convert without evidence of insurability provide the insured with complete protection against loss of insurability.[7] The conversion is usually effected at the policyholder's attained age, but it can also be made retroactive to his or her original age. For example, if the insured decides to convert the term policy to whole life at age 32, and to convert at the attained age, the premium on the whole-life policy will be the same as if it had been purchased at age 32—which, in fact, it is. However, the policy could also be converted at the original age of 25, and the premium rates on the converted policy will be those the insured would have paid if the whole-life policy had originally been purchased at age 25. However, the insured will be required to pay a lump sum to the insurer that is sufficient to bring the reserve on the converted policy to

[6] Other provisions of the *Internal Revenue Code* relating to life insurance are discussed in Chapter 16 (modified endowment contracts) and Chapter 19 (tax-free exchanges).

[7] To minimize the element of adverse selection, most companies impose a time limit within which the conversion must take place. In the 10-year term policy, the insured could be required to convert within 7 or 8 years after the date of issue of the original contract. If the policy is renewable, however, the only limitation is that conversion must take place before the limiting age for renewal or that it be converted within a certain period before the expiration of the last term for which it can be renewed.

the level it would have reached if originally purchased at age 25.

The right of conversion was once a virtually universal trait of term policies, but this is no longer the case. As price competition in term insurance has intensified, some insurers have determined that by eliminating the conversion privilege, or limiting it to the first five years of the policy, they can offer a lower-priced term product. The consumer should, of course, weigh the lower price of these products against the absence of convertibility.

Variations in Renewal and Conversion Privileges

Renewal and conversion provisions and the premium structure in term policies may be combined in a variety of ways, creating a myriad of different contracts. Many term policies permit renewal for another period at a level premium. Some term policies that start off with a level premium for 5, 10, or 20 years become annually increasing premium policies after that initial period. Still other policies have a *re-entry provision* that allows the insured to requalify through a somewhat abbreviated underwriting process, to continue the policy at a relatively low rate. If the insured does not qualify, he or she may keep the policy, but at a much higher premium. Often, this premium is a multiple of the prior premium: a guaranteed maximum that is stated in the policy. Because these subtle variations in renewability and conversion privileges can produce significant differences in protection and cost, they are important considerations in the selection of term insurance products. Understanding the differences among apparently similar contracts is a requisite for an informed decision.

Advantages and Disadvantages of Term Insurance

The advantages and disadvantages of term insurance stem from its dual character as pure protection and temporary protection. With respect to term's nature as pure protection, because the premium for term insurance covers protection only, term insurance provides the greatest amount of protection for a given dollar outlay. Because it is temporary protection, it may be better suited to meet temporary insurance needs than permanent insurance would be.

As in the case of its advantages, the disadvantages of term insurance also stem from its nature as pure protection and temporary protection. Term insurance is misused when it is used to meet permanent needs. In addition, because insurers are subject to a greater element of adverse selection in term policies than in policies that include an investment element, the cost of term insurance may be somewhat greater than the cost of death protection in permanent insurance.

Whole-Life Insurance

In our discussion of the difference between term insurance and cash value insurance, we used the whole-life policy as the representative of cash value-type contracts. This seems entirely appropriate, since the whole-life policy is the standard approach to permanent insurance, and other cash value policies may be described in terms of the way(s) in which they differ from whole life.

Straight Whole Life The term *straight whole life* refers to a contract in which the premiums are payable for the entire lifetime of the insured (i.e., until age 100). It is also called *continuous premium whole life.*

The principal advantage of straight whole life is that it provides permanent protection for permanent needs and can be continued for the entire lifetime of the insured. In addition, because it includes a cash value, it serves the dual function of protection and saving. The savings element in the policy can be borrowed for emergencies, or it can be used to pay future premiums under the policy.

Straight whole life has disadvantages when it is used to fill a need for which it was not designed. When it is used to meet a temporary need, the amount of coverage that may be purchased may be less than if the need were met with term insurance. On the other hand, there are permanent life insurance needs, and permanent insurance should be used to meet such needs. Insurance to provide liquidity for estate tax purposes, for example, is a permanent need that cannot be met by temporary life insurance contracts such as term insurance.

Limited-Pay Whole Life Limited-payment whole life is a variation of the whole-life policy, differing only in the manner in which the premium is paid. As in the case of a straight whole-life policy, protection under the *limited-pay whole-life policy* extends to age 100, but the premium payments are made for some shorter period of time. During the period that premiums are paid, they are sufficiently high to prepay the policy in advance. Thus, under a 20-payment life policy, during the payment period, one pays premiums that are high enough to permit one to stop payment at the end of 20 years and still enjoy protection equal to the face amount of the policy for the remainder of one's life.

Universal Life Insurance

Universal life insurance was introduced in 1979 by Hutton Life, a subsidiary of the stock-brokerage firm, E. F. Hutton. The essential feature of universal life, which distinguished it from traditional whole life, is that, subject to specified limitations, the premiums, cash values, and level of protection can be adjusted up or down during the term of the contract to meet the owner's needs. A second distinguishing feature is the fact that the interest credited to the policy's cash value is geared to current interest rates, but is subject to a minimum such as 4 percent.

In effect, the premiums under a universal life policy are credited to a fund (which, following traditional insurance terminology, is called the cash value), and this fund is credited with the policy's share of investment earnings, after the deduction of expenses. This fund provides the source of funds to pay for the cost of pure protection under the policy (term insurance), which may be increased or decreased, subject to the insurer's underwriting standards. Universal policyholders receive annual statements indicating the level of life insurance protection under their policy, the cash value, the current interest being earned, and a statement of the amount of the premium paid that has been used for protection, investment, and expenses.

Some insurers set the minimum amount of coverage for their universal life products at $100,000; other companies offer contracts with an initial face amount as low as $25,000. As in the case of other forms of permanent insurance, the policyholder may borrow against the cash value, but in the case of universal life, he or she may also make withdrawals from the cash value without terminating the contract.

To understand the excitement that universal life insurance (ULI) brought to the insurance market when it was introduced, it should be recalled that interest rates in this country reached a historic high in the early 1980s. The high rates of interest that were credited to universal life cash values, combined with the favorable tax treatment and the ability to withdraw a part of the cash value (as opposed to borrowing against the cash value), enhanced the contract's appeal. Universal life enjoyed a phenomenal growth throughout the 1980s.

Although ULI received a warm response in the insurance market when it was introduced, this was primarily a result of timing. It was not an accident that ULI products were first offered during the era of record-level interest rates in the late 1970s and early 1980s. Investors who purchased universal life policies in 1982, when the rate on money market funds reached 15 percent, thought that these rates would go on forever. They were wrong. When interest rates inevitably fell, so did the performance of ULI policies. Many insureds who had been mesmerized by unrealistic projections had purchased the policies with the expectation that the investment earnings would pay future premiums. When the investment earnings on the policy fell short, the insureds were compelled to pay unexpected premiums to continue their coverage.

Variable Life Insurance

Variable life insurance is a whole-life contract in which the insured has the right to direct how the policy's cash value will be invested and the insured bears the investment risk in the form of fluctuations in the cash value and in the death benefit. Variable life is patterned after the variable annuity, which has been available to groups since 1952 and to individuals for well over a decade.[8] Like the variable annuity, variable life is designed as a solution to the problem of the decline in the purchasing power of the dollar that accompanies inflation. Although several models were proposed for a variable life insurance policy, the plan that eventually emerged is patterned after the so-called ratio plan, a concept originally suggested by New York Life. Under this plan, the amount of the premium is fixed, but the face amount of the policy varies up and down, subject to a minimum, which is the original amount of insurance. The cash value of the policy is not guaranteed and fluctuates with the performance of the portfolio in which the premiums have been invested by the insurer. This fluctuating cash value provides the funds to pay for the varying amount of death protection. Some insurers offer policyholders a choice of investments, with the underlying fund invested in stock funds, bond funds, or money market funds.

[8] The variable annuity, which predated variable life insurance by over two decades, is discussed in Chapter 18. Briefly, however, it is an attempt to cope with the impact of inflation on retirement incomes by linking the accumulation of retirement funds to the performance of common stocks. The annuitant's premiums are used to purchase units in a fund of securities, much like an open-end investment company. These units are accumulated until retirement, and a retirement income is then paid to the annuitant based on the value of the units accumulated. The concept is based on the assumption that the value of a diversified portfolio of common stocks will change in the same directions as the price level.

Although variable life policies have been available in other countries for some time,[9] this type of insurance developed slowly in the United States, in large part because of the regulatory conflicts that had accompanied the emergence of the variable annuity. Although the NAIC approved model legislation providing for the sale of variable life policies in 1969 and recommended this legislation to the states, there remained the problem of the equity-based nature of the contract and the qualification requirements of the Securities and Exchange Commission (SEC). In 1972, seeking to avoid some of the difficulties that had been encountered in connection with the variable annuity, the insurance industry petitioned the SEC for an exemption on variable life. After conducting hearings, the SEC ruled that variable life would be treated as a security.[10] This meant that variable life policies could be sold only by agents registered as broker-dealers with the National Association of Securities Dealers.

Variable Universal Life The latest innovation, *variable universal life insurance,* was introduced in 1985. It combines the flexible premium features of universal life with the investment component of variable life. The policyholder decides how the fund will be invested, and the fund's performance is directly related to the performance of the underlying investments.[11]

Adjustable Life Insurance

The adjustable life policy was introduced in 1971[12] and was proposed as a solution to the dilemma posed by an individual's changing need for and ability to pay for life insurance. The *adjustable life policy* allows the buyer to adjust various facets of the policy over time as the need for protection and the ability to pay premiums change. Within certain limits, the insured may raise or lower the face amount of the policy and increase or decrease the premium over the life of the policy.

There is no rate manual as such for adjustable life, and the relationship between the initial face amount and the premium determine the nature of the policy issued. The insured selects an amount of coverage at inception and, within limits, the premium he or she can afford to pay. Based on this choice, the adjustable life policy may provide either lifetime protection (that is, whole life) or limited protection (term insurance), depending on the face amount and the premium at the insured's attained age. After issue, the premium and/or the face amount may be adjusted at any monthly policy anniversary. Increases in the amount of protection can be offset by increased premiums, and reductions in coverage will permit reduced premiums, but other options are also possible. When the premiums paid exceed the cost of protection, the policy cash value increases; when the cost of protection exceeds the premiums paid, the cash value diminishes.

Adjustable life predates universal life and was the first version of modern flexible premium policies. It differs from universal life insurance in several ways. First, changes in the premium of an adjustable life policy are more structured than is the case with universal life insurance. The insurer must be notified of the proposed change and once the change is made, the new premium must be paid until another formal change is made. In variable life, the premiums can vary according to the preference of the insured without prior specific notification to the insurer. In addition, in a universal life policy, the investment and protection elements are unbundled, and the insured receives annual reports concerning investment income, mortality cost, and other expenses. This transparency does not exist in adjustable life insurance.

Endowment Life Insurance

Although endowment policies were one of the victims of the changes in the tax code enacted in 1984, our discussion of life insurance policies would not be complete without at least a brief mention of these contracts.

Under *endowment life policies,* which, like term insurance, are issued for a period such as 10 years or 20 years, the insurer promises to pay the face of the

[9] Variable life insurance has been available in the Netherlands since the mid-1950s, where it was originally introduced by a Dutch insurance company, DeWaerdye, Ltd. Under the Dutch version of variable life insurance, the face amount, the cash value, and the premiums are all variable, based on a fund invested in common stocks.

[10] The SEC granted an exemption from the provisions of the Investment Company Act of 1940 with respect to the separate funds in which the insurer invested the assets generated by variable life policies, but the policy itself must be registered under the Securities Act of 1933, and agents selling variable life must be registered as broker-dealers under the Securities and Exchange Act of 1934.

[11] By 1996, variable universal life represented about 10 percent of new life insurance sold, while variable life was about 1 percent. Universal life sales were about 18 percent of new life insurance sold.

[12] Adjustable life was introduced by Minnesota Mutual in 1971 and was also offered shortly thereafter by Bankers Life of Des Moines, Iowa, which had independently developed the same concept. See Charles L. Trowbridge, "Adjustable Life—A New Solution to an Old Problem," *CLU Journal,* vol. 31, no. 4 (October 1977).

policy if the insured dies during the policy period, but also promises to pay the face of the policy if the insured survives until the end of the period. ("You win if you live and you win if you die.") Endowment policies are essentially investment instruments, which combine a pure endowment with a death benefit.[13] Because they require premiums far in excess of the amount required to fund the death benefit, they do not qualify as life insurance under the current provisions of the tax code.

Participating and Nonparticipating Life Insurance

Before leaving our discussion of the types of life insurance policies, we should note an additional differentiation among life insurance policies: the distinction between participating and nonparticipating types. A *participating policy* is one on which annual dividends are paid to the policyholder. Originally, such policies were issued only by mutual life insurers, but today many stock life insurers also offer them. Under a participating policy, a substantial margin of safety is built into the premium, sufficient to reflect a willful overcharge, but justified on the assumption that if the extra premium is not needed, it will be returned to the policyholder as a *dividend.*

Because of the long-term nature of life insurance contracts, companies must calculate premium charges under traditional policies on a conservative basis. Once the premium rate on traditional policies is established, it must be guaranteed for the entire policy. It cannot be altered, even if the basic factors used in the computation should change considerably. Over a long period, substantial shifts in the premium factors could occur: mortality rates may change; the expenses of operating the company may increase, particularly if the long-run trend of prices is upward; and interest rates may change, going down as well as up. If the current premium rates are to be sufficient to enable insurers to fulfill their obligations on contracts that may continue for many decades in the future, a safety mar-

gin must be used in calculating the premium. The participating concept permits the insurer to establish a more generous margin in the form of an intentional overcharge, which will be returned to the policyholder if not needed. The safety margin on nonparticipating policies is narrower, because the cost of the insurance to the policyholder cannot be adjusted at a later time. The gross premium charged on nonparticipating policies must reflect, at least for competitive reasons, the actual cost of providing the insurance. Any profit realized in the operation will be used to provide dividends to stockholders as well as surplus funds that may be used as a buffer for future adverse experience.

GENERAL CLASSIFICATIONS OF LIFE INSURANCE

There are four basic classes of life insurance, distinguished by the manner in which they are marketed:

- Ordinary life insurance
- Industrial life insurance
- Group life insurance
- Credit life insurance

Our discussion thus far has been concerned with ordinary life. It would not be complete without at least a brief description of the other three types.

Ordinary Life Insurance

Ordinary life insurance constitutes the oldest and largest of the classes. In ordinary life, individual policies are marketed with a face amount of $1000 or more. Their premiums are paid annually, semiannually, quarterly, or monthly. The main characteristics of ordinary life are purchase on an individual basis and policy amounts of $1000 or more. It currently accounts for 58.8 percent of all life insurance in force in the United States.

Industrial Life Insurance

In *industrial life insurance,* the face value of the policy is less than $1000, and the premiums are payable as frequently as weekly. The most distinctive feature is that the premiums are collected by a representative of the insurance company at the home of the insured. In most instances, industrial life insurance is

[13] A *pure endowment* is a contract that promises to pay the face amount of the policy only if the insured survives the endowment period. The benefits that each survivor receives are contributed to in part by the members of the group who do not survive to collect, for if the purchaser of a pure endowment dies before the end of the period, there is no return. Pure endowment policies trace their roots to *Tontine* policies, which provided payment to persons who survived until some deferred time, or until the other participants had died.

sold in premium units, not units of face amount. Generally, it is decided how much weekly premium the insured can pay, and the amount of insurance will depend on the amount of coverage this premium will purchase under the plan selected at the attained age of the insured. Generally, the premiums vary from $0.05 to $1.00 a week. The types of policies available include whole life with premiums payable to a specified age such as 65 or 70 and 20-payment life. As a general rule, the insurance is provided without medical examination.

The weekly premium and its collection at the insured's home are important factors in keeping the policies in force. Most people who purchase industrial insurance are not able to save the money necessary to pay a monthly or quarterly premium. Also, they are not likely to send the premium to the insurance company, as in ordinary insurance. But if a company representative calls each week at the home of the insured and collects, for example, the 25-cent premium, there is some assurance that the policy will be maintained.

It should be obvious that this method of distribution is expensive, and it follows that industrial life is also expensive insurance. The cost per unit of coverage is substantially higher than is that of ordinary or group life. Industrial life insurance currently represents less than two-tenths of 1 percent of all legal reserve life insurance in force as compared with more than 10 percent four decades ago. Its relative decline has been due primarily to the rising incomes of individual workers, increasing awareness of the need for more adequate life insurance, and the expansion of both group life insurance and the Social Security system.

Although industrial life insurance in its traditional configuration has diminished significantly over the past five decades, a variation of this product called Monthly Debit Ordinary (MDO) life insurance has emerged as its progeny. MDO life insurance—also known as *home service life insurance*—is a form of cash value life insurance that combines insurance protection with an investment element. The policies are written with relatively low face amounts and are characterized by high premiums, owing primarily to the method of distribution and premium collection. As in the case of industrial life insurance, agents call door-to-door on customers, both to sell MDO products and to collect premiums after the policy is issued.

Because the volume of MDO life insurance is included in insurance company reports as ordinary life, there is no dependable data on the magnitude of this segment of the life insurance market. There are a number of insurers that specialize in this field and others that write MDO in addition to other forms of ordinary life insurance.

Group Life Insurance

Group life insurance is a plan in which coverage can be provided for a number of persons under one contract, called a master policy, usually without evidence of individual insurability. It is generally issued to an employer for the benefit of employees, but may also be used for other closely knit groups. The individual members of the group receive certificates as evidence of their insurance, but the contract is between the employer and the insurance company. Group life insurance programs sponsored by an employer may be contributory or noncontributory. Under a contributory plan, which is the more common approach, employer and employees share the cost of the insurance. Under a noncontributory plan, the employer pays the entire cost.

In most states, the groups to which group life insurance may be issued are defined by laws patterned after an NAIC Model Group Life Insurance Law. The NAIC Model Group Life Insurance Law definition includes:

1. Current and retired employees of one employer
2. Multiple employer groups
3. Members of a labor union
4. Debtors of a common creditor
5. Members of associations formed for purposes other than to obtain insurance, provided the association has at least 100 members and has been in existence for at least two years
6. Members of credit unions

In addition to these standard groups defined in the NAIC model law, some state laws authorize "any other group approved by the commissioner," generally referred to as *discretionary groups*. The requirements for the first six groups are defined in the law, and no specific permission is required for the purchase of insurance by such groups. Discretionary groups require specific approval by the insurance commissioner, which will be granted only if the proposed coverage meets a balancing test set forth in the law. Generally, the laws state that the commissioner will approve such groups if the plan meets three conditions. First, the

issuance of the group policy must be judged not contrary to the best interest of the public. Second, the issuance of the group policy will result in economies of acquisition or administration costs. Finally, the benefits under the group policy must be reasonable in relation to the premium charged.

The basic feature of group life insurance is the substitution of group underwriting for individual underwriting. This means that there is no physical examination or other individual underwriting methods applicable to individual employees. The major problem of the insurance company is, therefore, that of holding adverse selection to a minimum, and many of the features of group life insurance derive from this requirement. For example, when the premium is paid entirely by the employer, 100 percent of the eligible employees must be included. When the plan is contributory, with the premium paid jointly by the employer and the employees, not less than 75 percent of the eligible employees must participate. Furthermore, the amount of insurance on each participant must be determined by some plan that will preclude individual selection. In most instances, either the amount of insurance is a flat amount for all employees, or it is determined as a percentage or multiple of the individual's salary. It should be obvious that if group life insurance were provided without any required minimum number or percentage of employees, and if the employees could choose to enter the plan or stay out, a disproportionate number of impaired individuals would subscribe to the insurance. If the employee could choose the amount of insurance, the impaired lives would tend to take large amounts, while those in good health would opt for only small amounts. For group insurance to be practical, safeguards must be provided to prevent and minimize the element of adverse selection.

The cost of group life insurance is comparatively low. The reasons are quite simple. First, the basic plan under which most group life insurance is provided is yearly renewable term insurance, which provides the lowest cost form of protection per premium dollar. For employer-sponsored plans, the flow of insureds through the group maintains a stable average age as older employees retire, die, or leave the firm and their places are taken by younger workers. In addition, the expenses of medical examinations and other methods of determining insurability are largely eliminated. Third, group life involves mass selling and mass administration, with the result that expenses per life insured will be less under group policies than under

the marketing of individual policies. Finally, when group life insurance is part of an employee's compensation, there are tax advantages that further reduce the cost. Under current federal tax laws, an employer may deduct as a business expense premiums on group term life insurance up to $50,000 per employee, and amounts paid by the employer for such insurance are not taxable as income to the employee. This means that the employees would have to receive something more in salary than the amount paid by the employer for the insurance to purchase an equivalent amount of life insurance individually.[14]

The coverage under group life insurance contracts is very liberal. There are no exclusions, and the insurance proceeds are paid for death from any cause, including suicide, without restrictions as to time. In addition, most policies include a conversion provision, under which the insured employee may, within 31 days after termination of employment, convert all or a portion of the insurance to any form of individual policy currently offered by the insurance company, with the exception of term insurance. Conversion would be at the attained age of the employee and could not be refused by the insurance company because of the worker's uninsurability.

Although the original group idea was to substitute group underwriting and group marketing for individual underwriting and marketing, group underwriting has changed somewhat since the beginning of group life insurance. Under the first group life insurance laws, the definition of *groups* for insurance purposes were restrictive, requiring a minimum number of members, usually 50 or 100 lives.[15] Over time, statutory requirements concerning the minimum number of individuals in a group have shrunk, and with the decrease in the number, the nature of group underwriting has changed. As the minimum number of members required for group coverage fell, insurers introduced elements of individual underwriting for smaller groups. Although group underwriting is still used for large groups, state laws often allow insurers the right to require evidence of individual insurability on groups. Whether an insurer will require evidence

[14] For example, an employee in a 28 percent tax bracket would have to receive $277 in before-tax income to pay the equivalent of $200 in premiums contributed by the employer for group life insurance.

[15] The first NAIC model group law, adopted in 1917, set the minimum for groups at 50. Many states reduced this to 25, and the number has gradually dropped to 10.

of individual insurability for group coverage depends on the size and nature of the group.

Group life insurance has become an important branch of life insurance today, accounting for 39.9 percent of all such protection in force in 2000. For many persons who would not be insurable under ordinary life insurance, it provides the only means for obtaining coverage. For others, the low-cost group life insurance is an excellent supplement to the individual life insurance program.

Credit Life Insurance

Credit life insurance is sold through lending institutions to short-term borrowers contemplating consumer purchases and through retail merchants selling on a charge account basis to installment buyers. It also includes mortgage protection life insurance of 10 years' duration or less that is issued through lenders.[16] The insurance protects both the lenders and the debtors against financial loss should the debtor die before completing the required payments. The life of the borrower is insured for an amount related to the outstanding balance of a specific loan, and the policy generally provides for the payment of the scheduled balance in the event of the debtor's death. The insurance is term insurance, generally decreasing in amount as the loan is repaid.

The major suppliers of credit life insurance, and the lenders who are usually involved as vendor-beneficiaries of this coverage, include commercial banks, sales finance companies, credit unions, personal finance companies, and retailers selling goods and services on a charge account or installment basis. More than 250 insurance companies, both stock and mutual, offer credit life insurance. Some companies specialize in writing credit life, while for other insurers, it represents only a small part of their total business. The coverage is sold on both an individual and group basis. In the former, borrowers receive individual policies. In the latter, a master policy is issued to the lending institution, and the individual borrowers receive certificates outlining their coverage. Approx-

imately 85 percent of the credit life insurance in force is written on a group basis.

Although credit life insurance was first introduced in 1917, its growth was modest until the end of World War II. Since then, however, it has grown rapidly, closely paralleling the increase in consumer debt. From an insignificant $365 million in coverage in 1945, it has increased to about $200 billion, or about 1.2 percent of total life insurance in force by 2000. Further evidence of its growing significance is that only about 7 percent of all outstanding consumer credit was protected by credit life insurance in 1945, but by 2000, the percentage had climbed to more than 80 percent.

Total Life Insurance in Force in the United States

Total life insurance in force in 2000 exceeded $15 trillion, well over twice the amount held a decade earlier. The bulk of this amount—more than 97.5 percent—was issued by legal reserve life insurance companies operating under state insurance laws specifying the minimum basis for the reserves that the company must maintain on its policies.[17] The remainder was issued by other private insurers and government insurers discussed in the paragraphs that follow. Table 12.2, which lists the insurance in force with legal reserve life insurance companies from 1900 through 2000, indicates the distribution of the insurance by class, and also depicts its growth and changing distribution by class over time.

Other Types of Life Insurance

In addition to the life insurance issued by legal reserve life insurance companies, a small amount (about 2.5 percent of all life insurance in force) is written by other types of insurers.

Savings Bank Life Insurance In three states—New York, Massachusetts, and Connecticut—the law authorizes mutual savings banks to issue life insurance policies under prescribed conditions to residents of the state and to persons regularly employed there. The law requires the banks to set up guarantee funds and limits the size of the policies and their provisions. Because savings bank life insurance is sold without agents, there are no commissions, and the cost is usually somewhat

[16] Credit life insurance is frequently sold in conjunction with a companion coverage, credit accident and health insurance. This insures against the disability of the borrower through accident or illness and provides benefits by meeting required payments for a specific loan during the debtor's disability. Benefits are commonly subject to some dollar maximum per payment and some maximum number of payments.

[17] Insurers that do not qualify as legal reserve life insurers include fraternals and assessment societies.

TABLE 12.2 **Life Insurance in Force in the United States, 1900–2000 (in millions)**

Year	Ordinary Number	Ordinary Amount	Group Number	Group Amount	Industrial Number	Industrial Amount	Credit Number[a]	Credit Amount	Total Number	Total Amount
1900	3	$6,124	–	–	11	$1,449	–	–	14	$7,573
1910	6	11,783	–	–	23	3,125	–	–	29	14,908
1920	16	32,011	2	$1,570	48	6,948	b	$4	66	40,540
1930	32	78,576	6	9,801	86	17,963	b	73	124	106,413
1940	37	79,346	9	14,938	85	20,866	3	380	134	115,530
1950	64	149,116	19	47,793	108	33,415	11	3,844	202	234,168
1960	95	341,881	44	175,903	100	39,563	43	29,101	282	586,448
1970	120	734,730	80	551,357	77	38,644	78	77,392	355	1,402,123
1975	134	1,083,421	96	904,695	70	39,423	80	112,032	380	2,139,571
1980	148	1,760,474	118	1,579,355	58	35,994	78	165,215	402	3,541,038
1985	142	3,247,289	130	2,561,595	44	28,250	70	215,973	386	6,053,107
1990	141	5,366,982	141	3,753,506	36	24,071	71	248,038	389	9,392,597
1994	140	6,835,239	143	4,608,746	29	20,145	59	209,491	371	11,673,621
1995	151	7,547,537	145	4,777,912	30	19,977	66	231,251	392	12,576,677
2000	163	9,376,370	156	6,376,127	c	c	50	200,770	369	15,953,267

[a] Includes group credit certificates.

[b] Fewer than 500,000.

[c] Included with ordinary life.

Source: American Council of Life Insurers, *Life Insurance Fact Book 2001.*

lower than that available from insurance companies. Nevertheless, the amount of savings bank life insurance in force in each of the states is a small percentage of the total insurance in force: about 3 percent in Massachusetts, 2.5 percent in New York, and less than 2 percent in Connecticut.[18]

Fraternal Life Insurance As we noted in Chapter 5, *fraternals* represent a special class of mutual insurers, usually associated with a lodge or fraternal order, that provide life insurance to their members. Most fraternals originally used the assessment principle, but the majority currently operate on a legal reserve basis. The total amount of insurance in force with fraternals at the end of 2000 was $279 billion.

Wisconsin State Life Insurance Fund The Wisconsin State Life Insurance Fund issues policies with a $1000 minimum and a $10,000 maximum to persons in the state at the time of issuance. Although the program has been in effect since 1911, the total amount of insurance in force under the program is less than 1 percent of all life insurance in force in the state.

Veterans' Life Insurance The Veterans Administration has sold life insurance to veterans since World War I. No veteran can own more than $10,000 in government life insurance under any one or combination of these plans.[19] The total amount of government life insurance in force under these programs was about $21.8 billion at the end of 2000. Only one of the programs—designed for veterans separated from the service with a service-connected disability—is still open to new issues, so it may be assumed that the amount of insurance of this type will decline in the future.

In addition to the veterans' life insurance programs in which the government itself acts as the insurer, there are two other programs supervised by the Veterans Administration and subsidized by the federal government: the Servicemen's Group Life

[18] In 1990, the Massachusetts legislature extended authority to market savings bank life insurance to commercial banks. Prior to 1990, only Massachusetts savings banks had this authority. In Massachussets, individuals may purchase up to $5000 in savings bank life insurance from any one bank with an aggregate of $64,000 in all banks. In New York, all insurance must be purchased from the same bank, and the maximum is $30,000. The maximum of such insurance allowable in Connecticut is $25,000.

[19] Servicemen's Group Life Insurance (SGLI) and Veterans Group Life Insurance (VGLI), which is sold by private insurers, are included in the private insurance industry totals in Table 12.2.

Insurance Program and the Veterans' Group Life Insurance Program. However, these are underwritten by the private insurance industry.

Members of the U.S. military, including cadets and midshipmen at the service academies, are automatically insured under Servicemen's Group Life Insurance (SGLI) for $100,000. Service members who wish to do so, may purchase an additional $100,000 or they may elect in writing to be covered for a lesser amount or not covered at all. Total life insurance in force under this program totaled $487 billion in 2000.

SGLI may be converted to five-year renewable term coverage known as Veterans' Group Life Insurance (VGLI). Coverage is limited to the amount that the service member had in force at the time of separation and may be continued in increments of $10,000 from $10,000 to $200,000. The VGLI may be renewed for an additional five-year term at the end of each five-year term or it may be converted to an individual permanent life insurance policy without evidence of insurability.

IMPORTANT CONCEPTS TO REMEMBER

term insurance	renewable term	participating life insurance
cash value life insurance	convertible term	nonparticipating life insurance
net premium	yearly renewable term	policy dividend
gross premium	straight whole-life insurance	ordinary life insurance
level premium	limited-pay whole-life insurance	industrial life insurance
policy reserve	universal life insurance	group life insurance
nonforfeiture value	variable life insurance	franchise life insurance
transfer for value	variable universal life insurance	credit life insurance
guideline premium test	adjustable life policy	savings bank life insurance
cash value corridor test	endowment life insurance	fraternal insurer
term to expectancy	pure endowment	

QUESTIONS FOR REVIEW

1. Distinguish between *term insurance policies* and *cash value policies.*

2. Explain what is meant by the statement that term insurance is *pure protection.*

3. Under a whole-life policy, the overpayment by the insured during the early years of the contract offsets underpayments in later years. This being the case, the reserve should reach a peak and then gradually decline. How do you explain the fact that it does not?

4. Under a whole-life policy, the amount payable in the event of the insured's death can be viewed as consisting of two parts. Explain this concept.

5. Describe the ways in which life insurance policies receive favorable tax treatment.

6. John Jones buys a *renewable, convertible, nonparticipating* term insurance policy. Explain the precise meaning of each of the italicized words.

7. Describe the distinguishing characteristics of *universal life, variable life,* and *adjustable life insurance.*

8. What is the difference between a *participating* and a *nonparticipating* life insurance contract? How do their premiums reflect this difference?

9. Life insurance may be classified according to the manner in which it is marketed. Identify the four classes of insurance based on this classification and explain the distinguishing characteristics of each.

10. Distinguish between *individual* and *group life insurance* arrangements and identify the sources of the cost advantage for group life insurance.

QUESTIONS FOR DISCUSSION

1. To what extent are the proceeds of a life insurance policy exempt from the claims of the creditors of the beneficiary? On what basis can such exemptions be justified?

2. The *Internal Revenue Code* provides certain tax advantages to life insurance. Some observers argue that this gives life insurance an unfair advantage over other savings vehicles, such as mutual funds. Do you agree or disagree? Why?

3. The life insurance policy reserve arises because of the overpayment of premiums in the early years of the policy. When a policy lapses, state laws require that the insurer return a part of that overpayment to the policyholder as a nonforfeiture benefit. There are other policies where a similar cost and premium structure exists, but insurers are not required to provide nonforfeiture benefits if the policy

lapses. For example, long-term care insurance (discussed in Chapter 22) is typically written without nonforfeiture benefits. Do you think insurers should be required to pay nonforfeiture benefits for these policies? Why or why not?

4. Dividends paid to policyholders on participating policies are treated by the IRS as a return of premium and are not subject to income tax. Dividends to shareholders in a stock company, however, are taxable income to the recipients. Do you believe this difference in treatment is justified? Why or why not?

5. Discuss the potential for adverse selection when insureds exercise the renewability or convertibility option in a term life insurance policy. Which is more likely to be affected by adverse selection?

SUGGESTIONS FOR ADDITIONAL READING

Black, Kenneth, Jr., and Harold D. Skipper, Jr. *Life Insurance,* 13th ed. Englewood Cliffs, N.J.: Prentice-Hall, 2000. Chapters 4, 5, 6.

Crawford, Muriel L. *Life and Health Insurance Law,* 7th ed. Homewood, Ill.: Richard D. Irwin, 1994.

Graves, Edward E., ed. *McGill's Life Insurance.* Bryn Mawr, Pa.: The American College, 1994. Chapters 2, 3, 4, 33.

Hallman, G. Victor, and Karen L. Hamilton. *Personal Insurance: Life, Health & Retirement.* Malvern, Pa.: American Institute for CPCU, 1994. Chapter 4.

WEB SITES TO EXPLORE

American College	http://www.amercoll.edu/
American Council of Life Insurance	http://www.acli.com/
American Society of CLU & ChFC	http://www.agents-online.com/ASCLU/web/index.html
Association for Advanced Life Underwriting	http://www.agents-online.com/AALU/
Insurance News Network	http://www.insure.com/
Life Office Management Association (LOMA)	http://www.loma.org/
Life-Line	http://www.life-line.org/
LIMRA	http://www.limra.com/aboutlim.htm
Newsedge News Page	http://www.newspage.com/browse/46622/
S.S. Huebner Foundation for Insurance Education	http://rider.wharton.upenn.edu/~sshuebne/

CHAPTER 13

THE ACTUARIAL BASIS OF LIFE INSURANCE

*An actuary is a mathematician with a kind of insanity so
rare as to be valuable.*

— ANONYMOUS

CHAPTER OBJECTIVES

When you have finished this chapter, you should be able to
- Differentiate between net premiums and gross premiums in life insurance
- Identify the three factors that are used in computing life insurance rates and explain how each enters into the computation
- Describe the nature of a mortality table and explain the nature of the entries for each age
- Describe the net single premium and explain the way it is computed
- Explain the relationship of the net single premium to annual level premiums and describe the way in which annual level premiums are computed
- Explain how the net premium for an annuity is computed
- Distinguish between benefit-certain life insurance contracts and benefit-uncertain contracts and explain the significance of the distinction

In this chapter we will briefly examine the manner in which the insurance company determines the premiums for the various types of contracts it offers. The purpose here is not to attempt to make the readers competent actuaries. The purpose is to help the reader gain an appreciation of the differences among the various contracts. As we will see, differences in premiums among the various forms reflect the differing probabilities of payment under the policies, the length of time for which protection applies, and the manner in which the premiums are to be paid.

LIFE INSURANCE PREMIUM COMPUTATION

There are three primary elements in life insurance rate making:

1. Mortality
2. Interest
3. Loading

The first two (i.e., mortality and interest) are used to compute the net premium, which measures only the cost of claims and omits the provision for operating expenses. The net premium plus an expense loading constitute the gross premium, which is the selling price of the contract and the amount the insured pays. For the most part, we will confine our discussion here to the net premium, realizing that the premiums we develop are in fact "net" and that an additional charge to cover expenses called the loading, must be added to arrive at the final premium.

Mortality

The mortality table is simply a convenient method of expressing the probabilities of living or dying at any given age. It is a tabular expression of the chance of losing the economic value of the human life. Since the insurance company assumes the risk of the individual, and since this risk is based on life contingencies, it is important that the company know within reasonable limits how many people will die at each age. Based on past experience, applying the theory of probability, actuaries are able to predict the number of deaths among a given number of people at some given age.

Tables 13.1 and 13.2 are mortality tables, specifically, the 1980 Commissioners' Standard Ordinary Tables (1980 CSO tables) for males and females.[1]

The mortality table is not, as its form might suggest, a history of a group of people from the year they were born until they all die. The information does not come to the actuary in the form shown. The actuary determines the rate of death at each given age (e.g., the number dying per thousand at ages 1, 2, 3, 4, and so on) and, based on this information, builds up a table with an arbitrary number of lives at the beginning age. The table starts with 10 million lives; this figure, known as the radix, is completely arbitrary. Any number could have been used, for it is the ratio of the number dying to the number living that is important. Tables 13.1 and 13.2 each contain five columns: (1) age; (2) the number living at each age out of the original 10 million; (3) the number of those living at the start of a given year who will die in that year; (4) the ratio of persons dying to persons living expressed as deaths per thousand; and (5) the number of years that those living at any given age can expect, on the average, to live.

Given the mortality table (the chance of loss), the problem of computing the insurance premium at any given age becomes a matter of simple arithmetic. According to the 1980 CSO table for female lives, for example, out of an initial 10,000,000 females, there are 9,810,509 alive at age 21. Of that number, 10,497 will die before reaching age 22. This represents a death rate of 1.07 per 1000. To insure each of the 9,810,509 members of the group alive at age 21 for $1000 for one year will require $10,497,000 (10,497 times $1000). If we collect $1.07 from each insured (9,810,509 times $1.07), we will have a sufficient fund to pay all claims. The $1.07 represents the net premium (the cost of the losses only) that each insured contributes:

$$\frac{\$10,497,000}{9,810,509} = \$1.0699 \ (\$1.07)$$

Interest

Thus far in our computation, we have not considered the factor of interest. All life insurance policies provide for the payment of the premium before the contract goes into effect, but the benefits will not be paid until some time in the future. Since the insurance company collects the premium in advance and does not pay claims until a future date, it has the use of the insured's money for some time, and it must be prepared to pay him or her interest on it. Life insurers

[1] The illustrations in this chapter use the 1980 CSO table for females. This is one of two tables (male and female) developed by a special committee of the Society of Actuaries. The tables are referred to as the 1980 Commissioners' Standard Ordinary Tables because they were completed in 1980 and have been adopted by the National Association of Insurance Commissioners for minimum reserve valuations on standard lives under ordinary policies. The tables are derived from the experience of a group of life insurers during the period 1970–1975 and contain a built-in safety margin, which overstates the death rate. In actual rate making, insurers use mortality tables reflecting up-to-date experience, often based on the company's own most recent experience.

TABLE 13.1 Commissioners' 1980 Standard Ordinary Mortality Table—Male Lives

Age	Number Alive	Number Dying	Deaths per 1000	Life Expectancy	Age	Number Alive	Number Dying	Deaths per 1000	Life Expectancy
0	10,000,000	41,800	4.18	70.83	50	8,966,618	60,166	6.71	25.36
1	9,958,200	10,655	1.07	70.13	51	8,906,452	65,017	7.30	24.52
2	9,947,545	9,848	0.99	69.20	52	8,841,435	70,378	7.96	23.70
3	9,937,697	9,739	0.98	68.27	53	8,771,057	76,396	8.71	22.89
4	9,927,958	9,432	0.95	67.34	54	8,694,661	83,121	9.56	22.08
5	9,918,526	8,927	0.90	66.40	55	8,611,540	90,163	10.47	21.29
6	9,909,599	8,522	0.86	65.46	56	8,521,377	97,655	11.46	20.51
7	9,901,077	7,921	0.80	64.52	57	8,423,722	105,212	12.49	19.74
8	9,893,156	7,519	0.76	63.57	58	8,318,510	113,049	13.59	18.99
9	9,885,637	7,315	0.74	62.62	59	8,205,461	121,195	14.77	18.24
10	9,878,322	7,211	0.73	61.66	60	8,084,266	129,995	16.08	17.51
11	9,871,111	7,601	0.77	60.71	61	7,954,271	139,518	17.54	16.69
12	9,863,510	8,384	0.85	59.75	62	7,814,753	149,965	19.19	16.08
13	9,855,126	9,757	0.99	58.80	63	7,664,788	161,420	21.06	15.38
14	9,845,369	11,322	1.15	57.86	64	7,503,368	173,628	23.14	14.70
15	9,834,047	13,079	1.33	56.93	65	7,329,740	186,322	25.42	14.04
16	9,820,968	14,830	1.51	56.00	66	7,143,418	198,944	27.85	13.39
17	9,806,138	16,376	1.67	55.09	67	6,944,474	211,390	30.44	12.76
18	9,789,762	17,426	1.78	54.18	68	6,733,084	223,471	33.19	12.14
19	9,772,336	18,177	1.86	53.27	69	6,509,613	235,453	36.17	11.54
20	9,754,159	18,533	1.90	52.37	70	6,274,160	247,892	39.51	10.96
21	9,735,626	18,595	1.91	51.47	71	6,026,268	260,937	43.30	10.39
22	9,717,031	18,365	1.89	50.57	72	5,765,331	274,718	47.65	9.84
23	9,698,666	18,040	1.86	49.66	73	5,490,613	289,025	52.64	9.30
24	9,680,626	17,619	1.82	48.75	74	5,201,588	302,680	58.19	8.79
25	9,663,007	17,104	1.77	47.84	75	4,898,908	314,461	64.19	8.31
26	9,645,903	16,687	1.73	46.93	76	4,584,447	345,209	70.53	7.84
27	9,629,216	16,466	1.71	46.01	77	4,239,238	326,930	77.12	7.40
28	9,612,750	16,342	1.70	45.09	78	3,912,308	328,243	83.90	6.97
29	9,596,408	16,410	1.71	44.16	79	3,584,065	326,329	91.05	6.57
30	9,579,998	16,573	1.73	43.24	80	3,257,736	321,995	98.84	6.18
31	9,563,425	17,023	1.78	42.31	81	2,935,741	314,858	107.48	5.80
32	9,546,402	17,470	1.83	41.38	82	2,620,883	307,299	117.25	5.44
33	9,528,932	18,200	1.91	40.46	83	2,313,584	296,740	128.26	5.09
34	9,510,732	19,021	2.00	39.54	84	2,016,844	282,862	140.25	4.77
35	9,491,711	20,028	2.11	38.61	85	1,733,982	265,213	152.95	4.46
36	9,471,683	21,217	2.24	37.69	86	1,468,769	243,948	166.09	4.18
37	9,450,466	22,681	2.40	36.78	87	1,224,821	219,917	179.55	3.91
38	9,427,785	24,324	2.58	35.87	88	1,004,904	194,218	193.27	3.66
39	9,403,461	26,236	2.79	34.96	89	810,686	168,031	207.29	3.41
40	9,377,225	28,319	3.02	34.05	90	642,655	142,522	221.77	3.18
41	9,348,906	30,758	3.29	33.16	91	500,133	118,522	236.98	2.94
42	9,318,148	33,173	3.56	32.26	92	381,611	96,719	253.45	2.70
43	9,284,975	35,933	3.87	31.38	93	284,892	77,522	272.11	2.44
44	9,249,042	38,753	4.19	30.50	94	207,370	61,361	295.90	2.17
45	9,210,289	41,907	4.55	29.62	95	146,009	48,177	329.96	1.87
46	9,168,382	45,108	4.92	28.76	96	97,832	37,621	384.55	1.54
47	9,123,274	48,536	5.32	27.90	97	60,211	28,913	480.20	1.20
48	9,074,738	52,089	5.74	27.04	98	31,298	20,593	657.98	.84
49	9,022,649	56,031	6.21	26.20	99	10,705	10,705	1,000.00	.50

Source: Commissioners' 1980 Standard Ordinary Mortality Table.

TABLE 13.2 **Commissioners' 1980 Standard Ordinary Mortality Table—Female Lives**

Age	Number Alive	Number Dying	Deaths per 1000	Life Expectancy	Age	Number Alive	Number Dying	Deaths per 1000	Life Expectancy
0	10,000,000	28,900	2.89	75.83	50	9,219,130	45,727	4.96	29.53
1	9,971,100	8,675	0.87	75.04	51	9,173,403	48,711	5.31	28.67
2	9,962,425	8,070	0.81	74.11	52	9,124,692	52,011	5.70	27.82
3	9,954,355	7,864	0.79	73.17	53	9,072,681	55,797	6.15	26.98
4	9,946,491	7,659	0.77	72.23	54	9,016,884	59,602	6.61	26.14
5	9,938,832	7,554	0.76	71.28	55	8,957,282	63,507	7.09	25.31
6	9,931,278	7,250	0.73	70.34	56	8,893,775	67,326	7.57	24.49
7	9,924,028	7,145	0.72	69.39	57	8,826,449	70,876	8.03	23.67
8	9,116,883	6,942	0.70	68.44	58	8,755,573	74,160	8.47	22.86
9	9,909,941	6,838	0.69	67.48	59	8,681,413	77,612	8.94	22.05
10	9,903,103	6,734	0.68	66.53	60	8,603,801	81,478	9.47	21.25
11	9,896,369	6,828	0.69	65.58	61	8,522,323	86,331	10.13	20.44
12	9,889,541	7,120	0.72	64.62	62	8,435,992	92,458	10.96	19.65
13	9,882,421	7,412	0.75	63.67	63	8,343,534	100,289	12.02	18.38
14	9,875,009	7,900	0.80	62.71	64	8,243,245	109,223	13.25	18.08
15	9,867,109	8,387	0.85	61.76	65	8,134,022	118,675	14.59	17.32
16	9,858,722	8,873	0.90	60.82	66	8,015,347	128,246	16.00	16.57
17	9,849,849	9,357	0.95	59.87	67	7,887,101	137,472	17.43	15.83
18	9,840,492	9,644	0.98	58.93	68	7,749,629	146,003	18.84	15.10
19	9,830,848	10,027	1.02	57.98	69	7,603,626	154,810	20.36	14.38
20	9,820,821	10,312	1.05	57.04	70	7,448,816	164,693	22.11	13.67
21	9,810,509	10,497	1.07	56.10	71	7,284,123	176,494	24.23	12.97
22	9,800,012	10,682	1.09	55.16	72	7,107,629	190,982	26.87	12.28
23	9,789,330	10,866	1.11	54.22	73	6,916,647	208,260	30.11	11.60
24	9,778,464	11,147	1.14	53.28	74	6,708,387	227,616	33.93	10.95
25	9,767,317	11,330	1.16	52.34	75	6,480,771	247,825	38.24	10.32
26	9,755,987	11,610	1.19	51.40	76	6,232,946	267,830	42.97	9.71
27	9,744,377	11,888	1.22	50.46	77	5,965,116	286,564	48.04	9.12
28	9,732,489	12,263	1.26	49.52	78	5,678,552	303,519	53.45	8.55
29	9,720,226	12,636	1.30	48.59	79	5,375,033	319,008	59.35	8.01
30	9,707,590	13,105	1.35	47.65	80	5,056,025	333,647	65.99	7.48
31	9,694,485	13,572	1.40	46.71	81	4,722,378	347,567	73.60	6.98
32	9,680,913	14,037	1.45	45.78	82	4,374,811	360,484	82.40	6.49
33	9,666,876	14,500	1.50	44.84	83	4,014,327	371,446	92.53	6.03
34	9,652,376	15,251	1.58	43.91	84	3,642,881	378,167	103.81	5.59
35	9,637,125	15,901	1.65	42.98	85	3,264,714	379,033	116.10	5.18
36	9,621,224	16,933	1.76	42.05	86	2,885,681	373,090	129.29	4.80
37	9,604,291	18,152	1.89	41.12	87	2,512,591	360,105	143.32	4.43
38	9,586,139	19,556	2.04	40.20	88	2,152,486	340,480	158.18	4.09
39	9,566,583	21,238	2.22	39.28	89	1,812,006	315,180	173.94	3.77
40	9,545,345	23,100	2.42	38.36	90	1,496,826	285,520	190.75	3.45
41	9,522,245	25,139	2.64	37.46	91	1,211,306	253,005	208.87	3.15
42	9,497,106	27,257	2.87	36.55	92	958,301	219,269	228.81	2.85
43	9,469,849	29,262	3.09	35.66	93	739,032	185,874	251.51	2.55
44	9,440,587	31,343	3.32	34.77	94	553,158	154,503	279.31	2.24
45	9,409,244	33,497	3.56	33.88	95	398,655	126,501	317.32	1.91
46	9,375,747	35,628	3.80	33.00	96	272,154	102,259	375.74	1.56
47	9,340,119	37,827	4.05	32.12	97	169,895	80,695	474.97	1.21
48	9,302,292	40,279	4.33	31.25	98	89,200	58,502	655.85	.84
49	9,262,013	42,883	4.63	30.39	99	30,698	30,698	1,000.00	.50

Source: Commissioners' 1980 Standard Ordinary Mortality Table.

collect vast sums of money, and since their obligations will not mature until some time in the future, they invest this money and earn interest on it. Since they do earn interest on the funds they collect, they do not need to collect the full amount of future losses from the members of the group. They can collect something less than the full amount of the losses, invest it, and then pay the losses out of the total fund of principal and interest. Thus, the present value of a future dollar discussed in Chapter 10 is an important concept in the computation of premiums. To simplify computation, we will assume that all premiums are collected at the beginning of the year and all claims mature at the end of the year.

The allowance for interest is made by discounting the future claims to obtain their present value. If we bring the interest into the computation of premiums, the net premium will be something less than would be necessary to charge each insured for his or her cost of the death claims of the group.

Returning to our example of $1000 worth of insurance for one year for each of the 9,810,509 females alive at age 21, and assuming interest at the rate of 4.5 percent, the cost of the claims for the group as a whole is $10,044,999 (compared with $10,497,000 without interest).[2] If we invest $10,044,999 at 4.5 percent, it will equal $10,497,000 at the end of one year. The cost per individual becomes $1.0239, or $1.02 ($10,044,999 divided by 9,810,509).

To recapitulate, a one-year term policy at age 21 without interest costs

$$\frac{\$10,497,000}{9,810,509} = \$1.0699 \ (\$1.07)$$

A one-year term policy at age 21 with interest costs

$$\frac{\$10,497,000 \times 0.95694}{9,810,509} = \$1.0239 = \$1.02$$

Now, if we want to insure the survivors for another year, we will find that the premium is higher, because there are fewer members left to pay the costs, and at the same time the number of deaths will have increased.

At age 22:

$$\$10,682,000 \times 0.95694 = \$10,222,033$$
$$\frac{\$10,222,033}{9,800,012} = \$1.0430 = \$1.04$$

At age 23:

$$\$10,866,000 \times 0.95694 = \$10,398,110$$
$$\frac{\$10,398,110}{9,789,330} = \$1.0621 = \$1.06$$

At age 24:

$$\$11,147,000 \times 0.95694 = \$10,667,010$$
$$\frac{\$10,667,010}{9,778,464} = \$1.090 = \$1.09$$

At age 25:

$$\$11,330,000 \times 0.95694 = \$10,842,130$$
$$\frac{\$10,842,130}{9,767,317} = \$1.110 = \$1.11$$

By the time the insureds reach age 65, the mortality table indicates that only 8,134,022 of the original 10,000,000 will still be alive and that 118,675 of those still alive will die before reaching 66. Thus, the net premium for the one-year term at age 65 will be:

$$\$118,675,000 \times 0.95694 = \$113,564,850$$
$$\frac{\$113,564,850}{8,134,022} = \$13.96$$

Because premiums are based on mortality, they increase as the group of insureds grows older, and as the insureds reach advanced ages, the cost becomes prohibitive. In general, it becomes advisable to level out the cost of protection by charging slightly more during the early years to offset a deficiency during the later ones.

The Net Single Premium

It is possible to compute a lump-sum payment, which, if made by the members of the group, will pay all mortality costs over a term longer than one year.

[2] As in the selection of the mortality table, the insurer has freedom in selecting the interest assumption for premium computation. The interest rate for computing policy reserves is set at 4.5 percent in most states (5.5 percent for single-premium policies). Because of the long-term nature of life insurance contracts, insurers use conservative interest assumptions.

The computation of all long-term policies makes use of this concept. The net single premium is a sum that, if paid when the policy is issued and if augmented by compound interest, will pay the benefits as they come due. Let us assume, for example, that instead of purchasing insurance annually, our 21-year-old and the other members of his or her group wish to purchase a five-year term contract. How much must we charge each individual at the beginning of the five-year policy to permit us to pay the death claims as they mature?

The process of computing the net single premium for a five-year term policy is much the same as that used in computing the annual premium. However, since the charge will be made at the inception of the policy and all claims will not have been paid until the end of the five-year period, the company will have the use of the money for varying lengths of time. To compensate for this, we simply compute the present value of future claims by discounting the claims due at the end of the first year for one year, those due at the end of the second year for two years, those due at the end of the third year for three years, and so on throughout the policy term. For example, we know from our previous computation that we need $10,044,999 now to meet the $10,497,000 in claims that will mature at the end of the first year. At the end of the second year, we can expect, according to the mortality table, claims in the amount of $10,682,000, but applying the discount factor for two years we find that we will need only $9,781,828 ($10,682,000 times 0.91573) at the beginning of the contract to meet the obligations that will mature in two years. Continuing the process for the full five years, we obtain the present value of all future claims:

Age	Number of Claims	Amount of Claims	Discount	Present Value of Claims
1	10,497	$10,497,000	$0.95694	$10,044,999
2	10,682	10,682,000	0.91573	9,781,828
3	10,866	10,866,000	0.87630	9,521,876
4	11,147	11,147,000	0.83856	9,347,428
5	11,330	11,330,000	0.80245	9,091,759
		$54,522,000		$47,787,890

During the five-year period, the company will be called on to pay $54,522,000 in death benefits. The present value of these claims is $47,787,890. In other words, $47,787,890 is the amount that when invested will, with the interest earned on it, permit the company to meet the total obligations during the policy period. This is the cost of claims for the group as a whole. To find the cost of claims for each individual in the group, we simply divide the present value of future claims by the number of entrants in the group:

$$\frac{\$47,787,890}{9,810,509} = \$4.8710$$

If you add the individual annual premiums ($1.02, $1.04, $1.06, $1.09, $1.11), you will notice that the net single premium for a five-year term policy is somewhat less than the summation of the annual premiums for the same five years ($4.87 compared with $5.32). The lower premium for the single-premium contract stems from two facts. First, the insurer has a part of the insured's premium for a longer period when the policy is paid in advance, and the cost is reduced by the greater amount of interest that is earned. In addition, in the five-year term policy, all insureds pay their full share of the five-year mortality costs in advance. In the annual premium case, some insureds will die before later premiums become due. In effect, those who die during the early years under the five-year term policy "overpay" their share of the mortality costs, which reduces the cost to the survivors.

Calculating the net single premium on any of the various policies we have discussed follows the same procedure. In the case of the whole-life policy, for example, all the future claims under the policy are discounted (clear to the end of the mortality table), ending at age 99, when we would expect $30,698,000 in claims. A summation of all the present value of future claims divided by the number of entrants at age 21 would give the net single premium for the whole-life policy. In a sense, a whole-life policy is a term policy to age 100, for the premium computation on the whole-life policy follows the manner described above. The only difference is in the number of years involved.

If we carry the computation out to the end of the mortality table, using the same technique as in the five-year policy, we obtain the present value of all future claims under a whole-life contract:

Year	Age	Number of Claims	Amount of Claims	Discount	Present Value of Claims
1	21	10,497	$10,497,000	$0.95694	$10,044,999
2	22	10,682	10,682,000	0.91573	9,781,828
3	23	10,866	10,866,000	0.87630	9,521,876
4	24	11,147	11,147,000	0.83856	9,347,428
5	25	11,330	11,330,000	0.80245	9,091,759
*	*	*	*	*	*
*	*	*	*	*	*
*	*	*	*	*	*
75	95	126,501	126,501,000	0.03682	4,657,767
76	96	102,259	102,259,000	0.03523	3,602,585
77	97	90,695	90,695,000	0.03371	3,057,328
78	98	58,502	58,502,000	0.03226	1,887,275
79	99	30,698	30,698,000	0.03087	947,647
					$1,052,972,752

The present value of future claims, $1,052,972,752, represents the amount the insurance company must have now to pay all death claims under the whole-life contract as they occur. Divided by the 9,810,509 entrants at age 21, the net single premium for the whole-life contract is $107.33:

$$\frac{\$1,052,972,752}{9,810,509} = \$107.33$$

The Net Level Premium

The net single premium is the basis for computing the level premium on long-term policies. Although some policies are sold on a single-premium basis, in the event of an early death, the cost of the insurance is high compared with the annual cost. In addition, most people cannot afford the single premium.

To determine the net level premium, we first compute the net single premium and then convert it to a series of annual payments, considering the number of premiums that can be expected and the year in which the expected premium will be paid. To do this we make use of the concept of the annuity due. Annu-

ities, as we have seen, are concerned with the number of survivors. The practical question we ask in computing an annuity due is, "How much must the insurance company charge now to be able to pay each member of the group $1.00 for a given number of years?" The same principles of mortality and compound interest apply, but in a somewhat reverse order. Obviously, the promise by the insurance company to pay $1 for the next five years to each of the 9,810,509 21-year-olds will involve the payment of something less than 9,810,509 times $5. Some entrants will die; in addition, the company will have the money to invest and will make some return on it. If we refer to the mortality table, we find that there will only be 9,800,012 members of the original group alive at age 22 to collect their $1.00. In addition, if we assume a 4.5 percent rate of return, the insurance company needs only about $0.956 now to pay each 22-year-old $1.00. Every year there are fewer members of the group; in addition, the company needs less per dollar of benefit the longer the time before the dollar must be paid. We compute the value of an annuity due of $1.00 for five years in the following manner.

Age	Number Living	Present Value of $1	Present Value of Benefits
21	9,810,509 × $1.00 due now	$1.00	$9,810,509
22	9,800,012 × $1.00 due in 1 year	0.95694	9,378,023
23	9,789,330 × $1.00 due in 2 years	0.91573	8,964,383
24	9,778,464 × $1.00 due in 3 years	0.87630	8,568,868
25	9,767,317 × $1.00 due in 4 years	0.83856	8,190,481
			$44,912,264

To be able to pay each of the entrants $1.00 each year for the next five years (paying only those entrants who are alive, of course), the insurance company will need $44,912,264 now. Dividing the amount needed by the number of entrants, we get the cost of an annuity due of $1.00 for five years for each entrant:

$$\frac{\$44,912,264}{9,810,509} = \$4.5779$$

Once we obtain the cost of an annuity due of $1.00 for five years, the problem of converting the net single premium on a five-year policy of any type into a level annual premium becomes one of simple proportion. Taking the premium we computed as the net single premium for a five-year term policy first, we get the following equation:

$$\frac{\$4.5779}{4.8710} = \frac{\$1.00}{X}$$

$$X = \$1.0640 = \$1.064$$

Since $4.5779 is the actuarial equivalent of $1.00 paid now plus $1.00 each year for the next four years, giving the insurer $1.064 now plus $1.064 each year for the next four years is the same as giving the insurer $4.87 at the beginning of the five years.

To convert the net single premiums for a whole-life contract to an annual level premium, we use the same approach, but use the value of a $1.00 annuity due for life rather than for five years. The value of a lifetime annuity due is computed in exactly the same manner as the five-year annuity due, except that the computation is carried out to the end of the mortality table as shown. The cost of a $1.00 lifetime annuity, therefore, is:

Age	Number Living	Present Value of $1	Present Value of Benefits
21	9,810,509 × $1.00 due now	$1.00	$9,810,509
22	9,800,012 × $1.00 due in 1 year	0.95694	9,378,023
23	9,789,330 × $1.00 due in 2 years	0.91573	8,964,383
24	9,778,464 × $1.00 due in 3 years	0.87630	8,568,868
25	9,767,317 × $1.00 due in 4 years	0.83856	8,190,481
*	*	*	*
*	*	*	*
*	*	*	*
95	398,655 × $1.00 due in 74 years	0.03848	15,340
96	272,154 × $1.00 due in 75 years	0.03682	10,021
97	169,895 × $1.00 due in 76 years	0.03523	5,985
98	89,200 × $1.00 due in 77 years	0.03371	3,007
99	30,698 × $1.00 due in 78 years	0.03226	990
			$203,363,389

$$\frac{\$203,363,389}{9,810,509} = \$20.7291$$

The net single premium for a whole-life policy was $107.24. Using the net premium for a $1.00 lifetime annuity due at age 21 of $20.7291, we convert this whole-life net single premium into annual installments:

$$\frac{\$20.7291}{107.33} = \frac{\$1.00}{X}$$

$$X = \$5.1777$$

The net level annual premium for whole life at age 21 is $5.18.

Computing the limited-pay whole-life policies also uses this basic procedure. A limited-pay whole-life policy is the actuarial equivalent of a straight life policy, except for the way in which the premiums are paid. To compute the premium for a 20-payment whole-life contract, we begin with the net single premium for a whole-life policy. Under a 20-payment policy, we will spread the premiums over a 20-year period rather than over the total lifetime of the insured. To make the conversion from a net single premium to 20 payments, we use an annuity due for

20 years. The net single premium for an annuity due for 20 years at age 21 is $13.46.

$$\frac{\$13.46}{107.33} = \frac{\$1.00}{X}$$

$$X = \$7.97$$

The net single premium of $107.33 is mathematically the same as a payment of $7.97 from each of the surviving members of the group for a 20-year period. In fact, each of the premiums for the whole-life policy that we have computed is the equivalent of the other two. It makes no difference to the insurer whether the insured makes a net single-premium purchase by paying $107.33, or agrees to pay $7.97 each year for 20 years, or $5.18 for as long as she lives.

RESERVES ON LIFE INSURANCE POLICIES

Under the level premium plan, the insured pays more than the cost of the protection during the early years of the contract. The difference between what the insured pays and the cost of the protection represents the policy reserve. This represents the prepayment of future premiums and is the basis for the cash value.

To illustrate the effect of the prepayment of costs under the level premium plan, Table 13.3 shows the reserve on five one-year term policies beginning at age 21, a five-year term policy on a single-premium basis, and a five-year term policy on a level premium basis. The table indicates the initial reserve and the terminal reserve for each policy for each year. The reserve on a policy at the end of the policy year is known as the terminal reserve, and the terminal reserve at the end of a year plus the net premiums for the next year is known as the initial reserve of that next year. The average of the initial and terminal reserves for any year is called the mean reserve for that year. It is the mean reserve for all policies in force that the insurance company is required by law to have on hand at all times.

As indicated in Table 13.1, under the one-year term option, the premiums collected at the beginning of each year are sufficient with interest income to pay the death claims for the year. When the five-year term policy is purchased on a single-premium basis, a

significant reserve is created at inception. Each year, interest is added and death claims are deducted, and the result is the terminal reserve for the year. The reserve gradually diminishes until the final year, when it is just sufficient to pay death claims. Under the level premium option, the reserve increases during the first three years, as the insureds overpay the cost of protection, and then diminishes as death costs exceed premium income and interest in the last two years.

Unlike the reserve on term policies, the reserves on whole-life policies, endowments, and limited-payment whole-life policies do not diminish, but continue to accumulate, eventually reaching the face amount of the policy. Since these reserves represent payments by members of the group that are more than the current cost of the insurance protection, members of the group have a vested interest in these reserves. In effect, the reserves represent a prepayment for future protection. If an individual decides to withdraw from the group and does not wish the future protection for which he or she has paid, that person is entitled to a return of a portion of his or her premiums. In a sense, the reserve "belongs" to members of the group, and a member who leaves the group is entitled to withdraw a portion of the reserve. Permanent insurance contracts such as whole-life, limited-payment, and endowment policies all develop a cash saving fund that is the property of the insured. On withdrawing from the group, the insured is entitled to a surrender value based on the policy reserve. Normally, a policy does not develop a cash value until after the second year, and its surrender value rarely equals the full amount of the policy reserve until it has been in force for 10 or 15 years. Obviously, the reserve required for any given policy depends on the age of the insured at the date of issue, the assumed rate of interest, and the type of policy. Since the reserve equals an amount that, together with all future premiums and interest on these premiums and the reserve, will equal future benefits, the lower the amount of future premiums and the higher the amount of future claims, the higher must be the reserve. A simple identity should prove helpful in understanding this relationship:

$$\text{Reserve} = \frac{\text{Present value of}}{\text{future benefits}} - \frac{\text{Present value of}}{\text{future premiums}}$$

A whole-life policy, if continued, will eventually be payable as a death benefit or as an endowment at age

TABLE 13.3 Policy Reserves—Net Single Premium and Net Level Premium for Five-Year Term Policy and Net Premium for Five Annual Term Policies

				Five One-Year Term Policies			
Age	Number Alive	Number Dying	Annual Premium	Initial Reserve	Reserve Plus Interest	Minus Death Claims	Terminal Reserve
21	9,810,509	10,497	1.023900	10,044,976	10,497,000	−10,497,000	$0
22	9,800,012	10,682	1.043061	10,222,010	10,682,000	−10,682,000	0
23	9,789,330	10,866	1.062186	10,398,086	10,866,000	−10,866,000	0
24	9,778,464	11,147	1.090865	10,666,986	11,147,000	−11,147,000	0
25	9,767,317	11,330	1.110039	10,842,105	11,330,000	−11,330,000	0
Total premiums paid:			5.330051				

				Net Single Premium			
Age	Number Alive	Number Dying	Single Premium	Initial Reserve	Reserve Plus Interest	Minus Death Claims	Terminal Reserve
21	9,810,509	10,497	4.871088	47,787,856	49,938,309	−10,497,000	$39,441,309
22	9,800,012	10,682		39,441,309	41,216,168	−10,682,000	30,534,168
23	9,789,330	10,866		30,534,168	31,908,206	−10,866,000	21,042,206
24	9,778,464	11,147		21,042,206	21,989,105	−11,147,000	10,842,105
25	9,767,317	11,330		10,842,105	11,330,000	−11,330,000	0
Total premiums paid:			4.871088				

				Net Level Premium			
Age	Number Alive	Number Dying	Annual Premium	Initial Reserve	Reserve Plus Interest	Minus Death Claims	Terminal Reserve
21	9,810,509	10,497	1.064028	10,438,655	10,908,394	−10,497,000	$411,394
22	9,800,012	10,682	1.064028	10,838,880	11,326,630	−10,682,000	644,630
23	9,789,330	10,866	1.064028	11,060,749	11,558,483	−10,866,000	692,483
24	9,778,464	11,147	1.064028	11,097,041	11,596,408	−11,147,000	449,408
25	9,767,317	11,330	1.064028	10,842,105	11,330,000	−11,330,000	0
Total premiums paid:			5.320139				

100. The accumulating reserve, which will be required for payment as an endowment at age 100, results in a decreasing amount of risk under the policy. For example, when Mr. X purchases $10,000 of whole-life coverage, he obtains $10,000 in immediate protection. As he pays on the policy, the cash value accumulates. After 10 years, the policy has a cash value of, say, $3000. The point that is often overlooked is that the actual amount of protection has declined and the insurance amounts to only $7000. If the insured dies, his beneficiary will collect $10,000, but $3000 of this amount consists of his investment.[3] Under the permanent forms of life insurance, the policyholder does not have $1000 in life insurance protection for each $1000 of face amount, but $1000 minus the insured's own accumulated cash value. The actual insurance, or "risk," of the insurance company is constantly being reduced.

The major differences among the various forms of cash value life insurance are simply the rates at which the reserve accumulates. Perhaps these differences and the relationship of the policy reserves under the various contracts can be shown better graphically. Figure 13.1 illustrates the reserve accumulation of various policies purchased by a female insured at age 21. The lines in the chart indicate the accumulation of the policy reserve for a whole-life contract, a 20-payment life contract, a 30-payment life contract, and a policy paid up at age 65. The most important line for our purposes is the one designated net single premium. If the insured purchases a whole-life contract

[3] An alternate approach would be to say that the beneficiary collects $10,000 and that the investment is forfeited to the company. The net effect is the same.

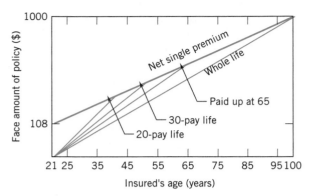

FIGURE 13.1 Reserve accumulation of cash value policies.

with a net single premium of approximately $108, this amount will be sufficient to equal the face of the policy at age 100. The interest on the net single premium will be credited to the reserve, and, together with this interest, the net single premium will be sufficient to pay death claims for members of the group and accumulate to the face of the policy at age 100. All the other reserve lines begin at zero, but as the insured overpays the premium, the excess is accumulated as the policy reserve. At any point in time at which the policy reserve equals the net single premium line, premium payments may be discontinued. Remember, there are no additional premium payments due under the net single premium contract, so if the reserve under any other form equals the net single premium line, interest on that reserve will then be sufficient, as in the case of the net single premium, to pay all death claims and still reach $1000 by age 100. Thus, under the 20-payment life policy, the reserve equals the net single premium line at age 41; under a 30-payment life policy, they are equal at age 51. Thus, other things being equal, the reserve on a 20-payment life and a 30-payment life will be the same at the end of 30 years, since the reserve on each policy must by that time be sufficient to pay all future benefits under the policy when credited with interest.[4]

[4] A policy is paid up when there are no further premiums due on it and the reserve is sufficient, with the interest on it, to pay all future claims under the policy. Since

$$\text{Reserve} = \frac{\text{Present value of}}{\text{future benefits}} - \frac{\text{Present value of}}{\text{future premiums}}$$

a policy is paid up when

$$\text{Reserve} = \frac{\text{Present value of}}{\text{future benefits}}$$

BENEFIT-CERTAIN AND BENEFIT-UNCERTAIN CONTRACTS

Thus far, we have seen that the procedure for the computation of the premium for all forms of life insurance is essentially the same. The present value of the future claims under the contract is summed, obtaining the net single premium. The net single premium is then distributed over the selected premium payment period, using the concept of an annuity due, which considers interest and survival probability.

The present value of the future benefits under a life insurance contract varies with the probability that the insurer will be required to make payment, which changes with the length of time for which the insurance is to be provided and also with the nature of the promise made by the insurer. If the insurer agrees to pay the face of the policy if the insured dies within a specified period, as in term insurance, the present value of future benefits will be the individual's share of the discounted death claims that are expected to occur during that period. The longer the period for which the insurance is to be provided, the greater will be the present value of future benefits. Suppose that the insurer agrees to pay the face amount if the insured dies within a specified period and also to make payment if he or she survives that period, as in the case of an endowment or whole-life policy. In that case the present value of future benefits will be the individual's share of the discounted death claims during the period and the discounted value of the endowment benefit. Assuming that the insured persists, the payment of the face of the policy is a certainty.[5]

All forms of permanent life insurance are benefit-certain contracts. If the insured continues to live, the face of the policy will inevitably be payable—the probability that the insurer will be required to make payment is 100 percent. Term contracts, on the other hand, are benefit-uncertain contracts, in that payment will be made only if the insured dies during the policy period. Since the probability of loss under these contracts is something less than 100 percent, the present value of future claims is less than that of the present value of future claims under the benefit-certain contracts.

In Chapter 12, we noted that the increasing probability of death at advanced ages makes the cost of

[5] A policy is mature when the face of the policy is payable. Thus, the whole-life policy matures at age 100.

insurance at those ages prohibitive. The net premium for a one-year term contract of $1000 face amount at age 70 for a female is $20.20, at age 80 it is $63.15, and at age 90 it is $182.53. Few people would be willing to purchase life insurance coverage at these rates, so the level premium plan was developed to avoid the impact of the increasing mortality.

The perceptive student will note, however, that the level premium contract does not avoid the costs inherent in the higher mortality at advanced ages. The actuarial equivalent of the increasing one-year term rate must be charged even under the level premium plan, but the higher costs are hidden by premium redistribution and the compound interest on the overpayments made during the early years of the contract. It makes no difference whether the premiums are paid on an annually increasing basis or if they are leveled out via the level premium; the costs are there. The real secret to the operation of the level premium plan and permanent forms of insurance is simply the magic of compound interest rather than the law of large numbers. The level premium plan does not avoid the higher mortality costs at advanced ages; it merely spreads them over a longer period.

Consider the probabilities found in the various forms of life insurance. A young man, age 21, may purchase a term-to-age-65 policy. The probability that he will die and that the insurance company will be required to pay the face of the policy is about 24 percent. If he could purchase a term-to-age-75 contract, the probability that the company would be required to pay the face of the policy is increased to 49 percent. Protection to age 85 involves a probability of 82 percent. What is the probability if a whole-life or endowment contract is purchased? Since the company will inevitably pay the face amount of these policies, the probability is 100 percent.[6]

[6] The probability of death after age 65 is much greater than is the probability of death up to age 65. In fact, the probability of death during the 10-year period from age 65 to age 75 exceeds the probability for the entire period from age 21 to age 65.

At some point, the death "risk" ceases to be a risk. The probability increases each year until the loss becomes a certainty. The exposure under term insurance contracts, on the other hand, is a true contingency—an event that may or may not occur. Mortality costs for the entire life span, that is, to the end of the mortality table, do not constitute an insurable risk. Mortality costs up to age 65, on the other hand, represent a reasonable approximation of the insurable risk.

There is some question whether insurance covering to the end of the mortality table is a proper application of the insurance mechanism. Insuring under a benefit-certain policy such as a whole-life policy involves the accumulation of an investment rather than a distribution of losses through the law of large numbers. As the insureds under permanent forms of life insurance continue their premium payments, the overpayment piles up and the compound interest on the overpayment accumulates, so that the insureds build up a fund that acts to reduce the risk facing the insurance company. While a rational person would probably refuse to purchase insurance at age 75, or 80, or 85, or 90, on an individual year-to-year basis, this is precisely what is done under the whole-life contract. However, since the costs associated with the high probabilities can be hidden by the redistribution of premiums and compound interest, the whole-life contract is a salable product, but the high cost is not avoided. The only way in which the cost of death at advancing ages can be avoided is by refusing to purchase coverage against death at advancing ages.

The most intriguing aspect of the distinction between the benefit-certain and the benefit-uncertain contracts is that it illustrates once again that there is nothing magical or mystical about the insurance equation. The insurance company must collect sufficient premiums to pay the claims it will incur. The benefit-certain contracts are possible only because of the compounding interest on the insured's overpayment of premiums during the early years of the contract.

IMPORTANT CONCEPTS TO REMEMBER

net premium	annuity due	mean reserve
gross premium	net single premium	initial reserve
mortality tables	net level premium	benefit-certain contract
loading	terminal reserve	benefit-uncertain contract

QUESTIONS FOR REVIEW

1. What are the primary elements in life insurance rate-making? Which are used in computing net premiums? The gross premium?

2. The insurer must estimate in advance both the mortality and the interest that will be earned on policyholders' premiums. How do insurers attempt to guard against deviations from these estimates?

3. The net single premium for a five-year term policy at age 21 is $4.87 (1980 CSO table, female lives, 4.5 percent interest assumption). Why can we not compute the annual premium for a five-year term policy by dividing $4.87 by 5?

4. Explain what is meant by the term present value. Ignoring the concept of present value, what is the net single premium for a whole-life policy?

5. At age 28, Mr. Jones purchased a whole-life policy, paying the premium in one single payment. On the same day, Mr. Smith bought a 20-pay whole-life policy identical in all other respects to the one purchased by Jones. At what point will the reserve on the two policies be equal? Why must they be equal at this point?

6. Under a whole-life policy, the actual amount at risk by the insurance company is constantly reducing. Explain what is meant by this statement.

7. In a given year, would you expect the initial reserve, the mean reserve, or the terminal reserve of a particular policy to be highest? In your answer, distinguish among the three measures. Which is most significant for regulatory purposes?

8. What is the difference between a policy that is paid up and one that is mature?

9. Briefly explain the distinction between benefit-certain and benefit-uncertain life insurance contracts.

10. You have been called on as a consulting actuary by a tribe of natives in an underdeveloped country. Due to warfare with the neighboring tribes, the mortality rate in the country is quite high. At the same time, the interest rate is also high. On the basis of the mortality and simplified discount tables given here, compute:

a. The one-year term rate for ages 21–25

b. The net single premium for a five-year term policy at age 21

c. The net single premium for a five-year endowment at age 21

d. The annual premium for the five-year endowment at age 21

Mortality Table

Age	Number Alive	Number Dying
21	1000	10
22	990	20
23	970	30
24	940	40
25	900	50

Compound Discount Table

Present value of $1		
	One year from now	= $0.90
	Two years from now	= $0.80
	Three years from now	= $0.70
	Four years from now	= $0.60
	Five years from now	= $0.50

QUESTIONS FOR DISCUSSION

1. An article on life insurance in a midwestern newspaper stated: "It makes good sense to purchase life insurance at an early age, since the cost of coverage increases the longer you wait." Do you agree or disagree with this statement?

2. Assume two groups of policies, each consisting of 1000 policies, issued at the same time to groups of the same age. One group consists of single-premium whole-life policies and the other of 20-payment whole-life policies. If mortality is less than anticipated, which group will show the largest mortality savings?

3. "A young man, age 21, may purchase a term-to-age-65 policy. The probability that he will die and that the insurance company will be required to pay the face amount of the policy is about 24 percent. If he could purchase a term-to-age-75 contract, the probability that the company

would be required to pay the face of the policy is increased to 49 percent. Protection to age 85 involves a probability of 82 percent." Reflecting on the rules of risk management discussed in Chapter 3, what conclusions can one draw concerning the purchase of benefit-certain contracts?

4. "Other things being equal, the lower the interest assumption used in the computation of the premium, the lower will be the reserve on a policy at any point in time." Do you agree or disagree? Why?

5. It has been shown that wide differences in cost exist among life insurers for the same type of policy. The three factors used in premium computation are the basis for these differences in cost. To which of the three factors would you attribute the widest differences in cost?

SUGGESTIONS FOR ADDITIONAL READING

Black, Kenneth, Jr., and Harold D. Skipper, Jr. Life Insurance, 13th ed. Englewood Cliffs, N.J.: Prentice-Hall, 2000. Chapters 27–29.

Chastain, James J. "The A, B, C's of Life Insurance Rate and Reserve Computation." Journal of Insurance, vol. 27, no. 4 (Dec. 1960).

Cooper, Robert W. "The Level Premium Concept: A Closer Look." CLU Journal, vol. 30, no. 2 (April 1976).

Gerber, Hans U. Life Insurance Mathematics. New York, N.Y.: Springer Verlag, 1990.

Harper, Floyd S., and Lewis Workman. Fundamental Mathematics of Life Insurance. Homewood, Ill.: Richard D. Irwin, 1970.

Mehr, Robert I., and Sandra G. Gustavson. Life Insurance: Theory and Practice, 4th ed. Austin, Tex.: Business Publications, 1987. Chapters 23–24.

WEB SITES TO EXPLORE

American Academy of Actuaries	http://www.actuary.org/
American Council of Life Insurance	http://www.acli.com/
Society of Actuaries	http://www.soa.org/

CHAPTER 14

THE LIFE INSURANCE CONTRACT—GENERAL PROVISIONS

■

Youngsters read it, grown men understand it, and old
people applaud it.

— CERVANTES
Don Quixote

CHAPTER OBJECTIVES

When you have finished this chapter, you should be able to
- Describe the common provisions of life insurance contracts
- Explain the purpose and importance of the incontestable clause in life insurance contracts
- Identify and explain the distinction among the various types of beneficiaries that may be designated in a life insurance contract
- Identify and describe the settlement options and explain the circumstances in which each of the settlement options might be used

Unlike many other insurance contracts, there is no standard policy form that must be used in life insurance. However, while there is no uniform contract, the states have enacted legislation that makes certain provisions mandatory in life insurance policies. The most commonly required provisions include the following:

1. The policy shall constitute the entire contract.

2. There must be a grace period of 30 days or 1 month.

3. The policy shall be contestable only during the first 2 years.

4. Misstatement of age shall be cause for an adjustment in the amount of insurance.

5. Reinstatement must be permitted.

6. Participating policies shall pay dividends on an annual basis.

7. Nonforfeiture values must be listed for at least 20 years.

8. The nonforfeiture values to which the insured is entitled must be listed after the payment of three premiums.

9. Loan values must be listed.

10. Installment or annuity tables shall show the amount of benefits to which the beneficiary is entitled if the policy is payable in installments or as an annuity.

Some of these provisions pertain only to certain types of policies, and do not, therefore, appear in all life insurance policies. For example, provisions relating to dividends are included only in participating contracts, while those relating to cash values are not found in term policies, where there is no cash value. To provide a systematic basis for analysis, we have divided life insurance policy provisions into two classes: Those that are included in every life insurance policy are discussed in this chapter; those that are included only in certain policies, or whose inclusion is optional, will be analyzed in Chapter 15.

INCEPTION OF THE LIFE INSURANCE CONTRACT

Coverage under the life insurance policy is effective as soon as the contract comes into existence. The fundamental question, then, is when does the policy come into existence. The answer hinges on a relatively small detail in the eyes of many insureds—whether the first premium accompanies the application for insurance. If the application is sent to the insurer without the premium, it is considered an invitation to the insurer to make an offer, which it does by issuing a policy. There is no contract until the applicant has accepted the insurer's offer, which he or she does by taking the policy and paying the first premium. If the insured should die during the period between making the application and receiving the policy and paying the first premium, no benefits will be paid, for the policy has not yet come into existence. For the most part, this is not the usual procedure.

Normally, the premium accompanies the application for insurance. The company acknowledges receipt of the premium with a *conditional binding receipt*. The typical binding receipt makes the policy effective as of the date of application, provided that the applicant is found to be insurable according to the underwriting rules of the company. If the individual does not meet the company's underwriting standards, it may offer a rated policy or a policy subject to limitations. This, in effect, represents a counteroffer by the insurer, and the applicant is again in the situation in which he or she may accept or reject the insurer's offer. A situation might arise in which the underwriter is forced to determine whether a deceased person would have qualified for insurance if he or she had not died. If the applicant would have qualified then the company is bound to pay the death benefit, since the policy went into effect conditionally at the time of the application.[1]

GENERAL PROVISIONS OF LIFE INSURANCE CONTRACTS

Although certain provisions are required by law, in many cases they are not spelled out exactly. However, the final wording adopted by the insurance company must be approved by the commissioner of insurance. In addition, even in the case of those provisions not required by law, competition generally forces them to be substantially similar. So, although there is no "standard" life insurance policy, the provisions discussed here are more or less common to all life contracts.

Entire Contract Clause

When the application is incorporated as a part of the policy contract, the representations of the insured become contractual provisions and can be used as evidence in a contest of the contract's validity. To prevent the use of other evidence, most states require the inclusion of a clause in life insurance policies stating that the policy and the application attached to it constitute the entire contract between the insurer and the insured. The typical policy expresses this provision as follows:

[1] Although the conditional binding receipt is the normal procedure, some companies use a binding receipt that is not conditional. Here coverage is effective immediately under *interim term insurance,* which continues until the contract is issued.

This policy and the application, a copy of which is attached when issued, constitute the entire contract. All statements in the application, in the absence of fraud, shall be deemed representations and not warranties. No statement shall void this policy or be used in defense of a claim under it unless contained in the application.

In declaring that the statements of the insured are to be considered representations and not warranties, the clause requires the insurer to prove the materiality of any misrepresentations by the insured. This provision is clearly beneficial to the insured.

Ownership Clause

A life insurance policy is a piece of property. The policy may be owned by the individual on whose life the policy is written, or by the beneficiary, or by someone else. In most cases, the insured is also the owner of the policy. The person designated as the owner has vested privileges of ownership, including the right to assign or transfer the policy, receive the cash values and dividends, or borrow against it. At the death of the insured, the beneficiary becomes the owner of the policy.

Beneficiary Clause

The beneficiary is the person named in the life insurance contract to receive all or a portion of the proceeds at maturity of the policy. The designation of the beneficiary is an important aspect of the policy and is designed specifically to reflect the insured's decisions concerning the disposition of his or her insurance. In an endowment or retirement income policy, the beneficiary may be the insured or, in the event of the insured's death, the estate, or a third party. In most instances, it is best not to name the estate as beneficiary, particularly when it is intended that the proceeds will go to certain individuals. If a specific beneficiary is named, the proceeds will be paid to the designated person or persons directly after the death of the insured, and they will not be subject to estate administration, with its accompanying probate costs and creditors' claims against the insured. But most important, if a specific beneficiary is named, the payment of the proceeds will not be delayed until the entire estate has been settled.

A beneficiary may be *primary* or *contingent*. A *primary beneficiary* is the person first entitled to the proceeds of the policy following the death of the insured. A *contingent beneficiary* is entitled to the policy benefits only after the death of the primary or direct beneficiary.

The customary type of beneficiary designation is the donee or third-party beneficiary. Here the beneficiary may be a specific individual or a class designation. To make certain that his or her intentions will be accomplished, the insured should designate the beneficiary or beneficiaries with care. For example, a man may wish that his current wife be the primary beneficiary and that his children by this wife are to be the class-contingent beneficiaries. Proper identification could be accomplished in this case by the designation of "my wife, Elizabeth Hallquist Jones" as the primary beneficiary and "the children of my marriage to Elizabeth Hallquist Jones" as the contingent beneficiaries. The children then would receive, and share equally, the proceeds if the wife should predecease the insured.[2]

There are many classifications of beneficiaries, but for our purpose the most important is that in which the insured may or may not reserve the right to change the designation. In this classification, beneficiaries may be *revocable* or *irrevocable*. In the former, the insured reserves the right to change the designation at any time; in the latter, the insured imposes a restriction on the use of this right.

The revocable designation is used in the vast majority of life insurance contracts today. As the owner of the contract, the insured has the right to designate anyone as the beneficiary, even if the person named has no insurable interest in the policyholder's life. If at the inception of the contract, the insured designates a beneficiary and reserves the right to change this designation, then the change may take place at any time and any number of times during the term of the policy. This means that the interest of a revocable beneficiary is nothing more than a mere expectancy subject to all the rights and privileges that the insured may exercise in the contract. The insured is the complete owner of the contract

[2] There are many reasons for the use of care in the designation of the beneficiary. For example, if the insured designates as beneficiary "my wife, Mrs. John Jones," to whom does he have reference? Is this his present or a former wife? Or if he designates "my children" as a class beneficiary, which children does he desire to include? Would adopted or illegitimate children be included? And what about children of a former wife? These difficulties may be avoided with a little care.

and the revocable beneficiary cannot interfere in any manner with the insured's exercise of these rights. The insured may borrow on the policy, surrender the contract for cash value, assign the policy, or anything else that he or she wishes, without any possible legal interference on the part of the beneficiary. The only time the beneficiary acquires a legal interest in the contract is at the death of the insured. But even here the right of the beneficiary to the proceeds is still subject to the conditions of any settlement options selected by the insured.

If the insured designates an irrevocable beneficiary, the right to exercise the privileges granted by the contract, except with the consent of the beneficiary, is lost; the insured loses complete ownership of the policy, which then becomes the joint property of beneficiary and insured. This means that the insured cannot change the designation of the beneficiary without the latter's consent and that the acquisition of a policy loan or an assignment of the contract will require the permission of the beneficiary. However, if the irrevocable beneficiary should predecease the insured, most policies today provide that the interest of the beneficiary shall terminate and that all rights in the contract will revert to the insured. As a consequence, the irrevocable beneficiary does not become the complete owner of the policy; this person's interest is conditionally vested along with that of the insured.

Collateral Assignment In the designation of the beneficiary, the insured (owner) designates the party to receive the policy proceeds at death. The insured can also assign a part of the policy proceeds to another party after the policy is issued. This is often done as security for a loan. Because the assignment of the policy proceeds serves as a collateral for the loan, the transaction is called a *collateral assignment*. Collateral assignment is a partial and usually temporary transfer of ownership rights to the lender (or other party).

Incontestable Clause

One unusual provision that is required in life policies is the *incontestable clause*. The usual policy provision reads as follows: "This policy shall be incontestable after it has been in force during the lifetime of the insured for two years from the date of issue."[3] This means that the validity of the contract cannot be questioned for any reason whatsoever after it has been in force during the lifetime of the insured for two years. The rational for this restriction is based on the long-

term nature of the life insurance contract. It is to assure the person insured and the beneficiary that they will not be harassed by lawsuits long after the original transaction and at a time in which all evidence of the original transaction has disappeared and original witnesses have died. The effect of the clause is not that of justifying a contract involving fraud. The courts justify the clause on the grounds that they are not condoning fraud, but that after an insurance company has been given a reasonable opportunity to investigate the validity of the contract, it should then relinquish its right on the grounds that the social advantages will outweigh the undesirable consequences.[4]

The clause is applicable for two years *during the lifetime of the insured.* This means that the death of the insured during the contestable period suspends the operation of the clause. If this were not the case, if the beneficiary knew that the insured had made material misrepresentations in the application, he or she could wait until the end of the two-year period before submitting the claim, and thus would be protected against voidance of the contract because of the insured's fraudulent acts.[5]

Misstatement of Age Clause

The incontestability clause does not apply to the misstatement of age by the insured. Since the amount of

[3] By statute in most states, the incontestable clause must be a provision in all life insurance contracts, and no state permits the period to exceed two years from the date of issue of the contract. Some insurers, perhaps for competitive reasons, have shortened the contestable period to one year, which is permissible under the law. However, courts have generally refused to uphold a provision that makes the contract incontestable from date of issue, particularly in those cases where fraud is involved.

[4] However, there are a few instances in which fraud would be so abhorrent that impossibility of nullification because of the incontestable clause would be a distinct violation of public policy. For example, courts will permit insurers to deny liability after the contestable period has terminated in those cases in which insurable interest did not exist at the inception of the contract. Liability could also be denied if it is discovered that a healthier person impersonated the applicant in the medical examination, particularly if this person would have been the beneficiary under the policy.

[5] In years past, the incontestable clause did not contain the language "for two years during the lifetime of the insured." In a celebrated case, *Monahan v. Metropolitan Life Insurance Company* (283 Ill. 136, 119 N.E. 68), an insured had died during the contestable period and the company denied liability, alleging breach of warranty. The beneficiary, however, waited until the two-year period had expired and then sued the company. The Supreme Court of Illinois held that the policy was incontestable and ordered the insurance company to make payment.

insurance a given premium will purchase varies with the age of the insured, there is a marked tendency on the part of applicants for insurance to understate their age.[6] The *misstatement of age clause* provides that in the event that the insured has misstated his or her age, the face of the policy will be adjusted to the amount of insurance that the premium paid would have purchased at the correct age. In other words, the amount of the policy is adjusted; the contract is not voided. The typical policy provision reads as follows: "If the age of the insured has been misstated, the amount payable shall be such as the premium paid would have purchased at the correct age."

For example, the premium on a certain policy is $20 per $1000 at age 40. The premium on the same policy is only $15 per $1000 at age 31. The insured in question was a particularly youthful-looking individual and convinced the agent and the insurance company that she was indeed 31 years old, when in reality she was 40. She purchased a $10,000 policy, paying the annual premium of $150. On her death, the insurance company discovered that she was in fact 40 years old when the policy was issued. In this event, the company would pay 15/20 of the face amount, or $7500. This is the amount of insurance the individual could have purchased for the premium that she paid if she had given her correct age.

Grace Period

We have already learned that the consideration for the insurance company's promise is the payment of the first premium by the insured. While subsequent premiums are not a part of the legal consideration, they must be paid when due or the contract will end. A premium due date is designated in the policy, and the premium should be paid on or before that date. The insured may pay the premium annually, semiannually, quarterly, or monthly.

If the insured does not pay the premium on the due date, technically the contract will lapse. The time

of lapsing, however, is subject to a modification that is in the nature of a *grace period* and that is almost universally required by statute. A typical statement of the grace period clause in a life insurance contract is as follows:

> A grace period of 31 days shall be allowed for payment of a premium in default. The policy shall continue in full force during the grace period. If the insured dies during such period, the premium in default shall be paid from the proceeds of this policy.

Thus, for example, if the premium due date is May 1, and the insured does not pay it on this date, the policy allows a grace period of 31 days before lapsing. If he or she should die on May 15, the proceeds of the policy will be paid, but minus the amount of the premium in default. If the insured pays the premium before the end of the grace period, the policy continues in effect as if payment had been on time. The purpose of this clause is not to encourage procrastination in the payment of premiums (although it does), but rather to keep the policy from lapsing when the owner of the policy inadvertently neglects to pay the premium.

Reinstatement

Practically all permanent life insurance contracts permit *reinstatement* of a lapsed policy. However, the reinstatement is subject to certain specific conditions. The provisions of a typical contract read as follows:

> This policy may be reinstated within five years after the date of premium default if it has not been surrendered for its cash value. Reinstatement is subject to (a) receipt of evidence of insurability of the insured satisfactory to the Company; (b) payment of all overdue premiums with interest from the due date of each at the rate of 6 percent per annum; and (c) payments or reinstatement of any indebtedness existing on the date of premium default with interest from that date.

It is apparent that reinstatement is not an unconditional right of the insured. It can be accomplished only if the risk has not changed for the insurance company and only if, by payment of the back premiums with interest, the reinstated policy would have the same reserve as it would have had if the policy had not been lapsed. The conditions necessary are

[6] For rating purposes, life insurers assume that the individual's age changes at the midpoint between birthdays. (Health insurers, in contrast, usually use the applicant's age at his or her last birthday until the next birthday is reached.) Insurers will often agree to backdate a life insurance policy to allow the insured to purchase the coverage at a lower age if the insured pays the premium for the backdated period of coverage. Most state insurance laws limit the period for which a policy may be backdated to not more than six months.

quite specific. First, reinstatement is possible only if at the time of lapsing the insured did not withdraw the cash value of the policy. Withdrawal of the surrender value in cash terminates the contract forever. Second, reinstatement must be effected within a specific time period, normally five years after the lapse. Third, the insured must provide proper evidence of insurability. Not only must his or her health be satisfactory, but other factors such as financial income and morals must not have deteriorated substantially. Fourth, it is obvious also that reinstatement can be effected properly only if the insured pays the overdue premium plus interest and pays or reinstates any indebtedness that may have existed. These conditions may appear burdensome, and some may appear unnecessary. However, they are required if the contract is to be maintained in its original form and are particularly important if the insurance company is to avoid what would otherwise be a substantial element of adverse selection.[7]

Suicide Clause

Almost universally, suicide during a stipulated period after inception of the contract is excluded. A typical *suicide exclusion* reads as follows: "If within two years from the date of issue the insured shall die by suicide, whether sane or insane, the amount payable by the Company shall be the premiums paid." Some companies, however, limit the suicide exclusion period to one year. The reason for the exclusion is, of course, that of protecting the insurer against a person who might purchase the insurance with the deliberate purpose of committing suicide.[8] The assumption of the two years is that during this length of time, if the insured has not committed sui-

cide, the reason for doing so will probably have disappeared. After the exclusion period is over, death by suicide becomes just another cause of death, and coverage is justified on the assumption that it should be provided for as a hazard of life to which practically all people are subject.[9]

Aviation Exclusions

At one time, virtually all life insurance policies excluded death resulting from aviation. Today, most policies cover loss from aviation accidents, although an additional premium may apply in the case of private pilots and the pilots and crews of commercial airlines. The single area in which *aviation exclusions* are still found is with respect to military aircraft, and even here the exclusion can usually be eliminated for an additional premium.

War Clause

During times of war, or when war appears imminent, insurance companies usually insert a clause in their policies that provides for a return of premium plus interest rather than payment of the face amount of the policy if the insured dies under excluded circumstances.

War exclusions may be divided into two classes: exclusions based on *status,* and exclusions of *results.* Under a status-type clause, death while serving as a member of the military is excluded, regardless of cause. Under the results-type exclusion, coverage is denied only if the death results directly from war.[10]

The purpose of the war clause is not so much to avoid payment to beneficiaries of insureds who are killed in the war as to prevent adverse selection. If the clause were not put into policies sold during wartime, those who faced a higher chance of loss would obtain larger amounts of insurance than they

[7] The question may arise concerning the application of the incontestability clause to the reinstated policy. Is the entire contract subject to contest for two years after the reinstatement, or is only the information concerning the reinstatement subject to contest, or is neither applicable? There is some difference of opinion in the courts. However, the majority opinion is that a reinstated contract is contestable for the same period as prescribed in the original contract, but only with respect to the information supplied for the reinstatement. Representations in the original application for the policy may not be contested.

[8] The courts have evolved the doctrine of *presumption against suicide,* which states that the love of life in and of itself is sufficient grounds for a presumption against suicide. The burden of proof of suicide is on the company, and the insurance company must prove conclusively that the death was a suicide or pay the face of the policy.

[9] Some states have statutes that impose restrictions on the right of the insurer to avoid liability if the insured commits suicide. In Missouri, for example, the law does not permit any exclusion at all. The insurer can deny liability only if it can prove that the insured contemplated suicide at the time the policy was purchased. Needless to say, this intent is difficult, if not impossible, to prove, so insurers in Missouri do not even attempt to do so.

[10] *Hazle v Liberty Life Insurance Company,* 186 S.E. 2d 245, 257 S.C. 456 (1972).

might otherwise purchase. The result would be selection against the company.[11]

SETTLEMENT OPTIONS

The average person, in thinking about the settlement of life insurance policies, normally thinks of a lump sum being paid to the beneficiary of the insured. While the vast majority of death claims are paid in a lump sum, a portion of life insurance death benefits is disbursed in some other manner. In addition to the lump-sum settlement, there are certain *optional modes of settlement* that may be used to pay out the proceeds of the policy. Normally, the owner (who in most cases is also the insured) elects the option under which the proceeds of the policy are to be paid. If no election is in force when the policy becomes payable, the beneficiary is entitled to select the option desired. Unless the insured (owner) has made provision that denies the right, the beneficiary may also change to some other mode of settlement.

Interest Option

Under the *interest option,* the proceeds of the policy may be left with the insurance company, to be paid out at a later time, in which case only the interest on the principal amount is paid to the beneficiary. A minimum rate of interest is guaranteed in the policy, but it should be noted that under participating options, many insurance companies pay excess interest above the guaranteed rate if additional interest is earned by the company.[12] Normally, the interest option is selected when there are proceeds from other policies available for income, and the principal of the policy is not needed until some later time.

Installments for a Fixed Period

The insured may specify (or the beneficiary may elect) to have the proceeds of the policy paid out over some specified interval. The insurance company simply computes how much it can pay out of the policy proceeds and the interest on them during each of the required periods so that the entire principal and interest will have been distributed by the end of the period. The rate of interest credited to the unpaid balance is specified in the policy, but, as in the case of the interest option above, excess interest may be payable under participating policies. The same is true of the other settlement options discussed in the paragraphs that follow. A typical schedule of *installments for a fixed period* is reproduced in Table 14.1. The longer the period of time for which the company promises to pay the installments, the smaller each installment must be. According to Table 14.1, a $100,000 policy would provide $1812 per month if paid over a 5-year period and only $983 if paid out over a 10-year period. These payments (and the other payments discussed below) are based on the contract's minimum guaranteed interest rate, which is 3.5 percent. If the insurer's investment earnings are higher than the guaranteed minimum, all installments will be increased to reflect the higher earned interest.

The fixed period selected may be any number of years, usually up to 30. This option is most valuable where the chief consideration is to provide income during some definite period, such as the child-raising years.

Installments of a Fixed Amount

The owner of the policy (or the beneficiary) may elect to have the proceeds of the policy paid out in payments of some fixed amount ($500, $1000, $1500, and so on) per month for as long as the principal plus interest on the unpaid portion of the principal will last. Since the amount of each installment is the controlling factor under this option, the length of time for which the payments will last will vary with the amount of the policy. In a sense, the *installment-of-fixed-amount option* is similar to the installment for a fixed period. Under one option, the amount to be paid determines the length of time the benefits will last, and under the other, the length of time for which the benefits are to be paid determines the amount of the benefits.

Life Income Options

In addition to the options listed, the policy gives the insured's beneficiary the right to have the proceeds paid out in the form of an annuity. In such cases, the proceeds of the policy are used to make a

[11] Deaths in past wars have not proved to be catastrophic for insurers. After each of the wars in which the United States has been engaged in the twentieth century, insurance companies found that they could cover the deaths that were excluded under the war clause of policies issued and paid the face amount of these policies retroactively.

[12] For example, while most policies issued today guarantee interest of 3 percent, 3.5 percent, or 4 percent, most companies are actually paying 7 percent or 8 percent. In addition, on some interest-sensitive policies (discussed in Chapter 16), higher rates may be payable.

TABLE 14.1 Installments for a Fixed Period

	Minimum Monthly Installments for Each $1000 of Net Proceeds				
Period (Years)	Monthly Payment	Period (Years)	Monthly Payment	Period (Years)	Monthly Payment
1	$84.65	11	$9.09	21	$5.56
2	43.05	12	8.46	22	5.39
3	29.19	13	7.94	23	5.24
4	22.27	14	7.49	24	5.07
5	18.12	15	7.10	25	4.93
6	15.35	16	6.76	26	4.84
7	13.38	17	6.47	27	4.73
8	11.90	18	6.20	28	4.63
9	10.75	19	5.97	29	4.53
10	9.83	20	5.75	30	4.45

single-premium purchase of an annuity. Although the various life insurance companies list many life income options, they may be classified into four basic categories.

Straight Life Income Under a *straight life income option,* the proceeds of the policy are paid to the beneficiary on the basis of life expectancy. The beneficiary is entitled to receive a specified amount for as long as he or she lives, but nothing more. If the beneficiary dies during the first year of the pay period, the company has fulfilled its obligations, and no further payments are made. Beneficiaries who live longer than the average are offset by those who live only a short time.

Life Income with Period Certain Under this option, the beneficiary is paid a *life income* for as long as he or she lives, but a minimum number of payments is guaranteed. If the beneficiary dies before the number of payments guaranteed has been made, the payments are continued to a contingent beneficiary. Normally, the *period certain,* as the time for which payments are guaranteed is known, is 5, 10, 15, or 20 years.

Life Income with Refund Under the *life income with refund option,* the beneficiary is paid a life income for as long as he or she lives, and if the policy proceeds have not been paid out by the time the beneficiary dies, the remainder of the proceeds will be paid to a contingent beneficiary. The life income with refund may be a life income with installment refund, in which case installments are continued until the contingent beneficiary has received the difference between the original policy proceeds and the amount

received by the direct beneficiary, or it may be a cash refund. Under the cash refund, installments do not continue to the contingent beneficiary, but instead that individual is paid a lump sum.

Joint and Survivor Income The *joint and survivor income option* is a somewhat specialized option, designed to provide income to two payees. The payments continue after the first of the two payees has died and only stops with the death of the second. A modification of this plan provides that the amount of the benefit will be decreased when the first of the two payees dies. The benefit to the surviving payee will then be either two-thirds or one-half (or some other fraction) of the original income amount. The benefit is computed on the basis of two lives, its amount depending on the age of both beneficiaries.

Payments The amount payable under any one of the life income options depends on the age and sex of the beneficiary, plus the plan selected. For obvious reasons, the company cannot afford to pay as high a monthly income if it also guarantees to pay it for some guaranteed period of time. When a period certain is selected, the mortality gains under the annuity are eliminated for whatever length the period certain is. Table 14.2 illustrates a typical life income option table for single lives and Table 14.3 details a joint and survivor life income option.

To illustrate the operation of Table 14.2, let us assume that the policy proceeds amount to $100,000 and that the beneficiary is a 65-year-old female. Since the life expectancy of women is greater than is that of men, a given number of proceeds dollars will provide a higher monthly income to a male than to a female. If our 65-year-old female beneficiary selects a life

TABLE 14.2 **Single Life—Life Income Payments**

	Minimum Monthly Life Income Payments per $1000 Proceeds								
Male	*Chosen Period (Years)*					*Chosen Period (Years)*			
Adjusted Age	*Zero*	*10*	*20*	*Refund*	*Female Adjusted Age*	*Zero*	*10*	*20*	*Refund*
55	$4.99	$4.91	$4.66	$4.73	55	$4.54	$4.51	$4.38	$4.40
56	5.09	5.00	4.72	4.81	56	4.62	4.58	4.44	4.47
57	5.20	5.10	4.78	4.90	57	4.71	4.66	4.51	4.54
58	5.32	5.20	4.85	4.99	58	4.80	4.75	4.57	4.62
59	5.44	5.31	4.91	5.08	59	4.90	4.84	4.64	4.70
60	5.57	5.42	4.97	5.18	60	5.00	4.93	4.70	4.78
61	5.71	5.54	5.04	5.29	61	5.11	5.03	4.77	4.87
62	5.86	5.67	5.10	5.40	62	5.23	5.14	4.84	4.96
63	6.02	5.80	5.16	5.51	63	5.36	5.25	4.91	5.06
64	6.20	5.94	5.22	5.63	64	5.49	5.37	4.98	5.17
65	6.38	6.08	5.28	5.76	65	5.64	5.50	5.05	5.28
66	6.54	6.23	5.33	5.90	66	5.79	5.63	5.12	5.39
67	6.70	6.38	5.38	6.04	67	5.94	5.77	5.19	5.52
68	6.87	6.54	5.43	6.19	68	6.09	5.91	5.25	5.65
69	7.05	6.71	5.48	6.35	69	6.25	6.07	5.32	5.79
70	7.21	6.87	5.52	6.52	70	6.42	6.23	5.37	5.94
71	7.40	7.05	5.55	6.69	71	6.59	6.40	5.43	6.09
72	7.58	7.21	5.59	6.88	72	6.78	6.58	5.48	6.26
73	7.77	7.40	5.62	7.07	73	6.96	6.76	5.52	6.44
74	7.95	7.57	5.64	7.28	74	7.16	6.95	5.57	6.63
75	8.14	7.75	5.66	7.49	75	7.35	7.14	5.60	6.83
76	8.32	7.92	5.68	7.72	76	7.56	7.34	5.63	7.04
77	8.49	8.09	5.70	7.96	77	7.77	7.54	5.66	7.26
78	8.84	8.26	5.71	8.21	78	7.97	7.74	5.68	7.51
79	9.18	8.42	5.72	8.47	79	8.18	7.94	5.70	7.76
80	9.51	8.57	5.73	8.74	80	8.37	8.13	5.71	8.03
81	9.84	8.71	5.74	9.04	81	8.57	8.32	5.72	8.32
82	10.18	8.85	5.74	9.34	82	8.93	8.50	5.73	8.61
83	10.49	8.97	5.75	9.65	83	9.28	8.67	5.74	8.93
84	10.82	9.09	5.75	9.98	84	9.62	8.83	5.74	9.27
85 and over	11.13	9.20	5.75	10.34	85 and over	9.96	8.97	5.75	9.62

income without a period certain, she will receive a guaranteed payment of $564 a month for life, but payments will cease on her death, regardless of the amount that has been paid out. She may select a life income with 10 years certain, in which case the policy will pay $550 a month for as long as she lives, but at least for 10 years. The slight decrease in the amount payable under the 10-year certain option as compared with the payment without a period certain results from the fact that there is no mortality gain to survivors during the first 10 years. If a 20-year period certain is selected, the amount of the monthly benefit is reduced even more. Under the 20-year certain option, the monthly benefit amount will be only $505. Finally, the woman might select a life income

with installment refund. Under this option, the insurer will pay her $528 a month for life, and at least until the full $100,000 has been paid out. Note that at the age specified, the amount payable under the installment refund option is slightly less than the amount payable under the life income with 10 years certain, but slightly more than the amount payable under the life income with 20 years certain. This is because the guarantee to pay 20 years certain calls for a commitment to pay for a greater number of years than would be required to consume the original $100,000.

Table 14.3 indicates the payment that will be made under a joint and survivor life income option. Under this particular agreement, the company will make

TABLE 14.3 **Joint and Survivor Life Income Option**

Minimum Monthly Joint and Survivor Life Income with Payments Certain for 10 Years per $1000 of Proceeds

Male Adjusted Age	Female Adjusted Age						
	55	60	65	70	75	80	85 and Over
55	$4.16	$4.34	$4.51	$4.65	$4.76	$4.84	$4.88
60	4.26	4.51	4.75	4.98	5.16	5.29	5.37
65	4.35	4.65	4.98	5.31	5.61	5.84	5.98
70	4.41	4.76	5.17	5.62	6.07	6.44	6.68
75	4.46	4.84	5.32	5.88	6.48	7.03	7.42
80	4.48	4.89	5.41	6.05	6.79	7.52	8.07
85 and over	4.50	4.92	5.46	6.15	6.99	7.85	8.53

payments of the specified amount until both individuals have died, but at least for 10 years. For example, assuming the same $100,000 in policy proceeds, with male and female beneficiaries both age 65, payment would be made in the amount of $498 a month. Payments would continue until the second payee has died—that is, jointly and to the survivor. If both payees die before the end of the 10-year period, payments will continue to a contingent beneficiary. Under other contracts, provisions might be made for a reduction in the benefit at the death of the first beneficiary.

Taxation of Policy Proceeds under Various Settlement Options

As a general rule, benefits payable to a beneficiary under a life insurance policy are not subject to taxation under the federal income tax, except insofar as the benefits are composed in part of interest on the policy proceeds. When a life insurer pays death benefits to a beneficiary in a series of installments (under one of the installment options or a life income option), a part of each payment is considered a nontaxable death benefit and a part is treated as taxable interest income.[13] For example, let us say that the proceeds of the insured's life insurance policy amounted to $100,000. The spouse elects to take the proceeds under an installment option and receives $11,796 a year for 10 years. The $1796 in excess of the death benefit received each year is taxable as interest.

When proceeds are payable under one of the life income options, the taxable interest is determined by computing the portion of each installment that represents payment of principle, based on the beneficiary's life expectancy as indicated by *gender-neutral* mortality tables prescribed by the IRS. The difference between the amount of the installment and the excludable principal is taxable as interest income.

[13] Prior to the Tax Reform Act of 1986 (TRA-86), the first $1000 in excess of the amount of the death benefit in any taxable year was excluded from gross income if paid to a surviving spouse. Under the new law, this $1000 interest exemption is repealed, and the entire amount of interest payable under installments is taxable.

IMPORTANT CONCEPTS TO REMEMBER

binding receipt
entire contract clause
incontestable clause
misstatement of age clause
primary beneficiary
contingent beneficiary
direct beneficiary

revocable beneficiary
grace period
reinstatement provision
suicide exclusion
settlement options
life income with period certain
life income with refund option

life income with installment refund
installments for a fixed period
installments of a fixed amount
interest option
ownership clause
straight life income option
joint and survivor income

QUESTIONS FOR REVIEW

1. Some life insurance contract provisions are designed for the protection of the insured and some for the protection of the insurance company. Indicate whether each of the following provisions is designed for the benefit of the insured, the company, or both: (a) the entire contract provision; (b) the incontestability provision; (c) the suicide provision; (d) the misstatement of age provision.

2. Explain the difference among the insured, the owner, and the beneficiary of a life insurance policy. Give a specific example in which each party might be a different person.

3. Briefly distinguish between a *direct beneficiary* and a *contingent beneficiary;* between a *revocable* and an *irrevocable beneficiary.*

4. Explain in detail the obligation of the insurer under a *straight life income option, life income with ten years certain,* and *life income with installment refund.*

5. Settlement options of life insurance policies include *lump sum, the interest option, installments for a fixed period, installments of a fixed amount,* and *life income options.* Explain each.

6. What are the rights of a person who is designated as an irrevocable beneficiary?

7. Describe the taxation of life insurance proceeds payable under the policy settlement options.

8. What is meant by reinstatement? Under what conditions may a policy that has been lapsed be reinstated?

9. At age 30, John Doe applies for a life insurance policy, stating that he is 28 years old. The misstatement is discovered at the time of his death. Does it make any difference if the misstatement is discovered before or after the end of the incontestability period? Why?

10. The settlement option providing a life income with cash or installment refund seems too good to be true. How can the insurance company agree to pay for as long as the beneficiary-annuitant lives and also agree to pay out at least the face amount of the policy?

QUESTIONS FOR DISCUSSION

1. The incontestability clause seems to permit fraud to go unpunished. Do you think that this exception is justified? On what grounds?

2. John Jones dies, leaving $100,000 in life insurance policy proceeds to his widow. Widow Jones elects to have the $100,000 paid out under the life income option. At the end of the first year, after having received $7176 in income, widow Jones is struck by a car and killed. Selection of a straight life income option was a foolish mistake on her part. Discuss.

3. The interest rate guaranteed under the settlement options of a life insurance policy seems incredibly low in comparison with alternatives available to the beneficiary. Does the guarantee of 3.5 percent or 4 percent constitute undue enrichment of the insurer at the expense of the beneficiaries?

4. The exposure of insurers to adverse selection is not restricted to the underwriting process. To what extent, if any, is the insurer subject to any form of adverse selection under policy settlement options?

5. On January 1, 1997, Sam Smith gave his application for life insurance to his agent, including his first premium payment. On the application, he neglected to notify the company of a mild heart attack he had suffered eight years earlier. On February 15, he received notification from the company that his application had been accepted. He failed to pay the premium due on January 1, 1999, and on January 30, 1999, he died of a massive coronary heart infarction. Discuss in detail the liability of the insurance company, with reference to specific clauses that apply in this instance.

SUGGESTIONS FOR ADDITIONAL READING

Black, Kenneth, Jr., and Harold D. Skipper, Jr. *Life Insurance,* 13th ed. Englewood Cliffs, N.J.: Prentice-Hall, 2000. Chapters 9, 10.

Crawford, Muriel L., and William T. Beadles. *Law and the Life Insurance Contract,* 6th ed. Homewood, Ill.: Richard D. Irwin, 1989.

Graves, Edward E., ed. *McGill's Life Insurance.* Bryn Mawr, Pa.: The American College, 1994. Chapters 10, 25.

Hallman, G. Victor, and Karen L. Hamilton. *Personal Insurance: Life, Health & Retirement.* Malvern, Pa.: American Institute for CPCU, 1994. Chapter 4.

WEB SITES TO EXPLORE

American Council of Life Insurance http://www.acli.com/
American Society of CLU & ChFC http://www.agents-online.com/ASCLU/web/index.html
Insurance News Network http://www.insure.com/
Newsedge News Page http://www.newspage.com/browse/46622/

CHAPTER 15

THE LIFE INSURANCE CONTRACT—OTHER PROVISIONS

■

Can we ever have too much of a good thing?

— CERVANTES
Don Quixote

CHAPTER OBJECTIVES

When you have finished this chapter, you should be able to

- Describe the nonforfeiture options in life insurance contracts and explain the source of these values
- Identify and describe the dividend options in life insurance policies and explain the source of dividends
- Explain the importance of the disability waiver of premium provision and the guaranteed insurability option

In addition to those provisions discussed in the last chapter that are included in all life insurance policies, there are a number of provisions that are included only in certain contracts or that are optionally included at the request of the insured. These provisions are the subject matter of this chapter. First, we will examine the *nonforfeiture values,* which are included in those policies that accumulate a cash value. In addition, we will discuss the *dividend provisions* that are found in participating contracts. Finally, we will consider a number of optional provisions that

can be inserted into most policies to provide additional benefits or to deal with special situations.

NONFORFEITURE VALUES

As you will recall from the discussion of the grace period in the preceding chapter, if the insured fails to pay the premium within the grace period, the policy will lapse. Years ago life insurance policies had no nonforfeiture values and, in the event of a missed

premium, the policy was terminated with no return to the insured. Some critics argued that, considering the overpayments that the insured had made under the level premium system, this was unfair to the policyholder and resulted in unjust enrichment of the insurer. Under the Standard Nonforfeiture Law, today, at any time after the policy has begun to develop a cash value, the insured may discontinue premium payments and obtain the return of a part of the overpayment. Normally, policies do not begin to accumulate a cash value until after the end of the second policy year, and although there is a relationship between the policy reserve and the cash value, the cash value of the policy rarely equals the full amount of the policy reserve until the policy has been in force for 10 to 15 years.

On deciding to stop payment of premiums, the insured is entitled to the cash value of the policy, which may be taken in one of three ways:

- The insured may take the cash listed in the table of nonforfeiture values.
- The insured may take a paid-up policy in some reduced amount. The amount of the reduced policy will be the amount the cash value would purchase as a net single premium.
- The policy may be continued in force as term insurance for as long as the cash value will permit. The cash value is used to make a net single-premium purchase of a term policy in the face amount of the policy. If the insured does not request another option, the company will normally provide extended term insurance.

Table 15.1 is a typical table of nonforfeiture options. It lists the guaranteed values at the end of each policy year. The law requires that these values be listed for at least the first 20 years of the policy, but they are also commonly given for advanced ages of the insured.

Cash Option

To illustrate the operation of the surrender provision, let us assume that Mr. X purchases an ordinary life policy with a face value of $100,000 at age 35. Let us further assume that he lapses the policy after 10 years and chooses to withdraw the *cash surrender value.* The insurance company would send him a

TABLE 15.1 **Nonforfeiture Table (Dollar Values per $1000 of Face Amount)**

End of Policy Year	Cash or Loan Value	Paid-Up Insurance	Extended Term Insurance	
			Years	Days
1	$ 0.00	$ 0	0	0
2	10.78	50	3	165
3	22.01	98	6	118
4	33.71	144	8	256
5	45.88	187	10	268
6	58.52	229	12	162
7	71.65	268	14	37
8	85.28	305	15	284
9	99.42	341	17	44
10	114.11	374	18	72
11	129.33	406	19	13
12	145.15	437	19	250
13	161.56	466	20	70
14	178.60	493	20	213
15	196.29	519	20	321
16	214.66	544	21	31
17	233.70	568	21	77
18	253.41	590	21	96
19	273.80	611	21	92
20	294.86	631	21	70
Age 60	383.28	718	19	302
Age 65	475.45	788	18	36
Age 70	567.41	844	16	48

Paid-up additions and dividend accumulations increase the cash values; indebtedness decreases them.

check for $11,411.[1] If he should decide to drop the policy and take the surrender value in cash at age 65, the guaranteed amount would be $47,545.[2]

The Standard Nonforfeiture Law requires that a surrender value be made available in cash, but it also permits a company to delay or postpone payment of the cash value for a period of six months after surrender of the policy. This is known as a delay clause and is now mandatory in all policies. Its purpose is to prevent

[1] Remember that the values in the table are for each $1000 of insurance, so if the insured has a $100,000 policy, the cash value and paid-up policy amount will be multiplied by 100.

[2] The student should note that the figures used are the guaranteed surrender values. If the policy is participating, that is, if dividends are paid on the contract, and if the dividends are left with the insurance company, the actual cash surrender value could be substantially greater than those shown in the table.

substantial investment losses in case many insureds cash in their contracts in a relatively short period, as might occur during a major economic recession. Insurers pay little attention to the clause and perhaps would use it only under the most unusual circumstances.

A typical policy provision specifying the *cash surrender value* is as follows:

> The cash value at any time when all premiums due have been paid shall be the reserve on this policy less the prescribed deduction, plus the reserve on any paid-up additions and the amount of any dividend accumulations. The owner may surrender this policy for its cash value less any indebtedness. The insurance shall terminate upon receipt at the Home Office of the policy and a written surrender of all claims. The Company may defer paying the cash value for a period not exceeding six months from the date of surrender. If payment is deferred 30 days or more, interest at the rate of 3 percent per annum from the date of surrender to the date of payment shall be allowed on the cash value less any indebtedness.

The six-month delay provision is statutory. It was adopted in 1934 when bank closings during the Great Depression led to fears that insurers would experience the same "runs" on cash values that had led to the closing of many banks.

If the insured surrenders the policy for its cash value, the entire contract is terminated and the company has no further obligations.[3]

Paid-Up Reduced Amount

The second surrender option is paid-up whole-life or endowment insurance. Here, in lieu of obtaining the cash surrender value in cash, with complete termination of any insurance, the insured will receive a reduced amount of paid-up insurance that will be payable under the same conditions as the original policy. The *paid-up policy of reduced amount* provision in a typical policy reads as follows:

> In lieu of the extended term insurance, this policy may be continued in force as participating paid-up life insurance. The insurance will be for such amount as the cash value will purchase as a net single premium at the attained age of the insured. Any indebt-

edness shall remain as a lien against the policy. Such paid-up insurance may be requested before or within three months after the date of premium default. A request shall be made by written notice filed at the Home Office.

Referring back to Table 15.1, if the insured lapses the $100,000 ordinary life policy at the end of 10 years, the cash value could be used as a net single premium at his or her attained age to purchase a paid-up whole-life contract with a face value of $37,400. At age 65, the reduced paid-up insurance would be $78,800. The paid-up contract will have a cash and loan value on the same general terms as those of the original policy. If the original policy is a limited-payment contract, the paid-up insurance of reduced amount will be whole life. But if the original contract is endowment insurance, protection in a reduced amount will be granted only for the remainder of the endowment period. If the insured survives the endowment period, the payment at that time will also be less.

This option perhaps has its greatest attraction for older insureds who no longer have a substantial need for life insurance protection. To be relieved of the burden of continued premium payments and still have a substantial amount of life insurance in force, the policy could be lapsed and the paid-up policy of reduced amount option selected.

Extended Term Insurance

The third surrender option is paid-up term insurance, and the benefit is commonly referred to as *extended term insurance*. Here, the amount of the term insurance will be the same as the face value of the original contract. The variable will be the length of the term period rather than the amount of the insurance, and the length of the period will be that which the cash value used as a net single premium will purchase at the insured's attained age. For example, Table 15.1 shows that if the insured lapses the policy at the end of the tenth year and chooses the extended term option, he or she would have a paid-up term policy with a face value of $100,000 for a term period of 18 years and 72 days. The contract could continue, then, into the insured's sixty-fourth year of age. If the policyholder should die during this term, the insurer will pay the $100,000 to the beneficiary. But if the policyholder outlives the term, the commitment of the insurance company will be terminated.

[3] At the time that the policy is surrendered, the excess of cash surrender value over net premiums paid is taxable as income.

The extended term option normally subjects the insurer to an element of adverse selection. Many insureds in poor health, who must discontinue premium payments, are inclined to select the extended term option. As a result, the death rates under extended term insurance tend to be greater than normal. For this reason, insurance companies are permitted to calculate net premiums for extended term on mortality factors higher than those shown in the mortality table. However, because of competition, most insurance companies have not taken advantage of this provision in the Standard Nonforfeiture Law.

Policy Loan Provisions

One of the most important secondary benefits of a life insurance contract is the *policy loan provision.* The insured may, at any time, obtain a loan from the insurance company, usually equal to the full amount of the cash surrender value, using the policy as collateral for the loan. The loan provision is subject to a *delay clause* similar to that previously discussed in connection with the cash surrender value, and under which the company may delay making the loan for up to six months. As in the case of surrender, the option of delay is rarely exercised.

The loan will bear interest at some percentage stipulated in the policy (5 or 6 percent in older policies but up to 8 percent in newer contracts) or the loan may be subject to a variable rate. During the 1970s, insurers experienced significant disintermediation as policyholders took cash value out of their life insurance policies to invest it elsewhere at higher rates.[4] Because life insurance rates explicitly consider the investment income that will be earned on prepaid premiums, the lower earnings realized on policy loans created a subsidy from nonborrowers to borrowers. In an effort to address this problem, the NAIC adopted a new *Model Policy Loan Interest Rate Law* in December 1980, which permits variable-interest-rate policy loans. Some variation of the model law has been enacted by every state. As

explained later, the existence of a loan under a participating policy may affect the policy dividends.

Although some insurers charge interest in advance, the more common practice is to charge interest at the end of the year. If the interest is not paid when due, it is added to the policy loan. If the insured dies while the indebtedness exists, the loan plus interest will be deducted from the proceeds of the policy.

An insured who becomes financially embarrassed and is in need of temporary funds may borrow on his or her life insurance policy. For example, turning back to Table 15.1, on the $100,000 ordinary life policy purchased at age 35, the insured could borrow as much as $11,411 if the policy had been in effect for 10 years and could do so merely by assigning the contract to the insurance company as security for the loan. The advantage of this right should be obvious. First, it would be practically impossible for the insured to borrow elsewhere and pay only a true annual rate of 6 to 8 percent interest. Compare this with the rate that one would have to pay the XYZ Finance Company; perhaps 18 percent or more. Second, the insurance company cannot refuse the loan, regardless of its purpose. Finally, there is no legal obligation to repay the loan, and the insured will not be hounded for repayment as might be the case with an overdue loan from a finance company.

The policy loan right also carries some substantial disadvantages. The most important is, of course, the ease with which the loan can be acquired and the lack of legal pressure for repayment. If the insured does not repay the loan, the indebtedness will constitute a lien against the contract to be subtracted from the proceeds when the insured dies. This, of course, could defeat the purpose of the life insurance.

Automatic Premium Loan

Most policies today contain an *automatic premium loan* provision. A typical provision reads as follows:

> A premium loan shall be automatically granted to pay a premium in default. A premium for any other frequency permitted by this policy shall be loaned whenever the loan value, less any indebtedness, is sufficient for such premium but is insufficient for a loan of the premium in default. A revocation or reinstatement of this provision shall be made by written notice filed at the Home Office.

If this provision is included in the contract and the insured does not pay the premium on the due

[4] The term *disintermediation* refers to the risk facing insurance companies, banks, savings and loan associations, and other financial intermediaries who derive their investable funds from depositors or other groups, and then invest those funds in longterm obligations. The "risk" is that the depositors may decide to withdraw their funds, requiring the institution to liquidate investments at a loss. For insurance companies, disintermediation risk arises from the possibility that policyholders may borrow the cash value in their contracts or cash the policies in to obtain funds for more attractive investments.

date, the company automatically will pay the premium and charge it against the cash value of the policy. The loan will bear interest at the rate applicable to policy loans as stipulated in the contract. The effect of the provision is to extend the original face amount of the insurance, decreased by the amount of the loan plus interest, for as long as the remaining cash value is sufficient to permit the advance of an additional premium. This provision may be very beneficial for the policyholder, particularly for one who forgets to pay the premium within the grace period or one who cannot pay the current premium because of financial difficulties. The most important aspect is that the policy does not lapse. When the insured is again financially able, he or she can start paying the premiums and will not be subject to the conditions imposed in the event of a reinstatement. Another advantage is that any special coverages such as double indemnity and disability coverages will remain in force.[5] In addition, if the policy is participating, dividends will continue to be paid, which would not be true under the extended term option. After the policy has been in effect for a period of time, it is possible for the increase in cash value each year to exceed the premium payment. In these cases, the policy is capable of sustaining itself, for a loan against the cash value to pay the premium permits an increase in the cash value that is sufficient to pay the next year's premium. Of course, the amount of protection provided by the policy is decreased by the amount of any loans outstanding, so the automatic premium loan provision must be considered as a device that can consume protection under the policy. There are also disadvantages in the automatic premium loan provision. Most important, if the premium payments are not resumed by the insured and the cash value of the policy is low, the contract may eventually terminate. It is even possible that the period in which the policy will remain in force under automatic premium loan will be shorter than under the extended term option, and the amount of insurance coverage will be considerably less. The automatic premium loan feature also has the disadvantage of being used on the slightest provocation. An insured who has the choice of paying the current premium or using the money to finance a Friday-night party may be inclined to choose the

party—of course, with the solemn promise that the loan will be paid off in the near future.

Most companies now offer this provision, but it is optional, and an election must be made at the time the policy is taken out or at least before the premium is in default. Various companies handle the option differently: Some specify that the insured must notify the company if he or she wants the provision to apply, while others make the provision automatic and the insured must specify if it is not wanted.

DIVIDEND PROVISIONS

Participating policies, as we have noted previously, are those under which the insured is entitled to participate in the divisible surplus of the company. Obviously, only participating policies on which dividends are payable will include the provisions discussed here. The dividends payable to the insured reflect the difference between the premium charged for a given class of policies and their actual cost based on the experience of the insurer. Favorable deviations from the assumptions used in the calculation of the gross premium are the source of the surplus from which the policy dividends are paid. The savings in mortality, the excess interest, and the savings in expenses will yield a surplus each year. A portion of this gain will be transferred to company surplus or to a special-contingency reserve to be used if necessary for future losses arising from adverse-mortality experience, extremely low interest earnings, or unusually high operating expenses. The balance will be distributed as dividends.

In some companies, the amount of the dividend payable on a particular policy may reflect the existence of a policy loan. Because policy loans transfer to policyholders funds that would otherwise be invested elsewhere, they represent an opportunity to cost to the insurer. Under a system called *direct recognition* the dividend is reduced by recognizing the difference between the interest on the policy loan and the amount of investment income that would otherwise be earned on the funds. When an individual has a fixed interest rate policy loan, and borrows at a rate lower than the insurance company can earn, direct recognition causes his or her dividends to decrease. If that same individual has a variable loan rate, the dividends generally continue as if no borrowing took place. Failure to reflect the existence of

[5] These coverages of the original contract will not remain in force in the surrender options of paid-up policies of reduced amount and extended term.

outstanding loans in the dividend scale would result in a subsidy from nonborrowers to borrowers.[6]

The policyholder is provided with several dividend options. The dividend may be taken in cash, applied toward the payment of the policy's current premium, applied to the purchase of paid-up additions to the policy, or left on deposit with the insurance company to accumulate at interest.

The policyholder normally makes an election as to the disposition of the dividends when purchasing the policy. However, a new election may be made at any time with just one possible qualification: If the insured does not elect to use the dividends to purchase paid-up additions to the face of the policy or one-year term insurance at the inception of the contract, he or she must then file evidence of insurability if this option is selected at some later date.

Several of the options are so simple as to require little explanation. If the insured chooses to receive the dividends in cash, the insurer will send him or her a dividend check, on each anniversary of the contract, the money to be used in any way at all. If the dividend is to be applied toward payment of the next premium, the insurer will indicate the amount of the dividend on the premium due notice and the insured will remit only the difference between the gross premium due and the amount of the dividend. If the insured chooses to use the dividend to purchase paid-up additions to the policy, the dividend will be used as a net single premium at his or her attained age to purchase whatever amount it could purchase at that age. The additions will be payable under the same conditions as the basic policy, that is, as whole-life or endowment insurance. The paid-up additions, like the basic policy, are participating, and they may be surrendered for their cash value at any time.

Some insurers offer still another dividend option—generally referred to as the *fifth dividend option*—under which dividends may be used as a single premium to purchase one-year term insurance at net rates. This is an attractive alternative to the insured, permitting an increase in protection at favorable rates.

The insured may also choose to leave the dividends on deposit with the insurance company. Interest at some guaranteed rate will be paid on the deposit and the insured will also share in the company's excess interest earnings.[7] If the insured should die, the accumulated deposits will be paid in addition to the face of the basic contract. If the policy is surrendered, the deposits will be added to the surrender value; they may also be added to the face amount of the paid-up policy of reduced amount or to extended term.

Should the dividends be left with the company either as deposits or to purchase paid-up additions, it is possible for the insured to convert the basic contract into a fully paid-up policy at an earlier date than that called for by the terms of the original contract. For example, an ordinary life policy might be fully paid up at age 55; a 20-payment life might be paid in 15 years; and an endowment at age 65, purchased at age 25, might be paid up by age 50.

A policy is considered to be fully paid up when the reserve of the basic contract plus the value of the dividend additions or deposits equals the net single premium for the policy in question at the insured's attained age. The insurance company will inform the policyholder when this point is reached. The insured will then surrender the paid-up additions or the deposits, and from this time on will have no premium payment obligation on the policy.

After the original policy has become fully paid up, it will continue to be participating. It is possible that, in time, the reserve value of the basic policy plus the reserve value of the dividend additions or deposits will equal the face of the policy. In this case, the policy matures as an endowment and the insured may obtain a check for the face of the policy if he or she so desires.

IMPORTANT OPTIONAL PROVISIONS

Disability Waiver of Premium Provision

The *disability waiver of premium provision* is one of the most important options available to a person purchasing life insurance. Under the provisions of this coverage, the company agrees to waive all premiums coming due after the insured has become totally and permanently disabled. The benefits of this provision should be obvious. Once an individual has

[6] Although most companies do not reduce dividends unless and until a policy owner borrows, some companies reduce the dividends on policies that have fixed loan interest rates, regardless of the actual borrowing that occurs.

[7] This interest will be taxable as income to the insured. The dividends themselves are obviously not taxable, for they are not income, but merely the return of an overcharge.

become disabled, it will undoubtedly be difficult, if not impossible, for the person to obtain insurance coverage; it is therefore essential to be able to continue the existing coverage. In essence, this benefit provides for the waiving of all premiums on the contract during the period of disability and the continuation of the contract as if the premiums were paid. This means that the cash value will increase and the dividends will be paid to the insured just as if payment of the premiums was continuing. The provision is so important and so desirable, while at the same time so inexpensive, that many companies include it automatically in their policies. If it is not an automatic provision, the insured should certainly elect to have it included.

The most difficult problem in connection with the disability waiver of premium provision is that of determining what constitutes total disability. A typical insurance clause reads as follows:

> Total disability means disability which (a) resulted from bodily injury or disease; (b) began after the issue date of this policy and before the policy anniversary nearest the insured's sixty-fifth birthday; (c) has existed continuously for at least six months; and (d) prevents the insured from engaging for remuneration or profit in any occupation. During the first 24 months of disability, occupation means the occupation of the insured at the time such disability began; thereafter, it means any occupation for which he or she is or becomes reasonably fitted by education, training, or experience. The total and irrecoverable loss of the sight of both eyes, or the use of both hands, or of both feet, or of one hand and one foot, shall be considered total disability even if the insured shall engage in an occupation.

Note first that the disability may arise from sickness or from *bodily injury*. For example, if the insured contracts a severe case of tuberculosis or has a complete mental breakdown, the disability benefits would be forthcoming. The same is true if the incapacity is the result of an automobile accident. The disability must occur before a specified age (our definition specifies age 65), although the customary limiting age in most contracts is now 55 or 60.[8] Furthermore, the

provision requires that the disability have lasted for six months.[9]

Disability is defined in this provision as the inability of the insured to engage in his or her own occupation during the first two years of incapacity. Thereafter, disability is defined in terms of an occupation for which he or she is reasonably fitted by education, training, or experience. For example, if a dentist should lose his or her right arm in an accident, he or she will be totally disabled in the occupation of dentistry, and the premiums on the policy will be waived. However, if a college professor teaching economics should lose his or her right arm, the loss presumably would have little effect on his or her ability to engage in that occupation. But after a period of two years, if the dentist is able to pursue some occupation for which he or she is reasonably fitted by education, training, or experience, or for which he or she becomes reasonably suited, the benefits would then cease. Therefore, if the dentist becomes a faculty member in a dental college or a sales representative for a dental supply firm, it would be a job for which education, training, or experience have prepared him or her.

By definition, there are certain circumstances in which the benefits will be paid regardless of the insured's ability to engage in an occupation. If the disability arises from the total and irrecoverable loss of the sight of both eyes, or the use of both hands, or of both feet, or of one hand and one foot, the disability shall be considered total, even if the insured can engage in an occupation. Therefore, if the dentist should lose not only an arm in the accident but also a leg, the disability benefits in the life insurance policy will be paid even though the dentist teaches in a dental college or works for a dental supply firm.

The disability waiver of premium benefit is not an indemnity benefit. That is, the benefit is payable even though the insured suffers no monetary loss because of the disability. In addition, the disability provision never becomes incontestable. This means that the insurance company has the right at any time to contest the validity of a claim under the provision. Finally, the normal exclusions are disabilities resulting from self-inflicted injuries, military service in time of war, and in some cases, violation of the law.

[8] The student should not confuse the time the disability must begin with the duration of the benefits. If the disability commences before the limiting age, then it could continue for the lifetime of the insured. However, if it should commence after the limiting age, the company would have no liability under the contract.

[9] At this point, the student will probably ask whether the benefits are paid during the six-month waiting period. In most instances the *waiver of premium* benefit is provided from the commencement of the disability. This means that premiums will be waived even for the first six months.

The disability income rider under a universal life policy deserves special scrutiny, since there are significant differences among insurers with respect to this provision. Under some contracts, the disability income benefit applies only to the charges for mortality and administrative expenses, and does not include an increment to the policy's cash value. Other insurers offer a disability income rider with their universal life policies under which the full amount of the premium the insured would have paid is waived, including the increment to the policy's cash value.

The application of the disability waiver of premium provision can also differ significantly among convertible-term policies. In some convertible-term policies, the conversion may take place while the insured is disabled, and if the term policy is converted to whole life, the premium on the whole life policy will also be waived. These policies are among the more expensive term products, but when the potential benefit is weighed against the premium, they may still be considered attractive.

Accidental Death Benefit

Another coverage, commonly known as *double indemnity,* can be added to a life insurance contract. Here, if the death of the insured is caused by accident, an additional sum equal to the face of the policy will be paid.[10] A typical clause providing this benefit would read as follows:

> The Company agrees to pay an Accidental Death Benefit upon receipt at its Home Office of due proof that the death of the Insured resulted, directly and independently of all other causes, from accidental bodily injury, provided that death occurred within 90 days after such injury and while this benefit is in effect. This benefit shall be in effect while this policy is in force other than under Extended Term Insurance, Paid-up Insurance, or Optional Maturity Date provisions, but shall terminate on the policy anniversary nearest the Insured's seventieth birthday.[11]

Payments will be made under the accidental death benefit provision according to the terms of the defini-

[10] The term *double indemnity* persists, even though the benefit is not always double the face amount of the policy. Some companies provide triple and quadruple indemnity.

[11] Disability and accidental death benefits are not provided under the surrender options of extended term and paid-up policies of reduced amount, even though they were applicable in the basic contract prior to its surrender.

tion only if three conditions are satisfied. First, death must have resulted, directly and independently of all other causes, from accidental bodily injury. This means that the accidental bodily injury must be the proximate cause of the death and that no other factor, such as sickness, was a cause. For example, if the insured is driving at 110 miles an hour and the car goes out of control and collides with a tree, the insured's death would be caused by accidental bodily injury. However, if the insured has a heart attack and as a result loses control of the car and crashes into a tree, the proximate cause of death would be the heart attack, a sickness, and not the bodily injury arising from hitting the tree. In other words, if the heart attack is the proximate cause of the death, the death was not caused directly and independently of all other causes by accidental bodily injury. Second, the death must occur within 90 days after the injury. This limitation is included to minimize the influence of other facts that could contribute to the death. Third, the accidental bodily injury and the death must occur before age 70. This restriction is necessary, because the probability of death from accident increases quite substantially in the older years, and if an age limitation were not imposed, the coverage would become too expensive relative to its value.

The double indemnity provision contains several exclusions. The two most typical are: (1) death by suicide, whether sane or insane, and (2) death resulting from or contributed to by bodily or mental infirmity or disease. In addition, even though death results directly and independently of all other causes from accidental bodily injury, coverage is excluded if any act of war causes the fatal injury. Death arising while riding in or descending from any kind of aircraft is also excluded if the insured is participating in training or in any duties aboard the aircraft, or if such aircraft is being operated by or for the armed forces.

There is little to commend and much to criticize in the accidental death benefit. There is no basic economic justification for its existence, since the termination of the insured's income through death is the same whether death is caused by an automobile accident or lung cancer. In addition, its existence will tend to create an illusion of having more insurance coverage than will be the case for most causes of death. In this respect, it is a contributing factor in many of the inadequate insurance programs people are counting on today.

Guaranteed Insurability Option

Many companies now permit an insured to purchase additional amounts of insurance at stated intervals without providing evidence of insurability. The option under which this is possible is known as *guaranteed insurability, additional purchase option,* or some similar designation, and is applicable only to the permanent types of contracts such as whole life and endowment. The insured has the option of purchasing additional insurance, regardless of his or her insurability, at three-year intervals and up to a specified maximum age, most commonly age 40. In most cases, the amount of the additional insurance is limited to the face amount of the basic policy or an amount stipulated in the policy for the additional purchase option, whichever is the smaller. Although the maximum amount of each option was originally $10,000, a number of companies now offer up to $25,000 per option date. The option requires an extra premium that is based on the company's estimate of the extra mortality that will be experienced on policies issued without evidence of insurability. The premium is payable to the last option date and, for the insured, is the cost of insuring his or her insurability.

For purposes of illustration, let us assume that the insured purchases a $10,000 ordinary life policy at age 21 and that the guaranteed insurability option is a part of the policy. The company automatically agrees to issue an additional policy on the life of this insured, without evidence of insurability, at each option date. The customary option dates are at ages 25, 28, 31, 34, 37, and 40. So if our insured desires, he or she can add $10,000 insurance at each of these six dates, despite having become uninsurable. This could result in the addition of $60,000 coverage to the original policy for $10,000.

The option is not standardized, and there is some variation in the provisions used by different insurance companies. One of the most important variations involves the *waiver of premium* and *accidental death benefit* provisions. Naturally, the question must arise as to whether the additional insurance will contain these benefits if they are included in the original contract. If the answer is "yes," will the *waiver of premium* benefit be applicable to the additional insurance in case the insured becomes totally disabled at the time the additional insurance becomes effective? The most liberal options automatically provide for the inclusion of the *waiver of premium* benefit, if it exists in the original contract. For example, the insuring clause may read as follows:

If the Waiver of Premium Benefit is a part of this policy at the time an additional policy is issued (1) an additional policy of Whole Life or 65 Life plan may contain the Waiver of Premium Benefit even though premiums are being waived under this policy. If premiums are being waived under this policy when such additional policy is purchased, premiums will also be waived under the additional policy. (2) An additional policy on other than the Whole Life or 65 Life plan may contain the Waiver of Premium Benefit only if the premiums are not being waived under this policy. The Waiver of Premium Benefit of such additional policy will apply only if total disability resulted from bodily injury or disease originating after the effective date of such policy.

The insuring clause will provide for waiver of premium benefits automatically on the additional insurance, and premiums will be waived on the additional insurance if they are being waived on the basic contract on the purchase option date. This is a liberal benefit that few insurers provide in the purchase option.

In many of the purchase options in use today, it is customary to provide for a change in the option date because of marriage of the insured or birth of a child. For example, one policy provides the right of change as follows:

If the insured is a male, upon his marriage or upon the birth of his child, the right to purchase an additional policy as of the next available Purchase Date may be exercised immediately. The additional policy shall be in lieu of the policy that otherwise might be purchased as of such date. Each such privilege shall expire on the ninetieth day after it becomes exercisable.

Some companies will also provide automatic term insurance, in an amount equal to what could be purchased as additional insurance, beginning on the date of marriage or of the birth of the child. The term insurance would then cease on the day preceding the expiration of the privilege to purchase the additional insurance. So if the insured gets married and does not exercise this option immediately and dies before the expiration of the 90-day period, the company would pay the proceeds of the basic contract, plus the proceeds of the term insurance.

The incontestable clause, in general, is not applicable to the additional purchase options, but only to the original contract. However, the suicide exclusion will be applicable to each additional policy and will be effective from the date of issue of each addition.

Common Disaster Clause

The widespread use of the automobile and the airplane have given rise to a circumstance that could vitally affect the rights of parties in the life insurance contract. What would happen if the insured and the beneficiary were both killed in the same accident? To whom would the policy proceeds be paid? The answer depends on the circumstances. If the insured survived the beneficiary, even for a moment, the policy proceeds would be payable to a contingent beneficiary or, in the absence of a contingent beneficiary, to the estate of the insured. On the other hand, if there is evidence that the beneficiary survived the insured, policy proceeds payable on a lump-sum basis become payable to the beneficiary and on the subsequent death of the beneficiary, to the beneficiary's estate. The latter arrangement may be totally contrary to the intent of the insured and may, in addition, subject the proceeds to unnecessary probate and estate tax costs. In addition to those situations in which it is clear that one party survived the other, there are many instances in which it is impossible to determine whether one outlived the other, so the only conclusion to draw is that they died simultaneously. To develop a rule for the disposition of insurance proceeds in such cases, the majority of states have adopted the provisions of the Uniform Simultaneous Death Act. With specific reference to life insurance, the act stipulated that where the insured and the beneficiary have died and there is not sufficient evidence that they died other than simultaneously, the proceeds shall be distributed as if the insured survived the beneficiary. However, even this does not totally solve the problem, since in some instances it is known that the beneficiary did survive the insured, if only for a short time.

The contingency is dealt with far more effectively in the life insurance policy itself through a provision called the *common disaster clause* or through the optional modes of settlement with designated contingent beneficiaries.

Under the common disaster clause (sometimes called the *time clause*), settlement of the policy proceeds is withheld for a designated number of days after the death of the insured (usually 30), and, for the purpose of making a settlement, any beneficiary surviving the insured but dying within that specified period is considered to have predeceased the insured.

Perhaps the most effective approach to the problem is the use of one of the optional modes of settlement (such as the interest option or an installment option) for the primary beneficiary, with contingent beneficiaries named. In this case, no matter when the primary beneficiary dies, any remaining proceeds under the policy will be payable to the contingent beneficiaries. This approach ensures that the policy proceeds will go to the persons the insured desires to be paid, and not to some distant relatives who share in the primary beneficiary's estate.

Spendthrift Clause

It is sometimes the practice to include a provision in the policy called the *spendthrift clause*, which denies the beneficiary the right to commute, alienate, or assign his or her interest in the policy proceeds. The provision is used only in conjunction with an installment settlement option. In addition to providing some protection against the beneficiary's extravagance that might result in the dissipation of the policy proceeds, the clause also provides some protection against claims made by creditors of the beneficiary. A typical spendthrift clause reads as follows:

> Unless otherwise provided in this settlement option agreement, no beneficiary may commute, anticipate, encumber, alienate, withdraw, or assign any portion of his share of the proceeds. To the extent permitted by law, no payments to a beneficiary will be subject to his debts, contracts, or engagements, nor may they be levied upon or attached.

It should be noted that the provision protects the policy proceeds only while they are being held by the company. Once the proceeds have been paid out to the beneficiary, creditors are free to attempt to obtain them.

Rights of Creditors to Life Insurance Proceeds

While on the subject of the claims of creditors, we should note that all states grant at least some exemption to the proceeds of life insurance policies from the claims of the deceased insured's creditors. While it has sometimes been maintained that this represents discrimination against creditors, it seems justifiable, since the insured also has certain obligations to dependents that are even more fundamental than are those to creditors. In some states, the exemption applies only if the benefits are payable to certain beneficiaries, such

as a spouse or children. The laws differ in scope, and the broadest laws exempt the proceeds of life insurance policies not only from the claims of the insured's creditors but also from the claims of the beneficiary's creditors. For example, Section 511.37 of the *Insurance Laws of Iowa* states that:

> A policy of insurance on the life of an individual in the absence of an agreement or assignment to the contrary shall inure to the separate use of the husband or wife and children of said individual, independently of his creditors.
>
> The proceeds of an endowment policy payable to the assured on attaining a certain age shall be exempt from liability for any of his debts.
>
> Any benefit or indemnity paid under an accident, health or disability policy shall be exempt to the assured or in case of his death to the husband or wife and children of the assured, from his debts.
>
> The avails of all policies of life, accident, health or disability insurance payable to the surviving widow shall be exempt from liability for all debts of such beneficiary contracted prior to the death of the assured, but the amount thus exempted shall not exceed $15,000.

Laws such as the Iowa law, which exempts the proceeds of an endowment policy from the debts of the insured, and the proceeds from a life or accident policy from the debts of the beneficiary, are rare. In most jurisdictions, the proceeds are subject to the claims of creditors of the beneficiary, but not of the insured.

Cost-of-Living Riders

As a result of chronic inflation in our economy, cost-of-living riders have become increasingly popular additions to permanent life insurance policies. Under the basic model of a *cost-of-living rider,* the insurer offers the insured additional coverage (for which the insured pays an added premium) when the consumer price index increases. The principal advantage of the cost-of-living rider is that the additional insurance is offered without evidence of insurability by the insured. However, to continue eligibility to additional insurance without evidence of insurability, the insured must accept each additional offering of coverage. If the insured rejects any of the increases, the insurer may require evidence of insurability for the next increase.

UNIVERSAL LIFE POLICY PROVISIONS

Universal life policies include many of the standard policy provisions noted in the preceding chapter. These include, for example, the misstatement of age provision, suicide provision, incontestability provision, reinstatement provision, and settlement options. The special nature of the universal life policy also requires certain specialized provisions that do not appear in traditional life insurance policies. For the most part, these provisions are unique to universal life policies, although some also appear in adjustable life and variable life policies. The most important universal life provisions are the following.

Premium and Cost of Insurance Provision

Universal life policies contain several provisions relating to premiums. First, universal life policies include a cost of insurance table that specifies the maximum rate per $1000 of insurance chargeable under the policy for the life insurance protection. The rates actually charged are usually below the specified maximum by a considerable margin.

Because premiums under universal life are variable at the option of the insured, most policies also make a distinction between *scheduled* or *planned* premiums and *unscheduled* additional premiums. The policy indicates when additional premiums may be paid and the procedure for changing the level of planned premiums.

Finally, universal life policies may include a cumulative premium limit table, setting a maximum to the premiums payable under the policy. The maximum premium payable in any given year is limited to the cumulative premium limit specified for the year less the sum of premiums paid in prior years.

Changes in the Amount of Insurance

Although various companies use different terminology, the universal life policy usually has a provision relating to changes in the amount of insurance. The provision generally requires proof of insurability and stipulates when the increased coverage is effective (usually the day following receipt of the request by the company). The insured is normally required to submit a supplemental application, which will become a part of the policy.

Decreases in the amount of insurance, like increases, are usually effective the day following receipt of the request. However, most policies stipulate a minimum level of coverage that must be continued under the policy. The following amounts used by one insurer are typical:

Insured's Age on Policy Date	Minimum Level of Coverage
0 through 54	$25,000
55 through 59	$20,000
60 through 64	$15,000
65 and older	$10,000

Death Benefit Provision

Some provisions in universal life policies are designed to maintain the policy's status as "life insurance" and avoid disqualification under the *Internal Revenue Code (IRC)* service tax code. Because interest earnings in excess of the guaranteed minimum increase the cash value of the policy, a part of the cash value must be withdrawn periodically or the amount of protection must be increased as the cash value increases. Otherwise, the excess accumulation in the cash value of the policy will result in disqualification. In this respect, universal life policies use two approaches. Under one approach, the policy includes a provision maintaining the required corridor between the cash value and the face amount of protection. Under the second approach, increases in the cash value in excess of the guaranteed minimum are payable as a death benefit. In some cases, policies provide death benefit options, under which the insured may select the manner in which the death benefit will be determined. For example, one insurer includes the following death benefit provision in its policies:

Death Benefit

If the insured dies while this policy is in force, this policy will provide a death benefit that depends on the following:

• The death benefit option in effect on the date of death.

• Any increases or decreases in the initial specified amount shown on page 3 of the policy.

Death Benefit Option

This policy offers two death benefit options.
Option 1: The death benefit will be the greater of
• The specified amount on the date of death, *or*
• The cash value on the date of death times the applicable percentage.
Option 2: The death benefit will be the greater of
• The specified amount plus the cash value on the date of death, *or*
• The cash value on the date of death times the applicable percentage.
The applicable percentage is indicated in Table A.

This provision is typical of universal life death benefit provisions. Note first that payment varies with the death benefit option that is in effect at the date of the insured's death. One or the other of the two options is selected at the time the policy is taken out. Thereafter, the insured may change from one option to the other on request.

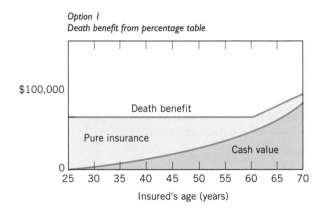

FIGURE 15.1 Universal Life Insurance Death Benefit Options

Under Option 1, the amount payable as a death benefit is the specified amount (i.e., face amount) of the policy or, if the cash value multiplied by an *applicable percentage* indicated in the policy produces a higher amount, the higher amount will be payable. Although policies issued prior to 1985 use a different schedule, the applicable percentage in policies issued since 1985 usually coincides with the percentage table in the *IRC,* which specifies the required corridor between cash value and the amount of insurance if the policy is to meet the code's definition of life insurance.

For the purpose of illustration, assume that Jones dies at age 55 and that the specified amount of his policy is $100,000. Assume also that the cash value of the policy is $48,000. Reference to the policy's *applicable percentage table* indicates an applicable percentage of 150 percent at age 55. Since $48,000 times 150 percent is $72,000, the specified amount will be payable. Had Jones' cash value been $70,000, $70,000 times 150 per-

cent, which equals $105,000, the $105,000 would have been payable. The provision for a death benefit based on the policy's cash value is designed to comply with the provisions of the tax code's definition of "life insurance." Under this provision, the corridor between cash value and the face amount of insurance required by the *Code* will always be maintained.

Death benefit Option 2 is also designed to comply with the provisions of the tax code. When the insured selects Option 2, the cash value of the policy is payable as an additional death benefit and the death benefit increases in an amount exactly equal to the increase in the cash value. As in the case of Option 1, this prevents disqualification of the contract the *IRC* definition of life insurance.

Figure 15.1 (see page 274) illustrates the difference in the two approaches and the manner in which the amount of life insurance varies with the option selected.

IMPORTANT CONCEPTS TO REMEMBER

nonforfeiture values	accidental death benefit	policy loan provision
paid-up reduced amount option	additional purchase option	automatic premium loan
extended term option	cost-of-living rider	renewable
delay clause	waiver of premium	convertible
dividend options	guaranteed insurability option	double indemnity
fifth dividend option	common disaster clause	cash surrender value
disability waiver of premium provision	Uniform Simultaneous Death Act spendthrift clause	

QUESTIONS FOR REVIEW

1. Joe Smith purchased a $10,000 whole-life policy with an accidental death (double indemnity) provision on December 1, 1989. He committed suicide on December 15, 1991. Discuss the liability of the insurance company.

2. What is the purpose behind the insertion of an automatic premium loan provision into a life insurance policy? What is its relation to the grace period?

3. Describe the nonforfeiture options. Under what circumstances would you advise the choice of each in preference to the other two?

4. John Jones has elected to permit the dividends under his participating whole life contract to accumulate, but is concerned because a friend informed him that this subjects the dividends to taxation. Advise Jones regarding the

taxation of dividends left to accumulate with the insurer.

5. It has been said that policy loans constitute "borrowing from widows and orphans." What is meant by this statement? Do you agree with it?

6. One week after taking out a policy loan, John Doe is in a fatal automobile accident. How much will be payable to the beneficiary of his policy?

7. What are the four standard dividend options available under a participating life insurance policy? What is the so-called *fifth dividend option?*

8. Historically, the disability waiver of premium provision was to provide benefits only if the disability was *total* and *permanent.* How have the terms *total* and *permanent* been interpreted?

9. Jones elected to use dividends under his whole-life policy to buy paid-up additions to the policy, but has now changed his mind and would like to prepay the policy as quickly as possible. Are the past dividends lost, or can they be applied to prepayment of the policy?

10. Describe the two approaches commonly used to adjust the death benefits of universal life policies to avoid tax disqualification.

QUESTIONS FOR DISCUSSION

1. Although there is no such thing as a standard life insurance policy, certain provisions may be required by law. In addition, some optional provisions or modifications may need to be added to the basic policy. Which of the optional provisions do you think should be considered essential by the insurance buyer?

2. To what extent does the *accidental death benefit* (or *double indemnity*) provision of a life insurance policy violate the rules of good risk management?

3. What, in your opinion, are the principal benefits of the disability waiver of premium provision in life insurance contracts? Of what significance is the fact that premiums are waived only until the insured's age 65?

4. It is often said that policyholders should not have to pay interest on policy loans since they are "borrowing their own money." Explain specifically the fallacy of this argument. Assuming that policyholders did not pay interest on any policy loans, what would happen?

5. The guaranteed insurability option is a valuable form of protection, permitting an individual to insure his or her insurability up to some multiple of the face amount of the policy to which the option is attached. What do you think of the idea of marketing the guaranteed insurability option by itself, without any form of current protection? Would it be marketable? Why or why not?

SUGGESTIONS FOR ADDITIONAL READING

Black, Kenneth, Jr., and Harold D. Skipper, Jr. *Life Insurance,* 13th ed. Englewood Cliffs, N.J.: Prentice-Hall, 2000. Chapters 9, 10.

Crawford, Muriel L., and William T. Beadles. *Law and the Life Insurance Contract,* 6th ed. Homewood, Ill.: Richard D. Irwin. 1989.

Hallman, G. Victor, and Karen L. Hamilton. *Personal Insurance: Life, Health, and Retirement.* Malvern, Pa.: American Institute for CPCU, 1994. Chapter 4.

WEB SITES TO EXPLORE

American Council of Life Insurance	http://www.acli.com/
American Society of CLU & ChFC	http://www.agents-online.com/ASCLU/web/index.html
Insurance News Network	http://www.insure.com/
Newsedge News Page	http://www.newspage.com/browse/46622/

SPECIAL LIFE INSURANCE FORMS

■

Variety's the very spice of life.

— WILLIAM COWPER
The Task

CHAPTER OBJECTIVES

When you have finished this chapter, you should be able to
- Describe the characteristics of the various special life insurance forms discussed in the chapter
- Explain the circumstances in which each of the specialized forms may be used
- Identify the economic conditions that led to the new generation of life insurance contracts
- Identify the advantages and disadvantages of specialized life insurance policies generally

In Chapter 12, we divided the life insurance products currently available into two broad categories: term insurance, which provides pure protection, and cash value life insurance, which combines protection and saving. In addition to this basic distinction, we also distinguished between the traditional forms of life insurance that have existed for many years (term, whole life, and endowment) and the innovative contracts that were introduced over the past two decades. In the innovative class, we identified universal life, adjustable life, and variable life as three additional types of contracts that may be considered "basic" today.

In addition to these contracts, life insurance companies offer a wide variety of policies that combine two or more of the basic types into one contract or that provide for an unusual pattern of premium payments. In this chapter, we will examine a few of these specialized contracts that have been developed to fill the particular needs of individuals. The discussion that follows is not intended to be exhaustive, but only to describe the more important of these special contracts.

SPECIALIZED LIFE CONTRACTS

Many life insurance policies have been designed to fit special situations, and while they may or may not offer the same degree of flexibility as the basic contracts,

they possess advantages that make them attractive in many situations. The important point to remember is that the forms discussed are merely combinations or modifications of the three basic types of life insurance, and the manner in which they may be combined is limited only by the imagination of the policy writers.

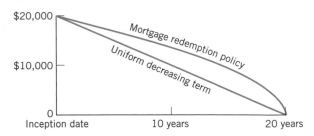

FIGURE 16.1 Mortgage Redemption Policy

Mortgage Redemption Policy

Actually, we could call any policy purchased for retiring a mortgage if the head of the household dies before it has been paid off, mortgage insurance. As the term is used in the insurance industry, a *mortgage redemption policy* (also called a mortgage protection policy) refers to a policy designed to provide protection in some amount sufficient to pay off the mortgage at any given time. Since the amount of the mortgage is constantly decreasing throughout its term, a policy designed to pay off the mortgage in the event of the death of the head of the family therefore may also decrease in face amount over its life. The mortgage redemption policy is written on a decreasing basis for the term of the mortgage. If the policyholder lives to pay off the mortgage, the policy expires without value at the same time the need for protection has disappeared.

Although some insurers refer to virtually any decreasing term policy as their "mortgage redemption policy," other insurers offer flexible contracts, with different time periods and amortization rates that facilitate a close match between the decreasing level of coverage and the amount of the unpaid mortgage.

The difference between a mortgage protection policy and a uniform decreasing term policy is illustrated in Figure 16.1. Because the insurance remains at a higher level for a longer period of time under the mortgage protection policy, the premium is also slightly higher. The premium on a 30-year uniform decreasing term policy for a male at age 25 with one company is $1.50 per $1000. The company's rate for a 30-year mortgage protection policy at the same age is $2.41 per $1000.

Joint Mortgage Protection Policy

Another contract that has appeal to young couples is the *joint mortgage protection policy,* under which decreasing term is written on the lives of two persons, with the insurance payable at the death of the first. Today, married couples often purchase a house based on their joint incomes. In the event that one of the two dies, the remaining spouse would find it difficult, if not impossible, to continue the mortgage payments. One solution is a joint mortgage protection policy. The cost for a joint mortgage protection policy is slightly less than the cost of a separate individual mortgage protection policy on each partner. With one company, for example, a husband and wife, each age 25, would pay about $220 a year for a $50,000 30-year joint mortgage protection policy. Separate policies on the husband and wife would cost $150 and $135, respectively, for a total of $285.

Survivorship Whole Life

Survivorship whole life or the *second-to-die* policy is a contract that insures two lives with the promise to pay only at the second death. Survivorship life was developed in response to the unlimited marital deduction under the federal estate tax law, under which an individual may leave his or her entire estate to a spouse without estate tax liability. Although the bequest of an individual's estate to his or her spouse avoids the estate tax, a tax will be payable on the death of the beneficiary spouse, resulting in a potentially immense tax liability if the couple have a large estate. Survivorship life insurance is a practical approach to this exposure; it automatically provides life insurance proceeds to cover the estate tax when it occurs—at the death of the second spouse. Because survivorship life is not payable until the second death, the premium is significantly lower than the cost of separate policies on the two individuals. One insurer, for example, charges a premium of $2831 for a $100,000 survivorship whole-life policy covering a male age 65 and a female age 62. If separate whole-life policies were purchased, the annual premiums

for the husband and wife would be $6935 and $4405, respectively.[1]

Family Income Policy

The *family income policy* also utilizes the concept of decreasing term insurance to fit a need for a decreasing amount of insurance. The family income policy is a combination of some form of permanent insurance (e.g., whole life), with decreasing term insurance. The term insurance makes provision for the payment of some stipulated amount per month from the date of the insured's death until some specific date in the future. The sum payable per month is typically 1 percent of the amount of permanent insurance, although many companies offer other options. To illustrate how the family income policy works, let us assume that the insured in question purchases a $100,000 whole-life policy with a 1 percent family income benefit. The insuring agreement of the family income policy promises to pay $1000 per month to the beneficiary from the date of death of the insured until a date 20 years from the inception of the policy. The normal family income period is 20 years, although other options such as 10 or 15 years are also available. If the insured outlives the period specified as the family income period, the decreasing term portion of the policy ceases. The insured then has the basic amount of permanent insurance on which premiums continue to be paid.

Figure 16.2 illustrates the family income policy graphically. The amount of whole-life insurance in this illustration is $100,000, and a $1000 per-month benefit will be paid from the date of the insured's death until the end of the 20th year after the inception date. The $160,000 in decreasing term represents the amount the insurance company must have in policy proceeds at the beginning of the family income period to pay $1000 per month for 20 years. As time goes by, the amount of insurance needed to make the $1000 monthly payments for the remainder of the 20-year period declines. The $1000 family income bene-

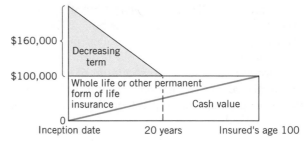

FIGURE 16.2 Family Income Policy

fit comes from two sources: One part comes from the decreasing term, and the other part comes from interest on the benefits left with the company. It is common under the family income policy to provide for the payment of the basic policy at the end of the income period. Thus, the interest from the basic policy helps to provide the monthly income payments.[2] In some instances, the insurance company will permit the beneficiary to take the commutation value of the monthly benefits at the time of the death of the insured. In either case, the amount payable will be reduced by the amount of interest forgone by the insurer.

Family Income Rider

The family income rider is merely a variation of the family income policy, but with somewhat more flexibility. The *family income rider* is a decreasing term rider that is attached to some permanent form of insurance. Some companies will even permit the use of the family income rider with a form of long-duration term, such as term to age 65 or term to expectancy.

While both the family income policy and the family income rider may provide for the payment of a specified amount (e.g., $1000 per month), the actual amounts of term insurance required to provide this amount may differ. The determining factor is the time at which the basic policy is payable. As we have seen, it is common under the family income policy to provide for the payment of the basic policy at the end of the income period. In the case of the family income rider, the term insurance is usually sufficient

[1] Special measures may be required with respect to the ownership of second-to-die policies if the incidents of ownership that will result in inclusion of policy proceeds in the insured's estate are to be avoided. Given the uncertainty as to which spouse will die first, the most logical plan is to have one of the couple's other heirs serve as owner of the policy. This will avoid incidents of ownership and the inclusion of the policy proceeds in the estate of the second spouse to die. If this is not practical for some reason, the policy may be owned by a trust.

[2] To provide funds for funeral expenses and the costs of the last illness, some family income policies allow the payment of a certain amount at the death of the insured if it should occur during the income period. In some contracts, this amount would be $200 per $1000 of the face amount.

to provide the full amount of the monthly benefit, without the interest from the basic policy. This means that the amount of the basic policy may be paid immediately at the death of the insured, it may be left at interest to increase the amount of the monthly benefit above the designated amount, or it may be left to accumulate at interest until the end of the income period.

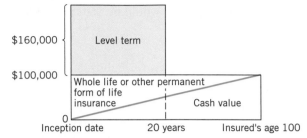

FIGURE 16.3 Family Maintenance Policy

Family Maintenance Policy

The *family maintenance policy* is another variation of the family income policy. Instead of paying a monthly income from the date of the insured's death until some date 10, 15, or 20 years from the inception of the policy as does the family income policy, the family maintenance policy pays the monthly income for a period of 10, 15, or 20 years from the date of the insured's death, provided that the insured dies during a specified period. For example, if X had purchased a $100,000 family maintenance policy at age 30, with an income period of 20 years, and had died at age 40, the income payments of $1000 per month would be paid to the surviving spouse for 20 years, that is, until the time the insured would have been 60. Then the face amount would be paid to the beneficiary. In all other respects the two contracts are the same.

The family maintenance policy consists of a basic policy, which is some form of permanent insurance, plus level rather than decreasing term. The term portion of the policy will furnish income for the number of years specified. The family maintenance policy is illustrated in Figure 16.3. Note that the amount of term insurance provided does not decrease. The term insurance remains level and provides a sum of $160,000 at the death of the insured, if the insured dies within the 20-year period. The $160,000 will be sufficient, together with the interest earned on that portion of the benefits held by the company, to pay $1000 per month for 240 months. Note also, however, that if the insured does not die within the 20-year period, the term expires, and premiums on this portion of the protection cease.

Family Protection Policy

The *family protection policy* is known by many names; almost every insurance company offers it in one form or another, and many refer to it by their own trade name.[3] This special form is an attempt to provide insurance on the entire family. The distinguishing characteristic is that insurance in predetermined proportions is provided for each family member. For example, the unit on the husband may be $5000 on an ordinary life basis, with $1000 term insurance on the wife (the term extending to the time the husband is 65) and $1000 term coverage on each child, with coverage to a designated age such as 21 years. Children born after the inception of the contract are covered automatically without notice to the insurance company on the attainment of a specified age, for example, 14 days. Surrender and loan values are provided, but paid-up insurance normally is provided only on the coverage applicable to the husband. It is also customary to permit conversion of the term insurance on the lives of the dependents on the expiration of the specified term. For example, many contracts provide for conversion of the coverage on the children up to as much as $5000 of permanent life insurance for each $1000 of term coverage and without evidence of insurability.

The premium on this form of insurance is based on the age of the husband, with an adjustment made for the additional risk the company accepts. The basic premium computation assumes that the wife is the same age as the husband. If she is not, the face amount of the term insurance covering her is adjusted. The younger the wife relative to her husband, the greater the amount of insurance coverage on her life.[4] The older the wife, the less her coverage. For example, if the standard program provides $1000 coverage on the wife, and a particular wife is one year older than her husband, her coverage might be

[3] Some insurers create *ad hoc* family protection policies through the use of riders that add a spouse or children to an individual policy.

[4] Although this is the standard approach, some insurers leave the amount of insurance on the wife at the standard $1000 and adjust the premium based on her age.

reduced to $900. If she is one year younger than the husband, it would be adjusted to $1100.

All members of the family must be insurable if the contract is to be issued. If the husband or wife should be uninsurable, the contract cannot be issued at all.[5] The only exception involves the children. If one child is uninsurable, the family protection policy may be issued, but with that child excluded from coverage.

The family protection policy is extremely popular with young married couples, since it provides some insurance on every member of the family. It can be, and often is, written with a family income rider that provides 1 percent of the amount of coverage on the father as monthly income during the family income period. One of the more attractive features of the policy is that it guarantees the insurability of the children in the family. In the event that a child should become uninsurable before reaching the conversion age, or if a child who was uninsurable were born to the marriage, this contract would guarantee that the child would be able to purchase at least some minimum amount of permanent insurance on reaching the conversion age.

Return-of-Premium and Return-of-Cash-Value Policy

Some individuals who lack an understanding of the level premium concept think that the insurance company should pay the face of the policy when the insured dies, plus the cash value. They reason that since the cash value is the insured's saving fund, it is inequitable to pay this to the beneficiary and call it a part of the death benefit. If the insured dies before the policy matures, these individuals think the company should be obligated to pay the face amount of the policy plus the cash value. Insurance companies attempt to create a product that is salable, and if people want a policy that will pay the face amount plus the cash value, they are certainly going to get it.

Policies have been issued that purport to pay, in addition to the face of the policy, the cash surrender value at the time of death. It should be obvious from what we have learned about the cash value and its relationship to the level premium that this is impossible unless an additional premium is charged. The policies that agree to pay the cash value plus the face of the policy are nothing more than a combination of two whole-life contracts. As

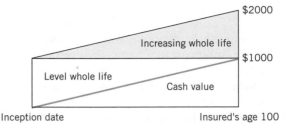

FIGURE 16.4 Return-of-Cash-Value Policy

Figure 16.4 indicates, there are two amounts of insurance in force at all times. The basic amount is level, being equal to the face of the policy the insured has purchased. The second portion, for which the insured, of course, pays an additional premium, is always sufficient to pay an amount equal to the cash value of the basic policy.

A variation of this idea is found in the *return-of-premium policy* (Figure 16.5). Most individuals like to think that they are getting something for nothing. The return-of-premium policy purports to pay the face amount of the policy at the death of the insured, plus all the premiums that have been paid, provided that the insured dies within a certain period of time. Like the *return-of-cash-value policy,* the return-of-premium policy is also composed of two amounts of insurance. The basic policy is whole life or some other form of permanent insurance. The second portion is actually increasing term insurance, with a face amount that is always sufficient to pay the total amount of premiums that have been paid for both portions. The insured must die within a certain period (normally 20 years) if the beneficiary is to receive both the face amount and the premiums paid. If the insured does not die until after the 20-year period has passed, the beneficiary will receive only the face amount of the basic policy, and the term portion of the policy expires without value.

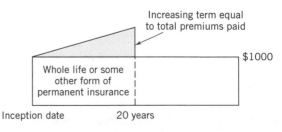

FIGURE 16.5 Return-of-Premium Policy

[5] With some insurers, a *parent's policy,* covering one parent and the insurable children, may be employed.

Modified Whole Life

The distinguishing characteristic of *modified whole life* is its premium arrangement. The premium for the first three or five years is slightly more than that on the same amount of term insurance. After the end of the three- or five-year period, the premium increases to a level that is slightly more than the whole-life premium at the age at which the policy was taken out, but also slightly less than the premium on permanent insurance at the attained age of the insured. One company quotes the following rates for five-year term, whole life, and modified whole life:

	First Five Years	Thereafter
Five-year term converted at the end of five years	$4.23	$14.99
Modified whole life	4.58	13.54

This policy is particularly attractive to college students and other individuals who think that their income will increase within a short time. They would like to purchase permanent insurance at their current age, but cannot afford to do so. If they wait until they can afford it, or if they purchase convertible term, the premium on the permanent insurance will be based on their age at conversion. The modified whole-life policy helps to solve this problem. If the insured knows he or she will be converting to permanent insurance within a short period of time, premium outlay will be lower over the long term if modified whole life is purchased instead of convertible term.

Actually, modified whole life is essentially equivalent to automatically convertible term. As in the case of term, during the first three to five years, there is rarely a cash value. Although there is a separate type of policy that is actually designated *automatic convertible term,* it is almost identical with modified life.

Graded-Premium Whole Life

Another contract closely related to modified whole life is graded-premium whole life. *Graded-premium whole life* is a contract in which the initial premium is quite low (say, $2 per $1000 at age 21) but increases yearly until it levels off sometime between the tenth and twentieth years. Cash values are not generally available until year 10, and even by year 20 the cash values are quite low.

Indexed Whole Life

Under *indexed whole-life insurance,* the face amount of the policy increases with increases in the Consumer Price Index. Two versions of the policy exist. Under one approach, the death benefit of the policy increases annually, and the premium is adjusted to reflect the higher level of protection. Under the second approach, the initial premium is loaded to compensate the insurer for the anticipated increases in the future amount of insurance. Under this approach, the premium does not increase with the annual increases in the amount of insurance.

Single-Premium Life

As its name suggests, a *single-premium life* policy is one in which there is a single premium; generally, the minimum premium is $5000 or more. This premium creates an immediate cash value in the policy. This cash value and the investment income earned on it are sufficient to pay the cost of the policy's benefits, which, to comply with the requirements of the *Internal Revenue Code (IRC)* must be 100 percent to 250 percent of the cash value, depending on the age of the insured. Single-premium life insurance is written on both a traditional whole-life and variable basis.

The rate of return on a single-premium whole-life policy is usually guaranteed for a period of from one to five years. Thereafter the rate is adjusted, either at the discretion of the insurer or according to a formula, but does not fall below a guaranteed minimum (e.g., 4 percent or 5 percent). The earnings on the cash value accumulate tax free until the policy is cashed in, at which time the earnings are taxable.

Unlike traditional forms of life insurance, single-premium life does not usually have a front-end "load." Although a commission is, of course, paid to the agent, the amount of the commission is not deducted from the premium in creating the policy's cash value. Instead, the policy is subject to a surrender charge, generally in the range of 5 to 10 percent, which is levied if the policy is cashed in during a specified period of time, usually 7 to 10 years. The surrender charge diminishes and eventually disappears after 7 to 10 years.

Modified Endowment Contracts Following the elimination of many traditional tax shelters by the Tax

Reform Act of 1986, sale of single-premium life insurance mushroomed. In 1987, the sale of single-premium life insurance soared to about $10 million, more than double the level the previous year. Ironically, this rapid growth served as the motivation for congressional action to modify its status under the tax laws. Because single-premium life policies were treated the same as any other contract that met the *Code* definition of life insurance, many buyers found them to be attractive investment shelters. Like other forms of life insurance, the cash value buildup is tax free until the policy is terminated. Also like other forms of life insurance, the insured could borrow from the cash value without tax liability, as long as the loans did not exceed his or her basis in the contract. This meant that large sums invested in single-premium life insurance could generate tax-sheltered investment income.

Although single-premium life insurance and certain other contracts with a high investment element met the standards established by the 1984 act, Congress considered the tax treatment of these contracts to be a loophole, which it acted to close in the Technical and Miscellaneous Revenue Act of 1988 (TAMRA). In this law, Congress instituted a new test, designed to further discourage the use of life insurance contracts with high premiums as an investment. TAMRA classifies any contract sold after June 21, 1988, that fails the test as a *modified endowment contract* (MEC). It then makes modified endowment contracts subject to a penalty if investment earnings are withdrawn by a cash surrender or loan before age 59 and $1/2$. The test, called the *seven-pay test,* compares the premiums paid for the policy during the first 7 years with seven annual net level premiums for seven-pay policy. The net level premium for a seven-pay policy is an artificial standard constructed by the IRS based on the guideline level premium concept introduced in the 1984 tax act.

Modified endowment contracts are subject to two important provisions. First, funds withdrawn from such contracts are subject to a *last-in first-out* treatment. This assumes that the investment income is withdrawn from the policy before the insured's basis. In addition to the last-in-first-out treatment, MECs are subject to a 10 percent penalty on any taxable gains withdrawn before age $59^1/2$. Like an annuity, the cash value buildup accumulates tax free unless it is withdrawn.

Juvenile Insurance

Historically, the primary purpose of most juvenile policies was thrift, and many policies were purchased to accumulate funds for the child's college education. Prior to the Deficit Reduction Act of 1984, the most popular forms of juvenile insurance were a 20-year endowment and an educational endowment at age 18, but these contracts have disappeared because of their inability to satisfy the cash-value corridor test. The most popular forms of juvenile insurance today are term contracts that automatically convert to whole life without evidence of insurability when the child reaches a stipulated age (such as 25) and whole-life policies with a guaranteed insurability option. Some policies combine the features of automatically convertible term with a guaranteed insurability option that permits the insured to incrementally increase the amount of insurance at specified ages.[6]

The major appeal of *juvenile* insurance is that it protects the insurability of the child. Should the child become uninsurable, a whole-life contract (or a convertible-term policy) with the guaranteed insurability option would ensure at least some minimum level of lifetime protection.

It is common in the case of juvenile policies to include a policy provision called the *payor clause,* which specifies that all future premiums under the policy will be waived if the premium payer, who is named in the endorsement attaching the payor clause, should die or become disabled. This provision guarantees completion of the payment on the child's policy if the payer should die or become disabled.

Juvenile insurance is an extremely specialized form of protection. In many cases it is misused. Far too many individuals purchase this kind of life insurance when they themselves are inadequately protected. In most cases the premium dollars used to purchase insurance on children would be better spent in providing protection on the head of the family. Although a child's death is certainly a tragedy, it does not bring with it the grave consequences for the family that the death of the breadwinner brings. Dollars spent to provide educational funds for the child can accomplish this purpose almost as well when they purchase insurance on the father's life.

[6] These policies are similar to, but not identical with, a policy form known as *jumping juvenile* that was popular prior to the introduction of the *modified endowment contract* penalty in the *IRC*. Jumping juvenile policies were whole-life contracts that automatically increased to some multiple of the face amount (usually five times) when the child reached age 21.

Indeterminate Premium Policies

The years from 1976 to 1985 marked a period in which interest rates climbed to unprecedented levels. These record rates combined with diversification strategies of firms in the financial services market to create a backdrop for a revolution in life insurance products. One of these was the universal life policy, but there were others as well.

As interest rates rose in the late 1970s, the insurance-buying public soon recognized that the investment elements in their cash value insurance policies were not earning competitive yields. (It was not uncommon during this time for traditional life insurance products to yield 3 to 5 percent on the investment element when alternative investments were returning 12 to 14 percent.) Often, especially when the guaranteed policy loan rate was low, policyholders borrowed their policy cash values at 5 percent to invest them at 12 percent. Other insureds went even farther and cashed their policies in, purchasing newer policies with lower premiums or higher yields or converted to term insurance and a separate investment. As a result, a significant turnover of policyholders resulted for many companies and extensive replacement of old policies with new ones. As interest rates rose, insurers found it difficult to meet the competition from universal life policies using traditional participating policies. What was needed, and what some insurers eventually devised, was a mechanism whereby insurers could adjust the premiums on existing policies to reflect changes in investment income; this led to the indeterminate premium policy.

The benefit structure of the *indeterminate premium policy* is the same as that for other policies, but the premium structure differs. Indeterminate premium policies have maximum guaranteed premium rates specified in the policy, but initial premiums are generally set at a level well below the maximums. The issuing company then reserves the right to change the initial premium up or down, subject to the specified maximum. The low initial premium is guaranteed for a specified period of time, usually ranging from 2 to 10 years. Generally, the longer the period for which the initial premium is guaranteed, the higher the initial premium. Although the earliest indeterminate premium policies were whole-life policies, indeterminate term soon followed. Indeterminate premium policies are also known as *variable premium life insurance.*

Interest-Sensitive Whole Life

Interest sensitive whole life, which is also called *current assumption*

whole life (CAWL) insurance is an indeterminate premium policy in which the policy's cash value is also variable, based on changes in the premium. Interest sensitive policies include a *redetermination provision* under which the insurer can, after an initial guarantee period, increase or decrease the premiums based on current interest and mortality. If the current assumption produces a lower premium the insured can pay the lower premium or continue to pay the old higher premium and thereby increase the cash value. Subject to evidence of insurability, the insured can use the difference between the old and new premiums to increase the death benefit. If the new premium is higher than the previous premium, the insured can pay the new premium, reduce the face amount of the policy, or use a part of the cash value to cover the difference.

Participating Policy Innovations The same competitive forces that prompted creation of indeterminate premium policies and interest sensitive policies also prompted insurers selling participating policies to create new approaches in allocating dividends. These new approaches that have been adopted are called collectively the *investment generation method* (IGM), a term broadly used in reference to any allocation procedure that recognizes the year (or generation of policies) during which money was invested by the policyholder in determining the dividend.

Under the traditional dividend allocation method (called the *portfolio average method*), excess investment earnings to be included in dividends are allocated to all policies, old and new, at a single rate, regardless of the pattern of premium payments over the years. Because a life insurer has a portfolio of investments with different inceptions, maturities, and rates, funds invested at different times earn different returns. The portfolio average method, as the name implies, produces an average return that is allocated to all policies. During periods of high interest rates, the average allocation produces a lower rate on new funds than is available elsewhere. To meet the competition from other interest-sensitive products, many companies switched from the portfolio average method of dividend allocation to IGM.

There are two distinct types of IGM. They are referred to as *partitioned-portfolio* IGM and *policy-based* IGM. The partitioned-portfolio approach establishes groupings (partitions) of policies by issue year (e.g., prior to 1979, 1980 to 1983, 1984 and later) and calculates a separate average rate of return for each partition. Conceptually, this approach breaks

the insurer's policyholders into several small companies corresponding to the issue-year groups. The portfolio average interest rate for each group is calculated from the earnings on the net cash flow of that group over the years. Thus, the generation of policies issued from 1980 through 1983 would have a considerably higher rate than would the generation of policies issued prior to 1980.

The policy-based IGM works differently. Each individual policy receives excess interest at rates reflecting the timing of deposits (such as premium payments) made in that policy. More specifically, generations of one or more years are defined, and the increase in policy reserve during each generation receives the rate earned on investments made during those years.[7]

Low-Load and No-Load Life Insurance

Low-load and no-load life insurance products are available from a limited number of insurers. The term *low-load* refers to a contract in which the commission for the first and subsequent years is lower than the traditional commission rates. A *no-load* policy is one on which no commission is payable.

Initially, low-compensation products were offered only by insurers that do not have a conventional distribution system (such as TIAA/CREF and mail-order insurers). Increasingly, however, both low-load and no-load life insurance has become available through specialty agents or brokers who charge a fee for placement. Most companies offering low-load and no-load products limit the market for these products through restrictions such as high minimum face amounts and high minimum premiums so that their traditional agents can coexist with the new products.

The interest in no-load and low-load life insurance products parallels the popularity of no-load mutual funds. Other things being equal, a product with a reduced load or no load should be less expensive than a fully loaded product. However, no-load and low-load policies sometimes carry backend loads (surrender charges) similar to those discussed in connection with the single-premium deferred annuity.

ADVANTAGES AND DISADVANTAGES OF SPECIAL FORMS

The special policy forms examined in this chapter have certain advantages and disadvantages, both of which arise from the fact that these policies are designed to meet special needs. Because they are narrowly designed, these special forms meet those needs better than any other policies, but by the same token they are often inflexible and meet other needs poorly. Each individual faces different circumstances, and the danger exists that one of the special policy forms may be used in a situation for which it is inappropriate. Of course, there are some needs that are almost universal. There is little chance of the family income policy being misused because of the general need for protection during the child-raising years. On the other hand, the juvenile insurance policies are often misused, eating up the premium dollars that would better be spent on the head of the family.

In addition to the special policy forms discussed in this chapter, there are a number of other, even more specialized contracts. The variety and type of special policies are limited only by the imagination of the marketing directors of the insurance companies. When properly used, the special policy forms are extremely useful tools for protecting the members of the insured's family against the financial consequences of premature death or for accumulating a fund for some specific future need such as retirement or education.

[7] Although the newer dividend formulas are effective tools for competition, they may be viewed negatively by older policy holders who are receiving dividends based on the lowest dividend interest rate, which can lead to further replacement activity. The question of which method of allocating dividends is proper is a matter of judgment, subject to honest differences of opinion. While equity is an important factor in setting the method of allocating investment income, the motivating force that led to IGM was competition.

IMPORTANT CONCEPTS TO REMEMBER

mortgage redemption policy
joint mortgage protection policy
family income policy
family income rider

family maintenance policy
family protection policy
modified whole-life policy
return-of-premium policy

return-of-cash-value policy
graded-premium whole-life
 insurance
jumping juvenile

payor clause single-premium life low-load insurance policy
indeterminate premium policy single-premium deferred annuity no-load insurance policy
interest sensitive whole life investment generation method
indexed whole-life insurance portfolio average method

QUESTIONS FOR REVIEW

1. Explain the difference between the *family income policy* and the *family income rider.* How would you expect their rates to differ and why?

2. Briefly describe the specialized policies that have been created to address the needs associated with mortgages.

3. The family income policy is simply a combination of whole-life insurance and decreasing term insurance. Explain.

4. Briefly explain the nature of the *family protection policy,* identifying the various components by type of protection.

5. Describe the situation for which *survivorship whole-life* or the *second-to-die policy* was developed. Are there any other situations for which it would be appropriate?

6. Explain why the economic environment of the late 1970s and early 1980s led to the creation of new types of life insurance policies.

7. Explain how *indeterminate premium* whole-life policies differ from *traditional* whole-life policies.

8. In what way does the treatment of acquisition expense under single-premium life insurance differ from that of other life insurance policies?

9. What are the principal uses of *juvenile life insurance?*

10. Explain how the investment generation method of determining dividends differs from the traditional portfolio average method.

QUESTIONS FOR DISCUSSION

1. Taking any combination of the basic forms of insurance out of which special policy combinations studied in this chapter are constructed, invent a new policy not discussed in the text and explain the circumstances under which it would be useful.

2. Many products are brought to the market because, in the words of the seller, "the consumer demanded it." Do you think that the return-of-premium policy or the return-of-cash-value policy were the response of the insurance industry to consumer demands, or do you feel that they were developed for competitive reasons? What is your opinion of these two policies?

3. During the high-interest-rate environment of the 1980s, many policyholders purchased vanishing-premium policies. Because interest rates dropped in subsequent years, premiums have not vanished as originally projected, and many consumers are dissatisfied. Some observers have proposed requiring that insurance companies and agents make projections only on the basis of the minimum guar-

antees in the policy. Do you agree or disagree with this proposal? Explain.

4. Although the family protection policy attempts to provide protection on the entire family, the insurance on the wife is generally low relative to that on the husband. In addition, the coverage on the wife is term insurance, while only the husband's coverage accumulates cash value. Design a policy that would provide maximum protection on both the husband and wife during the childraising years, with cash values at retirement that vary depending on whether the husband and wife are both alive or only one survives. Indicate the specific types of coverage you would use.

5. John Jones travels considerably in his occupation. Although he thinks that he needs more life insurance, he does not think he can afford it. However, he is considering a $100,000 travel accident policy on the grounds that it will provide at least some additional protection. How would you advise him?

SUGGESTIONS FOR ADDITIONAL READING

Bernstein, Ted S., and Timothy C. Pfeifer. "No-Load Products: The New Breed." *Best's Review* (October 1990).

Black, Kenneth, Jr., and Harold D. Skipper, Jr. *Life Insurance,* 13th ed. Englewood Cliffs, N.J.: Prentice-Hall, 2000. Chapters 5, 6.

Blease, Roger L., and Gary S. Pallay. "Survivorship Life Policy Survey." *Best's Review* (August 1990).

Conant, Roger B. "Inflation and the Variable Annuity." *Journal of the American Society of Chartered Life Underwriters,* vol. 30, no. 4 (October 1976).

Daily, Glenn S. *Low-Load Insurance Products* (International Publishing Corporation, 1990).

Graves, Edward E., ed. *McGill's Life Insurance.* Bryn Mawr, Pa.: The American College, 1994. Chapter 54.

Hallman, G. Victor, and Karen L. Hamilton. *Personal Insurance: Life, Health, and Retirement.* Malvern, Pa.: American Institute for CPCU, 1994, Chapter 4.

Schaeffer, Karen P. "Second-to-Die Plans: Why the Avalanche?" *Best's Review* (August 1990).

WEB SITES TO EXPLORE

American Council of Life Insurance	http://www.acli.com/
American Society of CLU & ChFC	http://www.agents-online.com/ASCLU/web/index.html
Insurance News Network	http://www.insure.com/
Newsedge News Page	http://www.newspage.com/browse/46622/

BUYING LIFE INSURANCE

■

The measure of choosing well, is whether a man likes what he has chosen.

— CHARLES LAMB

CHAPTER OBJECTIVES

When you have finished this chapter, you should be able to

- Identify the three major decisions that must be made in buying life insurance and the sequence in which the decisions should be made
- Identify the ways in which a consumer can determine the financial strength of a life insurer
- Discuss the relative merits of term insurance and cash value insurance for meeting financial security needs
- Explain how differences in cost among traditional life insurance policies can be compared
- Explain how differences in cost among universal and variable life insurance policies can be compared
- Discuss the deficiencies in the current price disclosure system used in the life insurance field
- Briefly summarize the advantages and disadvantages of life insurance as an investment

The purchase of life insurance differs in many ways from the other purchases that the average consumer makes day in and day out. In many ways, it also differs from the purchase of other forms of insurance, since it sometimes combines protection with savings. In addition, because of the long-term nature of most life insurance contracts, the decision normally calls for committing funds well into the future to pay for the policy. Such a long-term commitment obviously requires careful forethought and consideration of objectives. The fact that one out of every five life insurance policies purchased today is dropped within the first 2 years of its purchase is a clear indication of the consumer regrets sometimes associated with the purchase of life insurance. We turn now to the subject of buying life insurance.

DECISIONS IN BUYING LIFE INSURANCE

Three fundamental decisions must be made in the purchase of life insurance:

1. How much should I buy?
2. What kind should I buy?
3. From which company should I buy it?

In Chapter 10, we examined several approaches to answering the first question. Here we are concerned with the remaining two questions. As explained in the discussion that follows, the first and most important question to be addressed in the purchase of life insurance is the amount. Only after this question has been answered should the type of policy to be purchased be addressed.

Buy Term and Invest the Difference?

Buy term and invest the difference are the six most controversial words in the area of life insurance buying. They summarize the philosophy of those who have argued that the individual would be better off by purchasing term insurance and investing, separately, the difference in premiums between term and permanent insurance. The long-raging controversy between the proponents of permanent insurance as an investment and the advocates of insurance for the sake of pure protection will probably never be settled.

If it were not for the fact that the risk management process must also deal with the risk of outliving one's income, we could ignore the debate over term versus cash value life insurance. But the individual must be concerned with the possibility of living beyond the income-earning years and, recognizing this contingency, must plan to meet it. If one foresees that his or her income will cease at some time in the future while the need for income will remain, the logical course of action is to provide for the accumulation of a fund that can be used to replace the income. Life insurance can be one vehicle for amassing that fund, and we ought therefore to discuss the merits of this form of accumulation.

There are, as we have seen, two separate risks that can be met through life insurance: premature death and superannuation. Yet these two risks are diametrically opposed. If the individual dies before reaching retirement age, there is no need to have accumulated

a fund for retirement income. On the other hand, if he or she survives to enjoy retirement, the death benefits will have been unnecessary. Unfortunately, from an insurance-buying point of view, we do not know what the future holds, and so the individual must prepare for both contingencies.

Many persons do not have sufficient income to provide adequate death protection and simultaneously accumulate funds for retirement, forcing a choice between death protection and the savings element. As Table 17.1 indicates, there is an inverse relationship between the amount of insurance protection and the cash value of the various forms of life insurance. The higher the cash value, the lower the amount of death protection that can be purchased for a given number of premium dollars.

The decision to be made in the purchase of insurance should be divided into three separate and unrelated decisions. First, and this is the most important risk-management decision, what should be done about the risk of premature death? How significant is this risk relative to many others the individual faces? Measuring the loss potential here requires determination of the amount of insurance needed. If the potential loss that is beyond the family's margin for contingencies is $250,000 or $500,000, then this is the amount of risk that ought to be transferred to the insurance company.

The first question, then, is not what kind of life insurance should be purchased, but rather, how much is needed. Often, the answer to this first question will provide an answer to the second question, the type of insurance that should be purchased. If the amount of insurance needed is substantial, term insurance may be the only alternative. When the money available for

TABLE 17.1 Protection and Cash Values Available per $100 in Premium—Nonparticipating Rates

Type of Policy	At Age 25, a $100 Premium Will Purchase the Following Amount of Death Protection	Cash Value at the End of 20 Years Will Be
Yearly renewable term	$78,000	$ 0
Ten-year term policy	57,000	0
Whole-life policy	11,300	1,695
Paid up at age 65 whole life	10,250	1,671
Twenty-pay whole life	7,400	1,798

Source: Best's Flitcraft Compend (Oldwick, N.J.: A. M. Best Company, 1993).

life insurance is limited (and it usually is), the savings feature of permanent insurance forces the individual into a compromise in setting up protection for the family during the critical years. If one follows the proper techniques of risk management, one will seek to transfer that portion of the risk of loss of income-earning ability that his or her family could not afford to bear. If sufficient insurance is purchased to replace the income that would be lost, term insurance may be all that the individual can afford. In other words, as we have seen from our programming example, the arguments about term versus other forms of life insurance are meaningless for a substantial portion of the population, because with limited resources available to spend on insurance, there may be very little "difference" left after providing for complete protection.

In the cold realism of mathematics, we noted that the insurable value of a young man earning $30,000 a year might be as much as $300,000, or even more. If this individual chooses to purchase cash value coverage for this amount, the premiums would be more than $3000 a year. Even based on the needs approach, we saw that significant amounts of insurance may be required. The buyer opting for permanent life insurance must make a choice between savings and protection. This is not intended as a criticism of cash-value life insurance. It is a criticism of the misuse of cash-value life insurance and the violations of good risk-management practice that it entails. As a matter of fact, the major criticism that can be levied against cash-value life insurance is that it frequently leads to a violation of all three rules of risk management. With a limited number of dollars available for the purchase of life insurance, cash-value life insurance carries an opportunity cost in the death protection that must be forgone. As a result, many individuals leave their families inadequately protected. They fail to consider the odds by purchasing coverage against an event that is not a contingency at all, and in so doing, they risk more than their family can afford to lose. They risk a lot for a little by underinsuring their income-earning ability, leaving a serious exposure unprotected in exchange for interest on the funds that should have been used to protect against that exposure.[1] They

commit the great error of permitting the question of the type of policy to purchase to determine the answer to the question of how much to purchase instead of vice versa. The first and most important decision is the amount of protection needed, a decision that must be made without reference to the type of coverage that will be obtained to provide the protection.

In deciding on the form of life insurance to be purchased, we leave the area of risk management and enter the field of finance. The question of term insurance versus permanent cash value insurance is a separate issue, unrelated to the problems of risk management. Once the individual has decided to transfer the risk of the loss of $100,000 or $200,000 in income-earning ability to an insurance company, the rules and principles of risk management are no longer helpful. The choice of the type of insurance contract that should be used is an investment question and should be evaluated by the same standards that are used in ranking investments of other types. As a matter of fact, the question is not really one of term versus permanent insurance at all, but rather a choice between permanent insurance and alternative forms of investment. The only logical reason for the purchase of cash-value insurance is that it is superior to the other investment alternatives available to the insured for his or her purpose.[2]

Sometimes, the purveyors of life insurance attempt to pose the choice between term and permanent insurance in terms of *protection* rather than an investment decision by pointing out that term insurance cannot be continued beyond age 65 or 70. "Term insurance is only temporary protection," they criticize, as if there were something inherently good about insurance that is not temporary. When one recalls that the income-earning period and the economic life value of an individual are also temporary, it is *permanent* that takes on the undesirable connotation. By age 65, a person's economic value has declined to zero in most cases; in addition, by this time the economic responsibility to dependents is also normally fulfilled. One has little need for income-earning protection at this age; yet it is during the 35-year period following this age that the cost of life insurance becomes prohibitive. Nothing could

[1] Wouldn't it be absurd if an insurance company approached the owner of a $1 million building with the proposal that the owner purchase $100,000 in coverage on the building and use the premium saved for an investment program? Yet this is essentially what occurs in the life insurance field when individuals are persuaded to purchase high-premium, benefit-certain life insurance in an amount less than the required level of protection.

[2] We will defer our discussion of life insurance as an investment until the next chapter, which deals with the retirement risk.

more clearly be a violation of the principles of risk management than insuring an asset that no longer has value.[3]

Life Insurance as an Investment

The long-raging controversy between the proponents of permanent insurance as an investment and the advocates of insurance for the sake of pure protection will probably never be settled. There is a considerable amount of literature—much of it generated by vendors of competing investments—that condemns life insurance as an investment. The issue, however, is much more complex than this literature suggests, and anyone who states that "life insurance is a poor investment" is oversimplifying the issue. In fact, the assertion that any investment is "good" or "poor" rests on a variety of unstated assumptions that may or may not hold true for a particular set of circumstances. There are some situations in which life insurance may compare favorably with other investment alternatives, and the student should at least be aware of these situations.

The first feature that is often cited in support of life insurance as an investment is the compulsion it entails. Many people do not have the self-discipline and determination required to follow through with their plans for the regular accumulation of a savings fund. Once a policy is taken out, an individual usually will pay the premiums rather than deprive the family of the protection the policy gives, and paying the premiums means making regular contributions to the savings element of the contract. Frankly, this argument is not particularly compelling.

A more persuasive advantage of life insurance as an investment is the fact that it enjoys certain tax advantages that some other forms of investment do not enjoy. First, increments in the cash value are not taxable until actually received by the insured. At the time that the policy is surrendered, the excess of the cash surrender value over the premiums paid is taxable as ordinary income. Furthermore, the insured is permitted to deduct the total amount of premiums paid, which includes the cost of protection, in computing the gain. The advantage of the tax deferral lies not only in the fact that the individual's tax rate may be lower when the gain is eventually taxed, but more importantly in the fact that the accumulation of untaxed earnings will be greater than the accumulation of earnings that are taxed. To earn a net return on investments that do not share the tax advantage enjoyed by life insurance, the gross rate of return on the alternative investment must be higher than that available under the life contract.

Finally, there is a safety of principal not found in certain other investments. The major criticism usually leveled at life insurance as an investment is the relatively low rate of return—usually between 6 and 8 percent (but sometimes, depending on the company, much lower). Perhaps the rate of return is low, but low relative to what? Common stocks represent a riskier form of investment. The investor hopes to realize gains, but may also suffer losses. Traditional life insurance cash values are a guaranteed form of investment, with both safety of principal and a guaranteed minimum rate of return.[4] In addition, the newer interest-sensitive policies make it possible to realize significantly higher returns than those guaranteed in the policy. Finally, for the investor who prefers the appreciation potential of common stocks, variable life insurance offers the same tax-deferral as traditional cash value life insurance.

With respect to the return on life insurance policies, it should be noted that life insurance policies have a relatively high expense component. For many forms of life insurance, the front-end commission makes the return during the early years negative, and in the long run less attractive than alternative investments. The actual rate of return that will be earned on the investment element, then, depends on the time for which the policy is maintained. If it is to be considered as an investment, life insurance should be considered only as a *long-term* investment.

Besides the expense factor, another legitimate criticism of traditional life insurance as an investment is that inflation may seriously erode the value

[3] Another criticism of term insurance, which hardly deserves comment, is "You have to die to collect," undoubtedly the most absurd criticism that can be made. The implication is that if you do not collect under an insurance policy, you have somehow lost in the transaction. One might just as well say that your house has to burn down in the case of fire insurance or that you have to run over someone to collect under your automobile liability insurance. The best approach to use on someone who makes such a comment is to refer the person to any insurance textbook that explains the operation of the insurance principle. Perhaps he or she will learn that the insured receives something under an insurance policy even without collecting.

[4] In addition to the insurer's capital and surplus, life insurance cash values are guaranteed by state insolvency funds, virtually all of which guarantee cash values up to $100,000.

of the dollars contributed, but this is a legitimate criticism of all fixed-dollar instruments. When one makes judgments about the "goodness" or "badness" of a given type of investment in the long run, there is an implicit assumption about the future trends in the economy. If the future economy is marked by inflation and a rising price level, then traditional cash value life insurance (or any other fixed-dollar investment) will be less attractive than those investments that ride the inflationary trend.

The most appealing feature of life insurance as an investment is its complementary functions of providing protection against premature death at the same time it provides an accumulation that may be used if the individual does not die prematurely. If the individual has no need for protection against premature death, it is unlikely that life insurance will match other investment alternatives. At the risk of oversimplification, the premium for cash-value life insurance covers three things: the first part goes to pay the death benefits for those members of the group who die, the second part goes to pay insurer operating expenses (including agents' commissions), and the third part contributes to the accumulating savings element. The individual who has no need for death protection but purchases life insurance as an investment incurs costs for death benefits and commissions that are avoided with other investments. To the extent that life insurance is an attractive investment, its appeal is based primarily on its role in simultaneously meeting the diametrically opposed risks of premature death and superannuation.

For many individuals, traditional cash-value life insurance may be an attractive and dependable investment. On the other hand, there are many individuals who are not content with the fixed-dollar nature of traditional life insurance, preferring equity investments with their potentially greater return. The choice, however, is a matter of finance rather than of insurance.

Choosing the Company

In choosing from among the approximately 2000 life insurance companies doing business in the United States, the insurance buyer may consider many factors—some more important than others. Among the weightier considerations are the company's financial strength and integrity, its policy forms and their suitability to the insured's needs, and the cost.

Financial Strength and Integrity Since the life insurance policy represents a long-term promise on the part of the seller, the financial strength of the insurer and its ability eventually to meet its promise rank as the first consideration. Although consumers have generally taken the financial strength of life insurers for granted, this changed dramatically in 1991 when several large life insurers encountered financial difficulties. Throughout much of 1990, industry observers had warned that a number of life insurers were in a perilous condition. In April 1991, the California insurance commissioner seized the Executive Life Insurance Company, triggering speculation about the financial condition of other life insurers. The seizure sensitized consumers to the risk of life insurer insolvencies and, as policyholders lost confidence, caused *policyholder runs* on other life insurers. The seizure of Executive Life was followed by the failure of First Capital Life and Fidelity Bankers Life[5] and Monarch Life Insurance. Then, in July 1991, Mutual Benefit Life Insurance Company of Newark, New Jersey, the 18th largest life insurer in the country, with $13.8 billion in assets, submitted to the control of the New Jersey insurance department.

The financial problems afflicting life insurers in the early 1990s resulted from three causes. The first was a decline in the value of the insurers' bond portfolios. The second was the almost simultaneous souring of mortgage loans held by some insurers. The third factor was disintermediation—the "run on the bank"—which exacerbated the problems created by the first two.[6]

Many authorities argue that the difficulties encountered by some life insurers can be traced to the introduction of universal life and other interest-sensitive policies, which were sold on the basis of their rates of return. Insurers developed UL and other interest-sensitive policies in response to pressures caused by rising interest rates in the late 1970s and early 1980s. At that time, many insureds were borrowing cash values or cashing policies to invest the funds at higher rates elsewhere. Insurers felt pressured to

[5] First Capital Life and Fidelity Bankers Life are subsidiaries of First Capital Holdings Corporation, whose largest shareholder is Shearson Lehman Brothers, Inc., a subsidiary of American Express Company.

[6] The problem of disintermediation for life insurers arises from higher returns on alternative investments. It was intensified by the failure of a few large life insurers.

offer high rates of return on the investment element in life insurance policies. This led some insurers to invest in high-yield bonds (often called unrated bonds, or more commonly junk bonds) and real estate. When performance in the real estate and bond markets deteriorated, it affected the portfolios of a number of life insurers. Insurers might have weathered these adversities except for the policyholder runs. Withdrawals by insureds threatened to deplete the liquid assets of the insurers, forcing them to liquidate mortgages and real estate in a depressed market. Regulators stepped in to stem the outflow of insurers' cash before the assets were depleted.[7] Although many policyholders have recovered from state guaranty funds, the insolvencies illustrated that the insolvency of life insurers is a real threat.

In Chapter 3, we discussed the insurer ratings that are published by A. M. Best and other financial rating services. These rating agencies are far from infallible, as evidenced by their failure to anticipate the approaching difficulties of the companies that were taken over by regulators. Still, given the complexities in insurance company accounting, we believe that the insurer rating services are a valuable source of information. It makes sense to compare the ratings from several rating agencies. The higher the ratings and the more the rating services agree, the less is the likelihood that the company will encounter financial problems.

Types of Policies Available Here the matters of concern include not only the specific policy forms available (such as modified whole life, decreasing term, annual renewable term, family income policies, or special annuity forms), but also the availability of participating and nonparticipating contracts. Most major companies offer a wide range of policy forms, including those discussed in the preceding chapters plus many others. However, a given company may not write a particular form of coverage in which the buyer is interested.

The availability of participating and nonparticipating contracts may also be an important consideration. Mutual companies offer mainly participating policies, whereas some stock companies offer both kinds, and other stock insurers issue only nonparticipating forms. Under participating agreements, there is an opportunity cost to be considered in the excess payment that may be returned as a dividend. On the other hand, with nonparticipating policies, the insurer gets only one chance in pricing, and there is no provision for returning gains that may be realized from improved mortality experience or favorable investments. Although some people favor participating policies and others favor the nonparticipating kind, the preference of the buyer in this respect will be a determining factor in choice of company.

Cost Consideration Although most life insurance companies invest in approximately the same securities and start with similar mortality tables, there are significant differences in the premiums different companies charge for the same type of policy. This wide range of premiums makes the selection of a company and a policy a complicated process. The fact that the premium for a whole-life policy with Company A is $10 per $1000 and the premium for a whole-life policy with Company B is $12 per $1000 does not necessarily mean that Company A is offering the best "deal" and that Company B is overcharging its customers. The differences in premiums do not mean differences in cost. In the case of cash-value policies, the premium paid by the insured does not represent a true cost, since a part of the payment goes toward the accumulation of the cash value. The cash value of Company B's policy may increase more rapidly than that of Company A. In addition, the settlement options or other internal policy provisions may be more liberal.[8] Unfortunately, it is also true that the provisions of Company A's policy may be more liberal or its cash value may increase more rapidly.

One of the most common fallacies about differences in premiums among life insurance companies is that these variations can always be traced to actuarial differences in the benefits of the contracts, and

[7] Although the seizure of Executive Life was the formal trigger for widespread concern about life insurer insolvencies, there were earlier indications that a number of life insurers faced financial problems. In 1990, of the 1926 life and health insurers in the NAIC's data base, 482 had four or more IRIS ratios outside the usual ranges. See Joseph M. Belth, "A Watch List of Insurance Companies Based on the NAIC's 1990 IRIS Ratios," *The Insurance Forum,* vol. 17, no. 9 (September 1990). See also Joseph M. Belth, "Life Insurance Companies' Junk Bonds, Troubled Mortgages, Real Estate and Investment in Affiliates," *The Insurance Forum,* vol. 17, no. 8 (September 1990).

[8] The first point to recognize in comparing cost among companies is that the policy provisions of the contracts are probably not identical. Disregarding cash values and dividends for the moment, there are other differences of great importance, and a price comparison of two contracts is valid only if the two contracts are identical in other respects.

in the field of life insurance, you get exactly what you pay for. While some discrepancies in premiums among companies may be traced to differing rates at which the saving elements of the contracts accumulate, to differences in dividends, and to differences in the liberality of policy provisions, the dissimilarities may also be due to varying levels of expense and efficiency of operation. Since the company's operating expenses must eventually be borne by the insureds, the levels of these expenses are important determinants of price. Not only is internal efficiency important in price setting, but commissions and other acquisition costs may also differ significantly among companies, resulting in wide differentials in the actual costs to the insured. New companies in particular, which are attempting to grow rapidly, often pay substantially higher commissions to their agents, and these commissions must be passed on to the consumer as higher premiums. For this reason, many consumerists suggest avoiding new life insurance companies. Others recommend dealing only with companies licensed to do business in New York State, because New York imposes a statutory maximum on commission levels and requires companies operating in the state to observe this maximum in other states in which they operate as well. Most authorities recommend that consumers should avoid credit life insurance, because of its high commission expense and high premiums. It is a simple principle of mathematics that higher costs incurred by the company will mean higher costs to the consumer.

The popular misconception that "you get what you pay for in life insurance" is based on an unwarranted faith in the principle of competition. Some people maintain that the marketplace will effectively keep a company from overcharging the public and that competition will result in an equality of value among companies. But is competition truly an adequate device for the protection of the consumer in the field of life insurance? An increasing number of authorities maintain that there are excessive prices in the life insurance field, and to the extent that those excessive prices exist, competition is obviously not effective.[9] In other words, when purchasing life insurance, one cannot always be certain of getting what one is paying for or that more attractive alternatives

are not to be had. Competition is effective only when the consumer is aware of the alternatives, and the complexity of price analysis has generally precluded this condition in the past. Although improved methods of cost comparison have become available, this remains a challenging area for consumers.

Comparing Differences in Cost

The simplest cost comparison in life insurance is between two nonparticipating term policies. Since neither policy provides dividends or cash value accumulations, a simple and straightforward comparison is possible. Once dividends or cash values are introduced, the process of comparison becomes increasingly complicated. Differences in premiums may be offset by differing rates at which the cash values accumulate, or through dividends. With an increasing number of variables to be considered, and a complex pricing structure based on the variables, it is easy for the insurance buyer to be misled.

Traditional System of Net-Cost Comparisons

One method of selling life insurance widespread in the past uses an illustrative projected *net cost*. Such proposals are not only misleading, but the manner in which they are usually presented is fundamentally invalid as well. The basic technique is to make a summation of the total premiums paid over some period of time (usually 20 years), subtract projected dividends, then subtract the cash value, and call the answer the net cost of the policy. The fallacy in this technique is that it completely ignores the time value of money. An accurate appraisal of a proposed contract must include consideration of the opportunity costs involved.

To illustrate, let us consider two term contracts without cash values, one a nonparticipating contract with a $4 per $1000 premium and the other a participating contract at $6 per $1000. The net cost of the latter contract can be made to appear lower than that of the former: Company A charges $4 per $1000. The premium for a $50,000 policy will be $200 a year, and at the end of a 20-year period, the net cost will be $4000. Company B, on the other hand, charges $300 for the $50,000 policy and returns the *overcharge* at the end of the year as a dividend. It has the use of the $100 overcharge for a full year. Assuming that the company can earn 5 percent on the $100 overcharge, it can return a dividend of $105, making the *net cost* to the policy-holder $195 for the year and the net cost over the 20-year period $3900. Thus, the overcharge

9 For example, see Joseph M. Belth, *The Retail Price Structure in American Life Insurance* (Bloomington: Indiana University Press 1966), and *Life Insurance: A Consumer's Handbook* (Bloomington: Indiana University Press, 1973).

on participating policies can permit a net-cost comparison, which, ignoring the interest on the insured's overpayments, makes the cost appear lower. When dividends are left to accumulate, the opportunity cost becomes even greater. Although our illustration has used a nonparticipating policy and a participating policy for the purpose of simplification, it should be clear that the same distortion can result when both policies are participating, but have differing levels of overcharge.[10] The same approach may be used to distort comparisons of policies with different savings components.

Interest-Adjusted Method In response to the demand from many sources for a more accurate system of comparing life insurance costs, in 1969 the life insurance industry appointed a special committee, known as the Joint Special Committee on Life Insurance Costs. In its report, issued in mid-1970, this committee recommended an alternate cost comparison method known as the interest-adjusted method. As its name implies, the *interest-adjusted method* considers the time value of money by applying an interest adjustment to the yearly premiums and dividends.

In 1976, the National Association of Insurance Commissioners (NAIC) adopted a *Life Insurance Solicitation Model Regulation* and recommended it to the states for enactment. One part of this regulation requires that insurers provide buyers with a *surrender cost index* and a *net payment cost index,* which are two slightly different versions of the interest-adjusted measure of cost. The regulation also requires the insurer to provide the buyer with an equivalent annual dividend for the policy under consideration. Some insurers voluntarily comply with this regulation, even in states where it has not been adopted.

Surrender Cost Index The manner in which the interest-adjusted method differs from the traditional cost method can best be explained through an example. Assume that the policy under consideration is a $10,000 whole-life policy with a $240 annual premium. Projected dividends amount to $1300, and the cash value at the end of the twentieth year is $3420. The traditional cost calculation uses simple arithmetic:

Total premiums paid over 20-year period	$4800.00
Less: Dividends received during the 20 years	1300.00
Net premiums over the 20-year period	3500.00
Subtract year 20 cash value	3420.00
Net insurance cost	80.00
Net cost per year ($80/20 years)	4.00
Net cost per $1000	0.40

From this calculation, it appears that the insured's cost per $1000 of coverage over the 20-year period has been a mere 40 cents per $1000. As we have seen, this is misleading in that it ignores the time value of money.

Calculating the interest-adjusted cost index for the same policy calls for a more involved computation:

20 years' premiums accumulated at 5 percent interest	$8333.00
Less: 20 years' dividends accumulated at 5 percent	2256.00
Net premiums over the 20-year period	6077.00
Subtract year 20 cash surrender value	3420.00
Insurance cost	2657.00
Amount to which $1 deposited annually will accumulate in 20 years at 5 percent	34.719
For interest-adjusted surrender cost index, divide $2657 by $34.719	76.52
Interest-adjusted surrender cost index per $1000 per year at the end of year 20	7.65

By accumulating both the premiums paid by the insured and the dividends at interest, the interest-adjusted method considers the opportunity cost by reflecting the amount the premiums paid could generate at a conservative rate[11] over the years used in the comparison. Although we have used a 20-year period, the computation is also often made for 10 years. Subtracting the cash value from the accumulated

[10] Comparisons between participating and nonparticipating policies involve additional difficulties. Some allowance must be made for dividends under the participating policies, and since dividends usually increase under a policy as time goes by, they must be considered over the long run. At the same time, it should be recognized that future dividends cannot be guaranteed and are mere estimates based on past experience or future projections.

[11] The Joint Special Committee on Life Insurance Costs recommended 4 percent as the interest rate to be used because it felt that this was reasonably close to the after-tax rate that could be earned over a period of years on personal investments with the same security and stability of life insurance. The 5 percent rate used in our illustration has replaced the 4 percent rate.

premiums minus dividends indicates the insured's actual cost if the policy is terminated at the end of the 20 years, considering the time value of money. Dividing the cost by $34.719 indicates the number of dollars per year it would be necessary to invest and allow to accumulate at 5 percent to equal the $2657 cost of insurance.

Net Payment Cost Index The *net payment cost index* is a variation of the interest-adjusted method that attempts to overcome some of the criticisms that have been leveled at the surrender cost index. It differs from the surrender cost index only in the fact that the cash value is not deducted at the end of the 10 or 20 years used in the computation. In our example policy, the net payment cost index is computed by dividing the net premiums over the 20-year period ($6077) by the value of $1 annually at 5 percent ($34.719). The net payment cost index for the policy is $175.03, or $17.50 per $1000 per year.

Significance of the Indexes It should be clear that both the surrender cost index and the net payment cost index are meaningless in themselves; they merely provide a basis for comparing one policy with another, and it is the difference in the index between two policies that is important. Small differences that may be indicated between two companies by either index are probably not significant. The cost index is determined by the interest rate used, and a slightly different rate could result in a different cost advantage between two policies, particularly when the difference is small.

In addition, it is possible that some companies may manipulate their cash value tables for the tenth and twentieth years—the years for which the index is usually computed. This may make the policy appear more attractive at those points in time, while it is far less attractive at all other times. New model life insurance disclosure legislation recommended to the states by the NAIC in December 1983 seeks to address this problem. The NAIC new model legislation requires a notation in the disclosure document when an unusual pattern of premiums or benefits makes the comparison of the cost index with other policies unreliable. It also requires notation when the dividend illustration for a particular policy is not made in accordance with the contribution principles.

Despite these shortcomings, the interest-adjusted indexes represent a vast improvement over the traditional net-cost approach to comparing policies. Published information sources are available that list interest-adjusted cost data for all of the larger and better known companies.[12] For the consumer who is willing to spend the time and effort to compare costs, the interest-adjusted indexes represent an important source of information.

Other Cost-Comparison Techniques The interest-adjusted method represents one of two basic approaches designed to deal with the fact that the life insurance premium consists of a payment for protection and a contribution to savings. Under the interest-adjusted method, an assumption is made concerning the rate of yield on the savings, and the cost of protection is calculated. A second approach is to make an assumption concerning the cost of the protection, and then calculate the yield on the savings element. Several models have been devised under which the rate of return on the investment element of a life insurance policy is calculated by assuming that the cost of the protection is the same as the cost of an amount of term insurance equal to the difference between the face amount of the policy and an increasing investment fund.[13] The obvious advantage of this approach is that it provides a basis for comparisons not only between two cash value life insurance policies, but also between cash value life insurance and alternative investments. In 1995, the California Insurance Division adopted regulations requiring that consumers be given information on the annual rate of return on life insurance contracts at the time of sale. Whether other states will follow remains to be seen.

Premium Payment Options Although life insurance premiums represent the annual cost for the protection, most insurers offer installment options under which the purchaser can pay the premium semiannually, quarterly, or monthly. The monthly option is frequently based on a preauthorized check system, in which payments are automatically deducted from the purchaser's bank account. Although these installment arrangements represent a convenience to the insured, the cost for the convenience can be substantial. An insurer with an annual premium of $1000 has a

12 For example, see the current editions of *Best's Flitcraft Compend* (Oldwick, N.J.: A. M. Best Company) or Price Gains, *Interest Adjusted Index: Life Insurance Payment and Cost Comparisons* (Cincinnati: National Underwriter Company).
13 For example, see Michael L. Murray, "Analyzing the Investment Value of Cash Value Life Insurance," *Journal of Risk and Insurance,* vol. 43, no. 1 (March 1976), pp. 121–128.

monthly payment option in which the monthly payment is $95. Using a standard annual percentage rate formula, the cost of the installment "convenience" represents a 30 percent annualized charge. Consumer advocates such as Professor Joseph Belth[14] argue that arrangements of this type clearly call for a more rigorous system of price disclosure in the sale of insurance.

The NAIC Life Insurance Illustrations Model Regulation

The NAIC's Life Insurance Illustrations Model Regulation originated as a response to deceptive sales practices based on policy illustrations that are misleading and incomplete. Although deceptive illustrations have probably existed from the earliest days of life insurance, they intensified in the 1980s, when microcomputer software became available that permitted insurance agents to make policy projections using "illustrative" rates of return. A typical example was the so-called *vanishing premium policy,* a concept that was widely marketed in the 1980s. A vanishing premium policy was usually a participating whole-life policy with relatively high premiums and generous dividends. In theory, dividends would be allowed to accumulate until the accumulated dividends, plus anticipated future dividends were sufficient to pay all future premiums under the policy, at which point the premium would "vanish." Vanishing premium policies enjoyed their greatest popularity during the 1980s, when interest rates on such policies often reached 10 to 12 percent. The policy illustrations that were used in the sale of these policies projected interest rates of 10, 12, and 15 percent into the future, giving prospective buyers delusions of astronomical returns on their investments. In fact, in some instances, the agents represented the contracts as investments, retirement accounts, or even as pension plans. Once interest rates fell, premiums that "vanished" reappeared for many insurance buyers.[15]

In 1995, in response to alleged abusive practices in life insurance policy illustrations, the NAIC adopted a new Model Life Insurance Illustrations Regulation. By early 1998, it had been adopted in 24 states and 5 more were considering its adoption. Although the *model regulation* applies only in those states where it has been adopted, most major life insurers have elected to abide by the model. The model applies only to sales of nonvariable life insurance, but the NAIC is also drafting model regulations applying to variable life insurance products and to annuities.

The basic purposes of the model regulation is first, to ensure that life insurance policy illustrations do not mislead consumers, and second, to make illustrations more understandable. To achieve these goals, the law establishes standards that apply to all group and individual life insurance policy illustrations except variable life, credit life, and insurance with death benefits not exceeding $10,000.

For each policy it sells, the insurer must inform the commissioner of insurance whether the policy will be sold with or without illustrations. If a policy is identified as one to be sold without illustrations, no illustration may be used in its sale. For policies identified as those to be marketed with illustrations, specific standards apply to the illustration used. All illustrations must be certified annually by an *illustration actuary,* appointed by the insurer. The actuary must be qualified according to the Actuarial Standards Board requirements regarding education, experience, and familiarity with the model law. The illustration actuary must also be a member in good standing of the American Academy of Actuaries. The illustration actuary must certify that the assumptions in all illustrations used in marketing a policy comply with the model regulation and with the requirements of a new Actuarial Standard of Practice (ASOP), developed by the Actuarial Standards Board in cooperation with the NAIC's Life Insurance Committee.

Projected performance of a policy must be illustrated on three separate bases. First, performance is illustrated using the policy guarantees. Second, performance is illustrated under assumptions reflecting the *disciplined current scale,* an actuarial standard reflecting nonguaranteed elements that are reasonable, based on the actual recent historical experience of the insurer. The Actuarial Standards Board has developed the standards to be applied in the development of the disciplined current scale. It should reflect the most recently available experience on policies of the type illustrated, but may not include

[14] See Joseph M. Belth, "The Arguments Against Rigorous Disclosure," *The Insurance Forum,* vol. 22, no. 2 (February 1995). The majority of insurers will accept monthly premiums only if they are through an automatic fund transfer from the policy owner's account. Monthly premiums are normally 8.81 percent or 8.9 percent of the annual premium. This represents about 11.5 percent and 13.6 percent respectively.

[15] The disappointing return on vanishing premium policies generated thousands of lawsuits against the insurers that sold them, including class-action suits against Prudential, Metropolitan Life, New York Life, Crown Life, The Equitable, and other giants in the industry. The class-action suits purported to represent all the policyholders in the country or all the people in a particular state.

any projected or assumed improvements in experience.[16] Finally, a scale halfway between the guaranteed and disciplined current scale is illustrated.

Copies of illustrations provided to clients must be sent to the insurer along with the policy application. The copies must be signed by the applicant and by the agent. If an illustration is not used for a policy identified to the commissioner as one for which an illustration is used, the producer must inform the insurer and the applicant must acknowledge the absence of a policy illustration. An illustration must then be sent to the applicant.

In addition to illustrations provided at the time of sale, the insured must be given an annual report, indicating the current death benefit, annual premium, current cash value, dividends, and any policy loans. If the annual report does not include an updated policy illustration, the insured must be informed that one is available upon request and encourage the policyholder to request it.

Other areas addressed by the model law prohibit certain activities of an insurer, its producers, or other authorized representatives. These include representing a policy as anything other than a life insurance policy, making misleading use of nonguaranteed elements, or using future policy values that are higher than possible under the disciplined current scale of the insurer. The model also prohibits the use of the term *vanish, vanishing premium,* or similar terms that imply a policy will become paid up dependent on nonguaranteed elements.

NAIC Model Replacement Regulation

In June 1998, the Life Insurance Committee of the National Association of Insurance Commissioners adopted a new Life Insurance and Annuities Replacement Model Regulation, which is expected to be adopted by many states. The model regulation establishes a new regulatory scheme for replacements and *financed purchases* of life insurance and annuities. (A financed purchase occurs when policy values from an existing policy, such as the cash value, is borrowed or surrendered to provide funds to purchase another policy.) Under the model regulation, where the sale involves a potential replacement, the agent must provide a notice regarding replacements

that identifies some disadvantages of replacements and recommends the insured make a comparison between his or her current policy and the proposed policy. Insurance companies that are replacing an existing policy must provide the insured with a 30-day "free look" period, during which the policyholder can cancel that new policy and receive a full refund. Agents and insurers planning to replace a policy must provide written notification to the insurance company that issued the policy being replaced and, where requested, provide a copy of the policy illustration or policy summary for the proposed policy. The replacing company must provide credit for prior periods of coverage toward satisfying the suicide clause, and, where the replacing insurer is the same as the original insurer, must provide credit toward meeting the incontestability period. The model does not apply to sales of credit life insurance or to group life or annuities where there is no direct solicitation of individuals.

Industry Reform Initiatives

The alleged abuses in life insurance policy illustrations that prompted the NAIC to develop the model Life Insurance Illustrations and Life Insurance Replacement model regulations also served as the motivation for efforts within the industry to address this problem. Two efforts are noteworthy.

Insurance Marketplace Standards Association (IMSA) One industry response was the creation of the Insurance Marketplace Standards Association (IMSA), which has defined six Principles of Ethical Conduct for marketing life insurance and annuity products in the individual market. The principles address such areas as fairness and service to consumers, fair competition, advertising and sales materials, consumer complaints, and supervision of producers. An insurer that wishes to become a member of IMSA commits to abide by the principles and submits to a thorough self-assessment with respect to the principles, followed by a review by an independent assessor. If the applicant meets the requirements of the IMSA, the insurer is given a 3-year membership and is permitted to use the IMSA logo for marketing purposes.

Life Insurance Illustration Questionnaire Because of increasing awareness of the problem with life insurance illustrations, the American Society of CLU & ChFC developed a *Life Insurance Illustration*

[16] Some insurers, to improve their illustrations, have included assumptions about improving mortality and lapse rates.

Questionnaire (IQ), for use in evaluating life insurance illustrations. The IQ consists of five sections (General, Mortality, Interest or Crediting Rates, Expenses, and Persistency). Each section contains a series of questions designed to elicit information about nonguaranteed performance assumptions used in life insurance illustrations. Properly used, the IQ can help reveal whether misleading assumptions have been made in the illustration. Use of the IQ by insurance companies or agents, however, is voluntary.

Shopping for Universal and Variable Life

While universal life and variable universal life have widened the range of consumer choices, they have also compounded the difficulty in shopping for life insurance. In fact, there is a strong possibility that the increased flexibility of universal life and variable life will require consideration of so many variables that the decision process will become unmanageable. Before leaving the subject of buying life insurance, it seems appropriate that we at least touch on the subject of purchasing universal and variable life.

Factors to Consider in Universal and Variable Life Costs The same three factors that are used in rate-making in life insurance—interest, mortality, and loading—are the factors that must be considered in evaluating a universal life policy. Unfortunately, it may be very difficult to bring these elements into focus, since they are uncertain at the time the policy is purchased and are often interrelated. The expense charges, for example, will determine the portion of each premium that will be available for addition to the cash value. This, in turn, will determine the rate at which the cash value will increase.

Interest Although the minimum interest rate guaranteed in the policy is of some passing interest, it will not provide much in the way of information that can be helpful in evaluating the product. More important by far is the actual interest credited to the policy. (Interest earned and interest credited to policies may not be the same.) In most cases, the interest rate actually credited to universal life policies is determined by the insurer from time to time, subject to the minimum specified rate. Prospective customers should ask the agents for recent fund performance reports.

Mortality The charge for the life insurance protection under most universal life policies is usually competitive with that of other universal life insurers and with traditional insurers. Nevertheless, the prospective buyer should determine the level of these charges, as indicated by past and current practice of the insurer. While universal life policies indicate guaranteed mortality charges, these guaranteed rates are generally far more than the actual charges currently being made and are not of much use in evaluating the contract. Again, information on the insurers' current practice is of much greater significance than the guaranteed rates.

Loading The differences among insurers with respect to expense charges and the complexities such charges introduce into the analysis are almost overwhelming. One company may charge a fixed fee of, say, $30 to $50 a month for the first year of the policy with only modest charges thereafter (a front-end load). Some companies make no charge when the policy is sold, but charge a withdrawal fee when cash is withdrawn (a rear-end load). Another might charge 5 percent of each premium paid plus a charge for withdrawals. Sometimes the additional charge for withdrawals remains fixed, and sometimes it decreases over time. Some companies charge a monthly or an annual contract maintenance fee, others charge an investment adviser's fee, and some retain a part of the investment income generated. With such a wide range of approaches to the expense charges for a universal life policy, it seems clear that comparing differences among policies is exceedingly difficult.

Universal and Variable Life Benchmarks The complexities of universal and variable life have led one expert to conclude that it is impractical to search for the lowest possible price and that the best one can hope to do is determine whether the charges for mortality and expense on a policy being considered are reasonably priced. For this purpose, Professor Joseph M. Belth has developed a model for comparing the cost of a universal life or variable life policy against a *benchmark*. Basically, Belth's formula treats some funds as being *invested* in the policy and computes the cost of the insurance by assuming that these invested funds earn some assumed rate of interest. Belth's formula for computing the cost per $1000 of protection is:

$$YPT = \frac{(P + CVP)(1 + i) - (CV + D)}{(DB - CV)(0.001)}$$

where *YPT* is the yearly price per $1000 of protection, *P* is the annual premium, *CVP* is the cash value at the end of the preceding year, *i* is the assumed interest rate expressed as a decimal, *CV* is the cash value at the end of the year, *D* is the dividend (if any) for the year, and *DB* is the death benefit at the end of the year.

If we focus on the numerator in the formula, it is evident that this part of the formula computes the policy's total cost by comparing what the year-end fund would have been had it been invested at interest rate *i* with the actual funds available under the policy—the new cash value and the dividend. At the beginning of the year, the policyholder "invests" the cash value at the end of the previous year *(CVP)* and the premium *(P)*. Had the insured invested the cash value and premium elsewhere at a given interest rate *i,* they would have accumulated to $(CVP + P) \times (1 + i)$. Because he invested them in the insurance policy, he has a new cash value *(CV)* and a dividend *(D)*. The difference between what he would have had and what he does have represents the cost of the policy. The total annual cost for the year is then divided by the amount of pure life insurance protection (logically defined as the total death benefit minus the cash value) to determine the cost per $1000.

To illustrate the application of Belth's formula for computing the cost of insurance, assume that the policy in question has an annual premium of $1000, that the cash value at the end of the preceding year was $2900 and that the cash value at the end of the current year is $3759, that the annual dividend is $289, that the death benefit is $54,368, and that the interest rate is 8 percent. Inserting these values in the formula, we make the following computations:

(1) YPT
$$= \frac{(\$1,000 + \$2,900)\,(1 + .08) - (\$3,759 + \$289)}{(\$54,368 - \$3,759)\,(0.001)}$$

(2) $$YPT = \frac{\$4,212 - \$4,080}{(\$50,608)\,(0.001)}$$

(3) $$YPT = \frac{\$164.00}{\$50.61}$$

(4) $$YPT = \$3.24$$

The cost of protection per $1000 is $3.24. Once this cost has been determined, it can be compared with benchmark costs that were computed by Professor Belth using modest assumptions. According to Belth, if the yearly price per $1000 for the policy is the same or lower than the benchmark price, the combined mortality and loading are small. If the yearly price is higher than the benchmark, but less than 200 percent of the benchmark, combined mortality and expense charges are medium. If the yearly price for the policy is more than 200 percent of the benchmark price, the combined mortality and loading is large. The benchmark prices developed by Belth are indicated in Table 17.2.

To perform the computations, the prospective buyer will need, for the years to be measured: (1) the annual premium, (2) the cash value at the end of each year, (3) the annual dividend payable at the end of the year, and (4) the death benefit at the end of each year. An appropriate rate of interest must be assumed. Professor Belth recommends that the computation be continued up to and including age 74 for the individual.

Table 17.2 also includes front-end load multiples, which may be used to measure the size of the policy's front-end load. When the policy is front-end loaded, higher prices are charged in the first one or two years to cover sales and administrative expenses. If the policy is front-end loaded, the yearly price indicated by the computation will be substantially above the benchmark. However, if the front-end load for the policy is less than the multiple for the age as indicated in Table 17.2, the load is not unreasonable. When evaluating the size of a front-end load, the multiples for the first two years are combined. For example, if the front-end load is six times the benchmark in the first year and

TABLE 17.2 Universal Life—Variable Life Benchmarks

Age	Benchmark Price	Front-End Load Multiple
Under age 30	$ 1.50	10
30–34	2.00	9
35–39	3.00	8
40–44	4.00	7
45–49	6.50	6
50–54	10.00	5
55–59	15.00	4
60–64	25.00	3
65–69	35.00	3
70–74	50.00	3
75–79	80.00	2
80–84	125.00	2

Source: Insurance Forum, vol. 11, no. 6 (June 1984).

four times the benchmark in the second year, the policy multiple is 10.[17]

SOME ADDITIONAL TAX CONSIDERATIONS

Although the tax treatment of life insurance contracts generally was discussed in Chapter 12, and the special rules applicable to modified endowment contacts were discussed earlier in the chapter, there are two remaining areas relating to the tax treatment of life insurance that should be mentioned. The first is the tax treatment when one life insurance policy is exchanged for another. The second is the special rules that may apply to the tax treatment of life insurance purchased to meet obligations under a divorce decree.

Section 1035 Exchanges ("Rollovers")

Occasionally, an insured will decide to exchange an existing life insurance policy for a new contract, using the cash value of the old policy as the initial premium for a new contract. The question naturally arises concerning the tax treatment of any gain on the policy that is being terminated if the cash value exceeds premiums paid. As a general rule, the exchange of one life insurance policy for another life insurance policy will not result in recognition of a taxable gain for federal income tax purposes to the policyholder who exchanges the policy. The *Internal Revenue Code (IRC)*[18] provides that the following are tax-free exchanges:

1. The exchange of a life insurance policy for another life insurance policy or for an endowment or annuity contract

2. The exchange of an endowment contract for an annuity contract or for an endowment contract under which payments will begin not later than payments would have begun under the contract exchanged

3. The exchange of an annuity contract for another annuity contract

If an exchange involves life policies, the policies must be on the life of the same insured; or if an annuity is exchanged for another annuity, the contracts must be payable to the same person or persons. Otherwise, the exchange does not qualify as a tax-free exchange.

All other exchanges are taxable. This means that while the exchange of a life insurance policy for an endowment or annuity is not taxable, the reverse is not true. Nonrecognition of gain or loss does *not* apply to endowments or annuities that are exchanged for life insurance contracts and taxable gain or loss *will* be recognized if an endowment contract is exchanged for a life insurance policy, or if an annuity is exchanged for a life insurance or endowment policy.[19]

The government's position on taxable exchanges is based on the fact that life insurance death proceeds are exempt from income tax, while living benefits under endowment policies and annuities are subject to tax. If exchanges of endowments or annuities for life insurance were allowed tax-free, it would permit the individual to accumulate funds under an instrument subject to one set of tax rules (endowments and annuities) and then exchange it for an instrument subject to different rules (life insurance). Consequently, the *IRC* views any exchange that increases the possibility of eliminating the tax by extending the period of life insurance protection, or by providing life insurance protection where none existed, as a method of tax avoidance.

Note also that even in the case of the *tax-free* rollovers, the recognition of gain is merely deferred. For tax purposes, the policyholder's basis in the new policy must be reduced by the amount of gain that is realized, but not recognized, on the exchange. This means that the gain will be recognized when the second policy is surrendered in a taxable transaction.

For policies that are subject to outstanding loans, care must be taken to be sure that the loans do not result in a taxable event. If the loan on a policy is cancelled at surrender, the cancellation of the loan is treated as money received by the owner and can cause a part of the gain on the policy to be taxed. If the insurer issuing the new policy issues the policy with a loan equal to the outstanding loan on the old

[17] See Joseph M. Belth, "Universal Life and Variable Life—How to Evaluate the New Wave of Products," *Insurance Forum,* vol. 11, no. 6 (June 1984), pp. 21–24.
[18] *IRC* Section 1035(a); see also *Revenue Ruling* 68-23S, 1968-I CB 360 and *Revenue Ruling* 72-358, 1972-2 CB 473.

[19] Regulation Section 1.1035-1(c); *Revenue Ruling* 54-264, 1954-2 CB 57; *W. Stanley Barrett v Commissioner,* 348 F.2d 916 (1st Cir 1965) aff'd 42 TC 993.

policy, the new loan *cancels out* the taxable event that would occur if the old loan were simply extinguished.

Aside from tax concerns, it is wise for insureds to be cautious when replacing life insurance policies, for this is an area fraught with abuse. Because life insurance policies can be very complex, it is often difficult to compare two policies. An unscrupulous or unknowledgeable insurance agent can mislead a policyholder into replacing an old policy with a policy that is actually less attractive than the old one.

The issue of life insurance policy replacement has come under increasing scrutiny by the industry, consumers, and regulators. The term *churning,* originally used in the securities area to describe actions by brokers who engage in excessive trading of securities for customers, with the primary purpose of generating commissions, has recently been applied to describe the actions of some life insurance agents. Observers note that the commission structure in life insurance, where first-year commissions can be quite large, encourages agents to replace policies, thereby earning a new first-year commission. Some reformers have suggested that insurers should be permitted to pay a first-year commission only on the net increase in life insurance purchased. Others argue that this would reduce the incentive of agents to periodically review the life insurance policies of insureds and recommend changes when they are appropriate.

Life Insurance and Divorce Agreements

Before leaving the subject of buying life insurance, an additional topic deserves mention: the uses of life insurance in meeting obligations under a divorce decree or other qualified domestic relations order.[20] A divorce proceeding may require the purchase of new life insurance, it may require that existing life insurance be continued with the former spouse as beneficiary, or it may involve the transfer of ownership in existing life insurance policies to the former spouse. Each of these transactions can have tax ramifications for both spouses. In general, the tax treatment of premiums paid for life insurance in connection with a divorce settlement follows the rules applicable to alimony payments. If alimony payments are made on an informal basis, there is no tax consequence. The payer does not claim the payments as a deduction and the recipient does not treat them as taxable income. However, if certain conditions are met, the alimony payments are deductible by the payer and reported as income by the recipient. This will usually reduce the total tax bill, since the payer is usually in a higher tax bracket than the recipient.

Life Insurance Premiums as Alimony Payments

Under the rules applicable to divorce and separation agreements executed after 1984,[21] alimony is deductible by the payer, and taxable to the recipient as income if specified conditions are met. First, the payments must be required by an official agreement. In addition, the payments must be made by cash, check, or money order, and there is no liability to make payments after the death of the recipient spouse. Finally, the payments cannot be scheduled to change after children are grown or finish school. (Amounts designated as child support do not qualify as alimony and are not deductible.) The *IRC* specifically provides that payments made to a third party on behalf of the spouse can count as alimony if they are made under the terms of the divorce or separation instrument.

Often, only the income-earning spouse is covered with life insurance and, unless required otherwise by the divorce decree, the insured spouse will change the beneficiary of his or her life insurance. Frequently, a court will require that the beneficiary not be changed and may further require that the ownership of the life insurance be transferred to the dependent spouse as a part of the divorce settlement. When a life insurance policy transfer is incident to a divorce, no gain is recognized, the transferee is treated as having acquired the policy by gift. The transferor's basis is transferred to the spouse receiving the policy. Further, the transfer of an existing policy in connection with the termination of a marriage will not cause the proceeds of the insurance to be includable in the income of the recipient under the transfer-for-value rule.[22]

The divorce decree may also require the income-earning spouse to pay premiums on a policy designed

[20] A qualified domestic relations order is a judgment or order that relates to the provision of child support, alimony or property rights to a spouse, a former spouse, or a child and which is made under a state's community property or other domestic relations law.

[21] Tax laws were changed in 1984, creating different tax treatment for payments under a qualified domestic relations order before 1985 and after 1984. Transfers prior to 1985 are subject to rules that differ from those discussed earlier.

[22] *IRC* Section 1041.

to guarantee payments to the former spouse. Tax treatment of the life insurance premiums (and proceeds) in this case, depends on the ownership of the policy.

When the alimony-entitled spouse is the owner of the policy, premiums paid by an alimony-obligated spouse for term or whole-life insurance on his or her life, with a former spouse as beneficiary pursuant to a divorce or separation instrument (executed after December 31, 1984) qualify as alimony payments. The premium payments that qualify as alimony are generally deductible by the spouse making the payments.[23] This rule applies both to policies assigned to the alimony-entitled spouse and to newly purchased policies of which the alimony-entitled spouse is the owner. Policy proceeds to the alimony-entitled spouse as policy beneficiary are treated as life insurance proceeds, and are not taxable.

When the alimony-obligated (premium-paying) spouse retains ownership of the life insurance policy, the premiums are not deductible by him or her and are not taxable to the alimony-entitled spouse. At the time of the insured's death, installment payments of the policy's proceeds would be taxable as alimony to the divorced spouse. Also, payments from an insurance trust that is established to meet the obligations are fully taxable to the recipient. The same treatment applies when the alimony-entitled spouse's interest in the policy is contingent (e.g., where the policy will revert to the premium-paying spouse at the death of the alimony-entitled spouse).[24]

Funding Future Obligations by Annuity A spouse who is obligated to pay alimony can fund the payment of future alimony payments through the purchase of an annuity for the spouse to whom the payments are due. When an annuity is purchased to fund alimony payments under a divorce decree, payments under the annuity are fully taxable to the recipient beneficiary, and the beneficiary cannot recover the purchasing spouse's investment in the contract tax free. Further, the annuity purchaser cannot take an income tax deduction for the payments, even though they are taxable to the spouse. If, instead of transferring the annuity to the spouse, the individual who is obligated to make the alimony payments purchases an annuity but retains ownership, he or she can receive the annuity payments, deduct the basis under the annuity rules, and then make payment to the spouse entitled to alimony. The payments would be deductible to the party making them and taxable to the recipient.

[23] *IRC* Section 215, Temp Reg. § 1.71-1T, A-6.

[24] *IRC* Section 71 and 682.

IMPORTANT CONCEPTS TO REMEMBER

buy term and invest the difference
net-cost comparison
interest-adjusted method

surrender cost index
net payment cost index
vanishing premium policy

benchmark
NAIC Life Insurance Illustrations
 Model Regulation

QUESTIONS FOR REVIEW

1. List the three important considerations in selecting a life insurance company. How important is each relative to the other two?

2. Briefly outline the factors you would consider in deciding the answer to each of the three basic decisions involved in the process of buying life insurance.

3. Explain how the traditional *net-cost system* of life insurance cost comparison can be misleading to the consumer.

4. List and explain the most commonly offered objections to term insurance. How valid is each of these objections?

5. Briefly describe the tax advantage enjoyed by cash-value life insurance as an investment. Does it have any disadvantages? Explain.

6. Why is it more difficult to evaluate a universal life product than a traditional whole-life product?

7. Identify the three factors used in life insurance rate-making and explain how they are recognized in universal life insurance policies.

8. When selling universal life and other interest-sensitive life insurance policies, insurance agents frequently use a policy illustration, which projects accumulated premiums and investment income. Identify the difficulties in making these projections. What should an individual look for when evaluating a policy illustration?

9. Briefly discuss the taxation of life insurance policy exchanges.

10. "In life insurance, differences in premiums do not mean differences in cost." Explain this statement.

QUESTIONS FOR DISCUSSION

1. Income may be divided into two components: consumption and savings. Into which of these components do you think expenditures on insurance should be put?

2. What underlying assumptions are embodied in the advice, "Buy term and invest the difference"? What do you think of this advice?

3. When deciding on the type of insurance to buy, "the question is not really one of term versus permanent insurance at all, but rather a choice between permanent insurance and alternative forms of investment." In comparing permanent insurance with alternative forms of investment, what do you consider to be the most attractive features of insurance?

4. Some companies specialize in selling life insurance to college students. In many instances, the student is permitted to pay the first annual premium (and sometimes the second and third annual premiums) with a note. What do you think of this practice?

5. The guaranteed-insurability option is a valuable form of protection, permitting an individual to insure his or her insurability up to some multiple of the face amount of the policy to which the option is attached. What do you think of the idea of marketing the guaranteed-insurability option by itself, without any form of current protection? Would it be marketable? Why or why not?

SUGGESTIONS FOR ADDITIONAL READING

Auxier, Albert L. "A Test of the Usefulness of Policy Information in Ranking Life Insurance Alternatives." *Journal of Risk and Insurance,* vol. 43, no. 1 (March 1976).

Belth, Joseph M. "The Cost of Life Insurance to the Policyowner—A Single Year Attained Age System." *Journal of Risk and Insurance,* vol. 28, no. 4 (Dec. 1961).

———. *The Retail Structure in American Life Insurance.* Bloomington, Ind.: Bureau of Business Research, Graduate School of Business, Indiana University, 1966.

———. *Life Insurance: A Consumer's Handbook,* 2nd ed. Bloomington, Ind.: Indiana University Press, 1985. *Best's Flitcraft Compend.* Oldwick, N.J.: A. M. Best, annual.

Black, Kenneth, Jr., and Harold D. Skipper, Jr. *Life Insurance,* 13th ed. Englewood Cliffs, N.J.: Prentice-Hall, 2000. Chapters 11, 12.

Crowe, Robert M., and Charles E. Hughes, eds. *Fundamentals of Financial Planning,* 2nd ed. Bryn Mawr, Pa.: The American College, 1993.

Federal Trade Commission. Life Insurance Cost Disclosure: A Staff Report of the Federal Trade Commission. Washington, D.C.: 1979.

Gains, Price. *Interest Adjusted Index: Life Insurance Payment and Cost Comparisons.* Cincinnati, Ohio: National Underwriter Company, Annual.

Hallman, G. Victor, and Karen L. Hamilton. *Personal Insurance: Life, Health, and Retirement.* Malvern, Pa.: American Institute for CPCU, 1994. Chapters 3, 4.

Murray, Michael L. "Analyzing the Investment Value of Cash Value Life Insurance." *Journal of Risk and Insurance,* vol. 43, no. 1 (March 1976).

Reynolds, G. S. *The Mortality Merchants.* New York: David McKay, 1968.

WEB SITES TO EXPLORE

American Council of Life Insurance	http://www.acli.com/
American Society of CLU & ChFC	http://www.agents-online.com/ASCLU/web/index.html
Association for Advanced Life Underwriting	http://www.agents-online.com/AALU/index.htm
Insurance News Network	http://www.insure.com/
Newsedge News Page	http://www.newspage.com/browse/46622/

CHAPTER 18

ANNUITIES AND PENSION BENEFITS

I advise you to go on living solely to enrage those who
are paying your annuities.

— VOLTAIRE

CHAPTER OBJECTIVES

When you have finished this chapter, you should be able to

- Explain the general nature of annuities and describe the manner in which they can help to deal with the retirement risk
- Discuss the tax treatment of annuities, and explain the ways in which this tax treatment is advantageous to the purchaser
- Differentiate among the various classes of annuities, and explain the distinguishing characteristics of each class
- Explain the way in which employer contributions to a qualified pension plan are treated under federal tax laws and the way in which this treatment benefits workers covered under such plans
- Identify and explain the difference between the defined-contribution and defined-benefit approaches in qualified retirement plans
- Describe the basic features of qualified retirement plans, including benefits and vesting
- Explain the provisions of the *Internal Revenue Code (IRC)* relating to Individual Retirement Accounts (IRAs) and explain the benefits that arise both from deductible and nondeductible contributions to IRAs

In this chapter we leave our extended discussion of life insurance and turn to an examination of other products sold by life insurers: annuities. In addition, we will examine a related topic, pension benefits under qualified retirement plans, which generally make use of the annuity principle. Our discussion of pensions in this chapter focuses on those features of qualified retirement plans that are particularly relevant to the

employee's retirement planning. The administration and funding of qualified plans will be discussed in Chapter 23.

ANNUITIES

Annuities have been called *upside-down life insurance,* and in a sense they are a reverse application of the law of large numbers as it is used in life insurance. Whereas life insurance is a method of scientifically accumulating an estate, an annuity is a device for the scientific liquidation of an estate.

An *annuity* is a contract that provides periodic payments for a specified period of time, such as a number of years or for life. The payments may begin at a stated or contingent date and may be payable for a specified number of years or for the duration of a person's life or the lives of more than one person. The person whose life governs the duration of the payments is called the annuitant. If the payments are to be continued for a specified period but only for as long as the annuitant lives, the contract is known as a temporary life annuity. Because the temporary life annuity is used only infrequently, our discussion of annuities will concentrate on life annuities.

The basic function of a life annuity is that of liquidating a principal sum, regardless of how it was accumulated, and it is intended to provide protection against the risk of outliving one's income. It may involve the liquidation of a sum derived from a person's savings (including the annuity itself or the cash value of life insurance policies) or the liquidation of life insurance death benefits in the form of a life income to the beneficiary of the policy.

To illustrate the principle involved, let us assume that the ubiquitous Mr. X attains age 65, retires, and has exactly $100,000 to provide for his needs during the balance of his lifetime. How much of this $100,000 can he afford to spend each year so that the principal will be used up when he dies, but not before? Because X is uncertain as to how long he will live, he cannot answer the question.

If X decides to use only the interest on his $100,000, he might obtain $7000 or $8000 a year, which is inadequate for his needs. He decides that he must invade the principal, but the question is, at what rate? If he decides to draw $5000 plus the interest on the principal each year, he will have about $12,000 or $13,000 per year initially, but the interest component will diminish as the capital is consumed. Moreover,

he will have enough money to last only until age 85, but what will he do then?

If X uses his $100,000 principal as a single premium to purchase a life annuity, he will be guaranteed an income for life, with a payout rate that will maximize his withdrawals without premature dissipation of his capital. His income from this contract will be guaranteed at a rate of $8000 a year (and could be as much as $12,000), but more important, it will be guaranteed for the rest of his life, regardless of how long he lives.

Under the annuity principle, the law of averages operates to permit a lifetime-guaranteed income to each annuitant. Some people who reach age 65 will die before they reach 66. Others will live to be 100. Those who live longer than average will offset those who live for a shorter period than average, and those who die early will forfeit money to those who die later. Every payment the annuitant receives is part interest and part principal. In addition, each payment is part survivorship benefit, in that it is composed in part of the funds of group members who have died.

Insurance companies have found that annuitants live longer than most people. This is simply a result of adverse selection. People who feel that they have short life expectancies do not normally purchase annuities, while the individual whose parents and grandparents all lived to be 115 years old will probably look on an annuity as a good investment. The annuity principle favors the long-lived, and on the whole, these are the people who purchase these policies. For this reason, insurance companies use different mortality tables for computing the cost of annuities than they use for life insurance. Since the company promises to pay an income for the life of the annuitant, the longer he or she is expected to live, the higher will be the cost for a given amount of annual or monthly income. The older the annuitant, the lower the cost for a given amount of monthly income.[1] Obviously, there is no requirement that the annuitant be in good health.

In addition to their function in liquidating an accumulated principal, annuities may also serve as investment instruments through which the principal may be accumulated. When the commencement date for

[1] Since on average women live longer than men, life annuities are more expensive for women. The amount of monthly income produced by a given amount for a female at age 65 is approximately the amount produced for a male who is 60 years old.

annuity payments is set at some time in the future, the annuity principal may be accumulated by the periodic payment by the annuity purchaser. As in the case of life insurance, the investment income on the growing fund accumulates on a tax-deferred basis. The increments to the fund arising from investment income are not taxed until they are paid out to the annuitant.

If the annuitant dies during the accumulation period—that is, before the contract is annuitized—a death benefit is payable to a beneficiary or to the insured's estate. Annuities therefore represent a part of the individual's protection against premature death. The most common approach is to provide for a return of gross premiums without interest, or the cash value (whichever is larger).

Classification of Annuities

Annuities may be classified in various ways. Traditionally, annuities have been classified according to the following distinctions:

- Individual versus group annuity
- Fixed-dollar versus variable annuity
- Immediate versus deferred annuity
- Single-premium versus installment annuity
- Single life versus joint life annuity
- Pure life annuity versus annuity certain

Individual versus Group Annuities Annuities, like life insurance, are sold on both an individual and a group basis. Group annuities often serve as a funding mechanism for the qualified retirement programs discussed later in this chapter. Although the discussion that follows focuses primarily on individual contracts, the basic principles are essentially the same.[2]

Fixed and Variable Annuities Second, the annuity may be a *fixed-dollar annuity* or a *variable annuity.* Although most annuities are sold on a fixed-dollar basis, variable annuities have become increasingly popular. Under the variable annuity, premiums are generally invested in a portfolio of stocks, although policyholders may also have the option of directing their investment to a bond fund or a money market fund. Variable annuities are discussed in greater detail later in the chapter.

Immediate versus Deferred Annuities Annuities may be grouped according to when payments are to commence. With the *immediate annuity,* the first annuity payment is due one payment interval from the date of purchase, or it may be a *deferred annuity*—that is, there is a spread of several years between the date of purchase and the beginning of the annuity payments. An immediate annuity is purchased at retirement from funds accumulated in other investment instruments. A deferred annuity is purchased at some time before retirement and the purchase price is augmented by investment income during the interval between the time of purchase and the time the benefits commence.

Single-Premium versus Installment Annuities Annuities may also be classified according to the method of premium payment. They may be purchased with a single premium (the annuity to begin immediately or at some future date), or they may be purchased on an installment basis over a period of years. Installment premium annuities are always deferred annuities, while a single-premium annuity may be an immediate or deferred annuity.

Single Life versus Joint Life Annuities Annuities may be classified according to the number of lives that determines the duration of the payments. This classification covers the single life and the *joint-and-survivor annuities.* An annuity may provide payment for the lifetime of a single individual or it may provide payment until two (or more) annuitants have died. The amount payable after the death of the first annuitant may be the same as during the lifetime of both annuitants or it may be lower.

Joint-and-Last-Survivor Annuity Annuities may be designed for special purposes just as life insurance contracts have been. One specialized annuity form is the *joint-and-last-survivor annuity,* which is computed on the basis of two lives. Under the joint-and-last-survivor annuity, the insurance company promises to make payments until both annuitants have died, an especially attractive form of annuity for a retired couple. If, as is likely, one predeceases the other, annuity payments will be continued for the rest of the other's life. A variation of this form provides for a reduction in the income payments at the death of the first annuitant, with lower annuity payments (usually two-thirds of the original income payments) being continued until the death of the second annuitant.

Joint Life Annuity The *joint life annuity* is similar to, but should not be confused with, the joint-and-

[2] Group annuities are discussed in Chapter 23.

last-survivor annuity. Under the joint life annuity, payments cease on the death of the first annuitant; the other annuitant then receives no further benefits under the program. This form is useful when there is a secondary source of income that is sufficient to support one, but not both, of the annuitants.

Pure Life Annuities versus Period-Certain Annuities Finally, annuities may be classified according to the nature of the insurer's obligation. Under a *pure life annuity,* payments are made only for the balance of the annuitant's lifetime, regardless of how long or short this period might be. The annuity is considered fully liquidated at the annuitant's death, with nothing payable to his or her estate. On the other hand, the annuity may contain some sort of refund feature, with a specified amount to be paid to the estate or a beneficiary if the annuitant should die shortly after the payments begin. Even though the pure life annuity provides the maximum income per dollar of principal sum, some people object to placing a substantial sum into a contract that promises no return if death should occur shortly after the annuity payments begin. As a consequence, insurers have found it necessary to add refund features to annuities to make them more salable. One of the most common refund features is found in an annuity with a certain number of payments guaranteed, whether the annuitant lives or dies. With a principal of $100,000 at age 65, a man can purchase a pure life annuity that will yield a monthly income of about $1000 for life (guaranteed rate). For the same $100,000, a woman aged 65 will receive $925 per month for life. With a 10-year period certain, the man would receive $960 per month, and the woman would receive $900 per month, but the payments will be guaranteed for the 10-year period. If the annuitant should die at age 70, the insurance company will be obligated to continue the payments to a designated beneficiary or to the annuitant's estate for 5 more years. If the annuitant survives the guarantee period, the payments will continue for the balance of his or her lifetime.

Today, guarantee periods are available for 5, 10, 15, and 20 years. Naturally, the longer the guarantee period, the greater will be the cost of the annuity. For example, if you purchase an annuity with 20 rather than 10 years certain, the guaranteed annuity income would be reduced from the amount payable with a 10-year period certain.

Another popular refund feature is one that provides for annuity payments at least equal to the pur-chase price of the annuity. The balance will be paid to a beneficiary or to the annuitant's estate either in a lump sum or on an installment basis. If the balance is paid in continued installments, the contract is referred to as an *installment refund annuity.* If it is paid in a lump sum, the contract is a *cash refund annuity.* Under an installment refund annuity, $100,000 will provide about $970 per month to a male annuitant and $890 per month to a female annuitant.

Income Tax Treatment of Annuities

As in the case of life insurance, investment income earned on annuities during the accumulation period is not taxable until distributed to the policyholder.[3] Distributions are taxed to the extent that payments exceed the investment in the contract. In addition, a 10-percent premature penalty is imposed on early withdrawals from annuities. A *premature* (or *early*) *withdrawal* from an annuity is any distribution made prior to the time the annuitant reaches age $59^1/_2$. The penalty on premature distributions does not apply if the contract holder becomes disabled or if the distribution is over the life of the annuitant.[4]

The taxation of distributions requires apportioning the amounts received between recovery of capital and income. This is accomplished through an *exclusion ratio formula,* which excludes from taxable income the portion of each payment that the investment in the contract has to the expected return under the contract. The expected return is the annual amount to be paid to the annuitant multiplied by the number of years of life expectancy using annuity tables prescribed by the IRS. Separate tables are used for single life annuities and for joint-and-survivor annuities. The exclusion ratio formula is:

$$\text{Payment} \times \frac{\text{Investment in Contract}}{\text{Expected Return}} = \frac{\text{Nontaxable}}{\text{Return of Capital}}$$

To illustrate the operation of the formula, assume that Brown has purchased an annuity for $60,000 and

[3] The 1999 Clinton budget proposal announced in February 1998 contained a proposal to modify the tax treatment of annuities. Under the proposal, annuity owners would be allowed a single tax-free rollover from one annuity to another. Thereafter, any gain on the annuity would be taxable to the owner.

[4] The Tax Equity and Fiscal Responsibility Act of 1982 imposed a 5 percent penalty on premature withdrawal from annuities. The Tax Reform Act of 1986 increased this penalty to 10 percent.

that he is to receive $500 per month for life. He is 65 years old and has a life expectancy of 15 years, which means that he "expects" to receive $90,000 ($6000 per year for 15 years). Applying the exclusion ratio formula to the $6000 benefit Brown receives in the first year:

$$\$6,000 \times \frac{\$60,000}{\$500 \times 12 \times 15 \text{ years}} = \$4,000$$

The $4000 is a nontaxable return of capital and $2000 is taxable income. Once the annuitant has recovered the full amount of his or her investment in the contract, the exclusion ratio no longer applies and subsequent payments are fully taxable. If the annuitant dies before his or her basis is fully recovered, the unrecovered basis may be deducted from the decedent's final tax return. (In the case of contracts annuitized before January 1, 1987, the exclusion ratio applies to all payments, including those made after the annuitant's basis has been recovered.)

For variable annuities, the amount excluded from taxable income each year is also the total investment divided by the number of years the annuitant is expected to live. However, if losses on the underlying portfolio result in payments that are less than the excludable amount for that payment, the investment in the contract for future payments is recalculated. The amount of nontaxable return of principal that was not deductible is factored into the computation of taxable gain for future installments. Suppose, for example, that Brown is receiving a distribution under a variable annuity in which his basis is $300,000. He is 65 years old and his life expectancy is 15 years. Brown may exclude $20,000 of the variable payment he receives each year. After receiving benefits for 4 years, the variable benefit in the fifth year drops to $15,000, which is less than the excludable $20,000. The $5000 exclusion is not lost. At this point, Brown is 74 years old and has a life expectancy of 10.1 years. The $5000 exclusion that was not taken may be added to the initial $20,000 exclusion over the 10.1 years ($495.05 per year) making the new excludable amount $20,495.05.

If the contract holder dies after annuity payments have begun but before the entire interest has been distributed, the remaining portion of the annuity must be distributed at least as rapidly as the original method of distribution and will be taxable to the beneficiary. If the contract holder dies before the annuity starting date, the entire interest must be dis-

tributed within five years after the date of death or be annuitized within one year, unless the beneficiary of the annuity is a spouse. For a spousal annuity, the annuity contract may be continued (and the tax on the earnings deferred) until distribution of the benefits to or the death of the spouse.

Annuities and the Federal Estate Tax

Under a straight life annuity, there is no remaining value at the death of the annuitant. However, if the annuity provides a survivor benefit (as under a refund life annuity, a joint-and-survivor annuity, or a period-certain annuity), the taxation of the remaining value depends on whether the survivor benefit is payable to the decedent's estate or to a named beneficiary and, in the case of benefits payable to a named beneficiary, who purchased the annuity.

Internal Revenue Code Section 2039 provides that the gross estate of a decedent includes the value of payments made to a beneficiary under an annuity contract because the beneficiary survived the decedent.

- If the annuity is payable to the decedent's estate, the value of any survivor benefits is includable in his or her gross estate, as a property interest owned at the time of death. Payments included under this provision include lump-sum or annuity payments under a guaranteed period-certain or cash-refund contract.
- If survivor benefits are payable to a named beneficiary (under a joint-and-survivor annuity or under a period-certain or refund annuity), the inclusion or exclusion of the survivor benefits from the decedent's estate is determined by a premium-payment test. Under this test, if the decedent purchased the annuity, the value of the survivors' benefit is includable in the estate. If the decedent contributed only a part of the purchase price of the annuity, the value of the survivor benefits is includable in the decedent's gross estate only in the proportion that he or she contributed to the purchase price of the annuity.

Special rules apply to employee annuities under qualified pension and profit-sharing plans and to individual retirement accounts. However, for persons dying after 1984, the value of an annuity or other payment from a decedent's individual retirement account is includable in the decedent's gross estate. If the beneficiary of the annuity is the spouse of the

decedent, the survivor benefits qualify for the unlimited martial deduction of the federal estate tax.[5]

Specialized Annuities

As in the case of life insurance contracts, insurers have developed specialized and innovative annuity contracts. The following are some of these specialized annuity contracts.

Single-Premium Deferred Annuity The *single-premium deferred annuity* (SPDA), like single-premium life, has enjoyed a rush of popularity since 1986, when the Tax Reform Act of 1986 eliminated many tax shelters. As the appeal of other investments diminished, SPDAs became increasingly popular. Under current law, the SPDA enjoys the same tax treatment as other annuities, the principal feature of which is that earnings accumulate tax free until distributed. Some insurers sell SPDAs with a deposit premium as low as $2500, but a more common minimum is $10,000.

Market-Value-Adjusted Annuities *Market-value-adjusted annuities* are a cross between variable and fixed annuities. The interest rate is fixed for a specified period, but the cash surrender value fluctuates with the market value of the underlying securities if the policy is surrendered before the end of the period. At set intervals, such as every 5 or 10 years, a *window* opens, permitting withdrawals without a market-value adjustment.

Two-Tier Annuity The *two-tier annuity,* which appeared on the market in the late 1980s, is a dual-value, dual-interest-rate contract. The two values are an accumulation value and a surrender value. The accumulation value is equal to premiums paid plus interest, and the surrender value is always less. The surrender value is subject to a permanent, increasing surrender charge, designed to discourage lump-sum withdrawals. In contrast, in a conventional annuity, at the end of the surrender charge period, the surrender value is the same as the accumulation value. The accumulation value is available only under an annuity pay-out option. To receive the accumulation pay-out, the two-tier annuity must be annuitized over a minimum of 5 years. Insurers argue that purchasers' long-term commitment of funds permits them to credit higher investment earnings on the accumulation fund. Critics argue that the abnormal surrender charge, if the policy is terminated prior to being annuitized, prevents the purchaser from withdrawing funds to take advantage of more attractive alternatives that appear.

Equity-Indexed Annuities *Equity-indexed annuities* first appeared in early 1996 and quickly captured a significant portion of the annuities market. In 1997, equity-indexed annuity sales amounted to $3 billion, and by early 1998, most major annuities writers were offering a version of this product or preparing to offer one. Many observers believe this product could ultimately account for a third of all annuity sales in the United States.

An equity-indexed annuity is a fixed annuity that earns interest or provides benefits that are linked to the performance of an equity index, such as the S & P 500. Generally, the crediting rate is a function of the relative change in the index, the participation rate (i.e., the percentage of the index growth that is passed on to policyholders), and any caps imposed on the crediting rate. These annuities also typically have minimum interest guarantees and comply with the minimum nonforfeiture law.

Because of the wide variety in terms and conditions of equity-indexed annuities, individuals purchasing these products should carefully consider the design features. This includes the indexing method, the participation rate, any rate caps, whether the annuity pays compound or simple interest, and any administrative fees assessed. Consumers should also consider whether the equity index recognizes dividends paid on stock. Typically it does not, resulting in a lower interest rate than would be received if dividends were also considered.

Because of the complexity of equity-indexed annuities, the NAIC produced a buyers' guide in 1998 and encouraged companies to make it available to consumers considering a purchase.

Reversionary or Survivorship Annuity The *reversionary life insurance* policy (which is also called a survivorship annuity) is a seldom-used form, but in certain circumstances, it meets a special need far better than does any other form of life insurance. Basically, the reversionary policy is life insurance on one person, with benefits in an amount required to provide a lifetime annuity to another person. The premium is based on the life expectancy of both persons. The two individuals on whose lives the premium is based are

[5] *IRC* Sections 2033, 2039.

referred to as the *annuitant* and the *nominator*. The nominator is the individual insured, and the annuitant is the beneficiary of the policy. If the beneficiary dies before the insured, the policy expires without value. When this policy is written with a young person as the nominator and an older person as the annuitant or beneficiary, the premium is extremely low, since the beneficiary is likely to die before the nominator. In addition, since the amount of insurance required to provide a life income to the annuitant decreases as the annuitant grows older, the protection is written on a decreasing term basis. In computing the premium for this policy, the company estimates the life expectancy of the annuitant and then computes the premium on a decreasing term policy at the age of the nominator. The amount of the decreasing term policy will be the sum necessary to provide a life income to the annuitant at any given time, should the nominator die.

The Variable Annuity Although we have already mentioned the variable annuity briefly, given the importance of this annuity form, a few additional comments seem in order. After all, it was the variable annuity that set the pattern for many of the innovative life insurance contracts that were to follow. It is a classic example of an imaginative approach to a critical problem.

As we noted in Chapter 12, the variable annuity was designed as a means of coping with the impact of inflation on individuals' attempts to save for retirement. Under a fixed-dollar annuity, premiums paid by the annuitant are converted into a lifetime pay-out, and the annuitant is guaranteed a fixed number of dollars monthly or annually for the rest of his or her lifetime. While the number of dollars payable is guaranteed, those dollars may have reduced purchasing power. Under a *variable annuity,* the premiums are invested in common stocks or other investments and maintained in separate accounts by insurers. (Insurers have greater discretion with respect to the investment of funds in separate accounts.) The underlying philosophy of the variable annuity is that while the value of the dollar will vary over time, the value of a diversified portfolio of common stocks will change in the same direction as the price level. Variable annuities may be variable during the accumulation period and fixed during the payout period or variable during both the accumulation period and the payout period.

History of the Variable Annuity The variable annuity as we know it today was developed by the Teachers Insurance and Annuity Association of America

(TIAA), a nonprofit organization founded in 1918 by the Carnegie Foundation to provide college professors with retirement programs.[6] In 1952, TIAA created a companion organization, called the College Retirement Equity Fund (CREF). The fund issued its first variable annuity in 1952, and now serves over 3 million participants. Following CREF's innovative lead, private insurance companies became active in the field. The first variable annuities written by a private insurer were issued in 1954 by the Participating Annuity Life Insurance Company of Little Rock, Arkansas, which operated strictly on an intrastate basis. Late in 1955, the Variable Annuity Life Insurance Company (VALIC) was formed in Washington, D.C., and became the first interstate company (other than CREF) in this field. The two most active companies in the early stages of the variable annuity's development were VALIC and the Prudential Insurance Company of America. Their entry into the variable annuity field prompted the Securities and Exchange Commission (SEC) to intervene, leading to considerable litigation. The most important issue was whether variable annuities were insurance (and as such exempt from federal regulation under Public Law 15) or, as the SEC contended, securities. The litigation was eventually settled when the U.S. Supreme Court ruled that the variable annuity was a security and so subject to regulation by the SEC. This decision was vital to the SEC and established the pattern for control of the variable annuity. Variable annuities are currently regulated by both the SEC and the state insurance departments.[7] Agents who sell variable

[6] The TIAA originally wrote conventional fixed dollar annuities, until several faculty members at Harvard University, realizing how vulnerable their retirement program was to inflation, decided to invest a part of their retirement dollars in the Harvard Endowment Fund, which bought mainly common stocks. With a part of their retirement dollars in TIAA and a part in the Harvard Endowment Fund, these faculty members hedged against inflation and deflation. Shortly thereafter, TIAA began a study of the possibility of equity-funded retirement programs as a hedge against inflation. The conclusions of the study were published in 1951, William C. Greenough, *A New Approach to Retirement Income* (New York: Teachers Insurance and Annuity Association of America, 1951).

[7] Although the SEC has granted some exemptions in the case of certain group variable annuities, in general, the Commission treats the variable annuity as a security. Registration with the SEC is required before a variable annuity may be marketed, and a prospectus must be furnished to the buyer. The seller must be registered with the SEC as a broker-dealer and must comply with the rules of the Commission or the National Association of Securities Dealers (NASD). State insurance departments exercise control over the design of variable annuities, including mortality assumptions, and also oversee licensing of agents to sell variable annuities.

annuities must be licensed by state insurance departments for the sale of life insurance products and must be registered with the National Association of Securities Dealers (NASD).[8]

Operation of Variable Annuities Premiums paid into a variable annuity by the purchaser are converted into *accumulation units* as they are received by the insurer. The number of accumulation units credited to the purchaser depends on the current value of the accumulation units. The value of the accumulation units is determined in much the same way as the value of shares in a mutual fund – by dividing the current value of all securities in the insurer's accumulation fund by the total number of accumulation units outstanding. Over time, the value of the accumulation unit rises and falls with the market price of the securities held by the insurer. By contributing a fixed amount each month regardless of the fluctuations in the value of the securities, the annuity purchasers make use of the principle of dollar averaging.

Many companies selling variable annuities offer *self-directed annuities,* in which the purchaser has a choice of investments. Under a self-directed annuity, the insurer gives the purchaser a choice among several stock, bond, and money portfolios. The purchaser can allocate his or her premiums among the stock and bond options and can transfer the funds from account to account as conditions change. As the stock and bond markets change over time, the annuity's value also changes.

When the annuitant reaches retirement age, the accumulation units may usually be converted into a fixed or variable payout, using a special mortality table for annuitants. Under the variable payout, the number of annuity units does not change over the lifetime of the annuitant, but the income produced by each unit will reflect changes in the value of the investments, with the current value of the annuity unit determining the annuitant's income.

How Well Has it Worked? As a pioneer in the field of variable annuities, CREF has established a 40-year-plus record that is helpful in appraising the performance of variable annuities. The period since the inception of the CREF program has been marked by continued inflation. As an indication of the program's performance, the value of the CREF accumulation unit since 1952 is presented in Table 18.1.

Although the value of the CREF accumulation unit has generally moved in the same direction as the

TABLE 18.1 **Value of CREF Accumulation Unit, 1952–2001**

Year	Accumulation	Year	Accumulation
1952	1.02	1977	7.35
1953	1.05	1978	7.98
1954	1.56	1979	9.25
1955	1.95	1980	11.71
1956	2.14	1981	11.53
1957	2.04	1982	14.06
1958	2.88	1983	17.58
1959	3.28	1984	19.41
1960	3.39	1985	24.42
1961	4.02	1986	29.75
1962	3.44	1987	31.28
1963	4.07	1988	36.73
1964	4.59	1989	47.01
1965	5.40	1990	44.41
1966	5.15	1991	50.56
1967	6.35	1992	56.73
1968	6.74	1993	65.02
1969	6.37	1994	67.89
1970	6.17	1995	80.81
1971	7.41	1996	99.74
1972	8.68	1997	127.08
1973	7.11	1998	151.74
1974	4.91	1999	187.15
1975	6.48	2000	206.09
1976	7.85	2001	173.15

Source: TIAA-CREF, 2001 *Annual Report.*

Note: From 1952 until 1987, changes in the monthly value of CREF accumulation units reflected only market value changes. Dividends and other investment income received by CREF were credited to participants in the form of additional units, and were therefore not reflected in the value of the accumulation unit. During this period, the CREF unit increased from $10.52 to $101.49 by the end of 1986. Beginning January 1, 1987, the value of the CREF accumulation unit was changed to reflect the CREF portfolio's net total return, including not only changes in the market value of stocks, but investment income as well. Instead of buying additional accumulation units, investment income from CREFs common stocks is added to the market value of the stocks to determine the value of the accumulation unit. The value of an accumulation unit in 1952, $10.43 under the old method, was changed to $1. Simultaneously, the number of accumulation units in each account was decreased. The change in the method of computing accumulation units and the restatement of units had no effect on the dollar value of the total accumulation units, but makes it easier to track performance of a portfolio overtime.

[8] NASD registration requires passing either the NASD Series 6 limited registration examination or the Series 7 general securities examination.

cost of living, there have been periods during which the relationship has been imperfect. During the period from 1972 through 1974, for example, the value of the accumulation unit fell 43 percent, while the consumer price index increased 18 percent. The value of the accumulation unit did not again reach its 1972 level until 1979; during the same 5 year period, the cost of living had increased by 74 percent. Declines in the value of a variable annuity are always unwelcome, but they are especially so during periods of rising consumer prices. The 1972–1979 experience is a stark reminder to many annuitants that under the variable annuity, the annuitant assumes the investment risk, even though the insurance company guarantees a lifetime income.

By 1998, more than 15 million persons had variable annuities. Persons insured are about equally divided between group and individual plans, with about 51 percent of those insured covered under group plans. Over half of those insured in group plans are with CREF.

Annuities as Investments for Retirement

The return that will be earned over the life of an annuity depends on a variety of features. The most important of these are the interest rate, the surrender charge, and administrative expenses. In general, these features are similar to those discussed in connection with single-premium life. For example, a "current" rate of interest is guaranteed for a specified number of years during the accumulation period, after which the interest rate may be changed, but subject to a guaranteed minimum. The guarantee period may range from one year up to ten, and some insurers offer the buyer a choice as to the period for which the current rate will be guaranteed. Usually, the longer the period for which the rate will be guaranteed, the lower the rate. In the case of an annuity, there is also a guaranteed settlement option rate and a current settlement option rate during the payout period. The guaranteed rate is a contract minimum and is the interest assumption on which the minimum monthly installments are computed. If the current settlement option rate is higher than the guaranteed rate, the annuity benefit will be proportionately higher. The guaranteed settlement option rate is set on a conservative basis—usually 4 or 4.5 percent today. Actual payments reflect the higher rate that is actually earned—generally in the range of 8 to 9 percent over the past decade.

As in the case of other investment vehicles, a part of the premium for deferred annuities purchased on an installment basis goes to pay expense charges. Although some insurers still charge a front-end sales fee of 4 or 5 percent of the premium, most insurers have eliminated front-end commission charges on annuities and use a surrender fee for early withdrawals. The surrender fee usually begins at a high level (8 to 10 percent), and then diminishes until it disappears after a specified period (ranging from 7 to 15 years). In addition to the surrender charges, there is usually an annual maintenance fee of from $25 to $50 to cover administrative costs. For variable annuities, asset management fees similar to those levied by regular stock and mutual fund accounts are also assessed. These fees may range from 0.25 to 2 percent of the accumulated assets. The administrative fees are automatically deducted from the investment account.

QUALIFIED RETIREMENT PLANS

Although private pension plans in the United States have existed since the late 1800s, their greatest growth has taken place since World War II. In 1940, about 4 million people—less than 20 percent of all employees in government and industry—were covered by private pensions. By 2001, over 100 million persons, including about one-half of all workers in private business and three-fourths of all government workers, were enrolled in retirement programs other than Social Security. Qualified retirement plans are established by employers, and sometimes jointly by unions and employers, to provide individual workers with a retirement income that will supplement Social Security retirement benefits. The plan may be set up for the employees of a particular firm, or it may be a "multi-employer" plan, serving workers from several unrelated firms.

Retirement plans may be noncontributory, in which case the entire cost of the pensions is borne by the employer, or they may be contributory, with employees making contributions in addition to those of the employer. Employee contributions may be voluntary, or they may be required for participation. Although employee contributions are not *usually* deductible by the employees, the investment income on such contributions is exempt from federal taxes until distributed, which makes savings plans a form of tax-deferred compensation.

A General Overview of Qualified Plans

A *qualified retirement plan* is one that conforms to the requirements of federal laws and for which the *Internal Revenue Code (IRC)* provides favorable tax treatment. Employer contributions are a tax-deductible expense at the time they are made, and the employee is not taxed on the employer's contributions until benefits are actually received (usually at retirement). Also, during the accumulation period, investment income on accumulating funds is not subject to taxation and will be taxed only when paid out to the employee. This means that funds in a retirement plan will accumulate to a larger amount on an after-tax basis than funds held in other (nontax-deferred) forms.

Federal Regulation of Private Retirement Plans

Private retirement plans are regulated by the federal government. The major law relating to private plans is the *Employee Retirement Income Security Act of 1974* (ERISA). ERISA prescribes which employees must be included in a plan, establishes minimum vesting requirements, specifies the amounts that may be contributed, and sets forth minimum funding requirements. The act also requires extensive reporting and disclosure information about pension and welfare programs, their operations, and their financial conditions to the Secretary of Labor, the IRS, and to those covered by the plan and their beneficiaries.[9]

Qualification Requirements

For a plan to be qualified by the IRS, it must conform to certain standards specified in the *IRC*. In general, to be qualified, the plan must be designed for the exclusive benefit of employees and their beneficiaries, must be in writing and communicated to the employees, and must meet one of several vesting schedules. Contributions and benefit formulas cannot be designed to discriminate in favor of officers, stockholders, or highly compensated employees, and the plan must provide either for definite contributions by the employer or a definite benefit to the worker at the time of retirement. (Profit-sharing plans are an exception in which the contributions vary with the profits of the firm.) Life insurance benefits may be included in the plan only on an incidental basis.[10] Finally, top-heavy plans—plans that provide a disproportionate share of their benefits to owners or other highly paid executives—are subject to special requirements designed to guarantee that they provide minimum benefits or contributions for rank-and-file workers.[11]

Vesting Requirements

The term *vesting* refers to the right of a covered employee to retain a claim to the benefits accrued, even though his or her employment terminates before retirement. Under current law, qualified retirement plans are generally subject to the following vesting requirements.

1. No vesting for three years, with 100 percent vesting after three years (called *cliff vesting*).
2. After two years of service, 20 percent vesting, with 20 percent per year thereafter, so that 100 percent vesting exists after six years of service.

The vesting schedules are minimum requirements, and an employer may provide vesting at a more rapid rate.[12] Where the plan requires employee contributions, the employee contributions are always 100 percent vested.

Types of Qualified Plans

The *IRC* recognizes several types of qualified plans, including corporate plans, plans for self-employed persons and their employees and several "simplified" plans for small employers. In addition to the various plans offered by employers, federal tax law also provides tax-deferred treatment to *individual retirement accounts* (IRAs), under which individuals

[9] Pension plans are also subject to various provisions of the *Internal Revenue Code (IRC)* and the *Civil Rights Act of 1964*. The application of these statutes to qualified retirement plans is discussed in greater detail in Chapter 23. Here, we are concerned with qualified retirement plans from the perspective of the participant.

[10] Qualification requirements are discussed in greater detail in Chapter 23.

[11] Generally, a plan is top-heavy if at least 60 percent of the account balances or accrued benefits are allocated to a group of participants known as the *key employees*. A key employee is defined as any plan participant employee who, during the preceding plan year was (1) an officer earning over $130,000, (2) a 5-percent owner, or (3) a 1-percent owner earning over $150,000. Prior to EGTRRA-2001, the definition of key employees used a five-year look-back provision. It also included officers earning over $70,000 and one of the 10 employees earning more than $35,000 with the largest ownership interests in the employer.

[12] Prior to EGTRRA-2001, the current vesting schedule applied only to top-heavy plans. The requirements for all other plans were either 100 percent vesting for participants after five years of service or graded vesting at the rate of 20 percent after three years and an additional 20 percent each year thereafter, so that a participant will be fully vested after seven years of service.

may accumulate funds for retirement. IRAs are also used as funding vehicles for several types of simplified employer-sponsored qualified plans under which employers make contributions to an IRA plan on behalf of their employees. Finally, IRAs provide a basis for portable pensions. Regulations permit persons who terminate employment and receive a lump-sum distribution from a qualified plan to "roll over" the distribution into an IRA. This defers taxation until the proceeds are withdrawn from the IRA at a later date.

The various types of employer-sponsored plans differ in eligibility and in permissible limit on contributions imposed by the IRC. Although these plans may differ in design, the amount of benefits received by the employee at retirement under all plans is based on a formula applicable to all employees. All employer sponsored plans fall into one of two basic benefit formula categories: the defined contribution approach and the defined benefit approach.

Defined Contribution Pension Plan A defined contribution plan (also called *money purchase plans*), works exactly as its name implies. The employer's contribution to the plan is set as a percentage of compensation, such as, for example, 5 percent or 10 percent of the employee's wages. The employee's retirement benefit is simply the amount that the contributions and investment earnings on those contributions will provide at retirement age.

The employer's maximum annual contribution on behalf of any employee is limited to 25 percent of the individual's earnings for the year, subject to a dollar maximum, which is indexed for inflation. The dollar maximum was $40,000 in 2002 and is indexed for inflation in increments of $1000.[13] The compensation to which the contribution percentage applies is subject to a dollar maximum that is indexed for inflation in increments of $5000. In 2002, the dollar limit on income to which the contribution percentage could be applied was $200,000.[14] This means that a plan that provides an employer contribution equal to 10 percent of compensation would provide a $10,000

contribution for a person earning $100,000, but only $20,000 for a person earning $250,000.

Prior to EGTRRA-2001, Section 415 of the *IRC* imposed a limit on the amount of *annual additions* to an individual's account during the year that was the same as the limit on employer deductions (i.e., the dollar maximum or 25 percent of compensation). Effective for years after 2001, EGTRRA-2001 increases the limit on annual additions to an individual's account to the current dollar maximum (i.e., $40,000 in 2002) or 100 percent of compensation.

Defined Benefit Pension Plan Under a defined benefit pension plan, the employer promises to pay the employee a specific income at retirement. The benefit the employee will receive at retirement is specified in a benefit formula, and the employer's contribution is the amount that will be required, together with the investment earnings on the contributions, to provide the specified benefit and pay the expenses of the plan.[15] Benefit formulas for defined benefit plans are usually based on the employee's salary, the benefit accrual rate, and the employee's years of service. Under *final average salary plans*, the benefit depends on the salary earned in the later years of employment. For example, a plan may promise a monthly benefit equal to 1 percent of the average monthly salary during the last three years of employment for each year worked. An employee who worked for the employer for 40 years would receive a benefit equal to 40 percent of the final three-year average salary. Other plans are *career average salary plans*, and the benefit is a function of the salary earned in all years of employment.

The maximum deductible contribution to a defined benefit plan is expressed in terms of the maximum benefit that the contribution may provide. This maximum is 100 percent of the employee's earnings in the person's three consecutive years of highest earnings, subject to an inflation-adjusted dollar maximum. In 2002, the maximum annual benefit permitted under a defined benefit plan was $160,000, with future adjustments for inflation in increments of $5000. This maximum benefit is the amount that may be paid to participants age 62 to 65. If benefits are

[13] Prior to the changes enacted in EGTRRA-2001, the dollar maximum was $35,000 and was indexed in increments of $5000.

[14] In 1993, employers could consider up to $236,000 in employee compensation in computing pension benefits and contributions. The 1993 legislation cut the maximum to $150,000, which through inflation adjustments in $10,000 increments, had grown to $170,000 by 2001. Thus, the $200,000 maximum under EGTRRA-2001 is still below the permissible contribution limit in 1993.

[15] Some plans use a *target benefit plan*, which is a cross between a defined benefit and a defined contribution plan. The annual contribution is the amount needed each year to accumulate (at an assumed rate of interest) a fund sufficient to pay a defined retirement benefit (the *target benefit*) at retirement age.

paid earlier the maximum is reduced and if later it is increased.[16]

Qualified Profit-Sharing Plans A qualified profit-sharing plan is a form of defined contribution plan, since ultimate benefits depend on the amount contributed by the employer. A major difference between a qualified profit-sharing plan and a defined contribution pension is that the contribution under a profit-sharing plan need not be fixed; employers may vary the contribution from year to year (theoretically, according to profits). Although a profit-sharing plan does not require annual contributions, the IRS does require that recurring and substantial contributions be made (generally interpreted to mean that a contribution should be made at least once every three years). In addition, the plan must provide a formula for allocating the contributions that are made among employees on a nondiscriminatory basis. The most common approach is to allocate contributions according to the ratio of each employee's earnings to the earnings of the group.

Profit-sharing plans may be contributory or noncontributory. Because it is an oxymoron to speak of "employee contributions to a profit-sharing plan," when employees contribute their own funds into a plan, the plan is usually called a *thrift* or *savings plan.*

Historically, the contributions limit for profit-sharing plans was 15 percent of employee compensation. Effective for tax years beginning 2002, the allowable deduction is increased to 25 percent of the participant's compensation.

Employee Stock Ownership Plan An employee stock ownership plan (ESOP) is a qualified stock bonus plan closely related to the qualified profit-sharing plan. The principal difference is that under an ESOP instead of giving the employees a part of the profits of the firm, the employer gives them part of the firm itself, in the form of stock in the corporation. Although contributions to an ESOP may be made in cash or in stock, the accumulation in the employees' portfolio is based on the value of the employer's stock. Because an ESOP is basically a type of profit-sharing plan, it is subject to the same limits as those outlined previously for profit-sharing plans.

Keogh Plans Keogh plans are qualified retirement plans for self-employed persons and their employees. Self-employed persons are permitted to make tax-deductible contributions to a retirement plan, provided the plan includes coverage for all other eligible employees on a nondiscriminatory basis. A Keogh plan may be established as a defined benefit plan, a money purchase plan, or a profit-sharing plan, subject to essentially the same limitations, deductions, and benefits that apply to corporate pension or profit-sharing plans. A special definition of *earned income* is used to make contributions by a self-employed person correspond to those for a common-law employee. First, the self-employed business owner's net earnings must be reduced by the income tax deduction for one-half of the owner's self-employment (FICA) tax. In addition, the contribution percentage applies to the owner's net income *excluding* the contribution itself. For example, if a partnership establishes a 25 percent money purchase Keogh plan, and a partner earned $100,000, the deductible contribution on his or her behalf would be $20,000 (25 percent of earned income of $80,000), not $25,000.[17] With this adjustment, earned income for a self-employed person corresponds to a common-law employee's compensation. This special definition of earned income also applies to the contributions to self-employed persons under other noncorporate plans.

Section 401(k) Plans Section 401(k) plans, also referred to as *cash or deferred plans,* derive their name from the section of the *IRC* that outlines the rules for these plans. A 401(k) plan is a special type of profit sharing or stock bonus plan that permits employees to make contributions to the plan on a pre-tax basis. These plans provide a mechanism for accomplishing two apparently conflicting goals: increasing the retirement income of some employees, while increasing the current compensation of others. This is accomplished through a profit-sharing

[16] Under prior law, the $140,000 limit was decreased when benefit payments began before the normal Social Security retirement age (age 65 in 2001) and was increased when benefit payments start after this age. Under new rules introduced by EGTRRA-2001, the $160,000 amount (indexed for inflation) will be decreased when benefit payments begin before age 62 and increased when they start after age 65.

[17] For a common-law employee, the employer's contribution to a qualified retirement plan is added to earned income, creating a maximum for taxable income and nontaxable deferred income equal to 125 percent of earned income. This means that 80 percent of the total compensation is taxable and 20 percent is a nontaxable deferral. A self-employed person qualifies for the 2002 maximum contribution of $40,000 if he or she has $200,000 in earned income [25 percent of ($200,000–$40,000)].

plan under which employees *individually* elect whether to receive their contributions currently or have them deferred. In practice, the employees elect to contribute a portion of their income into a profit-sharing plan and instruct their employer to make contributions on their behalf. The *IRC* provides that the amounts an employee elects to defer under Section 401(k) are treated as contributions by the employer rather than by the employee. This makes all monies set aside in the plan deductible by the employer, and the contribution and its earnings are tax free to the employee until withdrawal. Although deferrals are subject to Social Security and Medicare taxes, they are not included in the employee's taxable income for income tax purposes.[18]

EGTRRA-2001 set the dollar limit on employee's elective deferrals to a 401(k) plan at $11,000 for 2002, with scheduled increases of $1000 annually through 2006, when the elective deferral limit will be $15,000. Thereafter, the limit will be indexed for inflation in $500 increments. In addition, for participants who are age 50 and older, EGTRRA-2001 authorizes additional *catch-up* deferrals. Beginning in 2002, the annual limit on catch-up contributions is $1000. This limit will increase in $1000 increments until it reaches $5000 in 2006, after which it will be indexed for inflation in increments of $500.

The employer may make matching contributions to a 401(k) plan and can also make contributions (other than matching contributions) without giving the employee the choice to take cash instead. The maximum employer contribution is 25 percent of employee compensation.[19] The employer's matching contributions that are allocated to a self-employed person (such as partners or a proprietor) are not considered elective employee contributions subject to the $10,000 limit. This puts self-employed persons and their employees on the same basis regarding contributions.

Simplified Employee Pension (SEP) Plans A *simplified employee pension* (SEP) permits employers to provide retirement benefits under a less complex arrangement than a qualified pension plan. Under a SEP, the employer contributes to a traditional IRA (individual retirement account or individual retirement annuity) that is owned and controlled by the employee. The employer makes contributions to the financial institution where the IRA is maintained. The maximum employer contribution to a SEP is 15 percent of employee compensation (up to the $200,000 limit, or $30,000). Employee contributions are not allowed and employer contributions are immediately vested.

Prior to 1997, SEPs could be established on a salary-reduction basis (much like a 401(k) plan) in which case the plan was referred to as an SARSEP. New SARSEPs have not been permitted since 1997 but the plans in existence before 1997 may continue to operate and can add new employees. The contribution limit to SARSEPs is the same as for a 401(k) plan and is scheduled to increase according to the same schedule, along with the catch-up deferrals for persons over age 50.

Section 403(b) Plans for Employees of Nonprofit Organizations The employees of certain nonprofit organizations (referred to in the *IRC* as Section 501(c)(3) organizations) are permitted to make before-tax contributions to tax-sheltered annuities under what are called 403(b) plans. As in 401(k) plans, the employee makes an agreement with the employer to reduce his or her salary by an amount equal to the contribution to the retirement plan. The contribution limits for 403(b) plans is the same as that for 401(k) plans, including the over-age 50 catch-up contribution limits.[20]

SIMPLE Plans The Small Business Job Protection Act of 1996 (SBJPA) introduced a new type of retirement plan known as a *Savings Incentive Match Plan for Employees* (SIMPLE). Eligibility is limited to employers with 100 or fewer employees that do not maintain any other type of employee retirement

[18] Because the cash or deferred plan is based on voluntary contributions by employees, Section 401(k) plans have also been referred to as *salary reduction plans.* For obvious reasons, at least from the employer's perspective, the term *cash or deferred* is a more appealing designation. Employees are likely to misconstrue the nature of the plans and perhaps be turned off by the designation "salary reduction plan."

[19] Because elective deferrals by participants are not considered part of the employer's contribution, the 25 percent limit applies only to the employer's matching or nonelective contributions to the plan. The maximum annual addition to the plan is the lesser of the employer's 25 percent of employee compensation plus employee deferrals or the dollar maximum indexed for inflation ($40,000 in 2002).

[20] Prior to EGTRRA-2001, a 403(b) plan participant's contributions for a year was limited by an *exclusion allowance,* which was 20 percent of the participant's compensation for the year, multiplied by the participant's years of service, less tax-excludable contributions in prior years to qualified plans maintained by the same employer. EGTRRA-2001 eliminated the exclusion allowance beginning in 2002.

plan. The key feature of a SIMPLE plan is its exemption from many of the complicated rules applicable to other qualified plans, such as the top-heavy rules and some of the more complex nondiscrimination rules. All employees with two years earnings of at least $5000 in each year and compensation of at least $5000 for the current year must be eligible to participate. The employer can choose to be less restrictive. Eligible employees make annual voluntary salary deferral contributions up to a statutory dollar maximum, regardless of their compensation level. The employer must either match employee contributions up to 3 percent of annual compensation or make nonelective contributions for all eligible employees of 2 percent of compensation. EGTRRA-2001 increased salary deferral maximum for SIMPLE plans from $6500 in 2001 to $7000 in 2002, with phased increases to $10,000 in 2005. After 2005, the limit adjusts for inflation in $500 increments. As in the case of 401(k) and 403(b) plans, individuals age 50 or older will be permitted to make additional catch-up contributions beginning in 2002. The catch-up contribution will be phased in gradually and will ultimately be $2500 by 2006. After 2006, the $2500 catch-up contribution will be indexed to inflation in $500 increments. The scheduled increases in the deferral limits for SIMPLE plans, along with the limits for Section 401(k), 403(b), and SAR-SEP Plans are summarized in Table 18.2.

Minimum Contribution or Benefit for Top-Heavy Plans Top-heavy plans are required to provide a minimum contribution on behalf of non-key employees. For defined contribution plans, the minimum annual contribution is 3 percent of the employee's compensation. In defined benefit plans, it is the amount required to provide a single life annuity beginning at the plan's normal retirement age, equal to 2 percent of the employee's average annual compensation during the five highest paid years with the employer, multiplied by the employee's years of service with the employer. However, the minimum benefit need not exceed 20 percent of such average annual compensation.

Roth Contributions to 401(k), 403(b) and SAR-SEP Plans Beginning in 2006, Section 401(k) plans and Section 403(b) plans can include provision for after-tax employee contributions to the plan. These contributions will be referred to as *Roth contributions,* after the member of Congress who introduced the concept of after-tax IRA contributions. The contributions and investment income on the accumulation will be withdrawn tax-free after the employee has completed five years of service and reaches age $59\frac{1}{2}$.

Integrated Benefit Formulas Although the rules of the tax code require that contribution rates be nondiscriminatory, employers may recognize the FICA payments made on behalf of employees and consider benefits under Social Security in establishing contribution levels. This process is referred to as *integration.* Defined benefit plans and defined contribution plans may both be *integrated* with Social Security.

In a defined contribution plan, the employer reduces the contribution to the pension plan on a

TABLE 18.2 **Scheduled Changes in Deferral Limits for Qualified Plans**

| | Maximum Deferral Limit | | | | | |
| | Section 401(k), 403(b), and SAR-SEP Plans | | | SIMPLE Plans | | |
Year	Under Age 50	Over Age 50 Catch-Up	Over Age 50 Total	Under Age 50	Over Age 50 Catch-Up	Over Age 50 Total
2001	$10,500	0	$10,500	$6500	0	$6500
2002	11,000	$1000	12,000	7000	$500	7500
2003	12,000	$2000	14,000	8000	$1000	9000
2004	13,000	$3000	16,000	9000	$1500	10,500
2005	14,000	$4000	18,000	10,000	$2000	12,000
2006	15,000	$5000	20,000	Indexed[a]	$2500	Indexed[a]
2007 and thereafter	Indexed[a]	Indexed[a]	Indexed[a]	Indexed[a]	Indexed[a]	Indexed[a]

[a] Increases indexed for inflation in $500 increments. The over-age 50 total contribution in 2007 and after is the total of the indexed basic and catch-up contributions.

part of wages subject to the FICA tax (the integration level). The integration level can be any amount up to the Social Security taxable wage base for the year. The amount contributed to the plan in excess of the integration level (the excess level contribution) cannot exceed the base contribution level by more than (1) the base contribution level itself or (2) the non-Medicare Social Security tax rate (6.2 percent in 2001). Thus, a plan with a base contribution level of 2 percent can have an excess contribution level of 4 percent, or a plan with a base contribution level of 5 percent can have an excess contribution level of not more than 10 percent. However, if the base contribution rate is 7 percent, the excess contribution rate cannot be more than 13.2 percent (i.e., the base contribution rate plus 6.2 percent).

In a defined benefit plan, integration is accomplished through a formula that replaces a higher percentage of earnings in excess of some level than is provided for earnings below that level. One of two approaches is used:

1. An excess plan, which provides greater benefits on compensation that exceeds the integration level than on benefits below that level. The excess-benefit percentage cannot exceed the base-benefit percentage by more than 0.75 percent for any year of service, or in total, 0.75 percent times the employee's number of years of service.

2. An offset plan, which provides benefits on the employee's full compensation, but then reduces the benefits by a percentage of the benefits received under Social Security. An offset provision cannot reduce the benefit by more than 50 percent of the benefit computed without the offset.

The offset method may not result in a reduction in private benefits to persons receiving a pension or disability benefit or to vested persons when Social Security benefits are increased in the future.

Although the provisions for integration initially appear to discriminate against lower-paid workers, they are designed to compensate for the fact that Social Security benefits provide for replacement of a higher percentage of a lower-paid worker's preretirement income than they do for the higher-paid employees. Integration formulas are designed to supply approximately the same percentage of income replacement after retirement for all workers.

Nonrefundable Tax Credit for Employee Contributions EGTRRA-2001 introduces an entirely new feature with respect to qualified retirement plans—a tax credit for certain low-income workers. The credit is available to employees with adjusted gross income below $50,000 for joint filers, $37,500 for head of household filers, and $25,000 for all other filers (excluding full-time students and any person who is claimed as a dependent by another taxpayer). The credit is a percentage of the first $2000 of the individual's annual contribution to a qualified retirement plan. The credit varies inversely with the individual's income as follows:

Joint Filers	Heads of Household
$0–$30,000	$0–$22,500
$30,000–$32,500	$22,500–$24,375
$32,500–$50,000	$24,375–$37,500
Over $50,000	Over $37,500

All Other Filers	Credit Rate
$0–$15,000	50%
$15,000–$16,250	20
$16,250–$25,000	10
Over $25,000	0

If the taxpayer does not have a tax liability prior to application of the credit, the credit is lost.

Significance of the Nature of the Employer's Promise

Defined contribution plans and defined benefit plans vary in the manner in which the employer's contribution is determined, but this difference creates other differences from the employee's perspective.

Investment Risk Under a defined contribution plan (which includes defined contribution pension plans, profit-sharing plans, ESOPs, Section 401(k) plans, and SEPs), the employer promises to make contributions to an account that earns investment income. The employer does not make any guarantee concerning the amount of the retirement benefit. The accumulated contributions will ultimately be available to provide a benefit to the employee. The amount of the benefit will depend on both the level of contributions and the amount of investment income. If investment

income is less than anticipated, the accumulation will be less than expected, and the retirement benefit will be lower. Similarly, a higher investment income will increase the retirement income available to the employee. Because the employer promises only to make contributions to the plan, but does not guarantee any level of benefits, the employee bears the investment risk in a defined contribution plan.

Since the employee bears the investment risk in a defined contribution plan, he or she is likely to have some say in how the funds are invested. Employers may provide a number of investment options from which the employee may choose. In an employee stock option plan, the employer is only required to allow the employee to direct the investment of a portion of his or her account balance (25 percent or 50 percent, depending on the situation). The remainder is typically invested in employer securities.

In a defined benefit plan, the employer's promise is to provide a certain level of retirement benefits to the employee, starting at normal retirement age. The employer determines the required contributions to the pension fund by making assumptions about the number of employees who will reach retirement age, the time for which benefits will be paid, and the rate of investment income earned on the pension fund. The higher the assumed investment income, the lower the employer's required contribution. If, however, investment income goes down and is therefore inadequate to fund the benefits, the employer must increase the contributions because the employer's obligation is to provide the promised benefits.

Advantages to Younger and Older Employees In addition to the difference between who bears the investment risk, defined benefit and defined contribution plans differ in their relative advantages to young and older employees. In general, a higher proportion of the ultimate retirement benefits are earned in the early years of participation in a defined contribution plan. This is because the contribution in early years will accumulate with investment income for a longer period than the contribution in later years. Hence, the accumulation at retirement will be larger, and the benefits it can purchase will be greater. On the other hand, the present value of the benefits promised to a young worker under a defined benefit plan tends to be small compared to the present value of the benefits promised when the worker is closer to retirement.

Forfeitures Finally, defined contribution and defined benefit plans may differ in how they deal with amounts forfeited by employees who terminate before being fully vested. In a defined contribution plan, amounts that are forfeited by employees who leave before being fully vested may be used to reduce future employer contributions, or they may be reallocated among remaining participants on a nondiscriminatory basis. In a defined benefit plan, gains from employee termination may be used only to reduce future employer contributions.

Protection for Inflation Given the long period between the time an employee begins to work for an employer and the time retirement benefits are paid, the employee would be wise to consider how the plan protects against the risk of inflation during the working years. Similarly, the individual may be retired for many years, and the effect of inflation during retirement on the purchasing power of the benefits should be considered.

Defined-benefit final-average salary plans provide the greatest protection against inflation during the employee's working years, since the retirement benefits are based on the employee's earnings during the period immediately preceding retirement. Careeraverage salary plans, on the other hand, base the benefits on the employee's salary throughout his or her career. Inflationary periods will reduce the value of the salary paid in early years, and hence the benefits based on those early salaries. Defined-contribution plans have, to some extent, a built-in protection against the risk of inflation, since the investment earnings on the funds are likely to be higher in inflationary periods. .

Some private plans provide cost-of-living adjustments during retirement years to protect against decreases in the purchasing power of benefits after retirement. This tends to be uncommon, however, and even where offered, the adjustment is subject to an annual cap.

The Shift to Defined Contribution Plans Since the mid-1970s, there has been a significant shift in the percentage of defined benefit and defined contribution plans. According to the U.S. Department of Labor, the percentage of workers covered by defined benefit plans declined from about 86 percent in 1975 to 50 percent in 1995, while the number of workers covered by defined contribution plans has increased from 13 percent to 50 percent. The trend to defined

contribution plans continues and appears to be increasing.

The are two reasons for the shift to the defined contribution approach. The first was passage of the Employee Retirement and Income Security Act of 1974 (ERISA), which required that employers insure defined benefit plans with the PBGC, thereby increasing their cost.[21] The second was the creation of the 401(k) account in 1978, which has become one of the most popular forms of pension funding. Many employees find the opportunity to defer taxes on part of their income appealing, because current taxable income is reduced, which can lower current personal taxes. At the same time, the pre-tax contribution means that the employee has more dollars working in the plan. In 1984, there were 17,303 plans with 401(k) features covering about 7.5 million workers. By 2000, the number of 401(k) plans had increased to 327,364, with 42 million covered workers.[22] The changes introduced by EGTRRA-2001 will make 401(k) plans even more appealing to employers and employees.

Other Benefits

Although the basic purpose of a pension plan is to provide retirement benefits, some plans include other features such as death benefits and disability benefits.

Preretirement Death Benefits A death benefit prior to retirement of the employee is an optional feature in pensions, except in the case of a contributory plan, where the employee's contribution is payable as a death benefit. Some employers also provide for a death benefit before retirement based on the employer's contributions. Federal regulations require that a qualified plan must provide that if a vested participant dies before the annuity starting date leaving a surviving spouse, benefits will be paid in the form of *a qualified preretirement survivor annuity*. In addition, some plans include preretirement death benefits via life insurance. As a rule, a defined contribution plan (e.g., a money purchase pension or a profit-sharing plan) can provide (1) term insurance, as long as the premiums are less than

25 percent of the allocation to the employee's account, or (2) permanent insurance, as long as premiums are less than 50 percent of the allocation.[23]

Postretirement Death Benefits Postretirement death benefits may be provided by annuities with joint and survivor options or by annuities with period-certain payments.

Required Joint and Survivor Option

ERISA required any participant who has been married for at least one year specifically to decline or else default to accepting a joint and survivor option of at least 50 percent of the participant's retirement benefit. The Retirement Equity Act of 1984 extended this requirement, mandating that qualified retirement plans provide automatic survivor benefits to the surviving spouse of a retiree or to the surviving spouse of a vested participant who dies before retirement. Spousal consent is required for a participant to elect out of joint-and-survivor annuity or preretirement survivor annuity coverage.

Period-Certain Payments

It is possible to arrange the benefits under a pension plan so a benefit is payable for some minimum period of time, regardless of the death of the beneficiary. So-called *period-certain* arrangements require the plan to pay for the lifetime of the beneficiary or for a specified period of time (such as 5 or 10 years), whichever is longer. Election of the period-certain option reduces the amount payable to the beneficiary on a lifetime basis.

Disability Benefits Some pension plans also make provision against the contingency of the employee's total and permanent disability. A plan may provide for the payment of disability benefits, as long as the cost of such benefits, when added to any life insurance protection provided by the plan, are subordinate (less than 50 percent of cost) to the retirement

[21] The insurance of pension plans by the PBGC is discussed in Chapter 23.

[22] Employee Benefit Research Institute, http://www.ebri.org.

[23] The cost of permanent life insurance protection is treated as a distribution from the plan and is taxable income to the employee for the year in which the premium is paid. The cost taxable to the participant is determined using one-year term insurance rates published by the IRS. In 2001, the IRS issued new rules regarding the tax treatment of life insurance under qualified plans and released a new table for the imputed cost of life insurance in such plans. The 2001 table replaces the previous P.S. 58 rates, which were somewhat higher than the new rates.

benefits. Under some plans, disability is simply treated as a form of early retirement, with a reduced retirement benefit payable. A more favorable approach provides for continued contributions to the plan on behalf of the disabled employee. The contributions are based on the compensation the employee would have received if he or she was paid the compensation earned immediately before becoming totally and permanently disabled.[24]

Distribution Requirements

The provisions that limit contributions and the accrual of benefits are supported by requirements regarding the time at which benefits may commence, the time at which they must commence, and also by a tax on excess contributions.

Commencement of Benefits Prior to the amendments made by the Small Business Job Act of 1996 (SBJPA), the *IRC* generally required that distributions from a tax-qualified retirement plan commence no later than April 1 of the calendar year following the calendar year in which an employee attained age $70^1/_2$. This meant that an employee who attained age $70^1/_2$ was required to commence distributions from the plan, even if the employee had not retired from employment with the employer maintaining the plan. Similar rules applied to an IRA and a section 403(b) contract (i.e., an annuity program). The SBJPA-96 amended the required beginning distribution date for most employees effective after December 31, 1996.[25] Under the new law, distributions may be deferred beyond age $70^1/_2$ until actual retirement. The eventual distributions must then be actuarially increased to take into account the period after age $70^1/_2$ in which the employee is not receiving distributions.[26]

When distribution begins, it must be made over one of the following periods:

- The life of the participant or the lives of the participant and a designated beneficiary *or*
- A period not extending beyond the life expectancy of the participant and his or her beneficiary

Under the first option, the accumulation is annuitized, and the plan administrator makes payments for the entire lifetime of the participant (and beneficiary if the joint life option is selected). The annuity may be based on one or two lives, and the annuitant may elect a minimum guaranteed number of payments. The key feature is that benefits are payable based on a life contingency.

Under the second option, distributions are *based* on the life expectancy of the individual (or the individual and his or her spouse), but cease when the funds are exhausted. If the entire accumulation is not paid out before the individual dies, the balance is paid to the designated beneficiary or the decedent's estate. The key feature in this arrangement is that the accumulation is distributed based on a life expectancy, but is not guaranteed for life.

Distributions From SIMPLE IRAs Generally, the same tax results apply to distributions from a SIMPLE IRA as to distributions from other plans. However, a special rule applies to a payment or distribution received from a SIMPLE IRA during the two-year period beginning on the date on which the individual first participated in a SIMPLE plan. Taxable distributions during this period are subject to a 25-percent penalty (rather than the 10-percent penalty applicable to other plans). Also, during the initial two-year period of participation, transfers from a SIMPLE IRA are permitted only to another SIMPLE IRA. Transfers to an IRA that is not a SIMPLE IRA do not qualify as rollover contributions.

Premature Withdrawals A 10-percent penalty applies to premature withdrawals that are made before the individual reaches age $59^1/_2$. The penalty does not apply to withdrawals that are rolled over into another qualified plan or an IRA. The penalty also does not apply if (1) the distribution is made on account of the employee's death or disability; (2) the distribution is used to pay deductible medical expenses; (3) the distribution is received as an annuity over the lifetime of the employee or under a joint life annuity including a beneficiary; or (4) the individual

[24] The election to continue deductible contributions on behalf of a disabled employee cannot be made for a disabled employee who is an officer, owner, or highly compensated employee.

[25] For employees who are 5-percent owners, the required beginning date remains April 1 of the calendar year following the calendar year in which the 5-percent owner attains age $70^1/_2$. The SBJPA amendments do not apply to the required beginning date for distributions from an IRA, including an IRA established in conjunction with a Simplified Employee Pension (SEP) or a SIMPLE Plan.

[26] The amount of the required minimum distributions generally are determined by using life expectancy tables established by the Internal Revenue Service in its regulations. A provision in EGTRRA-2001 requires the IRS to revise the life expectancy tables used in computing the minimum distributions after age $70^1/_2$ (or after retirement, if later) to reflect longer life expectancies.

is at least age 55 and meets the requirements of a plan that permits retirement at his or her age.[27]

Taxation of Distributions

Distributions from a qualified pension are taxable to the recipient when received, under special rules. In addition, if the participant dies, a distribution to his or her dependents is taxable as income and, in some cases, is also subject to estate taxes.

Income Taxes Most retirement plans provide for optional methods of receiving distributions. For example, a participant may receive plan benefits in a lump sum or in installments over his or her lifetime. The method of distribution determines the taxation.

Installment Distributions Retirement benefits have traditionally been paid to participants as lifetime annuities. Amounts distributed in installments will generally be taxable to the distributee under special annuity rules of *IRC* Section 72. Installment distributions are taxable only to the extent that they exceed the employee's investment in the contract. Every payment, beginning with the first, is considered part taxable income and part nontaxable. The nontaxable part consists of the portion of the payment that represents the employee's nondeductible contribution and is referred to as the *exclusion ratio.*[28]

Lump-Sum Distributions An employee who receives a lump-sum distribution can choose from among several alternatives. He or she can roll the distribution over into an IRA or another qualified retirement plan, in which case there is no tax on the distribution until it is eventually received from the IRA or other plan. As an alternative, within 60 days of receiving a lump-sum distribution, an employee may use the distribution to purchase a single-premium, nontransferable annuity and the distribution will be taxed under the annuity rules. At one time, lump-sum distributions from qualified plans were eli-

gible for five-year income averaging but this provision was repealed effective January 1, 2000.

Death Benefits If all or part of a plan's death benefits are payable from the proceeds of a life insurance policy, the excess of the face amount of the policy over its cash surrender value is excludable from income of the beneficiary (as life insurance proceeds). The distribution resulting from the death of a covered employee is usually taxed to the beneficiary in the same manner as it would have been to the deceased worker.

A surviving spouse can roll over to an IRA all or part of a lump-sum death benefit distribution received due to the deceased employee's death. The amount rolled over is not includable in the surviving spouse's taxable income, but will be taxed as ordinary income when it is subsequently distributed and will not be eligible for five-year averaging, even if paid in a lump sum.

If an employee dies before his or her entire interest is paid and a joint-and-survivor option is not in effect, or if payments are being made to a surviving spouse who dies before the entire interest is received, the balance will generally have to be distributed to beneficiaries within five years.

Estate Taxes Distributions from qualified plans are not subject to the estate tax if the benefits are paid to a surviving spouse. Other distributions are includable in the estate and are subject to the estate tax.

Limitations on Loan Transactions The substantial accumulation of funds in qualified pension plans has been an appealing source of loans to the plan participants. Such loans, however, are subject to restrictions imposed by the *IRC*. A loan from a qualified plan to an employee is treated as a distribution (and is therefore taxable) to the extent that it exceeds prescribed limits. Furthermore, a loan to a participant may not exceed the lesser of $50,000 or one-half of the participant's vested accrued benefit (but not less than $10,000). The loan must be repaid within five years, and the repayment must be on an amortized basis. An exception to the five-year payback rules applies to a loan used to acquire the principal residence of the participant.[29]

[27] Prior to 1997, there was a 15-percent excess tax on distributions from qualified retirement plans in excess of $155,000 (indexed). This penalty was suspended for three years in 1996. TRA-97 repealed the penalty for distributions after 1997 and for persons dying after 1996.

[28] Annuity payments beyond the individual's life expectancy will be fully taxable. Should the retired person die before reaching full life expectancy, his or her heirs may take a deduction on the deceased's final return for the amount of any unrecovered contributions.

[29] Prior to EGTRRA-2001, loans from qualified plans to owner-employees were not permitted, but EGTRRA-2001 makes owner-employees eligible to receive loans from qualified plans subject to the same limitations as other participants.

INDIVIDUAL RETIREMENT ACCOUNTS

The individual retirement account, often referred to as the IRA, was created by the Pension Reform Act of 1974. At that time, it represented the first new concept in pension planning since the introduction of Keogh plans in 1962. Although individual retirement accounts are not an employee benefit per se, they were originally intended as substitutes for employer-provided pensions. The original purpose of the IRA was to permit persons who were not covered under a qualified pension plan or government plan to establish their own pension program and accumulate funds for retirement on a tax-favored basis. The annual contributions to an IRA by an eligible individual was made tax-deductible by the individual and the tax on investment earnings was deferred until withdrawal after age $59^1/_2$.

IRA eligibility rules have been changed several times. From 1974 through 1981, IRAs were available only to individuals who were not participants in another pension plan. From 1982 until 1986, eligibility was extended to all persons with income, whether or not they were covered by an employer-sponsored plan. The Tax Reform Act of 1986 established a new sct of eligibility rules, with limits on the deductibility of contributions by persons who are covered by an employer-sponsored plan. The Tax Reform Act of 1997 created a new type of IRA, called the *Roth IRA,* which has been available since 1998. The distinguishing feature of the Roth IRA is that contributions are made only on a nondeductible basis and the tax benefit is realized when the funds are withdrawn. All earnings on the contributions compound tax-free as long as they are not withdrawn for at least five years and there are no taxes due when the funds are withdrawn for retirement (i.e., after age $59^1/_2$).

Traditional IRAs

For many years, the maximum deductible contribution to an IRA was $2000. Under EGTRRA-2001, the maximum annual contribution that may be made to any combination of traditional and Roth IRAs will be gradually increased from $2000 to $5000 by 2008. After 2008, the $5000 contribution limit will be indexed to inflation in $500 increments. Individuals age 50 or older by the end of the taxable year for which a contribution is made will be permitted to make additional catch-up contributions of $500 per year in 2002 through 2005 and $1000 a year in 2006 and thereafter. Unlike catch-up contributions to 401(k) plans, 403(b) plans, 457 plans, SEP-IRAs, and SIMPLE IRAs, the catch-up contribution for Traditional and Roth IRAs is not indexed for inflation but will remain at $1000 after 2006. The scheduled maximum contribution limits for IRAs is indicated in Table 18.3

Traditional IRA Eligibility Although it significantly increased the limits for deductible contributions, EGTRRA did not alter the eligibility rules with respect to deductible contributions. Under the current rules, a person who is not covered by an employer retirement plan can make deductible contributions to an IRA up to the lesser of the statutory maximum or 100 percent of compensation. A person who is covered by an employer-sponsored plan may still be entitled to a deduction, depending on his or her income. The deduction begins to decrease when the taxpayer's adjusted gross income (AGI) rises above a certain level and is eliminated altogether when it reaches a higher level. The eligibility phase-out limits currently in effect, established by the TRA-97, are indicated in Table 18.4.

A spouse who is not employed outside the home can make tax-deductible IRA contributions up to $2000 a year even if his or her partner is covered by an employer's retirement plan. In other words, if only one spouse is a participant in an employer's plan, the limitation only applies to that spouse. The deduction for such spousal contributions phases out

TABLE 18.3 **Traditional or Roth IRA Contribution Limits**

| Year | Maximum Contribution Limit | | |
	Under Age 50	Over Age 50	Over Age 50 Total
2001	$2000	0	$2000
2002	3000	$ 500	3500
2003	3000	500	3500
2004	3000	500	3500
2005	4000	500	4500
2006	4000	1000	5000
2007	4000	1000	5000
2008	5000	1000	6000
2009	Indexed	1000	Indexed

TABLE 18.4 Traditional IRA Income Phase-Out Limits

Year	Single Persons and Heads of Households	Married Filing Jointly
2002	$34,000–$44,000	$54,000–$64,000
2003	$40,000–$50,000	$60,000–$70,000
2004	$45,000–$55,000	$65,000–$75,000
2005	$50,000–$60,000	$70,000–$80,000
2006	$50,000–$60,000	$75,000–$85,000
2007 and after	$50,000–$60,000	$80,000–$100,000

for married couples with incomes between $150,000 and $160,000.[30]

To compute the permissible deductions for an individual who is covered by an employer plan and whose income is within the AGI phase-out range, the simplest approach is to deduct the individual's AGI from the upper limit of the phase-out bracket, and multiply the answer by 0.20. The result is the permissible contribution.[31] For example, if Mr. Smith has AGI of $56,000 for 2002 and files a joint return, his deductible contribution is $1600:

Maximum phase-out limit	$64,000
Adjusted gross income	46,000
Income below limit	$8,000
Partial deduction ($8000 × .20)	1,600

Nondeductible Contributions to Traditional IRAs

Taxpayers whose income exceeds the AGI phase-out levels for traditional or Roth IRAs can make nondeductible contributions to a traditional IRA up to the statutory maximum or 100 percent of compensation, whichever is less. Earnings on the contributions are not taxed until distributed.

If an individual contributes more to an IRA than the legal maximum, a 6-percent penalty is imposed on the excess contributions. The 6-percent tax is imposed each year until either the excess contribution is withdrawn or the taxpayer reduces the contribution to absorb the amount of excess contributions.

[30] Prior to the 1997 tax law changes, a nonworking spouse (or a working spouse not covered under an employer-sponsored plan) could not make a deductible contribution to an IRA if the other spouse participated in an employer-sponsored plan and the spouses had an income above a certain limit.

[31] The result is rounded to the next higher multiple of $10. If the amount is less than $200, a $200 deduction is permitted. When the AGI limits for persons filing jointly are fully phased in 2007, the difference between AGI and the phase-out limit of $100,000 should be multiplied by 0.10 to determine the permissible deduction.

Tax Treatment of IRAs

The tax on deductible contributions to an IRA and the investment income on both deductible and nondeductible contributions is not eliminated: It is merely deferred until distribution. Deductible contributions and investment income are taxable when distributed and premature distributions (i.e., distributions before age $59\frac{1}{2}$) are subject to a 10-percent tax penalty. At the time of distribution, a tax is imposed on the deductible contributions and on earnings that have not been taxed (i.e., earnings from both deductible and nondeductible contributions). Nondeductible contributions, however, are tax free when distributed. When the IRA is funded in part by deductible contributions and in part by nondeductible contributions, withdrawals are considered to consist in part of deductible and in part of nondeductible contributions, with the nondeductible contributions exempt from tax on the distribution. The part of distributions in any year that is considered to arise from nondeductible contributions (and which is therefore nontaxable) is determined by a formula under which the nontaxable portion of each distribution is equal to the ratio of the remaining nondeductible contributions to the IRA to the fair market value of the IRA at the time the distribution was made. The formula under which the computation is made is:

$$\text{Amount Distributed from IRA during Year} \times \frac{\text{Total Nondeductible Contributions All Years to IRAs} - \text{Tax Free Withdrawals in Prior Years}}{\text{Fair Market Value of all IRAs at End of the Year} + \text{Amount Distributed from IRA during the Year}}$$

Under certain circumstances, withdrawals prior to age $59\frac{1}{2}$ may be exempt from the 10-percent early withdrawal penalty. First, beginning in 1997, the Health Insurance Portability and Accountability Act of 1996 (HIP AA-96) allows penalty-free withdrawals to cover potentially devastating medical expenses. The medical costs must be that of the taxpayer, spouse, or dependents, and the expenses must exceed 7.5 percent of the taxpayer's adjusted gross income. The amount withdrawn is subject to income tax, but if the taxpayer itemizes, the income can be partially offset by the itemized deduction of the medical expense.

In addition, unemployed individuals may withdraw amounts for the payment of health insurance premiums without incurring the 10-percent penalty.

The 7.5-percent floor does not have to be met if the individual has received unemployment compensation for at least 12 weeks and the withdrawal is made in either the year that such unemployment compensation is received or the year immediately following. The exception ceases to apply once the individual has been reemployed for a period of 60 days.[32]

In addition, beginning in 1998, penalty-free (not income-tax-free) withdrawals from the traditional IRAs are permitted for qualified first-time home buyers or for the first home purchase by a spouse, child, or grandchild (subject to a $10,000 lifetime limit), and for qualified higher education expenses for individuals, their spouses, children, or grandchildren.

IRAs as Portable Pensions A special provision in the regulations applicable to IRAs creates a collateral benefit of the IRA by establishing a basis for portable pensions. A unique privilege under the act permits individuals who terminate employment and receive a lump-sum distribution from a qualified plan to avoid taxation on such proceeds until they actually withdraw it from an IRA in the form of benefits at some later date. Thus, an employee who receives a lump-sum distribution may establish an IRA and thereby avoid immediate taxation.

Partial IRA Rollovers Partial IRA rollovers have been permitted since 1982. Prior to that time, a taxpayer receiving a lump-sum distribution from a qualified pension could defer taxation on that distribution only by *rolling over* the entire distribution. Under the new law, it is possible for the taxpayer to roll over a part of the distribution and escape taxation on the portion rolled over. Only the part of the distribution not rolled over is taxed.

Deductible contributions and investment income are taxable when distributed and premature distributions (i.e., distributions before age $59^1/_2$) are subject to a 10-percent tax penalty. When the IRA is funded by both deductible and nondeductible contributions, withdrawals are considered to consist in part of deductible and in part of nondeductible contributions, with the nondeductible contributions exempt from tax on the distribution.

Generally, IRA accounts may be funded with any investments that are acceptable for other tax-qualified plans. The most common funding instruments are custodial accounts established by banks and retirement annuities. The *IRC* forbids IRAs to invest in life insurance contracts.

The Roth IRA

Annual contributions up to the lesser of 100 percent of compensation or the statutory maximum per individual are permitted for single taxpayers with annual income of up to $95,000 or couples filing jointly with annual income up to $150,000.[33] The contribution amount is gradually reduced to zero at income levels between $95,000 and $110,000 for single taxpayers, and $150,000 and $160,000 for couples. There is no requirement that withdrawals commence at $70^1/_2$ and contributions to a Roth IRA may continue after age $70^1/_2$ as long as the individual or spouse has earned income.

Taxpayers with adjusted gross incomes less than $100,000, whether single or joint filers, can roll over assets from traditional IRAs into a Roth IRA. Once rolled over, these assets continue to accumulate tax-deferred until withdrawn. Income taxes apply to the taxable amount that is rolled over, but there is no premature distribution penalty.

There is no penalty on early withdrawals of the after-tax contributions to a Roth IRA. Under the *IRC* provisions applicable to Roth IRAs, the first money taken out of the account is considered the after-tax contributions, rather than earnings. Premature withdrawals of earnings (i.e., before age $59^1/_2$) are taxable income, subject to a 10-percent penalty except in the event of death, disability, or a first-time home purchase. The first-time homeowner withdrawal is subject to a $10,000 one-time limit.

Individuals can have both a traditional IRA and a Roth IRA, but they cannot contribute more than the statutory maximum for a given year between both accounts. Individuals who are not eligible for deductible contributions to a traditional IRA or contributions to a Roth IRA may still make nondeductible contributions to a traditional IRA.

A CONCLUDING NOTE

This discussion of qualified retirement plans and IRAs illustrates the enormous complexity facing

[32] *IRC* Section 72(t).

[33] Unlike the dollar limits for other retirement programs, the IRA contribution phase-out AGI limits are not indexed for inflation.

individuals as they consider their options in planning for retirement. This is a highly technical area. It is complicated by the fact that a significant body of law applies to the design of these plans. It is further complicated because this law frequently changes, particularly as it applies to *IRC* requirements. Obviously, this discussion is only an overview, intended to acquaint students with the general characteristics of these plans and important elements to consider in evaluating their own retirement programs.

IMPORTANT CONCEPTS TO REMEMBER

fixed-dollar annuity	ERISA	SIMPLE IRA
variable annuity	defined benefit plan	simple 401(k) plan
immediate annuity	defined contribution plan	funding
deferred annuity	profit-sharing plan	final average salary plan
joint life annuity	employee stock ownership plan	career average salary plan
joint-and-last-survivor annuity	(ESOP)	maximum benefit limitations
installment refund annuity	Keogh plan	Social Security integration
cash refund annuity	simplified employee pension plan	individual retirement accounts
qualified retirement plans	Section 401(k) plan	Roth IRA
vesting	Section 403(b) plan	

QUESTIONS FOR REVIEW

1. It has been stated that an annuity is "upside-down" life insurance. Explain what is meant by this notion.

2. Identify the various ways in which annuities may be classified and list the different types of annuities in each classification.

3. Describe the variable annuity and explain the theory on which it is based. To what extent have the results produced by variable annuities been consistent with the theory?

4. Describe the tax treatment of annuities

a. During the accumulation period

b. When distributed

5. Distinguish between the *last survivor annuity* and the *survivorship annuity.*

6. Briefly distinguish between a *defined-benefit* pension plan and a *defined-contribution* plan. Which of these would a variable annuity be?

7. What is the purpose of a Keogh plan? What is the maximum deductible contribution that may be made on behalf of a self-employed person under a Keogh plan?

8. Who is eligible to establish individual retirement accounts? What is the maximum deductible contribution that may be made on behalf of participants under IRAs?

9. Describe the various provisions that may be included in a pension plan with respect to death or disability of a plan participant.

10. The obvious difference between defined-contribution plans and defined-benefit plans is in the formula by which the contribution is determined. Identify and explain the significance of the other differences between defined-benefit and defined-contribution plans.

QUESTIONS FOR DISCUSSION

1. A highly successful college athlete has just signed with a professional team and has received a $500,000 bonus. Prudently, he plans to invest the money and it has been suggested that he put the money in a single-premium deferred annuity. What are the advantages and disadvantages of this course of action?

2. Assume that you have reached age 65 and are about to retire. You have accumulated a fund of $300,000 and are considering the purchase of an annuity. A straight life annuity will pay you $1800 a month for life, and a life annuity with a 20-year certain period will pay you $1650 a month. Which would you select and why?

3. You are considering employment with two corporations and, among other things, you would like to compare their pension plans. What features of the two plans would you be most interested in?

4. Over the past 40 years, Carl's employer-funded defined-contribution retirement program has been invested in a variable annuity. Now that he has reached retirement age, he is elated by the fact that the value of the accumulation exceeds $1 million. He anticipates that the investment income on the accumulation will be between 7 and 8 percent annually. Because this amount is sufficient for his and his wife's needs, he looks forward to leaving his two children approximately a half-million dollars each. Advise him.

5. Why does ERISA require employers to insure defined benefit plans but not defined contribution plans?

SUGGESTIONS FOR ADDITIONAL READING

Allen, Everett T., Joseph J. Melone, Jerry S. Rosenbloom, and Jack L. VanDerhei. *Pension Planning,* 8th ed. Homewood, Ill.: Richard D. Irwin, 1997.

Beam, Burton T., Jr., and John J. McFadden. *Employee Benefits,* 3rd ed. Brookfield, Wis.: Dearborn Financial Publishing, 1994.

Black, Kenneth, Jr., and Harold D. Skipper, Jr. *Life Insurance,* 13th ed. Englewood Cliffs, N.J.: Prentice-Hall, 2000. Chapters 8, 21.

Hallman, G. Victor, and Karen L. Hamilton. *Personal Insurance: Life, Health, and Retirement.* Malvern, Pa.: American Institute for CPCU, 1994. Chapters 6, 7.

WEB SITES TO EXPLORE

Association of Private Pension and Welfare Plans	http://www.podi.com/appwp/retire.htm
Insurance News Network	http://www.insure.com/
International Foundation of Employee Benefits	http://www.ifebp.org/
Newsedge News Page	http://www.newspage.com/browse/46622/
Quicken InsureMarket	http://www.insuremarket.com/
TIAA-CREF	http://www.tiaa-cref.org/
U.S. Pension Law—Cornell University	http://www.law.cornell.edu/topics/pensions.html

MANAGING THE RETIREMENT RISK

The wise man saves for the future, but the foolish man spends whatever he gets.

— PROVERBS 21:20

CHAPTER OBJECTIVES

When you have finished this chapter, you should be able to

- Identify the factors that create the risks related to retirement
- Identify the two financial risks that arise in connection with the retirement risk
- Identify the three broad steps in the retirement planning process
- Identify the three lines of defense that constitute a well-designed retirement plan
- Identify and describe the two approaches that may be used to estimate retirement needs
- Explain the strategies that may be followed in managing the distribution of a retirement accumulation

In this chapter, we turn to the other side of the life contingency risk, the possibility of outliving one's income, the retirement risk. As we noted in Chapter 10, the retirement risk is the complement of the risk of premature death. If the individual dies prematurely, he or she will have no need for funds that were being accumulated for retirement. If the individual lives until retirement, provision made for premature death will not be used, but there is a need for retirement funds. Because there is a possibility of either outcome, the individual must make provision for both contingencies.

AN OVERVIEW OF THE RETIREMENT RISK

For the average college student, who has yet to begin a career, the time at which that career is likely to come to an end seems beyond the span of relevance.

It is difficult to imagine the time at which the working years will eventually come to an end. It is even harder to imagine that at the time they end, there might be too few assets to live comfortably for the remainder of one's lifetime. But this is the essence of the retirement risk.

Causes of the Retirement Risk

The retirement risk arises from uncertainty concerning the time of death. It is influenced by both physiological and cultural hazards. As a society, our current population tends to live longer after retirement than any previous generation. In 1935, a woman who reached age 65 in good health could plan on living another 13 years; for a man the life expectancy was about 12 years. By 1995, a woman who reached age 65 in good health had a life expectancy of 19 years, while a man had an expectancy of 16 years. For the current college-age population, life expectancies are even longer.

At the same time people are living longer, they are retiring earlier. People have quit working at earlier ages for several reasons. One is the advent of financial planning and the fact that more people are financially able to retire. In addition, many business firms are offering their employees attractive early retirement packages to make room for younger (and less expensive) workers. Many of today's college students will live 25 to 30 percent of their life span after they retire.

Two Risks Associated with Retirement

Although they are closely related, there are two distinguishable risks associated with retirement. The first is the possibility that insufficient assets will have been accumulated by the time the individual reaches retirement age. The second is the possibility that the individual may outlive the assets that have been accumulated. Even if sufficient assets have been accumulated to provide an adequate standard of living after retirement, uncertainty concerning the life expectancy raises a problem regarding the portion of the accumulation that should be consumed each year so that the accumulation will last for the individual's entire lifetime. This second problem is the easier of the two to address. The annuity principle, in which a principal sum is liquidated based on life expectancies, can be used to convert an accumulation into an income the individual cannot outlive. In Chapter 18, we discussed the specifics of different types of annuities. It should be clear from that discussion that annuities are essential tools in managing the retirement risk and that they provide a convenient solution to the second problem associated with retirement, the possibility of outliving the retirement accumulation.

Retirement Risk Alternatives

Some people attempt to avoid the risk of outliving their income by the simple expedient of not retiring. Although societal pressures and corporate policies sometimes mitigate against this strategy, there are many who continue working beyond the normal retirement age by preference or out of necessity. People who elect not to retire do not, however, totally avoid the risk that they may outlive their income. Even if the individual decides to continue working beyond the "normal" retirement age, the possibility of becoming disabled increases significantly beyond age 65. Since disability income policies do not provide full coverage beyond age 65, the individual may find him or herself in an involuntary retirement forced by disability. Although continued employment at retirement age does not, therefore, avoid the risk of outliving one's income, it clearly reduces the risk.

Transfer is also used as a technique for dealing with the retirement risk. A part of the retirement risk is transferred to that portion of the work force that will still be employed when the individual retires. Under the Social Security system, taxes paid by employed workers provide the funding for Social Security beneficiaries. In addition, annuities can be used to transfer the risk of outliving an accumulated sum to an insurer. Finally, some individuals transfer the retirement risk to their children or to society, by the simple expedient of not preparing for retirement.

Although the provision for one's retirement may combine the techniques of avoidance, reduction, and transfer, the primary technique for dealing with the retirement risk is retention. As in the case of other retention strategies, this requires the accumulation or identification of the funds that will be required to meet the loss when it occurs.

An Overview of the Retirement Planning Process

Retirement planning involves three steps that more or less parallel those that we have considered in planning life insurance needs.

- The first step is to estimate the future income need. This requires predicting the income needs that will exist after retirement, and then identifying the sources that will be available to meet these needs.

- The second is to determine how the funds required to meet the needs defined in the first step will be accumulated. This involves designing and implementing a plan to accumulate assets sufficient to fund the difference between the resources that will be needed and the resources that will be available to provide the required retirement income.

- The final step is to plan the manner in which the accumulation will be consumed. This requires consideration of the period over which the retirement accumulation will be consumed and the provision that should be made for a spouse.

Sources of Retirement Funding There are three broad sources of funding for the retirement need: Social Security, qualified pensions and profit-sharing plans, and private savings. These three sources of funding have traditionally been referred to as the *three legs* to the retirement stool.

The First Leg: Social Security For most people, the first source of retirement income will be Social Security. The adequacy of Social Security retirement benefits depends in large part on the standard of living the retiree wishes to maintain. Because Social Security benefits are computed in a manner that favors those in low-income classes, it provides about 60 percent of the retirement needs for minimum wage earners, but less than 30 percent of the retirement needs for those who earned the maximum Social Security taxable wage base. In addition to the smaller percentage of preretirement income that Social Security replaces for middle- and upper-income categories, there is reason to question whether it is reasonable to project present Social Security benefit levels into the future. Given the financial difficulties facing the system, we will likely see additional measures aimed at correcting the system's problems. Judging from the measures that have been adopted in the past, the changes could reduce the level of benefits for some retirees. As we saw in Chapter 11, the Social Security benefits of individuals (and couples) with significant income from other sources are now subject to the federal income tax. In addition, the retirement age at which full benefits will be payable is scheduled to increase gradually from its current level to age 67. Although the situation does not yet seem sufficiently precarious to warrant ignoring the Social Security benefits that will be available to the individual, it does suggest vigilance in monitoring the retirement program.

Even barring changes in the Social Security benefit structure, Social Security benefits are rarely adequate to continue the worker's preretirement standard of living. Income from Social Security must be supplemented by other sources of income. One possibility is for the worker to accept employment after the Social Security benefit has begun. Although this may be the only alternative, Social Security regulations relating to earnings of beneficiaries impose an enormous tax on postretirement earnings. As noted in Chapter 11, income that is earned by a Social Security beneficiary may reduce the Social Security benefit. Although beneficiaries over age 65 have no limit on their earnings, beneficiaries below age 65 can lose Social Security benefits if their earnings exceed specified levels. This means that a retired worker who finds it necessary to work to maintain a desired standard of living may suffer a reduction in benefit, which, combined with the Federal Insurance Contributions Act (FICA) and income tax on the earnings, will significantly diminish the benefit of the employment.[1]

The Second Leg: Qualified Pensions and Profit-Sharing Plans For some people, an employer-sponsored pension or profit-sharing plan will be available to supplement the benefits provided by Social Security. Although qualified retirement plans have traditionally been considered another keystone in the individual's retirement planning, only about 50 percent of the work force have any kind of pension plan. In addition, there has been a trend away from the defined-benefit plan to defined-contribution plans, which, as we have seen, place the investment risk associated with the plan on the employee. There has also been a shift to the increasingly popular 401(k) plans, in which employees defer income in tax-sheltered contributions. In some cases, the employer matches the employee's contribution to these plans, in other cases not. When the employer contributes to the plan, the individual's burden in constructing the third part of the program is less. When the employer

[1] A 62-year-old retired worker who receives a Social Security benefit of, say, $1500 a month and accepts employment at $2000 a month, will lose $4750 in Social Security benefits. FICA taxes will take an additional $1836 and federal income tax will be about $1575, making total deductions of $8161 of the $24,000 in wages.

does not contribute, the employee should still take advantage of the opportunity to shelter a part of his or her income.

The Third Leg: Personal Savings Except in unusual situations, the benefits provided by Social Security and an employer-sponsored pension will rarely provide a retirement income that is adequate for retirement needs. Depending on whether the individual is covered by a corporate pension plan, anywhere from 30 percent to 70 percent of the retirement income will have to come from savings that are generated during the individual's income-earning years.

An obvious question that arises in connection with the funds accumulated for retirement relates to the form in which these funds should be held. There are a variety of options, including life insurance and annuities, government bonds, corporate bonds, stocks, mutual funds, limited partnerships, and real estate. Financial planners have identified a number of criteria that should be considered in selecting the long-term investments that will be used in accumulating the personal savings component of one's retirement income. These include the rate of return, vulnerability to inflation, tax treatment, and safety of principal. Appropriate consideration should be given to each of these factors in selecting investments for the retirement portfolio. Annuities (and life insurance), because of their favorable tax treatment, deserve consideration for inclusion in the retirement accumulation.

There is an obvious relationship between the tax treatment of investments and their rate of return. Differences in tax treatment produce different rates of return over the accumulation period, which in turn influence the amount that a given dollar level of investment will produce. The different rates of return and their associated accumulations indicated in Table 19.1 show the dramatic effect of differences in rates of return on a growing fund. Obviously, if a part of the investment income cannot be reinvested because it must go to pay taxes, the realized rate of return will be lower. Investments on which the investment income accumulates tax free, or on which the taxation of the investment return is deferred, will accumulate more rapidly and provide a greater terminal value than when the increments are subject to current taxation.

Because of the differential rates of growth associated with different rates of return, the investment accumulation should make maximum use of tax-deferred vehicles. When permitted, voluntary contributions to an employer-sponsored plan will provide the desired tax deferral. Similarly, investment in an IRA, even on a nondeductible basis, will shelter the investment income from current taxation, thereby increasing the accumulation. Finally, annuities—under which investment earnings accumulate on a tax-deferred basis—also represent an attractive alternative. Unlike nondeductible contributions to an IRA, which are limited to $2000 (or $2250 if a spouse is included), there is no maximum on the amount that may be paid into an annuity. Given the wide range of options available in self-directed annuities, a portfolio of virtually any dimension can be constructed using a deferred installment annuity. Because the tax on the investment income from the instruments included in the self-directed portfolio is

TABLE 19.1 Accumulation of $1,000 Annual Investment

| Rate | Number of Years | | | | | | | |
	5	10	15	20	25	30	35	40
5%	$5802	$13,207	$20,579	$ 34,719	$ 50,113	$ 69,761	$ 94,836	$ 126,840
6%	5975	13,972	22,276	38,993	58,156	83,802	118,121	164,048
7%	6153	14,783	26,888	43,865	67,676	101,072	147,913	213,610
8%	6335	15,645	29,324	49,422	78,954	122,345	186,102	279,781
9%	6523	16,560	32,003	55,764	92,324	148,574	235,125	368,292
10%	6715	17,531	34,949	63,002	108,181	180,942	298,127	486,852
11%	6912	18,561	38,189	71,265	126,998	220,912	379,164	645,827
12%	7115	19,654	41,753	80,698	149,333	270,292	483,463	859,142
13%	7322	20,814	45,671	91,469	175,850	331,314	617,749	1,145,486
14%	7535	22,044	49,980	103,768	207,332	409,736	790,673	1,529,909
15%	7753	23,349	54,717	117,810	244,712	499,956	1,013,346	2,045,954

deferred, the tax treatment of these instruments becomes inconsequential. There is no need to limit investments to those that receive favorable tax treatment, since all investments in the annuity portfolio produce tax-deferred income.

Countering the Urgency Deficit

It has been suggested that an ambiguity in the terms *important* and *urgent* sometimes results in a distorted sense of priorities; importance and urgency do not always go together. Often, unimportant things get done because there is a sense of urgency, while important things are sometimes postponed to be done "later." Retirement planning is a good example. While most people would probably agree on the importance of retirement planning, the sense of urgency does not arise until the individual approaches retirement. Because there are many years until retirement at age 25 or 30 or 35, it is easy to delay designing and implementing a retirement program.

The importance of timing rests in the effect of compound interest on regular contributions to an accumulating fund. The sooner one begins to accumulate funds for retirement and the greater the amount set aside, the greater will be the accumulation when the individual retires. Consider again the accumulations at different rates of return indicated in Table 19.1, which indicates the impact that both time and the rate of return can have on the accumulating fund. The longer the time before retirement one begins to make regular periodic contributions toward a retirement fund, the greater will be the accumulation. Except in cases where provision for retirement has been assured by a generous employer-sponsored plan, the individual is responsible for planning his or her program, and then executing that plan. The sooner one begins, the greater the likelihood of achieving the retirement goals that have been set.

CONSTRUCTING A RETIREMENT PLAN

As previously noted, retirement planning involves three basic steps:

1. Estimating retirement needs
2. Planning the retirement accumulation
3. Planning the retirement distribution

As will be clear from the discussion that follows, the three steps are interrelated, and decisions in one step can influence choices in the other two. Estimating retirement needs involves choices that define the parameters for decisions in the second and third steps, but the financial realities encountered in steps two and three may require revisiting the decisions made in step one. We will begin our discussion with an examination of some issues that must be addressed in the first step of the process, estimating the retirement needs.

Estimating Retirement Needs

The purpose of estimating retirement needs is to provide a goal or objective for the second step in the process, which is to plan the manner in which funds for retirement will be accumulated. Defining the size of the retirement fund that must be accumulated involves two estimations: the total retirement income that will be needed and the part of that need that will not be met from existing resources.

Estimating the Aggregate Need With respect first to the total retirement income that will be needed, it is necessary to determine the amount of monthly income that will allow the individual and his or her spouse to live after retirement. The amount that will be required for a comfortable retirement will depend on the lifestyle to which the individual or couple aspires after retirement and on the rate of inflation.

There are two ways in which future income needs may be estimated. The first is to construct a budget for postretirement living, estimating the costs that will need to be met for housing, food and other necessities, medical expenses, and so on. The second approach, which we will follow, is to set the retirement income need at some percentage of the preretirement income. This second approach assumes that changes in the cost of living will be reflected by changes in the individual's income, and that postretirement income needs can be estimated from the individual's preretirement income. Because preretirement income will be influenced by inflation and other changes in income as the individual progresses through a career, the initial calculation is to project present income to retirement age. Consider, for example, a 25-year-old person with a present annual income of $36,000, who plans to retire at age 65. Projecting present income at a modest annual increase of 3 percent, the present income will increase to

slightly more than $114,000 by the time he or she reaches age 65. Assuming current tax rates, after-tax income will be about $90,000.

Once present income has been projected to a retirement-age income level, the income need at the beginning of rétirement is set as a percentage or fraction of the preretirement income. The fraction of preretirement income that is established as the retirement income need will depend on personal considerations, the first of which is the lifestyle to which the individual aspires during retirement. Although it is traditional to assume that postretirement income needs will be less than the income need during the working years, it is conceivable that for some persons the need might be greater. This is particularly true in the case of persons who plan to travel and engage in a variety of recreational activities during retirement. For the purpose of illustration, we will follow convention and assume that the retirement income need will be less than the income need during the working years. A reasonable fraction, for the purposes of our illustrations, is 75 percent of the preretirement income level. Using the projected after-tax income of $90,000 already suggested, this indicates an initial retirement income need of $67,500.

Retirement needs may be expected to increase after retirement due to inflation. Even at a modest inflation rate of 3 percent, prices will approximately double over a 25-year period and the purchasing power of a fixed annual income will fall by half. This means that in projecting retirement needs an allowance should be made for inflation that will occur both before and after retirement. The consumer price index indicates that the historical rate of inflation over the past 30 years has been about 5.6 percent annually. Although the inflation rate over the next 30 to 40 years may be more or less, selecting the rate is a judgment call. Although any inflation rate selected is subject to error, the greater error is in ignoring inflation, which in effect sets the inflation rate at zero.

In addition to the allowance for inflation, a second adjustment is to recognize the effect of taxes on postretirement income. Because retirement distributions will generally be taxable—at least in part—the retirement plan should be constructed to produce after-tax income in the amount required for postretirement needs. If the postretirement need is for say, $60,000 annually, the $60,000 should be converted into a pretax income. If the income will come from an accumulation composed of untaxed contributions (as in the case of a qualified plan), it is conceivable that the entire distribution will be subject to tax. In other instances, only the investment earnings on the accumulation will be taxable. Although tax rates and other features of the tax code are subject to change, a reasonable approximation of the pretax income that will be required to produce a given amount of after-tax income can be estimated using tax multipliers. Assuming a retired couple filing a joint return, with current tax rates, standard deduction, and exemptions, the after-tax income for various taxable distributions is indicated in the first two columns of Table 19.2.

More useful information, from a planning perspective, is contained in the third and fourth columns of the table. The final column indicates the multiplier that may be used to convert a given level of after-tax income need into a before-tax retirement distribution. As a consequence of the progressive tax rate, the higher the level of income needed, the greater

TABLE 19.2 **Taxes and Retirement Distributions**

Effect of Taxes on Retirement Distributions		Net to Gross Income Tax Multiplier	
Annual Retirement Distribution	After-Tax Income	Desired After-Tax Income	Tax Multiplier
$30,000	$27,923	$30,000	108%
35,000	32,173	35,000	110%
40,000	36,423	40,000	111%
45,000	40,673	45,000	111%
50,000	44,923	50,000	113%
55,000	49,062	55,000	115%
60,000	52,662	60,000	117%
65,000	56,262	65,000	119%
70,000	59,862	70,000	120%
75,000	63,462	75,000	121%
80,000	67,062	80,000	122%
85,000	70,662	85,000	123%
90,000	74,262	90,000	124%
95,000	77,862	95,000	126%
100,000	81,462	100,000	127%
105,000	85,062	105,000	127%
110,000	88,602	110,000	128%
115,000	92,052	115,000	129%
120,000	95,502	120,000	130%
125,000	98,952	125,000	131%
130,000	102,402	130,000	132%
135,000	105,852	135,000	133%
140,000	109,302	140,000	134%

the difference between the amount needed and the pretax retirement distribution.

Inventory of Available Resources Once the aggregate retirement need has been defined, the next step is to inventory the resources that will be available to meet this need. For most people, the first source of retirement income will be Social Security. For many, Social Security will be supplemented by the second layer of protection, a pension provided by the employer. If the individual is covered by a corporate pension or profit-sharing plan, the expected benefits from this source should be factored into the equation to determine the part of the postretirement need that will be met by Social Security and the pension.

This phase of the process is one fraught with uncertainty. Any attempt to estimate the level of future Social Security benefits is subject to inaccuracy, if for no other reason than the uncertainty about the future of the system itself. Despite the dire prophecies about the bankruptcy of the Social Security system, it is highly unlikely that politicians will ever be able to scrap the system. At the same time, the changes that will probably be required to save the system will most likely have their greatest effect on the benefits of persons in middle- and upper-income brackets. If one assumes that a solution to the system's problems will be found and that that solution will not alter the basic features of the system, Social Security benefits can be projected at the same rate of inflation as the projected increases in income. It is not unreasonable, however, to assume that in the future, Social Security benefits will be fully taxable.

The projected income at retirement from the pension or other qualified retirement plan will depend on the nature of the plan and the extent to which benefits are guaranteed. In the case of a defined-benefit plan, it is reasonable to project retirement benefits based on projected income. An adjustment should be made to reflect the nature of the plan (i.e., career average or final average salary). In the case of a defined contribution plan, assumptions will be required concerning the rate of future contributions and investment earnings. In making these assumptions, the prudent course is to estimate the level of retirement benefits based on conservative assumptions.

Summarizing the Unmet Need The preceding calculations indicate a monthly flow of income that will be needed after retirement. The next step is to convert this projected flow into a capital amount. The traditional technique for this is discounting. Ideally, the capital

amount should reflect the influence of both life expectancy and inflation. The problem is that while there are tools that reflect the influence of one or the other, there is no simple technique that considers both.

The influence of the life-contingency risk—the uncertainty of death and the period for which the needs should be projected—is easily addressed by using the purchase price for a life annuity at age 65 (or other retirement age). The cost of a life annuity at age 65 can be used to convert the monthly income required from private savings into a principal amount. For a male at age 65, the cost of a $10 monthly benefit is about $1100. For a female, it is about $1350. The cost of an annuity that will provide the required monthly amount is computed by dividing the monthly requirement by $10, to determine the number of $10 per month units that must be purchased. If the monthly need is say, $3000, the purchase price of an annuity that will provide $3000 per month to a 65-year-old female is $405,000:

$$\frac{\$3000}{\$10} = 300 \times \$1350 = \$405,000$$

The problem with this calculation is that it indicates the amount required to provide a fixed, unchanging, income of $3000 a month, rather than an income that increases with inflation.

To consider the effect of inflation, it is necessary to project the initial need at some assumed rate of inflation, and discount the projection to determine its present value. The problem with this method summarizing retirement needs is in determining the period for which the projection should be made. It is possible to compute a principal sum that will allow increasing withdrawals for any period selected, but in selecting any period, the planner makes an assumption about the retiree's longevity. This means that the computation will be valid only for that particular longevity. One approach is to compute the inflation-adjusted income need for a period at least equal to the person's life expectancy, and then deal with the life contingency problem separately through the purchase of a life annuity.

Illustrated Summary To illustrate the manner in which the factors already discussed may be considered in estimating retirement income needs, consider the following example. The subject is 25 years old and currently earns a modest but respectable salary of $36,000. Projecting the $36,000 at an assumed

TABLE 19.3 Inflation-Adjusted Retirement Need Projection

A	B	C	D	E	F	G	H
Age	After-Tax Need Projected at 3%	Tax Multiplier	Pretax Income Need	OASDI Benefits Projected at 3%	Projected Pretax Gap	Discount Rate (7.0%)	Discounted Pretax Need
64	$90,000			$47,505			
65	67,500	119%	$80,325	48,931	$31,394	1.000000	$31,394
66	69,525	119%	82,735	50,398	32,336	0.934579	30,221
67	71,611	120%	85,933	51,910	34,022	0.873439	29,717
68	73,759	120%	88,511	53,468	35,043	0.816298	28,606
69	75,972	121%	91,926	55,072	36,854	0.762895	28,116
70	78,251	121%	94,684	56,724	37,960	0.712986	27,065
71	80,599	122%	98,330	58,426	39,905	0.666342	26,590
72	83,016	122%	101,280	60,178	41,102	0.622750	25,596
73	85,507	123%	105,174	61,984	43,190	0.582009	25,137
74	88,072	123%	108,329	63,843	44,486	0.543934	24,197
75	90,714	124%	112,486	65,759	46,727	0.508349	23,754
76	93,436	124%	115,860	67,731	48,129	0.475093	22,866
77	96,239	126%	121,261	69,763	51,498	0.444012	22,866
78	99,126	126%	124,899	71,856	53,043	0.414964	22,011
79	102,100	127%	129,667	74,012	55,655	0.387817	21,584
80	105,163	127%	133,557	76,232	57,325	0.362446	20,777
81	108,318	127%	137,563	78,519	59,044	0.338735	20,000
82	111,567	128%	142,806	80,875	61,931	0.316574	19,606
83	114,914	128%	147,090	83,301	63,789	0.295864	18,873
84	118,362	129%	152,687	85,800	66,886	0.276508	18,495
85	121,913	130%	158,486	88,374	70,112	0.258419	18,118
86	125,570	131%	164,497	91,025	73,471	0.241513	17,744
87	129,337	131%	169,431	93,756	75,675	0.225713	17,081
88	133,217	132%	175,847	96,569	79,278	0.210947	16,723
89	137,214	133%	182,494	99,466	83,028	0.197147	16,369
Discounted Pretax Projected Need							$524,110

inflation rate of say, 3 percent, the subject's salary will reach $114,013 at age 65 with after-tax income of $90,000. Projecting a monthly Social Security benefit of $1250 for the same 40 years, the annual Social Security benefit is projected to be $47,505. These projections take us to the subject's retirement age. The additional calculations required to determine the total amount required to meet specified retirement needs are summarized in Table 19.3.

The after-tax income need in the first year of retirement (age 65) is set at 75 percent of the individual's preretirement (age 64), after-tax income of $90,000. The after-tax need is projected at an inflation rate of 3 percent (column B) and then converted to a pretax need using the tax multipliers that incorporate the exemptions, deductions, and tax rates of the current law (columns C and D). Social Security benefits, projected at the same 3 percent rate as inflation (col-

umn E), are deducted from the pretax need (column F), thus assuming that Social Security benefits will be fully taxable. If pension benefits are payable, they are deducted in the same manner. The remainder represents the pretax income gap. This projected pretax income need is discounted at 7 percent to reflect the anticipated earnings on the accumulation during distribution. This converts the projected before-tax income need into present values that can be summed to determine the present value of the future income need. The discounted inflation-adjusted before-tax income need is projected for a 25-year period. A shorter or longer period could have been selected, but the 25-year period seems reasonable.[2] Based on

[2] The longevity after retirement of participants in the TIAA-CREF program who retired at age 65 is 21 years for men and 24 years for women.

the assumptions of the illustration, it will require $542,110 to provide the desired income.

The computations in the illustration are based on numerous assumptions. The program assumes that income will increase at a specified rate and that OASDI benefits will increase at the same rate. It further assumes that tax rates will remain essentially as under current law and that the accumulation will earn 7 percent during the distribution period. Any (or all) of these variables are subject to change. The appeal of this process, however, is that the planner can select the assumptions. If the planner is uncomfortable with a particular assumption, it can be changed to relieve the anguish. Although summing the projection of inflation-adjusted needs is more complicated than converting a fixed monthly need into a principal amount, it is much more likely to yield a dollar amount that reflects the actual needs of the individual.

Planning the Accumulation

Once the accumulation that will be required to finance retirement has been estimated, we turn to the second step in managing the retirement risk, which is to design and implement a plan to accumulate that fund. Because the problem here is the future value of current contributions, the concept of compounding is again useful. We can compute the future value of $1 contributed each year to an accumulating fund and invested at a specified rate. Table 19.4 indicates the future value of a dollar invested each year at various rates of interest for various numbers of years. The future value of annual contributions is used in determining the contributions that will be required to meet an accumulation target. Suppose, for example, that Jones decides she would like to accumulate $550,000 for retirement, which is 40 years in the future. Table 19.4 indicates that $1 contributed each year for 40 years at 7 percent interest is $213.61. To accumulate $550,000 in 40 years, Jones must contribute $2575 a year, or about $215 per month, that is

$$\frac{\$550,000}{\$213.61} = \$2,574.78^3$$

The perceptive student will note that this funding approach assumes a constant contribution level throughout the accumulation period. Since it may be assumed that the individual's income and ability to save will increase over time, it seems more logical to base retirement funding on a variable (increasing) contribution. To achieve the same $550,000 accumulation with a contribution increasing at the same rate as income (i.e., 3 percent per year), the initial contribution required is $1757, increasing to $5564 in the last year before retirement. Since the initial $1800 represents 4.9 percent of the $36,000 monthly income, the individual might reasonably decide to contribute 5.0 percent of annual income to the retirement program, which will result in an automatic adjustment of the contribution as income changes over his or her career. If the assumptions on which the program is based hold true, this program will produce an accumulation of $563,963 by the time the individual reaches age 65. Obviously, if income increases at a higher or lower rate than assumed, or if earnings on the accumulation are higher or lower than the assumed rate of return, the accumulation will also vary.

As previously discussed, life insurance and fixed-dollar annuities should be considered as investment vehicles for the fixed-dollar component of the retirement accumulation. The tax-deferred nature of their investment earnings make them attractive instruments for the retirement accumulation. Because variable annuities share this tax-deferred advantage, they also deserve consideration as retirement funding instruments.

Managing the Distribution

The final step in planning for retirement is planning the distribution. Although it is obvious that determining the amount of income that will be needed for retirement and planning the manner in which these funds will be accumulated are critical steps, planning the manner in which the funds will be distributed is equally critical. In fact, decisions in this phase of the planning process may require adjustments in the earlier steps as the assumptions concerning needs and funding are tested against the assumptions in the distribution plan.

There are a number of decisions that need to be addressed regarding distribution of the retirement accumulation. The major decisions in this phase generally relate to the uncertainty regarding life expectancy of the retirees. They include the question

[3] Microcomputer software programs are available that perform the retirement planning calculations. Among the more popular programs (all available only for IBM compatible PCs) are *Vanguard's Retirement Planner,* Version 2.0, *Harvest Time, Fidelity's Retirement Planning Thinkware,* and *T. Rowe Price's Retirement Planning Kit.*

TABLE 19.4 Future Value of $1 Annually for N Years at Various Rates

Year	1%	2%	3%	4%	5%	6%	7%	8%	9%	10%	11%	12%	13%	14%	15%
1	$1.01	$1.02	$1.03	$1.04	$1.05	$1.06	$1.07	$1.08	$1.09	$1.10	$1.11	$1.12	$1.13	$1.14	$1.15
2	2.03	2.06	2.09	2.12	2.15	2.18	2.21	2.25	2.28	2.31	2.34	2.37	2.41	2.44	2.47
3	3.06	3.12	3.18	3.25	3.31	3.37	3.44	3.51	3.57	3.64	3.71	3.78	3.85	3.92	3.99
4	4.10	4.20	4.31	4.42	4.53	4.64	4.75	4.87	4.98	5.11	5.23	5.35	5.48	5.61	5.74
5	5.15	5.31	5.47	5.63	5.80	5.98	6.15	6.34	6.52	6.72	6.91	7.12	7.32	7.54	7.75
6	6.21	6.43	6.66	6.90	7.14	7.39	7.65	7.92	8.20	8.49	8.78	9.09	9.40	9.73	10.07
7	7.29	7.58	7.89	8.21	8.55	8.90	9.26	9.64	10.03	10.44	10.86	11.30	11.76	12.23	12.73
8	8.37	8.75	9.16	9.58	10.03	10.49	10.98	11.49	12.02	12.58	13.16	13.78	14.42	15.09	15.79
9	9.46	9.95	10.46	11.01	11.58	12.18	12.82	13.49	14.19	14.94	15.72	16.55	17.42	18.34	19.30
10	10.57	11.17	11.81	12.49	13.21	13.97	14.78	15.65	16.56	17.53	18.56	19.65	20.81	22.04	23.35
11	11.68	12.41	13.19	14.03	14.92	15.87	16.89	17.98	19.14	20.38	21.71	23.13	24.65	26.27	28.00
12	12.81	13.68	14.62	15.63	16.71	17.88	19.14	20.50	21.95	23.52	25.21	27.03	28.98	31.09	33.35
13	13.95	14.97	16.09	17.29	18.60	20.02	21.55	23.21	25.02	26.97	29.09	31.39	33.88	36.58	39.50
14	15.10	16.29	17.60	19.02	20.58	22.28	24.13	26.15	28.36	30.77	33.41	36.28	39.42	42.84	46.58
15	16.26	17.64	19.16	20.82	22.66	24.67	26.89	29.32	32.00	34.95	38.19	41.75	45.67	49.98	54.72
16	17.43	19.01	20.76	22.70	24.84	27.21	29.84	32.75	35.97	39.54	43.50	47.88	52.74	58.12	64.08
17	18.61	20.41	22.41	24.65	27.13	29.91	33.00	36.45	40.30	44.60	49.40	54.75	60.73	67.39	74.84
18	19.81	21.84	24.12	26.67	29.54	32.76	36.38	40.45	45.02	50.16	55.94	62.44	69.75	77.97	87.21
19	21.02	23.30	25.87	28.78	32.07	35.79	40.00	44.76	50.16	56.27	63.20	71.05	79.95	90.02	101.44
20	22.24	24.78	27.68	30.97	34.72	38.99	43.87	49.42	55.76	63.00	71.27	80.70	91.47	103.77	117.81
21	23.47	26.30	29.54	33.25	37.51	42.39	48.01	54.46	61.87	70.40	80.21	91.50	104.49	119.44	136.63
22	24.72	27.84	31.45	35.62	40.43	46.00	52.44	59.89	68.53	78.54	90.15	103.60	119.20	137.30	158.28
23	25.97	29.42	33.43	38.08	43.50	49.82	57.18	65.76	75.79	87.50	101.17	117.16	135.83	157.66	183.17
24	27.24	31.03	35.46	40.65	46.73	53.86	62.25	72.11	83.70	97.35	113.41	132.33	154.62	180.87	211.79
25	28.53	32.67	37.55	43.31	50.11	58.16	67.68	78.95	92.32	108.18	127.00	149.33	175.85	207.33	244.71
26	29.82	34.34	39.71	46.08	53.67	62.71	73.48	86.35	101.72	120.10	142.08	168.37	199.84	237.50	282.57
27	31.13	36.05	41.93	48.97	57.40	67.53	79.70	94.34	111.97	133.21	158.82	189.70	226.95	271.89	326.10
28	32.45	37.79	44.22	51.97	61.32	72.64	86.35	102.97	123.14	147.63	177.40	213.58	257.58	311.09	376.17
29	33.78	39.57	46.58	55.08	65.44	78.06	93.46	112.28	135.31	163.49	198.02	240.33	292.20	355.79	433.75
30	35.13	41.38	49.00	58.33	69.76	83.80	101.07	122.35	148.58	180.94	220.91	270.29	331.32	406.74	499.96
31	36.49	43.23	51.50	61.70	74.30	89.89	109.22	133.21	163.04	200.14	246.32	303.85	375.52	464.82	576.10
32	37.87	45.11	54.08	65.21	79.06	96.34	117.93	144.95	178.80	221.25	274.53	341.43	425.46	531.04	663.67
33	39.26	47.03	56.73	68.86	84.07	103.18	127.26	157.63	195.98	244.48	305.84	383.52	481.90	606.52	764.37
34	40.66	48.99	59.46	72.65	89.32	110.43	137.24	171.32	214.71	270.02	340.59	430.66	545.68	692.57	880.17
35	42.08	50.99	62.28	76.60	94.84	118.12	147.91	186.10	235.12	298.13	379.16	483.46	617.75	790.67	1,013.35
36	43.51	53.03	65.17	80.70	100.63	126.27	159.34	202.07	257.38	329.04	421.98	542.60	699.19	902.51	1,166.50
37	44.95	55.11	68.16	84.97	106.71	134.90	171.56	219.32	281.63	363.04	469.51	608.83	791.21	1,030.00	1,342.62
38	46.41	57.24	71.23	89.41	113.10	144.06	184.64	237.94	308.07	400.45	522.27	683.01	895.20	1,175.34	1,545.17
39	47.89	59.40	74.40	94.03	119.80	153.76	198.64	258.06	336.88	441.59	580.83	766.09	1,012.70	1,341.03	1,778.09
40	49.38	61.61	77.66	98.83	126.84	164.05	213.61	279.78	368.29	486.85	645.83	859.14	1,145.49	1,529.91	2,045.95

of annuitizing the distribution, preservation of principal, and joint-and-survivor options.

Capital Retention versus Capital Liquidation Strategies It is conceivable that the individual will have accumulated sufficient capital so that the investment income alone may be adequate to provide the income required. In this case, he or she may elect to pursue a capital retention strategy, and live on the investment income only. The choice between invading principal and living from the investment earnings will depend on the amount of principal available and the return that is earned on that principal.[4] In measuring whether a capital retention strategy is feasible, however, the requirements of the *Internal Revenue Code* concerning required distributions must be considered.

Required Distributions For most persons, the accumulated principal in a retirement program (i.e., a pension, an IRA, or an annuity) will include an accumulation of untaxed contributions to the retirement program, plus the untaxed earnings on those contributions. Because neither the contributions that created the accumulation nor the investment income on those accumulating contributions have been taxed, the *IRC* requires that the accumulation be distributed and taxed as income to the participant. The requirements in this respect are specific and inflexible. Although distribution can be delayed until April 1 of the year following the year in which the participant reaches age $70^1/_2$, or actual retirement, if later, at that time the accumulated funds must be paid out over a period that does not exceed the life expectancy of the participant or the combined life expectancy of the participant and his or her beneficiary.[5] IRS tables are used to calculate life expectancies. Failure to meet the *IRC* requirements regarding minimum distributions can result in a penalty tax equal to 50 percent of the amount by which the required minimum distribution exceeds the distribu-

tion that is actually made.[6] Although one can defer distribution of the accumulated principal until age $70^1/_2$, the distribution must then be distributed over a shorter life expectancy and will probably be taxed at a higher marginal tax rate.

Life Annuities and Installment Distributions A first major decision is whether the individual will choose to withdraw retirement funds from the retirement accumulation in the form of a life annuity or in installments.[7] Because the IRS requires a distribution no lower than one that would liquidate the principal over the individual's lifetime, there is a tendency to think of distributions in terms of a life annuity payout. As we saw in the last chapter, however, the distribution may be in the form of a life annuity, or it may be in the form of payments based on the expected lifetime of the participant (or the life expectancy of the participant and his or her beneficiary).

Although annuitizing the accumulation is one option, the second approach—withdrawing income in installments based on life expectancy—may be considered more attractive by some people. The appeal of this approach is that it guarantees that the entire accumulation will be paid out, even if the beneficiary should die prior to reaching his or her life expectancy. At the same time, if the individual outlives the expectancy, the principal will be exhausted and the individual will need another source of funding. (This source could consist of funds that were withdrawn but not spent during the distribution period.)

Minimum Distribution Option If the retiree does not want to annuitize the principal or begin the withdrawal at retirement, some insurers offer a minimum distribution option. Under this option, the insurer will calculate and distribute the minimum income required each year to avoid the confiscatory (50 percent) tax on less than the minimum distributions required by the *IRC*. This allows the individual to preserve the principal while still meeting the withdrawal provisions of the *IRC*.

Variable Annuity Variable annuities may be variable during the accumulation period and fixed during the payout period or variable during both the

[4] The higher the after-tax rate of return and the longer the period over which the capital will be withdrawn, the smaller the difference in monthly income produced by annuitizing the principal and preserving the capital intact. An individual in the 15 percent tax bracket with $500,000 invested at 8 percent could withdraw $40,000 annually ($34,000 after tax) and preserve the $500,000 intact. If interest and the total principal are withdrawn over a 25-year period, the principal required to produce the same $34,000 annually is about $444,070. An additional $56,000 in principal will produce the required $34,000 after-tax annual income without invading the principal.

[5] *IRC* Section 401 (a)(9)(A).

[6] *IRC* Section 4974.

[7] Although the *IRC* also allows withdrawal in a lump sum, except in unusual cases, tax treatment of installment or annuity distributions will be more favorable to the insured.

accumulation period and the payout period. With the variable payout option, when the participant reaches retirement, the accumulation units are converted into a lifetime income of annuity units, using a special mortality table for annuitants. The number of annuity units does not change over the lifetime of the annuitant, but the income produced by each unit will reflect changes in the value of the investments, with the current value of the annuity unit determining the beneficiary's income.[8]

We noted in the preceding chapter that changes in the value of annuity units do not always parallel changes in the price level. This was demonstrated rather dramatically during the 1970s, when the value of the CREF accumulation unit dropped 43 percent over a three-year period, during which the CPI increased 18 percent. Discontinuities of this type illustrate the risks involved in the withdrawal decision. Again, as during the accumulation period, diversification seems a prudent strategy.

Variable Distributions under Nonvariable Annuities Although the variable annuity provides one approach to a variable distribution, as noted above there is a danger in this approach. Recognizing that inflation over a period of 20 to 30 years can severely erode the purchasing power of annuity payments, insurers provide optional modes of settlement under which the payments increase over time. Although the terminology differs among insurers, the basic distinction is between a standard payment method and a graded payment method.

Under the *standard payment method,* the beneficiary receives the contractually guaranteed interest plus allocated excess interest (i.e., the interest earnings that exceed the guaranteed rate). Under the *graded payment method,* the annuity payments include the guaranteed interest and principal, but only a part of the excess interest. The remainder of the excess interest is reinvested to purchase additional annuity benefits for each year in the future. As additional purchases are made, the payments in future years are augmented by the proceeds from the additional annuities. Table 19.5 illustrates the difference in the payout rates under the standard payment method and the graded payment method.

It should be clear that there is a risk in the graded payment approach. The annuitant sacrifices current income for income in the future. Although the actual amount of income deferred will depend on the level of excess investment income, under the assumptions embodied in the illustration, it will take at least 15 years for the annuitant to "catch up" and recover the income sacrificed by accepting the lower payments under the graded system. When interest is considered, the break-even point will be even later.

With a part of the retirement payout invested in a variable annuity and a part invested in a fixed-dollar annuity, the retiree can hedge against inflation and against fluctuations in the equity-based variable annuity. Payments will be less during periods of high inflation than under a program in which the entire principal is invested in equities, but it will be higher during periods in which equities are decreasing.

Single or Joint Life Annuity A second major decision relates to the provision, if any, that will be made for a surviving spouse. Under the provisions of ERISA, qualified pension plans must provide a joint-and-survivor life income option. Further, rejection of this option by a plan participant requires an affirmative rejection by the spouse. Although a joint-and-survivor benefit guarantees a continuing income to a surviving spouse at the death of the primary annuitant, there is a cost. Because the joint-and-survivor option pays an income to the surviving spouse after the death of the first, payments during the joint lives of the spouses are lower than under a straight life annuity on a single person.

Pension Maximization The difference in the level of the monthly benefit under a joint-and-survivor annuity and a single life annuity led to a strategy known as *pension maximization.* This strategy is based on the ERISA requirement that pension participants accept a joint-and-survivor benefit unless the participant's spouse affirmatively rejects the option. Pension maximization developed as a means of maximizing the pension payout. Basically, the strategy consists of electing a single life annuity and using a part of the higher monthly benefit to purchase life insurance on the annuitant.

The amount of insurance should be sufficient to provide a lifetime annuity to the spouse equal to the survivorship benefit he or she would receive under the joint-and-survivor option. Under the right conditions—when the premium for insurance on the annuitant spouse is less than the after-tax difference in the

[8] The monthly amount usually remains the same throughout the year because the value of the retirement annuity unit is usually established on an annual basis.

TABLE 19.5 **Standard and Graded Annuity Payments**

Annuitant's Age	Standard Payment Method	Graded Payment Method	Annuitant's Age	Standard Payment Method	Graded Payment Method
65	$1000	$750	78	$1000	$1223
66	1000	779	79	1000	1270
67	1000	809	80	1000	1319
68	1000	840	81	1000	1369
69	1000	872	82	1000	1422
70	1000	905	83	1000	1476
71	1000	940	84	1000	1533
72	1000	976	85	1000	1592
73	1000	1013	86	1000	1683
74	1000	1052	87	1000	1716
75	1000	1093	88	1000	1782
76	1000	1135	89	1000	1850
77	1000	1178	90	1000	1921

benefits—pension maximization can increase total benefits to a couple. Although any form of permanent life insurance on which the insured can continue the premium will work, the reversionary or survivorship annuity is ideally suited to this exposure.

Obviously, pension maximization is available only if the individual is insurable or if he or she has life insurance purchased at an earlier age still in force. In addition, for retirees who have employer-sponsored postretirement health insurance, a surviving spouse is generally able to continue the health care plan only if he or she is receiving a retirement benefit. For this situation, a joint-and-one-fourth-or-one-third-survivor benefit may be an attractive compromise. This will guarantee a benefit to the spouse, if he or she survives, so the health care benefits will continue.

IMPORTANT CONCEPTS TO REMEMBER

This chapter relies heavily on material presented in earlier chapters, and few new concepts are introduced. Some concepts introduced earlier in connection with life insurance planning also have application in retirement planning. The important new concepts that are introduced in the chapter are the following:

minimum distribution option graded payment distribution pension maximization

QUESTIONS FOR REVIEW

1. Describe the factors that create the retirement risk.

2. Identify and describe the two risks associated with retirement and briefly describe the strategies that may be used in addressing these risks.

3. Identify and describe the three steps in the retirement planning process discussed in the text.

4. Identify the three sources of retirement funding. In your opinion, how important and how dependable (certain) is each?

5. Distinguish between the capital retention strategy and a capital liquidation strategy. What factors will determine the individual's choice between these two strategies?

6. Describe the distribution requirements of the *Internal Revenue Code* with respect to retirement accumulations.

7. Describe the minimum distribution option offered by some insurers. What is the purpose of this option?

8. Describe the graded distribution option available in connection with pension and annuity distributions. What are the advantages and disadvantages of this option?

9. What is pension maximization? Under what conditions is it feasible? Under what conditions is it advisable?

10. The estimate of postretirement income needs is usually based on a projected preretirement income level. Identify the two adjustments that are required in projecting the preretirement income to determine postretirement income needs.

QUESTIONS FOR DISCUSSION

1. What is the underlying motivation for the capital conservation strategy in planning a retirement distribution? What is your personal opinion of this strategy?

2. Under the graded payment method of distribution for an annuity, the annuitant accepts a reduced payment during the early years of distribution in exchange for an increasing benefit. Can an individual achieve the same results by accepting the standard payment method and judiciously investing the amount by which the standard payment method benefit exceeds the graded payment method benefit? Why or why not?

3. You have graduated from college and commenced a highly successful career. In fact, the major problem you now face is that your income has reached a point at which your combined state and federal marginal tax rate is nearly 50 percent. You are considering a flexible-premium deferred annuity as an investment, primarily because of the tax deferral on the accumulation. A friend has suggested that you can achieve the same results by investing in tax-exempt bonds. Describe the factors you would consider in choosing between these alternatives.

4. Since superannuation is one of the risks to which the individual is exposed, an income protection plan should provide for the contingency that the individual will reach retirement age. Considering the nature of cash-value life insurance, variable annuities, and alternative vehicles for accumulation, what do you think is a logical and reasonable approach to the problem of saving for retirement?

5. Given the predicted financial difficulties facing the Social Security system, to what extent do you think that Social Security benefits should be considered in the retirement planning process?

SUGGESTIONS FOR ADDITIONAL READING

Allen, Everett T., Joseph J. Melone, Jerry S. Rosenbloom, and Jack L. VanDerhei. *Pension Planning,* 7th ed. Homewood, Ill.: Richard D. Irwin, 1992.

Beam, Burton T., Jr., and John J. McFadden. *Employee Benefits,* 3rd ed. Brookfield, Wis.: Dearborn Financial Publishing, 1994.

Black, Kenneth, Jr., and Harold D. Skipper, Jr. *Life Insurance,* 13th ed. Englewood Cliffs, N.J.: Prentice-Hall, 2000. Chapters 8, 16, 21.

Graves, Edward E., ed. *McGill's Life Insurance.* Bryn Mawr, Pa.: The American College, 1994. Chapter 6.

Hallman, G. Victor, and Karen L. Hamilton. *Personal Insurance: Life, Health & Retirement.* Malvern, Pa.: American Institute for CPCU, 1994. Chapter 6.

Shilling, Dana. *Financial Planning for the Older Client,* 2nd ed. Cincinnati, Ohio: The National Underwriter Co., 1994.

WEB SITES TO EXPLORE

Institute of Certified Financial Planners	http://www.icfp.org/
Internal Revenue Service	http://www.irs.ustreas.gov/
International Association for Financial Planning	http://www.iafp.org/
National Senior Citizens Law Center	http://www.nsclc.org/

HEALTH INSURANCE: DISABILITY INCOME INSURANCE

He jests at scars that never felt a wound.

— WILLIAM SHAKESPEARE
Romeo and Juliet

CHAPTER OBJECTIVES

When you have finished this chapter, you should be able to

- Compare the severity of the risk of disability and the risk of premature death
- Describe the nature of disability income insurance and differentiate among the various types of disability income insurance contracts
- Identify and contrast the alternative definitions of total disability
- Identify ways in which benefits are provided for partial disabilities
- Explain how the maximum benefit period and the waiting period affect the cost of a disability income insurance policy
- List and explain the common continuance provisions of individual health insurance contracts and identify the uniform provisions
- Explain the way in which disability income needs can be estimated and how disability income insurance can be integrated with social insurance benefits

Few areas of insurance are as confusing to the average individual as the field of health insurance. One reason for this is the bewildering number of health insurance contracts available. Health insurance is a generic term, encompassing several types of insurance contracts that, although related, protect against different types of risk. Until recently there was little agreement on health insurance terminology. It was called *accident insurance, health insurance, accident and health insurance, accident and sickness insurance,*

and *disability insurance,* all of which are gradually yielding to the general term *health insurance.*

There are two separate types of insurance included in the generic term health insurance: *disability income insurance,* which provides periodic payments when the insured is unable to work because of sickness or injury, and *medical expense insurance,* which pays the costs of medical care that result from sickness or injury. In this chapter, we will deal with the first of these two forms of health insurance, disability income. Coverage for the expenses relating to health care will be discussed in the next chapter.

GENERAL NATURE OF DISABILITY INCOME INSURANCE

Disability income insurance is the oldest of the health insurance coverages and has been marketed for over a century. The coverage provides periodic payments to the person insured when he or she is unable to work because of injury or illness. Coverage may be provided for disabilities resulting from accidents only or for disabilities resulting from accidents or sickness. Coverage for disability resulting from sickness only is rarely written. Benefit eligibility presumes a loss of income, but in practice this is usually defined as the inability to pursue an occupation.

Types of Insurers

Disability income insurance is sold by property and liability insurers, life insurance companies, and specialty insurers that operate only in the health insurance field. Individual insurers in both the life insurance field and the property and liability field may write little or no disability income insurance, whereas for other companies in each class it is a major line. With the advent of all-line groups, many company fleets transferred the bulk of their health insurance operations from their property and liability affiliates to the life insurers in the group. In addition, larger employers often self-fund disability income benefits provided as a part of their employee benefit package.

Methods of Marketing

Disability income insurance is marketed in two principal ways: through groups and to individuals. Approx-imately four-fifths of the disability income insurance in the United States is sold on a group basis. Group underwriting in the disability income field employs much the same principle as does group life insurance. A minimum-sized group is required, and its nature must be such that insurance is incidental to its existence. In other words, the group cannot be organized primarily for the purpose of purchasing the group insurance. Most group disability income coverage is written under employer-sponsored employee benefit plans, but some is also written under association group plans. Association group disability programs are similar to the association group life insurance programs discussed in Chapter 12.

As in the case of group life insurance, there are economies in the group approach to disability income insurance. The insurer enjoys some freedom from adverse selection and the employer usually performs certain administrative functions. Finally, the agent usually receives a lower commission rate. Distinguishing features of group coverage are explained in the discussion that follows.

Need for Disability Income Insurance

We noted in Chapter 10 that the probability of disability at most ages before retirement is greater than the probability of death. Because disability can be both total and permanent, the exposure ranks in severity with the death of the wage earner. In fact, some authorities argue that loss-of-income protection should come even before life insurance. When a wage earner is disabled, his or her earnings stop just as surely as if death had occurred. This "living death" of disability can be economically more severe than actual death. If the breadwinner of the family dies, the family's income stops; if he or she is disabled, not only does the income stop, but expenses remain the same and usually increase. Because a disabled person—by definition—is one whose ability to work is impaired, he or she must depend on sources other than employment for income. When persons other than the disabled individual were also supported by the lost income, the problem is compounded.[1]

[1] In addition to a policy to cover living expenses, some self-employed persons carry *overhead* insurance, which is designed to pay business expenses, such as rent and clerical costs, while they are disabled. Disability policies can also be obtained with provision for a lump-sum settlement, rather than periodic payments, to be used in purchasing a disabled partner's interest in a business.

Protection Available from Other Sources In Chapter 11 we noted the protection that is available under social insurance programs for the disability risk. For disability that arises out of and in the course of employment, most injured workers are entitled to benefits under the workers compensation law of the state in which they are employed. The amount of these benefits is related to the worker's earnings at the time of the injury and are specified by law. In addition, workers in California, Hawaii, New Jersey, New York, Rhode Island, and Puerto Rico are covered for nonoccupational disabilities by compulsory programs, under which the benefits are also prescribed by law. Finally, workers who are totally and permanently disabled and who meet the special eligibility requirements for disability under the federal Old-Age, Survivors', and Disability Insurance program qualify for disability benefits under that program.

Although Social Security may provide some benefits in the event of a worker's disability, the qualification requirements for disability benefits are demanding. Social Security defines disability as the inability to engage in *any* substantial gainful activity by reason of any medically determinable physical or mental impairment that can be expected to result in death or that has lasted or can be expected to last for a continuous period of not less than 12 months. This is a demanding requirement, intended to include only disabilities that are total and permanent.[2] Not only must the individual be unable to perform the duties of the previous work, to qualify for OASDI disability benefits, the individual must be unable to engage in *any other kind* of substantial work.

Besides these government-sponsored or supervised programs, the most common source of recovery is through group or individual disability income policies. In some instances, employers self-insure a program of disability benefits for their employees, providing either cash benefits or paid sick leave. In others, the paid sick leave plans are integrated with disability income insurance purchased from commercial insurers.

Extent of Coverage for Disability Because there is some overlapping, it is difficult to measure precisely the extent of disability income coverage applicable to the labor force. Excluding the coverage under workers compensation laws and the OASDI program, approximately two-thirds of the U.S. labor force had some sort of disability income coverage by 1995. About 57 percent of nongovernment workers and self-employed persons were covered under short-term disability plans, including sick leave programs.[3] Of this total, about two-thirds were insured with commercial insurers.[4] At the same time, slightly less than 30 percent of the nongovernment labor force had long-term disability protection, all of which was provided through commercial insurers. Because some workers participate in both short- and long-term programs, total coverage is less than would be suggested by combining these two categories.

Short-Term versus Long-Term Disability Coverage

In addition to the distinction between group and individual marketing, a distinction among disability income coverage is drawn on the basis of the periods for which coverage is provided. *Short-term disability* insurance provides coverage for disabilities up to two years, whereas *long-term disability* protects the individual for a longer time, often until age 65 for illness and for life in the case of accident. Short-term disability policies are written with benefit periods of 13, 26, 52, or 104 weeks. Long-term disability policies, also called LTD policies, provide benefits for 5 years, 10 years, until age 65, or even for the lifetime of the insured.

The distinction between short-term disability and long-term disability is not merely in the length of time for which benefits are payable. The short-term/long-term distinction also reflects a difference in pricing, in underwriting, and in the breadth of coverage. The earliest forms of disability income coverage provided indemnity for 13 weeks. Gradually, the period was extended, first to 26 weeks and eventually to one year and finally to two years. The disinclination of insurers to provide coverage for longer periods reflects the caution insurers felt was required in a field in which the potential for both morale and

[2] According to the Social Security Administration, slightly less than half of those who apply for disability benefits under OASDI are approved for benefits. *Social Security Bulletin—Annual Statistical Supplement—1997.*

[3] When persons covered under the state compulsory temporary disability plans and railroad workers are excluded, the total covered for short-term disability is less than 50 percent of the nongovernment labor force.

[4] Health Insurance Institute, *Source Book of Health Insurance Data,* (New York: The Institute, 1995).

moral hazard exists. When long-term disability contracts were eventually placed on the market, it was with some apprehension on the part of insurers. In time, it became clear that the long-term disability exposure was an insurable one and that the underwriting considerations that had deterred insurers from offering the coverage could be addressed. Since most disabilities are short term, the insurer's risk decreases as the contract lengthens. A 26-week plan does not cost twice as much as one for 13 weeks. Most disabilities will not exceed 13 weeks, so the insurer does not have to pay out twice as much in benefits under a 26-week plan. The longer the contract, other things being equal, the lower the cost of the additional protection. Approximately 82 percent of the short-term disability coverage and 78 percent of the long-term disability coverage are sold through groups.

Disability Income Underwriting and Pricing

Disability income insurance is a field in which moral hazard and morale hazard are high. These hazards are reflected in insurers' underwriting and marketing practices and explain some of the unusual features in the disability income field. Insurers are cautious about the amount of coverage they are willing to allow on a given individual and exhibit a concern over adverse selection that to the detached observer seems to border on obsession.

Limiting disability coverage to a level that discourages malingering is a critical function in underwriting individual disability insurance. Insurer underwriting tables indicate the amount of monthly disability income coverage that can be purchased on specific earning levels, generally limiting coverage to an amount that approximates the after-tax personal income the insured would have received in the absence of the disability. Tables for individual policies generally reflect the fact that the individual is purchasing coverage with after-tax dollars, which means that benefits will not be taxable to the claimant.[5] The issue limits for most companies are now $4000 to $5000 per month, although some insurers offer coverage as high as $15,000 to $20,000 per month. In the case of application for high levels of

coverage, the required underwriting information may include documentation of past income, including tax forms.

Occupational Classes and Underwriting Nearly 150 years ago, one of the earliest insurers to offer insurance coverage with benefits to bodily injury that did not cause death, The Accidental Death Association, recognized the necessity for differences in rates for different occupations. Interestingly, its classification system divided risks into four classes: (1) professional, (2) master tradesmen doing no manual labor, (3) mechanics or operative classes, and (4) all others, who were considered the most hazardous.[6] After a century of experimentation with more sophisticated classification systems, modern insurers generally classify insureds into categories that are surprisingly similar. Although the defining characteristics may vary, the most common rating classes today divide risks into professional, white-collar, and blue-collar, in descending order of underwriting desirability. Not only do these occupational classes affect rates, they affect the breadth of the coverage that will be offered as well. Coverage for blue-collar workers may have more restrictive definitions of disability, provide coverage for a shorter period, and for lesser amounts.

Group versus Individual Coverage In the field of life insurance and group medical expense insurance, group policies tend to be more liberal in their provisions than individual policies, with fewer restrictions and a generally more liberal underwriting attitude. In the disability income field, group policies are often more restrictive in their coverage features than individual policies. Although group policies tend to be cheaper than individual policies, they are also likely to include restrictive provisions that are not imposed in individual policies.

Actually, the demarcation in liberality of policy provisions in disability income insurance is not the group-individual dichotomy, but rather between short-term and long-term coverage. Although the insurer's potential liability may be greater under a long-term disability policy than under a short-term policy, the different classes insured under short-term and long-term coverage and the difference in coverage features permit somewhat more liberal features in LTD policies.

[5] As a general rule, for disability income insurance, if the premium for the policy is paid on a tax-favored basis (e.g., deductible) the benefits will be taxed at the time of receipt. If the premium is paid with after tax dollars, benefits will be received tax free.

[6] Edwin J. Faulkner, *Health Insurance,* (New York: McGraw-Hill, 1960), pp 513–514.

Most short-term disability coverage is employer-provided group coverage, usually covering blue-collar workers. Group long-term disability coverage may be provided both to blue-collar and white-collar workers, although generally with different benefit periods. LTD for blue-collar workers is usually limited to 5 years, while coverage for white-collar workers can be provided to age 65 or lifetime.

DISABILITY INCOME CONTRACTS

Since there is no such thing as a standard disability income policy, the discussion of this kind of coverage must focus on the differences in the provisions likely to be included in such contracts. Individual disability income policies must include certain mandatory provisions discussed later in the chapter, but there are wide variations in both individual and group contracts.

Perils Covered

The disability income policy may provide coverage for loss of income caused by accident, or it may cover loss of income that results from either accident or sickness. Few companies are willing to sell disability income protection covering the peril of sickness only. The reason, of course, is the moral hazard involved. It is relatively easy to feign sickness, but it is more difficult to feign accidental injury. For the same reason, insurance companies will not sell disability income protection to home-makers; it is difficult to determine when a home-maker is disabled.

When a disability income policy is written to cover both sickness and accidents, the intervals for which benefits are payable may be different, depending on the cause of the disability. Thus, one policy will pay benefits for two years if the disability is brought on by illness and for 5 years if it results from accident. For individual long-term disability, coverage to age 65 or 70 is becoming the standard. Although lifetime benefits are still available from some insurers, increasingly, lifetime-benefit periods are being replaced with "to age 70" plans. Generally, the savings from reducing the benefit period to age 65 is 25 to 30 percent; from age 65 to 5 years, 30 to 60 percent.[7]

Occupational-Nonoccupational Disability Another important distinction in the disability insurance field is between policies that cover both occupational and nonoccupational disabilities and those that cover nonoccupational disabilities only. Some disability income policies exclude losses arising out of the occupation of the insured for which the insured is entitled to receive workers compensation benefits. These contracts are called *nonoccupational disability insurance.* Most short-term disability income coverage is written on a nonoccupational basis, but some policies provide workers compensation "wrap around" coverage, which supplements workers compensation benefits. In the event of occupational injury, the benefit is equal to the difference between the workers compensation payment and the payment under the policy for nonoccupational disabilities. This then provides the same income replacement for the individual whether the injury is occupational or nonoccupational.

Long-term disability may be written on a nonoccupational basis or may provide coverage for both occupational and nonoccupational disabilities *(24-hour coverage).* When coverage is written on an occupational basis, some insurers provide for a reduction in benefits equal to the amount received under workers compensation, while still others pay the full policy benefit regardless of the occupational or nonoccupational character of the injury.

Waiting Periods

The *waiting period* in disability income policies acts like a deductible, forcing the insured to bear a part of the loss. The purpose of the waiting period is to eliminate coverage for short-term disabilities of the "sniffle" type and to help to control the morale hazard. Waiting periods of 3, 7, 15, 30, 60, 90, 180, and 365 days are available. As might be expected, short-term disability coverage generally has shorter waiting periods than long-term coverage. Although coverage for losses resulting from an accident may be written without a waiting period, a 3-day waiting period is about as short as it is possible to purchase under sickness coverage. In addition, the waiting period in a given contract may differ for accident and sickness losses. One widely used plan in the short-term disability income field is the *1-8-26 formula.* This coverage provides benefits from the first day if the disability results from an accident, and from the eighth day if it is caused by illness. The *26* indicates the number of weeks for which benefits are payable.

[7] Jeff Sadler, *Disability Income: The Sale, The Product,* 2nd ed. (Cincinnati, Ohio: National Underwriter Co., 1995)

In the case of individual long-term disability, plans with 14-day and 30-day elimination periods are virtually extinct, and the 60-day elimination period is disappearing for the professional and executive disability classes. Lowering the cost of the plan by extending the elimination period has become an increasingly necessary strategy in recent years as the rates for disability income coverage have increased. Although some companies still offer elimination periods as short as 30 days, the high cost of elimination periods less than 90 days has made them unattractive for the average consumer.

Limitations on Amount of Coverage

Ideally, the disability income policy should restore the income of the incapacitated worker as closely as possible to what was earned before the disability. However, insurance companies typically limit the amount of coverage under short-term policies to about 60 percent of the worker's weekly wage. Under long-term contracts, coverage is sometimes written for as much as 70 percent of the worker's monthly wage, but most insurers impose a dollar limit (such as $3000 or $4000) on the maximum monthly benefit that will be provided. Such limits are considered necessary to prevent moral hazard. If a policy could be purchased that would pay as much as or more than the worker's regular income, there would be an incentive to feign illness and contrive accidents. In addition, the worker collecting benefits would have little reason to return to the job as quickly as possible.[8]

Because of the potential for morale hazard, LTD policies sometimes include a provision relating to income the policyholder may have from other sources. Other income might include, for example, Social Security benefits or disability benefits under a corporate pension plan. In some cases, income from such sources serves as an offset against the policy's benefits, and the amount of the income is subtracted from the benefits payable. In other instances, the policy may provide for a cap on benefits if income from all sources exceeds a percentage of the insured's pre-disability income (e.g., 70 percent). When an LTD policy includes an income offset or cap on total income received, there may be an exception for

Social Security benefits, called a *Social Security freeze*. The Social Security freeze provision provides a modest element of protection against inflation; it provides that increases in Social Security benefits after LTD payments have commenced will not reduce the LTD benefits.

Definitions of Disability Income Policies

The definitions are of utmost importance in disability income policies, for the broadness of the coverage is based on the definitions of *disability, injury,* and *sickness.*

Definition of Disability The traditional approach to disability income insurance has been to define disability as the insured's inability to engage in a designated occupation due to accident or sickness. *Disability* may be defined in various ways, but most definitions fall into one of four categories:

- The inability of the insured to engage in his or her own occupation
- The inability of the insured to engage in his or her own occupation and not working in any gainful [or reasonable] employment
- The inability of the insured to engage in any reasonable occupation for which he or she is or might easily become qualified
- The inability of the insured to engage in any occupation.

The most liberal, of course, is the one that defines disability as the inability of the insured to engage in his or her own occupation, and the narrowest, as the inability to engage in any occupation. Short-term disability coverage almost universally uses the *any* occupation definition.

Although the first definition (referred to as *own occupation*) provides the broadest coverage, unfavorable loss experience with this definition has caused many insurers to shift to the second definition (referred to as *modified own occupation*). Under this definition, if the insured cannot perform the duties of his or her own occupation, benefits will be payable unless the insured enters another occupation. The modified own occupation definition is becoming increasingly prevalent and, for most insurers, represents the current standard.

Some insurers use a two-part definition that defines disability as the inability of the insured to

[8] Insurers question the amount of an applicant's insurance in force with other insurers and, if the total exceeds the percentages cited, decline to insure the excess. If the applicant does not truthfully disclose the total amount of coverage, the insurer may attempt to void its contract on the grounds of fraud.

engage in his or her own occupation for some initial period (e.g., two years) and the inability to engage in any occupation for which he or she is suited or might become qualified after that period.

Loss of Income Coverage Approach The newest approach to the definition of disability abandons the effort to define the disability in terms of the cause of the loss (e.g., in the ability to engage in a defined occupation) and focuses instead on the result—which is the loss of income. Today, many insurers are offering a *loss of earnings (income replacement)* coverage that pays benefits based on the economic loss following a physical disability event, either an accident or sickness. The loss of income coverage simply provides for payment of benefits when the insured suffers a *loss of income due to illness or injury,* and the loss continues for the elimination period.

Because the level of income insured reflects the after-tax income underwriting limits of the insurer, the monthly limit is payable in the event of total disability, which occurs when the insured's income ceases. Coverage also applies for partial disabilities, measured by the reduction in income suffered by the insured. For partial disabilities, a percentage of the monthly benefit is payable, based on the percentage reduction in the insured's income. This approach, which focuses on the income loss, rather than on inability to perform functions of a specific occupation, is the only form of disability insurance that will pay a claim on a progressive disease such as multiple sclerosis or muscular dystrophy, before the insured is totally disabled.

In addition to those discussed already, there are several more restrictive definitions. When the disability results from sickness, some policies make it a requirement that the insured be confined indoors to collect full benefits for sickness. Some policies allow only reduced benefits if the insured is unable to pursue the occupation specified but is not confined to the house. The most restrictive contracts provide benefits only if the policyholder is hospitalized. Typically, these policies pay a specified benefit (e.g., $100 a day), regardless of expenses incurred and in addition to any other coverage the insured may have, for each day in the hospital. These contracts are frequently sold through the mail. It should be recognized that they represent an extremely limited form of coverage and hardly qualify as disability income protection.

Definition of Injury The most common definition of injury today is *accidental bodily injury,* which requires that the result (bodily injury) be accidental or unintended. Older policies sometimes used the definition of *bodily injury by accidental means,* which required not only that the result must have been accidental, but also that the cause of the injury must have been accidental.

Definition of Sickness The definition of *sickness* is often used to exclude preexisting conditions in individual disability contracts.[9] For example, the definition of sickness in one contract specifies that

> The company will pay the total disability benefit for total disability resulting from sickness first manifesting itself while the policy is in force.

Thus, coverage would be provided for a preexisting condition that did not manifest itself until after the inception of the policy. Some earlier contracts used a definition that covered *sickness contracted or commencing while the policy is in force.* In that case, there would be no coverage for a sickness or disease that the insured had at the inception of the policy, even if the condition were unknown to the insured. Since ailments can go undetected for many years, this is a severe limitation. Courts do not look favorably on those definitions. In most states, insurers may exclude only those preexisting conditions that manifested themselves during the five years prior to the inception of coverage.

Group disability income plans tend to have either no exclusions or less restrictive exclusions for preexisting conditions. A typical exclusion might eliminate coverage for a disability starting within one year of inception if the sickness was diagnosed or treated in the year prior to being covered.

Exclusions in Disability Income Contracts

While the coverage of the policy is generally defined and limited by the insuring agreement and the policy definitions, disability income policies also have exclusions. The number of exclusions is usually limited. Common exclusions include war, self-inflicted injuries, and normal pregnancies.[10] In some individual policies, preexisting conditions are eliminated by an exclusion

[9] Preexisting conditions are not normally excluded under group contracts.

[10] Although disability from a normal pregnancy may be excluded (depending on the state) in an individual policy, disability from complications of pregnancy would generally be covered. Some insurers insert a separate 90-day elimination period for pregnancy.

rather than by the definition of sickness. The trend is toward a reduction in the number of exclusions, but each policy should be examined individually.

In group contracts, the number of exclusions is even smaller. Nonoccupational contracts may bar work-connected injuries by an exclusion or in the insuring agreement. Pregnancy is generally not excluded in group plans. Federal and state laws require that disability plans offered by most employers treat disability from pregnancy or childbirth the same as any other disability.

Payments for Other Than Total Disability

Although disability coverage is usually payable only when the insured is totally disabled, some contracts provide for payment of a reduced benefit when the insured resumes work on a partial basis after a period of total disability. There are two approaches to the payment of such benefits: a *partial disability benefit* and a *residual disability benefit*.

Partial Disability Benefit Partial disability is usually defined as the inability to perform some specified percentage of the duties of the insured's usual occupation. A common definition of partial disability is

> the inability of the insured to perform some, but not all of the important duties of his or her occupation, or the inability to engage in his or her regular occupation for longer than one-half the time normally spent in performing the usual duties of the regular occupation.

If the individual cannot perform the duties of the job, it is presumed that his or her income will decrease, but partial disability does not base its benefits on the reduction in income. It is based on the inability to perform the specified percentage of the functions that constitute the person's normal job. The customary payment under a *partial disability benefit* is a monthly indemnity equal to one-half the monthly benefit for total disability. Usually, the partial disability benefit is payable for the period of partial disability, but not exceeding a specified term, such as five or six months. The provision usually states that it will be payable only for a partial disability that immediately follows a period of total disability for which benefits were payable. In fact, one of the motivations for offering partial disability coverage was as an encouragement for the insured to resume employment as quickly as possible, even on a part-time basis.

Residual Disability Benefit Increasingly, a somewhat different provision is used to provide benefits for partial disabilities. As in the case of the partial disability benefit, a *residual disability* benefit provides coverage for partial disabilities but focuses on the amount of income lost rather than on the physical inability to work. The residual disability benefit was introduced in the 1970s in response to deteriorating claim experience under policies that defined disability in terms of the insured's *own occupation*. Studies by insurance companies show that a very high percentage of disabled persons eventually returned to their own occupation. Because disability benefits under an *own-occupation* contract cease if the insured returns to work in his or her own occupation—even on a part-time basis—there was no incentive for a disabled insured to do so. Insurers concluded that a provision that pays benefits based on loss of earnings when the insured returns to his or her own occupation might encourage a quicker return to work.

There are two types of residual disability definitions: those that measure loss of earnings only and those that measure loss of earnings and require the inability to perform some functions of the regular occupation. Residual disability benefits written on an *own-occupation* basis typically require both loss of earnings and the inability to perform some functions of the regular occupation. For policies written on a *modified-own-occupation* basis, the residual disability benefit usually measures loss of earnings only. This is, of course, also true for policies written on the new *loss of income* basis. Residual disability benefits that measure the loss of income only (i.e., that do not also require the inability to perform functions of a particular occupation) are particularly appropriate for self-employed persons, who may suffer a loss of income after returning to work, even though they are now capable of performing all of the functions of their occupation (due to a loss of clients, for example).

Insureds must usually have a 20-percent income loss to be eligible for the residual disability income benefit. To determine the amount of income loss under the residual disability provision, a benchmark against which loss of earnings will be measured is needed. This benchmark is the amount of income earned while the insured was healthy. Usually, the insured has a choice of earning periods prior to disability to be used in determining the income base.

- The first choice is usually a monthly average for the 12-month period (sometimes 6 months)

immediately preceding the disability. Usually, the insured's highest earnings will have been during this period.

- If earnings were higher during an earlier period, the insured can use the highest average monthly earnings for any 24 consecutive months in the 60 months prior to disability.

The payment for residual disability is a percentage of the total disability benefit based on the percentage reduction in the insured's income. If the insured's income is reduced by 40 percent, 40 percent of the total disability monthly amount is payable. Some policies include a provision called *significant loss of earnings,* which provides that if the income loss reaches a stipulated percentage of prior earnings (75 or 80 percent), the disability will be deemed total. Although some policies require a prior total disability, it is increasingly common for residual disability benefits to cover income lost because of accident or sickness, even in the absence of prior disability.

Although there is a similarity between the partial disability benefit and the residual disability benefit, there are important differences. A partial disability benefit is payable in an amount equal to one-half the total disability benefit, regardless of the reduction in earnings. The residual disability benefit in contrast, is payable in proportion to the individual's reduced earnings. In addition, coverage under a partial disability benefit is limited to a specified period, such as five or six months. Residual disability benefits are usually not limited in duration, other than the maximum benefit period under the basic plan.

Although the distinction between the terms *residual disability* and *partial disability* was once clear, there has been a gradual blurring of the distinction. Some companies define the term *residual disability* in the same way that other companies define partial disability and vice versa. The actual wording of the provision must be reviewed to determine the exact nature of the coverage.

Rehabilitation Provision In addition to the partial disability and residual disability benefits, some long-term disability contracts include a *rehabilitation provision,* which provides for continuation of disability benefits or other financial assistance while a totally disabled person is retraining or attempting to acquire skills to return to work.

Presumptive Disability Some contracts include a provision entitled *presumptive disability,* which pro-

vides that loss of the use of two bodily members or the loss of sight will be considered as total disability, regardless of whether the insured can do any work for remuneration. In some contracts, presumptive disability may include the loss of speech or hearing. This means that an insured who suffers a stroke, for example, and loses the use of an arm and leg, would be entitled to full benefits under the policy, even though the crippling of these members did not affect the person's income-earning ability. Individual companies differ in their presumptive disability provisions. Some companies require the loss of hands or feet by severance, while others require only the loss of use. When coverage is provided for *loss of use,* some insurers require that the loss of use be permanent, while others provide benefits as long as the loss of use continues.

Optional Benefit Provisions

Some insurers offer additional benefits that liberalize the coverage of their disability income contracts. The following are among the more common optional benefit provisions.

Guaranteed Insurability Option Some insurers offer a guaranteed insurability option similar to the one available in life insurance contracts. The disability income version of the guaranteed insurability option permits an individual whose income increases after the policy is purchased to increase the amount of coverage at specified dates after the inception of the policy.

Cost-of-Living Adjustment Benefit The *cost-of-living adjustment benefit* is designed to offset the decline in purchasing power of disability benefits that result from inflation. Under this provision, disability benefits are increased by the lesser of the increase in the consumer price index or a percentage specified in the policy. The percentage specified is usually 5 to 10 percent, and the increase applies after disability benefits have been paid for a year.

Automatic Benefit Increases Some disability income insurers offer a feature (generally called an automatic benefit increase) that combines characteristics of the guaranteed insurability option and the cost-of-living rider. Under the automatic benefit-increase provision, the monthly benefit is automatically increased during the early years of the contract, usually by a set percentage, such as 5 percent. The premium is automatically adjusted to reflect the increased cost. Insureds may have the option of rejecting the

automatic increases. In some contracts, however, the increase is not an option, but occurs automatically.

Accidental Death and Dismemberment Some disability income policies provide a death benefit, expressed as some multiple of the weekly benefit specified in the policy (e.g., 200 weeks) to be paid to a beneficiary if the insured dies as a result of accidental bodily injury. The policy usually provides that death must occur within 90 days from the date of the accident claimed to be the cause of death. In addition to the principal amount payable in the event of death, a scaled-down benefit is usually payable for loss of sight or loss of a bodily member. For example, a policy might provide payment of a sum equal to 200 weeks indemnity in the event of the death, and a schedule such as the following for dismemberment:

Payable in the event of death by accidental bodily injury	200 weeks
Loss of two hands, feet, or sight of both eyes	200 weeks
Loss of one hand and one foot	200 weeks
Loss of one hand	100 weeks
Loss of one foot	100 weeks
Loss of sight of one eye	65 weeks
Loss of thumb and index finger	50 weeks

In addition to its inclusion in some disability income policies, this *accidental death and dismemberment* coverage may be written as a separate contract. In such cases, the face amount is expressed as a dollar limit rather than a number of weeks. The indemnity for loss of members or loss of sight is expressed as a percentage of the principal amount:

Payable in the event of death by accidental bodily injury	Principal sum
Loss of two hands, feet, or sight of two eyes	Principal sum
Loss of one hand and one foot	One-half of principal sum
Loss of one hand	One-half of principal sum
Loss of one foot	One-half of principal sum
Loss of sight of one eye	One-third of principal sum
Loss of thumb and index finger	One-fourth of principal sum

As in the case of the double indemnity provision of the life insurance policy, there is no logic whatsoever to this form of coverage. If an individual dies, his or her family's need is the same regardless of whether the death is caused by accident or otherwise.

Waiver of Premium Nearly all disability income policies include provisions that waive premiums if the insured becomes totally disabled and the disability lasts for some specified minimum period. The provision may waive premiums only while the insured is receiving benefits or for as long as the insured remains disabled. Premiums may also be waived during a residual disability.

Social Insurance Substitute Benefit Although Social Security and workers compensation provide benefits for disability, both forms of social insurance provide benefits only under specified circumstances, and it is difficult to predict whether benefits will be payable in the event of disability. First, there is the 5-month waiting period under Social Security, during which no benefits are payable. In addition, there is no coverage under Social Security for disabilities when it is clear that the disability will last less than 12 months. Finally, the demanding definition of "disability" under Social Security suggests the possibility that some longer-term disabilities may not be covered under Social Security, because disability is defined as the inability to engage in any occupation.

Like Social Security, workers compensation provides coverage for some disabilities, namely, those that arise out of injuries in the workplace. This means that workers compensation benefits will be payable in the case of some disabilities, but not payable in others. The uncertainty regarding whether workers compensation benefits will be payable, like the uncertainty concerning Social Security benefits, poses a problem regarding the amount of disability insurance that should be purchased. If the social insurance benefits are ignored, the amount of coverage purchased may be excessive in some cases. The *Social Insurance Substitute* (SIS) benefit offered by some commercial insurers permits the insured to coordinate the individual's disability insurance with the social insurance programs. When the insured receives social insurance benefits, SIS monthly benefits are reduced.

The SIS benefit is designed to serve as a contingency ("just in case") coverage to provide additional monthly disability benefits when Social Security or workers compensation benefits are not payable

under these social insurance programs. In a sense, the coverage is excess over any benefits provided by the social insurance programs. If social insurance benefits are not payable, the SIS benefit provides coverage. If social insurance benefits are forthcoming from OASDHI or workers compensation, the SIS benefit terminates or is reduced by the amount of the social insurance benefits. SIS permits private disability income insurance to *wrap around* the benefits provided by social insurance programs. Because it does not pay when social insurance benefits are paid, the premiums for SIS coverage are less expensive than coverage that does not include a social insurance offset.

If the insured purchases the amount of coverage required to meet family needs, the SIS benefit and Social Security will provide that level of benefits regardless of whether or not Social Security benefits are payable. The SIS benefit may have the same waiting period as the base policy, but it may also be written in conjunction with a *short-term additional monthly indemnity benefit* (discussed next), in which case it becomes effective at the end of the additional monthly benefit period.

Short-Term Additional Monthly Indemnity A *short-term additional monthly indemnity benefit* is an optional endorsement that may be added to long-term disability policies to provide for payment of an additional amount of monthly indemnity during the first few months of total disability. Usually, this additional monthly benefit is payable for a maximum of 5 or 6 months, which makes it ideally suited to dovetail with the Social Security waiting period. Some insurers offer the benefit for up to a full year. To protect against a disability of less than 12 months and to cover the loss during the five-month waiting period under Social Security, a one-year short-term additional monthly indemnity benefit equal to the expected Social Security benefit can be added to a long-term disability policy. Ideally, this benefit would be written in an amount approximately equal to the individual's expected family Social Security disability benefit. The coverage can be written to cover both sickness and accident, and it can also be written on an SIS basis, which means that it will pay only if Social Security benefits are not payable. This benefit, combined with the long-term disability coverage, will provide reasonably adequate protection against the loss connected with a short-term disability not covered by Social Security.

INDIVIDUAL HEALTH INSURANCE POLICY PROVISIONS

As we noted at the beginning of the chapter, there has never been a "standard" health insurance policy. Although group contracts differ one from another in various ways, the greatest variations are among the individual contracts. Thus far in our discussion, we have dealt with provisions that are used in group and individual contracts. The following provisions appear in individual contracts only.

Individual Health Insurance Continuance Provisions

The right to continue a health insurance contract may be crucial for the insured, particularly if he or she has become uninsurable. Since individual health insurance policies provide coverage for a specified term, the absence of a cancellation provision does not guarantee continuing protection, for even when it cannot cancel, the insurer may retain the right to refuse to renew the policy. Individual health insurance policies (including both disability and medical coverage contracts) have a variety of provisions stating the respective rights of the company and the insured to continue or discontinue the policy. There are three types of contracts that cannot be canceled during the term and in which a guarantee to renew is provided. In addition, there are three forms in which the contract may either be canceled or where there is no guarantee of renewability. The six main types of policies, classified according to their continuance provisions, are:

1. *Noncancelable.* Noncancelable policies provide the most liberal continuation provision. The noncancelable policy is a continuous-term contract guaranteeing the insured the right to renew for a stated number of years or to a stated age (normally 60 or 65), with the premium at renewal guaranteed. In trade jargon, these policies are called *noncan.* Although noncancelable LTD policies were once common, poor claims experience caused most disability income insurers to abandon this type of renewable provision. It is not the inability to terminate coverage that has been a problem for insurers, but the inability to adjust the rates on a particular block of business. In place of noncancelable provision, insurers have adopted a guaranteed renewable provision.

2. *Guaranteed renewable.* Under a *guaranteed renewable* policy, the insured is protected against cancellation and is guaranteed the right to renew the policy, but with a provision permitting the company to adjust the premium for an entire class of insureds. Although the premium rate for renewal is not guaranteed under the guaranteed renewable contract as it is under the noncancelable policy, the company may not increase the rate for a single individual, but only for an entire class.

3. *Conditionally renewable.* Conditionally renewable policies are continuous-term policies under which the insurer may terminate the contract by not renewing it under certain conditions stated in the contract. This form provides some guarantee of continuance, but *usually* less than either the noncancelable or the guaranteed renewable. There are exceptions, however, depending on what is conditioned. Some companies offer contracts that may be conditionally renewed beyond age 65 if the insured is still working full time. The premiums are based on the current rate for the insured's age at the time of renewal.

4. *Renewable at the company's option.* Some continuous term policies are renewable only at the option of the company. This in effect means that the insured has no guarantee whatsoever of continuation.

5. *No provision.* Policies that have no provision for continuation are simply single term policies. They provide coverage for the stated period only.

6. *Cancelable.* A contract that may be terminated by the insurer during its term is called a cancelable policy. The provision for cancellation usually requires the insurer to give the insured a specified number of days of notice. Under such a policy, not only does the insured lack a guarantee with respect to continuation at the expiration of the policy, but coverage may be terminated during the policy period as well.

For obvious reasons, the noncancelable policy is more expensive than the guaranteed renewable policy, and the guaranteed renewable policy is more expensive than a conditionally renewable one. Although it has been pointed out that only a very small percentage of the policies not written on a noncancelable basis are refused renewal, the loss of health insurance at the time it is most needed might be a serious financial blow.

Uniform Provisions

In an attempt to induce some uniformity in conditions and operating procedures in health insurance contracts, the various states have enacted laws requiring that certain uniform provisions recommended by the NAIC be included in all individual health insurance policies. These laws provide that policies submitted to the state insurance departments must be drafted according to the standards imposed by the uniform provisions put forward by the NAIC and must meet certain other requirements. (Some requirements of the laws have to do with style, arrangement, and size of type.)

There are 23 uniform provisions: Twelve of these are required and must be included in every contract. The other 11 are optional and may be included or omitted. An insurance company may reword any of the provisions, if the new wording is not less favorable in any respect to the policy-holder or the beneficiary. The mandatory uniform provisions are the following:

Provision 1: Entire Contract—Changes The policy, including endorsements and attached papers, if any, constitutes the entire contract of insurance. No change in the policy is valid until approved by an executive officer of the insurer and added to the policy by endorsement.

Provision 2: Time Limit on Certain Defenses Except for fraud, the policy is incontestable after it has been in force for three years. Although the uniform provisions law makes the policy incontestable after three years, most insurers liberalize this provision making the policy incontestable after two years.

Provision 3: Grace Period A grace period of not less than 7 days applies to policies on which premiums are payable weekly, 10 days for monthly policies, and 31 days for all other policies. A policy that contains a cancellation provision may add the qualification *subject to the right of the insurer to cancel in accordance with the cancellation provision hereof.*

Provision 4: Reinstatement Policies that have been lapsed by nonpayment can be reinstated by the acceptance of an overdue premium by the company or one of its agents unless a reinstatement application is required. When reapplication is required, the reinstatement does not take effect until approved by the insurer or until 45 days have passed and the applicant has not been notified that reinstatement has been refused. The reinstated policy covers accidents

occurring only after the reinstatement date and sickness originating 10 days or more after that date.

Provision 5: Notice of Claim

The policyholder is required to furnish the insurer with a notice of claim within 20 days after the occurrence or commencement of a loss, or as soon as reasonably possible. Notice to an agent is considered sufficient.

Provision 6: Claim Forms

The insurer must furnish claim forms to the insured within 15 days of the notification. If the forms are not furnished, the insured may comply with the proof of loss requirement by submitting written proof of loss in any reasonable manner.

Provision 7: Proof of Loss

The policyholder must furnish a written proof of loss within 90 days after the termination of the period for which the company is liable. However, failure to submit the proof of loss within the 90-day period does not invalidate the claim if it was not possible for the insured to file the document. Except in cases of legal incapacity, the proof of loss must be filed within one year from the date otherwise required.

Provision 8: Time of Payment of Claims

Benefits are payable by the insurer immediately on receipt of the proof of loss. Income benefits are to be paid at specified intervals not less frequent than monthly.

Provision 9: Payment of Claims

Death benefits are payable to the named beneficiary or, if no beneficiary has been named, to the insured's estate. Any balance due from benefits (other than death benefit) may be paid to the beneficiary or the estate of the insured at the option of the insurer. All other indemnities will be payable to the insured.

The insurer may add a *facility-of-payment* clause, permitting it to pay up to $1000 in proceeds to any relative by blood or marriage of the insured or beneficiary who the company believes is entitled to receive it. Another optional addition to this claims clause permits the insurer to make payment directly to a person or hospital rendering service.

Provision 10: Physical Examinations and Autopsy

The insurer may, at its own expense, have the policyholder examined at reasonable intervals during the period of the claim and have an autopsy performed when death benefits are payable, provided it is not prohibited by law.

Provision 11: Legal Action

No legal action may be brought to recover on the contract in the 60 days immediately following the proof of loss. In addition, no suit may be brought under the policy unless it is instituted within three years from the date the proof of loss is required to be filed.

Provision 12: Change of Beneficiary

Unless the policyholder has specifically denied himself or herself the right to change the beneficiary, the beneficiary may be changed or the policy assigned as the insured wishes.

Optional Uniform Provisions

Any or all of the 11 optional provisions listed next may be included in individual health insurance policies.

Optional Provision 1: Change of Occupation

If the insured changes to a more hazardous occupation, benefits will be reduced to the amount that the premium paid would have purchased at the more hazardous classification. If the insured changes to a less risky occupation, the premium rate is reduced accordingly and any overpayment will be refunded on request.

Optional Provision 2: Misstatement of Age

If the insured's age has been misstated, the benefits payable under the policy are adjusted to the amount that the premium paid will purchase at the correct age.

Optional Provision 3: Other Insurance in This Insurer

If the insured already has coverage with the insurer that, with the additional policy, provides benefits in excess of some maximum allowed by the company, only the maximum is payable and the excess premiums will be returned to the policyholder or his or her estate.

Optional Provision 4: Insurance with Other Insurer

If the policyholder has duplicate coverage on an *expense incurred basis* with other companies and does not notify the insurer of the other policy, the liability of the insurer is limited to its proportionate share of the expenses incurred. The premiums for the unused part of the coverage are refunded to the insured.

Optional Provision 5: Insurance with Other Insurer

This option is the same as Optional Provision 4, except that it relates to benefits other than expenses incurred. It is seldom used since the relation-of-earnings-to-insurance provision discussed next provides more effective protection against overinsurance.

Optional Provision 6: Relation of Earnings to Insurance

This provision is generally known as the average earnings clause and is used only in noncance-

lable and guaranteed renewable contracts. It protects the company from the moral and morale hazard that would arise if disability benefits payable were greater than the normal income of the insured. The wording provides that if, at the time disability commences, the insured's total disability income exceeds earned income, or average earned income for the preceding two years (which-ever is greater), the income benefits under the policy will be reduced proportionately. In no case, however, will the benefits under all policies be reduced to less than $200 per month. Premiums for the excess coverage are returned to the insured.

Optional Provision 7: Unpaid Premium This clause states that the company may deduct from a claim any unpaid premium that is due.

Optional Provision 8: Cancellation The cancellation clause gives the company the right to cancel at any time with at least 5 days' notice. Excess or unearned premiums must be refunded. Of course, cancellation does not affect any claim originating before cancellation.

Optional Provision 9: Conformity with State Statutes Although this is an optional provision, some states require that it be included. It amends the policy, if necessary, so that it will conform to minimum state requirements.

Optional Provision 10: Illegal Occupation The insurer is not liable for loss for which a contributing cause was the insured's commission of a felony or being engaged in an illegal occupation.

Optional Provision 11: Intoxicants and Narcotics This provision relieves the insurer of liability for losses while the insured is under the influence of liquor or narcotics. For many people this is a very restrictive provision.

PROGRAMMING AND BUYING DISABILITY INCOME INSURANCE

For the individual, disability income insurance is an essential coverage. For some fortunate individuals, the coverage will be provided by the employer as a part of an employee benefit package. Usually, such programs are integrated with the available social insurance coverages, and little or no decision will be required by the individual. When coverage is not provided by the employer, however, the individual will be responsible for decisions relating to the design of the disability income program and for purchasing the coverages designed to implement those decisions. In this section, we will consider some of the decisions relating to programming disability insurance and some of the additional considerations in the area of buying disability insurance.

Determining Disability Income Coverage Needs

Measuring needs for disability income insurance follows the same general principles discussed earlier in connection with life insurance. It involves predicting future income needs, measuring the extent these needs will be met by existing sources of recovery, and then designing an insurance that will fill the gap between the future needs and existing sources of protection.

Income Needs in the Event of Disability As explained in Chapter 10, the disability income need is fundamentally different from the life insurance need, where the absence of dependents may eliminate the need for insurance. A single person without dependents who is disabled still needs income to replace his or her wages. Because the single person does not have the cushion of a possible second family income, a greater percentage of the future income needs may have to be insured. In addition, since there are no family members to serve as care providers, the need for disability income is not diminished by the individual's marital status. The specific amount of income that would be needed in the event of disability is determined in essentially the same way as income needs are determined for life-insurance programming; by constructing a budget for the various expenditures that will be required.

Disability and the Retirement Risk Since insurers do not offer lifetime disability coverage for illness, a disability protections program should make provision for income when the disability income policies stop making payments at age 65. The need for income after age 65 will exist whether or not the person is disabled. Sufficient income should be provided in the disability protection program to allow the individual to complete the accumulation for retirement in the same manner as would have been

the case in the absence of the disability.[11]

Some insurers increase their maximum limits of income coverage to recognize contributions to a retirement program. If an individual is contributing to a pension or profit-sharing plan, all or a portion of the contribution may be added to the person's income in determining the monthly benefit amount that can be issued. For example, someone earning $100,000, who contributes $20,000 to a pension or profit-sharing plan over and above these earnings, will be eligible for coverage at earnings of $120,000 (rather than just $100,000) in determining the monthly level available.[12]

Evaluating Existing Sources of Protection

Once income needs have been determined, the existing sources of protection that may be available to meet those needs should be inventoried.

Sources of funds during a period of disability include, first, any sick leave or short-term benefits available in connection with the job. Many employers provide their employees with a salary continuation plan or sick leave. A standard model is to grant 2.5 days of sick leave a month, which the employee may accumulate up to 30 days a year. Some plans are more generous and some are less. There are some employments in which there is no sick leave and no salary continuation plan. Although some corporate pension plans provide disability benefits, unless the individual has a significant accumulation in his or her plan, or unless the disability benefits are separately insured, this is not likely to be of much help.

The next important source of protection is the coverage available under social insurance programs, such as Social Security and workers compensation. Because of the stringent definition of disability and the five-month waiting period, some "advisers" suggest that one disregard Social Security benefits in determining the amount of disability income benefits to purchase. In view of the significant benefits that may be payable under both Social Security and workers compensation, this makes little sense. The only problem is in finding a way to integrate other forms of protection into an overall program that incorporates Social Security disability benefits while at the same time avoiding unneeded duplication. As we noted earlier, there are several specialized forms of disability insurance—such as the social insurance substitute benefit and the short-term additional monthly indemnity benefit—that can be used to make private disability insurance dovetail with social insurance coverages.

As in the case of life insurance, the disability income program should be viewed as a potential flow of income, capable of replacing the income lost as a result of the inability to work. In determining the amount of insurance necessary, the same needs discussed in connection with life insurance are appropriate. In selecting the amount of weekly and monthly indemnity and the length of the waiting period, consideration should be given to other sources of income that may be available, such as sick leave, a qualified pension plan, and social insurance coverages. Inasmuch as it is impossible to determine in advance the length of the period of disability, protection should be provided for the worst possible eventuality, a disability that is permanent in nature. A disability policy should therefore provide benefits for life or until retirement age in an amount that will permit the individual to continue the accumulation of a retirement program in the same way as if he or she had not been disabled.

Taxation of Disability Income

The tax treatment of disability income benefits has an important effect on the amount of income that needs to be replaced. Benefits received from individually owned disability income policies are not subject to federal income tax. Since the individual will not have to pay taxes on the benefits, something less than 100 percent of the predisability income needs to be replaced. The amount of income that needs to be replaced is also affected by the reduction in expenses associated with employment (such as work, clothing, and transportation expenses); however, this reduction will probably be small. Premiums paid by individuals for disability income insurance are not deductible for federal income tax purposes.

The tax treatment of disability income benefits provided through employment is somewhat more complicated. Sick pay and other disability income payments that have been paid for by the employer

[11] Alternately, the insured may purchase cash value life insurance with a disability waiver of premium provision. The accumulation of cash values will then serve to provide funds to supplement Social Security benefits when the disability income benefits terminate at age 65.

[12] Both Paul Revere and UNUM have offered coverages that insure an individual's specific pension contribution.

are treated essentially the same as wages and are taxable to the employee. If the employee was required to contribute to the cost of the disability income plan as a condition for being covered, however, the portion of the benefits paid for by the employee is received tax free.

Cost of Disability Income Insurance

The cost of disability income insurance varies widely, depending on whether the coverage is purchased through a group or individually. Even among individual contracts, there can be wide variations in cost. The premium depends on the occupation, age, and sex of the insured, the length of time for which benefits are payable, the extent of the coverage, the amount of the weekly or monthly benefit, and the length of the waiting period.

Because most disabilities are short term in duration, coverage for longer periods of disability costs proportionately less than coverage for short periods. Depending on the individual's age, the differential in cost between short-term disability policies and long-term disability will be significant. For the age group into which most readers of this text will fall, the premium for a short-term policy providing two years of benefits is less than half the cost (about 40 percent) of a policy providing benefits until age 65. This difference in premiums can make the short-term policy appear attractive. On the other hand, a short-term policy will not address the financial consequences of a truly catastrophic loss.

Fortunately, the fact that most disabilities are short term in duration means that the waiting period under disability policies will also have a significant influence on cost. The longer the waiting period, the lower, other things being equal, will be the premium. The principles of risk management suggest that the appropriate trade-off is to accept the highest waiting period one can afford and purchase coverage for the longest duration available. Often, a higher waiting period will make it possible to purchase the longest duration coverage available, which pays benefits for lifetime in the event of accident and until age 65 for sickness. For example, a short-term disability contract written by one company on the 1-8-26 plan has an annual premium of $36.40 per $10.00 of weekly benefit. The cost of a $200-per-week benefit under this contract would be about $730 a year. On the other hand, a long-term contract providing $800 a month for life for accident, and until age 65 for sickness, can be obtained with a 30-day waiting period for about $475 per year. With a 180-day waiting period, the cost of the contract would be $385 per year.

For the lower-income family, a short waiting period may be a necessity. However, the individual should consider other disability income protection he or she may have, such as sick leave. If the length of the waiting period can be increased, the resulting premium reduction may well permit a substantial increase in the amount of benefits or the length of time for which benefits are payable. Families in the middle-income group ($25,000–$35,000) should consider a waiting period of at least two weeks. Families in higher income brackets should be able to carry themselves for three to six months, or even a year.

IMPORTANT CONCEPTS TO REMEMBER

short-term disability coverage	rehabilitation provision	average earnings clause
long-term disability coverage	sickness	misstatement-of-age provision
occupational disability	Social insurance substitute	facility of payment clause
nonoccupational disability	presumptive disability	overhead disability income
waiting period	preexisting condition	relation-of-earnings-to-insurance
accidental bodily injury	noncancelable	clause
bodily injury by accidental means	guaranteed renewable	renewable at insurer's option
disability	conditionally renewable	medical expense insurance
partial disability	uniform provisions	accidental death and
residual disability benefit	change-of-occupation provision	dismemberment

QUESTIONS FOR REVIEW

1. Identify the ways in which disability income insurance is marketed. Which approach accounts for the greatest percentage of disability income insurance sold?

2. What sources of protection other than disability income insurance may the individual have to protect against loss of earnings? Why is disability income insurance a necessary supplement to these forms of protection?

3. List the three definitions of *disability* that may be found in disability income contracts. Which is the most beneficial to the insured? Which is the narrowest form of coverage?

4. In your own words, explain the basic difference between the two common definitions of sickness contained in disability income policies. Explain which would be preferable from the insured's point of view and why.

5. Briefly distinguish between *long-term* and *short-term* disability income contracts.

6. Briefly distinguish between *occupational and non-occupational* disability income contracts.

7. Identify and briefly describe three optional benefits that may be included in disability income policies.

8. List and explain the alternative continuance provisions of individual health insurance policies.

9. What provisions may an insurer incorporate in an individual health insurance policy to guard against over-insurance and morale hazard?

10. Compare and contrast the uniform health insurance optional provisions that deal with a change in occupations by the insured and misstatement of age.

QUESTIONS FOR DISCUSSION

1. Joe Smith is considering the purchase of a disability income policy and is trying to decide between two policies sold by two different companies. Although both will pay until age 65 for disability arising out of sickness, and for lifetime for disability resulting from accident, the cost of one policy is almost twice that of the other. What provisions in the two contracts would you advise Smith to compare?

2. In this best seller, *Wealth Without Risk,* Charles J. Givens, the self-styled expert on "low-risk ways to achieve and hold on to wealth," offers the following advice as his *strategy #32:* "Buy disability insurance only if you are in poor health or accident prone." What is your reaction to this "strategy?"

3. Which type of hazard (physical, moral, or morale) do you believe would pose the greatest problem for an insurer writing disability income insurance?

4. You have been retained by an insurer to design a disability income policy covering both accident and sickness, but with appropriate provisions to protect against the special hazards associated with writing sickness coverage. What provisions or conditions would you incorporate into the policy?

5. One of the major problems facing a person who is permanently disabled is the possibility of erosion of purchasing power when price level changes occur during the period of disability. To what extent could the concept of variable annuity or variable life insurance be used in the field of disability income?

SUGGESTIONS FOR ADDITIONAL READING

Beam, Burton T., Jr., and John J. McFadden. *Employee Benefits,* 3rd ed. Brookfield, Wis.: Dearborn Financial Publishing, 1994.

Black, Kenneth, Jr., and Harold D. Skipper, Jr. *Life Insurance,* 13th ed. Englewood Cliffs, N.J.: Prentice-Hall, 2000. Chapters 7, 18.

Eilers, R. D. *Regulation of Blue Cross and Blue Shield Plans.* Homewood, Ill.: Richard D. Irwin, 1963. Chapters 1–5, 8–11.

Graves, Edward E., ed. *McGill's Life Insurance.* Bryn Mawr, Pa.: The American College, 1994. Chapter 7.

Health Insurance Association of America. *Annual Report 1990–1991.* Washington, D.C.: Health Insurance Association of America, 1991.

Price, Daniel N. "Cash Benefits for Short-Term Sickness." *Social Security Bulletin,* vol. 47, no. 8 (Aug. 1984).

Rosenbloom, Jerry S., ed. *The Handbook of Employee Benefits: Design, Funding and Administration,* 3rd ed. Homewood, Ill.: Richard D. Irwin, 1991.

WEB SITES TO EXPLORE

Association of Health Insurance Agents	http://www.agents-online.com/AHIA/
Health Insurance Association of America	http://www.hiaa.org
Insurance News Network	http://www.insure.com/
Quicken InsureMarket	http://www.insuremarket.com/

HEALTH INSURANCE: COVERAGE FOR MEDICAL EXPENSES

Physicians of the utmost fame
Were called at once; but when they came
They answered, as they took their fees,
"There is no cure for this disease."

— HILAIRE BELLOC

CHAPTER OBJECTIVES

When you have finished this chapter, you should be able to

- Identify and describe the major problems associated with the current health care system
- Identify the past efforts that have been made to address the problems associated with the financing of health care in the United States
- Distinguish between the traditional fee-for-service approach to health insurance and the capitation system of managed care providers
- Identify common cost-containment activities that have been adopted by health insurers
- Identify and describe the traditional forms of medical expense insurance, distinguishing between basic policies and major medical insurance
- Describe the nature of medical savings accounts and explain the way in which they are used
- Identify the three broad approaches that have been proposed as methods of providing universal health care in this country

A well-planned program for financing medical expenses is an important part of any personal risk management plan. Unexpected illnesses and injuries can result in catastrophic medical expenses for the individual and his or her family. In this chapter, we turn to the subject of insurance against the cost of medical expenses.

Medical expense insurance provides for the payment of the costs of medical care that result from sickness and injury. It helps to meet the expenses of physicians, hospital, nursing, and related services, as well as medications and supplies. Benefits may be in the form of reimbursement of actual expenses (up to a limit), cash payments, or the direct provision of services. Like disability income and life insurance, medical expense coverage is sold on both an individual and a group basis.

Although insurance is an important tool for financing health care expenditures, most health care costs are paid from sources other than private health insurance. State and federal governments cover a staggering 45.2 percent of health care expenses in the United States. Out-of-pocket expenditures and other payments from private resources cover about 20.6 percent of total expenditures for health care. Finally, private insurance, written by various types of insurers, provides financing for the remaining 34.2 percent of health care expenditures.[1]

BACKGROUND ON THE CURRENT HEALTH INSURANCE MARKET

Before turning to a discussion of health insurance, it will be helpful to examine the system of health care delivery in this country and the ways in which the delivery of health care is financed. Both will be useful in understanding some of the coverage features one encounters in the health insurance market.

Historical Development of Health Insurance in the United States

Health insurance is a phenomenon of the twentieth century. Although accident insurance was first offered in 1863, coverage for expenses associated with sickness did not become popular until after World War I. Interestingly, it was not traditional insurance companies that popularized medical expense coverage, but hospitals. Early in the 1920s, a number of innovative hospitals began to offer hospitalization on a prepaid basis to individuals.

Blue Cross and Blue Shield In 1929, a group of schoolteachers arranged for Baylor University to provide hospital benefits on a prepaid basis. This plan is considered the forerunner of Blue Cross plans, which were organized by a group of hospitals to permit and encourage prepayment of hospital expenses. They offered subscribers contracts that promised a semiprivate room in a participating hospital when the insured was hospitalized. In 1939, the first Blue Shield plan was organized by physicians in California to offer prepaid surgical expense coverage.[2]

Commercial Insurance Companies In the 1930s, commercial insurance companies began to market hospital and surgical expense insurance. Unlike the blues, commercial insurers provided coverage on a reimbursement basis, providing payment up to a specified dollar maximum per day while the insured is confined to a hospital, or a specific limit of coverage for various surgical procedures. In 1949, commercial insurers introduced a form of catastrophe medical expense coverage called major medical insurance. When written with basic hospital insurance and surgical expense insurance, this major medical insurance became the standard against which other health insurance plans were measured.

Fee for Service The health insurance provided by Blue Cross and Blue Shield organizations and insurance companies is now referred to as *fee-for-service* coverage. Under this approach, the insured had

[1] Health Care Financing Administration, *National Health Expenditures Tables;* see http://www.hcfa.gov/stats/NHE-OAct/tables/. Until 2001, the federal agency responsible for administering the Medicare and Medicaid programs was called the Health Care Financing Administration (HCFA). Although the agency's name was changed in 2001 to the Centers for Medicare and Medicaid Services (CMS), the HCFA website (http://www/hcfa.gov/) remained in operation early in 2002, along with two new CMS sites at http://www.medicare.gov/ and http://cms.hhs.gov/.

[2] The laws under which Blue Cross and Blue Shield plans were organized originally exempted the plans from the state insurance premium tax and from other provisions of insurance laws. A number of states have eliminated the exemption from the premium tax in recent years. Prior to the Tax Reform Act of 1986 (TRA-86), Blue Cross and Blue Shield plans were exempt from federal taxes, but TRA-86 repealed this exemption for years after 1986. In recent years, a number of Blue Cross/Blue Shield plans have converted to mutual insurance companies.

complete autonomy in the choice of doctors, hospitals, and other health care providers. Insureds were free to choose any specialist without getting prior approval and insurers did not attempt to decide whether the health care services were necessary. Insurers attempted to control costs through deductibles and share-loss provisions called *coinsurance,* under which the patient was required to bear a part of the cost.

Medicare In 1965, Congress amended the Social Security system by establishing the Medicare program to provide medical expense insurance to persons over age 65. The same legislation created Medicaid, a state–federal medical assistance program for low-income persons. During the years immediately following Medicare in 1965, the cost of health care (and of private health insurance) increased dramatically. Attention turned to the problems inherent in the "fee-for-service" system. Many experts argued that this system provided an incentive to overutilize health care. When the insurer (or government) paid the costs, insureds and providers had no incentive to reduce costs. In fact, it was argued, the provider stood to gain when more services were provided. Insurers, employers, and public policy makers began to look for ways to change the way in which health care is financed to give providers an incentive to control medical expenses.

Managed Care Organizations The solution was the concept of managed care, which represented a change not only in the financing of health care, but in its delivery as well. New types of "insurers" emerged that not only offered risk financing, but health care as well. The prototype for this type of organization was the *health maintenance organization,* which offered a more direct relationship between the provision of health care and its financing.

Health Maintenance Organizations The distinguishing characteristic of a health maintenance organization (HMO) is that the HMO not only provides for the financing of health care—as do commercial insurers and the blues—it also delivers that care. HMOs often operate their own hospitals and clinics and employ or maintain contracts with physicians and other health care professionals who deliver health care services. The insurance element in the operation of HMOs derives from the manner in which they charge for their services, which is called *capitation.* Under the capitation approach, subscribers pay an annual fee and in return receive comprehensive

health care. The HMO may be sponsored by a group of physicians, a hospital or medical school, an employer, labor union, consumer group, insurance company, or Blue Cross and Blue Shield plans.

Although HMOs have been around for at least as long as the Blue Cross and Blue Shield plans, it was not until 1970s that public and government attention was focused on them, bringing them their current popularity.[3] In 1971, the federal government adopted a policy of encouraging and promoting HMOs as an alternative to the fee-for-service approach to health care financing.[4] Two years later, Congress passed the Health Maintenance Organization Act of 1973, which provided funding for new HMOs and the expansion of existing ones. The law also required employers with 25 or more workers who are subject to the Fair Labor Standards Act to offer, as a part of its health benefit program, the option of membership in a federally qualified HMO if one is available.

During the period since 1973, HMOs have grown at a phenomenal rate. HMOs increased from about 25 in the early 1970s to more than 800 by the year 2001. Although the original organizations were independent plans, commercial insurers and the Blue Cross and Blue Shield organizations have embraced the idea. By 2001, insurance companies were administering over 200 HMO projects. Blue Cross and Blue Shield organizations have been equally active, with 89 HMOs in operation by 2001.

HMOs include a variety of arrangements, but consist mainly of three types: the *staff model,* the *group model,* and the *independent practice association* or IPA type. Under the staff model HMO, physician services are provided through a group of multispecialty physicians who are salaried employees of the HMO. Under the group model, physicians' services

[3] Although the roots of the HMO idea can be traced back to the 1800s, their modern history dates from 1938, when industrialist Henry Kaiser adopted the idea of prepaid group medical practice and capitation for his employees working on the Grand Coulee Dam. The idea spread to Kaiser shipyards and other Kaiser industries during World War II, and the result was the Kaiser Permanente Medical Care Program, the largest HMO in the country. Other early HMOs include the New York Health Insurance Plan (HIP), the United Mine Workers' Plans, the Ross-Loos Medical Group in Los Angeles, the Metro Health Plan of Detroit, and the San Joaquin Plan.

[4] In that year, Elliott L. Richarson, secretary of HEW, described the administration's health care strategy: the HMO was central to the core of that strategy. Elliott L. Richarson, *A White Paper: Toward a Comprehensive Health Policy for the 1970s.* Washington, D. C.: Department of Health, Education and Welfare, May 1971.

are provided by a group of physicians independent of the HMO, but who contract with the HMO to provide service. The physicians primarily serve members of the HMO, but may serve other patients as well. The physicians' group is compensated on a capitation basis. Finally, the individual practice association (IPA) type of HMO involves physicians who practice in their own offices, but agree to provide medical services to the HMO. IPA physicians are reimbursed on a fee basis within agreed ranges by the association and the association provides comprehensive health care to its enrolled population on a capitation basis.[5]

Whatever the arrangement with the physicians, from the subscriber's point of view, the fee-for-service system is replaced by a system of capitation. In return for a fixed monthly fee, the individual receives virtually all the medical care required during the year. There may be a nominal charge, on the order of $5, paid by the participant when visiting the physician, but this charge is the same regardless of the service rendered. The subscriber is required to choose a primary-care physician (also known as the *gatekeeper*), who is responsible for determining what care is received and when the individual is referred to specialists. If the primary care physician decides the patient requires the services of a specialist, the patient is referred to a specialist in the HMO network. If the network does not include a specialist of the type required, referral is made to a specialist outside the network. Emergency care services are provided outside the network when there is a sudden onset of an illness or injury, which, if not immediately treated, could jeopardize the subscriber's life or health.

Preferred Provider Organizations Given the successes of HMOs in controlling costs, commercial insurers began to look for ways to copy their success. Noting that many individuals objected to the limitations placed on their ability to select the physicians and hospitals, insurers sought other ways they could reduce costs by contracting with providers, while still allowing insureds the option to choose their provider. This led to the development of *preferred provider organizations* (PPOs). A preferred provider organization is a network of health care providers (doctors and hospitals) with whom an insurance company (or an employer) contracts to provide medical services. The provider typically offers to discount those services and to set up special utilization review programs to control medical expenses. In return, the insurer promises to increase patient volume by encouraging insureds to seek care from preferred providers. The insurer does this by providing higher rates of reimbursement when the care is received from the network. The insured is still permitted to seek care from other providers, but will suffer a penalty in the form of increased deductibles and coinsurance.

This arrangement preserves the employee's option to choose a provider outside the network, should he or she desire. When the insured stays in the network, the discounted fees to providers should provide some cost savings, although the potential for savings is lower than with an HMO. In 2001, over 1000 preferred provider organizations were operating countrywide.

Point-of-Service Plans Eventually some HMOs adopted procedures that made them more like PPOs, using what are known as *point-of-service plans* (POS). In one respect, a POS plan operates like a PPO, since the employee retains the right to use any provider, but will have to pay a higher proportion of the costs when he or she uses a provider outside the network. On the other hand, a POS plan is like an HMO, since care received through the network is managed by a primary care physician, or "gatekeeper". In fact, the first POS plans were created when HMOs allowed their subscribers to use non-network providers. The penalties for using a non-network provider are usually greater than the penalties under a PPO. It is hoped that the use of the gatekeeper approach in POS plans will provide greater cost control than that provided by a PPO arrangement.

Provider-Sponsored Organizations The newest type of managed care insurer is the *provider-sponsored organizations* (PSO). A *provider-sponsored organization* (PSO) is essentially an HMO that is organized by a partnership of health care providers, such as a hospital and a group of physicians. The terminology for *provider-sponsored organizations* has been revised several times, as health care reformers reinvent the concept. At various times and in different proposals, provider-sponsored organizations have been called *physician-hospital organizations* (PHOs) and *organized delivery systems* (ODSs). The PSO designation is

[5] In addition to the three main types of HMOs, there are two additional models; the *network model* and the *direct contract model*. The network model is similar to the group practice model, except that the HMO enters into contracts with several multispecialty groups of physicians. Under the direct contract model, also called an *open-ended HMO,* physicians who are not affiliated with the HMO may provide services.

used in the Tax Reform Act of 1997 in connection with new Medicare options and is likely to become the standard designation for these organizations.

Dominance of Managed Care Collectively, HMOs, PPOs, and POS plans are referred to as *managed care plans*. Although there are important differences among these plans, greater similarities do exist. All managed care plans involve an arrangement between insurers and a selected network of providers and they offer policyholders significant financial incentives to use the providers in the network. The term *managed care* is also used to refer to the variety of case management procedures that are now used by virtually all health insurers as cost control measures. Even when indemnity plans are offered, they now contain cost-containment features that encourage efficient provision of care.

The dramatic growth in popularity of HMOs, PSOs, PPOs, and POS plans can be seen by examining the trends in enrollment in recent years. Thirty years ago, 90 percent of individual employees were covered under traditional fee-for-service plans offered by commercial insurers and Blue Cross and Blue Shield plans. By 2001, that number had fallen to less than 20 percent. Approximately 32 percent of employees are enrolled in PPOs, 33 percent are enrolled in HMOs, and 17 percent are enrolled in POS plans. Fee-for-service plans now cover about 18 percent of insured individuals.

ERISA A final event of significance in the evolution of our current health care financing system occurred in 1974 with the passage of the Employee Retirement Income Security Act (ERISA). Although the primary focus of ERISA was employee retirement plans, it also included a broad preemption of state regulation for employee welfare benefit plans, specifically providing that states may not regulate self-funded health insurance arrangements as insurance. As a result, group health insurance in the United States has evolved into two separate but unequal parts—one subject to regulation by the state insurance departments and the other almost free of regulation. Employers that self-fund the costs of employee health care are exempt from most state laws regulating health insurance.

Current Deficiencies in the System

Rapidly rising costs, inadequate health care services for some segments of the population, and the failure of past measures to solve the problems of health care have contributed to a growing dissatisfaction with the health care financing system. Critics point out that although U.S. medical research in most fields is the most advanced in the world, and although many of our hospitals are the best equipped in the world, the United States has been slipping behind other nations in key indexes of national health. These critics argue that other countries spend a smaller percentage of their gross national product on health services than our 13-plus percent, and that in return they get better medical care, lower infant mortality rates, and longer life expectancies, with fewer people dying in their productive years.[6] Although they are manifest in many ways, the U.S. health care system faces two main problems: access to health care and cost.

Access to Health Care A part of the dissatisfaction with the present system results from the uneven distribution of health care. It is estimated that 38.7 million Americans have no health insurance coverage.[7] Individuals may be uninsured for a number of reasons. About three-fourths of the uninsured are employees and their dependents. About half of these workers have insurance available at their place of employment, but elect not to purchase it. Many of the uninsured are low-income workers. Some of the uninsureds are unemployed and about one-third have incomes at or below the poverty level and do not qualify for Medicaid. Others are between jobs or have taken early retirement and are not yet eligible for Medicare.

The problem of access is not limited to the economically disadvantaged. It also exists for persons who, because of personal hazards, are unable to obtain health insurance in the standard market. Persons who must purchase insurance individually

[6] Despite the high expenditure on health care, infant mortality in the United States is higher than most western European countries, and life expectancy is about average. Some people argue that these differences in mortality rates are not an accurate measure of the relative effectiveness of the health delivery systems. They point out that our diet, work habits, and leisure activities are all different from other peoples' and that there is very little about our lifestyles that is the same as that of other countries.

[7] The indicated 38.7 million persons who do not have health insurance is for 2000 and is somewhat lower than previous estimates. The number of uninsured persons was reported to have peaked at 43.9 million persons (18.4 percent of the population) in 1998. A March 2000 study by the Census Bureau indicated that the 1999 estimate of 42.6 million uninsured persons was too high by 3.3 million persons, suggesting that previous estimates have also been too high. See Charles T. Nelson and Robert J. Mills, *The March CPS Health Insurance Verification Question and Its Effect on Estimates of the Uninsured* (U.S. Census Bureau: August 2001).

sometimes find that they cannot obtain it. It is estimated, however, that only 3 percent of uninsured lack insurance because they are unable to obtain it from a provider.

High Cost of Health Care Ensuring access to health care for the poor is only part of the problem. For insured and uninsured persons alike, the most distressing problem is cost—not only the absolute level of health care costs, but their escalation from year to year. National expenditures for health care, as a percentage of GNP, have increased from 4.4 percent of GNP in 1950 to over 13 percent by 2000. For consumers, the increases in the cost of health care have come in two ways. The first is the annual increase in premiums, which at times in the past has been 15 to nearly 20 percent a year. A second increase in costs has come in the form of increased deductibles and cost-sharing features adopted by employers. Although these measures reduce the employer's cost, the reduction is achieved by shifting the cost to employees.

The increasing cost of health care is due to many causes. These include an aging population, improved technology, excess capacity, and defensive medicine.[8] In addition, the use of insurance tends to worsen some problems.

The Aging Population One factor that contributes to increasing health care costs is our aging population. People are living longer, and in doing so incur increased costs for health care. Older persons tend to experience more frequent and more costly need for medical services. The Medicare system made access available to the elderly, but in doing so has acted as a cost driver.

Improved Medical Technology By far the greatest cause of escalating health care costs is the high cost of medical technology and the advances in medical knowledge. Medicine is constantly learning new procedures, but seldom does the new medical miracle save money over the old method of treatment. Human organ transplants such as heart, liver, and kidney transplants have become more common, and their enormous cost intensifies the problems of financing health care.

[8] The Centers for Medicare and Medicaid Services estimates that population growth accounts for about 10 percent of health care cost increases between 1980 and 1993, technology-driven increases in utilization account for 26 percent, general inflation accounts for 44 percent, and other health-care inflation accounts for 21 percent.

Excessive Capacity Although advances in medical technology create justifiable increases in cost, they can also be a source of waste and inefficiency. When new technology comes onto the market, it tends to spread rapidly throughout the medical community. Once an expensive machine is purchased, the incentive to use it to recoup the investment, combined with the desire to improve medical care, work naturally to increase health care costs.

Defensive Medicine The increasingly litigious atmosphere in the country, evidenced by an epidemic of malpractice suits, encourages physicians to practice "defensive medicine," an inclination that compounds the impact of technology on costs. Advances in technology create increasingly expensive testing equipment with vastly expanded diagnostic powers; the threat of malpractice suits strengthens the physician's inclination to use the equipment to perform more and higher-cost diagnostic testing. Patients rarely object to more testing, especially if it is covered by insurance, because it might do them some good, even if it is not cost effective for society as a whole.

Insurance as a Complicating Factor Despite the varied causes of the problems in the health care financing system, the insurance mechanism has become a focal point in the debate. Based on what we know about how insurance operates, this was probably inevitable. The health care financing problem is brought into focus and perhaps worsened by the ways in which insurance operates to spread risk.

Insurance-Encouraged Utilization Medical expense insurance has a natural tendency to increase utilization of health care services, because it alters the cost barriers for consumers. Individuals who have full coverage essentially face a price of zero at the time health care service is delivered. When deductibles and coinsurance exist, they pay some price, but not the full cost of the service. There is a tendency for people to use more health care when someone else is paying the cost. Although the problem is less pronounced in managed care plans than in fee-for-service plans, it is pervasive.

Segmentation and Adverse Selection Another problem with a free, competitive health insurance market is the tendency toward risk segmentation—the classification of insureds into groups that reflect their hazards. The reason this is a problem is the highly skewed distribution of health expenditures. The most expensive 1 percent of our population

accounts for 30 percent of all health spending. The most expensive 50 percent of the population produces 97 percent of total national health spending, meaning that the least expensive 50 percent account for only 3 percent of spending.[9]

In a private insurance market, competitors have incentives to identify and compete for insureds with lower than average expected losses, which they do by offering these insureds lower premiums. This inevitably results in segmentation of the market. In every insured group, there are some individuals whose predictable losses are less than the average of the group. These better-than-average insureds are those who are most likely to be attracted to a competing insurer whose rates better reflect their hazard. When the better-than-average insureds are removed from a group, the average loss of the remaining population increases. While risk segmentation of the insurance market provides benefits for low-risk populations, higher risk populations may find it prohibitively expensive or impossible to obtain insurance for themselves or their families.

The distribution of health costs across the population also suggests a significant potential for adverse selection. Some people have an incentive to not buy insurance because they have lower than average expected loss costs. The problem with this is that today's healthy person may be tomorrow's sick person. Those who do not feel that they need health insurance change their minds after the onset of a serious illness and would then like to join the mechanism that spreads the high cost of health care.

Dominance of Employer-Sponsored Health Insurance Another feature of the current health insurance environment that is helpful in understanding some of the problems the system faces is that the overwhelming majority of the population covered by health insurance obtain their coverage under group plans, usually sponsored by an employer. These plans cover the worker and his or her dependents. Slightly fewer than 10 million persons, less than 5 percent of the total population, obtain their health insurance coverage under individually purchased policies.

There are two reasons for the overwhelming dominance of the group approach. The first is that most people obtain their health insurance as an employee benefit. The economies of the group approach make group coverage cheaper than individually written coverage. The potential for cost savings inherent in the operation of the group mechanism was discussed in Chapter 12. Group insurance provides opportunities for cost savings because of lower underwriting expenses, reduced agents' commissions, and the reduced potential for adverse selection. Where the individual is insured as a member of a group, the premium tends to be lower than if the individual had purchased the insurance on his or her own.

The second major reason that medical expense insurance is typically provided through an employment relationship is taxes. Contributions made by an employer as payment for health insurance premiums for employees are deductible as a business expense for the employer, but the amount of premiums is not taxable as income to the employee. This means that the employee would have to receive something more than the amount of premiums paid by the employer as additional compensation to purchase the same level of benefits. The employee is not taxed on benefits received under such a program if they are reimbursement of medical expenses actually incurred.[10]

Group health insurance plans, like group life insurance, were originally distinguished from individual health insurance in the fact that group underwriting and group rating are substituted for individual underwriting and individual rating. As in the case of group life insurance, the nature of group health insurance changed from this original concept. Over time, statutory requirements concerning the minimum number of individuals in a group have shrunk, and with the decrease in the number, the nature of group underwriting changed. As the minimum number of persons required for group coverage fell, state laws were modified to allow insurers to require evidence of individual insurability on groups. Although group underwriting and rating continued for large groups, individual underwriting became the norm for smaller groups. This led to availability problems for members of smaller groups, and sometimes for the smaller groups themselves.

Insurance Market Reform Options Historically, insurers could refuse to issue coverage to groups or

[9] M. Berk and A. Monheit, "The Concentration of Health Expenditures; An Update," *Health Affairs* (Winter 1992)

[10] Some experts suggest that the favorable tax treatment of employer-provided health insurance encourages employees to seek and employers to offer more generous health insurance benefits. They also point out the inequity that exists because premiums for individual health insurance are deducted only to a limited extent, as discussed later in the chapter.

individuals based on their past health care use or general indicators of their health status. Insurers could also refuse to renew policies based upon previous years' claims experiences, and could deny coverage for preexisting illnesses or conditions. In response to the problems encountered by insurance buyers, there have been continuing attempts to reform the market in ways that will make insurance available to those who have difficulty in obtaining it. These efforts generally take the form of restrictions on the ability of insurers to select from among prospective buyers. These reforms, which tend to be grouped together in reform proposals are *guaranteed issue, renewability, portability, limits on preexisting condition exclusions,* and *mandated benefits.*

Guaranteed issue is a requirement that insurers sell health insurance to any eligible party that agrees to pay the applicable premiums and to fulfill the other plan requirements. It can be thought of as a "take all comers" rule. Guaranteed issue does not regulate the premium charged to a given individual or group. This means that for some buyers, the guaranteed issue coverage could be prohibitive in cost.

Guaranteed renewability ensures that those currently insured cannot have their coverage discontinued by their insurer in a subsequent year as long as the insurer continues to do business in that particular market. As with the guaranteed-issue, guaranteed renewability alone does not limit the premium that can be charged a covered group or individual.

Preexisting condition exclusions disallow coverage related to any previous conditions. Without such restrictions, there would be no incentive to purchase insurance until the onset of an illness or injury. Recognizing that a complete elimination of preexisting conditions exclusions would create chaos, reform proposals generally limit the time for which preexisting conditions can be excluded, usually for six to 12 months.

Portability refers to the ability to change insurers without encountering a gap in coverage. Reforms relating to portability take the form of limits on preexisting condition exclusions. Under the proposed reforms, individuals maintaining continuous coverage are exempt from all preexisting condition exclusions applying to new policies. The objective of such a rule is to decrease the problem of "job-lock," the limit on worker mobility that results from the potential loss of insurance coverage if the worker changes jobs.

Mandated benefits laws are an attempt to guarantee that particular health services are covered in every insurance product sold in a state. The rationale for mandating particular benefits is to avoid segmentation of persons who are subject to the illness or medical needs that are mandated and thereby spread the cost of treatment. Mandated benefits include such diverse benefits as inpatient alcohol and drug abuse programs, infertility treatment, coverage for mental health, and the services of chiropractors and podiatrists. Mandated benefits provisions, by forcing coverage of particular services, have the potential for spreading risk. Mandated benefits may also increase the incentives for insurers to select risks, worsening the degree of risk segmentation, as insurers attempt to write those who are least likely to have need for the mandated benefits.

Previous Attacks on the Access Problem

The problems in health care delivery and financing have existed for many years. In view of the critical importance of medical expense insurance, it is not surprising that both the state and federal governments have enacted legislation that addresses access and cost problems of health insurance.

State Efforts to Improve Access Most states have attempted to address the problem of availability of health insurance by creating subsidized state health insurance pools for the uninsurable.[11] Individuals who are not eligible for Medicare or Medicaid and who cannot buy private health insurance obtain coverage from the pools, usually at a subsidized rate. Although the plans differ in detail, the pools provide comprehensive medical coverage that includes in-hospital services, skilled nursing facility care, and prescription drugs. Although the pools are subsidized, even with the subsidy, premiums range from 125 to 200 percent of the state's average premiums. Costs in excess of the premiums are covered by a subsidy. The source of the subsidy varies by state, and includes state general revenues, a tax on hospital revenues, and assessments on health insurers. Most states fund their plans with an assessment on health insurers.

[11] By 2002, the following 32 states had created such pools: Alabama, Alaska, Arkansas, California, Colorado, Connecticut, Florida, Georgia, Idaho, Illinois, Indiana, Iowa, Kansas, Kentucky, Louisiana, Maine, Minnesota, Mississippi, Missouri, Montana, Nebraska, New Hampshire, New Mexico, North Dakota, Oklahoma, Oregon, South Carolina, Texas, Utah, Washington, Wisconsin, and Wyoming.

In addition, during the 1990s, many states passed "small-group reform" laws, which require insurers to offer plans to small groups on a guaranteed issue basis. The insurer may not exclude individual employees and may exclude preexisting conditions only for a limited period. Having met the preexisting conditions requirement in one plan, coverage must be "portable," that is, a new insurer may not impose a new preexisting conditions requirement. Rating rules limit the rate the insurer may charge and also limit annual rate increases. Insurers are allowed to nonrenew only for certain specified reasons.

Federal Legislation to Increase Access Federal legislation has been enacted to ensure, to some extent, access to health care.

COBRA The Consolidated Omnibus Budget Reconciliation Act of 1986 (COBRA) requires that employees and certain beneficiaries be allowed to continue their group health insurance coverage following a qualifying loss of coverage. The law applies to the employers with group plans covering 20 or more persons and permits continuation when coverage would otherwise end as a result of termination of employment, divorce, legal separation, eligibility for Medicare, or the cessation of dependent-child status. The employer must provide the coverage for up to 18 months for terminated employees and up to 36 months for spouses of deceased, divorced, or legally separated employees and for dependent children whose eligibility ceases. Generally, the COBRA participant pays a premium based on the existing group rate. Many states have COBRA-like laws that apply to employers with fewer than 20 employees.

The Health Insurance Portability and Accountability Act of 1996 (HIPAA) The second federal attempt to address access was the Health Insurance Portability and Accountability Act of 1996, also known as Kassebaum-Kennedy, which became effective on July 1, 1997. Although most states had already enacted small group and individual insurance reforms similar to those contained in HIPAA, HIPAA was significant because, for the first time, minimum federal standards were enacted for all plans nationally, including self-insured plans. HIPAA imposed reforms on the large group market (employers with more than 50 employees), the small group market (employers with 2 to 50 employees), and the individual market.

Reforms in the group market (both large and small) include guaranteed renewability, limitations on preexisting conditions, and portability. Preexisting conditions (defined as a medical condition diagnosed or treated within the previous six months) may not be excluded for more than 12 months. Credit toward satisfying the preexisting condition exclusion must be granted for prior coverage (with no gap greater than 63 days).

In the small group market (2 to 50 employees), insurers must provide all products on a guaranteed-issue basis and may not single out an individual in the group to be charged higher premiums or excluded from coverage. Insurers may use underwriting requirements such as minimum employee enrollment or minimum employer contribution levels.

In the individual market, policies must be guaranteed renewable. Also, certain *eligible individuals* must be given access to coverage in the individual market. An eligible individual is a person who has at least 18 months of prior health insurance coverage, with the most recent coverage being employer-provided, and no break in coverage greater than 63 days. HIPAA permits states to use one of two approaches in meeting this access requirement; the *federal fallback approach* (so-called because it applies if the state does nothing) and an *approved alternative mechanism*. Under the federal fallback approach, all insurers who operate in the individual market must offer eligible individuals a choice between at least two health plans. Most states (37 plus the District of Columbia) opted to use an approved alternative mechanism. The most common choice is a qualified high-risk pool (chosen by 22 states), which many states already had in place. Thirteen states implemented the "federal fallback" standards.

Significantly, the federal fallback standards did not contain rating reforms. Although insurers are required to provide individual insurance to eligible individuals, there is no limit on the premium they can charge. Not surprisingly, a GAO report issued in early 1998 questioned the effectiveness of the reforms in the federal fallback states, noting that many consumers who lost group coverage experienced difficulty obtaining individual market coverage or paid significantly higher rates for the coverage, reportedly up to 600 percent of the standard rate.

Efforts to Reduce Costs

Efforts to reduce cost have come mainly in the form of managed care initiatives that were pioneered by HMOs, but that have been adopted by other insurers.

Covering Alternative Sites of Care Originally, hospital insurance policies covered only care administered in a hospital. Today, most policies recognize that there may be less costly alternatives, but still appropriate, sites for delivering care. Policies are likely to cover outpatient surgery and ambulatory care. Birthing facilities are often covered as a less expensive alternative to in-hospital maternity care. Policies are also likely to cover care delivered in skilled nursing facilities, home health care, and hospice care (i.e., services to terminally ill patients, with emphasis on pain relief and other support).

Addressing Utilization A number of policy provisions adopted by insurers are designed to encourage the cost-effective delivery of care. *Second surgical opinion* programs will pay for the cost of a second opinion prior to surgery, with the belief that this might reduce the incidence of unnecessary surgeries. *Preadmission certification* programs require the insured to receive approval of the insurer prior to being admitted to the hospital for certain conditions. The object is to prevent unnecessary admissions for ailments that can be treated on an outpatient basis. Under a *concurrent review* program, the insurer reviews the care while the insured is in the hospital to determine whether continued hospitalization is necessary. It authorizes an appropriate length of confinement and may authorize more inpatient days if the patient's condition requires it. Many companies have *case management programs* under which cases that have very high medical expenses are reviewed individually, with an attempt to design a plan of care that will reduce overall costs. This plan may result in the insurer covering expenses that are otherwise excluded but that will result in the elimination of other unnecessary costs.

Medical Savings Accounts Medical savings accounts are a reform initiative that has been proposed as a way of reducing health care costs by giving consumers a stake in the level of expenditures.[12] The basic idea of the MSA is to allow individuals to make tax-sheltered contributions to a fund that is used to cover medical expenses. This fund is used with a high deductible health insurance policy and covers the expenses that fall within the policy deductible. It is hoped that MSAs will serve as an incentive to con-

sumers to control medical care expenses.

As a pilot experiment, HIPAA authorized up to 750,000 MSAs for employees of small businesses and self-employed persons who purchase high-deductible health insurance. This program (discussed later in this chapter) was scheduled to end in 2000, but has been extended through 2002.

THE HEALTH INSURANCE MARKET

The ability to segment the insurance market has created a multitiered system of coverage. Coverage is found in both the public and private sector, although public sector coverage is limited to particular categories of individuals.

The Public Sector

Persons whose health care financing is provided by government includes those covered by Medicare, Medicaid, and a new Children's' Health Insurance Programs (CHIP).

Medicare The Medicare program covers most persons over age 65 and disabled persons who meet specific eligibility requirements. Approximately 60 percent of Medicare-covered persons purchase private insurance to supplement the protection under Medicare. The Medicare program is discussed in greater detail later in the chapter.

Medicaid Title XIX of the Social Security Act, popularly known as Medicaid, is a federal–state program of medical assistance for needy persons that was enacted simultaneously with the Medicare program. It provides medical assistance to low-income persons and to some individuals who have enough income for basic living expenses but cannot afford to pay for their medical care. States administer the program and make the payments, which are then partially reimbursed by the federal government. The federal proportion of the cost is based on a formula tied to state per-capita income and varies from about 50 percent to 80 percent, with the poorest states receiving the greatest proportion.[13]

Child Health Assistance Program The Balanced Budget Act of 1997 (BBA-97) introduced a new

[12] The idea of Medical Savings Accounts has been around at least since 1965. See Thomas L. Wenck, "Financing Senior Citizen Health Care: An Alternative Approach," *Journal of Risk and Insurance,* vol. 32, no. 2, pp. 165–175.

[13] Medicaid is discussed later in the chapter.

Child Health Assistance Program (Title XXI of the Social Security Act), from fiscal year 1998 through fiscal year 2007. The law committed new federal spending of $24 billion over five years for children's health, with a total commitment to expend more than $48 billion for the initiative over the next 10 years. The funding will allow states to provide health insurance coverage to poor uninsured children who do not qualify for Medicaid. States can provide the coverage by expanding coverage under Medicaid or providing insurance under a *State Children's Health Insurance Program* or a combination of the two approaches. The federal funds can be used to purchase coverage under group health or individual insurance plans.

Federal CHAMPUS Program All active and retired military personnel and their dependents are eligible for medical treatment in any Department of Defense installation medical facility. In addition, the Department of Defense operates an insurance program called *Civilian Health and Medical Program of the Uniformed Services* (CHAMPUS) for those who cannot obtain required medical treatment at a military medical facility. In 2000 the CHAMPUS program covered approximately 8.4 million persons.

The Private Sector

As noted earlier, the vast majority of those insured in the private sector are covered by group insurance plans, usually sponsored by an employer. Generally, the choice of the insurer for such plans rests with the employer, not the employee covered under the plan. This is significant because the objectives of the employer and the employee may differ regarding the scope of coverage and the cost of the plan. The coverage in the private sector is provided by several types of insurers, including employers that self-insure.

ERISA Plans The largest group of workers covered by group plans consists of those covered by ERISA-exempted plans—that is, self-insured plans that are exempt from state regulation. It is estimated that more than two-thirds of large employers are self-insured, with programs covering over 60 million persons. Employers favor the ERISA preemption of state insurance laws because it allows them to avoid state premium taxes (usually 2 to 3 percent of premiums) and the costs associated with state-mandated benefits.

MEWAs Originally, the ERISA exemption from state regulation applied to self-insured plans of a limited number of large employers. Over time, smaller and smaller employers have shifted to self-insurance, often as a part of a *multi-employer welfare arrangement* (MEWA). Multiple employer welfare arrangements (MEWAs) are group programs that provide health and welfare benefits under the ERISA exemption. When Congress enacted the ERISA in 1974, it included a broad preemption of state regulation for employee benefit plans, specifically providing that states may not treat certain self-funded employee benefit arrangements to be insurance. The decision to exempt these plans from state regulation proved ill advised. After a number of MEWA failures due to the absence of regulatory oversight, the 1982 amendments to ERISA authorized states to regulate self-funded MEWAs.[14] The U.S. Department of Labor and the states now have concurrent jurisdiction for regulation of MEWAs. Unfortunately, due to the complex and confusing provisions of ERISA, there is still some ambiguity concerning regulatory responsibility for MEWAs. Although MEWAs generally self-insure their members' medical expense exposures, they may also purchase insurance from commercial insurers.

Capitating Health Care Providers Capitating health care providers include health maintenance organizations (HMOs) and provider-sponsored organizations (PSOs). HMOs insure an estimated 60.4 million persons, including about 8.7 million persons enrolled in HMOs operated by commercial insurance companies and 9 million enrolled in Blue Cross/Blue Shield HMOs. Because PSOs are relatively new, they presently insure a small number of persons.

Commercial Insurance Companies Private commercial insurance companies selling medical expense protection include property and liability insurers, life insurers, and monoline health insurers. These insurance companies cover about 78.4 million persons. This includes 38 million persons covered under fully insured

[14] In 1994, Secretary of Labor Robert Reich cited a General Accounting Office report showing that fraudulent MEWAs had left at least 398,000 health plan participants with more than $123 million in unpaid claims between January 1988 and June 1991. Reich went on further to say that "we have every reason to believe that problem has gotten worse since then." *Labor Secretary Reich Files Lawsuits to Raise Pressure on Fraudulent MEWAs,* Health L. Rep. (BNA). April 7, 1994.

group plans and 7.2 million persons covered under individual policies. The remainder are persons in programs that are fully or partially self-insured by employers and administered by insurance companies.

Blue Cross and Blue Shield Plans Blue Cross and Blue Shield organizations insure an estimated 67.1 million persons, a part of whom represent participants in employer self-funded plans that are administered by the Blue Cross and Blue Shield organizations.

Distribution of Insurance Buyers

Approximately 203.7 million persons, or slightly more than 70 percent of the population, are insured by the private sector. Government programs (Medicare and CHAMPUS) cover 46.1 million. Because there is some overlapping between private and government programs, the total insured population is about 249.9 million, or roughly 86 percent of the total population. About 38.7 million persons, or 13.8 percent of the population, are uninsured. Many uninsured persons receive reimbursement for medical expenses under the Medicaid program. Table 21.1 summarizes the distribution of the U.S. population according to the source of health insurance protection. Because there is some overlap among the categories, it is difficult to be precise in measuring the percentages of the population in each category. Self-insured plans, for example, are partially insured by commercial insurers. In addition, about 60 percent of those persons covered by Medicare also purchase private insurance.

THE INSURANCE PRODUCT

Medical expense policies are not standardized. There are, however, certain benefits that are common to all policies. For these common benefits, the major differences among plans is in the percentage of the costs that are paid.

Traditional Forms of Medical Expense Insurance

Traditional medical expense insurance available from private insurers is divided into four major classes: hospital expense coverage, surgical expense coverage, physicians expense coverage, and major medical coverage. Today, these four classes of coverage are generally merged into a single package of health care benefits.

TABLE 21.1 Distribution of Health-Insured Population

	Persons Insured (millions)	Percentage of Population
Insured coverage	143.0	50.83
Self-insured plans	60.7	21.57
Total private sector	203.7	72.40
Medicare	39.0	13.86
CHAMPUS	8.4	3.0
Total government	47.4	16.86
Total insured population	249.9	86.25
Uninsured	38.7	13.75
Medicaid	36.0	10.4
Total population	281.4	100.00

Base Plan Coverage Hospitalization, surgical expense coverage, and physician's expense coverage are generally written together and referred to as a base plan or sometimes as basic coverage. The coverage is provided in two ways: expense reimbursement contracts marketed by insurance companies, and service contracts, originally offered by Blue Cross and Blue Shield organizations. Either type may be written to cover the individual or an entire family.

Hospitalization Insurance Blue Cross service plans provide a semiprivate room in a participating hospital for a stated number of days, rather than a cash benefit. The number of days varies, but generally ranges from 70 to 365 days. If the subscriber desires a private room, he or she may reimburse the hospital for the difference between the cost of the private room and the charges paid by Blue Cross. The Blue Cross plan pays the hospital a fee for each day the subscriber is in the hospital, based on a pre-negotiated contract rate. Not all hospitals are members of Blue Cross, and when a subscriber is admitted to a nonmember hospital, the insured is reimbursed for the Blue Cross organization's cost of a semiprivate room in a member hospital.

Hospital expense policies offered by commercial insurers reimburse some or all of the cost of room and board when the insured is confined to a hospital. Like Blue Cross plans, coverage applies for a stated number of days. Early contracts paid a maximum daily benefit (e.g., $100, $200, or $300), with charges in excess of the daily benefit paid by the insured. Although this approach is still used, many policies have dropped the dollar limit and instead pay benefits based on "reasonable and customary" charges. Under this arrangement, the policy pays a benefit

based on the prevailing charges for hospitals in the region. These plans operate very much like service benefit policies.[15]

In addition to the room benefit, policies of both Blue Cross and commercial insurance companies cover incidental hospital expenses such as the use of the operating room, X rays, drugs, anesthesia, and laboratory charges. These services and facilities are generally referred to as hospital miscellaneous expenses or incidental hospital expenses.

Surgical Expense Insurance Two types of basic coverages pay for physicians' fees. *Surgical expense insurance* provides coverage for surgeons' fees, and *physicians' expense insurance* covers nonsurgical doctors' fees. Blue Shield plans cover surgical and physicians' services in much the same way that Blue Cross plans provide hospital benefits. Blue Shield organizations agree to pay the physician's usual, customary, and reasonable charges. Surgical expense contracts sold by insurance companies originally reimbursed the policyholder according to a schedule that assigned a dollar value to different types of operations, but most commercial insurers have switched to the "reasonable and customary" basis of coverage.

Usual, customary, and reasonable (UCR) charges means the *usual* fee charged by the provider for the particular service, the *customary* or prevailing fee in that geographic area, and a *reasonable* amount based on the circumstances. The usual, customary, and reasonable standard is a statistically determined value, based on surveys of what doctors and hospitals charge. The UCR level is set at a percentile of what providers charge. For example, if the UCR is set at the 85th percentile and the UCR for a particular operation is $1500, this means that 85 percent of doctors charge $1500 or less for the procedure. If the patient patronizes one of the 15 percent of doctors who charge more than $1500 for the procedure, the patient must absorb the difference.

Physician's Expense Insurance *Physician's expense insurance* (formerly called regular medical expense insurance) covers a physician's fees for nonsurgical care in a hospital, home, or doctor's office, usually with a limit per visit (e.g., $25 to $50) and a maximum number of calls per sickness or injury. This coverage is not written alone, but only as an adjunct to hospitalization or surgical expense coverage in a base plan.

Major Medical Policy The major medical policy is designed to provide coverage for catastrophic medical expenses. The distinguishing characteristics of the major medical policy is the high limit per loss and the relative absence of exclusions. Major medical policies are commonly written with a limit as high as $500,000 or $1 million. The policy maximum may apply to each accident or illness, or it may apply as a lifetime maximum. Some policies, especially group contracts, are written without a maximum limit on the amount payable. Some major medical policies include internal limitations, restricting the amount payable for specific types of expense (e.g., mental illness).[16] In general, however, major medical policies go beyond the usual health insurance contracts, providing payment for blood transfusions, prescriptions and drugs, casts, splints, braces and crutches, and durable medical equipment such as artificial limbs or eyes, and even the rental of wheelchairs.

A second characteristic of the major medical policy is its deductible, which may be $100, $200, $250, $300, $500, or even higher. The application of the deductible differs from contract to contract. Most policies make the deductible applicable to a time period, such as a calendar year. Under this form, the deductible applies only once per member of the family during the stated period. Other policies apply the deductible on a disability basis, requiring that the deductible be paid only once for any disability. Many policies have both individual and maximum family deductibles.

Finally, the major medical policy also requires the insured to share a part of the loss in excess of the deductible. For example, the insurance company may pay 80 percent of the loss in excess of the deductible, with the insured paying the other 20 percent. The insurer may pay a lower percentage for certain classes of expenses (e.g., mental illness). There is usually a cap on out-of-pocket costs borne by the insured—

[15] A third type of hospitalization coverage is the cash payment policy, which is also referred to—somewhat illogically—as a hospital indemnity policy. These contracts agree to pay a specified amount per day, regardless of expenses incurred, when the insured is hospitalized, up to a maximum number of days stated.

[16] The Mental Health Parity Act of 1996 (MHPA) barred health plans from imposing lower limits for mental illness than for other disorders. The requirements did not apply to group health plans of employers with not more than 50 employees or if their application would result in an increase in the plan's cost of at least 1 percent. The MHPA included a sunset provision under which the MHPA requirements expired on September 30, 2001.

commonly $2000 or $3000—beyond which the insurance pays 100 percent of covered expenses up to the policy limit.

Historically, major medical contracts were either *supplemental major medical policies* or *comprehensive major medical policies.* A supplemental major medical policy is written with a base plan and subject to a corridor deductible, which represents out-of-pocket expenses the insured must incur before the major medical plan applies. With the transition to managed care, medical expense insurance increasingly resembles the comprehensive major medical policy, which combines the best features of a base plan and the major medical contract into a single policy. Although some supplemental major medical policies still exist in the marketplace, the comprehensive major medical policy has become the standard approach that most insurers now follow.

Originally, comprehensive major medical plans applied the deductible and coinsurance provision to all covered medical expenses, including hospital and surgical expense. Current versions have eliminated the deductible for hospital charges, and sometimes for surgical charges as well. They provided for payment of these expenses without a coinsurance provision up to some specified maximum, with coinsurance applicable above this limit. The initial level of deductible-and coinsurance-free coverage—usually from $2500 to $5000 or $6000—reflects the base plan origins of these policies. A sample comprehensive major medical plan is depicted in Figure 21.1.

To illustrate the elements in the comprehensive major medical depicted in Figure 21.1 and the operation of major medical policies generally, assume that the insured under this program incurs expenses as follows

	Expenses	Insured Pays	Insurer Pays
Hospital and surgical expenses	25,000	2000	23,000
Rehabilitation therapy	13,000	500	12,500
Total medical expenses	38,000	2,500	35,500

The first $5000 in hospital and surgical expenses is covered without a deductible and without coinsurance. Expenses in excess of this initial $5000 are subject to 80 percent coinsurance, up to a $2000 out-of-pocket maximum. Expenses other than hospital and surgical expense are subject to the $500

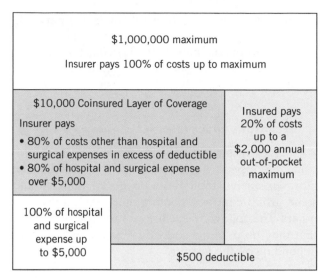

FIGURE 21.1 Comprehensive Major Medical

deductible and the 80 percent coinsurance provision. Because the insured's share of the hospital and surgical expense above $5000 satisfies the out-of-pocket maximum on coinsured losses, coverage for the rehabilitation therapy in the example is subject only to the $500 deductible.

HMO Contracts

In HMO contracts, hospital room and board and in-hospital physicians' medical and surgical services are provided on a fully prepaid basis with no limit on the number of days covered. In addition to these basic benefits, managed care plans often include additional benefits such as preventive care and checkups, well-baby care, and similar health care services.

Subscribers are encouraged to have regular medical checkups and see their physician as often as necessary. Outpatient services, such as visits to a doctor's office for diagnostic services, treatment, and preventive care (i.e., routine physical examinations) may be subject to a nominal co-payment charge (e.g., $10 or $15), with no limit on the number of visits. The co-payment charge is usually the same, regardless of the service rendered. Some HMOs provide prescription benefits as a part of the capitation fee. Prescriptions are usually subject to a $10 or $15 co-payment applicable to each 100-day supply of a drug. There is no lifetime maximum dollar limits under the coverage of an HMO.

Virtually all care is provided within the network. The major exceptions are when the primary care physician refers the patient to a specialist outside the network or when the subscriber requires emergency services.

Exclusions under Health Insurance Policies

All health insurance policies are subject to exclusions. Exclusions in individual policies tend to be more extensive than those in group policies and some group contracts contain more exclusions than others. The following exclusions are typical of those that may be in either individual or group contracts, depending on the insurer.

1. Expenses payable under workers compensation or any occupational disease law
2. Personal comfort items (e.g., television, telephone, air conditioners)
3. Elective cosmetic surgery
4. Routine medical care (e.g., annual physical exams, birth control, well-baby care)
5. Hearing aids and eyeglasses
6. Dental work
7. Experimental procedures
8. Expenses resulting from self-inflicted injuries
9. Expenses resulting from war or any act of war
10. Expenses incurred while on active duty with the armed forces
11. Services received in any government hospital not making a charge for such services
12. Expenses arising out of mental or nervous disorders. (Some policies cover mental and nervous disorders subject to a lower maximum or only for a percentage of the costs covered.)

Most policies contain limitations on coverage for preexisting conditions. These tend to be less restrictive in group policies, which are subject to the requirements of state small group reform laws and HIPAA.

Maternity benefits may or may not be included in individual contracts. If they are included, they usually have a specified maximum payment. It is also customary to include maternity benefits in individual contracts only after the dependent has been covered under the policy for 9 or 10 months.

Under group contracts, maternity benefits are usually covered on the same basis as any other condition.[17] The Newborn and Mothers Health Protection Act of 1996 (NMHPA) requires all health plans that provide maternity coverage to allow new mothers and their infants to stay in the hospital at least 48 hours after a normal birth and 96 hours after a Caesarian birth.[18]

Other exclusions not listed here may be found in the policies issued by a particular insurer. Similarly, some of the exclusions listed here may not be present. It is increasingly common for policies to cover preventive health care, such as annual physical exams. Each policy must be examined individually to determine the extent of the coverage.

Coordination of Benefit

With the increase in the two-income family, situations often arise in which a married couple will both be covered under medical expense policies provided by their employers. When an employer-provided policy includes coverage on dependents, one or both partners may be covered under two policies: the policy provided by their own employer and that provided by their spouse's employer.

Insurers developed the *coordination of benefits provision* to eliminate double payment when two policies exist and to establish a coverage priority for payment of losses. Under a standard coordination of benefits provision, if a wife is covered by her employer and as a dependent under her husband's policy, her policy applies before the husband's policy. The husband's policy pays nothing if the wife's policy covers the total cost of the expenses. Children are covered under the policy of the parent whose birthday is earliest in the year.

[17] The Pregnancy Discrimination Act of 1975 amended the Civil Rights Act of 1964 to prohibit employment discrimination with respect to pregnancy, childbirth, or related medical conditions. All employer-sponsored health and disability insurance plans must provide equal benefits for pregnancy-related conditions and other medical conditions.

[18] The *Taxpayer Relief Act of 1997* (TRA-97) prohibits a group health plan from giving rebates to mothers who shorten their hospital stays or reducing payment to health care providers who follow these timeframes. *IRC* Section 9811.

OTHER MEDICAL EXPENSE COVERAGES

Besides the various forms of medical expense coverage we have discussed, there are several other health contracts with which you should be familiar. In general, these contracts meet specialized needs or are limited contracts providing coverage for particular losses or losses from specific causes.

Limited Health Insurance Policies

Some health insurance contracts provide protection only for certain types of accidents or certain types of disease. They are referred to as limited policies and often bear the admonition on the face of the policy, "This is a limited policy. Read the provisions carefully."

Travel accident policies are a good example of the limited health contract. These policies cover situations if the insured is killed or suffers serious injury while a passenger on a public transportation facility; others provide payment in the event of death from an automobile accident.

The *dread-disease policy* is an example of a limited sickness policy. This contract provides protection against the expenses connected with certain diseases such as polio, cancer, meningitis, and others.

In general, limited health insurance contracts are a poor buy. More important, they represent a logical inconsistency and a violation of the principles of risk management. If the individual cannot afford the loss associated with any of the dread diseases covered under such policies, for example, he or she also cannot afford the loss associated with other catastrophic illness not so covered. Remember, a proper approach to risk management emphasizes the effect of the loss rather than its cause.

Dental Expense Insurance

Dental expense insurance is a specialized form of health expense coverage, designed to pay for normal dental care as well as damage caused by accidents. Most of the coverage is written on a group basis. It is offered by insurance companies, the Blue Cross and Blue Shield organizations, and dental service corporations, similar in nature to the blues. The blues and dental service corporations provide benefits on a service basis. The coverage may be integrated with other medical expense coverage (integrated plans)

or it may be written separately from other health care coverages (nonintegrated plans).

Dental expense coverage is written on a scheduled or nonscheduled basis. Scheduled plans provide a listing of various dental services, with a specific amount available for each. Unscheduled plans generally pay on a *reasonable and customary* basis, subject to deductibles and coinsurance.

Usually, dental expense insurance distinguishes among several classes of dental expenses, and provides somewhat different treatment for each. The coverage is usually subject to a calendar year deductible of $50 or $100 and a coinsurance rate that varies with the type of service provided. In addition, a dollar maximum per insured person is usually applicable on a calendar-year basis, except for orthodontia services, which may be subject to a lifetime maximum. A typical dental insurance plan might provide the following benefits with the indicated limits and coinsurance provisions:

Category	Limit	Deductible	Coinsurance
Preventive and diagnostic services	$1000 annual	none	90%/10%
Basic services	Included in annual	$100	80%/20%
Major services	Included in annual	$100	60%/40%
Orthodontia	$1000 lifetime	$250	50%/50%

Routine care and preventive maintenance are often covered without a deductible and with a modest coinsurance requirement, such as 90 percent. This part of the coverage includes payment for routine examinations and teeth cleaning once a year, full-mouth X rays once every three years, and topical fluoride treatments as prescribed. The absence of a deductible and low coinsurance provision is intended to encourage preventive maintenance. Basic services include endodontics, periodontics, and oral surgery, including anesthesia. These services are subject to a slightly higher coinsurance provision and to the annual maximum. Major services include restorative services, such as crowns, bridges, and dentures. These services are subject to still higher coinsurance requirements, usually in the range of 60 percent to 40 percent. Orthodontic care is subject to a separate maximum and a separate deductible, which may differ from the deductible for restorative care. It is also subject to the highest coinsurance provision, under which the insured is required to pay 50 percent of the cost of treatment.

Limited Policies—Prescription Drugs

Prescription drug insurance is a limited form of health insurance designed to cover the cost of drugs and medicines prescribed by a physician. The coverage is written on a group basis, often as an adjunct to other types of health care coverage. Coverage is written on a reimbursement basis, under which payment is made for the usual and customary charges for covered drugs and prescriptions. Often, there is a coinsurance or deductible arrangement, under which the insured is required to bear a part of the cost. The typical deductible is from $2 to $5 for generic drugs and from $5 to $20 for name-brand drugs. Today, among the most common is $5 for generic and $10 for name brand. Under an alternate approach, the coverage is subject to an annual deductible, such as $25 or $50. Coverage may be subject to an annual maximum.

An alternative to reimbursement coverage is coverage for prescription drugs from a service plan, which operates in a manner similar to the Blue Cross-Blue Shield organizations. Under this approach, the insurer makes payment directly to participating pharmacists or, sometimes, to a third-party administrator. When drugs or prescriptions are obtained from a nonparticipating pharmacy, payment is limited to the amount that would have been payable to a participating pharmacy. Coverage under both reimbursement plans and service plans typically excludes contraceptive drugs, dietary supplements, beauty aids, and cosmetics.

Medical Savings Accounts

Among the various changes in the health insurance scene enacted by HIPAA-96, one of the most potentially significant is the authorization for a limited number of *medical savings accounts* (MSAs). Medical savings accounts have long been proposed as a strategy that can reduce health care costs by discouraging utilization. By giving the consumer a stake in the level of expenditures, it is hoped that MSAs will encourage consumers to control medical care expenses. The idea of medical savings accounts has been around for more than three decades and fiercely debated by those who favor and those who oppose the concept.[19]

The basic idea of the MSA is to allow individuals to make tax-sheltered contributions into a fund to be used to cover medical expenses. Generally, this fund is used in connection with a high deductible health insurance policy and covers the expenses that fall within the policy deductible.

It is hoped that MSAs will serve as an incentive to consumers to control medical care expenses. Critics of MSAs argue that they may discourage people from seeking needed health care. They also argue that individuals with poor health are more likely to elect lower deductibles, while the healthier insured population will elect the MSA approach. In that case, premiums for low-deductible plans will increase and may become unaffordable for some insureds.

HIPAA-96 established a MSA pilot experiment for small business employees (50 or fewer employees) and self-employed individuals. The MSA pilot program was scheduled to end in the year 2000 or, if earlier, when the limit on the number of MSAs has been exceeded. In 2001, Congress extended the MSA pilot through 2002 and renamed the project in recognition of Representative Bill Archer (R-Texas). Medical savings accounts are now called Archer MSAs.

An individual is eligible for an MSA if he or she is covered under a high-deductible health plan and not under any other health plan that provides coverage for the same type of expenses under the high-deductible health plan. The high-deductible plan must be established by the employer of the individual or his or her spouse or by a self-employed person. In 2002, for individual-only coverage, the minimum deductible is $1650 and the maximum is $2500, with a $3300 out-of-pocket limit. For family coverage, the minimum and maximum are $3300 and $4950 and the out-of-pocket limit is $6050. These amounts have been adjusted for inflation since 2000.

MSA Contributions Generally, MSA contributions may be made by either an individual or an employer. If made by an employer, these contributions are excluded from the employee's income. If made by the individual taxpayer, the MSA contributions are deductible from income. An individual with an MSA may deduct an amount equal to the aggregate amount paid in cash into the MSA during the taxable year subject to a maximum limitation of 65 percent of the annual deductible for individual coverage and 75 percent of the annual deductible for family coverage. The MSA deduction cannot exceed an employee's compensation or a self-employed individual's earned income.

[19] The idea of medical savings accounts has been around at least since 1965. See Thomas L. Wenck, "Financing Senior Citizen Health Care: An Alternative Approach," *Journal of Risk and Insurance,* vol. 32, no. 2, pp. 165–175. Prior to enactment of HIPAA-96, 13 states had enacted MSA legislation and more than 40 had considered such legislation.

The procedure for establishing an MSA is similar to that for establishing an IRA. Any insurance company or bank can be an MSA trustee. In addition, any organization already approved by the IRS to act as an IRA trustee or custodian is automatically approved to act in the same capacity for MSAs. Eligible individuals and small employers may establish MSAs with qualified trustees and custodians without obtaining permission from the IRS.

MSA Distributions Distributions from an MSA that are used to pay for qualified medical expenses are not taxed to the MSA holder. In contrast, any distribution that is not used in this manner must be included in income. Further, any distribution that is includable in income is also subject to a penalty tax of 15 percent of the includable amount. Includable distributions received after an MSA-holder becomes disabled, dies, or reaches Medicare eligibility are not subject to the 15-percent penalty tax.

Funds may be rolled over from one MSA to another provided that the distribution is placed into the new MSA within 60 days of its receipt. MSA-to-MSA rollovers are permitted only once a year. Additionally, an MSA may be transferred without income taxation from one spouse to another if the transfer is incident to a divorce or separation.

At the death of an MSA holder, if a surviving spouse of the MSA holder is designated as the MSA beneficiary, the MSA is treated as if the spouse were the owner. If the MSA is acquired by anyone other than a surviving spouse, it ceases to be an MSA and the fair-market value of the assets in the MSA must be included in income.

Medicaid

Title XIX of the Social Security Act, popularly known as Medicaid, is a federal–state program of medical assistance for needy persons that was enacted simultaneously with the Medicare program. It provides medical assistance to low-income persons and to individuals who have enough income for basic living expenses, but cannot afford to pay for their medical care. The program is jointly financed by the federal and state governments. The federal government establishes regulations and minimum standards related to eligibility, benefit coverage, and provider participation and reimbursement. States have options for expanding their programs beyond the minimum standards, subject to federal criteria.

States administer the program and make the payments, which are then partially reimbursed by the federal government. The federal proportion of the cost is based on a formula tied to state per-capita income and varied from about 50 percent to 80 percent in 1998, with the poorest states receiving the greatest proportion.

Eligibility Federal statutes require state Medicaid programs to cover people who are receiving welfare payments or Supplemental Security Income (SSI), and persons who meet certain requirements that previously applied to the Aid to Families with Dependent Children (AFDC) program. Prior to enactment of the Personal Responsibility and Work Opportunities Act of 1996, individuals who received AFDC cash assistance were automatically eligible for Medicaid. In addition, various rules of the AFDC program were used to establish Medicaid eligibility for other Medicaid-only eligibility groups (e.g., pregnant women and children whose eligibility is related to the poverty level, optional groups of children and caretaker relatives who do not receive AFDC, and the medically needy.) The 1996 welfare reform law eliminates the AFDC cash assistance program and replaces it with a block-grant program called Temporary Assistance for Needy Families (TANF). However, families who met the AFDC eligibility criteria prior to welfare reform are eligible for Medicaid. In addition to SSI and AFDC recipients, federal legislation, beginning in 1984, expanded required coverage to individuals who are not receiving welfare payments or cash assistance. The expansions of coverage included certain low-income pregnant women, children under age six, and certain Medicare beneficiaries.[20]

Individuals can become eligible because their income is below the standard or they can "spend down" to Medicaid eligibility levels. A spend-down occurs when an eligible person has medical expenses that reduce income to below the payment standard. The spend-down can apply to both AFDC and SSI participants.

Medicaid Benefits Medicaid benefits are generally quite comprehensive. They include the services traditionally included in a commercial group-health-insurance package, as well as some services, such as

[20] The eligibility requirements for Medicaid are extensive and complex. Students who are interested in a more detailed description of eligibility requirements are referred to the Health Care Financing Administration (HCFA) Web site (http://www.hcfa.gov).

long-term care, that are not. As with eligibility, some benefits are federally mandated, while others are optional. The general-benefit package is fairly similar from state to state. The mandatory benefits required of all states include inpatient outpatient hospital services, physician services, rural health clinics, prenatal care, family planning, nurse midwife, early and periodic screening, diagnosis, and treatment (EPSDT) for children, laboratory and X-ray services, nursing facility for adults over 21, and home health care. Optional services that are not required by the federal statute, but that most states offer, include outpatient prescription drugs, prosthetic devices and hearing aids, intermediate care facilities for the mentally retarded, optometric services, eyeglasses, and dental services.

States can require certain recipients to share nominally in the cost of their Medicaid coverage through premiums, deductibles, co-payments, coinsurance, enrollment fees, or other cost-sharing provisions. However, significant cost sharing is prohibitive for recipients and is therefore prohibited by federal regulations. Cost sharing is limited to one form per service, and the state must specify and disclose all cost-sharing provisions to the federal government.

Efforts to control Medicaid costs have led many states to consider reductions or further limitations to covered services. Although a state cannot arbitrarily deny or reduce the amount, duration, or scope of care because of diagnosis or the type of illness or condition, it can restrict services to those that are medically necessary. States are permitted to incorporate reasonable utilization management provisions in their Medicaid programs. Some states have implemented fairly restrictive limits on the amount, duration, and scope of care without conflicting with the federal requirements.[21]

Child Health Assistance Program The Child Health Assistance Program (Title XXI of the Social Security Act), introduced by the Balanced Budget Act of 1997 was initiated by federal funding commit-

ment of $48 billion for the initiative over the ten-year period from 1998 through 2007. The funding will allow states to provide health insurance coverage to poor uninsured children who do not qualify for Medicaid. States can offer the coverage by expanding coverage under Medicaid or by providing insurance under a *State Children's Health Insurance Program* or by a combination of the two approaches. The federal funds can be used to purchase coverage under group health or individual insurance plans.[22]

State plans must be submitted to the Secretary of the U.S. Department of Health and Human Services (HHS) for approval, but the states will determine the eligibility of children and the benefits package under their *Children's Health Insurance Program*. The plan must maintain Medicaid eligibility for children that was in effect on June 1, 1997, and private insurers may not exclude coverage of otherwise-insured children who might be eligible for the new state program. Low-income children who are under 19 years of age and whose family income is below 200 percent of the federal poverty line and who are ineligible for Medicaid may be eligible for the state children's health program. Eligibility for assistance may not be denied based on preexisting conditions or diagnosis, although group health plans may limit services, as under current law. States must screen applicants for Medicaid eligibility and ensure that Medicaid-eligible children are enrolled in Medicaid.

The state plan must provide benefits equivalent to those provided in a benchmark plan (the standard Blue Cross/Blue Shield plan for federal employees, the largest commercial HMO in the state, or the state employee health plan) or coverage of benefits that have the same actuarial value as one of the benchmark packages. States may also propose another benefit plan for approval by the Secretary of HHS.[23]

Under a state children's health insurance plan, children with family incomes at or below 150 percent of poverty cannot be required to pay more than the

[21] The state of Oregon, in a revolutionary but controversial experiment, obtained a waiver that allows the state to cover a list of services, based on a ranking of the assessed value of each service. Various medical treatments are ranked according to their effectiveness and cost, and those that ranked low (e.g., life-saving measures for very-low-weight premature babies) will not be covered. State budget constraints determine which services will be covered, based on their ranking. Critics argue that this results in health care rationing to Medicaid recipients. Proponents counter that it is necessary to extend the benefits of Medicaid to all of Oregon's needy population at a cost the state can afford.

[22] Ninety percent of a state's allocation must be spent on health insurance, either through Medicaid or a new state program. Up to 10 percent can be spent on a combination of administrative costs, outreach programs, direct health services for children, and other children's health initiatives.

[23] States are not required to provide a mental health benefit under the new children's health insurance program, but if the benefit package is based on the actuarial value of one of the three benchmark plans, the children's plan must include 75 percent of any actuarial value for mental health coverage in the benchmark plan. In addition, mental health benefits must be subject to the same annual and lifetime aggregates as other illnesses.

premiums, deductibles, coinsurance, co-payments, and out-of-pocket institutional costs permitted for adults under Medicaid. Children with family incomes above 150 percent of poverty may be charged on a sliding scale developed by the state, but total charges may not exceed 5 percent of family income. Well-child, well-baby care, and immunizations must be exempt from all cost sharing.

BUYING HEALTH INSURANCE

Sometimes, the decisions relating to health insurance coverage of the individual and his or her family are simple: when the employer provides a noncontributory plan, there is no decision to make concerning that coverage. Usually the employee's only concern is whether the program provided is adequate for the family's needs or if a supplement is needed. Sometimes, when the option is provided, the individual may have to choose between a traditional form of health insurance and membership in a health maintenance organization. Such decisions are generally a matter of personal preference.

In those cases in which the employee must pay part or all of a group plan, or when the insurance must be purchased individually, there are several considerations, all of which serve to complicate the decision.

First-Dollar Coverages

During recent years, the first-dollar insurance coverages have been increasingly condemned as an improper application of the insurance principle. In the case of health insurance, this criticism may not apply. Because group insurance plans can achieve economies for participants through managed care and participation in a PPO network, the cost of health care acquired through an insurance plan is generally less expensive than when the same services are purchased by the individual consumer on a fee-for-service basis. For insurance obtained as a part of a large group, administrative fees are extremely modest and can be more than offset by the reduction in loss costs.

Taxes and Health Care Costs

Decisions regarding the purchase of first-dollar coverages are complicated to a certain extent by the federal tax code. As already noted, employer-paid premiums for employee health insurance are deductible as a business expense by the employer and are not taxable to the employee as income. The employee is not taxed on benefits received under such a program as specified reimbursement of medical expenses actually incurred.

For the individual, medical insurance premiums receive no special tax treatment. They are considered simply another medical expense that, combined with other medical costs, are deductible to the extent that the total exceeds 7.5 percent of the individual's adjusted gross income.

The Tax Reform Act of 1986 introduced a new tax deduction for medical expenses of the self-employed, allowing self-employed persons to deduct 25 percent of the cost of health insurance premiums from their gross income. Subsequent legislation increased this 25 percent to 70 percent by 2001, with the deduction increasing to 100 percent in 2003 and later years. The deduction is not available to a self-employed person who is eligible to participate in a subsidized health plan maintained by his or her spouse's employer.

THE FUTURE OF HEALTH INSURANCE

The Failure of Past Efforts

Despite these efforts, health care costs continue to rise, and the uninsured population continues to grow. (The number of uninsured is estimated to have increased from 32.6 million in 1988 to 38.7 million in 2000.) In addition, although the rate of growth in health care costs slowed in the late 1990s, it began to accelerate again in 2000 and 2001. The cost of health care continues to increase in the face of the efforts of the federal government, insurers, and managed care consultants. Although it can be argued that the situation would be worse without past efforts, the attempts that have been made to address the problems of the system have failed to correct its deficiencies. No single party is totally to blame, and none are totally free from blame.

Both the fee-for-service system and managed care contain built-in incentives to practice bad medicine. Under the fee-for-service system, the incentive is to provide unneeded services. Under the managed care approach, there is an incentive to deny needed services. Insurance companies and employers continue to support managed care as the most effective approach to cost control, but increasingly they are standing

alone. Although it is indisputable that the growth of managed care has had a positive effect on medical inflation, cost controls have come at a price.

The Attack on Managed Care

By 1999, the health care financing problem had become even more complex, as consumer dissatisfaction with the cost-saving features of managed care programs turned the focus of reformers to the quality of the health care being delivered. Managed care, which was once heralded as the solution that promised affordable health insurance to most Americans, became the target of a consumer backlash.

Managed care came into being out of a desperate need to cut health care costs. It was conceived as one answer to the increasing level of health care costs in the country. Measured against this goal, managed care has been reasonably successful in controlling utilization and associated costs, but the cost controls have been accompanied by changes in the traditional relationship between patients and providers. Physicians and hospitals have become disenchanted with the discounting arrangements of preferred provider organizations and other network organizations. Health care providers complained about the interference of "outsiders" in medical decisions, such as the appropriate hospital stay for a particular illness or procedure. Arbitrary decisions by the claims personnel of insurance companies and third-party administrators became the new crusade for consumer activists. The crusade was fueled by congressional hearings and daytime talk shows, where HMO patients recited horror stories about HMOs denying care to patients, resulting in serious injury or death. Newspapers and magazines attacked health maintenance organizations over the allegations of bonus payments to physicians for not treating patients and for blocking people from even seeing their doctors.

Patients' Bill of Rights Legislation Eventually, the debate culminated in legislative proposals to address patients' rights, which were introduced in Congress in 1998.[24] Democrats and Republicans offered different versions. Congress failed to reach agreement on a bill, and new versions were introduced in 1999 and again in 2000. In 2001, Congress again considered two versions of a patients' bill of rights. Senators John Edwards (D-N.C.), Edward Kennedy (D-Mass.), and John McCain (R-Ariz.), introduced the Democrats' bill, the *Bipartisan*

Patient Protection Act of 2001 (S 872). Companion legislation in the House was sponsored by Reps. John Dingle (D-Mich.), Greg Ganske (R-Iowa), and Charles Norwood (R-Ga.). The Republican bill, the *Bipartisan Patients' Bill of Rights Act of 2001* (S 889) was sponsored by Senators John Breaux (D-La.), Bill Frist (R-Tenn.), and James Jeffords (I-Vt.) and was supported by the White House.

Both bills included provisions to provide better access to physicians, coverage for services outside the network in case of emergencies that would cause a prudent person to seek medical care, increased information for patients, the elimination of "gag clauses" in contracts with participating physicians, and improved appeal processes for patients who have complaints.[25] The major difference in the legislation was the provision in the Democrats' *Bipartisan Patient Protection Act of 2001* to repeal a provision in ERISA that exempts employers and fiduciaries of employee benefit plans from tort liability in connection with such plans. The Democrat bill would allow suits against benefit plans in state courts and permit recovery for pain and suffering and punitive damages. The Republican bill would allow suits against benefit plans, under certain circumstances, for denial of coverage, if independent outside review held that the treatment should have been covered. Such lawsuits could be brought in federal court, but only after all internal and external review of the decision had been exhausted. Payment for noneconomic damages (pain and suffering) would be capped at $500,000 and punitive damages would not be allowed.

The right of patients to sue their HMOs and their employers and benefit plan fiduciaries over the denial of treatment has been the most divisive issue in the debate over the patients' bill of rights. Patients who receive what they consider to be substandard care want to sue someone, but have often found that their ability to sue their HMO or their employer is restricted by federal law. The reason is the ERISA preemption of

[24] State legislatures have been ahead of congress in the area of patients' rights, and many states have adopted "Patient Protection Acts" incorporating quality of care protections such as those embodied in the congressional proposals. At the time the first patients' bill of rights was introduced in congress in 1998, 14 states had mandated that managed care organizations provide an external review process. By 2002, the number had increased to 42.

[25] With respect to patients' rights generally, the legislation follows the general recommendations of an Advisory Commision on Consumer Protection and Quality in Health Care, appoined by President Clinton in 1997.

state law discussed earlier in the chapter. Congress established ERISA as an exclusive remedy for claims against employers and employee welfare plan fiduciaries. This ERISA preemption of state law[26] was included in ERISA primarily because Congress wanted to encourage employers to establish health plans and pension plans without being exposed to expensive litigation. The ERISA preemption, which was intended to protect *employers* and other *fiduciaries* from suit, made sense in 1974, before the growth of HMOs, where the fiduciary is also the provider of health care. When the fiduciary is also a health care provider (as in the case of an HMO), the issues become cloudy indeed. Nevertheless, many people, including some members of Congress, believe that the preemption may still make sense. There are instances in which the denial of a particular treatment is totally consistent with the terms of the plan. In this case, it is not a medical decision that is flawed, but the design of the plan. Extending the concept of tort liability to include decisions in the design of a health care plan, in the view of many, would open a Pandora's box with effect far worse than the present situation.

Proposals for National Health Insurance

Some critics of our current system point out that the one thing the United States lacks that every other industrialized country has is some form of national health insurance. These critics argue that the solution to the health care crisis in this country is a national health insurance program, coupled with more emphasis on coordinated planning of health services. Whether the United States is likely to have a national health insurance plan depends in part on how one defines national health insurance. Although many approaches have been suggested, most fall into three broad categories.

Single-Payer Plan One approach to a national health insurance scheme is a government-run and financed health insurance similar to Medicare, but applicable to the entire population. Under this approach, a universal system of comprehensive health insurance would be funded by taxes and administered by a federal agency. It would eliminate private health insurance and substitute a federal insurance system with benefits for hospital, dental,

optometric, home, and nursing care. The federal agency would establish a national budget for health care and set the fees paid to providers. One clear advantage of this approach is that it would supply universal coverage. Proponents also argue that it would be more efficient than the current privately financed system. Critics, on the other hand, argue that this approach would involve the most dramatic change from the current system and would result in a massive restructuring of the way health care is delivered, giving excessive control to a government agency. They believe this would ultimately reduce the quality of care, since the current price-based system of allocating health care would be replaced by another form of rationing. Finally, they argue that this dramatic change is not necessary to solve problems that affect only a few and point to the moderating rate of increase in private plans as evidence that the current system can be fixed.

Employer-Mandated Health Insurance A second group of proposals for reforming health care would build on the current employment-based system. In its basic form, employers would be required to provide health care for their employees or pay a payroll tax that would help fund benefits provided by a government program. This is often referred to as the *play-or-pay approach.* Persons who did not receive insurance from their employer may be required to purchase insurance either individually or from the government program.

Individual Mandates This approach places the burden for purchasing health insurance on the individual. All individuals would be required to purchase insurance for themselves and their dependents. They would be permitted to arrange this through their employment, other group plans, or individual insurance. Those who could not afford health insurance would be eligible for tax credits to subsidize the cost. Typically, this plan would also eliminate the current tax advantage of employer-provided plans, up to a certain level. A change in the tax treatment of employer-provided health insurance is intended to increase employee awareness and concern about price and encourage price competition across plans.

The Clinton Administration Health Security Act In 1993, President Clinton announced his health care reform program in the Health Security Act of 1993. It involved a variety of health care benefits, including not only universal health insurance coverage, but

[26] ERISA 514(a); 29 U.S.C. 1144(a).

long-term care benefits, Medicare drug benefits, and subsidies to low-income workers and their employers. Financing for the reforms was to come from savings in Medicare and Medicaid expenditures, a "sin" tax on tobacco, and savings in other federal programs.

Initially, the reaction to the plan was mixed. As might have been expected, legislators reacted to the proposed law following party lines, with Democrats generally praising the law and Republicans condemning it. Public reaction was also divided, with some constituencies expressing unbridled approval of the program and others rejecting it as unworkable. Gradually, as the details of the program were publicized and better understood, public opposition grew. As this opposition was communicated to the Congress, it became clear that the Clinton plan was not the solution to the problem.

The most objectionable feature of the Clinton plan was the proposal for *purchasing alliances* that would be operated as government monopolies (technically *monopsonies*). All consumers would have been required to purchase their health insurance through a single alliance operating in their area.[27]

[27] The purchasing alliances of the Clinton plan were based loosely on the idea of *health insurance purchasing cooperatives* or *HIPCs*, which were central to the *Consumer Choice Plan* developed by Professor Alain C. Enthoven. See Alain C. Enthoven, "Consumer Centered vs. Job Centered Health Insurance," *Harvard Business Review* (January-February 1979).

The public was also skeptical of the claim by the Clintons and their top health care strategist Ira Magaziner that the reforms included in the plan could be financed almost entirely from savings, without new taxes and with enough left over to reduce the federal deficit. Eventually, public opposition made it clear that the public was ready to wait for a different approach to solving the problems of the health care delivery and financing system.

The Future

Many people in the United States believe that a comprehensive national health insurance program for all Americans is an idea whose time has come. Regardless of whether some form of national health insurance is eventually adopted, however, one point is clear: our health-care financing system will continue to change. The pressure of health care costs, both for the individual and for society as a whole, will force us to take steps to deal with the problem.

The challenge in designing a health care system to meet the nation's future needs is to somehow reconcile two competing objectives. Ideally, we would have a system that provides quality health care to everyone who needs it, while at the same time containing costs at a level society can afford. Unfortunately, there is no simple solution to this problem, and the health care debate will continue into the future.

IMPORTANT CONCEPTS TO REMEMBER

fee-for-service benefits
service benefit contract
reimbursement contract
usual, customary, and reasonable (UCR) contract
surgical-expense contract
benefit schedule
physician's expense insurance
major medical policy
coinsurance
corridor deductible
comprehensive major medical
health maintenance organization (HMO)

capitation
primary care physician
gate keeper
preferred provider organization (PPO)
point-of-service (POS) plan
cost containment
coordination of benefits provision
dental expense insurance
medical savings accounts
Medicaid
first-dollar coverage
single-payer plan
insurance-encouraged utilization

defensive medicine
cost shifting
mandated benefits
Consolidated Omnibus Budget Reconciliation Act (COBRA)
Health Insurance Portability and Accountability Act (HIPAA)
small-group reform
employer-mandated health insurance
individual mandates
physician hospital organization (PHO)
national health insurance

QUESTIONS FOR REVIEW

1. Identify the major problems associated with health care listed in the chapter. What measures have been taken in the past to address these problems?

2. Compare and contrast the typical provisions and benefits of a commercial hospitalization policy with a Blue Cross contract, and a commercial surgical expense contract with a Blue Shield contract.

3. Explain what is meant by an ERISA-exempt health insurance plan. Why are these plans popular with employers?

4. Briefly describe the distinguishing characteristics of a comprehensive major medical policy.

5. Give reasons for the coinsurance feature and the deductible in the major medical policy. Are both really necessary?

6. Briefly describe the distinguishing characteristics of a health maintenance organization (HMO). How does an HMO differ from the other insurers operating in the health insurance field?

7. To what do you attribute the rapid increase in the number of HMOs throughout the country?

8. In what ways does the operation of the private insurance mechanism complicate the problem of health care access?

9. To what extent can the provisions of the tax code influence the decision to insure or retain the health care exposure? Your answer should include a discussion of the provisions of the code with respect to

a. Employer-paid medical expense insurance

b. Premiums paid by the individual for medical expense insurance

c. Costs incurred directly by the individual for health care

10. Explain what is meant by the term *limited health insurance policies*. To what extent do such contracts violate the rules of good risk management?

QUESTIONS FOR DISCUSSION

1. Movie audiences cheered when the heroine in the movie *As Good as It Gets* referred to her HMO with an expletive. Do you agree or disagree with the sentiment expressed by the audiences? Why?

2. Briefly explain the basic features of each of the three approaches that have been suggested for a national health insurance plan. Which do you prefer, and why?

3. In a 1999 survey, a significant percentage of physicians stated that they would misrepresent a patient's symptoms to an insurer if the misstatement would result in payment for treatment that would otherwise be denied. In your opinion, is this a positive or a negative phenomenon?

4. State mandates are intended to spread the cost of covering certain procedures such as infertility treatments. Do you agree or disagree with the exemption of ERISA plans from these mandates?

5. "Much of the increase in the cost of medical care can be attributed to unnecessary and undesirable overutilization of health services, often prompted by the existence of insurance." Do you agree or disagree? What policy provisions have been designed to control overutilization of health services?

SUGGESTIONS FOR ADDITIONAL READING

Ahmad, Khurshid, et al. "Long Term Care: An Insurance Industry Perspective," *Journal of the American Society of CLU/ChFC,* 62 (March 1992).

Beam, Burton T., Jr., and John J. McFadden. *Employee Benefits,* 4th ed. Brookfield, Wis.: Dearborn Financial Publishing, Inc., 1996.

Black, Kenneth, Jr., and Harold D. Skipper, Jr. *Life Insurance,* 13th ed., Englewood Cliffs, N.J.: Prentice-Hall, 2000. Chapters 19, 20.

Bowen, Howard R., and James R. Jeffers. *The Economics of Health Services.* New York: General Learning Press, 1971.

Crowell, Michael J., and Walter H. Hoskins. *AIDS, HIV Mortality and Life Insurance.* Itasca, Ill.: Society of Actuaries, 1987.

Eilers, R. D. *Regulation of Blue Cross and Blue Shield Plans.* Homewood, Ill.: Richard D. Irwin, 1963. Chapters 1–5, 8–11.

Enthoven, Alain C. "Consumer Centered vs. Job Centered Health Insurance." *Harvard Business Review* (Jan.–Feb. 1979).

Gorham, William. *Medical Care Prices:* A Report to the *President.* Washington, D.C.: U.S. Department of Health Education, and Welfare (Feb. 1967).

Health Insurance Association of America. *Group Life and Health Insurance Parts A and B,* 5th ed. Washington, D.C.: Health Insurance Association of America, 1994.

———. *Group Life and Health Insurance Parts C,* 4th ed. Washington, D.C.: Health Insurance Association of America, 1994.

Richardson, Elliott L. *A White Paper: Toward a Comprehensive Health Policy for the 1970's.* Washington, D.C.: U.S. Department of Health, Education, and Welfare (May 1971).

Rosenbloom, Jerry S., ed. *The Handbook of Employee Benefits: Design, Funding and Administration,* 4th ed. Homewood, Ill.: Richard D. Irwin, 1996.

U.S. Bipartisan Commission on Comprehensive Health Care. *Access to Health Care and Long-Term Care for All Americans,* Recommendations to the Congress, 101st Congress, 2d Session, Washington, D.C.: U.S. Government Printing Office, 1990.

WEB SITES TO EXPLORE

American Association of Health Plans	http://www.aahp.org
American Association of Managed Care Providers	http://www.aapso.com/
Association of Health Insurance Advisors	http://www.ahia.net/
Blue Cross/Blue Shield Association	http://www.bluecares.com/
Centers for Medicare and Medicaid	http://cms.hhs.gov/
Consumer Insurance Guide	http://www.insure.com/health
Health Care Financing Administration	http://www.hcfa.gov/
Health Insurance Association of America	http://www.hiaa.org
Insurance News Network	http://www.insure.com/
International Association of Health Funds	http://www.fhf.com/
Managed Care Magazine	http://www.managedcaremag.com/
Medicare	http://www.medicare.gov/
Money Magazine	http://www.pathfinder.com/money/depts/insurance/
National Senior Citizens Law Center	http://www.nsclc.org/
Quicken InsureMarket	http://www.insuremarket.com/

HEALTH INSURANCE FOR THE ELDERLY

■

If I'd known I was going to live so long,
I'd have taken better care of myself.

MICKEY MANTLE

CHAPTER OBJECTIVES

When you have finished this chapter, you should be able to
- Describe the benefits provided by the traditional Medicare program
- Explain how Medicare supplement policies dovetail with traditional Medicare coverage
- Explain the alternatives to the traditional Medicare coverages that were added to the Medicare program by the Medicare+Choice coverage options
- Describe the features of long-term care insurance
- Identify and briefly explain the alternatives to long-term care insurance
- In general terms, identify the qualification requirements for Medicaid and explain the way in which the Medicaid program provides for financing of long-term care needs
- Explain what is meant by Medicaid planning and describe the legislative restrictions that have been imposed on the process

In this chapter, we turn our attention to health insurance for the elderly. We believe that the health insurance needs of the elderly, and the manner in which it is provided, are sufficiently different from the needs and health insurance options for the population generally to justify a separate discussion.

Because they often need more extensive care than other members of society, and because their resources are often limited, senior citizens face special problems in the area of health care costs. Three broad types of coverage exist for insuring the health care needs of the elderly:

- Medicare
- Medicare supplement (or Medigap) policies
- Long-term care insurance

These three distinct forms of coverage developed over time, and represent pieces of the health insurance programming puzzle for older persons. In addition to these forms of social and private insurance, the federal Medicaid program also provides financing for the health care needs of senior citizens.

Medicare is a federal social insurance program enacted by Congress in 1965 to address the problem facing senior citizens in the area of health care financing. Although the program provides extensive benefits, it is subject to both deductibles and coinsurance provisions. To fill the gaps between the cost of medical care and the reimbursement under Medicare, commercial insurers and Blue Cross and Blue Shield organizations have developed special policies, usually called *Medicare supplement policies* or *Medigap* policies.

Medicare and Medicare supplement policies provide coverage for a wide range of health care–related costs. They do not, however, cover long-term care, which is yet another exposure facing senior citizens. Although Congress considered including long-term care in the Medicare program, the idea was rejected, and Medicare provides coverage only for intermittent care and for periods of limited duration. Long-term care insurance developed in response to the need of senior citizens for protection against the catastrophic costs of nursing homes and other types of custodial care.

Because the Medicare program applies to virtually ally all persons over 65, it serves as the foundation of health care coverage for the elderly. We will begin our discussion of health insurance for senior citizens with a brief overview of this government social insurance program.

MEDICARE

The Social Security Act of 1935 stands as the most comprehensive piece of social legislation of its kind in the history of this country. It became an even more significant feature in our national social environment in 1965 when it was amended to include the Medicare Program. The Medicare program became effective on July 1, 1966. It introduced two forms of essential health insurance to virtually all citizens over 65 and to certain disabled persons. The first coverage, designated Part A, is compulsory hospitalization insurance, financed by payroll taxes levied on employers and employees. Part B is voluntary medical insurance, designed to help pay for physicians' services and other medical expenses not covered by Part A. This supplementary coverage is financed by monthly premiums shared by the participants and the federal government.

Although the Medicare program provides comprehensive health insurance to most persons over 65, its recent history has been characterized by efforts to "save" it from the financial difficulties that have afflicted it because of the growing number of beneficiaries and the increases in health costs generally. The 1997 Annual Report of the Medicare Trust Fund trustees stated that, barring some change in the finances of the program, the Medicare Trust Fund would be broke by the year 2001. In the wake of that report, Congress enacted the most recent effort to "save Medicare"—*The Balanced Budget Act of 1997* (BBA-97). The BBA-97 introduced the most significant changes in the Medicare program since its inception in 1965. BBA-97's provisions included both changes in financing and in the coverage options. It is anticipated that the spending reductions will keep the Medicare Hospital Insurance Trust Fund solvent to 2010. The growth in Medicare spending was slowed by $115 billion over 5 years, from 1998 to 2002. Of the anticipated $115 billion savings, $100 billion came from reduced payments to hospitals, physicians, home health care providers, and medical equipment suppliers. Medicare beneficiaries also bore a part of the cost reduction.[1]

In addition to changes in the financing of Medicare that are designed to address the program's solvency, the BBA-97 added a new Medicare option, Medicare Part C, also known as Medicare+Choice. Because Medicare+Choice is a new alternative to the traditional Medicare program, we will begin with a discussion of that traditional program.

The Traditional Medicare Program

Eligibility Almost all persons 65 or over are eligible for Part A—Hospital Insurance—under the

[1] For additional information on Medicare, see the Web site for the Centers for Medicare and Medicaid at http://www.medicare.gov/default.asp and the Web site for the Health Care Financing Administration (the former designation of the Centers for Medicare and Medicaid at http://www.hcfa.gov/.)

Medicare portion of OASDHI.[2] *Medicare Part A* is financed by part of the Social Security payroll tax paid by workers and their employers, and by self-employed persons. Persons who are entitled to benefits under Social Security or the Railroad Retirement system, or who worked long enough in federal, state, or local government employment to be insured, do not pay any premium for Part A. In addition to those over 65, all persons who have received OASDI disability benefits for at least two years are entitled to Medicare benefits. Finally, chronic kidney patients requiring dialysis or renal transplant, who are fully and currently insured or who are dependents of a fully and currently insured worker, are also eligible for Medicare Part A coverage.[3]

Persons who are eligible for Part A of Medicare have the option of purchasing *Part B,* supplemental medical insurance (SMI). SMI is a voluntary coverage financed jointly by monthly premiums paid by persons who elect the coverage and a contribution for each participant by the federal government. Enrollment is automatic for the elderly and disabled as they become eligible for hospital insurance, but they are given the opportunity to decline the coverage. For the 12-month period beginning January 1, 2002, the Medicare Part B premium was $54.[4] Although the purchase of Part B is not required, most individuals do purchase the coverage, which is subsidized to the extent of about 70 percent of the program costs. Even persons who do not qualify for premium-free Part A, can generally purchase Part B if they are 65 years of age or older.

Medicare Enrollment Periods The initial enrollment period for Part B and premium Part A runs for 7 months, beginning 3 months before the month in which the individual reaches age 65. If a person does not enroll during this initial 7-month period, he or she must wait until the next *general enrollment period.* These enrollment periods occur each year, from January 1 through March 31. Coverage begins the following July 1.

Premiums for both Part A and Part B generally will be higher if the individual waits to enroll during a general enrollment period. The Part B premium goes up 10 percent for each 12 months the individual delays after the initial enrollment period. This means, for example, that a person who waits for, say two years before enrolling in Part B will pay a 20-percent higher premium. For persons who pay a Part A premium, the increase is 10 percent, regardless of the delay period.[5]

Employer Group Medicare Coverage Under certain circumstances, persons who are eligible for Medicare but who are still employed must be given the option of enrolling (with their spouses) in their employer's health insurance plan. Federal law requires that employers with 20 or more employees must also offer the same health benefits, under the same conditions, to employees age 65 or over and to their spouses who are 65 or over, that they offer to younger employees and spouses. Employers must also offer health care coverage to employees' spouses who are between 65 and 69, even if the employee is under age 65. The employee may accept or reject coverage under the employer group health plan. If the individual accepts the employer plan, it will be the primary payer and Medicare becomes excess. If the individual rejects the plan, Medicare will be the primary payer for Medicare-covered health services that he or she receives. If the employee rejects the employer plan, an employer cannot provide a plan that pays supplemental benefits for Medicare-covered services, nor can it subsidize such coverage. An employer may, however, offer a plan that pays for health care services not

[2] The amendment that added Medicare extended coverage to almost all persons who reached age 65 before 1968, regardless of whether they were entitled to retirement benefits. The requirement for Part A of Medicare is now the same as for old-age retirement benefits (i.e., fully insured).

[3] The 1972 amendments permit the aged who are not eligible for Medicare to enroll in Part A of the program by voluntarily paying a monthly premium. The premium was initially $33 a month in 1972. The monthly Part A premium in 2002 is $175 for persons who had had at least 30 quarters of Medicare-covered employment but fewer than 40 quarters and $319 for persons with fewer than 30 quarters or no quarters of covered employment. Because the premium is based on the full cost of hospital care for a high-risk group and is automatically adjusted, it will continue to increase. In addition to persons over 65 who do not qualify for Part A, disabled persons who were previously entitled to Medicare under the disability provisions but whose benefits have been terminated because of work and earnings, but whose disability continues can also purchase Part A.

[4] Historically, Part B premiums have increased according to the cost-of-living adjustments in Social Security. The BBA-97 scheduled accelerated increases to $67 a month in the year 2002, but the change generated so much opposition that it was repealed.

[5] Under some circumstances, a beneficiary can delay Medicare enrollment without penalty. A person age 65 or older who has group health insurance based on his or her current employment (or the employment of a spouse) may enroll during the eight-month period beginning with the month he or she stops working or is no longer covered under the employer plan, whichever comes first. If the individual does not enroll during the eight-month period, he or she must wait until the next general enrollment period.

covered by Medicare, such as hearing aids, routine dental care, and physical checkups.[6]

Medicare Cost Controls The cost of the Medicare program has been a problem for Congress since the program began in 1965, and the Social Security Administration has conducted a continuing campaign to control costs. Medicare limits the reimbursement for services to the lower of the reasonable cost determined under Medicare, or the customary charges to the general public. Since 1984, payments to hospitals under Medicare have been determined under the *prospective payment system (PPS),* based on *diagnostic-related groups (DRGs).*[7] Under this system, the hospital is paid a flat amount based on the patient's diagnosis, rather than an amount that varies with the number of days the patient is hospitalized. The flat amount is based on the *average* resource use for the patient's diagnostic-related group. It is hoped that this will give hospitals an incentive to provide care efficiently, since they are not compensated for excessive use of health care resources.[8]

In addition to the limits on payments to hospitals determined by DRGs, payments to doctors are also subject to cost controls. The 1989 changes in Medicare revised the Medicare physician payment system and instituted the *Resource-Based Relative Value Schedule (RBRVS).* The schedule is based on a value scale that measures the time, training, and skill required to perform a given service, adjusted for overhead costs and geographic differences. The new fee schedule was phased in over the period 1992 through 1997.

Part A—Hospital Insurance Coverage The basic benefits under the Hospital Insurance coverage fall into four broad categories: (1) hospital care, (2) care in a nursing home or extended care facility, (3) home health services, and (4) care in a hospice.

Hospital Insurance (Part A) Benefits Medicare Part A helps pay for medically necessary inpatient care in a general hospital, skilled nursing facility, psychiatric hospital, or hospice care. In addition, Part A pays the full cost of medically necessary home health care and 80 percent of the approved cost for wheelchairs, hospital beds, and other durable medical equipment (DME) supplied under the home health care benefit. Coverage is also provided for blood after the first three pints, when furnished by a hospital or skilled nursing facility during a covered stay.[9]

When the beneficiary is hospitalized, Medicare will pay for all covered hospital services during the first 60 days of a benefit period, except for the deductible. The Part A deductible in 2002 was $812 per benefit period. A benefit period begins the day the beneficiary is hospitalized. It ends after the beneficiary has been out of the hospital or other facility that primarily provides skilled nursing or rehabilitation services for 60 days in a row. If the beneficiary is hospitalized after 60 days, a new benefit period begins. With each new benefit period, Part A hospital and skilled nursing facility benefits are renewed, except for any lifetime reserve days or psychiatric hospital benefits used. There is no limit to the number of benefit periods a beneficiary can have for hospital or skilled-nursing-facility care.

In addition to the deductible, if the beneficiary is hospitalized for more than 60 days in a benefit period, he or she is responsible for a share of the daily costs. For the sixty-first through the ninetieth day, Part A pays for all covered services except for coinsurance, which is paid by the beneficiary. In 2002, the coinsurance for the sixty-first through the ninetieth day was $203 a day.

Under Part A, beneficiaries have a lifetime reserve of 60 days for inpatient hospital care. These lifetime reserve days may be used whenever the individual is in the hospital for more than 90 days in a benefit period.

[6] The Tax Equity and Fiscal Responsibility Act of 1982 required employers with more than 20 employees to offer workers between ages 65 and 69 the choice of enrolling in the corporate plan or sticking with the federal Medicare program for their health care coverage. If these older workers had spouses who also were between 65 and 69, employers had to offer the corporate health care plan to the spouses. The Deficit Reduction Act of 1984 further requires employers to offer health care coverage to employees' spouses who are between 65 and 69 even if the employee is under age 65.

[7] Medicare DRGs are derived by taking all possible diagnoses identified in the International Classification of Diseases system, classifying them into major diagnostic categories (MDCs) based on organ systems, and further breaking them into distinct groupings (DRGs).

[8] Provisions in the system allow hospitals to receive additional payments for outliers—patients who remain significantly longer than the average or incur significantly greater than average costs.

[9] The 1988 amendments to the Social Security Act, the Medicare Catastrophic Coverage Act (MCCA), substantially expanded the benefits under Medicare, but the changes in the law were repealed before they became effective. The MCCA significantly expanded Medicare Part A and Part B benefits effective January 1, 1989, and January 1, 1990, respectively. The MCCA also established a new Medicare supplemental premium, based on the individual's taxable income. In November 1989, responding to a public outcry against the legislation, Congress voted over-whelmingly to repeal the law.

Once used, the reserve days are not renewed. When a reserve day is used, Part A pays for all covered services, except for coinsurance of $406 a day in 2002.

Medicare Part A helps pay for no more than 190 days of inpatient care in a Medicare-participating psychiatric hospital in the individual's lifetime. Once the 190 days have been used, Part A does not pay for inpatient care in a psychiatric hospital. Psychiatric care provided in a general hospital, rather than in a psychiatric hospital, is not subject to the 190-day limit. Persons who are patients in a psychiatric hospital on the first day of their entitlement to Medicare are subject to different limitations with respect to inpatient psychiatric care. For these persons, inpatient care in a psychiatric care facility is subject to the same terms and conditions as other Medicare inpatient hospital care.

Skilled Nursing Facility Care Medicare Part A can help pay for up to 100 days of skilled care in a skilled nursing facility during a benefit period. All covered services for the first 20 days of care are fully paid by Medicare. All covered services for the next 80 days are paid by Medicare, except for a daily coinsurance amount. The daily coinsurance in 2002 was $101.50. Persons who require more than 100 days of care in a benefit period are responsible for all charges beginning with the 101st day.

Coverage for care in a skilled nursing facility is limited to the special kind of facility that primarily furnishes skilled nursing and rehabilitation services. It may be a separate facility or a distinct part of another facility such as a hospital. A skilled nursing facility is different from a nursing home, and Medicare will not pay for the confinement if the services received are primarily personal care or custodial services, such as assistance in walking, getting in and out of bed, eating, dressing, bathing, and taking medicine.

Home Health Care Medicare pays the full cost of medically necessary home health visits by a Medicare-approved home health agency. These services are usually provided on a periodic basis by a visiting nurse or home health aide. To qualify for coverage, the individual must require intermittent skilled nursing care, physical therapy, or speech therapy, be confined to his or her home, and be under a physician's care. There is no deductible or coinsurance, and no prior hospitalization is required for home health care benefits. Coverage is also provided for a portion of the cost of *durable medical equipment (DME)* provided under a plan of care set up and periodically reviewed by a physician.

To help extend the solvency of the Medicare Part A Trust Fund, the BBA-97 shifted a portion of home health care spending from Medicare Part A to Medicare Part B Payments for home health care that follow a three-day hospital stay or a skilled nursing facility stay will remain in Part A (up to 100 visits per spell of illness). Home health visits that do not follow a 3-day hospital or skilled nursing facility stay and visits beyond 100 per spell of illness will be moved to Part B. The transfer of costs from Part A to Part B will be phased in over a period of 6 years from 1998 to 2003.

Hospice Care Medicare pays for *hospice care* for terminally ill beneficiaries who choose to receive hospice care rather than regular Medicare benefits for management of their illness. Under Medicare, hospice is primarily a program of care generally provided in the patient's home by a Medicare-approved hospice. The focus is on care, not cure. Medicare Part A covers hospice care for individuals with a life expectancy of six months or less. Benefits are provided for up to two 90-day periods, plus one 30-day period, plus one extension period of unlimited length.

Part B—Supplementary Medical Insurance The coverage under the supplementary medical insurance is much like a major medical contract. Benefits begin after a deductible ($100 in 2002), and nothing is paid until this initial expense has been met by the insured. Medical insurance pays 80 percent of the covered expenses in excess of the deductible, provided that the charges are *reasonable* (based on customary and prevailing charges). Covered expenses include the following:

1. Physicians' and surgeons' services, no matter where rendered, including those in a hospital, clinic, doctor's office, or even in the home

2. Home health services, even if the insured has not been in the hospital, up to 100 visits during the calendar year

3. Diagnostic tests, surgical dressings, splints, and rental or purchase of medical equipment

4. All outpatient services of a participating hospital, including diagnostic tests and treatments

In addition to the foregoing expenses, medical insurance will pay 100 percent of the cost of radiological and pathological services when the insured is an inpatient in a participating hospital. These

expenses are not subject to the deductible or coinsurance provision.[10]

Although Part B generally does not cover outpatient patient prescription drugs, it does cover some oral anti-cancer drugs, certain drugs for hospice enrollees, and drugs that cannot be self-administered but are provided as part of a physician's services. Certain drugs furnished during the first year after an organ transplantation and epoetin for home dialysis patients are also covered, as well as antigens and vaccines for flu, pneumococcal, and hepatitis B. Coverage is also provided for blood after a three-pint annual "deductible." Note that both Part A and Part B of Medicare cover blood, and if the beneficary meets the three-pint blood deductible under one part it need not be met under the other part.

Since 1991, Medicare Part B has provided coverage for screening mammography—the radiological procedure used for the early detection of breast cancer in women. The BBA-97 expanded access for Medicare beneficiaries to preventive services, including screening mammography, pelvic exams, pap smears, prostate and colorectal cancer screening, vaccines for influenza and pneumonia, and diabetes self-management. Although some of the tests will be available only for those at high risk for the disease, other tests may be obtained regularly without the Medicare deductible requirement.[11] The BBA also makes reimbursement for telemedicine available to individuals residing in rural areas.

Besides the deductible and coinsurance, the individual may have additional out-of-pocket costs if the physician or medical supplier does not *accept assignment* of the Medicare claim and charges more than

Medicare's *approved amount.* The difference to be paid is called the *excess charge.*

Assignment refers to the arrangement in which a physician agrees to accept the Medicare-approved amount as full payment for services and supplies covered under Part B. If the physician does not agree to accept assignment, Medicare imposes a maximum (called the limiting charge) on the amount a physician may charge a Medicare beneficiary for a covered service. The limit on these excess charges is 15 percent above the fee schedule amount for nonparticipating physicians (which is 95 percent of the amount for participating physicians who accept assignment). This means that when the physician refuses to accept assignment, the beneficiary must pay 20 percent of the approved amount (which is 95 percent of the approved amount for physicians who accept assignment), plus the amount of any excess charges, which are limited to 15 percent above the fee schedule amount for nonparticipating physicians.

Besides avoiding excess charges, another advantage of using physicians or suppliers who accept assignment is that they are paid directly by Medicare, except for the deductible and coinsurance amounts, for which the beneficiary is responsible. Physicians who do not accept assignment collect the full amount of the bill from the patient. Medicare then reimburses the beneficiary for its share of the approved amount for the services or supplies received. Regardless of whether physicians and suppliers accept assignment, they are required to file the Medicare claim for the beneficiary.

Physicians who do not accept assignment for elective surgery are required to give the patient a written estimate of the cost before the surgery if the total charge will be $500 or more. If the written estimate is not provided, the patient is entitled to a refund of any amount paid in excess of the Medicare-approved amount. In addition, a nonparticipating physician who provides services that he or she knows or has reason to believe Medicare will determine to be medically unnecessary (and thus will not pay for), is required to inform the patient in writing before performing the service. If written notice is not given, and the patient did not know that Medicare would not pay for the service, the patient cannot be held liable for payment for the service.

[10] The 1990 changes in the law eliminated a 210-day limit that had applied to hospice benefits if the physician recertifies that the individual is terminally ill.

[11] Annual mammograms are available to all women who are eligible for Medicare and over the age of 40, without having to meet the Part B deductible. Annual pap smears and pelvic exams will be available to high-risk women, while non-high risk women will have coverage provided every third year. Screening for colon cancer will be available to all beneficiaries over age 50 on a frequency to be determined by the secretary of Health and Human Services. Also added by the BBA-97 are new coverages for diabetes outpatient self-management training services, blood-glucose monitors and testing strips, and expanded coverage of bone-mass measurement for high-risk beneficiaries. Annual prostate-cancer screening tests (previously not covered at all by Medicare) are available to male Medicare beneficiaries over age 50 from the year 2000 and after.

Traditional Program Medicare Supplement Policies

Although enactment of the Medicare program in 1965 greatly reduced the need for individual health policies for persons over 65, the Medicare program is subject to both deductibles and coinsurance provisions. To fill the gaps between the cost of medical care and the reimbursement under Medicare, commercial insurers and Blue Cross and Blue Shield organizations have developed special policies—usually called Medicare supplement policies or Medigap policies. Unfortunately, abuses developed in the sale of these contracts. Some contracts sold as supplements to Medicare have been both overpriced and inadequate in the protection they provide. In addition, a small number of unscrupulous agents have preyed on older people, selling them multiple policies with duplicate coverage. As a result, both the states and the federal government have enacted legislation to regulate the sale of Medicare supplement policies.

Regulation of Medigap Insurance Most states adopted an NAIC model act for regulating the sale of Medicare supplement policies, with provisions relating to both sales practices and policy benefits. Despite these laws, however, abuses persisted. In 1990, as part of the *Omnibus Budget Reconciliation Act* (OBRA), Congress enacted measures to encourage the states to regulate Medicare policies more rigidly. Among other standards, in an effort to deal with the myriad of policy types that consumers faced, OBRA required the NAIC to promulgate a "core" of basic benefits that must be included in all Medigap policies, plus not more than nine optional benefit packages that may be added to the core benefits. In any state that fails to adopt the model legislation proposed by the NAIC, the federal standards will apply.

Standard Medigap Contracts Responding to the federal mandate, the NAIC set standards for 10 levels of coverage under Medicare supplement policies. The standard Medigap policies are assigned letter designations ranging from *A* through *J,* with Plan *A* being the most limited and Plan *J* the most comprehensive. Plan *A* comprises the basic benefits core of five coverages:

1. Reimbursement for insured's share of hospital charges (coinsurance) under hospital insurance (Part A coverage) for days 61 through 90 and days 91 through 150
2. Coverage for all charges for an additional 365 days in hospital
3. Reimbursement for Hospital Insurance blood deductible (3 pints)
4. Reimbursement for Medical Insurance (Part B) blood deductible (3 pints)
5. Reimbursement for insured's 20-percent share of expenses covered under Part B

Each of the other nine plans includes the basic package plus a different combination of additional benefits, as indicated in Table 22.1. Insurance companies may not change the combination of benefits or the letter designations of any of the plans.

TABLE 22.1 Medicare Supplement Policies

Benefits Included	Plan									
	A	B	C	D	E	F	G	H	I	J
Basic Medicare supplement benefits	yes	yes	yes	yes	yes	yes	yes	yes	yes	yes
Hospital deductible ($812 in 2002)		yes	yes	yes	yes	yes	yes	yes	yes	yes
Skilled-Nursing-Facility Coinsurance, days 21–100 ($101.50 in 2002)		yes	yes	yes	yes	yes	yes	yes	yes	yes
Emergency care while traveling overseas			yes	yes	yes	yes	yes	yes	yes	yes
Doctors' services deductible ($100 in 1994)			yes			yes				yes
Excess doctors' charges					100%	80%		100%	100%	
Health care services provided at home				yes			yes		yes	yes
Prescription drugs—$250 deductible, 50% coinsurance							$1250	$1250	$3000	
Preventive medical care					yes					yes

Each state must allow the sale of Plan A and all Medigap insurers must make Plan A available if they are going to sell any Medigap plans in a state.[12] Although not required to offer any of the other nine plans, most insurers offer several plans to pick from, and some offer all 10 plans. Insurers can independently decide which of the optional plans they will sell, as long as the plans they select have been approved for sale in the state.

The limitation on the number of plans and the standardization of plans from insurer to insurer is designed to make it easier for consumers to make informed choices. Medigap insurers must use the same format, language, and definitions in describing the benefits of each of the Medigap plans and must use a uniform chart and outline of coverage to summarize the benefits. Because each company's products are alike, insurers must compete on the basis of service, reliability, and price.

Other Federal Standards In addition to the standardizing policies, OBRA also requires that state regulation of Medicare supplement policies meet the following standards.

- Medigap insurers must accept all applicants for coverage within the first 6 months after they enroll in Medicare after age 65, regardless of their health. No one can be rejected because of illness, injury, or a preexisting condition.
- Preexisting conditions may not be excluded. A probationary or waiting period for preexisting conditions may not exceed 6 months.
- A waiting or probationary period may not apply to a policy that is purchased to replace a similar existing one.
- Medigap policies must be guaranteed renewable.
- The benefits under Medigap policies that are designed to cover cost-sharing features of Medicare must change automatically to coincide with any changes in the Medicare deductible and coinsurance percentages. Insurers are permitted to change the premiums to reflect the changes in coverage.

- The contract must provide coverage for accident and sickness on the same basis, and may not include any exclusions, limitations, or reductions that are not consistent with the exclusions, limitations, or reductions permissible under Medicare.
- Selling duplicative policies is prohibited. Insurance agents are required to obtain, in writing, a statement from the buyer about his or her eligibility for Medicare and whether he or she has other Medicare supplement insurance.[13]
- Insurers must achieve a minimum loss ratio of 65 percent on individual Medigap policies and a 70 percent loss ratio on group policies.

Finally, in addition to the other requirements, Federal law requires the seller to deliver a *Medicare Supplement Buyer's Guide* to purchasers. Buyers are granted a *30-day free look,* during which the policy can be canceled and returned for a full refund.

Unlike some types of health coverage that restrict where and from whom the insured can receive care, Medigap policies generally pay the same supplemental benefits regardless of the beneficiary's choice of health care provider. If Medicare pays for a service, wherever provided, the standard Medigap policy must pay its regular share of benefits.[14]

Medigap Premiums Although the benefits are identical for all Medigap plans of the same type, the premiums may vary from one company to another and from area to area. Insurance companies use three different methods to calculate premiums: issue age, attained age, and no-age rating. Under the issue age method, the premium varies with the insured's age at which the contract was purchased, but does not increase as the insured becomes older. Under the attained age method, the premium is based on the

[12] Some states have limited the number of plans available in the state. For example, Delaware does not permit the sale of Plans C, F, G, and H, and Vermont prohibits the sale of Plans F, G, and I. Medigap plans sold in Minnesota, Massachusetts, and Wisconsin are different from those sold in other states. This is because these states had alternative Medigap standardization program in effect before the federal legislation standardizing Medigap was enacted. Therefore, these states were not required to change their Medigap plans.

[13] Although OBRA-90 made it illegal to sell seniors policies that duplicate coverage they already have, Congress amended this provision in 1994, establishing new rules that allow the sale of duplicate coverage. Under the 1990 law, retirees with inadequate health coverage from a former employer could not supplement it by buying a Medigap policy, because some of the coverages would overlap. Under the rules enacted in 1994, insurers can market policies that overlap with Medicare but are required to disclose the fact. Further, the insurer cannot deny coverage based on the duplication.

[14] Medicare Select Policies are an experiment authorized by OBRA-90. The only difference between Medicare Select and standard Medigap insurance is that under Medicare Select policies insureds must use a preferred provider organization (except in emergency situations) to receive full benefits. Originally, Medicare Select policies were available only in 15 states. Congress extended authorization for Medicare Select policies to all 50 states in 1995.

insured's current age and increases as he or she grows older. Under no-age rating, everyone pays the same premium regardless of age.

Medicare and Medicaid Recipients State Medicaid offices offer two programs that are designed specifically to help certain low-income Medicare beneficiaries meet their health care costs. One is called the *Qualified Medicare Beneficiary (QMB) program* and the other is called the *Specified Low-Income Medicare Beneficiary (SLMB) program.*

The QMB program pays Medicare's premiums, deductibles, and coinsurance amounts for certain elderly and disabled persons who are entitled to Medicare Part A, whose annual income is at or below the national poverty level, and whose savings and other resources are very limited.

The SLMB program is for persons entitled to Medicare Part A whose incomes do not exceed the national poverty level by more than 20 percent in 1998. Persons who qualify for assistance under the SLMB program receive a subsidy in which the state pays their Medicare Part B premium. SLMB-eligible persons remain responsible for Medicare's deductibles, coinsurance, and related charges.

Traditional Medicare Program and HMOs As an alternative to receiving benefits under Medicare Parts A and B and purchasing a Medicare Supplement policy, some Medicare beneficiaries have the option of enrolling in a federally approved HMO. In this case, the beneficiary does not require a Medigap policy, since the HMO plan will cover the Medicare deductibles and coinsurance.[15]

In August 1997, more than 5.5 million Medicare care beneficiaries were enrolled in a total of 398 managed care plans, accounting for 14 percent of the total Medicare population. The Medicare and Medicaid programs combined make HCFA the largest purchaser of managed care in the country, accounting for about 19 million persons. According to HCFA, the majority of Medicare beneficiaries in managed-care plans are concentrated in six states: Arizona, California, Florida, Hawaii, New York, and Oregon.

HCFA contracts with HMOs have been of two types: *risk contracts* and *cost contracts.* HMOs operating under either approach are required to provide all of the Medicare benefits generally available in the plan's service area. They may also provide additional benefits, depending on the contract with the HCFA. Risk-contract plans have been paid a per-capita premium set at approximately 95 percent of projected average expenses for fee-for-service beneficiaries in the area. Cost plans have been a paid a predetermined monthly amount per beneficiary based on a total estimated budget. Adjustments to that payment are made at the end of the year for any variations from the budget.[16]

Medicare+Choice

A major initiative in the BBA-97 was the introduction of the Medicare+Choice option for beneficiaries (also called Medicare Part C), which some have characterized as the "privatization" of the Medicare system. Medicare beneficiaries may continue to participate in the program's traditional fee-for-service program, or they may elect one of several alternatives to the traditional Medicare program. These new options may be classified into three broad categories.

- Coordinated care plans
- Private fee-for-service Medicare
- Medical Savings Accounts (MSAs)

Except in the case of MSA plans, Medicare+Choice plans must provide the same services and benefits (other than hospice care) as are covered under Parts A and B of original Medicare. MSA plans must provide reimbursement for items and services covered under Parts A and B after the beneficiary reaches the deductible. In addition, Medicare+Choice Plans, other than MSA plans, will be required to pass on to beneficiaries in the form of additional benefits any "savings" they achieve because their costs are less than the Medicare payment. As defined by BBA-97, the "additional benefits" include both the health care services covered under the plan that are in addition to regularly covered Medicare services and any reductions in premiums or cost-sharing for Medicare covered services. Plans may also offer

[15] HMOs with a point-of-service (POS) option allow participants to go outside the plan, but will pay only a part of the charges and the participant is responsible for the part of the cost that is not paid by the POS plan.

[16] Under the BBA-97, HCFA is precluded from entering into new HMO risk-sharing contracts after the date it establishes standards for Medicare+Choice plans and cannot renew risk contracts after January 1, 1999. HCFA cannot enter into any cost contracts after August 5, 1997, the date of enactment of the BBA, although contracts may be renewed through the end of 2002.

supplemental benefits for which they charge a separate premium, though the premium may be combined with the premium representing the charge for Medicare copayments and deductibles.

Goals of Medicare+Choice The goal of the Medicare+Choice initiative is to contain costs in Medicare by injecting private competition into the system and encouraging more beneficiaries to enroll in managed care plans. Health care in the United States has been transformed by the HMO-based managed care plan and Medicare+Choice is an attempt to move Medicare in the same direction.

Observers speculate that at least initially, most beneficiaries will elect to stay in the traditional fee-for-service Medicare plan. Over time, however, the other options, which may offer more benefits at a lower cost, might attract an increasing number of beneficiaries. Some authorities have suggested that the Medicare+Choice option will create a multi-tiered system within Medicare, in which wealthy beneficiaries will opt for fee-for-service, healthy individuals will shift into managed care plans, and sicker and more expensive beneficiaries will stay in the traditional fee-for-service plan.

Coordinated Care Plans As used in the BBA-97 and now in the Medicare program, *coordinated care plans* consist of what have traditionally been referred to as *managed care plans.* They include but are not limited to health maintenance organzation plans (with or without POS options), preferred provider organization plans, and plans offered by provider-sponsored organizations (PSOs). HMOs and PPO-like arrangements were previously available as Medicare options, but PSOs will be new. Also new to Medicare is the Religious Fraternal Benefit Society plan, a type of coordinated care plan offered by a religious fraternal benefit society. Coverage is offered only to members of a church, convention, or affiliated group and all members must be allowed to enroll without regard to health status.

Health Maintenance Organizations Prior to the BBA-97, the Medicare program permitted only managed care plans that are state-licensed HMO or POS plans to participate in its private plan option. POS plans were added in 1996 and allow beneficiaries to go out of the HMO network for care, but with higher cost sharing.

Preferred Provider Organizations Under Medicare+Choice, the PPOs will contract directly

with Medicare. Generally, a group of providers will form their own network, like an HMO, to enroll and treat beneficiaries for a fixed amount. These plans will provide Medicare benefits independent of insurance companies.

Provider-Sponsored Organizations PSOs are provider-owned and sponsored ventures that operate much like HMOs. In some instances, the PSO enters into a full-risk contract with an existing licensed HMO. In other instances, the PSO may seek to contract directly with employers or government payers, simultaneously assuming the risk and responsibility for providing health care services. BBA-97 includes provisions establishing PSOs as an alternative to federally qualified HMOs and competitive medical plans for Medicare beneficiaries.

A major concern is whether the PSOs will be regulated by the states like other health-financing organizations, or if they will be exempt from such regulation. Currently, states differ in their regulation of PSOs. Most states require that a PSO be licensed as an HMO. A few states do not require any direct government oversight. Several states have adopted laws regulating PSOs in a category distinct from other managed care entities such as HMOs, indemnity insurers, and health services corporations.[17]

HCFA was required to publish rules relating to the solvency and capital adequacy of PSOs by April 1, 1998, which it did. BBA-97 also created a federal waiver process, under which a PSO could seek to be exempt from state solvency regulation if a state attempts to impose solvency requirements that exceed the federal requirements. The waiver process expired January 1, 2001.

Operational Aspects of the Coordinated Care Option To choose managed care, Medicare recipients will file an enrollment form with a particular plan, and HCFA will contribute a Medicare+Choice capitation amount directly to that plan. To be eligible for enrollment in a Medicare+Choice plan, a beneficiary must participate in both Part A and Part B of the Medicare program. Individuals with end-stage renal disease are ineligible to participate in the new

[17] To bring some consistency to this patchwork, the National Association of Insurance Commissioners has established the CLEAR (Consolidated Licensure of Entities Assuming Risk) program to develop a series of model laws on health plan regulation. The premise of CLEAR is to regulate entities performing the same or similar functions under the same rules.

Part C choices. Beneficiaries who fail to make an election will remain in the traditional Medicare fee-for-service program.[18] A Medicare+Choice plan may not deny enrollment to an eligible individual based on health status or other factors described by HIPAA.

Initially, beneficiaries who enroll in a Medicare+Choice plan will be allowed to change to another plan monthly. Eventually, this movement between managed care and fee-for-service—and between managed care plans—will be restricted. Beginning in 2003, beneficiaries may disenroll from a Medicare+Choice plan and choose another plan or return to Medicare fee-for-service only one time during the first three months of the calendar year. Beneficiaries will be effectively locked in to their Medicare+Choice plan for the remaining nine months.

Payments to Organizations The secretary of Health and Human Services (HHS) will make advance monthly payments to coordinated care plans for each individual covered by the organization under Medicare+Choice. The payment will be made from the Federal Hospital Insurance Trust Fund and the Federal Supplementary Medical Insurance Trust Fund in the proportion that the secretary of HHS determines reflects the relative weight that benefits under Part A and under Part B represents to the actuarial value of the coordinated care plan benefits.

The payment will be 1/12 of the annual Medicare+Choice capitation rate for the particular area. The BBA-97 changed the capitation rate formula for payment to coordinated care plans. The previous system had been criticized for perpetuating wide payment disparities to HMOs based on local differences in fee-for-service spending. The new payment formula increases payments to HMOs in rural counties and other low-cost areas where rates are below the national average and reduces future payment increases in high-payment urban areas. Local payment rates are blended with a national average payment rate, gradually phased in over 6 years to a blend of 50 percent local and 50 percent national, which is intended to reduce the wide geographic disparity in

payments.[19] Plans will receive a minimum payment increase of 2 percent annually. The BBA-97 sets a national minimum payment floor of $367 per beneficiary per month. Rates in many rural areas have been below $300 per month.

Coordinate Care Plan Patient Protection Provisions The BBA-97 added several patient-protection requirements for beneficiaries dealing with Medicare managed care plans. These include full disclosure, emergency services, quality assurance, appeals and grievance procedures, and a gag-rule prohibition. The term *gag rule* refers to the policies reportedly adopted by some managed care organizations that forbid their doctors from recommending or mentioning certain types of treatment because the treatment may be expensive.

Private Fee-For-Service In addition to "original" fee-for-service, BBA-97 allows Medicare beneficiaries to enroll in a private indemnity insurance plan offering unrestricted use of participating physicians. The plans will pay providers a specified amount for each service, and physicians will be limited to charging their patients up to 15 percent above the plan's payment. Medicare will make monthly payments to these plans to cover traditional Medicare benefits and the participating Medicare beneficiaries will pay the difference between the full cost of coverage and the Medicare payment. There will be no limit on the premiums that insurers can charge beneficiaries.

Private Contracts Outside Medicare In addition to the provision for Medicare+Choice Private-Fee-for Service option, Section 4507 of the BBA-97 allows doctors to opt out of Medicare and to enter into private contracts with beneficiaries to provide Medicare-covered services at a rate set by the doctor. Neither the beneficiary nor the physician will be able to obtain Medicare reimbursement for the services. In exchange for the right to charge a fee in excess of 115 percent of the Medicare-approved rate, the doctor is barred from participating in the Medicare program for two years.

The original Medicare act did not specifically forbid private contracting, but HCFA policies and subsequent changes to the Medicare law have worked

[18] The BBA-97 required HCFA to conduct a special campaign in November 1998 to educate beneficiaries about the new Medicare+Choice options and the new election procedures. Thereafter, HCFA will conduct an annual coordinated election period during which all Medicare beneficiaries will have to choose between the traditional Medicare program and one of the Medicare+Choice options.

[19] The blending began in 1998 with a 90 percent local and 10 percent national weighting. The local component drops by 8 percentage points per year (e.g., 82 percent-18 percent blending in 1999) until the blending becomes 50 percent local and 50 percent national in 2003.

toward eliminating the practice. In the late 1980s, HCFA threatened doctors with fines if they administered Medicare-covered treatment to Medicare beneficiaries without sending the bill to the government. The controversy eventually ended in the courts, where the case was dismissed.[20]

The argument over private contracting is based on HCFA's contention that private contracting will undermine Medicare's cost-control efforts. The opposing argument is that individuals should have the right to contract outside the Medicare system without penalty.[21]

Medical Savings Accounts

The BBA-97 introduced an option that has been widely discussed and that many believe has the potential to produce positive results—the *Medicare Medical Savings Account (MSA)*. Under a demonstration project, up to 390,000 Medicare beneficiaries will be able to establish an MSA to pay for qualified medical expenses.[22] Beneficiaries who choose this option will purchase a high-deductible (up to $6000) catastrophic health insurance policy to accompany their medical savings account.

For individuals with a new MSA plan, the contribution to the Medicare+Choice MSA on behalf of the individual for the first month and all successive months in the year is to be deposited during that first month. The BBA-97 requires that the secretary of HHS establish a procedure for the recovery of deposits attributable to the remaining months of the year if the MSA election is terminated before the end of a year.

Medicare contributions will be used to pay the premium for the high-deductible/catastrophic plan, with any remainder deposited into the beneficiary's

MSA. The catastrophic plan will provide coverage for at least the services that are available under Medicare Parts A and B, after the deductible has been met. Interest accrued and withdrawals from an MSA to pay medical expenses will not be taxable. However, withdrawals for nonmedical purposes will be subject to income tax, and in some circumstances, a 50 percent penalty. The 50 percent penalty applies to withdrawals that reduce the MSA fund below 60 percent of the annual deductible for the high-deductible policy. However, if a beneficiary allows the amount in the account to accumulate to more than 60 percent of the annual deductible level, the amounts above 60 percent can be withdrawn penalty-free for any purpose (although these amounts would be treated as taxable income). Thus, over time, Medicare dollars could be used for any consumer purchase.

Medicare+Choice Medicare Supplement Insurance

The BBA-97 added a new guaranteed-issue requirement for Medicare supplement plans, which is designed to allow persons returning to regular Medicare from a Medicare+Choice plan to enroll in a Medigap plan without the imposition of preexisting-condition exclusions. Effective for policies issued on or after July 1, 1998, Medigap policies must guarantee issue within six months of an individual's attainment of age 65 or making other allowed changes in coverage. The individual must seek enrollment in a Medigap policy not later than 63 days after the date of the termination of enrollment in a previous plan. If the beneficiary was enrolled in the previous plan for a period of less than six months, and if the policy excludes benefits based on a preexisting condition, the preexisting-condition exclusion must be reduced by the applicant's period of previous continuous coverage. The provision applies to Medigap/Medicare supplement policies that have a benefit package classified as Plan A, B, C, or F under existing Medigap standard policy provisions.

The BBA-97 also added two additional benefits to the 10 standard packages by specifying that a high deductible feature is added to Plans F and J. A high deductible feature is one that requires the beneficiary of the policy to pay annual out-of-pocket expenses (other than premiums) before the policy begins payment of benefits, and covers 100 percent of covered out-of-pocket expenses once such a deductible has been satisfied in a year. The deductible amount for

[20] *Stewart v. Sullivan,* 816 F. Supp. 281 (D.N.J., 1992).

[21] Senator Jon Kyl (R-AZ) and Representatives Bill Archer (R-TX), and Bill Thomas (R-CA) have introduced legislation known as the *Medicare Beneficiary Freedom to Contract Act of 1997,* aimed at changing the provision in Section 4507 of the BBA-97. The House bill, HR 2497, is cosponsored by Reps. Bill Archer (R-TX), chairman of the House Ways and Means Committee, and Bill Thomas (R-CA). The Senate bill is S 1194. Both bills would remove the 2-year Medicare claim filing limitation.

[22] Enrollments in Medicare+Choice MSAs will not be allowed after the number of persons enrolled reaches 390,000 or after January 1, 2003. The secretary of HHS is required to report to Congress no later than March 1, 2002, on whether the time limit for enrollment in MSAs should be extended or removed and whether the numerical limit should be ended.

1998 and 1999 was $1500, and will be increased by the CPI in subsequent years.

The Future of Medicare

Whether the changes in the Medicare program enacted by the BBA-97 will have a positive effect on the program's costs remains to be seen. The transition to a managed care environment and the new MSAs have both advocates and critics. As we noted earlier, some observers have argued that the changes are likely to create a multitiered Medicare program, with healthier persons enrolling in the new options, and those with health problems remaining under the traditional Medicare program.

Although the Congressional Budget Office predicts that the BBA-97 changes will ensure the solvency of Medicare through 2007, the longer-range problem remains. Future Medicare cost increases will reflect more beneficiaries, increases in the cost of medical services, and increases in the utilization and intensity of medical services. Beginning in 2010, the demographic shift that will occur with the retirement of the baby-boom generation is projected to significantly exacerbate the expected imbalance between expenditures and revenues. After that point, a larger proportion of our population will be eligible for Medicare, and a correspondingly smaller percentage will be paying the taxes that support the Health Insurance (HI) trust fund.

The 1997 Medicare Trustees Report made two recommendations. The first was that prompt, decisive, and effective action be taken to ensure short-term HI trust fund solvency. The BBA-97 was the congressional response to this recommendation. The second recommendation was the establishment of an advisory group to address long-term solvency. In response, Congress included a provision in HIPAA establishing a new 17-member *National Bipartisan Commission on the Future of Medicare,* which was to report to Congress with recommendations for restoring financial solvency of the Medicare Trust Funds, establishing an appropriate financing structure for Medicare and creating the appropriate balance of benefits and beneficiaries' contributions.

The Commission was scheduled to issue its report to the Congress and the Administration by March 1, 1999. U.S. Senator John Breaux (D-La.) and U.S. Representative Bill Thomas (R-Calif.) jointly chair the commission. The Commission missed the 1999 deadline and could not garner the necessary majority to forward a recommendation for its main proposal, a *premium support program* based on the Federal Employee Health Benefits Program.

Prescription Drugs An additional issue facing the Medicare system and its elder beneficiaries is the high cost of prescription drugs and the absence of coverage under Medicare for such drugs. When Medicare was enacted in 1965, the central core of health care treatment consisted of hospital inpatient procedures. The development of several hundred new medicines since 1965 has changed the focus of modern medicine to rely more on pharmaceuticals to treat and prevent illnesses. As a result, there has been agitation for expanding basic Medicare coverage to include prescription drugs. During the presidential election of 2000, the issue of prescription drug coverage under Medicare was hotly debated. Democrats pushed for legislation to add prescription drugs to the Medicare benefit package, while Republicans argued for a need-based program. Seldom mentioned during the debate is the fact that two-thirds of the nation's 40 million Medicare beneficiaries already have outpatient prescription drug coverage (from an employer, under a Medicare Supplement policy, or through a Medicare HMO).

In January 2001, Senator Tom Daschle (D-S.D.) and Edward Kennedy (D-Mass.) introduced the Medicare Prescription Drug Coverage Act of 2001. The bill would add a new Part D (Outpatient Prescription Drug Benefit Program) to Medicare. Coverage for prescription drugs would be provided subject to a $250 deductible (waivable for generic drugs) and a sliding co-payment provision. A 50 percent co-payment would be required on the cost of drugs up to $3500, 25 percent up to $4000, and no co-payment for the cost of drugs above $4000.

Senators Breaux (D-La.) and Frist (R-Tenn.) have sponsored two proposals to address the problem of access to prescription drugs for seniors, referred to as Breaux-Frist I and Breaux-Frist II. Breaux-Frist I, introduced in 1999, was an ambitious reform program that would have allowed Medicare beneficiaries to buy health insurance—including prescription drugs—from the traditional Medicare program or from private insurers. The more recent proposal, Breaux-Frist II, would give Medicare beneficiaries a subsidy to buy supplemental coverage, including coverage for prescription drugs, from private insurance companies and HMOs. Seniors with income over 150 percent of the federal poverty level would pay a premium of

$200, while those with incomes below this level would pay a lesser amount. Persons with income below 135 percent of the poverty level would receive full coverage for drugs without premium.

In June 2001, President Bush proposed a four-year $48-billion "helping hand" plan to help low-income seniors pay for prescription drugs, but also indicated his willingness to abandon the proposal if Congress acted quickly on Medicare reform that helped all elderly pay their drug costs.

Medicare Fraud One area on which there is general agreement that a problem exists is *Medicare fraud.* According to the General Accounting Office, fraud and abuse in the Medicare system cost about $17 billion a year, or about 10 percent of the program's costs. Fraudulent Medicare practices include fraudulent and negligent billings to Medicare recipients for services that were never provided, double billings for treatment, or charges that are disproportionate and severely marked up. Fraud also occurs in the overpricing of durable medical equipment.

HIPAA requires HCFA to establish a fraud-reporting hotline modeled after the whistle-blower program already in place at the Internal Revenue Service. The hotline solicits information from anyone about possible false claims or other fraud (excluding kickbacks) that involves amounts in excess of $100. If the disclosure leads to government recovery, the whistle-blower will receive a share of that recovery. Because fines can reach $10,000 per violation and triple-damages penalties can raise those amounts to $30,000, the rewards for disclosure can be substantial.

Another important anti-fraud measure in HIPAA is increased funding for enforcement. HIPAA authorized increased Medicare fraud-enforcement funding of $115 million to the Department of HHS, to be increased by about $15 million annually to a funding level of $150 million by 2002. It also authorized $47 million to the FBI for 1998, to be increased by $13 million annually to $114 million by 2002.

Other anti-fraud provisions in the HIPAA include a lifetime exclusion for any provider convicted of defrauding the program five times and the requirement of a $50,000 surety bond for new providers.

LONG-TERM CARE INSURANCE

Long-term care (LTC) insurance is a recent innovation, prompted by the enormous costs that can be associated with the health care needs of the aged. With the increase in life expectancy and improved medical care, Americans age 65 and older are increasing more rapidly than the remainder of the population. The number of persons age 85 and older has grown at an even faster rate than that for the 65-and-older group. For a variety of social and economic reasons, an increasing number of our aged are spending their final days in nursing homes and extended care facilities, with annual costs of $40,000 to $90,000 per year. It is not a criticism of the long-term care industry to observe that the cost of long-term care has reached a point at which few individuals can afford the cost out of personal resources.

Nature of the Long-Term Care Exposure

Although there is a tendency to think of long-term care insurance in the traditional terms of *accident* and *sickness,* the need for long-term care is different from the need for other types of medical care. Many people who require long-term care are not "sick" in the traditional sense. They are old and frail, and while they may not require traditional types of medical services, they do need assistance with the activities of daily living.

Two kinds of long-term care may be delineated—in-home care and institutional care (nursing homes). Although some elderly persons require care that can be provided only in an institution, other elderly persons do not need institutional care. Their needs can be met *in the community,* by people with a variety of skills, including health care professionals and others who provide assistance with the activities of daily living. Although the earliest versions of LTC insurance provided coverage only when care was provided in a skilled nursing facility following confinement, increasingly LTC policies also provide coverage for care delivered in the community.

Inadequacy of Medicare for Long-Term Care Needs

Although Medicare addresses two facets of the long-term care need (nursing home and home health care), it does so on a very restrictive and limited basis. With respect to the nursing home environment, coverage under Medicare is limited to skilled care, which, as already noted, may not be the level of care required by a person who is not sick in the traditional sense, but who needs assistance with the activities of daily

living. In addition, home care is covered only if it occurs within 30 days of a three-consecutive-day hospital stay for the same condition that requires admission to the nursing facility. Further, a physician must certify the need for the skilled care on a daily basis and the skilled nursing home facility must be certified by Medicare. (According to the HCFA, only about 50 percent of skilled nursing facilities are certified.)

If all four requirements have been met, up to 100 days of skilled nursing care benefits are provided. For the first 20 days, Medicare will pay 100 percent of the approved amount. For days 21 through 100, the patient is required to make a copayment ($101.50 per day in 2002). Medicare benefits terminate after 100 days and the patient becomes responsible for all costs. Most important, there is no coverage for intermediate care or custodial care.

For *home health care,* Medicare will pay the cost of medically necessary home health visits that meet specified conditions. Only part-time or intermittent home care is covered (defined as care that is required at least four or fewer times a week). Further, the patient must be house-bound, unable to leave the house except with assistance. The patient must be under a physician's care and the physician must certify the need for home health care. Finally, as in the case of nursing home care, the home health care agency must be certified by Medicare.

Medicare supplement policies issued by private insurers supplement Medicare, but do not provide coverage for extended care. The need therefore exists for a form of insurance that will assist in meeting the costs of long-term care for the aged. Long-term care coverage was developed by insurers to meet this need.

Development of LTC Insurance

The introduction of long-term care insurance created a challenge for insurers and insurance regulators. The exposure is new, and the manner in which coverage is structured and priced is still evolving. Some features in the earliest LTC policies produced complaints from consumer groups, which led to specific regulations for this form of coverage. The earliest contracts, for example, usually required prior hospitalization before benefits were payable. This requirement was criticized because many persons in need of nursing home care do not have recent hospital confinement. Other policies limited coverage to skilled nursing facilities, and provided no protection to persons

whose primary LTC need was custodial. Recent policies have eliminated these defects, due both to competition among insurers and to the imposition of regulatory requirements.

The NAIC Model Law The NAIC has adopted a model law for consideration by the states, specifying minimum standards for LTC policies. The NAIC model law requires that long-term care policies be guaranteed renewable, which, as we have seen, means that the renewability must be guaranteed and that the premium may be changed at renewal only for an entire class of long-term insureds. Although the NAIC model law permits cancellation under extreme circumstances, the causes for cancellation are spelled out in the law. The policy must be incontestable on the basis of misrepresentations after two years. The only allowable illnesses or conditions that may be excluded are those arising from preexisting conditions, war, attempted suicide, participating in a felony, service in the armed forces, aviation as a non-fare-paying passenger, or mental or nervous disorders. Coverage for Alzheimer's disease must be included. Insurers are required to offer an inflation-protection option. It may provide for annual increases in benefit levels or for the right to purchase increased benefits without evidence of insurability. Finally, the model law specifies a minimum loss ratio for LTC policies of 60 percent.[23]

HIAAP Long-Term Care Provisions Until 1996, the tax treatment of premiums paid for long-term care insurance was uncertain. HIPAA added a new section to the *IRC,*[24] extending the same tax treatment to long-term-care insurance premiums as has existed for other types of medical expense insurance. For tax years beginning after 1996, HIPAA grants favorable tax treatment to premiums for and recoveries under tax-qualified long-term care insurance (TQ-LTCI). Although the favorable tax treatment is similar to that provided to other forms of health insurance, it is subject to limitations.

For employer-provided plans, LTC insurance will now be treated as an accident and health plan, which means that premiums will not be includable in the gross incomes of the employees. Similarly, LTC insurance premiums are now eligible for deduction from

[23] By 1996, 43 states had adopted some version of the NAIC model Long-Term Care Coverage Act. Seven additional states adopted standards that differ significantly from the NAIC model law.
[24] *IRC* Section 7702B.

income by self-employed persons, up to the allowable limits discussed in Chapter 21.

For individuals, premiums paid on qualified LTC policies are deductible as medical expenses for itemized-deduction purposes. The annual amount of premiums deductible as medical expenses is limited, depending on the insured's age: If the taxpayer is not more than 40 by the end of the 2002 tax year, the annual limit is $230; age 41 through 50, $430; 51 through 60, $860; 61 through 70, $2290; 71 or older, $2860. The annual dollar limits are indexed to reflect increases in health care costs.

Benefits payable under a qualified LTC insurance contract are treated as amounts received for sickness and personal injuries, which are generally excludable from income. However, the new *IRC* provisions place a cap on the amount of qualified LTC benefits that may be excluded from income. Generally, if the total periodic long-term care payments received from all policies exceed a per-diem limitation, the excess must be included in income.[25] The per-diem limitation is the greater of $200 or the costs incurred for qualified LTC services provided for the insured. The $200 per day ($73.000 per year) limit applies in 2002 and will be adjusted for inflation in later years.[26]

Tax-favored status is granted to all existing LTC insurance policies issued before January 1, 1997, if they complied with state standards. Tax-favored status is granted to LTC insurance policies issued after January 1, 1997, only if they meet the new federal standards outlined in HIPAA.

Under the provisions of HIPAA, a qualified LTC insurance is an insurance contract that provides only coverage of qualified LTC services. The contract:

1. Must be guaranteed renewable

2. Must not provide for a cash surrender value or other money that can be paid, assigned, pledged, or borrowed

3. Must not provide refunds other than refunds on the death of the insured, or complete surrender or cancellation of the contract, and dividends under the

contract may be used only to reduce future premiums or increase future benefits

4. Generally must not pay or reimburse expenses incurred for services or items that would be reimbursed under Medicare, except where Medicare is a secondary payer, or the contract makes per diem or other periodic payments without regard to expenses

In addition to clarifying the tax treatment of LTC insurance, HIPAA established new coverage standards for TQ-LTCI. Many LTC policies currently provide superior coverage to the TQ-LTCI standard and therefore do not qualify as TQ-LTCI (unless they were purchased prior to HIPAA).

Coverage of LTC Policies

The typical LTC policy provides coverage for care in a skilled, intermediate, or custodial nursing home. Policies pay a specified amount per day for a designated period or incurred expenses up to an aggregate limit, subject to a waiting-period deductible. Within this broad framework, there are a variety of permutations among the policies offered by different insurers.

Benefit Limits There are two broad approaches to the benefit structure of LTC policies. Under the earliest approach—which still predominates—coverage is provided for a specified limit per day, with benefits payable for from one to five or six years and, in the case of some insurers, for life. The maximum daily limit available in 2002 varied by company, but daily limits up to $400 were available from some insurers. Some policies pay the full daily benefit selected, regardless of the actual charges for the long-term care services provided. Other policies pay the actual charge incurred for the long-term care services up to the daily limit selected.

The second type of benefit period available is not measured in days, months, or years, but in dollars. It is called a *pool of money concept* and is becoming popular among insurers. Rather than specify a period of time, benefits for LTC services are paid from a single lifetime maximum number of dollars. A $100-per-day benefit payable for 5 years represents $182,500 (365 × 5 × $100). Under a *pool of money* policy, a $182,500 policy limit is available to pay for whatever long-term care expenses are incurred and benefits are payable for as long as the maximum amount lasts, regardless of the time period.

[25] Periodic payments received under long-term care contracts by reason of the death of the insured are also considered taxable income. *IRC* Section 101(g).

[26] That portion of a life insurance policy (i.e., a rider) that provides LTC coverage is treated as a separate contract under the *IRC*. Any refund given upon cancellation or complete surrender of the policy will be includable in income to the extent that any deduction or exclusion was allowable with respect to the premium.

Increasingly, home care benefits are included in LTC policies. The NAIC model law does not require that LTC policies include home care benefits, but if the policy does include home care, it may not be subject to a step-down requirement (a requirement that the insured was previously confined in a hospital or skilled nursing facility to be eligible for home care benefits). Further, home care benefits cannot reduce the duration of institutional care provided by the policy. When home care benefits are provided, they must include services provided by custodial care workers and agencies that are not certified by Medicare. The daily benefit for home care, when it is not subject to the same limit as for nursing-home care, is usually 50 or 60 percent of the daily limit for nursing-home care. An increasing number of policies, however, pay the same amount for home care as for nursing-home care.

In addition to licensed nursing homes, some policies provide coverage for *assisted living facilities,* in which a lesser level of care is provided to residents. As in the case of the home care limit, some companies pay the same amount for assisted living facilities as for nursing home care, while others pay a reduced benefit, normally 50 or 60 percent of the nursing-home limit. Finally, some policies now include benefits for respite care. *A respite care benefit* provides payment for substitute care given when the primary caregiver (usually a relative) takes a vacation or break from the caregiving task.

Waiting Periods As noted in Chapter 20, for disability income policies, waiting periods shorter than 90 days have either disappeared from the market or have become too expensive for serious consideration by the knowledgeable buyer. For LTC policies, however, waiting periods as short as zero (first-day coverage) are available. In addition to the zero-day elimination period, LTC elimination periods are also available for 15, 20, 30, 60, 90, 100, 120, 150, 180, and 365 days. A 20-day elimination period is a common choice, because Medicare's skilled nursing coverage ceases 100 percent payment beginning the twenty-first day. Some policies use separate elimination periods for nursing home confinement and home health care, usually with a shorter elimination period for home health care, which tends to be the more common need.

LTC Coverage Trigger Prior to HIPAA, most LTC policies used three definitions for benefit eligibility:

1. The inability to perform a certain number of activities of daily living (ADLs)

2. Suffering from a cognitive impairment, such as Alzheimer's or Parkinson's disease

3. A medical necessity, as prescribed by a physician, for LTC services

The *activities of daily living* (ADLs) are a set of self-maintenance activities designed to measure one's ability to perform routine personal-care functions. LTC policies have traditionally defined eligibility for benefits in terms of the insured's inability to perform a specified number (one or two) of the ADLs listed in the policy (usually five to seven). Because LTC policies are not standardized, they have differed in the number of ADLs listed and in the number the insured must be unable to perform to receive benefits. The greater the number of ADLs listed and the fewer required for benefits, the broader the coverage. The activities usually listed include eating, bathing, dressing, walking (sometimes called mobility), toileting, transferring (moving from one place to another, such as from a bed to a chair), and continence (the ability to control one's bowel and bladder functions). Some insurers have also considered taking medicine an ADL.[27]

HIPAA defines TQ-LTCI as insurance that provides necessary diagnostic, preventive, therapeutic, curing, mitigating, and rehabilitative and maintenance or personal services to a *chronically ill person.* A chronically ill person is a person who has been certified as unable to perform, without substantial assistance, at least two activities of daily living for at least 90 days. The activities of daily living defined by HIPAA are (1) eating; (2) toileting; (3) transferring; (4) bathing; (5) dressing; and (6) continence.

Like pre-HIPAA contracts, the new *IRC* standard includes coverage for Alzheimer's by classifying a chronically ill person as one "who requires substantial supervision to be protected from threats to health and safety due to severe cognitive impairment."

There are two areas in which coverage standards of TQ-LTCI policies are narrower than most policies

[27] It seems unlikely that Congress intended to restrict or diminish the scope of coverage under LTC policies. A more plausible explanation is that the coverage standards were based on an inadequate understanding of the LTC policies on the market or existing state requirements. Many states have minimum standards that exceed those of HIPAA. To comply with federal standards, these states will be required to lower standards already in place. A more logical approach would be to make the TQ-LTCI standards a minimum and allow the states to set state standards, subject to the federal minimum.

being sold in 1997. The first is the reduced number of ADLs as compared with many pre-HIPAA LTC policies. The second is the absence of *medical necessity* as a trigger for benefits in TQ-LTCI policies, which was included in most pre-HIPAA policies. The absence of this coverage trigger is a narrowing of coverage. Although coverage can exist under a TQ-LTCI contract when a physician certifies that someone needs LTC services, the certification will have to be attributable to ADL-deficiency or cognitive impairment, rather than to medical necessity.[28]

Inflation Protection The NAIC model law requires that insurers offer some type of escalator clause or option to address the problem of inflation. One permissible option is a provision that automatically increases benefit levels at a compound rate of at least 5 percent annually. In some policies, the increase is on a simple, rather than compound, basis. As an alternative, the insured may be granted the option of periodically increasing benefit levels without evidence of insurability, as long as the option for the previous period has not been declined. Policies that agree to cover a specified percentage of actual reasonable charges without a specified maximum limit also meet the inflation protection requirement. When offering a contract with inflation protection, the insurer must provide the applicant with a comparison of the increasing benefit levels and a policy under which benefits do not increase, along with a comparison of the premiums for coverage with and without increasing benefits.

Unintentional Lapses Because buyers of long-term care policies may include persons who tend to be forgetful, the NAIC model law includes provisions designed to provide at least some protection against such inadvertent termination of coverage. Before issuing a long-term care policy, the insurer must give the applicant the option of designating at least one person (in addition to the applicant) who will be notified of an impending lapse for nonpayment of premium or a written waiver dated and signed by the applicant electing not to designate any additional persons to receive such notice. In addition, long-term policies may not lapse for nonpayment of premium unless the insurer, at least 30 days before the effective date of lapse, has given notice to the insured and to those persons designated by the insured. Finally, long-term care policies must also include a reinstatement provision, permitting reinstatement after lapse if the insurer is provided with proof of cognitive impairment or the loss of functional capacity.

LTC Renewability The NAIC established the guaranteed renewable provision as the minimum standard for LTC policies, meaning that virtually all LTC plans have conformed to this requirement. Given the problems that insurers encountered writing disability insurance on a noncancelable basis, there has been no movement by insurers to go beyond the guaranteed renewable basis required by the NAIC model law.

Nonforfeiture Provisions One of the problems in marketing long-term care policies has been the difficulty in spreading losses across age groups, despite the fact that premiums vary with the age of the insured. The disinclination of younger consumers to purchase LTC insurance is perhaps understandable. Unlike permanent life insurance, most long-term care policies have not had nonforfeiture or refund provisions, and the insured who lapses his or her policy forfeits the early premiums paid for protection. Most state laws allow a return of premium or cash value (nonforfeiture) benefit in LTC policies. Policies with a nonforfeiture feature generally cost about 20 percent more than policies without the option. As previously noted, however, HIPAA imposes limits on cash value and nonforfeiture provisions in TQ-LTCI.

One of the newest offerings in the LTC insurance arena is a limited-pay policy, similar to the limited-pay life insurance contracts. As the contract is designed, the insured can pay the premium in several large installments, which will pay for the policy for life in a few short years. This gives buyers the opportunity to purchase a paid-up LTC policy before retirement when their income and assets are higher. It would seem that as long as such contracts do not include provision for withdrawal of the prepayment, they could still qualify for favorable tax treatment.[29]

[28] Another difference in the requirements for qualified policies and plans previously marketed is the HIPAA requirement that cognitive impairment must be "severe." It is not yet clear how significant the addition of this qualifier will be interpreted. Many authorities believe that it is a difference without a distinction.

[29] Innovations in the field of long-term care insurance continue to occur and the configuration of LTC policies is still evolving. For a review of the latest in LTC policy design, *Life Association News* publishes an annual survey of LTC products, usually in July.

Cost of LTC Insurance

The cost of LTC insurance varies widely among companies, so any attempt to cite specific costs is challenging. However, the Health Insurance Association of America reports the following *average* premiums for LTC coverage in 1997. Regrettably, it does not differentiate in its average price summary among policies with different benefit durations or waiting periods. The indicated premiums are for a $100 daily benefit (50 percent home care):

	Age 50	Age 65	Age 79
Basic premium	$378	$1,010	$4,148
With 5 percent compound inflation protection	798	1,881	5,889

Source: Health Insurance Association of America, *Source Book of Health Insurance Data 1997–1998.*

Some insurers offer a two-policy discount (usually 10 or 15 percent) when two spouses purchase coverage. The discount may be applied to the cheaper of the two policies or to both policies.

The Life Insurance Accelerated Benefits Alternative to LTC

Although cash values in life insurance policies can provide a source of cash in the event of a terminal illness or the need for long-term care, cash values may be limited or nonexistent. An alternative is an agreement by the insurer to advance the policy proceeds under a provision known as *living benefits.* Living benefit riders agree to pay a part of the policy death benefit to policyholders who choose this way of paying nursing home or other bills.

Living benefit riders are usually offered in connection with permanent life insurance, under an *accelerated benefits rider* that stipulates the conditions under which the benefit is triggered. These usually include a designated catastrophic illness, a terminal illness, or the need for custodial or nursing-home care that occurs after the insured has reached a specified age ranging from 65 to 85. Most policies specify a maximum limit for the benefit, expressed as a dollar amount, a monthly benefit, or a percentage of the death benefit. The most common approach is a monthly benefit equal to a percentage of the face amount of insurance (e.g., 1 percent or 2 percent per month). Generally, the benefit is treated as a lien against the death benefit. Most companies charge

interest on the amount of benefits paid and add the unpaid interest to the lien against death benefits.

Initially, many companies charged from 10 percent to 15 percent of the basic premium for the coverage. More recently, however, a number of companies have announced the availability of living benefit riders on all new and existing policies as a no-additional-cost benefit.

Until 1996, the tax treatment of accelerated death benefits was subject to some uncertainty. HIPAA addressed this uncertainty, as well as the tax treatment of amounts received for the sale or assignment of a policy to a viatical settlement provider, by adding *Code* section 101(g). Generally, this new provision states that any amount received under a life insurance contract on the life of a terminally ill insured or a chronically ill insured will be treated as an amount paid by reason of the death of the insured. However, amounts paid to a chronically ill person are subject to the same limitations that now apply to long-term care benefits added to the *Code* in Section 7702B(d). Accelerated death benefits paid to terminally ill individuals are not subject to this limit.

Viatication

Another alternative with respect to life insurance policy proceeds is *viatication.*[30] Viatication refers to the sale of a terminally ill person's life insurance policy to a business firm that specializes in such transactions. These firms are generally referred to as viatical settlement companies.

Historically, the companies that engaged in this practice have not been regulated. In 1993, however, the NAIC adopted a model act on viatical settlements, placing viatical settlement companies under the jurisdiction of the state insurance department. The model act requires viatical settlement companies to file a plan of operation with the state insurance department, and also requires disclosure to prospects of the alternatives to viatication and the tax consequences of the transaction.

Although the question of the tax treatment of viatical settlements had been unclear, HIPAA codified the tax treatment of viatical settlements. Newly

[30] The term comes from the Latin word *viaticum,* meaning money or supplies provided as traveling expenses to an officer on an official journey in ancient Rome. The suggested meaning is that the proceeds from the sale of the life insurance policy provide "supplies" for the individual's final journey.

added *IRC* Section 101(g) provides that if any portion of the death benefit under a life insurance contract on the life of a terminally or chronically ill insured is sold or assigned to a viatical settlement provider, the amount paid for the sale or assignment will be treated as an amount paid under the life insurance contract by reason of the insured's death. In other words, such an amount will not be included in income.[31]

MEDICAID PLANNING

"Medicaid planning" is a euphemism used by some attorneys who encourage upper-middle-class people to become artificially impoverished by direct transfers of assets (i.e., signing over their life assets) and become eligible for long-term care Medicaid benefits. Medicaid is a program designed to provide benefits for the indigent and impoverished; it was created specifically to help those with limited resources gain access to, among other things, long-term health care. People who do not wish to spend their own assets on long-term care expenses have legally avoided doing so, but in the process they siphon dollars away from the licit poor who need care and exacerbate the problem of funding care for the needy.

Statutory Restrictions

Many members of Congress thought that the process of *Medicaid planning* subverted the underlying philosophy of the Medicaid program and acted to discourage the practice. In 1996, the HIPAA introduced a provision criminalizing the transfer of assets for the purpose of gaining eligibility to Medicaid. The law, effective January 1, 1997, received much criticism within the press and came to be known as the "Granny Goes to Jail Law." The political fall-out led Congress to amend the provision, replacing the controversial provision with a new one in the Balanced Budget Act of 1997 (BBA-97).

> Whoever, for a fee, knowingly and willfully counsels or assists an individual to dispose of assets in order for the individual to become eligible for Medicaid, if

disposing of the assets results in the imposition of a period of ineligibility for Medicaid shall be guilty of a misdemeanor and upon conviction thereof fined not more than $10,000 or imprisoned for not more than one year, or both.[32]

The amendments now make it a crime not to transfer assets to become eligible for Medicaid, but to counsel or assist an individual to make certain asset transfers for a fee. In other words, instead of Granny going to jail, her attorney or financial planner goes instead.

The "period of ineligibility" referred to in the statute is a period during which Medicaid benefits are not available because an individual or his/her spouse disposed of assets for less than fair-market value during a *look-back* period.[33] Under current federal and state law, when someone applies for Medicaid, the Medicaid agency looks back at all transfers of assets made in the prior 36 months (60 months for transfers to or from a trust). If a transfer of assets was made during the look-back period by either an applicant or his/her spouse and it does not fall within a stated exemption, then a period of ineligibility for Medicaid is calculated, beginning with the month following the date of the transfer. The number of months for which Medicaid benefits are denied is equal to the amount that was transferred divided by the average monthly cost of nursing home care in the region. For example, if the regional rate is $3000 per month and the individual transfers $30,000 in assets, he or she would lose Medicaid eligibility for 10 months. There is no limit to the length of the penalty period, but the look-back period is limited to 36 or 60 months.[34]

The new provision that criminalizes providing advice on Medicaid planning creates a dilemma for elder-law attorneys and financial planners. Under current Medicaid law, and for more than the past 10 years, it is not illegal to transfer assets for the purpose of achieving Medicaid eligibility. Yet it is now illegal for professionals to advise clients with respect to such transfers. Lawyers and financial planners therefore have a conflict that arises from their clients' right to know civilly permissible options and

[31] In addition to those firms that purchase life insurance policies, a growing number of companies have been formed that make loans against the policy's death benefit. For example, see http://www.viaticalbroker.com/options.html.

[32] 42 U.S.C. §1320a-7b(a).

[33] Section 1917(c) of the Social Security Act; *U.S. Code* Reference 42 U.S.C. 1396p(c).

[34] Prior to the Budget Reconciliation Act of 1993, the look-back period was 30 months and the maximum reduction in benefits was also 30 months.

the statutory prohibition against providing advice on the subject. Some lawyers and financial planners will undoubtedly continue to at least explain the options to their clients, without advising them of the course of action they should take.[35]

Spousal Impoverishment Provisions

The law allows the community spouse—that is, the spouse who is not institutionalized—to retain a certain level of income and assets. This concession dates from 1988, when Congress enacted provisions to prevent what is referred to as *spousal impoverishment,* meaning leaving a spouse who is still living in the community with little or no income or assets.[36] When the couple applies for Medicaid, an assessment of their resources is conducted. The couple's resources are combined and exemptions for the home, household goods, an automobile, and burial funds are made. The result is the spousal resource amount, from which the community spouse is allowed to retain a set dollar amount and still allow the institutionalized spouse to be eligible for Medicaid. In 2002, the community spouse was allowed to keep a minimum of $17,856 or one-half the couple's assets up to $89,280.[37] The federal law allows states to raise the $17,856 minimum, and several states have enacted a higher minimum level.

Estate Recovery

The Omnibus Budget Reconciliation Act of 1993 (OBRA-93) made a significant change in the rules for Medicaid eligibility that can affect asset-transfer decisions. Under the rules introduced by this law, states must recover from the probate estate of a deceased Medicaid recipient amounts paid on behalf of the individual while alive. Some property that was exempt in the eligibility determination will be included in the probate estate. The probate estate consists of property passing under a will or under the state's intestacy law. In addition, the state may seek recovery against any other assets that the deceased recipient held at interest at the time of his or her death, which could include assets not in the probate estate. Property not in the probate estate includes property owned with a right of survivorship, property in certain trusts, insurance proceeds, retirement death benefits, and life estates.

Medicaid Partnerships

In five states—California, Connecticut, Indiana, Iowa, and New York—the state legislatures have approved programs designed to protect citizens' assets from Medicaid spend-down requirements when the individual is covered by an approved long-term care policy. These LTC policies are called *partnership policies,* after the *Partnerships for Term Care* programs they were designed to implement. The partnerships are public/private arrangements between state governments and insurance companies designed to encourage citizens to plan for their long-term care needs in old age by purchasing private long-term care insurance. If the insurance benefits are used to pay for long-term care, the amount of the payments will exempt assets that would otherwise be considered in the determination of eligibility for Medicaid.

The first of the five state plans was enacted by Connecticut and formally approved by the federal government in 1991. It allows the state Medicaid authority to disregard individual assets equal to payments by private LTC insurance policies when establishing an individual's eligibility for Medicaid. The partnership policies provide LTC coverage in a lump-sum amount. Upon entry into a nursing home, costs are reimbursed from this lump sum until the individual recovers or the funds are exhausted. When the policy's benefits are exhausted, the individual may then apply for Medicaid. However, individuals need no longer spend down all their assets to qualify for Medicaid, since assets equal to the amount paid out by private insurance are protected.[38] The Connecticut plan is referred to as a *dollar-for-dollar* model, since one dollar of assets is protected for every one dollar of benefits paid under the private insurance plan.

[35] The penalty under BBA-97 applies only "if disposing of assets results in the imposition of a period of ineligibility for such assistance". If an individual transfers assets and then waits until the end of the look-back period before making application for Medicaid benefits, the action would not fall within or be subject to the penalties of Section 1320(a). This interpretation was upheld in the dismissal of *Peebler & Nay v. Reno,* Civ 97-256-HA (U.S. District Court for Oregon, April 25, 1997).

[36] Section 1924 of the Social Security Act; *U.S. Code* Reference 42 U.S.C. 1396r-5.

[37] These dollar amounts are adjusted for inflation on January 1 of each year.

[38] Connecticut's plan was developed under a planning grant from the Robert Wood Johnson Foundation, the nation's largest health care philanthropy, which has supported initiatives in eight states to promote long-term care insurance for the elderly.

Note that while the plan exempts assets from the Medicaid requirements, income requirements continue to apply. Like Connecticut, California, Indiana, and Iowa also use the dollar-for-dollar model.

New York uses the *total assets* model. Under this approach, certified policies must cover 3 years in a nursing home or 6 years of home health care. Once the benefits are exhausted, the Medicaid eligibility process will not consider assets at all. However, like the dollar-for-dollar model, the individual's income is devoted to the cost of care.

Paradoxically, while the partnership programs appear to have worked well in the four states in which they have been implemented, federal law discourages other states from enacting such programs. Federal legislation enacted as part of the *Omnibus Reconciliation Act* of 1993 provides that future state programs, if approved, may provide for protection of assets only during a person's lifetime. After the Medicaid recipient's death, the states must recover from the estate whatever was spent on Medicaid.[39] The federal restrictions on partnership programs were enacted in 1993, and may reflect the congressional expectation that the 1993 Clinton health care initiative would emerge as *the* solution to the health care problem generally. It may also reflect a fear on the part of some members of Congress that an expansion of private LTC insurance to other states might become a *de facto* substitute for a universal government health insurance plan, which remains the ultimate goal of some legislators and social reformers.

[39] Some states have enacted legislation for creation of partnership programs if the restrictive provisions in OBRA-93 are repealed. The states that have some type of modified partnership program in place or enabling legislation that allows for the creation of a program include Colorado, Illinois, Maryland, Massachusetts, Michigan, Missouri, North Dakota, Ohio, Rhode Island, and Washington. The Massachusetts program was approved before the cut-off date of May 14, 1993, but does not provide the broad protection of the five existing programs.

IMPORTANT CONCEPTS TO REMEMBER

Medicare
Medicare Supplement policy
Medigap insurance
long-term care insurance
The Balanced Budget Act of 1997
Medicare Part A
Medicare Part B
Medicare Part C
Medicare+Choice
prospective payment system (PPS)
diagnostic-related groups (DRGs)
Resource-Based Relative Value Schedule (RBRVS)
lifetime reserve days
skilled-nursing facility care
home health care
durable medical equipment (DME)

hospice care
accept assignment
approved amount
excess charge
Medicare Supplement Buyer's Guide
30-day free look
Qualified Medicare Beneficiary (QMB) program
Specified Low-Income Medicare Beneficiary (SLMB) program
HCFA risk contract
HCFA cost contract
coordinated care plans
Medical Savings Accounts (MSAs)
Provider-Sponsored Organizations
Medicare Private Fee-For-Service
Private contracts outside Medicare

Medicare Medical Savings Accounts (MSAs)
National Bipartisan Commission on the Future of Medicare
Medicare fraud
NAIC model long-term care law
respite care benefit
activities of daily living
nonforfeiture provision
living benefits
accelerated benefits rider
viatication
Medicaid planning
look-back period
period of ineligibility
spousal impoverishment
partnership policies

QUESTIONS FOR REVIEW

1. Identify and briefly distinguish between Part A and Part B of the traditional Medicare program.

2. Explain the relationship between Medicare and employer-provided health insurance for employees who are age 65 and over.

3. Describe the changes in Medicare that were enacted as

Part C, Medicare+Choice. In what fundamental way does Medicare+Choice differ from the coverage under the traditional Medicare program?

4. Your father and mother will soon reach age 65, the age at which they will become eligible for Medicare. They have asked you to advise them on the advantages

and disadvantages of a Medicare Medical Savings Account. Describe the essential nature of a Medicare MSA and explain to them what you consider to be the advantages and disadvantages of these plans.

5. Explain how life insurance policies can provide an alternative to long-term care insurance.

6. Explain the triggers that may be included in a long-term care insurance policy to determine eligibility for policy benefits.

7. Periodic surveys have indicated a significant misunderstanding on the part of the public concerning the benefits available under Medicare to cover long-term care. What specific limitations in the Medicare benefit structure make Medicare an undependable source of funding for the long-term care exposure?

8. Explain what is meant by a viatical settlement and the tax treatment of such transactions.

9. Briefly explain the eligibility requirements for Medicaid as they apply to expenses for long-term care.

10. Describe the difference in coverage triggers between a TQ-LTCI policy and the policies that were on the market at the time the HIPAA was adopted.

QUESTIONS FOR DISCUSSION

1. What arguments would you offer to support the decision to adopt the Medicare+Choice provisions of the BBA-97? What arguments would you offer to oppose the decision?

2. Under what circumstances would you recommend a Medicare Medical Savings Account to a person eligible for Medicare? For which persons would a Medicare MSA be inadvisable?

3. A noted insurance authority has said, "Because the financing of long-term care is inconsistent with insurance principles, it is a problem that does not lend itself to solu-tion through insurance." In what ways is the financing of long-term care inconsistent with insurance principles? What, in your opinion, is the solution to the problem of financing long-term care?

4. "Medicaid planning represents a fraud on one's fellow taxpayers. It is asking me to pay your bills, so you can leave your money to your children." Do you agree or disagree? Why?

5. To what extent do you believe that the cost of medical care for the aged is at the heart of the difficulties facing the nation with respect to financing health care expenses?

SUGGESTIONS FOR ADDITIONAL READING

Ahmad, Khurshid et al. "Long-Term Care: An Insurance Industry Perspective." *Journal of the American Society of CLU/ChFC,* vol. 62 (March 1992).

Beam, Burton T., Jr., and John J. McFadden. *Employee Benefits,* 3rd ed. Brookfield, Wis.: Dearborn Financial Publishing, Inc., 1994.

Hagen, Ronald D. "Long-Term Health Care." *Journal of the American Society of CLU/ChFC,* vol. 62 (March 1992).

Hallman, G. Victor, and Karen L. Hamilton. *Personal Insurance: Life, Health & Retirement.* Malvern, Pa.: American Institute for CPCU, 1994. Chapters 1, 2.

Neldo McCall. "Insurance Regulation and the Partnership for Long-Term Care." *Journal of Insurance Regulation,* vol. 16, no. 1 (Fall 1997), pp. 73–101.

Rejda, George E. *Social Insurance and Economic Security,* 5th ed. Englewood Cliffs, N.J.: Prentice-Hall, 1994, Chapters 9 and 10.

Sadler, Jeff. *The Long-Term Care Handbook.* Cincinnati, Ohio.: The National Underwriter Co., 1996.

U.S. Bipartisan Commission on Comprehensive Health Care. *Access to Health Care and Long-Term Care for All Americans,* Recommendations to the Congress, 101st Congress, 2d Session, Washington, D.C.: U.S. Government Printing Office, 1990.

WEB SITES TO EXPLORE

Centers for Medicare and Medicaid	http://cms.hhs.gov/
Health Care Financing Administration	http://www.hcfa.gov/
Health Insurance Association of America	http://www.hiaa.org/
Medicare	http://www.medicare.gov/
National Senior Citizens Law Center	http://www.nsclc.org/
Quicken InsureMarket	http://www.insuremarket.com/

---■---

CHAPTER 23

===

EMPLOYEE BENEFITS AND OTHER BUSINESS USES OF LIFE AND HEALTH INSURANCE

---■---

And they call these "fringes."

— WILL ROGERS

CHAPTER OBJECTIVES

When you have finished this chapter, you should be able to

- Identify the major classes of employee benefits that are provided by employers to their employees, and describe the tax treatment of these benefits
- Explain the statutory requirements that must be met by qualified retirement programs
- Identify and explain the characteristics of the funding alternatives available to employers with respect to qualified retirement plans
- Explain the nature of the business-continuation exposure facing business owners and describe the measures that may be used to address this exposure
- Explain the nature of the key-person exposure facing a business organization and describe the measures that may be used to address this exposure
- Explain the purpose and operation of nonqualified deferred-compensation programs and describe the characteristics that distinguish them from qualified programs

In addition to the uses we have examined for individuals, life and health insurance is also used extensively in the business world. In previous chapters, we discussed the various types of life and health insurance policies and how they could be used to meet the personal risks faced by individuals. This chapter will discuss the ways businesses use life and health insurance to meet their objectives.

Businesses use life and health insurance for two general purposes. First, most businesses make some

insurance available to employees of the business. It is common for an employer to offer an employee some life insurance, health insurance, or retirement benefits in the employment setting. In many cases, the employer pays a part of the cost. This may be viewed as another form of compensation, since it benefits the employee. These arrangements fall under the broad classification of *employee benefits*.

In addition to their use in employee benefits, employers may use life and health insurance arrangements to protect against risks faced by the business. These may involve loss to the business from death or disability of a key employee. Businesses may also use life insurance to arrange the continuation of the business following the death of the owner.

EMPLOYEE BENEFITS GENERALLY

There is no uniform definition of what constitutes employee benefits. The Chamber of Commerce defines employee benefits broadly, to include virtually any benefit provided to employees by an employer other than wages and salary for work performed. This definition also includes the employer's share of legally required payments for employee security, such as workers compensation, unemployment compensation, and Social Security. In addition to insurance benefits, this broad definition would include such things as vacation benefits, subsidized parking, child care assistance programs, tuition benefits, employee discounts on the firm's products, etc. Using this definition, it is estimated that U.S. employers spend roughly 40 percent of payroll on employee benefits. A more narrow definition focuses on those benefits offered voluntarily by the employer.[1] Clearly, the main components of this are those programs designed to assist the employee with his or her personal risks of premature death, disability, superannuation, and unemployment.

Regardless of the definition, it is clear that employee benefits represent a significant part of the compensation of many employees. Medical expense coverage for most employees and their dependents is obtained through an employer-sponsored health insurance plan. More than one-half of all employees are covered by employer-sponsored retirement plans. More than two-thirds of all employees are covered by life insurance offered by their employer. Although private disability insurance is less likely to be offered by an employer, it is estimated that about one of every four employees is covered by employer-sponsored long-term disability plans.

There are several reasons for the prevalence of employer-sponsored insurance benefits. First, employees may find it advantageous to accept insurance as part of their compensation. As described in Chapters 12 and 21, this is because wages are taxable income to the employee, while some insurance benefits are not. In addition, most life and health insurance provided by employers is part of a group insurance contract, which, as we have seen, tends to be less expensive than individual insurance. There are several reasons for this, including lower underwriting expenses and administrative costs, as well as reduced costs from adverse selection. In addition to the fact that employees may find insurance benefits to be an attractive form of compensation, employers may have other objectives for offering employee benefits. Some plans are established in the hope that they will improve employee morale and motivation. Plans may be designed to address certain specific goals, such as reducing employee turnover or encouraging early retirement.

Levels of benefits vary by type of industry and number of employees. Employee benefits are more likely to be offered by large employers than by smaller employers. In addition, employers typically differentiate between full-time and part-time employees in the design of their plans. Often, full-time employees are eligible for a variety of benefits for which part-time employees are not eligible. Waiting periods for participation may be imposed, so that seasonal and short-term employees are eliminated from the various plans.

The design of an employer's plan must carefully consider the employer's objectives and employee's needs, the various options available, and their cost. Typically, the employer will want to consider how its employee benefit plan compares to other firms that it competes with for employees. In addition, the employer must decide how the plan will be financed (whether through insurance or some other mechanism) and who will administer the plan. Finally, the employer must effectively communicate the plan to employees if it is to have the intended impact. Frequently, the employer will retain a consultant to assist in this process. The specific benefits offered by employ-

[1] This is generally consistent with the more narrow definition of employee benefits used by the Social Security Administration in its annual review of employee benefit plans.

ers under various life, health, and retirement plans were described in previous chapters. In this chapter, we will discuss other considerations that are important to employers in designing their benefit plans.

GROUP LIFE AND HEALTH INSURANCE AS EMPLOYEE BENEFITS

Both group life and group health insurance are widely used as part of the compensation package to workers. In part, the growth of group life and health has been encouraged by collective bargaining and the demands of unions. However, a more important impetus has probably been the favorable tax treatment of contributions made by the employer for such coverage. We have already noted that the employer's contribution to the cost of health insurance, including both disability income and medical expense coverage, is deductible as an expense by the employer and is not taxable to the employee. This favorable tax treatment results in a net saving to the employees, since in the absence of such treatment, the coverage would have to be purchased with after-tax income.

Group Term Life Insurance

The most common life insurance benefit offered to employees is group term life insurance. *Internal Revenue Code (IRC)* Section 79 exempts the premium paid by an employer on the first $50,000 of group term life insurance from the taxable income of employees. Like group health insurance, the premium for such coverage is deductible by the employer as a business expense, but is not taxable to the employee as income. The coverage must be provided on a nondiscriminatory basis.

A group term life insurance plan is considered nondiscriminatory if it does not discriminate in favor of key employees as to eligibility and amount of benefits. A plan is nondiscriminatory if it benefits 70 percent or more of all employees; if at least 85 percent of all employees who are plan participants are not key employees; or if the plan benefits employees who qualify under a classification established by the employer and found by the IRS not to discriminate in favor of key employees.[2]

The requirement that the group term insurance benefits not discriminate can be satisfied if the amount of insurance bears a uniform relationship to total compensation of the persons covered. This means that a formula that provides life insurance equal to, say, two times the individual's annual salary is nondiscriminatory, even though it produces a higher amount of life insurance for more highly compensated individuals.

Group term life insurance need not be limited to $50,000 per employee; higher amounts may be provided, but only the first $50,000 is granted favorable tax treatment. For each $1000 of coverage in excess of $50,000, the employee must include as income an amount that represents the taxable value of the premium paid by the employer. The taxable value of group term life insurance in excess of $50,000 is not the amount actually paid by the employer, but an imputed cost contained in IRS regulations.[3]

Group Ordinary Life Insurance

As its title suggests, group ordinary life insurance is group permanent insurance with an accumulating cash value. The premium for the insurance is divided into two parts. Usually, the employer pays that part of the premium that represents the cost of group term insurance and that is deductible under Section 79. (The part of the premium that qualifies for deduction is established by an IRS table.) The employee pays the remainder of the premium, which represents the cash value element of the policy. If the employer pays the entire premium, the employee is taxed on the nonterm portion of the premium.

Group Paid-Up Life Insurance

Group paid-up life is designed to provide a limited amount of permanent insurance to employees at retirement. This is usually achieved through the purchase of paid-up units of single-premium whole-life insurance during the employee's working years in combination with decreasing term insurance. The whole-life units are purchased by the employee's contribution. As the amount of paid-up whole life

[2] If a group term insurance plan discriminates in favor of key employees, the key employees are taxed on the value of the benefits, but the benefits remain tax exempt to other workers.

[3] In 2001, the IRS issued new rules regarding the tax treatment of life insurance under qualified plans and released a new table for the imputed cost of life insurance in such plans. The 2001 table replaces the previous P.S. 58 rates, which were somewhat higher than the new rates.

increases, the employee's contribution is usually reduced. At retirement, the employee may withdraw the cash value, or leave the policy in force for the remainder of his or her life.

Group Universal Life

Group universal life is similar in most respects to individual universal life, and differs primarily in the same ways that other forms of group life differ from individual contracts. Coverage is usually written without evidence of insurability, and is usually subject to lower administrative costs than individually written universal life. There is no tax advantage in employer funding, and premiums are generally paid by employees.

Survivor Income Benefit Insurance

Survivor income benefit insurance (SIBI) is life insurance payable to dependents as a monthly benefit rather than in a lump sum. The coverage is unique because payment of the benefit depends on the beneficiary's status. For example, the monthly benefit to a surviving spouse terminates if the spouse remarries. Otherwise, benefit payments continue until the spouse reaches a specified age (usually 65) or until he or she dies. SIBI benefits are payable to children until they reach a specified age, usually age 19 or until age 23 if attending school on a full-time basis. The child's benefit also terminates if the child dies or marries. SIBI may be written as a rider to another form of group life insurance, or it may be written as a separate contract.

Retired Lives Reserve

Usually, the employer's deductible contribution for group term insurance for employees terminates when the employee retires. Retired lives reserve is a mechanism for funding the continuation of yearly renewable term after the employee's retirement. The employer makes contributions to a trust fund during the employee's working years in an amount sufficient to fund the cost of term insurance after the worker retires. Since the Tax Reform Act of 1984, retired employees are taxed on the value of term life insurance exceeding $50,000, the same as active employees.

FUNDING ISSUES

The alternatives available to an employer for financing its life and health benefits for employees range from a fully insured plan to a fully self-funded plan, with many variations in between. Throughout this text, we have examined the proper role of insurance in the risk management plan of an individual. Recall that there are four alternatives available for dealing with a pure risk faced by an individual or firm: transfer, retention, avoidance, and loss control. The factors that influence the choice of each alternative were discussed in Chapter 3. We noted that insurance tends to be an expensive mechanism for treating risk, since it involves expenses beyond the payment for losses (insurer marketing expenses, premium taxes, insurer profit, etc.). Where the risk is characterized by a high frequency and low severity and, therefore, relatively predictable expenses, insurance is not likely to be as cost-effective. Retention, on the other hand, is likely to be appropriate where expenses are highly predictable.

These same considerations will affect an employer's choice of funding mechanism for its employee benefit plans. Where losses tend to be unpredictable and there is a potential for large-severity losses that would adversely affect the firm, self-funding is unlikely to be an attractive option. On the other hand, where losses are stable and relatively predictable, self-funding may be attractive. In addition to these general considerations, specific tax and other legal considerations may affect the choice of funding vehicle. Finally, if an employer decides to self-fund, it must also decide whether to administer the plan itself or to retain an outside administrator to make benefit determinations.

Because of potential loss severity, historically only very large employers self-insured their medical expense plans. Some smaller employers obtained employee health insurance under programs that involve partial self-funding, such as a retrospective rating plan (discussed in Chapter 7) or a *minimum premium plan* (MPP). Under a minimum premium plan, the employer retains liability for small claims and pays these directly. The insurer pays claims only above the stated level. Because most states level premium taxes only on premiums actually received by the insurer, the MPP arrangement avoids taxes on a significant part of the benefit costs, those paid directly by the employer. As health care costs have increased, it has become increasingly common for smaller employers to engage in more extensive self-funding arrangements, while capping their exposure with stop-loss insurance.

Stop-loss insurance puts a limit on the amount of loss the employer is required to fund. One common

form of stop-loss insurance is *aggregate stop-loss.* With aggregate stop-loss insurance, the employer agrees to pay all claims up to an agreed on limit for the year, and the insurer pays for all the claims beyond the limit. In a sense, the stop-loss limit acts as an annual deductible, and the policy caps the employer's loss exposure for the year. The employer self-funds losses within the limit, but is protected if losses exceed the limit. Frequently, the stop-loss limit is set at 120 to 140 percent of the employer's expected losses. Stop-loss policies are increasingly made available to small employers and have fueled a dramatic growth in self-funding among this employer group. An alternative form of stop-loss insurance, *specific stop-loss,* caps the amount of claims for one individual. When the claims of one employee or dependent exceed the stop-loss limit, any excess is covered by the insurer. The use of stop-loss insurance by small employers has grown significantly in recent years in response to the increased interest of small employers in self-funding their medical expense benefits.

The reasons for the greater interest in self-funding in recent years are numerous. Some observers point to the fact that self-funded plans are not subject to state insurance laws, thanks to a preemption in the Employee Retirement Income Security Act (ERISA). They see the increasing growth of self-funded plans as driven by a desire to escape state regulation. Most states have mandated-benefits laws requiring certain benefits to be provided in insured plans. Self-insured plans are not subject to these mandates. In addition, most states have passed small-group reform laws that impose rate limitations, require guaranteed issue of small employer policies, and limit preexisting-conditions exclusions. Although these reforms make insurance more available and less expensive for those firms where employees have health problems, they also tend to increase the cost modestly for other firms. These other firms might find it more attractive to escape the insured market and thereby avoid the mandated subsidy of the poorer risks under small-group reform.

There has been an attempt by some groups to modify the ERISA preemption, but these attempts have been opposed by large employer groups. Many employers argue that ERISA preemption is necessary because of the burden that would exist if employers operating in multiple states were forced to comply with the wide variety of health insurance laws in the states. At the moment, the states are attempting to stem the flow of small employers to the self-funded market by limiting the use of stop-loss insurance. Current proposals would prohibit stop-loss insurance with a loss limit of less than $20,000. Many small employers would be unable to self-fund at that level.

With the exception of very large employers, most employers that decide to self-fund their medical expense benefits will seek the assistance of an outside administrator. Administering a medical expense plan requires significant expertise, and the employer is often not interested in developing and maintaining that expertise internally. In addition, some employers are concerned that internal administration creates the possibility for conflict between the employer and employee over benefit decision. A third-party administrator (TPA) is often retained to make benefit determinations, pay benefits, assist in plan design, and otherwise administer the plan. The administrator may be an insurer or a TPA. Where the employer arranges stop-loss insurance, it is common for the insurer to be the administrator. Where the plan is fully self-funded, the contract between the administrator and employer is often called an *administrative-services-only* (ASO) agreement, in recognition of the fact that no insurance is being provided.

In the area of disability income, most employers offer sick-leave plans to employees, and pay the benefits out of corporate assets. For obvious reasons, it is less likely for an employer to self-fund life insurance and long-term disability insurance. The potential severity in both areas would preclude self-funding except in the case of very large employers.

Funding through a 501 (c)(9) Trust

An employer who self-funds certain employee benefits may establish a 501 (c)(9) trust vehicle. Section 501(c)(9) of the *IRC* allows employers to establish a voluntary employees' beneficiary association (VEBA) and to use the trust to fund certain benefits for members. Benefits that may be funded through a 501(c)(9) trust include those payable because of death, medical expenses, disability, legal expenses, and unemployment. Retirement and deferred-compensation benefits may not be funded through this vehicle. These funds may be used to prefund retiree life insurance or medical benefits subject to special rules.

Certain additional requirements apply. Membership in the trust is limited to employees, former employees who are retired, disabled, or laid-off, and their dependents. Benefits must not discriminate in

favor of highly compensated individuals (although benefits may be based on a uniform percentage of compensation). If the plan requires contributions, membership in the trust must be voluntary on the part of employees.

In any year, contributions to the trust are limited to the sum of (1) direct benefit costs for that year, (2) additional amounts necessary to fund benefits that were incurred but have not yet been paid, and (3) administrative costs. Excess contributions may not be deducted by the employer and may result in adverse tax consequences.

Accounting for Retiree Health Care Costs

An additional issue related to funding employee benefits involves the accounting for health benefits that are provided to retired workers. Although a relatively small percentage of all employers (about 4 percent) offer retiree medical benefits, 43 percent of companies with more than 500 employees offer retiree health coverage.[4] Historically, most employers have accounted for these benefits as the costs are incurred. In 1990, however, the Financial Accounting Standards Board (FASB) adopted a new standard, requiring that retiree health care costs be accrued while the employee is still working.[5] Starting in 1997, a company's balance sheet must reflect a liability equal to the unfunded obligations to retirees. At the time the new standard was adopted, benefit analysts estimated the unfunded liability for post-retirement health care benefits at more than $400 billion.[6] It is much higher today.

PENSIONS

Although private pension plans in the United States have been in existence since the late 1800s, their greatest growth has taken place since World War II. In 1940, about 4 million people—less than 20 percent of all employees in government and industry—were covered by private pensions. By 2001, over 100 mil-lion persons, including about one-half of all workers in private business and three-fourths of all government workers, were enrolled in retirement programs other than Social Security. Sixty million of these were covered by plans insured or administered by insurance companies.

Pension plans are established by employers, and sometimes jointly by unions and employers, to provide individual workers with a retirement income that will supplement Social Security retirement benefits. The plan may be set up for the employees of a particular firm, or it may be a "multi-employer" plan, serving workers from several unrelated firms.

Legislation Affecting Pension Plans

Two major pieces of legislation stand out in the history of pensions in the United States: the Employee Retirement Income Security Act of 1974 (ERISA) and the Tax Equity and Fiscal Responsibility Act of 1982 (TEFRA). In addition, several other acts establish conditions that must be observed by an employer in establishing retirement plans for their employees.[7]

Employee Retirement Income Security Act of 1974 Any discussion of private pension plans in the United States today must begin with the *Employee Retirement Income Security Act* (ERISA) of 1974,[8] which embodied the most sweeping overhaul of private pensions in the history of the country. The act was passed in response to a growing concern over the soundness and equity of the pension system. Although few pension plans had actually failed, there were many instances in which workers lost the benefits they had been counting on for retirement.[9] Funding provisions of many plans were unsound and the vesting requirements, under which an employee's right to the pension was established, were often severe. To correct these and other deficiencies in the existing pension system, Congress passed ERISA to establish standards for pension programs that would provide a better guarantee to the workers they covered.

[4] Health Insurance Association of America, *Group Life and Health Insurance—Part C* (Washington, D.C.: HIAA, 1994), p. 92.

[5] Financial Accounting Standards Board, "Employers Accounting for Post-Retirement Benefits Other Than Pensions," February 4, 1989.

[6] Lee Berton, "FASB Rule of Retirees to Cause Furor," *The Wall Street Journal,* February 9, 1989, p. A2.

[7] Other recent legislation includes the Deficit Reduction Act and the Retirement Equity Act of 1984 and the Tax Reform Act of 1986, all of which modified the rules related to qualified plans.

[8] P.L. 93–406.

[9] A well-publicized example of this occurred when the Studebaker auto factory closed in 1963. Although pensions for workers age 60 and older were paid, pension rights of workers under age 60 (some of which were vested) were lost.

The goal of ERISA was to increase the rate of national participation in pension plans, prevent loss of benefits by persons who terminate employment before retirement, establish minimum standards for funding and vesting, and provide for the overall control of new and existing pension plans. While the law does not require an employer to establish or maintain a pension plan, if such a plan exists, it must conform to the provisions of the law. ERISA prescribes which employees must be included in a plan, establishes minimum vesting requirements, specifies the amounts that must be contributed, and sets forth minimum funding requirements. The act also requires extensive reporting and disclosure information about pension and welfare programs, their operations, and their financial conditions to the Secretary of Labor, to the Internal Revenue Service, and to those covered by the plan and their beneficiaries.

Tax Equity and Fiscal Responsibility Act of 1982
The second major law affecting pension plans was the *Tax Equity and Fiscal Responsibility Act* (TEFRA) of 1982.[10] With respect to qualified retirement programs, TEFRA had two basic objectives: to require more equal treatment of highly compensated employees and rank-and-file workers and to make noncorporate retirement plans and corporate plans more similar. To achieve these two goals, Congress modified the rules for both corporate pension plans and Keogh plans. The maximum limits for contributions to corporate plans were reduced, and the limits for individual plans were increased. In addition, both corporate and individual plans were made subject to new rules with respect to *top-heavy* plans, that is, plans that discriminate in favor of stockholders, key employees, or highly paid executives.

Title VII of Civil Rights Act of 1964 In addition to the requirements of the *IRC,* pension plans are also subject to laws relating to employment practices, and the U.S. Supreme Court has ruled that the design of a pension plan may violate the equal employment provisions of the Civil Rights Act of 1964. In a 1978 case, the court ruled that when benefits to men and women under a pension plan are equal, it is illegal for an employer to require higher contributions to the plan by women than by men.[11] In another case, the Supreme Court ruled that when men and women make equal contributions to a pension plan (or when equal contributions are made by the employer on their behalf), women cannot receive a smaller monthly benefit than men, either directly from the plan or under an annuity purchased by an insurer selected by the employer.[12] The net effect of the Supreme Court's decisions is that a retirement plan cannot pay women lower retirement benefits and cannot require women to make higher contributions because of their generally longer life expectancy.

Qualification Requirements

For a plan to be qualified by the IRS, it must conform to certain standards specified in the tax code. In general, to be qualified, the plan must meet the following standards:

1. The plan must be designed for the exclusive benefit of employees and their beneficiaries. Officers and stockholders who are *bona fide* employees may participate in the plan.

2. Contributions and benefit formulas cannot be designed to discriminate in favor of officers, stockholders, or highly compensated employees.

3. The plan must be in writing, and a written description of the plan must set forth all the provisions necessary for qualification.

4. The plan must be communicated to the employees. Plan administrators must furnish participants with a written description summarizing the major provisions and clearly describing their rights and obligations.

5. The plan must specifically provide for nondiversion of contributions, making it impossible for the employer to divert or recapture contributions made until all liabilities under the plan have been satisfied.

6. The plan must provide either for definite contributions by the employer or a definite benefit to the worker at the time of retirement.[13]

[10] P.L. 97–248.

[11] *City of Los Angeles Department of Water and Power v. Manhart* (435 U.S. 702).

[12] *Norris v. Arizona Governing Committee for Tax Deferred Annuity and Deferred Compensation Plans.* This 1983 ruling on defined contribution plans was limited to future retirees, to avoid the risk of bankrupting pension plans nationwide if retroactivity were invoked.

[13] Employers who do not want to commit to a defined contribution rate or a defined benefit at retirement may establish a qualified profit-sharing plan under which the contributions may (but need not) vary with the profits of the firm.

7. The plan must be permanent, and while modifications in the plan over time are permitted, the employer cannot terminate the plan except for *business necessity.*

8. Vesting must be provided. (See discussion of vesting later in this chapter.)

9. Life insurance benefits may be included in the plan only on an incidental basis.[14]

Prior to ERISA, many plans provided that employees were not eligible to participate in the pension plan until they had been employed by the firm for long periods of time. The obvious intent was to reduce the employer's cost by eliminating benefits for persons involved in the firm's labor turnover. ERISA set standards for participation in qualified pension plans, requiring that all employees with one year of service who had reached age 25 be included in the plan, and that years of service after age 22 be counted for vesting purposes. The Retirement Equity Act of 1984 reduced the age at which employees must be allowed to participate to 21, and the Tax Reform Act of 1984 required that years of service after age 18 be considered for vesting purposes.[15]

Top-Heavy Plans The most far-reaching feature of TEFRA in the area of retirement programs was a new set of rules applicable to so-called *top-heavy plans,* those plans that do not provide what Congress considered a sufficient portion of their benefits to rank-and-file workers. If a plan is top heavy, it must satisfy several special requirements designed to ensure that it provides a floor of benefits to non-key employees. In particular, top-heavy plans are subject to special minimum vesting provisions and minimum benefits or contributions for non-key employees.

In general, a top-heavy plan is one that provides a disproportionate share of its benefits to *key employees* (owners and certain other highly compensated employees). More specifically, a pension plan is top heavy if more than 60 percent of the accumulated account balances or 60 percent of the present value of all accrued benefits are for key employees. The top-heavy test for any plan year usually is made as of the last day of the preceding plan year. Benefits derived from both employer contributions and employee contributions (voluntary and mandatory) are considered in determining the present value of accumulated accrued benefits under a defined benefit plan and the sum of the account balances under a defined contribution plan. In addition, the account balances and present value of the accrued benefits generally include amounts distributed to the participant during the year prior to the determination date. The proportion of the benefits that are vested is of no significance in determining whether a plan is top heavy.

Top-heavy plans are required to provide minimum contributions for non-key employees. For *defined contribution plans,* the minimum annual contribution is 3 percent of the employee's compensation. In defined benefit plans, it is the contribution necessary to provide a life annuity at the plan's normal retirement age, equal to 2 percent of the employee's average annual compensation during the 5 highest-paid years of employment, multiplied by the number of years employed by the firm. However, the minimum benefit need not exceed 20 percent of such average annual compensation.

Funding Pensions

The term *funding* refers to the preparation the employer makes for provision of the benefits under the plan. In a funded plan, monies are set aside in advance of the date that they are payable, normally as the liability for the benefits accrues. ERISA now requires full funding for currently incurred liabilities. Liability for past service (i.e., for benefits due to workers for service before the adoption of the plan or the establishment of the fund) must be amortized over a period of not more than 30 or 40 years. An employer failing to meet the funding requirement is subject to an excise tax equal to 5 percent of the unfunded liability. If the deficiency is not corrected within a period allowed after notice by the IRS, a 100 percent tax is imposed on it.

Two principal types of funding agencies are used for pension plans: trustees and insurance companies. In either case, the employer's contributions are paid to the funding agency, where they accumulate with investment earnings until they are paid to the pen-

[14] Life insurance is considered incidental if the cost of the life insurance is less than 25 percent of the cost of providing all benefits under the plan. Under a *defined benefit plan,* the requirement is life insurance benefits not exceed 100 times the expected monthly retirement benefit. Under a defined contribution plan, less than 50 percent of the total contributions may go toward the purchase of ordinary life insurance. See *Rev. Rul.* 68–453, 1968-2 CB 163.

[15] Part-time employees who work less than 1000 hours a year need not be included in the plan. Plans with immediate vesting may require three years of employment as a prerequisite to participation.

sion plan participants. The use of two or more agencies for the funding of a single pension plan is called *split funding*. Usually, split funding takes the form of a partial funding through insurance, with another part of the employer's contribution paid to a trustee for investment in equities.

Trust Fund Plans Under a *trust fund plan,* the employer usually retains a consulting actuary to determine the contributions necessary to fund the benefits specified in the plan. Contributions by the employer (and by employees in a contributory plan) are paid to a trustee, usually a bank or trust company, that holds and invests the contributions and pays benefits according to the terms of the trust agreement and the pension plan provisions. The funds are invested in a variety of instruments, including some issued by insurance companies. Since the 1970s, many trust fund plans have invested in instruments called *guaranteed investment contracts,* or GICs, issued by insurance companies. GICs are similar to the certificates of deposit (CDs) issued by commercial banks; they are generally issued for a fixed and fairly short period, such as 2 to 5 years, and bear a guaranteed rate of interest. Unlike bonds, the value of GICs does not fluctuate with the interest rate; their value does, however, depend on the financial strength of the issuer. A number of trust fund plans suffered losses on their GIC portfolios when insurers encountered financial difficulties in the early 1990s.

Although a trustee holds the assets, trust fund plans are self-insured by the employer, who is ultimately responsible for the payment of benefits under the plan. The trustee makes no guarantee as to the adequacy of the employer's contributions to meet the obligations under the plan.

Insured Plans For *insured plans,* the funding agency is an insurance company. Although funding through insurers once provided little flexibility, insurers now offer a variety of approaches for funding pension plans.

Individual Policies Individual cash-value life insurance and annuity policies are sometimes used by smaller employers as funding devices. When individual contracts fund a pension plan, the employer's (and employee's) contributions are paid to an *individual policy pension trust,* a trustee who arranges for the purchase of the individual policies, serves as a custodian, and pays the premiums. The cash values that accumulate provide the retirement benefits under the policy settlement options.

Group Permanent Plans Group permanent life insurance, which consists of cash-value life insurance written on a group basis, may also be used as a funding vehicle for a pension plan. When group permanent life insurance funds a pension plan, the amount of life insurance is usually set at $1000 per $10 of annuity benefits.

Group Deferred Annuities When a *group deferred annuity plan* is chosen, the annual contributions are used to purchase a deferred annuity for each employee each year. Under both the defined-benefit and defined-contribution plans, a paid-up unit of benefit is purchased with each year's contribution. Thus, under the defined-contribution plan, the annual contribution is used to purchase a single-premium deferred annuity, payable to the employee at retirement. A defined-benefit plan might purchase an annuity equal to 2 percent of the employee's current income; over a period of, say, 30 years, the cumulative value of such annuities would equal 60 percent of the employee's average earnings.

Unallocated Funding Instruments Individual policy pension trust programs, group permanent life insurance, and group deferred annuities are collectively referred to as *allocated funding instruments,* because the contributions of the employer are specifically allocated to the individual participants. A second approach to funding pension benefits through life insurance involves *unallocated funding instruments,* in which funds paid to the insurer are not allocated to individual plan participants, but reside in an aggregated pool until they are required for the payment of benefits. Unallocated funding instruments used by insurers for pension funding include deposit administration plans, immediate participation guarantee plans, and separate accounts.

Under a *deposit administration plan,* a single fund is established by the insurer for all participants under a pension plan. Contributions are not allocated to specific workers until retirement, when a withdrawal is made from the fund to purchase a single-premium immediate annuity sufficient to provide the retirement benefits due the employee. The insurer guarantees the interest rate that will be credited to the account for the first five years and also guarantees the annuity rates for five years, but both are changeable annually thereafter. The insurer does not guarantee the adequacy of the unallocated account to meet the accrued liabilities under the plan. It does, however, guarantee the benefits payable to retired employees for whom annuities have been purchased.

Immediate participation guarantee (IPG) plans are a variation of the deposit administration plan in which the gains or losses from mortality or investment of the account are segregated from the rest of the insurer's operations, giving the employer an "immediate participation" in the favorable (or unfavorable) experience of the plan. There is no guaranteed rate of interest credited to the fund; instead, the fund receives its share of the actual investment earnings of the company. In addition, annuities are not purchased for retiring workers as under the basic deposit administration plan; instead, annuity payments are made directly out of the IPG fund. As in deposit administration plans, the insurer makes no guarantee regarding the adequacy of the fund to meet the plan's obligations. If at any time the amount of the fund falls to a level required to purchase annuities for already retired workers, annuities are actually purchased for such workers.

Deposit administration plans and IPG plans were created by insurers to compete with trusteed plans. By permitting the plan sponsor to directly and immediately participate in mortality gains and losses, the plans represent a type of partial self-insurance by the plan sponsor. The appeal of these plans to pension sponsors is indicated by the fact that they account for a significant portion of the $322 billion in pension assets in insurance company general accounts.

Given the success insurers had achieved in marketing deposit administration and IPG plans, and the acceptance they had received in the market, the industry was stunned in 1993 when the U.S. Supreme Court ruled that the sale of these plans made insurance companies fiduciaries under ERISA. The decision that rocked the insurance industry—in *John Hancock Mutual Life Insurance Co. v. Harris Trust & Savings Bank (Harris Trust)*—held that some of the general account assets of insurers selling deposit administration and IPG plans were pension plan assets, subject to the fiduciary requirements of ERISA.[16] The decision was shocking because insurers had considered themselves exempt from the fiduciary standards of ERISA since the law's inception, based on an interpretative bulletin published by the U.S. Department of Labor in 1975.[17]

Under ERISA, a person is a fiduciary with respect to an employee benefit plan "to the extent that he exercises any discretionary authority or control respecting management of disposition of such plan or its assets."[18] Although it is clear that insurance companies do exercise discretionary control over plan assets they manage, Congress included a provision in ERISA exempting insurers from fiduciary responsibilities with respect to certain types of contracts sold to pension plans. ERISA provides that if an insurance company issues a "guaranteed benefit policy" to a pension plan, the assets of the plan are deemed to include the policy, but not any of the general assets of the insurer.[19]

In its decision, the Court held that a contract qualifies as a "guaranteed benefit policy" only to the extent that it allocates the investment risk to the insurer. Accordingly, deposit administration and IPG plans did not qualify for exemption from ERISA under the "guaranteed benefit policy" exclusion. This, in turn, meant that insurers with such plans in their portfolio were fiduciaries with respect to the funds associated with those assets.

The significance of the *Harris Trust* decision rests on the duties imposed on fiduciaries under ERISA and the potential conflicts between those duties and an insurance company's responsibilities to other policyholders and stockholders. The obligations imposed on a fiduciary under ERISA are stringent and demanding. They require the fiduciary to act for the exclusive benefit of plan participants—an obligation that an organization such as an insurance company, with other customers and stockholders—would find it difficult to meet. Indeed, since *Harris Trust* applied retroactively, a major concern was the possibility that insurers might be subject to litigation for violating the ERISA fiduciary responsibilities in any transaction after 1974.

In response to the *Harris Trust* decision, Congress amended ERISA to clarify the application of ERISA to insurance company general accounts. Congress also enacted legislation directing the Department of Labor to publish regulations that would retroactively provide limited relief to insurers from law-suits alleging breach of past fiduciary duties. As issued, the regulations apply to contracts issued before December 31, 1998. Contracts issued after that date that are not "guaranteed benefit policies" make a life insurer a fiduciary under ERISA.

[16] *John Hancock Mutual Life Insurance Co. v Harris Trust & Savings Bank,* 114 S. Ct. 517 (1993).

[17] *Interpretive Bulletin,* 75-2, 29CFR 2509.75-2 (1975).

[18] 29 *U.S.C.* Section 1002 (21)(A).

[19] 29 *U.S.C.* Section 1101(b)(2)(B); *ERISA* Section 401(b)(2).

As a consequence of the *Harris Trust* decision, insurers have made adjustments in the deposit administration and IPG plans by amending these plans to include minimum annuity rate guarantees and a minimum guaranteed return. Another alternative, discussed next, has been to shift deposit administration and IPG plans into separate accounts.

Separate Accounts One type of arrangement that was not jeopardized by the *Harris Trust* decision was the *separate account*. A *separate account* is a fund held by an insurance company apart from its general assets, to be used for investment of pension assets in equities. These accounts are "separate" in the sense that the funds are not commingled with the insurer's other funds, but contributions from a particular pension plan are usually commingled with those of other plans. Separate accounts were designed by insurers to compete with trusted plans, which had always had the advantage of investing in equities. They are permitted under special legislation enacted by the states in the 1960s. One likely result of the *Harris Trust* decision is a shift in emphases by insurers and an increase in the use of separate accounts for pension funding.

ERISA PENSION PLAN TERMINATION INSURANCE

In addition to the other provisions designed to increase the security of benefits under pension plans, ERISA also established the Pension Benefit Guarantee Corporation (PBGC) within the Department of Labor. All employers with defined-benefit plans are required to insure the benefits of their plan with the PBGC, paying a premium that varies with the nature of the plan. In 1995, the rate for multi-employer plans was $2.60 per participant. For single-employer plans, a variable rate applies. In 1995, the premium was $19 per plan participant, with an additional charge of $9 per participant for each $1000 of underfunding. Prior to 1995, the premium was limited to a maximum of $72. As a result of legislation enacted in 1994, this cap was phased out gradually and eliminated completely in 1997.

The benefits of a covered pension are guaranteed up to 100 percent of the average wages of the worker during his or her five highest-earning years, subject to a dollar maximum. The dollar maximum was originally set at $750 per month, but varies with the Social Security taxable wage base.[20] By 2002, the maximum coverage per employee had increased to $3579 per month.

Although the original provisions of ERISA that established the PBGC permitted voluntary termination of any single-employer pension plan on the grounds of *business necessity,* the provisions regarding terminations were significantly strengthened by the Single Employer Pension Plan Amendments Act of 1986 (SEPPAA). Under the provisions of SEPPAA, terminations in which the plan assets are insufficient to pay accumulated nonforfeitable benefits or *distress terminations* are permitted only if the sponsor can prove financial distress. *Standard terminations,* in which the plan assets are sufficient to pay benefits due may still be terminated for business necessity. If a plan is terminated with insufficient assets, the employer must reimburse the PBGC for the deficiency. This *contingent employer liability* is limited to 30 percent of the net worth of the employer plus 75 percent of the remaining liability. The PBGC must permit the employer to pay the additional 75 percent under commercial reasonable terms. The SEPPAA makes provision for the PBGC to appoint a trustee to collect additional payment from the employer over future years. The payments collected are paid to the plan beneficiaries along with the assets from the plan.

In 1994, motivated by increasing concern about the financial condition of the PBGC, Congress enacted a pension reform package that significantly strengthened the funding requirements for private pension plans. Over the years, the PBGC had accumulated a deficit of $2.9 billion from pension plans that terminated with insufficient funding. Features of the 1994 law, which was enacted as part of the General Agreement on Tariffs and Trade (GATT), would reduce underfunding by requiring companies to use more conservative mortality and interest assumptions when valuing plan liabilities and to accelerate contributions to underfunded plans.[21] The results have been

[20] The original $750 limit is increased by the same percentage as the Social Security taxable wage base increases over the 1974 wage base of $13,200.

[21] Employers will be required to use the 1983 Group Annuity Mortality Table (GAM 83) to calculate life expectancies of plan participants, and the Treasury Department will develop a new mortality table to be used beginning in 2000. With respect to the interest rate assumptions, employers were previously required to use an interest rate between 90 percent and 110 percent of the four-year weighted average rate for 30-year treasury bonds. The top of that range will gradually fall to 105 percent by 1999.

dramatic. In 1996, after more than 20 years of continuous deficits, the PBGC reported a modest surplus. The surplus continued to increase until 2000, when it reached $9.7 billion. The improvement resulted from the 36 percent increase in premiums for covered plans, the absence of major pension failures in recent years, and unusually strong investment income during a bull market. In 2001, owing to the failure of several major plans, the surplus fell to $7.7 billion.

CAFETERIA EMPLOYEE BENEFIT PLANS

A *cafeteria plan* is an employee benefit plan that meets the design conditions outlined in Section 125 of the *IRC,* and in which employees have the right to choose from among a range of benefits. Cafeteria plans have become popular because they permit employees to select the benefits that are most appropriate to their needs.

The normal approach to a cafeteria plan is a program that grants employees credits that may be used to "buy" benefits. Credits can be based on salary, years of service, or a combination of factors, but cannot discriminate in favor of key employees. The employee then selects benefits most appropriate to his or her need from the choices offered, which can include most nontaxable benefits, such as group term life insurance, health insurance, dependent care, or participation in a group legal service plan. The HIPAA provides that long-term care insurance may not be offered as a qualified benefit under a cafeteria plan. The employer may also permit the employee to take some or all of the credit in the form of additional cash compensation (but not as taxable benefits).[22] Section 401 (k) cash or deferred profit-sharing or stock-bonus plans can be included in the list of choices. Other deferred compensation plans, such as pensions, must be provided separately from the flexible program.

In some cases, flexible benefits are funded directly through salary reduction; employees can reduce their salaries by a certain amount and use the money tax free to pay for certain benefits. Such arrangements, while technically cafeteria plans, are called *flexible spending accounts.*

As in the case of other qualified employee benefits, a cafeteria plan may not discriminate in favor of highly compensated participants as to benefits or contributions. Under a restriction added by the Tax Reform Act of 1984, key employees will be taxed on otherwise nontaxable benefits in any year for which the qualified benefits for key employees exceed 25 percent of such benefits for all employees under the plan.[23]

SOME SPECIALIZED USES OF LIFE INSURANCE IN BUSINESS

In addition to providing protection to employees under the fringe benefit programs and funding retirement benefits, life insurance serves several other functions in the business firm. They include funding business purchase agreements, protecting the firm against the loss of a key employee, and providing additional compensation to executives and other valuable employees.

Business Continuation Insurance

The death or disability of the owner of a business, a member of a partnership, or a stockholder of a close corporation may create serious problems for that business. If it is a sole proprietorship, it may be necessary to liquidate and sell the specific assets rather than the going concern. Any value based on goodwill or earnings may be wiped out. In the case of a partnership, the executor of the deceased partner's estate may find it necessary to sell the estate's interest at the best offer obtainable from surviving partners. Finally, in the case of a corporation, the corporation will continue, but either the heirs of the deceased stockholder may not desire to continue their ownership or the remaining stockholders may not wish to share ownership and control with the heirs.

The ideal solution to those problems is to make arrangements for the sale of the individual's interest in the business prior to death through a buy-and-sell agreement under whose terms each owner agrees that his or her share of the business is to be sold to the remaining owners at death, and each owner

[22] Originally, participants under cafeteria plans were offered a choice from a wide range of nontaxable benefits, taxable benefits, and cash. Since 1988, cafeteria plans may include only cash or nontaxable benefits, such as coverage under group health insurance, group term life insurance, or other qualified benefits.

[23] *IRC* Section 125(b)(2).

agrees to buy the shares of a deceased owner. In a proprietorship, the parties to the purchase agreement may be the owner and an employee or the owner and a competitor. The buy-and-sell agreement should contain a formula for setting the value of the business at the time of the sale, thus eliminating later difficulties regarding the value.

It is possible to have a business purchase agreement without a funding arrangement. The partners may have sufficient cash or liquid assets to enable a survivor to purchase the interest of the decedent for cash. But this would be a very unusual situation, particularly in a growing business, where the partners have been plowing back the profits. The most satisfactory method of funding is to purchase business life insurance on the lives of the owners. The partners, partnership, stockholders, or the corporation—whoever is to be the purchaser—would pay the premiums and receive the proceeds of the policy on the life of the party whose interest in the business is to be purchased.[24]

The operational aspects of the funding may vary, depending on the circumstances. Under the arrangement known as a *cross-purchase plan,* each partner or stockholder carries enough life insurance on the lives of the others to permit the purchase of a proportionate share of the deceased member's interest. For example, if Abner, Baker, and Cole each own one-third of a business valued at $300,000, Abner would buy $50,000 in life insurance on Baker and $50,000 on Cole, Baker would buy $50,000 on both Abner and Cole, and Cole would buy $50,000 on Abner and Baker. If one partner dies, the remaining two will receive sufficient proceeds from their policies to permit them to purchase the decedent's interest.

As an alternative, the policy on each owner could be purchased by the firm itself. Under this arrangement, known as the *entity plan,* the firm owns the policies and is the beneficiary. Premiums paid by the firm are not a deductible expense, but the policy proceeds are exempt from income taxation. Under the entity plan, the partnership or corporation purchases the interest of the deceased owner, and the interest of the survivors is increased proportionately.[25]

Key-Person Insurance

One of the most valuable assets of any business is the skill of its employees. Since every employee contributes to the success of a business, the death of any one of them is a source of loss to the firm. The extent of this loss varies with the individual's part in the firm's success. Those employees who make a critical contribution to this success are key employees, and sometimes the risk of their loss may be sufficient to warrant *key-person insurance* protection. The key person may be a crucial factor in sales, production, finance, management, or some combination of these functions. In some cases, the key worker may be the owner, in others, it will be a partner or an employee. It may even be a stockholder. Whatever the case, when the death of an individual associated with the business might cause a financial loss through imperiled credit, loss of leadership, lower profits, or reduced ability to secure new business, the firm has an insurable interest in that individual.

One of the most difficult aspects of insuring key personnel is the determination of their value. The valuation may be based on an estimate of the probable loss of income that might result from the employee's death or an estimate of the additional expenses of obtaining a replacement. In the last analysis, the value will be an educated guess, based on a combination of factors.

Split-Dollar Plan

Split-dollar insurance is an arrangement by which an employer and employee share the cost of an insurance policy on the life of the latter. The two parties usually enter into an agreement under which the employer agrees to pay that portion of each annual premium equal to the increase in the cash value resulting from such premium payment. The employee pays the balance of the premium. The employer is usually the owner of the policy and is also a beneficiary to the

[24] Although this discussion describes the need and solution in the event of death, the same problems apply to disability. Business continuation disability policies are available that pay a lump-sum benefit for use in purchasing a disabled owner's interest. Another approach would be to provide sufficient disability income insurance for the firm to continue the income of the disabled owner, partner, or stockholder without imposing a financial burden on the firm itself.

[25] A stock-retirement agreement is a contract between stockholders and the corporation by which the corporation agrees to purchase the stock in the corporation owned by an employee on the employee's death. The stock may then be held by the corporation or canceled. A stockholders' buy–sell agreement is an agreement for the purchase and sale between stockholders, under which survivors agree to buy the stock of a deceased shareholder.

extent of the cash value. The employee's spouse or other personal beneficiary is designated as beneficiary to the extent of the balance of any death proceeds. Under the basic split-dollar plan, the employer may not change the portion of the beneficary designation dealing with the insured's personal beneficiary without the consent of the insured.

Split-dollar insurance is intended to give the employee an incentive to remain with the firm. It permits the employee to obtain additional life insurance with a minimum outlay of personal funds and, because it is permanent insurance, it can be continued beyond retirement age. One drawback to the basic split-dollar plan is that the amount payable to the insured's personal beneficiary decreases year by year as the cash value of the policy and the employer's interest increase. However, in the case of participating policies, this drawback can be partially offset through the use of dividends to purchase one-year term insurance (the fifth dividend option).

A split-dollar plan can be characterized in one of three ways. First, it may be viewed as a loan. Under this view, the employer's payment to the policy is viewed as a loan to the employee, which requires imputed interest. The employer receives taxable interest income and a deduction for employee compensation, while the employee receives additional compensation equal to the imputed interest and is also entitled a deduction for interest (subject to limitations). Under the second characterization (the traditional view of split-dollar plans), the employer is the owner of the policy and the employee receives imputed compensation equal to the value of the insurance, reduced by premium payments he or she makes to the plan. Under the third view, the employer pays the premiums on the policy, but does not acquire ownership in the policy. In this case, the entire premium paid by the employer is viewed as compensation to the employee.[26]

Deferred Compensation

Deferred compensation is an arrangement in which the employer agrees to make future payments to an employee after retirement or future payments to the

employee's spouse if the worker should die before retiring. Such an arrangement usually results from the employer's desire to retain the services and loyalty of key personnel. The employee also derives a benefit, since some income is deferred until a time when the tax burden is usually lower. The employee incurs no federal income tax liability prior to retirement under an orthodox deferred compensation agreement, because the employer's mere promise to pay, not represented by notes or secured in any way, is not regarded as the receipt of income by a cash-basis tax-payer.

Employers often find it advisable to obtain a life insurance policy on the life of the employee to fund the deferred-compensation agreement. If the employee lives to retirement age, the employer will use the cash surrender value of the policy to make monthly payments to the retiree. The employer may not deduct the premiums paid for the insurance, and the cash value is taxable when received to the extent that it represents a return over the premiums paid. If the employee dies before retirement, the proceeds of the life insurance policy provide the funds that will be paid to the employee's dependents. The death proceeds, which are received by the employer upon the death of the employee, are not taxable as income. Amounts paid to either the employee or surviving dependents are a deductible expense to the firm if reasonable in amount. Sums payable to the employee are fully taxable when received, and sums paid by the employer to the employee's surviving dependents if the employee dies are also taxable income.

SUMMARY

Our discussion of life and health insurance and pensions in the business firm has been very limited. These are highly technical fields, and generally require management decisions with long-range implications. The tax aspects of the business life and health area and of qualified pension plans call for the advice of competent tax and legal technicians. No attempt has been made to deal with all facets of these complicated areas, but it is hoped that the student has a better appreciation of the intricacies in the area and a foundation for further study.

[26] National Underwriter, *Taxline.* vol. 2001, no. 2 (February 2001).

IMPORTANT CONCEPTS TO REMEMBER

employee benefits	501 (c)(9) trusts	separate account
group life insurance	split funding	Pension Benefit Guarantee
group health insurance	group deferred annuity	Corporation (PBGC)
group term life insurance	Tax Equity and Fiscal Responsibility	cafeteria plan
employee death benefit	Act (TEFRA)	allocated funding instrument
group ordinary life	top-heavy plan	unallocated funding instrument
group paid-up life insurance	trust fund plan	cross-purchase plan
group universal life insurance	guaranteed investment contract	deferred compensation
survivor income benefit insurance	(GIC)	key-person life insurance
retired lives reserve	insured plan	entity plan
stop-loss insurance	deposit administration plan	split-dollar insurance
aggregate stop-loss insurance	immediate participation guarantee	
flexible spending account	plan	

QUESTIONS FOR REVIEW

1. Identify and briefly describe the employee benefits discussed in the chapter for which the tax code provides favorable tax treatment.

2. Explain the advantages granted to employees under the tax laws governing

a. Health insurance plans for which the employer pays the premium, and

b. Contributions made by an employer for life insurance on the lives of employees.

3. Identify and briefly explain the requirements for a pension plan to be "qualified" under ERISA. What are the advantages of qualification?

4. Identify and explain the differences in the funding agencies that an employer may use for funding a qualified pension plan.

5. What is the basic difference between *allocated funding instruments* and *unallocated funding instruments?*

Identify the funding instruments that fall into each category.

6. The PBGC guarantees insured plan participants against loss of benefits that can result from funding deficiencies. How can funding deficiencies arise?

7. In what way does the employer assume a greater element of risk under an immediate participation guarantee pension plan than under a group deferred annuity?

8. Briefly describe the special requirements that apply to a top-heavy plan. Why were these requirements enacted?

9. Briefly outline the provisions of the tax code relating to deductibility of premiums and taxation of policy proceeds in key-person life insurance.

10. In what way(s) does the Pension Benefit Guarantee Corporation protect (a) employees and (b) employers?

QUESTIONS FOR DISCUSSION

1. Many of the decisions relating to pension plans were formerly regarded to be management prerogatives, but are now dictated by federal regulations. To what extent does ERISA violate the freedom of choice of business managers with respect to pension plans? Is this violation justified?

2. The text notes that the business continuation exposure involves the possibility of the death or the disability of owners. From the perspective of other owners, in what ways is the effect of the disability of an owner the same as and different from the risk of the death of an owner?

3. For what reasons might an organization decide to establish a nonqualified deferred compensation program? Has the number of nonqualified programs increased or decreased since enactment of ERISA? Why?

4. A self-employed chiropractor has three full-time employees and is considering establishing a qualified retirement plan. What are the options with respect to the type of plan that she should establish and the features that will be included in the plan?

5. Employee benefits are sometimes referred to as "fringe" benefits, suggesting that they represent a form of

somewhat gratuitous compensation granted by an employer. This view considers pensions as a reward for long and faithful service. The opposing view is that employee benefits are a part of a total compensation package and that pension benefits are simply deferred compensation accepted by the employee in lieu of higher current wages. With which of these views are the provisions of ERISA consistent? To what extent are the provisions of ERISA fully consistent with this view?

SUGGESTIONS FOR ADDITIONAL READING

Allen, Everette T., Joseph Y. Melone, Jerry S. Rosenbloom, and Jack L. Vanderhei. *Pension Planning,* 8th ed. Homewood, Ill.: Richard D. Irwin, 1997.

American Council of Life Insurance. *Pension Facts.* Washington, D.C.: American Council of Life Insurance, published annually.

Beam, Burton T., Jr. *Group Benefits: Basic Concepts and Alternatives,* 4th ed. Bryn Mawr, Pa.: The American College, 1991.

Black, Kenneth, Jr., and Harold D. Skipper, Jr. *Life Insurance,* 13th ed. Englewood Cliffs, N.J.: Prentice-Hall, 2000. Chapter 19–20.

Brahs, Stuart J. "Tax Reform in 1986; What It Means for Employee Benefits." *Benefits Quarterly,* vol. 3, no. 1 (First Quarters 1987).

Cross, Mark L., Steven M. Flory, and Thomas J. Phillips, Jr. "Implications of the FASB Proposal for Accruing Post-retirement Health Care Benefits." *Benefits Quarterly,* vol. 5, no. 3, 1989.

Doyle, Robert J., Jr., et al., *The Financial Services Professional's Guide to the Tax Reform Act of 1986.* Bryn Mawr, Pa.: American College, 1986.

Fundamentals of Employee Benefit Programs, 4th ed. Washington, D.C.: Employee Benefit Research Institute, 1990.

Hallman, G. Victor, and Karen L. Hamilton. *Personal Insurance: Life, Health, and Retirement.* Malvern, Pa.: American Institute for CPCU, 1994. Chapters 7, 8.

Leimberg, Stephan R., et al. *The Financial Services Professional's Guide to the State of the Art,* 2nd ed. Bryn Mawr, Pa.: The American College, 1991.

Liscio, John. "Safe GICs: Everyone Wants Them But Do They Exist?" *Barrons* (July 29, 1991).

Rosenbloom, Jerry S., ed. *The Handbook of Employee Benefits: Design, Funding and Administration.* Homewood, Ill.: Richard D. Irwin, 1984.

Wood, Glenn L., Claude C. Lilly, III, Donald S. Malecki, Edward E. Graves, and Jerry S. Rosenbloom. *Personal Risk Management and Insurance,* 4th ed., vol 2. Malvern, Pa.: American Institute for Property and Liability, 1989. Chapters 12, 13, 14.

WEB SITES TO EXPLORE

American Society of Pension Actuaries	http://www.aspa.org/
Association of Private Pension and Welfare Plans	http://www.podi.com/appwp/retire.htm
Benefit Links	http://www.benefitslink.com/
Employee Benefit Research Institute	http://www.ebri.org
Employee Benefits Survey	http://www.bls.gov/ebshome.htm
Health Insurance Association of America	http://www.hiaa.org/
Integrated Benefits Institute	http://www.ibiweb.org
International Foundation of Employee Benefit Plans	http://www.ifebp.org/
Pension and Welfare Benefit Administration	http://www.dol.gov/dol/pwba/
Pension Benefit Guarantee Corporation	http://www.pbgc.gov/
U.S. Pension Law—Cornell University	http://www.law.cornell.edu/topics/pensions.html

CHAPTER 24

THE HOMEOWNERS POLICY—GENERAL PROVISIONS

A combination and a form indeed.

— WILLIAM SHAKESPEARE
Hamlet

CHAPTER OBJECTIVES

When you have finished this chapter, you should be able to

- Explain the general nature of the homeowners program
- Identify and distinguish among the homeowners forms and describe the individual for whom each form is designed
- Explain the difference between named-peril and open-peril coverage
- Identify the coverage parts of the homeowners policy
- Identify coverage features of each Section I coverage part

THE HOMEOWNERS POLICY PROGRAM

The home is one of the most important, and probably the most expensive, investments that the average consumer will ever make. Understandably, protection against damage to the dwelling is a central part of every family's insurance program. Insurance protection on the individual's personal property is also an important aspect of a personal insurance program. Finally, but by no means of lesser importance, is the liability coverage needed to protect against the financial consequences of legal liability. In this chapter, we will begin our study of the homeowners policy, which is a package policy approach to insuring these exposures.

Historical Development

The homeowners policy is a product of the multiple-line transition, which resulted from the removal of the legal barriers that separated property insurance from casualty insurance. One of the significant effects of the multiple-line transition was the package policy, in which property and casualty coverages are combined in a single contract. The homeowners policies, which combine fire insurance coverages with theft insurance and personal liability insurance, are the most widely sold and by far the best known of the package policies. The homeowners program was introduced in 1958. Within a short time after their introduction, the homeowners forms had become the standard approach to insuring residential property.

The program has been revised several times since its introduction. A significant revision occurred in 1976, when the Insurance Services Office (ISO) took the progressive step of dramatically simplifying the language. The 1976 homeowners program introduced simplified-language contracts to the field of insurance, eliminating much of the legalistic wording that had characterized insurance contracts, and replaced it with an easier-to-read "English translation." Throughout the policy, the insurance company is referred to as "we," and the insured (who presumably is reading the contract) is addressed as "you." The following discussion is based on the year 2000 edition of the homeowners program.

It should be noted that although the following discussion details the characteristics of the standard ISO 2000 Homeowners program, particular provisions may vary from state to state, depending on the unique characteristics of state law. This is particularly true in areas such as the cancellation provision.

General Nature of the Homeowners Program

In most jurisdictions, there are six standard homeowners forms:

HO 00 02, Homeowners 2 Broad Form

HO 00 03, Homeowners 3 Special Form

HO 00 04, Homeowners 4 Contents Broad Form

HO 00 05, Homeowners 5 Comprehensive Form

HO 00 06, Homeowners 6 Unit-Owners Form

HO 00 08, Homeowners 8 Modified Coverage Form

Four of these forms (2, 3, 5, and 8) are designed for individuals who own their homes, one (form HO-4) is designed for tenants, and one (form HO-6) is designed for condominium unit-owners.[1]

There are strict eligibility requirements under the program. Forms 2, 3, 5, and 8 may be written only for the owner-occupant of a one-to-four family dwelling used exclusively for private residential purposes (although the rules permit incidental office or professional occupancy, such as a physician who may have an office in his or her home). Homeowners form HO-4 may be written for a tenant who lives in a rented dwelling or an apartment or for a homeowner who owns a dwelling that does not meet the eligibility requirements for one of the other forms (i.e., because it contains more than four families). Form HO-6 may be written only for condominium unit-owners and members of cooperatives. (Members of cooperatives are eligible for either form HO-4 or HO-6.) Dwelling owners who are not eligible for form HO-2 or HO-3 may obtain coverage under form HO-8, which is intended for older homes or low-valued dwellings. The eligibility requirements of form HO-8 are less rigorous than those of the other forms, and the coverage is more limited.

All the forms include two sections: Section I, which provides coverage on the insured's own property, and Section II, which provides liability and medical payments coverage. The coverage under Section II is identical under all the forms, and it is only with respect to Section I that the forms differ. The provisions of Section II will be discussed in Chapter 27. Here we are concerned only with the coverage under Section I.

HOMEOWNERS SECTION I COVERAGE

The Section I coverages of the homeowners forms provide coverage on the insured's own property, and the forms differ from one another in the protection they provide. Differences exist both in terms of the items covered under some of the forms and in the perils insured.

[1] Earlier versions of the homeowners program included another form, the Homeowners Basic Form (HO-1). The Homeowners Basic Form is being phased out nationally and was still used in only six states in 1994. The Homeowners Comprehensive Form (HO-5) was eliminated in 1984, but was resurrected in the 2000 revision.

Section I Coverages: An Overview

There are four items of coverage under Section I, designated A, B, C, and D. As noted, the basic philosophy of the homeowners program is to require certain minimum amounts of coverage with a mandatory relationship among the minimums for the various coverages.

Coverage A provides protection on the dwelling and is included only in forms HO-2, HO-3, and HO-5. Form HO-4 does not cover the dwelling and does not include Coverage A. Under Form HO-6, Coverage A provides $1000 on the condominium unit-owner's building items. This nominal amount may be increased if there is a need for greater coverage.

Coverage B provides a specific amount of insurance on other structures (such as a garage) on the premises, equal to 10 percent of the amount on the dwelling. The insurance on other structures may be increased above this standard 10 percent when there is a need.

Coverage C provides coverage on personal property or *contents*. Under Forms 4 and 6 the minimum coverage on personal property is $6000. Under the other forms, it is 50 percent of the amount on the dwelling. The coverage on personal property may be increased when its value exceeds the standard 50 percent, or it may be reduced, but not below 40 percent of dwelling coverage.

Coverage D, designated *Loss of Use,* covers indirect loss. It provides payment for additional living expense and loss of rental income when the insured property cannot be used because of damage by an insured peril. The standard limit for the loss of use coverage is 30 percent of the amount on the dwelling under forms HO-2, HO-3, and HO-5 and 10 percent of the amount on the dwelling under Form 8. The limit for Coverage D under form HO-4 is 30 percent of personal property coverage, and under form HO-6 it is 50 percent of the amount on personal property.

In addition to the four coverages designated A, B, C, and D, each form also includes several extensions, called *Additional Coverages,* that further broaden the coverage. The additional coverages are discussed later in the chapter.

Perils Insured

As explained earlier, there are two broad approaches to insuring property: *named-peril* coverage and *open-peril* coverage. Under the named-peril approach, the specific perils for which coverage is provided are listed in the policy. Under the *open-perils* approach, the insurer agrees to pay for damage by any peril except those specifically excluded.[2] The coverage under homeowners policies is available on both a named-peril and open-peril basis.

Modern property insurance is generally available with three levels of coverage, referred to as *basic coverage* (or sometimes, depending on the contract, *standard coverage*), *broad form coverage,* or *special coverage.* Basic form coverage provides a minimum level of protection, with named perils, usually limited to the perils of fire, extended coverage, and vandalism. Coverage may be broadened to include additional named perils, in which case the coverage is referred to as *Broad Form* coverage. Finally, coverage may also be written under a *Special Form,* which provides coverage on an *open-peril* basis. The homeowners forms are based on these three standard levels of property coverage (*basic, broad,* and *special*), and also include the peril of theft, a coverage not generally covered in traditional "fire insurance" perils. With the exception of Homeowners Form 8, which is designed for older homes that do not quality for the "normal" homeowners policy, coverage under the homeowners forms is on a broad or special basis[3]—that is, coverage is on a broad named-peril basis or on an open-peril basis. The *broad named-peril* coverage includes 16 perils, with wording that is essentially identical from form to form. HO Form 2 covers buildings and contents on a broad named-peril basis. HO Forms 4 and 6 cover contents only, for the same broad named perils. HO Form 3 covers contents for the same named perils as do forms HO-2, HO-4, and HO-6, but covers buildings on an open-peril basis. Finally, form HO-5 covers both buildings and contents on an open-peril basis.

For the convenience of the reader, the coverage of the six homeowners forms used nationally, the minimum amounts of coverage, and the perils insured are summarized in Table 24.1.

[2] Historically, this coverage has been called *all-risk* coverage. However, there is a concerted effort by the insurance industry to abandon the term "all-risk," primarily because it is misunderstood by insureds.

[3] The Homeowners 8 Modified Coverage Form and the Homeowners 1 Basic Form, which is still used in a limited number of states, provide coverage for a smaller number of named-perils.

TABLE 24.1 Homeowners Forms

Coverage	Form HO 00 02	Form HO 00 03	Form HO 00 04	Form HO 00 05	Form HO 00 06	Form HO 00 08
A: Dwelling	Covered	Covered	Not covered	Covered	$1,000	Covered
B: Other Structures	10% of A	1-% of A	Not covered	10% of A	Part of A	10% of A
C: Personal Property	50% of A	50% of A	$6000 minimum	50% of A	$6000 minimum	50% of A
D: Loss of Use	30% of A	30% of A	30% of C	30% of A	50% of C	10% of A
	Fire or Lightning	OPEN PERIL on Building		OPEN PERIL on Building		Fire or lightning
	Windstorm or Hail					Windstorm or hail
	Explosion					
	Riot or Civil Commotion	Same perils as Form 2 on contents	Same Perils as Form 2	OPEN PERIL on Contents	Same perils as Form 2	Explosion
	Aircraft					Riot or civil commotion
	Vehicles					Aircraft
	Smoke					Vehicles
	Vandalism					Smoke
	Theft					Vandalism
	Falling Objects					Theft
	Weight of Ice, Snow, or Sleet					Volcanic eruption
	Accidental discharge or overflow of water or steam					
	Sudden and Accidental tearing apart, cracking, burning or bulging					
	Freezing of plumbing, heating, air-conditioning systems or appliances					
	Damage from artificially generated electricity					
	Volcanic eruption					

Dwelling and Other Structures Coverage

With a few exceptions noted in the following discussion, all the forms that provide coverage on the dwelling and other structures (i.e., Forms 2, 3, 5, and 8) contain the same definitions with respect to this property.

Coverage A: Dwelling Coverage A specifies that "dwelling" includes structures attached to the dwelling and also covers material and supplies located on the premises or adjacent to the premises, which are intended for use in construction, alteration, or repair of the dwelling. The extension of coverage to cover construction materials is important because the homeowners policy can be used to cover a dwelling under construction. (The dwelling must be intended for occupancy by the insured.) The form specifically states that land is not covered.

Coverage A of form HO-6, the Unit-Owners form, covers the condominium unit-owner's *building items,* with a $1000 limit. This coverage, discussed in greater detail later, may be increased if greater coverage is required.

Coverage B: Other Structures The coverage on other structures applies only to structures separated from the dwelling by a clear space. It includes buildings, such as a detached garage, but also includes nonbuilding structures, such as fences, patios, or even swimming pools. The coverage on other structures excludes buildings that are rented to anyone other than a tenant of the residence unless used solely as a private garage. Other structures used to store business property are also excluded. Here, an exception applies for business property owned by an insured or a tenant of the building, provided such business property does not include gaseous or liquid fuel (other than fuel in a vehicle parked in the structure).

Replacement Cost Coverage The coverage on the dwelling and other buildings under the homeowners forms is on a *replacement cost* basis. It provides that if at the time of a loss the amount of insurance covering a building is at least 80 percent of the building's replacement cost, the loss will be paid on a replacement cost basis (without deduction for depreciation) rather than on an actual cash value basis. In determining compliance with this 80 percent requirement, the insured is permitted to deduct the cost of excavations and pipes, wiring, or foundations that are below the basement (or below the ground if there is no basement). The replacement cost provi-

sion applies only to buildings; personal property is covered for its actual cash value. In addition, the replacement cost provision does not apply to carpeting, domestic appliances, awnings, outdoor antennas, and outdoor equipment.

In its simplest aspect, the extension eliminates depreciation in settling losses, if the insured has maintained the required insurance equal to 80 percent of replacement cost. In effect, the extension permits the insured to purchase insurance on the depreciation the building has suffered. If the amount of insurance is less than 80 percent of the replacement cost, the company will pay the larger of the following two amounts:

- The actual cash value
- The proportion of the replacement cost of the loss that the amount of insurance bears to 80 percent of the replacement cost value of the building.

If the loss is more than $2500 or 5 percent of the amount of insurance, the building must actually be repaired or replaced before the insured can collect on a replacement cost basis.

It might be well here to discuss some problems in determining insurance value of real property. The fact that most insureds have a somewhat distorted notion of what is meant by insurable value often results in improper insurance coverage. There are two basic measures of insurable value in dwelling property: replacement cost and actual cash value. Replacement cost is simply the cost of rebuilding the structure with materials of like kind and quality at current prices. Actual cash value, on the other hand, means *replacement cost less depreciation.*

Some insureds think of insurable value in terms of some other inappropriate measure such as loan value or market value. The mortgagee usually requires insurance equal to its interest in the property, reinforcing the mistaken notion that market value somehow coincides with insurable value. There is no reason that market value will be the same as either actual cash value or replacement cost; there is even good reason to assume that it will not. Market value is based on the supply and demand for a particular type of real estate. It includes the value of the land on which the building stands, yet the land value is not a part of the insurable worth.

To illustrate the operation of the replacement cost provision (and at the same time indicate the effects of the misconceptions about insurable value), consider a

dwelling built 30 years ago at an original cost of $50,000. The owner has just purchased this dwelling for $120,000, and insures it for the purchase price of $120,000. Now assume that a loss occurs, causing damage to the roof in the amount of, say, $8000. In adjusting the loss, the adjuster determines that the current replacement cost of the building is $200,000. The roof on the building is determined to be 10 years old, with a life expectancy of 20 years. In settling the $8000 loss to the roof, the insurer will pay the greater of the actual cash value of the loss (50 percent of $8000, or $4000) or that proportion of the loss that the amount of insurance carried bears to 80 percent of the replacement cost. Since 80 percent of the replacement cost is $160,000 and only $120,000 in coverage has been purchased, the insurer will pay 120/160 of the $8000 loss, or $6000. The policyholder will be forced to bear $2000 of the loss personally. If the insured had purchased insurance equal to 80 percent of the replacement cost, payment for the same $8000 loss would have been made in full without a deduction for depreciation or a penalty for underinsurance.[4]

Note that the recovery in this example is greater than the actual cash value of the loss and that without the Replacement Cost provision, the insured would have received only the actual cash value of the loss, or $2000. This demonstrates that even if the insured is underinsured, he or she is better off with Replacement Cost coverage.

Coping with Inflation Maintaining adequate insurance on a dwelling requires continuing attention. Two approaches have been developed to help insureds in addressing this problem.

The Inflation Guard Endorsement The *Inflation Guard Endorsement* is an option that automatically increases the amount of insurance under the policy by some percentage of the original face amount every quarter. The insured may select a quarterly percentage increase in the amount of insurance (e.g., 1, 2, or 3 percent, and so on) with the premium for the endorsement varying with the percentage increase selected. The purpose of the endorsement is to help the insured to meet the provisions of the replacement cost condition and protect against underinsurance, which might result from inflation and increasing construction costs. The increase applies not only to the building but to other items of coverage as well.

Guaranteed Replacement Cost The most attractive approach to coverage on the dwelling is an option offered by some insurers for *guaranteed replacement cost* coverage. The standard ISO endorsement for this coverage is called *Additional Limits of Liability for Coverage A, B, C, and D* (HO 0411). The endorsement provides that the insured must notify the insurer of additions or improvements to the dwelling that increase its replacement cost by 5 percent or more within 30 days of the completion of the improvements. The insurer agrees to pay for the repair or replacement of the dwelling even if the cost to do so exceeds the limit for Coverage A shown in the declarations. In effect, the limit for Coverage A is increased retroactively to equal the current replacement cost of the building. Coverages B, C, and D limits are increased by the same percentage as the increase in the Coverage A limit. The premium is also adjusted to reflect the higher limits of coverage.

Under a second endorsement, *Specified Additional Amount of Insurance for Coverage A— Dwelling* (HO 04 20), the insured may choose 25 or 50 percent of the Coverage A limit as an additional amount of insurance on the dwelling, to be used for payment of dwelling losses that exceed the limit listed in the declarations.

Personal Property Coverage

The limit for personal property is 50 percent of the dwelling limit under Form 2, 3, and 5. This limit may be increased when there is a need for greater coverage. The limit may be decreased if the insured does not own personal property equal to 50 percent of the value of the dwelling, but it cannot be decreased below 40 percent. Under form HO-4 and form HO-6, the minimum coverage on personal property is $6000. The Personal Property coverage can, of course, be increased under any of the forms if the need exists.

The personal property insuring agreement of all forms is identical:

> We cover personal property owned or used by any insured while anywhere in the world.

[4] It should be noted that while the form requires only 80 percent of the replacement cost to be insured, this does not and should not preclude the insured from purchasing 100 percent replacement cost coverage. When the insured purchases coverage equal to 80 percent of the replacement cost of the building, losses are paid with a deduction for depreciation, but, in the event of a total loss, the insured is underinsured to the extent of 20 percent of the value of the building.

Note, first, that coverage is provided on both owned and borrowed property. For example, if an insured borrows property from a friend, and the property is damaged or lost as a result of an insured peril, the homeowners policy will cover the property as if it had been owned by the insured.

The reference to property owned or used *by any insured* grants coverage for the property of all persons that fall within the definition of *Insured*. The policy definition defines "Insured" to include the named insured ("You"), residents of the named insured's household who are relatives of the insured, and other persons under the age of 21 who are in the care of the named insured or a resident relative. The definition of insured also extends to full-time students who were residents of the household before moving out to attend school if they are under age 24 and related to the insured, or under 21 and in the care of the insured or a resident relative.

The entire personal property coverage applies "anywhere in the world," subject to one exception. Coverage on personal property located at a secondary residence is limited to 10 percent of the Coverage C limit, subject to a $1000 minimum. For example, if the insured has a summer cottage, coverage on personal property at the cottage is limited to 10 percent of the total Personal Property coverage.[5] With this exception, property located elsewhere than on the premises is covered up to the full limit specified for personal property.

If the insured requests at the time of loss, coverage also applies to property owned by others while on that part of the premises occupied by an insured or to the property of a guest or residence employee while in any residence occupied by an insured. The requirement that the insured request coverage on the property of others is intended to protect the insured in case the value of property of others that is damaged or destroyed, when combined with the insured's destroyed property, exceeds the limit of coverage.

Personal Property Replacement Cost Although replacement cost coverage on buildings has been available since the inception of the homeowners program, personal property is covered on an actual cash value basis. The optional *Personal Property Replacement Cost Endorsement* converts coverage on personal property to a replacement cost basis. Like the replacement cost on building items in the homeowners form, the personal property replacement cost provision agrees to pay losses to the subject property without a deduction for depreciation. When the replacement cost of the loss is over $500, payment is made on a replacement cost basis only if the property is actually replaced. Coverage applies not only to personal property insured under Coverage C, but to items scheduled under the Scheduled Personal Property endorsement.

Four classes of property are not eligible for replacement cost coverage under the endorsement: (1) antiques, fine arts, and similar property, (2) memorabilia, souvenirs, collectors items, and the like, (3) property not kept in good or workable condition, and (4) obsolete articles that are stored or not being used. The first two classes of property are excluded because of the difficulty in determining replacement cost. These items are more appropriately scheduled in the Scheduled Personal Property endorsement (HO 04 61) and insured on a valued basis. The last two classes of property are excluded from the replacement cost condition because to provide coverage on such property would violate the principle of indemnity and could result in an increased moral hazard.

In addition to the replacement cost coverage on personal property, the endorsement provides replacement cost coverage on certain building items that are specifically excluded from the replacement cost coverage applicable to buildings: awnings, carpeting, household appliances, outdoor antennas, and outdoor equipment.

Property Excluded under Personal Property Coverage The personal property insuring agreement provides coverage on a *blanket* basis. This means that all personal property owned or used by the insured is covered by a single amount of insurance. Blanket coverage is contrasted with specific or scheduled coverage, in which items are listed and insured individually. Some types of property, such as jewelry, furs, guns, and other property with high values, are commonly insured on a scheduled basis, usually for broader perils than the perils applicable to property covered on a blanket basis. The blanket coverage of the homeowners forms excludes or limits coverage on certain classes of property for which coverage is available on a scheduled basis or under other more specialized contracts. The following property is excluded:

[5] The 10 percent limit on property at a secondary residence does not apply to property at a newly acquired principal residence for 30 days after the insured begins to move property to that location. Neither does it apply to property that has been moved while the principal residence is being repaired, renovated, or rebuilt and is not fit to live in or store property in.

1. Articles that are separately described and specifically insured under the homeowners or any other insurance

2. Animals, birds, or fish

3. Motor vehicles, their accessories, equipment and parts, and electronic apparatus designed to be operated *solely* by the vehicle's electrical system and tapes, discs or other media for use with such equipment, while in or on the vehicle

4. Aircraft and their parts (except model or hobby aircraft)

5. Hovercraft and their parts

6. Property of roomers, boarders, and other tenants not related to the insured

7. Property in an apartment regularly rented or held for rental to others by the insured, except as provided under the landlord's furnishings additional coverage

8. Property rented or held for rental to others away from the premises

9. Business data, including such data stored in books of account, drawings, paper records, and electronic data processing (EDP) software media

10. Credit cards, electronic fund transfer cards, or access devices use for deposit, withdrawal or transfer of funds (except as provided under Additional Coverages)

11. Water or steam

Most of these excluded classes are self-explanatory, but a few may require comment.

First, the exclusion of property separately described and specifically insured eliminates coverage on scheduled items and property insured under other policies from the blanket coverage on personal property to avoid duplication of coverage.[6]

The exclusion of motor vehicles and their equipment excludes not only automobiles, motorcycles, motorscooters, and the like, but also go-carts, minibikes, golf carts, and snowmobiles. An exception to the exclusion of motor vehicles provides coverage on vehicles not required to be registered for use on public roads that are used *solely* to service an insured's residence (such as riding lawnmowers or garden tractors) or that are designed to assist the handicapped.[7] Coverage is also available on owned golf carts by endorsment.

The motor vehicle exclusion extends to the vehicle's equipment and accessories only while in or on the vehicle. This means that the theft of a tire from the vehicle is excluded, while theft of the same tire while stored in the insured's garage would be covered. The exclusion of motor vehicle electronic apparatus includes tape players, CB radios, cellular telephones, fax machines, or any other electronic equipment only if it can be operated *solely* by the vehicle's electrical system. Electronic equipment that can be operated by the power system of the vehicle, but which can also be operated from other power sources, is not excluded, but is subject to a dollar limit discussed in a later section.

The exclusion of hovercraft and their parts was added to the policy in the 2000 revision, to address an ambiguity over whether hovercraft were motor vehicles or watercraft.

Exclusions 6 and 7 are related. Property of roomers and boarders who are not members of the insured's family is excluded along with the property of other tenants. Furnishings owned by the insured in that part of the premises rented to roomers or boarders is covered. Furnishings in an apartment (a living unit with its own cooking and bathing facilities) are limited to the amount of coverage provided by the landlord's furnishings additional coverage.

Exclusion 8 eliminates coverage on property rented or held for rental to others away from the premises. Such property represents a business exposure beyond the scope of the homeowners policy.

The exclusion of business data stored in records and electronic data processing media eliminates coverage for the cost of reconstructing the information that is lost. The cost of blank or unexposed records and media is covered. Coverage is also provided for standard software such as word processing or spreadsheet programs available in the retail market.

The exclusion of water and steam is intended to make clear that water or steam delivered through public water mains is considered a utility and, therefore,

[6] The reasons for obtaining specific insurance on certain items will become apparent later in this chapter. The coverage provided when items are specifically insured will be discussed in Chapter 25.

[7] The requirement that lawnmowers and such vehicles be used *solely* to service an insured's residence was added in the 2000 revision. Some observers have expressed concern that the use of a mower or similar vehicle to cut a neighbor's lawn could conceivably jeopardize the coverage on such vehicle. It is unlikely that this was the intent and the "glitch" will probably be changed in a future revision.

not owned by the insured. Coverage will not apply, for example, for the loss of water or steam through a broken pipe on the premises that results in a massive increase in the insured's utility bill.

Personal Property Subject to Dollar Limits In addition to excluding certain classes of property just described, the homeowners forms impose dollar limits on other classes of property. Some of these limits may be increased for an additional premium. In other cases, the property may be scheduled with a higher limit of coverage or insured under another policy. The property subject to dollar limits is indicated in Table 24.2

The $200 limit on money applies not only to currency, but to coin collections, scrip, stored value cards, and smart cards. Stored value cards are instruments like prepaid phone cards with a magnetic strip or computer chip that are loaded with some amount

of spendable credits. Smart cards can also be loaded with spendable credits, but serve other functions as well. The limitation on such cards reflects their increasing role as substitutes for cash. The $200 limit may be increased to $500 for an additional premium.

The coverage on boats applies to any boat and its equipment (including a trailer), but is limited to $1000. Boats valued at more than this amount should be specifically insured.

Note that the dollar limitations for jewelry and furs, silverware, and firearms and related equipment (classes 6, 7, and 8) apply only to loss by theft. Property of these types valued at more than the specified limits may be scheduled for their full value.

Coverage on business property ("property used primarily for business purposes") is limited to $2500 while on premises.[8] Coverage on business property away from the premises is limited to $500. The limit for business personal property on premises may be increased by endorsement up to $10,000 for an additional premium. When the on-premises business property limit is increased, the off-premises limit is increased to 20 percent of the on-premises limit.

Two separate provisions limit coverage on electronic apparatus (including accessories, antennas, tapes, discs, or other media) that is equipped to be operated by the power system of a vehicle, but that retains the capacity of being operated by another source. The first limit on such equipment is $1500 while it is in or on a motor vehicle. The second provision imposes a $1500 limit on the same types of equipment while it is away from the premises, but not in an auto, if the equipment is used primarily for business purposes. Although the distinction between the two limitations is perhaps confusing, the intent is to limit coverage on such property that is used for both personal and business purposes to $1500 while it is in a vehicle. Electronic apparatus that is used for business is also limited to $1500 while it is away from the insured premises whether or not it is in a vehicle. This $1500 limit supersedes the $500 limit on business property away from the premises.

When specific insurance is obtained on any of the classes to which dollar limits apply, the property should be scheduled for its full value since the coverage on

TABLE 24.2 Dollar Limits on Specified Types of Personal Property

Item	Class of Property	Dollar Limit
1.	Money, bank notes, bullion, coins, medals, scrip, stored value and smart cards	$200
2.	Securities, manuscripts, personal records, stamp collections, and valuable papers	1500
3.	Watercraft of all types, including their trailers, equipment, and motors	1500
4.	Other trailers or semitrailers	1500
5.	Loss of jewelry, watches, furs, and precious and semiprecious stones by theft	1500
6.	Loss of firearms and related equipment by theft	2500
7.	Loss of silverware, silver-plated ware, goldware, gold-plated ware, and pewterware by theft	2500
8.	Property on the residence premises used primarily for business purposes	2500
9.	Property away from the residence premises used for business purposes	500
10.	Electronic apparatus that may be powered by electrical system of a motor vehicle but which retains its capability of being operated by other sources, while in or on a motor vehicle	1500
11.	Electronic apparatus that may be powered by electrical system of a motor vehicle but which retains its capability of being operated by other sources if used primarily for business purposes, while away from the premises	1500

[8] The HO-91 program limited coverage for "personal property used at any time or in any manner for any business purpose." The 2000 wording broadens coverage since the limitation would no longer apply for an insured who, for example, owns a personal computer and only occasionally uses it for business purposes.

such property under the blanket personal property coverage of the homeowners policy no longer applies once the item has been specifically insured. An individual with a $2500 stamp collection, for example, cannot depend on the homeowners insurance to provide $1000 on the collection when it is scheduled; it must be scheduled for the full $2500, not merely $1500.

Loss of Use Coverage

The *Loss of Use* Coverage, designated Coverage D, provides protection against loss involving both the part of the premises occupied by the insured and any part rented to others. For the part of the premises occupied by the insured, the *additional living Expense Coverage* pays for the necessary increase in living expenses incurred by the insured to continue as nearly as practicable the normal standard of living of the household when the premises are rendered uninhabitable by an insured peril. Payment is made only for the period required to repair or replace the damage or, if the insured permanently relocates, for the period required to settle the household elsewhere.

For damage to a part of the premises rented to others, coverage applies for the fair rental value. Again, coverage applies for the shortest period in which the property could be repaired or replaced. Under form HO-4 and form HO-6, Coverage D applies not only for loss arising out of damage to covered property (i.e., personal property) but also for loss to the building containing the covered property that makes the building uninhabitable.

Additional Coverages

The homeowners forms include supplementary extensions of coverage under Section I, called *Additional Coverages*. Although most of the additional coverages are common to all forms, a few of the additional coverages are included in some forms but not others.

Debris Removal The *Debris Removal* additional coverage covers expenses incurred in removing the debris of insured property damaged by an insured peril. Coverage also applies for the expense of removing ash, dust, or articles from a volcanic eruption that has caused direct damage to the building or insured personal property. If the policy limit is exhausted by payment for damage to the property, the debris removal additional coverage provides up

to 5 percent of the limit applicable to the property damaged as an additional amount of insurance to cover the removal of debris.

The Debris Removal additional coverage also covers the removal of certain fallen trees from the premises, up to $500 per tree, with a $1000 aggregate. Coverage is provided for the removal of trees that have been "felled" by the perils of windstorm, hail, the weight of ice, snow, or sleet, and trees belonging to a neighbor that are felled by any of the named perils applicable to Coverage C (the contents coverage) if, in falling, the tree damages a covered structure, blocks a driveway denying access to the premises, or blocks a ramp or fixture designed to assist a handicapped person entering or leaving the premises. As explained later, these are not perils for which damage to trees is covered and there is no indemnity for the loss of the tree itself. In other words, the extension applies only for the removal of trees that are not insured (i.e., a neighbor's tree) or that suffer damage that is not insured.

Reasonable Repairs The policy requires the insured to take all reasonable steps to protect and preserve the property at and after a loss (under the Conditions section of Section I). Under the *Reasonable Repairs additional coverage*, the insurer agrees to pay the costs incurred by the insured in providing such protection. This extension is not additional coverage, but the cost of reasonable repairs is included in the amount of loss payable, up to the policy limit.

Trees, Shrubs, Plants, and Lawns An extension is also provided to cover trees, shrubs, plants, and lawns. Under Forms 2, 3, 5, and 8, the extension is 5 percent of the amount on the dwelling. Under Forms 4 and 6, it is 10 percent of the amount of coverage on personal property. The coverage is subject to its own specific perils (fire, lightning, explosion, riot or civil commotion, aircraft, non-owned vehicles, vandalism and malicious mischief, and theft). A $500 limit applies per tree, shrub, or plant, except in Form 8, where the limit is $250.

Fire Department Service Charge Many municipal fire departments will respond to calls outside the city limits, but a charge is usually made, which can amount to several hundred dollars. The *Fire Department Service Charge coverage* provides up to $500 to cover the insured's liability under a contract or agreement for fire department charges when the fire department is called because the property is

threatened by an insured peril (normally fire).

Property Removed Insured property may be damaged while attempting to preserve it from destruction by removing it from a building that is threatened by an insured peril. It would be grossly unjust to penalize the insured for attempting to prevent a loss to the property or to reduce the amount of loss if the property were somehow damaged in the process. For this reason, the homeowners forms (and most other property insurance policies) provide coverage for damage to property that is being removed to protect it from one of the perils insured against. Coverage applies for loss by any cause during the process of removal and also for 30 days following the removal.

Credit Card, Electronic Fund Transfer Card or Access Device, Forgery, and Counterfeit Money This additional coverage provides protection up to $500 for losses resulting from the unauthorized use of a credit card, electronic fund transfer card, or other electronic access device issued or registered to any insured.[9] It makes no difference whether the card was stolen, lost, or simply misplaced, as long as the loss results from its unauthorized use. Coverage is also provided for depositor's forgery, which protects against loss resulting from the forgery or alteration of any check drawn on or by the insured, up to the $500 limit. In addition, the insured is protected up to $500 against loss sustained through the acceptance of bogus paper currency. Finally, this coverage agrees to defend the insured and pay court costs arising in connection with any of the covered losses.

Increased limits of coverage—up to $10,000—are available by endorsement for insureds that need increased protection. In measuring the possible need for increased limits, it should be noted that the policy provides that all losses resulting from a series of acts committed by any one person or in which any one person is implicated are considered to be a single loss.

Loss Assessment Coverage *Loss assessment* coverage provides payment for assessments against the insured by a condominium association or a corporation or association of property owners. Separate Loss Assessment coverages apply to Section I and Section II of the policy. With respect to Section I, coverage applies up to $1000 per loss for assessments resulting from direct loss to property owned by all members collectively, when such damage is caused by a peril insured under the policy. Increased limits are available by endorsement.

Collapse Prior to 1984, Collapse was included in many property insurance forms as an insured peril, a logical inconsistency, since collapse is not a peril, but a result that is caused by some peril. Collapse is now defined as an additional coverage and is covered only if it results from specific causes. The Collapse *additional coverage* is included in all homeowners forms except Form 8 (and Form 1, where still in use). Collapse is defined to mean the abrupt falling down or caving in of a building or part of the building with the result that it cannot be occupied. Coverage applies only if the collapse is caused by a specific group of perils. The specific perils that must cause collapse for coverage to exist are

1. The perils insured against in Coverage C

2. Decay that is hidden from view, unless the insured knew of such damage

3. Insect or vermin damage that is hidden from view, unless the insured knew of such damage

4. Weight of contents, equipment, animals, or people

5. Weight of rain on a roof

6. Defects in materials or methods used in construction, if the collapse occurs during the course of the construction

Coverage applies for damage to all insured property that results from a covered collapse.

Glass or Safety Glazing Material The *glass or safety glazing material additional coverage* was added in the 1990 revision, and replaces a *glass breakage peril* that was included in earlier forms. The change makes sense, since breakage of glass is a type of loss rather than a peril. Like the peril it replaces, the Glass or Safety Glazing Material additional coverage does not require that the breakage result from a specific cause, but covers breakage of glass constituting a part of the building, including glass in storm doors and windows, by any cause and limited only by the

[9] Federal legislation effective since October 1970 provides a maximum limit of $50 for a credit card holder's liability in the event of the unauthorized use of the card. Even though the limit applies to each card, it has reduced the possible severity of credit card losses.

amount of insurance.[10] There is no coverage for breakage if the building has been vacant for over 60 days, but a building under construction is not considered vacant. Loss for breakage is settled based on the replacement with safety glazing material when such replacement is required by law.

Landlord's Furnishing The *Landlord's Furnishings additional coverage* is included in Form 2 and Form 3. It provides $2500 to cover appliances, carpeting, and other household appliances in each apartment on the residence premises that is rented or held for rental to others. The perils for which landlord's furnishings are covered are identical under Form 2 and Form 3: the broad named perils applicable to contents, but excluding theft.

Ordinance or Law In many cities, building codes specify that new buildings must meet certain construction requirements. Owners of buildings that do not conform to the code provisions (because they were constructed before these laws were passed) face a special exposure. Usually, the building code requires that if a structure is destroyed, it must be replaced with one that meets code provisions. This is normally more costly than replacing the existing building. The building codes also provide that if a nonconforming building is damaged beyond a specified percentage (e.g., 40 or 50 percent), it cannot be repaired. This creates a gap in coverage, since the 40 or 50 percent loss would be only a partial loss under the property policy, but would be a total loss to the insured.

Historically, property insurance forms have excluded any increase in the amount of a loss that is due to the enforcement of building codes. Like other property forms, the homeowners forms contain an *Ordinance or Law exclusion* (discussed later in the chapter), which excludes any increase in the amount of loss due to the enforcement of building laws. In 1994, the Insurance Services Office (ISO) added a new additional coverage to the homeowners forms, which provides, as additional insurance, 10 percent of the Coverage A limit of liability to pay for certain increased costs of construction made necessary by the enforcement of an ordinance or law. Coverage applies for the increased cost of construction or the demolition or reconstruction of the undamaged part

of a covered building, due to the enforcement of a building law, when the building is damaged by an insured peril. This 10 percent may be increased to 25, 50, 75, 100 percent or more of the Coverage A limit. In Form HO-4, the Ordinance or Law additional coverage is 10 percent of the Building Additions and Alterations coverage.

Grave Markers Grave markers, including mausoleums, on or away from the premises, are covered up to $5000. Coverage is provided for loss caused by the perils insured against under Coverage C. This extension was added to the policy in the 2000 revision.

Homeowners Deductibles

In most states, there is a $250 deductible under the homeowners policy that applies to loss by any of the perils under Section I, including Loss of Use coverage. However, the deductible does not apply to scheduled items or to the Credit Card, Forgery, and Counterfeit Money coverage. In many states, the deductible may be reduced to $100 for an additional premium. If the insured desires a higher deductible, options of $500, $1000, and $2500 are provided under the ISO rules, with substantial rate reductions.

OTHER PROVISIONS

There is a set of conditions applicable to Section I of the policy, a separate set for Section II, and a set of General Conditions applicable to the entire contract. Here we will briefly discuss the Section I conditions and the General Conditions. Section II conditions are treated in Chapter 28.

Section I Conditions

Generally, the Section I conditions relate to loss settlement; they specify the obligations of the insured and of the company at the time of loss, and they impose restrictions and limits on the amounts payable.

Insurable Interest and Limit of Liability The insurer will not be liable for more than the insured's interest in the property, or for more than the limit of liability under the policy.

Your Duties after a Loss The insured is required to give notice to the company in the event of loss, protect the property from further damage, prepare

[10] Coverage for loss under the *Glass or Safety Material additional coverage* of Form 8 is limited to $100.

an inventory of the damaged property indicating the items damaged or destroyed and the amount of loss, and submit a signed statement within 60 days of the company's request. In addition, the insured is required to notify the police in the event of a theft loss and notify the credit card company in the event of a loss under the credit card coverage. Compliance with the conditions relating to loss settlement is a requisite to payment by the insurer.

Loss Settlement The *Loss Settlement provision* specifies the basis for payment under the policy. It provides that loss to personal property or to structures that are not buildings will be on an actual cash value basis, but not exceeding the cost to repair or replace the property. With respect to buildings, the condition sets forth the replacement cost provision previously discussed.

Loss to a Pair or Set The *Loss-to-a-Pair-or-Set clause* establishes conditions relating to the situation in which a single item in a pair or set is lost or destroyed. Under such circumstances, the insurer may repair or replace the lost part, restoring the pair or set to its value before the loss, or it may elect to pay the difference between the actual cash value of the property before and after the loss. The net effect of this provision is to prevent the insured from collecting for a total loss when a part of a pair or set is lost.

Appraisal The *Appraisal provision* of the homeowners policy establishes a framework for the settlement of losses in those instances in which the company and the insured cannot agree on the amount of loss. In this event, the policy provides that each party shall select an appraiser. Together, the two appraisers select an umpire. If the appraisers cannot agree on an umpire, one will be appointed by the court. The appraisers then evaluate the loss, each setting their value on the loss. Their differences are submitted to the umpire, and an agreement in writing of any two of the three persons is binding on both parties. Each appraiser's fee is paid by the party represented and the umpire's fee is paid by both parties. The appraisal provision is not used when the insurer and insured disagree over whether a loss is actually covered under the policy. Such disputes can be settled through the courts.

Other Insurance The insurer agrees to pay that proportion of the loss that the limit of liability under the policy bears to the total insurance covering the loss. The policy provides coverage in excess of any

amounts payable under a home warranty or other type of service agreement.

Suit Against Us The homeowners forms set forth conditions that must be met before the insured can sue the insurer. The insured must have complied with all of the provisions of the policy, and the suit must be brought within one year of the loss or damage.

Our Option Normally, the insurer pays for the loss in cash, but this condition permits the company to repair or replace the damaged property at his or her option. In most situations, the insurer exercises the cash option, but the right to repair or replace operates as a safeguard against unreasonable cash claims.

Loss Payment The *loss payment clause* requires the insurer to pay a loss within 30 days after an agreement on the amount of loss has been reached with the insured.

Abandonment of Property Although the insurer has a right to take salvage after payment for a total loss, this provision stipulates that the insurer need not accept salvage and that property cannot be abandoned by the insured.

Mortgagee Clause A mortgagee occupies an unusual position in the homeowners policy (and many other property insurance contracts). Although not involved in the formation of the contract, a mortgagee listed in the policy becomes a party to the contract with rights distinct from those of the insured.[11] The Mortgage Clause grants those rights and imposes certain conditional obligations on the mortgagee. The rights of the mortgagee are:

- To receive any loss or damage payments to the extent of its interest in the property, regardless of any default of the insured with respect to the insurance.
- To receive separate written notice of cancellation.
- To sue under the policy in its own name.

The right of the mortgagee to recover regardless of any default of the insured means that the mortgagee's

[11] The mortgagee could, if it so desired, take out a separate policy covering its interest in the mortgaged property. However, this would result in a duplication of coverage, since the owner-mortgagor would insure the property to the extent of his or her insurable interest, which includes not only the owner's equity but also the obligation to the mortgagee for the unpaid loan balance. The normal practice is for the owner to purchase a policy naming the mortgagee as an insured under the standard mortgage clause.

protection under the policy is unaffected by any violations of the policy provisions or breach of the contract by the insured. The mortgagee's interest would still be covered even if the insured committed arson.

The mortgage clause also provides that policy conditions relating to Appraisal, Suit-Against-Us, and Loss Payment provisions apply to the mortgagee. As a separate party to the contract, the mortgagee's rights are distinct from those of the insured, and these include the right of a separate legal action against the insurer.

The obligations imposed on the mortgagee are:

- To notify the insurer of any change in occupancy, or substantial increase in hazard of which the mortgagee is aware.
- To render proof of loss to the insurer if the owner fails to do so, and to thereafter abide by the policy provisions with respect to appraisal, time of payment, and bringing suit.
- To pay premiums due if the owner fails to do so.
- To surrender to the insurer any claim it has against the mortgagor to the extent that it receives payment in those cases where the company has ruled that no coverage exists for the owner.

Note that these are conditional obligations. They must be met only if the mortgagee wishes to enjoy the coverage of the policy; they are not conditions the mortgagee can be required to keep.

No Benefit to Bailee Because the Personal Property coverage of the homeowners forms applies both on premises and off premises, situations may arise in which insured property is in the custody of a bailee, such as a laundry, dry cleaner, or storage firm. *The No Benefit to Bailee* provision denies coverage for any person or organization having custody for a fee (i.e., a bailee for hire).

Nuclear Hazard Clause The *Nuclear Hazard clause* excludes loss under Section I of the policy that is caused directly or indirectly by the nuclear hazard. Nuclear hazard is defined as any nuclear reaction, radiation, or radioactive contamination, whether controlled or uncontrolled. An exception to the exclusion provides coverage for direct loss by fire that results from the nuclear hazard.

Recovered Property If property for which a loss payment has been made to the insured is recovered by either party, the insured may elect to have the property returned or may relinquish ownership to the insurer. If the insured elects to have the property returned, the loss payment will be adjusted based on the amount that was paid for the recovered property.

Volcanic Eruption Period The *volcanic eruption provision* defines the coverage of the volcanic eruption peril. The provision simply states that one or more volcanic eruptions that occur within a 72-hour period will be considered as a single volcanic eruption. This prevents the application of multiple deductibles when a series of eruptions occur within a short period.

Concealment or Fraud The concealment or fraud provision of the homeowners forms was revised in 1994 to differentiate the effect of misrepresentations under Section I and Section II of the policy. Separate provisions relating to concealment or fraud apply to Section I and to Section II. With respect to Section I, any concealment or fraud by an insured—any insured—voids coverage for all insureds. This is the much-debated provision that affects the "innocent spouse." Under Section II, coverage is denied only for the insured who has concealed, misrepresented, or engaged in fraudulent conduct.

Loss Payable Clause If a loss payee is listed for insured personal property, the definition of insured is changed to include the loss payee. In case of cancellation or nonrenewal, the loss payee will be notified in writing.

General Conditions Applicable to Sections I and II

In addition to those conditions that apply separately to the Section I or Section II coverages, the homeowners forms include a third set of conditions, applicable to the entire policy. These conditions deal with such items as cancellation, subrogation, and the death of the insured—areas that are of importance to both the property coverage and the liability section coverages.

Policy Period Coverage applies only to the losses that occur during the policy period. The inception time of the homeowners policy is 12:01 A.M.

Liberalization Clause The *Liberalization clause* is included in most property insurance policies. It provides that if the insurer adopts a new form or endorsement during the term of the policy that would

broaden the policy without additional premium, such change is automatically made a part of the policy.

Waiver or Change-of-Policy Provisions Provisions like the homeowners *Waiver* or *Change-of-Policy Provisions* condition have been the subject of conflicting court opinions. The condition provides that no waiver affecting the policy is valid unless expressed in writing. Some courts have upheld the provision, while others have maintained that not only are oral waivers by the agent valid, but that the agent can waive the very clause that says that he or she cannot waive any of the provisions of the policy.

Cancellation Provision is made for cancellation of the contract by either party. The insured can cancel effective immediately on request. The insurer, on the other hand, can cancel only under certain conditions and must give the insured advanced written notice. In either case, the insured is entitled to a refund of the unearned premium on a pro rated basis.

The right of the insurer to cancel is limited by the provisions of the cancellation clause and may be exercised only under specified circumstances:

- The insurer may cancel for nonpayment of premium, but must give 10 days' written notice of cancellation.
- The insurer may cancel a new policy for any reason during the first 60 days after inception. After a policy has been in effect for 60 days or more, or in the case of a renewal effective immediately, the insurer may cancel only if there was a material misrepresentation by the insured or if the risk has changed substantially since the policy was issued. Thirty days' written notice of cancellation is required.
- When a policy is written for a period in excess of one year, it may be canceled for any reason on the policy anniversary. Thirty days' written notice of cancellation is required.

Nonrenewal In addition to the restrictions on cancellation, the policy also sets forth procedures that must be followed by the insurer in the case of nonrenewal. When the insurer decides not to renew, written notice must be mailed to the address shown in the declarations 30 days prior to expiration.

Assignment Clause This clause stipulates that "assignment of the policy shall not be valid unless we give our written consent." While we often speak of the property as being insured, the insurance contract is a personal contract, agreeing to indemnify a specific individual in the event of loss. Coverage does not transfer to the new owner of property when it is sold; moreover, through this clause, the insurance company reserves the right to decide if it wishes to continue the insurance for the new owner.

Subrogation The *Subrogation clause* requires the insured to assign his or her right of recovery against a third party to the insured, to the extent of the payment made under the policy. Under the homeowners forms, the subrogation provision also grants the insured permission to waive right of recovery against a third party before a loss, as long as the waiver is in writing. Landlords sometimes waive rights of recovery against tenants in the lease, to the extent that a loss is covered by insurance. This protects the tenant from subrogation by the insurer and is specifically permitted under the terms of the subrogation provision.

Death Some provision must be made for the possibility that the insured might die. Coverage is provided for the legal representative of a deceased named insured (or spouse) with respect to insured property. In addition, resident relatives continue as insureds under the policy. Finally, any person having custody of insured property pending appointment of a legal representative is also an insured.

IMPORTANT CONCEPTS TO REMEMBER

package policy
Homeowners Form 1 (Basic)
Homeowners Form 2 (Broad)
Homeowners Form 3 (Special)
Homeowners Form 4 (Tenant's)
Homeowners Form 5
 (Comprehensive Form)

Homeowners Form 6
 (Condominium Unit-Owner's
 Form)
Homeowners Form 8 (Modified
 Coverage)
Dwelling Coverage
Other Structures Coverage

Personal Property Coverage
Loss-of-Use Coverage
additional living expense
rental value
replacement cost
Collapse Additional Coverage
Inflation Guard endorsement

Debris Removal Additional
　Coverage
Property Removed Additional
　Coverage
Loss Assessment Additional
　Coverage
Landlord's Furnishings Additional
　Coverage
Building Additions and Alterations
　Additional Coverage
Ordinance or Law Additional
　Coverage
improvements and betterments

fire
extended coverage
named-peril coverage
open-perils coverage
actual cash value
assignment clause
appraisal provision
subrogation provision
mortgage clause
Pair and Set clause
liberalization clause
Ordinance or Law exclusion
Earth Movement exclusion

Power Failure exclusion
Neglect exclusion
Scheduled Personal Property
　endorsement
Earthquake Damage Assumption
　endorsement
Special Personal Property Coverage
　endorsement
additional amounts of coverage
　endorsements
sinkhole collapse

QUESTIONS FOR REVIEW

1. Identify and briefly describe the four coverages under Section I of the homeowners policy.

2. What procedure is followed when the insured and the insurer disagree on the amount of loss under the homeowners policy? What if they disagree as to whether the loss is covered?

3. List the classes of personal property that are (a) excluded from the definition of covered property under the homeowners forms, and (b) subject to dollar limitations.

4. Of what significance is the wording *owned or used by the insured* in the definition of insured personal property under homeowners forms?

5. Briefly explain the exclusion pertaining to motorized vehicles under Section I of the homeowners policy. What vehicles are excluded? Which are covered?

6. Briefly explain the distinction between named-peril coverage and open-perils coverage.

7. Briefly describe the provisions of the homeowners Inflation Guard Endorsement. To which of the Section I coverages do the provisions of this endorsement apply?

8. Although the entire contents coverage of the homeowners forms applies away from the premises, there are certain limitations. What exclusions have been encountered so far with respect to personal property while it is away from the premises?

9. Explain the extent to which business property owned by an insured is covered under the homeowners forms. Be specific.

10. Rosie La Rue has just purchased a 20-year-old dwelling for $80,000. The mortgagee insists that she purchase an amount of insurance at least equal to the $70,000 mortgage. Rosie protests that the lot on which the dwelling is located is worth $20,000, making the value of the house itself a mere $60,000. The mortgagee is adamant. Finally, Rosie comes to you for advice. Advise her.

QUESTIONS FOR DISCUSSION

1. John Jones carries a Homeowners Policy on his dwelling, with Easy Money Mortgage Company listed as a mortgagee. Jones tells his agent to cancel the policy because the property has been sold. The agent cancels the policy and Jones obtains a return of the premium. About 6 months later, when the building burns, Easy Money Mortgage Company makes claim for recovery. Investigations reveal that the dwelling was not sold, and that Jones canceled the policy without the knowledge of the mortgage company. Discuss the liability of the insurer and the agent.

2. Although replacement cost coverage on buildings has been available since the inception of the homeowners program, replacement cost coverage on contents is a recent innovation. Do you feel that this is a logical extension of the replacement cost principle or does it violate the principle of indemnity to a greater extent than does the replacement cost coverage applicable to the dwelling?

3. Jones Jr. and his wife, Mary, store their household goods at his parents' home while they are looking for an apartment. A fire at the parents' home damages $3000 worth of their property. Assuming that the parents have a

Form 3, explain whether or not coverage would be provided under the parents' policy for the $3000 loss.

4. Jane Smith borrows a boat worth $1300. The boat is stolen from her garage and Smith reports the theft to the police and to the insurer. The adjuster agrees that the boat is covered, but subject to the $1000 limit and further subject to the $250 deductible, making recovery under the policy $750. Smith argues that the deductible applies to the $1300 loss, and the $1000 limit is then applied. Who is correct?

5. The coverage on the dwelling under the Homeowners Special Form is considerably broader than the coverage on contents. It therefore becomes important at the time of a loss to determine if a particular item is part of the building or of the contents. Do you believe that wall-to-wall carpeting should be considered a part of the building or its contents? What evidence can you find in the policy form to support your position?

SUGGESTIONS FOR ADDITIONAL READING

Fire, Casualty and Surety Bulletins. Personal Lines Volume. Cincinnati: National Underwriter Company. (Loose-leaf manual service with monthly supplements.) See "Dwellings" section.

Gwertzman, Max J. *A Legal Analysis of the Standard Fire Policy.* New York: Insurance Advocate, 1964.

Hamilton, Karen L., and Donald S. Malecki. *Personal Insurance: Property and Liability.* Malvern, Pa.: American Institute for CPCU, 1994. Chapter 2.

Huebner, S. S., Kenneth Black, Jr., and Bernard L. Webb. *Property and Liability Insurance,* 4th ed. Englewood Cliffs, N.J.: Prentice-Hall, 1995. Chapter 30.

Launie, J. J., George E. Rejda, and Donald R. Oakes with Anita W. Johnson. *Personal Insurance.* Bryn Mawr, Pa.: Insurance Institute of America, 1991. Chapters 2–4.

Policy, Form and Manual Analysis Service, Property Coverages Volume. Indianapolis: Rough Notes Company. (Loose-leaf manual service with monthly supplements.) See "Homeowners Policy Program" section.

Taylor, Barbara. *How to Get Your Money's Worth in Home and Auto Insurance.* New York: Insurance Information Institute, 1991. Chapters 5, 6.

Vaughan, E. J. "What Is Insurable Value?" *American Agency Bulletin* (Sept. 1965).

Wood, Glenn L., Claude C. Lilly, III, Donald S. Malecki, Edward E. Graves, and Jerry S. Rosenbloom. *Personal Risk Management and Insurance,* 4th ed., vol. 1. Malvern, Pa.: American Institute for Property and Liability Underwriters, 1989. Chapter 4.

WEB SITES TO EXPLORE

Best's Review—Property/Casualty Edition	http://www.ambest.com/review/lh/index.html
Consumers Guide to Homeowners Insurance	http://www.iiaa.iix.com/homeguid.htm
Independent Insurance Agents of America, Inc.	http://www.iiaa.org
Insurance News Network	http://www.insure.com/
Newsedge News Page	http://www.newspage.com/browse/46622/
Quicken InsureMarket	http://www.insuremarket.com/
Rough Notes Company	http://www.roughnotes.com/

THE HOMEOWNERS
POLICY FORMS

■

You pays your money and you takes your choice.

— PUNCH, vol. X, No. 16, 1846

CHAPTER OBJECTIVES

When you have finished this chapter, you should be able to

- Interpret loss-settlement provisions
- Recognize significant exclusions and limitations in the homeowners Section I coverage
- List and describe the optional coverages available to broaden the homeowners forms

In this chapter, we continue our review of homeowners forms, turning now to a discussion of the perils against which coverage is provided under the forms. As we noted in the last chapter, there are differences in the perils for which the forms provide coverage. In this chapter, we will examine those differences more closely.

DIFFERENCES AMONG HOMEOWNERS FORMS

The differences in the homeowners policies are designed to accommodate the insurance needs of different types of property owners. Thus, there are sepa-

rate forms of dwelling owners, tenants, and condominium unit-owners. In addition to the differences traceable to the different status of insureds, some forms differ with respect to the scope of their coverage, as determined by the perils against which protection is provided.

In reviewing the differences among the homeowners forms, we will focus on a single form, homeowners form HO-3. It includes both the broad named-peril coverage applicable under forms HO-2, HO-4, and HO-6, and the open-peril coverage applicable to the dwelling and other structures under forms HO-3 and HO-5. It is therefore a convenient way of reviewing both the named peril and open-peril approaches to coverage.

Homeowners 2 Broad Form

Homeowners 2 Broad Form covers damage to buildings and personal property and loss of use arising out of damage to such property against loss by 16 named perils. We will defer the detailed discussion of these perils until we reencounter them in Homeowners 3 Special Form, discussed next. In this respect, it is important to keep in mind that the only difference between homeowners form HO-2 and HO-3 is in the coverage on the dwelling, other structures, and loss of use coverages. These are covered on an named-peril basis under HO-2, and on an open-peril basis under HO-3. The coverage on personal property is on a named-peril basis under both forms, with identical coverage for the 16 broad named perils that also apply in forms HO-4 and HO-6.

Homeowners 3 Special Form

The essential difference between the homeowners form HO-3 and most other forms is the open-peril coverage on the dwelling and other structures. We will begin our review of this form with this feature, the dwelling coverage.

Open-Peril Coverage—Dwellings and Other Structures Coverage on the dwelling and other structures under homeowners form HO-3 is on an "open-peril" basis, with coverage provided against all physical loss except by those causes that are specifically excluded. In addition, the Loss of Use coverage also applies on an open-peril basis. The open-peril insuring agreement of form HO-3 is simple and straightforward:

> We insure against risk of direct loss to property described in Coverages A and B only if that loss is a physical loss to property. We do not, however, insure for loss:…

A list of excluded losses for which coverage is not provided then follows. Any loss that does not fall within one of the exclusions is covered. The number of exclusions required in an open-peril form is usually extensive, since all uninsurable perils must be excluded. The exclusions that immediately follow the open-peril Dwelling and Other Structures insuring agreement include the general Section I exclusions (designated exclusion a), losses involving collapse, except as covered under the Collapse Additional Coverage (designated exclusion b), and a group of thirteen exclusions—combined as exclusions c(1) through c(6)—that are more or less standard exclusions in all open-peril contracts.

General Section I Exclusions The General Section I exclusions are divided into two groups designated A.1. through A.9. and B.1. through B.3. These exclusions are included in all homeowners forms.

A.1. Ordinance or Law. With the exception of the 10 percent extension for Ordinance or Laws provided under the Additional Coverage previously discussed (and any increase in this extension added by endorsement), the form excludes loss caused by the enforcement of any ordinance or law regulating construction, repair, or demolition of any building.

A.2. Earth Movement. The Earth Movement exclusion eliminates coverage for loss caused by earth movement except direct loss by fire, explosion, theft, or breakage of glass. Earth movement is defined in the policy to include earthquake, including land shock waves or tremors before, during, or after a volcanic eruption; landslide; mine subsidence, mudflow, and other types of earth movement such as earth sinking, rising, or shifting. Coverage for earthquake and other types of earth movement is available by endorsement for an additional premium.

A.3. Water Damage. The Water Damage exclusion eliminates coverage for certain types of enumerated water, including flood in all its forms, water or waterborne material that backs up through sewers or drains or overflows from a sump, and water or waterborne material below the surface of the ground that seeps through basement walls, foundation floors, and similar structural components. An exception to the exclusion provides coverage for loss by fire, explosion, or theft that is caused by any of the excluded forms of water. In most jurisdictions the exclusion of water and water-borne material that backs up through sewers or drains can be deleted by endorsement for the payment of an additional premium. The *Water Back Up and Sump Discharge or Overflow* endorsement provides coverage up to $5000 for loss resulting from such backup.

A.4. Power Failure. The Power Failure exclusion denies coverage for losses resulting directly from interruption of power or other utility service, if the interruption takes place away from the residence premises. The exclusion contemplates a special form of consequential loss damage that may result from power interruption. The best example as it applies to the dwelling risk is food in a deep freezer. If lightning

strikes the dwelling, and burns out the motor on the freezer, food in the freezer may spoil as a result. The damage to the food in the freezer results from the "interruption of power." The net effect of the Power Interruption exclusion is to provide coverage for such consequential losses when equipment on the premises is damaged by an insured peril and to deny coverage for such losses when the damage takes place away from the premises.

A.5. Neglect. The policy excludes loss resulting directly or indirectly from neglect of the insured to use reasonable means at or after a loss to save the property. The insured cannot collect for damage that he or she has a reasonable chance to prevent. Note, however, that neglect of the insured before a loss does not affect coverage. The exclusion merely relieves the insurer from liability for that part of the loss attributable to the insured's neglect *at or after* a loss (i.e., when a loss occurs).

A.6. War. As do most forms of property insurance, the homeowners forms exclude loss caused by war in all its forms, including undeclared war, insurrections, rebellion, or revolution. Any discharge of a nuclear weapon—even though accidental—is excluded under this provision. Following the terrorist attack on the World Trade Center on September 11, 2001, questions arose concerning the application of this exclusion to such acts of terrorism. The consensus is that the war exclusion does not apply to acts of terrorism.[1] Since the attack on the World Trade Center, some insurers have inserted a separate terrorism exclusion in their policies, although the practice has generally been limited to commercial rather than personal policies.

A.7. Nuclear Hazard. The nuclear hazard exclusion refers to loss defined in the Section I conditions and provides that losses from such hazards are not covered. The nuclear hazard includes nuclear reactions, radiation, or radioactive contamination. The one exception is direct loss by fire, which is covered even if it results from the nuclear hazard.

A.8. Intentional Loss. The homeowners policy excludes coverage for intentional loss "by or at the direction of an insured" and "with the intent to cause a loss." While this exclusion aims at eliminating payment to persons who commit arson losses, it goes beyond

this. It also eliminates payment to other persons insured, who were not involved in the intentional act. These could include an innocent spouse or even a person with an interest in the dwelling who has been added as an additional insured under the policy.[2]

A.9. Government Action. Loss resulting from government actions—such as the destruction, seizure, or confiscation of property by order of any government authority—is excluded. This could include property illegally held or used for illegal purposes. Sometimes, government authorities will seize or confiscate not only illegal substances, but the structure in which such property is located. The exclusion does not apply to acts of destruction taken to prevent the spread of fire.

B.1–B.3. Concurrent Causation Exclusions. Exclusions B.1 through B.3, usually referred to as the "concurrent causation" exclusions, were added to the policy (and to most other broad form and special form property contracts) in the 1980s in response to a series of adverse court decisions.[3]

Exclusion b.1 applies to loss caused by weather conditions that contribute to an otherwise excluded peril. For example, landslide caused by excessive rain or rain combined with wind is excluded. Loss caused directly by the weather condition such as windstorm damage would be covered.

Exclusion b.2 applies to loss caused by acts or decisions, including failure to act or decide, of any person, group, organization, or governmental body. Loss resulting from failure of a governmental body to maintain flood control structures or failure to enforce zoning or building codes would be excluded.

Exclusion b.3 relates to loss caused by faulty, inadequate, or defective activities such as planning, design,

[2] In 1998, the NAIC adopted a model law that, when adopted by a state, nullifies the intentional loss exclusion of the homeowners policy with respect to damage suffered by a victim of domestic abuse and caused by a co-insured. The model law prohibits insurance companies from denying, canceling, or nonrenewing coverage based on abuse status and requires insurers to pay claims filed by innocent co-insureds.

[3] These exclusions were added to the policy in 1984 in response to a doctrine adopted by some courts called *concurrent causation,* which held that when a loss results from two causes—one of which is excluded and the other not excluded—the loss is covered. This stretched the coverage of broad form and special form contracts beyond the intent of its drafters, providing coverage for flood and earthquake losses on the grounds that although these causes of loss were excluded, they were concurrently caused by perils that were not excluded (zoning laws that allowed structures to be built in flood or earthquake areas or negligence of a contractor in not making the structures earthquake resistant). The concurrent causation exclusions merely bring the scope of the coverage back to its original intent.

[1] A leading case in this area states "War refers to and includes only hostilities carried on by entities that constitute governments at least de facto in character." *Pan American World Airways v. Aetna Casualty and Surety,* U.S. Second Circuit Court of Appeals (1974).

maintenance, or faulty materials. Loss resulting solely from inadequate design of a building would not be covered, but the ensuing loss such as by fire arising from faulty installation or repair would be covered.

Dwelling and Other Structures Exclusions The remaining exclusions applicable to Coverages A and B fall into two broad classes. First, four exclusions—designated c.(1) through c.(4)—relate to perils that are covered as named perils in the other homeowners forms. These exclusions relate to freezing of plumbing, and damage to fences, pavements, patios, and certain other property by freezing, thawing, or the pressure of water or ice, theft in or to a dwelling under construction, and vandalism and any ensuing loss if the building has been vacant for more than 60 days. We will discuss these exclusions when we examine the named-peril coverage applicable to personal property.

The second class of exclusions—c.(5) and c.(6)—are a series of open-peril exclusions that appear in virtually all open-peril contracts. They exclude losses that are considered uninsurable, either because they are inevitable or because it is difficult to fix the time at which the damage takes place. The first of these exclusions—c.(5)—excludes loss caused by mold, fungus, or wet rot. An exception applies to loss caused by mold, fungus, or wet rot that is hidden in walls, ceilings, or floors that results from accidental discharge, leakage, or overflow of water from the plumbing system or domestic appliances. Despite the specific exclusion of mold damage, the exception to the exclusion for hidden mold caused by burst pipes has triggered litigation in several parts of the country, with juries sometimes finding coverage that was not intended.[4] In 2000 and 2001, insurance coverage for damage by mold became a national issue, intensified by the intense interest of the media and the legal profession. Some members of the legal profession have dubbed toxic mold "the asbestos of the new millennium." Many insurers have responded with new language to further clarify the mold exclusion. Conceivably, some insurers may decide to cover mold claims and price their policies accordingly, while others may offer coverage for damage caused by mold for an additional premium.

The remaining open-peril exclusions are grouped together as exclusion c.(6) and include the following:

(a) Wear and tear, marring, or deterioration

(b) Mechanical breakdown, latent defect, inherent vice or a quality in property that causes it to damage or destroy itself

(c) Smog, rust or other corrosion

(d) Smoke from agricultural smudging or industrial operations

(e) Discharge, release, or dispersal of contaminants or pollutants, unless caused by one of the named perils for which personal property is insured

(f) Settling, cracking, shrinking, bulging, or expansions of pavements, patios, foundations, walls, floors, or ceilings

(g) Birds, vermin, rodents, or insects

(h) Animals owned or kept by an insured

Any ensuing loss to property insured under Coverages A and B that is not excluded by another provision of the policy is covered. For example, if a mechanical breakdown resulted in a fire, the resulting fire would be covered.

Coverage C—Personal Property Perils Insured Homeowners form HO-3 covers damage to personal property against loss by 16 named perils. Because the coverage on personal property under form HO-2, 4, and 6 covers loss by the same 16 perils, the following discussion of the perils covered under this form will also serve to illustrate the coverage under these other forms. A complete analysis of these perils requires a close examination of the form itself, but the following explanation provides an indication of the scope of their coverage.

Fire and Lightning The basic peril against which coverage is provided in virtually all property insurance forms is *fire*. Surprisingly, the term *fire* is nowhere defined in the policy. Although the term is not defined, court decisions over many years have established that the fire contemplated in insurance policies is of a specific type. Fire, according to the courts, is "combustion proceeding at a rate rapid enough to generate flame, glow, or incandescence."[5] In other words, there must

[4] In 2001, a Texas District Court jury awarded an insured $32 million for mold damage to a 22-room mansion and mental anguish, finding that the insurer had mishandled a Homeowners policy claim for mold damage. (See *Mary Belinda Ballard et al. v. Fire Insurance Exchange, a member of the Farmers 7Insurance Group.* No. 99-05252, 354th Judicial District Court, Travis County, Texas).

[5] *Western Woolen Co. v. Northern Assurance Co.,* 139 Fed. 637 (1905).

be light. Mere smoke, scorching, or charring is not sufficient to constitute a fire.

Not all fires are covered under the fire peril. The courts distinguish between a *friendly fire* and a *hostile* or *unfriendly* fire. A friendly fire is one that is within the confines for which it was intended; the friendly fire was intentionally kindled and burns where it is supposed to. A hostile fire, on the other hand, has escaped its intended confines. Only hostile or unfriendly fires are covered under the named-fire peril.

In addition to the destruction by the actual fire itself, the "direct loss by fire" peril provides coverage for any damage that results from the smoke from a hostile fire, or is caused by water or attempts by firefighters to extinguish a hostile fire.

Windstorm and Hail The wind and hail insuring agreement excludes damage caused by rain, snow, sleet, sand, or dust to the interior of the building unless the exterior walls or roof are first damaged by direct action of the wind or hail. Thus, if an insured leaves a window open and the wind blows rain into the house, damaging the contents, there is no coverage. However, if the window were first broken by the wind, damage to the contents would be covered.

In addition to the exclusion relating to damage to the interior of the structure, there is an exclusion of damage by wind or hail to watercraft, their trailers, or equipment, unless such items are inside a fully enclosed building.

Explosion Explosions are covered whether they originate within or outside the building. There are no exceptions or exclusions.

Riot or Civil Commotion Damage caused by rioters and persons engaged in civil commotion is covered, subject to few exceptions. Even "pillage and looting" are covered, if they occur during and at the place of the riot. The only area in which an issue has arisen is in the distinction between a riot (which is covered) and an insurrection (which is excluded as a form of war). The courts have differentiated between the two: an insurrection is distinguished by its intent—to overthrow duly constituted authority. A riot, in contrast, is a "tumultuous disturbance of the peace"—something that happens in response to police brutality, civil unrest, or sometimes after a loss at the NCAA basketball tournament game.

Aircraft The aircraft peril provides coverage against damage to insured property caused by aircraft, including self-propelled missiles or spacecraft. This includes damage resulting from direct physical contact of the insured property with aircraft, but could also include damage resulting from objects falling from aircraft or even "sonic boom."

Vehicles Coverage applies for damage to insured property caused by vehicles, including vehicles owned or operated by an insured.

Smoke Although the fire peril includes coverage for damage caused by smoke from a hostile fire, the smoke peril broadens this to include coverage for sudden and accidental smoke damage from other sources, including the emission or puffback of smoke, soot, fumes, or vapors from a furnace or boiler. Smoke from agricultural smudging and industrial operations are excluded.

Vandalism and Malicious Mischief Vandalism and malicious mischief refers to the willful and malicious damage to or destruction of property. Loss by vandalism is not covered if the building has been vacant for over 60 days.[6] The policy also provides that a dwelling under construction is not considered "vacant."

Theft Except for forms HO-5 and HO-8, the theft coverage of the homeowners forms is identical.[7] The theft peril provides coverage for theft, including attempted theft or loss of property from a known location when it is likely that the property has been stolen. The phrase "loss of property from a known location when it is likely that the property has been stolen" is intended to reduce the insured's burden of establishing that the loss actually resulted from theft where there is no conclusive proof. The policy requires the insured to give immediate notice to the police if an article is stolen.

There are two sets of exclusions applicable to the theft peril: a set of general theft exclusions and a set that applies only to property that is away from the insured premises.

General Theft Exclusions. There are three general theft exclusions.

[6] Insurance contracts frequently reduce or exclude coverage when the insured property is "vacant" and some contracts restrict coverage in case of "unoccupancy." A building is vacant when it has neither occupants nor contents. It is unoccupied when it has contents, but no occupants.

[7] Theft coverage under Forms 5 and 8 is discussed later in the chapter.

1. Theft committed by any insured

2. Theft in or from a dwelling under construction or of materials or supplies for use in the construction until the dwelling is completed and occupied

3. Theft from any part of a residence rented by an insured to anyone except another insured

With respect to the first, theft from one family member by another is not covered. In addition, while the definition of the dwelling includes lumber, materials, and appliances on the premises and intended for use in construction, the second general theft exclusion eliminates insurance against the stealing of such items. The exclusion with respect to theft from any part of the dwelling that is rented relates not only to portions of the house that may be let to roomers and boarders, but also to the occasional rental of that portion of the dwelling customarily occupied by the insured. Such a situation might arise, for example, if the insured were leaving town for an extended period and decides to rent out the residence.

Off-Premises Theft Exclusions. Three exclusions apply to property while away from the premises.

First, theft of property from any residence owned, rented to, or occupied by any insured is not covered for loss by theft except while an insured is actually residing at the location. For example, if the policyholder owns a summer cottage, its contents are covered for other perils (subject to the 10 percent limitation on contents at a secondary residence), but the theft coverage does not apply except while the individual is actually residing at the cottage. An exception to this exclusion provides that coverage will apply to the property of a student residing away from home if the student has been at the residence at any time during the 60 days immediately preceding the loss. Although there would be no coverage for loss by theft on property left at a dormitory, sorority, or fraternity over an entire summer, coverage would apply on other occasions such as spring break, Christmas, or Thanksgiving, when students leave the campus.

The second off-premises exclusion excludes theft of watercraft or their furnishings, equipment, and outboard motors, and the third exclusion eliminates coverage for campers or trailers stolen while away from the premises.

Falling Objects This peril covers damage caused by falling objects such as tree limbs, but is not limited to this. Contents of a building are not covered for loss by falling objects unless the exterior of the building first sustains damage. Also, damage to the falling object itself is excluded. The exclusion of "damage to the falling object itself" eliminates coverage for damage to contents items that are damaged by being dropped or otherwise falling. Thus, if a heavy mirror fell from the wall, damaging the interior of the building and itself, there is no coverage under the "Falling Objects" peril.

Weight of Ice, Snow, or Sleet Damage caused by the weight of ice, snow, and sleet is covered, but the damage must actually result from the *weight*. Melting snow that leaks into the dwelling causing damage would not be covered. Damage to awnings, fences, patios, pavement, swimming pools, foundations, retaining walls, bulkheads, piers, wharves, or docks is also excluded.

Accidental Discharge or Overflow of Water or Steam Coverage is provided for the accidental discharge, leakage, or overflow of water from a plumbing, heating, or air-conditioning or automatic sprinkler system or from within a domestic appliance. This includes not only burst or leaking pipes, but overflow of plumbing fixtures such as bathtubs, or appliances such as automatic dishwashers. Coverage includes the cost of tearing out and replacing part of the building to make repairs, but the loss to the system or appliance itself is excluded.

Sudden and Accidental Tearing Apart, Cracking, Burning, or Bulging of Heating or Air-Conditioning Systems This insuring agreement provides coverage against loss caused by "Sudden and accidental tearing apart, cracking, burning or bulging of a steam or hot water heating system, an air-conditioning system or of a household appliance." Damage to steam or hot water heating systems of the type specified can occur if the water level for such systems becomes too low and damage of this type was the original rationale for this coverage. Damage of the types specified, from any cause, is covered.

Freezing of Plumbing, Heating, and Other Systems and Appliances Loss resulting from freezing of plumbing, heating, or air-conditioning or automatic sprinkler systems or domestic appliances is covered, provided the insured has used reasonable means to maintain heat in the building or unless the water has been shut off and the system has been drained. (If the building is protected by a sprinkler system, draining is not an allowable option.) Unlike the water

leakage peril, coverage applies for damage to a system or appliance damaged by freezing.

Sudden and Accidental Damage from Artificially Generated Electrical Current　Sudden and accidental injury to wiring and appliances from artificially generated currents is covered as an insured peril. The major exclusion with respect to artificially generated electricity is damage to tubes, transistors, electronic components, or circuitry, which are excluded. Although damage to television sets, stereos, and the like that is caused by artificial electricity is excluded, the same damage, if caused by lightning (natural electricity), is covered.

Volcanic Eruption　The Volcanic Eruption peril covers "above-ground" effects of volcanic eruption, such as damage caused by lava and debris from an earthquake. As noted earlier, the general exclusions exclude damage by shock waves and ground tremors caused by volcanic eruption.

Homeowners 4 Contents Broad Form

The Homeowners 4 Contents Broad Form (HO 00 04), which is designed for tenants, provides protection against the same named perils as does the contents coverage of Homeowners Form HO-3. The only difference in the insuring agreement of the various perils is in connection with the Glass Breakage peril and the Additional Coverage titled Building Additions and Alterations.

The Building Additions and Alterations coverage applies to building additions, alterations, fixtures, improvements, or installations made by the insured in a rented apartment or dwelling. This coverage, also sometimes called *tenant's improvements and betterments,* covers the insured's "use value" in such improvements. A tenant who installs extensive renovations in rented property does so in the expectation that he or she will have the use of the property for a period of time. If the property is destroyed, the tenant loses the use of the additions or improvements. The Building Additions and Alterations additional coverage provides compensation for this loss. The coverage on Building Additions and Alterations is limited to 10 percent of the coverage on contents.

Glass breakage under Form HO-4, as in Form HO-2, applies to glass that is a part of the building, including storm doors and storm windows. Under Form HO-4, the glass or Safety Glazing Additional

Coverage applies as a part of the Building Additions and Alterations coverage.

Coverage on personal property insured under Form HO-4 may be extended to an open-peril basis by the *Homeowners Special Personal Property Coverage—Form HO 00 04 Only Endorsement.* The open-peril coverage of this endorsement parallels the open-peril coverage on personal property under Form HO 00 05 discussed next.

Homeowners 5 Comprehensive Form

Virtually from the introduction of the homeowners program until 1991, there has been a homeowners program package that provides open-peril coverage on both buildings and personal property. In the 1991 revision of the program, the Homeowners Comprehensive Form HO-5 was withdrawn. In its place, an endorsement was introduced to provide open-peril coverage on personal property under HO-3, thereby creating the equivalent of the HO-5. After several years with this arrangement, ISO reintroduced the Homeowners Comprehensive Form HO-5 in the 2000 revision of the program. The new Homeowners HO-5, like its predecessor, provides open-peril coverage for buildings and personal property. In addition, the Loss of Use coverage is triggered by direct losses that fall within the scope of the open-peril coverage.

Exclusions under Form HO-5　As in the case of open-peril forms generally, coverage under HO-5 is defined and limited by the exclusions. Some of these exclusions have already been encountered in our discussion of HO-3. Others are specific to the open-peril coverage on personal property.

Form HO-5 includes, first, the Section I exclusions that appear in all of the homeowners forms and that apply to all coverages (Building Laws, Earth Movement, Water Damage, Power Interruption, Neglect, War, Nuclear Hazard, and Intentional Loss). However, HO-5 modifies the Earth Movement exclusion, making it applicable only to the Dwelling coverage and Other Structures coverage. In addition, the Water Damage exclusion of HO-5 does not apply to personal property while away from the premises. Besides these general exclusions, there are three other groups of exclusions.

The first of the three sets of exclusions consists of the same open-perils exclusions that apply to the building under the unendorsed Homeowners 3 Special

Form. These exclusions apply to *all* coverages under Section I.

The second group of exclusions applies only to the Dwelling and Other Structures coverage. These consist of the standard exclusions of Vandalism and Malicious Mischief or Glass Breakage if the building has been vacant for more than 60 days, constant or repeated seepage or leakage of water that takes place over a period of time, and collapse (other than as provided in the Collapse Additional coverage).

The final group of exclusions applies only to the Personal Property coverage. These exclusions applicable to personal property have not been encountered in the other forms examined and, therefore, deserve somewhat more detailed attention. There are seven exclusions applicable to the open-peril contents coverage, designated a through f.

a. Breakage of eyeglasses, glassware, statuary, marble, bric-a-brac, porcelains, and similar fragile articles (other than jewelry, watches, bronzes, cameras, and photographic lenses), unless caused by a specifically named peril. The specific perils for which breakage of fragile articles is covered include fire, lightning, perils of extended coverage, vehicles, vandalism and malicious mischief, collapse of a building, earthquake, water not otherwise excluded, theft or attempted theft, or sudden and accidental tearing apart, cracking, burning or bulging of a steam or hot water heating system, air conditioning system, or appliance for heating water.

b. Dampness of atmosphere or extremes of temperature unless the direct cause of loss is rain, snow, sleet, or hail

c. Refinishing, renovating, or replacing property other than watches, jewelry, and furs

d. Collision other than collision with a land vehicle, sinking, swamping, or stranding of watercraft, including their trailers, furnishings, equipment, and outboard motors

e. Destruction, confiscation, or seizure by order of any government or public authority

f. Acts or decisions, including the failure to act or decide, of any person, group, organization, or governmental body

The form qualifies these exclusions by stating that any ensuing loss to property described in Coverage C not excluded or excepted in the policy is covered.

Theft Coverage under Form HO-5 Because theft is not covered as a specifically named peril, questions sometimes arise in connection with the theft coverage of Form HO-5. The broad open-perils nature of HO-5 includes coverage for loss of real or personal property by theft. The theft coverage of Form HO 5 is subject to a single exclusion: theft in or to a building under construction until the structure is completed and occupied. The other exclusions of the named-peril forms—theft by an insured, theft from unlocked vehicles or watercraft away from the premises, and theft from a secondary residence—do not appear in the form and such losses are therefore covered. Furthermore, the form restates the limits on jewelry, furs, silverware, and firearms, making it clear that coverage applies not only to loss by theft, but to loss by *misplacing or losing* the property as well.

Homeowners 6 Condominium Unit-Owners Form

Homeowners form HO-6 is designed to cover the special exposures of a condominium unit-owner. To understand these special exposures, it may be helpful first to review the nature of a condominium.

Basically, a condominium is a multiple-occupancy building in which individuals own units of living space—a cube of air formed by the four walls, ceiling, and floor. The common areas of the building are jointly owned by all unit owners as tenants-in-common. These common areas include the basic structure, the grounds, halls, stairways, and other facilities. Because the condominium arrangement involves two kinds of ownership—individual and joint—the responsibility for insurance is also divided. The individual unit owners grant the right to purchase insurance on the common elements of ownership to a condominium association. This avoids difficulties that might arise from nonconcurrency, rebuilding of the damaged premises, and so on, if each owner attempted to insure his or her part of the common elements. Although the condominium association purchases insurance on the common elements of ownership, the unit-owner is generally responsible for the insurance on additions to his or her own unit. The exact definition of the unit-owner's responsibility varies with state law, and sometimes with the bylaws of the association. In some instances, the unit-owner is responsible for all real property within the confines of the perimeter of the condominium unit. This could include interior partitions, appliances, and

even plumbing fixtures and the interior décor, such as wallpaper, paneling, and carpeting. In addition to the need for coverage on unit-owners additions, the condominium unit owner needs coverage on his or her own personal property. Form HO-6 is designed to meet both needs.

Coverage of Form HO-6 The coverage under the *Homeowners 6 Unit-Owner's* form generally parallels the coverage of Form HO-4, providing protection against loss by the broad named perils discussed in detail earlier. However, Form HO-6 also contains special provisions tailoring it to the needs of the condominium unit-owner. These special provisions, which deal with the condominium exposure and differentiate this form from the tenants form, relate to the unit owner's additions to the condominium unit.

Unit-Owner's Building Items Although the building policy purchased by the condominium association covers the common elements of ownership, the unit-owner is generally responsible for additions to his or her own unit. The exact definition of the unit-owner's responsibility varies with state law, and sometimes with the bylaws of the association. In some instances, the unit-owner is responsible for all real property within the confines of the perimeter of the condominium unit. This could include interior partitions, appliances, and even plumbing fixtures. In addition, the interior decor is also usually the responsibility of the unit-owner. Wallpaper, paneling, and carpeting are only a few of the items that may be included in the definition of the unit-owner's additions and alterations.

Unit-owners' additions are automatically covered under Coverage A of Form HO-6 for a flat $1000. This standard limit of coverage may be increased when there is a need, which there usually will be.

Coverage A of homeowners Form HO-6 (which like Coverage A of Form HO-2 or Form HO-3 is designated *Dwelling Coverage*) covers building alterations and additions, plus certain other items of real property identified in the Dwelling insuring agreement. The definition of insured property under the Dwelling Coverage includes (1) alterations, appliances, fixtures, and improvements that are a part of the building contained within the residence premises; (2) items of real property that pertain exclusively to the insured's premises; (3) property that is the insured's responsibility under the condominium association agreement; and (4) structures owned by the insured, other than the condominium unit.

The first item of coverage includes the insured's individual interest in the condominium unit, consisting principally of the interior finishings of the unit. As previously noted, this includes the interior decor and real-property furnishings of the unit.

The second element of the coverage covers other types of real property that pertains to the premises. This might include, for example, structures such as balconies or patios, but it could also include trees, shrubs, or plants.

The extension to property that is the unit owner's responsibility under the association agreement is not defined or limited and could include almost any property for which the unit-owner is responsible under the agreement.

Finally, the coverage on structures owned solely by the insured is this form's equivalent of the Other Structures coverage (Coverage B) of the other homeowners forms. It could include a garage, tool shed, or other structure, provided such structure is owned solely by the insured.

Endorsements to Form HO-6 Although the Unit-Owner's form provides basic coverage for the owner of a condominium, it may be modified by endorsement to provide broader coverage and coverage tailored to the specific needs of the unit-owner.

Open-Perils Coverage on Unit-Owner's Building Items The coverage on unit-owner's additions, like the coverage on the contents, is on a broad named-peril basis. However, the coverage on real property may be extended by endorsement to an open-perils basis, providing essentially the same coverage on unit owner's additions as is provided on the building under homeowners Form HO-3.

Open-Perils Coverage on Personal Property In addition to the option of extending the coverage on building items to an open-peril basis, the condominium unit-owner's form may also be endorsed to provide open-peril coverage on personal property. The Unit-Owners Coverage C Special Coverage Form (HO 1731) provides essentially the same coverage on contents as that discussed earlier in connection with HO-5.

Rental Unit Coverage Special provision is also made for those situations in which the condominium unit is rented by the owner to other persons. Many condominium units, particularly those in recreational areas, are purchased with the intention of renting the property, at least for parts of the year. When the

Rental Unit coverage endorsement is added to the policy, the definition of *personal property* is amended to provide coverage on property in the residence premises regularly rented or held for rental to others. (The Basic form covers personal property only if *"occasionally"* rented to others.) In addition, coverage is added for theft of personal property from any part of the residence premises rented to other than an insured, an exposure that is excluded under the Basic form without the endorsement. The Theft coverage, however, excludes theft of money, gold, silverware, and items of a similar nature from the residence premises when rented to others.

Assessment Coverage As in the case of the other homeowners forms, Loss Assessment is automatically included as an Additional Coverage under Form HO-6. Increased limits of Assessment coverage are available by endorsement under Form HO 04 35. Like the basic Loss Assessments coverage, the increased limits provide coverage under Section I for losses resulting from damage by perils insured under the unit owner's own policy and under Section II for losses that arise out of liability suits that are covered under the terms of Section II of the policy. A provision in the Loss Assessment Endorsement sets a $1000 limit on payment for assessments that arise from a deductible in the association's property insurance policy.

Homeowners 8 Modified Coverage Form

The homeowners forms were conceived as a program for superior exposures in the dwelling field. The discount offered for packaging of coverages contemplates high insurance to value and reduction of adverse selection by the fixed relationships among the property coverages. Although this concept has operated satisfactorily in most instances, there have always been some insureds who, for one reason or another, were not able to obtain coverage under the homeowners package. One major class of buyers who could not obtain coverage under the homeowners forms consisted of owners of certain types of older property. Some dwellings, for example, were built many years ago, when labor-intensive techniques characterized the home-building industry. These dwellings often involve obsolete types of construction or are too large in relation to the insured's needs. In most instances, the replacement cost of such structures far exceeds their market value. It is not unusual for an older obsolete dwelling to have a replacement cost of $500,000 or more, while the market value is $100,000 or $200,000. Owners of such property often do not see any sense in insuring the building for twice its purchase price. In addition, many insurers are reluctant to provide replacement cost coverage for the full replacement cost of such buildings.

To meet this dilemma, the Insurance Services Office (ISO) introduced a new homeowners form in 1978, the Homeowners Modified Coverage Form 8. The coverage of Form 8 is similar to that of Form HO-2, but there are several important limitations. The two most important differences between Form 8 and the other homeowners forms are the following:

- The policy does not include the standard replacement cost provision contained in other homeowners forms, but substitutes a unique *functional replacement cost* approach to building losses.
- Theft coverage applies on premises only, and is limited to $1000 per occurrence.

Form 8 Loss Settlement Provisions Because many dwellings insured under Form 8 are older dwellings constructed during periods when labor-intensive methods characterized the building trades, actually replacing parts of a damaged building could be prohibitive in cost. Instead, for partial losses, the contract agrees to make "functionally equivalent repairs." The insurer agrees to pay the amount necessary to repair the damage, but not more than the cost of using common construction materials and methods that are functionally equivalent to but less costly than obsolete, antique, or custom construction materials and methods. This means that hand-plastered walls will be replaced with plasterboard, and marble will be replaced by Formica. If the building is not repaired, payment is limited to the lowest of (a) the limit of insurance, (b) the market value of the property (excluding the land), or (c) the actual cash value of the loss. There is no functional replacement formula like the replacement cost formula in other homeowners forms.

Although the coverage of Form 8 is more limited than that of the other homeowners forms, the introduction of this form has made package buying available to many personal insurance buyers who previously were forced to purchase individual packages. Despite the limitations of the form, Form HO-8 represents a more attractive alternative than the separate contracts that

would otherwise be required to provide the same coverage.

HOMEOWNERS SECTION I OPTIONAL COVERAGES

Although the homeowners forms constitute an attractive package of protection for the average family, several optional coverages are also available by endorsement. We have already noted some of these—the inflation guard and guaranteed replacement cost endorsements, and the replacement cost endorsement for personal property. In addition, the following are noteworthy optional endorsements.

Optional Perils

Four endorsements are available to extend the coverage of the policy to include additional perils: the Sinkhole Collapse Endorsement, the Earthquake Endorsement, Refrigerated Property Coverage endorsement, and the Water Back Up and Sump Overflow endorsement.

Sinkhole Collapse *Sinkhole Collapse* coverage was made available as an optional peril in 1986. All homeowners forms except Form HO-4 and Form HO-6 may be endorsed to provide coverage against sinkhole collapse. The sinkhole collapse peril covers damage to insured property caused by underground erosion of limestone or similar rock caused by water. The cost of filling the sinkhole is not covered.

Earthquake The *Earthquake endorsement* modifies the basic Earth Movement exclusion of the policy, reimbursing for loss to insured property resulting from earthquake or volcanic eruption, excluding only loss by flood or tidal wave generated by these catastrophes. The coverage does not, of course, apply to damage to land itself, and it is subject to a percentage deductible. In most jurisdictions, the deductible is 5 percent of the value of each item insured. In some jurisdictions, where the earthquake hazard is severe, a 10 percent deductible is used.

Refrigerated Property Coverage The *Refrigerated Property Coverage Endorsement* (HO 04 98) covers damage to property stored in freezers or refrigerators against loss caused by the interruption of electrical service to the refrigeration unit or by the mechanical failure of the unit. The coverage is sub-

ject to a $500 limit and is subject to a $100 deductible.

Water Back up and Sump Overflow The Water Damage exclusion of all homeowners forms specifically denies liability for water damage, which is defined to include "water which backs up through sewers or drains and which overflows from a sump." In most jurisdictions, this exclusion can be eliminated by endorsement for an additional premium. The *Water Back Up and Sump Overflow* endorsement (HO 04 95) provides up to $5000 in coverage for direct physical loss, not caused by the negligence of an "insured," to covered property that is caused by water that backs up through sewers or drains or water that overflows from a sump. Coverage for water damage that overflows from a sump applies even if the overflow results from the mechanical breakdown of the sump pump. Damage to the sump pump or related equipment that is caused by mechanical breakdown is excluded. The coverage is subject to a $250 deductible. The deductible does not apply to loss under Coverage D, Loss of Use.

Other Endorsements

Other endorsements are available to provide coverage for exposures that are not common and for which the average insured may not require coverage. Making coverage for such exposures available as an option isolates the costs associated with the exposure so that only those who need the coverage are required to pay for it.

Other Members of Your Household The growth of nontraditional households has prompted the insurance industry to change some of its policy provisions. The definition of insured in the homeowners policy, for example, does not extend coverage to a resident of the named insured's household who is not a relative and is not a person under age 21 in the care of an insured. In the year 2000 revision of the program, ISO introduced a new endorsement titled *Other Members of Your Household* (HO 04 58) that addresses this problem. The endorsement may be used to modify the definition of Insured to include a person of any age or gender living with the named insured to share expenses or in a personal relationship. The effect is similar to providing a HO-4 policy for the person named; coverage applies to personal property owned or used by the insured under Section

I, and the individual is an insured for the liability coverage under Section II. There is an additional premium for the endorsement.

Assisted Living Care Coverage A second area in which changing family patterns are recognized concerns elderly. Often the insured must place a relative (who need not be a household resident) into a care facility. A new *Assisted Living Care Coverage* endorsement (HO 04 59) extends the definition of insured to provide coverage on personal property of such relatives. Internal limits apply on personal property for items such as hearing aids, eyeglasses, wheelchairs, and false teeth. Coverage is also provided for additional living expense in the event of loss or damage to the assisted living facility. Finally, the endorsement extends the Section II liability coverage of the policy to provide comprehensive personal liability coverage for the designated relative. There is a premium charge for the endorsement.

Scheduled Personal Property Endorsements The *Scheduled Personal Property Endorsements* (HO 04 60 and HO 04 61)) are used when specific open-peril coverage is to be provided on valuable items such as jewelry and furs, silverware, musical instruments, cameras, and stamp and coin collections. The coverage available under these forms is discussed in the next chapter.

Nonbuilding Replacement Cost The HO-91 covered "other structures that are not buildings" at actual cash value. Examples of such structures include fences, mailboxes, light poles, satellite dishes, and swimming pools. The HO 2000 offers an endorsement—*Replacement Cost Settlement for Certain Non-Building Structures* (HO 04 43)—to convert some of these structures to replacement cost loss settlement,

for a 2 percent premium surcharge. To qualify, the other structure must be constructed of reinforced masonry, metal, fiberglass, or plastic materials. Structures made of wood do not qualify.

Coverage on Computers Computers are not scheduled under the Scheduled Personal Property Endorsement, but may be insured under a special computer coverage endorsement (HO 04 14). Although there is no specific exclusion of computers under the blanket personal property, the named-peril coverage for sudden and accidental damage by artificially generated electrical current specifically excludes damage to tubes, transistors, electronic components or circuitry, eliminating coverage for a major cause of loss to computers and their equipment. The Special Computer Coverage Endorsement provides open-peril coverage on the insured "computer equipment." A new exclusion of mechanical breakdown has been added to the endorsement in the 2000 revision. It is not clear how this will impact the coverage, which heretofore has followed the pattern of machinery coverage.

Owned Golf Carts Coverage is available for physical damage to owned golf carts by endorsement to the homeowners policy. The *Owned Motorized Golf Cart—Physical Loss Coverage Endorsement* (HO 05 28) covers loss to an owned motorized golf cart, including permanently installed accessories and equipment, scheduled in the endorsement. Coverage is on an open-peril basis, with the option of including or not including collision. Coverage is subject to a $500 deductible. Physical damage coverage on other recreational motor vehicles is usually written under a recreational motor vehicle policy, which combines physical damage coverage with liability coverage.

IMPORTANT CONCEPTS TO REMEMBER

vacancy
unoccupancy
consequential damage
Loss Assessment additional
 coverage
Ordinance or Law additional
 coverage

Scheduled Personal Property
 Endorsement
Earthquake Damage Assumption
 Endorsement
Ordinance or Law exclusion
Earth Movement exclusion
Power Failure exclusion

Neglect exclusion
Special Personal Property Coverage
 Endorsement
sinkhole collapse
hostile fire
friendly fire

QUESTIONS FOR REVIEW

1. Without going into great detail, explain the essential difference among the *Homeowners 2 Broad Form,* the *Homeowners 4 Tenant's Form,* and the *Homeowners 3 Special Form.*

2. For each of the following losses, indicate whether coverage would or would not be provided under the *Homeowners 3 Special Form:*

a. Explosion of a hot water heater

b. Damage to the garage by the insured's automobile

c. Vandalism damage to trees

d. Damage caused by freezing of pipes

e. Theft of a set of snow tires from the garage

3. With respect to each of the following losses, indicate whether coverage would or would not be provided under the *Homeowners 2 Broad Form:*

a. A delivery truck backs over the insured's prize cherry tree

b. The insured backs his or her car over a 10-speed bicycle

c. Damage to kitchen ceiling caused by overflow of a bathtub

d. Theft of an airplane ticket from the insured's motel room

e. Damage to the picture tube of a television set caused by lightning

4. Identify the perils included in the *Homeowners 2 Broad Form* that are not contained in the *Homeowners 8 Modified Coverage Form.* With respect to those perils that are included in both forms, indicate the manner in which the coverage under the Broad form is broader than the coverage for the same peril under the Basic Form.

5. Due to a power transformer burnout, the entire city in which you live is without power for four days. There is some inconvenience, but your greatest loss is the damage to your freezer when the meat within it spoils. The freezer is no longer usable, and the meat is a total loss. Would you expect the loss of either the freezer or the meat to be covered under the Homeowners 2 Broad Form? Why or why not?

6. Your parents are planning a two-month trip to Europe. Your father, assuming that you are now an expert in the field of insurance, asks you if the fact that the house will be empty for two months will affect the coverage under his homeowners policy. You examine the policy and find that it is a Form HO-3. What do you tell him?

7. Briefly explain the doctrine of concurrent causation. In what ways have the homeowners policies been modified in response to this doctrine?

8. The theft coverage under the homeowners policies is subject to a number of exclusions and other limitations. Identify the exclusions applicable to the theft peril, and any other limitations imposed by the homeowners forms with respect to theft losses. For each of the exclusions or limitations identified, indicate the manner in which additional protection might be obtained.

9. List and briefly explain the general exclusions under Section I of the homeowners forms. Which of these exclusions can be deleted or modified?

10. Explain the special exposures of a condominium unit-owner that led to the development of a separate homeowners form for such individuals. Explain the manner in which these exposures are handled under *the Condominium Unit-Owner's form.*

QUESTIONS FOR DISCUSSION

1. Your homeowners policy is about to be renewed. It is written to cover your dwelling for its original construction cost. The policy is a Homeowners Form HO-3, and is standard in all respects: The coverages are all standard percentages and there are no endorsements or modifications to the policy. What changes to this basic contract should you consider?

2. Josh Jones is insured under a Homeowners Form HO-3, with $50,000 in coverage on the dwelling and standard amounts on all other coverages. Jones borrows a neighbor's camping trailer and, while attempting to back it into his garage, hits the garage door. The damage to the borrowed trailer is $425 and to the garage door, $300. Unfortunately, the neighbor is an impoverished college student and does not have any insurance on the trailer. Indicate,

with reference to the specific policy provisions applicable, whether Jones's policy will apply to the trailer and to the garage.

3. The Homeowners Special Form insures the dwelling on an open-peril basis. What perils that are not covered under the Broad Form would be covered under the Special Form?

4. Sue and Mary share a small apartment. Some of the property in the apartment belongs to Sue and some belongs to Mary, while some items are owned jointly. Mary purchases a Homeowners 4 Contents Broad Form (tenant's form), with herself as the named insured. What coverage is provided under this form for the personal property owned by Mary, by Sue, and by the two jointly?

5. A distant uncle dies, leaving you his $150,000 condominium unit in Aspen, Colorado. It is rented to skiers during the winter months, and managed by a local realtor. You elect to spend your summers living in the unit yourself. Upon investigation you find that the uncle has been insured under a Homeowners Form HO-6, with $25,000 in coverage on the contents of the unit. All other features of the policy are standard. What modifications in this policy would you consider?

SUGGESTIONS FOR ADDITIONAL READING

Fire, Casualty and Surety Bulletins. Personal Lines Volume. Cincinnati: National Underwriter Company. (Loose-leaf manual service with monthly supplements.) See "Dwellings" section.

Hamilton, Karen L., and Donald S. Malecki. *Personal Insurance: Property and Liability.* Malvern, Pa.: American Institute for CPCU, 1994. Chapters 2, 3.

Launie, J. J., George E. Rejda, and Donald R. Oakes with Anita W. Johnson. *Personal Insurance.* Bryn Mawr, Pa.: Insurance Institute of America, 1991. Chapters 2–4.

Policy, Form and Manual Analysis Service. Property Coverages Volume. Indianapolis: Rough Notes Company. (Loose-leaf manual service with monthly supplements.) See "Homeowners Policy Program" section.

Taylor, Barbara. *How to Get Your Money's Worth in Home and Auto Insurance.* New York: Insurance Information Institute, 1991. Chapters 5, 6.

Vaughan, E. J. "What Is Insurable Value?" *American Agency Bulletin* (Sept. 1965).

WEB SITES TO EXPLORE

Best's Review—Property/Casualty Edition	http://www.ambest.com/review/lh/index.html
Consumers Guide to Homeowners Insurance	http://www.iiaa.iix.com/homeguid.htm
Independent Insurance Agents of America, Inc.	http://www.iiaa.org
Insurance News Network	http://www.insure.com/
National Association of Professional Insurance Agents	http://www.pianet.com/
Newsedge News Page	http://www.newspage.com/browse/46622/
Quicken InsureMarket	http://www.insuremarket.com/
Rough Notes Company	http://www.roughnotes.com/

CHAPTER 26

OTHER PERSONAL FORMS OF PROPERTY INSURANCE

Like—but oh how different!

— WILLIAM WORDSWORTH
"Yes, It Was The Mountain Echo"

CHAPTER OBJECTIVES

When you have finished this chapter, you should be able to

- Describe the purpose and uses of the monoline dwelling forms
- Explain how coverage under the mobilehome program differs from coverage on dwellings under the homeowners program
- Identify the coverage limits on residential property available under the National Flood Insurance Program
- Explain the reasons that an individual might choose to purchase scheduled coverage under an inland marine floater
- Identify the classes of property that may be insured under the scheduled coverage endorsement to the homeowners forms
- Explain the coverage features of watercraft policies

Although the homeowners policy does an adequate job of protecting the assets of persons eligible for coverage under the program, some properties are not eligible for a homeowners policy. In addition, while the homeowners policy protects many types of personal property owned by individuals, some property is excluded and the coverage on other classes is limited. Finally, while the homeowners policy protects against a wide range of perils, it does not cover flood, and protection against this peril must be obtained separately. For these reasons, additional forms of coverage are often needed by persons with specialized exposure.

In this chapter, we conclude our discussion of property insurance for the individual and the family with a brief look at several additional forms of protection. The specific coverages that remain to be considered

include the monoline fire dwelling policies, the Mobilehome Policy, the Federal Flood Insurance Program, and inland marine coverages designed for personal exposures. In addition, we will briefly discuss title insurance. Although title insurance is a considerably different form of insurance coverage from those encountered thus far, it represents an important part of the property owner's protection and is, therefore, appropriate to include in this section. Finally, we will examine the process of purchasing property insurance and provide some additional guidelines in this area, applying the principles originally encountered in Chapter 3.

MONOLINE FIRE DWELLING PROGRAM

Although the homeowners forms represent the most attractive approach to insuring residences and their contents, many dwellings are not eligible for coverage under one of these forms. Such properties must be insured under *monoline fire forms*, which have less demanding eligibility requirements. The monoline fire forms used to insure residential property are referred to as *dwelling forms.* As monoline forms, the dwelling policies have traditionally differed from the homeowners policies in that they do not provide personal liability insurance or personal theft coverage. (Theft coverage and personal liability coverage are now available under the dwelling policies by endorsement.) Although the coverage of the dwelling policies is still somewhat narrower than that of the homeowners policies in certain respects, the dwelling policies provide an alternative for those property owners whose buildings are not eligible for one of the homeowners forms.[1]

Current Dwelling Program

There are three forms in the Dwelling '89 program, designated the *Dwelling Property 1 Basic Form* (DP 00 01), *Dwelling Property 2 Broad Form* (DP 00 02), and the *Dwelling Property 3 Special Form* (DP 00 03).[2] The principal difference among the forms is with respect to the covered causes of loss. As its title indicates, the *Basic Form* provides the most limited coverage available on dwellings and their contents. The form makes provision for three levels of coverage. The first level consists of coverage for loss by fire, lightning, and *internal explosion.* For an additional premium, coverage may be extended to include eight additional perils (windstorm and hail, explosion, riot or civil commotion, aircraft, vehicles, smoke, and volcanic eruption).[3] For yet an additional premium, coverage is extended to include vandalism and malicious mischief. The *Broad Form* includes the perils of the Basic Form, plus additional named perils. The *Special Form* insures the dwelling and other structures on an open-perils basis and insures personal property for the same perils as the Broad Form. All three forms may be endorsed to include coverage for loss by theft. In addition, personal liability coverage may also be added by endorsement.

Eligibility

The dwelling forms may be used to insure most dwelling property, including dwellings in the course of construction, whether or not owner occupied. While farm dwellings are not eligible, most other residences are. Even trailer homes may be insured, provided they are at a fixed location and meet other eligibility requirements.[4]

[1] Residential property may be ineligible for coverage under the homeowners program for a variety of reasons. One major class of dwellings that is not eligible for homeowners coverage consists of rental property. All jurisdictions require that dwellings insured under homeowners forms must be owner occupied. Another class of ineligible dwellings consists of rooming and boarding houses. The homeowners program permits not more than two roomers or boarders per family. A residence insured under the dwelling program may have up to five roomers or boarders. Finally, many low-valued dwellings and older structures that do not meet the strict underwriting requirements of the homeowners program may also be insured under the dwelling policies.

[2] Originally, monoline fire insurance coverage on dwellings was provided by endorsement to the Standard Fire Policy, with forms that differed by jurisdiction. In 1978, the ISO introduced a uniform national program, the Dwelling '77 program, written in simplified terminology and following the format of Section I of the simplified homeowners policies. The Dwelling '77 program was replaced by the Dwelling '89 program in 1990.

[3] Although volcanic eruption was not an insured peril under the separate Extended Coverage Endorsement, it is included in the extended coverage perils of DP 00 01.

[4] More specifically, a dwelling policy may be used to insure a dwelling building used exclusively for dwelling purposes (except permitted incidental occupancies) with not more than four apartments and with not more than five roomers or boarders in total. Incidental occupancies permitted include business or professional occupancies and other occupancies such as barber shops, beauty parlors, photographers' studios, with not more than two persons at work at any one time.

Coverages under the Dwelling Program

There are five insuring agreements used in the Dwelling '89 policies:

Coverage A	Dwelling
Coverage B	Other Structures
Coverage C	Personal Property
Coverage D	Rental Value
Coverage E	Additional Living Expense

All forms include coverages A, B, C, and D, and the terminology affecting these coverages is identical under all three forms. Coverage E (Additional Living Expense) is included only in the Broad and Special Forms, but is available by endorsement to the Basic Form. In addition to these coverages, each of the forms also contains extensions entitled *Other Coverages,* which parallel the *additional coverages* of homeowners policies.

Differences between Dwelling Forms and Homeowners Forms
Our previous analysis of the homeowners program and the forms that are contained in that program permit a somewhat briefer discussion of the dwelling program forms. In general, each of the three dwelling forms parallels the homeowners form with the same designation, subject to the following exceptions.

1. The dwelling forms do not include the peril of theft of personal property. Coverage for loss by theft is available by endorsement.

2. The dwelling forms do not include personal liability coverage (as provided under Section II of the homeowners policy). Personal liability coverage is available as an option for an additional premium.

3. Coverage on property away from the insured premises is limited to 10 percent of the on-premises limit under all three forms.

4. In addition to the classes of personal property excluded under the homeowners forms, the Dwelling Basic Coverage Form excludes boats other than rowboats and canoes.

5. The dwelling forms do not provide coverage on money or valuable papers.

6. The dwelling forms do not contain the special limits of liability for certain types of personal property (money, watercraft, trailers, jewelry, firearms, silverware) that are found on homeowners forms.

A special provision in the definition of personal property provides automatic transfer of coverage for 30 days at a new location, which is to be used as the residence of the insured. Coverage applies at the new location and ceases to apply at the older location. During the period of removal, the property at each location is covered on a pro rata basis. Property in transit is covered only to the extent of the 10 percent off-premises extension.

Endorsements to the Dwelling Program Forms

A variety of endorsements are available to modify the Dwelling '89 forms. They include Automatic Increase in Insurance endorsement, Sinkhole Collapse endorsement, Dwelling Under Construction endorsement, Condominium Unit-Owners Coverage endorsement, and a Loss Assessment endorsement, whose coverage parallels the coverage under the homeowners program.

Modified Loss Settlement Endorsement (DP 00 08)
The *Modified Loss Settlement endorsement* (DP 00 08) is used only with the Dwelling Property 1 Basic Form to provide coverage equivalent to Form DP-8, which was withdrawn in the 1989 revision. It modifies the loss settlement provisions of the Basic Form to coincide with those of the Homeowners 8 Modified Coverage Form. In the event of a partial loss, payment is made on a functional cost basis—that is, the cost to replace the damaged property using common construction methods and materials. In the event of a total loss, coverage is limited to the lesser of the cost to repair the property or the market value of the property exclusive of land.

Dwelling Program Theft Endorsements
Prior to the 1989 revision of the dwelling program, theft coverage for residential exposures was available only under the homeowners policy or under separate personal theft policies. With the introduction of the 1989 dwelling program, the individual theft policies were withdrawn and two new endorsements were introduced that add theft coverage to the dwelling forms.

Broad-Form Theft Coverage Endorsement The *Broad-Form Theft Coverage Endorsement* (DP 04 72) may be used with any dwelling policy written on a dwelling, co-op, or condominium unit that is owner-occupied. In addition, the endorsement may be written for a named insured who is a tenant in

an apartment. The insured may elect on-premises coverage only or on-premises and off-premises coverage, but off-premises coverage is not available alone. The minimum limit for either on- or off-premises coverage is $1000.

The Broad-Form Theft Coverage Endorsement provides essentially the same theft coverage as does the Homeowners Broad Form (HO-2). The endorsement contains its own definition of insured property, and excludes the same classes of property that are excluded by the homeowners forms.[5] In addition, the endorsement imposes the same dollar limits on property as are contained in the homeowners forms.[6]

Limited Theft Coverage Endorsement The *Limited Theft Coverage Endorsement* (DP 04 73) is designed to insure personal property of landlords located in dwellings, co-ops, condominiums, or apartments that are occupied by others. Coverage is limited to property owned or used by the insured or a spouse, and applies only on-premises. In addition to those items excluded under the Broad Form, the Limited Form excludes money and valuable papers, jewelry and furs, and silverware. The Limited Form includes the same dollar limits as the Broad Form on watercraft and their trailers, other trailers, and firearms. Finally, the Limited Theft endorsement excludes losses caused by a tenant, roomer or boarder, members of the tenant's household, or employees of any of these persons.

Personal Liability Supplement to Dwelling Policies Prior to the 1989 revision of the dwelling policies, individuals who purchased a dwelling policy instead of a homeowners policy had to purchase personal liability coverage under a separate policy. Under the Dwelling '89 program, personal liability coverage is available as an endorsement to the dwelling forms under the Personal Liability Supplement.

MOBILEHOME PROGRAM

It has been estimated that one-half of the new homes being sold today are mobilehomes. In view of the increasing popularity of this type of dwelling, it is not surprising that a special program has been developed to meet the special insurance needs of mobilehome owners. Numerous packages were developed in the 1960s for the growing mobilehome segment of the insurance market. Most programs provided coverage for named perils based on the Homeowners Broad Form but otherwise followed the approach used in providing auto physical damage insurance. This *automobile approach* to insuring mobilehomes based the premium on the age and original price of the mobilehome structure. As a corollary, loss settlement was based on the actual cash value of the structure at the time of loss, and losses were settled in much the same way as auto physical damage claims.[7]

ISO Mobilehome Program

After many years of treating mobilehomes like automobiles, the homeowners underwriting approach for mobilehomes was adopted by the ISO in its *mobilehome supplement* to the homeowners program in 1984. Under this program, coverage for mobilehomes is provided by endorsement to a homeowners policy. This means that mobilehomes are basically accorded the same coverage treatment as conventional dwellings, modified by a number of essential provisions. The rules allow combining a Homeowners 2 Broad Form or Homeowners 3 Special Form with Mobilehome Endorsement MH 04 01. The *Mobilehome Endorsement* tailors the homeowners forms to accommodate the needs of mobilehome owners. In addition, the Homeowners 4 Contents

[5] The excluded classes of property are aircraft and their parts, motor vehicles, their equipment and accessories, property held as a sample or for sale or delivery after sale, business property, animals, birds, fish, and property of tenants who are not related to an insured. There is also an exclusion of credit cards or fund transfer cards and property separately described and specifically insured by other insurance. Some property is excluded only while away from the premises: property at a location owned, rented to or occupied by an insured, except while the insured is residing there, property in the custody of a laundry, cleaner, tailor, presser or dyer, and property in the mail.

[6] The classes of property and the dollar limits are: $1000 on watercraft, their trailers, furnishings, equipment and outboard motors, $1000 on other trailers, $2000 on firearms, $200 on money, bank notes and precious metals, $1000 on securities and valuable papers, $1000 on jewelry, watches, and furs, and $2500 on silverware, silver-plated ware, goldware, gold-plated ware, and pewterware.

[7] The difference in treatment of mobilehomes is due in large part to the loss experience associated with such units. Because of their construction, fire and windstorm losses are likely to be more severe in the case of mobilehomes than for other dwellings. According to a Federal Emergency Management Agency analysis of the National Fire Protection Association's 1981 National Fire Experience Survey, mobilehomes were involved in 25,715 fires that resulted in $841,330,000 in property loss, an average loss of $33,653. By comparison, the average fire loss to conventional homes was $3069 (522,175 fires causing a $1,602,693,000 property loss).

Broad Form may be used without endorsement for a tenant of a mobilehome.

The change from the *automobile approach* to insuring mobilehomes rests on the premise that modern mobilehomes, in general, tend to increase in value over time, as do conventional homes, rather than depreciate, as cars do.

Eligibility

A Mobilehome Policy may be written on a mobilehome that is designed for portability and year-round living and that is not less than 10 feet wide and 40 feet in length. These requirements are imposed to eliminate from eligibility the small trailers of a *camper type* that may be pulled by private passenger automobiles. Such trailers are insured under the auto policy. To be eligible for coverage under the Mobilehome Policy, the unit must be a trailer; that is, it must be a portable unit, designed and built to be towed on its own chassis, comprised of a frame and wheels, and must be designed for year-round living.

Coverage on the Mobilehome

Coverage A provides protection on the mobilehome described in the declarations. The Mobilehome Endorsement amends the definition of *dwelling* in the homeowners form to include utility tanks attached to the mobilehome and permanently installed floor coverings, appliances, dressers and cabinets, and other built-in or attached items of a similar nature. When coverage is written for at least 80 percent of replacement cost value, coverage applies on a replacement cost basis. The policy can be endorsed to provide coverage on an actual cash value basis. The mobilehome endorsement adds a provision deleting the ordinance or law additional coverage of the homeowners policy to which the endorsement is attached.

A special provision related to loss settlement has been added, reflecting the difficulties that can arise in repairing a mobilehome when part of a series of panels used in the construction of the unit are damaged. In the event of damage to pieces or panels of the mobilehome, the insurer agrees to pay:

> The reasonable cost of repairing or replacing the damaged part to match the remainder as closely as possible, or
> The reasonable cost of providing an acceptable decorative effect or utilization as circumstances may warrant.

This means if the repairs to the unit result in a mismatch (appearance damage), the insurer will pay for recovering (or perhaps painting?) the unit.

Coverage on Personal Property The basic limit of personal property coverage under the mobilehome program is 40 percent of the limit on the mobilehome rather than the standard 50 percent under other homeowners forms. The justification for the reduced limit of contents coverage is the fact that a substantial number of normal contents items are "built in" in mobilehomes. The coverage on contents may be increased if the need exists.

Additional Living Expense Additional living expense coverage has been revised to provide up to 20 percent of the mobilehome's insured value to pay for additional living expense. (The previous forms paid up to $15 per day for a maximum of 45 days.)

Property Removal Property removal coverage is provided in the amount of $500, with option to purchase a higher limit up to $2500 (in increments of $250). The property removal coverage provides payment for the expense of moving the mobile home, when such movement is required to escape damage from an insured peril.

Transportation/Moving Endorsement Coverage for damage to the mobilehome while being moved is covered under the *Transportation/Moving* endorsement (MH 04 03). This endorsement extends the policy for 30 days to cover collision, upset, stranding, or sinking while being moved to a new location. An additional premium is required.

Lienholders Single Interest Endorsement When the mobilehome is financed by a dealer on a time payment basis or when there is a lienholder interested in the unit, special coverage protecting the interest of such parties may be provided under the *Lienholders Single Interest Endorsement* (MH 04 04). This endorsement, which insures the interest of the vendor or lienholder only, provides protection against loss resulting from collision, conversion, embezzlement, or secretion of the mobilehome by the insured.

FLOOD INSURANCE

Until enactment of the 1968 Housing and Urban Development Act (HUD), which initiated the National Flood Insurance Program, flood insurance

on fixed location property was available only on an extremely limited basis. The HUD Act of 1968 created a federally subsidized flood insurance program, under which flood insurance is available to both individuals and businesses.

General Nature of the Program

The National Flood Insurance Program (NFIP) is under the jurisdiction of the Federal Insurance Administration in the Federal Emergency Management Agency (FEMA). Flood policies are issued both by the NFIP itself and by private insurers, participating in the cooperative program referred to as the Write-Your-Own Program. Private insurers issue flood insurance policies on behalf of the NFIP and are reinsured 100 percent against loss. Private insurers participating in the Write-Your-Own Program are reimbursed by the NFIP for losses that are not covered by premiums and the investment income on those premiums. Coverage written by both the private insurers and the federal government is sold by private insurance agents who are paid a commission for the coverage sold.

Eligible Communities The National Flood Insurance Program is open to any community that pledges to adopt and enforce land control measures designed to guide the future development of the community away from flood-prone areas. Cities, counties, or other governmental units seeking approval for the sale of flood insurance must take the initiative and submit an official statement to FEMA indicating a need for the insurance and a desire to participate in the program. To become eligible for the insurance, the community must agree to adopt certain land use and flood control measures, including zoning ordinances that prohibit new construction in areas where there is more than a 1 percent chance of flooding each year.

Once the community has agreed to adopt the specified controls, it becomes eligible for the *Emergency Program.* Under this program, coverage is available on eligible properties, up to specified limits, at subsidized rates. Although the program originally provided coverage only for residential property, the eligibility has gradually been expanded. Today, virtually all residential, industrial, commercial, agricultural, and public buildings are eligible for coverage.

Subsidized coverage is available under the emergency program for up to $35,000 on single family dwellings and up to $100,000 on other eligible structures, and up to $10,000 on residential contents and $100,000 on nonresidential contents. The cost of flood insurance under the Emergency Program is identical for all eligible cities and towns, and the rates for the additional coverage under the Regular Program vary with the loss probability of the particular area.

A community enters the *Regular Program* when the detailed flood risk study has been completed (or waived by FEMA) and the community adopts floodplain management ordinances. Increased amounts of coverage are available once the community enters the Regular Program. Under the Regular Program, available coverage is classed as *Basic Insurance Limits* and *Additional Insurance Limits.* Basic Limits are similar to (but not identical with) the limits under the Emergency Program. Rates under the Regular Program are actuarially determined and differ for the Basic Insurance Limit and the Additional Insurance Limit. The amounts of coverage under the Emergency Program and the Basic and Increased amounts under the Regular Program are summarized in Table 26.1.

Rate Maps The additional amounts of insurance available under the Regular Program are not at subsidized rates, but are actuarial rates calculated to consider the probability of loss in the community. Maps of participating communities indicate the

TABLE 26.1 Limits on Residential Property Under Federal Flood Insurance Program

	Emergency Program	Basic Insurance Limits	Additional Insurance Limits	Total Insurance Available
Single family residential	$ 35,000	$ 50,000	$200,000	$250,000
2–4 family dwelling		50,000	200,000	250,000
Other residential	100,000[a]	135,000	115,000	250,000
Residential contents	10,000	15,000	85,000	100,000

[a] Single family residential in Alaska, Guam, Hawaii, and U.S. Virgin Islands is $50,000, and other residential is $150,000.

Source: National Flood Insurance Manual, 2000.

degree of flood hazard so that actuarial premium rates can be assigned on properties. The initial map of a community is known as the Flood Hazard Boundary Map, and the official map detailing the actuarial risk for the community is called the Flood Insurance Rate Map (FIRM).

Other Important Provisions The 1973 law amended several provisions of the original law in an attempt to make flood insurance more available and more desirable. The most important amendment requires the purchase of flood insurance in *Special Flood Hazard Areas* as a condition to receiving any form of federal financial assistance for acquisition or construction purposes. This means that property owners in those communities where flood insurance is available and whose property is located in a Special Flood Hazard Area must purchase the flood insurance in order to qualify for federal loans or federally assisted or insured loans (VA, FHA, FDIC, and so on). A *Special Flood Hazard Area* is specifically designated land within a community in the flood plain that is most likely to be subjected to severe flooding. If the property is not in a Special Flood Hazard Area, the flood insurance is not a prerequisite to obtaining a loan but the property may, of course, still be insured.

Following the floods of 1993, the *National Flood Insurance Reform Act of 1994* significantly strengthened the compliance requirements for lenders. Federally regulated lenders and Federal agency lenders must now require flood insurance when making, increasing, extending, or renewing a loan, and the coverage must be maintained for the term of the loan. Lenders are required to notify, in writing, the purchaser or lessor of property that is in a Special Flood Hazard Area of the requirement for flood insurance in advance of the signing of the purchase agreement or lease. If the borrower has not purchased flood insurance within 45 days of the notification, the lender must purchase flood insurance on behalf of the borrower.

The 1973 legislation also eliminates the possibility of receiving federal disaster funds following a flood in any area identified as having a special flood hazard, unless the property owner has purchased flood insurance. The law specifically prohibits any federal agency from approving financial assistance to victims for reconstruction following a flood, if the individual did not purchase flood insurance. This prohibition applies regardless of whether or not the community has become eligible for the flood insurance program.

The Residential Flood Insurance Policy

The Residential Flood Insurance Policy is a simplified language form that generally follows the format of contracts used by private insurers for property insurance coverages. There are, however, a number of significant differences, outlined below, which are dictated by the nature of the flood peril.

Protection under the flood policy is provided under three items, designated Coverages A, B, and C, which insure the dwelling, contents, and debris removal respectively. Coverage may be purchased on the dwelling, its contents, or on both. The debris removal coverage is included in the limit of liability applicable to the property insured, although it is set forth in a separate insuring agreement.

Insuring Agreement The residential flood policy provides coverage for "direct physical loss by or from flood" as defined in the contract. Flood is defined in the policy as

> A general and temporary condition of partial or complete inundation of normally dry land areas from overflow of inland or tidal waters or from the unusual and rapid accumulation or runoff of surface waters from any source.

Losses caused by flood-related erosion and damage caused by mudslides (i.e., mudflows), as specifically defined in the policy, are also covered.

Flood must be a general condition; this is reinforced by specific exclusions of damage by water that stems from sources on the insured's own property or within the insured's control, or from a condition that does not cause general flooding in the area. This means that the policy will not cover as *flood damage* inundations from a broken or stopped-up sewer or a faulty sump pump in the insured's basement. Neither would accumulations of water on the insured property caused by the slope of the lot be covered in the absence of general flooding in the area.

Building Coverage The definition of the dwelling generally follows that of the dwelling and contents forms used with the fire policy. Materials and supplies intended for construction, alteration, or repair of buildings are covered, but only if they are inside a fully enclosed shelter. The building item includes a 10-percent extension to cover appurtenant structures on the premises, but only those that are fully enclosed. In addition, the extension does not provide

an additional amount of insurance. The basic policy is on an actual cash value basis, but replacement cost coverage is available for any one-to four-family dwelling occupied by the owner for at least 80 percent of the year. Like the homeowners forms, replacement cost coverage under the Residential Flood Insurance Policy requires that the structure be insured for 80 percent of its replacement cost. Although the policy does not include an ordinance or law extension, coverage for this exposure is available as an option.

There is a specific exclusion of land values, lawns, trees, shrubs, and plants. Fences and outdoor swimming pools and waterfront structures (e.g., docks and wharves) are excluded, as are walks, driveways, or other paved surfaces outside the building. Underground structures (like wells) and equipment outside the foundation walls of the dwelling (such as an air-conditioning unit) are also excluded. Finally, flood policies also exclude certain property in basements, including finished walls, floors, ceiling, or other similar construction or improvements and contents, building machinery, and equipment located in the basement area or below the lowest elevated floor of an elevated building. Enclosures and building components located below the lowest elevated floor of an elevated building (except utility connections and the footing, foundation, posts, pilings, piers, or other foundation walls and anchorage system as required for the support of the elevated building) are also excluded.[8]

Increased Cost of Construction Although the NFIP did not make provision for coverage equivalent to the Ordinance or Law additional coverage of the homeowners forms, an Increased Cost of Construction provision was added by the 1994 changes in the program. The Increased Cost of Construction coverage pays the cost of complying with land use and control measures for elevating structures that are damaged to 50 percent of the structure's value (or structures that have experienced flood losses on multiple occasions). Land-use ordinances required of communities for participation in the program require that structures that suffer such damage be elevated

or otherwise made flood-proof. This can involve significant additional costs to the property owner, over and above the replacement cost value of the property. The addition of this feature significantly enhances the coverage of the program.

Contents Coverage When residential contents are insured under the flood policy, the coverage applies to household and personal property usual or incidental to the occupancy of the premises as a dwelling. Coverage is provided on personal property owned by the insured and members of his or her family, or for which the insured may be liable. At the option of the policyholder, the contents coverage may be extended to cover the property of guests or servants on the premises. Perhaps the most important provision in this coverage is the stipulation that contents are covered against loss by flood only while inside a fully enclosed building on the premises. There is no off-premises extension.

Property defined as personal property includes clothes washers, clothes dryers, food freezers, air-conditioning units, portable dishwashers, carpeting installed over a finished floor, regardless of whether or not it is permanently installed, carpeting not permanently installed over unfinished flooring, outdoor equipment and furniture stored inside the dwelling or another fully enclosed building, and portable microwave ovens and cook-out grills.

The policy contains an extensive list of *Property Not Covered*. In addition to money, securities, and valuable papers, the form excludes animals, birds, fish, aircraft and motor vehicles, trailers, watercraft (including their furnishings and equipment), and business property. In addition to those classes of property that are completely excluded, there are two additional groups of property subject to dollar limits. The policy imposes a $250 aggregate limit on fine arts, such as statuary, paintings, antiques, and similar articles, and a separate $500 aggregate limit on jewelry, watches, articles of gold, silver, platinum, and furs.

Tenant's improvements and betterments are covered up to 10 percent of the amount of coverage on the contents, but like the appurtenant structures extension, this is not an additional amount of insurance.

Removal Although property removed from the premises to protect it from the insured peril is covered pro rata at its new location for up to 30 days, the coverage during removal and for the 30 days afterwards is not open-perils coverage as in the case of the homeowners and dwelling program policies. However, the

[8] An exception is made for buildings constructed (or substantially improved) before October 1, 1983. In these cases, coverage is provided for sump pumps, well water tanks, oil tanks, furances, hot water heaters, heat pumps, and electric junction and circuit breaker boxes in the basement.

policy does include specific coverage reimbursing the insured for reasonable expenses of moving insured contents to a safe area and temporary storage not exceeding 45 days when such property is in imminent danger of flood. The property removal expense reimbursement coverage is limited to $750. No deductible applies to removal expense reimbursement.

Debris Removal The coverage for debris removal applies only to removal of debris *of* or *on* the property insured. This is an important limitation. The property owner may incur significant expense in clearing away debris after a flood, but the cost is covered only to the extent of removing the debris of the covered property itself or removing other debris from the covered property. Reimbursement for debris removal is a part of, and not in addition to, the coverage provided on the dwelling or the contents.

Exclusions The policy asserts the standard exclusions of war, nuclear reaction, the operation of building codes, and neglect of the insured to protect and preserve the property at the time of a loss. A variation of the standard consequential loss exclusion eliminates coverage for damage resulting from power, heating, or cooling failure, unless such failure results from damage to equipment on the premises by flood. Finally, there is a specific exclusion of loss caused by fire, windstorm, explosion, erosion, earthquake, landslide, or other earth movement except mudslide.

Deductible The Residential Flood Insurance Policy is subject to a deductible that applies separately to the building and to contents. For dwellings insured under the Emergency Program or for dwellings that are located in certain zones where the rates used to compute the premium date from before the publication of the Flood Insurance Rate Map, the deductible is $750. In all other cases, it is $500. An additional $250 deductible applies separately to each building and content loss for payments for land subsidence, sewer backup, or seepage of water. Higher optional deductibles have been available, ranging from $1000 up to $5000, in increments of $1000.

Inception of Coverage and Cancellation Provision There is a 30-day waiting period, after application and the payment of the premium, before a flood insurance policy becomes effective. This waiting period is subject to two exceptions. The waiting period does not apply to the initial purchase of flood insurance in connection with making, increasing, extending, or renewing a loan. The waiting period also does not

apply to the initial purchase of flood insurance if the purchase occurs during the 13-month period following the revision or update of a Flood Insurance Rate Map.

The policy may be canceled by the insurer only for nonpayment of premium, and even in this case 20 days' written notice of cancellation is required. The policy may be dropped by the insured at any time, but if the insured retains title to the property, the premium for the current term is considered fully earned and there is no premium refund. If the insured disposes of the property, the return premium is calculated on a short-rate basis. Finally, if the community in which the insured property is located ceases participation in the NFIP during the term of the policy, the policy is deemed voided effective at the end of the policy year in which the cessation occurred and will not be renewed.

Condominium Master Policy A condominium association may purchase insurance coverage on a residential building and its contents under an NFIP Condo Master Policy with a *Residential Condominium Building Association Policy* (RCBAP) form. For condominiums that are not eligible for the RCBAP, coverage may be written under a Condominium Association Policy on the General Property Form. Individual unit owners may purchase contents coverage under the Residential Policy.

INLAND MARINE COVERAGE FOR THE INDIVDIUAL

Although the homeowners forms do a reasonably adequate job of insuring the personal property of the average individual, in some cases it may be desirable to specifically insure certain items of personal property under Inland Marine Forms. Obvious examples would include items of property that are specifically excluded under the homeowners insurance, such as automobiles and recreational motor vehicles or items on which the coverage afforded under the homeowners policy is limited. For example, coverage on boats and trailers is limited to $1500, and the theft peril does not apply away from the premises. Theft coverage on jewelry and furs under the homeowners is limited to $1500 per loss. Perhaps not so obvious is the need for broader coverage on certain classes of property than that afforded under the named-peril coverage of the homeowners or for valued coverage in the case of fine

arts or antiques. In this section, we will examine some of the inland marine forms that can be used as supplements to the Homeowners forms in providing coverage on the property of the individual or family. In addition to the various inland marine floater forms, we will also examine insurance for watercraft.

Personal Inland Marine Floaters

The term *floater* originally suggested a coverage that protected property while away from the insured's premises. Prior to the introduction of the homeowners forms, coverage on personal effects was provided under monoline dwelling forms, which offered only limited coverage on property away from the premises. With the introduction of the worldwide coverage of the homeowners forms, the term *floater* has lost some of its original significance, since the coverage on personal property under the homeowners forms also "floats;" that is, it provides coverage not only on the premises, but off premise as well. Nevertheless, the term *floater* retains its original meaning of an inland marine form that provides coverage on property that by its nature is mobile.

In addition to the fact that inland marine policies were originally designed to cover property away from the insured's premises, a second feature of these forms is that they generally (but not always) provide coverage on an open-peril basis. This is obviously an attractive feature, since it permits the insured to obtain broad coverage on items of a valuable nature. Today, floater coverage on personal property is provided under inland marine forms purchased as a separate *Personal Articles Floater* or by endorsement to the homeowners policy. We will not attempt to discuss all the personal floater policies available, but will limit our discussion primarily to those coverages that may be included in the Homeowners Scheduled Personal Property Endorsement.

Scheduled Personal Property Endorsement

The Homeowners *Scheduled Personal Property Endorsement* provides open-peril coverage on nine classes of property under the same terms as if separate contracts were purchased for each type of property.[9] Regardless of whether the coverage is purchased

as a separate floater policy or by endorsement to the Homeowners, it is extremely broad and provides an attractive means of insuring valuable types of personal property. The following discussion is based on the coverage under the Homeowners *Scheduled Personal Property Endorsement*. Coverage under this form is virtually identical with the coverage on the same items under a separate Personal Articles floater.

Valuation Options There are two versions of the Scheduled Personal Property Endorsement, one that provides coverage on a valued basis and one that provides coverage on either an *actual cash value* basis or on a *replacement cost basis*. Prior to the year 2000 revision, there was a single version of the endorsement, titled the Scheduled Personal Property Endorsement (HO 04 61), which covers all property on an *actual cash value* basis, except antiques and fine arts, which are insured on a *valued basis*. When the Homeowners policy to which the endorsement is attached includes replacement cost coverage on personal property, the Personal Property Replacement Cost endorsement stipulates that the replacement cost coverage it provides applies both to the blanket personal property coverage of Coverage C, and to scheduled items under the Scheduled Personal Property Endorsement. The second endorsement, *Scheduled Personal Property Endorsement (With Agreed Value Loss Settlement)* (HO 04 60) was introduced as part of the year 2000 revision, and provides coverage on all scheduled property on a valued basis. Under this arrangement, the amount for which an item is insured is agreed to be the value of the item for loss settlement purposes.

Scope of Coverage All property is covered on an open-peril basis anywhere in the world, with exclusions for different types of property that reflect the nature of the property. Generally, each item insured is scheduled, with an amount of insurance applicable to each. Insurers often require an appraisal of each article before it is insured; however, the sales slip on a recently purchased garment is sufficient to establish a value. The coverage is worldwide.

For some classes of property, additionally acquired property of an insured class is covered automatically, subject to a limitation of 25 percent of the amount of insurance scheduled or $10,000, whichever is less, and with the requirement that the acquisitions be reported within 30 days and an additional premium paid. However, the automatic coverage applies only

[9] Jewelry, furs, cameras, musical instruments, silverware, golfers' equipment, fine arts (including antiques), stamp collections, and coin collections.

to the specific classes of property already insured at the time the property is acquired.

Personal Furs Items eligible for coverage under the insuring agreement for furs include garments made of fur or trimmed with fur. It must be the dressed pelt of an animal and not a manmade fabric. As in the case of other scheduled property, an appraisal or recent sales slip is usually required and each garment is insured for a stated value. Coverage may be written on an actual cash value basis, for replacement cost, or on a valued basis, depending on which of the two Scheduled Personal Property Endorsements is used.

Coverage on personal furs typifies the coverage on property insured under the Scheduled Personal Property endorsement. The breadth of the coverage is indicated by the fact that there are only three exclusions. The first eliminates loss caused by wear and tear, gradual deterioration, insects, vermin, or inherent vice (a quality within a good that causes it to destroy itself); the second excludes loss by nuclear radiation or radioactive contamination; and the last excludes war. Coverage is worldwide.

Additionally acquired property is insured automatically, but subject to a limit of 25 percent of the amount of insurance or $10,000, whichever is less. The acquisitions must be reported within 30 days and an additional premium paid. (When coverage is provided under the Scheduled Personal Property Endorsement, automatic coverage applies only to newly acquired property of a class already insured. The automatic coverage on newly acquired property also applies to jewelry, cameras, and musical instruments under the Scheduled Personal Property Endorsement.)

Personal Jewelry Personal jewelry is covered on essentially the same basis as furs. Each item must be scheduled with an amount of insurance applicable to each and the indemnity may be on actual cash value, replacement cost basis, or on a valued basis. Again, an appraisal is usually mandatory, or at least some verification of the cost price must be established.

In addition to the normal exclusions, this contract has a *pairs and sets* clause that is an important condition. This clause prevents the assured from collecting for a total loss if one item in a pair or set is lost or destroyed. The loss payable then becomes a fair proportion of the total value of the set, giving consideration to the importance of the article or articles. This coverage is also worldwide. As in the case of the coverage on furs, additionally acquired property is cov-

ered up to 25 percent of the amount of insurance or $10,000, whichever is less. The acquisitions must be reported within thirty days and an additional premium paid.

Silverware Another class of property that may be insured under the Homeowners Scheduled Personal Property Endorsement or under a separate Inland Marine Floater is silverware. Coverage is provided on valuable silverware, silver-plated ware, and the like. The coverage is essentially the same as that provided for jewelry as described previously. The major difference is that there is no automatic coverage on additionally acquired items.

Golfer's Equipment Golfer's equipment may also be insured under a separate policy, or it may be covered under the Homeowners Scheduled Personal Property Endorsement. Either form provides coverage for golfing equipment, including clubs, golf clothing (but excluding watches and jewelry), and other clothing that is contained in a locker in a clubhouse or other building used in connection with the game of golf. The description of eligible property is quite broad and could even include a motor-driven golf cart. The coverage is on an open-peril basis for most items of property and most generally is written on a blanket basis. However, the coverage for golf balls is not open-peril, but is limited to the perils of fire and burglary.

Cameras Eligible equipment under the cameras insuring agreement includes not only cameras, projection machines, moveable sound equipment, and films, but binoculars and telescopes as well. As usual, the various items are scheduled and a blanket item may be included to provide coverage for miscellaneous articles such as sunshades, filters, and so on. Additionally acquired property is insured automatically, but subject to a limit of 25 percent of the amount of insurance or $10,000, whichever is less. The acquisitions must be reported within 30 days and an additional premium paid. The only exclusions are those of the wear and tear variety, war, and radioactive contamination.

Fine Arts and Antiques Coverage under the *Fine Arts and Antiques* insuring agreement is written to protect objects of art such as paintings, statuary, rare manuscripts, and antiques. The coverage is open peril with the usual exceptions. In addition to the standard open-peril exclusions of wear and tear, gradual deterioration or inherent vice, and insects or vermin, coverage on fine arts and antiques is subject to three

additional exclusions: the first excludes damage caused by repairing, restoration, or retouching process; the second excludes breakage of certain fragile articles, unless the breakage is caused by specifically named perils. Fragile articles specifically listed in the contract to which the breakage exclusion applies include art glass windows, glassware, statuary, marble, bric-a-brac, and porcelains. The exclusion is not limited to these; however, it also applies to other *similar fragile articles*. The specifically named perils for which coverage by breakage is provided are fire and lightning, explosion, aircraft, collision, windstorm, earthquake, flood, malicious damage or theft, and derailment of a conveyance. Coverage for breakage from causes other than these named perils is available for an additional premium. When the insured wishes to eliminate the exclusion of breakage, an entry is made in the declarations section of the endorsement.

The final exclusion applicable to antiques and fine arts eliminates coverage for loss by any cause to property on exhibition at fair grounds or premises of national or international expositions unless the premises are covered by the policy. The purpose of this exclusion is to alert the insurer to situations in which an unexpected concentration of insured values might occur. The exclusion requires the insured to notify the insurer when property will be exposed to loss at such locations.

It is customary to insure antiques and fine arts on a valued rather than an actual cash value basis. Since this means that the insurance company agrees to the value of each item insured and that this is the value paid in the event of a loss, appraisals are usually mandatory. Some insurance companies retain art appraisers to advise them on values. Each insured item is scheduled with an amount of insurance applicable. Newly acquired property is covered automatically, but subject to a percentage limitation relative to the aggregate amount of the schedule. However, reports of additional items must be made within 90 days and the proper pro rata additional premium paid.

Postage Stamps and Rare and Current Coins

The property eligible for coverage under the stamp and coin insuring agreement consists of postage stamps including due, envelope, official, revenue, match and medicine, covers, locals, reprints, essays, proofs, and other philatelic property owned by or in the custody or control of the insured, including the books, pages, or mountings. The eligible coins include rare and current coins, medals, paper money, bank notes, tokens of money, and other numismatic property owned by or in the custody or control of the insured, including coin albums, containers, frames, cards, and display cabinets in use with such collection. The property in both cases may be insured on a schedule or on a blanket basis. There are no automatic coverages of newly acquired property.

In addition to the customary exclusions, several are unique to this contract. For example, damage resulting from fading, creasing, denting, scratching, tearing, thinning, transfer of colors, or damage arising while the property is being worked on is excluded. The policy also excludes mysterious disappearance of individual stamps unless the item has been specifically scheduled or unless mounted in a volume and the page to which the stamp is attached is also lost. Loss by theft from an unattended automobile is also excluded except while being shipped by registered mail. The policy also contains a limit of no more than $250 on any unscheduled stamp, pair, block, or series, and $1000 on unscheduled numismatic property. Failure on the part of the insured to schedule high-valued items can result in a significant gap in coverage.

Musical Instruments Musical instruments may be scheduled under the Homeowners Scheduled Personal Property Endorsement or insured under a separate contract, with either approach providing open-peril coverage. The only unusual condition in this coverage involves an agreement on the part of the insured that none of the instruments insured will be played for remuneration during the term of the policy unless permitted by endorsement and the payment of an additional premium. The purpose of this condition is to separate amateur and professional musicians for rating purposes. Experience indicates that the loss experience of professional musicians is worse than that of individuals who are not engaged in performing for hire.

As in the case of the fur floater, jewelry floater, and camera floater, additionally acquired property is automatically covered up to 25 percent of the amount of insurance or $10,000, whichever is less. The acquisitions must be reported within 30 days and an additional premium paid.

The Personal Property Floater

The Personal Property Floater (PPF) predates the Homeowners program by several decades. It was

developed to provide open-peril coverage on personal property owned or used by an insured, on a worldwide basis. With the introduction of Homeowners endorsement HO 0424, which converts the named peril coverage of the Homeowners Tenant Form HO-4 to an open-peril basis, it is likely that the PPF will become a historical footnote.[10]

Wedding Present Floater

Wedding presents can add up to a considerable value, and the *Wedding Present Floater* is designed to provide coverage for the gifts during the temporary period in which they are accumulated before the bride and her new husband are settled in their home. The presents are considered the property of the bride, and she purchases the contract. Coverage commences at the time the presents begin to accumulate and continues up to a maximum of 90 days after the wedding. It is the usual open-peril coverage; in addition to the customary exclusions, certain types of property are denied coverage. The classes of property excluded consist of realty, animals, automobiles, motorcycles, aircraft, bicycles, boats, money, notes, securities, and stamps. Unlike the other floater classes that have been discussed, there is no provision for insuring this class of property in the Homeowners Scheduled Personal Property Endorsement.

Insurance on Watercraft

Although homeowners policies provide some coverage on watercraft and their equipment, this coverage is limited to $1000 and excludes coverage for loss by theft away from the premises. Because of this $1000 limit, and to lesser degree because of the theft exclusion, many boat owners will need specific coverage on their boats. In addition, boat owners need coverage for liability arising out of the operation of watercraft. Although Section II of the homeowners forms provides coverage for some liability arising out of use of watercraft, the coverage is limited and applies only to smaller watercraft. Liability coverage for other watercraft must be extended by endorsement

on the homeowners policy or be specifically insured under a separate contract.

Policies used to insure boats are not standardized, but they fall into two general classes: yacht policies, which are used to insure larger vessels, and boatowners policies. The distinction between the two has become somewhat blurred, but yacht policies are considered to be ocean marine coverages, while the Boatowners Policy was developed by combining liability coverage with an inland marine form, Outboard Motor and Boat Policy.[11] The complex nature of ocean marine policies in general is beyond the scope of this course, so we will focus primarily on the Boatowners Policy.

The Boatowners Policy The *Boatowners Policy* is a package contract that, similar to an auto policy, provides coverage for liability, physical damage, medical payments, and uninsured watercraft. The Boatowners Policy sold by most companies includes two sections:

| Section I | Physical Damage Coverages |
| Section II | Liability Coverages |

The Section I coverage includes a *Perils Insured* section, exclusions, and conditions applicable to Section I only. Section II includes separate insuring agreements for watercraft liability, medical expenses, and uninsured boaters.

Section I: Physical Damage Coverages Physical damage coverage on the boat is designated Coverage A in the Boatowners Policy. It includes coverage for the actual cash value of the described boat and motors, equipment and accessories manufactured for marine use, and any trailer described in the declarations. Coverage is on an open-perils basis, subject to the usual exclusions of wear and tear, gradual deterioration, inherent vice, and mechanical breakdown. Some policies also exclude loss when the boat is used to carry persons or property for a fee, while the boat is rented to others, or while a boat (other than a sailboat) is being operated in an official race or speed contest.

Some companies include special valuation provisions. The coverage may be written on an *agreed-*

[10] The *Personal Effects Floater* is another contract that is sometimes confused with the Personal Property Floater because of the similarity in their titles. The Personal Effects Floater is a specialized contract that provides open-perils coverage on a traveler's baggage on a worldwide basis. When written for a person who has a Homeowners policy, the Personal Effects Floater provides excess coverage.

[11] When watercraft liability is insured under the homeowners policy, the boat owner may obtain broader physical damage coverage on boats under an inland marine Outboard Motor and Boat Policy, which provides open-perils coverage on boats and their trailers.

value basis, under which the face amount of insurance is payable in the event of a total loss. Other insurers offer replacement cost coverage, similar to the replacement cost option on contents under the homeowners forms.

Section II: Liability Coverages The Section II coverages of the Boatowners Policy parallel the coverages of the Personal Auto Policy. They include

A. Watercraft liability
B. Medical payments
C. Uninsured boaters

Watercraft Liability Watercraft liability coverage provides protection up to a specified limit, for claims or suits against an insured for damages because of bodily injury or property damage caused by a watercraft occurrence. The term *insured* under liability coverage is broadly defined, and usually includes not only family members, but other persons while operating the insured watercraft with permission of the insured.

The liability coverage excludes (1) bodily injury or property damage which is expected or intended by the insured, (2) liability of any person using a watercraft without permission, (3) damage to property owned by or in the care, custody, and control of the insured, (4) injury to persons eligible for workers compensation benefits, and (5) liability of a person engaged in the business of selling, repairing, storing, or moving watercraft. Some policies also exclude liability arising out of any watercraft, other than a sailboat, while being used in any official race or speed test. Finally, the policy also includes the standard war and nuclear exclusions.

Medical Payments Coverage Most boat policies include medical payments. This coverage pays for medical expenses resulting from boating accidents when a person (including the named insured and family members) is injured "in, upon, getting into or out of the insured watercraft." The broadest policies include medical payments coverage for persons who are water-skiing.

Uninsured Boaters Coverage Uninsured watercraft coverage is a special form of accident insurance, which is available under the Boatowners Policy as an option. It provides payment up to a specified limit—usually $10,000—when the insured or a family member suffers bodily injury that is caused by an uninsured boater.[12]

Navigation and Territorial Definitions Most policies limit usage of the insured watercraft to a specified territory. The broadest policies cover the watercraft while being operated on any inland body of water within the continental United States, Canada, and coastal waters of the same areas, up to a limit of from 10 to 25 miles. The most restrictive policies provide coverage only on a specified body of water and within a narrow parameter around that particular area. Between these extremes, some policies only provide coverage in inland lakes, or only in certain states, and some provide coverage options to extend coverage to areas such as the Bahamas. Many policies provide no coverage for offshore waters, such as the Gulf of Mexico.

BUYING PROPERTY INSURANCE FOR THE INDIVIDUAL

Pricing and Cost Considerations

Before discussing the purchase of property insurance for the individual or family, a brief review of the factors that affect the cost of such insurance seems in order. Aside from the differences in prices among companies, there are differences in cost based on the characteristics of the individual exposure.

As the reader will recall, the *rate* is the cost per unit of insurance. In the property field, rates are generally stated as the cost per $100 or $1000 of coverage. The premium is determined by multiplying the amount of insurance purchased by the rate. The rate varies with the scope of the perils insured against and the loss potential carried by those perils. The loss potential (i.e., the likelihood that a loss will occur and the extent of damage if one does) is a function of the property itself and is measured in part by the characteristics of the item. For example, the type of construction is an important consideration in some perils: The rate for fire insurance is lower on a brick or masonry building than on a wood building. Rates also vary with the loss experience of each locality. Again, in the case of fire insurance, rates vary with

[12] Uninsured Boaters coverage is patterned after the automobile insurance coverage, *uninsured motorists coverage,* which is discussed in Chapter 29.

the fire protection provided by the city. Cities and towns are evaluated on certain critical factors such as the fire department and water supply and are placed in 1 of 10 classifications, numbered 1 through 10, with class-1 towns being the lowest rated and class-10 towns the highest.[13] The rates for other coverages also vary by locality: Extended coverage rates are higher in those areas subject to severe loss experience (e.g., from windstorms) just as crime rates are usually higher in large cities, reflecting the greater incidence of crime.

For dwelling property, rates are based on three major factors: the type of construction, the number of families, and the fire protection of the city.[14] Under the homeowners program, the same three considerations are involved, but package policies use an *indivisible premium* concept, in which the premium is the cost of the entire package, without allocation of parts of the premium to the different sections of coverage.

Choosing the Form

If the residence is eligible, the building and personal property should be purchased under a homeowners policy. The choice of a particular form to be purchased is somewhat more complicated and could be subject to debate. The difference in cost between Form 2 and Form 3 is so small that the choice of a Form 2 seems like false economy. Form 3 is only slightly more costly than Form 2, but it provides open-perils coverage on the dwelling. If the higher cost of Form 3 is a problem, the insured might consider a higher deductible. Table 26.2 indicates the premium credits available for increased deductibles under the homeowners policies. The choice of a Form 3 with a $500 deductible in preference to a Form 2 with a $250 deductible follows the principles of risk management. Since each additional peril insured against reduces the possibility of an uninsured catastrophe, the insured should prefer broader coverage with a high deductible to narrower coverage with a low deductible. By sacrificing coverage on the potential $250 difference in deductibles, the purchaser

[13] These classifications are assigned by the Insurance Services Office.

[14] There are four factors used in the determination of fire rates: construction, occupancy, protection, and exposure. The fourth, *exposure,* which reflects the hazard created by neighboring property, is used in the rate structure for nonresidential property.

TABLE 26.2 **Homeowners Deductible Premium Credits**

Insurance on Dwelling	$500 Deductible	$1000 Deductible	$2500 Deductible
$10,000–59,999	9%	17%	25%
60,000–99,999	7%	15%	25%
100,000–250,000	5%	12%	25%

Source: Insurance Services Office, Inc.

secures coverage against disastrous losses caused by perils not listed in Form 2 but covered under Form 3.

Tailoring the Coverage under the Homeowners Policy

The greatest errors in purchasing insurance on the dwelling and its contents are usually in the amount of insurance. As we have noted previously, the dwelling should be valued on its replacement cost. If it is relatively new, determining the replacement cost should not pose a great problem. Original cost may be inflated to current replacement cost using a construction price index. In the case of older dwelling property, replacement cost may be calculated with the aid of a replacement cost estimator, available from many insurance agents and companies. These replacement cost estimators are simple to use and permit a reasonable approximation of the value of a person's dwelling by the application of stated cost factors to the various items of construction. In most cases, the cost estimators make provision for differing types of construction and regional differences in cost, resulting in a fairly accurate estimate.

Even though the replacement cost condition requires that the amount of insurance on the dwelling be 80 percent of the full replacement cost value, it is good practice to insure for 100 percent of the replacement cost value. This cushion, plus the Inflation Guard Endorsement, should prevent possible underinsurance from inflation and increases in the cost of construction. An even more attractive option is the guaranteed replacement cost coverage.

The homeowners forms provide coverage on the contents equal to 50 percent of the value of the dwelling. Yet there is no reason to think that the actual value of contents will be this amount, and the insurance buyer should estimate the value of his or her personal property to avoid underinsurance. The problem of estimating insurable value of contents is even more difficult than estimating building replacement

cost. It requires an inventory of personal property, with the replacement cost value of each item. Although personal property is insured on an actual cash value basis under the homeowners forms, replacement cost coverage is a highly desirable option and the policy should be endorsed to provide this coverage. Although replacement cost coverage on contents is not an *essential* coverage, it certainly ranks as *important.*

The inventory of personal property compiled in estimating the value of contents should also note any valuable jewelry and furs or other items on which open-perils scheduled coverage is needed. Specific insurance should be purchased on those items of personal property not covered under the homeowners policy (such as snowmobiles and golf carts) or on property with a higher value than the limits under the homeowners policy (e.g., boats or trailers valued at more than $1500).

Finally, the insured should consider adding other perils or broadening those that are included under the form selected. For example, the earthquake peril should be added to the homeowners form through the use of the Earthquake Damage Assumption endorsement. It protects against a potentially catastrophic loss at an extremely reasonable (in most areas) premium.

Flood Insurance

Property owners in special flood hazard areas may have no choice in the purchase of federal flood insurance. If the real estate is financed through one of the specified types of lending institutions, flood insurance will be required as a condition of the loan. When the property is not in a flood hazard area, the purchase of the coverage is optional with the property owner. However, flood insurance, even in the minimal amount provided for the minimum $75 policy premium, seems like a sound way of protecting a substantial investment.

TITLE INSURANCE

Before leaving the subject of insurance for the home, we should briefly mention title insurance, which is a form of property insurance designed to protect against losses resulting from a defective title to land and improvements. The legal principles in the transfer of title to real estate are complicated, and because of the technicalities, it is possible for a defective title to be transferred in a real estate transaction. A person may purchase a home and after many years find that the one who conveyed the title to him or her was not the rightful owner, and did not in fact have the right to transfer the title. If a person with a superior claim to the land comes forward to exert this right, the purchaser who received the defective title may suffer.

Defects in a title may result from a number of causes, including forgery of titles, forgery of public records, invalid or undiscovered wills, or liens and encumbrances. All rights in real property, such as encumbrances, liens, and easements, are generally recorded in the public records of the jurisdiction in which the real estate is located. One approach to dealing with the risk of defective titles is therefore the examination of these public records. When buying real estate one may protect oneself by procuring an abstract of title, which is a summarized report of the history of the title as shown by the records, together with a report of judgments, mortgages, and similar recorded claims against the property. An attorney is generally retained to render an opinion on the accuracy and validity of the abstract. The major shortcoming of this procedure is that it only partially reduces the possibility of loss. Even if the abstractor or attorney is careful in the examination, there may be defects that are not discovered, such as a right to the property granted in a lost will or a forged transfer document that appears genuine. If the abstractor or lawyer is free from negligence, he cannot be held liable even if it is later determined that the title was defective.[15]

If no other alternative is available, an examination of the abstract and a title search serve as a means of loss prevention. However, in some areas, title insurance may be available as a more attractive alternative. Title insurance companies generally insure titles only within a limited territory, a natural result of the nature of title insurance. The basic asset of the title insurance company is the *abstract plant,* which consists of an index of the various plots of land in the area and the history of each. All transactions and transfers that affect the title to the property are noted in the records of the company on a day-to-day

[15] If the abstractor or attorney was negligent, the property "owner" who suffered the loss would have a right of action and could sue for damages.

basis, so that when an application for insurance is received, most of the information regarding the title to the property is already on hand. When an application is received, the title insurance company engages in a title search, attempting to determine if the title is valid. Any defects in the title that are discovered by the title insurance company in its research are listed in a schedule included in the policy. A contract is then issued under which the title insurance company agrees to indemnify the insured for any loss arising out of undiscovered defects in the title. Those defects scheduled in the policy are excluded from coverage.

This guarantee by the insurer differs from most other lines of insurance in that it relates to occurrences in the past rather than in the future. If an undiscovered defect later causes financial loss to the insured, the insurer will pay an indemnity. The remedy to the insured in the event of a defective title is a dollar indemnification and not possession of the property. In addition, the insurer agrees to defend the buyer in the event of legal action against him or her in connection with losses that are not excluded under the policy.

A single premium is payable for the title insurance policy, and it is fully earned once it is paid. The policy term is indefinite, terminating only when the property is again sold. For obvious reasons, title insurance may not be transferred to a new purchaser, but the latter may obtain a policy at a reduced reissue rate if purchase is within a short period after the previous policy was issued.

Torrens System

We should perhaps mention briefly an alternative to the system of title insurance just described, the *Torrens system,* originally developed in Australia by Robert Torrens. It provides that title to the property is vested in the purchaser. Fees are collected at the time that the title is registered and are deposited in an insurance fund. If someone can later show a claim to the property, the claimant is reimbursed for his or her loss out of the fund, and the title remains with the person who has registered. Many persons feel that this system is superior to the alternatives discussed earlier, because the purchaser of the property is granted a clear title. Torrens laws, which provide for the operation of the funds and establish the statutory basis on which they can operate, exist in 15 states. Despite the number of states that have authorized the system, Torrens funds operate only in Hawaii, Illinois, Massachusetts, and Minnesota.[16]

[16] California, Colorado, Georgia, Illinois, Massachusetts, Minnesota, New York, North Carolina, Ohio, Oregon, South Dakota, Utah, Virginia, and Washington. See Alfred A. Ring and Jerome Dasso, *Real Estate Principles and Practices* (Englewood Cliffs, N.J.: Prentice-Hall, 1977), p. 173.

IMPORTANT CONCEPTS TO REMEMBER

monoline fire forms	golfer's floater	stamp and coin collection floater
Dwelling Property Basic Form	Scheduled Personal Property	musical instrument floater
Dwelling Property Broad Form	endorsement	wedding present floater
Dwelling Property Special Form	personal furs floater	personal property floater
Mobilehome endorsement	personal jewelry floater	title insurance
Collision endorsement	silverware floater	abstract of title
Lienholder's Single Interest	camera floater	reissue rate
endorsement	fine arts and antique floater	Torrens system

QUESTIONS FOR REVIEW

1. Briefly describe the difference in coverage on the insured's own property under Section I of the homeowners forms and the coverage on that property under the equivalent monoline dwelling forms.

2. Under what circumstances might dwelling property be insured under one of the monoline dwelling forms rather than under one of the homeowners forms?

3. Briefly describe the provisions of the flood insurance policy relating to inception of coverage and cancellation.

4. What limits of coverage are currently available to residential applicants under the Federal Flood Insurance Program?

5. In what fundamental respect is the coverage on personal property owned by the insured under the mobile-home policy different from the coverage under the homeowners policies?

6. Describe the general nature of the Lienholder's Single Interest Conversion endorsement. Why would a mobile-home owner elect this coverage?

7. What factors, other than the value of the property insured, determine the cost of coverage under the monoline dwelling policies and the homeowners forms?

8. Is an examination of the abstract of title an adequate substitute for title insurance? Why or why not?

9. List and briefly describe the coverages that may be included in the boatowners policy.

10. For what reasons might an individual decide to insure property under the homeowners Scheduled Personal Property Endorsement?

QUESTIONS FOR DISCUSSION

1. Most people elect the standard percentage of coverage on contents when purchasing a homeowners policy, yet there is no reason to suppose that the value of contents for a given family will be equal to 50 percent of that of the dwelling. Unfortunately, few people have any idea what the true value of their contents is. How do you believe one should go about determining the amount of contents coverage to be purchased? What additional benefits might be derived from the technique you recommend?

2. The cancellation provisions of the Federal Flood Insurance Policy are different from those of any contracts previously encountered in the text. In what ways do these provisions seem necessary for the protection of (1) the insured, and (2) the insurer?

3. Do you believe that persons owning property in the city in which you live should purchase the Earthquake Assumption endorsement to their homeowners policies? Why or why not?

4. If you lived in an area where both title insurance and a Torrens system were available, which would you elect? Why?

5. The *open-perils* coverage of inland marine policies is generally subject to exclusions of damage caused by wear and tear, gradual deterioration, insects, vermin, and inherent vice. For what reason are these causes of loss excluded? Are these causes of loss uninsurable or, in your opinion, are they excluded for some other reason?

SUGGESTIONS FOR ADDITIONAL READING

Fire, Casualty and Surety Bulletins. Personal Lines Volume. Cincinnati, Ohio.: National Underwriter Company. (Loose-leaf manual service with monthly supplements.) See "Dwellings" section.

Hamilton, Karen L., and Donald S. Malecki. *Personal Insurance: Property and Liability.* Malvern, Pa.: American Institute for CPCU, 1994. Chapter 6.

Huebner, S.S., Kenneth Black, Jr., and Robert S. Cline. *Property and Liability Insurance,* 3rd ed. Englewood Cliffs, N.J.: Prentice-Hall, 1982. Chapter 27.

Johnson, Harry Mack. "The Nature of Title Insurance." *Journal of Risk and Insurance,* vol. 33, no. 3 (September 1966).

Johnstone, Q. "Title Insurance." *Insurance Counsel Journal* (July 1959).

Launie, J. J., George E. Rejda, and Donald R. Oakes with Anita W. Johnson. *Personal Insurance.* Bryn Mawr, Pa.: Insurance Institute of America, 1991. Chapter 5.

Policy, Form and Manual Analysis Service. Property Coverages Volume. Indianapolis, Ind.: Rough Notes Company. (Loose-leaf manual service with monthly supplements.) See "Homeowners Policy Program" section.

Shick, Blair, and Irving H. Plotkin. *Torrens in the United States.* Lexington, Mass.: D. C. Heath and Co., 1978.

Taylor, Barbara J. *How to Get Your Money's Worth in Home and Auto Insurance.* New York: McGraw-Hill, 1990.

WEB SITES TO EXPLORE

Best's Review – Property/Casualty Edition	http://www.ambest.com/review/lh/index.html
FEMA National Flood Insurance Program	http://www.fema.gov/nfip/
Independent Insurance Agents of America, Inc.	http://www.iiaa.org
Insurance News Network	http://www.insure.com/
National Association of Professional Insurance Agents	http://www.pianet.com/
Rough Notes Company	http://www.roughnotes.com/

NEGLIGENCE AND LEGAL LIABILITY

That man may err was never yet denied.

— JOHN DRYDEN
The Hind and the Panther

CHAPTER OBJECTIVES

When you have finished this chapter, you should be able to

- Distinguish between criminal acts and torts and define negligence, giving the requirements to support a claim of negligence
- Explain what is meant by vicarious liability
- Explain the obligations of property owners to those on their property
- Identify and describe the types of damages that may be awarded to an injured party and explain how each is determined
- Explain the defenses to negligence
- Apply the law of negligence to specific fact situations
- Explain the problems in the tort system and identify the proposals for change

A risk confronting almost every person or business is that of behavior that could result in an injury to another person or damage to property of others. The basis of the risk is the liability imposed by law on one responsible for injury or damage to other people or their property. It is a risk that can, and in many instances has, attained catastrophic proportions, and one that can materialize at any time. There is no way of estimating the amount of legal liability in advance.

It may be a mere thousand dollars, or a half-million. It is a risk that has no maximum predictable limit.[1]

[1] For many risks, the maximum predictable loss can be calculated precisely. For example, owning a car entails the possibility of the loss of the value of the auto itself, a loss with a maximum limit equal to the value of the car. But with respect to the legal liability arising from driving it, the loss will depend on the severity of the accident and the amount the jury is willing to award the injured parties.

Before we study the role of insurance in protecting the individual from the legal liability hazard, we will examine the hazard itself, with emphasis on the doctrines of negligence that give rise to the liability exposure.

CRIMINAL AND TORTIOUS BEHAVIOR

Basically, a person can commit two classes of wrongs: public and private. A public wrong is a violation of one of the laws that govern the relationships of the individual with the rest of society; it is called a crime and is the subject of criminal law. Crimes include a wide range of acts: treason, murder, rape, arson, larceny, trespass, disorderly conduct, assault, vagrancy, and so on. Criminal acts are prosecuted by the state as the moving party (plaintiff) against any citizen for violation of a duty prescribed by statute or common law. They are punishable by fine, imprisonment, or death.

A private wrong, on the other hand, is an infringement of the rights of another individual. A private wrong is called a tort, and the person who commits such a wrong is called a *tort feasor*. Commission of a tort may give the person whose rights were violated a right of action for damages against the tort feasor. Such an action is called a *civil action*. Torts may be subdivided into intentional and unintentional. *Intentional torts* include such infringements on the rights of others as assault and battery, libel, slander, false arrest or imprisonment, trespass, or invasion of privacy. Persons who suffer injury as a result of these intentional torts have the right to sue for damages.[2] *Unintentional torts* are those that result from negligence or carelessness. In these cases the injured party may also be entitled to damages in a civil action even though the tort feasor had no malicious intent, as in an intentional tort.

Liability insurance is rarely concerned with the legal penalties resulting from criminal behavior or intentional torts. It is considered against public policy to protect an individual from the consequences of an intentional injury he or she inflicts. Although insurance is available to protect against loss resulting from some intentional torts, most liability policies exclude injury or damage caused deliberately or at the direction of the insured. In liability insurance, we are concerned primarily with unintentional torts or losses arising from negligence.

Negligence and Legal Liability

We have already determined that there are many causes of legal liability.[3] The most important, and the most significant for insurance, is that of *negligence*. While many of the doctrines relating to the law of negligence are found in statutes, its primary development has been through common law. The basic principle of common law is that most people have an obligation to behave as a reasonable and prudent individual would. Failure to behave in this manner constitutes negligence, and if this negligence leads to an injury of another, or to damage of another's property, the negligent party may be held liable for the damage. Legal liability is imposed by the courts when it has been established that all the following occurred:

- There was negligence.
- There was actual damage or loss.
- The negligence was the proximate cause of the damage.

There Must Be Negligence

The basic concept of our law holds that unless a party is at fault—unless he or she has unreasonably and unlawfully invaded the rights of another—he or she is not liable.[4] The basic question in all cases concerning legal liability must be, "Has there been negligence?" Negligence is defined as the failure of a person to exercise the proper degree of care required by the circumstances.

Who May Be Held Liable? To be held legally negligent, it must be established that the individual

[2] It is possible for an act to be both a crime and a tort. If Smith assaults Jones, he commits a crime and he may go to jail, but in addition he has committed a tort and he may be liable for civil damages if Jones decides to sue.

[3] Liability may also arise from contracts. Civil law is composed of two branches: the law of contracts and the law of torts. Here we are concerned primarily with the area of torts.

[4] The concept of tort liability grew out of the ancient and deep-rooted *lex talionis*—the law of retaliation. Originally, absolute liability was the rule, and it was harshly applied. If a stone fell from a building and killed an occupant, the builder was put to death. Later, it seemed to make more sense to make the builder support the dead man's widow instead of killing him, and the idea of compensation developed. Gradually, the courts shifted away from the concept of absolute liability, under which liability was imposed regardless of fault, to the doctrine of negligence, under which a person cannot be held responsible unless proven negligent or at fault.

had a duty to act and that he or she failed to act or acted incorrectly. The duty to act is the first of the prerequisites.

At the beginning of this discussion, we stated that "most people have an obligation to behave as a reasonable and prudent individual would." The question arises, "What persons do not have this obligation?" There are certain classes of individuals and certain institutions who are excepted from the obligation.

Infants To be duty-bound to behave in a reasonable and prudent manner, the individual must be capable of determining what is reasonable. The person must have, in the terms of the law, reached the *age of reason.* In some states this has been set by law at seven years of age; in other jurisdictions the court determines the age at which the individual can distinguish between right and wrong. While children below this age are immune from legal liability, a minor who has attained the age of reason may be held legally liable for his or her own negligent acts.[5] Although minors can be held legally liable, the degree of care demanded of a child is often different from that required of an adult.

Mentally Incompetent For obvious reasons, certain mentally incompetent persons are not expected to exercise the care required of the sane. In the eyes of the law, a mentally incompetent person is approximately the same as an "infant." However, if it can be shown that the deficient person could have been expected to exercise some degree of care, the courts will hold the individual to that degree of caution.

Government Bodies At common law, sovereign powers can be sued only with their permission. Any government unit that shares in the sovereignty is immune from liability unless it is engaging in proprietary functions. When performing strictly government functions, it is normally immune from liability. This government immunity is based on the old common law maxim that "the king can do no wrong." The doctrine has been modified significantly—both by statute and by court decision. One of the most important qualifications is the Federal Tort Claims Act,[6] which provides that the United States shall be liable

for money damages to the same extent as a private individual. Government immunity also has been modified at the state level in many jurisdictions by similar statutes. Finally, in a growing number of instances, the courts have attempted to find exceptions to the doctrine of government immunity, and some have rejected it entirely.[7]

It should be noted that even in those areas where the doctrine has not been abrogated, the immunity does not extend to the employees of the government unit who are acting in their capacity as employees. If Mr. Smith is struck by a city vehicle and the damage is the result of the negligence of the vehicle's driver, the city itself may not be held liable, but the driver does not enjoy the same immunity.

Charitable Institutions Formerly there was a distinct difference between the liability exposure of a charitable institution and that of a profit-making one, but this distinction has gradually disappeared. At one time, the courts were reluctant (and some still are) to hold charitable institutions liable, but the recent trend has been to treat them in the same manner as profit-making institutions.

What Constitutes Negligence? As we noted previously, negligence is defined as the failure of a person to exercise the proper degree of care required by the circumstances. As a rule, the duty to exercise care is owed to anyone who might suffer injuries as a result of a person's breach of duty, even if the negligent party could not have foreseen a risk of harm to someone because of the behavior.

One of the major problems is to determine what constitutes correct action in any given situation. To make this determination, the courts apply what is known as the *prudent man rule,* which seeks to ascertain what would have been a reasonable course of action under the circumstances. The mere fact that some other course of action might have avoided the accident does not make the individual liable. The negligent person is entitled to have his or her actions judged by this "prudent man standard" rather than

[5] In addition to confusion over the liability of children themselves, the liability of parents for the acts of their children is often misunderstood. Fundamentally, parents are not liable for their children's acts. This point will be discussed in greater detail later in the chapter.

[6] Title 28, *United States Code,* Sections 1346(b), 2401, and 2671–2680.

[7] States in which government immunity has been substantially affected by statute include Alaska, Hawaii, Illinois, Iowa, Kansas, New York, Oregon, Rhode Island, Utah, Vermont, and Washington. The doctrine has been judicially invalidated in the states of Arizona, California, Colorado, Idaho, Indiana, New Jersey, New Mexico, Pennsylvania, and Wisconsin. In some states, the immunity is waived if insurance is in effect; these include Georgia, Maine, Mississippi, Missouri, Montana, North Carolina, North Dakota, Ohio, and Tennessee.

hindsight. The judge and jury are not permitted to look back at the situation in light of what happened and judge liability on whether some other course of action would have prevented the accident. The action must be judged by what a reasonable and prudent person, confronted with the same situation, might normally and properly have done.

Since the standard is rather vague and the variety of circumstances and conditions precludes hard-and-fast rules, in the final analysis whether the duty has been breached will be for a court of law to decide.[8] Normally, the burden of proof of negligence is on the injured party. However, there are certain doctrines that impose liability by statute or shift the burden of proof from the injured party to the defendant.

Negligence Per Se In many circumstances, what constitutes the standard of care to be met by an individual is set arbitrarily by statute. For example, speed limits in most states set the rate of speed for driving an automobile. These speed limits amount to the establishment of a rule that no reasonable person should violate. If the law is violated, it is referred to as *negligence per se* (negligence in itself), and the injured party is relieved of the obligation to prove that the speed was unreasonable.

Absolute Liability Under certain circumstances, liability may be imposed simply because "accidents happen," and it is imposed regardless of whether anyone was at fault. In such cases we have the application of the rule of strict or *absolute liability*. The injured party will be awarded damages even though there was nothing legally wrong in what the other person was doing or the manner in which it was done.

One of the most important examples of absolute liability is employment-connected injuries. All the states have enacted workers compensation laws that impose absolute liability on employers for injuries to employees who are covered under the laws. In this sense, there is a departure from the basic laws of negligence in the case of an injured worker, because there is no need for the worker to prove negligence on the part of the employer. Workers compensation laws, then, represent an exception to the rule that there can be no liability without fault, and the injured worker is entitled to indemnity regardless of the negligence or lack of it on the part of the employer.

The second application of the rule of strict liability is with respect to extra hazardous activities. The principle is that one who maintains a dangerous condition on his or her premises, or who engages in an activity that involves a high risk to the person or property of others in spite of all reasonable care, will be strictly liable for the harm it causes. Customary examples are keeping wild animals,[9] blasting, explosives manufacture, oil-well drilling, crop spraying by airplane, and containment of water.

Res Ipsa Loquitur A significant doctrine in the operation of the law of negligence is that of *res ipsa loquitur.* This means that "the thing speaks for itself" and is concerned with circumstances and types of accidents that afford reasonable evidence, in the absence of some specific explanation, that negligence existed. The accident is of a type that normally does not occur without someone's negligence and the doctrine recognizes the persuasive force of a particular kind of circumstantial evidence. The characteristics of the event constitute an inference or *prima facie* evidence of negligence. In the operation of the doctrine, the law reverses the burden of proof. When the instrumentality causing the damage was under the exclusive control of the defendant, and the accident is the type that would not usually happen in the absence of negligence, the law holds that the very fact the accident happened is proof that the defendant was negligent. For example, if Mr. Smith walks down the sidewalk and a 2000-pound safe being lowered by a rope falls on him, he is not required to prove that the person or persons lowering the safe failed to exercise due care. The fact that the safe fell on him (or that he is 18 inches shorter) is evidence of this. The burden of proof is shifted, and the defendants must prove that care *was* exercised.

For the doctrine to be applicable, certain conditions are generally required. First, the event must be

[8] Not all situations arising from negligence, particularly those in which insurance is involved, become subjects of court litigation. Adjusters can determine the existence or nonexistence of legal liability in the vast majority of cases without court action. Only those in which the facts or issues are debatable reach court, and these constitute a relatively small percentage of the total.

[9] Pets represent a separate case. Up until a few years ago, most states still operated under the English common law doctrine that permitted a dog "one free bite." According to the doctrine of *scienter* (knowledge), the owner of the animal is liable for the injuries caused by the animal only if the animal is known to be vicious. Hence the one "free bite." How could the owner know that the dog bites people until it has bitten one? Recently, however, this doctrine has been changed in most jurisdictions. The prevailing current rule holds that anyone who keeps a pet that he or she knows or should know to be dangerous can be held strictly liable for any injuries caused by the animal. This doctrine of the owner's liability is known as the doctrine of *vicious propensity.*

of a type that normally does not occur in the absence of negligence. Second, the instrumentality causing the injuries must be shown to have been under the defendant's exclusive control. Finally, the injured party must in no manner have contributed to his or her own injuries. The injured party must be completely free from fault.

There Must Be Actual Damage or Loss

The mere fact that carelessness existed is not sufficient cause for legal liability. Actual injury or damage must have been suffered by the party seeking recovery. In most cases it is not difficult to prove that injury or damage has occurred, but establishing the amount of damages is often extremely difficult.

The tort may result in two forms of injury to another: bodily injury and property damage. In the case of property damage, the extent of the loss is relatively simple to determine. Generally, it is measured by the actual monetary loss to the injured party. If, for example, another driver negligently collides with your auto and "totals" it, it is relatively simple to place a value on the car. Market or depreciated value is the normal measure. An additional loss could involve the loss of use of your car. If you needed an auto in your business and had to rent one, the rental expenses would be included in the damages. The loss of use of property could amount to a large sum if, for example, a large building were destroyed. In some cases, punitive damages (discussed shortly) may also be awarded for property damage.

In the case of bodily injury, fixing damages can be considerably more complicated. Bodily injuries may lead to claims for medical expenses, lost income (present and future), disfigurement, pain and suffering, mental anguish, and loss of consortium.[10] Three classes of damages may be awarded:

1. Special Damages. *Special damages* are designed to compensate for measurable losses, such as medical expenses and loss of income caused by the injury.

2. General Damages. *General damages* compensate the injured party for intangible losses, such as pain and suffering, disfigurement, mental anguish, and loss of consortium. Determination of the amount that should be awarded for these damages is clearly subjective.

3. Punitive Damages. *Punitive damages* are amounts assessed against the negligent party as a form of punishment when the injury resulted from gross negligence or willful intent. They are intended not only as punishment, but also to deter others from similar behavior in the future.[11]

The great difficulty in determining the award for each of these types of losses should be fairly obvious. First, although the medical and hospital expenses incurred by an injured party are subject to fairly accurate measurement, an injury that will require expenditures for many years into the future can pose valuation problems at the time damages are determined. The same is true with respect to loss of future earnings. If the injury will prevent the victim from ever working again, the problem becomes one of determining the present value of his or her probable future earnings.

In determining the amounts that should be awarded as general damages, we enter the world of fantasy. What, for example, is the "price" for the pain and suffering and mental anguish over the loss of an arm or leg? The best answer is, "The amount that an attorney can convince a jury it is worth."

Finally, with respect to punitive damages, there is no necessary relationship between the extent of the injured party's loss and the amount awarded. Punitive damages tend to vary with the conduct of the negligent party rather than with the extent of the injured party's loss and, in a sense, represent a windfall to the injured party.

Collateral Source Rule It should be noted that damages for bodily injury can be assessed against the negligent party even when the injured person recovers the amount of his or her loss from other sources. A

[10] Loss of *consortium* originally referred to the loss of a wife's companionship. Under a common law rule still retained in most states, a husband has the right to the services and consortium of his wife. A husband has an ancillary cause of action against a negligent party who is responsible for the loss of his wife's services and consortium, as well as for reasonable expenses incurred for her recovery. Originally, loss of consortium applied only to the husband's right to sue for loss of the wife's services, and a wife had no corresponding right *vis-à-vis* her husband's services, but most jurisdictions now permit damages for loss of consortium by either husband or wife.

[11] The subject of punitive damages has been subject to considerable debate. Although some states do not allow punitive damages, in 1991 the U.S. Supreme Court upheld punitive damages (*Pacific Mutual Life Insurance Company v Cleopatra Haslip, Cynthia Craig, Alma M. Calhoun and Eddie Halgrove,* U.S. Supreme Court, No. 89–1279).

basic principle of common law, the *collateral source rule,* holds that the damages assessed against a tort feasor should not be reduced by the existence of other sources of recovery available to the injured party, such as insurance or a salary continuation plan provided by an employer. If X is injured by Y and X has full insurance to compensate for the injury, he or she can still sue Y for the amount of medical expenses and lost income he or she would have incurred had there been no insurance.

Negligence Must Be the Proximate Cause of the Damage

The negligence must have been the proximate cause of the damage if the injured is to collect. This means that there must have been an unbroken chain of events beginning with the negligence and leading to the injury or damage. The negligence must have been the cause without which the accident would not have happened.

The negligent person is usually held to be responsible not only for the direct consequences of his or her action, but for the consequences that follow naturally and directly from the negligent conduct. Even if an intervening force arises, the negligent party may still be held responsible for the damage if the intervening force was foreseeable. For example, suppose that Smith decides to burn his leaves but takes no precautions to confine the fire. The wind begins to blow (an intervening cause), and the flying embers set Smith's neighbor's house on fire. The negligence began the direct chain of events, and in spite of the intervening cause, Smith could be held liable. The wind is an intervening cause, but one that Smith should have foreseen and for which he should have provided.[12]

Vicarious Liability There are circumstances in which one person may become legally liable for the negligent behavior of another person. This type of liability is known as "imputed" or *vicarious liability* and is based on the common law principle of *respondeat superior,* "let the master answer." For example, principals are liable for the negligent acts of their agents. Employers are liable for the negligence of

their employees when they are acting within their capacity as employees. In some instances, vicarious liability is imposed by statute. For example, in many states a car's owner is held liable for the negligent acts of anyone driving it with his or her permission. Note that this is not liability without negligence; there is negligence, but the negligence of one person makes another person liable.

To illustrate the principle of vicarious liability, let us assume that an employee owns her own automobile, has no automobile liability insurance, and is using the car in the business of her employer. Through her negligent driving, a pedestrian is injured seriously. The injured party has a right of action against both the employee and the employer, and any judgment would be binding on both.[13] If the employee is financially irresponsible, the vicarious liability rule will obligate the employer to pay the damages.

Under English common law, a husband was liable for the torts of his wife. This is no longer recognized, and today the wife is liable for her own torts. As a rule, parents are not liable for torts committed by their children. Here, again, the child is liable for his or her own carelessness. While this is true as a basic principle, there are some circumstances in which the parents may be held liable for the acts of their children. First, the parent may be held liable if it can be shown that the parent himself or herself was negligent in supervising the child. For example, if a parent was aware that his child's hobby was breaking picture windows and did not at least tell the child to stop, the courts would probably consider this to be negligence on the part of the parent. In the same manner, in allowing a child to possess a dangerous weapon, the parent may be deemed negligent and be held liable for any injuries caused by the child with the dangerous weapon.[14] As a consequence, it might not be too desirable to give your child a machete or a 16-foot blacksnake whip for a birthday present. In addition, the parents may be held liable under the doctrine of *respondeat superior* if the child is acting as an agent of the parent. Several states have enacted

[12] In addition to an intervening cause, the chain of casualty can be interrupted by a "superseding" cause. A superseding cause is one that is more immediate to the event and "replaces" a prior event as the proximate cause. The doctrine of last clear chance discussed later in the chapter is an example of a superseding cause.

[13] The injured pedestrian will probably sue both or, in legal parlance, "everybody in sight." The purpose of the doctrine of *respondeat superior* is to permit the inclusion of other parties who probably will be better able to pay for the injury. Note that vicarious liability does not relieve the agent of liability. It merely makes it possible to impute his or her negligence to additional persons.

[14] An automobile is not considered a "dangerous weapon" in this context. The subject of legal liability arising out of the ownership and use of autos will be discussed in Chapter 28.

statutes that hold that the child is considered to be acting as an agent of the parent when driving the family car. Finally, many states have passed special laws that impose liability on the parents for willful and malicious destruction of property by their children. For example, the legal code in Nebraska reads as follows:

> The parents shall be jointly and severally liable for the willful and intentional destruction of real and personal property occasioned by their minor or unemancipated children residing with them, or placed by them under the care of other persons.[15]

The statutes may impose liability without limit, as in Nebraska, or the vicarious liability of the parent may be subject to a maximum, as in Kansas, where the limit is $300.

Joint-and-Several Liability Instances sometimes occur in which the negligence of two or more parties contributes to the injury or damage. In such cases, the question of who is to be held liable is of critical importance. One of the important doctrines in this area is the concept of *joint-and-several liability*. A liability is said to be joint and several when the plaintiff obtains a judgment that may be enforced against multiple tort feasors collectively or individually. In effect, this doctrine permits an injured party to recover the entire amount of compensation due for injuries from any tort feasor who is able to pay, regardless of the degree of that party's negligence. If A and B are both negligent and C is injured, the doctrine of joint and several liability permits C to collect the entire amount of damages from either A or B, even if A were 98 percent at fault and B were 2 percent at fault. The doctrine has been attacked by critics who argue that it is merely a manifestation of the "deep pocket" theory of recovery.

More than two-thirds of the states have passed laws since 1986 to abolish or modify the doctrine of joint-and-several liability,[16] replacing it with several liability or a system for apportionment of damages based on the degree of fault.

Obligations of Property Owners to Others As a general rule, the occupier of land has the right to do as he or she pleases with that land, but it is important to note at the outset that the owner of property or its occupant has an obligation to persons who come onto it. The degree of care that must be exercised depends on the status of the person coming onto the land and on the specific circumstances. Common law generally recognizes four classes of persons with differing degrees of care due them: trespassers, licensees, invitees, and children.[17]

Trespassers A *trespasser* is a person who comes onto the property without right and without consent of the owner or occupier. As a rule, the land occupant has no duty to exercise care to protect trespassers on his or her land from injury. Trespassing children (discussed shortly) and "discovered trespassers" are exceptions. Once a trespasser has been discovered, the occupier must exercise ordinary care for the trespasser's safety. Otherwise, the only obligation is to avoid doing the intruder intentional injury.[18]

Licensees A *licensee* is a person who comes onto the property with the knowledge or toleration of the owner but for no purpose of, or benefit to, the latter. This classification includes door-to-door salespeople, business visitors who have strayed from the part of the premises they were invited or authorized to enter, and perhaps visiting friends and relatives.[19] As

[15] Section 43–801, *Revised Statutes of Nebraska*, Reissue of 1960. Unemancipated means that the child is not freed; an emancipated child is one who has left home and is self-supporting.

[16] Alaska, Arizona, California, Colorado, Connecticut, Florida, Georgia, Hawaii, Idaho, Illinois, Indiana, Iowa, Kentucky, Louisiana, Michigan, Minnesota, Mississippi, Missouri, Montana, Nebraska, Nevada, New Hampshire, New Jersey, New Mexico, New York, North Dakota, Ohio, Oregon, South Dakota, Texas, Utah, Vermont, Washington, Wisconsin, and Wyoming.

[17] The once firmly established distinction among trespassers, licensees, and invitees has been modified by the courts in some jurisdictions. For example, courts in California and Hawaii have abolished the distinction. See W. Page Keeton, General Editor, *Prosser and Keeton on the Law of Torts,* 5th ed. (St. Paul, Minn.: West, 1984), p. 432ff.

[18] The fact that the person was a trespasser is not a defense for injuries caused intentionally; intentional injury to another is permitted only in self-defense. The rule is that one is privileged to use force likely to cause death or serious bodily harm only if there is reason to believe the behavior of the other party would cause one's death or serious bodily harm. For example, if someone were coming at you in an insane frenzy with a meat cleaver in one hand and a double-bitted axe in the other, you would be privileged to defend yourself with force that could inflict serious bodily harm on the other party. In addition, if someone intrudes on your land, you have the privilege to use force not likely to cause death or serious bodily harm if you have demanded that the intruder leave or desist and the demand has been ignored.

[19] The situation with respect to social guests varies in different jurisdictions. The majority of the courts hold that a social guest is a licensee, although some courts have held that a social guest is an invitee.

with trespassers, the property owner must avoid intentional harm to a licensee. In addition, the owner must warn the licensee of, or make safe, conditions or activities posing risk or harm that would not be obvious to a reasonable person coming onto the land. For example, the land occupier has a duty to protect licensees from wild or domestic animals on the premises that he or she knows or should know are dangerous. Therefore, if the family dog has a nasty disposition and has displayed this characteristic previously, the occupier of the premises must take care to protect licensees from this animal, or face strict liability.

If the land occupant knows that persons continuously or habitually trespass on his or her land, then the occupant has a higher degree of responsibility to such persons than to ordinary trespassers. This is based on the principle that if the owner knows that persons are in the habit of trespassing and does nothing to stop it, the toleration gives implied consent to the presence of the trespassers, changing their status to licensees. Perhaps the best evidence of this implied consent is a beaten path. The land occupier might overcome the implied consent by posting "no trespassing" signs.

Invitees An *invitee* is a person who has been invited in or onto the property for some purpose of the owner. If the person coming onto the premises of the land occupier is a business visitor—an invitee—rather than a licensee, the degree of care required of the land occupier is significantly increased. Invitees, as a classification, include customers and any person on premises open for admission to the general public, free or paid—such as theaters, churches, railroad stations, and the like. It also includes letter carriers, delivery people, workers, garbage collectors, and similar persons, who come onto the land to further the use to which the land occupier is putting the premises. With respect to invitees, the person occupying the land has a duty to inspect and discover the presence of natural and artificial conditions or activities carrying any risk of harm, and should exercise due care to warn invitees of such dangers or make them safe. This is a more onerous burden than the care one is obligated to exercise with respect to licensees, since it applies to more than just extraordinary or unusual hazards. Any condition that could cause harm to an invitee is a possible source of legal liability.

Children The law imposes a greater responsibility in the degree of care that must be exercised with regard to children. It is an accepted fact that children do not always act prudently. This being the case, the law requires the property owner to protect children from themselves, regardless of their status as trespassers, licensees, or guests. Under the doctrine of an *attractive nuisance,* a high degree of care is imposed on the land occupier for certain conditions on the land—attractive nuisances—that might attract and injure a child of tender years. The doctrine is based on the principle that there is a greater social interest in the safety of children than in the land occupier's right to do as he or she pleases with the land. For the doctrine to be applicable, the child must be so immature as to be unable to recognize the danger involved. Or it must be something the land occupant would realize could involve an unreasonable risk of harm to such children.[20]

In the application of the doctrine, the land occupier is obligated to use due care to discover children on the property. If he or she discovers them, or is charged with such knowledge, then the occupant is bound to warn them or to protect them from conditions threatening death or serious bodily harm. Many types of artificial conditions have been held to be attractive nuisances. However, there does not appear to be any consistent criterion that the courts have utilized. Unattended vehicles have been considered in this category. Explosives, guns, window wells in basements, trees, construction machinery, and fences have all been held to qualify. In fact, almost anything in or about premises has at one time or another been considered as qualifying. We might note that it is difficult to eliminate the possibility of legal liability from an attractive nuisance even by dying, because even gravestones have qualified under the doctrine.

Defenses to Negligence

Thus far in our discussion of negligence, we have been concerned with the existence of a duty owed to others and a breach of that duty. But an individual's negligent behavior does not necessarily mean that a person has a legal liability. For many torts predicated on negligence alone, the presumed negligent parties may have certain defenses that could free them from legal liability in spite of the negligent behavior.

Assumption of Risk An excellent defense to tort actions is that of *assumption of risk* by the injured

[20] The courts regard the doctrine either as an exception to the general rules of negligence, or as an application of the rules of negligence to a special class of persons, that is, children. The doctrine, however, is rarely applicable to a child over age 12.

party. If one recognizes and understands the danger involved in an activity and voluntarily chooses to encounter it, this assumption of the risk will bar any recovery for injury caused by negligence. Perhaps the most common application of this doctrine is attendance at certain types of sporting events such as baseball and hockey. Courts have held that in seeking admission, a spectator must be taken to have chosen to undergo the well-known risk of having his or her face smashed by a baseball or a hockey puck. Another common example is the guest passenger in an automobile. If the car is driven in a grossly negligent manner and the guest fails to protest the dangerous driving, he or she may be considered to have assumed the risk of injury.

Negligence on the Part of the Injured Party Negligence on the part of the injured party may also serve as a bar to recovery or, in some jurisdictions, reduce the amount to which the injured party is entitled as damages. Two doctrines have developed: contributory negligence and comparative negligence.

Contributory Negligence As an outgrowth of the idea that every person has an obligation to look out for his or her own safety and cannot blame someone else for damage where personal negligence is to blame, the common law principle of *contributory negligence* developed.[21] To collect, the injured party must come into court with clean hands. Under the doctrine of contributory negligence, any negligence on the part of the injured party, even though slight, will normally defeat the claim. Note that the degree of contributory negligence is of no consequence. Its existence on the part of the injured party, even though slight, will defeat the claim.

Contributory negligence is an important and effective defense, but it is an extremely harsh doctrine to apply in modern society. It seems unfortunate that some courts continue to follow the common law maxim of refusal to apportion blame. For example, one could seriously question the virtue of a legal doctrine under which a person who is 90 percent to blame for an accident should be free of liability just because the injured party was 10 percent responsible.[22]

The number of instances in which contributory negligence has qualified as a defense is practically infinite. One of the most common examples in automobile liability is jaywalking. Failure to signal a turn could be contributory negligence on your part, even though your car was rear-ended by an oncoming automobile. Being drunk, running down poorly lighted stairs, teasing an animal, and horseplay have all qualified at one time or another, to name just a few examples of contributory negligence.

Comparative Negligence Because of the harshness of the contributory negligence doctrine, the majority of the states have adopted a somewhat more lenient doctrine, that of *comparative negligence*. Here contributory negligence on the part of the injured party will not necessarily defeat the claim, but will be used in some manner to mitigate the damages payable by the other party. Comparative negligence rules divide into two broad types. One is the so-called *pure rule*, sometimes called the *Mississippi rule* because it was first adopted by that state in 1910. Under this rule, any defendant who is only partly at fault must still pay in proportion to his or her blame.[23] Most other states follow the *Wisconsin rule*, first asserted in 1933, under which the defendant who was least at fault is not required to pay at all.[24] By 1995, all but seven states had adopted one or the other of these rules.

To illustrate the difference between the two approaches, and to provide a contrast with the common law principle of contributory negligence, assume that Smith and Jones are injured in an accident, each suffering losses in the amount of $10,000. Assume also that Smith is 40 percent and Jones 60 percent at fault. Recovery under each of the systems would be as indicated by the following table.

[21] Contributory negligence is a defense only to tort actions based on negligence. It is not a defense to intentional torts such as assault and battery or to any tort predicated on strict liability.

[22] Because of the obvious and unjust harshness of the doctrine, some courts by judicial interpretation use the rule of comparative negligence discussed next. In practice, many courts are inclined perhaps to ignore slight degrees of contributory negligence.

[23] States following the *pure comparative negligence rule* are Alaska, California, Florida, Illinois, Louisiana, Michigan, Mississippi, Missouri, New Mexico, New York, Rhode Island, and Washington.

[24] States that follow the *Wisconsin rule* may be divided into two classes: those that permit recovery when the injured party's negligence is *less than that of the other person* (the 49 percent rule) and those that permit recovery when the injured party's negligence is *not greater than the other person's* (the 50 percent rule). States that follow the *less than rule* are Arkansas, Colorado, Georgia, Idaho, Kansas, Maine, North Dakota, Utah, West Virginia, and Wyoming. In addition, Arizona, Nebraska, South Dakota, and Tennessee have a special version of the *less than rule* and use the terms *slight* and *gross* negligence. States following the *not greater than rule* are Connecticut, Hawaii, Indiana, Iowa, Massachusetts, Minnesota, Montana, Nevada, New Hampshire, New Jersey, Ohio, Oklahoma, Oregon, Pennsylvania, Texas, Vermont, and Wisconsin.

The comparative negligence principle has much to commend it. It has the effect of tempering the harshness of the contributory negligence doctrine, particularly in situations in which only a slight degree of contributory negligence will defeat an injured party's claim. It seems unfair to disallow a claim in cases in which the negligence of the injured party is slight, but it also seems illogical to allow one to recover complete damages in such instances. If the jury can separate degrees of negligence, the comparative negligence principle will produce logical and fair results.

	Recovery under Common Law (18 states)	Recovery under Wisconsin Law (6 states)	Recovery under Mississippi Rule (26 states)
Smith, 40 percent at fault, $10,000 loss	0	$6,000	$6,000
Jones, 60 percent at fault, $10,000 loss	0	0	4,000

Last Clear Chance The *doctrine of last clear chance* is an additional modification of the doctrine of contributory negligence. Under this tenet, as utilized in practically all legal jurisdictions, it is recognized that the contributory negligence of an injured party will not bar his or her recovery if the other party immediately prior to the accident had a "last clear chance" to prevent it but failed to seize that chance. Its logic is obvious. If one can avoid an accident and does nothing to prevent its occurrence, one should be legally liable for damages, regardless of the contributory negligence of the injured party.

To illustrate the doctrine, let us assume that X drives onto a highway after stopping at a stop sign. He gets partially onto the highway, when his automobile stalls. He tries frantically to get the car started, but to no avail. A car driven by Ms. Y is speeding down the highway. Although Y notices X's car well in advance of the accident, she slows down very little and makes no attempt to drive to the other side of the road. From the resulting collision, X may be entitled to collect a considerable amount in damages, even though he had no right to be on the highway and even though he knew that his car was in the habit of stalling. Here, Y was negligent because of her failure to use reasonable care in driving her car. She saw X's predicament and could have avoided the accident by slowing down, or, if necessary, by coming to a halt. She could also have driven to the other side of the road if it had been clear of oncoming traffic. One of the most difficult lessons for a driver to learn is that having the right-of-way does not mean that one is permitted to use this right without reasonable regard for the safety of others, even though the others have placed themselves negligently in situations that may imperil their persons or property.

Survival of Tort Actions Under common law, tort actions do not survive the death of the person committing the injury or the person injured. This obviously prevents any recovery by the deceased individual's estate or personal representative. The responsible person could be held criminally but not civilly responsible. It is clear, therefore, that this rule had the unusual characteristic of making it more profitable to kill a person than to maim him or her. In almost every jurisdiction, this rule has been changed to some extent. Some statutes declare merely that cause of action for damage to property survives the death of either the plaintiff or the defendant. But most go further and allow the survival of causes of action for personal injuries as well.

Every jurisdiction now has some sort of statute of wrongful death. The most common creates a new cause of action for the benefit of particular surviving relatives—usually the spouse, children, or parents—which permits the recovery of the damage sustained by such persons. The new cause of action, however, does not eliminate any defenses available to the responsible party. Thus, the decedent's contributory negligence, assumption of risk, or a release executed by him or her before death for the full recovery of a judgment by the deceased are all held to bar wrongful death actions in most states.

Legal Liability and Bankruptcy The risk of legal liability is one fraught with potential catastrophic

losses. With all the various factors used in determining damages in an action for negligence added together, the result could be astounding. Naturally, the question must arise as to whether the guilty party, confronted with a large judgment, has any alternative but to pay, even if it takes the balance of his or her lifetime to make complete settlement. Bankruptcy is, of course, an alternative, and perhaps is the only possible course of action. The negligent party will lose most of what he or she has accumulated up to this point in life, but will be released from the balance of the judgment. The discharge of the judgment may appear to be desirable to the guilty party, but the stigma of bankruptcy will be lifelong and will hamper practically all his or her future business and personal activities.

A judgment for liability arising from a willful or malicious tort, on the other hand, cannot be discharged by bankruptcy. The guilty party will be obligated to pay the judgment if it takes the rest of his or her life. That bankruptcy will not discharge a judgment arising from a willful or malicious act is a fact that should be appreciated, particularly by young people who are inclined to drive in a manner that could amount to willful and malicious behavior.

POSSIBLE CHANGES IN THE TORT SYSTEM

In the 1980s, a debate over the tort system, which had begun with dissatisfaction over the "automobile problem," moved from the auto field into the field of general liability. Initially, agitation for reform came from the medical profession, whose members complained that the costs of insuring against tort losses had become an unbearable burden. Later, manufacturers complained that liability suits involving defective products had also reached an unbearable level. Eventually, the high cost of insuring against liability losses produced what many called a liability insurance crisis, affecting classes as diverse as day care centers, recreational facilities, medical practitioners, architects, product manufacturers, governmental bodies, and the officers of major corporations. Dissatisfaction with the system reached a peak in the period from 1985 to 1987, when many buyers faced astronomical increases for liability insurance, which the insurance industry blamed on a tort system out of control. Pressure for reform came from a coalition of

insurance buyers and the insurance industry. Opposition to reform has come principally from the American Trial Lawyers Association and other groups representing the plaintiff's bar.

The changes in the tort system that are collectively considered to be tort *reform* include

1. Alternative dispute resolution mechanisms, such as binding arbitration for small claims to reduce the cost of litigation

2. Elimination of the doctrine of joint-and-several liability

3. Establishing a sliding fee schedule for plaintiffs' attorneys in place of the contingency system

4. Limitations or "caps" on awards for noneconomic damages (pain and suffering)

5. Elimination of the collateral source rule (subtracting from the award for economic damages any reimbursement from other sources, such as personal health insurance)

6. Periodic payment of awards (also called structured settlements) in place of lump-sum awards

7. Elimination of punitive damages or making punitive damages payable to the state rather than to the injured party

In response to the pressure, most states have enacted some elements of tort reform. In general, however, the impact of reform on liability insurance costs has been modest. The limited impact of the reform measures that have been adopted thus far is blamed on two factors.

First, the reforms were virtually all at the state level, which means that their impact would be localized. Those who advocate serious tort reform have always been skeptical that state-by-state reform would solve the problem. In the case of products liability, for example, they point out that we are a national market, and that only a national system of product liability tort reform will eliminate the problems that underlie the crisis.

Furthermore, because insurers had not maintained loss data in a form that indicates the proportion of liability losses attributable to pain and suffering, punitive damages, or contingency fees, they have had difficulty in judging the amount by which the reforms were likely to reduce future losses. As a result, many states enacted legislation requiring insurers to accumulate loss data according

to categories that will permit measurement of such factors in the future.

Although the impact of tort reform on insurance prices has not met consumer expectations, there is evidence that even the regional changes in the tort system had a positive effect on insurer losses and on premiums. The limitations on joint-and-several liability, pain and suffering, and punitive damages did reduce insurers' losses, and the reductions were passed on to buyers in the form of premiums that were lower than otherwise would have been the case.[25]

[25] See Glenn Blackmon and Richard Zeckhauser, "State Tort Reform Legislation: Assessing Our Control of Risks," *Tort Law and the Public Interest* (New York: The American Assembly, W. W. Norton, 1991).

SUMMARY

Although we have surveyed only the more fundamental aspects of legal liability, the tremendous exposure that the individual faces in this area should be evident.[26] The catastrophic proportions that the liability loss can assume suggest that the appropriate risk management technique for this exposure is transfer. This is accomplished for the most part by transfer of the risk to an insurance company through the purchase of liability insurance, the subject of Chapter 28.

[26] The tort system is an evolving body of legal doctrines. It has undergone significant change in the past and is likely to change in the future. Changes in the tort system as it relates to automobiles are discussed in Chapter 29.

IMPORTANT CONCEPTS TO REMEMBER

tort
intentional torts
unintentional torts
negligence
lex talionis
law of retaliation
sovereign immunity
negligence *per se*
absolute liability
res ipsa loquitur

scienter
vicious propensity
consortium
proximate cause
special damages
general damages
punitive damages
collateral source rule
vicarious liability
joint-and-several liability

respondeat superior
trespassers
licensees
invitees
attractive nuisance
assumption of risk
contributory negligence
comparative negligence
last clear chance

QUESTIONS FOR REVIEW

1. What conditions must exist before an individual may be held legally liable in a tort action?

2. Distinguish among *invitee, licensee,* and *trespasser,* and describe a property owner's responsibilities to each.

3. Give an example of each of the following legal doctrines: *res ipsa loquitur, scienter,* and negligence *per se.*

4. Explain fully what is meant by the term *vicarious liability,* giving examples of several situations in which vicarious liability is likely to exist.

5. Identify the defenses that may be used against a tort action.

6. To what extent may parents be held liable for the acts of their minor children? Be complete and specific.

7. Distinguish between the concepts of *contributory negligence and comparative negligence.* Which doctrine is used in your state? Which do you feel is the more reasonable, and why?

8. What factors are considered in determining the amount of damages to which a person who suffers bodily injury is entitled in a tort action?

9. What is meant by the term *absolute liability?* Give three examples of absolute liability.

10. To what extent are the risk management techniques of *avoidance, reduction,* and *retention* suitable and adequate techniques for dealing with the liability risk?

QUESTIONS FOR DISCUSSION

1. At one time, it was felt that liability insurance would undermine the tort system, which has as its central theorem the concept that the individual responsible for injuring another should be made to pay for that injury. Do you think that the existence of liability insurance causes one to be less careful than he or she might otherwise be?

2. Schwartz had been troubled by burglars, so he installed a trap in his building with a shotgun rigged to fire when an intruder opened the door. Sam Burglar broke into the building and lost both legs when the shotgun discharged. Sam thereupon brought suit against Schwartz for damages. What defenses might Schwartz offer? Do you believe that a court would permit recovery under such circumstances?

3. Bodily injury awards have increased at a significant rate during the past two decades. To what do you attribute this increase? Were previous awards inadequate, or are the current ones excessive?

4. Because of a rash of liability suits and high judgments, many municipalities and other government subdivisions have had difficulty in obtaining liability insurance for a decade. This seems ironic in view of the fact that only a short time ago, such entities were immune from liability. To what do you attribute the reversal?

5. What major liability-exposures do you as an individual in your current status as a student face? How are your exposures likely to change after you have completed your education?

SUGGESTIONS FOR ADDITIONAL READING

Anderson, R. A. *The Insurer's Tort Law.* Ocean City, N.J.: Insurance Press, 1964.

Athearn, James L., Travis Pritchett, and Joan T. Schmit. *Risk and Insurance,* 6th ed. St. Paul, Minn.: West Publishing, 1989. Chapter 15.

Huebner, S. S., Kenneth Black, Jr., and Robert S. Cline. *Property and Liability Insurance,* 3rd ed. Englewood Cliffs, N.J.: Prentice-Hall, 1982. Chapter 29.

Keeton, Robert E. *Basic Text on Insurance Law.* St. Paul, Minn.: West Publishing, 1971.

Kulp, C. A., and John W. Hall. *Casualty Insurance,* 4th ed. New York: Ronald Press, 1968. Chapter 4.

Lorimer, James J., et al. *The Legal Environment of Insurance,* 3rd ed., vol. 2. Malvern, Pa.: American Institute for Property and Liability Underwriters, 1987.

Prosser, William L., et al. *Handbook on the Law of Torts,* 5th ed. St. Paul, Minn.: West Publishing, 1984.

WEB SITES TO EXPLORE

American Tort Reform Association	http://www.aaabiz.com/ATRA/default.html
American Trial Lawyers Association	http://www.atlanet.org/
Arbitration Forum	http://www.arb-forum.com/
Best's Review – Property/Casualty Edition	http://www.ambest.com/review/lh/index.html
Independent Insurance Agents of America, Inc.	http://www.iiaa.org
Insurance News Network	http://www.insure.com/
National Association of Professional Insurance Agents	http://www.pianet.com/

GENERAL LIABILITY INSURANCE FOR THE INDIVIDUAL

He that scatters thorns, let him not go barefoot.

— BENJAMIN FRANKLIN
Poor Richard's Almanac, 1736

CHAPTER OBJECTIVES

When you have finished this chapter, you should be able to

- Explain the distinction between a denial of payment by an insurer because there is no liability and denial because there is no coverage
- Identify the coverage features under Section II of the homeowners forms
- Describe the insuring agreements of liability insurance contracts generally and explain the insurer's obligation to defend the insured
- Explain the insuring agreement of the Section II Personal Liability coverage
- Explain the insuring agreement of the Section II Medical Payments coverage
- Recognize significant exclusions under the homeowners Section II
- Describe the personal umbrella liability contracts, including qualification requirements and typical exclusions
- List the available endorsements for broadening Personal Liability coverage

LIABILITY INSURANCE IN GENERAL

In Chapter 26, we examined the principles of negligence that give rise to the legal liability exposure. We noted that the risk of legal liability is a pervasive aspect of the life of every individual and that it is a risk of catastrophic potential. In this chapter, we turn to liability insurance, the form of coverage designed

to protect against the financial consequences of negligence, legal liability.

In its simplest form, liability insurance undertakes to assume the obligations imposed on the negligent party in the event of legal liability. The liability insurance policy agrees to pay the sums that the insured becomes legally obligated to pay, up to the limit of the policy, when such liability arises out of acts of the insured that are included in the definition of coverage. It is commonly called *third-party coverage* because it undertakes to compensate someone who is not a party to the contract, the injured person to whom the insured is liable. It is important to recognize that this "third party" is not an insured under the policy and has no direct claim against the insurer. Contractually, the insurer has no legal obligation to the injured third party unless and until the insured's liability has been established in a court of law.

Besides the promise to pay sums that the insured becomes legally obligated to pay, most liability policies also include a promise by the insurer to defend the insured in suits involving the type of liability covered under the policy. Thus, automobile liability policies will provide defense for suits alleging negligence in the operation of an automobile, while a premises liability policy will pay defense costs related to insured premises. The basic principle is that the insurer must pay defense costs if it would be obligated to pay damages if the insured should be held liable.

As a practical matter, few liability claims reach trial. Insurers realize that the best interests of all concerned will be served if a settlement can be reached without litigation, and the insurer normally seeks an out-of-court settlement with the injured party. Most liability policies reserve this right to the insurer. Although the insurance company often deals directly with the injured party, it is not obliged to do so under the contract.

An area frequently misunderstood by the public is the distinction between the liability of the insured and coverage under the liability policy. When presented with a claim, an insurer may attempt to negotiate a settlement, or it may refuse to consider payment. The insurer's denial of payment may be based on two different reasons. One is that the loss is not covered under the policy. Here, the insured must assume his or her own defense and, if held liable, must pay the claim. An entirely different situation exists when the company denies payment because it does not feel that the insured is legally liable for the damage or injury. In this instance, the insurer is obligated to defend the insured, and if the insured is eventually found to be liable, the insurer will pay for the loss up to the policy limits.

TYPES OF LIABILITY INSURANCE

Most people realize the liability exposure inherent in driving a car. The size of the judgments we see in newspapers acts as a constant reminder of this risk. Recognizing this, most individuals purchase automobile liability insurance to protect themselves against this exposure. At the same time, many fail to recognize that the basis of the liability exposure—that is, the negligent act—also underlies liability for acts that have no connection with an automobile. The individual needs protection against the consequences of any negligent act, not just those connected with the automobile. Several forms of liability insurance are available to meet the liability exposure from various sources. For convenience in discussion, we may divide liability insurance into three classes:

- Automobile liability
- Employers liability and workers compensation
- General liability

Usually, these three types of liability insurance are provided under separate contracts. Most general liability policies exclude liability arising out of automobiles and liability for injuries to employees. Liability arising out of the operation of automobiles is insured under a separate automobile liability policy, and coverage for injury to employees is available under the Workers Compensation and Employers Liability Policy. The discussion in this chapter is concerned primarily with the field of general liability.[1] General liability insurance can be subdivided further into coverages designed (1) to protect business firms and other institutions and (2) to protect the individual. We will confine our discussion to coverage for the individual.

COMPREHENSIVE PERSONAL LIABILITY COVERAGE

The general liability coverage designed to protect the individual is called *Comprehensive Personal Liability* (CPL) insurance. The coverage is "comprehensive"

[1] As we will see in the following discussion, comprehensive personal liability coverage is an exception to the general principle since it includes coverage for injuries to domestic employees.

in the sense that it insures against all types of liability hazards falling within a broad insuring agreement, except those that are specifically excluded. In general, the coverage is intended to protect against the nonbusiness, nonautomobile exposures of the individual or family unit. Protection exists for legal liability arising out of the premises and also for liability arising out of the personal activities of the insured or family members, both on and away from the premises. In addition, the coverage includes employers liability coverage for injury to domestic employees in those jurisdictions where such workers are not subject to the workers compensation laws. In some states, the policy can be endorsed to provide workers compensation coverage for domestic employees.

Comprehensive Personal Liability coverage may be purchased as a monoline contract, it may be added to monoline dwelling forms by endorsement, and it is automatically included as Section II of the homeowners policy.[2] Since the most widely used means of obtaining the coverage is under the homeowners forms, we will use Section II of the homeowners policy as the basis for our discussion.

General Nature of the Coverage

There are two basic coverages under Section II of the homeowners, designated Coverage E, Personal Liability, and Coverage F, Medical Payments to Others. There are also four supplementary insuring agreements, called additional coverages. A brief overview of the coverages may be helpful in the detailed discussion of the individual coverages that follows.

1. *Coverage E, Personal Liability.* Under the insuring agreement of this coverage, the company promises to pay, up to the limit of liability set in the policy, all payments that become the insured's legal obligation because of bodily injury or property damage falling within the scope of the coverage. The standard limit of liability, which may be increased, is $100,000.[3]

2. *Coverage F, Medical Payments to Others.* The Medical Payments coverage provides payment for medical expenses incurred by persons who are injured while on the premises with the permission of any insured or who are injured away from the premises if the injury results from an activity of the insured or a member of the insured's family. Coverage for medical payments applies regardless of the insured's liability. The basic limit under the homeowners policy for this coverage is $1000, which may be increased.

3. *Additional Coverages.* The Additional Coverages of Section II provide payment for certain additional expenses that may be incurred by the insured in the event of injury or damage to the person or property of others. These include claim expenses, first aid expense, limited payment for damage to property of others when the insured is not liable, and loss assessment coverage.

Personal Liability Coverage

The Personal Liability coverage is the major coverage of the CPL coverage. Its insuring agreement is simple and straightforward:

> If a claim is made or a suit is brought against any insured for damages because of bodily injury or property damage to which this coverage applies, we will:
> a. pay up to our limit of liability for the damages for which the insured is legally liable; and
> b. provide a defense at our expense by counsel of our choice. We may make any investigation and settle any claim or suit that we decide is appropriate. Our obligation to defend any claim or suit ends when the amount we pay for damages resulting from the occurrence equals our limit of liability.

This is a fairly typical liability insuring agreement. In addition to the promise to pay sums that the insured becomes legally obligated to pay, the agreement also promises defense, and reserves to the company the right to make an out-of-court settlement.

Persons Insured One of the most important parts of any liability policy is the definition of "persons insured" because the insurer promises to pay damages or defend under the liability coverage "if a claim is made or suit is brought against *any* insured." Like most liability policies, coverage is provided for certain individuals other than the person listed in the declarations

[2] Personal liability coverage is available as an endorsement to the dwelling forms under the Personal Liability Supplement. The same endorsement is combined with a set of conditions and a declarations page to form a separate monoline personal liability policy.

[3] Under a *single limit* of liability, the insurance company will pay up to that limit for either bodily injury or property damage arising out of a single occurrence. This is in contrast with *split limits* such as those used in some automobile policies. Automobile limits of $10,000/$20,000/$5000 mean that the insurance company will pay up to $10,000 for each person injured, up to $20,000 for all persons injured, and up to $5000 for property damage arising out of a single occurrence.

of the policy. In Chapter 24, we noted that the definition of *Insured* under the homeowners policy includes the named insured and resident relative, other persons under age 21 in the case of the insured, and certain student enrolled in school full-time who were residents of the household before leaving to attend school. (Insured students include persons under age 24 related to the insured and students under age 21 who were in the care of an insured.) These persons are also insureds under Section II of the policy. In addition, for Section II coverages only, the homeowners policy contains the following definition:

Under Section II, "insured" also means:

c. with respect to animals or watercraft to which this policy applies, any person or organization legally responsible for these animals or watercraft which are owned by you or any person included in 5.a. or 5.b. above. "Insured" does not mean a person or organization using or having custody of these animals or watercraft in the course of any "business" or without consent of the owner.

d. with respect to a "motor vehicle" to which this policy applies,

(1) Persons while engaged in your employ or that of any person included in 5.a. or 5.b. above; or

(2) Other persons using the vehicle on an "insured location" with your consent.

Under both Section I and II, when the word "an" immediately precedes the word "insured," the words "an insured" together mean one or more "insureds."

The inclusion of persons legally responsible for animals or watercraft to which the insurance applies extends coverage for persons to whom the insured may have loaned such animals or watercraft or who have custody for other reasons. If a neighbor takes care of the insured's dog while the insured is on vacation, the neighbor would be covered under the policy in the event of any suit arising out of the dog's actions. However, the exclusion of anyone having custody of an animal or watercraft in the course of business denies coverage to organizations such as kennels or marinas. The exclusion of persons having custody without permission is self-explanatory.

Finally, the definition of persons insured includes certain persons while operating a vehicle to which the insurance applies. As we will see shortly, this is limited to unlicensed motor vehicles, such as those used for the maintenance of the premises, and recre-

ational vehicles. The intent is to provide coverage, for example, to a gardener operating a riding lawn mower. Coverage applies for "any other person using the vehicle on an insured location with your (the named insured's) permission."

Severability of Insureds One of the conditions in the policy states: "This insurance applies separately to each 'insured.' This condition shall not increase our limit of liability for any one 'occurrence.'" Since the insurance is stated to apply separately to each insured, it is conceivable that one insured under the policy might injure another insured person and have coverage for the resulting liability. While intrafamily suits are, as explained later, specifically excluded, other suits by an insured against an insured are possible. A residence employee, who is covered while operating an insured vehicle, a person having custody of an animal owned by the insured, or someone using an insured watercraft are all insureds under the policy. If any of these persons were injured by another insured, they could bring suit and, if the suit were successful, collect under the policy.

Liability Exclusions Two sets of exclusions are applicable to the liability coverage. One set of twelve exclusions (designated 1 through 4 and 5.a through 5.h) applies to both liability and medical payments, and a second set of six exclusions (designated 6.a through 6.f) applies to liability coverage only.

1. Motor Vehicle Liability Liability arising out of motor vehicles owned or operated by any insured is excluded in a complex and somewhat wordy series of provisions. These include the exclusion itself (which denies coverage for "motor vehicle liability"), the definition of "motor vehicle," and a definition of "motor vehicle liability." There have been attempts in the past (mostly unsuccessful) to find coverage under the homeowners policy for automobile liability losses through claims against an insured other than the operator of the auto. These attempts were usually based on the argument that a parent was negligent, not in the operation of an auto, but in supervising a minor or by negligently entrusting someone with the auto. In an effort to address these arguments, in addition to excluding liability arising out of the ownership, maintenance, occupancy, operation, use, loading, and unloading of a motor vehicle, the policy also excludes liability arising out of entrustment, failure to supervise, or negligent supervision or vicarious liability for the actions of a child or minor involving a motor vehicle. The exclusions of watercraft,

aircraft, and hovercraft include similarly worded provisions.

The motor vehicle exclusion distinguishes between motor vehicles that are registered for use on public roads or property (or that should be so registered) and other vehicles. These are completely excluded. Other vehicles, which are not registered and are not required to be registered, may be excluded or covered, depending on the vehicle. Unregistered vehicles are excluded if they are operated in (or practicing for) any prearranged or organized race, speed contest, or other competition. Unregistered vehicles rented to others, used to carry persons or cargo for a charge, or used for business purpose are also excluded.

Unregistered motor vehicles for which coverage exists include a motor vehicle in dead storage on an insured location, motor vehicles used solely to service an insured's premises, and motor vehicles designed to assist the handicapped if actually being used for this purpose or parked at the time of the occurrence.

Recreational motor vehicles such as snowmobiles, all-terrain vehicles, go-carts, and other land motor vehicles designed for recreational use off public roads are divided, for coverage purposes, as owned and non-owned. Non-owned recreational motor vehicles are insured on and off premises. Owned recreational motor vehicles are covered only when on an insured location.

Motorized golf carts owned by an insured are covered while at a golfing facility and parked or stored there, or when being used by an insured to play golf or for other recreational activities allowed by the facility. The golf cart must be designed to carry no more than four persons and cannot have been modified after manufacture to exceed 25 miles per hour. Coverage also applies while the cart is being used for travel to and from an area where motor vehicles or golf carts are parked or while crossing public roads at designated points to access other parts of the golf course. Finally, owned golf carts are covered while on a private residential community (e.g., "Sun City") where the insured's residence is located. If it is legal for golf carts to travel on the public roads of the private community, coverage applies to such usage.

2. Watercraft Liability Watercraft exclusion 1.g excludes liability (including negligent entrustment, negligent supervision, and vicarious liability) arising out of the following types of boats.

- Inboard or inboard-outboard motorboats with more than 50 horsepower owned by or rented to an insured
- Sailing vessels (with or without auxiliary power) over 26 feet in length owned by or rented to an insured
- Any boats powered by an outboard motor or motors in excess of 25 horsepower if such motor or motors were owned by the insured at the inception of the policy and not listed or reported to the insurer

Note that the exclusion concerning outboard motors, unlike that about inboards or sailing vessels, does not apply to rented motors. Coverage applies to boats below these limits, and the exclusion of larger units may be removed by endorsement for an additional premium. The policy also provides that none of the exclusions relating to watercraft apply while the watercraft is stored.

3. Aircraft Liability Next, legal liability arising from the ownership, maintenance, or use of aircraft (including negligent entrustment, negligent supervision, and vicarious liability) is excluded by exclusion 1.h. If the insured owns or rents a private airplane, he or she must purchase aircraft insurance specifically designed for this purpose. The policy defines an aircraft as "any contrivance used or designed for flight, except model or hobby aircraft not used or designed to carry people or cargo." In addition to airplanes, the exclusion eliminates coverage for ultralights and hang gliders.

4. Hovercraft Liability The Hovercraft Liability exclusion was introduced in the year 2000 revision to address the ambiguity regarding the nature of these vehicles. Although the policy excluded aircraft, motor vehicles, and watercraft, it was argued that hovercraft were technically none of these. The wording of the hovercraft liability exclusion parallels the wording of the motor vehicle exclusion.

5.a. Intentional Injury It is considered contrary to public policy to protect an individual from the consequences of intentional injury to another. For this reason, the policy excludes coverage for bodily injury or property damage that is either expected or intended from the standpoint of the insured. The exclusion goes on to state that the exclusion applies "even if the injury or damage is of a different kind ... or is sustained by a different person than originally expected or intended."

If Joe throws a bottle at Bill and hits Sherrie, the insurer would likely invoke this exclusion.[4]

5.b. Business Activities The Personal Liability coverage of the homeowners policy is designed to provide coverage for legal liability arising from the dwelling premises and personal activities of the insured. It is not designed to provide coverage for business or professional activities. Exclusion 5.b makes this clear; it excludes liability "arising out of or in connection with a 'business' conducted from an insured location or engaged in by an insured." The exclusion applies not only to a business owned by the insured, but a business by which the insured is employed as well. The scope of the exclusion is defined, in part, by the policy definition of "business." "*Business*" means a trade, profession, or occupation engaged in on a full-time, part-time, or occasional basis. It also means any other activity engaged in for money or other compensation. Four types of activity are excluded from the definition of business (and are therefore covered). These include volunteer activity for which no money is received (other than payment for expenses), providing day care services without compensation (other than the mutual exchange of service), and providing home day care services to a relative of the insured. The final exception is any activity (other than the first three) for which no insured received more than $2000 in compensation in the 12 months before the inception of the policy.

In addition to the qualifications in the definition of "business," there are two exceptions to the business exclusion itself. The first relates to rental activities.

The definition of "business" is sufficiently broad to include rental activities of an insured. The rental activities exceptions to the business exclusion provide coverage for (1) the occasional rental of an insured's residence, (2) rental of part of the insured premises for use as a residence only (but with no more than two roomers or boarders per family), or (3) rental of part of the residence as an office, school, studio, or private garage.

The first exception is self-explanatory. The insured is permitted to rent the insured residence to others on a short-term or temporary basis (e.g., while the insured is on a temporary assignment in another city). The second exception permits rental of a single-family unit in the residence (provided there are no more than two roomers or boarders per single-family unit). Finally, a part of the insured residence may be rented to others for use as an office, school, studio, or private garage. Other rental activities may be covered by endorsement to the homeowners policy or under a separate business general liability policy.

Coverage for Business Activities Coverage is available by endorsement to the homeowners policy for some types of business activities, including businesses conducted from the residence premises. There are four separate endorsements, designed for different business exposures.

Employees who want liability coverage for their activities as employees (as opposed to business owners) may obtain coverage under the *Business Pursuits Endorsement*. This endorsement is available to clerical office employees, salespersons, collectors, messengers, and teachers. Although the liability insurance purchased by one's employer usually extends coverage to employees, an employee might desire coverage for exposures not covered by the employer's policy or where the employer's coverage is considered inadequate. The endorsement excludes coverage for acts of the insured in connection with a business owned by the insured and injury to fellow employees.

The homeowners program rules allow coverage on dwellings with certain "incidental" business occupancies (an office, studio, or school). When a homeowners policy is written for one of these permissible "incidental" occupancies, the business exclusion is modified to provide on-premises liability coverage relating to the incidental occupancy by attaching the *Permitted Incidental Occupancies (Residence Premises)* endorsement (HO 04 42).

The *Home Day Care Coverage* endorsement modifies the business activity exclusion to provide coverage for liability arising out of a home day care business operated in the dwelling or another building on the premises.[5]

[4] Some courts have found coverage in instances when an insured shot at one person and hit another. This led to the rewording about injuries "of a different kind" or sustained "by a different person" in the 2000 revision. In addition, the earlier version excluded loss "expected or intended by *the* insured," while the new wording excludes loss "expected or intended by *an* insured." *In Arenson v. National Automobile and Casualty Insurance Co.,* 286 PC. 2d, 816 (1976), the court held that coverage applied where the parent was held liable for the son's intentional damage, despite the exclusion of damage caused intentionally by the insured. The court based its decision on the fact that the insured who was held liable (the parent) had not caused the damage intentionally. It remains to be seen how courts will interpret the new wording.

[5] A mandatory endorsement (HO 04 96, *No Section II—Liability Coverage for Home Day Care Business: Limited Section I—Property Coverage for Home Day Care Business*) is attached to the policy when the Home Day Care Coverage endorsement is not used.

Finally, coverage may be added to the homeowners policy for certain other home businesses under a new *Home Business Coverage Endorsement* (nicknamed the HOBIZ™) introduced by ISO in 1997. This endorsement provides coverage for business property, loss of business income, and general liability coverage appropriate for the home business activity. The business must be owned by the named insured (or by the named insured and a resident relative) or the named insured and a partner who is a resident of the household. Three types of businesses are eligible: offices, service businesses, and sales. Businesses engaged in the manufacture, sale, or distribution of food products or personal care products (e.g., cosmetics) and businesses eligible for coverage under either the Permitted Incidental Occupancy or the Home Day Care Coverage endorsements are ineligible. The business may have no more than three employees and must have receipts of less than $250,000 annually.

When a business exposure exists that cannot be insured under one of these four endorsements, it must be insured under a business liability policy.

5.c. Professional Liability Exclusion 5.c excludes professional liability, such as the liability that might be incurred by a physician, accountant, lawyer, or other professional. The intent of this exclusion is the same as the business pursuits exclusion discussed earlier. The excluded professional exposures must be insured under separate professional liability policies.[6]

5.d. Uninsured Premises A specific exclusion (1.e) eliminates liability arising out of any premises owned or rented to any insured that is not an "insured location." The definition of insured location found in the general conditions states:

4. "Insured location" means
 a. the residence premises.
 b. the part of any other premises, other structures, and grounds used by you as a residence and which is shown in the declarations or which is acquired by you during the policy period for your use as a residence.
 c. any premises used by you in connection with the premises included in 4.a. or 4.b.
 d. any part of a premises not owned by any insured where any insured is temporarily residing.
 e. vacant land owned by or rented to any insured other than farmland.
 f. land owned by or rented to any insured on which a one- or two-family dwelling is being constructed as a residence for any insured.
 g. individual or family cemetery plots or burial vaults of any insured.
 h. any part of a premises occasionally rented to any insured for other than business purposes.

This definition includes, first, the listed residence premises and all other residence premises listed in the policy. This portion needs little analysis.[7] In addition to the residence premises listed, any other residential premises acquired by the insured during the policy term are also included.[8] Premises used in connection with any of the foregoing, such as a garage located elsewhere, are also included as insured premises.

The part of the definition that refers to a part of premises not owned by any insured in which an insured is temporarily residing extends the definition of insured premises to include a hotel or motel room, or perhaps a cabin on a lake that has been rented to the insured for a summer vacation.

The definition also includes vacant land, other than farmland, owned by or rented to any insured. Thus, legal liability arising in connection with a vacant lot owned by the insured is covered automatically in the policy, and there is no requirement that it be listed. Coverage on vacant land even continues following the start of construction of a one- or two-family dwelling on such land, if the dwelling is intended as a residence for an insured.

The next portion of the definition includes individual or family cemetery plots or burial vaults. Since the plot is owned by the insured, if somebody should be hurt there, the insured could have a legal liability.

The final section of the definition—"any part of a premises occasionally rented to any insured for other than business purposes"—would include, for example, a hall rented by an insured for the purpose of holding a reception or a party.

[6] Professional liability insurance is discussed later in the chapter.

[7] In the Condominium Unit-Owners Form 6 only, there is an important difference in the definition of residence premises. Instead of the limitation for other than one- or two-family residences to "that part of (the) building where you reside," the definition reads "a condominium unit where you reside shown as the 'residence premises' in the Declarations."

[8] Coverage on additional premises acquired during the policy period is automatic. However, a small additional premium must be paid by the insured for each one of the premises.

Any premises not falling within any of the sections of this definition are "uninsured locations." However, the best example of an uninsured location would be any residence owned by the insured at the inception of the policy and not declared.

5.e. War The next exclusion (5.e) eliminates coverage for bodily injury or property damage arising out of war, civil war, insurrection, rebellion, revolution, and similar forms of conflict.

5.f. Communicable Disease The communicable disease exclusion (5.f) eliminates coverage for liability arising out of the transmission of a communicable disease by an insured. Prior to the addition of this exclusion, courts had held that such losses are "bodily injury" within the meaning of the policy coverage and that the bodily injury was not expected or intended by the insured.

5.g. Sexual Molestation or Abuse Exclusion 1.k was added to the homeowners policy in the 1990 revision. It excludes bodily injury arising out of sexual molestation, corporal punishment, or physical or mental abuse. Prior to the 1990 revision, the sexual molestation and abuse exclusion was used only in an endorsement that provided liability coverage for the operation of a child care business in the home.

5.h. Controlled Substance Exclusion 5.h. was added in the 1990 revision of the homeowners policy. It excludes liability arising

> out of the use, sale, manufacture, delivery, transfer or possession by any person of a Controlled Substance(s) as defined by the Federal Food and Drug Law at 21 U.S.C.A. Sections 811 and 812. Controlled Substances include but are not limited to cocaine, LSD, marijuana and all narcotic drugs. However, this exclusion does not apply to the legitimate use of prescription drugs by a person following the orders of a licensed physician.

The severity of this exclusion for some people and some lifestyles does not require explanation.

6.a. Assessments and Contractual Liability In addition to the liability that arises out of negligence, liability may be incurred through contractual agreements. For example, a common clause in many leases shifts the liability in connection with premises from the landlord to the tenant or from the tenant to the landlord. Such agreements are called "hold-harmless agreements" because one party agrees to hold the other harmless from liability arising out of the premises. Brown, a tenant, may agree to hold Smith, the landlord, harmless from liability arising out of the premises. Jones is injured as a result of a defect in the premises and brings suit against Smith as the owner. Smith is held liable and is ordered to pay a judgment of $25,000. Under the terms of the hold-harmless agreement, Brown will be required to reimburse Smith. The homeowners forms provide coverage for this exposure through an exception to an exclusion.

Under exclusion 6.a.(1), loss assessments charged against the insured as a member of an association, corporation, or community of property owners is excluded, except to the extent that such loss is covered under the Section II Additional Coverage for Loss Assessment (discussed later in this chapter). Such assessments are a type of contractual liability (since the association would not have the authority to level such assessments in the absence of an agreement by the insured).

Exclusion 6.a.(2) excludes other liability assumed under contract. Then, in two important exceptions to the exclusion, provides a broad form of contractual liability to the insured. The exclusion of liability assumed under contract does not apply to (1) written contracts that relate directly to the ownership, maintenance, and use of an insured location or (2) contracts in which the liability of others is assumed by the insured prior to an occurrence. The first exception provides coverage for the types of assumption discussed in our Smith–Brown example. The second exception provides coverage for other contractual assumptions, as long as the agreement is executed prior to the damage for which liability is assumed and one of the other exclusions of the policy does not apply.

6.b. Property Owned by an Insured Section II of the homeowners, like most liability insurance contracts, excludes property damage to property owned by the insured. This exclusion prevents family members from suing one another for damage to their property.

6.c. Property Rented to, or in the Care of the Insured Damage to property occupied or used by the insured or rented to or in the care, custody, or control of the insured is excluded. Property of others in the insured's custody may be insured under Section I of the homeowners policy (or another form of first-party coverage). This exclusion has one important qualification. An exception to the exclusion

makes it inapplicable to property damage caused by fire, smoke, or explosion. This exception provides what is known as *Fire Legal Liability Insurance,* a special form of coverage designed to protect renters or lessees from claims arising out of fire damage to the rented or leased premises. The fact that the *care, custody, and control exclusion* does not apply to damage caused by fire, smoke, or explosion could be important to an insured who has rented a dwelling or apartment. Coverage would apply both to the building and to furnishings.[9]

6.d. Workers Compensation and Other Statutory Benefits

Exclusion 6.d eliminates payment for bodily injury to persons who are eligible for benefits under a workers compensation, nonoccupational disability, or occupational disease law.[10] The exclusion applies whether the benefits are required by law or the employer has voluntarily purchased workers compensation insurance. Note, however, that only liability under workers compensation is excluded, not injuries to employees. Although workers compensation benefits are excluded, coverage exists for suits by residence employees in jurisdictions where such employees are not covered by the workers compensation law. Residence employees are those employees whose duties relate to the maintenance of the premises, butlers, maids, gardeners, cleaning persons, baby-sitters, and domestic employees. Coverage is provided automatically for two full-time residence employees in the basic premium. An additional premium applies for each employee over two.

6.e. Nuclear Exclusion

The nuclear exclusion was inserted in virtually all liability policies very early in the development of nuclear energy as an alternate source of power and has been subject to much misinterpretation. The exclusion states that the policy does not apply to

> "bodily injury" or "property damage" for which an "insured" under this policy is also an insured under a nuclear energy liability policy...

Note that the exclusion applies only if the insured is also an insured under a nuclear energy liability policy. The initial conclusion might be that the exclusion would, therefore, rarely apply, since homeowners seldom purchase Nuclear Energy Liability policies. However, the Nuclear Energy Liability policy purchased by the nuclear facilities includes an extremely broad definition of persons insured. It includes not only the firm or organization purchasing the policy, but also *anyone* else who might be sued because of a nuclear incident. This means that, in the remote contingency of a suit against an individual, such individual would be protected by the policy carried by the nuclear facility. In short, an insured under the homeowners policy will always be an insured under a Nuclear Liability Policy.

6.f. Injuries to Insured Persons

The injury-to-insured persons exclusion (6.f) eliminates coverage for bodily injury to the named insured, resident relatives, other persons under the age of 21 in the care of the insured and those students who qualify as insureds under the policy. Coverage for suits by one insured against another insured would encourage such suits in situations in which they would not otherwise occur.[11]

Medical Payments to Others

The Medical Payments coverage provides payment for medical expenses incurred by persons who are injured while on the premises with the permission of

[9] The tenant who negligently sets fire to the apartment or dwelling might be sued by the landlord. On the other hand, the landlord may not sue, but collect instead from his or her fire insurance company. What do you suppose the fire insurer will do?

[10] In most states, domestic servants in a private home are not subject to the workers compensation law, but the employer may voluntarily bring them under the law by purchasing the appropriate insurance. In California, New Hampshire, New Jersey, and New York, workers compensation insurance is required for all residence employees, and the coverage may be added to the homeowners policy under a Workers Compensation Endorsement. Other states (Colorado, Connecticut, Delaware, Hawaii, Iowa, Kansas, Kentucky, Maryland, Minnesota, Missouri, New Jersey, Ohio, Oklahoma, South Dakota, Utah, and Washington) also require workers compensation insurance for residence employees working some minimum number of hours or with certain minimum earnings. In these states, the coverage is usually provided under a separate Workers Compensation Policy.

[11] Intrafamily suits were covered before 1984, and insurers were often called on to pay judgments when one family member injured another. Usually, such suits involved actions in which a parent brought suit on behalf of an injured child against the other parent who negligently caused the injury. Sometimes, when permitted, an injured spouse would sue the negligent partner who caused the injury. Although the common-law rule is that one spouse may not sue the other for tort, this rule has been modified in some states. Those states in which a suit may be brought by one spouse against the other are Alabama, Arkansas, California, Colorado, Connecticut, Hawaii, Idaho, Kansas, Kentucky, Minnesota, New Hampshire, New York, North Carolina, North Dakota, Ohio, Oklahoma, South Carolina, South Dakota, and Wisconsin. In Louisiana, a spouse cannot sue the other, but may sue the other's insurer.

any insured or are injured away from the premises if the injury results from an activity of the insured or a member of the insured's family. Coverage for medical payments applies regardless of the insured's liability. The basic limit under the homeowners for this coverage is $1000 per person, which may be increased. The insuring agreement provides that medical payments will be paid under a variety of circumstances:

> We will pay the necessary medical expenses that are incurred or medically ascertained within three years from the date of an accident causing "bodily injury." Medical expenses means reasonable charges for medical, surgical, X-ray, dental, ambulance, hospital, professional nursing, prosthetic devices, and funeral services. This coverage does not apply to you or regular residents of your household except "residence employees." As to others, this coverage applies only:
> 1. to a person on the "insured location" with the permission of an "insured"; or
> 2. to a person off the "insured location," if the "bodily injury":
> a. arises out of a condition on the "insured location" or the ways immediately adjoining;
> b. is caused by the activities of an "insured";
> c. is caused by a "residence employee" in the course of the "residence employee's" employment by an "insured"; or
> d. is caused by an animal owned by or in the care of an "insured."

Medical payments coverage applies regardless of fault. Furthermore, anyone injured within the scope of the coverage may claim directly under the policy. They do not have to have the consent of the named insured to enter a claim. The insuring agreement specifically provides that coverage does not apply to the insured or residents of the insured's household, *other than residence employees*. Residence employees are covered under medical payments for bodily injuries incurred on the premises or off premises if the injury arises out of or in the course of their employment by the insured.

The scope of covered medical expenses is inclusive, including even funeral expenses. The only requirements are that the expenses be "necessary" and that they be incurred or medically ascertained within three years of the accident.

Medical Payments Exclusions The Liability exclusions relating to intentional injuries, business pursuits, professional acts, uninsured premises, aircraft, motor vehicles, watercraft, and war also apply to the

Medical Payments coverage. In addition, four other exclusions apply to the Medical Payments coverage.

7.a. Residence Employees Away from the Premises Medical Payments coverage does not apply to injuries sustained by domestic servants or residence employees when they are away from the insured premises and the injury does not arise out of or in the course of their employment by the insured.

7.b. Workers Compensation and Other Statutory Benefits Just as the Liability section of the policy excluded liability imposed under any workers compensation law, medical benefits payable or required to be paid under any workers compensation, nonoccupational disability, or occupational disease law are excluded. This exclusion applies to any person eligible to receive such benefits, including, for example, workers who come on the premises and who are covered under a Workers Compensation Policy purchased by their employer.

7.c. Nuclear Exclusion …The Nuclear exclusion under Medical Payments excludes coverage for bodily injury resulting from any nuclear reaction, radiation, or radioactive contamination.

7.d. Persons Residing on Premises …The final Medical Payments exclusion excludes coverage for any person other than a residence employee regularly residing at the insured location. The purpose of this exclusion is to eliminate Medical Payments coverage for roomers or boarders and the tenants of an apartment on the premises. However, coverage would exist under the liability section if such persons were injured and brought suit.

Additional Coverages

The Additional Coverages of Section II provides payment for certain additional expenses that may be incurred by the insured in the event of injury or damage to the person or property of others. There are four Additional Coverages under Section II of the homeowners policy: Claim Expenses, First Aid Expenses, Damage to Property of Others, and Loss Assessment.

Claim Expense The insurer promises to pay, in addition to the limit of liability, all expenses incurred in the defense of any suit under the policy, interest on judgments, plus certain other legal costs. These include expenses incurred by the insured in cooperating with the insurer in defending a suit, including loss of earnings up to $50 a day.

First Aid Expenses The *First Aid Expenses coverage* promises to pay expenses incurred by the insured for first aid related to any bodily injury covered under the policy. First aid expenses, like defense costs, are payable in addition to the policy limit.

Damage to Property of Others Coverage *Damage to Property of Others coverage,* like Medical Payments, is not a "liability" coverage. It provides some insurance for damage to the property of others that is caused by an insured, but for which he or she would not be legally liable. It is intended to permit some payment for damage for which the insured feels a moral obligation, even though there is no legal one. It pays, up to $1000, for damage to the property of others that is caused by an insured, regardless of the insured's legal liability. The $1000 limit cannot be increased.

The insuring agreement of this coverage states

> Damage to Property of Others: We will pay up to $1000 per "occurrence" for property damage to property of others caused by an "insured."

Note that the harm must be caused by an insured and that the property must have actually been damaged. If the insured borrows a neighbor's golf clubs and loses one, the loss would not be covered.

Damage to Property of Others Exclusions There are four exclusions relating to this coverage:

Losses Covered under Section I. First, the policy excludes under the damage-to-property-of-others coverage any loss to the extent of any amount recoverable under Section I of the policy. As you will no doubt recall, the definition of insured property under Section I includes not only owned property, but also any property that is used by an insured. If the insured borrows personal property, it may be considered insured property just as if it were owned by the insured. If such property is damaged by one of the perils insured against under Section I, the insured may collect for the damage under that section of the policy. However, subject to the coverage limit, payment can be made under Section II for any part of the loss (including the deductible) that is not covered under Section I. The Damage to Property of Others coverage is excess over Section I, but it permits payment up to the limit for the coverage of any part of the loss not covered by Section I.

Intentional Damage. The coverage does not apply to property damage or destruction that is caused intentionally by any insured who has attained the age of 13. The Intentional Damage exclusion under the liability coverage does not specify any age limit, thus eliminating all intentionally caused damage. Under the Damage to Property of Others coverage, there is coverage up to a limit ($1000) for deliberate damage by insureds under the age of 13.

Owned and Rented Property. Damage to property owned by or rented to any insured, any resident of the insured's household, or any tenant of the insured is also excluded. This is less restrictive than the exclusion of Damage to Property in Care, Custody, or Control of the Insured in the Liability coverage. The Damage to Property of Others exclusion, like the Liability coverage exclusion, cites damage to property owned or rented, but it does not mention property in the care, custody, or control of the insured. This means that coverage would exist for damage to borrowed property up to $1000.

Business Pursuits, Uninsured Locations, and Vehicles. The fourth exclusion relating to this insuring agreement has three parts. It excludes completely any damage from business pursuits of the insured. It also excludes damage resulting from acts or omissions in connection with uninsured owned or rented premises. Finally, it excludes all damage resulting from the ownership, maintenance, or use of a motor vehicle, aircraft, hovercraft, or watercraft. An exception to this last exclusion provides that the exclusion does not apply to non-owned motor vehicles that are not subject to motor vehicle registration.

Loss Illustrations Several illustrations will clarify the intent of this coverage of damage to property of others. First, let us assume that the insured borrows a neighbor's power lawn mower. While mowing the lawn, he inadvertently runs over a large rock and damages the machine extensively. Our insured will be legally liable for the damage, but his liability insurance will not cover the loss because of the Care, Custody, or Control exclusion. But since the loss stemmed from physical damage to the property of others and was caused by an insured, the Damage to Property of Others coverage will be applicable up to $1000. The insurance is thus designed to provide coverage for property damage for which the insured is liable, but that is excluded elsewhere in the contract.

The student, however, should recognize that not all losses involving property of others in the care, custody, or control of the insured are covered. To illustrate, if the borrowed lawn mower had been placed in

the insured's garage overnight and had been stolen, the loss would not be paid, because there would have been no physical injury or destruction caused by an insured. Or if lightning had struck the garage and burned it to the ground, destroying the lawn mower, this loss would not be paid for the same reason.[12]

As a second example, assume that the insured and her two-year-old son are visiting friends. While the adults are talking, the child finds a bottle of laundry bleach, brings it into the living room, and before anyone can react, slams the bottle down on a glass-topped coffee table. The table is broken, as is the bottle, and the bleach damages a part of the rug. The facts would strongly imply that there is no legal liability on the part of the child or his parents, but still the parents might feel a strong moral obligation to pay for the property damage. Unless an insured is legally liable, the liability coverage of the policy would not apply. However, since the loss was caused by an insured (the son), payment would be made up to $1000 under the Damage to Property of Others coverage. The coverage is designed to indemnify for moral obligations like this one, even though no responsibility exists.

As a final illustration, suppose that the insured's tcn-year-old son has a fight with a neighboring child. In revenge, the boy heaves a brick through the neighbor's plate-glass picture window. This loss would not be paid under the liability coverage because it was an intentional act by the insured. However, the coverage for Damage to Property of Others would pay up to $1000, since only intentional acts of insureds who have reached the age of 13 are excluded.

In summary, the coverage provides a limited amount of protection (up to $1000) for Damage to the Property of Others that the insured may have in his or her care, custody, and control. In addition, it provides limited restitution for intentional damage caused by the insured's minor children, provided that they are under 13 years of age. Finally, it serves as some coverage in those cases where there is no legal liability, but in which the insured feels a moral obligation.

Loss Assessment Coverage The Section II Loss Assessment coverage, like the Section I coverage, applies to assessments against the insured by a condominium association or other cooperative body of property owners. Coverage applies for assessments arising out of legal liability of a type that is covered under the terms of the homeowners liability coverage. Coverage is limited to $1000, but an increased limit of coverage is available by endorsement. Coverage is included for the liability of the insured as an elected, uncompensated officer, director, or trustee of the corporation or association of property owners. However, the coverage excludes assessments charged against the insured or the group by any government body.

Section II Conditions

Section II of the homeowners policy is subject to its own set of conditions as well as to the general conditions applicable to both Section I and Section II.

Limit of Liability The Limit of Liability provision states that the limit of liability shown in the declarations for Coverage E is the maximum payable, regardless of the number of insureds involved, claims made, or persons injured. The maximum payable for all medical expenses of one person as the result of one accident will not be more than the limit listed for Coverage F in the declarations.

Severability of Insurance The insurance applies separately to each insured. Historically, this has been interpreted to mean that it is possible for one insured to bring suit against another under the policy. Under the Comprehensive Personal Liability (CPL) form, however, suits by the named insured and residents of the household are specifically excluded.

Duties after Loss In the event of loss, the insured must cooperate with the insurer in several ways. In addition to giving notice of loss to the insurer with information concerning the loss (e.g., name of the claimants and witnesses if possible), the insured is required to forward promptly to the insurer every notice, demand, summons, or other process relating to the loss and, at the company's request, cooperate in making settlement, attending trials, and so on. In addition, the insured may not admit liability or voluntarily make payment or assume any obligations at the time of a bodily injury, other than first aid.

Duties of Insured Persons—Coverage F—Medical Payments to Others A person seeking payment under the medical payments coverage must give written proof of loss, authorize the insurer to obtain medical records, and submit to a physical examination by a doctor of the insurer's choice.

[12] Both the stolen lawnmower and the one destroyed in the fire would be covered under the, Section I property coverage of the insured's homeowners policy.

Payment of Claim—Coverage F Payment of a claim under the Medical Payments coverage is not to be taken as an admission by the insurer of liability on the part of an insured.

Suits against Us No legal action may be brought against the insurer unless the insured has complied with the terms of the policy. Furthermore, a claimant does not have the right to bring the insurer into an action to determine the liability of the insured. The insurer cannot be sued by a claimant until the liability of the insured has been established, either by judgment or by agreement with the insurer.

Bankruptcy of Insured Bankruptcy or insolvency of a covered person does not relieve the insurer of its obligation under the policy. If the insured is sued and declares bankruptcy, thereby discharging his or her portion of a judgment, the insurer is still obligated to pay the part of the judgment that is covered by insurance.

Other Insurance—Coverage E The liability coverage is excess over any other valid and collectible insurance, except for umbrella liability policies or other excess policies that are written specifically to cover on an excess basis.

Cost of Personal Liability Insurance

The cost of *Comprehensive Personal Liability* (CPL) coverage is far less than one might imagine. Although the premium for the liability section of the homeowners policy is included in the basic premium for the policy, the cost per year of a separate CPL policy with the basic $100,000 limit for liability and $1000 for medical payments is about $25. Increasing the limits of liability increases the cost of the policy only slightly. A $300,000 limit raises the cost to about $33, and a $500,000 limit increases the cost only to about $37. Higher limits of coverage are also available from most companies, but when limits in excess of $300,000 or $500,000 are desired, an Umbrella Liability policy is generally used. In view of the catastrophic potential of the liability exposure and the low cost of increased limits, the sophisticated insurance buyer should elect the higher limits.

Optional Personal Liability Endorsements

Although the liability coverage afforded under the homeowners contract satisfactorily insures most of the non-automobile liability exposures of the average individual, a number of optional endorsements are available to broaden the coverage or to deal with the specialized exposures of particular individuals. One of these, the Business Pursuits Endorsement, has already been discussed. A few of the other optional endorsements are discussed in the paragraphs that follow.

Personal Injury Liability Endorsements The basic insuring agreement of the liability section of the homeowners policy, like the separate CPL policy, provides protection against losses resulting from "bodily injury," which is defined as "bodily harm, sickness or disease, including required care, loss of services, and death resulting therefrom." This means that there is no coverage for losses from tort actions such as libel, slander, defamation of character, false arrest, or invasion of the right of privacy, none of which involves bodily harm. Coverage for such suits is provided under a separate form of coverage referred to as Personal Injury Liability. Coverage is provided for three groups of hazards:

1. False arrest, detention, imprisonment, or malicious prosecution

2. Libel, slander, defamation, or violation of the right of privacy

3. Wrongful entry or eviction, or other invasion of the right of private occupancy

The coverage is subject to several exclusions, none of which should cause problems for the average insured. Exclusions apply with respect to (1) liability assumed under contract, (2) violation of law by or with the knowledge of the insured, (3) injury to employees of the insured, (4) business pursuits of the insured, or (5) any civic or public activities performed by an insured.

Premises Rented to Others In the discussion of "insured locations," we noted that all residence premises owned by the insured at the inception of the policy must be declared and an additional premium paid for each. When the insured is the owner of rental property, the basic terms of the policy must be altered to provide liability insurance for bodily injury or property damage arising out of such premises. Separate endorsements are available for additional residences that may be rented and also to extend the insuring agreements to portions of the insured's own residence that are rented to others.

Watercraft and Snowmobile Endorsements
When the insured owns watercraft excluded by the basic provisions of the homeowners policy or a recreational motor vehicle, such as a snowmobile, there is a need for additional liability coverage on these items. Endorsements are available for adding coverage on both watercraft and snowmobiles under the homeowners policy. However, these endorsements provide only liability coverage and do not allow for any reimbursement for the loss of the boat or snowmobile itself. For this reason, the liability coverage for these items is not usually added to the homeowners policy, but it is carried under a separate policy that also provides physical damage coverage.

Homeowners Pollution Endorsements Three new pollution endorsements were introduced in 1997 to address the problem of pollutants such as escaped liquid fuels (e.g., heating oil). The endorsements are designated *Property Remediation for Escaped Liquid Fuel and Limited Lead and Escaped Liquid Fuel Liability Coverages* and differ with respect to the HO form with which they are used.[13] All three endorsements provide both first-party coverage on the owned property and liability insurance.

The first-party coverage provides a $10,000 limit for loss caused by the escape of liquid fuel from a storage system with a minimum capacity of 100 U.S. gallons. Higher limits of coverage are available at an increased cost. Coverage applies for temporary repairs to prevent further escape or to stop the spread of fuel, and for expenses to test, monitor, or assess the effects of escaped fuel that is required by an outside source (such as the EPA or a similar state agency). The loss of market value to a structure is not covered, nor is the loss of liquid fuel or damage from the escape of fuel from a motor vehicle or watercraft.

The liability coverage applies to bodily injury or property damage liability arising out of lead and escaped fuel contamination. Coverage is limited to $50,000, regardless of the policy's Section II limit, but higher levels of coverage are available for an increased premium.

PROFESSIONAL LIABILITY INSURANCE

The term *professional liability* refers to liability arising from a failure to use due care and the degree of skill expected of a person in a particular profession. In cases where there is exposure to bodily injury (as with physicians, surgeons, and dentists), professional liability insurance is normally called malpractice insurance. In instances where the risk involves property damage (including intangible property), the coverage is referred to as errors and omissions insurance; this is applicable to such professions as insurance agents, attorneys, accountants, architects, and real estate agents.[14]

Malpractice Insurance

Malpractice insurance, which is written for physicians, surgeons, dentists, and hospitals, provides the best example of professional liability insurance. The need for such protection is obvious. In addition to liability that may arise because of a professional mistake or error, members of these professions are subject to suits alleging assault and battery for actions taken without the consent of the patient, libel and slander in connection with a breach of professional confidence, false imprisonment or wrongful detention, and invasion of privacy through undue familiarity. There are special forms of coverage available for anesthetists, barbers, beauticians, chiropractors, dental hygienists, masseurs, morticians, nurses, opticians, pharmacists, psychiatrists, radiologists, surgeons, and veterinarians. Time and space do not permit a detailed analysis of the various coverages that are designed to insure the various classes, but a brief examination of Physicians', Surgeons', and Dentists' Professional Liability coverage should suffice to illustrate their nature.

Although there is a standard bureau form of Physicians', Surgeons', and Dentists' Professional Liability coverage, most of the coverage is written by a limited number of companies using their own special forms. Many of the provisions of these forms have been changed in the recent past, primarily as a result of the difficulties encountered by insurers in this field.

[13] HO 05 80 is used for all forms except HO 00 04 and HO 00 06. HO 05 81 is used with HO 00 04 only, and HO 05 82 is used with HO 00 06 only.

[14] Some authors would prefer to treat professional liability coverages in the chapter on commercial contracts.

Several features of these forms deserve comment. First, the policy is not limited to bodily injury or property damage; it includes liability for personal injury losses such as mental anguish where there is no bodily injury. There is not even an exclusion of intentional acts—a logical feature—since the act that gives rise to the liability may be precisely the act that the physician or dentist intended.[15]

At one time, most policies were written to cover errors or mistakes made during the policy period, with no time limit on the discovery of the injury. This resulted in a phenomenon known as the "long tail on losses." If a surgeon left a sponge in a patient and the error was not discovered for 20 years, the insurer providing the insurance at the time of the original operation would be responsible for the loss. This made the pricing of the coverage extremely difficult, particularly in view of the rapidly increasing levels of malpractice awards. Many companies found themselves paying 1970 losses with 1950 premiums. To counter the difficulties resulting from these so-called occurrence form policies, many insurers changed to a *claims-made form,* in which the policy in effect at the time a claim is reported responds for the loss, regardless of when the error was made.

A second feature that has been modified by many insurers is the provision regarding defense and settlement. Under the older policy forms, the insurer was required to obtain the consent of the insured before settling any claim out of court. The reason, of course, was to protect the reputation of the doctor. A voluntary payment of a claim by the insurance company could be interpreted as an admission of fault and could be injurious to the reputation of the physician. Most of the newer policies have deleted the requirement that the insurer obtain consent of the insured before making an out-of-court settlement.

Errors and Omissions Insurance

There is a wide range of professions with a possibility of property damage resulting from the rendering or failure to render professional services. Included within this group are such varied occupations as abstractors, accountants, insurance adjusters, archi-

tects, county clerks and recorders, engineers, insurance agents and brokers, lawyers, real estate agents, stockbrokers, and travel agents. In the case of these professions, errors and *omissions insurance* coverage is available to pay for liability arising out of the performance of the professional duties. Coverage is tailored to the needs of the specific profession. The modern trend is to provide such coverage on a claims-made basis and to delete previous requirements with respect to consent of the insured for out-of-court settlement.

UMBRELLA LIABILITY POLICY

Many persons, particularly professional and well-to-do members of our society, are subject to liability claims of catastrophic proportions. These claims may stem from personal activities or professional or business pursuits and can exceed the limits of the basic liability forms by hundreds of thousands of dollars. The affluent are subject to high jury awards since they are always regarded as fair game for large settlements. To provide catastrophe liability protection for such individuals, insurance companies have developed a personal catastrophe liability contract or, as it is more commonly called, *Umbrella Liability Policy.* Although there is no standard form for the umbrella liability policy, in general it may be described as a broad form of liability insurance, covering both general liability and automobile liability, which is purchased in addition to the separate basic liability contracts.

To qualify for an Umbrella Liability Policy, the insured is required to purchase certain underlying liability insurance. For example, the insurer may require automobile liability insurance with limits of $100,000/$300,000/$50,000 and CPL coverage in the amount of $300,000. If other special exposures exist, coverage will be required for these also in the basic program. For example, if the applicant owns watercraft of the type excluded under the basic CPL, such craft must be insured. The umbrella policy is then written as excess coverage over the limits of the basic policies. The limit of liability under the umbrella may range from $1 million to $5 million.

The Umbrella Liability Policy performs two separate functions, the net effect of which is to superimpose a blanket or umbrella of protection on the individual's other liability coverages. The first function is that of providing "excess coverage" in those

[15] The injury must arise out of rendering or failure to render professional service. Liability arising from other causes is not covered, which means that professional liability coverage is not a substitute for other forms of liability insurance. It is a coverage that is purchased in addition to other general liability coverage.

instances in which a liability loss covered under the basic policies exceeds the limit of those policies. For example, if the insured is the object of a liability claim for $500,000 that is covered by either the homeowners policy or automobile insurance, the basic liability policies involved would respond for the first $300,000, and the umbrella would pay the remaining $200,000.

The second function of the umbrella is to establish broader coverage than that provided under the basic contracts. Although there is no standard umbrella contract and it is, therefore, difficult to generalize, most such policies are written with broad insuring agreements and are subject to fewer exclusions than the basic policies, so that many losses normally excluded under the basic contracts are covered under the umbrella. For example, the automobile liability coverage applies worldwide, with no restrictions regarding the type or use of the automobile.[16] In addition, the coverage is usually written to include personal injury hazards and blanket contractual liability.[17]

When a liability claim is covered under the umbrella, but not by one of the underlying contracts, the umbrella will respond, subject to a self-insured retention or deductible. The size of this deductible varies considerably among companies. On most personal umbrellas, it was originally $5000 or $10,000, but several companies now market policies with a

retention as low as $250. It should be noted that this deductible applies only where the loss is not covered by the basic contracts. If the loss is covered under the basic contracts, the umbrella responds from the first dollar once these policies are exhausted.

Exclusions under the Umbrella Liability Policy

Although the coverage under the Umbrella Liability Policy is far broader than that of the individual contracts, it does not cover all risks. There are exclusions, and some of them are rather important. There is an exclusion of owned or leased aircraft, watercraft of the type excluded under the basic homeowners policy, business pursuits, and professional services—unless coverage for these exposures has been provided in the underlying insurance program. If such coverage is afforded by the underlying program, these exposures are covered by the umbrella. In addition, workers compensation obligations are generally excluded; however, as in the case of the underlying CPL or homeowners policy, employers liability coverage is provided. Any act committed by, or at, the direction of the insured with the intent to cause personal injury or property damage is excluded also. With the exception of aircraft or watercraft, there is no exclusion of property rented to or in the care, custody, and control of the insured; however, damage to rented or borrowed aircraft and watercraft is excluded. Finally, damage to property owned by the insured is excluded.

Cost of the Umbrella

Despite the high limits and the extreme broadness of the insuring agreement, the cost of the Umbrella Liability Policy is not excessive. Although the premium will vary somewhat with the occupation of the insured and certain other variables such as the number of automobiles in the family, usually the annual cost is less than $100.

[16] As the reader will become aware of in Chapter 29, the automobile policy limits coverage to the United States and Canada and imposes restrictions on the type and use of automobiles that are covered.

[17] The breadth of umbrella liability policies is (perhaps) illustrated by the fact that two personal umbrella policies paid $1.5 million of the legal bills incurred by former President Clinton in the Paula Jones case. Umbrella liability policies were issued to the Clintons by State Farm Insurance Company and Pacific Indemnity Insurance Company (a subsidiary of Chubb Group Insurance). See http://www.washingtonpost.com/wp-srv/politics/special/pjones/stories/pj091097.htm and http://www.spectator.org/archives/96-06_york.html.

IMPORTANT CONCEPTS TO REMEMBER

third-party coverage	motor vehicles	care, custody, and control exclusion
general liability insurance	negligent entrustment	Medical Payments to Others
business pursuits	Comprehensive Personal Liability	coverage
Business Pursuits endorsement	contractual liability	personal injury
insured location	fire legal liability insurance	single limit of liability

communicable disease exclusion
intrafamily suits
damage to property of others
claim expense
first aid expense
Loss Assessment coverage

Personal Injury Liability
professional liability
errors and omissions
Umbrella Liability Policy
professional liability insurance
malpractice insurance

long tail
occurrence form
claims-made form
errors and omissions insurance

QUESTIONS FOR REVIEW

1. Why is liability insurance sometimes called *third-party* coverage?

2. Briefly explain the definition of the term *premises* as used in the homeowners policy with respect to Section II (liability) coverages.

3. Who is included within the definition of "persons insured" under Section II of the homeowners policy?

4. Briefly describe the coverage provided under the Medical Payments coverage under Section II of the homeowners policy. To whom does the coverage apply? To whom does it not apply?

5. Jones is playing golf and runs over her partner's foot with a rented golf cart. Will the Personal Liability coverage or the Medical Payments coverage respond for the injury?

6. What coverage exists under Section II of the homeowners policy for those situations in which the insured feels a moral obligation but where no legal obligation exists?

7. Jones owns a vicious German shepherd. The dog bites a mail carrier about three blocks away from Jones' premises. Discuss fully the coverage under Section II of the homeowners policy for this occurrence.

8. Briefly describe the Fire Legal Liability coverage found in Section II of the homeowners policy. To whom does it apply? What factors create the need for this coverage?

9. Explain the nature of the personal umbrella liability policy. In your explanation, be sure to point out the relationship of the umbrella to the underlying coverage and the application of the deductible.

10. Distinguish between a *claims-made* malpractice policy and an *occurrence* policy. What factors prompted the development of the most recent of the two?

QUESTIONS FOR DISCUSSION

1. For each of the following losses, indicate whether or not coverage would exist under Coverage E, the liability coverage, of Section II of the homeowners policy:

a. A young lady of the insured's acquaintance brings suit against him because of scurrilous remarks that he made about her virtue.

b. A cleaning lady slips on the wet bathroom floor in the insured's home and brings suit to collect for her injuries.

c. The insured throws a party at which one of the guests has too much to drink and injures a pedestrian while driving home. The injured party brings suit against the insured because the driver became intoxicated at the insured's party.

d. The insured borrows a motorboat powered by an 85-horsepower outboard motor and runs over a water-skier, who then brings suit.

e. The insured's wife borrows a friend's mink stole and negligently burns a hole in it with a lighted cigar. The friend demands payment.

2. For each of the following losses, indicate whether or not coverage would exist under Coverage F, the Medical Payments coverage, of Section II of the homeowners policy:

a. The insured's 65-year-old mother-in-law, who is living in his house, falls down the basement stairs and is injured.

b. The insured's dog playfully nips a mail carrier, whose wounds require 14 stitches.

c. The insured's cleaning lady mistakes a bottle of cleaning fluid for gin and has to have her stomach pumped.

d. The insured's babysitter slips on a loose throw rug while carrying the insured's child, and both are injured.

3. For each of the following losses, indicate whether or not coverage would exist under the supplementary coverage for Damage to the Property of Others.

a. The insured borrows a neighbor's lawn mower; while it is left outside overnight, it is stolen.

b. The insured's nine-year-old son pours sugar in his teacher's gas tank, resulting in extensive damage to the auto's engine.

c. The insured accidentally spills a glass of bourbon on his neighbor's dress, which is ruined as a result of the chemical reaction.

d. The insured backs his car over a neighbor's child's wagon, and although it is hardly worth a lawsuit, the insured would like to pay for the damage.

4. A friend, explaining his position with respect to liability insurance, states, "I don't feel that I really need high limits of liability, because I don't make that much money. If I were a doctor or a lawyer, I would carry higher limits of liability coverage, but since I am not, the $100,000 minimum included in my homeowners policy is enough." Do you agree or disagree? Why?

5. Mary Somers babysits for working mothers. She has 11 small children, ages two to four, in her care. She is concerned about potential liability if one of the children should be injured and wonders if her homeowners policy provides any coverage. What advice would you give her?

SUGGESTIONS FOR ADDITIONAL READING

Fire, Casualty and Surety Bulletins. Personal Lines Volume. Cincinnati, Ohio: National Underwriter Company. (Loose-leaf manual service with monthly supplements.) See "Dwelling" section.

Hamilton, Karen L., and Donald S. Malecki. *Personal Insurance: Property and Liability.* Malvern, Pa.: American Institute for CPCU, 1994. Chapter 3.

Launie, J. J., George E. Rejda, and Donald R. Oakes with Anita W. Johnson. *Personal Insurance.* Bryn Mawr, Pa.: Insurance Institute of America, 1991. Chapter 5.

Policy, Form, and Manual Analysis Service. Personal Lines Volume. Indianapolis, Ind.: Rough Notes Company. (Loose-leaf manual service with monthly supplements.) See "Dwellings" section.

Wood, Glenn L., Claude C. Lilly, III, Donald S. Malecki, Edward E. Graves, and Jerry S. Rosenbloom, *Personal Risk Management and Insurance,* 4th ed., vol 2. Malvern, Pa.: American Institute for Property and Liability Underwriters, 1989. Chapter 4.

WEB SITES TO EXPLORE

Best's Review-Property/Casualty Edition	http://www.ambest.com/review/lh/index.html
Independent Insurance Agents of America, Inc.	http://www.iiaa.org
Insurance News Network	http://www.insure.com/
National Association of Professional Insurance Agents	http://www.pianet.com/
Rough Notes Company	http://www.roughnotes.com/

THE AUTOMOBILE AND ITS LEGAL ENVIRONMENT

It's the Model T Ford made the trouble.

— MEREDITH WILSON
The Music Man

CHAPTER OBJECTIVES

When you have finished this chapter, you should be able to

- Explain the special provisions of tort law applicable to automobiles
- Explain the principles of vicarious liability and the special provisions applicable to guests
- Explain the legal requirements imposed by the states regarding automobile liability insurance
- Explain the no-fault concept and the basic philosophy on which this concept is based, and evaluate the arguments for and against no-fault laws
- Explain the differences among the approaches to reform of the automobile reparations system that have been adopted by the states
- Discuss the various systems for providing insurance to high-risk drivers
- Discuss the automobile insurance classification system and how rates are affected by various underwriting factors

The automobile is the most widely owned major asset in the United States. It is also one of the chief sources of economic loss. The ownership or operation of an automobile exposes the individual to many sources of loss: A person may be killed or injured while operating a car, or being struck by one, with resulting medical expenses and loss of income; one may also be held legally liable for injuries to others or for damage to the property of others; the car itself may be damaged, destroyed, or stolen.

In this chapter, we begin our study of automobile insurance with an examination of the legal principles governing the operation of the automobile, including a brief discussion of the no-fault laws that have been adopted by many states. In the next chapter, we will look at the automobile insurance policy itself.

Before turning to the legal environment, it may be helpful to review briefly the general nature of the automobile coverages available to protect against loss arising out of the automobile.

A BRIEF OVERVIEW OF AUTOMOBILE COVERAGES

For the purpose of our discussion that follows, it will be helpful if the reader will keep in mind the distinctions among the following four automobile insurance coverages: Automobile liability insurance, medical payments coverage, physical damage coverage, and uninsured motorists coverage.

Automobile Liability Insurance

Automobile liability insurance protects the insured against loss arising from legal liability when his or her automobile injures someone or damages another's property. This coverage is usually written today with a single limit similar to that of the homeowners policy, but it is also written subject to "split limits," usually expressed as $10,000/$20,000/$5000, or more simply as $10/$20/$5. The first two figures refer to the bodily injury liability limit, and the third refers to the property damage limit. Thus, $10/$20/$5 means that coverage is provided up to $10,000 for injury to one person and up to $20,000 for all persons injured in a single accident, and that property damage up to $5000 is payable for a single accident.

Medical Payments Coverage

Automobile medical payments coverage reimburses the insured and members of the insured's family for medical expenses that result from automobile accidents. The protection also applies to other occupants of the insured's automobile. Like the medical payments of the homeowners policy, automobile medical payments coverage is distinct from the liability coverage; it applies as a special form of accident insurance. Unlike the homeowners insurance, the coverage applies specifically to the insured and members of his or her family. It is written with a maximum limit per person per accident, which usually ranges from $500 to $5000.

Physical Damage Coverage

Automobile physical damage coverage insures against loss of the policyholder's own automobile and in this sense resembles Section I of the homeowners program. The coverage is written under two insuring agreements, (1) Other Than Collision (formerly called Comprehensive) and (2) Collision. Collision, as the name implies, indemnifies for collision losses; Other Than Collision is a form of open-perils coverage that provides protection against most other insurable perils. Physical damage coverage applies to the insured auto regardless of fault. If the other driver is at fault, the insured who carries collision coverage has the option of proceeding against the other driver or collecting under his or her own collision and permitting the insurance company to subrogate. If the other driver is held liable, his or her property damage liability coverage will pay the loss.

Uninsured Motorists Coverage

Uninsured motorists coverage is an imaginative form of auto insurance, under which the insurer agrees to pay the insured, up to specified limits, the amount the insured could have collected from a negligent driver who caused injury, when that driver is uninsured or is guilty of hit and run. Uninsured motorists coverage usually has the same limits as the bodily injury coverage in the liability section of the policy.

Understanding the following discussion will be much easier with a firm grasp of the distinctions among these four coverages.

LEGAL LIABILITY AND THE AUTOMOBILE

The liability of the owner or operator of an automobile is largely governed by the principles of negligence discussed in Chapter 27. However, special laws affecting automobile liability have been enacted to modify some of the basic principles of negligence. Several of these statutes relate to the responsibility of others when the driver is negligent. In addition, some laws deal with the liability of the operator toward passengers.

Vicarious Liability and the Automobile

As you will recall from Chapter 27, vicarious liability describes a situation in which one party becomes liable for the negligence of another. When one thinks of being held liable for the operation of a motor vehicle, one normally has in mind a situation in which he

or she is the driver. However, because of vicarious liability laws and doctrines, it is possible for an individual to be held liable in situations where someone else is the operator. First, if the driver of the automobile is acting as an agent for another person, the principal may be held liable for the acts of the agent. In addition to this imputed or vicarious liability, the owner of an auto that is being operated by someone else may be held liable because of his or her own negligence, either in furnishing the auto to someone known to be an incompetent driver or in lending a car known to be unsafe. In addition to these situations based on common law principles, vicarious liability laws have been enacted by various states that greatly enlarge the exposure of imputed liability in connection with the automobile.

Under the *family purpose doctrine,* applicable in 18 states and the District of Columbia,[1] the owner of an automobile is held liable for the negligent acts of the members of his or her immediate family or household in their operation of the car. The family purpose doctrine is basically a part of the principal-agent relationship, in that any member of the family is considered to be an agent of the parent-owner when using the family car, even for the driver's own convenience or amusement. Somewhat related to the family purpose doctrine, about half the states[2] impose liability on the parents of a minor or on any person who signs a minor's application for a driver's license for any damage arising out of the operation of any automobile by that minor. Note that in this situation it is not only driving of the family car, but of any car, that gives rise to the vicarious liability. Other states[3] have enacted statutes that go farther and make any person furnishing an auto to a minor responsible for the negligent acts of that minor in the operation of the automobile. The most sweeping vicarious liability laws are the *permissive use statutes,* enforced in 12 states and the District of Columbia, which impose liability on the owner of an automobile for any liability arising out of someone's operating it

with the owner's permission, regardless of the operator's age.[4]

One point bears mention again. The vicarious liability laws and doctrines do not relieve the driver of responsibility; they merely make the other party (owner or parent) jointly liable.

Guest Hazard Statutes

The second statutory modification of the principles of legal liability affecting the automobile defines the liability of a driver or owner toward passengers in the car. At one time, most states had so-called *guest laws,* which restricted the right of a passenger in an automobile to sue the owner or the driver.[5] The original reason for such laws was the allegation of insurers that suits by passengers presented an opportunity to defraud insurance companies. Without such laws, it was alleged, the guest in an automobile who is injured might easily induce the driver to admit liability in return for a portion of the settlement the driver's insurance company might make with the injured guest.

Under a standard guest law, the injured guest can collect from the negligent driver only if the driver was operating the auto in a grossly negligent manner or, in some jurisdictions, if the driver was intoxicated. Gross negligence is a "complete and total disregard for the safety of oneself or others." Even in the case of gross negligence, the guest may be denied recovery if he or she assumes the risk involved in it. Some laws provide that the failure of the guest to protest against the grossly negligent manner in which the auto is being operated constitutes acceptance of the risk.

Although there is room for disagreement, many observers believe that the guest statutes are ill-conceived laws. They were the result of a rash of state legislation in the 1920s and 1930s, the fruit of vigorous lobbying by the insurance industry. Although a few collusive suits may have been prevented over the years, tens of thousands of "guests" have been denied

[1] Arizona, Colorado, Connecticut, Georgia, Kentucky, Michigan, Minnesota, Nebraska, Nevada, New Jersey, New Mexico, North Carolina, North Dakota, Oregon, South Carolina, Tennessee, Washington, West Virginia, and the District of Columbia.

[2] Alaska, Arizona, Arkansas, California, Colorado, Delaware, Florida, Hawaii, Idaho, Indiana, Kentucky, Maryland, Mississippi, Montana, Nevada, New Mexico, North Dakota, Ohio, Oklahoma, Rhode Island, South Carolina, Tennessee, Texas, Utah, and Wisconsin.

[3] Delaware, Idaho, Kansas, Maine, Pennsylvania, and Utah.

[4] California, Connecticut, Florida, Idaho, Iowa, Massachusetts, Michigan, Minnesota, New York, North Carolina, Rhode Island, Tennessee, and the District of Columbia.

[5] States that have enacted guest laws include Alabama, Arkansas, California, Colorado, Delaware, Florida, Idaho, Illinois, Indiana, Iowa, Kansas, Michigan, Montana, Nebraska, Nevada, New Mexico, North Dakota, Ohio, Oregon, South Carolina, South Dakota, Texas, Utah, Vermont, Virginia, Washington, and Wyoming. In addition, the doctrine is applied by the courts in Georgia, although there is no statutory provision.

access to the courts for recovery of compensation for their injuries. No U.S. state has adopted a new guest law for many years; in many states the laws have been repealed or declared unconstitutional.[6] In those states where they still exist, the courts are now tending to construe them more narrowly.

Automobile Liability Insurance and the Law

As late as 1971, only Massachusetts, North Carolina, and New York had *compulsory automobile liability insurance laws.* However, with the enactment of the no-fault laws discussed later in this chapter, many legislatures also made automobile liability insurance compulsory. By 2002, 48 states and the District of Columbia had laws requiring the owners of automobiles registered in the state to have liability insurance or, sometimes, an approved substitute form of security.[7]

Before the widespread enactment of compulsory auto insurance laws, most states attempted to solve the problem of the financial responsibility of drivers through what are known as *financial responsibility laws.* These laws require a driver to show proof of insurance (or some other approved form of security) when he or she is involved in an accident. Because they require proof of "financial responsibility" only after an accident, these laws are sometimes called *free-bite laws.* Most states that have enacted compulsory auto insurance laws retained their financial responsibility law, and drivers are subject to the requirements of both.[8]

In most states, the financial responsibility laws take the form of a "security-type" law. It provides that any driver involved in an auto accident that causes bodily injury or damage to the property of others (the latter must exceed a specified minimum, usually $100 or $200) must demonstrate the ability to pay any judgment resulting from the accident or lose his or her license. If a driver's license is suspended, then security for future accidents must be posted before it will be restored. The financial responsibility laws apply to all parties in an accident, even those who do not appear to have been at fault.

The requirements of the law will be met if an insurer files a certificate (called an *SR-21*) indicating that, at the time of the accident, the driver had liability insurance with limits that meet the state's requirements. The limits of liability required by the various states and Canadian provinces in 2002 are indicated in Table 29.1. If the driver cannot provide evidence of insurance, the requirements of the law can be met by depositing security (money) with the specified authority in an amount determined by the authority. A person who does not have liability insurance and cannot make any other arrangements for settlement of the loss will lose his or her driving privileges.[9] Driving privileges remain suspended until any judgment arising out of the accident is satisfied and until proof of financial responsibility for future accidents is demonstrated. Judgments are deemed satisfied, regardless of the amounts awarded, when the payment equals the required liability limits. The requirement that any judgment be satisfied may also be met by filing with the authority (1) signed forms releasing the driver from all liability for claims resulting from the accident, (2) a certified copy of a final judgment of nonliability, or (3) a written agreement with all claimants providing for payment in installments of an agreed amount for claims resulting from the accident. Financial responsibility for future accidents normally is proven by the purchase of automobile liability insurance in the limits prescribed by the state. The insurance company then submits a certificate, an *SR-22,* showing that the insurance is in force. Financial responsibility may also be demonstrated by posting a surety bond or, as a final resort, by the deposit of a stipulated amount of cash or securities (for instance, $25,000 or $50,000) with the proper authorities. The length of time for which proof is required varies from state to state, but the usual time is 3 years.

In many states, a person's driver's license may also be revoked or suspended if a person is convicted of

[6] Vermont was the first state in 33 years to repeal a guest law, which it did in 1970. After the California Supreme Court's unanimous opinion in *Brown v. Merlo* (506 P. 2d 212 Cal., 1973), the laws of the following states were repealed or declared unconstitutional: Arkansas, Colorado, Florida, Idaho, Iowa, Kansas, Michigan, Montana, New Mexico, North Dakota, Ohio, Oregon, South Dakota, Vermont, Virginia, Washington, and Wyoming.

[7] The states without compulsory auto insurance laws are New Hampshire and Wisconsin.

[8] All states except Kansas, Maryland, Massachusetts, and Minnesota have some form of financial responsibility law (and these four states have compulsory insurance laws).

[9] The financial responsibility law of a particular state applies to nonresidents who have accidents in the state. The suspension of the license and registration of a nonresident normally affect driving privileges only in that state. But some states have reciprocal provisions, and if the nonresident's home state has reciprocity, his or her license and registration will be suspended in the home state as well.

TABLE 29.1 **State Financial Responsibility Limits, 2002**

United States: States	Liability Limits[a]	United States: States	Liability Limits[a]
Alabama	$20/40/10 or 50,000	Montana	$25/50/10
Alaska	50/100/25 or 125	Nebraska	25/50/25
Arizona	15/30/10	Nevada	15/30/10
Arkansas	25/50/15	New Hampshire	25/50/25
California	15/30/5[b]	New Jersey	15/30/5
Colorado	25/50/15	New Mexico	25/50/10
Connecticut	20/40/10	New York	25/50/10[c]
Delaware	15/30/10	North Carolina	30/60/25
District of Columbia	25/50/10	North Dakota	25/50/25
Florida	10/20/10 or 30	Ohio	12.5/25/7.5
Georgia	25/50/25	Oklahoma	10/20/10
Hawaii	20/40/10	Oregon	25/50/10
Idaho	25/50/15	Pennsylvania	15/30/5
Illinois	20/40/15	Rhode Island	25/50/25
Indiana	25/50/10	South Carolina	15/30/5
Iowa	20/40/15	South Dakota	25/50/25
Kansas	25/50/10	Tennessee	25/50/10
Kentucky	25/50/10 or 60	Texas	20/40/15
Louisiana	10/20/10	Utah	25/50/15
Maine	50/100/25	Vermont	25/50/10
Maryland	20/40/10	Virginia	25/50/20
Massachusetts	20/40/5	Washington	25/50/10
Michigan	20/40/10	West Virginia	20/40/10
Minnesota	30/60/10	Wisconsin	25/50/10
Mississippi	10/20/5	Wyoming	25/50/20
Missouri	25/50/10		

Canada: Provinces	Liability Limits[a]	Canada: Provinces	Liability Limits[a]
Alberta	$200,000	Nova Scotia	$200,000
British Columbia	200,000	Ontario	200,000
Manitoba	200,000	Prince Edward Island	200,000
New Brunswick	200,000	Quebec	50,000
Newfoundland	200,000	Saskatchewan	200,000
Northwest Territories	200,000	Yukon	200,000

[a] The first two figures refer to bodily injury liability limits and the third figure to property damage. For example, $25/50/10 means coverage up to $50,000 for all persons injured in an accident, subject to a limit of $25,000 for one individual and $10,000 coverage for property damage.

[b] Requirements for low-income drivers in Los Angeles and San Francisco who are covered by the California Automobile Assigned Risk Plan are 10/20/3, effective July 1, 2000, to January 1, 2004.

[c] $50/100 for wrongful death.

certain traffic violations. After the period of suspension, the restoration of the license requires proof of financial responsibility. This can be accomplished as was just discussed. Offenses leading to suspension vary among the states. Practically all states suspend licenses for driving while intoxicated, reckless driving, conviction of a felony in which a motor vehicle was used, operating a car without the owner's permission, or for a series of lesser offenses.

Insurance for High-Risk Drivers

For most American motorists, purchasing automobile insurance is fairly routine. Although the cost of the insurance may be irritating, there are many insurers that are willing to take the insured's premium dollars. There are some people, however, who find that insurers are generally unwilling to assume their risk and who have difficulty in obtaining auto-

mobile insurance. This is particularly true of youthful male drivers and some people who must demonstrate financial responsibility under state laws. It is also true of people whose poor driving records mark them as more hazardous risks than the average of the classification to which they would otherwise belong.

Automobile insurance companies, like most other businesses, want to make a profit, or at least cover all expenses of their business operations. They cannot do this if they accept a large number of applicants whose probability of loss is greater than the average. Yet if these high-risk drivers were to remain uninsured, their presence on the road would represent a financial risk not only to themselves but also to others who might be involved in the same accident.

The insurance industry has been concerned that if it does not provide coverage for high-risk drivers, a government plan might be instituted to do so. If the state undertook to insure high-risk drivers, it might decide to insure standard drivers as well, and private automobile insurance might disappear altogether. For these and other reasons, the insurance industry has established mechanisms to provide the necessary coverages for drivers who are unable to buy insurance through normal market channels. The most successful and widely used method of providing auto insurance to high-risk drivers is the *Automobile Insurance Plan,* now in operation in 42 states and the District of Columbia. Essentially, these are applicant-sharing plans under which each automobile insurance company doing business in the state accepts a share of the state's high-risk drivers. These systems were originally used in all states, but since 1972, eight states have introduced other methods for providing such insurance.

Automobile Insurance Plans An Automobile Insurance Plan is a risk-sharing pool in which all auto insurers operating in a particular state share in writing those drivers who do not meet normal underwriting standards.[10] It serves two functions. The first is to make auto liability insurance (and often other forms of auto insurance as well) available to those who cannot obtain it through normal channels. The second is to establish a procedure for the equitable distribution of these insureds among all the auto liability insurers in the state.[11]

With respect to the first function, the applicant must certify on a prescribed form that he or she has attempted, within 60 days before the application, to obtain liability insurance, but without success. In 38 states, coverage is provided to any applicant who presents a valid driver's license. In the remaining states, certain applicants, like habitual traffic violators, are ineligible. If the applicant is eligible, a company will be assigned to underwrite the insurance. The designated insurer will be obligated to provide coverage with limits equal to the financial responsibility requirements of the state law. In most states, the insurer will provide limits higher than the minimum required by state law. In addition, although the plans were originally designed to provide only liability insurance, all the plans provide medical payments (or no-fault benefits) and most states offer Physical Damage coverage on the insured's own car.

An applicant cannot be assigned to a company for longer than 3 years, and the insurer may cancel an assigned risk under certain circumstances. The right to cancel is usually permitted only for nonpayment of premium, loss of the driver's license, or a number of major offenses while operating a motor vehicle.

The second function of the plan is to distribute the risks equitably among all automobile insurers operating in the state. This is accomplished by assigning to a particular insurer the percentage of the assigned-risk premiums that its total liability premiums bear to the total liability premiums of all automobile insurers operating in the state. Thus, if a particular company has 1/20 of all liability premiums written in the state, it would be assigned 1/20 of the risks. While this is only one of the methods of distribution available, it appears to be working reasonably well.

Alternate Approaches Although the Automobile Insurance Plans exist in 42 states, 8 states use alternate systems for insuring high-risk drivers. In Maryland the insurance is available through a state-operated fund. The remaining seven states use one of two loss-sharing plans.

[10] These plans were originally called *Assigned Risk Plans,* but the name was changed to eliminate the stigma of being insured through a mechanism with "risk" in its title.

[11] Automobile Assigned Risk Plans were organized by insurers as voluntary risk-sharing mechanisms, but were later made compulsory. A U.S. Supreme Court decision in 1951 upheld the constitutionality of compulsory assigned risk plans in *California State Automobile Association Inter-Insurance Bureau, Appellant, v John R. Maloney, Insurance Commissioner,* 340 U.S. 105; 71 Sup. Ct. 601; 95 Law Ed. 788.

- **Reinsurance Pools.** In Massachusetts, New Hampshire, North Carolina, and South Carolina, all auto insurers participate in statewide automobile reinsurance pools, generally called the *facility*. Under this reinsurance system, every company accepts all applicants—good and bad. If the company considers a particular driver a high risk, it may place that driver in the statewide reinsurance pool. When this is done, all premiums paid and losses incurred by that driver are absorbed by the pool, but the policy is serviced by the originating company. The chief advantages to this system are that the stigma of purchasing insurance through an "assigned risk plan" is eliminated and the consumer may deal with the company of his or her choice.

- **Joint Underwriting Associations.** Three states—Florida, Hawaii, and Missouri—use a *joint underwriting association* approach to the problem of providing insurance for high-risk drivers.[12] Under this system, each agent or broker has access to a company that has been designated as a servicing company for high-risk drivers. A limited number of companies provide statewide service and claim handling facilities for the high-risk drivers, but all automobile insurers in the state share in the losses. Like the reinsurance facility plans outlined, the joint underwriting association operates on the principle of sharing losses rather than sharing applicants.

Experience under the Plans As might be expected, the automobile insurance plans and the alternate loss-sharing arrangements have consistently experienced heavy dollar losses, currently more than $1 billion a year. These financial losses are passed on to other drivers in higher auto insurance rates. In a sense, the various plans all represent a continuing subsidy to problem drivers by other insureds.

Distress Risk Companies Although Automobile Insurance Plans provide a mechanism for insuring high-risk drivers, there are some drivers who are uninsurable even by the Automobile Insurance Plans and the alternative facilities in the other states. To purchase insurance coverage to meet the requirements of the state financial responsibility law, these persons must turn to what is commonly known as a distress risk company. Usually, these insurers specialize in insuring high-risk drivers. They have special ratings in which the premiums can attain almost incredible proportions and special policy forms that may be very limited. The distress risk companies perform a service, at least to the extent that they are making automobile liability insurance possible at some price.

THE AUTOMOBILE INSURANCE PROBLEM AND CHANGES IN THE TORT SYSTEM

It is not at all unusual to hear complaints about automobile insurance today. Almost everyone connected with the automobile insurance business has what they consider to be a legitimate grievance. Insurance companies complain that they are losing money because of inadequate rates. The buyers complain that the rates are already too high. Young drivers (and to some extent older ones) complain that they frequently have difficulty in obtaining coverage. Finally, many who have suffered losses maintain that the settlements do not measure up to the economic loss. With all this dissatisfaction, it is not surprising that proposals for change have found widespread support.

Criticisms of the Traditional System

Dissatisfaction with auto insurance generally has fueled a debate that has been going on now since the mid-1960s. The debate has culminated in the passage of automobile *no-fault laws* or other legislation reforming automobile accident reparation in about half the states. While a part of the criticism has been aimed at insurance, some of the critics contend that the problem today is not so much with insurance as such, but rather with our method of compensating the injured. These critics maintain that our tort system is wasteful, expensive, unfair, and excessively time consuming, and they recommend that we abolish it for automobile accidents.

The effectiveness and rationale of the negligence approach have been questioned since the *Columbia Report* of 1932,[13] which pointed to many shortcom-

[12] New Jersey established a type of joint underwriting association known as the New Jersey Automobile Full Underwriting Association in 1984, but replaced it with an Automobile Insurance Plan in 1990.

[13] Columbia Council for Research in the Social Sciences, *Report by the Committee to Study Compensation for Automobile Accidents* (New York: Columbia University, 1932).

ings of the tort system. One major criticism of that report, and also of today's critics, is that many persons who are injured remain uncompensated or are inadequately compensated. The accident victim may be unable to obtain reimbursement because he or she was contributorily negligent, because the guilty party is insolvent, or because the guilty party is unknown, as in the case of a hit-and-run driver. Additionally, the amount of compensation that is awarded may depend more on the skill of the victim's attorney than on the facts. Other criticisms of our traditional system attack the high cost of operating the insurance mechanism, the contingency fee system, and the congestion of the courts that results in long delays before the injured are finally compensated. Furthermore, the critics maintain that the traditional system is inequitable and that insurers overpay small claims to avoid litigation, but resist large claims in which the victim is seriously injured. Finally, the critics contend, the system is too expensive, paying more for the operation of insurance companies and the work of attorneys than it delivers to those who are injured.

For these reasons, the tort system has been under attack, and many proposals have been made to substitute a no-fault compensation system. Such proposals are not new, but they have generated increased interest since the middle of the 1960s, and, as noted, many states have actually adopted no-fault laws.

The No-Fault Concept

The easiest way to understand the no-fault idea is to contrast it with the traditional tort system. Under the tort system, if you are involved in an accident and the accident is your fault, you may be held liable for injury to others or damage to their property. If you are found liable, you will be required to compensate the injured party through payment of damages. If you have liability insurance, your insurance company will pay for the other party's injuries. If the other party is found to have been negligent, his or her company will pay for your damages. If you are injured through your own negligence, you must bear the loss yourself, either out of existing resources or under some form of first-party insurance where the insurance company makes direct payment to you.

Under a *no-fault system,* there is no attempt to fix blame or to place the burden of the loss on the party causing it; each party collects for any injuries sustained from his or her own insurance company. Under a pure no-fault system, the right to sue the driver who caused an accident would be entirely abolished, and both the innocent victim and the driver at fault would recover their losses directly from their own insurance. Compulsory first-party coverage would compensate all accident victims regardless of fault.[14] Although some no-fault proposals have included abolition of tort actions for damage to automobiles, the principal focus has been on bodily injuries.

Differences among Proposals Although the basic no-fault concept is simple enough, several modifications of the idea have developed, and there are significant differences among the various proposals. We can distinguish among three different approaches.

1. *Pure No-Fault Proposals.* Under a pure no-fault plan, the tort system would be abolished for bodily injuries arising from auto accidents. (Some proposals would also abolish tort actions for damage to automobiles.) Anyone suffering loss would seek recovery for medical expenses, loss of income, or other expenses from his or her own insurer. Recovery for general damages (pain and suffering) would be eliminated.

2. *Modified No-Fault Proposals.* Modified no-fault proposals would provide limited immunity from tort action to the extent that the injured party was indemnified under a first-party coverage. Tort action would be retained for losses above the amount recovered under first-party coverage. In some modified no-fault plans, payment for pain and suffering would be limited or eliminated.

3. *Expanded First-Party Coverage.* In this case there is no exemption from tort liability. Instead, the injured party collects benefits under a first-party coverage, retaining the right to sue for losses more than the amount paid by the first-party coverage. Most important, the responsibility of the negligent driver is

[14] No-fault insurance is frequently described as being "just like workers compensation insurance." Those who draw this analogy misunderstand the no-fault concept or the nature of workers compensation insurance (or perhaps both). As the student will recall, workers compensation involves absolute liability and requires the employer to compensate injured workers without regard to fault. No-fault is almost diametrically the opposite; the person suffering the injury is responsible for his or her own loss. No-fault would be "just like workers compensation" if individual workers were required to purchase insurance to protect themselves against injuries suffered on the job, and the employer were released from all liability.

retained by permitting subrogation by the insurer paying the first-party benefits.

Unfortunately, the "no-fault" label is sometimes applied to all three classifications. It is clearly a misnomer to refer to the expanded first-coverage approach as no-fault. Plans in this category, which do not change the tort system, cannot be called nofault plans any more than fire insurance, health insurance, or even life insurance are no-fault plans. Before a plan qualifies as "no-fault," the requirement that motorists carry first-party coverage to protect themselves against medical expenses and loss of income must be accompanied by some restriction or outright elimination of the right to sue, together with the elimination of subrogation rights by the insurer making payment.

Existing State Laws By 1998, 25 states and the District of Columbia had enacted laws that modify the automobile reparation system. None of the laws that have been passed thus far is of the pure no-fault variety. All the laws that have been enacted are either modified no-fault laws, under which the right to sue is not totally abolished but is subject to some restriction, or are laws that simply require some form of expanded first-party coverage.

Massachusetts became the first state with a compulsory no-fault automobile law when its legislature enacted the Personal Injury Protection (PIP) Plan as an amendment to the state's compulsory automobile insurance law in August 1970.[15] The law, a modified no-fault plan, became effective January 1, 1971. Although it did not go nearly as far as many plans that had been proposed or that have been enacted since, it did contain many elements that were included in early proposals, and set a pattern that other states followed. The first-party coverage of the Massachusetts PIP plan provides coverage up to $2000 for medical expenses, lost wages, and loss of services. Reimbursement is limited to the "net loss" of wages, with a deduction to allow for the tax-free nature of the benefits. Loss of services includes coverage for reasonable expenses to replace services the injured person would have performed without pay (housekeeping, for example). The plan provides

immunity from tort action up to the $2000 limit. One feature of the Massachusetts law later copied by other states was the provision for suits for general damages (pain and suffering) when the accident results in loss of a body member, disfigurement, or death, and when medical expenses exceed a specific dollar amount called a "threshold." The Massachusetts law originally set its threshold at $500; it has since been raised to $2000.

By 1995, a total of 16 states plus Puerto Rico and the District of Columbia had passed compulsory no-fault laws. Three states (Connecticut, Georgia, and Nevada) later repealed their laws and two states (Pennsylvania and New Jersey) changed their laws to optional no-fault laws. The Pennsylvania law, which had been in effect since 1975, was repealed in 1984, and then replaced by a "freedom of choice" no-fault law in 1990.[16] In addition to the 11 compulsory no-fault laws that remain, there are three "choice" optional no-fault laws, under which drivers who elect no-fault coverage are granted a partial tort exemption. In addition, 10 other states have laws that are frequently called "no-fault" but that in reality are *expanded first-party coverage systems*. In three states the first-party coverages are compulsory; in the remaining states it is optional. Table 29.2 lists the no-fault laws and other automobile reparation statutes in effect in 2002 on a state-by-state basis.

As can be seen, there is considerable diversity in the laws. In six states, the first-party coverage is optional and there is no restriction on tort suits. Three states require the first-party coverage, but still without restrictions or exemptions for tort suits. All these plans provide for subrogation by the insurer paying the first-party benefits.

There are also vast differences among the modified no-fault laws, not only in benefit levels, but also in the tort exemption. Benefits range from $8000 to unlimited medical expenses and wageloss benefits. Most of the existing laws follow the Massachusetts pattern and permit accident victims to sue for general damages when medical costs exceed a certain threshold level. In five states the threshold is $2500 or less. Florida, Michigan, and New York do not use a dollar threshold, but permit

[15] Although Massachusetts enacted the first state law, Puerto Rico had a government-administered and tax-supported no-fault system in 1969. The Social Protection Plan of Puerto Rico provides unlimited medical expenses and modest loss of income benefits. Private insurers do not participate in the plan.

[16] The 1990 Pennsylvania law requires motorists to select between a full-tort alternative, under which they are allowed to seek compensation through the courts for both economic and noneconomic loss, and a limited-tort alternative under which they may sue for noneconomic loss only in the event of serious injury.

TABLE 29.2 Automobile No-Fault and Automobile Reparation Reform Laws, 2002

State	Effective Date	Type of Law	Maximum Benefits	Tort Exemption	Suits for Pain and Suffering	Dollar Threshold
Arkansas	1974	Optional First-Party	$20,920	No	No limitation	
Colorado	1974	Compulsory First-Party	125,829	Yes	Serious injury[b]	$2,500
Delaware	1972	Compulsory First-Party	15,000[a]	No	No limitation	
D.C.	1983	Optional No-Fault	128,000	Choice	Serious injury	
Florida	1972	Compulsory No-Fault	10,000	Yes	Serious injury	
Hawaii	1974	Compulsory No-Fault	15,000	Yes	Serious injury	Variable[c]
Kansas	1974	Compulsory No-Fault	15,180	Yes	Serious injury	2,000
Kentucky	1975	Choice No-Fault	10,000	Yes	Serious injury	1,000
Maryland	1973	Compulsory First-Party	2,500	No	No limitation	
Massachusetts	1971	Compulsory No-Fault	8,000	Yes	Serious injury	2,000
Michigan	1973	Compulsory No-Fault	Unlimited	Yes	Serious injury	
Minnesota	1975	Compulsory No-Fault	40,000	Yes	Serious injury	4,000
New Jersey	1990	Optional No-Fault	260,580	Choice	Serious injury	
New York	1974	Compulsory No-Fault	50,000	Yes	Serious injury[d]	
North Dakota	1976	Compulsory No-Fault	30,000	Yes	Serious injury	2,500
Oregon	1972	Compulsory First-Party	46,425	No	No limitation	
Pennsylvania	1991	Optional No-Fault	177,500[e]	Choice	Serious injury	
South Carolina	1974	Optional First-Party	1,000	No	No limitation	
South Dakota	1972	Optional First-Party	15,120	No	No limitation	
Texas	1973	Optional First-Party	2,500	No	No limitation	
Utah	1974	Compulsory No-Fault	27,800	Yes	Serious injury	3,000
Virginia	1972	Optional First-Party	7,200	No	No limitation	
Washington	1994	Optional First-Party	77,000	No	No limitation	

[a] $30,000 per occurrence.

[b] State laws differ, but serious injury usually includes death, dismemberment, disfigurement, or permanent disability.

[c] Variable annually.

[d] 90 days disability during 180 days following injury.

[e] Optional $1,100,000 medical.

recovery for pain and suffering when disability exceeds 90 days or when there is "significant permanent injury." These thresholds, above which tort action is permitted for general damages, represent legislative compromises with the no-fault principle. In addition to suits when medical expenses exceed the threshold, all states permit suits for serious injuries such as those resulting in death, disability, dismemberment, or disfigurement. Some states use both a dollar threshold and a verbal threshold. For all practical purposes, the dollar threshold controls in these states. Dollar thresholds and verbal thresholds, above which tort action is permitted for pain and suffering, both represent legislative compromises with the no-fault principle.

In most states, the no-fault statutes apply only to private passenger automobiles, excluding both trucks and motorcycles. Only one state applies the no-fault principle to property damage. In Michigan, vehicle owners are responsible for damage to their own automobiles, with suits between drivers for recovery of collision damage forbidden. Damage to property other than automobiles in Michigan remains under the tort system.

Cost Experience in No-Fault States There is an understandable interest in the cost experience of those states with no-fault plans, but it is difficult to compare costs over time because of other changes in the insurance environment. Premium reductions were mandated in many states when the no-fault laws were first passed, but like premiums elsewhere, rates have increased. Opponents of no-fault laws point to the rate increases and argue that although the plans were sold on the promise that they would cut premiums, the reverse has happened. Some supporters blame the increases on inflation and maintain that costs are still less than they would be without no-fault. Other

advocates of no-fault maintain that premium costs are a relatively insignificant consideration, and that the real issue is which plan—tort or no-fault—provides the greater benefits for the largest number of policyholders.

Prospect of Further No-Fault Legislation At the state level, only the District of Columbia and the state of Washington have enacted new auto reparation laws in the past two decades. The District of Columbia enacted an optional no-fault law in 1983, and Washington passed an optional first-party coverage law in 1995. As already noted, the states of Connecticut, Georgia, and Nevada have repealed their no-fault laws and New Jersey and Pennsylvania have changed from compulsory to optional no-fault laws. Still, interest in the automobile no-fault idea endures. In November 1988 an initiative for no-fault appeared on the California ballot as an alternative to Proposition 103.[17] California voters chose Proposition 103. In 1996, California voters again considered and rejected a no-fault initiative.[18]

After a two-decade hiatus, the subject of a national no-fault system has resurfaced. Twenty-five years ago, there was serious discussion of a national no-fault system, and members of Congress introduced several bills to create a national no-fault system during the period 1970 to 1978. By the mid-1990s, the idea of a federal no-fault plan seemed to have been forgotten. Then, in 1997, legislation was introduced in Congress based on the no-fault approach known as *freedom of choice no-fault*.[19] The *Auto Choice Reform Act of 1997* (S. 625, HR 2021) would create a "choice" auto

insurance system under which states would have the option of opting. Although the legislation was sponsored by leading Republicans (especially House Majority Leader Dick Armey, R-Tex.) it drew bipartisan sponsorship. In addition to Representative Armey and Senator Mitch McConnell (R-Ky), democratic sponsors included Senators Daniel Patrick Moynihan (D-NY), and Joseph Lieberman (D-CT) and Representative James Moran (D-Va).

In addition to the choice by states as to whether they will adopt the system, consumers within electing states would be allowed to choose one of two options, which generally parallel the existing tort system and a no-fault system. The principal difference will be with respect to recovery for noneconomic damages (intangible losses such as permanent disfigurement, impairment of a bodily function, loss of a limb, or pain and suffering).

Under the Personal Protection Insurance (PPI) option, consumers would opt out of coverage for pain and suffering. These drivers would recover economic damages from their own insurers up to the limits of their policy and could sue negligent drivers for any amount that exceeds their policy limits, but such suits would be permitted for economic damages only. PPI-insureds could not sue or be sued for noneconomic damages unless the injury was intentional or was a result of alcohol or drug abuse.[20]

For those consumers who do not want to relinquish their right to collect for noneconomic damages, the *tort maintenance option* would allow them to retain this right by purchasing a new form of coverage called *tort maintenance coverage* (TMC). TMC drivers would recover both economic damages and noneconomic damages from their own insurance companies up to the limits of their policies, based on who was at fault. In effect, TMC drivers would retain the option to recover noneconomic damages, but they would recover them from their own insurer up to their TMC limits. TMC is a form of *inverse liability coverage* that operates in much the same way as uninsured motorist coverage. TMC drivers not at fault in an accident would be permitted to sue negligent drivers for any damages that exceed the limits of their TMC coverage. Both TMC and PPI drivers would retain their rights to sue (and to be sued) for noneconomic damages if injuries are inflicted intentionally or as a result of drug or alcohol abuse. Also,

[17] Proposition 104, which was sponsored by the Association of California Insurance Companies, would have enacted a no-fault system with $10,000 in medical expense benefits, $15,000 wageloss benefit, and $5000 funeral benefit. The initiative also limited attorney contingency fees in auto cases to 33.3 percent of awards up to $50,000, 25 percent of the next $50,000, and 15 percent of any award amounts above $100,000. The right to sue would have been retained for losses in excess of the no-fault benefits and where there was serious injury or death.

[18] The 1996 California no-fault initiative was one of three propositions defeated in the election: the no-fault initiative (Proposition 200), a loser-pays initiative aimed at frivolous shareholder laws (Proposition 201), and a limit on attorneys' contingency fees (Proposition 202). Proposition 200—the no-fault initiative–was rejected by 65 percent of the voters. Opponents of the three measures were bankrolled almost exclusively by trial lawyers in the state. See G. Pascal Zachary, "California's Defeat of Legal, Insurance Overhaul Raises Questions About Tort Reform Nationwide," *Wall Street Journal* (March 28, 1996).

[19] Freedom of choice no-fault was proposed by Jeffrey O'Connel, one of the authors of the Keeton-O'Connel *Basic Protection* plan, in 1965 and Robert H. Joost in a 1986 article in the *Virginia Law Review*.

[20] "Feds Poised to Pounce on Auto Insurance Reform," *National Underwriter, P&C*, September 1, 1997, p. 20.

both PPI drivers and TMC drivers could claim economic and noneconomic damages from an unlawfully uninsured motorist based on fault.

California Proposition 213 Although it is not in the same variety as a no-fault law, in 1996 California voters enacted Proposition 213, which limits tort recoveries for injuries that are caused by the injured person's commission of a felony or flight from the scene of an accident. Proposition 213 was adopted at the general election held on November 5, 1996, by 78 percent of the voters. Challenges to the constitutionality of the law were rejected by the California Supreme Court in 1998.

COST OF AUTOMOBILE INSURANCE

Some of the dissatisfaction over automobile insurance relates to the manner that insurers use to spread the cost of accidents over the insured population. Many of the traditional rating factors are being challenged, and it seems appropriate that we examine those factors.

One of the most distressing aspects of automobile insurance, as far as youthful drivers are concerned, is the difficulty in obtaining adequate coverage and the cost of that coverage. Because youthful drivers have a greater proportion of accidents, their premium rates are considerably higher than those of adults. Many factors enter into the determination of the premium for a specific individual. Understanding these factors can be helpful in purchasing insurance.

Insurance Services Office Automobile Rating Systems

The rating system used in most states for automobile insurance was adopted by the Insurance Services Office in 1965. Although individual companies use systems that differ in detail from this standard system, the factors considered under the various systems generally follow the pattern of the Insurance Services Office (ISO) system.

Most automobile rating systems begin with three basic factors:

- Age and sex of the driver
- Use of the automobile
- The driver's record

In addition to these factors, the rates vary with the territory in which the automobile is principally garaged, the limits of coverage desired, and, for physical damage coverages, the value of the automobile and the deductible selected.

The starting point in the ISO system is a base premium for each coverage, which varies with the territory, the policy limits, and, for physical damage coverages, the value of the automobile. This is the premium charged for an automobile with no youthful drivers that is used for pleasure only. All other drivers and uses are expressed as a percentage of this base premium. Each driver is assigned a rating factor that expresses the percentage of the base premium that individual is to be charged. Thus, a rating factor of 1.55 means that the driver would pay 155 percent of the base premium, and a 3.30 rating factor would require a premium equal to 330 percent of the base. The rating factor for each individual is based on a number of variables, including the driver's age, marital status, and past driving record; the use of the automobile; and the type of automobile.

Driver Classifications There are ten general driver classifications under the Insurance Services Office rating plan; five for adult operators and five for youthful operators. The lowest-rated classes are drivers in the older age groups—from age 65 to 74 and age 75 and older. Female operators age 30 to 49 are the next lowest-rated class, followed by all other adult drivers. Youthful drivers are divided first by sex and then according to whether they are a principal or occasional driver of the vehicle.[21] Youthful male operators who are married are assigned to a separate category. Married youthful female operators are rated at the all-other-adult category.

Use Classifications In addition to the age of the principal operator, rating factors also vary with use. There are five use categories for those classes with no youthful operators:

1. *Pleasure Use:* The auto is not used in business and is not customarily driven to work or school more than 3 miles each way. (Persons who participate in car pools and drive fewer than 15 miles each way are

[21] The question may arise as to which classification applies when there is more than one occasional or incidental operator in the family. The basic rule is that the highest-rated operator class applies. If there is more than one automobile in the family, the highest-rated operator is assigned to the automobile with the highest basic premium, unless the driver is actually the owner or driver of another automobile.

classed for pleasure, provided the car is not used more than two days a week or two weeks in each five-week period.)

2. *Drive to Work Fewer than 15 Miles:* The auto is not used in business but is driven to work or school more than 3 miles and fewer than 15 miles.

3. *Drive to Work More than 15 Miles:* The car is not used in business but is driven to work or school more than 15 miles each way.

4. *Business Use:* The car is customarily used in business.

5. *Farm Use:* The car is principally garaged on a farm or ranch and is not used in any other business and is not driven to school or any other work.

For youthful drivers, there are only two use categories. Pleasure and Farm Use are combined into a single class, as are the Drive-to-Work classes and the Business Use category.

The rating and use classifications and their corresponding rating factors are indicated in Table 29.3.

Youthful Operator Discounts The automobile rating system contains two features that work to the benefit of some underage drivers. The first of these is the driver training credit. If the youthful driver has completed an approved driver-training course, the

rating factor is reduced by 5 to 35 points, depending on the basic classification factor.

A second feature of considerable interest to youthful drivers is the good student discount, which applies to full-time students, 16 years of age or older, on certification that the student, for the preceding semester or comparable period:

1. Ranked in the upper 20 percent of his or her class, or

2. Had a B average or higher, or

3. Had a three-point average or higher, or

4. Was on the dean's list, honor roll, or similar list.

As does the discount for driver training, the good student discount varies with the individual's basic rating factor. The discount results in a reduction in the rating factor by 10 to 65 points, depending on the basic classification factor. This credit is in addition to the driver training credit. Table 29.4 indicates the rating factors for youthful drivers with and without drivers training and the good student discount. These factors are for the pleasure use category and would be surcharged by the appropriate factor for drive-to-work and business use. Also, the rating factors listed in the table apply if the driver has not had any chargeable accidents in the past three years. If there are chargeable

TABLE 29.3 Driver and Use Rating Factors

Adult Driver	Age	Pleasure Use	Less than 15 Miles	15 Miles or More	Business Use	Farm Use
Principal operator	75 or over	.80	.90	1.00	1.10	.65
Principal operator	65 to 74	.90	.90	1.00	1.10	.65
Principal operator	50 to 64	.90	1.00	1.10	1.20	.75
Only operator female	30 to 49	.90	1.00	1.10	1.20	.75
Other Nonyouthful drivers		1.00	1.10	1.20	1.30	.85

Youthful Drivers Without Discounts	Age	Pleasure or Farm Use	Drive to Work or School or Business Use
Unmarried female, not owner/principal operator	Under 21	2.15	2.30
	21 thru 24	1.35	1.45
Unmarried female, owner/principal operator	Under 21	2.15	2.30
	21 thru 24	1.45	1.60
Unmarried male, not owner/principal operator	Under 21	2.50	2.65
	21 thru 24	1.45	1.60
Unmarried male, owner or principal operator	Under 21	3.30	3.45
	21 thru 24	1.95	2.10
Married male operator	Under 21	1.85	2.00
	21 thru 24	1.40	1.55

Source: Insurance Services Office, Inc.

TABLE 29.4 Youthful Driver Discounts

| Youthful Driver Class | Age | Without Good Student Discount | | With Good Student Discount | |
		No Driver Training	With Driver Training	No Driver Training	With Driver Training
Unmarried male, owner or	Under 21	3.30	2.95	2.65	2.40
principal operator	21 thru 24	1.95	1.95	1.60	1.60
Unmarried male, not owner	Under 21	2.50	2.30	2.10	1.95
or principal operator	21 thru 24	1.45	1.45	1.35	1.35
Unmarried female, owner	Under 21	2.15	2.00	1.85	1.75
or principal operator	21 thru 24	1.45	1.45	1.35	1.35
Unmarried female, not	Under 21	1.80	1.70	1.60	1.55
owner or principal operator	21 thru 24	1.35	1.35	1.25	1.25
Married male	Under 21	1.85	1.70	1.60	1.50
Married male	21 thru 24	1.40	1.40	1.30	1.30

Source: Insurance Services Office, Inc.

accidents and the insurer uses the safe-driver rating plan, additional surcharges will apply.

Safe-Driver Rating Plan The safe-driver rating plan or a variation of it is used by most automobile insurers. This plan is based on the assumption that the past driving record is a valid indicator of the individual's future experience. The experience period is the three years immediately preceding the date of the application for the insurance or the inception of the renewal policy. Points are assigned for traffic violations and certain accidents. Three points are assigned for a conviction for drunken driving, driving under the influence of drugs, failure to stop and report when involved in an accident, and homicide or assault arising out of the operation of a motor vehicle or for driving with a suspended or revoked license. Two points are assigned for an accumulation of points under a special state system of motor vehicle points or from a series of convictions requiring evidence of financial responsibility under a state financial responsibility law. One point is assigned for any other conviction or any other motor vehicle law violation for which one's operator's license is suspended or revoked, and for which the filing of financial responsibility is required as of the effective date of the policy. One point also is assigned for each accident causing bodily injury or death, or $500 or more in property damage. One point is also assigned if there were two or more accidents during the experience period, each of which resulted in damage to property in an amount of $500 or less. (No points are assigned if the insured's auto was legally parked at the time of the accident, if the damage was caused by a hit-and-run driver, or if the other driver was at fault

for the accident.) Finally, one point is assigned to any principal operator who has been licensed less than two years.

If the insured has 1 point under the plan, his or her rating factor is increased by 40 points. For the second point, there is an additional surcharge of 50 points. The third point calls for a further 60-point surcharge, and the fourth point 70 more points. Thus, a driver with 4 points would incur a total surcharge of 220 percentage points.

Number and Type of Automobiles When a person insures two or more automobiles with the same company, a special multicar discount applies. The rating factor applicable to each automobile is reduced by 0.20 points. In addition, any points developed under the safe-driver plan are applied to both automobiles, with the penalty developed divided in half and charged equally to each car.

The type and value of the automobile insured are obviously factors in the determination of collision and comprehensive premiums, but in some instances they affect all coverages. For 1971 and later-model automobiles, the revised system imposes a 0.15 factor point surcharge on sports cars and intermediate-performance cars and a 0.30-point surcharge on high-performance automobiles.

The Rating System and Equity

The various factors that are considered in determination of the final premium under the revised rating system can yield wide differences in premiums for different drivers, with some insureds paying considerably more for their insurance than others. For

example, rating factors may range from 0.65 (for a driver over age 65, living on a farm, with no points and driving a standard performance automobile with the multicar discount) to 5.50 (for a 17-year-old male operator with his own high-performance car who has accumulated 4 points and is not entitled to the driver's education or good student discounts). Although the system is complex, it results in a more equitable allocation of insurance costs among drivers. Most people agree that the system is fair, since it has been established quite conclusively that the operator who cannot drive a car without accidents or traffic violations, as demonstrated in the past, will likely be no different in the future.

THE SHIFTING VIEW OF AUTO INSURANCE

The increasing cost of automobile insurance and the difficulty that some drivers have in obtaining coverage have raised automobile insurance to the status of a major social problem in this country. At least a part of this problem stems from the seldom mentioned shift in the way that society views automobile insurance.

Originally, auto liability insurance—like personal liability insurance—was designed to protect the person insured against financial loss arising out of torts. When legislatures acted to make liability insurance compulsory, the motivation was not a paternalistic attempt to make sure that drivers were protected against lawsuits. It was an attempt to provide injured persons with a defendant who is worth suing. Imperceptibly, the function of auto liability insurance changed. Although it still provides protection for insureds against liability losses, compulsory auto liability insurance is also viewed as a form of protection for accident victims. With this shift in objectives, there has been an understandable shift in the attitude of consumers toward auto insurance.

Under the compulsory auto insurance system, some people are forced to purchase a product they don't want and don't need. They purchase insurance not for their own protection but for the benefit of those they might injure. Economically disadvantaged people in particular have developed an animosity toward automobile insurance. It is a product from which they derive little benefit. After all, a person who doesn't have anything can afford to lose it. In the absence of a legal requirement, people who have little to lose in a lawsuit would "take their chances" driving without insurance.

Ironically, compulsory auto insurance doesn't really solve the problem. The compulsory levels of protection are inadequate to protect many people who might be injured, especially persons with higher incomes. Despite the compulsory laws, many people must purchase coverage to protect against losses they might suffer that are in excess of the auto limits carried by drivers with minimum limits.

IMPORTANT CONCEPTS TO REMEMBER

automobile liability insurance	insurance laws	no-fault
automobile medical payments coverage	financial responsibility laws	modified no-fault
	free-bite laws	expanded first-party coverage
automobile physical damage coverage	SR-21	threshold level
	SR-22	freedom of choice no-fault
uninsured motorists coverage	Automobile Insurance Plan	tort maintenance option
family purpose doctrine	Assigned Risk Plans	base premium
permissive use statutes	facility	rating factor
guest laws	joint underwriting associations	safe-driver rating plan
compulsory automobile liability	distress risk company	

QUESTIONS FOR REVIEW

1. What are the three major classes of loss associated with the ownership or operation of an automobile? What types of insurance coverage protect against each? What automobile coverages protect against each?

2. Briefly describe the general provisions of a financial responsibility law. Why are these laws often called "free-bite laws"?

3. Briefly distinguish between an SR-21 and an SR-22 that must be filed with the state department of motor vehicles under a financial responsibility law.

4. What is the purpose and general nature of an Automobile Insurance Plan?

5. Outline the various ways in which one may be held vicariously liable in the operation of an automobile.

6. Describe the distinguishing characteristics of the four approaches currently used to provide automobile liability insurance to drivers who are unacceptable to insurers in the normal course of business.

7. Briefly describe the criticisms of the tort system that led to the enactment of automobile no-fault laws.

8. In what way is the automobile no-fault concept similar to workers compensation? In what way is it different?

9. List and briefly explain the differences among the three major approaches that automobile accident reparation reform legislation may take.

10. Briefly explain the factors that are considered in determining the premium for automobile liability insurance. What additional factors are considered in the rating of comprehensive and collision coverages? What factors apply in the case of youthful drivers that are not considered in the case of other drivers?

QUESTIONS FOR DISCUSSION

1. How do you personally think that we should cope with the problem of bad drivers who have difficulty in obtaining insurance through normal market channels?

2. Some states still have guest hazard statutes. Do you think that these laws are a logical extension of the assumption of risk doctrine, or should they be repealed?

3. What, in your opinion, is the strongest argument in favor of a no-fault system for compensating the victims of automobile accidents? What is the strongest argument against such a system?

4. Many people in the property and liability insurance industry complain about the "automobile problem." Actually, the "automobile problem" consists of a series of interrelated problems. What factors have combined to produce a problem in the automobile insurance area?

5. The insurance mechanism is based on the principle of loss-sharing, with those who do not suffer losses paying to meet the costs of those who do. In view of this principle, would it make more sense to group all ages together for rating purposes, with older drivers subsidizing the cost of the losses incurred by younger drivers? Explain why insurance companies divide drivers into different classifications with preferential rates for some groups.

SUGGESTIONS FOR ADDITIONAL READING

Consumer Federation of America, Consumers Union, National Insurance Consumer Organization, and Public Citizen. *Reducing Auto Insurance Rates: A Comprehensive Program.* Washington, D.C.: Consumer Federation of America, 1989.

Department of Transportation. *State No-Fault Automobile Insurance Experience 1971–1977.* Washington, D.C.: U.S. Government Printing Office, 1978.

Fire, Casualty and Surety Bulletins. Personal Lines Volume. Cincinnati, Ohio: National Underwriter Company. (Loose-leaf manual service with monthly supplements.) See "Auto" section.

Hallman, G. V. *Unsatisfied Judgment Funds.* Homewood, Ill.: Richard D. Irwin, 1968.

Hamilton, Karen L., and Donald S. Malecki. *Personal Insurance: Property and Liability.* Malvern, Pa.: American Institute for CPCU, 1994. Chapter 5.

Keeton, Robert E. *Insurance Law: Basic Text.* St. Paul, Minn.: West Publishing, 1971.

———, and Jeffrey O'Connell. *After Cars Crash.* Homewood, Ill.: Dow Jones-Irwin, 1967.

————, and Jeffrey O'Connell. *Basic Protection for the Traffic Victim.* Boston: Little, Brown, 1965.

Launie, J. J., George E. Rejda, and Donald R. Oakes with Anita W. Johnson. *Personal Insurance.* Bryn Mawr, Pa.: Insurance Institute of America, 1991. Chapter 9.

Mooney, Sean. *Auto Insurance: Critical Choices for the 1990s.* New York: Insurance Information Institute, 1989.

O'Connell, Jeffrey, and Robert H. Joost. "Giving Motorists a Choice Between Fault and No-Fault." *Virginia Law Review,* vol. 72 (1986).

Policy, Form and Manual Analysis Service. Personal Lines Volume. Indianapolis, Ind.: Rough Notes Company. (Loose-leaf manual service with monthly supplements.) See "Personal Auto" section.

Trends in Auto Bodily Injury Claims. Oak Brook, Ill.: Insurance Research Council, 1990.

Witt, Robert C., and Jorge Urrutia. "An Overview and Assessment of No-Fault Plans." *CPCU Journal,* vol. 37, no. 1 (March 1984).

WEB SITES TO EXPLORE

Best's Review—Property/Casualty Edition	http://www.ambest.com/review/lh/index.html
Free Advice Web Site	http://freeadvice.com/law/595us.htm
Highway Loss Data Institute	http://www.hwysafety.org
Insurance Information Institute	http://www.iii.org/
Insurance Institute for Highway Safety	http://www.hwysafety.org
Insurance News Network	http://www.insure.com/
Maryland State Auto Insurance Fund	http://www.mdarchives.state.md.us/msa/mdmanual/25ind/html/07autof.htm
National Highway Traffic Safety Adminstration	http://www.nhtsa.org
National Safety Council	http://www.nsc.org
Quicken InsureMarket	http://www.insuremarket.com/
Rough Notes Company	http://www.roughnotes.com

THE PERSONAL AUTO POLICY

■

Accidents will occur in the best regulated families.

— CHARLES DICKENS
David Copperfield

CHAPTER OBJECTIVES

When you have finished this chapter, you should be able to

- Determine if an automobile is eligible for coverage under the Personal Auto Policy (PAP)
- Identify and explain the four coverage sections of the PAP
- Describe the coverage features of the PAP liability coverage, including the persons and automobiles for which coverage is provided
- Describe the scope of coverage under the medical payments coverage of the PAP, including the persons to whom the coverage is applicable
- Describe the scope of coverage under the uninsured motorists coverage of the PAP, including the persons to whom the coverage is applicable
- Describe the scope of coverage under the Damage to Your Auto coverage of the PAP
- Identify and explain the Duties After Loss and general provisions of the PAP

In this chapter, we continue our study of automobile insurance, turning now to an examination of one of the contracts under which auto insurance is provided, the Insurance Services Office (ISO) Personal Auto Policy (PAP). The PAP is only one of several auto forms currently in use. Some insurers have developed their own contracts, which differ in detail from the ISO form. Still, the PAP is the most widely sold of the various auto insurance forms and serves as a standard against which other policy forms may be compared.

GENERAL NATURE OF THE PERSONAL AUTO POLICY

The Personal Automobile Policy was introduced in 1977. It is written in the simplified terminology that

has become common in the insurance field, but at the time of its introduction, it was considered a remarkable departure from the existing contracts. The policy has been revised several times, and the following discussion is based on the 1998 edition of the policy.[1]

The automobile insurance policy is one of the most complicated of all insurance contracts. The complicated nature of the contract results from the need to provide a contract that will provide coverage against different types of losses under diverse circumstances. The ownership or operation of an auto involves three types of loss:

1. Legal liability
2. Injury to the insured or members of the insured's family
3. Damage to or loss of the auto itself

The *Personal Auto Policy* is a package policy, providing protection against all three of these types of loss. It may be used to provide liability coverage, medical payments coverage, uninsured motorist coverage, and physical damage insurance. It may be endorsed to provide no-fault benefits in those states where such laws exist.

Besides covering various types of loss, the policy must provide protection in various situations. Most people in our society operate autos, and often the vehicle being driven is not owned by the operator. Jones may borrow Brown's car, and, as we have seen, Brown may be held liable with Jones if the latter is negligent. It is therefore necessary to devise a contract that will protect the owner when someone else is operating his or her auto. In addition, it is desirable that the contract protect the insured when he or she is driving someone else's car. Both requirements add to the complexity of the contract. In addition, the broadness of coverage in a policy designed to meet these various situations makes insurers limit its availability to specific classes. Before turning to an analysis of the policy itself, we will briefly examine the eligibility rules of the PAP.

Eligibility

The PAP is available only to certain eligible classes of persons and to cover specified types of vehicles.

First, the auto must be owned by an individual or by a husband and wife who are residents of the same household.[2] Autos owned by partnerships, corporations, or by two or more individuals who are not resident relatives of the household are not eligible.[3] For the purposes of eligibility and coverage, a vehicle that is leased under a written agreement for at least six months is treated as if it were owned.

Furthermore, the auto must be of a specific type. The first class of eligible vehicles consists of *private passenger automobiles,* defined as "a four-wheel motor vehicle, other than a truck type, owned or leased under contract for a continuous period of at least six months." The vehicle may not be used as a public or livery conveyance, and it may not be rented to others.

A pickup or van may also be eligible for coverage under the PAP if it is owned by an individual (or by a husband and wife who reside in the same household), depending on its size and use. The pickup or van must have a gross vehicle weight of less than 10,000 pounds and may not be used for the delivery or transportation of goods and materials. An exception to this "use" limitation permits delivery or transportation of goods or materials that are incidental to the business of installing, maintaining, or repairing furnishings or equipment, or use that is for farming or ranching.

Finally, the PAP may be used to provide coverage on motorcycles, motor homes, golf carts and similar type vehicles, and snowmobiles. The vehicle must be owned by an individual, husband and wife, or two relatives who are residents of the same household. A special endorsement is used to modify the coverage of the policy when it is used for these types of vehicles.[4]

Policy Format

The PAP follows the modern insurance contract style, and is written in simplified terms. "You" and

[1] The Personal Auto Policy is a direct descendant of the Family Automobile Policy, the standard bureau auto policy that preceded it, and which is still used by a few companies. The Family Automobile Policy, as its name implies, was developed to provide auto insurance for the entire family.

[2] Autos owned jointly by resident relatives who are not husband and wife (e.g., father and son) may also be insured, but the coverage is limited by a special endorsement.

[3] There is one exception to this rule: A motor vehicle owned by a family farm co-partnership or family farm corporation is eligible as long as it is principally garaged on a farm or ranch and otherwise meets the eligibility requirements.

[4] The changes in the policy provisions when the PAP is used to insure motorcycles and other miscellaneous vehicles are so pronounced that it is almost a different contract than the standard PAP. Coverage for motorcycles and other miscellaneous types of vehicles is discussed later in the chapter.

"your" are used throughout the policy to refer to the named insured and spouse, and "we," "us," and "our" are used to refer to the insurer. Wherever possible, awkward terminology has been removed and the legalistic phrases that once characterized insurance contracts have been removed. The policy is divided into six parts, designated as follows:

1. Part A, Liability Coverage
2. Part B, Medical Payments Coverage
3. Part C, Uninsured Motorists Coverage
4. Part D, Coverage for Damage to Your Auto
5. Part E, Duties After an Accident or Loss
6. Part F, General Provisions

Parts A through D are the four separate coverages that may be included in the policy. Each part has its own insuring agreement and exclusions. The parts are made effective by an indication in the declarations that the appropriate premium has been paid and that the coverage applies. Parts E and F apply to all sections of the policy. A specimen of the PAP should be referred to in the following discussion.

LIABILITY COVERAGE

The liability part of the PAP, designated Part A, provides the most important coverage of the policy. It contains the liability insuring agreement, supplementary payments, liability exclusions, and special conditions applicable to the liability coverage.

Liability Insuring Agreement

The liability insuring agreement obligates the insurer to pay, up to the policy limit, damages for which any "insured" becomes legally responsible because of an accident. Coverage for bodily injury and property damage is provided with split limits, with separate per person and per accident bodily injury limits and a separate limit for property damage. The minimum limits available vary with the financial responsibility law of the state. In most states the minimum bodily injury limits are $25,000/50,000, and the minimum property damage limit is generally $10,000 or $20,000, but these limits can be increased. The bodily injury limits may be increased to $50,000/100,000, $100,000/200,000 or $100,000/300,000, $250,000/500,000 or higher. The property damage limit can be increased to $25,000,

$50,000, $100,000, and higher. As in the case of most liability contracts, the insurer also agrees to defend the insured, but reserves the right to make any settlement it considers appropriate. The insuring agreement makes it clear that the company's obligation to defend ends when the policy limits are exhausted.

Persons Insured under Liability Coverage Since the policy agrees to pay sums an insured becomes obligated to pay, the definition of *insured* is a critical determinant of coverage. The PAP defines an insured as follows:

"Insured" as used in this Part means:

1. You or any "family member" for the ownership, maintenance or use of any auto or trailer.

2. Any person using "your covered auto."

3. For "your covered auto," any person or organization but only with respect to legal responsibility for acts or omissions of a person for whom coverage is afforded under this Part.

4. For any auto or "trailer," other than "your covered auto," any person or organization but only with respect to legal responsibility for acts or omissions of you or any family member for whom coverage is afforded under this part. This provision (B.4.) applies only if the person or organization does not own or hire the auto or "trailer."

Although the provision is written in simplified terminology, it considers a variety of situations and is therefore necessarily complex. A brief analysis of the definition should help to simplify it.

Initially, coverage is provided for "you" or any family member for the use of any auto or trailer. Reference to the policy definitions reveals that "you" means the named insured listed in the declarations, and his or her spouse if a resident of the same household. In a new provision added in the 1998 revision, the policy definition of "you" is expanded to include a spouse who ceases to be a resident of the household. This new provision is intended to eliminate short-term gaps in coverage arising from changes in relationships that existed under earlier forms. Coverage is provided for a spouse who leaves the residence for 90 days after changing residency or until he or she obtains a separate policy, or until the policy period ends, whichever comes first. The definitions section also indicates that the term "family member" means a person related to the named insured by blood, marriage, or adoption,

including a ward or foster child, who is a resident of the named insured's household.

For the named insured and resident relatives, coverage applies to *any auto,* which means both the auto designated as the covered auto[5] as well as borrowed or rented non-owned autos. There is no restriction on the type of auto that may be borrowed or rented and it could include, for example, a bus or truck. Although the definition of *insured* states that coverage applies to the named insured and resident relatives for any automobile, the contract must be interpreted as a whole, and this broad statement is subject to qualification by other provisions of the policy. Certain types of autos are eliminated from coverage by the exclusions that will be discussed shortly. In addition, while the definition of *Insured* does not refer to a requirement of permission, one of the exclusions (discussed shortly) eliminates coverage for anyone operating a vehicle without a reasonable belief that he or she is entitled to do so.

Persons other than the named insured and family members are covered while using the "covered auto" subject to the requirement that the use be with the reasonable belief that the person has a right to do so.

The extension of coverage to persons or organizations held vicariously liable is divided into two parts: One applies to the owned auto, and the other applies to non-owned autos.

Part 3 of the definition extends coverage to anyone vicariously liable for the operation of the owned auto. This would include, for example, the employer of any person operating a covered auto as an insured.

Part 4 of the definition extends coverage to anyone held vicariously liable for the operation of a nonowned auto by the named insured or a family member.

Note that for non-owned autos under Part 4 of the definition, there is no coverage for the owner of the non-owned auto, even if he or she is held vicariously liable for the acts of the named insured or the resident relative operating the vehicle. To illustrate the coverage for vicarious liability with respect to owned and non-owned autos, consider the following example. Smith, an insured under a PAP, uses her car in her occupation. In the event of a loss in which her employer is joined in the suit, Smith's policy will provide coverage for both Smith and her employer. If Smith borrows a friend's car to use in her occupation, Part 4 of the definition provides coverage for the vicarious liability of Smith's employer. However, Smith's policy will not extend coverage to the friend if he is sued as the owner of the car. The owner must look to his own policy for protection.

Because the PAP provides coverage for the named insured and family members while operating borrowed autos, and also provides coverage for other persons while operating the covered auto, situations will exist in which two policies will apply to the same loss. For example, if White borrows Brown's auto, Brown's policy will provide coverage for both Brown and White in the event of a loss. Brown is covered as you (the named insured), and White has coverage as a permissive user. In addition, White has coverage under his own policy as a "you" (named insured) while using a borrowed auto with permission. When two or more policies apply in the same loss, the policy on the auto being driven is primary, and the policy of the permissive user is excess.

The "Covered Auto" As is true of the definition of *insured,* the definition of insured autos is an important determinant of coverage. Because of its importance, the definition of *covered auto* is reproduced here in its entirety:

> **J.** "Your covered auto" means:
> 1. Any vehicle shown in the Declarations.
> 2. A "newly acquired auto."
> 3. Any "trailer" you own.
> 4. Any auto or "trailer" you do not own while used as a temporary substitute for any other vehicle described in this definition which is out of normal use because of its:
> a. breakdown
> b. repair
> c. servicing
> d. loss; or
> e. destruction
>
> This provision (J.4.) does not apply to Coverage for Damage to Your Auto.

A vehicle listed in the declarations is, of course, a covered auto. Certain newly acquired autos are also covered autos, as explained in greater detail in the paragraphs that follow. A trailer owned by the insured is also covered. There is no requirement that the trailer be listed, as long as it meets the policy definition of "trailer." Finally, any non-owned auto is covered while used as a temporary substitute for a

[5] The term *covered auto* is defined in the policy and has a precise meaning. For the present, we may consider the covered auto to be the auto described in the policy.

covered auto while the covered auto is withdrawn from use because of breakdown, repair, servicing, loss, or destruction.

The inclusion of a "newly acquired auto" in the definition of "your covered auto" provides coverage for autos acquired during the policy period, but on a qualified basis. First, the auto must be one that meets the eligibility requirements of the PAP (i.e., it must be a private passenger auto or a pickup or van that does not exceed the gross vehicle weight limitation and is not used for delivery or transportation of goods except as allowed by the eligibility requirements). Separate provisions apply for coverages other than physical damage and for the physical damage coverages. For liability, medical payments, and uninsured motorists coverages, replacement autos are automatically covered for the remainder of the policy period, without notice to the insurer. For additional vehicles, the insurer must be notified and coverage must be requested within 14 days of the date of acquisition for these coverages. Note that, if a loss were to occur during the 14-day grace period and before notice is given to the company, coverage applies. This means that the liability, medical payments, and uninsured motorists coverages apply to replacement autos for the remainder of the policy period, even without notice to the company.

For physical damage coverages, newly acquired autos—replacement vehicles and additional vehicles—are automatically covered for 14 days, for whatever physical damage coverage (Collision Coverage and/or Other Than Collision Coverage) is already provided by the policy for at least one insured auto. During this 14-day period, the newly acquired auto has the broadest physical damage coverage that is provided by the policy. For example, if the policy covers two automobiles, one with physical damage coverage and one without, any newly acquired vehicle is automatically covered for the physical damage coverage for 14 days.[6] The same feature will apply when one vehicle has Collision Coverage and the other does not or when two vehicles are insured with different deductibles. If the policy does not include physical damage coverage on any of the covered autos, newly acquired autos are automatically covered for 4 days. This automatic coverage is subject

to a $500 deductible that is applicable to either Collision Coverage or Other Than Collision Coverage. If the insured does not request coverage within the grace period provided, coverage for a newly acquired auto begins at the time coverage is requested.

Liability Exclusions

There are 13 exclusions applicable to the liability coverage. Nine of these exclusions (designated *A.*) eliminate coverage for certain persons. The other 4 (*B.*) exclude specified vehicles.

Exclusion A.1. is self-explanatory. It excludes coverage for any insured who intentionally causes bodily injury or property damage. It would be contrary to public policy to provide protection against the financial consequences of injuries or damage caused intentionally.

Exclusion A.2. excludes coverage for damage to property owned or being transported by an insured. Damage to owned property or property being transported should be covered under a property insurance form, such as the homeowners policy, or a floater policy.

Exclusion A.3. is the PAP version of the *care, custody, and control exclusion* found in most liability contracts. It excludes coverage for any insured for damage to property rented to, used by, or in the care of that insured, thus excluding damage to borrowed or rented property.

While Exclusion A.2. eliminates coverage on owned property and property being transported by the insured, A.3. goes further, and excludes coverage on rented property and property in a bailment status even when it is not being transported. If the insured negligently backs over a borrowed bicycle, he or she might be held liable, but the auto policy will not respond. However, an exception to the exclusion states that it does not apply to damage to a residence or private garage.

Exclusion A.4. eliminates coverage for injuries to employees in the course of their employment, except domestic employees in those states where workers compensation laws do not apply to domestic employees. This provision eliminates coverage for the driver's employer (who is otherwise covered for vicarious liability) if the liability involves injury to an employee of that employer.

Exclusion A.5. excludes coverage for liability while the auto "is being used as a public or livery conveyance." An exception to the exclusion makes it

[6] It should be noted that the coverage on newly acquired pickups and vans applies only if the vehicle meets the eligibility requirements for the PAP.

clear that it does not apply to shared-expense car pools.[7]

Exclusion A.6. eliminates coverage for any insured employed in the automobile business. However, the exclusion does not apply to the owned auto while being operated by the named insured or a family member (or by a partner, agent, or employee of the named insured or family member). Thus, if the named insured or a family member is operating the owned auto in the auto business, coverage will apply. However, there is no coverage for persons in the auto business (other than the named insured and family members) while operating the owned auto. Also, if the named insured or family member operates a non-owned auto while employed in the auto business, there is no coverage. If Abner takes his auto to a garage for a tune-up, there is no coverage under Abner's policy for Baker, the mechanic, while test-driving the car. If Baker has a PAP, neither will his policy cover him while operating Abner's car. The excluded exposures may be covered under a special business automobile policy called the *garage policy*.

Exclusion A.7. is a "business pursuits" exclusion. Its purpose is to eliminate coverage for business use of commercial vehicles, but it does so through a curious combination of exclusions, exceptions, and cross-references. Initially, the exclusion eliminates coverage for any insured using an auto in any business except farming or ranching (or in the auto business, which, as noted, is subject to a separate Exclusion A.6.). The provision then excepts private passenger autos, pickups and vans, and trailers used with these types of autos from the exclusion. This grants coverage for both owned and non-owned autos of these types used in business. What remains excluded are trucks (other than pickups and vans) while used in business.

Note that the exception for farming or ranching applies to the entire exclusion. This means that not only are pickups and vans covered if used in farming, other types of trucks are also covered.

Exclusion A.8. eliminates coverage for any insured using a vehicle without a reasonable belief that he or she is entitled to do so. Although the provision requires only that the individual have a "reasonable belief" that he or she is entitled to use the auto, the

exclusion can create dangerous gaps in coverage. For the sake of example, assume that Brown Jr. has his parents' car at school. White, another resident of the dorm, takes the car without permission and is involved in a spectacular accident. Many people are injured and the lawsuits promise to be astronomical. White appears to be in serious trouble. Although the policy covering Brown's car protects anyone operating it with "a reasonable belief" that he or she is entitled to do so, there is no basis for such belief and therefore no coverage. If White's parents have a PAP, the same exclusion will eliminate coverage under that policy.[8] In the 1998 revision, a provision was added to exclusion A.8. stipulating that the exclusion does not apply (and coverage is therefore provided) to a family member while using a covered auto belonging to the insured.

The last exclusion in group A—Exclusion A.9.—eliminates coverage for any insured who is also insured under a nuclear energy liability policy or who would be an insured under such a policy except for the exhaustion of its limits.

Exclusion B.1. eliminates coverage for liability arising out of motorcycles or other self-propelled vehicles with fewer than four wheels or vehicles designed mainly for use off public roads (such as an all-terrain vehicle). The exclusion is subject to three exceptions. First, it does not apply if the vehicle is being used by an insured in a medical emergency. Second, it does not apply to trailers. Finally, the exclusion does not apply to any non-owned golf cart. This means that the individual's PAP will provide liability coverage for borrowed or rented golf carts (but not for use of the insured's owned golf cart).

Exclusion B.2. eliminates coverage on vehicles that are owned by or furnished for the regular use of the named insured, other than the Covered Auto. Automobiles owned by the insured at the inception of the policy and not declared are, of course, excluded. Less obvious to some insureds is the exclusion of autos furnished for regular use. For example, a person may be furnished a company car by his or

[7] A livery conveyance is a vehicle used indiscriminately in conveying the public, without limitation to certain persons or particular occasions or without being governed by special terms (*Elliott v Behner*, 150 Kan. 876 96 P.2d 852, 857). A public conveyance is one that holds itself out as a common carrier (*Merchants Parcel Delivery v Pennsylvania Public Utility Commission, 150 Pa. Super. 120, 28 A.2d 340, 344*).

[8] Some students may say. "That may all be very true, but the only thing necessary is for Brown to say that he had given permission; if he is willing to do this, both policies will apply." As you will recall from the discussion of vicarious liability as it relates to the auto, the owner of an auto may be held liable for its operation by anyone who is operating it with the owner's permission. Since by admitting that White had his permission Brown would leave himself open for a substantial amount of liability, he may be reluctant to do so.

her employer. In the event of an accident, the employee must look to the employer's policy for coverage, since this exclusion eliminates coverage under the employee's policy.[9] Normally, the employer will have coverage to protect the employee. However, an individual who wants to arrange coverage on an auto that is furnished for his or her regular use may do so under the Extended Liability Endorsement to the PAP, which provides coverage for autos furnished for regular use.

Exclusion B.3. is related to Exclusion B.2. but differs in one important respect. This exclusion eliminates coverage for liability arising out of autos owned by or furnished for the regular use of family members. An exception to the exclusion states that it does not apply to the named insured or spouse. The intent is to exclude resident relatives for autos they own or that are furnished for their regular use. However, if the named insured or spouse should use an auto that is owned by or furnished for the regular use of a family member, coverage applies for the named insured or spouse. In the absence of this important exception to the exclusion, the coverage of the policy would never apply to an auto owned by another family member. This would be a serious gap in coverage for the parent with high limits of coverage who occasionally operated a son's or daughter's auto with low limits.

Exclusion B.4. excludes coverage for any vehicle located inside a facility designed for racing for the purpose of competing in or practicing or preparing for any prearranged or organized racing or speed contest. (Although the insured's souped-up stock car is covered while being used on streets and highways, it is not covered while being raced at the fair grounds.)

Other Liability Coverage Provisions

In addition to the liability insuring agreement and exclusions, Part A contains the following additional provisions applicable to the liability coverage.

[9] A seldom recognized facet of this exclusion is that it does not apply to a non-owned auto furnished for the regular use of the named insured if that vehicle is being used as a *temporary substitute* for any other Covered Auto. Suppose that Brown is furnished a company car by his employer. Normally, Brown's PAP will not apply to that company car. However, if the company car is being used as a temporary substitute for Brown's personal car, coverage will apply. This quirk results from the inclusion of a "temporary substitute auto" in the definition of "Your Covered Auto," which is excepted from this exclusion.

Supplementary Payments In addition to the promise to pay sums that the insured is legally obligated to pay and the cost of defending suits, the insurer promises to pay certain other costs under the Supplementary Payments section:

1. First, the policy promises to pay the cost of bail bonds required of the insured because of an accident, provided the accident results in bodily injury or property damage covered under the policy. The limit of payment for such bonds is $250.

2. Premiums on appeal bonds and bonds to release attachments in suits covered under the policy are covered in full.

3. Interest on a judgment after the judgment has been entered is covered.

4. Loss of earnings up to $200 a day while attending hearings or trials at the company's request is covered.

5. Other reasonable expenses incurred at the request of the insurer are covered.

Amounts payable under the supplementary payments provision are payable in addition to the liability limit.

Out of State Coverage One of the conditions of Part A, designated Out of State coverage, provides two important qualifications to the liability insuring agreement when the insured auto is involved in an accident in another state. First, if the state in which the accident takes place requires higher limits under its financial responsibility law than those of the policy, the policy automatically adjusts to provide the higher required limits. In addition, if the state has a compulsory insurance law that applies to nonresidents (such as a no-fault law), the policy changes automatically to include the minimum amounts of coverage required.

Limits of Liability The Limit of Liability provision stipulates that the per person and per accident bodily injury limits apply, and the per accident property damage limit is the most the insurer will pay, regardless of the number of insureds, claims made, vehicles insured under the policy, or vehicles involved in an accident. This section also states that no one will be entitled to receive duplicate payments for the same elements of loss under liability coverage and under medical payments coverage, uninsured motorists coverage, or under-insured motorists coverage provided by the policy.

MEDICAL PAYMENTS COVERAGE

Medical payments coverage is a special form of accident insurance, providing coverage for medical expenses incurred by insured persons in automobile-related injuries. The basic limit of liability for medical payments coverage is $1000 per person, with no maximum per accident. For a small additional premium (a few dollars a year), this limit can be increased to $5000 or $10,000 per person, again with no aggregate per accident.

Medical Payments Insurance Agreement

The Medical Payments Coverage insuring agreement is simple and straightforward:

> We will pay reasonable expenses incurred for necessary medical and funeral services because of "bodily injury":
>
> **1.** Caused by accident.
> **2.** Sustained by an "insured."
>
> We will pay only those expenses incurred within 3 years from the date of the accident.

The definition of *bodily injury* means "bodily harm, sickness or disease, including death that results." In the case of fatalities, funeral expenses are paid, again up to the limit for the coverage.

As in the liability insuring agreement, the definition of *insured* is an important determinant of coverage. Coverage applies to two classes of persons.

First, coverage applies to the named insured and to any family member who suffers bodily injury caused by accident while occupying a covered auto. The term *occupying* is defined to include "in, upon, getting in, on, out, or off." This broad definition of occupying means that the fairly common injuries caused by slamming car doors on hands and fingers are covered under the medical payments coverage.

Coverage also applies to the named insured and family members if, while a pedestrian, they are struck by any motor vehicle designed for use on public roads or by a trailer of any type. A child of the insured might be struck by an auto while crossing the street; in such a case, the medical payments coverage would pay for medical expenses incurred, up to the limit for the coverage. Under this "struck by" facet of the coverage, the injured party might be injured while a pedestrian. Although the insuring agreement makes specific reference to "pedestrian," an Insurance Services Office clarification states that there was no intent, by use of the term "pedestrian," to limit coverage to insureds when struck by a vehicle while walking. In other words, for example, an insured struck by a motor vehicle while riding a bicycle is entitled to Medical Payments coverage under the "pedestrian" provision.

Persons other than the named insured and family members are also covered for medical payments, but only while occupying the insured's covered auto. Persons injured while occupying a non-owned auto may have coverage for medical payments under the coverage on the non-owned auto or under their own policies.

Medical Payments Exclusions

Like the liability coverage, the medical payments coverage is subject to its own set of exclusions. Several of the exclusions are almost identical with those of the liability section, and it is therefore unnecessary to repeat their discussion here. The exclusions under the liability section that also apply to the medical payments coverage are those that relate to

- Vehicles with fewer than four wheels (1)
- Autos used as a public or livery conveyance (2)
- Autos (other than a covered auto) owned by or furnished for the regular use of the named insured (5)
- Autos (other than a covered auto) owned by or furnished for the regular use of family members (6)
- Autos operated without a reasonable belief that the user is entitled to do so (7)
- Trucks being used in business (8)

Exclusion 3 excludes coverage for injuries sustained while occupying a vehicle that is located for use as a residence or premises. Since the definition of *covered auto* includes a trailer owned by the insured, this exclusion is required to prevent the policy from becoming a general accident policy in those instances in which the insured owns and occupies a house trailer.

Exclusion 4 applies to individuals injured in the course of their employment and eliminates coverage if benefits are either available or required under a workers compensation law.

Exclusion 7, which involves vehicles used without permission, contains the same exception as the similarly worded liability exclusion, stating that it does not apply to a family member while using a covered auto belonging to the insured.

The next two exclusions under the medical payments coverage—Exclusions 9 and 10—eliminate coverage for injuries caused by the discharge of nuclear weapons, war, civil war, insurrection, rebellion or revolution, and injuries caused by nuclear reaction, radiation, or radioactive contamination.

Exclusion 11 excludes injuries sustained while occupying a vehicle located at a facility designed for racing for the purpose of competing in or practicing or preparing for an organized racing or speed contest.

Limitations Applicable to Medical Payment Recoveries

The Medical Payments section of the PAP is subject to several provisions that limit the insured's recovery. First, the Limit of Liability provision stipulates that duplicate payments will not be made for the same loss under the medical payments coverage and the uninsured or underinsured motorists coverage (discussed shortly).

Recovery under medical payments is further limited by the Other Insurance clause. This clause provides that Medical Payments coverage of the policy is excess with respect to any non-owned auto, and that when other auto medical payments coverage exists, payment is made on a pro rata basis, based on the medical payment limits.

Finally, the medical payments coverage is subject to a subrogation clause. The general provisions require the insured to assign to the insurer any right of recovery against a third party to the extent that he or she receives payment from the insurer.

UNINSURED MOTORIST COVERAGE

In spite of the financial responsibility laws and the dictates of common sense, some people still drive without auto liability insurance. *Uninsured motorist coverage,* designated Part C in the PAP, is designed to protect the insured and his or her family for injuries sustained as a result of being struck by an uninsured or hit-and-run driver or a driver whose insurance company has become insolvent.[10]

[10] In most states, Uninsured Motorist coverage applies to bodily injury only, but in California, Delaware, Georgia, Indiana, New Jersey, New Mexico, North Carolina, Rhode Island, South Carolina, Tennessee, Texas, Virginia, Washington, West Virginia, and the District of Columbia, it also includes property damage. In these states, the property damage part of the coverage is subject to a deductible ranging from $100 to $300. In other states property damage caused by uninsured motorists is covered by the Collision coverage of the Damage-to-Your-Auto part.

Uninsured Motorist Insuring Agreement

In its simplest terms, the uninsured motorist coverage insuring agreement promises to pay the amount that an injured insured could have collected from the insurer of an uninsured driver if such driver had carried auto liability insurance. As in the case of the liability coverage, uninsured motorist coverage is written with split limits of liability applicable per person and per accident. The standard limit for the coverage is the minimum limit required under the state's financial responsibility law, but higher limits are available. Increased limits may be purchased up to the limit carried under the liability section (Part A) of the policy.

Coverage applies when an insured is injured by an "uninsured motor vehicle." *Uninsured motor vehicle* is defined to include (1) a motor vehicle that is not covered for bodily injury liability insurance or for which the bodily injury limits are less than the limits required by the state law, (2) a hit-and-run vehicle, and (3) a vehicle that was insured at the time of the accident, but the insurer becomes insolvent. The policy specifically excludes from the definition of "uninsured motor vehicle" vehicles owned by or furnished for the regular use of the named insured or family members and vehicles owned or operated by qualified self-insurers or government bodies. In addition, farm-type tractors or equipment designed for use off public roads while not on public roads and vehicles operated on rails or crawler treads are also excluded.

Persons Insured The definition of *Insured* under uninsured motorist coverage includes three classes of persons: (1) the named insured and any family member, (2) any other person occupying the insured's covered auto, and (3) any person for damages that person is entitled to recover because of injury to a person described in (1) or (2). The named insured and family members are covered even when they are not occupying an auto and could recover if injured by an uninsured motorist as a pedestrian or, say, on a bicycle. Other persons are covered only if injured while occupying the insured's covered auto.

Uninsured Motorist Exclusions In addition to the previously noted exclusions of certain types of vehicles from the definition of "uninsured motor vehicle," the policy also contains eight additional exclusions. Two of these are grouped as Exclusion A, three are grouped as Exclusion B, and the remaining two are designated Exclusions C and D.

Exclusion A.1. excludes injuries sustained while occupying an owned vehicle that is not insured for uninsured motorist coverage under the policy. Exclusion A.2. excludes bodily injury sustained by any family member while occupying or if struck by a vehicle owned by the insured and covered on a primary basis under another policy. This provision is designed to eliminate pyramiding of uninsured motorist coverage limits.

Exclusion B.1. excludes coverage under uninsured motorist coverage if the injured person settles with the negligent party without the insurer's consent. This is to preserve the insurer's right to recovery against the negligent uninsured motorist, which would be impaired by such settlement.

Exclusion B.2. is the standard exclusion of an auto being used as a public or livery conveyance, and B.3. is the exclusion of vehicles used without a reasonable belief that the person is entitled to do so. The exclusion requiring reasonable belief that the person is entitled to use a vehicle, like the same exclusions under liability coverage and medical payments coverage, does not apply to a family member using a covered auto.

Exclusion C stipulates that the coverage shall not apply directly or indirectly to benefit any insurer or self-insurer under any workers compensation, disability benefits, or similar law. This means that such an insurer or self-insurer would not be subrogated to the injured party's right of recovery under the uninsured motorist coverage if the injury were sustained in the course of employment and the insurer paid workers compensation benefits to the injured insured.

Exclusion D excludes coverage for punitive or exemplary damages under the uninsured motorist coverage. It was added to the policy in response to court decisions in some states that ruled that punitive damages were covered because they were not specifically excluded.

Limitations on Payment The Uninsured Motorist Coverage's Limit of Liability provision establishes certain limitations on the amount payable under the coverage. It provides that amounts otherwise payable under the coverage will be reduced by all sums paid by or on behalf of the party who is legally responsible (i.e., the uninsured motorist). Payment under uninsured motorist coverage is also reduced by amounts payable under a workers compensation law, disability benefits law, or any similar law. Finally, payments under uninsured motorist coverage are reduced by amounts the recipient is entitled to receive under the Liability section of the policy.

The Other Insurance Provision of the uninsured motorist coverage makes coverage excess over the coverage on any non-owned automobile. In addition, recovery under all policies is limited to the highest applicable limit for any one vehicle under any insurance providing either primary or excess coverage.

Basis for Settlement Although the insuring agreement stipulates that the company will pay damages a covered person is legally entitled to recover from the owner or operator of an uninsured motor vehicle, the policy also states that the question of whether the injured person is entitled to collect from the uninsured motorist and, if so, the amount to which he or she is entitled, is to be decided by agreement between the covered person and the company. If the covered person and the company are unable to agree on either point, either party may request arbitration of the matter. If both parties agree to the arbitration, each party selects an arbitrator, and the two arbitrators select a third. The three arbitrators then settle the matter. If the arbitrators cannot agree on an umpire within 30 days, one is appointed by the court of jurisdiction. Each party pays the cost of his or her arbitrator, and they share the cost of the umpire.

Underinsured Motorist Coverage

Those insureds who purchase uninsured motorist coverage are eligible for an additional coverage, underinsured motorist coverage. Underinsured motorist coverage, which is added to the PAP by endorsement, covers bodily injuries sustained by an insured when the negligent driver has insurance, but the limits are less than the limits of the underinsured motorist coverage. As is true in uninsured motorist coverage, the injured party's insurer agrees to pay the amount that the insurer of the other driver would have paid, if he or she had been adequately insured.

It should be understood that the underinsured motorist coverage does not in any sense duplicate or overlap with uninsured motorist coverage. Uninsured motorist coverage applies only when the other driver does not carry insurance, is a hit-and-run driver, or is insured by an insurer that becomes insolvent. In the case of underinsured motorist coverage, the other driver has insurance, but the limits of coverage are less than the amount to which the injured party would be entitled based on his or her injuries.

As in the case of uninsured motorist coverage, determination of the amount to which the injured party is entitled is decided by agreement between the insurer and the injured party or by arbitration.[11]

Underinsured motorist coverage may be written only when the insured has purchased increased limits for uninsured motorists coverage. The underinsured motorists coverage must be written for the same limit as the uninsured motorists coverage.

PHYSICAL DAMAGE COVERAGE

The physical damage coverage of the PAP, Part D, is designated *Coverage for Damage to Your Auto.* Like the liability, medical payments, and uninsured motorist parts, the physical damage coverage includes its own insuring agreement, exclusions, and special conditions.

Physical Damage Insuring Agreement

There is a single physical damage insuring agreement, which provides coverage on an open-perils basis. However, the insuring agreement provides that loss by collision is covered only if the declarations section so indicates:

We will pay for direct and accidental loss to "your covered auto" or any "non-owned auto," including their equipment, minus any applicable deductible shown in the Declarations. If loss to more than one "your covered auto" or "non-owned auto" results from the same collision, only the highest applicable deductible will apply. We will pay for loss to "your covered auto" caused by:

1. Other than "collision" only if the Declarations indicate that Other Than Collision Coverage is provided for that auto.
2. "Collision" only if the Declarations indicate that "Collision" coverage is provided for that auto.

If there is a loss to a "non-owned auto," we will provide the broadest coverage applicable to any "your covered auto" shown in the Declarations.

Earlier forms of auto physical damage coverage, such as the family auto policy, divided physical dam-

age coverage into two separate insuring agreements: comprehensive and collision. Although the PAP refers to loss by collision, the term *comprehensive* is not used. The open-perils coverage excluding collision will undoubtedly continue to be referred to as *comprehensive* as well as by its newer designation, *other than collision.*

Loss Other Than by Collision The coverage for loss *other than by collision* is essentially an open-perils type of property coverage. Coverage applies to all losses except those that are specifically excluded. The policy specifically designates several perils as "not considered collision":

breakage of glass, loss caused by missiles, falling objects, fire, theft or larceny, explosion, earthquake, windstorm, hail, water, flood, malicious mischief or vandalism, riot or civil commotion, or contact with a bird or animal.

Because these losses are not considered collision losses, they are covered as *comprehensive* losses. Because the collision deductible is normally higher than for other losses, this is beneficial to the insured.

The policy also provides that the insured may, at his or her option, consider breakage of glass to be loss due to collision. This will be advantageous in two situations. First, if the insured carries collision, but does not carry comprehensive insurance, coverage would exist for glass broken in a collision. In addition, if glass is broken in a collision, the insured benefits by having the glass breakage subject to a single deductible with other damage to the vehicle, rather than subject to a separate comprehensive deductible.

Collision Coverage *Collision* is defined as "the upset of your covered auto or its impact with another vehicle or object." Coverage for loss by collision applies to the covered auto regardless of fault and will respond when the insured cannot recover from another party because his or her personal negligence was the cause of the damage. But collision coverage can also be valuable in those cases where the insured is not at fault.

In those cases where the driver of the other auto is to blame, we would expect his or her Liability coverage to respond for damages to the owned auto. However, the other party may not have insurance. The innocent driver with Collision coverage can collect the amount of the loss (less any deductible) and then leave the job of collecting from the negligent driver

[11] In some states, uninsured motorist coverage and underinsured motorist coverage are merged into a single coverage.

to the insurance company. The PAP includes a subrogation provision under which the insured is required to assign to the insurer the right of claim against a negligent third party to the extent that he or she collects under the policy. Also, where the insured is at fault, the Collision coverage will pay for damage to his or her auto.

Physical Damage to Non-owned Autos We have already noted that the physical damage coverage of the PAP applies not only to the insured's covered auto, but to a non-owned auto as well. This means that when the individual has purchased physical damage coverage on his or her own auto, such coverage is extended to non-owned autos being used by or in the custody of the insured or a family member. If there is a loss to a non-owned auto, the insurer will provide the broadest coverage that is applicable to any covered auto shown in the declarations. If, for example, a policy insures one owned auto for collision and comprehensive and another owned auto for comprehensive only, a non-owned auto will be covered for both comprehensive and collision if a loss occurs.

The definition of "non-owned auto" under the physical damage section is an important determinant of coverage. A *non-owned auto* is defined as follows:

"Non-owned auto" means

1. Any private passenger auto, pickup, van or "trailer" not owned by or furnished or available for the regular use of you or any "family member" while in the custody of or being operated by you or any "family member"; or

2. Any auto or "trailer" you do not own while used as a temporary substitute for "your covered auto" which is out of normal use because of its
 a. breakdown
 b. repair
 c. servicing
 d. loss; or
 e. destruction

Note that the term *non-owned auto* includes two parts. The first refers to a private passenger auto, pickup, van, or trailer not owned by, or furnished, or available for the regular use of the named insured or any family member, while in the custody of or being operated by the named insured or any family member. The second part includes any non-owned auto or trailer used as a temporary substitute for a covered auto that is out of normal use because of its breakdown, repair, servicing, loss, or destruction.

Coverage on non-owned autos is subject to the same insuring agreements as owned autos. Non-owned autos are also subject to three specific exclusions (discussed next). One of these exclusions eliminates coverage for loss to a non-owned vehicle when used by an insured without a reasonable belief that the user is entitled to do so.

The question of permissive use also arises in connection with the owned auto. The policy's subrogation clause states that the insurer does not have the right to subrogate against a person who uses a covered auto with a reasonable belief that he or she is entitled to do so. This means, conversely, that the insurer may subrogate against a person operating the vehicle without permission after making payment for damage arising out of such operation.

The physical damage coverage on non-owned autos is excess over other coverage applicable to the non-owned auto. If Brian borrows Joan's car and demolishes it, Joan's policy will apply if she carries collision coverage. If Joan does not carry collision on her car, Brian's collision coverage will apply. The same is true with respect to a borrowed trailer. The definition of non-owned auto includes "trailer," so coverage applies to rented or borrowed trailers. The Limit of Liability provision imposes a $500 limit on payment for damage to non-owned trailers.

One situation in which coverage for damage to non-owned autos can be important is the rental of an automobile. National car rental companies such as Hertz and Avis provide the renter with auto insurance covering liability, medical payments, and uninsured motorist coverage (plus no-fault benefits in those states with such laws), but do not provide the renter with physical damage coverage. Collision damage waiver (CDW) is offered at a cost of $9 or $10 per day. For those persons who carry comprehensive and collision on their own cars, the extension of physical damage coverage to non-owned autos under the PAP provides coverage on rented cars, subject to the policy deductible.[12]

[12] The National Association of Insurance Commissioners has developed a *Collision Damage Waivers Act,* which provides for the regulation of rental companies when issuing CDWs. The act provides definitions and establishes standards to which rental companies must adhere and makes certain practices unfair or deceptive practices under the statutory provisions on fraud.

Physical Damage Exclusions

In view of the fact that the physical damage coverage is on an "open-perils" basis, the number of exclusions in this section of the policy is surprisingly small. There are 14 exclusions: 5 of these (exclusions 1, 2, 3, 7, and 13) exclude loss to both owned and nonowned vehicles and their equipment under specified circumstances, 3 apply only to nonowned autos (exclusions 9, 12, and 14), and 6 eliminate certain types of property from coverage (4, 5, 6, 8, 10, and 11). We will begin our examination of the exclusions with the 5 exclusions that deal with specific loss situations.

Exclusion 1 is the now-familiar exclusion of loss while the auto is being used as a public or livery conveyance.

Exclusion 2 eliminates coverage for damage due and confined to wear and tear, freezing, mechanical or electrical breakdown or failure, and road damage to tires. Losses of this nature are inevitable or at least controllable by the insured. However, the exclusion does not apply if the damage results from total theft of the insured auto.

Exclusion 3 eliminates coverage for damage caused by radioactive contamination or by the discharge of a nuclear weapon and war in all its forms.

Exclusion 7 excludes the total loss of an auto by destruction or confiscation by government or civil authorities. The exclusion was added in response to the increasingly frequent confiscation of vehicles by law enforcement agencies and decisions holding that such confiscation was a covered loss under the policy, because it was not excluded. The exclusion does not apply to the interests of a loss payee under the policy.

Exclusion 13 excludes any owned or nonowned auto while located inside a facility designed for racing, for the purpose of competing in or practicing for a prearranged or organized racing or speed contest.

Three exclusions (9, 12, and 14) apply to non-owned autos. Exclusion 9 excludes coverage for damage to a non-owned vehicle being used without a reasonable belief that the user is entitled to do so. It is similar in wording and intent to the permissive use exclusion discussed in connection with the liability coverage.

Exclusion 12 is a business-related exclusion applicable to non-owned autos. It eliminates coverage for damage to non-owned autos being used by any insured while employed in the automobile business. This eliminates coverage for damage to a non-owned auto while being operated by the named insured or a relative who is employed in the automobile business.

Exclusion 14 excludes coverage for loss to a rental vehicle, if the rental company is precluded from recovering for the loss because of the provisions in the rental agreement or in the applicable state law.

Exclusions 4, 5, 6, 8, 10, and 11 exclude damage to or loss of specific types of equipment. The first of these, Exclusion 4, deals with sound systems that may be installed in the auto, such as radios and stereos, tape decks, and compact disc players. The exclusion does not apply to such equipment if it is permanently installed in the vehicle. Equipment that is permanently installed is excepted from the exclusion and is therefore covered. In addition, equipment that is a component of a permanent housing unit and that is powered by the covered auto's electrical system is covered if it is in or upon a covered auto when the loss occurs. Under the physical damage limit of liability, there is a $1000 sublimit for sound reproducing equipment and accessories that are permanently installed in a covered auto in a location not used by the auto manufacturer for such equipment. Such equipment might include, for example, a CD player or a set of humongous speakers that are installed in the trunk.[13]

Exclusion 5 excludes coverage for electronic equipment, capable of sending or receiving data signals, such as CB radios, telephones, video and audio cassette recorders, and computers. Accessories for such equipment is also excluded. The exclusion does not apply to equipment that is part of an auto's operating system or to telephones which are permanently installed and powered by the covered auto's electrical system.[14]

Exclusion 6 eliminates coverage on tapes, records, discs or other media designed for use with the equipment excluded by exclusions 4 and 5.[15]

Exclusion 8 deletes coverage on camper bodies, trailers, or motor homes not listed in the declarations and facilities or equipment used with such vehicles.

[13] Coverage for loss to such types of equipment can be bought back on a stated amount basis by endorsement for an additional premium.

[14] Coverage for electronic equipment designed for transmission and reception of signals can be bought back by endorsement for an additional premium.

[15] When specific coverage on sound-reproducing equipment is added by endorsement, coverage is automatically provided for $200 on tapes, records, or discs. When coverage on equipment is not purchased, coverage on tapes, records, and discs up to $200 may be separately purchased by endorsement for an additional premium.

Facilities and equipment include, but are not limited to, cooking, dining, plumbing and refrigeration facilities, and awnings or cabanas. There are two exceptions to the exclusion. First, it does not apply to non-owned trailers or camper bodies (including facilities and equipment). (Under the Limit of Liability provision of the physical damage section, there is a $500 limit for loss to non-owned trailers, but there is no dollar limit on camper bodies.) In addition, the exclusion does not apply to newly acquired trailers or camper bodies. The insurer must be notified of the acquisition within 14 days.

Exclusion 10 excludes loss to equipment designed or used for the detection or location of radar (i.e., "fuzz-busters") or laser devices.

Exclusion 11 eliminates coverage on custom furnishings or equipment in or on any pickup or van. The exclusion cites carpeting and insulation, furniture or bars, facilities for cooking and sleeping, height-extending roofs, or custom murals, paints, or other decals or graphics.[16] An exception to the exclusion extends coverage to caps, covers, and bedliners, which are covered while in or upon a pickup.

Diminished Value Exclusion In some states, when a vehicle is involved in a collision requiring repairs in excess of stated amount, say $3000, a notation of the damage and repair is made on the auto title. This can affect the trade-in or sale value at a later time. This loss (or potential loss) in the value of the vehicle is referred to as *diminished value,* a concept that has sparked considerable debate between consumers and insurers. In 1999, ISO filed a new endorsement— *Coverage for Damage to Your Auto Exclusion* (PP 13 01), which excludes diminished value. The endorsement adds a new definition to the policy for *diminution in value,* and a new exclusion eliminating coverage for such loss to owned and non-owned autos. Insurers are free to use or not use the diminished value endorsement and it remains to be seen to what extent it will find acceptance.

Other Physical Damage Provisions

In addition to the insuring agreement and exclusions, the physical damage section includes a number of other important provisions.

Limit of Liability—Payment of Loss The company's liability under the physical damage coverage is limited to the lesser of (1) the actual cash value of the stolen or damaged property or (2) the amount required to repair or replace the property with other property of like kind and quality. The 1994 edition of the policy adds a new provision, stipulating that an adjustment for depreciation and physical condition will be made in determining the actual cash value in the event of a total loss. The contract further provides that if repair or replacement results in betterment to the insured, the insurer will not pay for the betterment.

The Payment of Loss provision gives the insurer the option of deciding how to settle the claim. The company reserves the right to repair the damage, replace the auto, or to pay for the loss in cash. In the event of theft, the insurer has the right to return the stolen auto. If the stolen auto has been damaged, the company must, of course, pay for the repair of the damage.

The After-Market Parts Issue In November 1999, a Marion, Illinois, jury awarded a $1.2 billion judgment against State Farm, the nation's largest insurer, for their use of non-original equipment manufacturer (OEM) parts (also sometimes called *after-market parts* or *competitive parts*). Competitive parts, or non-OEM parts, are large collision replacement parts, usually made of sheet metal or plastic and are built by a manufacturer other than the original automaker. Competitive parts were initially developed to address the problem of skyrocketing costs to replace car parts, which were previously available only from the manufacturer of the auto. Insurers argue that the use of competitive parts is a proven tool to encourage competition that provides consumers better products and lower prices. They also argue that the lawsuits to prohibit the use of competitive parts could create an artificial monopoly where competition has provided consumers with choice and lower costs. The jury in the State Farm case evidently felt otherwise.[17]

Transportation Expense Coverage is provided for temporary transportation expenses (the cost of renting a car or using public transportation) incurred by the insured in the event of loss to the covered auto or

[16] Coverage for such property is available by endorsement for an additional premium.

[17] The Certified Automotive Parts Association (CAPA) a non-profit organization with membership including collision repairers, distributors, and the insurance industry was established in 1987 to certify quality of after-market parts. For CAPA's view on the State Farm verdict, see http://www.capacertified.org.

a non-owned auto. Coverage applies for loss by collision only if collision coverage has been purchased, and for loss other than collision if comprehensive coverage has been purchased. The limit for this coverage is $20 per day with a maximum of $600.[18] The coverage applies to expenses incurred by the insured for loss to an insured owned auto. For a non-owned auto, Transportation Expenses coverage applies for the loss of use expense for which the insured is legally liable. Except for losses caused by theft, coverage applies to expenses beginning 24 hours after the auto has been withdrawn from use. Coverage for transportation expenses resulting from theft begins 48 hours after the theft, and ends when the auto is returned to use or the insurer pays for the loss.

Towing and Labor Costs Coverage Towing and Labor Costs coverage can be added to the PAP by endorsement. Limit of liability options of $25, $50, and $75 are available. When purchased, Towing and Labor Costs coverage applies to both "your covered auto" and a "non-owned auto."

POLICY CONDITIONS

The two final parts of the contract, designated Part E and Part F, contain the general policy provisions, some of which have already been noted in passing.

Part E—Duties after an Accident or Loss

Part E of the PAP lists the duties of the insured and other persons seeking coverage under the policy in the event of loss. An introductory statement requires that the insurer be notified promptly of how, when, and where the accident or loss happened. In addition, a person seeking coverage under any of the provisions of the policy must

1. Cooperate with the insurer in the investigation, settlement, or defense of any claim.

2. Promptly send the insurer copies of any notices or legal papers received in connection with the accident or loss.

3. Submit to physical examinations by physicians selected by the insurer as often as the insurer reasonably requires. The insurer pays the cost of the examinations. A person seeking coverage under the policy must agree to submit to examination under oath if required by the insurer.

4. Authorize the insurer to obtain medical reports and other pertinent records.

5. Submit a proof of loss when required by the insurer.

A person seeking coverage under the Uninsured Motorist Coverage must also promptly notify the police if a hit-and-run driver is involved.

With respect to the Physical Damage coverages (Damage to Your Auto), the insured must take reasonable steps after the loss to protect the auto and its equipment from further loss. The insurer will pay any expenses incurred by the insured in providing such protection. The insured must also notify the police if the covered auto is stolen. Finally, the insured must permit the insurer to inspect and appraise the damaged property before it is disposed of or repaired.

Part F—General Provisions

There are nine general provisions in the PAP, some of which are similar or identical in wording with their similarly titled counterparts in the Comprehensive Personal Liability form already discussed.

Bankruptcy Bankruptcy or insolvency of an insured does not relieve the insurer of its obligation under the policy. If the insured is sued and declares bankruptcy, discharging his liability, the insurer is still obliged to pay that part of the judgment covered by the insurance.

Changes The terms of the policy cannot be changed or waived except by endorsement. If a change requires a premium adjustment, the premium will be adjusted as of the effective date of coverage. This provision also includes a liberalization clause; if the insurer revises its policies to provide broader coverage without additional premium, existing policies are automatically broadened to include the new coverage.

Fraud The fraud provision stipulates that the insurer will not provide coverage for any insured who has made fraudulent statements or engaged in fraudulent conduct in connection with any accident or loss. Like most other policy provisions dealing with fraud or misrepresentation, this provision merely affirms in the contract the right the insurer

[18] The limit of coverage may be increased by endorsement for an additional premium.

would have at common law.

Legal Action Against Us No legal action may be brought against the insurer until the insured has complied with all the terms of the policy. Furthermore, a claimant does not have the right to bring the insurer into an action to determine the liability of the insured. (Some states have laws that permit an injured party to sue both the insured and his or her insurer. In these jurisdictions this provision is invalid.)

Our Right to Recover Payment This is the subrogation clause. It applies to all coverages under the policy, and requires the insured to assign any right of recovery against a third party to the insurer, to the extent that payment is made to that insured. The insured is required to do whatever is necessary to enable the insurer to exercise its right of recovery and may do nothing to prejudice that right.

Policy Period and Territory The policy applies only to accidents and losses that occur during the policy period (shown in the declarations) and within the policy territory. The policy territory is the United States, its territories or possessions, or Canada. Coverage also applies for accidents or losses while the covered auto is being transported between ports of the United States, its territories or possessions, or Canada. Note that there is no coverage under the policy in Mexico. If the insured drives into Mexico, he or she must obtain coverage from an insurance company licensed to write auto insurance in Mexico.[19]

Termination The termination provision outlines the conditions under which either the insured or the company may cancel the policy and the rights of both parties with respect to nonrenewal, and related provisions.

First, the named insured may cancel the policy at any time, either by returning the policy to the company or by giving written notice of the date of cancellation.

The insurer's right to cancel depends on the period for which the policy has been in force. If the policy has been in force for less than 60 days, the company may cancel by giving 10 days' written

notice. However, once the policy has been in force for 60 days, the insurer can cancel only for non-payment of premium, if the named insured or any resident relative has his or her driver's license suspended or revoked, or if the policy was obtained through material misrepresentation. Cancellation for nonpayment requires 10 days' written notice. Cancellation for revocation or suspension of license requires 20 days' written notice. Renewal policies (or extensions of direct billed policies) are considered to have been in force for more than 60 days, and are therefore cancelable only for nonpayment of premium, revocation or suspension of license, or material misrepresentation in obtaining the policy.

While the company's right to cancel is limited after the policy has been in force for 60 days, the company may still choose not to renew a policy. If the company elects not to renew the policy, it must give the insured at least 20 days' written notice of its intent not to renew. Furthermore, on policies that are written for less than a full year, nonrenewal may take place only on the anniversary of the original effective date.

This condition also makes provision for automatic termination in the event that the company offers to continue or to renew the policy and the insured does not accept. Failure to pay the required premium when due is considered failure of the insured to accept the offer to renew.

Finally, the termination provision states that any state laws concerning cancellation of auto insurance take precedence over the policy provisions. If laws in the state where the policy is sold impose greater restrictions on the insurer's right to cancel or to refuse renewal, the state law applies.

Transfer of Your Interest in This Policy This provision is an assignment clause, and stipulates that the named insured's rights and duties under the policy may not be assigned without the written consent of the insurer. Automatic coverage is provided, however, if the named insured dies, for the surviving spouse or the named insured's legal representative.

Two or More Auto Policies This special "other insurance" clause provides that when an insured has two or more policies with the same company applicable to the same accident, the maximum payable under all policies will not exceed the highest applicable limit of liability under any one policy. For example, if Jones has two autos insured with the same company and has an accident while using a non-owned

[19] Failure to purchase Mexican insurance can lead to serious complications in the event of loss. In Mexico, jurisdiction for criminal and civil law rests in a single court. It is customary to impound the vehicle and hold the driver in jail until an investigation is completed and a court hearing is held. If the driver has insurance with a Mexican-licensed insurer, the arresting officer has the authority to waive the incarceration and impounding of the auto.

auto, the maximum payable under the two policies will be the highest limit under those policies.

ENDORSEMENTS TO THE PAP

The Personal Auto Policy may be modified by endorsement to meet special needs or to reflect the statutory requirements of individual states. The following are a few of the more important endorsements available for use with the PAP. Although these endorsements represent only a small fraction of those available, they are among the most important and reflect the extreme flexibility of the PAP.

Extended Liability Coverage

The PAP may be extended by endorsement to cover certain non-owned autos that would otherwise be excluded. The need for broadened *drive-other-car* coverage arises from the restrictions in the PAP that eliminate coverage on certain types of non-owned autos. These include, as you will recall:

1. Autos furnished for the regular use of the named insured

2. Autos furnished for the regular use of resident relatives

3. Non-owned autos that are not private passenger autos used by the named insured or resident relatives in business

4. Non-owned autos used by any insured in the garage business

In each excluded case, the intent is that the excluded auto be covered under its own policy and that coverage for the named insured and resident relatives while operating such autos be provided by the non-owned auto's policy. However, there are instances in which the individual who has occasion to use a non-owned auto of the excluded types desires his or her own coverage, which will apply as excess over the specific coverage on the non-owned auto.

The Extended Liability Coverage endorsement (PP 03 06), designed for use with the PAP may be used to extend the drive-other-car coverage of the policy to include coverage for all the excluded types of non-owned autos except those used in the garage business. Coverage applies for the individual named

in the endorsement as the insured, and a separate premium is required for each person for whom coverage is provided.

Named Non-Owner Policy

Occasions sometimes arise in which an individual who does not own an auto desires coverage for those instances in which he or she may borrow an auto. As the reader may recall, under such circumstances, coverage for the borrower is provided under the auto policy applicable to the borrowed car, provided the borrower had permission of the named insured under that policy. However, the possibility always exists that the borrowed auto might not be insured, or that the limits of liability on the borrowed car might be inadequate. When borrowers have their own policy, coverage under their policy will apply on an excess basis, but for the individual who does not own an auto there could be a serious deficiency.

A special form of coverage, called Named Non-Ownership coverage may be written for a person who does not own an auto, but who desires his or her own coverage in the event that a borrowed auto is inadequately insured. Coverage is normally provided under the PAP, with a special endorsement called the Non-Owner Endorsement. Coverage applies for the named insured only and does not extend to any other person—even a resident spouse—unless specifically named. Coverage is provided for liability arising out of the use of any auto not owned by the named insured or spouse or by any member of the named insured's household. The coverage is excess over any other coverage applicable to the borrowed auto, and does not apply to the owner of the auto. However, as in the PAP, other persons or organizations held vicariously liable for the operation of the borrowed auto by the named insured or spouse are covered.

Although the endorsement is designed to provide coverage on non-owned autos, it also provides automatic coverage for 30 days on a private passenger auto or a pickup, panel truck, or van not used in business other than farming, which is acquired by the insured during the policy period.

Miscellaneous Type Vehicle Endorsement

The increasing popularity of motorcycles and motorscooters has brought about a corresponding

increase in demand for insurance for such vehicles. At the same time, recreational motor vehicles such as go-carts, minibikes, and all-terrain vehicles have increased in popularity, creating a demand for insurance suited to the needs of their owners.

Initially, both the liability and physical damage exposure of recreational motor vehicles were handled in a variety of ways. Specialty insurers developed specialized policies for each of the various types of recreational motor vehicles, usually based in one way or another on the automobile policy. Thus, one company offered a *Snowmobile Policy,* while another insurer offered an *All-Terrain Vehicle Policy,* and another offered a *Go-Cart Liability Policy.* Although these contracts are still available through specialty insurers, there is now a standard *Miscellaneous Type Vehicle Endorsement* available for use with the PAP to provide protection for the owner of a recreational motor vehicle.

The *ISO Personal Vehicle Manual* includes rules for insuring various types of vehicles that are not otherwise eligible for coverage under the PAP through the use of the Miscellaneous Type Vehicle Endorsement. The types of vehicles that are eligible under this rule include motor homes, trailers designed for use with private passenger autos, motorcycles, mopeds, motorscooters, motorbikes, gocarts, and other similar vehicles, snowmobiles and all-terrain vehicles, dune buggies, golf carts, antique autos, and classic autos.

When the PAP is used to insure these vehicles, it is modified by endorsement. The Miscellaneous Type Vehicle Endorsement is used for all of the listed types of miscellaneous vehicles except snowmobiles and antique or classic autos. Separate endorsements are used for insuring these type vehicles. In addition, a second endorsement is used with the Miscellaneous Type Vehicle Endorsement when coverage is written on a motor home.

The Miscellaneous Type Vehicle Endorsement may be used to provide all of the standard PAP coverages on the miscellaneous-type vehicle, including liability coverage, medical payments, uninsured motorist coverage, and physical damage coverage. The endorsement may be added to a PAP that is used to insure vehicles that meet the standard eligibility requirements of the PAP. This means that private passenger autos and miscellaneous-type vehicles may be insured in the same policy. Provisions pertinent to private passenger automobiles remain in full

effect and apply to any private passenger autos insured under the contract.[20]

"Your Covered Auto" Redefined The Miscellaneous Type Vehicle endorsement adds a new definition of *your covered auto* to the contract, corresponding to the particular type of vehicle that is being insured. Coverage is extended to include newly acquired miscellaneous-type vehicles of the same type as shown in the schedule or declarations, subject to the same reporting requirements for additional and replacement autos under the regular personal auto policy. This means that a newly acquired motorcycle is covered only if the vehicle described in the policy is also a motorcycle.

In addition to the coverage on newly acquired vehicles of the type scheduled in the endorsement, the endorsement also provides coverage for any newly acquired private passenger auto, pickup, panel truck, or van (not used in any business other than farming). The owner of a motorcycle insured under the PAP has automatic coverage for 14 days in the event he or she acquires an eligible automobile.

The definition of *your covered auto* also includes any temporary substitute auto while used for a covered auto that has been withdrawn from use because of mechanical breakdown, servicing, repair, loss, or destruction. There is no restriction as to the type of vehicle that qualifies as a temporary substitute; a temporary substitute may be a vehicle of the type insured or it could be a private passenger auto or a truck.

Coverage Features Perhaps the most significant provision of the endorsement is the definition of covered persons. With respect to the scheduled vehicle ("your covered auto"), coverage applies for the named insured, family members, and other persons, subject to the usual exclusion of anyone using an auto without a reasonable belief of being entitled to do so. In addition, the endorsement covers the vicarious liability of any person or organization for the acts or omissions of another insured person. While coverage is provided for this range of persons with respect to the owned vehicle, there is no coverage for

[20] The Miscellaneous Type Vehicle Endorsement is also used when the PAP is used to insure a passenger-type auto that is owned by two or more relatives other than husband and wife or by two or more individuals who reside together.

anyone—including the named insured—for non-owned vehicles. The only exception is that coverage applies for the named insured while using a non-owned vehicle as a temporary substitute for a vehicle described in the endorsement.

Liability Exclusions The exclusions applicable to miscellaneous-type vehicles differ from those in the PAP in two respects. First, the standard PAP exclusion of any vehicle with less than four wheels is modified so that coverage is provided for the type of vehicle scheduled in the endorsement. The similarly worded exclusion applicable to medical payments is also modified to include coverage for vehicles with less than four wheels.

The second exclusion is an optional exclusion of liability to passengers. It is activated by an indication in the endorsement. A 20-percent premium credit is granted for the passenger liability exclusion for liability written with a single limit. When the policy is written with split limits, a 40-percent credit applies. The exclusion of liability to passengers is obviously an undesirable feature, and should, of course, be avoided.

Physical Damage Coverage Physical damage coverage may be written to include collision coverage and loss other than by collision (comprehensive).[21] Physical damage coverage on the insured miscellaneous type vehicle applies to non-owned vehicles only when being used as a temporary substitute only when being used as a temporary substitute vehicle and not otherwise.

Motor Home Endorsement When the Miscellaneous Type Vehicle Endorsement insures a motor home, an additional endorsement is attached to the policy, entitled *Miscellaneous Type Vehicle Amendment (Motor Homes)*. This endorsement excludes liability, medical payments, and physical damage coverage on the motor home when the named insured rents or leases it to others. Full liability coverage for rental situations can be bought back in the same endorsement. The additional premium for buyback of the rental coverage exclusion varies with the number of weeks per year for which the motor home is rented.

In addition to the exclusion of damage or loss to the motor home while rented (which may be eliminated for an additional premium), the motor home endorsement also excludes loss due to dishonest or fraudulent acts by a person to whom the motor home has been rented or loaned. This exclusion cannot be removed.

Finally, the motor home amendment endorsement excludes medical payments coverage for any person for bodily injury sustained while occupying the motor home while it is rented or leased to any organization or any person other than the named insured.

Snowmobile Endorsement The Insurance Services Office has developed a *Snowmobile Endorsement* for use with the PAP in insuring snowmobiles. A "snowmobile" is defined as a land motor vehicle designed for use mainly off public roads on snow or ice and propelled by wheels, crawler treads, or belts. A vehicle powered by airplane-type propellers or fans is specifically stated not to be a snowmobile.

The principal difference between the Snowmobile Endorsement and the Miscellaneous-Type Vehicle Endorsement relates to coverage on newly acquired vehicles. Unlike the Miscellaneous-Type Vehicle Endorsement (and the PAP itself), notice to the insurer is required within 30 days from the date of acquisition for both replacement vehicles and for additional vehicles.

Coverage is provided for a temporary substitute used by an insured when the covered snowmobile is withdrawn from use because of mechanical breakdown, servicing, or repair. As in the case of the PAP, a temporary substitute may not be owned by the named insured.

Two additional exclusions under the Snowmobile Endorsement must be noted. The first excludes coverage on any snowmobile while rented or leased to any person or organization other than the named insured. This means that there is no coverage age if the covered snowmobile is leased or rented to others. Coverage would apply, however, to a snowmobile leased to the named insured. Although the named insured has coverage while operating a leased or rented snowmobile, other family members do not. The second exclusion eliminates coverage for any snowmobile operated or used in practice or preparation for any racing or speed contest, regardless of

[21] Some insurers offer named-peril physical damage coverage for the perils of fire, theft, and Combined Additional Coverage. *Combined Additional Coverage* (which is also sometimes written on autos) includes windstorm, hail, earthquake, explosion, riot, civil commotion, aircraft, flood, malicious mischief and vandalism, and external discharge or leakage of water.

whether the contest is prearranged or organized. In addition to the exclusion of leased or rented snowmobiles and the racing or speed contest exclusion, there is an optional exclusion of liability to any passenger on the snowmobile. This exclusion leaves the insured with a serious uninsured exposure and is not an acceptable restriction in coverage. Coverage for the passenger hazard is an essential coverage and should be included in all snowmobile policies.

Antique and Classic Automobiles

Another specialized vehicle exposure that is sometimes encountered is the antique or classic automobile. The major consideration in connection with such vehicles relates to valuation. As you will recall, the PAP does not usually provide a specified dollar limit on the vehicle for physical damage coverages. It merely stipulates that coverage will apply up to the actual cash value of the vehicle. Because the value of an antique or classic auto can vary significantly, depending on the condition of the vehicle, a different approach is deemed necessary for such vehicles.

An antique auto is a motor vehicle of the private passenger type that is 25 years old or older and is maintained primarily for use in exhibitions, club activities, parades, and other functions of public interest. It may occasionally be used for other purposes. A classic auto is a motor vehicle of the private passenger type that is 10 years old or older and may be used on a regular basis. Its value is usually higher than the average value of other autos of the same make and model year because of its rarity and condition.

The major problem that arises in insuring both antique autos and classic autos is the question of the vehicle's value. When the PAP is written to cover an antique or classic auto, the policy is endorsed with the Coverage for Damage to Your Auto (Stated Amount Maximum Limit of Liability) Endorsement. The endorsement specifies a maximum dollar limit for the vehicle and provides, under the Limit of Liability provision that:

Our limit of liability for loss will be the lesser of the:

1. Stated amount shown in the Schedule or in the Declarations;

2. Actual cash value of the stolen or damaged property; or

3. Amount necessary to repair or replace the property.

Note that although the endorsement contains a specific dollar limit for physical damage coverage, the coverage is not on a valued basis. The limit merely serves as a maximum limit of recovery. The actual cash value of the vehicle is determined with appropriate consideration of depreciation and the vehicle's condition.

BUYING AUTOMOBILE INSURANCE

There is little doubt that auto insurance can be costly, and it promises to become more so in the future. While it is dissatisfying to pay the large premiums we are required to pay to insurers, it is distressing to do so and then find at the time of a loss that the coverage purchased is inadequate for the need.

Purchasing auto insurance should follow the principles of risk management and insurance buying we originally encountered in Chapter 4. There, you will recall, we established a priority ranking for insurance coverages, based on the financial impact that each exposure might have. Those exposures that have the potential to generate losses that might result in bankruptcy are critical, and insurance against these exposures is essential. Those that would require one to borrow rank next in order, and insurance against these losses is important. The last category—the possible losses that could be met out of existing assets or current income—represent optional coverages. We will begin our discussion with the essential auto coverage, the liability coverage.

Liability Coverage

In purchasing auto insurance, one logically begins with liability coverage. The question is not whether to buy liability coverage, but rather how much to buy. While it is difficult to say "how much is enough," it is clear that the minimum limits of coverage required by the financial responsibility laws fall short of adequate protection.

One of the poorest ways to save premium dollars in buying auto insurance is to purchase only the minimum required limits of liability. Fortunately, the cost of increased limits of liability coverage is far less proportionately than the basic limits. Table 30.1 indicates the increased limit factors for the liability coverage of the PAP. For example, the $20,000/40,000 basic limit can be increased to $100,000/300,000 for an additional 41 percent in premium and the $15,000

TABLE 30.1 Premium Factors for Increased Liability Limits: Personal Auto Policy

Bodily Injury Liability Limits	Rate Factor	Property Damage Liability Limit	Rate Factor
$20,000/40,000	1.00	$15,000	1.00
25,000/50,000	1.07	25,000	1.02
50,000/100,000	1.27	50,000	1.05
100,000/300,000	1.41	100,000	1.10
250,000/500,000	1.53	250,000	1.17
500,000/1,000,000	1.57	500,000	1.19

Source: Insurance Services Office, Inc.

property damage limit can be increased to $100,000 for an additional 10 percent. Although there is no scientific way to determine exactly what level of protection is adequate today, it makes good sense to purchase as much as you can reasonably afford (or the amount required as underlying coverage when a personal umbrella is purchased). The relatively small premium required for the higher limits of protection is a small price to pay for the security it provides.

Medical Payments Coverage

Automobile medical payments coverage represents something of a dilemma in the application of risk management principles. From one point of view, it can be argued that it violates the principles of risk management by focusing on the cause of a loss rather than on the effect. Clearly, protection against catastrophic medical expenses is important, but such protection is needed for medical expenses from any source, not just those caused by auto accidents. If an individual has purchased proper health insurance coverage to protect against catastrophic medical expenses, the auto medical payments coverage represents a duplication.

There is, however, an argument in favor of the coverage. Automobile medical payments coverage protects not only the insured and family members, but guests in the auto as well. Responsible motorists feel a sense of obligation to their passengers, and medical payments coverage serves as a mechanism for meeting this obligation. In some jurisdictions a guest statute may prevent a passenger from collecting medical expenses sustained as a result of the driver's negligence. Even where there is no guest statute, medical expense coverage may eliminate the need to make a federal case out of the accident. Adequate medical payments coverage may even serve as a loss-prevention device, reducing the possibility of a liability suit when a guest is injured. One of the main reasons for carrying auto medical expense coverage, then, is to provide for the payment of medical expenses incurred by guests or passengers.

Like the cost of increased liability limit, the cost of higher medical payments is relatively low. For example, in a midwestern city in mid-2001, the cost of medical payments coverage was as follows:

If $1000 medical payment limit costs $11, then $2000 costs $19, and $5000 costs $30. A $50,000 limit costs $58 and $100,000 costs $61.

The individual needs a comprehensive medical expense program to provide coverage for medical expenses from all sources, not just those associated with the auto. In view of the fact that the cost of the coverage is low, it is probably a good idea to purchase medical payments coverage. But the coverage is not an essential one and certainly should not be purchased at the expense of adequate liability coverage.

Physical Damage Coverage

The decision to purchase or not to purchase auto physical damage insurance is influenced by a variety of factors. If the car is financed, the lender may insist on insurance to protect its financial interest. In this case, the only decision the buyer must make is with respect to the deductibles. In the case of an older car, insurers may be unwilling to provide the coverage. While some car owners have little choice in the matter, there are many owners who must make a decision on the physical damage coverage.

Obviously, the value of the auto and the other financial resources of the individual are important factors. For some, an auto is a major asset, representing perhaps a half a year's salary. In such cases, the loss of the auto can be a serious financial blow, and although it does not have the same grave implications as does a liability suit, the loss can be a heavy one.

In those cases where the loss of the auto would be a serious loss beyond the individual's margin for contingencies, the risk management concept dictates that coverage should be purchased against as wide a range of perils as possible, which means that both comprehensive and collision would be purchased. Although the advice may seem wearisome at this point, the judicious use of deductibles can generate

TABLE 30.2 **Personal Auto Policy Physical Damage Deductible Credits**

Deductible	Comprehensive Percentage of $100 Deductible Premium	Collision Percentage of $200 Deductible Premium
None	118%	—
$50	109%	—
100	100%	105%
200	88%	100%
250	83%	98%
500	66%	89%
1000	49%	74%

Source: Insurance Services Office, Inc.

substantial economies. Table 30.2 indicates the premium credits available for differing levels of deductibles for both comprehensive and collision coverage. Because the credits are a percentage centage of the premium, larger deductibles will be most attractive to persons with high-priced autos or high rating classifications. In general, however, you should select as large a deductible as you can afford.

Uninsured Motorist Coverage

Uninsured Motorist coverage (and Underinsured Motorist coverage) represent a somewhat different dilemma from the medical payments coverage. Because it provides coverage based on the cause of loss rather than the effect, it falls short of the ideal from a risk management perspective. On the other hand, it covers a potentially catastrophic loss and is the only way in which some losses related to auto accidents can be covered. Although complete life insurance, disability coverage, and major medical insurance would cover a part of the loss caused by an uninsured driver, it would not cover disfigurement, physical impairment, or general damages (such as pain and suffering) for which a negligent uninsured driver might be liable. Most informed authorities treat Uninsured Motorist coverage as an essential form of protection and recommend that the highest limits possible be purchased.

Cost Differences among Companies

As a final note, it should perhaps be repeated that there are wide variations in price among automobile insurers. Although a comparison of costs should not be the sole criterion in selecting a company, the insurance buyer should at least investigate alternate sources and their costs. Although those companies with the lowest premiums are usually ultraselective, there are also wide differences in prices among insurers with similar underwriting philosophies, differences that result from different efficiencies and differences in expenses.

SUMMARY

Automobile liability insurance is an essential coverage for every driver. The contract under which this coverage is provided may also be used to provide Medical Payments coverage, Uninsured Motorists coverage, and Physical Damage coverage on the vehicle itself. Given the range of coverages that may be included in the auto policy and the variety of circumstances under which it provides coverage, the provisions of the contract are necessarily complex. Despite the complexities, if you have mastered the material in this chapter, you will have a good grasp of the technical aspects of automobile insurance.

IMPORTANT CONCEPTS TO REMEMBER

Personal Auto Policy (PAP)
private passenger automobiles
insureds
your covered auto
split limit of liability
supplementary payments

occupying
physical damage coverage
comprehensive
collision
transportation expense
non-owned auto

uninsured motorist coverage
underinsured motorist coverage
Named Non-ownership coverage
Miscellaneous Type Vehicle
 Endorsement

QUESTIONS FOR REVIEW

1. Briefly describe the four basic coverage sections of the Personal Auto Policy and explain the nature of the coverage under each section.

2. Who is included in the definition of *Insured* with respect to the owned automobile under the Personal Auto Policy? Who is included in the definition of *Insured* with respect to non-owned automobiles?

3. What coverage is provided under the Personal Auto Policy for individuals or organizations held vicariously liable? Under what circumstances is there no coverage for a person who is held vicariously liable?

4. The definition of insured property under the homeowners policy includes property owned or "used by an insured." Briefly describe the coverage under the Personal Auto Policy that parallels this provision.

5. Ed Jones drives to work every day and carries two fellow employees, who pay him $10 per week for this service. He has been told that this voids his automobile liability insurance and comes to you for advice. What do you tell him?

6. Jones Jr. borrows a friend's pickup truck and is involved in a collision in which both the pickup and another car are demolished. Although Junior does not have an automobile himself, he lives with his parents who have a Personal Auto Policy, written to include liability and "Coverage for Damage to Your Auto." Describe the coverage that may be applicable to this situation, indicating the specific policy provisions that will control whether or not coverage applies.

7. Smith is injured by an uninsured driver. She sues the driver and obtains a $100,000 judgment. Will the Uninsured Motorist coverage of her Personal Auto Policy pay this amount? Why or why not? Explain the manner in which amounts payable under the Uninsured Motorist coverage are determined.

8. Why might a person who does not own an automobile want to purchase automobile liability insurance? How can such a person obtain this protection?

9. John Jones has a motorcycle insured under a Personal Auto Policy that has been endorsed with the Miscallaneous Type Vehicle endorsement. What coverage exists under John's policy for the following situations?

a. John borrows a friend's private passenger auto for a date, and loans his motorcycle to the owner of the borrowed car. The friend's car is uninsured.

b. John borrows a pickup truck to use while his motorcycle is in the shop for repairs.

10. Under what circumstances is it advisable that the Extended Liability Coverage endorsement be added to the Personal Auto Policy?

QUESTIONS FOR DISCUSSION

1. The agent delivering a Personal Auto Policy tells a client, "This policy will cover you when you are driving my car, and it will cover anyone when they are driving your car." How accurate is this statement?

2. Cassandra owns a late-model car that is insured under a Personal Auto Policy, with a $300,000 liability limit, $5000 medical payments, $100 deductible comprehensive, $200 deductible collision, and $300,000 uninsured motorist coverage. Which of the coverages would apply to each of the following losses? (If there is no coverage, indicate why not.)

a. Cassandra parks the car on a riverbank, but forgets to set the brake or put the car in park. It rolls into the river and the damage amounts to $800.

b. Cassandra is changing a tire when the car slips off the jack and breaks her leg.

c. Thieves break into the car and steal the car radio, a spare tire, and an overnight bag full of clothing.

d. Cassandra borrows a trailer from a neighbor (who has no insurance). While backing the car up to the trailer, Cassandra misjudges the clearance and smashes into the trailer. Damage to the car amounts to $300 and the damage to the trailer is $250.

3. Robert and Francesca are not married, but live together. Robert owns an automobile, which they both use, and which is insured under a Personal Auto Policy. Are there any special dangers related to the automobile coverage of which they should be aware?

4. Robert carries full coverage on his automobile under a Personal Auto Policy, including liability, medical payments, physical damage, and uninsured motorist coverage. He enjoys a financial windfall and decides to purchase a second car. He drives the new car home and parks it in the driveway, then goes into the house to call his insurance agent and report the purchase. Cassandra, who is driving Robert's old car, wheels into the driveway and is unable to stop, colliding with the new car and causing extensive damage to both vehicles. Robert is heartbroken because the agent's line was busy, and he had not yet completed his call. Attempt to console him.

5. In what sense does the purchase of automobile medical payments coverage violate the principles of risk management? Is the same criticism valid with respect to Uninsured Motorist coverage? Why or why not?

SUGGESTIONS FOR ADDITIONAL READING

Fire, Casualty and Surety Bulletins. Personal Lines Volume. Cincinnati, Ohio: National Underwriter Company. (Loose-leaf manual service with monthly supplements.) See "Personal Auto" section.

Hamilton, Karen L., and Donald S. Malecki. *Personal Insurance: Property and Liability.* Malvern, Pa.: American Institute for CPCU, 1994. Chapter 4.

Hashmi, Sajad A. "Uninsured Motorist Coverage." *CPCU Annals,* vol. 20, no. 2 (June 1967).

Huebner, S. S., Kenneth Black, Jr., and Robert S. Cline. *Property and Liability Insurance,* 3rd ed. Englewood Cliffs, N.J.: Prentice-Hall, 1982. Chapter 34.

Launie, J. J., George E. Rejda, and Donald R. Oakes with Anita W. Johnson. *Personal Insurance.* Bryn Mawr, Pa.: Insurance Institute of America, 1991. Chapters 7–8.

Policy, Form, and Manual Analysis Service. Casualty Coverages Volume. Indianapolis, Ind.: Rough Notes Company. (Loose-leaf manual service with monthly supplements.) See "Auto Liability" section.

Taylor, Barbara J. *How to Get Your Money's Worth in Home and Auto Insurance.* New York: McGraw-Hill, 1990.

WEB SITES TO EXPLORE

Best's Review—Property/Casualty Edition	http://www.ambest.com/review/lh/index.html
Independent Insurance Agents of America, Inc.	http://www.iiaa.org
Insurance News Network	http://www.insure.com/
National Association of Professional Insurance Agents	http://www.pianet.com/
Nine Ways to Lower Your Auto Insurance Costs	http://www.iii.org/consumer/nineways.htm
Rough Notes Company	http://www.roughnotes.com/

COMMERCIAL PROPERTY INSURANCE

By a small sample, we may judge of the whole piece.

— MIGUEL DE CERVANTES
Don Quixote

CHAPTER OBJECTIVES

When you have finished this chapter, you should be able to

- Identify the seven broad classes of property and liability insurance for business firms
- Identify and distinguish among the four broad classes of commercial property insurance, and explain the distinguishing characteristics of each class
- Describe the general nature of coverage available to business firms with respect to fixed location property
- Distinguish between direct damage property insurance coverages and indirect loss coverages
- Identify and explain the general nature and uses of indirect loss (time element coverages) and explain the circumstances in which each type of coverage is needed
- Describe the general nature of the coverage available to business firms with respect to property that is not at a fixed location
- Explain the principal features of boiler and machinery insurance and the feature that distinguishes it from other types of insurance
- Identify the two broad classes of commercial crime insurance

Our discussion throughout this book has focused primarily on insurance coverages designed for the individual and the family unit. Although a detailed discussion of the coverages available for business firms and other organizations is beyond the scope of this text, it seems appropriate that we at least describe the insurance coverages that are available to cover the exposures of business firms. In this chapter and the next, we will examine the insurance coverages that are available to meet the property and

liability insurance needs of businesses and other organizations. The wide range of insurance coverages available for commercial enterprises, generally referred to as "commercial line insurance," can be classified into the following seven broad categories:

1. Commercial property insurance
2. Boiler and machinery insurance
3. Transportation insurance
4. Crime insurance
5. Commercial liability insurance
6. Commercial automobile insurance
7. Workers compensation and employers' liability insurance

This chapter treats the first four classes. The remaining three classes will be discussed in the next chapter. Although we will discuss the coverages treated in these two chapters separately for the purpose of clarity, many of the coverages are available under package policies. These package policies combine several coverages into a single contract, thereby eliminating gaps in coverage and possible overlapping. While the trend toward commercial package policies continues to gain momentum, commercial insurance packages are a case in which the whole is equal to the sum of the parts. Commercial package policies are simply combinations of the individual monoline coverages, which means that one learns about commercial package policies by studying the individual types of insurance that are combined to create the package.

COMMERCIAL PROPERTY COVERAGE

The evolution in commercial property insurance was characterized by the separate parallel development of several diverse types of insurance that protect against different types of property losses. This was a natural result of the monoline structure of the industry and underwriting attitudes of insurers. Commercial fire insurance forms, for example, traditionally provided coverage only at the insured's premises, creating a need for a form of coverage—the marine forms—to protect property while it is away from the premises. Other forms of property insurance, such as crime insurance and boiler and machinery coverage, also developed as separate fields of insurance.

In January 1986, the Insurance Services Office (ISO) implemented a long-planned overhaul of most commercial insurance forms with the introduction of its *portfolio program*. This program introduced simplified policy language forms for most commercial property insurance lines, including the fire insurance, plate glass, boiler and machinery, inland marine, and crime insurance.[1]

Although considerable progress had been achieved in simplifying and standardizing personal line policies, until the introduction of the portfolio program, commercial line forms were a hodgepodge, with each line of insurance following a different format, style, and terminology. The portfolio program attempts to introduce an element of standardization into commercial line forms through innovations that were originally developed for commercial package policies. These include modular forms and standard policy conditions.

All portfolio commercial coverages (fire and allied lines, plate glass, boiler and machinery, crime, inland marine, auto, and general liability) follow the same general format, and the structure of the policy is essentially the same regardless of the type of coverage. A commercial portfolio policy includes a standard Common Declarations part, Common Conditions part, and forms applicable to the particular line of insurance. The Common Declarations part contains information about the insured, the inception date and term of the policy, and the premium for the coverages in the policy. The Common Policy Conditions Form contains items common to all (or most) types of coverage, eliminating the need to restate the same provision in each of several separate policies. In addition, for each type of coverage, there is a separate declarations form (e.g., Property Insurance Declarations Form, Crime Insurance Declarations Form, and so on) and a coverage form or forms for the particular type of insurance. The portfolio forms may be used to create monoline contracts, or they may be combined to create package policies; the same forms are used in either case. If the policy includes both property and liability insurance, it becomes eligible for a package discount.

[1] Officially, the portfolio program is called the Commercial Lines Policy Rating and Simplification Project. The program was introduced and became effective January 1, 1986. Many of the property forms were revised in 1988, 1990, 1995, and again in 2000. The discussion is based on the 2000 edition of the forms.

COMMERCIAL PROPERTY DIRECT LOSS COVERAGES

We will begin our discussion with the commercial property coverages for direct loss.[2] ISO's commercial property coverage program consists of those lines of insurance that were traditionally known as *fire and allied lines.* *Allied lines* referred to coverages such as earthquake and sprinkler leakage that were often allied with fire insurance coverage. Actually, the term *fire insurance* itself was something of a misnomer, because coverage for loss by fire was rarely written alone. Generally, coverage for loss by fire was combined with coverage against other perils; the perils of extended coverage mentioned in Chapter 24 usually represented the minimum coverage package.

Commercial Property Coverage Policies

A commercial property coverage policy is created from modular parts, which include a standard Common Policy Conditions Form, a Commercial Property Conditions Form, a Commercial Property Coverage Part, and a Causes of Loss Form. A monoline property insurance contract is illustrated in Figure 31.1.

Commercial Property Coverage Forms Different coverage forms are used for different types of property and are designed to provide protection against different types of losses. There are 12 property coverage forms designed for use under the Property Coverage part of the portfolio program:

CP 00 10 Building and Personal Property Coverage Form
CP 00 17 Condominium Association Coverage Form

CP 00 18 Condominium Commercial Unit Owner's Coverage Form
CP 00 20 Builders' Risk Coverage Form
CP 00 30 Business Income Coverage (and Extra Expense) Form
CP 00 32 Business Income Coverage (Without Extra Expense) Form
CP 00 40 Legal Liability Coverage Form
CP 00 50 Extra Expense Coverage Form
CP 00 60 Leasehold Interest Coverage Form
CP 00 70 Mortgage Holder's Errors and Omissions Coverage Form
CP 00 80 Tobacco Sales Warehouses Coverage Form

Some of these forms provide coverage for direct loss; others, such as the business income and extra expense forms, are indirect or consequential loss coverages. The property coverage forms must be used with one of several standard causes-of-loss forms that specify the perils for which coverage is provided, along with the relevant exclusions. Because the perils for which protection is provided are added by another form, the basic coverage is the same regardless of the perils package selected.

Although we will not attempt to examine all of these forms, we can provide a general understanding of their nature and provide some insight by an examination of the most commonly used forms.

Building and Personal Property Coverage Form

The *Building and Personal Property Coverage Form* (BPP) is the standard form for insuring most types of business property. It may be used to provide direct damage coverage on completed buildings and structures or business personal property, including personal property of others. Coverage may be written on buildings only, personal property only, or on both in the same contract. In addition, the form can be used to provide coverage on specific classes of property (such as stock, tenants improvements and betterments, or machinery and equipment) by endorsements or by describing the property in the declarations. The coverage is provided under three insuring agreements: Building, Your Personal Property, and Personal Property of Others. Each of the three insuring agreements defines the property that is insured under that item and specifically excludes other property from coverage.

[2] *Commercial property coverage* is the term used by the Insurance Services Office to designate those fields that were previously known as "fire and allied lines." Because the term *Commercial property insurance* (or *commercial property coverage*) is also used in reference to the range of coverages that provide protection on property of commercial risks (i.e., fire and allied lines, boiler and machinery, plate glass, marine, and crime insurance), this creates a potential for ambiguity. To minimize the confusion, we will follow the ISO's usage of the term *commercial property coverage* to refer to the traditional fields of fire and allied lines, and will use the term *commercial property insurance* when referring to the broad field of property insurance coverages.

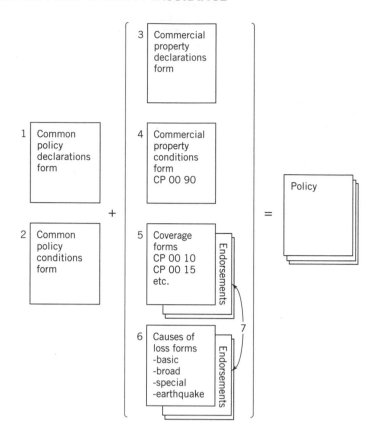

FIGURE 31.1 Commercial Property Coverage Policy

Building The building coverage defines *building* to include the structure described, completed additions, permanently installed fixtures, machinery and equipment, outdoor fixtures, personal property used to maintain or service the building, and materials and supplies for use in additions, alterations, or repairs of the structure.

Your Personal Property The definition of *Your Personal Property* includes furniture and fixtures, machinery and equipment, stock, and all other personal property owned by the insured and used in the business. The insured's use interest in tenant's improvements and betterments is also included in the definition of personal property. As in the case of other items of property for which coverage is not desired, improvements and betterments may be excluded by endorsement. Finally, the latest version of the BPP includes coverage for leased personal property which the insured is contractually obligated to insure, unless such property is insured under the Personal Property of Others insuring agreement.

Personal Property of Others The *Personal Property of Others coverage* applies to property of others

that is in the insured's care, custody, or control, and which is located in or on the building described in the declarations. Coverage also applies to property in the open, or on a vehicle within 100 feet of the described premises.[3]

Replacement Cost Option Replacement cost coverage is available for all three classes of property (buildings, your personal property, and personal property of others). New language added to the replacement cost provision in the 2000 edition clarifies that replacement cost coverage, if selected, applies to tenants' improvements and betterments. Replacement cost coverage on personal property of others applies only when the insured is legally liable.

Additional Coverages The BPP includes certain extensions of coverage; some of these are referred to as *Additional Coverages,* while others are referred to

[3] Although personal line forms such as the homeowners policies automatically extend coverage to property of others in the insured's custody, commercial line policies generally do not. If coverage is required on the property of others, it must be specifically purchased.

as *Coverage Extensions*. There are five Additional Coverages.

Debris Removal The Debris Removal additional coverage provides payment for the expense of removing the debris of covered property damaged by an insured peril. Coverage for debris removal is limited to 25 percent of the amount paid for direct loss plus the amount of the deductible under the policy. For example, if direct damage to insured property is, say, $6000, and the deductible is $250, the insurer will pay $5750 for the direct loss and up to $1500 for debris removal (25 percent of $5750 + $250). In the event that the cost of debris removal exceeds this limitation, an additional $10,000 is provided for debris removal under the Limit of Insurance provision. An important exclusion under the Debris Removal coverage eliminates coverage for the cost of removing pollutants. Limited coverage for removal of pollutants is provided under a separate Pollutant Cleanup and Removal additional coverage.[4]

Preservation of Property Coverage for removal of covered property is now provided by the preservation of property additional coverage. This coverage is on an open-perils basis and runs for 30 days.

Fire Department Service Charges The Fire Department Service Charge additional coverage is similar to the same coverage in the homeowners forms. Coverage under the BPP is provided up to a $1000 limit with no deductible.

Pollutant Cleanup and Removal The Pollutant Cleanup and Removal additional coverage provides limited protection, up to $10,000, for the insured's expense in extracting pollutants from land or water at the described premises when the discharge or release of the pollutants was caused by a covered cause of loss. The $10,000 limit may be increased by endorsement for an additional premium.

Increased Cost of Construction This additional coverage was added to the form in the 2000 revision. It provides coverage for increased cost of construction resulting from building laws enforcement up to

the lesser of $10,000 or 5 percent of the limit of insurance on the building. It does not provide coverage for the cost of demolishing undamaged parts of the building, loss of undamaged parts of the building, or the cost of upgrading undamaged parts of the building. Full coverage for building ordinance loss exposures is available under the *ordinance or law coverage* endorsement, CP 04 05.

Coverage Extensions The coverage extensions, like the additional coverages, provide added coverage for specified exposures. However, unlike the previous additional coverages, the coverage extensions apply only when the policy is written with 80 percent or higher coinsurance.

Newly Acquired Buildings The Newly Acquired Building extension provides automatic coverage on newly acquired or newly constructed buildings, subject to a $250,000 cap (which can be increased by endorsement).

Newly Acquired Personal Property Newly acquired personal property at existing locations, newly acquired locations, and newly constructed buildings at existing locations is automatically covered, subject to a $100,000 maximum for 30 days. The 30-day coverage period begins on date of acquisition or start of construction of a portion of the building qualifying as covered property.

Personal Effects and Property of Others There is an extension to cover the personal effects and property of others, such as the personal effects of employees and members or managers of limited liability companies. The limit on this extension is $2500.

Valuable Papers and Records Coverage applies up to $2500 per location to cover the cost of labor to research and reconstruct information in business records, when such records are destroyed by an insured peril. Coverage applies only if duplicate records do not exist.

Property Off Premises Coverage applies to personal property while away from the premises, up to $10,000. Coverage applies while the property is off premise for any reason. If the on-premises coverage is open peril, the off-premises coverage applies on the same basis. In the 2000 revisions, this extension was expanded to apply to stock, property in storage at newly leased locations, and property at fairs, trade shows, or exhibitions, all of which were not previously covered.

[4] The exclusion of the cost of removing pollutants in the debris removal coverage was introduced in response to court decisions that held insurers liable for extensive pollution cleanup expense under the debris removal provision. Water used to extinguish a fire at a chemical plant, for example, can result in the dispersal of chemicals into the land or water. Under earlier forms, insurers were held liable for such costs up to the face amount of the policy.

Outdoor Property Certain forms of outdoor property are also covered by extension. The extension includes outdoor trees, shrubs, plants, fences, detached signs,[5] and antennas. A limit of $1000 applies, subject to a $250 sublimit per tree, shrub, or plant. Coverage applies only to loss caused by fire, lightning, explosion, riot or civil commotion, or aircraft.

Non-Owned Detached Trailers Coverage Extension It is common for trucking companies delivering goods to insureds to leave the trailer for unloading by the insured and return later to pick up the empty trailer. During the period the trailer is left at the insured's premises, the insured may be responsible for any damage to or theft of the trailer. The *non-owned detached trailers coverage extension* (which was added in the 2000 revision) is designed to respond to these loss exposures. It provides $5000 of automatic coverage on non-owned trailers used in the insured's business, but only if the insured is contractually obligated to pay for the loss or damage. A higher limit may be purchased.

Perils Insured The insured may choose from a range of perils. There are four causes-of-loss forms that are used in connection with the BPP: Basic Causes of Loss, Broad Causes of Loss, Special Causes of Loss, and Causes of Loss Earthquake Coverage Form. The first three forms more or less parallel the coverage of the similarly titled homeowners forms.

Causes of Loss—Basic Form The Causes of Loss—Basic Form covers fire, lightning, explosion, windstorm or hail, smoke, aircraft or vehicles, riot or civil commotion, vandalism, sprinkler leakage, sinkhole collapse, and volcanic action. Windstorm or hail, vandalism, and sprinkler leakage can be excluded. The coverage of these perils is similar to that of the homeowners forms.

The Basic Form excludes building ordinance, earth movement, governmental action, nuclear hazard, utility services, war and military action, water (e.g., flood and other types of water losses), electrical apparatus, leakage or discharge of water or steam from appliances other than sprinkler systems, and rupture of water pipes.

Causes of Loss—Broad Form The Causes of Loss—Broad Form includes all Basic Form perils plus breakage of glass ($100 per plate and $500 per occurrence), falling objects, weight of snow, ice, or sleet, and water damage. Collapse is included as an additional coverage and subject to the special concurrent causation exclusions. There is no exclusion for leakage or discharge of water or steam from an appliance or rupture or bursting of water pipes.

Causes of Loss—Special Form The Causes of Loss—Special Form provides coverage on an open-perils basis for risks of direct physical loss; it provides additional coverage for collapse and additional coverage extensions for property in transit ($1000 limit for personal property for certain named perils) and water damage (costs to repair damage to buildings to fix system). The special form excludes pollutants and contaminants and transfer of property due to unauthorized instructions. A theft exclusion endorsement is available.

Causes of Loss—Earthquake Form The Causes of Loss—Earthquake Form insures against earthquake and volcanic eruption, explosion, or effusion (from earthquakes or volcanoes that begin during the policy period, even if direct physical loss occurs within 168 hours of the expiration of the policy period).

Spoilage Coverage The Spoilage Coverage endorsement was introduced by the ISO in 1988. It extends the BPP to cover damage to perishable stock owned by or in the insured's care, custody, or control and at the described premises. Spoilage coverage is effected by the addition of two covered causes of loss: breakdown or contamination and power outage. Breakdown or contamination is defined to include a change in temperature or humidity resulting from mechanical failure of refrigerating, cooling, or humidity-control equipment at the described premises. Power outage includes a change in temperature or humidity that results from interruption of electrical power, either on or off the described premise, caused by conditions beyond the control of the insured.

Other Provisions In addition to those provisions previously outlined, the coverage part is subject to several other important provisions.

Deductible The standard deductible under the form is $250, but larger deductibles are available and may be scheduled in the declarations. The deductible

[5] In addition to the extension for detached signs, the BPP also covers signs attached to the building, subject to a $1000 limit per occurrence.

applies *per occurrence,* regardless of the number of buildings affected.

Vacancy Condition The vacancy condition provides that 60 days' vacancy bars recovery for loss by vandalism, sprinkler leakage, glass breakage, water damage, theft, and attempted theft. For all other perils, vacancy beyond 60 days results in a 15 percent loss-payment penalty.

Valuation Condition The valuation condition provides that covered property will be valued at actual cash value. Building losses of $2500 or less are payable at replacement cost, provided the insured meets the coinsurance requirement. Glass is covered at the cost to replace with safety glazing material if required by law. When duplicates of valuable papers and documents exist, coverage is provided for the cost of transcribing valuable papers and documents. Prepackaged computer software is valued at its actual cash value.

Mortgage Holders Condition The Mortgage Holders condition sets forth the agreement between the insurer and any mortgagee named in the policy. The provisions are virtually identical to those already examined in our discussion of the homeowners forms.

Coinsurance The Building and Personal Property Coverage Form—like many other commercial property forms—contains a coinsurance clause. Because the coinsurance clause and the principle on which it is based are critical elements in many forms of property insurance, we will stop to examine it more closely. However, before turning our attention to the policy provision itself, it will be helpful to examine the underlying rationale for the coinsurance principle.

Rationale for Coinsurance To understand the logic of the coinsurance concept, one must begin by recognizing that most fire losses are partial. ISO loss statistics indicate that about 85 percent of all fire losses are for less than 20 percent of the value of the property, while only about 5 percent result in damage over 50 percent of the property's value. Since fire insurance rates are based on the ratio of losses to the total values insured, the rate will be higher if owners insure a lower percentage of their property values than if they insure the property to some high percentage of its value. This relationship can be illustrated by an example.

Assume that an insurance company insures 10,000 buildings worth $10,000 each for 100 percent of their value. On the basis of past experience, the company projects the following losses:

30 partial losses at $1000 each	$30,000
2 total losses at $10,000 each	20,000
	$50,000

Since the company can expect $50,000 in losses on $100,000,000 worth of buildings, it computes the pure rate to be $0.05 per $100.00:

$$\frac{\$50,000}{\$100,000,000} = 0.0005 \text{ per } \$1, \text{ or } \$0.05 \text{ per } \$100$$

If the insurer assumes that the loss ratio will be 50 percent of gross premiums, it will add a loading, making the gross rate $0.10 per $100.00 of coverage.

If the same buildings are each insured for 50 percent of their value, the rate per $100 will be considerably higher. Assuming the same losses,

30 partial losses at $1000 each	$30,000
2 total losses at $5000 each	10,000
	$40,000

$$\frac{\$40,000}{\$50,000,000} = 0.0008 \text{ per } \$1, \text{ or } \$0.08 \text{ per } \$100$$

Again assuming that the loss ratio will be 50 percent of gross premiums, the gross rate is $0.16 per $100 of coverage.

Since insurance to value has a definite relationship to equity in fire rates, some concession must be made in the rating structure to those who insure their property for a high percentage of its value. The coinsurance clause was invented to support a concession in rates for policyholders who purchase insurance equal to a high percentage of the value of the property.[6] It is designed to enforce the insured's agreement to insure the property for a specified percentage of its value, which is made in return for a lower rate.

[6] The coinsurance principle is used primarily in the commercial area, and the coinsurance clause and rates are not generally applicable in the field of dwelling property. Although some people incorrectly refer to the replacement cost provision of the homeowners forms as a *coinsurance* provision, it is not. It is an extension of coverage that totally or partially eliminates any deduction for depreciation in loss settlement. Under a coinsurance clause, the insured may collect less than the actual cash value of the loss. Under the homeowners insurance replacement cost provision, the insured will never collect less than the actual cash value of the loss.

Coinsurance Clause Under the provisions of the coinsurance clause, the insured agrees to maintain insurance equal to some specified percentage of the value of the property (e.g., 80 percent, 90 percent, 100 percent) in return for a reduced rate. In effect, the coinsurance rate is a quantity discount. If the insured fails to maintain insurance to value as agreed, he or she may suffer a penalty at the time of a loss. A simplified language version of the coinsurance clause states that

> All property covered by this form must be insured for at least 80 percent of its total value at the time of "loss" or you will incur a penalty. The penalty is that we will pay only the proportion of any "loss" that the Limit of Insurance shown in the Declarations for the property bears to 80 percent of the total value of the property at the premises as of the time of "loss."

More simply, at the time of a loss, the company will make payment on the basis of the following formula:

$$\frac{\text{Amount of Insurance Carried}}{\text{Amount of Insurance Required}} \times \text{Amount of Loss} = \text{Amount Paid}$$

The application of the provision is simple. As long as the insured carries insurance equal to the required percentage, all losses covered by the policy will be paid in full up to the face amount of the policy. If the insured fails to maintain insurance to value as required, only a part of the loss will be collected.

Coinsurance Clause Illustrated To illustrate, let us assume that the insured has purchased coverage on a $100,000 building, subject to an 80 percent coinsurance clause. In keeping with the requirement of the clause, $80,000 in coverage has been purchased. In the event of a $5000 loss, the company would pay

$$\frac{\text{Amount Carried (\$80,000)}}{\text{Amount Required (\$80,000)}} \times \$5000 = \$5000$$

Now let us assume that as time goes by, construction costs go up, increasing the value of the building, but the insured continues to carry $80,000 in coverage. When the next $5000 loss occurs, it is found that the actual cash value of the building is $200,000. To comply with the 80 percent coinsurance clause, the insured should now be carrying $160,000 in coverage.

In this case, the insured becomes a coinsurer and suffers a penalty equal to the coinsurance deficiency:

$$\frac{\text{Amount Carried (\$80,000)}}{\text{Amount Required (\$160,000)}} \times \$5000 = \$2500$$

Two important points are illustrated by the examples. First, the coinsurance requirement applies at the time of the loss, and the amount of coverage required for compliance is based on the value of the property at the time of loss—not the value of the property when the insurance is purchased. Second, the burden of maintaining the proper amount of insurance is on the insured. The insurance company does not check to see if the insured has kept his or her promise until a loss takes place.

Deductibles and Coinsurance Although the simplified ISO portfolio property forms stipulate that the deductible is to be applied after the application of the coinsurance penalty, if any, this represents a break with tradition. Prior to the introduction of the portfolio forms, and in many other forms in use today, the deductible is applied to the loss and the coinsurance penalty is applied to the after-deductible portion of the loss. Because contracts differ in this respect, they must be examined individually to determine the manner in which the deductible applies.

Optional Coverages Three optional coverages are available for use with the BPP: Agreed Value, Inflation Guard, and Replacement Cost. The Inflation Guard coverage and Replacement Cost coverage are essentially the same as their personal line counterparts examined in connection with the homeowners policies. The *Agreed Value optional coverage* suspends the coinsurance provision for a one-year period, guaranteeing that the insured will not suffer a coinsurance penalty. The insurer will grant agreed value coverage after verifying the values insured.

Specialized Valuation Endorsements Although the actual cash value and replacement cost valuation provisions are suitable for most property, there are some situations in which it is desirable to modify the basis on which property is insured. Several standard endorsements exist for this purpose.

Ordinance or Law Coverage Endorsement An *Ordinance or Law Coverage endorsement* is used to provide three types of coverage related to the enforcement of building codes. The endorsement provides essentially the same coverage as that provided

by the Ordinance or Law additional coverage in the homeowners policy. Coverage is provided for three types of losses.

First, the endorsement permits a building owner to purchase insurance for an amount required to replace a substandard building with one that will meet code requirements. An increased cost of construction limit is listed in the endorsement. In addition, under the terms of the endorsement, the insurer agrees to pay as a total loss any partial loss in which building code provisions prevent the owner from using the undamaged parts of the building in reconstruction. Finally, coverage may be included for the cost to demolish undamaged parts of a building following damage by an insured peril, when such demolition is required by the building code. Payment for damage to the structure and the cost of demolition cannot, however, exceed the limit of insurance. A limit is indicated in the endorsement for the cost of demolition.

Functional Building Valuation Endorsement Situations sometimes exist in which, because of advances in technology or architecture, it is possible to replace an existing structure with one that performs the same function, but at a lower cost than would be required to duplicate the existing building. The *Functional Building Valuation Endorsement* insures buildings for the cost of repairing with less costly materials, but in the architectural style that existed before the loss. For total loss, coverage applies for the cost of replacing the building with a less costly, but functionally equivalent building. The coinsurance provision does not apply to buildings insured on a functional valuation basis.

Functional Personal Property Valuation (Other Than Stock) Coverage on personal property may also be written on a functional valuation basis. In this case, coverage applies to specifically described property which can be replaced with similar property that performs the same function as the original, when replacement with identical property is impossible or unnecessary. If the property is repaired or replaced, payment is made for replacement with the most closely equivalent property available. If the property is not repaired or replaced, coverage is limited to the lowest of (a) the amount of insurance, (b) the market value of the property, or (c) the actual cash value of the property.

Manufacturer's Selling Price Clause A manufacturer with finished goods on hand faces a loss not covered under the standard BPP form, and that is the loss of the expected profits on the goods destroyed. The policy provides coverage on stock for its actual cash value—the replacement cost less depreciation—not the selling price. Coverage for this potential loss can be obtained under the *manufacturer's selling price* endorsement, which provides that the value of finished stock shall be the price at which it would have sold had no loss occurred. The manufacturer's selling price endorsement is applicable only to the finished stocks of manufacturers and is not available to wholesalers and retailers.[7]

Blanket Insurance

Thus far, we have discussed only one approach to fire insurance, that form known as *specific insurance,* which applies a definite amount of coverage to a stated item. Coverage may also be in the form of *blanket insurance,* under which one amount of insurance covers more than one type of property or property at more than one location. For example, a firm with a number of buildings may purchase specific insurance on each, but it can also them on a blanket basis, with a single amount of insurance applicable to all. When coverage is written on a blanket basis, 90 percent coinsurance is usually required.

There are significant advantages in the blanket approach. The major advantage is that the blanket limit is available to cover loss to any of the individual items insured. For example, suppose that the XYZ Company owns 10 buildings, each worth $100,000. If the properties are insured on a blanket basis, subject to a 90 percent coinsurance clause, XYZ must purchase $900,000 in blanket coverage. In the event of a loss, coverage would apply to any building up to the full $100,000 of its value, provided that XYZ meets the coinsurance requirement at the time of the loss. If the same 10 buildings were insured for $90,000 each on a specific basis, recovery would, of course, be limited to the $90,000 applicable to each. Contents at different locations may also be insured on a blanket basis, or buildings and contents can be insured in this way.

Reporting Form Coverage

Reporting forms are designed to meet the needs of business firms whose stocks of merchandise fluctuate

[7] Retailers and wholesalers do not face the same exposure. They can normally replace their stock within a short time, and the income lost on sales during the period required to replace the stock is covered under the Business Interruption Form used for mercantile firms.

over time. A reporting form is written with a maximum limit sufficient to cover the highest values expected during the year, and the amount of insurance moves up and down with the values exposed to loss, subject to this maximum. The insured makes periodic reports (monthly or quarterly) of current values on hand and is charged on the basis of these reports, paying only for the values exposed to loss, not the limit of liability. The premium cannot be known until the year is over, so a provisional premium is paid at the inception of the policy and then adjusted at year's end to reflect the true cost of the protection provided.[8]

The insured must report 100 percent of the values of the property insured. Late reports or underreporting of values, intentional or otherwise, may result in a penalty at the time of a loss. In the event of a late report, the amount of insurance is limited to the values contained in the last previous filing. In addition, the *full value reporting clause* (also called the *honesty clause*) provides that if the insured underreports, the insurer's liability is limited to that percentage of loss that the last stated values bear to the values that should have been reported. Thus, if the insured reports a value of $100,000, when the actual value of the property on hand was $200,000, recovery would be limited to 100/200, or 50 percent of the loss sustained. In effect, the full value reporting clause is a 100 percent coinsurance clause.

Builder's Risk Coverage Form

When a building under construction is to be insured, it is normally covered under a specialized contract known as the Builder's Risk Form. There is a single *Builder's Risk Form* under the commercial property portfolio program, which provides coverage on a *completed value* basis. Under this form, coverage is written for the final full value of the building, and a premium based on 55 percent of the 100 percent coinsurance builder's risk rate is charged. Coverage continues during the process of construction but terminates automatically when the structure is completed and occupied. If the insured desires, the coverage can be converted to a reporting basis by endorsement. Builder's risk coverage may be written to cover the interests of the building owner, the general contractor,

and subcontractors, all of whom have an insurable interest in the building under construction.

Condominium Association Coverage Form

The Condominium Association Coverage Form is used in place of the BPP when buildings and contents are insured in the name of a condominium association. The form states that certain types of property will be covered or not covered depending on whether the condominium association agreement requires the association or the unit-owner to insure it. This provision avoids the need to include a specific description of this property in the declarations and permits the form to be used with either a *bare walls* or *all included* type of condominium agreement.

Condominium Commercial Unit-Owner's Coverage Form

The Condominium Commercial Unit-Owner's Coverage Form dovetails with the Condominium Association Coverage Form. It excludes fixtures, improvements, alterations, and appliances in units unless the association agreement places responsibility for insuring them on the unit-owner. When association and unit-owner's coverage responds to the same loss, the unit-owner's coverage is excess.

Standard Property Policy

The Standard Property Policy is a self-contained property damage form that is used to insure buildings and personal property on a somewhat more restrictive basis than the BPP. It is used to insure property assigned to the insurer under FAIR plans or for other properties that do not meet high underwriting standards. The Standard Property Policy is similar to the BPP, but provides coverage only for the perils of the Causes of Loss Basic Form. The provisions regarding cancellation, increase in hazard, and vacancy are more restrictive than those of the BPP.

Plate Glass Insurance

Until 2001, the ISO portfolio of property coverage forms included a special form to cover plate glass, called the Glass Coverage Form, providing what has traditionally been referred to as *plate glass coverage*. Under earlier property coverage forms, breakage of glass by causes other than fire and a number of other

[8] When the fluctuation in value is limited to an identifiable period, a peak season Endorsement may be used. Here the amount of insurance is increased pro rata for a specified period to cover the increased values, and a pro rata premium charge is made for the added coverage.

specified perils was limited to $100 per pane and $500 per occurrence. This limitation was eliminated in the 2001 revision of commercial property forms and glass breakage is now covered on the same basis as any other loss.

Although ISO has withdrawn its version of the plate glass coverage form, some insurers (including a number that specialized in plate glass insurance) continue to offer plate glass coverage as a stand-alone form of protection. Coverage under plate glass policy applies for accidental glass breakage (except by fire) and damage caused by acids or chemicals accidentally or maliciously applied to specifically insured glass. Lettering and ornamentation are not covered unless they have been specifically insured. The policy also covers the cost of repairing or replacing frames or sashes and boarding up or installing temporary plates in broken windows.

COMMERCIAL PROPERTY COVERAGE FOR INDIRECT LOSS

Unlike the dwelling forms, commercial property forms do not provide coverage for the indirect loss resulting from damage to the insured property. Such protection must be obtained under a separate form for an additional premium. The major consequential loss coverages are business interruption insurance, extra expense insurance, contingent business interruption and contingent extra expense insurance, and leasehold interest coverage.[9]

Business Interruption Insurance

Business interruption insurance indemnifies business firms for loss of income during the period required to restore property damaged by an insured peril to useful condition. It pays the expenses that continue and the profits that would have been earned during a period of interruption. Although a valued form of coverage is available, most business interruption is written on an indemnity basis.

Business Income Forms Under the portfolio program two business interruption forms are available:

the *Business Income Coverage (And Extra Expense) Form* and the *Business Income Coverage (Without Extra Expense) Form.* Coverage under either form is written subject to a coinsurance provision that requires coverage equal to 50 percent, 60 percent, 70 percent, 80 percent, 90 percent, or 100 percent of the firm's annual earnings for the 12-month period of the policy. For those situations in which the business could be shut down for over a year, a 125 percent coinsurance option is available.

Both business income forms require a choice of three income coverages: business income including rental value, business income excluding rental value, and rental value only. *Rental value* is the anticipated rental income from tenants at the described premises minus expenses that do not continue or the fair rental value of any part of the premises occupied by the insured. The option selected determines the scope of *business income* for which payment is made.

If the business is interrupted, payment is made for the *loss of business income,* defined as the net profit that would have been earned (including or excluding rental income) and the necessary expenses that continue during the *period of restoration.* The period of restoration is defined as the period that should be required to repair or replace the property with reasonable speed. An additional coverage called *Extended Business Income* extends the form to also cover a reduction in income during the 30 days following the restoration of the property that was damaged or destroyed.

In determining the amount of loss, the insurer considers the insured's experience before the loss and probable future experience if no loss had occurred. The definition of business income may be modified to delete or limit coverage on ordinary payroll (roughly, the payroll for rank-and-file workers) if the insured does not wish to collect for this expense in the event of interruption.

Loss of income coverage may be written to provide coverage against the same perils as the direct damage coverages, and payment is made only if the interruption results from an insured peril. The damage must occur during the policy period, but the period of indemnity is not limited by expiration of the policy.

Resumption of Operations If damage to property triggers an interruption, the *resumption of operations provision* requires the insured to resume operations as soon as possible, even on a partial basis, using dam-

[9] Coverage for loss of rents or rental value was written as a separate form in the past. Under the portfolio program, loss of rents or rental value are viewed as simply another form of business interruption and may be insured under the Standard Business Income Form.

aged or undamaged property at the described premises or elsewhere. If operations are not resumed when it is possible to do so, the insurer will reduce payment for loss of income by the amount that resumption of operations would have reduced the loss.

Expense to Reduce Loss/Extra Expense The principal difference between the two business income forms is in the additional coverages. The *Without Extra Expense* form includes *Expense to Reduce Loss* as an additional coverage, which provides payment for expenses incurred to resume operations or otherwise reduce the amount of the business interruption loss. Expenses incurred to continue operations are payable under the expense-to-reduce-loss additional coverage only to the extent that they actually reduce the business interruption loss. Under the *and extra expense* business income form, the additional coverage is called *extra expense.* Payments are made under this additional coverage for expenses incurred to continue operations whether or not such expenses reduce the business interruption loss. In effect, under the form that includes the extra expense additional coverage, the entire amount of insurance is payable for either business interruption or extra expense.

Optional Coverage Provisions The optional coverage provisions permit activation of the more popular time element coverage options. There are four optional coverages:

1. *Maximum Period of Indemnity.* The *Maximum Period of Indemnity* optional coverage replaces the coinsurance clause with a 120-day limit on the period for which indemnity is payable. There is no limit on the amount payable per month within the 120-day period.

2. *Monthly Limit of Indemnity.* The *Monthly Limit of Indemnity* optional coverage replaces the coinsurance clause with monthly limits on recovery expressed as fractions of the limit of insurance. Under this option, the insured may collect a specified fractions of the amount of insurance during any month for which the business is totally or partially interrupted. Options are available to permit collection of 1/3, 1/4, or 1/6 of the face amount of coverage.

3. *Agreed Value.* The *Agreed Value* optional coverage of the Loss of Income Form, like the Agreed Value Coverage of the BPP, suspends the coinsur-

ance provision and guarantees that the insured will not suffer a coinsurance penalty on a partial loss.

4. *Extended Period of Indemnity.* The *Extended Period of Indemnity* optional coverage increases the 30-day period in the coverage extension to a longer period entered in the declarations.

Extra Expense Insurance

Under some circumstances, it may be necessary for a business to continue operations after destruction of its facilities. For example, a bank's earnings, which are derived from loans and investments, would not be affected by destruction of the bank's premises, but the bank would need other facilities to continue to service its accounts. Extra expense insurance is an alternative to business interruption insurance for those enterprises that can continue operations with other facilities. It provides payment for expenses above normal costs when such expenses are incurred to continue operations after damage to the premises by an insured peril.

The Extra Expense Only Form contains a schedule of cumulative monthly limits, expressed as a percentage of the face amount of the policy, and the insured's recovery is limited to these percentages. The most commonly used schedule permits the policyowner to collect up to 40 percent of the face of the policy during the first month following damage, up to 80 percent during the first two months, and up to 100 percent for three months or more. An insured anticipating a more extended period requiring extra expenses can select a smaller monthly limitation (for example, 10 percent during the first month, 20 percent in the first two months, and so on). The rate for the coverage decreases as the percentage of the face amount collectible in the first and succeeding months decreases.

Contingent Business Interruption and Extra Expenses

Contingent business interruption insurance and contingent extra expense insurance protect a firm against interruption and extra expense losses resulting from damage caused by an insured peril to property that it does not own, operate, or control. There are four situations in which these coverages are used:

- When the insured depends on a single supplier or a few suppliers for materials, the firm on which the insured depends is called a *contributing property*.
- When the insured depends on one or a few manufacturers or suppliers for most of its merchandise, the firm on which the insured depends is called the *manufacturing property*.
- When the insured relies on one or a few businesses to purchase the bulk of its products, the firm to which most of the insured's production flows is called the *recipient property*.
- When the insured counts on a neighboring business to help attract customers, the neighboring firm is called a *leader property*.

The contingent business income coverage under the portfolio program is provided by endorsement to the Loss of Income Form. There are two versions of the Contingent Business Income endorsement: a broad form and a limited form. The broad form endorsement provides coverage in addition to the direct business income coverage and for the same limit. The limited form endorsement provides coverage when contingent interruption coverage is written without direct business income coverage or when it is written for a different limit.

Contingent extra expense insurance operates in much the same way as does the contingent business interruption insurance, but the former is designed for the firm that would incur increased costs as a result of damage to a contributing or recipient firm's property.

Leasehold Interest Insurance

Leasehold interest coverage protects against loss due to the termination of a favorable lease caused by fire or other insured peril. Consider, for example, a property leased for $1000 a month, subject to a lease that may be canceled in the event of fire or other damage to the premises. When prevailing conditions make it impossible to secure similar quarters at less than, say, $2500 a month, the existing contract would create a leasehold interest of $1500 a month for the remaining period of the lease.

The amount of coverage under leasehold interest coverage decreases month by month, with the amount of insurance always approximately equal to the insured's interest in the lease. In the event of a loss that terminates the rental agreement, the insured is paid a lump sum equal to the discounted value of the leasehold interest for the remaining months of the lease. Discount rates ranging from 5 percent to 15 percent are available.

Rain Insurance

Before leaving the subject of business interruption, we should briefly note another specialized indirect loss coverage, rain insurance. Rain insurance is a consequential loss coverage. It does not protect against damage to property, but against loss of income or the incurring of extra expenses due to rain, snow, sleet, or hail. It is usually sold to cover outdoor events scheduled for a certain day and dependent on favorable weather for success. The coverage may be written on an indemnity basis to cover the loss of income suffered or additional expenses incurred, or it may be written on a valued basis. Some contracts specify the amount of rain that must fall before payment will be made; in other contracts any amount of rain will require payment by the insurer. The policy must usually be taken out at least seven days before the event and is not subject to cancellation by either party. Although rain insurance is a specialty coverage and many companies design their own forms, the Crop-Hail Insurance Actuarial Association has developed a standardized form for its member companies.

BOILER AND MACHINERY INSURANCE

Boiler and machinery insurance originated from the efforts of a group of engineers in Hartford, Connecticut, who offered an inspection service for steam boilers and, for a small additional charge, guaranteed their inspection by providing insurance against loss up to some limit selected by the client. The inspection service that originally served as the basis for this type of insurance remains an important part of the service provided by boiler and machinery insurers today. The boiler and machinery line is a highly specialized field, and insurers who offer this coverage employ trained engineers who seek to discover faulty conditions and mechanical weakness before such defects can cause accidents. A large percentage of the boiler and machinery premium goes to pay inspection costs.

Although it is common to think of boiler and machinery insurance primarily in terms of steam, boil-

ers, there are many types of equipment to which the insurance applies: boilers, pressure containers, refrigerating systems, engines, turbines, generators, and motors. The inspection service that proved so beneficial for steam boilers has established its worth for other types of objects as well. Large and small businesses now rely on a range of equipment that was not imagined when boiler and machinery insurance was invented. These include computers, PBX systems, copier, duplicating, and fax machines, as well as production equipment with computer-based components.

Although the inspection service is a critical part of the boiler and machinery product, payment for damage from losses that do occur is an equally important feature of this insurance. Hazards associated with boilers and machinery are usually excluded from other forms of property insurance, so boiler and machinery insurance is needed to fill this gap. Similarly, coverage for damage caused by artificially generated electricity, usually excluded in other property forms, is covered by the boiler and machinery forms.

The ISO Breakdown Protection Coverage Form

In 2000, Insurance Services Office, Inc. (ISO) revised and modernized its boiler and machinery insurance program. In addition to several changes in coverage, the basic Boiler and Machinery Coverage form was renamed and is now called the Breakdown Protection Coverage Form.[10] The new name and the changes in coverage are indicative of the broadening nature of equipment exposures.

The new form incorporates the most common boiler and machinery coverages that were previously insured by separate forms into a single coverage form. Ten coverages, designated A through J, are printed in the form. A particular coverage is effective only if a limit or the word "included" is entered in the declarations for that coverage. The ten coverages are

A. Property Damage
B. Expediting Expenses
C. Business Income and Extra Expense—Extra Expense Only

D. Spoilage Damage
E. Utility Interruption
F. Newly Acquired Premises
G. Ordinance or Law Coverage
H. Errors and Omissions
I. Brands and Labels
J. Contingent Business Income and Extra Expense—Extra Expense Only Coverage.

Although the order in which the coverages are listed does not suggest any particular relationship, six of the coverages (A, B, F, G, H, and I) relate to direct damage and four (C, D, E, and J) provide indirect loss coverage.

Direct Damage Equipment Coverages

Open peril commercial property (fire and allied lines) forms usually exclude damage caused by artificially generated electrical current, mechanical breakdown, and explosion of steam boilers owned, leased, or operated by the insured. Like its predecessor boiler and machinery forms, the Breakdown Protection Coverage Form dovetails with these exclusions by covering losses from explosion of steam pressure vessels and damage to a wide range of mechanical or electrical equipment.

Property Damage Coverages A (Property Damage) pays for damage to covered property caused by breakdown of covered equipment. There is a single covered cause of loss under the Breakdown Protection Coverage Form—*breakdown* to *covered equipment.* "Breakdown" is defined to include mechanical failure, electrical failure (including arcing), and failure of pressure or vacuum equipment.[11] The definition specifically excludes several types of damage or equipment failure, such as leakage, damage to vacuum or gas tubes, brushes, and the functioning of safety devices. For machines with electronic or automated components, the definition also excludes defects, erasures, errors, limitations, or viruses in computer equipment and programs. Finally, in addition to the restrictions in the definition of breakdown, there are specific exclusions that eliminate coverage for depletion, deterioration, corrosion, erosion, and wear and tear.

[10] The new ISO Breakdown Protection Coverage Form, BM 00 20, replaces three separate coverage forms: Boiler and Machinery Coverage Form, BM 00 25; Small Business Boiler and Machinery Coverage Form, BM 00 40; and Small Business Boiler and Machinery Broad Coverage Form, BM 00 45. The new form is designed for use by organizations of any size, type, or industry.

[11] The earlier boiler and machinery coverage forms insured against an "accident" to an "insured object," and required that the breakdown be sudden and accidental and that it manifest itself by physical damage at the time the breakdown occurred.

Covered equipment is defined as equipment that has been built to operate under internal pressure or vacuum, electrical or mechanical equipment used for the generation, transmission, or utilization of energy and communication and computer equipment.

Covered property includes all property owned by the named insured or in the named insured's care, custody, or control and for which it is legally liable. *Covered equipment* refers to the specific boiler and machinery items whose breakdown is insured. The distinction between covered property and covered equipment is important because damage caused by a breakdown can extend beyond the equipment itself. A boiler explosion, for example, can destroy an entire building. Equipment breakdown coverage protects against damage *to* insured equipment and also covers damage to other property that is caused *by* breakdown of such equipment.[12]

The Expediting Expense coverage (Coverage B) provides payment for the reasonable extra cost of temporary repairs and the cost of expediting permanent repairs. Expediting expense might include, for example, the cost of having parts delivered by air or the cost of overtime for workers. Coverage is limited to $25,000, but may be increased.

The Newly Acquired Premises Coverage—Coverage F—provides automatic coverage for equipment at newly acquired premises for 90 days or the number of days designated in the declarations.

There are two optional coverage enhancements available under the direct damage coverage. The *Ordinance or Law Enforcement* coverage—Coverage G in the form—is similar to the comparable coverage under the commercial property program. Coverage is triggered when loss is increased by the enforcement of laws or ordinances that regulate the demolition, construction, repair, or use of the building or structure. The *Brand and Labels* Coverage—Coverage I—relates to the value of salvage. Under this coverage, the insured may require an insurer taking undamaged property to remove the brand name and labels from salvaged property. This reduces the value of the salvaged property to the insurer, but avoids the situation in which the manufacturer's products would be offered in the market with the brand and labels intact.

Hazardous Substances and Other Limitations
Unless a higher limit is stated in the declarations, a separate $25,000 limit applies to each of the following losses: expenses for the cleanup of hazardous substances, damage caused by ammonia contamination, and damage by water caused by breakdown of refrigerating or air-conditioning equipment.

Indirect Loss Boiler and Machinery Coverages

There are three indirect loss boiler and machinery coverages printed in the Breakdown Protection Coverage Form: Business Interruption and Extra Expense, Spoilage Damage, and Utility Interruption coverage.

Business Income and Extra Expense Business income coverage under BM 00 20 pays for the actual loss of business income and the extra expense the insured incurs to continue operations during the period of restoration. Extra expense coverage may also be purchased without business income. Business income and extra expense are defined in exactly the same way as under the ISO commercial property program. The period of restoration begins at the time of the breakdown and ends five days after the damaged property is repaired or replaced with reasonable speed and similar quality. The five-day period may be extended by entering a greater number of days in the declarations.

The insured must complete an annual report of business income values, which is used to determine the premium for business income and extra expense coverage. If the report is not filed as required, a coinsurance provision is applicable.

Spoilage Damage Spoilage damage coverage provides payment for direct damage caused by the lack or excess of power, light, heat, steam, or refrigeration. Coverage also applies for the necessary expenses incurred to reduce the amount of loss under the spoilage damage coverage, limited, however, to the amount of loss that otherwise would have been payable. A freezing plant, a meat locker, or a florist might purchase spoilage damage coverage for loss resulting from the breakdown of its freezing or heating equipment.

Utility Interruption Utility interruption coverage extends business income and extra expense and spoilage coverages to cover loss caused by interruption of electrical power, communication, sewer, air

[12] Because other forms of property insurance generally exclude steam boiler explosion, the limit on insured boilers should be high enough to cover all damage to owned property that may result from an accident. The standard policy covers on a repair or replacement basis (i.e., on a replacement cost basis), but actual cash value coverage is available by endorsement.

conditioning, heating, gas, water, or steam, resulting from breakdown of covered equipment owned, operated, or controlled by a utility or distributor that provides these utility services to the insured premises.

Deductibles

The policy provides for five different deductible possibilities: a dollar deductible, a time deductible applicable to business income and extra expense, a multiple of daily value deductible[13], a percentage of loss deductible, and a minimum or maximum deductible. The minimum or maximum deductible may be used in connection with the multiple of daily value or the percentage of loss deductible.

Suspension

The boiler and machinery policy contains a unique provision permitting the insurance company to suspend coverage on any or all insured objects found to be in a dangerous condition. Any insurance company representative may execute suspension by handing notice of suspension to the insured or by mailing the notice to the insured's address stated in the policy or to the location of the object on which coverage is to be suspended. The suspension becomes effective immediately on delivery without prior notice or waiting period. When coverage has been suspended, it may be reinstated only by endorsement to the policy.

TRANSPORTATION COVERAGES

The property forms used to insure business firms do not generally include off-premises coverage like that of the Dwelling or Homeowners forms; for this reason, special provision must be made for business property away from the premises. Ocean marine and inland marine forms are designed to provide this coverage.

Ocean Marine Insurance

Despite the technological advances in marine transportation, ocean disasters remain an ever-present hazard for those engaged in foreign trade. Ocean marine insurance provides coverage against four types of losses, corresponding to the four major classes of ocean marine insurance:

1. *Hull Insurance.* Hull insurance protects the owner of a vessel against loss to the ship itself. The coverage is written on a modified open-perils basis. A special provision in the hull policy called the *running-down clause* provides a form of property damage liability applicable to damage to other ships.

2. *Cargo Insurance.* Cargo insurance, which is written separately from the insurance on the ship, protects the owner of the cargo from financial losses that result from its destruction or loss.

3. *Freight Insurance.* Freight insurance is a special form of business interruption insurance. When a vessel is lost, this coverage indemnifies the shipowner for the loss of income that would have been earned on completion of the voyage.

4. *Protection and Indemnity.* Protection and indemnity coverage is essentially liability insurance that protects the owner of the ship from the consequences of negligent acts of his or her agents.

These contracts are written in a strange and antiquated language and are governed by principles derived from ancient maritime practice and admiralty law. Ocean marine insurance is a fantastically complicated field, so we will include just a brief discussion of a few major concepts.

Perils Insured The ocean marine insuring instrument is an open-perils agreement—with certain limitations. Damage arising from *perils of the seas* is covered, including damage caused by waves, sinking, stranding on reefs or rocks, lightning, collisions, or any number of other causes associated with transportation by water. The policy also provides coverage for *perils on the seas,* which are specifically listed, including fire, pirates, thieves, jettisons, barratry,[14] and all other like perils. Note that this is not truly all risk; the perils must be of the same nature as those specifically listed. In addition to the speci-

[13] The daily value deductible is determined by dividing the business income that would have been earned during the period of interruption by the number of days the business would have been open, and then multiplying that amount by the number of days shown in the declarations.

[14] Jettison is the voluntary act of destruction in which cargo is cast overboard to save the ship. In barratry, the master and/or mariners steal the ship and its cargo, willfully sink or desert the ship, or imperil the vessel by disobeying instructions.

fied perils, marine policies are frequently expanded to include others.[15]

Certain perils that would otherwise be included in the broad insuring agreement are specifically excluded. The *Free of Capture and Seizure* (FC & S) clause excludes war in all its aspects. A separate war risk policy may be purchased to obtain coverage for the perils of war. The *Strike, Riot, and Civil Commotion* (SR & CC) clause excludes loss or damage caused by acts of strikers, rioters, or persons engaged in civil commotion. This exclusion may be deleted if the underwriter is willing to assume the risk.

Valuation Almost all ocean marine policies are valued policies, and the face amount of insurance is payable in the event of total loss. In addition, although the policy does not contain a 100 percent coinsurance clause, the legal custom of 100 percent insurance to value has been in existence for so long that it is considered a condition of the contract, and policies are interpreted as if they did contain a 100 percent coinsurance clause.

Average Conditions The term *average* is considered by many people to be the most important single word in the terminology of ocean marine insurance. It is synonymous with *partial loss.*[16] *Average* (or partial loss) under an ocean marine policy may be a *particular average* or *general average.*

Particular Average A *particular average* is defined as a partial loss to property of a particular individual. Cargo insurance is often written "free of particular average unless caused by the vessel being stranded, sunk, burnt, on fire, or in collision," which means that partial losses from other causes are excluded. In some cases, a hull contract or a cargo policy may provide that coverage is "free of particular average under 3 percent." In this case, the clause acts as a franchise deductible. If the loss is less than 3 percent (or some other percentage specified), it is not covered; if it exceeds 3 percent of the amount of insurance, it is covered in full.

General Average A *general average* loss is one borne by all parties to the venture. It is based on the ancient maritime law that requires all persons participating in a venture to share the loss when one person's goods are sacrificed to save the venture. The simplest example is the jettison of cargo to lighten the ship in time of stress. If goods belonging to one party are thrown overboard to save the ship and the attempt is successful, all other parties, including the shipowner and the other cargo owners, will share in the loss of the jettisoned cargo with its owner, based on the proportion of the total value of the venture each owns. Under the terms of the ocean marine policy, the company insuring each of the participants will pay its insured's share of the general average loss. Amounts payable for general average and salvage charges[17] are in addition to the amounts payable for loss of the insured's property.

Warehouse-to-Warehouse Clause Unless the policy designates the contrary, coverage is provided only from the time goods are actually loaded on the ship. However, policies may be endorsed to cover goods during transportation to and from the vessel. In these cases, it is customary to endorse the policy with the warehouse-to-warehouse clause to provide coverage for the entire exposure from the time goods leave the premises of the shipper until they arrive at the premises of the consignee, including transit over land.

Inland Marine Insurance

Inland marine insurance developed as an extension of the warehouse-to-warehouse clause in ocean marine policies. Historically, ocean marine insurers have been exempt from state regulation, primarily on the grounds that regulation would impede their ability to compete in an international market. Exercising their freedom from regulation, marine insurers began to write coverage on goods in transit not only by water, but overland

[15] A good example is the *Inchmaree clause,* which covers bursting of boilers and latent defects in machinery or errors in navigation or management of the vessel by the master or crew. The clause is named after the ship *Inchmaree,* which suffered loss because of breakage of a pump through negligence in maintenance by the crew. The British House of Lords decided that the loss was not covered since it was not of the same nature as the *perils on the sea* listed. To counteract this decision, the Inchmaree clause was added to hull policies.

[16] The English word *average* comes from the French noun *avarie* meaning "damage."

[17] Salvage charges are expenses payable to third parties known as salvors for assistance rendered in saving property exposed to loss. Such charges may be incurred under contract, or they may be incurred to parties acting independently of any contractual obligation. For example, the shipowner and cargo owners might be assessed salvage charges if the ship was in danger of sinking and was forced to accept help from another vessel to reach port.

as well. Eventually, they turned to writing coverage on fixed location property. In 1933, the NAIC promulgated its *Nationwide Marine Insurance Definition*, specifically defining the types of insurance marine insurers were permitted to write. The definition was revised in 1953 and again in 1977 and assumed the more modest role of defining those types of insurance that are considered marine insurance for rate filings and for the reporting of statistics. The 1977 version of the definition recognizes six broad classes of property that may be insured under marine contracts:

1. Imports
2. Exports
3. Domestic shipments
4. Means of transportation
5. Personal property floater risks
6. Commercial property floater risks

The first two classes—imports and exports—are strictly limited to the ocean marine category. Export property is considered to be in the course of transportation and thus eligible for marine coverage as soon as it is designated or prepared for export. Imports are eligible until they reach their intended destination.

For purely *inland* marine risks, the definition recognizes four categories: domestic shipments, means of transportation, personal property floater risks, and commercial property floater risks. Although the first two classes (domestic shipments and means of transportation) consist of fairly homogeneous groups of contracts, the commercial property floater risks class includes a smorgasbord of property coverages. For the purpose of analysis, it is helpful to divide the NAIC's commercial property floater risks class into four subclasses (business floater policies, dealers' forms, bailee forms, and miscellaneous policies) and to consider the commercial inland marine field as being divided into six general classes:

1. Transportation forms, which insure shipments of goods by rail, motor carrier, and air carrier. These include forms that cover the legal liability of the carrier and forms to protect the owner of the goods against loss or damage of the merchandise.[18]

2. Means of transportation forms, which include policies written to cover instrumentalities of transportation and communication, including mobile property such as railroad rolling stock, but also fixed objects such as bridges, tunnels, pipelines, power transmission lines, and radio and television transmitting equipment. Although some of this property is not mobile in nature, its inclusion in the field of inland marine insurance was justified on the grounds that it is subject to the perils of transportation.

3. Business floater forms, which cover personal property (such as construction equipment) that is mobile in nature and, therefore, subject to damage by the perils of transportation.

4. Dealers forms, which cover the merchandise of certain types of businesses, such as jewelers, furriers, camera dealers, and musical instrument dealers. These forms cover the merchandise while it is on the insured's premises and also provide incidental off-premises coverage.

5. Bailee forms, designed to cover goods that are in the custody of someone other than the owner to whom the goods have been entrusted.[19]

6. Miscellaneous policies, which include unrelated and anomalous types of inland marine coverages such as accounts receivables and valuable papers coverages as well as electronic data processing policies.

Before turning to a discussion of the specific policy forms that are used in the inland marine field, a few preliminary observations on the nature of inland marine policies will be helpful.

Controlled and Uncontrolled Forms One often encounters the terms *controlled* and *uncontrolled* in connection with inland marine forms. *Controlled forms* (C) are those that are filed with the state insurance departments by insurers or on their behalf by bureaus. The controlled forms are subject to the rules contained in the inland marine section of the *Commercial Lines Manual* (or other approved manual) and cannot be changed, except to the extent that modification is permitted by the rating rules approved by the state insurance department. Controlled forms are a part of the ISO portfolio program. As in the case of the portfolio property coverages previously

[18] The transportation forms designed to protect common carriers against liability losses arising out of damage to property being transported will be treated in the next chapter with the liability coverages.

[19] Bailee forms are treated in greater detail in the next chapter.

discussed, the portfolio inland marine policy is constructed through the use of common coverage parts and declarations and inland marine specific forms.

Uncontrolled forms (U), on the other hand, are not standardized by a rating bureau, but are developed by individual insurers. The terms of uncontrolled forms can differ from insurer to insurer, depending on underwriting philosophy. Some uncontrolled forms are written on a manuscript basis, with provisions tailored to meet the insured's needs, and the rates tailored to meet the provisions. Both the rates and provisions of the uncontrolled forms are determined by the underwriter's judgment. In the discussion that follows, controlled and uncontrolled forms are distinguished by the designations (C) and (U), respectively.

Transportation Forms The owner of goods may ship them by common carrier or by contract carrier, or on the firm's own trucks. Regardless of the means used, insurance may be needed. For example, even though the liability of a common carrier for merchandise in its custody may be extremely broad, there are some instances in which the carrier may not be liable for damage to goods in its care. In addition, carriers frequently make use of a *release bill of lading,* limiting their responsibility to, say, 50 cents per pound. Even in those instances in which the common carrier may be liable, the owner may find it more convenient to collect from his or her own insurer and permit the insurer to subrogate against the common carrier.

There are two standard approaches to insuring goods in transit, depending on whether common carriers or the firm's own trucks are used. Goods shipped by common carrier are usually insured under the Annual Transit Policy (U) designed to cover all shipments in a given year.[20] Policies are written to meet the requirements of the individual firm and may be modified to meet the specific situation. For example, coverage may be provided on incoming shipments, outgoing shipments, or both. There are forms for insuring property in the custody of railroads and coastwise shipping firms, on trucks used to connect with railroads and steamers, solely by truck, or by air cargo. Coverage is normally on a named-peril basis, covering fire and lightning and the perils of extended coverage (except strike, riot, and

civil commotion, which are optional), plus the *perils of transportation,* which include flood, collision, overturn of a vehicle, bridge collapse, derailment, earthquake, and landslide. Theft coverage is also available by endorsement.

Goods shipped on the owner's own trucks are usually insured under a Motor Truck Cargo Owner's Policy (U) (although such goods may also be insured under a version of the Annual Transit Policy). Coverage under the Motor Truck Cargo Policy is essentially the same as under the Annual Transit Policy. It is subject to a limit of liability on any one truck or in any one place, with a further limit on any single disaster.

Other transportation forms include the Parcel Post Policy (U), designed for firms that make frequent parcel post shipments and prefer commercial to government insurance, and the Mail Coverage Form (C), designed for banks and other businesses that regularly ship securities, money, or other valuable property by registered mail or express. The Mail Coverage Form covers valuable property such as bonds, stock certificates, certificates of deposit, money orders, checks, drafts, warehouse receipts, and other property of a similar nature when sent by first class mail, certified mail, U.S. Postal Service express mail, or registered mail. The form may also be used to cover bullion, platinum, other precious metals, currency, unsold travelers' checks, jewelry, watches, precious and semiprecious stones, and similar valuable property when sent by registered mail.

Business Floater Policies Merchandise being shipped is not the only business property exposed to damage away from the business premises. There are many classes of property that are mobile in nature and, so, vulnerable to risk. To meet the need for protection on these classes, there are a large number of inland marine floater policies. In general, these floaters fall into one of three categories:

1. *Equipment Floaters.* These are designed to cover business property not held for sale or on consignment that is in the hands of the owner for its intended purpose. Examples include the contractors' equipment floater (U), agricultural equipment and livestock floater (C), and salesmen's sample floater (U).

2. *Processing and Storage Floaters.* These insure property in temporary storage and property undergoing processing outside the owner's premises. A good example is the garment contractor's floater (C),

[20] A Trip Transit Form is available to insure specified lots of goods for a particular trip.

which covers the stock of a manufacturer that has been sent off premises for processing.

3. *Consignment and Sales Floaters.* These policies protect goods being held for sale under consignment, being installed, or being sold under an installment plan. Examples include the installment sales floater (U), which covers goods sold on an installment basis; the Floor Plan Merchandise Form (C), which covers stock pledged as collateral under a *floor plan* arrangement; and the installation floater (U), which covers machinery and equipment in transit for installation in a building and while being installed.

The coverage of these forms may be written on both an open-perils or named-peril basis, and the coverage varies under the different forms. In several classes, the insured has a choice between open-perils and named-peril coverage. In addition, the coverage may be written on a schedule or blanket basis.

Dealers Forms Dealers forms represent something of an anomaly in inland marine insurance. Although inland marine forms generally cover property that is mobile and that is commonly away from the owner's premises, the dealers forms provide coverage on a dealer's stock of goods. Although coverage applies on- and off-premises, the major exposure is on-premises. Dealers forms are available only for specific classes of dealers. They include jewelers, furriers, musical instrument dealers, camera dealers, equipment dealers, fine arts dealers, and stamp and coin collection dealers. The policies for jewelers and furriers are referred to as the Jeweler's Block Policy (C) and the Furrier's Block Policy (C).[21] The other forms are referred to simply as dealer's forms, for example, Musical Instrument Dealer's Form (C), Camera Dealer's Form (C), and so on. The Equipment Dealers Coverage Form is typical of these policies. The Equipment Dealers Coverage Form insures the stock in trade of dealers in agricultural equipment and implements and contractors equipment. Motor vehicles designed for highway use are not eligible for coverage under the form. In addition to the

dealer's stock, the form also covers property of others in the custody of the dealers. Such property of others would consist of customers' equipment in the dealer's custody for servicing or repair.

Miscellaneous Inland Marine Forms The miscellaneous class of inland marine commercial policies includes unrelated and unusual types of inland marine coverages such as accounts receivable and valuable papers coverages and electronic data processing policies. Accounts receivable insurance and valuable papers insurance are the most common of these coverages.

Accounts Receivable (C) Accounts receivable insurance protects against the inability to collect amounts owed to the insured because of destruction of records by fire or other insured perils. The coverage is written on an open-perils basis, on either a reporting basis or, subject to an 80 percent coinsurance provision, on a nonreporting basis. The coverage is on an indemnity basis and compensates the insured for any amounts that are uncollectible because of the destruction of the accounting records (with allowance for bad debts). In addition, payment is made for expenses incurred to reconstruct the records, for collection expenses above normal costs, and for the interest charges on loans taken out by the insured to offset the impaired collections.

Valuable Papers Insurance (C) Valuable papers coverage may be written to insure various types of important records, including maps, film, tape, wire or recording media, drawings, abstracts, deeds, mortgages, and manuscripts. Coverage is on an open-perils basis and can be either blanket or scheduled. Items specifically insured are covered for an agreed amount, whereas papers covered on a blanket basis are insured for their actual cash value.

EDP Policy (U) With the rapid spread of electronic data processing (EDP) equipment and its software, a need quickly developed for insurance coverage to protect against losses arising out of damage to or destruction of this costly equipment. The coverage was originally written by insurers with an extensive background in inland marine insurance usually on inland marine forms. The coverage is written on an open-perils basis and generally provides coverage under separate insuring agreements for damage to hardware, software, and extra expense or business interruption.

[21] The term *block* as used in connection with the jeweler's block and furrier's block policies comes from the French phrase *en bloc*, meaning "all together." Thus, block policies are intended to cover all the property of the business in a single contract.

Manufacturers Output Policy The Manufacturers Output Policy was developed as an inland marine form to cover manufacturers' stocks of merchandise being shipped to dealers. The earliest versions of the policy covered automobiles being shipped from the factory to dealers and covered property only while away from the insured's premises. The standard form excludes property at any manufacturing location owned by the insured, but the policy is usually endorsed to provide open-perils coverage both on- and off-premises.

Difference-in-Conditions Coverage Difference-in-conditions insurance, generally referred to as DIC coverage, is a special form of open-perils coverage written in conjunction with basic fire coverage age and designed to provide protection against losses not reimbursed under the standard fire forms. It is always written as an adjunct to separate policies covering against fire, extended coverage, and vandalism and malicious mischief (plus sprinkler leakage when the exposure exists) and does not provide coverage against losses caused by these perils. It does, however, provide coverage for most other insurable perils, including flood and earthquake. There is no coinsurance clause and no pro rata clause, and the policy may be written for an amount different from the basic policies it complements. The coverage is subject to a deductible, which is usually substantial, ranging upward from $10,000. Protection against earthquake and flood may be subject to limits and deductibles that differ from the remainder of the policy. Each DIC policy is individually rated. The coverage was originally available only to giant firms, but some insurers have recently developed mini-DIC forms for medium to small businesses. In some instances, consequential and transit coverages are included.

THE NATIONAL FLOOD INSURANCE PROGRAM

The general nature of the National Flood Insurance Program (NFIP) and the coverage available for residential property, under the program were discussed in Chapter 26. As in the case of residential property, the program provides different amounts of coverage under the Emergency Program and the Regular Program. New limits of coverage were implemented March 1, 1995. The maximum limits now available are indicated in Table 31.1. As in the case of the residential program, the additional amounts of insurance available under the Regular Program are not at subsidized rates, but are actuarial rates calculated to consider the probability of loss in the community.

The General Property Form Flood Insurance Policy

The National Flood Insurance Program consists of a policy jacket and a form. The flood policy used to insure commercial property is called the General Property Form. Many of the provisions of this form—such as the definition of flood, inception and cancellation, and the debris removal and property removal provisions—parallel those of the Residential Flood Policy already discussed. Replacement Cost coverage is not available under the General Property Form. In addition, the General Property Form includes a special *Other Insurance* provision.

Federal Flood—Other Insurance Provision The General Property Form provides that if there is other flood insurance applicable to a covered loss, the NFIP's share of the loss is limited to the percentage of the loss that the NFIP coverage bears to the total insurance covering the loss. The General Property

TABLE 31.1 Limits on Nonresidential Property under the Federal Flood Insurance Program

	Emergency Program	Basic Insurance Limits	Additional Insurance Limits	Total Insurance Available
Nonresidential buildings	$100,000[a]	$150,000	$350,000	$500,000
Small business buildings		150,000	350,000	500,000
Nonresidential contents	100,000	130,000	370,000	500,000
Small business contents		130,000	370,000	500,000

[a] Nonresidential buildings insurance limit in Alaska, Guam, Hawaii, and U.S. Virgin Islands is $150,000.

Form provides that excess insurance will not be considered in determining the total amount of insurance applicable to the loss. *Excess Insurance* is defined in the policy as "insurance of such part of the actual cash value of the property as is in excess of the maximum amount of insurance permitted [under the NFIP for the particular property]."

For the purpose of illustration, assume that an insured has a NFIP covering contents for $200,000 (the maximum allowable under the NFIP). Assume also that the individual has excess flood insurance purchased under a contract from a private insurer written under a DIC (or other) form. In the event of a $100,000 loss, the insured will collect the full $100,000 from the NFIP.

In contrast, assume that the insured purchases only $100,000 in contents coverage from the NFIP and purchases a DIC policy with a $100,000 deductible applicable to flood. In this case, the DIC coverage is not "excess." The NFIP share of the loss is determined by the formula:

$$\frac{\text{NFIP Coverage Carried}}{\text{NFIP Coverage Available}} \times \frac{\text{Amount}}{\text{of Loss}} = \text{Payment}$$

In case of a $100,000 loss, the NFIP would pay only $50,000. The excess policy would not respond. Ironically, if the DIC coverage had not been purchased, the NFIP policy would have paid the entire $100,000 loss.

Nonresidential Condominiums

Nonresidential condominium buildings and their commonly owned contents may be insured in the name of the association under the General Property Form. A unit owner of a nonresidential condominium unit may not purchase flood insurance on his or her unit, but may purchase contents coverage under the General Property Form.

INSURANCE AGAINST DISHONESTY

The broad field of dishonesty insurance includes all instances in which the cause of the loss is the wrongful taking of property belonging to the insured. Historical factors led to two distinct classes of dishonesty insurance: fidelity bonds, which cover employee dishonesty, and crime insurance, designed to cover dishonest acts of persons who are not employees of the insured. Each by itself provides incomplete protection against the perils of dishonesty.

Coverage for some nonemployee crime losses is included in the open-peril commercial Property Coverage Form. Property other than money and securities, for example, if not excluded, is covered for loss by burglary, robbery, or theft under the Special Cause of Loss Form. The expansion of fire insurance coverages to include crime perils has reduced the demand for monoline crime coverages on property other than money and securities. At the same time, most property forms exclude loss to money and securities, which are exposed to loss not only by theft, but from other perils (e.g., fire) as well. Coverage on money and securities for perils other than dishonesty is usually combined with dishonesty perils in commercial crime forms.

Dishonesty Insurance Coverage Triggers

There are two approaches to the coverage trigger in crime insurance, called *loss sustained coverage* and *discovery coverage*. The distinction originated in the field of employee crime, where losses can occur over an extended period of time and may not be discovered until long after they occur. More recently, the distinction is applied to both employee and nonemployee crime coverages.

Under the loss sustained forms, coverage for employee theft (as well as all other insuring agreements) applies only to loss resulting from acts committed during the policy period, and that are discovered during the policy period or within a *discovery period* that ends one year after termination of the policy. Under the discovery forms, coverage for employee theft (as well as all other insuring agreements) applies to loss resulting from acts committed at any time, provided that the loss is discovered during the policy period or a specified discovery period.

The discovery period under the loss sustained coverage forms is one year. Under the discovery forms, it is 60 days after the end of the policy period, or for up to one year after the end of the policy period with respect to employee benefit plans. Under both the loss sustained forms and the discovery forms, the discovery period terminates immediately upon the inception of replacement insurance.

Continuity of Coverage Under the ISO crime program, the *Loss Sustained* forms include a provision

titled *Loss Sustained During Prior Insurance*. It states that any loss that would have been covered under prior insurance is covered under the current bond, provided there has been no lapse in coverage from the old bond to the new one. The provision applies whether the current insurer or another insurer wrote the prior bond.[22] Without such a provision, a loss that occurred during a previous policy period would be uninsured if it were not discovered until after that policy had terminated and its discovery period had expired. The insurer that issued the previous policy would not be obligated to pay since its policy's discovery period had expired, and the present insurer would not be obligated to pay because the acts causing the loss did not occur during its policy period.[23]

The ISO Crime Insurance Program

Historically, the Surety Association of America (SAA) and the Insurance Services Office, Inc. (ISO) served as advisory organizations for employee and nonemployee crime, respectively. In 2002, the commercial crime insurance program that was jointly administered by ISO and the SAA was replaced by a new ISO program. Individual insurers may elect not to adopt the ISO program and continue to use the forms and endorsements of the joint ISO/SAA program. However, in most states, ISO no longer files the ISO forms and endorsements that were part of the ISO/SAA program on behalf of its affiliates.

Structure of New Program As indicated in Table 31.2, there are ten *coverage* and *policy forms* under the ISO commercial crime program. The differences between several of these forms, however, are more cosmetic than substantive. There are three basic crime policies: the Commercial Crime Policy, the Government Crime Policy, and the Employee Theft and Forgery Policy. There are two versions of each of

TABLE 31.2 ISO 2000 Commercial Crime Program Forms

Loss Sustained Forms	Discovery Forms
CR 00 21, Commercial Crime Coverage Form (Loss Sustained Form)	CR 00 20, Commercial Crime Coverage Form (Discovery Form)
CR 00 23, Commercial Crime Policy (Loss Sustained Form)	CR 00 22, Commercial Crime Policy (Discovery Form)
CR 00 25, Government Crime Coverage Form (Loss Sustained Form)	CR 00 24, Government Crime Coverage Form (Discovery Form)
CR 00 27, Government Crime Policy (Loss Sustained Form)	CR 00 26, Government Crime Policy (Discovery Form)
CR 00 29, Employee Theft and Forgery Policy (Loss Sustained Form)	CR 00 28, Employee Theft and Forgery Policy (Discovery Form)

these three policies— a *loss sustained* version and a *discovery* version, which accounts for six of the ten forms. In addition to these six forms (referred to as *policy forms*), there are four *coverage forms,* which are identical in their coverage with four of the *policy forms.* The policy forms are designed for use as monoline stand-along policies, while the coverage forms are designed for use in a package policy. The only difference between the similarly titled coverage forms and policy forms is that the provisions of the common policy conditions form (IL 00 17) are included in the policy forms, but omitted from the coverage forms.

Insuring Agreements The ISO crime coverage forms contain provisions for both employee and nonemployee crime coverages. With two exceptions, all the forms contain the following seven insuring agreements, and coverage applies only to those insuring agreements for which a limit of insurance is indicated in the declarations.

A.1. Employee Theft

A.2. Forgery or Alteration

A.3. Inside the Premises—Theft of Money and Securities

A.4. Inside the Premises—Robbery or Safe Burglary of Other Property

A.5. Outside the Premises

[22] If the amounts of the bonds differ and the current insurer also wrote the prior insurance, the higher penalty applies. If a different insurer wrote the prior insurance, the lower penalty will apply.

[23] Before the introduction of the portfolio program, fidelity bonds were written on a continuous basis until canceled. This continuous term was adopted because embezzlement losses can occur over an extended period of time, and a continuous contract maintained the continuity required to cover losses that were not discovered for many years. Portfolio bonds are written for annual periods, but achieve continuity of coverage through the *Loss Sustained During Prior Insurance* provision.

A.6. Computer Fraud

A.7. Money Orders and Counterfeit Paper Currency

The two employee theft and forgery forms (i.e., loss sustained and discovery) contain only the two insuring agreements indicated in their title. They are designed for insureds that elect to purchase these two coverages only.

Employee Crime Coverages

Employee crime coverages, also called *fidelity bonds,* protect against loss resulting from employees' dishonesty and cover loss of money, securities, or other property resulting from fraud, forgery, embezzlement, or theft by the person bonded, up to the face amount of the bond, which is called the *penalty.* The penalty under a bond is never cumulative, and a series of thefts by one person is considered a single loss. In addition to the distinction between *loss-sustained forms* and *discovery forms,* fidelity bonds are also classified as *schedule* bonds and *blanket* bonds.

1. *Schedule Bonds.* Schedule bonds cover the specific person or position that is listed in the policy. When several individuals are listed in a single bond, it is called a name schedule bond. Under a position schedule bond, positions to be covered are listed rather than the individuals. If a person leaves the firm or moves to another position, his or her successor is covered in the scheduled position. When more individuals occupy a scheduled position than the number originally specified, all are covered, but on a decreased basis. For example, if the bond provides for two cashiers with a $100,000 penalty on each, and there are actually four cashiers, loss by any of the four would be covered, but only up to $50,000 each.

2. *Blanket Bonds.* The broadest form of fidelity coverage is provided under blanket bonds that are designed to cover all employees, regardless of position, with new employees covered automatically.

A.1.—Employee Theft The ISO employee theft insuring agreement (coverage A.1. of the Commercial Crime Policy) provides blanket coverage and applies to theft by any individual meeting the definition of "employee" without any need to list the names of individual covered employees or covered positions. The limit of insurance shown in the declarations for employee theft applies to *each loss,* regardless of how many employees were involved in causing the loss, and regardless of whether the employees causing the loss can be identified.[24]

Coverage applies for loss of money, securities, and other tangible property by employee theft. An *employee* is defined as an individual in the insured's service who the insured has the right to direct and control while he or she is performing services for the insured, who is compensated directly by the insured with salaries, wages, or commissions. Such individuals are considered employees for 30 days after their service terminates. The definition of "employee" can also be amended to include certain nonemployees such as partners, limited liability company managers, directors and trustees, agents, leased workers, and data processing service providers.

Exclusions All the ISO crime forms for commercial entities contain seven exclusions that apply to all insuring agreements, plus a number of others applicable only to particular insuring agreements. The following seven exclusions are applicable to all coverages under the commercial crime forms.

Exclusion 1, *Theft by an Insured, Partner, or Member,* excludes loss caused by dishonest acts of the insured, a partner, or member of a limited liability company (LLC). Coverage is available by endorsement to protect innocent partners and LLC members, but only for loss in excess of the value of the dishonest partner's or member's interest in the business and amounts owed to that partner or member.

The second general theft exclusion, *Theft by Any Employee Except Under Employee Theft,* divides the coverage of the policy into employee and nonemployee components.

Exclusion 3, *Indirect Loss,* precludes coverage for indirect losses such as the loss of income that may result from loss by theft, liability for damages (other than compensatory damages, or expenses incurred in establishing the existence or the amount of a loss).

Exclusion 4, *Legal Expense,* eliminates coverage for expenses related to any legal action, except when

[24] Scheduled employee dishonesty coverage is available by endorsement, using the employee theft-name or position schedule endorsement, CR 04 08. When this endorsement is attached to the form, the limit of insurance for employee theft applies per employee for each *identified* employee involved in causing the loss whose name or position is shown in the endorsement schedule.

covered under the forgery or alteration insuring agreement.

Exclusions 5, 6 and 7, *War, Nuclear Hazards and Government Authority,* are the virtually universal exclusions of war, nuclear hazards, and seizure or destruction of property by order of governmental authority.

In addition to the seven exclusions applicable to all coverages, there are four exclusions applicable to the employee theft coverage. The first of these, *Employee Cancelled Under Prior Insurance,* eliminates coverage for loss caused by an employee of the insured (or of a predecessor in interest of the insured) for whom similar insurance was canceled and not reinstated. This exclusion is more far-reaching than is sometimes realized. Another policy provision, titled *Cancellation as to Any Employee,* states that coverage is canceled with respect to an individual employee immediately on discovery by the insured or a partner, officer, director, or trustee of the insured (or, if the insured is a limited liability company, a member or manager) of any dishonest act committed by that employee.[25] The provision, sometimes called the prior dishonesty clause, applies not only to employee theft, but also to any other instance of employee dishonesty, including acts committed before the employee is hired.

The *Inventory Shortage Exclusion* precludes coverage for claims that are based solely on inventory computation or profit and loss figures. Inventory shortages can arise from employee or nonemployee theft, and without some evidence that indicates what caused the loss, there is no coverage. If the insured can establish through evidence other than inventory records that the loss was caused by employee theft, inventory records can be used to support the amount of the loss.

The final two exclusions applicable to the employee theft coverage eliminate coverage for loss resulting directly or indirectly from trading, and losses resulting from fraudulent activities related to warehouse receipts.

Employee Benefit Plan Provisions The Employee Retirement Income Security Act (ERISA) requires that those handling funds of an employee welfare or benefit plan subject to its provisions be bonded. The required amount of insurance is 10 percent of the funds handled, subject to a $1000 minimum and a $500,000 maximum. These ERISA requirements can be satisfied simply by including the employee benefit plans as named insureds under the crime policy. When an employee benefit plan is so named, the 60-day extended reporting period of the discovery forms is extended to one year (as required by ERISA) with respect to employee benefit plans insured under the employee theft insuring agreement.

Nonemployee Crime Coverages

Policies designed to cover against loss of money or other property through dishonest acts of persons other than employees are classified according to peril. There are policies to protect against burglary, robbery, theft, forgery, and so on. Only the specified type of criminal activity indicated is covered, and coverage exists only when the loss meets the definition of the particular type of crime covered. For example, burglary consists of stealing property when the premises are not open for business and requires forcible entry into the premises. Insurance policies covering loss by burglary typically require visible evidence of forcible entry into the premises or forcible exit. Robbery, on the other hand, consists of taking property by violence or threat of violence. Theft is much broader in meaning than is either burglary or robbery and includes an illegal taking of property, thus embracing both burglary and robbery. All nonemployee crime forms exclude employee fidelity losses.

A.2. Forgery or Alteration Insuring Agreement
The forgery or alteration insuring agreement protects an insured against loss due to the forgery or alteration of checks, bank drafts, promissory notes, and similar documents drawn on the insured's bank account. The forgery coverage conditions provide that mechanically reproduced signatures are considered the same as handwritten signatures. Also, the coverage territory for this coverage is worldwide. The only exclusions applicable to the forgery coverage are the seven exclusions applicable to all coverages.

Coverage also applies to legal expenses incurred in defending a suit that results from the insured's refusal to pay a covered instrument believed to be forged or altered. Amounts paid under this extension are in addition to the forgery or alteration limit of insurance. The insured must have the written consent of the insurer to defend against the suit.

[25] In the government crime forms, discovery by "an official or employee authorized to manage, govern or control your employees" (rather than by a partner, officer, etc.) cancels coverage with respect to the dishonest employee.

A.3. Inside the Premises Theft of Money and Securities Most commercial property insurance forms exclude loss of money and securities. For organizations that have substantial amounts of money and securities, the solution is to purchase coverage under a commercial crime form. Despite its title, this insuring agreement covers not only theft, but also disappearance or destruction of money and securities. In effect, it provides open-peril coverage on money and securities. Coverage applies only on the insured's premises, but coverage for the off-premises money and securities exposure is available under insuring agreement A.5.

Coverage also applies for damage to the exterior of the building during the actual or attempted theft if the insured is the owner or is legally liable for the damage. Damage to locked safes, vaults, cash registers, cash boxes and cash drawers inside the premises that are damaged during a theft or a theft attempt are similarly covered.

Exclusions In addition to the seven general exclusions applicable to all coverages under the crime policy, insuring agreement A.3. is subject to eight additional exclusions, which also apply to insuring agreements A.4. and A.5.

The *Accounting or Arithmetical Errors or Omissions* exclusion eliminates coverage for mistakes in bookkeeping, such as underbilling an account.

The *Exchanges or Purchases* exclusion excludes losses such as a salesperson's undercharging on a purchase, error in making change, or giving of an unwarranted refund.

Two exclusions (*Fire* and *Motor Vehicles and Their Accessories*) exclude damage to property other than money and securities caused in the commission of a theft. Burglars often torch premises they have burglarized; such loss, even though caused by theft, is covered under the firm's property (fire) coverage. Damage to property other than money and securities, even if caused by theft, is covered under the firm's property (fire) coverage form. Similarly, the exclusion of damage to vehicles contemplates damage that would be covered under the vehicle's physical damage coverage.

The *Money-Operated Devices* exclusion provides that loss of property from a money-operated device is covered only when a continuous recording instrument in the device keeps a record of the amount of money deposited.

The *Transfer or Surrender of Property* exclusion eliminates coverage for loss of money and securities

as a result of their transfer or surrender to a person or place outside the insured's premises (or banking premises) based on unauthorized instructions or because of a threat of bodily harm or property damage. This exclusion is aimed primarily at losses resulting from computer fraud and extortion, both of which can be covered under other insuring agreements.

The *Voluntary Parting of Title to or Possession of Property* exclusion eliminates coverage in situations in which the insured has willingly entered into a business transaction that turns out to be fraudulent. Such losses have traditionally been regarded as avoidable by the victim and, therefore, uninsurable.

Finally, a *Vandalism* exclusion excludes loss by vandalism to the interior or exterior of the insured premises or to a safe, vault, cash register, cash drawer, or to other property. The vandalism exclusion does not apply to covered money and securities.

A.4. Inside the Premises—Robbery or Safe Burglary of Other Property This insuring agreement covers loss to property other than money and securities from actual or attempted robbery of a custodian inside the premises and actual or attempted safe burglary. Coverage also applies to resulting damage to the premises or the exterior of the premises and resulting loss of or damage to a locked safe or vault inside the premises.

"Robbery" is defined as the taking of property from the care and custody of a person by one who has either caused or threatened bodily harm to that person, or committed an obviously unlawful act witnessed by that person.

"Safe burglary" means either the taking of covered property from within a locked safe or vault inside the premises (as evidenced by marks of forcible entry on the safe or vault) or removal of the safe or vault itself from inside the premises.

Exclusions Coverage under the Inside the Premises—Robbery or Safe Burglary of Other Property insuring agreement is subject to the seven exclusions applicable to all coverages and the eight exclusions that were discussed under the Theft of Money and Securities—Inside the Premises insuring agreement.

A.5. Outside the Premises Insuring Agreement This insuring agreement provides essentially the same coverage away from the premises as agreement A.3 provides coverage for on-premises theft, disappearance, or destruction of money and securities.

Coverage applies while the insured property is outside the premises in the custody of a messenger or an armored motor vehicle company. The coverage is subject to the same exclusions discussed earlier in connection with the Inside the Premises – Theft of Money and Securities insuring agreement.

A.6. Computer Fraud This insuring agreement covers the loss of money, securities, and other property caused by the use of a computer to fraudulently transfer covered property from inside the insured's premises or a banking premises to a person or place outside those premises. A fraudulent transfer of money from the insured's bank account to a thief's bank account is an example of computer fraud. Other kinds of computer-related loss, such as computer vandalism, are not covered. In addition to the seven general exclusions, the computer fraud coverage is subject to an exclusion of loss for which proof of its existence or amount is dependent on inventory or profit and loss computations.

A.7.Money Orders and Counterfeit Paper Currency The insuring agreement provides coverage for loss caused by acceptance of counterfeit paper currency and money orders issued by a post office, express company, or bank that are not paid on presentation. The term "counterfeit" is defined in the definitions section to mean "an imitation of an actual valid original which is intended to deceive and to be taken as the original." Although currency of any nation is covered, territory is not worldwide—only the United States, its territories, Puerto Rico, and Canada are included. Coverage under this insuring agreement is subject only to the seven general crime exclusions.

PACKAGE POLICIES FOR BUSINESS FIRMS

Although the package policy began with the homeowners contract, the concept was soon applied to the field of commercial insurance. Eventually, two standard bureau package programs designed for businesses and institutions evolved: the Special Multi-Peril (SMP) Program and the Businessowners Policy (BOP). In addition to these programs, many insurers also developed their own commercial packages, although the independently filed packages usually paralleled the bureau forms. With the introduction of the new portfolio program, the ISO SMP program was replaced by a new Commercial Package Policy.

Commercial Package Policy

One of the progressive features of the portfolio program is the use of the same standardized forms for both monoline policies and for a multi-line package policy, called a *Commercial Package Policy* (CPP). The contents of a monoline policy differs from that of a package policy only in the number of coverage parts included. Because the CPP uses the same forms as the monoline coverages, the coverage is identical with the separate monoline forms.

Like the SMP before it, the CPP is a multiline policy in the truest sense of the term, and it provides both property and liability insurance in a single contract. In fact, the new program goes further in this respect than did the SMP. Commercial auto insurance, which was not included in the SMP may now be included as a part of a package policy.

Package Modification Factor One of the principal features of package policies has been a discount for the packaging. The CPP follows this principle, providing a *package modification factor,* which in effect discounts the premiums for individual coverages when they are combined in a qualified package. This discount is allowed only if the policy contains both property and liability coverage, applicable to the same premises. Usually, this will consist of coverage on the insured's building and/or contents under the Building and Personal Property Coverage Form, together with general liability coverage for the insured's premises and operations. Package discounts are not available for properties rated under certain specialized rating schedules (such as a highly protected risk rating plan), earthquake coverage, earthquake sprinkler leakage insurance, and personal liability coverage. Although these coverages may be included in the package, they are not eligible for the package discount.

Businessowners Policy

The *Businessowners Policy* (BOP) is a package policy approach to insurance for business firms similar to the CPP but designed for smaller firms. The program was introduced in 1976 and extensively revised in 1987 and again in 1997. The 1987 and 1997 versions generally resemble the format of the simplified portfolio program, but the BOP is not a part of the CPP.

It is an independent policy, complete with its own separate forms. Like the homeowners policy and the SMP policies, the BOP provides property and liability coverage in a single policy. The program was originally available for small and medium apartments, offices, mercantiles, and processing firms. The 1997 revision extended eligibility to contractors, certain restaurants (those with limited cooking and fast-food types), convenience stores without gasoline pumps, and laundry or drycleaning operations. For those firms that are eligible, the program provides an extremely broad package of coverage on a simplified basis.[26]

Property Coverage Property coverage is provided under one of two forms, the Standard Property Coverage Form and the Special Property Coverage Form. Coverage under the standard form includes the perils of fire and extended coverage, vandalism, sprinkler leakage, sinkhole collapse, volcanic action, and transportation. Coverage under the special form is on an open-perils basis, subject to the standard open-perils exclusions.

While the businessowners forms are similar in most respects to the simplified portfolio property forms, they differ in the following ways:

1. Coverage on both buildings and contents is for replacement cost and there is no coinsurance provision. Furthermore, coverage on the building automatically increases by 8 percent a year, unless a higher option has been elected.

2. If contents coverage equals 100 percent of the average monthly values for the preceding 12 months, an automatic 25 percent increase in contents coverage is provided to offset seasonal variations in stock value.

3. Business income and extra expense coverage are automatically included. There are no limits of liability and no coinsurance clause, and the insured may collect for reduced earnings up to 12 months.

4. Property that is off-premises and/or in transit is covered up to $1000.

5. Full open-perils coverage for exterior glass on all floors of the building.

6. $100,000 automatic coverage for personal property at newly acquired locations.

7. $5000 coverage on accounts receivable and $5000 coverage on valuable papers.

8. $5000 or 5 percent of the building limit for increased cost of construction due to ordinance or law.

9. $1000 coverage on money orders and counterfeit paper currency.

10. $2500 coverage for forgery and alteration.

Optional coverages under both froms include contingent business interruption coverage, employee dishonesty, and mechanical breakdown. Burglary and robbery coverage is an option under the Standard Form (and is automatically included in the Special Form). Other options include higher limits on both accounts receivable and valuable papers coverages over the $5000 basic limit, increased limits on forgery crime coverage, and coverage for loss caused by utility services equipment failure.

Liability Coverage In general, the Liability coverage of the Businessowners Policy is similar to the simplified CGL *occurrence* form. Coverage is provided for premises and operations, products and completed operations, advertising and personal injury liability, fire legal liability, and medical payments. There are separate limits for medical expenses ($5000), fire legal liability ($50,000), and liability and medical expenses combined ($300,000, which may be increased to $500,000 or $1 million). There are two aggregate limits. The products and completed operations aggregate is the same as the liability and medical expense limit, and the general aggregate is equal to two times the liability and medical expense limit. Firms that do not own automobiles may cover their non-owned automobile exposure under an optional hired and non-owned auto liability endorsement.

SUMMARY

Although our discussion of the commercial property and liability coverages in this chapter has been brief, it should serve to illustrate the general nature of the property coverages available to the business firm for the protection of its assets. In addition to the forms discussed, other, more specialized forms have been developed to fit specific needs.

[26] Eligible properties include apartment buildings of six stories or fewer with no more than 60 units and 25,000 square feet or less, office buildings of six stories or fewer and up to 100,000 square feet, and mercantile, processing and service firms with up to 25,000 square feet. Eligibility is limited to firms with gross sales of $3 million or less. For restaurants, the square footage limitation is 7500 and maximum gross sales are capped at $1 million.

IMPORTANT CONCEPTS TO REMEMBER

portfolio program
commercial property coverage
Building and Personal Property
 Coverage Form
coinsurance
Causes of Loss—Basic Form
Causes of Loss—Broad Form
Causes of Loss—Special Form
Causes of Loss—Earthquake Form
blanket insurance
reporting forms
full-value reporting clause
Agreed Value coverage
Ordinance or Law coverage
Condominium Association
 Coverage Form
Condominium Commercial Unit
 Owner's Coverage Form
business interruption insurance
business income
Business Income Coverage (And
 Extra Expense) Form
Business Income Coverage (Without
 Extra Expense) Form

Resumption of Operations provision
contingent buiness interruption
contributing property
manufacturing property
recipient property
leader property
Builder's Risk Coverage Form
Extra Expense Coverage Form
leasehold interest coverage
demolition cost coverage
Boiler and Machinery Coverage
 Form
consequential damage
ocean marine
hull coverage
cargo coverage
freight coverage
protection and indemnity
perils of the seas
particular average
general average
warehouse-to-warehouse clause
inland marine
perils of transportation

equipment floaters
processing and storage floaters
consignment and sales floaters
dealer's forms
accounts receivable insurance
valuable papers insurance
controlled forms
uncontrolled forms
difference-in-conditions insurance
National Flood Insurance Program
burglary
robbery
Employee Dishonesty Coverage
 Form
discovery period
Robbery and Safe Burglary
 Coverage Form
Theft, Disappearance and
 Destruction Form
premise burglary coverage
Combination Crime – Separate
 Limits Option
Commercial Package Policy (CPP)
Businessowners Policy (BOP)

QUESTIONS FOR REVIEW

1. List and briefly describe the extensions of coverage under the Buildings and Personal Property Coverage Form used to insure commercial buildings.

2. The Widget Manufacturing Company insures its plant against loss by fire for $900,000, under a policy with an 80 percent coinsurance clause. At the time that a $600,000 loss takes place, it is determined that the building is worth $1,250,000. How much will the insurer pay? How much would be paid in the event of a total loss?

3. Briefly describe the provisions of a reporting form that apply in the event that the insured (a) is late in filing a report, or (b) underreports the values on hand.

4. Give two specific examples in which contingent business interruption insurance would be needed.

5. List and briefly distinguish among the four coverages that are written as a part of an ocean marine policy.

6. Identify and briefly describe the six broad classes into which inland marine coverages may be divided.

7. Distinguish between a general average loss and a particular average loss in ocean marine insurance. What is a *free of particular average* clause?

8. The Widget Manufacturing Company purchased an Employee Dishonesty Coverage Form (Portfolio Crime Form A) with a $10,000 penalty on June 1, 1995, and canceled the bond on June 1, 1997. Which of the following losses would be covered and to what extent?

a. Employee A embezzled $5000 in 1994 and $5000 in 1996, the total $10,000 loss being discovered in January 1997.

b. Employee B embezzled $15,000 in 1992, but the loss was not discovered until January 1998.

c. Employees C and D embezzled $7500 each in a collusive loss during 1996, but the loss was not discovered until May 1998.

9. Briefly distinguish between *burglary* and *robbery*.

10. Briefly describe the four coverages of the *Boiler and Machinery Coverage Form*. What consequential loss coverages are available by endorsement?

QUESTIONS FOR DISCUSSION

1. Insurance-to-value is of paramount importance in the operation of the insurance mechanism. Describe the technique used to induce the insured to carry insurance-to-value in each of the following fields of coverage: (a) fire insurance, (b) extended coverage, (c) fire insurance reporting forms, (d) business interruption insurance, (e) extra expense insurance, (f) boiler and machinery insurance.

2. With respect to each type of coverage discussed in this chapter, indicate whether the coverage would probably be considered "essential," "important," or "optional" in programming insurance for the largest bookstore on or near your campus.

3. What elements of the employee dishonesty exposure make it difficult to estimate the size of the loss that can occur? In what way does the fidelity exposure differ from other property exposures?

4. Why might a business firm that purchases fire and extended coverage on its buildings and personal property also need to purchase inland marine insurance?

5. The Businessowners Policy is a standard package approach to insuring small businesses. Briefly describe the general nature of the Businessowners Policy program, and identify the coverages that are included on a mandatory basis. if you were asked to develop improvements to the Businessowners Policy, what additional coverages would you include?

SUGGESTIONS FOR ADDITIONAL READING

Brunck, Arthur E., Victor P. Simone, and C. Arthur Williams, Jr. *Ocean Marine Insurance,* vol. 1 and vol 2. Malvern, Pa.: Insurance Institute of America, 1988.

Fire, Casualty and Surety Bulletins. Casualty and Surety Volume. Cincinnati, Ohio: National Underwriter Company. (Loose-leaf manual service with monthly supplements.) See "Burglary," "Power Plant," and "Miscellaneous Casualty" sections.

———— Fire and Marine Volume. Cincinnati, Ohio: National Underwriter Company. (Loose-leaf manual service with monthly supplements.) See "Commercial Multi-Peril," "Fire," "Miscellaneous Fire," "Business Interruption," "Inland Marine," and "Consequential" sections.

Hillman, Bruce. *Commercial Property Coverage Guide.* Cincinnati, Ohio: National Underwriter Co., 1997.

Jorgensen, James R. *Business Income Insurance—How It Works,* 3rd ed. Boston, Mass.: The John Liner Organization, 1991.

Krause, George E. *Businessowners Policy Coverage Guide.* Cincinnati, Ohio: National Underwriter Co., 1997.

Malecki, Donald S., Ronald C. Horn, Eric A. Wiening, and James H. Donaldson. *Commercial Liability Risk Management and Insurance,* 2nd ed., vols. 1 and 2. Malvern, Pa.: American Institute for Property and Liability Underwriters, 1986.

McNamara, Roderick, Robert A. Laurence, and Glenn L. Wood. *Inland Marine Insurance,* vol. 1 and vol. 2. Malvern, Pa.: Insurance Institute of America, 1987.

Morrison, Robert M., Alan G. Miller, and Stephen J. Paris. *Business Interruption Insurance: Its Theory and Practice.* Cincinnati, Ohio: National Underwriter Company, 1986.

Policy, Form and Manual Analysis Service. Casualty Coverages Volume. Indianapolis, Ind.: Rough Notes Company. (Loose-leaf manual service with monthly supplements.) See "Boiler and Machinery," "Crime Insurance," and "Glass" sections.

———— Property Coverages Volume. Indianapolis, Ind.: Rough Notes Company. (Loose-leaf manual service with monthly supplements.) See "Fire and Allied Lines," "Inland Marine," "Ocean Marine," "Multiple Line," and "Miscellaneous" sections.

Rodda, William H., James S. Trieschmann, Eric A. Wiening, and Bob A. Hedges. *Commercial Property Risk Management and Insurance,* 3rd ed., vol. 1 and vol. 2. Malvern, Pa.: American Institute for Property and Liability Underwriters, 1988.

Trieschman, James D., Eric A. Wiening, Bob A. Hedges, Jerome Trupin, and Arthur L. Flitner. *Commercial Property Insurance and Risk Management,* 4th ed., vol. 1 and vol. 2. Malvern, Pa.: American Institute for CPCU, 1994.

Webb, Bernard L., Stephen and Arthur L. Flitner. *Commercial Insurance,* 2nd ed. Malvern, Pa.: Insurance Institute of America, 1990.

Winter, W. D. *Marine Insurance,* 3rd ed. New York.: McGraw-Hill, 1952.

Youd, James D. *A Practical Approach to Inland Marine Insurance.* Boston, Mass.: Standard Publishing Company, 1979. *Your Guide to the ISO Commercial Line Policies,* 3rd ed. Boston, Mass.: John Liner Organization, 1991.

WEB SITES TO EXPLORE

Best's Review—Property/Casualty Edition	http://www.ambest.com/review/lh/index.html
Business Insurance Magazine	http://www.businessinsurance.com/
National Fire Protection Association	http://www.nfpa.org
RISKWeb	http://www.RISKWeb.com/
Rough Notes Company	http://www.roughnotes.com/

COMMERCIAL LIABILITY INSURANCE

If you have known one, you have known them all.

— TERRENCE
Phormoi

CHAPTER OBJECTIVES

When you have finished this chapter, you should be able to
- Identify and differentiate among the three broad categories into which liability insurance for business firms may be divided
- Identify the coverage elements in a Workers Compensation and Employers Liability Policy and explain the exposure that each is designed to cover
- Identify and explain the general liability exposures facing a business
- Identify the major coverages of a Commercial General Liability Policy
- Explain the purpose and intent of each of the exclusions in a Commercial General Liability Policy
- Explain the difference between an occurrence general liability policy and a claims-made liability form
- Identify and differentiate among the four types of commercial automobile insurance policies
- Identify and differentiate among the three broad classes of automobiles that may be insured under a Business Auto Policy
- Explain the liability of a common carrier and explain how this exposure is generally insured
- Identify and differentiate among the types of bailment and explain the liability associated with each class
- Explain how bailee liability coverages differ from other forms of liability insurance
- Describe the characteristics of commercial excess liability policies and commercial umbrella liability policies

The liability exposures arising from business operations are both numerous and varied, and for the business firm as for the individual, there is virtually no calculable limit to the losses that can arise from legal liability. The sources from which liability can result multiply with the complexity of the business, and as a result, the field of commercial liability is significantly more complicated than the field of liability coverages for the individual.

As noted earlier, liability coverages can be conveniently divided into three classes: employers liability and workers compensation, automobile liability, and general liability. In addition to these three standard classes of liability insurance, we will also discuss bailee liability coverages and liability insurance for common carriers in this chapter.[1]

EMPLOYERS LIABILITY AND WORKERS COMPENSATION

Earlier, we focused on the social insurance role of the workers compensation laws, viewing them primarily as a technique for providing income to wage earners in the event of occupational disability. Here we consider the other side of the coin: the obligations that these laws impose on the employer. All states require the employer to insure the workers compensation exposure or to qualify as a self-insurer. Usually, only the largest firms self-insure, and even in these instances, some form of catastrophic coverage is normally purchased.

In addition to the liability imposed on the employer under the workers compensation laws, injury to employees may be a source of liability in still another way; a suit at common law. Although the workers compensation system was intended as an exclusive remedy for injured workers, there are several situations in which an employer may be sued for injury to an employee. Some form of coverage is needed to defend the employer in the event of such suits, and also to pay any resulting judgments. Protection for employers liability is provided as a part of the standard workers compensation policy.

[1] Bailee liability coverages and the liability coverages for common carriers are classed as inland marine insurance and are traditionally treated with the floater policies discussed in the preceding chapter. The authors feel that they are more appropriately treated in this chapter with other liability coverages.

Workers Compensation Policy

The *Workers Compensation and Employers Liability Policy* is written in simplified language and includes two standard coverages, Workers Compensation and Employers Liability. An optional coverage, Other-States Insurance, is printed in the policy and is made applicable by an entry in the declarations. Other coverages may be added by endorsement.

Part One: Workers Compensation Insurance The workers compensation insuring agreement obligates the insurer to pay the benefits for which the insured is liable under the workers compensation law of the state or states listed in the declarations. The commitment is extremely broad. There are no exclusions under the workers compensation coverage, and there is no maximum limit on the insurer's liability.

In a legal sense, the workers compensation section of the policy is not simply an agreement to pay benefits on behalf of the insured; it goes beyond merely indemnifying the insured and makes the insurer directly and primarily liable to employees who are entitled to benefits, even though such employees are not named in the policy. A special *statutory provision* in the policy in effect incorporates the provisions of the workers compensation law of the designated state into the contract, just as if it had been fully written out in the policy. The insurer's obligation to employees is not affected by any default of the insured under the policy or the failure of the insured to comply with the policy provisions. In other words, as respects the insurer's obligation to employees for benefits under the law or laws listed in the declarations, it is never a defense to a claim that the policy is not written broadly enough to cover the loss or that the insured violated a policy provision. The only matter to be determined is whether or not the employer is liable to the employee under the law. When a claim is proved, the insurer makes direct payment to the worker or dependents. The insurer may seek recovery from the employer for amounts that would not have been paid except for the unique position of the employee as a direct beneficiary under the policy. Although the insurer's liability to the employee is governed by the workers compensation law, the insurer's obligation to the employer is governed by the policy terms.

Part Two: Employers Liability Insurance The Employers Liability insurance provides protection for common lawsuits by employees who suffer bodily

injury. The coverage is subject to a per-accident limit and a separate per-employee occupational disease limit. In addition, there is a policy aggregate for occupational disease. The standard limits for Employers Liability Coverage, which may be increased for an additional premium, are $100,000 per accident, $100,000 per employee for occupational disease, and $500,000 aggregate for occupational disease.

Originally, Employers Liability coverage was included in the Workers Compensation Policy primarily as a defense coverage. Because workers compensation was intended as an exclusive remedy, suits by employees were once considered unlikley. Moreover, if an injured employee brought suit, the legal principles generally favored the employer. Nevertheless, it was argued, the cost of defending the suits could be expensive, and the Employers Liability coverage provided such defense.

Recently, the exclusive remedy theory of workers compensation has been subject to attack and is being eroded. As a result, Employers Liability coverage can no longer be considered merely a defense coverage, but instead an increasingly important component of the liability insurance program.

Attacks on the exclusive remedy theory of employer protection have come in several forms. Some states permit the spouse of an injured worker to bring action against the employer for his or her loss (as opposed to the loss suffered by the injured worker). Another approach is the so-called *third-party over suit*. Third-party over suits arise when an employee is injured in the course of employment by a negligent third party and, in addition to collecting workers compensation benefits, brings suit against that party. The third party, when found liable to the employee, then seeks to pass a part of the liability on to the employer, usually arguing that the employer's negligence was partly responsible for the injury.[2]

Another doctrine under which employees have been permitted to recover from their employer in a tort action is *dual capacity*. The dual capacity doctrine permits the employee to bring action against the employer if the employer was acting in a different capacity at the time of the injury. A classic illustration of this doctrine arose when a worker employed by a hospital received medical treatment at the hospital following a work-related injury. The court held that the employee had two relationships with the hospital: that of employee and that of patient. Although the employee was barred from bringing suit as an employee, he could sue as a patient.[3] The doctrine has also been applied to incidents in which the worker was injured by a product manufactured by the employer, when the injury occurred in the course of employment.[4]

The insuring agreement of the Employers Liabilty section of the policy makes specific reference to these types of suits, stating that coverage is provided for damages under the doctrine of dual capacity, third-party over suits, and for loss of care and consequential bodily injury to relatives of the injured employee.

The Employers Liability coverage is subject to several important exclusions. These include punitive or exemplary damages because of injury to persons employed in violation of the law, bodily injury caused or aggravated intentionally by the insured, and damages arising out of discharge, coercion, or discrimination against an employee in violation of the law. Liability assumed under contract is also excluded. Bodily injuries occurring outside the United States, its territories or possessions or Canada are also excluded, except to a citizen or resident of the United States or Canada who is temporarily outside these areas. Finally, there is an exclusion of any obligation under a workers compensation, occupational disease, unemployment compensation or disability benefits law, or any similar law. The exclusion of workers compensation and occupational diseases simply makes it clear that coverage under Part One and Part Two are separate and distinct.

Part Three: Other States Insurance Other States Insurance provides coverage that was previously available by an endorsement called the *Broad Form All States Endorsement*. The coverage is designed to protect against liability under the workers compensation laws of states in which the employer does not expect to have employees, but

[2] The landmark case in this area is *Dole v Dow Chemical Company,* 331 N.Y. Supp. 2d 382 N.E.2d 288 (1972). Here the court ruled that the employer was liable to a manufacturer who had been held liable to an injured employee.

[3] *Tatrai v Presbyterian University Hospital,* 439 A. 2d 1162 (1982).

[4] In an Ohio case, a truck driver was injured when his tire blew out and he brought a tort action against the employer, who was the manufacturer of the tire. See *Mercer v Uniroyal,* 49 Ohio 279 (1977). In a well-known California case, an employee who was injured on a scaffold manufactured by his employer successfully brought suit against his employer in its capacity as the scaffold manufacturer. *Douglas v E. and J. Gallo Winery,* 69 Cal. App. 3d 103 (1977). See also *Bell v Industrial Van Gas,* 110 Cal. App. 3d 463 (1980).

where a workers compensation obligation could conceivably be incurred.[5]

Initially, the employer should list all states in which the firm has employees. The Other States Insurance may then be used to further broaden the policy to provide workers compensation benefits in any state listed in the declarations for other-states coverage if the employer becomes liable under the law of such state. Rather than listing other states individually, it is common to use a blanket designation, stipulating that coverage applies to "all states except…" The states excepted are those with monopolistic state funds (North Dakota, Ohio, Washington, West Virginia, and Wyoming) and the state or states designated for Part One coverage. Some insurers also exclude those states in which they are not licensed to write insurance.

U.S. Longshoremen's and Harbor Workers Compensation Act Persons (other than sailors) who are engaged in maritime employment on navigable waters are covered under a federal workers compensation statute, the U.S. Longshoremen's and Harbor Workers Compensation Act (LHWCA). Although this is a complex area of law, in general a worker is covered under the LHWCA only if he or she meets a *situs* and a *status* test. The injury must occur on the navigable waters or on an adjoining wharf, pier, dock, or similar facility used in loading, unloading, building or repairing vessels. In addition, the individual must have been engaged in maritime employment when injured. Because the LHWCA is a federal statute, it does not fall within the scope of the workers compensation insuring agreement. When coverage is required for the LHWCA, it may be added to the policy by endorsement.

Voluntary Compensation Insurance Voluntary compensation insurance is an optional coverage that may be added to the policy by endorsement, using the *Standard Voluntary Compensation and Employers Liability Coverage Endorsement.* This endorsement is used when an employer wishes to provide workers compensation benefits to employees even though the law does not require payment of benefits. The insured selects a state law (usually the state of employment), and in the event of injury to a member of the class of employees for whom voluntary compensation is provided, the policy will provide benefits as if the employee were subject to the law.

GENERAL LIABILITY INSURANCE

Before examining the various general liability contracts that protect the firm against the peril of legal liability, it may be helpful to examine the major risks for which these contracts are designed. In general, these liability forms provide protection against nonautomobile liability that involves injuries to persons other than employees of the insured.

General Liability Exposures

Because business firms vary greatly in their activities, their liability exposures also vary, but every business firm is subject to one or a combination of the following liability exposures.

Ownership and Maintenance of Premises The basic exposure of the individual in owning property also threatens the business firm. The owner or tenant of a building may be held liable for damages if a member of the public is injured, or if property of others is damaged because of a condition in or arising out of the premises. There is almost no end to the list of possible defects that may cause injury; the student's imagination will provide an adequate substitute for a listing of such defects.

Conduct of Business Operations Besides the liability exposure from premises occupied, the firm may be liable if a member of the public or property of others is injured on or away from the premises by an activity of the owner or an employee. For example, employees of a contractor may injure someone at some place other than the firm's premises. The liability arising out of the ownership and maintenance of the premises and the conduct of business operations both on and away from the premises is covered under the general liability coverage entitled *Premises and Operations coverage.*

[5] Most workers compensation laws are *extraterritorial* which means that the provisions of the law apply to injuries to employees while in the state and also while traveling outside its boundaries. In addition, some laws have further extraterritorial effect in that they impose liability on an employer who is located in another state if an employee is injured in a state where he or she is working. For example, the employee of an Iowa firm who is injured while working in Illinois may bring action for workers compensation benefits under the Iowa law. In addition, however, the injured worker may decide to bring action under the law of the state where he or she was injured, particularly if the benefits of that state are higher. The worker in our example may elect benefits under either the Iowa law or the Illinois law, and the employer will be obligated to make payment in either case.

Products The legal liability exposure of a seller does not end when the product is sold and delivered to the customer. The manufacturer or distributor of a faulty product that injures someone or damages property may be held legally liable, and such liability may be established on one of three bases: negligence, breach of warranty, and strict liability.

If a product is negligently made or improperly designed, or if proper warning is not given to the consumer about its dangerous qualities, the manufacturer may be judged negligent and can be held responsible for the resulting injury or damage. Liability can also arise under the doctrine of *breach of warranty*. When a product is sold, there is an implied warranty that it is fit for the purpose intended. If it should prove defective and injurious in use or consumption, the warranty is breached and liability can result. Breach of warranty is a type of contractual liability.[6] Finally, product liability can also arise under the strict liability doctrine. Under the doctrine of strict liability, a "seller engaged in the business of selling such products" may be held liable if a defective product is sold and causes injury to the consumer, even in the absence of a warranty of suitability.[7]

Product liability losses mushroomed during the 1970s, as both the number of losses and the size of the awards mounted. In 1971, the average product liability award was $195,020. By 1986, it had increased to $1,161,522.[8] In many cases, manufacturers were held liable for injuries caused by machines manufactured 10, 20, or 30 years prior to the time of the injury. Faced with an increasing number of losses and escalating judgments, insurers reacted by increasing their premiums. For most buyers, the cost of product liability insurance skyrocketed, and in some instances the protection was difficult or impossible to obtain.

In the wake of this product liability crisis, many proposals were made during the 1970s for changes in the tort system as it relates to product liability. These proposals suggested modification of statutes of limita-tions, adoption of the rule that manufacturers be held responsible only to the extent of the "state of the art" at the time the product was originally produced, and even a no-fault approach to products liability. By 1998, two-thirds of the states had actually enacted leg-islation that in one way or another limited the injured party's right to sue or provided a defense for the man-ufacturer.[9] Although the exact nature of the laws dif-fers, most include a *period of repose* doctrine, which requires that the suit must be brought within a certain time from the manufacture or sale of the product, a statute of limitations, ranging from 2 years to 11 years, consideration of the state of art when the product was manufactured, and mitigation of damages in cases involving misuse or alteration of the product. In spite of the changes, however, the product liability expo-sure remains a severe one.

Completed Operations The completed opera-tions exposure is similar to the products exposure and consists of the possibility of liability arising out of work that has been performed. Such work is, in a sense, the product of the firm, and any damage arising out of it may result in liability if it is defective. The legal liability arising out of products or out of work performed is covered under a form of insurance called *products and completed operations* coverage.

Contingent Liability An individual or a business can sometimes be held liable because of work per-formed by independent contractors. As a rule, the principal does not control the actions of an inde-pendent contractor and is, therefore, generally not liable for the negligence of such contractor; however, there are important exceptions. In instances where the work being performed by the independent con-tractor is unlawful in itself, or the work is inherently dangerous, or where the principal exercises any supervision, the principal may be held liable. In addi-tion, the principal may also be held liable because there are certain duties and obligations that cannot be delegated. These conditions all create situations in which the negligence of an independent contractor may be imputed to the owner of property who has engaged that contractor. This means that every firm

[6] Under common law, the seller or distributor of a product could be liable for breach of warranty only to those with whom he or she was in *privity of contract* (i.e., with whom the seller had a direct contractual relationship). However, most courts have abandoned the requirement of privity of contract and permit suits based on breach of warranty to be brought against the manufacturer as well as the retailer and permit persons other than the direct purchaser to bring action based on the breach of warranty doctrine.

[7] Restatement, Second Torts, Section 401-A.

[8] *Insurance Facts,* 1986–1987 (New York: Insurance Information Institute, 1987).

[9] Alabama, Arizona, Arkansas, California, Colorado, Connecticut, Florida, Georgia, Idaho, Illinois, Indiana, Iowa, Kansas, Kentucky, Louisiana, Maine, Michigan, Minnesota, Missouri, Montana, Nebraska, New Hampshire, New Jersey, North Carolina, North Dakota, Oregon, Rhode Island, South Carolina, South Dakota, Tennessee, Texas, Utah, and Washington. The Alabama law was held to be unconstitutional.

that hires contractors or subcontractors has a *contingent liability* exposure. Insurance for this exposure is called *independent contractor coverage* and *owner's and contractor protective coverage*. Coverage for independent contractors is automatically included in premises and operations coverage, but it may also be written separately.

Contractual Liability In certain instances, a business firm (or an individual) may, by means of a written or oral contract, become liable for the negligent acts of another. Here the legal liability for the negligent behavior of someone else is assumed by a *contractual* agreement. For example, construction contracts often include a provision in which one party agrees to hold the other harmless for all claims for injuries arising out of the performance of the work. In such cases, the *indemnitor* (the individual who assumes the liability) promises to pay any judgment arising out of the work that might be entered against the other party (the indemnitee). Coverage for liability assumed under contract is covered by contractual liability insurance, now included as a part of premises and operations coverage.

Miscellaneous Exposures In addition to these major exposures, which may be covered under the liability coverages mentioned, there may be additional exposures that result from gaps or exclusions in the contracts. For example, most general liability policies contain the same *care, custody, or control* exclusion we saw in the homeowners policy. This exclusion can be particularly troublesome for the business firm whose primary function involves working on the property of others. In addition, other exposures may result from specialized activities of the firm. Some specialized coverages may be added to the general liability policy by endorsements, and specialized forms of coverage are available for other businesses with individualized needs.

Commercial General Liability Coverage

General liability coverage for organizations is provided under the *Commercial General Liability Policy* (CGL), which was introduced by the Insurance Services Office (ISO) in January 1986 as a part of the commercial lines simplification program, also known as the portfolio program. The Commercial General Liability forms replaced the Comprehensive General Liability Policy (which was also known as the CGL).

The new CGL—like the old CGL—is designed to insure those general liability exposures that are common to most organizations: premises and operations, products and completed operations, liability arising out of independent contractors, and contractual assumptions of liability. However, the new CGL form offers two approaches to the provision of this coverage: an *occurrence form* and a *claims-made form*. Under the older program, most general liability policies were written on an *occurrence basis*, which means that they covered injuries and damage that occurred during the policy period, regardless of when a claim was made or suit was brought. Under a claims-made form, coverage applies to injury or damage for which claim is made during the policy period.

Occurrence-form liability policies, which cover losses arising out of *occurrences* during the policy period, have served the marketplace well, virtually from the inception of liability insurance. When the injury is of an obvious nature and is recognized when it occurs, there is no problem. Unfortunately, however, there are some types of injuries that are not discovered until long after they occur. These are referred to as *latent injuries*. Latent injuries have required insurers to pay losses under occurrence policies long expired, because the injury or damage was not discovered until long after it had occurred.

The phenomenon of latent injury is best illustrated by asbestosis, an occupational lung disease incurred by workers in a variety of industries. Persons who suffer asbestosis may not discover the injury until long after it occurs. Employees who began working with asbestos in the 1950s did not discover they had contracted the disease until the 1970s or 1980s. The insurers who provided the products liability coverage for asbestos manufacturers in the 1950s on an *occurrence* basis found themselves paying for losses in the 1980s on policies that had long since expired. The problem was compounded by conflicting court decisions as to precisely when the occurrence covered under the policy occurs.[10]

[10] In what has been called the *triple trigger,* courts ruled that the occurrence that "triggers" the insurer's liability was the initial inhalation of asbestos fibers, the continued exposure to the hazard, or the diagnosis of the disease. This decision said that all insurers that had provided coverage from the time of inhalation through manifestation of an asbestos-related disease are liable for defense and indemnification costs. In some cases, the firms had been uninsured for extended periods, and the courts sought an interpretation that would find coverage under any (or all) of their expired contracts. *Insurance Company of North America v Forty-Eight Insulations, Inc.,* 633 F.2d 1212 (6th Cir., 1980) cert. denied 102 S. Ct. 686 (1981); *Eagle-Picher Industries, Inc. v Liberty Mutual Insurance Co.,* 523 F. Supp. 110 (D. Mass., 1981): *Keene Corporation v Insurance Company of North America,* 667 F.2d 1034 (D.C. Cir., 1981).

ISO and its member companies believed that a new approach to liability insurance was needed to counter the legal theories adopted by the courts in long-term exposure cases. The solution was the introduction of a new claims-made form for the general liability field, under which coverage applies, not based on the time at which the injury or damage occurs, but on the time that the claim is filed with the insurer. Although some insurers argued for a complete shift to claims-made coverage, ISO developed two new forms, one written on the claims-made basis and the other written on the traditional occurrence basis. At the time it was introduced, there was concern that the claims-made form would be widely used and that it might even replace the occurrence form. In fact, its use has been limited. Despite the lower cost of the claims-made form, few insureds have chosen to purchase it. In addition, insurers have insisted on using the claims-made form only in those situations in which the latent injury exposure is significant.

Because the occurrence form remains the most common approach to general liability insurance, we will concentrate on its provisions. We can then examine the specific differences between the two forms.

Coverage of the CGL Both versions of the CGL policy provide coverage against two major exposures: premises and operations, and products and completed operations. The insuring agreement for these coverages is designated Coverage A, for Bodily Injury and Property Damage Liability. In addition, coverage is provided for Personal and Advertising Injury Liability as Coverage B, and for Medical Payments as Coverage C.

Like its predecessor, the Comprehensive General Liability Policy, the Commercial General Liability Policy automatically covers new exposures. The premium for the CGL begins with an advance payment determined at inception. After the policy period, an audit is performed to determine what, if any, additional exposures have developed, and an additional charge is made for these.

Insuring Agreements The Coverage A insuring agreement contains the different terminology to provide coverage on an occurrence basis or a claims-made basis. The occurrence insuring agreement states that:

> We will pay those sums that the insured becomes legally obligated to pay as damages because of "bodily injury" or "property damage" to which this insur-

ance applies. The "bodily injury" or "property damage" must be caused by an "occurrence." The "occurrence" must take place in the "coverage territory." We will have the right and duty to defend any "suit" seeking those damages.

The claims-made form adds the statement

> This insurance applies to "bodily injury" or "property damage" only if a claim for damages because of "bodily injury" or "property damage" is first made against any insured during the policy period.

These broad insuring agreements, which provide coverage for liability "to which this insurance applies," are modified by the exclusions in the contract.

In 2001, the Insurance Services Office, Inc. (ISO) introduced a series of changes to the CGL policy designed to limit the scope of the contract's coverage involving Internet exposures. One major change was to redefine property damage to make clear that electronic data is not tangible property, and liability arising from its loss is therefore not covered by the form.

A second change in the 2001 form addressed the issue of when injury or damage must occur for coverage to apply. Traditionally, this has not been a problem; under the occurrence form, coverage applies to damage that occurs during the policy period, or so it was thought. Then, in 1995, in a bizarre interpretation of the plain language CGL, the Supreme Court of California ruled that the policy covers damage that occurred and was known to the insured to have occurred prior to the inception of the contract (*Montrose Chemical Corporation v. Admiral Insurance Company,* California S.C, July 1995). The court reasoned that because the insured's legal obligation to pay third party claims for damage that occurred before the inception of the policy had not yet been established, there remained a potentially insurable risk. In response to the Montrose Chemical case, ISO introduced mandatory endorsements in 1999 specifically eliminating coverage for loss or damage known to have existed at the inception of the policy. The 2001 edition of the CGL incorporates the provisions of the 1999 endorsement.

Exclusions There are 15 exclusions in the CGL, designated a. through o. Coverage for some of the excluded exposures is available under other forms of coverage, such as the auto policy or workers compensation insurance. Other exclusions eliminate coverage for exposures that require an additional premium,

and provision is made for a "buy-back" of the coverage. Finally, some of the excluded exposures are simply considered uninsurable by insurers. The following are the exclusions of the CGL form.

a. *Expected or Intended Injury.* The policy excludes bodily injury or property damage that is either expected or intended by the insured. An exception to the exclusion states that it does not apply to the use of reasonable force to protect persons or property.

b. *Contractual Assumptions.* Liability assumed under contracts is excluded, but there are several important exceptions. Coverage applies to *insured contracts* (leases, sidetrack agreements, easement agreements, agreements and contracts pertaining to the insured's business under which the insured assumes the tort liability of another). In addition, the exclusion does not apply to liability that the insured would have in the absence of the contract or agreement.

c. *Liquor Liability.* The policy excludes liability imposed under a liquor liability statute or at common law for causing or contributing to the intoxication of any person, or furnishing alcoholic beverages to a person under legal drinking age or who is intoxicated. The exclusion applies only to organizations in the business of manufacturing, selling, or distributing alcoholic beverages, and the courts have interpreted it narrowly. Courts have refused to apply the exclusion, for example, to injuries arising out of the sale or serving of alcoholic beverages by churches or other nonprofit organizations at social functions or fund-raising activities, on the grounds that these organizations are not in the business of serving or selling alcoholic beverages. In response to these decisions, the ISO developed an optional endorsement that insurers can add to the policy when they anticipate a liquor liability exposure. The *Amendment of Liquor Liability Exclusion endorsement* (CG 21 50) expands the exclusion to eliminate coverage for anyone who serves alcoholic beverages for a charge, whether or not the activity is for the purpose of financial gain. This includes a variety of fund-raising and social activities sponsored by nonprofit organizations. If the insurer is willing, the exposure can be covered by scheduling the specific functions at which

the liquor will be sold using the *Amendment of Liquor Liability Exclusion—Exception for Scheduled Activities endorsement* (CG 21 51).

d. *Workers Compensation.* There is an exclusion of benefits payable under any workers compensation, disability benefits, or unemployment compensation law.

e. *Employers Liability.* The policy excludes bodily injury to employees of the insured arising out of and in the course of employment. As in the workers compensation exposure, losses of this type are intended to be covered under the Workers Compensation and Employers Liability Policy.

f. *Pollution Exclusion.* The pollution exclusion has two parts. In addition to an exclusion of bodily injury and property damage arising out of the discharge, release or escape of pollutants, the policy separately excludes liability for cleanup costs. Unlike earlier policies, in which the exclusion did not apply if the emission was sudden and accidental, the new form excludes all forms of pollution. The only exception is with respect to the products or completed operations hazard. Even here, however, the exclusion of cleanup costs applies.

As discussed later in the chapter, the policy may be endorsed to provide pollution coverage and two pollution liability coverage forms are available.

g. *Aircraft, Autos, and Watercraft.* This exclusion eliminates liability arising out of the ownership, maintenance, use, or entrustment to others of aircraft, motor vehicles, and watercraft that are owned or operated by or rented or loaned to any insured. Nonowned watercraft of less than 26 feet in length are covered by an exception to the exclusion. The definition of motor vehicle does not include *mobile equipment* (bulldozers, farm machinery, forklifts, and other vehicles designed for use principally off public roads), which means that coverage is provided for vehicles of this type.

h. *Mobile Equipment.* Mobile equipment is excluded while being transported by an auto, or while being used in any racing, speed, or demolition contest, or while practicing for such activities.

i. *War Exclusion.* Liability arising out of war is excluded, if such liability is assumed in a contract. (No one knows why, so don't ask your instructor.)

j. *Care, Custody, and Control.* This exclusion excludes property damage to property owned by, rented to, or in the care, custody, and control of the insured. It also excludes damage to premises sold, given away, or abandoned unless such premises are the insured's work (formerly called the *alienated premises*). The exclusion of property in the insured's care, custody, and control applies only to personal property. Finally, property damage is excluded for the particular part of real property on which the insured or any subcontractor is working or the particular part of any property that must be restored, repaired, or replaced because work was incorrectly performed on it.[11]

k. *Damage to the Insured's Product.* The policy excludes property damage to the insured's product arising out of the product. Many people find this exclusion confusing, but the concept is simple enough. If a service station sells a defective tire to a customer and it blows out, there is no coverage for the loss of the tire. If, on the other hand, the blowout causes the customer to lose control of the car and demolishes it or other property, everything except the tire would be covered. The basic point is that the products coverage is designed to cover damage caused *by* the product and not damage to the product.

l. *Damage to the Insured's Work.* The exclusion of damage to the insured's work is similar in intent to the exclusion of damage to the insured's product. Although the situation is somewhat more complicated, the principle remains the same. The exclusion of damage to the insured's work applies only under the products and completed operations coverage, which means that it applies only after the work is completed. In addition, an exception to the exclusion makes it inapplicable if the damaged work or the work out of which the damage arises was performed on the named insured's behalf by a subcontractor.

m. *Property Damage to Impaired Property.* The policy excludes loss arising out of *impaired property* (property not actually injured or damaged) arising out of a defect, deficiency, or condition in the insured's work or product or delay or failure by the insured to perform a contract or agreement in accordance with its terms. The term *impaired property* distinguishes property that is diminished in value or usefulness from property that has actually been damaged. It is property that cannot be used or is less useful because of a defect in the insured's product or work, but the situation is correctable. If, for example, the insured manufactures aviation navigation equipment, defects in such equipment might result in grounding of aircraft in which it has been installed. The aircraft are not damaged; they are impaired property. The distinction between *impaired* property and *damaged* property is whether the property can be restored by removal or replacement of the insured's product, or by the insured fulfilling the terms of the contract or agreement.

n. *Product Recall.* The policy excludes liability for damage or claims arising out of the withdrawal or repair of products that are, or are believed to be, defective. The cost of recalling defective products can be considerable, and coverage for this exposure is available from specialty insurers on a limited basis.

o. *Employment-Related Practices.* The policy may be modified by endorsement to exclude coverage for bodily injury arising out of employment practices. Suits by employees alleging wrongful termination, sexual harassment, and discrimination proliferated during the 1980s and 1990s. Although such offenses do not meet the policy definition of bodily injury, some plaintiffs argued successfully that the employment practices caused bodily injuries such as emotional distress, trauma, and anxiety. Efforts to deny such claims based on the employee injury exclusion also failed as courts ruled that the employment-related activities fell outside *the course of employment.* Responding to these decisions, ISO developed the *Employment-Related Practices Exclusion Endorsement* (CG 21 47) that may be added to the policy. The endorsement excludes bodily injury arising out of any refusal to employ, termination, coercion, demotion, evaluation, reassignment, discipline, defamation, harassment, humiliation discrimination, or other employment-related practices, policies, acts, or omissions. Although the

[11] The care, custody, and control exclusion of the CGL form is both long and complex. It incorporates a number of provisions that were previously available only by endorsement and generally broadens the coverage in this area from that of earlier forms.

endorsement is designated as an optional modification, it is almost universally included in the CGL policies.

Coverage B: Personal and Advertising Injury Liability Personal injury and advertising injury liability were originally available as optional coverages under the CGL form. They are now included as standard components of the coverage. *Personal injury* is defined to include:

1. False arrest, detention, or imprisonment

2. Malicious prosecution

3. Wrongful entry into or eviction of a person from a room, dwelling, or premise that the person occupies

4. Oral or written publication of material that slanders or libels a person or organization or disparages a person's or organization's goods, products, or services

5. Oral or written publication of material that violates a person's right of privacy

Advertising injury means injury arising out of oral or written publication of materials that slanders or libels a person or an organization, that disparages a person's or organization's goods, products, or services, or that violates a person's right of privacy. It also includes misappropriation of advertising ideas or style of doing business or infringement of copyright, title, or slogan. The trigger of coverage for personal and advertising injury liability is on an occurrence basis in the occurrence form and on a claims-made basis in the claims-made form.

There are relatively few exclusions. Liability assumed under contract is excluded, as is personal or advertising injury arising out of the willful violation of a penal statute. Libel, slander, or defamation committed by the insured before the inception of the policy or done by or at the direction of the insured with knowledge that the statements were false is also excluded. As in the case of the Bodily Injury coverage, Personal Injury coverage may be endorsed to exclude personal injury arising out of employment practices.

As in the case of the bodily injury and property damage coverage, the Personal and Advertising Injury Liability coverage was modified in 2000 to address new exposures related to the Internet. Exclusions under the Personal and Advertising Injury Liability, previously applicable only to those in the publishing business, were extended to "Insureds in Media and Internet Type Businesses" (i.e., firms that design or determine content of Web sites for others and Internet search, access, content, or service providers). New exclusions have also been added for liability arising out of chat-rooms of bulletin boards that the insured owns or controls.

A newly added exclusion eliminates coverage for claims arising out of the infringement of copyright, patent, trademark, trade secret, or other intellectual property rights except infringement of copyright, trade dress, or slogan in the named insured's advertisement. Also excluded is liability for the unauthorized use of another's name or product in the insured's domain name, e-mail address, domain name, or metatag (i.e., a part of the Internet computer code that tells a browser about the subjects found on the Web-site page) or any other similar tactics to mislead another's potential customers.

The coverage territory has been broadened to cover personal and advertising injury offenses that take place through the Internet or similar electronic means of communication. However, the previous requirement that suit be brought in the United States, its territories or possessions, Puerto Rico, or Canada continue to apply.

Coverage C: Medical Payments Coverage The medical payments coverage is similar in nature and intent to the medical payments coverage examined in the Homeowners forms. It pays reasonable medical expenses incurred within three years of an accident to persons injured on the premises, regardless of liability. The medical payments coverage excludes injury to all insureds (instead of just the named insured). In addition, for tenants in residence, coverage applies only with respect to nonoccupied areas.

Other Coverages Several coverages that were previously available only by endorsement are now incorporated into the basic policy by virtue of the absence of exclusions. Two of these are fire legal liability and contractual liability insurance.

Fire Legal Liability One of the special problems created by the *care, custody, and control* exclusion is the lack of coverage for damage to property rented or leased to the insured. If a tenant (or an employee of the tenant) negligently sets fire to a leased or rented structure, the owner (or the owner's insurer) may seek to recover the amount of the loss from the

tenant. Fire legal liability coverage is covered by virtue of an exception to the care, custody, and control exclusion. The coverage applies only to real property and is subject to a separate limit of liability stated in the declarations. Exclusions c. through o. do not apply to damage by a fire to premises rented to the insured.[12]

Contractual Liability Coverage Under earlier versions of the general liability forms, a separate contractual liability coverage part was used to provide protection for liability arising out of contractual assumptions. The exceptions to the contractual exclusion we noted earlier automatically provide coverage for contractual liability without a separate form or insuring agreement. The coverage for liability assumed under contract is subject to the other exclusions of the form. This means, for example, that contractual assumptions of liability involving motor vehicles are excluded and must be covered elsewhere. (The Business Auto Coverage Form includes coverage for contractual liability related to motor vehicles.)

In the early 1990s, a controversy arose regarding coverage for contractually assumed defense costs, such as those that arise when an insured agrees to "defend and indemnify…" the other party in a contract. The disagreement was whether such costs are subject to the policy limit or, like defense costs payable on behalf of the insured, are payable in addition to the policy limit. Responding to the ambiguity that triggered the dispute, ISO modified the CGL provisions relating to contractual liability.

The 1996 edition of the CGL incorporates two alternative extensions of coverage to indemnitees who have been promised a defense in an insured contract. The first provides that contractually assumed defense costs—attorney fees and litigation expenses—are considered "damages" when they are part of an "insured contract" and are incurred in legal proceedings against the insured's indemnitee

for bodily injury or property damage covered by the policy. By considering such defense costs as damages, the coverage provided under this alternative is subject to the policy's limits.

Under the Supplemental Payments provision, the insurer agrees to provide the insured's indemnitee with a defense under specified and limited circumstances. Defense costs under this provision are not subject to the policy's limit of insurance. An indemnitee's defense costs are payable under Supplemental Payments only when a specific assumption of the *indemnitee's* defense or defense costs has been contractually agreed to by the insured in an insured contract. Further, the obligation to defend the indemnitee applies only when the insured and the indemnitee are both being sued in the same action.

There must be no apparent conflict of interest between the insured and the indemnitee, and the insured and the indemnitee must request the defense and agree to the assignment of the same counsel to defend both parties. The indemnitee must further agree to cooperate with the insurer in defending the suit. Finally, the indemnitee must agree to notify any other insurer whose coverage is available to the indemnitee and to cooperate in "coordinating" such other coverage.

Policy Limits The application of the policy limits differs from previous forms in several ways. A combined single limit applies to bodily injury and property damage on a *per-occurrence* basis. In addition, an aggregate limit applies to the products or completed operations hazard, with a separate aggregate limit applicable to all other coverages combined. Finally, separate sublimits apply on a *per-person* basis to personal and advertising injury liability, *per person* to medical payments, and *per fire* to fire damage legal liability.

Occurrence Form Compared with Claims-Made Version The major difference between the occurrence and claims-made versions of the CGL is, of course, the difference in the trigger of coverage, but this difference dictates other differences as well. The claims-made trigger is the date when a claim is "reported and recorded" by the insured or the company, for injury or damage that occurred after the policy's *retroactive date.*

A *retroactive date* in a claims-made liability policy is a coverage restriction. It limits coverage to claims arising out of events that occur after the specified retroac-

[12] Fire legal liability coverage may also be purchased separately under the commercial property coverage portion of the portfolio program. The separate coverage may be purchased by attaching a legal liability form to a portfolio property insurance policy. The coverage may be limited to real property, or it may include personal property as well. Although the standard liability form applies to fire only, the fire policy version may be written to include additional perils such as internal explosion and, in some areas, extended coverage.

tive date.[13] Initially, the retroactive date will be the date on which a claims-made form first replaces an occurrence form. Thus, if an occurrence policy is replaced by a claims-made policy on June 1, 2001, the retroactive date of the claims-made form will be June 1, 2001. This is a natural approach to eliminating duplication of coverage between a claims-made form and an occurrence form. The retroactive date eliminates coverage for claims arising out of occurrences before inception, since such losses will presumably be covered under the expired occurrence policy that was replaced. Ideally, renewals of claims-made policies should have the same retroactive date as the policy being renewed, which would be the same as the first claims-made policy (and the expiration of the last occurrence policy).

If all claims-made policies subsequent to the first are issued with the same retroactive date as the initial claims-made policy, coverage will be provided on an uninterrupted basis from the last occurrence form up to the latest claims-made form. Losses that occurred prior to the retroactive date (that is, before inception of the first claims-made form) will be covered under the occurrence forms that preceded the change to a claims-made basis. Coverage for losses that occurred after the retroactive date will be provided by the claims-made form in effect at the time the claim is made.

As long as the retroactive date in claims-made forms remains the same as the date the last occurrence policy expired, there is no gap in coverage. If the retroactive date in any renewal of a claims-made policy is advanced, however, a gap in coverage is created.[14] The expired claims-made policy will not cover claims that are filed after its expiration, and the new claims-made policy will not cover claims arising out of occurrences prior to its retroactive date (inception). Thus, a claim made during the renewal policy arising out of an occurrence during the expired policy would not be covered.

The traditional solution to this gap in claims-made policies has been for the insured to purchase an extended reporting date endorsement (commonly called *tail* coverage) for the expiring policy. An *extended reporting period* provision stipulates that any claim reported within the designated extended reporting period will be deemed to have been reported during the policy and will be covered.

Extended Reporting Period Provisions The revised version of the claims-made form includes three extended reporting provisions. Two are built into the basic policy, and together are called *Basic Extended Reporting Period Coverage.* The third provision is provided by endorsement for an additional premium, and is referred to as the *Supplemental Extended Reporting Period Coverage.*

The *basic extended reporting period* begins when the policy period ends and is activated when there is an interruption in claims-made coverage—that is, when the policy is canceled or nonrenewed, renewed with an advanced retroactive date, or replaced with an occurrence policy. The basic extended reporting period has two elements. First, claims arising out of occurrences after the retroactive date but before the policy expiration are covered if reported during the 60-day period following expiration. In addition, the policy covers claims reported within five years of the expiration of the policy, which arise out of occurrences reported to the insured or the insurer during the policy period or within 60 days following expiration.[15]

Claims covered under the basic extended reporting period provisions are subject to the policy limits, and the limits are not increased or reinstated with respect to claims under these provisions. In addition, the coverage applies only in the absence of future insurance that applies to the claims or that would apply except for the exhaustion of limits.

The insured may elect, within 60 days of the expiration of the policy, to purchase a *Supplemental Extended Reporting Period Endorsement* for an additional premium. The endorsement extends the reporting period indefinitely. Unlike the provisions

[13] Although it is possible to write a claims-made form without a retroactive date, most claims-made policies will be written with a retroactive date. The insurer may eliminate the retroactive date feature of the coverage by entering "none" in the policy declarations entry entitled *retroactive date.*

[14] The claims-made form allows the insurer to advance the retroactive date in a renewal under specified conditions: (1) when there is a substantial change in the insured's operations that increases the hazard; (2) when the insured fails to provide the insurer with information known or that should have been known to the insured about the nature of the risk; (3) with the agreement of the insured; and (4) when there is a change in insurer.

[15] The five-year extended reporting period seems peculiar without an explanation of its rationale. In the first version of the claims-made form, an actual claim for damages had to be received during the policy period to trigger coverage. Insurance buyers argued that an insurer, learning of an occurrence that had not yet generated an actual claim, might advance the retroactive date or decline to renew, forcing the insured to purchase the optional extended reporting period coverage for an additional premium. Responding to the criticism, ISO added the five-year tail for claims arising out of occurrences reported during the policy period or within 60 days of the end of the policy.

of the basic extended reporting period, the coverage of the Supplemental Extended Reporting Period Endorsement applies even if the loss is covered by other insurance. Also, when the Supplemental Extended Reporting Period Endorsement is purchased, the original policy limits are reinstated.[16]

Other Portfolio Liability Coverages

In addition to the two CGL forms, there are a number of other specialized forms of liability coverage under the new program. Although products and completed operations, coverage is included in the CGL, instances arise in which the coverage must be written separately, and separate occurrence and claims-made forms of the coverage are available. *Owners and Contractors Protective Liability Coverage* is also available under a separate coverage part to insure liability arising out of independent contractors.[17] *Railroad Protective Liability Coverage* is a special form of contractual liability required for those who perform construction or demolition work on or near railroad property.

Miscellaneous General Liability Coverages

In addition to the CGL and those liability coverages that have been noted, there are a number of specialized liability coverages designed to meet specific exposures. Some of the more interesting of these are discussed in the paragraphs that follow.

Liquor Liability Coverage Another exclusion of the CGL creating a need for a specialized coverage is that of liability arising out of the business of manufacture, sale, or serving of alcoholic beverages. Many states have special statutes, called *dram shop* laws, that provide a right of action against the seller in the event that the purchaser injures a third party. The laws vary greatly in their detail. Some apply only when the injury results from sale to a minor or intoxicated person, whereas others have no such qualification. Some laws provide for liability only to those

injured by the intoxicated person, whereas others permit liability for loss of support by dependents of the intoxicated party or even injuries sustained by the intoxicated person. Even in those states where such laws do not exist, similar liability may be imposed under common law.[18] When the expanded liquor liability exclusion endorsement is attached to the policy, coverage is excluded not only for insureds in the liquor business, but for anyone who serves alcoholic beverages for a charge, whether or not the activity is for the purpose of financial gain. This would include a variety of fund-raising and social activities sponsored by nonprofit organizations. These activities may be covered by endorsement to the CGL, or they may be covered under a *Dram Shop or Liquor Liability Policy* in the same manner as firms in the business of manufacturing, selling, or distributing alcoholic beverages. Occurrence and claims-made liquor liability coverage forms were introduced as a part of the portfolio general liability program. Both cover liability arising out of the selling, serving, or furnishing of alcoholic beverages but differ in the coverage trigger. Coverage provisions of the claims-made version generally parallel those of the claims-made CGL already discussed.

Pollution Liability Insurance Coverage As we noted in our discussion of the CGL, the latest version of the CGL excludes all liability arising out of pollution. An endorsement is available under which an insurer can add pollution coverage to the CGL, but most insurers have been unwilling to extend the policy.

In addition to the pollution liability endorsement, ISO introduced two simplified pollution liability forms as a part of the portfolio revision. The two new pollution liability forms are designated Pollution Liability Coverage Form—Designated Sites and Pollution Liability Limited Coverage Form—Designated Sites. The principal difference between the two forms is that the limited form does not provide coverage for "mandated off-site cleanup costs," whereas coverage for such costs is specifically insured in the standard form.

[16] The premium for the extended reporting period is limited to 200 percent of the final annual premium of the terminated policy. Factors considered in determining the premium for the endorsement include the exposures insured, the previous types and amounts of insurance, the limits purchased, and "other related factors."

[17] Liability arising out of independent contractors is covered under the CGL, but the exposure is sometimes insured under a separate contract to isolate the cost of the insurance and shift it to the independent contractor.

[18] Dram shop liability laws exist in Alabama, Alaska, California, Colorado, Florida, Georgia, Illinois, Iowa, Maine, Michigan, Minesota, New Mexico, New York, North Carolina, North Dakota, Ohio, Oregon, Pennsylvania, Rhode Island, Utah, Vermont, and Wyoming. Liability has been imposed on sellers of alcoholic beverages under common law in Arizona, Colorado, Hawaii, Idaho, Indiana, Kentucky, Louisiana, Massachusetts, Mississippi, Missouri, New Jersey, New Mexico, North Carolina, South Dakota, Washington, Wisconsin, and Wyoming.

Federal law requires owners and operators of certain hazardous properties, such as landfills, land treatment facilities, and similar surface impoundments, to carry environmental liability coverage for nonsudden occurrences of at least $3 million per occurrence and $6 million aggregate. These limits are in addition to a requirement of $1 million per occurrence and $2 million annual aggregate limits of coverage for sudden and accidental occurrence. The coverage is available only from a limited number of insurers.[19]

Underground Storage Tank Liability Policy In response to the Environmental Protection Agency's finalizing regulations on financial responsibility for pollution, the ISO developed an Underground Storage Tank Liability Policy (CG 00 42). Coverage is provided for loss arising out of an underground storage tank incident, greater than the deductible, for damages and corrective action costs, subject to the amount of the actual damages/corrective action costs or the UST incident limit, whichever is least.

Pension Fiduciary Liability The Employee Retirement Income Security Act of 1974 (ERISA) imposed new responsibilities on employers and fiduciaries supervising pension plans and group life and health insurance programs, holding them liable to beneficiaries for violation of the prudent man rule in the supervision of such a plan. Pension fiduciary liability insurance protects against this exposure. The coverage is sometimes written to include employee benefit errors and omissions coverage, which protects against liability arising from errors in advising employees and from other types of mistakes related to a fringe benefit program.

Directors and Officers Errors and Omissions Insurance A special form of coverage known as Directors and Officers Errors and Omissions insurance is available to protect corporate officers and directors from suits alleging mismanagement. Such suits may be brought by stockholders or by persons outside the firm. The coverage is subject to a deductible and the insured is usually required to bear 5 percent of any loss in excess of the deductible. The coverage excludes losses based on alleged personal

gain by the insured and losses resulting from failure to purchase proper insurance coverage.

Variations of this coverage are available to protect elected and appointed public officials. These include the Board of Education Liability Policy and the Public Official Liability Policy. Like the officers and directors coverage, above, there is no standard form for these coverages, and they are usually sold by specialty insurers.

Employment Practices Liability Coverage The 1990s witnessed an exponential rise in the incidence of claims alleging wrongful employment practices. Suits alleging discrimination in the workplace, wrongful termination, and sexual harassment have grown at an exponential rate for a variety of reasons. One reason has been the growth in federal legislation that specifically outlaws various types of discrimination in the workplace.[20] Although risk-management principles suggest that this exposure should be addressed by loss prevention and control, not all claims can be prevented. The increase in the number of successful suits alleging employment related practices therefore led to a demand for a new form of insurance to cover the exposure.[21]

A limited number of insurers offer employment practices liability policies, which cover discrimination, sexual harassment and wrongful termination. Fines and criminal penalties are universally excluded.[22] Some insurers include coverage for punitive damages and some do not. In most cases, defense costs are included in the policy limit, rather than "outside"

[19] ISO introduced a pollution liability policy in 1982. In 1984, a Pollution Liability Insurance Association (PLIA) was formed for the purpose of handling the pollution liability insurance written by its 49 member companies. The PLIA was dissolved in 1989 after the number of participating members had fallen to 14.

[20] Title VII of the Civil Rights Law of 1964, the Equal Pay Act, the Age Discrimination in Employment Act of 1967, the Rehabilitation Act of 1973, the Pregnancy Discrimination Act of 1978, the Americans with Disabilities Act of 1990, the Older Workers Benefit Protection Act of 1990, the Civil Rights Act of 1991, and the Family and Medical Leave Act of 1993.

[21] Although it was sometimes possible to find coverage for employment-related practices liability under other forms of liability insurance in the past, the vestiges of coverage were generally unintended and have been removed. General liability insurers, workers compensation insurers, and umbrella liability insurers have all added the Employment-Related Practices Liability Exclusion endorsement to their policies.

[22] Initially, there was a serious debate over whether insurance for employment-related practices—which are illegal—violates public policy. The Civil Rights Act of 1964 recognizes two distinct types of discrimination: that of *disparate treatment* and that of *disparate impact*. The former is where you treat people differently and it is an intentional act. The latter is where treatment is actually the same, but results in *de facto* discrimination. This may not be an intentional act. In addition, coverage is deemed permissible for the vicarious liability of an employer even when the act committed by an employee is criminal.

the policy limit as in the case of the CGL and most other liability contracts. Coverage is written on a claims-made basis with a retroactive date and a limited discovery period. Extended reporting coverage is available for an additional premium if coverage is canceled or nonrenewed by the insurer. Deductibles range upward from a low of $1000 to $25,000. In addition to the deductible, policies also include a coinsurance provision, which functions as a copayment provision. The insured must usually share a percentage of defense and settlement costs, normally ranging from 5 percent to 25 percent, with most being either 5 percent or 10 percent.

In 1997, ISO filed a new standardized Employment Related Practices Liability (ERPL) Form with state regulatory authorities. This means that an increasing number of insurers will likely offer this coverage in the future. Like the existing contracts on the market, the ISO form is written on a claims-made basis, with defense costs included in the policy limit. The ISO ERPL Form is designed to be written as a stand-alone policy or as part of a commercial package policy. The basic limit under the ISO form is $100,000 with the option to increase the limit to $10 million. Presumably, the ISO form will provide a means by which smaller insurers can enter the employment practices liability insurance market.

COMMERCIAL AUTOMOBILE INSURANCE

In those cases in which a business is organized as a proprietorship, a *business* automobile may be insured under a Personal Auto Policy. However, if the firm is a partnership or corporation, or if the automobile itself is not eligible for a personal auto form, coverage must be provided under a commercial auto form. There are four commercial automobile forms designed to cover different types of commercial automobile exposures. The four forms are the Business Auto Coverage Form, the Garage Coverage Form, the Truckers Coverage Form, and the Motor Carriers Coverage Form. These forms may be used to create a monoline auto policy, or they may be included with other coverage forms in a package policy. Some general observations on each are in order.

Business Auto Coverage Form

The standard form for insuring commercial automobiles is the Business Auto Coverage Form (BAC).

This form may be used to provide liability coverage, medical payments, physical damage coverage, and uninsured motorist coverage. It can also be endorsed to provide no-fault benefits in states where such coverage is required.

Liability Coverage The BAC liability insuring agreement is similar in most respects to the liability insuring agreements that have been examined thus far. It begins with the traditional wording in which the insurer states:

> We will pay all sums an "insured" legally must pay as damages because of "bodily injury" of "property damage" to which this insurance applies, caused by an "accident" and resulting from the ownership, maintenance or use of a covered "auto."

The form then goes on to add a unique insuring agreement, under which the insurer agrees to pay for certain pollution costs:

> We will also pay all sums an "insured" legally must pay as a "covered pollution cost or expense" to which this insurance applies, caused by an "accident" and resulting from the ownership, maintenance or use of covered "autos." However, we will only pay for the "covered pollution cost or expense" if there is either "bodily injury" or "property damage" to which this insurance applies that is caused by the same "accident."

Covered pollution cost or expense is defined in the policy to mean the cost or expense arising out of any request, demand, order, or claim or suit by or on behalf of the government demanding that the insured clean up the pollutants. The coverage for covered pollution cost or expense means that under the defined conditions (i.e., when there is a covered bodily injury or property damage loss), the BAC will cover not only damage caused by pollutants, but the cost of cleaning up such pollutants when such cleanup is mandated by government order.

Covered Auto In describing those autos that are covered for each of the coverages the insured selects, the BAC uses the term "Covered Auto." A series of numerical designations, each representing a class of autos, is entered in the declarations opposite the various coverages, indicating the types of autos covered under the policy. There are nine numerical symbols that designate the autos for which the policy provides coverage:

1 = Any Auto

2 = Owned Autos Only

3 = Owned Private Passenger Autos Only

4 = Owned Autos Other than Private Passenger Autos Only

5 = Owned Autos Subject to No-Fault

6 = Owned Autos Subject to Compulsory Uninsured Motorists Law

7 = Specifically Described Autos

8 = Hired Autos Only

9 = Non-owned Autos Only

Historically, auto liability insurance for commercial insureds has recognized three classes of autos: owned autos, hired autos, and non-owned autos. The classes hired autos and non-owned autos are mutually exclusive. *Hired autos* include those that are leased, hired, rented, or borrowed, excluding autos that are owned by employees. Autos leased, hired, rented, or borrowed from employees are considered *non-owned autos*. Thus, the distinction between a *hired* and *non-owned automobile* does not depend on whether payment is made for the use of the auto, but rather on whether it is owned by an employee. This somewhat artificial distinction exists primarily for the purpose of rating and premium determination.

The preferred approach is symbol 1, Any Auto (also referred to as comprehensive auto liability coverage). When comprehensive auto liability coverage is written, coverage is provided for liability arising out of the ownership, maintenance, or use of all owned, non-owned, and hired autos, including replacements and additionally acquired autos. All owned and hired autos are scheduled at the inception of the policy, and additional exposures are automatically covered. After the policy, an audit of the exposure that developed is made and any additional premium due to the company is charged.

In some situations, the insurer is unwilling to provide coverage on a comprehensive basis, in which case the insured must accept coverage on specifically described autos (symbol 7). When Specifically Described Auto coverage is selected, newly acquired autos are covered only if the company insures all autos owned by the insured or if the newly acquired auto replaces a described auto. Notice to the company is required within 30 days. Also, when owned autos are insured on a specifically described basis, hired autos and non-owned autos should be covered by entering symbols 8 and 9 in the declarations of the policy.

Persons Insured The BAC includes coverage for the named insured, permissive users, and persons or organizations vicariously liable for acts or omissions of the named insured or permissive users. As in the case of the Personal Auto Policy, coverage for those held vicariously liable does not apply to the owner of a nonowned vehicle.

Exclusions Twelve exclusions apply to the liability coverage of the Business Auto Coverage Form: (1) expected or intended injury, (2) contractual, (3) workers compensation, (4) employers liability, (5) fellow employee, (6) care, custody, and control, (7) handling of property, (8) movement of property by mechanical device, (9) operation of mobile equipment, (10) completed operations, (11) pollution, and (12) war. Most of the exclusions are similar to their counterparts in the CGL. Several, however, deserve special comment.

The handling of property, movement of property by mechanical device, and operation of mobile equipment exclusions eliminate duplication with the CGL, which is designed to cover these exposures.

The pollution exclusion contains an exception that adds back coverage for pollution resulting from the discharge or leakage of fuels, lubricants, exhaust gases, or similar pollutants from the vehicle itself. The principal thrust of the remainder of the pollution exclusion is to exclude only pollution arising out of property being transported (i.e., cargo). This means that neither liability for bodily injury and property damage, nor *covered pollution cost or expense* is provided with respect to pollutants that are being transported by the insured. Coverage for this exposure may be added by endorsement.

Physical Damage Coverage Physical Damage coverage for owned and non-owned automobiles is available under the BAC, which provides essentially the same forms of protection that are available for personal autos. The insured may select from among three options with respect to the perils insured against, and different classes of vehicles may be insured for different perils. The available coverages include Comprehensive coverage, Specified Perils coverage, and Collision coverage. Numerals corresponding to the class of autos for which each coverage is desired are entered in the appropriate sections of the policy declarations.

The comprehensive and collision insuring agreements and exclusions parallel those of the Personal Auto Policy. The Specified Perils coverage is an

alternative to the Comprehensive coverage and provides protection against the perils of fire or explosion, theft, windstorm, hail, earthquake, flood, vandalism and malicious mischief, and the perils of transportation (sinking, burning, collision, or derailment of any conveyance transporting the covered auto).

Medical Payments and Uninsured Motorists Coverage The BAC may be written to include medical payments and uninsured motorists coverage. Because employees who are injured while operating an insured auto will normally be covered by workers compensation, these coverages are not as widely sold in commercial policies as in personal policies.

Coverage Territory The coverage territory of the BAC is the United States, its territories and possessions, Puerto Rico, and Canada. The 2001 edition of the policy makes coverage worldwide for private passenger autos that are leased, hired, or borrowed without a driver for 30 days or less. For the worldwide coverage to apply, the insured's liability must be determined in a suit in the normal coverage territory or in a settlement to which the insured agrees.

Business Auto Coverage Form Endorsements There are a wide range of endorsements available to modify the BAC. Several of these endorsements are particularly noteworthy.

Commercial Auto Drive Other Car Coverage Endorsements Instances occasionally arise in which an individual does not own a personal auto, and in which the only coverage available to a person is that of the BAC form. In such cases, a potential gap in protection exists in the case of non-owned autos that may be used by such individuals outside of their business pursuits. The BAC may be endorsed to provide coverage for the use of nonowned vehicles by the named insured or family members using the *Individual Named Insured* endorsement (CA 99 17) or *the Drive Other Car Coverage—Broadened Coverage for Named Individuals* endorsement (CA 99 10).

Under the *Individual Named Insured* endorsement, coverage is extended for the use of non-owned automobiles by the named insured and resident relatives. It is used when the named insured under policy is an individual. When the named insured is not an individual, drive-other-car coverage may be added for specifically named persons, using the *Drive Other Car Coverage—Broadened Coverage for Named Individuals* endorsement (CA 99 10).

Limited Mexico Coverage CA 01 21 This optional endorsement, introduced in 1998, extends the coverage territory to include Mexico on a limited basis. It was introduced as a result of the implementation of the North American Free Trade Agreement (NAFTA) on January 1, 1994, and the resulting increase in business travel and commerce with Mexico by Americans. Coverage under the endorsement applies to accidents that occur within 25 miles of the U.S. border during trips into Mexico that do not exceed 10 days. Coverage applies only to autos that are principally garaged and used in the United States and to insureds that are U.S. residents. Coverage applies on an excess basis and requires that physical damage losses be paid in the United States, unless the repairs are required to drive the auto.

Employee Hired Autos CA 20 54 The Employee Hired Autos (CA 20 54) endorsement provides liability coverage for an employee who rents a vehicle without a driver, in his or her own name for use in the employer's business. In addition to liability coverage, it also provides protection for physical damage to that vehicle.

Fellow Employee Endorsements The *Fellow Employee Coverage* endorsement (CA 20 55) deletes the fellow employee exclusion (No. 5 in the liability exclusions section) in its entirety. A somewhat different endorsement *Fellow Employee Coverage for Designated Employees/Positions* (CA 20 56) deletes the exclusion of injury to fellow employees with respect to specifically designated fellow employees or classes of fellow employees. It is used as an alternative to the *Fellow Employee Coverage* endorsement when coverage is not desired for all fellow employees, but only for some employees, such as executive officers.

Garage Coverage Form

The Garage Coverage Form is designed to provide comprehensive liability coverage for businesses commonly known as garages, and other automotive firms such as automobile sales agencies, repair shops, service stations, storage garages, and public parking places. Like the BAC, the Garage Coverage Form is a self-contained document that provides both liability and physical damage coverages.

The basic premium for the policy includes coverage for legal liability arising out of three classes of hazards: premises and operations, products and completed operations, and automobile liability. In addition, the

contract may be used to provide physical damage coverage on owned and hired automobiles, including the stocks of automobiles held for sale by automobile dealers.

The premises and operations as well as the products and complete operations coverage of the Garage Coverage Form are essentially the same as the separate coverage parts providing these forms of protections and with the same exclusions. The care, custody, and control exclusion causes an inordinate number of problems in this class of business, because it excludes damage to automobiles of customers that are in the care of the insured.

Garagekeeper's Coverage Since most garages take custody of customers' cars, there is a need for a special form of bailee liability insurance. The Garage Coverage Form includes a coverage known as *Garagekeeper's Coverage* which provides coverage on customers autos while in the care of the garage. The coverage is made effective by payment of the required premium.

Perils Insured Coverage may be written to provide coverage on several bases. First, the insured can choose from among Collision, Comprehensive, or Specified Perils coverage (Specified Perils includes fire, explosion, theft and vandalism, and malicious mischief). Loss to the customer's automobile must fall within the definition of the coverage or coverages selected.

Basis of Coverage Besides selecting the perils to be covered, the insured may also select the basis on which the coverage will apply. Three options are offered: legal liability basis, direct coverage—primary basis, and direct coverage—excess basis. Under the first of these three options, coverage applies only if the garage is legally liable for damage. Under the second option, the Garagekeeper's coverage becomes primary with respect to the customer's automobile and regardless to the liability of the garage. Under the third option, the Garagekeeper's coverage responds regardless of liability, but only if the customer has no physical damage coverage.

Truckers Coverage Form

The Truckers Coverage Form is a modified version of the Business Auto Coverage Form (BAC), designed to meet the special needs of truckers. ISO rules define a *trucker* as "a person, firm or corporation in the business of transporting goods, materials, or commodities for another."

The form adapts the provisions of the BAC to deal with the special practices of the trucking industry and the insurance requirements imposed by those practices. Because entry into the trucking business is controlled, those firms that hold licenses or certificates authorizing them to operate in a particular area often permit unlicensed independent *owner–operators* (who own a tractor or trailer, but who do not have a license), to use the licensed carrier's permit by leasing the independent operator's equipment. Since both state and federal regulatory authorities require the licensed trucker to provide insurance for all vehicles being used under their permits, the insurance coverage of the licensed trucker must be written to cover the equipment of the owner–operators that the licensed carriers lease. This means that unlike most forms of auto liability insurance, the Truckers Form provides coverage on hired autos, not only for the named insured, but for the owner of the hired vehicle as well. The definition of persons insured extends coverage to owner–operators who lease their vehicles to a certified carrier under the following provision:

> The owner or anyone else from whom the named insured hires or borrows a [covered auto] is an insured ... while the [covered auto] is being used exclusively in the named insured's business as a trucker (i.e., motor carrier for hire) and while it is being used pursuant to operating rights granted to the named insured by a public authority.

This means that the owner–operator is covered by the liability coverage of the lessee's policy to the same extent as the lessee that has been granted the operating certificate to serve a particular route.

Coverage for Owner–Operators An owner–operator who leases vehicles to a licensed trucking firm is covered under the lessee's policy while the equipment is being operated over routes the licensee is authorized to serve. However, owner–operators must generally obtain insurance to cover liability when they are not operating under the certificate of a licensed carrier. Nontrucking use of a tractor without a trailer is called *bobtailing*. Operating a tractor with an empty trailer is known as *deadheading*. Coverage for bobtailing and deadheading is provided for owner–operators under a special endorsement to the BAC, *Truckers Insurance for Non-trucking Use*. As its title indicates, this form provides coverage only

when the vehicle is not being used to carry goods.

Trailer Interchange Coverage The loan of trailers between truckers is usually accomplished under a *trailer interchange agreement* that requires the borrower to assume responsibility for damage to the trailer. The Truckers Coverage Form includes a special type of contractual liability coverage, Trailer Interchange coverage, which provides protection for losses involving damage to leased or rented trailers for which liability is assumed under contract.

The Motor Carrier Coverage Form

The Motor Carrier Coverage Form was introduced in response to the changing regulatory environment in the trucking industry. Changes in the federal regulatory oversight of the trucking industry began with the Motor Carrier Act of 1980, which reduced the authority of the Interstate Commerce Commission over some of the truckers it regulated. Deregulation continued with the Trucking Industry Regulatory Reform Act of 1994 (TIRRA) and the ICC Termination Act of 1995 (ICCTA). TIRRA eliminated the requirement that motor carriers file their rates with the Interstate Commerce Commission (ICC), and ICCTA eliminated the ICC.[23]

Traditionally, truckers (or, as they were designated in regulatory jargon, motor truck carriers) fell into one of three categories: common carriers, contract carriers, and private carriers. Common carriers held themselves out to the public to provide carriage for hire and were usually authorized to do so only after demonstrating a need for their services in a particular area or over a particular route. Contract carriers provided motor carriage for compensation under continuing agreement with one or more persons either by assigning vehicles for their exclusive use or by otherwise serving their distinct needs. Private carriers carried their own goods on their own trucks. In addition to these three classes, exempt carriers were truckers that were exempt from regulation while

engaged in interstate hauling because of the type of commodities they carried (e.g., ordinary livestock, agricultural commodities, poultry feed).

With federal deregulation of interstate trucking, the differences between common carriers and contract carriers have been less pronounced. In fact, the ICCTA makes no distinction between common and contract motor carriers. Rather, it defines motor carrier as "a person providing motor vehicle transportation for compensation." With the erosion of the distinction between common carriers and contract carriers, the stricter regulation of common carriers has eased. Applicants for new or expanded common carrier operating authority to transport property (other than household goods) are no longer required to demonstrate "public convenience and necessity," a standard that was originally conceived as a measure to prevent excessive capacity in the industry. Applicants for authority as a motor carrier are now required to demonstrate only that they have the ability to comply with all statutory and regulatory safety requirements and that they can meet the statutory financial responsibility requirements, usually in the form of adequate liability insurance or by meeting statutory self-insurance requirements.

With the deregulation of the trucking industry, truckers may now enter into hauling operations that would not have been possible prior to deregulation. For example, current regulations allow the mixing of exempt and regulated commodities as long as the motor carrier has authority to haul the regulated commodities.

The Motor Carrier Coverage Form was developed to respond to the needs of both regulated and unregulated motor carriers. The Truckers Coverage Form is structured as if all motor carrier operations were subject to exactly the same regulations and all operations were conducted in accordance with operating rights granted by a public authority. It automatically presumes that in all but specifically excepted cases, the liability insurance of the motor carrier under whose authority the transportation is being conducted will be primary for the benefit of owners of leased commercial vehicles, for example, owner–operator units. The Motor Carrier Coverage Form, on the other hand, makes no reference to such regulations. It addresses the needs of both ICC-regulated motor carriers and private motor carriers.

Coverage of the Motor Carrier Coverage Form
Many of the coverage features of the Motor Carrier

[23] Regulation of interstate trucking was originally the responsibility of the Interstate Commerce Commission (ICC). The ICC Termination Act of 1995, Pub. L. No. 104-88, which was enacted in 1995 and took effect on January 1, 1996, abolished the ICC and transferred certain functions to the Surface Transportation Board (STB). The insurance-related functions previously performed by the ICC are now the responsibility of the STB. Section 101 of the ICC Termination Act provides that references to Interstate Commerce Commission in existing legislation are deemed to refer to Surface Transportation Board.

Coverage Form are exactly the same as those of the Truckers Coverage Form. Like the Truckers Form, the Motor Carriers Form includes coverage for trailer interchange exposures. In addition, the definition of "Who is Insured" provides a means for the liability insurance of the motor carrier to be primary for the benefit of owner–operators. Under the Motor Carriers Coverage Form, liability coverage is extended to

> The owner or anyone else from whom the named insured hires or borrows a [covered auto] is an insured while the [covered auto] is leased to the named insured under a written agreement (if the written agreement does not require the lessor to hold the named insured harmless) and then only when the leased unit is used in the named insured's business as a motor carrier for hire.

Unlike the similarly worded provision of the Truckers Coverage Form, the extension of liability coverage is not limited to situations in which the vehicle is being used "pursuant to operating rights granted to the named insured by a public authority." Coverage extends to the owner–operator regardless of the usage in the lessee's business as a motor carrier for hire.

Flexibility of the Motor Carrier Coverage Form
The Motor Carrier Coverage Form may be used in any circumstance in which the Truckers Coverage Form would otherwise be appropriate. It may also be used in circumstances where the Truckers Coverage Form could not be used, for example, private motor carriers. A motor carrier may transport only its own property and still be eligible for coverage under a Motor Carrier Coverage Form, but would not be eligible for coverage under a Truckers Coverage Form. Prior to the introduction of the Motor Carrier Form, such an entity would only be eligible for coverage under a BAC. Likewise, an entity that transported its own property and also transported property for others would have formerly purchased a BAC.

The introduction of the Motor Carrier Coverage Form may have a significant impact on the use of the Truckers Coverage Form. In fact, there is a distinct possibility that it will eventually replace it entirely. Any firm that previously purchased its auto coverage under the Truckers Coverage Form can obtain its coverage under the Motor Carrier Coverage Form. The Motor Carrier Form is more appropriate for the needs of exempt carriers or carriers that haul both

exempt and regulated commodities than the Truckers Form because not all of their operations are conducted pursuant to rights granted by a public authority.

However the type of carrier that will most benefit from having the motor carrier coverage form available is the private carrier who hauls for him or herself and also hauls for others either occasionally or on a regular basis. For these insureds, coverage is simplified under the Motor Carrier Coverage Form since it applies in the same manner regardless of whether a loss occurs while it is transporting for itself or for others.

AVIATION INSURANCE

The importance and rapid growth of the aviation industry make it desirable to include at least a brief discussion of aviation insurance. The most common coverages are aircraft liability insurance and hull coverage.

Aircraft Liability Insurance

Aircraft liability coverges are similar to those for automobile liability, with one major difference. The bodily injury liability is divided into two coverages: passenger liability and bodily injury excluding passengers. Some contracts cover bodily injury to passengers, bodily injury excluding passengers, and property damage liability with a single limit to cover all three exposures.

Admitted Liability Admitted Liability coverage, also known as *voluntary settlement coverage,* is issued only with passenger legal liability. It is written on a per-seat basis and provides a specified sum for loss of life, limb, or sight by a passenger. When payment is offered under Admitted Liability coverage, a release of liability against the insured is obtained from the passenger. If the injured party refuses to sign the release, the offer of payment is withdrawn and the injured party must bring suit against the insured, who is protected by the Passenger Bodily Injury coverage.

Medical Payments Medical Payments coverage is also available with aircraft liability insurance. The coverage is similar to that of the automobile policy, except that the injury must be sustained while in, entering, or alighting from the insured aircraft. Medical Payments coverage is available only when the

policy includes Passenger Bodily Injury liability.

Hull Coverage

There are two basic forms of hull insurance: one that provides open-perils coverage both on the ground and in flight, and another that provides open-perils coverage on the ground with limited coverage in flight. Under the more limited form, coverage in flight is limited to the perils of fire, lightning, and explosion, but excludes crash or collision.

LIABILITY INSURANCE FOR COMMON CARRIERS

One of the important implications of the distinction between common carriers and contract carriers is in their differing liability for the goods in their custody for transportation. Although the distinction between common carriers and contract carriers is being eroded in the regulatory framework at the federal level, it remains an important part of state law applicable to intrastate transportation of goods.

The Liability of a Common Carrier

The legal liability of a common carrier for damage to goods that it carries is quite strict, going far beyond liability resulting from negligence. The common carrier is responsible for all damages to the goods it carries, except when the damage is caused by one of a few specified causes:

1. Acts of God
2. Acts of a public enemy
3. Order of public authority
4. Neglect of the shipper
5. Inherent vice

Acts of God are, of course, such things as floods, tornadoes, earthquakes, and the like. Damage by *acts of a public enemy* reflects consequences of war. Damage caused by *order of public authority* might include many types of losses. For example, a government authority might order a dike cut to prevent flooding of a city downriver. Water from the cut dike might damage goods in the custody of a common carrier, but the carrier would be excused from liability. *Neglect of the shipper* is concerned primarily with

faulty packing of the goods by their shipper. *Inherent vice* is a quality in a good that causes it to destroy itself. For example, there will be a normal amount of spoilage of fresh fruit and vegetables shipped by the carrier, and the carrier is not held liable for such loss.

Even in the case of the five exceptions, a common carrier may not be absolved absolutely from liability. It is still required to take all precautions possible to prevent loss if disaster threatens. For example, a flood is an act of God, but if a railroad could have moved the freight cars from the path of a flood and failed to do so, its negligence becomes a contributing factor and it could be held liable for the resulting damage.

Limitations on Carrier Liability Because of this broad liability, common carriers frequently limit their liability by a *released bill of lading,* under whose terms the carrier specifies the maximum amount for which it will be held liable. For example, a common carrier may use a bill of lading with the stipulation that its liability will be limited to a specified dollar amount per pound or per shipment. Under the terms of the Interstate Commerce Act, a common carrier could limit its liability if it provided for a difference in rates, offering a lower rate to those who accepted the limitation in the bill of lading. Although interstate common carriers have limited their liability by contract for decades, with deregulation, their ability to do so has increased significantly. Prior to deregulation, the carriers had to seek permission from the ICC to reduce liability. They are now free to decide the extent to which they will be liable for the goods they transport. Increasingly, they have limited their liability under the terms of their contracts for carriage.[24]

Insurance Requirements

Historically, the ICC regulated two aspects of trucking operations related to insurance. The first was the requirement for bodily injury and property damage liability insurance previously discussed. The second related to cargo insurance on the goods being carried. Under the provisions of the Motor Truck Cargo Act of 1935, trucking firms operating in interstate

[24] Since deregulation, the carrier's responsibility for loss or damage has become a point of contention between shippers and carriers. Carriers have sought to limit their liability and the most often mentioned figure is $2.50 per pound without a declaration of higher value by the shipper. Shippers want the carriers to continue to provide full liability as required by the amended ICC act.

commerce have been required to purchase cargo liability insurance covering damage to property being shipped up to $5000 on the contents of any one vehicle and $10,000 for aggregate losses at any one time or place. Similar insurance requirements are imposed on intrastate truckers by state regulatory authorities. In actual practice, most trucking firms carry limits of coverage substantially higher than these prescribed amounts, the limit depending on the type and value of the merchandise being carried.

Motor Truck Cargo Policy—Trucker's Form

Truck cargo forms are designed to insure public truckers against losses resulting from damage to merchandise in their possession. The policy is used by both common carriers and contract carriers. The truckers form is a liability policy in the truest sense of the word: it pays only when the trucker is legally obligated to pay for the damages, and only to the extent of the trucker's liability.

Coverage is available on a named-peril basis and also under an open-perils form. The named-peril form protects against damage caused by fire; flood; windstorm; collision or overturn of vehicles; collapse of bridges; and the perils of the sea, lakes, rivers, or inland waters while on ferries. Coverage for loss by theft may be added; the insurer generally requires a sizable deductible. Usually, only theft of an entire shipping package is covered, thus excluding loss by pilferage. Coverage applies to the cargo while loaded for shipment or in transit, and if it is desired while the cargo is off vehicles in terminals or other locations, it must be endorsed onto the policy.

Interstate Commerce Commission Endorsement Motor truck cargo policies issued to comply with the insurance requirements of the STB must contain a special endorsement prescribed by the Board. (A similar endorsement is used in most states in the regulation of intrastate carriers.) The endorsement (which continues to be known as the *ICC endorsement*) makes the insurer responsible for any liability of the insured trucker for damage to property being carried, *regardless of cause,* up to the limits

of $5000 per truck and $10,000 per occurrence.[25] If a loss occurs because of a peril not covered under the basic policy, the insurer is required to make payment to the owner of the goods, but may then seek reimbursement from the trucker for the amount paid. Insurance companies seldom pay a loss under the ICC endorsement and then recover from the insured. In actual practice, the trucker usually reports losses to the insurer only when they are covered under the basic policy, paying the customer directly for other losses.

INSURANCE FOR BAILEES

A bailment consists of the delivery of property of one person, the *bailor,* to another, the *bailee,* for some specific purpose. The property may be in the care of the bailee to be worked on, as in the case of an automobile being repaired, or in storage, or for some other purpose. If property in the hands of a bailee is damaged or destroyed, the bailee may be liable to the owner.

Bailee Liability

In general, there are three types of bailment, and the degree of care that the bailee must exercise in protecting the property depends on the nature of the bailment. The first is gratuitous bailment for the benefit of the bailor. For example, you may ask your neighbor to take care of your cat while you are on vacation. In this situation, perhaps *slight care* is all that is necessary, since the bailment is gratuitous and for the benefit of the bailor. The second type of bailment is also gratuitous, but here it benefits the bailee. For example, if you borrow your neighbor's lawn mower, you must exercise *extraordinary care* to protect it from loss. The third type of bailment is bailment for mutual benefit. Here the bailment may be gratuitous, or in the case of most business firms, it involves bailment for hire. For example, if you store your auto in an overnight parking garage, the situation is a bailment for mutual benefit, but it is also bailment for hire. In general, bailees in mutual benefit bailments must use *reasonable care*—that is, the same degree of care they would exercise with respect to their own property. However, the degree of care that must be used is greater in bailment for hire than for gratuitous bailment.

[25] This is the limit of the company's liability under the ICC endorsement regardless of the limits of the policy to which it is attached.

A bailee may extend or limit its liability for the bailed property by contract or advertisement. The bailee may assume complete responsibility for damage to property of customers, regardless of negligence. A bailee may also, by contract, limit its liability. For example, the bailee may specify that its total liability for a single fur coat in storage will be $200. Normally, it is legal for the bailee to limit its liability. However, the courts frown on attempts of a bailee to relieve itself of liability completely. The decided trend of modern decisions is against the validity of exculpatory clauses or provisions of parking lots, garages, checkrooms, and warehouses, where business firms undertake to protect themselves against liability by posting signs or printing limitations on the receipts delivered to the bailor-owner at the time of bailment.

Bailee Liability Coverages

The need for specialized coverages to protect against liability as a bailee arises because of the care, custody, and control exclusion of the general liability policies. If it were not for this exclusion, the bailee's liability because of damage to customers' goods would be covered under the general liability policies. Bailed property has traditionally been insured under property insurance forms, most frequently under inland marine contracts.[26]

Bailee liability coverages sometimes depart from the other liability coverages we have noted in a very fundamental respect. Under some bailee forms, payment is made by the insurer regardless of the liability of the bailee, as long as the cause of the loss is a peril under the policy. This approach is the result of the demand of customers that their property be returned to them in good condition, regardless of the liability of the bailee. A merchant who refused to reimburse a customer for the loss of property because of not being liable under the specific set of circumstances might soon find him-or herself without customers. Although some bailee coverages provide for payment only when the insured is legally liable, these are the exceptions rather than the rule.

Bailee's Customer Policy The Bailee's Customer Policy is the basic policy for bailees' customer insurance. It is completed by the attachment of a special form designed for the particular class of business. Coverage may be provided under these forms for such businesses as laundries, dyers and dry cleaners, processors, and service-type firms. There are special forms for appliance repair stores, radio and television repair stores, and other similar establishments.

In general, the Bailee's Customer Policy covers all kinds of lawful goods and articles that are the property of customers in the custody of the insured. Coverage applies regardless of the bailee's liability. The normal perils insured against include fire, lightning, windstorm, riot, earthquake, sprinkler leakage, burglary, robbery, and confusion of goods caused by any of the perils insured against.[27] In addition, the usual perils of transportation are covered and coverage applies to the property while in transit or at the insured's premises. The normal exclusions are loss while the goods are in the custody of other processors, unless specifically endorsed onto the policy; loss due to shortage (unless caused by burglary or holdup); loss resulting from delay, misdelivery, or mysterious disappearance; and losses from infidelity, nuclear energy, and war.

Other Bailee Forms In addition to the Bailee's Customer Policy, there are more specialized bailee forms for certain business classes. There is a Furrier's Customer Policy, which covers customers' coats in storage; a Cold Storage Locker Bailee Floater, which covers customers' property in public freezers; and a special form for hotels and motels, the Innkeepers Liability Policy. In some instances, the coverage applies regardless of the bailee's liability. In others, it applies only when the insured is actually liable. In some cases, such as the garage keeper's coverage, the insured may elect coverage on either basis. Each of these forms has special provisions necessary to tailor the protection to the unique exposures of the business involved.

EXCESS LIABILITY AND UMBRELLA LIABILITY COVERAGE

The average size of liability claims has increased steadily over time and will undoubtedly continue in

[26] The bailor may, of course, insure his or her property under all conditions, including the period while it is in the custody of the bailee, but the general principle is that coverage purchased by the bailor shall not benefit the bailee. If the bailor collects from his or her insurance company, the insurer may then subrogate against the bailee.

[27] Confusion of goods refers to the inability to identify the ownership of the goods even though they are not destroyed, but the confusion must result from an insured peril.

this direction in the future. The occasional gigantic liability claims that appear in the newspapers are stark reminders of the catastrophic proportions the liability risk may assume.[28] To provide protection against the devastating losses that businesses may suffer in this area, excess liability policies and the blanket catastrophe excess liability policy (frequently called the *umbrella*) were developed.

Excess Liability Distinguished from Umbrella Liability Contracts

The term *umbrella liability policy* was originally intended to describe a blanket excess liability policy, which provides broadened excess coverage over a schedule of underlying contracts. Unfortunately, there is no official definition of an *umbrella,* and the term is also used loosely to describe not only contracts with the original characteristics, but narrower excess contracts as well.

There is no "standard" umbrella or excess liability policy. Each insurer draws up its own contract, and while most of the contracts are similar in nature, there may be substantial differences. Because insurers use the term *umbrella* to designate contracts with difference characteristics, the true nature of a particular contract can be determined only by a detailed analysis of the specific contract being considered. In general, umbrella and following form excess policies fall into one of three broad classes:

1. *Following-Form Excess Liability Policies.* The first of the three types of policies, the *following-form* excess liability policy, is subject to all the terms and conditions of the scheduled underlying policies. It provides coverage identical to that of the underlying contracts, although sometime this type of policy includes a few terms and conditions of its own that may further restrict the coverage.

2. *Excess Umbrella Liability Policy.* This is the contract that most agents have in mind when refering to an *umbrella*. The distinguishing feature of this type is a self-insured retention (SIR) in areas of no underlying insurance, which indicates that the policy is broader, at least in some areas, than the underlying coverage.

3. *Combination Umbrella and Following-Form Excess.* This is sometimes called the *two-step* umbrella. It combines the two preceding types, with the umbrella provisions applying to some aspects of the program, and other areas of the insurance subject to following-form coverage only. Not only does it provide a combination of agreements, but it also may be a combination of occurrence and claims-made forms, depending on the coverages for which it is used as excess.[29]

Umbrella Liability Policies

The umbrella policy is a form of excess liability insurance and differs from primary liability insurance in that the insurer promises to indemnify insureds for their ultimate net loss in excess of some retained limit. The policy limits are quite high, ranging upward from $1 million. When purchased in conjunction with the liability policies normally purchased by the business firm, the umbrella serves three functions:

1. *Excess coverage.* The umbrella policy applies as excess coverage over the other liability coverage purchased by the insured. It takes over when the limits of the basic policies are inadequate to pay any judgment against the insured.

2. *More comprehensive coverage.* Certain losses that are not covered by the underlying insurance may be included within the broad scope of the umbrella liability policy. In these instances, the umbrella provides protection subject to a deductible called a *self-insured retention* or SIR usually ranging from $10,000 upwards. It should be noted that the deductible or SIR applies only in cases where the loss is not covered by the underlying coverage. In other words, there is no corridor deductible on those losses that are covered by underlying coverage.

[28] Product liability suits, in particular, have produced losses of catastrophic proportions. In 2001, fatalities and injuries resulting from accidents involving Ford Explorers equipped with Firestone tires alleged triggered a series of liability claims against both companies. The losses will likely total in the billions. Previous product liability losses resulted in bankruptcy of the Manville Corporation, the asbestos manufacturer, A.H. Robins, maker of the Dalkon Shield contraceptive device, and Dow Corning, the maker of silicone breast implants filed for bankruptcy. The largest civil liability loss in U.S. history was the 1998 agreement by forty-six states to accept $246 billion from the tobacco industry in a suit to recover public-health costs linked to smoking.

[29] In addition to excess liability policies and umbrella liability, there is a third form, known as a *bumbershoot,* which covers marine liability as well as nonmarine liability.

3. *Drop-down coverage.* If the underlying coverage is exhausted, the umbrella becomes the underlying coverage, subject to the terms and conditions of the underlying contracts.

Underlying Insurance Requirements In general, the umbrella liability policy is written only for insureds that have a broad and substantial program of underlying coverage. Normally, the insurer requires comprehensive general liability coverage with bodily injury limits of $250,000/$500,000, property damage limits of $100,000, and automobile liability coverage with the same limits. Employers' liability coverage is required, usually in the amount of $100,000 (although some insurers have begun to require a $500,000 limit). In addition, when the exposure exists, bailee liability and aviation liability coverage may also be required. The policy conditions call for the maintenance of the underlying coverage, and the liability of the umbrella insurer is determined as if the underlying coverage were in force, whether or not it is.

Defense Coverage In some contracts, the policy limit includes defense and investigation costs. In other policies, the defense coverage is in addition to the policy limit. Other policies may not include defense coverage at all. Individual policies must be examined to determine the manner in which defense coverage is treated. Practically all umbrella liability contracts have a provision that, in effect, provides that the insurer may take over or participate in the defense of a claim in which it may be involved.

Coverage under the Umbrella Liability Policy There is no standard form of commercial umbrella liability insurance. Each insurer draws up its own contract, and while most of the contracts are similar in nature, there are substantial differences. These can be identified only through a detailed analysis of the specific contract being considered. In general, the insuring agreements are broad and comprehensive in nature. It is common to provide coverage under three sections:

1. Personal injury liability

2. Property damage liability

3. Advertising liability

Although some umbrella policies separate coverage for *bodily injury* and *personal injury,* the most common approach is to include bodily injury in the personal injury insuring agreement. In the broadest contracts, *personal injury* is defined to include bodily injury, mental injury or mental anguish, sickness, disease, disability, false arrest or imprisonment, wrongful eviction, detention, malicious prosecution, and humiliation, plus libel, slander, defamation of character, and invasion of rights of privacy that are not the result of advertising activity. One type of action that is usually excluded is discrimination.

Exclusions While the coverage under the umbrella liability policy is far broader than that of standard general liability and automobile liability contracts, it is not all-risk. There are exclusions and many of the exclusions are quite important. Some of the more common exclusions contained in the current umbrella liability contracts are the following:

1. The policies exclude any liability arising out of any workers compensation, unemployment compensation, or disability benefits law. As in case of the underlying contracts, this exclusion does not apply to liability of others assumed by the insured under contract. Employers' liability, however, is covered.

2. The policies exclude liability arising out of claims against the insured for repairing or replacing any defective products manufactured, sold, or distributed by the insured, or for the cost of repairing or replacing defective work performed by the insured.

3. Most policies exclude liability arising out of the ownership, maintenance, use, loading or unloading of any aircraft owned by or chartered without a pilot by the insured. Some policies totally exclude liability arising out of aircraft, including both owned and nonowned.

4. There is an exclusion of liability of any employee with respect to liability for injury to or death of a fellow employee.

5. Most umbrella policies also exclude any error or omission, malpractice or mistake of a professional nature committed by or alleged to have been committed by or on behalf of the insured.

6. All umbrella policies exclude liability for damage to property owned by the insured.

7. Most policies include some variation of the *Care, Custody, and Control exclusion.* Usually, only property with respect to which the insured is obligated to provide property insurance is excluded.

Some policies also exclude damage to aircraft, water-craft, or automobiles in the insured's care, custody, and control.

8. Increasingly, umbrella liability policies include a sweeping pollution liability exclusion generally patterned after the pollution exclusion of the 1986 version of the CGL form.

9. Finally, some umbrella insurers include an exclusion of punitive damages.

The recent trend has been toward higher and higher liability suits, particularly in the case of the individual versus the corporation. The liability contracts discussed in this chapter represent the major forms of coverage that are available to businesses to protect against this exposure. The Umbrella Liability Policy is a part of the total framework of liability protection and constitutes a critical part of the overall protection of the business firm.

IMPORTANT CONCEPTS TO REMEMBER

workers compensation
statutory provision
employers liability
third-party over suit
dual capacity
Other States Insurance
U.S. Longshoremen and Harbor Workers Compensation Act
Voluntary Compensation Insurance
breach of warranty
product liability
completed operations
contingent liability
Independent Contractor coverage

Commercial General Liability Policy (CGL)
occurrence form
claims-made form
insured contract
mobile equipment
triple trigger
impaired property
personal and advertising injury liability
retroactive date
Dram Shop or Liquor Liability Policy
Business Auto Coverage Form

admitted liability
common carrier
Garage Coverage Form
Garagekeepers' coverage
Truckers Coverage Form
Motor Carrier Coverage Form
voluntary settlement coverage
released bill of lading
bailee liability
Bailee's Customer Policy
commercial umbrella policy
aggregate limit

QUESTIONS FOR REVIEW

1. Why does the Workers Compensation and Employers Liability Policy not contain a specific statement of the benefits which it provides?

2. What is the purpose of the Other-States Coverage optionally available under the Workers Compensation and Employers Liability Policy? Why is it needed?

3. What basic forms of general liability insurance are included in the Commercial Liability Policy?

4. What conditions led to the introduction of the claims-made form to the general liability field?

5. Why is it advisable for an employer to purchase employers' non-ownership automobile liability coverage, even though the firm's employees may carry their own insurance?

6. What three basic types of liability insurance are provided under the Garage Coverage Form?

7. Under what circumstances is a common carrier liable for damage to goods in its custody?

8. What is the purpose of the Interstate Commerce Commission Endorsement to the Truckers Coverage Form?

9. Distinguish between the coverage provided by the Garage Coverage Form and that provided by Garagekeepers' Coverage.

10. Joe Smith has been in the plumbing business as a sole proprietor for the past 35 years and is now planning to retire. His insurance agent has told him that he should continue to carry Products and Completed Operations Liability coverage. Do you agree with the agent's recommendation? Why or why not?

QUESTIONS FOR DISCUSSION

1. The liability exposures of a business firm are far more complex than those of an individual. What characteristics of the business firm make this so?

2. The *care, custody, and control* exclusion continues to cause difficulties in the field of liability insurance. Assume that a business firm carries a Commercial General Liability Policy. What additional coverages, endorsements, or techniques should it consider to eliminate the loss potential in connection with property in its care, custody, and control?

3. Three housewives decide to go into business publishing cookbooks. They form a corporation, having been told that the corporate form of ownership carries limited liability. They decide not to purchase any form of liability insurance for the corporation, on the grounds that their loss in the event of an uninsured liability loss will be limited to the amount of their initial investment. Is there a fallacy in their logic?

4. Of the liability exposures discussed in this chapter, which do you suspect are the most frequently overlooked in programming liability insurance for business firms?

5. You have just opened a new motel with an attached restaurant and cocktail lounge. What liability coverage will you consider essential in your insurance program?

SUGGESTIONS FOR ADDITIONAL READING

Fire, Casualty and Surety Bulletins. Casualty and Surety Volume. Cincinnati, Ohio: National Underwriter Company. (Loose-leaf manual service with monthly supplements.) See "Public Liability" and "Auto" sections.

—. Fire and Marine Volume. Cincinnati, Ohio: National Underwriter Company. (Loose-leaf manual service with monthly supplements.) See "Inland Marine" section.

Garthe, David J. "Occurrence: Coverage Problem of the 80's." *CPCU Journal,* vol. 36, no. 3 (Sept. 1984).

Gentile, Willard J. *The Workers Compensation and Employers Liability Policy,* 7th ed. New York: Insurance Advocate, 1974.

Malecki, Donald S., Ronald C. Horn, Eric A. Wiening, and Arthur L. Flitner. *Commercial Liability Insurance and Risk Management,* 3rd ed., vol. 1 and vol. 2. Malvern, Pa.: American Institute for CPCU, 1996.

Malecki, Donald S., and Arthur L. Flitner. *Commercial General Liability,* 6th ed. Cincinnati, Oh.: National Underwriter Co., 1997.

McCormick, Roy C. *Guide to Liability Insurance.* Indianpolis, Ind.: Rough Notes Company, 1988.

Peeples, James W. "Asbestos Litigation and Theories of Insurance." *Federation of Insurance Counsel Quarterly.* Iowa City, IA.: Federation of Insurance Counsel, vol. 32, no. 4 (Summer 1982), pp. 323–359.

Policy, Form and Manual Analysis Service. Casualty Coverages Volume. Indianapolis, Ind.: Rough Notes Company. (Loose-leaf manual service with monthly supplements.) See "Liability-General" and "Workers Compensation" sections.

Prior, Derek. "Products Liability in the Modern Era." *Best's Review,* Property/Casualty Insurance Edition (April 1988).

Whiteaker, Raymond E. "Exclusive Remedy Doctrine under Siege." *For The Defense,* vol. 1984, no. 3. Milwaukee, Wisc.: Defense Research Institute, 1984.

Woodward, W. Jeffrey. "The 1996 ISO CGL Program," *The Risk Report,* vol. 18, no. 5 (January 1996).

WEB SITES TO EXPLORE

Aviation Association Underwriters	http://www.aau.com/
Best's Review—Property/Casualty Edition	http://www.ambest.com/review/lh/index.html
Business Insurance Magazine	http://www.businessinsurance.com/
Defense Research Institute, Inc.	http://www.dri.org
RISKWeb	http://www.RISKWeb.com/
Rough Notes Company	http://www.roughnotes.com/

SURETY BONDS AND CREDIT INSURANCE

He that is surety for a stranger shall smart for it.

— PROVERBS, 11:14–15

CHAPTER OBJECTIVES

When you have finished this chapter, you should be able to

- Identify the three parties to a surety contract and describe their roles
- Distinguish between suretyship and insurance
- Identify and describe the five main categories into which surety bonds may be classified
- Describe the coverage provided by credit insurance policies and distinguish between "extraordinary coverage" and "general coverage"
- Describe the purpose of credit enhancement or financial guarantee insurance

Although surety bonds and credit insurance might seem completely unrelated, there is a basic similarity between the two: both are designed to protect against financial losses from default by someone on whom the insured depends.

When a business firm or a government organization hires a contractor to erect a building or perform some other work, it is assumed that the building will be put up according to plan or that the work will be completed. This is not always the case. The contractor may go bankrupt and be unable to complete the job. When a business extends credit to one of its customers, it assumes that the customer will eventually pay for the goods—but credit losses do arise. Insofar as these possibilities exist, risk exists, for such failures may produce serious financial loss.

One approach to dealing with these exposures is, of course, loss prevention. Care in the selection of clients to whom credit is granted and investigation of the financial stability of the contractor are steps to avoid loss. Another alternative is retention, and the individual or business faced with these risks may elect or have no choice but to retain the risk. The coverages discussed in this chapter represent a third alternative—that of transferring the risk to a professional risk bearer.

In addition to the treatment of surety bonds and credit insurance, this chapter also includes a discussion of a new area of financial guarantees, credit enhancement insurance. Basically, credit enhancement insurance is a type of financial guarantee in which the insurer guarantees the payment of interest and principal on debt instruments. Although the relationship among the parties is somewhat different, credit enhancement insurance is similar to both surety bonds and credit insurance.

SURETY BONDS

Technically, all bonds are surety bonds, including the fidelity coverages discussed in Chapter 31. However, the term *surety* is generally reserved for the nonfidelity field. Fidelity bonds are more closely related to insurance coverages than they are to suretyship as discussed here.

As noted in Chapter 4, suretyship is the practice of guaranteeing obligations through a three-party contract. Under the provisions of such a contract, one party (the *surety*) agrees to be held responsible to a second party (the *obligee*) for the obligations of a third party (the *principal*). Under a surety bond, the surety lends its name and credit to guarantee the obligation of the principal. The surety guarantees principal's performance; if the principal fails to perform, the surety is responsible to the obligee for the amount of the bond, called the "penalty".

Originally, the surety was a friend or a relative. When there was doubt about the ability of a person to perform some task, the individual to whom the obligation was due required a friend or relative to guarantee the performance.[1] Personal suretyship frequently proved to be unsatisfactory, both to the obligee and to the surety, and the natural result was corporate suretyship, which developed in England in about 1842.

Surety bonds are used today in situations in which one of the parties insists on a guarantee of indemnity if the second party fails to perform a specified act. Such a requirement may arise in connection with construction contracts, court procedures, or other situations in which there may be doubt concerning ability to perform.

Suretyship Distinguished from Insurance

Suretyship differs from insurance in several ways. The most frequently stated distinction is that a surety bond is a three-party contract, involving surety, principal, and obligee, whereas the insurance policy is a two-party contract, between the insured and insurer. The most important distinction, however, is one of basic philosophy regarding losses. In the field of insurance, the insurer generally expects losses. In the surety field, no losses are expected, primarily because the surety will not issue the bond if a loss appears likely. For example, before issuing a bond for the completion of a construction project by a contractor, the surety will examine the contractor's financial resources, manner of operation, and past history. If it appears that the contractor has the financial strength and the technical skill required for the completion of the project, the surety will issue the bond. This bond is a certificate of character, ability, and financial worth of the principal. In essence the surety says, "We have examined the financial statements and the performance record of this principal, and we are convinced that he or she has the financial resources and skills to complete the project for which he or she intends to contract; if we are wrong in our opinion, we will be held responsible." This is an unusually strong guarantee, and a bond will be issued only when the surety has the utmost confidence in the ability of the principal to perform. If there is any question about that ability, the bond will not be issued. Sometimes, the surety may require the principal to put up collateral equal to the amount of the maximum possible loss under the bond. Thus, whereas actuarial science is the basis for insurance rates, the fee for a surety bond is primarily a payment for the investigation and certification, with only a small element to cover inevitable losses.

It is important to note that although the purchaser of the bond is normally the principal, a surety bond is issued for the benefit of the obligee. As proof of this, in the event of a loss under the bond, the surety has a right to collect from the principal any amount that the surety has been obligated to pay to the obligee. In other words, when a loss is paid by the surety, the surety obtains full rights of recovery against the principal.

[1] One of the earliest forms of suretyship was the hostage. A debtor might offer as security for a debt a hostage, who was usually a close relative. When the debt was paid, the hostage was released. If the debt was not paid, the hostage was likely to be in for a hard time.

The main categories into which surety bonds may be divided are

1. Contract bonds
2. Court bonds
3. License and permit bonds
4. Public official bonds
5. Miscellaneous bonds

A brief discussion of the more important bonds under each of these classifications should serve to illustrate more fully the nature of suretyship.

Contract Bonds

The general purpose of the contract bond is to guarantee that the principal, who is normally a contractor or supplier, will fulfill his or her commitment according to specifications under the contract. For this reason, many of these bonds are designated performance bonds. *Performance bonds* provide for indemnification if the principal fails to perform on the contract.

Construction Contract Bonds This type of bond is designed for use in connection with contracts to build real property. Under a construction bond, the surety agrees to indemnify the obligee if the principal fails to complete the construction according to specifications in the contract. If the contractor cannot, for one reason or another, finish the agreed project, it is up to the surety to see that it is done. The construction contract bond may be written to include the terms of a labor and materials bond, which is discussed next.

Labor and Materials Bond Under the labor and materials bond, the surety guarantees that the principal will pay all bills for labor and material in connection with the contract, thus assuring the obligee that the work completed will be free of all mechanics' or other types of liens. It may be written separately or it may be included in a construction contract bond.

Supply Contract Bond This bond guarantees faithful performance under a contract to supply goods or materials. The bond guarantees that the principal will furnish the obligee with the goods contracted for according to the specifications in the contract to supply goods.

Completion Bond Here the obligee is normally a lender who has furnished funds to a contractor in connection with construction work. It guarantees the obligee that the principal (who is the borrower) will use the money according to the terms of the contract and will complete the work undertaken.

Bid Bond In many cases where a contract is being let for public bids, the agency letting the contract requires all bidders to furnish a bid bond. This is necessary to establish that the bid is a bona fide offer by the one required to post the bond. It protects against loss resulting from failure of the bidder to accept the contract. If the bidder who is awarded the contract fails to sign the contract, or is unable to provide the required performance bond, the contract may then be awarded to the next lowest bidder. The surety on the bid bond then becomes liable for the difference between the bid of its principal and the next lowest bidder. A point of frequent misunderstanding has to do with the obligation of the surety under a bid bond. The surety on such a bond is not required to furnish its principal with a performance bond if he or she is awarded the contract; however, if the principal cannot obtain a performance bond, the surety on the bid bond becomes liable.

Court Bonds

In many court proceedings, some form of bond may be required by the court. There are two basic forms of court bonds:

- *Fiduciary bonds* are required when an individual is appointed by the court to hold, control, or manage the property of others; examples of persons who are required to post fiduciary bonds are executors and administrators of estates, guardians, and receivers.

- *Litigation bonds* are required of a person who wishes to bring action in a court of law or equity; normally, these bonds are required when the person bringing suit wishes to tie up the assets of the other party in the suit or restrain the other party from doing something.

Fiduciary Bonds A *fiduciary* is a person appointed by the court to hold, control, or manage the property of others. The fiduciary bond guarantees that the fiduciary (who is the principal under the bond) will faithfully perform the duties of the trust. Usually, the form of the bond is prescribed by the court, which also sets the face amount of the bond (the *penalty*).

To protect itself, the surety frequently asks for joint control of the assets of the estate. Under this arrangement, all the estate funds are kept in a joint account, and disbursements are made only with the signature of both the principal and the surety. The major subclassifications of fiduciary bonds are described next.

Executor's Bond This is the bond required of the person named in the will of the deceased to administer the estate.

Administrator's Bond When a person dies without a will, the court appoints an administrator, whose duties are similar to those of an executor. The obligee under both the *executor's bond* and the *administrator's bond* is the state or the court for the benefit of the beneficiaries.

Guardian's Bond This is required when it becomes necessary to appoint someone to administer property belonging to a minor. The guardian is normally appointed by the court, which then requires a bond guaranteeing the faithful performance of the guardian. The obligee is the state for the benefit of the minor.

Bonds in Trust Estates These are called for when the owner of property directs that the property be held in trust for his or her heirs, either for a given period of years or until the death of the heirs. Such a trust may be established by will (testamentary trust) or it may be established during the lifetime of the owner of the property (*inter vivos* trust). In either case, when a trust is established, the property must be turned over to a trustee, who is then responsible for its administration. The trustee's bond guarantees the faithful performance of the trustee.

Committee Bonds These are required when a person is not competent to handle his or her own affairs and the court appoints someone (known as the *committee*) to protect the person's property. A *committee bond* guarantees the faithful performance of the committee.

Miscellaneous Fiduciary Bonds In addition to those already discussed, there are a number of other bonds of similar nature that are required of persons who have custody or control over the property of others. Examples of such bonds are *receiver's bonds,* which are required of a court-appointed receiver in bankruptcy proceedings; *trustee's bonds,* which are also appointed in bankruptcy proceedings; and bonds that are demanded of conservators or liquidators of business firms or partnerships.

Litigation Bonds Litigation bonds are the second major class of court bonds. The bonds in this class are required for the purpose of obtaining some restriction on property of others or releasing property from such restrictions. If a person bringing action seeks to attach property and loses the case, the person whose property was attached might maintain that the action injured him or her and caused damages. The bonds that are required in litigation will pay any such damages. In addition, under certain circumstances, the person bringing suit must furnish security to guarantee the payment of court costs. The more common types of litigation bonds are described next.

Attachment Bonds These are required when property is attached before the court decision to prevent its disposal by the person having custody of it. The bond guarantees reimbursement for damages if the attachment is unjustified.

Garnishment Bonds These are necessary when the plaintiff wishes to attach wages or financial assets in the hands of a third party. It is much the same as an attachment bond, except that the assets distrained are in the hands of a third party.

Replevin Bonds These are similar to attachment bonds, except that the plaintiff is suing to recover specific property. The replevin bond guarantees that the property will be returned to the defendant in proper condition if the plaintiff loses the suit.

Bonds for Distraint of Rent A landlord who seeks to have a tenant's personal property seized in an action to recover rent must provide one of these bonds.

Release of Attachment Bond This enables the defendant, whose goods have been attached, to recover possession of the goods. It also guarantees that the property will be available and will be turned over to the plaintiff should the defendant lose the suit.

Appeal Bonds These are required of individuals who have lost a suit and wish to appeal and suspend execution of the judgment pending the decision of a higher court. The bond guarantees payment of the costs of appeal.

Removal Bonds In certain cases when the defendant who is being sued in a state court wishes the suit

to be removed to a federal court, or from the court of one state to another state, these bonds are required. The bond guarantees the payment of court costs by the principal if it is found that the case was improperly removed to the new court.

Nonresident Cost Bonds These are sometimes required when a nonresident of a state, city, or county wishes to institute action against a resident. The bond guarantees payment of costs in the event of failure of the suit.

Injunction Bonds These are required when the plaintiff alleges that he or she is being injured by the actions of the defendant and requests the court to restrain the defendant from further action. If an injunction is granted, a bond is required of the plaintiff that guarantees payment of damages if the injunction proves to be unwarranted.

Discharge of Mechanic's Lien Bond The owner of property can obtain removal of a lien before trial by furnishing a bond that promises to indemnify the claimant if the claimant wins the suit.

License and Permit Bonds

Many state and federal licenses are required for manufacturing, tax, and occupational purposes. In many cases the applicant for a license is required to post a bond guaranteeing faithful performance of duties or payment of taxes collected. The purpose of these bonds is to protect the state and the public from damages arising out of the manner in which the business is conducted or to guarantee the payment of taxes collected by the license holder. The major classes of license and permit bonds and some classes of individuals who require the bonds are

1. Federal license bonds for manufacturers.

2. State tax bonds, required in connection with the sale of gasoline, cigarettes, liquor taxes, sales taxes, and so forth; these guarantee that the principal will deliver to the state all taxes collected.

3. Occupational bonds, required for securities salespeople, liquor stores, undertakers, collection agencies, warehouse workers, and a vast array of other occupational classifications; these guarantee honest and faithful performance by the principal.

4. License bonds, required for placing or construction of materials that might cause injury or inconvenience to the public. In many cities permit bonds are required for signs and billboards, or street obstructions; these guarantee indemnity to anyone who is injured because of the construction or materials.

Public Official Bonds

The law requires that certain persons elected to fill positions of trust must furnish bonds that guarantee their faithful performance of duties. The public officials are generally held to be liable for the faithful accounting for all money they receive. If for any reason public officials cannot turn over to the state all the money they have received, or if they dissipate assets belonging to the government unit they serve, they are personally liable. Public official bonds are designed to guarantee payment of funds that the public official has not turned over or that he or she has dissipated. These bonds are designed to protect against dishonesty, negligence, and even lack of ability.

Most public official bonds are referred to as *statutory,* because they are required by law. The surety cannot reduce its liability by inserting provisions in the bond; the provisions spelled out by statute take precedence. These bonds are normally written for the term of the elected or appointed official and are noncancelable during the term. Usually, the cost of the bond is paid out of public funds.

Public Employees Bond The public employees bond is closely related to the public officials bond. It is available to cover employees who are not required by law to post a bond, which includes most workers in public service other than tax collectors and treasurers. The minimum amount for which this bond may be written is $2500. The coverage may be written to cover honesty of the public employees, or it may be written to cover *faithful performance.* The faithful performance form will pay losses resulting from dishonesty of the bonded person, and in addition will pay for losses resulting from negligence or lack of ability.

Miscellaneous Bonds

In addition to the bonds discussed already, there are others that do not fall into any of the described categories.

Lost Instrument Bonds These bonds, which are also called *lost securities bonds,* are required of an individual who has lost or accidentally destroyed securities or other valuable papers and wishes to obtain

duplicates. The lost instrument bond guarantees that the principal will reimburse the issuer of a duplicate instrument if the original security or instrument later turns up and its holder is able to collect on it.

Workers Compensation Bonds In many states, the workers compensation law permits certain employers to self-insure their workers compensation exposure. To make certain that the benefits to which an injured worker is entitled will be paid, the self-insurer is required to post a *self-insurer bond,* which guarantees payment of benefits to workers who are injured and entitled to workers compensation benefits under the workers compensation law.

CREDIT INSURANCE

Most business firms deal with the risk of financial loss from bad debts and credit losses through loss prevention techniques and risk retention. They are careful in choosing customers to whom credit is to be extended and make allowances in the budgeting process for normal bad debt losses. In some cases, these approaches may be inadequate, particularly when outstanding credit is a large item in the firm's balance sheet or when questionable accounts must be carried. In instances where the credit risk is great, the firm may prefer to transfer the risk through credit insurance, which provides protection against abnormal credit losses. Credit insurance, which is sold only to manufacturers and wholesalers and is not available to retail establishments, protects against loss resulting from the inability to collect accounts due to insolvency or unwillingness or inability to pay.[2] Policies may be written to cover losses arising out of defaults occurring during the policy term, without regard to the time of the sale, or they may be issued to cover losses that arise from sales during the term of the contract, regardless of when the default occurs. Policies that cover losses arising out of defaults during the policy period are referred to as back coverage policies, and those covering losses stemming from

sales during the policy period are called forward coverage policies. Both types are written with a maximum amount of coverage on each account.

Credit insurance is a highly specialized field, and the coverage is only written by a limited number of insurers. The bulk of the credit insurance sold in the United States is sold by two companies, the American Credit Indemnity Company and the London Guarantee Company. The American Credit Indemnity Company writes approximately 75 percent of the coverage sold and the London Guarantee Company writes most of the remainder.[3]

Types of Policies

In addition to the distinction between forward coverage and back coverage policies already noted, credit policies may also be subdivided according to the accounts insured. In general, there are two types of contracts. The first type, known as *extraordinary coverage* (or specific coverage), reimburses for losses involving specific customers of the insured and is generally limited to one or a few accounts. It is used when the outstanding balances of a single customer or a few customers represent a serious exposure to the firm, and it is generally purchased by companies that deal with a limited number of buyers. It is issued only after an investigation of the individual debtors and acceptance of each one by the insurer. Under this form of coverage, the insurer is permitted to cancel coverage as to future shipments to any debtor, but must give written notice of such cancellation.

The second type of coverage is known as the *general coverage* policy; it includes protection on all policyholder's customers with a credit rating as specified in the policy. Investigation of the individual customers is not necessary under the general policies, because they describe the amount of coverage and the quality-of-accounts coverage by reference to mercantile credit ratings such as those published by Dun & Bradstreet, Inc. Each account insured must have a capital and credit rating, which express the net worth of the company and its credit standing. The

[2] It is important at the outset of our discussion to distinguish clearly credit insurance from accounts receivable coverage discussed in Chapter 30. As the reader will recall, the accounts receivable coverage provides indemnification of the insured in the event of a loss resulting from the destruction of accounts receivable records as a result of an insured peril. In the case of credit insurance, the peril insured against is insolvency or default of a debtor to whom credit has been extended.

[3] In 1998, American Credit Indemnity was acquired by the Paris-based EULER Group, the world's largest business credit insurer. EULER purchased 50 percent ownership in the company from Dun and Bradstreet in 1996 and acquired the remaining 50 percent interest from co-owner Securitas Capital, LLC. In 2001, the St. Paul Insurance Companies announced an agreement to purchase the Toronto-based London Guarantee Insurance Company.

coverage on each account is determined by a table of mercantile ratings, selected by the insured and incorporated into the contract.[4] Only debtors whose credit rating comes within the limitations of the ratings adopted by the insured are covered. For example, the insured might select coverage on accounts having a general credit rating of "high" or "good," and with a net worth of over $500,000. Sales to customers outside these classifications is at the insured's own risk. The total amount of coverage for each debtor is dependent on the rating of that debtor. For example, the policy might specify that the maximum amount of coverage for an account with a Dun & Bradstreet rating of AA-A1 is $50,000, and the maximum for an account with an AA-1 rating is $40,000. If the insured suffers a credit loss of $75,000 on an account with an AA-A1 rating, only $50,000 of that loss will enter into the computation of the amount recoverable.

Coinsurance and the Normal Loss

Every credit insurance policy provides that the insured shall assume the first portion of each net loss through the application of a coinsurance percentage. This coinsurance percentage works in essentially the same way as that of the major medical policy; that is, it provides that the insured bear a specified percentage of each loss. The normal coinsurance percentages are 10 percent and 20 percent, but higher figures may be used when the risk is great, as in the case of a debtor with an inferior credit rating.

In addition to the coinsurance percentage, the policy also includes an annual deductible, known as the primary loss (or normal loss). This equals the normal bad debt write-off experienced by most business firms. The normal loss is calculated from the previous experience of the firm insured or as a percentage of the firm's net annual sales from tables that express bad debt ratios for various industries. It is not insurable and is generally adjusted at each renewal. The insurer relies on the coinsurance percentage and the normal loss to induce the insured to exercise care in the extension of credit. Thus, credit insurance is not a substitute for a sound credit policy. In fact, without a

proper credit policy it will be very difficult for a firm to obtain credit insurance.

Loss settlement is made on an annual basis, with the coinsurance percentage applied to each loss before the application of the normal loss deductible. In addition, losses in excess of the coverage on individual accounts are excluded prior to loss computation.

To illustrate, assume that the credit insurer limits coverage to $50,000 on accounts receivable with a Dun & Bradstreet rating of AA-A1. If the amount owed by such an account is $50,000, the most that the creditor could lose on this account (over and above the primary loss) would be $5000, assuming a 10-percent coinsurance provision. If the amount owed were $70,000, the insurance company would admit $50,000 of this account for coverage purposes and assume 90 percent of that amount. All such losses during the year would then be subject to the normal loss deductible. The loss computation here should serve further to illustrate the process.

	Amount of Debt	Admitted Loss	Less Coinsurance
Account with AA-A1 rating	$70,000	$50,000	$45,000
Account with AA-1 rating	50,000	40,000	36,000
			$81,000
Less: Primary loss			−10,000
Recoverable from credit insurer			$71,000

Collection Service

Although not all credit policies include provision for collection of past due accounts by the insurer, many contracts do, and the collection service is one of the most attractive aspects of credit insurance. Contracts differ in their provisions for collection. In some contracts, the insured is required to turn past due accounts over to the insurer for collection. In other contracts, it is optional. A third group of contracts makes no provision for collection by the insurer. In those instances where the insured is required or permitted to turn past due accounts over to the insurer, accounts that are overdue a stated period (say, 60 days) under the original terms of sale are turned over to the insurer for collection. If the insurer succeeds, a small service charge is made for the collection. If the insurer is unsuccessful, the account becomes a loss

[4] Normally, the policies are written based on Dun & Bradstreet, Inc., ratings, but some other trade mercantile agencies are also acceptable.

under the policy and payment is made in the usual manner.

CREDIT ENHANCEMENT INSURANCE

Credit enhancement insurance—also called financial guarantee insurance—has been around since about 1971, when the American Municipal Bond Assurance Corporation, a subsidiary of Municipal Guaranty Insurance Company (MGIC), began to offer municipal bond guarantee insurance, guaranteeing the payment of principal and interest on bonds issued by municipalities. Until the early 1980s, however, few other insurers ventured into this field. This changed in the early 1980s, when the field of financial guarantees expanded rapidly and traditional insurers entered the field, offering innovative coverages and serving a pseudobanking function for insureds.[5]

Financial guarantee or *credit enhancement insurance* are terms used to describe a field of coverages that combines elements from the fields of suretyship and insurance. Basically, credit enhancement insurance is an arrangement by which an insurer guarantees the payment of principal and interest in connection with debt instruments issued by the purchaser. The insurer "insures" the purchaser of bonds and other debt instruments that the debt will be paid and, in a sense, substitutes its financial strength for the financial strength of the borrower. Although generally referred to as "insurance," the coverages are actually more closely related to suretyship, since they guarantee an obligation to third parties and the insurer retains a right of recovery against the insured purchaser of the coverage.

Municipal Bond Guarantee Insurance

The leading example of credit enhancement insurance is municipal bond guarantee insurance, a form of coverage that has been around for about 20 years. The coverage is sold to municipalities issuing debt instruments and guarantees the payment of interest and principal on bonds issued. Municipal bonds are rated by Moody's and by Standard & Poor's rating

services. The lower the rating of the bond, the higher will be the interest that the municipality must offer to sell the bonds. When the bonds being issued are covered by bond guarantee insurance, the rating is based on the insurer's financial strength rather than the municipality's. The insurance makes the bonds more attractive to potential borrowers, because of the lower potential for default, which allows the municipality to issue the bonds at a lower rate. The premium, in effect, is the sharing of a reduced interest cost with the insurance company.

Municipal Lease Insurance

Municipal lease insurance is a related credit enhancement coverage. It guarantees the prompt payment of principal and interest on municipal lease financing. It assures the lessor that debt service will be paid on a lease by the insurer if the lessee fails to pay due to default or nonappropriation. This insurance affords a high-grade investment rating on the lease so the investing public gains additional security and will invest in the guaranteed tax-exempt leases.

Commercial Paper Insurance

Commercial paper insurance guarantees the timely payment of principal and interest on commercial paper issued by corporations. It assures the borrower of a high-grade investment rating, which lowers the borrowing cost and assures the investor of prompt redemption of the maturing notes if the issuer should fail to pay.

Industrial Development Bond Insurance

Like municipal bond insurance, industrial development bond insurance is designed to reduce the cost of issuing bonds by increasing their attractiveness to investors. It guarantees the prompt payment of principal and interest on industrial development bonds and provides nonrated business a high-grade investment rating that makes the bonds salable in the open market and provides financing at a reduced cost.

Money Market Fund Insurance

Insurance protection against speculative risks associated with investments in money market funds was also introduced in the early 1980s. Money market funds are not insured by a federal agency as are com-

[5] These included major property and liability insurers, such as the American International Group, Continental Insurance Company, CIGNA, Aetna Casualty & Surety, General Reinsurance. Fireman's Fund, Chubb, CNA, Reliance, St. Paul, Travelers, and Industrial Indemnity.

mercial banks, savings and loan associations, or credit unions. The Money Market Fund Association, which represents money market mutual funds, arranged to provide insurance to its members that protects an investment principal against default. The program protects insured investors in the group's money market mutual fund in case the fund collapses or if issuers of investments held by the fund default.

IMPORTANT CONCEPTS TO REMEMBER

surety	court bonds	extraordinary (or specific) coverage
obligee	fiduciary bonds	general coverage
principal	litigation bonds	primary loss
contract bonds	license and permit bonds	credit enhancement insurance
performance bonds	public official bonds	municipal bond guarantee insurance
labor and materials bond	public employees bond	municipal lease insurance
supply contract bond	lost-instrument bonds	commercial paper insurance
completion bond	back coverage policy	money market fund insurance
bid bond	forward coverage policy	

QUESTIONS FOR REVIEW

1. Briefly distinguish between an insurance contract and a surety bond.

2. In what way is the underwriting process different for surety bonding and fire insurance?

3. Who is the obligee under a labor and materials bond? Who, in addition to the obligee, benefits from the existence of a labor and materials bond?

4. What determines the scope of the surety's obligation under a construction contract bond?

5. Describe the purpose of a lost instruments bond and explain the relationship among the parties in this bond.

6. Explain the purpose of a joint-control provision used in connection with surety bonds. With what types of bonds is this provision required?

7. Describe the purpose and function of a probate bond, indicating the principal and the obligee(s).

8. Describe the difference between the dishonesty form and the faithful performance form of the public official bond.

9. There are five bidders on a construction job. The average bid on the job is $2.5 million, and the bids of four bidders range from $2.4 to $2.6 million. The fifth bidder submitted a bid of $2 million and has been awarded the contract and is now applying for a bond. What will be the reaction of the underwriter?

10. For which type of bond would the underwriting standards be more severe, a bid bond or a construction contract bond?

QUESTIONS FOR DISCUSSION

1. A property and liability insurance agent is generally authorized to bind coverage. This is not true with respect to surety coverages. Why not?

2. Joe Schwartz is the principal stockholder in a small construction company specializing in concrete work. He needs a performance bond to obtain a contract to build a swimming pool for the city. However, the surety company has refused to issue the bond unless Schwartz personally signs a co-indemnity agreement under whose terms he will personally be responsible for the obligation assumed by his corporation. He feels that this defeats the whole purpose of a corporation and main-

tains the surety company is being unreasonable. What do you think?

3. Is the treatment of suretyship and credit insurance in the same chapter a logical combination? What is the similarity or dissimilarity in their natures on which you base your answer?

4. The Widget Manufacturing Company has a credit insurance policy with a $5000 normal loss and a 90-percent coinsurance clause. The limits are $40,000 for AA-Al accounts and $30,000 for AA-1 accounts. Two debtors go bankrupt, each owing $35,000. One is AA-Al and the other is AA-l. What will Widget recover under its credit policy?

5. In most states certified public accountants licensed by the State Board of Accountancy are required to post a surety bond or show evidence of an accountant's professional liability policy. Based on your understanding of surety bonds, what do you think is the basic difference between the protection provided by the professional liability policy and the accountant's bond?

SUGGESTIONS FOR ADDITIONAL READING

Clapp, Wallace L. "Credit Enhancement Insurance Featured at Symposium." *Specialty Coverage Market Reports.* Indianapolis, Ind.: Rough Notes Company, June 1984.

Crist, G. W. *Corporate Suretyship,* 2nd ed. New York: McGraw-Hill, 1950.

Fire, Casualty and Surety Bulletins. Casualty and Surety Volume. Cincinnati, Ohio: National Underwriter Company. (Loose-leaf manual service with monthly supplements.) See "Bonds" section.

Insurance Services Office. *Insurer Profitability: A Long-Term Perspective.* New York: ISO, 1987.

Levi, A. *Credit Insurance.* Baltimore, Md.: American Credit Indemnity Co., 1960.

Lewis, Richard C. *Contract Suretyship: From Principles to Practice* New York, John Wiley & Sons, 2000.

Morgan, W. D. "The History and Economics of Suretyship." *Cornell Law Quarterly,* (1926–1927).

Phelps, C. W. *Commercial and Credit Insurance as a Management Tool.* Baltimore, Md.: Commercial Credit Company, 1961.

Policy, Form and Manual Analysis Service. Casualty Coverages Volume. Indianapolis, Ind.: Rough Notes Company. (Loose-leaf manual service with monthly supplements.) See "Bonds" section.

Porter, David. *Fundamentals of Bonding,* 6th ed. Indianapolis, Ind.: Rough Notes Company, 1978.

Remmen, Albert. *The Contract Bond Book.* Cincinnati, Ohio: National Underwriter Company, 1977.

CHAPTER 34

INSURANCE IN THE FUTURE

─────── ■ ───────

We should all be concerned about the future
because we will have to spend the rest of our lives there.

— CHARLES F. KETTERING

CHAPTER OBJECTIVES

When you have finished this chapter, you should be able to

- Outline the most likely changes in the future environment of insurance
- Identify the continuing problems of the insurance industry and the possible solutions to those problems
- Discuss career opportunities in insurance and the necessary training to prepare for those opportunities

Since the end of World War II, the insurance industry has experienced remarkable growth. Concurrent with this growth, it has undergone significant change. The multiple-line transition, the introduction of package policies, the variable annuity and variable life insurance, universal life, changes in the regulatory framework, adoption of automobile no-fault laws, continued expansion of the Social Security system, and the involvement of government as a provider of private insurance are all a part of the changing environment within which insurance operates. This final chapter examines the implications of future economic and social changes for the insurance industry. Just as the industry has had to adjust in the past to developments in its environment, future changes undoubtedly will be demanded.

Projecting past trends to predict a future environment is always subject to error, for things may not continue to happen in the future as they have in the past. Still, we can gain some insight into the probable future of the insurance industry and the nature of the industry itself by extrapolating some developments of the current environment within which the insurance industry operates.

SOCIAL INSURANCE PROGRAMS

The growth of the private insurance sector is influenced by the extent to which the government acts as a source of financial security for citizens. Although some social insurance is sold by private insurers

(most notably workers compensation), most social insurance programs in the United States are operated by the government.

The Social Security System

The problems afflicting the Social Security system were discussed in Chapter 10. As noted in that discussion, the system faces long-range financial problems. These problems are likely to come to a head shortly after the turn of the century. The growing imbalance between workers and beneficiaries and the automatic increases in benefits have put the system on a collision course with insolvency. Although several solutions (such as reducing benefits and increasing the retirement age) have been suggested in the past, Congress has seemed unwilling to make the tough decisions that are required. As the 1990s came to a close and the armageddon for OASDI seemed nearer, congressional attention became more focused. In addition to the time-worn suggestions for reducing and deferring benefits, serious discussion about the possibility of privatizing Social Security began. Although many favor this approach, there are some legislators who fear even a modest degree of privatization, viewing it as a first step toward full privatization and the loss of Social Security's income redistribution effects.

Medicare

The Medicare system faces problems that mirror those of the OASDI program. Although Medicare's condition has improved somewhat in recent years, it still faces difficulties that will come sooner and that are more severe than those facing Social Security. Although both programs face the demographic problem of growing beneficiaries and fewer workers per beneficiary, Medicare costs are increasing faster than wages. The system will reach a crisis stage when costs exhaust the HI Trust Fund, probably about 2029. Although it is conceivable that the solution to the nation's general problem of financing health care (discussed next) may address the Medicare problem, most of the proposals for reform of health care financing generally have assiduously avoided suggesting changes in Medicare. Numerous changes in the system have been legislated over the years in attempts to save the system. The most recent changes were enacted as a part of the *Balanced Budget Act of 1997*, which added the new Medicare Part C, also known as Medicare+Choice, to the program. Medicare+Choice will extend the costsaving features of managed care to the

Medicare system. Although these changes will defer the time at which the imbalance between income from taxpayers and outgo to beneficiaries occurs, financing the Medicare system remains a problem in search of a solution.

Health Insurance

Although health insurance is a private form of insurance, we have witnessed a shift in national attitudes toward the risks associated with medical expenses. Our current philosophy is that the risk of health care costs is a fundamental risk, and that a national policy is needed to define the ways in which this risk will be addressed. The Congress and the nation are engaged in deliberations over how this risk will be managed.

In Chapter 21, we identified problems facing the nation with respect to health care delivery and financing: access to health care and the increasing cost of health care. These problems are among the most troublesome areas facing both the insurance industry and society today. For the insurance industry, the influence of runaway health care costs is pervasive. In addition to the obvious impact on health insurance, the costs of hospital and physicians' services are a significant factor in the price of automobile insurance, general liability insurance, and workers compensation insurance. For society, the lack of adequate health care by some segments of the population and the ever-increasing cost in the United States have caused public concern and a search for solutions.

Despite the attention focused on the problem, health care financing and health insurance remain problems in search of a solution.

CHANGES IN THE LEGAL ENVIRONMENT

Changes in the laws of society have always had a significant impact on the insurance industry, and this will remain so in the coming decades. To a large extent, the growth of the insurance industry will be determined by the legal environment within which it operates. Legislation in many areas affects the need for security and the manner in which that security is provided.

Changes in the Tort System

The automobile no-fault laws enacted during the 1970s are an example of how legislation can influence the insurance industry. Not only did these laws

alter the structure of benefits payable for automobile accidents, thereby affecting insurer losses, they also created a legal requirement for automobile insurance where none had previously existed. Before 1971, only three states had compulsory automobile liability insurance laws. State legislatures have increased this number to 48. During the 1990s, the notion of automobile no-fault legislation was resurrected at the federal level in the form of choice no-fault, discussed in Chapter 29. Congressional response was lukewarm and nothing significant occurred on this front.

In recent years, the debate over tort reform has moved from no-fault auto to other areas. In the 1990s, virtually every state enacted some type of tort reform, usually involving limitations on joint and several liability, pain and suffering, and punitive damages. Almost immediately, the constitutionality of these reforms was challenged in court.[1] The challenges to state tort reform statutes intensified the efforts of those who believe that tort reform is required at the federal level.[2] Pressure for federal reform in the tort system (and resistance to that pressure) will undoubtedly continue. Two major areas of focus will be products liability and medical malpractice.

In 1996, after a decade of lobbying by manufacturers, doctors, drug companies, and other business groups, Congress finally passed national tort reform legislation, the *Common Sense Product Liability Reform Act of 1996,* only to see President Clinton veto it. An attempt by the House to override the veto failed. The act embodied a group of changes that advocates of tort reform had long sought. It established a federal product liability standard, allowing punitive damages only when proven by a strict, "clear-and-convincing-evidence" standard. It would have limited a defendant's liability for noneconomic damages to its degree of negligence and would have capped punitive damages in all civil and product liability cases at $250,000 or three times the plaintiff's economic damages (whichever is larger). A 15-year statute of repose would have barred cases against manufacturers of durable goods and workplace goods more than 15 years old. Finally, the bill would have applied the so-called "loser pays rule," in which the unsuccessful party in a suit pays the attorneys' fees of the prevailing party. In 1998, an effort to enact a more limited version of product liability reform failed to gain passage. No product liability reform activity occurred in Congress in 1999.

In 2001, Congress considered liability reform legislation (H.R. 1805 and S. 865) that would limit the liability of small businesses with fewer than 25 full-time employees. The bill would cap punitive damages at the lesser of $250,000 or three times the compensatory damages. Punitive damages would be recoverable only if the plaintiffs prove by "clear and convincing evidence" that the defendant acted with "a conscious flagrant indifference to the rights and safety of others" and that the defendant's actions were the proximate cause of the damage and injury.

The debate over tort reform will continue and changes will undoubtedly occur at the state level. Although public sentiment seems to support national tort reform, plaintiff's lawyers and Ralph Nader's Public Citizen organization have taken the lead in opposing legal reform. According to those who oppose legal reform, the current system gives those who are injured access to the court system to which they might otherwise be denied. The eventual resolution of the debate over the tort system will have an important effect on the price and availability of liability insurance for these exposures.

Pollution and Environmental Impairment Liability Another pressing problem for insurance buyers today is the need for liability coverage to meet obligations with respect to environmental impairment. More than a dozen federal statutes establish regulations relating to the environment and pollution, and many states have added their own laws in this area.[3] The Environmental Protection Agency (EPA) has identified 38,000 hazardous waste sites in need of cleanup or containment. These and other inactive and abandoned hazardous waste disposal sites are the subject of the Comprehensive Environmental Response, Compensation, and Liability Act (CERCLA, also known as *Superfund*), which was passed in

[1] A study of challenges to state tort reform laws conducted by the American Tort Reform Association found that 72 decisions since 1985 overturned the reform laws, while 140 decisions sustained the laws. American Tort Reform Association, *The Reformer* (Winter 1997–1998) vol. 2, no. 4.

[2] Tort reform was one of the prominent features in the Republican "Contract with America" that was central to the Republican election strategy in the fall of 1994.

[3] These include, for example, the Resource Conservation and Recovery Act, the Clean Water Act, the Clean Air Act, the Safe Drinking Water Act, the Toxic Substances Control Act, and the Comprehensive Environmental Response, Compensation, and Liability Act (Superfund).

late 1980 and renewed in 1986 and 1991. The original act established a $1.6 billion fund, principally from taxes on the chemical industry, to be used to clean up old waste dumps, and the 1986 act increased the fund to $8.5 billion. In 1991, an additional $5.1 billion was appropriated.

Where responsible parties (an owner and operator, the transporter who selected the site, or the generator of the waste) can be identified, that party is responsible for the cleanup cost. If the parties responsible for a particular site fail to respond, the government can fund the cleanup and then sue for reimbursement plus punitive damages equal to three times the cleanup costs. When the companies or people responsible for contamination at Superfund sites cannot be found, or cannot perform or pay for the cleanup work, cleanup costs are paid from the Superfund Trust Fund. Until 1995, the Trust Fund money came mainly from taxes on the chemical and petroleum industries. In 1991, Congress extended Superfund until 1995, but the authority for Superfund taxes expired in 1995 and no revenues from taxes have been collected since that time. By the year 2001, despite attempts by every Congress since 1994 to pass renewal legislation, Superfund remains in limbo.

In 2001, Congress proposed the *Recycle America's Land Act of 2001,* a bill to amend CERCLA and reauthorize Superfund. The 2001 act would exempt small businesses (those with no more than 100 employees) from liability for cleanup costs associated with dumping municipal solid waste (such as paper and normal household trash) at a Superfund site. In addition, the Small Business Liability Relief Act of 2001, as the act was titled, would exempt companies of any size that disposed of less than 110 gallons or less than 200 pounds of material containing hazardous waste at a Superfund site from cleanup costs. Only disposals that occurred before April 1, 2001, would be exempt. No companion legislation was introduced in the Senate.[4]

In the 20 years since Congress created it, Superfund has become the world's most expensive environmental program. Instead of cleaning sites, the bulk of Superfund monies have gone to lawyers, consultants, and administrative expenses. The reason, according to critics, is Superfund's retroactive, strict, joint-and-several liability mechanism, which allows responsibility for cleanup costs to be shifted to any

party whose activity involved wastes found at a site. By mandating a system under which liability may be assigned to any potentially responsible party (PRP)—regardless of that party's degree of fault—Congress created a system under which litigation was inevitable. Further, by making liability retroactive in cases involving pre-1980 sites (that were operated under different disposal laws than those now in force), Congress created a liability exposure that is incompatible with the functioning of insurance markets. Insurers for parties held liable under Superfund's retroactive liability provisions are unable to pass cleanup-related costs on to insurance buyers because the policies under which coverage is provided expired many years ago.

Almost from the inception of Superfund, insurers have engaged in a debate with both industry and government over the responsibility of polluters under the act and the coverage for pollution cleanup costs under the CGL. In 1986, after several unsuccessful attempts to limit coverage for pollution losses to those that are accidental and unexpected, insurers added a total pollution exclusion to the CGL policy, specifically excluding pollution cleanup costs. Whether cleanup costs are covered under the pre-1986 general liability occurrence forms is unsettled. The supreme courts in several states have addressed the question of whether government-mandated cleanup costs constitute "damages" under the policy and have reached conflicting conclusions.[5] In many instances, however, insurers have been held liable under policies long expired, some dating back to the 1940s.

The future of Superfund remains an area of significant concern in the insurance industry and in society. Estimates of the industry's ultimate burden from these claims have ranged from $40 billion to $1 trillion, with a large portion of the costs representing legal expenses.[6] In large part, the resolution of the pollution liability problems depends on the provisions Congress includes in any new Superfund legislation.

[4] *Business Insurance,* May 28, 2001.

[5] State supreme courts in California, Iowa, Massachusetts, Minnesota, North Carolina, and Washington have ruled that pollution cleanup costs fall within the definition of "damages" under pre-1986 CGL policies. State supreme courts in Maine and New Hampshire have ruled that they do not.

[6] A report published in October 1995 by Standard and Poor predicted that the cost would be approximately $40 billion, or more than 20 percent of the industry's capital and surplus. See *Standard and Poor's Creditweek,* October 30, 1995, p. 43.

Workers Compensation Laws

Some observers are questioning the fragmentation of our system for compensating the disabled. Workers compensation laws provide coverage for work-related disability and private health insurance covers other types of disability. Since the need for income is the same for work-related disabilities and other disabilities, some people believe that it would make sense to eliminate the distinction and cover all disabilities under expanded public and private programs. One authority has recommended that the reliance on workers compensation as the primary payer of benefits for work-related injuries be reduced.[7] There is an increased interest in the notion that some form of 24-hour coverage should be adopted as an alternative to separate coverage for occupational disabilities under workers compensation and coverage for other disabilities under health insurance disability policies.

Some impediments to 24-hour coverage are structural in nature. The workers compensation system was accepted by employers because of the exclusive remedy doctrine. Employers and their insurers are reluctant to relinquish the exclusive remedy protection of workers compensation due to a fear that litigation would increase costs. Currently, a few states have enacted enabling legislation that allows employers and their insurers to adopt 24-hour coverage as an alternative to workers compensation. Many observers believe that 24-hour coverage is both desirable and inevitable.

Protection for Catastrophe Exposure

As a result of increased population density and associated capital investment, the concentration of asset values in some areas has increased the potential for catastrophe losses. Simulation studies indicate that the potential for a mega-catastrophe—ranging upward to $100 billion or more—exists in several areas on both the East and West Coasts. Insurance companies have become increasingly concerned as the magnitude of catastrophe losses that have occurred has increased. This concern was heightened by the $15.5 billion insured losses of Hurricane Andrew in 1992, followed by the $12.5 billion in losses from the Northridge, California, earthquake in 1994. With the increased concentration of values, it is argued, it is only a matter of time before a mega-catastrophe occurs. Every earthquake and hurricane that occurs is inevitably followed by dire predictions that "the next one could be worse."

State Solutions In the wake of devastating natural disaster losses suffered in the first half of the 1990s, California, Florida, and Hawaii created state catastrophe funds to provide direct insurance or reinsurance for hurricane and/or earthquake losses. The Hawaii catastrophe fund, created in 1993 (the year after Hurricane Iniki), provides hurricane insurance directly to consumers, via a separate policy. The Florida catastrophe fund, created in 1994, is primarily a reinsurance mechanism that reimburses insurance companies when disaster-related losses exceed certain levels. The California program, the California Earthquake Authority, was created in 1996 to write residential earthquake coverage for the policyholders of insurers that contributed capital to fund the program. (An earlier California state-operated earthquake insurance program created in 1990 was repealed effective January 1, 1993, shortly before the massive Northridge quake of 1994.) Other states that have considered state catastrophe funding programs include New York, Texas, Louisiana, and North Carolina.

Federal Reinsurance Despite the creation of the state disaster funds, there has been a growing interest in a national disaster reinsurance program. The first proposal for a federal reinsurance program came in 1990, the year after the Loma Prieta earthquake in California. Not surprisingly, this proposal was for an earthquake reinsurance program, structured as a public/private partnership between the insurance industry and the federal government. Legislation to create a program of this type was introduced in 1991 and again in 1992. In 1993, the year following the $15.5 billion Hurricane Andrew, the bill was changed from a *national earthquake* initiative to a national *disaster* one. National disaster plan initiatives have been introduced in every session of Congress since that time.

The most recent proposal for a federal disaster reinsurance plan is the Homeowners Insurance Availability Act of 2000 (H.R. 219), originally introduced by Representative Rick Lazio (R-NY) and about 100 other representatives in 1999. In November 1999 the act was passed by the House Banking and Insurance Committee by a vote of 34–18.

[7] See Michael L. Murray, "Workers Compensation—A Benefit Out of Time," *Benefits Quarterly,* vol. 1, no. 2 (Second Quarter 1985).

H.R. 219 would establish a federal program to provide for reinsurance of state disaster insurance programs. The act would authorize the Treasury to auction excess-of-loss reinsurance contracts to public and private catastrophe risk-bearers, insurers, and state funds. Coverage under the contracts would be triggered by a loss exceeding the larger of $2 billion or the estimated magnitude of a one-in-100-year event in the particular state or region. For contracts sold to state catastrophe funds, the trigger would be the state program's current claim-paying capacity. The reinsurance contracts would pay 50 percent of the eligible loss in excess of the trigger limits. The Secretary of Treasury would be responsible for managing the program so that the aggregate liability would be unlikely to exceed $25 billion.

The bill was opposed by the Consumers Federation of America, National Taxpayers Union, Citizens Against Government Waste, Americans for Tax Reform, the Coast Alliance, Citizens for a Sound Economy, US PIRG, the U.S. Business and Industry Council, the Competitive Enterprise Institute, the Coast Alliance, the Environmental Defense Fund, and many organizations within the insurance industry. The prospects for action on the bill were not enhanced by a March 2000 study by the U.S. General Accounting Office (commissioned by the House Banking Committee) concluding that the industry could handle most major catastrophes. There are many in the industry who believe that the idea of a federal disaster reinsurance program is a bad idea. They believe that a different approach—embodied in the *Policyholder Disaster Protection Act of 2001* (HR 785)—makes infinitely more sense. This bill would amend the *Internal Revenue Code* to allow insurers to establish pre-tax reserves by creating disaster protection funds for claims arising from future catastrophic events. Income allocated to the catastrophe reserves would be taxable as income only when withdrawn for the payment of losses.

Federal Tax Laws

Provisions of the federal tax laws—especially those relating to the taxation of life and health insurance, annuities, pensions, and other qualified retirement programs—have important implications for the insurance industry and insurance consumers. In 2001, when Congress passed and the president signed the Economic Growth and Tax Relief Reconciliation Act of 2001, a new level of uncertainty concerning a vari-

ety of issues arose. As discussed in Chapter 10, EGTRRA-2001 phases out and then repeals the federal estate tax, effective 2010. Then, owing to a sunset provision in the law, in 2011, unless a future Congress makes the changes permanent, everything reverts back to the way that it was in 2001. A future Congress could, of course, make the changes permanent. A future Congress could also slow the rate at which the estate tax is phased out or stop the progress completely. Whatever the decision, it will have a profound effect on the demand for life insurance.

EGTRRA-2001 also made significant changes in the rules applicable to qualified retirement program, including not only employer-sponsored plans, but Individual Retirement Accounts as well. These changes are likely to increase the flow of funds into qualified plans administered by insurance companies as well as to trusteed plans. As in the case of the provision related to the federal estate tax, a sunset provision in the law will return things to the 2001 state unless a future congress acts to make the changes permanent.

Possible Changes in the Pattern of Regulation

Although changes in insurance regulation are likely in several areas, two major issues relating to regulation dominate the current environment: proposals to amend or repeal the McCarran-Ferguson Act and modernizing state regulation. Besides these issues, there are several other developments on the horizon whose future depends on the resolution of these first two issues.

Repeal or Modification of McCarran Ferguson Virtually from the time it was enacted, there have been proposals for the repeal of McCarran Ferguson Act. Interest comes and goes and agitation for repeal or modification of McCarran Ferguson Act is greater at some times than at others. Pressure for repeal was intense throughout the 1970s and 1980s, but waned somewhat during the 1990s.[8] Then, in 2000, pressure

[8] During the 1980s, three legislators in particular pushed for repeal or modification of McCarran-Ferguson; Senator Howard M. Metzenbaum (D-OH), Representative Jack Brooks (D-TX) and Representative John Dingell (D-MI). Senator Metzenbaum did not seek reelection in 1994 and Representative Brooks was defeated in the November 1994 election. Congressman Jack Brooks—a former plaintiff's attorney—had been the most persistent proponent of federal regulation, and had introduced a series of bills throughout the 1980s, all aimed at shifting the regulation of insurance from the state to the federal level. Although Representative Dingell was reelected, he lost his chairmanship of the House Energy and Commerce Committee; and so his influence as a member of the congressional minority is greatly diminished.

for modification of McCarran–Ferguson returned, primarily from those who are regulated (or will now be regulated) by the state system. As noted in Chapter 5, the repeal of the *Glass–Steagall Act* and the authorization of bank-insurer affiliations by the *Financial Services Modernization Act* in 1999 is likely to result in a wave of such affiliations during the next few years. To the extent that banks affiliate with insurers, there will be pressure to modify the state system of regulation. Large national banks are accustomed to a dual regulatory system. State banking regulators coexist with national banking regulators, and banks have some freedom to elect the system they prefer. Many national banks have openly expressed their preference for a dual regulatory system over the current state-based insurance regulatory system. Banks and many large insurers complained about the costs and inefficiencies of dealing with multi-state product approvals, licensing and other regulations.

In 2001, the American Bankers Association Insurance Association (ABAIA) released its draft of legislation for a national insurance commissioner. The National Insurance Act of 2001 would establish a dual chartering system modeled after regulation in the banking industry, where state and federal regulation has existed for decades. Under the law, an insurer could choose to be regulated at the state level. The American Council of Life Insurers (ACLI) drafted its own proposal for a dual chartering system as did the American Insurance Association (AIA).

Erosion of State Regulatory Authority Regardless of what happens with respect to McCarran–Ferguson, there are other developments that have the potential to significantly diminish the states' authority to regulate insurance. These developments involve a type of creeping federal regulation created by Congress and, in some instances, by the courts. The erosion of state authority has resulted from legislation that preempts state authority in specific limited areas and court decisions that give federal agencies preeminence in resolving state-federal jurisdiction conflicts.

One area that illustrates the potential for erosion of state authority involves the regulation of the insurance-related activities of commercial banks. Although this threat has diminished with enactment of the Gramm–Leach–Bliley *Financial Services Modernization Act* (GLBA), it illustrates the ways in which state authority can slip away. During the 1990s, two U.S. Supreme Court decisions ruled that the Office of the Comptroller of Currency, the federal

regulator of national banks, has primary authority for regulating certain insurance-related activities of national banks.[9] These decisions were compounded by the *Chevron* doctrine, according to which the courts will give deference to the federal regulator when interpreting federal law.[10] GLBA mandated function regulation in the financial services industry, meaning generally that banks will be regulated by banking authorities, securities firms will be regulated by the Securities Exchange Commission (SEC), and the states will retain their traditional role as regulators of insurance. More important, GLBA ended the deference to federal regulators that had threatened to make McCarran–Ferguson moot.

A second area in which the authority of the states to regulate insurance has been significantly eroded is health insurance. As explained in Chapter 16, the enactment of ERISA created a dual regulatory structure in this country for health insurance and health benefits. Although subsequent legislation gives states authority to regulate MEWAs, self-insured, single-employer plans that cover an estimated 48 million persons remain exempt from state regulation under ERISA. Despite the past problems associated with MEWAs, several of the health insurance reform proposals in Congress in recent years would authorize a new variety of MEWA, association health plans (AHPs), which would be exempt from all state mandated laws.

In addition to the PWBA (which regulates health insurance and pension plans) and the OCC (which regulates the insurance activities of national banks), other agencies in the federal bureaucracy that have oversight of private insurers and private insurance markets include the Federal Emergency Management Agency (flood insurance) and the Department of Agriculture (federal crop insurance). The proposed U.S. Treasury reinsurance program would further involve the federal government in the insurance industry.

Although the future regulation of insurance is uncertain, it appears that if the states' authority to

[9] United States Supreme Court—No. 94-1837 *Barnett Bank of Marion County, N. A., Petitioner v. Bill Nelson, Florida Insurance Commissioner, et al.* [March 26, 1996]. *NationsBank of North Carolina v. Variable Annuity Life Insurance Co.,* 115 S.Ct. 810 (1995). The *Barnett* case dealt with the sale of insurance by banks in violation of state law. *NationsBank* involved the sale of annuities as agents without regard to state insurance laws.

[10] *Chevron U.S.A. Inc. v. Natural Resources Defense Council, Inc.,* 467 U.S. 837(1984).

regulate the insurance industry is further diminished, it will be the result of the gradual preemption of that authority by the courts and the Congress, rather than by the repeal of McCarran–Ferguson.

NAIC Statement of Intent Recognizing the increasingly global nature of the industry, the competition insurers face from other sectors of the financial services industry, and the increasing complaints from the insurance industry about the state-based system, the NAIC and the states embarked on an ambitious agenda to modernize the state regulatory system. The reform agenda was endorsed by the states in the "Statement of Intent on the Future of State Insurance Regulation," adopted in March 2000. Areas for reform include producer licensing, company licensing, rate and form regulation, market conduct, and solvency oversight.

In general, the Statement of Intent initiatives seeks more uniformity among the states and greater coordination in regulatory oversight, to reduce the duplication of dealing with multiple states. In the producer licensing areas, for example, the NAIC urged states to adopt the Uniform Producer Licensing Model Act to achieve greater uniformity in state laws and the creation of a national electronic system for nonresident producer licensing. By January 2002, significant progress had been made in creating a national producer licensing system.

Insurers had long complained about the difficulty of getting approval for products in all states. In response, the NAIC undertook a two-pronged effort to improve "speed to market." The first of these focuses on the processes and standards within each state and seeks to create a more uniform product filing process, greater transparency in requirements, maximum review times, and the elimination of unnecessary differences in regulations across states.

The second major "speed-to-market" effort was the creation of the Coordinated Advertising, Rate and Form Review Authority (CARFRA), a coordinated multi-state product review process, designed to eliminate the need for a company to deal with a separate review of its products in every state. CARFRA began as a pilot project in May 2001 with ten states and three products. Additional states and products were expected to be added in 2002.

During 2001, it became clear that state deviations from the CARFRA national product standards limited CARFRA's effectiveness. While CARFRA provided a single multi-state approval process, the deviations prevented insurers from marketing a single product nationally. To address this "deviation problem", in March 2002, the NAIC announced that it will work with state legislators to draft an interstate compact for the approval of life insurance and annuity products. Using an interstate compact, a state would recognize CARFRA as a standard-setting body for national filings, and products approved by CARFRA could be sold in the state. The NAIC is currently working on governance issues and the conditions under which a state could opt out of the CARFRA standards. Draft interstate compact legislation will be exposed in June, with consideration by the membership in September. Some observers believe that the NAIC's 2002 interstate compact initiative, if successful, could be the most significant change in state regulation in history.

Market-based Regulation of Commercial Line Rates In 1998, a committee of the National Association of Insurance Commissioners endorsed the concept of market-based regulation of rates and forms for some segments of the property and liability commercial lines insurance market. In a white paper adopted by the Special Committee on Regulatory Reengineering in March 1998, the NAIC introduced the concept of "exempt commercial policyholders" or ECPs, meaning those commercial insurance buyers who are relatively sophisticated, understand insurance markets, and are unlikely to need regulatory protection. Policies sold to ECPs would be exempt from rate and form regulation. Under the white paper's guidelines, a company would have to meet any two of the following criteria to be considered an ECP: have a net worth of more than $50 million; have net revenues/sales of more than $100 million; employ more than 500 people; use a risk manager; have aggregate premiums of more than $500,000; be a nonprofit or public entity with an annual budget or assets of at least $45 million; or be a municipality with a population exceeding 50,000.

In addition to a full exemption from rate and form regulation for policies sold to ECPs, the white paper endorsed a move toward more competitive rating systems in the commercial lines market. The NAIC white paper recommends that the NAIC draft a model law on rate and form regulation incorporating the concepts of the white paper that would replace existing NAIC model laws.

The Unregulated Market A new regulatory concern grew out of the proliferation of risk-retention groups and purchasing groups under the Risk Reten-

tion Act of 1986. Some regulators and industry executives have expressed concerns about the long-term implications of the alternatives to commercial insurance such as captives and risk-retention groups on state insurance regulation and the conventional insurance market. The decade of the 1980s witnessed a substantial increase in the number of premium dollars to these mechanisms and away from the regulated environment. Captives and risk-retention groups are more loosely regulated than insurers in the conventional market. As a growing part of aggregate premium dollars moves to the unregulated sector, the incidence of failure is likely to be greater. This problem is exacerbated by the fact that state guaranty funds are not applicable to the nontraditional mechanisms. Insurers are also concerned over the prospect that more and more of the better-than-average insureds will move to the alternative mechanisms. This could create a burden for regulated insurers, which will be required to provide coverage to the residual pool of insureds.

CHANGES IN THE INSURANCE INDUSTRY

Not only will the environment within which the insurance industry functions change in the future, but there will undoubtedly also be changes within the industry itself. From the consumer's perspective, the most significant changes within the industry are likely to be shifts in the pattern of distribution and the development of new forms of protection.

Changes in Industry Structure

The number of insurance companies continues to change and will undoubtedly change in the future. During the past decade, there have been a number of mergers, acquisitions, and consolidations that have been defining characteristics in the insurance industry. These consolidations are occurring not only nationally, but also internationally. Some reflect the convergence in the three segments of the financial services industry,[11] while others represent market

positioning within the insurance industry. Among the major property and liability insurers, there have been more than 500 mergers, acquisitions, and consolidations over the past decade.

Besides the decrease in the number of insurers, a number of insurers have changed their organization structure, either by demutualizing or reorganizing under mutual holding company laws enacted by the state. It is likely that the number of insurers in both the life insurance field and in the property and liability field will continue to decline as mergers and consolidations continue.

Changes in Distribution Patterns

In the future there will undoubtedly be further changes in the distribution patterns within both the property and liability and the life and health insurance fields. The major changes in this area will involve the system of compensating agents and banks in insurance.

Changes in Agents' Compensation Although the practice has been restricted primarily to larger accounts, there is a movement within the industry toward a fee system of compensating agents and brokers for their services in lieu of the traditional commission system. The concept has met serious opposition from some quarters, but for larger accounts it has considerable merit. The traditional system of paying the agent or broker by commission ties the compensation to the hazard faced by the insured, which seems illogical. It seems difficult to justify a higher compensation to the agent for handling one account simply because the insured has a frame building, when the work involved is no greater (and may be less) than that done for another account where the insured owns a brick building. The challenges to antirebating laws discussed in Chapter 6 are likely to increase, which may speed the movement toward a net pricing system.

Convergence of Financial Services Market Globally The debate over the combination of banking and insurance in the United States occurred against a backdrop of a convergence of financial services globally. Few other countries have legislation similar to our Glass–Steagall Act and in many nations the consolidation of banking and insurance operations has been occurring at a rapid pace. In fact, the combination of banking and insurance in Europe has given rise to a phenomenon known as *bancassurance,* the full integra-

[11] In April 1998, Citicorp and the Travelers Group announced plans to merge, a consolidation that was technically illegal at the time it was announced. Had it not been for the repeal of the Glass-Steagall Act, after a two-year grace period under the Bank Holding Company Act, Travelers would be required to divest itself of the activities that conflicted with the Glass-Steagall Act. In 2001, Citicorp announced its decision to divest itself of Travelers' property and liability operations.

tion of retail banking and insurance operations.[12] Competition from foreign banks that can freely underwrite and distribute insurance products gave these insurers a competitive advantage over U.S. insurers, which could not offer the same wide mix of insurance, commercial banking, and investment banking services. With the passage of GLBA, this will now change.

The convergence of the financial services industry in other countries has occurred in two waves, the first of which involved the merger of insurance and security brokerage firms.[13] Many large U.S. life insurers owned or were affiliated with securities broker-dealers prior to the enactment of GLBA. The second wave of mergers—primarily outside the United States—involved the merger of banking and insurance. Whether the convergence follows the same pattern in the U.S. remains to be seen.

Changes in Forms of Coverage

The future will undoubtedly witness a variety of new forms of coverage to address emerging and still-unrecognized exposures related to e-commerce. E-commerce, the umbrella term for the technologies and processes that automate business operations, has produced a variety of new risks, both for businesses and individuals. The Internet, by design, is inherently insecure, which facilitates the flow of information between computers. This design allows knowledgeable people who have the proper tools to intercept and modify data during transmission. In addition, the interconnectivity of the system exposes data storage systems to compromise. Risks related to the Internet and e-commerce include the destruction, altering, or theft of data by hackers, unscrupulous vendors, and former or present disgruntled employees. They also include viruses and other malicious programs that can infect the data storage and operating systems and cause enormous loss.[14]

Finally, the Internet raises the specter of a whole range of new potential e-commerce liability claims. Businesses operating through the Web are in the publishing business, whether or not they realize it. This means that they are subject to the same exposures that were previously limited to traditional publishing companies: copyright and trademark infringement, libel, and invasion of privacy.

Most standard forms of business coverage were created long before the internet became a business tool. As a result, policy provisions do not address the types of risk that have developed with the information age. In those instances in which the wording of the contract provides coverage where none was intended, insurers are moving to remove the ambiguities (and the coverage). At the same time that insurance companies have been rewriting existing policy forms to specifically exclude cyber-risk exposures, they have also been developing new forms of coverage to address these exposures.

New policies designed to protect organizations conducting business via the Internet have already appeared. Typically, these policies protect against claims for fraudulent use of customers' credit and debit cards, infringement of copyright and other intellectual property rights, and misuse of confidential information. Other specialized policies protect against claims for damage to Web sites by third parties, loss caused by unauthorized access to Web sites by persons outside the organization, and liability claims.

This is new territory for insurers, in which the full nature and scope of the exposures are still emerging. The challenges in meeting these risks will undoubtedly involve a period of trial and error and some experimentation. Because the old risks will remain, the period of challenge will also be a period of enormous opportunity for the industry.

GLOBALIZATION OF INSURANCE

Although the United States has traditionally dominated the world insurance market, its domination has declined over the past three decades as insurers outside the United States have increased their share of the world premium volume. In 1970, the United States controlled 70 percent of the world premium volume. By 2000, it had fallen to 32 percent. The three largest insurance companies in the world are Japanese.

[12] ING Group, the largest financial services group in the Netherlands, is often cited as a *bancassurance* success story. Although many European banks now sell insurance, ING was the first to implement wholesale mergers between banks and insurers.

[13] Among the more important 1997 acquisitions and mergers, Travelers acquired Salomon Brothers, Inc.; the Swiss insurer, Zurich Group, acquired Kemper Corporation and Scudder Stevens and Clark. Shortly after these acquisitions, the Zurich Group and B.A.T. Industries agreed to merge their insurance and financial services operations.

[14] According to a report by Swiss reinsurance, of the $10.6 billion in catastrophe losses incurred by the insurance industry in the United States in 2000, nearly one-fourth resulted from a single man-made event—the "I love you" computer virus.

A part of the growing percentage of world premiums written by foreign insurers is simply a reflection of the growth in the gross national product of foreign countries relative to the United States. As economic activity increases in a nation, the premiums written to protect assets against loss also increase. Thus, a part of the decreased share of world premiums indicated for the United States results not from a decrease in U.S. premiums, but from an increase in premiums in other nations. Individuals and businesses in a particular country tend to purchase their insurance from domestic insurers and the growth of other economies has brought a corresponding growth in the insurance premiums in other countries.

Multinational Corporations

A point that is sometimes ignored in the discussion of changing shares in the world insurance market is the role that the growth of U.S. corporations abroad has had on the distribution of insurance expenditures. Many of what we think of as U.S. corporations are actually multinational corporations. A multinational corporation (MNC) is one that not only sells, but produces in foreign markets. It is contrasted with what may be called a *limited international corporation,* whose commitment to the international market is limited and whose major activity in the world economy is exporting. The U.S. corporations operating overseas customarily do so through subsidiaries, often incorporated in the various countries where they carry on business. Although U.S. corporations abroad would often prefer to purchase their insurance from U.S. insurers, regulatory restrictions and trade barriers have sometimes prevented this. Recently, however, the regulatory barriers that precluded international insurance transactions, like other international trade barriers, have been gradually disappearing.

Financial Services Trade Barriers

Governments worldwide are deregulating and privatizing, and, with deregulation, barriers to trade have also fallen. European countries, in particular, have been working for years to promote competition through the continent by removing their various national trade barriers. The leader in this movement

is the European Union, whose fifteen member nations have agreed to a phased-in mutual reduction of restrictive laws and regulations. For insurance and other financial services, the European Commission in Brussels has issued a series of twenty-one directives to harmonize insurance regulations in member countries. Since these directives became effective in 1994, an insurer licensed and regulated by one member nation has authorization to operate anywhere in the European Union.[15]

In 1997, a World Trade Organization pact, known as the General Agreement on Trade in Services (GATS), further opened international markets for insurance and financial services generally. The pact is the first multilateral, legally enforceable agreement covering trade and investment in financial services. As such, it provides a framework to reduce or eliminate government barriers that prevent financial services from being freely provided across national borders or that discriminate against firms with foreign ownership.[16] Liberalization in many cases will be phased in over several years after the agreement goes into effect in 1999. Provisions of the WTO agreement became effective for China insurance markets after the People's Republic of China became a member of the WTO late in 2001.

In November 1997, the Japanese Prime Minister announced that Japan would undertake an extensive deregulation of Japan's financial system. The exact nature of the reforms and the timetable for implementation are uncertain, but, if it occurs, the deregulation will open financial markets to foreign competitors and will likely end the compartmentalization of Japanese financial services.

Foreign Insurers in the United States

Coincident with their preparations to capitalize on the opening of European markets, some foreign insurers moved to expand their writings in the

[15] The second phase of the European Union occurred on January 1, 1999 when it became the European Monetary Union (EMU) and the participating countries began to adopt a common monetary unit, the *euro.* The *euro* officially replaced domestic currencies for all purposes on January 1, 2002. The introduction of the euro will create a quasi-unified monetary economy larger than the United States, one potentially worth $8.6 trillion 1998 dollars.
[16] John Jennings, "WTO Agreement: Not Perfect But Good Enough," *National Underwriter, Property & Casualty/Risk Management Edition* (December 22, 1997), p. 1.

United States. Although foreign insurers wrote only about 8 percent of the total premiums in the United States in 1999, many authorities are predicting that the U.S. market will experience major competition from international insurers, including companies from the United Kingdom, France, Germany, and the Netherlands. Companies in these nations are well capitalized, and are seeking areas for expansion. One way in which foreign companies can enter the United States is by acquiring U.S. insurers. Foreign insurers have made a number of significant acquisitions during the 1990s.[17]

Although few Japanese insurers have indicated an inclination to enter the U.S. market, there are signs that this could change. Tokyo Fire and Marine and Nippon Life have both acquired U.S. subsidiaries. With the expansion of Japanese investment in the United States, Japanese insurers will probably increase their presence in the United States to provide coverage for U.S. subsidiaries of Japanese companies they insure in Japan.

U.S. Insurers Abroad

Although less than 5 percent of the U.S. insurance industry's premium writings is generated in foreign countries, there are 60 to 70 U.S. insurers that have established a significant presence abroad. At the top of this list is the American International Group (AIG). AIG is the largest commercial and industrial insurer in the United States, and over one-half its total operating income comes from foreign sources. AIG is the largest non-Japanese life insurance operation in Japan, as well as the largest non-Japanese property and liability insurance operation. Other leading U.S. insurers with a significant presence in the overseas and international market include CIGNA, Chubb, New York Life, the Principal Finan-

cial Group, and the St. Paul Fire and Marine Insurance Company. One motivation of U. S. insurers that establish an overseas presence is the desire to serve U.S. corporations operating abroad. An equally important goal is to participate in the premium growth that will occur in a number of foreign countries in the near future, which will by far exceed the growth in U.S. premiums. A number of countries have privatized or are considering privatizing their national retirement schemes, generating intense interest from U.S. life insurers.

Major U.S. brokerage firms have also established a presence in many foreign countries, and have contracts with the foreign insurers. In fact, with a few exceptions, such as AIG, U.S. brokers have become international at a faster rate than U.S. insurers. Even brokers who do not have offices in foreign countries have established working relationships with affiliate agencies abroad, giving them access to foreign markets and providing a network through which they can serve the foreign insurance needs of their U.S. clients.

The globalization of insurance will undoubtedly accelerate with the changes in the financial services industry and the elimination of restrictions on cross-border insurance sales. The extent to which U.S. insurers will participate in the international premiums that will now become available remains to be seen.

A NEW PROBLEM—THE TERRORISM EXPOSURE

It has been said, without exaggeration, that the events of September 11, 2001 forever changed America. Like so many other sectors of the economy, the insurance industry faces new problems as a result of the September 11 attack. Estimates of the insured losses arising from the attack range from $20 billion to $70 billion and included not only property and liability coverages, but life insurance losses as well. The implications for the insurance industry and insurance buyers, however, go far beyond the losses that insurers sustained in the attack.

Shortly after the events, the insurance industry began to react to the existence of the potentially catastrophic exposure from terrorism, previously unrecognized in insurance underwriting and pricing. Although many forms of insurance exclude acts of war, as noted in Chapter 25, legal precedent holds that acts of terrorism do not fall within the war exclusion. Almost immediately after the attack, reinsurers

[17] These acquisitions include the purchase in 1990 of Fireman's Fund for $3.3 billion by Germany's $54 billion-in-assets Allianz. In addition to this major acquisition, Zurich Insurance of Switzerland acquired Maryland Casualty Insurance Company, Winterthur of Switzerland acquired General Casualty, and Home Insurance Company was acquired by the Trygg-Hansa Group of Sweden and Industrial Mutual of Finland. In 1993, financially troubled Mutual Benefit Life Insurance Company sold its group health, accident, and life business to the Belgium-based N.V. AMEV, through its U.S. subsidiary, AMEV Holdings, Inc. During the 1990s, the Netherlands' ING Group purchased Equitable of Iowa, Aetna's life insurance operations, and Reliastar. AXA, an insurance group based in France, purchased the Equitable Life Assurance Society of the United States.

world-wide announced that they would exclude terrorism from their reinsurance contracts in the future, most of which were scheduled for renewal on January 1, 2002. Faced with the prospect of catastrophic losses from future attacks, the insurance industry lobbied congress for some type of backstop reinsurance program that would cap industry losses from terrorism in the future. Uncertain about the prospect of congressional action, insurers also sought approval of terrorism exclusions from state insurance departments. The two leading advisory organizations, the Insurance Services Office and the American Association of Insurance Services, created optional endorsements for use by insurers, which were subsequently filed in all states. Most state insurance departments withheld action on the exclusions, pending resolution of the congressional debate.

Legislation to create a federal terrorism reinsurance program was passed by the House. Although there was considerable activity in the Senate, no bill emerged and Congress adjourned in December without enacting legislation. Immediately after Congress adjourned, the NAIC recommended that states begin approving terrorism exclusions for commercial line policies. Recognizing that Congress might act when it returned in January 2002, the NAIC recommended that the approval be conditional, subject to withdrawal 15 working days after the President signed legislation for a federal terrorism backstop program.

The NAIC recommendation attempted to differentiate between the potentially catastrophic type of terrorism that occurred on September 11 and the more isolated terrorist acts that have been covered in the past (e.g., bombing of abortion clinics and acts of radical animal rights groups). More specifically, the NAIC recommended that a terrorism exclusion apply only when total industry-wide losses from the terrorist event exceeds $25 million or where the terrorist act includes nuclear materials or the dispersal of biochemical materials. In the case of commercial liability policies, terrorist acts would also be excluded if 50 or more people were killed or seriously injured. Due to the statutory nature of the benefits under workers compensation insurance, an exclusion cannot be used with workers compensation policies. In addition, the laws in many states require that ensuing fire be covered.

By mid-January 2002, 47 jurisdictions (including Puerto Rico and the District of Columbia) had begun approving the terrorism exclusions for commercial lines, essentially adopting the NAIC's recommendations. The exclusions remained under consideration in five states (California, Florida, Georgia, New York, and Texas).

The terrorism exclusion is optional and insurers can, of course, continue to provide broader coverage. A limited market for terrorism insurance began to develop early in 2002, with some U.S. insurers, Lloyds of London, and some Bermuda-based insurers offering limited amounts of coverage.

Although the prospects for federal legislation appear questionable, it is conceivable that congress will act to provide some type of reinsurance backup program for the terrorism exposure. If legislation is enacted, it could include a sunset provision, after which the program will terminate. Thereafter, the problem of insurance against international terrorism will need to be addressed by the industry.

The arguments for and against a federal reinsurance program have developed along two lines. Those who favor a federal reinsurance solution argue that international acts of terrorism such as occurred on September 11—like war—is a fundamental risk. It is uncontrollable by the individual and the potential magnitude of losses exceeds the insurance industry's capital capacity. Only the federal government, with its ability to tax, has the capacity to address losses of the magnitude that now threaten the nation.

Those who oppose a federal reinsurance program argue that businesses of all types are exposed to loss from terrorism and that a federal reinsurance program would represent a bailout of the insurance industry.

The exposure to terrorism losses creates a variety of issues that will need to be resolved. If reinsurance is not available from private insurers or from the government, insurers will be reluctant to provide coverage, a possibility that has serious consequences not only for property owners but for creditors and lenders as well.

SOME PERSISTENT PROBLEMS

Although the future of the insurance industry appears bright, a number of unresolved problems remain. In general, these problems have existed for a long time, but they have increased somewhat in recent years.

The AIDS Problem

One serious issue facing the life and health insurance segments of the industry in the immediate future is the

growth of acquired immunodeficiency syndrome or AIDS and the difficulties that both life insurers and health insurers will have in dealing with the problem.

The most immediate difficulty arising out of the spread of AIDS is the cost of medical expenses associated with the disease, a problem that has serious implications for the health insurance field. Victims of AIDS who do not have health insurance at the time they contract the disease find it almost impossible to obtain coverage except through state insurance pools. Even here, however, the cost is sometimes prohibitive.

The spread of AIDS is also a serious problem for the life insurance industry. Infection with AIDS carries an additional mortality risk of 2000 to 6000 percent, which is significantly greater than the risk for virtually any other health impairment. AIDS ranks as the tenth leading cause of death in the country. For persons in the 25 to 44 age group, it is the third leading cause of death. Because persons infected with AIDS incur abnormally high mortality, they are generally considered uninsurable by private insurers, and underwriting for life insurance has become a focal point in the debate over AIDS and insurance.

A study published by the Society of Actuaries in 1987 concluded that the life insurance industry is facing a financial burden conservatively estimated to be $50 billion in life insurance claims for AIDS-related deaths on life insurance already in force. The study adds that if the insurance industry is prevented from screening for AIDS virus, claims from newly written insurance will double this figure, threatening the solvency of some insurers. A survey by the American Council of Life Insurance and the Health Insurance Association of America suggests that insurers are subject to an element of adverse selection by persons who are subject to the AIDS virus.[18]

Given the potential for adverse selection, insurance companies are concerned that the result of the debate may be the loss of their traditional right to evaluate applicants and reject those who have an abnormally high loss potential. The conflicting view is that some precautions are required to ensure that insurers do not unfairly discriminate in their efforts to avoid the AIDS burden. For example, since a large percentage of infected people are male homosexuals, regulators are concerned that insurers will attempt to shortcut the underwriting process and underwrite on the basis of sexual preference, rather than attempting to determine if the applicant is actually infected. In 1987, the NAIC adopted underwriting guidelines that prohibit consideration of a person's sexual preference in underwriting insurance. The guidelines were endorsed by the American Council of Life Insurance and the Health Insurance Association of America, which had hoped that in return for this endorsement the NAIC could be persuaded to recognize the need for insurers to be able to test for infection by the AIDS virus.[19]

AIDS-related claims will remain an important problem for the life and health insurance industry as long as the disease itself remains a problem for society, reflecting once again the way in which the problems facing the insurance industry mirror those facing society.

Genetic Testing

In recent years, researchers have made great strides in understanding the structure of human DNA and, in particular, identifying genes that contribute or cause physical conditions. With this increased information, it will become possible for insurers to use genetic testing to identify individuals likely to contract particular diseases. The potential impact on life and health insurance underwriting is enormous.

Some critics argue that insurers should not be permitted to use the information gathered from genetic testing in their underwriting decisions. Their rationale is similar to that used by some states when they attempted to prohibit insurers from testing for the AIDS virus. If insurers have access to information that identifies a genetic disorder, they may charge a higher premium, exclude coverage for the condition, or simply reject the application. In addition to the affordability and availability implications, there are confidentiality concerns when third parties have access to the results of a genetic test.

When insurers are denied access to this information, of course, significant adverse selection will

[18] The survey reported that the average AIDS-related claims for individual and group life insurance were $30,500 and $27,300, respectively, compared with average claims of $7300 and $13,800 for all life insurance claims. Michael J. Crowell and Walter H. Hoskins. *AIDS, HIV Mortality and Life Insurance* (Society of Actuaries, Schaumburg, Ill.: 1987).

[19] Insurance departments in California, Massachusetts, New York, and the District of Columbia adopted regulations prohibiting the use of the AIDS antibody test (also known as ELISA, HTLV-III, or the HIV test) as an underwriting tool. The regulations were challenged by the insurance industry and overturned by the courts.

result. Individuals who have undergone genetic testing and become aware that they face a high risk of illness will seek to buy large amounts of insurance. Without access to that same information, the premium charged by insurers would not appropriately reflect the risk being assumed. The result is inadequate pricing and cross-subsidization between those with and without genetic disorders.

Crime and Its Associated Costs

Most Americans today rank crime as a major problem for the nation. Because much of the property that is damaged by vandalism, arson, and looting is covered by insurance, crime is a major concern for the property and liability insurance industry.

Arson According to the National Fire Protection Association, arson accounts for roughly one out of every seven structural fires (as opposed to vehicle or outdoor fires). Some of these fires were intentionally set to defraud insurers, but others were set by persons with no direct financial interest in the property. In fact, less than 15 percent of arson suspects are motivated by a desire to defraud an insurer. The major cause of arson is vandalism, which is attested to by the fact that the majority of those arrested for arson are young people. Fires caused by arson cost the insurance industry literally billions of dollars annually.[20]

Vehicle Thefts According to the FBI, vehicle theft is the fastest-growing type of crime in the United States. Combined with automobile insurance fraud, it has caused insurance costs to escalate sharply.

Crimes Against Property Crime against property—burglary, robbery, and theft—is growing faster than the population. In addition to the loss of property that is taken or destroyed, many criminal acts also result in bodily injury to the victims of the crime. Damage and theft of property and the attendant bodily injuries inflate insurers' loss ratios and account for a significant part of total insurance claims.

Insurance Fraud In addition to criminal acts against property such as arson and theft, insurers also suffer losses as a result of fraudulent claims by professional criminals. Insurance fraud has been rampant in the area of health insurance, where unethical physicians collaborate with the criminals to document fictitious claims. Staged automobile accidents are another scam that has been prevalent in some parts of the country.

Although criminal acts are clearly a problem for insurers, they are also a problem for insurance buyers. Based on what the reader has learned about the way in which insurance operates, it should be clear that the increased loss costs that result from criminal activity such as arson, vehicle theft, and crimes against property are passed on to insureds by insurance companies in the form of higher rates. Policyholders pay for losses resulting from these criminal acts in the same way that they pay for the inflated claims by ordinary policyholders who exaggerate their claims. Law-abiding citizens who would never think of stealing sometimes have no qualms about inflating a property damage claim so that the recovery will be sufficient to cover the deductible that would otherwise apply. For insurers and their policyholders, the result is the same as the losses occasioned by arson and other overt criminal acts.

Availability and Affordability of Insurance

Another troublesome issue facing the property and liability insurance industry today is the high cost of insurance for some segments of the insurance-buying public and the response that this high cost has generated among those buyers and among certain other groups. Increasingly, the demand is heard that insurance must be made available to all who want and need it and that it must be made available at affordable rates.

Although the main issue for some people today is still the question of the method we should use to provide the subsidy to those who demand availability and affordability, the entire debate has prompted a reappraisal of the systems that have been used in the past to subsidize some buyers. Increasingly, it is recognized that the distinctions among the approaches to subsidization are artificial and that in the last analysis it makes little difference if the subsidy is granted through an industry pool, through the tax system, or through the rating system. In each case, one group in society pays a part of the costs that would—without government interference—fall on a

[20] Although insurers rightfully deny payment to arsonists when arson can be proved, the provisions of property policies related to mortgagees that we discussed in Chapter 24 allow the mortgagee or other lender to collect for a loss, even when it is established that the owner torched the property. In addition, as explained in Chapter 25, the NAIC model law aimed at preventing discrimination against domestic abuse victims requires an insurer to pay claims to an innocent abuse victim for intentional property damage caused by a third party, even when that party was a coinsured under the homeowners policy.

different group. The issue of subsidies in insurance remains a little-understood subject.

Lack of Consumer Sophistication

Another persistent problem facing the insurance industry is the lack of sophistication on the part of consumers. Although many insurance buyers have become more knowledgeable over the past few decades, the majority of consumers misunderstand the purpose of insurance, and this misunderstanding creates widespread difficulties for the insurance industry.

Much of the dissatisfaction with insurance is based on a faulty idea of insurance and how it operates. With little notion of the way insurance works or the principles of risk management, many consumers feel that an insurance policy is not worthwhile unless it covers every possible small loss. They find buying insurance a frustrating experience and are frequently disappointed or dissatisfied with their purchase. They complain that the cost of insurance is too high, that deductibles are simply a scheme developed by insurers to get out of paying their just claims, and that the entire insurance mechanism is some sort of "rip-off."

By this time, it is hoped that the reader has gained a sufficient understanding to see just why many criticisms are unjustified. As we have learned, insurance operates on a very simple principle: Individuals exposed to loss contribute to a fund, and those who suffer losses are compensated out of this fund. Cutting away the complicated details of the mechanism, it is a system in which the losses of a few are shared by the many. There is nothing magical or mysterious about it, unless one considers the law of averages to be magical or mysterious. When losses are high, rates must also be high. The insurance industry is very much like a conduit or pipe. Money is paid into one end of the conduit and flows out the other. Most of the complaints have focused on the amount of money going in, ignoring the fact that the money going in is a function of the money going out. In a sense, insurance is merely a mirror that reflects the loss experience throughout the economy. Although considerable progress has been made in consumer education, much remains to be done.

Unwarranted Criticism of the Insurance Industry

The insurance industry is a convenient target, and criticism of the industry abounds. Much of this criticism is contradictory. Some complain that the insurance industry makes excessive profits; others complain that many insurers are on the brink of insolvency; still others allege both, apparently oblivious to the contradiction.

The most common criticism is the allegation that property and liability insurers operate as a cartel, fixing prices and raising rates in concert with impunity. This theory is exemplified in the following comments of one industry critic:

> The commercial liability crisis of the mid-1980s was preceded by a medical malpractice insurance crisis in the mid-1970s, and by an automobile liability insurance crisis in the mid-1960s. The well-recognized pattern of hard markets giving way to soft markets and back and forth is facilitated by the McCarran-Ferguson antitrust exemption. The 1945 law allows insurers to raise rates in concert without the threat of federal prosecution.[21]

Industry critics are particularly fond of the charge that because of its exemption from the federal antitrust laws, the industry operates as a cartel, engaging in conspiracies to increase prices. The allegation ignores the obvious fact that if insurers conspire to increase rates, they must also conspire to decrease them. Periods in which insurance prices increase significantly usually follow periods of intense price cutting, when competition drives rates below their actuarial level. When insurance prices decrease below actuarially sound levels, insurers are accused of mismanagement. When premiums increase during the hard phase of the cycle, they are accused of gouging consumers or of conspiracy.

The conspiracy idea is a favorite explanation of industry critics for high insurance costs, availability problems, and underwriting cycles, which they attribute to collusion and intrigue within the industry. There is a much simpler and more believable explanation: that the industry is fiercely competitive and that it therefore exhibits the characteristics of a competitive industry.

The most frustrating complaint to many within the industry is the criticism directed at the industry when it attempts to price its products on an actuarial basis. The simple fact is that there are some types of insurance that are demonstrably unprofitable for insurers.

[21] Linda Lipsen, "The Evolution of Products Liability as a Federal Policy Issue," *Tort Law and the Public Interest* (New York: The American Assembly, W. W. Norton, 1991).

Given the choice between insuring exposures on which they are virtually guaranteed to lose money and those on which they can reasonably expect to earn money, insurance companies logically choose the latter. One criticism of which some critics are especially fond is that "insurance companies refuse to write some types of insurance simply because those lines are unprofitable." It is a commentary on the complexity of the issues and the confusion in which society finds itself that this criticism goes unanswered.

Those who criticize the reluctance of insurers to write unprofitable classes of business when their overall profitability is satisfactory are, in effect, arguing for cross-subsidies. They would like to make the insurance industry a mechanism for taxing and redistributing wealth. The question is really whether insurers should overcharge buyers of homeowners insurance to subsidize the cost of product liability insurance, or whether premiums for fire and marine insurance should be loaded to cover losses under malpractice insurance. These questions involve complex value judgments that should not be made lightly.

It is undeniable that the insurance industry—like virtually all segments of society—includes some ethically challenged individuals who have few qualms about engaging in dishonest or questionable practices detrimental to consumers. Identifying and eliminating these undesirables is an important responsibility, both for regulators and other members of the industry. It is of no help, in this respect, when bogus criticism of legitimate business strategies, based on the law of averages, are mischaracterized as a nefarious conspiracy to exploit consumers. Whether the misplaced criticism stems from ignorance on the part of the critics about how insurance works, or from some hidden agenda, it obstructs and interferes with efforts to deal with the real crimes and misdemeanors that may actually occur.

CAREER OPPORTUNITIES IN INSURANCE

Economists predict substantial increases in this nation's gross national product and personal income over the next two decades, with corresponding increases in per capita income. Rising population, housing, businesses, and income will be accompanied by a heightened awareness of the need for financial security. Given the long-range growth expected throughout the economy, with new advances in technology, new products, and higher personal incomes,

the continued expansion of the insurance industry seems assured. Regardless of possible inroads by government, the future of the industry appears bright indeed. Increased security needs and the ability to pay for them point to a tremendous growth for the insurance business. This will lead to an increase in the industry's employment needs, and the nation's insurers will be offering thousands of career opportunities to college graduates.

Today's insurers carry on a growing number of activities: rehabilitation of the injured, product safety, industrial hygiene, and medical research. Because the industry serves the needs of consumers in many ways, a broad variety of career positions has been created to provide these services. It would be difficult to find another industry that offers such diversified positions as mathematician, nurse, lawyer, computer analyst, and engineer in addition to the more traditional insurance careers in sales, investments, underwriting, and claims. Regardless of whether the individual's academic work has been in business administration, engineering, economics, mathematics, or computer applications, he or she is likely to find an attractive career in the highly diversified insurance industry.

Broadly speaking, employment opportunities in the insurance field may be divided into two major categories: sales and nonsales. Positions within each of these categories exist in both the property and liability industry and the life and health insurance fields. In addition to jobs within the insurance industry proper, employment opportunities also can be found in the growing field of risk management and corporate insurance buying.

Opportunities in the Insurance Sales Field

Sales positions in the property and liability field exist with direct-writing companies and with independent agencies. Most direct-writing companies recruit on college campuses, seeking sales representatives at the same time they hire other specialists. Although independent agencies have a continuing need for personal lines and commercial lines producers, most agencies do not have a sophisticated personnel recruitment programs and so do not recruit on college campuses. Positions with independent agencies therefore must be sought out by the prospective applicant.

Life insurance general agents and district sales managers generally conduct intensive recruiting campaigns on college campuses. Because the turnover rate

in life insurance sales is high, there is a constant need for new agents. Many companies have had moderate success in reducing the turnover rate through more intensive selection procedures and better training.

Sales positions in the insurance field demand a high degree of expertise. Insurance agents do not sell a standard tangible product, but a special kind of financial security that must be tailored to meet the needs of the individual policyholder. In many situations, the role of the agent is far removed from the stereotype of the high-pressure, fast-talking sales type. The professional agent functions as an adviser to his or her clients, filling a role similar to that of the attorney or accountant.

Although the demands on those who enter the field of insurance sales are great, so also are the rewards. Insurance sales positions with pay based on a commission rather than salary rank among the highest in the nation in potential earnings.

Nonsales Opportunities in the Insurance Industry

Although many insurance agencies employ nonsales personnel, the person seeking a nonsales position within the insurance industry would be best advised to seek employment with an insurance company.

In the property and liability field, insurance companies recruit actuaries,[22] underwriters, claims personnel, and marketing representatives in addition to the more traditional noninsurance positions found in every business. Underwriters, as the reader will recall, are charged with the responsibility of deciding which of the various applicants for insurance should be accepted. Claims persons handle the delicate problems of loss adjustment. Marketing representatives generally serve as a link between the company and its agency force, although in the case of direct-writing companies, the marketing representative may deal directly with the consumer.

Life insurance companies offer positions similar to those of the property and liability firms. Many life insurance companies have their own staff of actuaries. Special marketing representatives are also employed by the life insurance companies to deal with group programs and pension plans and to assist the company's agents in the technical details of more complicated life insurance cases.

Positions with both property and liability insurers and life insurers are challenging and rewarding. Increasingly, the insurance company employee is performing a decision-oriented job, requiring independent judgment and a greater degree of individual responsibility at every level. Executives in the insurance field have traditionally risen from within the industry. This practice of internal promotion is an additional advantage to people choosing the insurance business as a career. Capable people have a greater probability of rapid promotion because of the great expansion the industry foresees during the next 20 years, which is going to result in a shortage of managerial personnel.

Salary levels in both the property and liability field and the life and health insurance field vary with each company and in each region of the country. These positions typically pay less than insurance sales positions, but the U.S. Department of Labor reports that starting salaries for professional workers in the insurance industry are generally comparable with those for similar positions in other industries.

Another important factor to most employees is the industry's stability. Insurance buyers regard insurance as a necessity even during periods of economic recession, and to a large measure the insurance industry is immune to the up-and-down fluctuations of the economy.

Opportunities in the Risk Management Field

Risk management positions are sometimes difficult for the new college graduate to obtain. Many companies seeking to fill staff risk management positions prefer to hire seasoned and experienced personnel from the insurance industry itself. Although occasionally the risk management department of a large corporation will hire a trainee, these positions, like those in independent agencies, must generally be sought out by the applicant.

CONCLUDING OBSERVATION

The field of insurance continues to be an exciting one. It constantly faces new problems and challenges, somehow coping with each and surviving to go on to meet new problems. The changing nature of the industry makes it all the more attractive as a field of

[22] Larger property and liability insurers have their own staff of actuaries, while smaller companies usually use actuarial consultants.

endeavor. Few industries hold out the opportunity and excitement of a career in insurance today. Besides the challenging and rewarding work itself, the industry also offers many of the intangible factors that young men and women are seeking: the opportunity to render a worthwhile service to society, a socially useful career with high prestige, and greater than average personal rewards.

IMPORTANT CONCEPTS TO REMEMBER

Comprehensive Environmental Response, Compensation, and Liability Act (CERCLA)

Superfund
unregulated market
net pricing system

globalization of insurance
European Union

QUESTIONS FOR REVIEW

1. Explain the problems facing the Social Security system, Medicare, and health insurance in the future. In what way(s) are the problems related?

2. Identify and describe the changes in the tort system that may affect the insurance industry during the next decade.

3. Identify the features of the *Comprehensive Environmental Response, Compensation, and Liability Act* (CERCLA) that have made the Superfund program ineffective. What problems does the industry face with respect to environmental losses? What proposals have been made to address these problems?

4. Describe the major features of the proposals for addressing the insurance industry's exposure to catastrophe loss.

5. What are the significant changes that may be expected in the regulation of insurance during the next decade?

6. Describe the way in which future congressional action of EGTRRA-2001 has implications with respect to the demand for insurance.

7. Explain the significance of the Gramm, Leach, Bliley *Financial Services Modernization Act of 1999* to the insurance industry.

8. Describe the issues that face the life and health insurance industry as a result of advances in genetic testing.

9. Identify and describe the factors that are contributing to the globalization of insurance.

10. What is the impact of crime and fraud on the insurance industry?

QUESTIONS FOR DISCUSSION

1. Which of the factors discussed in this chapter do you personally believe will have the greatest impact on the insurance industry during the next decade? Why?

2. One of the chronic problems facing the insurance industry is the lack of consumer sophistication and the misconceptions on the part of insurance buyers regarding the purpose of insurance. What, in your opinion, can the insurance industry do to remedy this problem?

3. Do you think that there is a solution to the conflict between "capital's need for an adequate return and the public's entitlement to the security of the insurance product"? Should insurance companies be permitted to refuse to write those lines of insurance that are unprofitable?

4. What do you think of the employment outlook in the insurance industry? Do you think that it will be better, about the same, or worse than the situation in other fields?

5. What do you think is the most important principle you have learned in this course? Why?

SUGGESTIONS FOR ADDITIONAL READING

Brockmeier, Warren G. (ed.). *The Impact of Consumer Activism on the Insurance Industry.* Malvern, Pa.: Society of CPCU, 1991.

Ennsfellner, Karl C., and Mark S. Dorfman, "The Transition to a Single Insurance Market in the European Union." *Risk Management and Insurance Review,* vol. 1, no. 2 (Winter 1998).

Focus on the Future: The Insurance Industry Looks Toward the 21st Century. Malvern, Pa.: Society of Chartered Property Casualty Underwriters, 1987.

Huber, Peter. "The Environmental Liability Dilemma." *CPCU Journal,* vol. 40, no. 4 (December 1987).

Hutchin, James W. "Managing Risks in a Global Environment." *The John Liner Letter* (Fall 1995).

Insurance Services Office. *Long-Term Profitability: The Risk-Return Tradeoff.* New York: Insurance Services Office, 1990.

Long, John D. *Ethics, Morality, and Insurance.* Bloomington: Bureau of Business Research, Graduate School of Business, Indiana University, 1971.

Skipper, Harold D. Jr. *International Risk and Insurance: An Environmental-Managerial Approach.* Irwin, N.Y.: McGraw-Hill, 1998.

Slattery, Thomas J. "Globalization a Necessity for Insurers." *National Underwriter Property and Casualty Edition* (June 24, 1991).

WEB SITES TO EXPLORE

Coalition Against Insurance Fraud	http://www.insurancefraud.org
Environmental Protection Agency	http://www.epa.gov/
Global Risk Management Network	http://www.grmn.com/pages/welcome.asp
Institute for Global Insurance Education	http://www.igie.org/
Insurance Fraud Bureau	http://www.ifb.org/
Insurance Information Institute—Superfund	http://www.iii.org/media/SUPERFND.HTM
International Association of Insurance Fraud Agencies, Inc.	http://www.iaifa.org
National Disaster Coalition	http://www.naturaldisaster.org
National Insurance Crime Bureau	http://www.nicb.com
Risk World	http://www.riskworld.com/
The Insurance Job Center	http://connectyou.com/talent/

GLOSSARY

Abandonment the act of surrendering to the insurer all interest in the thing insured; it is generally conceded that damaged property cannot be abandoned to the insurer. One notable exception to this general rule occurs in ocean marine, where abandonment is merely one step in proving a loss.

Absolute Liability a legal doctrine under which one can be held liable even in the absence of negligence having been proven, as in the case of workers compensation.

Accelerated Benefits an optional benefit under life insurance policies under which the insurer agrees to prepay a part of the death benefit if the insured is stricken by a catastrophic illness or is confined to a nursing home.

Acceptance agreeing to terms by means of which a bargain is concluded and the parties are bound; the binding of an insurance contract by the insurer.

Accident an event or occurrence that is unforeseen and unintended.

Accident Insurance a form of health insurance against loss by accidental bodily injury.

Accidental Bodily Injury injury to the body of the insured as the result of an accident.

Accidental Death Benefit a provision added to a life insurance policy for payment of an additional benefit in case of death by accidental means; it is often referred to as "double indemnity."

Accidental Means appearing in some policies, the unexpected or undesigned cause of an accident; the "means" that caused the mishap must be accidental in order to claim policy benefits.

Accommodation Risk insurance written for an applicant that would normally be rejected by the insurer, but that is provided as a concession to the agency or a valued insured.

Accumulation Period a specified period of time, such as 90 days, during which the insured person must incur eligible medical expenses at least equal to the deductible amount in order to establish a benefit period under a major medical expense or comprehensive medical expense policy.

Acquisition Cost that portion of an insurance premium that represents the cost of producing the insurance business; it includes the agent's commission, the company field expense, and other related expenses.

Act of God Bond see Catastrophe Bonds.

Activities of Daily Living (ADL) everyday living functions such as eating, bathing, dressing, walking (sometimes called mobility), moving from place to place, toileting, and continence that serve as coverage triggers for long-term care insurance when the insured is unable to perform a specified number.

Actual Cash Value the limit of indemnification under the Standard Fire Policy and other property contracts; in most cases it is replacement cost minus depreciation.

Actuary a person professionally trained in the technical aspects of insurance and related fields, particularly in the mathematics of insurance such as the calculation of premiums, reserves, and other values.

Additional Interest one who may claim under, or is protected by, an insurance policy issued to another, as a mortgagee named in a fire policy.

Additional Living Expense insurance paying the extra expense involved in living elsewhere during the period of time it is impossible to remain in a dwelling that has been damaged by fire or another insured peril.

Adjustment Bureau an organization that contracts with insurers to provide loss settlement services on behalf of those insurers.

Adjustable Life Insurance a type of life insurance that allows the policyholder to change the plan of insurance, raise or lower the face amount of the policy, increase or decrease the premium, and lengthen or shorten the protection period.

Adjuster one who settles insurance claims; may be a salaried employee or an independent operator.

Administrative Services Only (ASO) Plan an arrangement under which an insurance carrier or an independent organization will, for a fee, handle the administration of claims, benefits, and other administration functions for a self-insured group.

Administrator a person authorized to administer the estate of a deceased person by the court; his or her duties are to collect assets of the estate, pay its debts, and distribute the residue to those entitled: he or she resembles an executor, who is appointed by the will of the deceased—the administrator is appointed by the court and not by the deceased and therefore must give security for the administration of the estate, called an administration bond.

Admiralty involving maritime law; concerning the high seas or navigable waters.

Admitted Assets those assets of an insurer that under state law can be taken into account in representing the financial position of the company.

Admitted Company an insurer of another state or country licensed under the laws of a state to do business in that state.

Advance Premium Mutual an insurance company owned by its policyholders that charges an advance premium that is expected to cover losses and expenses; policies may be assessable or nonassessable.

Adverse Selection the tendency of persons with a higher than average probability of loss to seek or continue insurance to a greater extent than do persons with an average or below average probability of loss.

Advisory Organization a cooperative rate-making body that is supported by member companies; advisory organizations collect loss statistics and publish trended loss costs.

Age Limit in accident, life, or automobile insurance, the age below which or above which an insurer refuses to insure an applicant.

Agent in property and casualty insurance, an individual authorized by an insurance company to create, modify, and terminate contracts of insurance; in life insurance a sales and service representative who is also called a "life underwriter."

Aggregate the greatest amount recoverable on account of a single loss or during a policy period, or on a single project.

Aggregate Indemnity in disability insurance, the maximum dollar amount that may be collected for any disability, period of disability, or under the policy.

Agreed Amount Endorsement a provision in fire insurance whereby the coinsurance clause is suspended if the insured carries an amount of insurance specified by the company (normally 90% or more of the value).

AIDS acquired immune deficiency syndrome. A fatal, incurable disease caused by a virus that can damage the brain and destroy the body's ability to fight off illness.

Alien Company an insurance company organized under the laws of a foreign country.

Alimony Insurance insurance designed to protect the insured against default in connection with payment of child support and alimony.

All-Risk a term commonly used by insurance people to describe broad forms of coverage; it is misleading because no property or liability insurance policy is truly an all-risk coverage. There is a concerted effort to eliminate use of this term and to replace it with the term *open peril*.

Allied Lines a term that has been adopted to refer to the lines of insurance that are allied with property insurance; these coverages provide protection against perils traditionally written by fire companies, such as sprinkler leakage, water damage, and earthquake.

Allocated Benefits in health insurance, coverage for which the maximum amount payable for specific services is itemized in the contract.

Allowable Charge in health insurance, the lesser of the actual charge, the customary charge and the prevailing charge. It is the amount on which Medicare will base its Part B payment.

Alternate Delivery Systems health services provided in other than an inpatient, acute-care hospital, which are designed to provide needed services in a more cost-effective manner.

Alternative markets mechanisms used to fund self-insurance. This includes captives, which are insurers owned by one or more non-insurers to provide owners with coverage. Risk-retention groups, formed by members of similar professions or businesses to obtain liability insurance, are also a form of self-insurance.

Ambulatory Care medical services that are provided on an outpatient (nonhospitalized) basis; services may include diagnosis, treatment, and rehabilitation.

Amendment a formal document changing the provisions of an insurance policy signed jointly by the insurance company officer and the policyholder or his authorized representative.

American Agency System the term applied to the system of insurance marketing in which the agent is an independent business operator rather than an employee of the company.

Amortized Value the amount at a given point in time to which the purchase price of a bond purchased at a discount or premium has been increased or decreased.

Annual Statement an insurer's financial report to insurance departments issued at the end of the year. The report is required by the various state insurance departments and is made according to a form agreed upon by the supervising authorities.

Annuitant the person during whose life an annuity is payable, usually the person to receive the annuity.

Annuity a contract that provides an income for a specified period of time, such as a number of years or for life.

Annuity Certain a contract that provides an income for a specified number of years, regardless of life or death, to the insured if living or to his or her beneficiary if deceased.

Application a statement of information made by a person applying for life insurance: it is used by the insurance company to determine the acceptability of the risk and the basis of the policy contract.

Apportionment a division according to the interests of the various parties therein, as the apportionment clause in a fire policy.

Appraisal an estimate of value, loss, or damage; see Arbitration.

Arbitration the submitting of a matter in dispute to the judgment of a specified number of disinterested persons called *arbitrators,* whose decision, called an *award,* is binding upon the parties.

Arson the criminal act of maliciously burning or attempting to burn property.

Assault an intentional, unlawful threat of bodily injury to another by force, or force unlawfully directed toward the person of another, under such circumstances as create wellfounded fear of imminent peril, coupled with apparent present ability to execute the attempt; see also Battery.

Assessable insurance to which the policyholder may be required to contribute in the event the company becomes unable to pay its losses; confined to certain mutual companies.

Assessment a charge sometimes levied against policyholders by certain types of companies.

Assessment Mutual an insurance company owned by its policyholders that issues policies under which the policyholders may be assessed for losses and expenses.

Assigned Risk an applicant for automobile or workers compensation insurance declined by one or more companies; such a risk may be assigned to designated companies as directed by recognized authority. The operation is called an "assigned risk plan."

Assignment the legal transfer of one person's interest in an insurance policy to another person.

Assured a person who has been insured by an insurance company or underwriter against loss.

Attachment a statutory legal remedy whereby one party may prevent removal of property belonging to another party, pending determination of a court action.

Attorney-in-Fact one appointed to act for another; the chief administrative officer of a reciprocal insurance group, who uses his or her power of attorney to commit the members of the group as insurers of each other; also one who executes a surety bond on behalf of the company being represented.

Attractive Nuisance a dangerous place, condition, or object that is particularly attractive to children; in these cases the courts have frequently held that where "attractiveness" exists, the owner is under a duty to take steps to prevent injury to those who may be attracted and the owner may be held liable for failure to do so.

Audit Premium the additional premium to which an insurer is entitled or the return premium to which the insured is entitled after an audit and refiguring of the base on which the original or deposit premium was charged.

Automatic Premium Loan a provision in a life insurance policy authorizing the insurer to pay automatically by means of a policy loan any premium not paid by the end of the grace period.

Automatic Treaty a reinsurance contract under which risks written by the reinsured are automatically assumed by the reinsurer subject only to the terms and conditions of the treaty.

Automobile Insurance Plan a state pool in which each automobile insurer in the state accepts a portion of the undesirable automobile insurance applicants; formerly called "assigned risk plans."

Automobile Liability Insurance a form of liability insurance that is specifically designed to indemnify for loss incurred through legal liability for bodily injury and damage to property of others caused by accident arising out of ownership or operation of an automobile.

Average Clause a coinsurance clause; a clause requiring an insured to purchase insurance for a stipulated portion of the entire value of the thing insured; see General Average; Particular Average.

Bail a deposit or assignment guaranteeing appearance of a defendant for a trial and which is forfeited if the defendant fails to appear at the stipulated time.

Bailee one who has possession of property belonging to another.

Bailment a delivery of goods or personal property by one person to another in trust for the execution of a special object upon or in relation to such goods. Bailment may be for the benefit of the bailee, for the benefit of the bailor, or for mutual benefit. In addition, bailment may be gratuitous or may be a bailment for hire.

Bailor the owner of property that has been delivered to and is in the possession of another.

Battery any unlawful beating or other wrongful physical violence or constraint inflicted upon a human being without his or her consent; see Assault.

Beneficiary one for whose benefit a contract is made: the person to whom a policy of insurance is payable.

Beneficiary, Contingent the person or persons designated to receive the death benefit if the primary beneficiary dies prior to the death of the insured.

Beneficiary, Irrevocable a beneficiary that cannot be altered by the insured, the insured having relinquished the right to change the beneficiary designation.

Beneficiary, Primary the person or persons designated to receive the benefits under the policy.

Betterment an improvement rendering property better than mere repairs would do.

Bid a proposal or offer.

Binder a written agreement (sometimes oral) whereby one party agrees to insure another party pending receipt of, and final action upon, the application.

Binding Receipt in life insurance, a receipt for a premium that accompanies the application for insurance. It binds the company if issuance is approved, to make the policy effective from the date of the receipt.

Blanket in property and liability, used to designate insurance that extends to more than one location, or one class of property or one employee.

Blanket Medical Expense (health) a provision for the payment of actual expense of hospital, nurse, surgical, and medical care subject to an overall maximum for all such expense.

Blue Cross an independent, nonprofit membership corporation providing protection against the costs of hospital care in a limited geographical area.

Blue Shield an independent, nonprofit membership corporation providing protection against the costs of surgery and other items of medical care in a limited geographical area.

Bodily Injury physical injury to a person.

Boiler and Machinery Insurance coverage for loss arising out of the operation of pressure, mechanical, and electrical equipment; it may cover loss suffered by the boiler and machinery itself and may include damage done to other property, as well as business interruption losses.

Bond a written agreement of obligation under seal; the person to whom the obligation is owed is called the "obligee"; the person liable for the undertaking is called the "obligor" or "principal," if a third party guarantees performance of the agreement, he is called the "surety."

Bottomry in the early days of marine insurance, a ship owner would borrow money on a mortgage on the ship, and the mortgage would provide that if the ship were lost, the borrower would not have to repay the loan. This was bottomry, which thus combined money lending with insurance. When cargo instead of hull was involved, it was called "respondentia."

Breach of Contract failure to comply with the terms or conditions incorporated in an insurance policy, frequently resulting in a restriction of coverage or a voiding of a policy itself.

Broker an individual who arranges and services insurance policies on behalf of the insurance buyer: he or she is the representative of the insured, although the broker receives compensation in the form of a commission from the company.

Bureau see Advisory Organization.

Burglary felonious abstraction of property from within premises by persons making felonious entry by force of which there are visible marks on the exterior.

Business Interruption insurance covering the loss of earnings resulting from, and occurring after, destruction of property; also called "use and occupancy insurance."

Business Life Insurance life insurance purchased by a business enterprise on the life of a member of the firm: it is often bought by partnerships to protect the surviving partners against loss caused by the death of a partner, or by a corporation to reimburse it for loss caused by the death of a key employee.

Businessowners Policy a multiple-line package policy for small businesses that includes property and liability coverages.

Cafeteria Plan an employee benefit arrangement under *Internal Revenue Code* Section 125 whereby an individual is allowed to select among certain employee benefits on a pretax basis rather than an after-tax basis.

Calendar Year Deductible in health insurance, the amount of expense that must be borne by the insured during a calendar year before the health insurance policy makes payment for loss.

Capital Sum a lump sum payable for dismemberment and sight losses.

Capitation a method of payment for health services in which a physician or hospital is paid a fixed, per capita amount for each person served regardless of the actual number of services provided to each person.

Captive Agent an agent who, by contract, represents only one company and its affiliates.

Captive Insurer an insurance company established by a parent firm for the purpose of insuring the parent's exposures.

Case Management The process by which all health related matters of a case are managed by a physician or nurse or designated health professional in an effort to match the intensity of services with the patient's need over time.

Cash Surrender Value the amount available in cash upon voluntary termination of a policy before it becomes payable by death or maturity.

Cash Value Accumulation Test one of two tests used in determining if a contract is a life insurance policy for the purpose of the *Internal Revenue Code;* see Cash Value Corridor Test.

Cash Value Corridor Test one of two tests used in determining if a contract is a life insurance policy for the purpose

of the *Internal Revenue Code;* see Cash Value Accumulation Test.

Casualty Insurance a classification of insurance coverages used in the monoline era consisting of workers compensation, liability, crime, glass, and boiler coverages, used to distinguish such coverages from "fire" or property coverages.

Catastrophe Bonds Bonds issued by an insurance company with the repayment terms linked to the company's losses from disasters, or acts of God. A loss exceeding a certain size automatically produces changes in the bonds' structure designed to the issuing insurer's capital base. Also known as "cat bonds" or "act of God bonds."

Catastrophe Loss a loss of unusual size; a shock loss; a very large loss.

CATEX A New York computer-based electronic market for the exchange of insurance risks by insurance companies and reinsurers.

Ceding Company a company that has placed reinsurance as distinguished from the company that has accepted the reinsurance.

Certified Professional Public Adjuster (CPPA) professional designation granted to public adjusters who pass a rigorous examination and meet specified eligibility requirements.

Cession the amount of a risk that the insurance company reinsures; the amount passed on to the reinsurer.

Change of Occupation Clause standard provision in health insurance policies that reduces benefits if the insured changes to a more hazardous occupation.

Chartered Life Underwriter (CLU) professional designation granted to persons in the life insurance field who pass a series of rigorous examinations and meet specified eligibility requirements.

Chartered Property Casualty Underwriter (CPCU) professional designation granted to persons in the property and liability insurance field who pass a series of rigorous examinations and meet specified eligibility requirements.

Civilian Health and Medical Program of the Uniformed Services (CHAMPUS) part of the Uniformed Services Health Benefits Program, which supplements the medical care available for families of active, deceased, and retired military personnel.

Claim notification to an insurance company that payment of an amount is due under the terms of a policy.

Claims-made Form a liability insurance policy under which coverage applies to claims made during the policy period; see Occurrence Form.

Class Rating an approach to rate-making in which a price per unit of insurance is computed for all applicants with a given set of characteristics. For example, the rate may apply to all persons of a given age and sex, to all buildings of a certain type of construction, or to all businesses of a certain type.

Closed panel A managed care plan that contracts with physicians on an exclusive basis for services and does not allow those physicians to see patients for another managed care organization. Examples include staff and group model HMOs. Could apply to a large private medical group that contracts with an HMO.

CLU see Chartered Life Underwriter.

Coinsurance in property and casualty insurance, a clause or provision in an insurance policy requiring a specified amount of insurance based on the value of the property insured; normally, there is a premium reduction for purchasing insurance to some percentage of the value of the property—if the insured fails to comply with the clause, he or she will suffer a penalty in the event of partial loss; in health insurance, a policy provision requiring the insured to share a given percentage of the loss.

Collateral Source Rule a legal principle applicable in the area of tort liability, which holds that the plaintiff's measure of damage should not be mitigated by payments received from sources other than the tort feasor.

Collusion a compact between persons, usually to the detriment of other persons or for some improper purpose.

Combined Ratio a rough indication of the profitability of a property and liability insurer's underwriting operations, generally computed by adding the ratio of losses incurred to premiums earned and expenses incurred to premiums written.

Commercial the opposite of personal; of a business nature, usually mercantile or manufacturing.

Commercial Paper Insurance a form of credit enhancement insurance that guarantees the timely payment of principal and interest on commercial paper issued by corporations.

Commission the fee paid by the insurance companies to agents for the sale of policies.

Common Carrier a firm that offers to transport merchandise for hire and must accept shipments from anyone who wishes to use its services. Different laws and rules govern common carriers than those applicable to private or contract carriers that only transport the goods of those with whom they have made agreements.

Common Law distinguished from law created by enactment of statutes; common law comprises the body of principles and rules of action, which derive their authority solely from the judgments and decrees of the courts or from usages and customs of immemorial antiquity.

Community rating the rating methodology required of federally qualified HMOs and of insurers under some state laws in which premiums do not vary by age, sex, contract size, or other traditional rating variables but are determined by the geographic region's health and demographic profile.

Comparative Negligence a modification of the principle of contributory negligence. In those jurisdictions that follow

the principle of comparative negligence, negligence on the part of the injured party will not necessarily defeat the claim, but will be considered in determining the amount of damages.

Compensation wages, salaries, awards, fees, commissions, financial returns of any kind.

Completed Operations a commercial liability insurance coverage applicable to liability arising out of work performed by the insured after such work has been finished.

Comprehensive a loosely used term signifying broad or extensive insurance coverage.

Comprehensive General Liability (CGL) a business liability policy that covers a variety of exposures in a single contract.

Comprehensive Major Medical Insurance a policy designed to give the protection offered by both a basic and major medical health insurance policy; it is characterized by a low "deductible" amount, coinsurance feature, and high maximum benefits ($500,000, $1 million, or more). Some policies are written without a maximum limit.

Comprehensive Personal Liability Insurance a type of insurance that reimburses the policyholder if he or she becomes liable to pay money for damage or injury he or she has caused to others; this form does not include automobile liability but does include almost every activity of the policyholder except business operations.

Concealment deliberate failure to reveal material facts that would affect the validity of a policy of insurance.

Concurrent covering the same kind of property at the same location under the same terms and conditions, with the same types of coverage, as two or more insurance policies.

Concurrent Causation a legal doctrine in property insurance that makes the insurer liable for damage when property is damaged by two causes, one of which is excluded and the other covered.

Concurrent review A case management technique that allows insurers to monitor an insured's hospital stay and to know in advance if there are any changes in the expected period of confinement and the planned release date.

Conditionally Renewable a continuation provision in health insurance under which the insurer may not cancel the policy during its term but can refuse to renew under specified circumstances.

Conditions those provisions in insurance contracts that qualify the insurer's promise of indemnity or impose obligations on the insured.

Confining Sickness that which confines an individual to his or her home or a hospital (visits to physicians and hospitals are generally considered as not terminating confinement).

Conglomerate a group of corporations engaged in widely varied activities. In the insurance industry a conglomerate refers to a group of companies with noninsurance interests that purchases an insurance company.

Consequential Loss loss occurring after, and as a result of, some other loss, as loss of profits resulting from a fire or a loss of frozen foods resulting from electrical failure.

Consideration price, token, or other matter used as an inducement for the completion of a contract, as an insurance premium.

Constructive Total Loss a loss of sufficient amount to make the cost of salvaging or repairing the property equal to or greater than the value of the property when repaired.

Contingent conditional; depending on another happening; a contingent beneficiary is one next in line after the first named.

Contingent Beneficiary in life insurance, a beneficiary who is entitled to receive proceeds if the primary beneficiary has died.

Contract Bond a surety bond issued to support the obligation of one who is engaged to perform under a contract.

Contractual Liability legal liability assumed under contract.

Contribution a participation, as two insurance policies in the same loss.

Contribution by Equal Shares an "other insurance" provision under which two or more policies share equally in a loss until the limit of one policy is exhausted, with the unexhausted policy paying the loss in excess of this amount.

Contributory Negligence the lack of ordinary care on the part of an injured person, which combined with the defendant's negligence and contributed to the injury as a proximate cause. In some jurisdictions, contributory negligence on the part of an injured party will defeat his or her claim.

Convention Blank see Annual Statement.

Conversion wrongful appropriation to one's own use of property belonging to another.

Conversion Privilege privilege granted in an insurance policy to convert to a different plan of insurance without providing evidence of insurability.

Convertible Term Insurance term insurance that can be exchanged, at the option of the policyholder and without evidence of insurability, for another plan of insurance.

Coordinated Care Plans term used under the Medicare + Choice program to refer to what have traditionally been called *managed care plans*.

Coordination of Benefits Provision a group health insurance policy provision designed to eliminate duplicate payments and provide the sequence in which coverage will apply when a person is insured under two contracts.

Copay an arrangement in which the covered person pays a specified amount for various services and the health care provider pays the remainder. Similar to coinsurance, except that coinsurance is usually a percentage of certain charges where the co-payment is a dollar amount.

Corridor Deductible in health insurance, a deductible under a major medical policy that applies after coverage under a base plan is exhausted.

Cost Containment the control or reduction of inefficiencies in the consumption, allocation, or production of health care services that contribute to higher than necessary costs.

Cost Contract A managed care contract payment method by which the Health Care Financing Administration (HCFA) pays for the delivery of health services to members based on the managed care organization's reasonable costs.

Cosurety a personal or corporate guarantor of a surety obligation on which one or more of the sureties are directly responsible for the same obligation.

Counter Signature an additional signature required in most states to comply with resident agency laws; applies when a producer in one state controls business located in, or operating in, another state.

Coverage the insurance afforded by the policy.

CPCU see Chartered Property Casualty Underwriter.

CPPA see Certified Professional Public Adjuster.

Credit Enhancement Insurance a form of coverage in which the insurer guarantees the payment of interest and/or principal of the insured in connection with debt instruments issued by the insured.

Credit Insurance a form of guarantee to manufacturers and wholesalers against loss resulting from default on the part of debtors.

Credit Life Insurance term life insurance issued through a lender or lending agency to cover repayment of a specific loan, installment purchase, or other obligation in case of the debtor's death.

Crime a wrong against public laws or customs punishable by fine, imprisonment, or death after trial in a criminal court.

Crop-Hail Insurance protection for monetary loss resulting from hail damage to growing crops.

Crummey Rule a doctrine established by court decision in 1968 that holds annual contributions to the trust by the grantor will qualify as gifts as long as the trust beneficiaries are given the right to withdraw the contributions. If not withdrawn, the contributions are used to pay the premiums on life insurance on the grantor that is owned by the trust.

Currently Insured under OASDHI, the status of a worker who has at least 6 quarters of coverage out of the last 13 quarters and whose beneficiaries are entitled to "currently insured" benefits.

Custodial care care that is primarily for meeting personal needs such as help in bathing, dressing, eating or taking medicine. It can be provided by someone without professional medical skills or training but must be according to doctor's orders.

Daily Report a copy of that portion of an insurance contract dealing with the description of the risk and the amount of insurance, which is sent to the home office of the insurance company and retained in the agent's files.

Damages the amount claimed or allowed as compensation for injuries sustained or property damaged through the wrongful acts or the negligence of another; an award.

Declarations that part of an insurance policy containing the representations of the applicant.

Declination the rejection by a life insurance company of an application for life insurance, usually for reasons of the health or occupation of the applicant.

Deductible a provision whereby an insured may be required to pay part of a loss, the insurance being excess over the amount of the deductible.

Deferred Annuity an annuity providing for the income payments to begin at some future date, such as in a specified number of years or at a specified age.

Deferred Group Annuity a type of group annuity providing for the purchase each year of a paid-up deferred annuity for each member of the group, the total amount received by the member at retirement being the sum of these deferred annuities.

Defined-Benefit Plan a pension plan in which the retirement benefit is defined and in which the employer's contribution is a function of that benefit.

Defined-Contribution Plan a pension plan under which the payments into the plan are fixed, but the retirement benefit is variable; also called a money purchase plan.

Demutalization the process whereby a mutual insurance company converts to a capital stock company. Policyholders are generally offered a choice between stock in the new corporation or cash.

Dental Insurance a type of health insurance that covers dental care expenses.

Dependency Period the period during which children will be dependent on a surviving parent.

Deposit Administration a type of group annuity providing for the accumulation of contributions in an undivided fund out of which annuities are purchased as the individual members of the group retire.

Deposit Premium an original premium paid by the insured at the inception date of the policy; estimated premium, subject to later adjustment; see Audit Premium.

Depreciation the lessening of value through age, deterioration, and obsolescence.

Derivative a financial instrument whose price is derived from the value of commodity prices, interest rates, stock market prices, foreign exchange rates, or insurance indexes.

Deviate to file or use a rate that is based upon but departs from a standard bureau rate.

Diagnosis-Related Groups (DRGs) standard categories of treatment used in a system that reimburses health care

providers fixed amounts for all care given in connection with specific treatments.

Difference In Conditions (DIC) Insurance a broad form of open-perils property insurance written as an adjunct to policies that cover named perils.

Direct Loss loss resulting directly and immediately from the hazard insured.

Direct Recognition a system of life insurer dividend distribution in which dividend on a policy is reduced by recognizing the difference between the interest on outstanding policy loans and the amount of investment income that would otherwise be earned on the funds.

Direct Writer an insurance company that deals directly with the insured through a salaried representative, as opposed to those insurers that use agents; also used to refer to insurers that operate through exclusive agents; in reinsurance, the company that originally writes the business.

Disability inability to perform all or part of one's occupational duties because of an accident or illness; see Total Disability and Partial Disability.

Disability Benefit a provision added to a life insurance policy for waiver of premium, and sometimes payment of monthly income, if the insured becomes totally and permanently disabled.

Disability Income Insurance a form of health insurance that provides periodic payments to replace lost income when the insured is unable to work because of illness or injury.

Discovery Period the period after termination of an insurance policy or bond, or after the occurrence of a loss, within which the loss must be discovered to be covered.

Dismemberment accidental loss of limb or sight.

Distress Insurer an insurance company specializing in substandard risk, usually in the field of automobile insurance.

Dividend in insurance contracts, the refund of a part of the premium paid at the beginning of a year that still remains after the company has made deductions for losses, expenses, and additions to reserves.

Dividend Addition an amount of paid-up insurance purchased with a policy dividend and added to the face amount of the policy.

Domestic Insurer a name given to a company in the state of its incorporation, as an Iowa company is domestic in the state of Iowa, foreign as to all other states, and alien as to all other countries.

Double Indemnity a provision under which certain benefits are doubled when an accident is due to specified circumstances, such as public conveyance accidents; in a life insurance policy, a provision that the face amount payable on death will be doubled if the death is a result of an accident.

Dread Disease Policy a limited form of health insurance that pays for treatment of specified diseases such as cancer.

Dram-Shop Law a state statute that imposes liability on sellers of alcoholic beverages in the event that the buyer causes bodily injury to another or in some cases, to himself or herself.

Duplication of Benefits overlapping or identical coverage of the same insured under two or more health plans, usually the result of contracts of different insurance companies, service organizations or prepayment plans; also known as multiple coverage.

Early warning system a system of measuring insurers' financial stability set up by insurance industry regulators. An example is the Insurance Regulatory Information System (IRIS), which uses financial ratios to identify insurers in need of regulatory attention.

Earned Premium premium for which protection has been provided. When a premium is paid in advance for a policy period, the company "earns" a portion of that premium only as time elapses during that period.

Economatic Ordinary Life See Enhanced Ordinary Life.

Education IRA a mechanism for saving for the cost of higher education created by the Tax Reform Act of 1997, under which nondeductible contributions compound free from taxes and for which withdrawals for education expenses are also tax free.

Effective Date the date on which the policy is put in force; the inception date.

Effective Benefit a benefit payable in lieu of another (e.g., a lump sum benefit may be allowed for specified fractures or dislocations in lieu of weekly indemnity).

Eligibility Period in group insurance, a period during which group members may enroll in the plan without providing evidence of insurability.

Elimination Period see Waiting Period.

Employee Retirement Income Security Act (ERISA) a 1974 federal statute that establishes minimum standards for pension plans.

Employers Liability legal liability imposed on an employer making him or her responsible to pay damages to an employee injured by the employer's negligence. Generally, replaced by "workers compensation," which pays the employee whether the employer has been negligent or not.

Employment Practices Liability Coverage liability insurance for employers that covers wrongful termination, discrimination, or sexual harassment toward the insured's employees or former employees.

Endorsement a written amendment affecting the declarations, insuring agreements, exclusions, or conditions of an insurance policy; a rider.

Endowment Insurance insurance payable to the insured if he or she is living on the maturity date stated in the policy, or to a beneficiary if the insured dies prior to that date.

Enhanced Ordinary Life a type of participating life insurance that uses policy dividends to provide some form of level constant coverage at a relatively low premium. Usually, dividends are used to purchase paid-up whole-life additions as the face amount of insurance automatically reduced. The policies are offered under names such as "Economatic" or "Extra Ordinary Life."

Environmental Impairment Liability (EIL) liability arising out of pollution.

Equipment Value Insurance (EVI) insurance designed to protect businesses against a decline in the value of certain types of property.

Equity Indexed Annuity a fixed annuity that earns interest or provides benefits that are linked to the performance of an equity index, such as the S & P 500.

Equivalent Level Annual Dividend the average of annual life insurance policy dividends for a specified period, adjusted for interest at a specified rate.

Errors and Omissions Insurance professional liability insurance for individuals in professions such as accounting, insurance, law, or real estate, where the exposure is primarily a property damage one as opposed to bodily injury.

Estate possessions of a deceased person; possessions of a minor or incompetent person; possessions of a bankrupt person or corporation; worldly goods of anyone.

Estoppel an admission or declaration by which a person is prevented from proving the contrary.

Evidence of Insurability any statement of proof of a person's physical condition and/or other factual information affecting his/her acceptance for insurance.

Excess that which goes beyond, as excess insurance, over and above a primary amount.

Excess of Loss Reinsurance a form of reinsurance whereby the reinsuring company reimburses the ceding company for the amount of loss the ceding company suffers, over and above an agreed aggregate sum in any one loss or in a number of losses arising out of any one event.

Exclusion that which is expressly eliminated from the coverage of an insurance policy.

Exclusive Agency System an insurance marketing system under which the agent represents a single company or company group.

Expectation of Life (life expectancy) the average number of years of life remaining for persons of a given age according to a particular mortality table.

Expected Loss Ratio the percentage of the final rate allocated for the payment of losses.

Expense Ratio the proportionate relationship of an insurer's expenses to premium expressed as a percentage.

Experience Rating an insurance pricing system in which the insured's past experience determines the premium for the current protection.

Expiration the date on which an insurance policy terminates unless continued or renewed by an additional premium.

Exposure unit of measurement to which an insurance rate is applied.

Extended Coverage Insurance a standard package of perils usually sold in conjunction with the peril of fire; includes the perils of windstorm, hail, smoke, explosion, riot, riot attending a strike, civil commotion, vehicle, and aircraft.

Extended Term Insurance a form of insurance available as a nonforfeiture option; it provides the original amount of insurance for a limited period of time.

Extended Unemployment Insurance Benefits additional unemployment benefits under a state-federal program payable during periods of high unemployment to workers who have exhausted their regular benefits.

Extra Expense Insurance a form of indirect loss property insurance that pays for the increased costs of continuing operations following damage to property by an insured peril.

Face Amount the amount stated on the face of a life insurance policy that will be paid in case of death or at the maturity of the contract; it does not include dividend additions, or additional amounts payable under accidental death or other special provisions.

Factory Mutuals a group of mutual companies, principally located in New England, specializing in the insurance of manufacturing properties.

Facultative Reinsurance reinsurance effected item by item and accepted or declined by the reinsuring company after scrutiny as opposed to reinsurance effected by treaty.

FAIR Plan—Fair Access to Insurance Requirements state pools designed to provide insurance to property owners who are unable to obtain property insurance because of the location of their property or other factors over which they have no control.

Family Income Policy a life insurance policy, combining whole life and decreasing term insurance, under which the beneficiary receives income payments to the end of a specified period if the insured dies prior to the end of the period, and the face amount of the policy either at the end of the period or at the death of the insured.

Family Maintenance Policy life insurance that pays, in addition to the face of the policy, a monthly income for a period commencing with the insured's death and continuing for the number of years specified; the period is most often 10, 15, or 20 years.

Family Policy a life insurance policy providing insurance on all or several family members in one contract, generally whole-life insurance on the wage earner and smaller

amounts of term insurance on the spouse and children, including those born after the policy is issued.

Family Purpose Doctrine a legal doctrine that imposes vicarious liability on the head of the family for operation of a family car by family members.

Federal Crime Insurance Program a program administered by the Federal Insurance Administration that provides for the sale of Federal Crime insurance in any state where adequate and affordable crime insurance is not available.

Federal Flood Insurance a federally subsidized flood insurance program enacted in 1968 under which flood insurance is available in areas that meet specific conditions.

Federal Insurance Administration a government office responsible for the supervision of insurance programs such as the Federal Riot Reinsurance Program, Federal Flood Insurance Plan, and Federal Crime Insurance Program.

Fee-for-service in health insurance, a financing arrangement under which physicians and other providers receive payment from an insurer based on their billed charges for each service provided.

Fellow Servant one who serves and is controlled by the same employer; also those engaged in the same common pursuit under the same general control.

Fellow Servant Rule rule that a master is not liable for injuries to a servant caused by the negligence of a fellow servant engaged in the same general business and where the master has exercised due care in the selection of servants.

Fidelity Bond a contract of fidelity insurance; a guarantee of personal honesty of the person furnishing indemnity against defalcation or negligence; a form of insurance or suretyship that protects a party against loss from the dishonesty of employees.

Fiduciary a person or corporation having the duty created by undertaking to act primarily for another's benefit in matters connected with such undertaking, or an agent handling the business of another when the business he or she transacts or the money or property being handled is not his or her own or for his or her own benefit.

Field Supervisor a salaried employee of an insurance company, whose responsibilities are (1) production of new business through existing agents, (2) the appointment of new agents, (3) general supervision of the company's affairs in his or her territory.

File and Use Law a system of rate regulation in which rates may be used immediately by an insurer once they are filed with the state regulatory authority. The supervisory authority may later disapprove and rescind the rates.

Financial Guarantee Insurance a form of coverage in which the insurer guarantees the payment of interest and/or principal of the insured in connection with debt instruments issued by the insured.

Financial Responsibility Law a statute that requires motorists to show evidence of financial responsibility following an accident that involves bodily injury or property damage in excess of some amount; normally, proof of financial responsibility is given through a valid policy of insurance.

Fire as used in insurance contracts, combustion proceeding at a rate rapid enough to generate a flame, glow, or incandescence.

Fire Insurance coverage for losses caused by fire and lightning, as well as the resultant damage caused by smoke and water.

Fire Legal Liability a form of liability insurance that covers damage to leased or rented property caused by fire or other specified perils.

Fleet a group, as of automobiles.

Flexible Benefits under a cafeteria plan, selected benefits that qualify for pretax treatment.

Floater a marine or fire policy, the coverage of which follows the movement of the property insured.

Flood overflow of water from its natural boundaries. More specifically defined by the National Flood Act of 1968 as "a general and temporary condition of partial or complete inundation of normally dry land areas from (1) the overflow of inland or tidal waters, or (2) the unusual and rapid accumulation or runoff of surface waters from any source."

Foreign Insurer an insurance company that is chartered in another state.

Franchise Insurance a class of life insurance in which individual policies are issued to members of a group, with an employer or other body collecting and/or remitting the premiums.

Fraternal Insurance certain fraternal organizations have a form of cooperative life or disability insurance that is available to members of the fraternal organization.

Friendly Fire a fire confined to the place it is supposed to be in (e.g., in a stove or similar place).

Fronting an arrangement in which a primary insurer acts as the insurer of record by issuing a policy, but then passes the entire risk to a reinsurer in exchange for a commission. Often, the fronting insurer is licensed to do business in a state or country where the risk is located, but the reinsurer is not.

Fully Insured under OASDHI, the status of a worker who has 40 quarters of coverage or one quarter of coverage for each year after 1950 or after age 21, if later, and who is entitled to "fully insured" benefits.

Gatekeeper in health care, a primary care physician who performs initial diagnosis and refers the participant to specialist members of a provider network.

General Average in marine insurance, a loss that must be borne partly by someone other than the owner of the goods that were lost or destroyed; for example, if it is necessary to jettison cargo to save a ship, the owners of the ship and the rest of the cargo that is saved will share in the loss of the goods that were intentionally sacrificed.

General Damages amounts awarded in litigation to compensate for pain and suffering and other noneconomic loss.

Grace Period the period of time following the due date of a policy premium during which the payment of the premium will continue the policy and during which the policy is in full force and effect.

Graded Commission a reduced commission justified by the size of the premium.

Graded Expense a reduced expense item for the insurance company justified by the size of the premiums.

Graded Premium Whole Life a whole-life contract for which the initial premium is low, but increases yearly until it levels off sometime between the tenth and twentieth years.

Gramm–Leach–Bliley Act the Financial Services Modernization Act of 1999, which removed Depression-era prohibitions against the combination of commercial banking and investment-banking activities. It allows insurance companies, banks, and securities firms to engage in each others' activities and own one another.

Gratuitous made without a consideration, as a gift requiring nothing in return.

Gross Premium the premium for insurance that includes the provision for anticipated losses (the pure premium) and for the anticipated expenses (loading).

Group Annuity a pension plan providing annuities at retirement to a group of persons under a single master contract, with the individual members of the group holding certificates stating their coverage; it is usually issued to an employer for the benefit of employees.

Group Insurance any insurance plan under which a number of employees and their dependents are insured under a single policy, issued to their employer, with individual certificates given to each insured employee; the most commonly written lines are life and accident and health.

Guaranteed Investment Contract (GIC) investment instruments issued by insurers to pension plans that are similar to the certificates of deposit issued by commercial banks.

Guaranteed Renewable Policy a policy that the insured has the right to continue in force by the timely payment of premiums to a specified age (usually age 50), during which period the insurer has no right to make unilaterally any change in any provision of the policy while the policy is in force, but may make changes in premium rates by policyholder class.

Guest Laws state statutes that limit the right of action of an injured guest passenger in an automobile against the driver to instances of gross negligence or willful and wanton negligence.

Hard Market a seller's market in which insurance is expensive and in short supply.

Hazard a condition that creates or increases the probability of a loss.

Hazard, Moral the increase in the chance of loss caused by dishonest tendencies on the part of an insured.

Hazard, Morale the increase in the chance or loss or in the amount of loss that results from an attitude of carelessness or indifference simply because the loss will be paid by insurance.

Health Employer Data and Information Sets (HEDIS) a standardized set of performance measures that assess managed care plans' performance on a number of elements, including such things as financial stability, access and quality of care. HEDIS enables purchasers and consumers to readily compare the performance of managed care plans. It is sponsored, supported, and maintained by the National Committee for Quality Assurance (NCQA).

Health Insurance a generic term applying to all types of insurance indemnifying or reimbursing for losses caused by bodily accident or sickness or for expenses of medical treatment necessitated by sickness or accidental bodily injury.

Health Maintenance Organization (HMO) a prepaid medical group practice plan for the provision of health care, in which individual subscribers pay an annual fee in return for entitlement to a wide range of health services. HMOs are both insurers and providers of health care.

Hold-Harmless Agreement a contract usually written such that one party assumes legal liability on behalf of another party.

Home Service Life Insurance See Monthly Debit Ordinary Life Insurance.

Hospital Indemnity a form of health insurance that provides a stipulated daily, weekly, or monthly indemnity during hospital confinement without regard to the actual expense of hospital confinement.

Hostile Fire a fire burning where none is intended.

Hull Insurance in ocean marine and aviation insurance, coverage for physical damage to a vessel or aircraft.

Immediate Participation Guarantee (IPG) Plan a type of insured pension plan under which gains and losses from mortality or investments are segregated from the rest of the insurer's operations and credited directly to the employer's account. See Harris Trust Decision.

Improvements and Betterments Insurance insurance that protects a tenant against loss to improvement made by him or her to property in which he or she is a tenant.

Incontestable Clause a provision that prevents the insurer from challenging the coverage because of alleged misstatements by the insured after a stipulated period has passed, usually two or three years.

Incurred Losses losses actually sustained during a fixed period, usually a year. Incurred losses are customarily computed by the formula: losses paid during the period, plus outstanding losses at the end of the period, less outstanding losses at the beginning of the period.

Indemnity, Principle of a general legal principle related to insurance that holds that the individual recovering under an insurance policy should be restored to the approximate financial position he or she was in prior to the loss.

Independent Adjuster one who adjusts losses on behalf of companies but is not employed by any one. He or she is paid by fee for each loss adjusted.

Independent Agent a person operating under the American Agency System, representing several property and liability insurers, and dividing the policies he or she writes among the various companies represented.

Independent Contractor one who performs work for another in his or her own manner and method, and who is not subject to the control or direction of the party for whom the work is performed; he or she is not an employee of the party for whom the work is performed.

Indeterminate Premium Life Insurance life insurance in which the premium may be adjusted upward or downward after inception, subject to a maximum premium stated in the policy.

Indirect contingent; that which happens only after something else has occurred.

Individual Policy Pension Trust a type of pension plan, frequently used for small groups, administered by trustees who are authorized to purchase individual level premium policies or annuity contracts for each member of the plan; the policies usually provide both life insurance and retirement benefits.

Individual Retirement Account (IRA) a tax-sheltered retirement plan established by an individual under which earnings accumulate tax free until distributed. Contributions up to $2250 are deductible for some persons.

Industrial Development Bond Insurance insurance designed to guarantee prompt payment of principal and interest on industrial development bonds.

Industrial Life Insurance life insurance issued in small amounts, usually less than $1000, on a single life exclusive of additional benefits, with premiums payable on a monthly or more frequent basis, and generally collected at the insured's home by an agent of the company.

Inherent Vice a characteristic depreciation such as the fading of ink, a cracking of parchment, the graying of hair.

Injury Independent of All Other Means an injury resulting from an accident, provided that the accident was not caused by an illness.

Inland Marine Insurance a broad type of insurance, generally covering articles that may be transported from one place to another; the essential condition is that the insured property be movable, though bridges, tunnels, and similar instrumentalities of transportation are also considered inland marine.

Insolvency Fund state plans created by law to guarantee payment of liabilities of insolvent insurers.

Inspection an examination by those having authority; right usually reserved by an insurance company with respect to any property it insured.

Insurable Interest an interest that might be damaged if the peril insured against occurs; the possibility of a financial loss to an individual that can be protected against through insurance.

Insurance an economic device whereby the individual substitutes a small certain cost (the premium) for a large uncertain financial loss (the contingency insured against) that would exist if it were not for the insurance contract; an economic device for reducing and eliminating risk through the process of combining a sufficient number of homogeneous exposures into a group in order to make the losses predictable for the group as a whole.

Insurance Purchasing Group a group of firms or other organizations that band together under the provisions of the Risk Retention Act of 1986 for the purpose of buying insurance collectively.

Insurance Regulatory Information System (IRIS) a computerized model designed by the National Association of Insurance Commissioners for the detection of potential insurer insolvencies before they occur through analysis of selected audit ratios.

Insurance Services Office (ISO) the principal ratemaking organization for property and liability insurers.

Insured in life insurance, the person on whose life an insurance policy is issued; in property and liability insurance, the person to whom or on whose behalf benefits are payable under the policy.

Integrated Delivery System (IDS) a joint venture in which physicians and hospitals combine to provide a full range of health care services to subscribers for an annual fee (capitation); also sometimes called a Physician Hospital Organization (PHO).

Integration a coordination of retirement or disability benefits with benefits payable under Social Security, through a specific formula.

Interest-Adjusted Method a means of measuring differences in cost among life insurance policies that considers the time value of money.

Interest-Sensitive Whole Life a participating life insurance policy in which the dividends are geared to current money rates. Some insurers guarantee a particular rate for the first few years of the policy.

Internet Liability Insurance coverage designed to protect businesses from liabilities that arise from the conducting of business over the Internet, including copyright infringement, defamation, and violation of privacy.

Intestate leaving no will at death.

Investment Generation Method (IGM) a dividend allocation approach used in life insurance that recognizes the year (or generation of policies) during which money was invested by the policyholder in determining the dividend; See Portfolio Average Method.

Invitee a person having an express or implied invitation to enter a given location.

Irrevocable Beneficiary a beneficiary designation that may be changed only with the consent of the beneficiary.

Irrevocable Life Insurance Trust A type of living trust used to avoid the incidents of ownership in a life insurance contract that makes the insurance proceeds taxable under the federal state tax. The basic function of the trust is to own life insurance policies covering the grantor.

Joint Insured one of two or more persons whose names or interests are insured under the same or identical contracts.

Joint-and-Last-Survivor Annuity an annuity issued on two lives under which payments continue in whole or in part until both have died.

Joint-and-Several Liability a judgment obtained against multiple tort feasors that may be enforced against the tort feasors collectively or individually; permits the injured party to recover the entire amount of compensation due for injuries from any tort feasor who is able to pay, regardless of the degree of that party's negligence.

Joint-Life Annuity an annuity issued on two lives under which payments cease at the death of either of the two persons.

Joint Mortgage Protection Policy decreasing term life insurance written on the lives of two persons, with the insurance payable at the death of the first.

Joint Underwriting Association (JUA) a loss-sharing mechanism used in some states to provide insurance to high-risk drivers.

Judgment the decision of a court or the reason for such decision.

Judgment Rating the process of determining the rate for a coverage without the benefit of extensive loss experience or statistical information.

Judicial Bond a surety bond required in court proceedings.

Jumbo Risk a risk requiring exceptionally high benefit limits.

Jumping Juvenile Insurance permanent life insurance on children under which the face amount automatically increases to a multiple of the initial amount when the child reaches a specified age.

Keogh Plan a tax-qualified retirement plan for self-insured individuals similar in most respects to qualified corporate pensions.

Key-Persons Insurance a life insurance program designed to cover the key employees of an employer; it may be written on a group or individual policy basis.

Kidnap/Ransom Insurance insurance that cover the cost of ransom or extortion payments and related expenses. Policies generally require that the policyholder not reveal the coverage's existence.

Lapse termination of a policy due to failure by the insured to pay the premium as required.

Lapsed Policy a policy discontinued for nonpayment of premiums; the term is technically limited to a termination occurring before a life insurance policy has a cash or other nonforfeiture value.

Last Clear Chance an exception to the doctrine of contributory negligence that makes a person who has a final opportunity to avoid an accident and fails to do so legally liable.

Law of Large Numbers the theory of probability that is the basis for insurance; the larger the number of exposure units, the more closely will the actual results obtained approach the probable results expected from an infinite number of exposures.

Leasehold Interest an intangible use interest that exists when the provisions of a lease stipulate a rental that is greater or less than the prevailing market price of renting similar facilities.

Legal Reserve Life Insurance Company a life insurance company operating under state insurance laws specifying the minimum basis for the reserves the company must maintain on its policies.

Level Premium Insurance life insurance for which the cost is distributed evenly over the premium paying period: the premium remains constant from year to year, and is more than the actual cost of protection in the earlier years of the policy and less than the actual cost in the later years; the excess paid in the early years accumulates the reserve.

Liability a debt or responsibility; an obligation that may arise by a contract made or by a tort committed.

License and Permit Bond a surety bond required of persons who obtain certain licenses and permits that guarantees that the individual will comply with laws and regulations pertaining to the license or permit.

Licensee a person on one's property with stated or implied permission but not to further the purposes of the landholder. The property owner is obligated to warn a licensee of any dangers the licensee might not be expected to know about.

Life Annuity a contract that provides an income for the life of the annuitant.

Lifetime Disability Benefit a benefit for loss of income payable as long as the insured is totally disabled, even for life.

Limited Payment Life Insurance a form of whole-life insurance on which premiums are payable for a specified number of years less than the period of protection, or until death, if death occurs before the end of the specified period.

Limited Policies those that cover specified accidents or sickness.

Limits the value or amount of a policy; the greatest amount that can be collected under the policy.

Livery in automobile insurance, the carrying of passengers for hire.

Living benefits rider a rider attached to a life insurance policy that provides LTC benefits or benefits for the terminally ill. The benefits provided are derived from the available life insurance benefits.

Lloyd's a voluntary unincorporated association of individuals organized for the purpose of writing insurance; normally refers to Lloyd's of London, a group of individual underwriters and syndicates that underwrite insurance risks severally, using facilities maintained by the Lloyd's of London Corporation.

Loading that part of an insurance rate designed to cover expenses, profit, and a margin for contingencies: in some instances, an additional amount added to an insurance rate because of some extraordinary hazard or expense.

Local Agent a producer of insurance whose activities are purely of local extent.

Long-Term Care Insurance health insurance coverage designed to cover the cost of custodial care in nursing homes or extended care facilities.

Long-Term Disability a generally accepted period of time for more than two years—can vary according to company standards.

Loss the unintentional decline in, or disappearance of, value due to a contingency.

Loss Frequency the number of claims on a policy during a premium period.

Loss Ratio the proportionate relationship of incurred losses to earned premiums expressed as a percentage.

Loss Reserves an estimated liability in an insurer's financial statement, indicating the amount the insurer expects to pay for losses that have taken place but which have not yet been paid.

Losses Incurred But Not Reported (IBNR) losses resulting from accidents that have taken place but on which the company has not yet received notice or report of the loss.

Low-Load Life Insurance a life insurance contract on which the commission for the first and subsequent years is lower than the traditional commission rates.

Major Medical Expense Insurance policies especially designed to help offset the heavy medical expenses resulting from catastrophic or prolonged illness or injury; they provide benefit payments for 75–80 percent of all types of medical treatment by a physician above a certain amount first paid by the insured person and up to the maximum amount provided by the policy—usually $500,000, $1 million, or more. Some policies are written without a maximum limit.

Malpractice alleged professional misconduct or lack of ordinary skill in the performance of a professional act. A practitioner is liable for damage or injuries caused by malpractice.

Managed Health Care a system of health care delivery that tries to manage the cost of health care, the quality of that health care, and access to that care. Features typically include a panel of contracted providers that is less than the entire universe of available providers, some type of limitations on benefits to subscribers who use noncontracted providers (unless authorized to do so), and some type of authorization system.

Mandated benefits in health insurance, benefits required by state or federal law.

Manual a book of rates, rules, and coverages usually available for each kind of insurance.

Marine pertaining to the sea or to transportation; usually divided as to "ocean marine" and "inland marine"; the insurance covering transportation risks.

Mass Merchandising the sale of group property and liability insurance, generally through an employer.

Material Fact information about the subject of insurance that if known would change the underwriting basis of the insurance, and that would cause the insurer to refuse the application or charge a higher rate.

Medicaid state programs of public assistance to persons regardless of age whose income and resources are insufficient to pay for health care. Title XIX of the federal Social Security Act provides matching federal funds for financing state Medicaid programs.

Medical Information Bureau (MIB) an organization to which life insurers report health impairments of applicants for life insurance; the information is then available to member companies for underwriting purposes.

Medical Payments an additional coverage included in some liability contracts under which the insurer agrees to reimburse injured persons for medical expenses.

Medical Savings Account a fund into which individuals make tax-sheltered contributions to cover medical expenses that is used in connection with a high deductible health insurance policy to cover the expenses that fall within the policy deductible.

Medicare hospital and medical expense insurance provided under the Social Security system.

Medicare Select Policy a Medicare Supplement policy under which insureds must use a preferred provider organization (except in emergency situations) to receive full benefits.

Medicare+Choice a major initiative in the Balanced Budget Act of 1997 (also called Medicare Part C), under which Medicare beneficiaries may select from among several managed care options or a Medical Savings Account.

Medicare Supplement Policy Medical expense insurance designed to dovetail with and supplement insurance under the federal Medicare system.

Medigap private health insurance products that supplement Medicare insurance benefits.

MET see Multiple Employer Trust.

MEWA see Multiple Employer Welfare Arrangement.

Minimum Premium Plan in group health insurance, a cost-plus arrangement in which an employer pays the insurer only a portion of the premium which is to be used for administration costs. The remainder is placed in a bank account which is then used by the insurer to pay claims.

Miscellaneous Hospital Expense a provision for the payment on a blanket basis or schedule basis of hospital services (other than room and board, special nursing care, and doctors fees) up to a stipulated maximum amount.

Misrepresentation a misstatement: if done with intent to mislead, it may void the policy of insurance.

Misstatement of Age Clause in life and health insurance, a policy provision requiring an adjustment in the amount of insurance when the insured has misstated his or her age.

Modified Endowment Contract (MEC) a life insurance contract that does not meet the requirements specified in the *Internal Revenue Code* and on which a withdrawal of investment earnings by a cash surrender or loan before age 59 1/2 is subject to penalty.

Modified Own Occupation a coverage definition in disability income policies under which benefits are payable if the insured cannot perform the duties of his or her own occupation and is not working in any gainful employment.

Modified Whole Life a form of whole-life insurance with a lower than usual initial premium that increases after 3 to 5 years.

Money Market Fund Insurance private insurance that protects insured investors in a money market mutual fund against loss in the event the fund fails or the issuers of investments held by the fund default.

Monthly Debit Ordinary (MDO) Life Insurance a marketing approach similar to industrial life insurance, characterized by relatively low face amounts of cash value life insurance with high premiums where the agents call door-to-door on customers both to sell the products and to collect monthly premiums. Also called home service life insurance.

Moral Hazard a dishonest predisposition on the part of an insured that increases the chance of loss.

Morale Hazard a careless attitude on the part of an insured that increases the chance of loss or causes losses to be greater than would otherwise be the case.

Morbidity The incidence and severity of sickness and accidents in a well-defined class or classes of persons.

Morbidity Table a statistical table showing the probable incidence and duration of disability.

Mortality Table a statistical table showing the probable rate of death at each age, usually expressed as so many per thousand.

Mortgage a deposit or conditional transfer to secure the performance of some act; the person who makes the transfer is called the "mortgagor," the other party, the "mortgagee"; sometimes an intermediary called a "trustee" is appointed.

Multiple Employer Trust (MET) a legal trust established by a plan sponsor that brings together a number of small, unrelated employers for the purpose of providing group medical coverage on an insured or self-funded basis.

Multiple Employer Welfare Arrangement (MEWA) a multiple employer trust that provides health and welfare benefits to the employees of a number of employers under the provisions of the Employee Retirement Income Security Act (ERISA).

Multiple-Line Insurance policies that combine many perils previously covered by individual policies of fire and liability companies; the homeowners policy is one example; other examples are the commercial portfolio package policy and the farm coverage program.

Municipal Bond Guarantee Insurance a form of coverage sold to municipalities under which the insurer guarantees the payment of interest and principal on bonds issued by the municipality.

Municipal Lease Insurance a form of coverage sold to municipalities that ensures the municipality's lessors the prompt payment of principal and interest on municipal lease financing.

Mutual Insurance Holding Company an organization form under which a holding company organized as a mutual owns a capital stock insurers. Mutual insurance holding companies are organized under special state mutual insurance holding company laws.

Mutual Insurance Company a nonprofit insurer, without capital stock, that is owned by the policyholders; it may be incorporated or unincorporated.

Named Insured the person designated in the policy as the insured, as opposed to someone who may have an interest in a policy but not be named.

Named Peril Coverage property insurance that covers losses that result from specifically named causes; see Open Perils.

National Association of Insurance Commissioners a national organization of state officials who are charged with the regulation of insurance; although the organization has no official power, it exerts a strong influence through its recommendations.

National Committee for Quality Assurance (NCQA) a nonprofit organization that evaluates and accredits managed care plans. It is also responsible for implementing the Health Employer Data and Information Sets (HEDIS) data reporting system, that provides standardized performance measures for managed care plans.

Nationwide Marine Definition a classification of insurance coverages developed by the National Association of Insurance Commissioners to delineate marine insurance from other lines of insurance.

Negligence failure to exercise the degree of care that would be expected from a reasonable and prudent person.

Net Payment Cost Index in life insurance, a measure of cost of a life insurance policy maintained in force until death, with allowance for interest at some rate.

Net Retention the final amount of insurance retained by the insurance company after reinsuring such amounts as it did not wish to retain.

No-Fault Insurance a form of first party insurance written in conjunction with a no-fault law. Under a no-fault law, the person causing injury is granted immunity from tort action and the person injured must collect for his or her loss from his or her own insurer.

No-Load Life Insurance a life insurance policy on which no commission is payable; available from a limited number of insurers.

Nonadmitted Insurer an insurer that has not been licensed to write insurance in a given jurisdiction.

Noncancelable or Noncancelable and Guaranteed Renewable Policy a continuous term health insurance policy that guarantees the insured the right to renew for a stated number of years or to a stated age (usually 60 or 65), with the premium at renewal guaranteed.

Nonconcurrency a condition that exists when two or more policies covering the same property are written subject to different provisions.

Nonconfining Sickness a sickness that does not confine the insured to his or her home or a hospital.

Noncontributory Plan a group insurance or pension program under which the employer pays the entire cost.

Nondisabling Injury an injury that does not cause total or partial disability.

Nonforfeiture Option privilege available to the policyholder based upon his or her interest in the contract or once cash value has been created.

Nonoccupational Policy one that does not cover loss resulting from accidents or sickness arising out of or in the course of employment or covered under any workers compensation law.

Nonparticipating Insurance policy insurance on which the premium is calculated to cover as closely as possible the anticipated cost of the insurance protection and on which no dividends are payable to the insured.

Obligee the person in favor of whom some obligation is contracted, whether such obligation be to pay money, or to do, or not do something; the party to whom a bond is given.

Obligor the person who has engaged to perform some obligation; one who makes a bond; the bonding company.

Occupational Disease a disease or condition of health that results from performance of an occupation; examples include psittacosis, mercury poisoning, dust collection in the lungs, and the like; in most states occupational disease is now covered as part of the workers compensation exposure.

Occupational Safety and Health Act of 1970 (OSHA) a federal statute establishing safe and healthy working conditions on a nationwide basis. The act sets job safety and health standards enforced by Labor Department safety inspectors and also provides for compilation of relevant statistics on work injuries and illness.

Occurrence a happening that occupies some length of time, as an individual catching cold after sitting in a draft in a theater all evening; sometimes a series of accidents; see Accident.

Occurrence Form a liability insurance policy under which coverage applies to injuries or damage sustained, during the policy period, regardless of when the claim is made; see Claims-made Form.

Ocean Marine Insurance coverage on all types of vessels, including liabilities connected with them, and on their cargoes; the cargo coverage has been expanded to protect the owners from warehouse to warehouse, inclusive of all intermediate transit by rail, truck, or otherwise.

Omnibus Clause archaic term formerly used to refer to a provision in liability contracts that extends coverage to other persons not named in the policy.

Open Form a continuous policy written on a reporting basis.

Open Perils a term used to describe a broad form of property insurance in which coverage applies to loss arising from any fortuitous cause other than those perils or causes specifically excluded. This is in contrast to other policies that name the peril or perils insured against; see All-Risk.

Optionally Renewable in health insurance, a contract in which the insurer reserves the right to terminate coverage at an anniversary or premium-due date.

Ordinary Life Insurance a form of whole-life insurance usually issued in amounts of $1000 or more with premiums payable on an annual, semiannual, quarterly, or monthly basis to the death of the insured or to the end of the mortality table employed, whichever occurs first and at which time (benefits) proceeds are due; the term is also used to mean straight life insurance.

Organized Delivery System see Integrated Delivery System.

Outage Insurance a boiler and machinery consequential loss coverage covering loss during the period a specified object is inoperable as a result of an accident.

Overhead Disability Insurance a type of short-term disability income contract that reimburses the insured person for specified, fixed monthly expenses, normal and customary in the operation and conduct of his/her business or office.

Own Occupation in disability insurance, a term that defines the most liberal wording of the total disability requirement. It applies a single test in determining whether the insured is totally disabled; whether the insured is able to perform the duties of his or her own occupation.

Ownership of Expiration exclusive right on the part of a property and casualty insurance agent operating under the American Agency System to the records of dates and details of expiring policies.

P & I Insurance see Protection and indemnity insurance.

Package Policy a combination of the coverages of two or more separate policies into a single contract.

Paid-up Insurance insurance on which all required premiums have been paid; the term is frequently used to mean the reduced paid-up insurance available as one of the non-forfeiture options.

Parol Evidence Rule when the parties to a contract have purported to embody their contract in writing, that writing is the contract and all of the contract; therefore no evidence is admissible to prove any terms of the contract different from, or in addition to, those set forth in writing.

Partial Disability a provision generally found in accident and occasionally in sickness policies designed to offer some weekly or monthly indemnity benefit if the insured cannot perform all the important daily duties of his or her occupation.

Participating Insurance policies that entitle the policyholder to receive dividends reflecting the difference between the premium charged and the actual operating expenses and mortality experience of the company; the premium is calculated to provide some margin over the anticipated cost of the insurance protection. If expenses and mortality are lower than anticipated so that an excess of premium has been collected, a portion of the excess available is returned to the insured in the form of dividends.

Particular Average a term meaning an accidental and usually a partial loss suffered by one interest and not chargeable against others; see General Average.

Paul v Virginia a U.S. Supreme Court decision of 1869 in which the court ruled that insurance was not commerce and therefore not interstate commerce, thereby exempting the industry from federal control. This decision was reversed in the South Eastern Underwriters Association case of 1944.

Payor Benefit a provision generally included in juvenile life insurance policies waiving future premiums if the payor (usually the parent who pays the premium on the policy) becomes disabled or dies before maturity of the policy.

PCS Option an insurance futures option traded on the Chicago Board of Trade (CBOT) for which the value is determined from an index of insurance catastrophe estimates provided by the Property Claim Services (a division of American Insurance Services Group, Inc.).

Penalty the limit of an insurer's or surety's liability under a fidelity or surety bond.

Percentage Participation Clause in health insurance, a provision that requires the insured to bear a percentage of expenses in excess of the deductible; also called coinsurance.

Peril the cause of possible loss; the event insured against.

Permanent Life Insurance a phrase used to cover any form of life insurance except term; generally insurance, such as whole life or endowment, that accrues cash value.

Permissible Loss Ratio the maximum percentage of premium income that can be expended by the company to pay claims without loss of profit.

Personal Auto Policy a simplified language automobile policy designed to insure private passenger automobiles and certain types of trucks owned by an individual or husband and wife.

Personal Injury in law, a term used to embrace a broad range of torts that includes bodily injury, libel, slander, discrimination, and similar offenses. Also a standard insurance coverage that protects against a more limited group of torts (false arrest, detention or imprisonment, malicious prosecution, wrongful entry or eviction, and libel, slander, or defamation).

Personal Injury Protection Coverage/PIP a form of automobile coverage that covers the treatment of injuries to the driver and passengers of the policyholder's car used in states that have enacted no-fault laws or other auto reparation reform laws.

Personal Producing General Agent a life insurance agent who has established a record of successful production and

who is granted a contract that gives them greater compensation than they received as agents. These agents absorb all their own expenses, including office facilities, clerical staff, and other overhead expenses.

Physical Hazard a condition of the subject of insurance that creates or increases the chance of loss, such as structural defects, occupancy, or similar conditions.

Physician-Hospital Organization a joint venture in which physicians and hospitals combine to provide a full range of health care services to subscribers for an annual fee (capitation); also sometimes called an Integrated Delivery System (IDS).

Plaintiff a party to a lawsuit who brings charges against another party called the defendant.

Point-of-Service Plan in health insurance, a cost-containment approach in which care provided through a network of providers is managed by a primary care physician or *gatekeeper.*

Policy the written contract of insurance that is issued to the policyholder insured by the company insurer.

Policy Dividend a refund of part of the premium on a participating life insurance policy reflecting the difference between the premium charged and actual experience.

Policy Fee an additional charge placed on the initial premium designed to offset a portion of the expense of policy issuance.

Policy Loan a loan made by an insurance company to a policyholder on the security of the cash value of his or her policy.

Policy Period the term for which insurance remains in force, sometimes definite, sometimes not.

Policy Reserve the amounts that a life insurance company allocates specifically for the fulfillment of its policy obligations; reserves are so calculated that, together with future premiums and interest earnings, they will enable the company to pay all future claims.

Policyholders Surplus total capital funds as shown in an insurer's annual statement. Consists of capital, if any, unassigned funds (surplus) and any special funds that are not in the nature of liabilities.

Pollution the contamination of the environment that includes air pollution, noise pollution, water pollution, and disposal of waste materials.

Pool a risk-sharing mechanism in which the members of a group agree to be collectively responsible for losses.

Portfolio Average Method a dividend allocation approach used in life insurance in which excess investment earnings to be included in dividends are allocated to all policies, old and new, at a single rate, regardless of the pattern of premium payments over the years; see Investment Generation Method.

Postselection Underwriting an insurer's practice of reevaluating the desirability of insureds at or prior to the renewal of their policies.

Pre-admission authorization A cost containment feature of many group medical policies whereby the insured must contact the insurer prior to a hospitalization and receive authorization for the admission.

Preauthorized Check Plan a plan by which a policyholder arranges with his bank and insurance company to have his or her premium payments drawn, usually monthly, from his checking account.

Preexisting Condition a physical condition that existed prior to the effective date of the policy.

Preferred Provider Organization (PPO) a health care delivery organization composed of physicians, hospitals, or other health care providers that contracts with subscribers to provide health care services at a reduced fee.

Premises and Operations a commercial liability coverage that protects against liability arising out of the ownership or maintenance of premises or out of the activities of employees away from the premises.

Premium the payment, or one of the periodical payments, a policyholder agrees to make for an insurance policy.

Premium Loan a policy loan needed for the purpose of paying premiums.

Premium Period the length of time covered by the premium, usually identical with the policy period but frequently not.

Prepaid Group Practice Plan a plan under which a person pays in advance for the right to specified health services performed by participating physicians and institutions.

Primary basic, fundamental; an insurance policy that pays first with respect to other outstanding policies.

Primary Beneficiary the individual first designated to receive the proceeds of an insurance policy; see Contingent Beneficiary.

Primary care physician the designated contact for a patient in health insurance plans that require members to select and seek treatment from a specific physician who either renders treatment or refers the member to an appropriate specialist within the approved health care network.

Principal the applicant for, or subject of, insurance: the one from whom an agent derives his or her authority.

Principal Sum a term used to refer to the lump sum amount payable for accidental death, dismemberment, or loss of sight.

Prior Approval Law a system of rate regulation in which rates must be filed with the state regulatory authority and approved before they may be used.

Prior authorization in health insurance, a cost containment measure that provides full payment of health benefits only when the hospitalization or medical treatment has been approved in advance.

Private Insurance voluntary insurance programs available from a private firm or from the government by which

an individual may obtain protection against the possibility of loss due to a contingency.

Pro Rata Apportionment a division of loss according to the interest of the various companies providing insurance; thus, if Company A has insured the property involved for $10,000 and Company B has insured the property for $20,000, Company A will pay one-third of any loss and Company B will pay two-thirds.

Pro Rata Cancellation cancellation with a return of premium charged for the period of time the policy was in force equal to the ratio of the total premium to the total policy period; see Short Rate Cancellation.

Pro Rata Distribution Clause a clause that provides that the face amount of the insurance will be divided between the objects insured in the proportion that the value of each bears to the value of all.

Probationary Period (also sometimes called "waiting period") a period of time from the policy date to a specified date, usually 15–30 days, during which no sickness coverage is effective; it is designed to eliminate a sickness actually contracted before the policy went into effect—occurs only at the inception of a policy.

Producer an agent for an insurance company.

Professional Review Organization (PRO) an organization in which practicing physicians assume responsibility for reviewing the propriety and quality of health care services provided under Medicare and Medicaid.

Prohibited Risks those not written by a company because of an unusual occupational exposure or uninsurable physical or moral conditions.

Proof the act of substantiating another act, such as a claim for insurance payment.

Proposal an application for insurance or the facts contained in it; a recommendation.

Prorate Clause in health insurance, an optional policy provision designed to protect the company when an insured changes to a more hazardous occupation and does not have his or her policy amended accordingly; the company may pay only such portion of the indemnities provided as the premium paid would have purchased at the higher classification, subject to the maximum limits fixed by the company for such more hazardous occupation; it also protects the insured when he or she changes to a less hazardous occupation by providing for a return premium.

Prospective payment system a system of Medicare reimbursement for Part A benefits that bases most hospital payments on the patient's diagnosis at the time of hospital admission.

Protection and Indemnity (P & I) Insurance liability insurance coverage in an ocean marine policy.

Provider-Sponsored Organizations under Medicare+ Choice, provider-owned and -sponsored ventures that operate much like health maintenance organizations.

Provisions the terms or conditions of an insurance policy.

Proximate Cause the immediate or actual cause of loss under an insurance policy.

Public Adjuster one who represents the policyholder instead of the company.

Public Guarantee Insurance Programs compulsory quasi-social insurance programs designed to protect lenders, investors, or depositors against loss in connection with the failure of a financial institution or other type of fiduciary: for example, the Federal Deposit Insurance Corporation.

Public Law 15 an historic piece of legislation passed by Congress in 1945 whereby insurance was exempted from the operation of federal antitrust laws "to the extent that it is regulated by the various states." Certain other restrictions were added such as a prohibition of coercion; also known as the "McCarran Act."

Punitive Damages damages awarded separately and in addition to the compensatory damages, usually on account of malicious or wanton misconduct, to serve as a punishment for the wrongdoer and possibly as a deterrent to others.

Pure Premium that part of the premium that is sufficient to pay losses and loss adjustment expenses but not including other expenses. Also, the premium developed by dividing losses by exposure disregarding any loading for commission, taxes, and expenses.

Pure Risk a condition in which there is the possibility of loss or no loss only.

Quota Share Reinsurance a reinsurance contract that reinsures an agreed fraction of every risk of the kind described in the contract, which the ceding company writes.

Rate the cost of a unit of insurance.

Rated Policy an insurance policy issued at a higher-than-standard premium rate to cover the extra risk involved in certain instances where the insured does not meet the standard under-writing requirements; for example, impaired health or a particularly hazardous occupation.

Rating Bureau see Advisory Organization.

Reasonable and Customary Charge a charge for health care, which is consistent with the going rate or charge in a certain geographical area for identical or similar services.

Rebate the return of part or all of a premium to a policyholder.

Reciprocal Exchange an association of individuals who agree to exchange insurance risks—each member of the association insures each of the other members and in turn is insured by each of the other members; see Attorney-in-Fact.

Recurring Clause a period of time during which a recurrence of a condition is considered as being a continuation of a prior period of disability or hospital confinement.

Reduced Paid-up Insurance a form of insurance available as a nonforfeiture option; it provides for continuation of the original insurance plan, but for a reduced amount.

Refund Annuity an annuity that provides that the difference between the original cost and payments made to the annuitant will be paid to a beneficiary.

Regional Agent a district agent; the grade between local and general agent.

Regular Medical Expense Insurance coverage for services such as doctor fees for nonsurgical care in the hospital or at home, X-rays, or laboratory tests.

Rehabilitation Benefit in disability policies, a provision that provides for continuation of disability benefits or other financial assistance while a totally disabled person is retraining or attempting to acquire skills to return to the work force.

Reimbursement Benefits those for which the insured is reimbursed on an actual expense-incurred basis.

Reinstatement the restoration of a lapsed policy.

Reinsurance insurance placed by an underwriter in another company to cut down the amount of the risk assumed under the original insurance.

Relation of Earnings to Insurance Clause in disability insurance, a provision that reduces payment to the proportion of policy benefits that the insured's earnings at the time of disability (or average earnings for two years prior to disability) bear to total disability benefits under all policies; also called the average earnings clause.

Release a discharge, as from further liability under an insurance policy.

Renew to continue; to replace, as with new policy.

Renewable at Insurers Option in health insurance, a continuance provision that reserves to the insurer the right to refuse to renew the contract.

Renewable Term Insurance term insurance that can be renewed at the end of the term, at the option of the policyholder, and without evidence of insurability, for a limited number of successive terms; the rates increase at each renewal as the age of the insured increases.

Rental Value Insurance insurance arranging to pay the reasonable rental value of property that has been rendered untenantable by fire or some other peril insured against, for the period of time that would be required to restore the property to tenantable condition.

Replacement Cost Insurance property insurance that pays for damaged or destroyed property without a deduction for depreciation.

Reporting Form insurance that depends upon regular reports from the insured to determine the amount of insurance or the premium or both.

Representation statements made by an applicant in the application that he represents as being substantially true to the best of his or her knowledge and belief, but which are not warranted as exact in every detail.

Res Ipsa Loquitur (the thing speaks for itself) rebuttable presumption that the defendant was negligent: the presumption arises on proof that the instrumentality causing the injury was in the defendant's exclusive control, and that the accident is one that ordinarily does not happen in the absence of negligence.

Reserve liability set up for particular purposes.

Residual Disability Benefit a provision in disability income policies that grants benefits based on a reduction in earnings, as opposed to inability to work full time.

Residual Market Plan a mechanism through which high-risk insureds who cannot obtain insurance through normal market channels are insured.

Residuary the balance remaining, as in an estate after specific bequests and debts have been paid.

Respondeat Superior (let the master answer) the principal is liable in certain cases for the wrongful acts of his agent; the doctrine does not apply where the injury occurs while the servant is acting outside the legitimate scope of his or her authority.

Respondentia an early form of marine insurance on cargo; similar to bottomry, the equivalent on hulls.

Restoration reinstatement, as the amount of coverage after a loss.

Retention the act of retaining an exposure to loss; also that part of the exposure that is retained.

Retroactive Conversion conversion of term life insurance into whole-life insurance at the insured's original age at issue rather than at the insured's attained age at conversion.

Retrocession the amount of risk that a reinsurance company reinsures: the amount of a cession that the reinsurer passes on.

Retrospective Rating the process of determining the cost of an insurance policy after expiration of the policy, based on the loss experience under the policy while it was in force.

Return Premium an amount due the insured upon cancellation of a policy.

Revival the reinstatement of a lapsed policy by the company on receipt of evidence of insurability and payment of past due premiums with interest.

Revocable Beneficiary a beneficiary designation that may be changed by the policy owner without the consent of the existing beneficiary.

Rider a document that amends the policy; it may increase or decrease benefits, waive a condition or coverage, or in any other way amend the original contract—the terms *rider* and *endorsement* are often used interchangeably.

Risk in the abstract, used to indicate a condition of the real world in which there is a possibility of loss; also used by insurance practitioners to indicate the property insured or the peril insured against.

Risk-Based Capital a financial-analysis model adopted by the National Association of Insurance Commissioners for judging the adequacy of insurers' capital, based on the specific risks facing an insurer, including underwriting risk, investment portfolio risk, and other risks not reflected in these factors.

Risk Contract a managed care contract payment method in which the Health Care Financing Administration (HCFA) pays a fixed monthly payment (sometimes supplemented by a payment from the enrollee) in return for the delivery of all Medicare-covered services medically necessary to members.

Risk Management a scientific approach to the problem of dealing with the pure risks facing an individual or an organization in which insurance is viewed as simply one of several approaches for dealing with such risks.

Risk Retention Act A 1986 federal statute that exempts risk retention groups and insurance purchasing groups from a substantial part of state regulation.

Risk Retention Group group-owned insurer formed under Risk Retention Act of 1986, whose primary activity consists of assuming and spreading the liability risks of its members.

Robbery the unlawful taking of property by violence or threat of violence.

Roth IRA a type of IRA established by the Tax Reform Act of 1997 under which contributions made only on a nondeductible basis and for which withdrawals are free from taxes.

Salvage value recoverable after a loss: that which is recovered by an insurance company after paying a loss; see Subrogation.

Schedule a list of coverages or amounts concerning things or persons insured.

Schedule Rating a system of rating in which debits and credits are added and subtracted from a base rate to determine the final rate for a particular insured.

Second-Injury Fund in workers compensation, a state fund that pays the increased benefits when a second work-related injury combined with a previous injury results in greater disability than would be caused by the second injury only.

Second-to-Die Policy a life insurance contract that insures two lives with the promise to pay only at the second death; also called survivorship whole-life insurance.

Securitization of Insurance Risk the process of converting insurance risk into securities that can be sold in financial markets. See Catastrophe Bond and PCS Option.

Self-funded plan synonymous with self-insured; an employee benefit plan in which the employer pays the claims rather than an insurance company.

Self-Insurance a risk-retention program that incorporates elements of the insurance mechanism.

Senior Professional Public Adjuster (SPPA) professional designation granted to public adjusters with 10 years' experience who pass a rigorous examination and meet other specified eligibility requirements.

Separate Account funds held by a life insurer that are segregated from the other assets of the insurer and invested for pension plans.

Settlement Option one of the ways, other than immediate payment in a lump sum, in which the policyholder or beneficiary may choose to have the policy proceeds paid.

Seven-Pay Test a test applied to life insurance contracts under the *Internal Revenue Code* that is designed to determine if the contract is primarily an investment instrument rather than a life insurance contract. Premiums during the first 7 years of the contract may not exceed seven annual net level premiums for a 7-pay policy; see Modified Endowment Contract.

Short Rate Cancellation cancellation with a less than proportionate return of premium; see Pro Rata Cancellation.

Short-term Additional Monthly Benefit in disability policies, a monthly benefit payable during the first months of total disability. The benefit may be payable for up to 12 months, depending on the insurer.

Short-term Disability a generally accepted period of time for 2 years or less; can vary according to company standards.

Sickness Insurance a form of health insurance against loss by illness or disease.

SIMPLE Plan a simplified approach to pensions created by the Small Business Job Protection Act of 1996 (Savings Incentive Match Plan for Employees Plan) under which individual pensions are established for each employee using an IRA or 401(k) plan. Depending on the approach, the plans are referred to as either a SIMPLE IRA or a SIMPLE 401(k).

Single Premium Whole Life a whole-life policy in which the initial premium, together with interest earnings, is sufficient to pay the cost of the policy over its lifetime.

Single Premium Deferred Annuity an annuity under which the initial premium accumulates together with investment income to create a fund that will be paid out to the annuitant at some time in the future.

Social Insurance compulsory insurance, in which the benefits are prescribed by law and in which the primary emphasis is on social adequacy rather than equity.

Social Insurance Substitute Benefit in disability policies, an optional benefit that is payable when the individual is

disabled under the policy terms, but does not qualify for Social Security disability benefits. Also sometimes called a *Social Security Offset Rider.*

Social Security Offset Rider see Social Insurance Substitute Benefit.

Soft Market a buyer's market in which insurance is relatively inexpensive and in plentiful supply.

South-Eastern Underwriters Association (S.E.U.A.) case U.S. Supreme Court decision in 1944 that reversed the decision in *Paul v Virginia* and held that insurance is interstate commerce.

Special Agent a representative of an insurance company who travels about a given territory dealing with agents and supervising the company's operations there.

Special Damages amount awarded in litigation to compensate for specific identifiable economic loss.

Speculative Risk a condition in which there is a possibility of loss or gain.

Split Funding a technique in which a part of the contributions to a pension plan is paid to a life insurer and a part is invested separately under a pension trust.

SPPA see Senior Professional Public Adjuster.

Sprinkler Leakage Insurance insurance against loss from accidental leakage or discharge from a sprinkler system due to some cause other than a hostile fire or certain other specified causes.

Staff Adjuster one who adjusts losses and is paid a salary by one company for all his or her time.

Standard Provisions (health insurance) a set of policy provisions prescribed by law setting forth certain rights and obligations of both the insured and company; these were originally introduced in 1912 and have now been replaced by the Uniform Provisions.

Standard Risk a person who, according to a company's underwriting standards, is entitled to insurance protection without extra rating or special restrictions.

Statutory Accounting accounting prescribed by regulatory authorities for insurance companies. Under the statutory account system, GAAP (Generally Accepted Accounting Principles) are not followed, but statutory conventions replace GAAP.

Statutory Profit the profit of an insurer computed under the statutory system of accounting.

Stock Insurance Company an insurance company owned by stockholders, usually for the purpose of making a profit.

Stop-loss insurance a type of reinsurance purchased by a health plan or self-funded employer plan. Coverage can be written to cover losses over a specified amount either on a specific or individual basis, or on a total basis for the plan over a period of time such as one year.

Straight Life Insurance whole-life insurance on which premiums are payable for life.

Structured settlement legal agreement to pay a designated person, usually someone who has been injured, a specified sum of money in periodic payments, usually for his or her lifetime, instead of in a single lump sum payment.

Subrogation an assignment or substituting of one person for another by which the rights of one are acquired by another in collecting a debt or a claim, as an insurance company stepping into the rights of a policyholder indemnified by the company.

Substandard (impaired risk) risks that have some physical impairment requiring the use of a waiver, a special policy form, or a higher premium charge.

Suicide Clause life insurance policy provision that limits the insurer's liability to the return of premiums if the insured commits suicide during the first 2 years of the policy.

Superfund a federal environmental cleanup fund created principally from taxes on the chemical industry intended for use in cleaning up waste dumps.

Summary Plan Description a recap or summary of the benefits provided under a health insurance plan most often used for employees covered by self-funded plans.

Supplementary Contract an agreement between a life insurer and a policyholder or beneficiary by which the insurer retains the proceeds payable under an insurance policy and makes payments in accordance with the settlement option chosen.

Supplementary Medical Insurance (SMI) optional insurance under the Medicare program that covers physicians' fees and other specified medical services.

Surety a guarantor of a duty or obligation assumed by another.

Surety Bond an agreement providing for monetary compensation should there be a failure to perform certain specified acts within a stated period: the surety company, for example, becomes responsible for fulfillment of a contract if the contractor defaults.

Surgical Expense Insurance health insurance coverage that provides benefits toward the physician's or surgeon's operating fees, usually with a scheduled amount for each surgical procedure.

Surplus Line commonly used to describe any insurance for which there is no available market to the original agent or broker, and which is placed in a nonadmitted insurer in accordance with the Surplus or Excess Line provisions of state insurance laws.

Surrender Cost Index in life insurance, a measure of the cost of a policy, including interest foregone, if the policy is surrendered for its cash value at the end of a specified period.

Survivorship Whole Life a life insurance contract that insures two lives with the promise to pay only at the second death; also called the "second-to-die" policy.

Tail Coverage an extended reporting period extension under claims-made liability policies that provides coverage for losses that are reported after termination of the policy.

Tax-Qualified Long-Term Care Insurance (TQ-LTCI) Long-term care insurance policies that meet the requirements established by the Health Insurance Portability and Accountability Act of 1996.

Tender Offer Defense Expense Insurance insurance designed to reimburse a publicly held corporation for defense expenses in resisting takeover attempts.

Term the length of time covered by a policy or a premium.

Term Insurance insurance payable to a beneficiary at the death of the insured, provided death occurs within a specified period, such as 5 or 10 years, or before a specified age.

Theft the unlawful taking of property of another: the term includes such crimes as burglary, larceny, and robbery.

Third Party someone other than the insured and insuring company.

Third-Party Administration administration of a group insurance plan by some person or firm other than the insurer or the policyholder.

Third-Party Insurance liability insurance, so called because it undertakes to pay to a third party sums that the insured becomes legally obligated to pay.

Title Insurance insurance that indemnifies the owner of real estate in the event his or her clear ownership of property be upset by the discovery of faults in his or her title: largely written by companies specializing in this class alone.

Tort an injury or wrong committed against an individual.

Total Disability disability that prevents the insured from performing all the duties of his or her occupation or any occupation: the exact definition varies among policies.

Travel Accident Policies those that are limited to paying for loss arising out of accidents occurring while traveling.

Trespasser one who enters property of another without permission. A property owner generally is obligated to avoid intentional injury to trespassers and do so by a full disclosure of all information material to the proposed contract.

Trust transfer of property right to one person called a "trustee" for the benefit of another called a "beneficiary."

Trust Fund Plan a pension plan administered by a trustee rather than by an insurance company.

Twisting the act of switching insurance policies from one company to another, to the detriment of the insured.

Uberrimae Fidei literally, of the utmost good faith. The basis of all insurance contracts—both parties to the contract are bound to exercise good faith and do so by a full disclosure of all information material to the proposed contract.

Umbrella Liability Insurance a form of excess liability insurance available to corporations and individuals protect-ing them against claims in excess of the limits of their primary policies or for claims not covered by their insurance program. This latter coverage requires the insured to be a self-insurer for a substantial amount ($10,000–$25,000).

Unallocated Benefit in health insurance, a policy provision providing reimbursement up to a maximum amount for the cost of all extra miscellaneous hospital services, but not specifying how much will be paid for each type of service.

Underinsured Motorist Coverage a form of automobile coverage that pays for bodily injury to insured persons by a motorist who has insurance that meets the requirements of the financial responsibility law, but is insufficient to cover the loss sustained by the insured.

Underwriter an individual who decides whether the insurance company will issue coverage and, in some cases, the rate at which it will be issued.

Underwriting the process by which an insurance company determines whether and on what basis it will accept an application for insurance.

Unearned Premium that portion of the original premium for which protection has not yet been provided because the policy still has some time to run before expiration. A property and liability insurer must carry unearned premiums as a liability on its financial statement.

Uniform Provisions statutory policy provisions that specify the rights and obligations of the insured and company.

Uninsured Motorist Coverage a form of automobile insurance that pays for bodily injury to an insured person by a motorist who is uninsured, a hit-and-run driver, or a driver whose insurer becomes insolvent.

Universal Life Insurance a flexible premium life insurance policy under which the policyholder may change the death benefit from time to time (with satisfactory evidence of insurability for increases) and vary the premium payments. Premiums (less expense charges) are credited to a policy account from which mortality charges are deducted and to which interest is credited at rates that may change from time to time.

Unsatisfied Judgement Fund a state fund created to reimburse persons injured in automobile accidents who cannot collect damages awarded to them because the responsible party is either insolvent or uninsured. Such funds are often financed by an addition to the regular automobile registration fee and will only pay unsatisfied judgments up to fixed limits.

Usual, Customary, and Reasonable (UCR) Charges in health insurance, an approach to benefits under which the policy agrees to pay the "usual, customary and reasonable" charges for a procedure, rather than a stipulated dollar amount.

Utilization Review a cost control mechanism by which the appropriateness, necessity, and quality of health care is monitored by both insurers and employers.

Valued Policy an insurance contract in which the value of the thing insured and the amount to be paid in case of total loss is settled at the time of making the policy.

Valued Policy Law a state statute that specifies that in the event of a total loss, the insured shall receive in payment the full amount of the policy, regardless of the principle of indemnity.

Vanishing Premium Policy a participating whole-life policy on which dividends are allowed to accumulate until accumulated dividends plus future dividends are sufficient to pay all future premiums under the policy.

Variable Annuity an annuity contract under which the amount of each periodic payment fluctuates according to the investment performance of the insurer.

Variable Life Insurance life insurance under which the benefits are not fixed but relate to the value of assets behind the contract at the time the benefit is paid.

Variable Universal Life a form of life insurance (also called Universal Life II) that combines the flexible premium features of universal life with the investment component of variable life.

Vesting a provision that a participant in a pension plan will, after meeting certain requirements, retain the right to the benefits he or she has accrued.

Viatical Settlement Company a business that specializes in the purchase of life insurance policies from terminally-ill persons.

Viatication the sale of a terminally ill person's life insurance policy to a business firm that specializes in such transactions.

Vicarious Liability in law, liability arising out of imputed negligence.

Void of no force or effect; null.

Waiting Period (also sometimes called "elimination period" or "probation period") a provision designed to eliminate disability claims for the first number of days specified for each period of disability; the waiting period may run from 3 days to as long as 1 year: this term is also sometimes used to refer to a period of time after policy issuance during which specified conditions are not covered.

Waiver the voluntary relinquishment of a known right.

Waiver of Premium a provision that waives payment of the premium that becomes due during a period of covered total disability that has lasted for a specified period of time, usually, 3 to 6 months.

Warranty a statement concerning the condition of the item to be insured that is made for the purpose of permitting the underwriter to evaluate the risk; if found to be false, it provides the basis for voidance of the policy.

Whole Life Insurance insurance payable to a beneficiary at the death of the insured whenever that occurs; premiums may be payable for a specified number of years (limited-payment life) or for life (straight life).

Workers Compensation a system of providing for the cost of medical care and weekly payments to injured employees or to dependents of those killed in industry in which absolute liability is imposed on the employer, requiring him or her to pay benefits prescribed by law.

Written Premiums the premiums on all policies that a company has issued in some period of time, as opposed to "earned premiums."

AUTHOR INDEX

■

SUBJECT INDEX

■

663